THE DICTIONARY OF
CLASSICAL MYTHOLOGY

THE DICTIONARY OF
CLASSICAL MYTHOLOGY

Pierre Grimal

Translated by
A. R. Maxwell-Hyslop

Blackwell Reference

English translation © Basil Blackwell Ltd 1986

First published in French as *Dictionnaire de la Mythologie*
Greque et Romaine
© 1951 Presses Universitaire de France, Paris

English translation first published 1986
Reprinted with corrections 1987
Reprinted 1987, 1988

Basil Blackwell Ltd
108 Cowley Road, Oxford OX4 1JF, England

Basil Blackwell Inc.
432 Park Avenue South, Suite 1503
New York, NY 10016, USA

British Library Cataloguing in Publication Data
Grimal, Pierre
The dictionary of classical mythology
(Blackwell Reference)
1. Mythology—Dictionaries
I. Title   II. Dictionnaire de la mythologie
Grecque et Romaine, *English*
292′ .13′ 0321   BL715
ISBN 0–631–13209–0

Library of Congress Cataloging in Publication Data
Grimal, Pierre, 1912—
The dictionary of classical mythology

(Blackwell Reference)
Translation of: Dictionnaire de la mythologie
grecque et romaine.
Includes index.
1. Mythology, Classical — Dictionaries.
I. Title.
BL715.G713   1985   292′ .13   85–7387
ISBN 0–631–13209–0

The endpapers show a view of the Greek theatre at Taormina, Sicily.
Photograph: James Austin

Typeset by Katerprint Typesetting Services, Oxford
Printed in Great Britain by
Butler and Tanner Ltd, Frome

Contents

Acknowledgements

The Translator and Publishers would like to thank Francis Boothroyd, Carole Martin-Sperry, Charles Milne and Christopher Robinson for their assistance with the translation; Michael Trapp and Jonathan Powell for their painstaking efforts with the references and genealogical tables; and Peter Clayton for his help and advice with the photographs.

The Translator and Publisher are grateful to the following for permission to reproduce plates on the following pages:

Ashmolean Museum Oxford 64, 343, 345, 419, 422, 465; James Austin 110, 273, 386, 415, 464; Peter Clayton 20, 45, 53, 69, 118, 141, 152, 156, 169, 175, 197, 198, 209, 216, 241, 244, 252 (2), 255, 291, 295 (2), 319, 320, 338, 360, 390, 391, 412, 425, 433; Hirmer Verlag Munich 48, 388; Michael Holford 130, 199, 231, 242, 292, 307, 355, 446, 449; The Mansell Collection 11, 28, 54, 67, 94, 125, 132, 146, 164, 175, 185, 201, 210, 249, 269, 298, 332, 350, 375, 458; Mauro Pucciarelli Rome 49, 74; Werner Forman Archive 9, 90, 406.

Translator's Preface

A translation as long as this cannot be produced in a reasonable time without the help of many people who have been associated with it in different ways, and I am deeply grateful to all of them, hastening to add that the order in which I have named them bears no relation to my degree of gratitude.

I owe a great deal to my fellow translators who managed, in spite of their many preoccupations, to complete their tasks within the stipulated time; to Michael Trapp and Jonathan Powell; to the Principal and Fellows of Jesus College, Oxford for allowing me to use their Senior Common Room where I could work in beautiful and quiet surroundings; to John Griffith who helped me with classical queries; to Dr Pilkington whom I consulted on questions of French; to Lord Sackville who put the library at Knole at my disposal; to Mr and Mrs Christopher Huntley; to Mrs Burnett of Chipping Norton who typed the first part of the translation; to John Davey, Janet Godden and Gillian Forrester of Basil Blackwell who were always helpful and accessible; and finally to Rachael, my wife, and Hilary, our younger daughter, who more than once rescued me when I was in imminent danger of drowning in a sea of paper.

I could not have hoped for a better band of helpers; any mistakes are mine and mine alone.

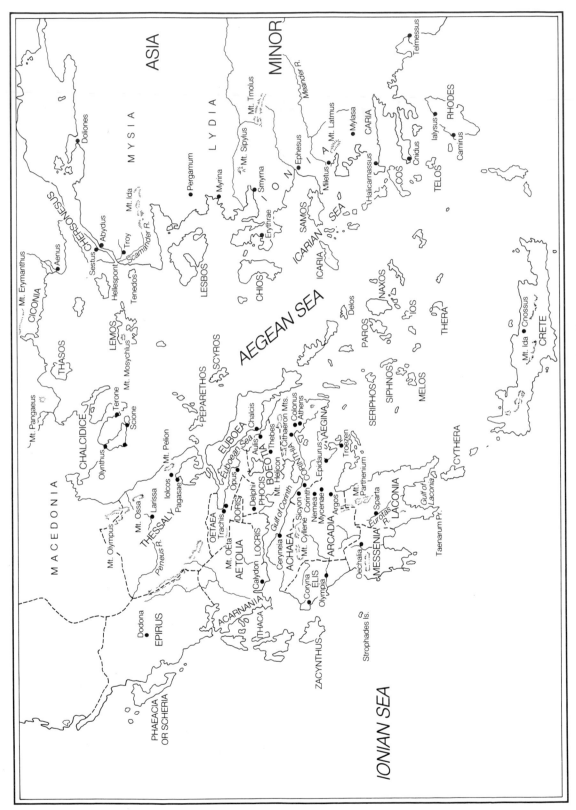

Greece – the mythological world

Italy and Sicily – the mythological world

A

Abas (Ἄβας) There are three heroes of this name but they are not easily distinguishable.

1. The earliest Abas gave his name to the Abantides, a tribe in Euboea which is mentioned in the *Iliad*. He is said to have been the son of Poseidon and the nymph Arethusa, goddess of a spring near Chalcis, but a late Athenian myth makes him a descendant of Metion, the son of Erectheus, and therefore the son of Chalcon who was the son of Metion. Abas had two sons, Chalcodon and Canethus.

2. The best known Abas was the king of Argos, son of Lynceus and Hypermestra. In his veins flowed the blood of the two feuding brothers, Danaus and Egyptus and he was the ancestor of Perseus and his family (Table 31). He was considered to be the founder of the Phocian town of Abae. With his wife Aglaea, Abas had twin sons, Acrisius and Proetus, and a daughter, Idomene, who married Amythaon (Table 1). He is also said to have had an illegitimate son Lyrcus, who gave his name to the district of Lyrceia in the Peloponnese.

3. Yet another Abas was the son of Melampus, the grandson of Amythaon and consequently the great-grandson of the preceding Abas. He is said to have been the father of Lysimache, the wife of Talaus and mother of Adrastus (Table 1), the soothsayer Idmon and of Coeranus (see POLYIDUS).

Aborigines The earliest inhabitants of central Italy, according to Roman legends, and supposedly sons of the trees. They lived as nomads, without laws or fixed habitations, and their food was wild fruit. Their name is generally taken to mean 'the original population'. When Aeneas arrived in Latium at the head of the Trojans the Aborigines were ruled by Latinus. Once they were united with the Trojans they formed the Latin race, so called in honour of LATINUS.

Acacallis (Ἀκακαλλίς) One of the daughters of Minos, loved first by Hermes, by whom she had Cydon, and then by Apollo by whom she had three sons: Naxos (who gave his name to the island), Miletus and Amphitemis who was also known as Garamas. While Acacallis was waiting for the birth of Amphitemis, Minos, in a fit of anger, banished her from Crete and sent her to Libya where her son became the progenitor of the nomadic people the Garamantes. Acacallis had also fled from her father's anger before the birth of her third son Miletus. She sought refuge in the woods, where she gave birth to Miletus and, unable to rear him herself, she left him at the foot of a tree. In obedience to Apollo, the she-wolves in the forest suckled him until some shepherds found him, took him in, and brought him up.

Acacallis is sometimes called Acacalle, which in Greek means 'the Egyptian tamarisk' (see PHILANDRUS).

Acacos (Ἄκακος) The son of Lycaon and founder of the town of Acacesion in Arcadia. According to some traditions he was the foster-father of Hermes.

Academus (Ἀκαδήμος) An Attic hero who disclosed to Castor and Pollux exactly where Theseus was holding their sister Helen prisoner when they were searching for her throughout Greece. His tomb was on the outskirts of Athens beyond the Ceramicus district and was surrounded by a sacred wood in which Plato set up his Academy. The name Academy is sometimes said to be derived from that of Echedemus, an Arcadian who accompanied Castor and Pollux in their search for Helen.

Acalanthis (Ἀκαλανθίς) One of the nine daughters of Pierus, king of Macedonia. With her sisters she challenged the Muses to match her at singing, and in indignation the goddesses changed all nine girls into birds. Acalanthis became a goldfinch (which in Greek means a thorn). (See PIERIDES).

Acamas (Ἀκάμας) The name of several heroes.

1. A Trojan, the son of Antenor and Theano, who played a particularly brilliant part in the attack on the Greek camp. He was killed by Meriones.

2. The uncle of CYZICUS, who also fought for the Trojans, and was leader of a Thracian contingent. He was killed by Ajax, the son of Telamon.

3. The son of Theseus and Phaedra and the most

famous Acamas. He gave his name to the Attic clan of the Acamantides. This particular Acamas does not feature in the Homeric epic, though legends created after the composition of the *Iliad* give him, together with his brother Demophon, a part in the capture of Troy. Acamas is said to have accompanied Diomedes to Troy before the war broke out in an attempt to demand the return of Helen. While there he was seen by Priam's daughter Laodice, who fell in love with him. She confided her feelings to Philobia, the wife of Perseus, who immediately decided to help. Philobia persuaded her husband, who ruled the town of Dardanus in the Troad, to invite the two young people to a feast separately and to make them sit side by side, Laodice pretending to be a member of Priam's harem. By the end of the feast Laodice had become Acamas' wife. Their marriage resulted in a son, Munitus, who was brought up in Priam's palace by his great-grandmother Aethra, the mother of Theseus, who was at that time Helen's prisoner. After the fall of Troy Munitus returned to Acamas and they set out for Attica, together with Aethra who had finally regained her freedom. Munitus died on the way after being bitten by a snake while hunting at Olynthus.

There is a story that Acamas was one of those inside the wooden horse at the capture of Troy and that as his share of the booty he received the captured Clymene. On his way home from Troy he spent a long time in Thrace on account of his love for Phyllis. Later he founded a colony in Cyprus where he is said to have died when his horse fell and he was impaled on his own sword. This legend is more generally thought, though, to refer to Acamas' brother DEMOPHON.

According to still other legends, Acamas took part in the capture of Troy with Demophon and returned with Aethra to Attica, where he reassumed power and reigned peacefully.

Acanthis (Ἀκανθίς) The daughter of Autonous and his wife Hippodamia, who also had four sons, Anthus, Erodius, Schoeneus and Acanthus. Acanthis was also known as Acanthyllis. The family farmed a large area of land but it was not very fruitful since they did not work hard and their fields were always full of thistles and rushes. This was appropriate to the names of two of the sons, Schoeneus and Acanthus, whose names in Greek mean respectively 'rush' and 'thistle'. Their main occupation was horse breeding and they were in the habit of leaving mares to graze on the marshes. One day Anthus went to fetch the mares and they, not wanting to leave their grazing, reared up in anger and fell on him crushing him to death. The whole family was cast into such despair by this dreadful death that Zeus and Apollo, out of pity for their passionate grief, turned them all into birds. Autonous became a bittern, Hippodamia a crested lark, and Anthus, Erodius, Schoeneus, Acanthus and Acanthis birds of uncertain identification, which were called by the same names. Acanthus and Acanthis probably became two varieties of goldfinch (see ACALANTHIS) and Erodius probably a heron.

Acarnan (Ἀκαρνάν) One of the two sons of Alcmaeon, the son of the Theban soothsayer Amphiaraus by Callirhoe ('the lovely spring') who was a daughter of the river Achelous (Table 1). The name of the other son was Amphoterus. At some time during his adventures Alcmaeon had given offence to Phegeus, the king of Psophis in Arcadia, and he was eventually killed by Phegeus' children. When Callirhoe learnt of her husband's death she asked Zeus, who loved her, to cause her two small sons to grow miraculously so that they could avenge their father. Zeus agreed to this request, enabling Amphoterus and Acarnan to kill Pronus and Agenor, the sons of Phegeus, whom they met in the house of King Agapenor. They subsequently made their way to Psophis and killed Phegeus himself. The inhabitants of the town pursued them but they managed to escape and took refuge near Agapenor at Tegea in Arcadia. At the command of their grandfather Achelous, Amphoterus and Acarnan then went to Delphi to dedicate the necklace of Harmonia, which lay behind a long chain of murders and in particular had been the indirect cause of the deaths of their father Alcmaeon and their grandfather Amphiaraus (see ERYPHILE). After completing their mission they next made their way through Epirus where they enlisted some companions and founded the colony of Acarnania, whose inhabitants, formerly called the Curetes, took their new name from that of Acarnan.

According to one tradition, Acarnan was killed while trying to wed HIPPODAMIA, the daughter of Oenomaus, who put her suitors to death.

Acastus (Ἄκαστος) The son of Pelias, king of Iolcos, and Anaxibia (Table 21). Acastus took part in the voyage of the Argonauts against his father's wishes, Pelias having conceived the expedition simply as a means of getting rid of Jason whom he regarded as a threat to his throne. Acastus also took part in the hunt for the wild boar of Calydon. After the murder of his father by MEDEA Acastus reigned in Iolcos.

Acastus played an indirect part in the legend of PELEUS, father of Achilles. During the hunt of the Calydonian boar Peleus accidentally killed Eurytion, one of the hunters, and to purify himself after this killing he went to the court of Iolcos. While he was there Astydamia, the wife of Acastus, fell in love with him. When Peleus rejected her advances she sent a message to his wife saying that her husband was about to leave her in order to marry Sterope, the daughter of Acastus. Peleus' wife hanged herself in despair. Astydamia did not think that she had yet exacted sufficient revenge, and in the presence of Acastus accused Peleus of trying to seduce her. Acastus believed the story and, not daring to kill his guest whom he had only just purified after a murder, lured Peleus to the hunt on Pelion where he left him asleep, hiding his sword in cow's dung to make sure that he would not be able to protect himself from the wild beasts or other evil creatures on the mountain. The unarmed Peleus was almost put to death by the Centaurs who lived on the mountain but one of them, the wise Chiron, woke him in time and gave him back his sword.

When Peleus returned to his kingdom he thought about means of revenge. In some accounts he renewed the attack against Iolcos, either alone or with the help of Jason, Castor and Pollux, capturing the town, killing Astydamia, and scattering her limbs all round the town so that his army could march between the various limbs of the dismembered body. He also killed Acastus.

Other writers claim that Peleus, left defenceless during the Trojan war as his son Achilles was in Asia, was attacked by Acastus and forced to flee. There is also a tradition that besides Astydamia, Acastus had another wife, Hippolyta Cretheis, the daughter of CRETHEUS.

Acca Larentia During the reign of Romulus or possibly of Ancus Martius, the keeper of the temple of Hercules in Rome invited the god to join in a game of dice on a feast day, the winner to give his opponent a feast and a beautiful girl. Hercules accepted the invitation and won the match: the keeper offered him a feast in the temple and the favours of Acca Larentia, the loveliest girl of the period in Rome. When Hercules gave Acca up he advised her, by way of compensation, to put herself at the disposal of the first man she should meet. This man happened to be an Etruscan named Tarutius, who married her. He was extremely rich and shortly afterwards died; Acca Larentia inherited his large estates near Rome, which she bequeathed to the Roman people on her death. This version of the legend was clearly devised to give full legal entitlement to the ownership of areas claimed by Rome. In her old age Acca vanished without trace to Velabria where another Larentia, wife of Faustulus, was buried.

Another legend tells of an Acca Larentia, the wife of a shepherd named FAUSTULUS. She had twelve children, as well as Romulus and Remus whom she adopted. The college of the twelve Arval Brothers was said to have been constituted in memory of the twelve children of Acca Larentia.

Acestes See AEGESTES.

Achaemenides (Ἀχαιμενίδης) One of the companions of ODYSSEUS. The latter made such a hasty departure from the land of the Cyclops in his efforts to escape the rocks which the giants, incited by Polyphemus, were hurling at his ships that he forgot to take Achaemenides on board. However, Achaemenides managed to save himself by going into hiding and he was subsequently rescued by Aeneas.

Achates (Ἀχάτης)
1. A Trojan, the faithful friend of Aeneas and companion on his travels until he reached Italy. There is a tradition that Achates killed Protesilaus, the first Greek to land on Trojan soil.
2. The name given by Nonnus in his *Dionysiacs* to one of the companions of the god. This Achates was said to be a Tyrrhenian.

Achelous (Ἀχελῷος) The name both of the largest river in Greece (in Boeotia) and of the river god. Achelous was said to be the son of Oceanus and Tethys, that is to say, of one of the most ancient couples known to Greek theogonies. He was regarded as the oldest of the three thousand river gods who were his brothers.

Different legends say that Achelous was the son either of Helios and Earth, or one of the sons of Poseidon (in these versions the river is called Phorbas). One day Achelous was fatally wounded by an arrow while crossing the river. He fell in and the river was later called after him.

Achelous is said to have had various affairs, first with Melpomene, by whom he was believed to have been the father of the Sirens, and then with some of the other Muses. He was also regarded as the father of several streams: of Pirene in Corinth, of Castalia at Delphi, and of Dirce in Thebes. Callirhoe ('the lovely spring') who married Alcmaeon was said to be his daughter, but no tradition records her mother's name (see ALCMAEON and ACARNAN).

Achelous was closely involved in the cycle of the Labours of Heracles. As a neighbour of Oeneus, king of Calydon in Aetolia, he asked for the hand of Oeneus' daughter Deianeira. Being both god and river Achelous was endowed with the gift of assuming whatever shape he liked, such as that of a bull or a dragon, but Deianeira was not at all attracted by the idea of having such a disquieting husband and when Heracles presented himself at Oeneus' court, and asked for her hand she immediately accepted him. Nevertheless, Heracles had to win her by force from Achelous who did not lightly allow himself to be sup-planted, and in the ensuing battle between the two claimants Achelous used all his resources and Heracles all his strength. In the course of the struggle Achelous turned himself into a bull and Heracles tore off one of his horns, at which point Achelous considered himself defeated, and sur-rendered. He conceded to Heracles the right to marry Deianeira but demanded the return of his horn. Heracles gave him back a horn of the she-goat AMALTHEA, the nurse of Zeus, who spread fruit and flowers far and wide. Other authors claimed that this miraculous horn belonged to Achelous himself.

The Echinades Islands, lying at the mouth of the river, were reputed to have been miraculously created by Achelous. While four nymphs of the country were sacrificing to the divinities on the river banks of the Achelous they omitted to include the god of the river himself and in his anger he caused the waters to rise and sweep them down into the sea where they became islands. The fifth island in the group, Perimele, was a girl whom the god loved and whose virginity he had taken by force. Her father Hippodamas cast his daughter into the river as she was about to give birth to a child. In answer to her lover's prayers the girl was changed by Poseidon into an island.

The modern name of the Achelous, which flows into the Ionian Sea at the entrance to the gulf of Patras, is the Aspropotamo.

Acheron (Ἀχέρων) The first mention of the river Acheron occurs in the *Odyssey*, where it is described in the subterranean world of Hell, together with Pyriphlegethon and Cocytus. The Acheron is the river which souls have to cross to reach the empire of the Dead. A ferryman, CHARON, has the duty of carrying them from one side to the other. The river is almost stagnant and its banks are thick with reeds and heavy with mud. According to tradition Acheron was a son of Earth (Gaia), condemned to stay underground as punishment for having allowed the Giants, who were thirsty after their struggle with the Olympians, to drink his waters. By Orphnea, the Nymph of Darkness or, in another version, by Gorgyra, Acheron had begotten ASCALAPHUS, the youth who was changed by Demeter into an owl.

There was a river Acheron in Epirus, on the western side of the Greek mainland, which ran through wild countryside and after flowing for some distance, disappeared into a deep cleft. When it surfaced again, near its mouth, it formed an unhealthy marsh set in a barren landscape. An etymological mistake (according to which its name was thought to be derived from the Greek word for sorrow) as well as the characteristics of the river in Epirus undoubtedly contributed to the birth of the idea that it was associated with Hell, and its earthly features were transferred to the subterranean world.

In the mystical beliefs current under the Roman Empire the Acheron was regarded as lying some-where near the South Pole, among the constella-tions of the Antipodes.

Achilles (Ἀχιλλεύς) The legend of Achilles is among the richest and oldest in Greek mythology. It owes its fame largely to the *Iliad*, which has as its main theme not the capture of Troy itself but the wrath of Achilles during the campaign which almost led to the loss of the Greek army. Other poets and popular legends seized on the figure of Achilles and strove to complete the story of his life by inventing legends to fill the gaps left by the Homeric accounts, and so an Achilles cycle gradu-ally came into being, overlaid with incidents and legends which, though frequently inconsistent with each other, continued to be an inspiration to tragic and epic poets throughout antiquity until the Roman period.

Childhood Achilles was the son of Peleus, king of Phthia in Thessaly. On his father's side he was a direct descendant of Zeus, while his mother was the goddess Thetis, daughter of Oceanus (Table 30). There are varying accounts of his upbringing.

One version depicts him as being brought up by his mother in his father's house, under the guidance of his teacher Phoenix or the Centaur Chiron, while another says that he was the involuntary cause of a quarrel between his father and mother and tells how, after Thetis had left her husband, Achilles was put in the care of the Centaur Chiron, who lived on the mountain of Pelion. The match between Thetis, a goddess, and Peleus, a mortal, could not last, for too many differences separated them. Achilles was said to have been the seventh child of the marriage and Thetis had tried to purge each of her offspring in turn of the mortal elements which indicated that Peleus was their father. She did this by thrusting them into a fire and so killing them, but when she came to the seventh child Peleus awoke and saw her actually engaged in this dangerous enterprise. He snatched the child from her and Achilles was found to have suffered nothing worse than the scorching of his lips and of a small bone in his right foot. Thetis, in her anger at such behaviour, went back to live with her sisters in the depths of the sea. Peleus asked the Centaur Chiron, who was skilled in the art of medicine, to replace the scorched bone and to meet this request Chiron exhumed the body of a giant called Damysus, who in his lifetime had been a notably swift runner, and replaced the missing bone with the corresponding one from the giant. This explains the runner's gifts which Achilles possessed to an extraordinary degree. Another legend asserts that in his infancy Achilles was bathed in the Styx, the river of Hell, whose waters had the power of making invulnerable all who were steeped in them, but the heel by which Thetis was holding him was untouched by the magical waters and remained vulnerable.

On Mount Pelion Achilles was looked after by Chiron's mother Philyra and his wife the Nymph Chariclo. When he was older he began to practise hunting and breaking horses as well as medicine. In addition he learned to sing and play the lyre and talked with Chiron about the ancient virtues – contempt for worldly goods, a horror of lying, a sense of moderation, resistance to evil passions and grief. He was fed on nothing but the entrails of lions and wild boars (to instil in him the strength of these animals), honey (intended to give him gentleness and persuasiveness) and bear's marrow. Chiron named him Achilles: previously he had been called Ligyron.

Departure for Troy According to the *Iliad*

Achilles decided to take part in the Trojan expedition in response to an invitation brought to him personally in Thessaly by Nestor, Odysseus and Patroclus. He led a fleet of fifty warships sailed by a body of Myrmidons and was accompanied by his friend Patroclus and his teacher PHOENIX As he left, Peleus made a vow to dedicate the hair of his son to the River Spercheius (which flowed through his kingdom) if he returned safe and sound from the expedition. Thetis, for her part, warned Achilles of the fate which awaited him: if he went to Troy he would win a dazzling reputation but his life would be short, whereas if he stayed at home his life would be long but inglorious. Achilles had no hesitation in choosing the former alternative. This is the Homeric version of the story but later poets, and especially the tragic ones, give a very different account. According to them an oracle had disclosed to Peleus (or, in some versions, Thetis) that Achilles was fated to die at the gates of Troy. When the Greeks were discussing whether to go to Asia to fight against Priam's city, Peleus (or Thetis) had the idea of hiding the young Achilles by dressing him in women's clothes and making him live at the court of Lycomedes, king of Scyros, where he shared the life of the king's daughters. He is said to have stayed there for nine years. He was known as Pyrrha (the red-haired girl) because of his fiery auburn locks and while in this disguise he married Deidamia, one of Lycomedes' daughters, by whom he had a son, Neoptolemus, who was later to take the name of Pyrrhus. This disguise was of no avail in trying to cheat Fate however as Odysseus had learned from the soothsayer Calchas that Troy could not be taken without the active help of Achilles. He immediately set himself the task of seeking Achilles and eventually learned where he had taken shelter. Odysseus then presented himself at the court of Scyros and, offering a pedlar's pack, made his way into the women's quarters. The woman chose some embroidery implements and materials but Odysseus had mixed up some valuable weapons with them and these were the immediate choice of 'Pyrrha'. Odysseus had no difficulty in persuading the young man to reveal his identity. In another version Odysseus, in order to compel Achilles to disclose his warlike instincts, arranged for the sound of the trumpet to be heard in the middle of the harem of Lycomedes. While the women fled in terror, Achilles, so strong was his martial spirit, stood his ground and called for weapons. Peleus and Thetis had therefore to resign themselves to what was beyond their power to prevent, and Achilles' warlike vocation was no longer thwarted. On his departure from Aulis, where the Greek fleet had assembled, Thetis gave the hero a divine suit of armour, given by Hephaestus to Peleus as a wedding gift, and she added the horses which Poseidon had given on the same occasion. In a final effort to change the course of fate, she placed near her son a slave whose only duty was to prevent Achilles from killing a son of Apollo; for an oracle had affirmed that Achilles was bound to die a violent death if with his own hands he killed a son of Apollo (who was not further described).

The First Expedition   According to the *Iliad*, the Greek army made its way directly from Aulis to Troy, but later legends speak of a first attempt at landing which completely failed. The first time the fleet left Aulis to attack Troy there was a mistake in the navigation and instead of landing on the Troad the army came ashore much further south, in Mysia. Under the impression that they were in the Troad the Greeks set about laying the country waste, but Telephus, the son of Heracles and king of the country, advanced to meet them and a battle ensued in the course of which Achilles wounded Telephus with his spear. The Greeks then realized their mistake and re-embarked to head for Troy but a storm scattered the fleet and each contingent found itself back where it had started. Achilles, among others, was driven ashore on Scyros, near his wife and son. The Greeks made a fresh start and reassembled at Argos, and there Telephus, on the advice of the oracle of Delphi, came to ask Achilles to heal the wound he had inflicted, for, according to the oracle, only Achilles' spear could heal the wounds it had made.

The Second Expedition   From Argos the Greek fleet made its way to Aulis where it lay becalmed, an event said by Calchas to have been caused by the goddess Artemis who demanded the sacrifice of Agamemnon's daughter Iphigenia. Agamemnon agreed to this demand and in order to transport his daughter to Aulis without arousing the suspicions of herself or her mother Clytemnestra, he pretended that he wanted to betroth her to Achilles. By the time the unwitting Achilles discovered what the king had planned Iphigenia had arrived at Aulis and it was too late to take any action. He tried hard to resist the sacrifice, but the soldiers, roused in opposition to him, would have stoned him to death, and he was forced to resign himself to the inevitable. This episode seems to have been treated in unusually great detail by the tragic

poets. Favourable winds sprang up and the army, led by Telephus, arrived at the island of Tenedos where during a feast Achilles and Agamemnon fell into a quarrel for the first time. It was also in Tenedos that Achilles killed Tenes, a son of Apollo, whose sister he tried to abduct. Realizing too late that he had fulfilled the oracle which his mother had warned him of, he arranged a magnificent funeral for Tenes and he killed the slave whose duty it had been to prevent the murder.

The Greeks besieged Troy for nine years before the events which form the story of the *Iliad* began. These years were full of exploits, some of which were familiar to the writer of the *Iliad* while others were invented at a later date. The *Iliad* speaks of a whole range of deeds of piracy and brigandage against the islands and cities of Asia Minor, in particular against Thebes in Mysia which was captured by Achilles who killed King Eetion, the father of Andromache, together with his seven sons, and abducted the queen. To the same group of stories belongs the episode of the campaign against Lyrnessos during which Achilles captured Briseis while Agamemnon captured Chryseis in the Theban operation. With Patroclus, Achilles attempted a raid on the herds of oxen which Aeneas grazed on Mount Ida. Other episodes connected with the skirmishes of the first nine years include those which took place during the Greek disembarkation when the Trojans, initially victorious, were routed by Achilles who killed Cycnus, the son of Poseidon. It was also said that Achilles, who was not among the suitors of Helen before Menelaus was chosen as her husband, was curious to see her and that Aphrodite and Thetis arranged for them to meet in a remote spot. No one, though, seems to have tried to portray Achilles as Helen's lover.

The real Homeric stories and the quarrel over Briseis begin with the tenth year of the war. When a plague caused widespread destruction among the Greek ranks the soothsayer Calchas revealed that this calamity was a manifestation of the wrath of Apollo, sent at the request of his priest Chryses whose daughter Chryseis had been abducted and allotted to Agamemnon as his share of the booty of Thebes. Achilles summoned the chiefs to meet and compelled Agamemnon to surrender the girl. In retaliation Agamemnon demanded that Achilles should give back his own prize, Briseis. Achilles retired to his tent and refused to take any part in the struggle as long as anyone contested his right to the girl. When the heralds came to reclaim her from him he returned her, but made a solemn protest against this injustice. Then, going to the seashore, he appealed to Thetis who advised him to let the Trojan attack get as far as the ships, in order to prove the indispensability of his presence for, as she well knew, he was the only man who could inspire enough terror in the enemy to prevent them from attacking the Greeks effectively. Thetis, re-ascending into heaven, went to Zeus and asked him to grant the Trojans victory as long as Achilles kept well away from the fighting. Zeus agreed and for several days the Greeks suffered a series of defeats. Agamemnon in vain sent a mission to appease Achilles, promising him Briseis and a magnificent ransom, as well as twenty of the most beautiful women in Troy and the hand of one of his own daughters, but Achilles remained unmoved. The battle came close to the camp but Achilles watched from the upper part of the deck of his ship. Patroclus could eventually hold out no longer and asked Achilles to let him help the Greeks, whose ships were in danger of being burnt. Achilles agreed to lend his armour, but Patroclus (after a certain degree of success, which lasted as long as the Trojans believed him to be Achilles) fell under the weight of Hector's blows. Achilles was overcome by indescribable grief. His cries were heard by Thetis, who hastened to him and promised him a fresh suit of armour in place of that which Hector had just stripped from Patroclus' body. Though unarmed, Achilles arrived on the scene of the battle and his voice put to flight the Trojans who were struggling against the Greeks for possession of the corpse of Patroclus.

The next morning Achilles asked Agamemnon to regard their quarrel as over and said that he was ready to fight at his side. Agamemnon in his turn asked Achilles' forgiveness and returned Briseis, whom he had not harmed; Achilles soon rejoined the fighting, whereupon his horse Xanthus ('the Chestnut'), which had been miraculously and momentarily endowed with the gifts of prophecy and speech, foretold the imminent death of his master. Achilles, disdainful of this warning, advanced to fight and the Trojans fled before him; Aeneas alone, under the inspiration of Apollo, stood up to him. Achilles' spear pierced Aeneas' buckler; Aeneas brandished a huge stone and Poseidon rescued both of them by enveloping them in a cloud. Hector also wanted to attack Achilles, but in vain: the gods were against it and fate for the moment did not allow the two heroes to meet face to face. Achilles continued his advance towards Troy. After fording the river

Scamander, he took twenty young Trojans prisoner intending to sacrifice them at Patroclus' tomb. The river god wanted to stop the bloodshed and kill Achilles, whose victims were blocking his course. The river became swollen, overflowed its banks and pursued the hero, but Hephaestus obliged it to return to its course. Achilles continued his attack towards the gates in order to cut off the Trojan retreat. He was diverted into a fruitless pursuit of Apollo, and when he finally began to make his way towards Troy he had lost his opportunity. Hector was alone in front of the Scaean Gate, but, just as Achilles was drawing close and they were on the point of fighting, he took fright and Achilles chased his enemy round the walls until at last Zeus, raising the scales of fate, weighted Achilles' lot against Hector's, whose scale tipped towards Hades. This was the moment at which Apollo abandoned Hector. Athena appeared and, assuming the likeness of his brother Deiphobus, she inspired Hector with the fatal wish to confront his opponent; he was quickly disillusioned and soon killed, uttering a warning to Achilles that he himself had not long to live. On the point of death he asked Achilles to return his corpse to Priam, but Achilles refused and, after piercing his heels and binding them with a leather thong, he dragged the corpse behind his chariot into the Greek camp. Such were Patroclus' obsequies.

Each day Achilles dragged round the camp the corpse of the enemy who had robbed him of his friend Patroclus, for whom he wept. After twelve days Thetis was bidden by Zeus to let Achilles know that the gods were angry at his lack of respect for the dead, and when Priam came to ask for Hector's body, he was kindly received by Achilles, who gave him back the corpse though he demanded a heavy price for it. That is the story told in the *Iliad*.

In the *Odyssey* we find Achilles in Hades, where he wanders with long strides over the fields of asphodel. He is surrounded by heroes, his friends during the war – Ajax, the son of Telamon, Antilochus, Patroclus and Agamemnon. The last of these told Odysseus of the death of Achilles, but he did not give the name of his killer. The *Odyssey* gives an account of the games held to commemorate Achilles' funeral, and the subsequent quarrel caused by the way in which the hero's arms were awarded (see AJAX, son of TELAMON and ODYSSEUS).

The later stories in the Homeric poems bring the cycle to its close. First there is the tale of the struggle against Penthesilea, the queen of the Amazons who, having come to help Troy, arrived just as the funeral of Hector was taking place. Initially she forced the Greeks to retreat to their camp, but Achilles gave her a mortal wound and just as she was on the point of death he exposed her face. Confronted by such beauty he was stricken with a sorrow so obvious (for he was incapable of concealing his emotions) that Thersites derided his love for a corpse. With a single blow of his fist Achilles killed him.

A further story records Achilles' struggle against Memnon, the son of Aurora, which took place in the presence of their respective mothers Thetis and Eos. Finally comes the tale of Achilles' love for Polyxena, one of Priam's daughters. After he set eyes on Polyxena during the recovery of Hector's body Achilles fell so deeply in love with her that he promised Priam that he would betray the Greeks and come over to the side of the Trojans if he would agree to give her to him in marriage. Priam accepted these terms and the agreement was to be signed in the temple of Apollo Thymbrius which stood not far from the gates of Troy. Achilles came to the appointed place unarmed and there Paris, hidden behind the statue of Apollo, slew him. The Trojans seized his corpse and demanded the same ransom for it as they had had to pay to recover Hector's body.

This romantic version of the hero's end seems to be a late one: other authors say that Achilles met his end in battle at a moment when he had once again driven the Trojans right back to the walls of their city. Apollo confronted him and ordered him to withdraw and, when he refused to obey, killed him with an arrow. In some versions the actual archer is said to be Paris, but Apollo is said to have guided the arrow to strike Achilles at his only vulnerable place, his heel. A struggle took place round Achilles' body, no less bloodthirsty than that which had marked Patroclus' death. Ajax and Odysseus eventually managed to intimidate their enemies and were able to carry the body back to the camp. The funeral was celebrated by Thetis and the Muses, or the Nymphs. Athena anointed the body with ambrosia to preserve it from decay. Later, after the Greeks had erected a tomb in Achilles' honour beside the sea, there was a story that Thetis removed his body to the White Island at the mouth of the Danube where he had a mysterious existence. Sailors passing close to the island heard by day the incessant clashing of weapons and by night the clinking of cups and songs from a feast that never ended. And in the Elysian Fields Achilles is said to have married Medea, or Iphigenia, or Helen, or Polyxena. There is also a tale that, after Troy had been taken but before the Greeks had left the country, a voice from Achilles' tomb had been heard demanding that Polyxena should be sacrificed in his memory.

The memory of Achilles remained very fresh in the popular Greek imagination and his cult was widely practised in the islands, as well as on the Asiatic mainland, the scene of his achievements.

As depicted by Homer Achilles was a very handsome young man, fair-haired, with flashing eyes and a powerful voice, who did not know the meaning of fear. His greatest passion was fighting: he was impetuous and loved glory above all else, but he also had qualities of mildness and even tenderness. He was musical and could charm away care with lyre and song; he loved his friend Patroclus, and shared a loving life with Briseis. He could be cruel, as he was when he ordered the execution of the captured Trojans, and when, from beyond the grave, he demanded that Polyxena should be sacrificed at his tomb, but he was nevertheless hospitable and could weep with Priam when the latter came to recover his son's body. In the Elysian Fields he rejoiced to learn that his son Neoptolemus was a man of courage. He revered his parents, confided in his mother, and, when he knew the gods' will, lost no time in carrying it out. Despite all these civilized characteristics, Achilles was taken by Hellenistic philosophers, and by the Stoics in particular, for the archetype of the man of violence, a slave to his emotions, and they were very ready to contrast him with Odysseus, the perfect example of the man of judgement. We also know of the cult consecrated to Achilles by Alexander who took him as his pattern. Both of them died young.

Achilles was the source of inspiration of many works of ancient literature, starting with the *Iliad* and ending with the *Achilleid* of Statius. He plays a part in many tragedies, notably Euripides' *Iphigenia in Aulis*.

Acis (Ἄκις) The god of the river of the same name, near Etna. He was supposed to be the son of the Italic god Faunus and the Nymph Symaethis. Before being a river, he had loved the Nymph Galatea who was also loved by the Cyclops Polyphemus, but with no hope of success. In his intense jealousy, Polyphemus tried to crush his rival under some rocks, but Acis turned himself into a river, and thus escaped from the giant.

The Parthenon (the temple of Athena Parthenos) at sunrise. This temple was built on the highest part of the Acropolis at Athens; it was begun in 447 BC and dedicated in 438 BC.

Acontius (Ἀκόντιος) A very handsome young man from the island of Chios who belonged to an affluent though not noble family. One year he went to the festivals in Delos, where he saw a girl accompanied by her nurse who had also come to worship the gods of Delos. She was so lovely that Acontius instantly fell in love with her. Her name was Cydippe and she was the daughter of a distinguished man who was at the time passing through Delos. Acontius followed Cydippe right to the temple of Artemis, where she sat down while the sacrifice was taking place. Then Acontius picked a quince and on it scratched with the point of a knife 'I swear by the temple of Artemis that I will marry Acontius'. Then he adroitly threw the quince towards the girl. The nurse picked it up and handed it to Cydippe who innocently read the writing on it out loud. On realizing the meaning of the words she was uttering, she blushed and quickly threw it a long way from her, but she had,

though quite unintentionally, uttered a form of words which bound her to Acontius. Moreover, the goddess Artemis was a witness of the oath. Acontius returned to his native Chios, consumed by love for the girl whom he regarded as his betrothed. Cydippe's father, however, was preparing for her engagement to a husband of his choice. When the celebrations began Cydippe fell so suddenly and seriously ill that the engagement had to be postponed till later. The girl immediately recovered, but three times, at each attempt to arrange the betrothal, her mysterious illness returned. News of these happenings reached Acontius, who hurried to Athens (Cydippe was an Athenian) and hourly and daily asked about the health of his loved one, to the point where he became the talk of the town. People began to think that he had bewitched the girl. Her father went to consult the oracle at Delphi and the god disclosed to him that Cydippe was bound by an oath and that she was punished by the anger of Artemis each time she was on the point of committing perjury. When her father learned the truth in this way he made enquiries about the family of Acontius which seemed to him to be entirely suitable to be united with his own, and soon a happy marriage rewarded the young man's trick. (See also HERMOCHARES).

Acrisius (Ἀκρίσιος) Abas, king of Argos, the son of Lynceus and Hypermestra, was the father of twin sons, Proetus and Acrisius (Table 31). The two children, who were a reincarnation of the hatred between their ancestors Aegyptus and Danaus, fought each other while they were still in their mother's womb, and when they grew up their antagonism was as strong as ever. They openly declared war on each other to find out which of them should succeed to the throne of Argos, which their father had left them at his death. The story goes that it was during this war that round shields, which were destined to be so widely used in warfare in antiquity, were first invented. Eventually, after a long struggle, victory went to Acrisius, who expelled his brother; the latter went to Lycia where he married Anteia, who was known to the tragic poets as Stheneboea. Her father King Iobates, at the head of a Lycian army, restored Proetus to the Argolid and set him up at Tiryns, which the Cyclops had fortified for him with huge stones. At this point the brothers decided to come to an agreement whereby Acrisius reigned at Argos and Proetus at Tiryns, thus dividing the kingdom of the Argolid into two equal parts.

Acrisius had a daughter, Danae, by his wife Eurydice, the daughter of Lacedaemon. He wanted to have a son and consulted the oracle, who told him that his daughter would bear a son, but that the latter would kill him. In order to thwart the oracle's prediction, Acrisius had an underground room built of bronze, where he kept Danae under strict guard, but it was ineffective in preventing Danae from being seduced. Some say that her uncle Proetus was the culprit, but the majority attribute the deed to Zeus who seduced her in the form of a shower of gold which fell through a crack in the roof and thereby into her womb. When Acrisius heard of Danae's seduction he refused to believe in its divine origin and put her and her baby into a chest which he left to its fate on the sea. The child was the hero PERSEUS. Dictys rescued him from the beach at Seriphos, where the flood tide had cast him up. Later

Perseus wanted to see his grandfather again and in order to do so he returned to Argos with his mother and Andromeda, his wife. When Acrisius learned that Perseus was preparing to come and see him he was afraid that the oracle's prediction would be fulfilled and left for Larissa in Thessaly, in the land of the Pelasgians, at the furthest point of Greece, equally far from Seriphos and Argos and well away from the road between them. When he arrived at Larissa he found that King Teutamides was holding games in honour of his father, and that Perseus had come there to compete. At the very moment of Perseus throwing the discus a violent wind sprang up, the discus was unfortunately diverted and struck Acrisius a fatal blow on the head. Perseus, realizing that the prediction had in spite of everything come true, buried Acrisius outside the city and returned to Argos.

Acron King of the Sabine town of Caenina. After the rape of the Sabines he was the first person to take up arms against Romulus. He accepted the latter's challenge and their duel took place before the two armies. Acron was killed by Romulus, who stripped him of his armour and dedicated it to Jupiter Feretrinus on the Capitol. This was the origin of the ceremony of the Opimian Spoils.

Actaeon (Ἀκταίων) Aristeus, son of Apollo and the Nymph Cyrene, had by Antonoe, Cadmus' daughter, a son named Actaeon; he was brought up by the Centaur Chiron who taught him the art of hunting. One day Actaeon was devoured by his own dogs on Mount Cithaeron. There are differing accounts of his death: some say that this was his punishment from Zeus for having tried to rob him of the love of Semele, but most authors ascribe it to the wrath of the goddess Artemis, incensed at having been seen naked by Actaeon when she was bathing in a spring. The goddess incited his pack of fifty hounds to fury and she set them on him. They ate him without recognizing him, then hunted for him in vain throughout the forest, which echoed with their howls. Finally their search brought them to the cave where the Centaur Chiron lived and he made a statue in the semblance of Actaeon to calm them down.

Actor (Ἄκτωρ)
1. A Thessalian hero, sometimes said to be the son of Myrmidon and Pisidice who was one of the daughters of Aeolus (see MYRMIDON), and some-

Artemis inciting Actaeon's hounds to tear the hunter to pieces to punish him for having seen her bathe naked. Crater by the Pan painter c. 470 BC. Boston, Museum of Fine Arts.

times said to be a Lapith, the son of Phorbas and Hyrmine, the daughter of Epeius (Table 23) and Helios. In the latter version Actor was accordingly the father of Augias (Table 14). The traditions about his descendants are as variable as those about his ancestry. Sometimes he is regarded as the father of Menoetius, and consequently the grandfather of Patroclus, and sometimes he is taken to be the human father of the Molionidae Eurytus and Cteatus and the dynasty of Elis (see THALPIUS). Like many of the Thessalian heroes he had a Peloponnesian double. Actor reigned at Pheres in Thessaly and Peleus came to him when, after being banished by his father for having killed

Phocus, he was searching for someone who was willing and ready to purify him. Actor agreed to do so, kept Peleus near him, and on his death bequeathed him his kingdom. According to this version of the legend Actor was said to have had a son, EURYTION (3), who took part in the Calydonian hunt, and a daughter, Philomela.
2. Another Actor, from Orchomenos, was a descendant of Phrixus (Table 33).

Admete (Ἀδμήτη) The heroine of a Samian legend. She was the daughter of Eurystheus and great-granddaughter of Perseus (Table 31), and lived at Argos where she was the priestess of Hera. One version of the legend of the Amazons says that it was for her that Heracles went to search for the girdle of the Queen of the Amazons. Admete performed her religious duties for fifty-eight years, but when her father died she had to flee from Argos and sought refuge in Samos, taking with her the cult statue of the goddess which had been entrusted to her charge. In Samos she discovered a very ancient shrine of Hera, founded in the distant past by the Leleges and the Nymphs, and there she put the statue.

The Argives were dismayed by the disappearance of the statue and commissioned Tyrrhenian pirates to go in search of it. Moreover they hoped that the Samians would hold Admete responsible for the statue and would punish her if it had been stolen. As the temple in Samos had no door the pirates had no difficulty in taking the statue away, but when they tried to set sail they found they could not cast off and they understood from this that the goddess wanted to stay in Samos. Accordingly they placed the sacred statue on the shore and offered a sacrifice to her. Meanwhile, Admete had become aware that the statue had vanished and she alerted the inhabitants who looked everywhere for it. Eventually they found it, abandoned on the shore by the departing pirates. They consequently supposed that the goddess had come there on her own initiative and they bound the statue in rushes. When Admete arrived she unfastened it, purified it and consecrated it afresh, for it had been sullied by being touched by human hands, then she brought it back to its temple. As a reminder of this episode the inhabitants of Samos celebrated an annual festival during which the statue of Hera was carried to the shore freshly consecrated and given offerings.

Pausanias claims that the Argive statue of Hera was brought to Samos not by Admete but by the Argonauts.

Admetus (Ἄδμητος) King of Pheres in Thessaly, the son of the Pheres after whom the country was named and Periclymene. In his youth he took part in the hunt for the wild boar of Calydon and in the expedition of the Argonauts. On his father's death he became king, and fell in love with Alcestis, daughter of Pelias, the king of Iolcos, who had determined to give his daughter only to a man whose chariot should be drawn by a lion and a wild boar yoked together. Apollo, who was at that time Admetus' drover, provided his master with the necessary pair of animals, perhaps in gratitude for the good treatment he had received

during his period of servitude, or perhaps because he was himself enamoured of Admetus.

Having won the hand of Alcestis in this way thanks to the god's help Admetus omitted to offer a sacrifice to Artemis during the marriage celebrations and in her anger she filled the bridal chamber with snakes. Apollo promised Admetus that he would appease his sister and at the same time he asked the Fates on Admetus' behalf that he should not die on the day fixed by Destiny, if he found someone who would agree to die in his stead. To win this favour Apollo resorted to a subterfuge and made the Fates drunk, but when the day came on which Admetus was due to die, no one was willing to give their life for his except his wife. But Heracles, Admetus' former comrade on the expedition of the Argonauts, happened to be passing through Pheres at the very moment of Alcestis' death. Seeing no one save mourners in the palace and hearing cries of grief on all sides, he asked the cause of it and on hearing that the queen was dead he went down into the Underworld and brought back Alcestis, younger and lovelier than ever. This was the tradition followed by Euripides in his *Alcestis*. According to another version Heracles played no part in rescuing her but Persephone in admiration for her self-sacrifice returned her spontaneously to the light of day. Admetus had three children, Eumelus, Perimele and Hippasus (Table 21).

Adonis (Ἄδωνις) The fable of Adonis is derived from a Syrian legend, mentioned as early as Hesiod. The most generally accepted version is as follows. Theias, king of Syria, had a daughter, Myrrha or Smyrna, who was impelled by the wrath of Aphrodite to want to commit incest with her father. With the help of her nurse Hippolyta she succeeded in deceiving Theias, with whom she spent twelve nights, but on the twelfth night Theias realized how his daughter had deceived him and armed with his knife pursued her with the aim of putting her to death. Myrrha put herself under the protection of the gods, who changed her into a myrrh tree. Ten months later the bark of the tree rose and burst open and a child emerged, who was called Adonis. Aphrodite, moved by the infant's beauty, sheltered it and entrusted it secretly to Persephone to bring up, but she too was so taken by the child's beauty that she did not want to give it back to Aphrodite. This argument between the two goddesses was settled by Zeus (another version says by the Muse Calliope in the name of Zeus) and it was decided that

Adonis should spend one-third of the year with Aphrodite, one-third with Persephone and one-third wherever he chose, but Adonis always spent two-thirds of the year with Aphrodite and only one-third with Persephone. Later, the anger of Artemis (provoked for reasons which are not exactly known) caused him to be gored by a wild boar during a hunt, and he was fatally injured.

This first outline of the myth, which can be seen as symbolic of the mystery of natural growth, embodied in this child who is born of a tree, spends a third of the year underground and for the remainder comes into the daylight to join forces with the goddess of springtime and love, was subsequently both embellished and elaborated. The reason often given for the curse of Artemis upon Myrrha is that Cenchreis, mother of Smyrna, and wife of Cinyras (who here takes the place of Theias) had offended the goddess by claiming that her daughter was more beautiful; Smyrna's desire for an illicit love was a punishment for Cenchreis' presumption. As soon as she realized the incestuous nature of her passion, Smyrna wanted to hang herself but her nurse advised her to satisfy her love. Once incestuous intercourse had taken place the girl hid herself in shame in a forest where Aphrodite, taking pity on her victim, changed her into a tree. Smyrna's father who cleft the bark of the tree with his sword, thus bringing the baby Adonis into the world, but in yet another version it was a wild boar which freed the child from the protecting tree by opening it up with his tusks, thus foretelling the young man's death. It pleased the imagination of Hellenistic poets to think of Adonis as having been brought up by the Nymphs, hunting or leading his flocks in the country or the forest. The tragedy which led to his death was sometimes said to have been caused not by Artemis but by the jealousy of Ares, Aphrodite's lover, or, on yet another hypothesis, by the vengeance of Apollo on Aphrodite who had blinded ERYMANTHUS, the god's son, because he had seen her bathing naked.

The Adonis legend is set sometimes on Mount Idalion, sometimes in Lebanon. A river called the Adonis flowed through Byblos, its waters coloured red every year on the day when the death of Adonis was celebrated.

The story of Adonis provides a basis for several legends about flowers, not merely the mythical origin of myrrh (the tears of Myrrha) but also that of the red rose, which was originally white. As Aphrodite was running to the assistance of her wounded friend she pricked her foot on a thorn

and the flowers dedicated to him were coloured by her blood. Anemones too were said to be born of the blood of the wounded Adonis. The idyllic poet Bion tells that the goddess shed as many tears as Adonis shed drops of blood; from each tear sprang a rose and from each drop of blood an anemone.

In honour of her friend, Aphrodite established a funeral feast, celebrated each spring by the Syrian women. Vessels and boxes were planted with seeds, which were watered with warm water to make them grow very quickly, and they were called gardens of Adonis. Plants thus brought on unnaturally quickly, died soon after they appeared above the surface, thus symbolizing the fate of Adonis, and the women uttered ritual laments over the fate of the youth beloved of Aphrodite.

The Semitic roots of this legend are plain to see, even the name of the god can be traced back to a Hebrew word meaning 'lord'. Adonis is found depicted on Etruscan mirrors, and his cult spread throughout the Mediterranean world in the Hellenistic period.

Adrastus (Ἄδραστος) An Argive king whose legend is closely linked to that of the Expedition of the Seven against Thebes. Ever since Proetus had shared the kingdom of Argos between himself and the two sons of Amythaon, Bias and Melampus (see the legend of Proetus and the Proetids, under MELAMPUS and Table 1), three families jointly ruled the country, but soon disagreements broke out between the three. During a riot Amphiaraus, the descendant of Melampus, killed Talaus, the father of Adrastus, who was one of the descendants of Bias (or, in some versions, the victim is Pronax, one of the sons of Talaus). Adrastus thereupon fled to Sicyon, near his maternal grandfather, the king Polybus (Table 22), who died without male children and left him the kingdom. Once he was king of Sicyon, Adrastus' first move was to make peace with Amphiaraus and he then returned to the throne of Argos, but at heart Adrastus had never forgiven his cousin for the murder of his father. He gave Amphiaraus the hand of his sister Eriphyle and it was agreed that any further dispute between them would be left to her decision. Adrastus felt confident that in this way he would one day have the means of exacting his revenge, but it so happened that Polynices, Oedipus' son, was forced to leave Thebes by his brother Eteocles and at the same time Tydeus, son of Oeneus, King of Calydon, was exiled by his father because of a murder. One stormy night the two heroes appeared together to seek asylum in Adrastus' palace and they began to quarrel in the palace forecourt. Adrastus, who was woken up by the noise, made them both come inside and started by cleansing Tydeus of the dirt with which he was covered. Afterwards, realizing that the two heroes had fought like lion and wild boar (or perhaps seeing the two animals depicted on their armour) he remembered an ancient oracle to the effect that he would give his daughters in marriage to a lion and a wild boar. He gave the elder, Argia, to Polynices, and the younger, Deipyla, to Tydeus, and promised to take them both back to their countries and restore their rights. That was the start of the Expedition of the Seven against Thebes, in which the descendants of Bias and Melampus, as well as those of Proetus, that is, the three ruling houses of the Argolid, took part. According to later additions to this original legend, allies also came from Arcadia and Messenia, that is, from the rest of the Peloponnese with the exception of the Myceneans, whose princes, Agamemnon and Menelaus, the descendants of Atreus, foresaw that the war was bound to end in disaster. Under the leadership of Adrastus the seven chiefs were Amphiaraus, Capaneus, Hippomedon, Adrastus' nephew Parthenopaeus (sometimes said to be Adrastus' brother), Tydeus and Polynices. On their way the chiefs halted at Nemea, where they offered funeral games in honour of the young Archemorus who had been killed by a snake before their eyes (see AMPHIARAUS). This was the origin of the Nemean Games. On the river Ismenos the seven gained their first victory against the Thebans and drove them inside their walls, but when they attacked the city, their whole army was exterminated. Adrastus alone escaped with his horse Areion, conspicuous for his black mane. After this the story takes different forms. In one, Adrastus, a skilful orator, managed to persuade the Thebans to hand over the bodies of their victims; in the other – and this is the Athenian version – Adrastus fled to Athens, without resting on the way, to place himself under the protection of Theseus. The latter was said to have taken the field against Thebes, regained the bodies by force and buried them at Eleusis.

Wholly undeterred by the outcome of the first expedition, Adrastus is said to have undertaken a fresh war against Thebes ten years later with the sons of those who had died in the earlier venture. His army was not so large but the omens were favourable. The Epigoni (the name given to the sons of those who had died earlier) took Thebes and established Polynices' son Thersandrus on the throne. But Adrastus lost his own son, Aegialeus, who was killed by Laodamas, the son of Eteocles. The aged Adrastus died of grief at Megara. There is also a story that, in obedience to an oracle of Apollo, he cast himself into the fire. Adrastus had six children by his wife Amphithea, the daughter of Pronax. His four daughters, Argia, Hippodamia, Deipyle and Aegiale married respectively Polynices, Pirithous, Tydeus and Diomedes.

Aeacus (Αἰακός) The most pious of the Greeks, the son of Zeus and the Nymph Aegina, the daughter of the river Asopus. He was born on the island of Oenone, later called Aegina after his mother. Aeacus wanted some companions and a population to rule over, and he asked Zeus to change the numerous ants on the island into human beings. Zeus complied with this request and the people were named Myrmidons by Aeacus, from the Greek (μύρμηκες) meaning 'ant'. Aeacus subsequently married Endeis, the daughter of Sciron and fathered two sons, Telamon and Peleus (see also CYCHREUS). Some writers, who apparently give the earliest version of the legend, do not recognize any relationship between Telamon and Peleus and cite only the latter as the son of Aeacus.

Later, Aeacus coupled with Psamathe, the daughter of Nereus, and fathered a son. Psamathe who like most sea and river divinities possessed the gift of changing her shape, had turned herself into a seal to escape from Aeacus' pursuit, but this was to no avail and the son conceived by this union was given the name of Phocus which recalled his mother's metamorphosis. The son was exceptionally athletic and this made his two brothers Peleus and Telamon so envious that they killed him by throwing a discus at his head and then buried his body in a wood. When Aeacus discovered that this murder had taken place he exiled his sons from Aegina. Aeacus' reputation for piety and justice, demonstrated by his stern judgement against his own sons, resulted in his being chosen out of all the Greeks, to address a solemn prayer to Zeus at a time when fields were barren. This aridity was due to Zeus who was angry with Pelops for dismembering his enemy Stymphalus, the king of Arcadia and scattering his body over the land. Aeacus succeeded in placating Zeus.

It is said that after his death, Aeacus judged the

spirits of the dead in the Underworld, but this belief is comparatively late. Homer knew nothing of it, for he mentions only Rhadamanthys as the judge. Plato is the first source to cite Aeacus in this context. Another legend concerning Aeacus claims that together with Apollo and Poseidon he took part in building the walls of Troy. After the walls had been built, three serpents made their way to the top of them. When two of the serpents approached the sections built by the two gods, they fell dead but the third was able to slide over the section built by the mortal Aeacus. Apollo interpreted this omen as forecasting that Troy would be taken twice, first by a son of Aeacus (meaning the capture by Heracles, together with Telamon and Peleus) and secondly, three generations later, by Neoptolemus, the great grandson of Aeacus and the son of Achilles.

Aechmagoras (Αἰχμαγόρας) Phialo, the daughter of Alcimede of Arcadia, was loved by Heracles by whom she had a son, Aechmagoras. Alcimede told his daughter to expose him to die and abandoned both her and the child on the mountain. A nearby jay heard the infant's cries and tried to imitate them. Heracles heard echoes of the jay's cries and came to the place where he found his lover and his son. He freed the girl from her bonds and saved them both. A neighbouring spring took the name of Cissa ('the spring of the jay').

Aedon (Ἀηδών) According to the *Odyssey*, Aedon was the daughter of Pandareus and the wife of the Theban Zethus (the brother of Amphion). She had only one son and envied the number of children born to her sister-in-law Niobe, Amphion's wife. Driven by her jealousy she tried to kill Niobe's eldest son, Amaleus, in his sleep, but by mistake she killed her own son, Itylus. In her grief she begged the gods' pity and they transformed her into a nightingale (αηδῶν in Greek). There is an alternative legend, no less tragic and equally marked by murders, about the nightingale: in this Aedon was the daughter of Pandareus of Miletus and the wife of the artist Polytechnus. They lived together at Colophon, in Lydia, and had a son, Itys. So long as they honoured the gods Polytechnus and Aedon were happy, but their good fortune filled them with pride and they boasted that they were more closely united than Hera and Zeus. The former sent Eris or Discord to punish them, and they were filled with the desire to outdo each other. Both set to work, he building a chariot, she weaving, the first to complete their task having to give the other a serving maid. With the help of Hera, Aedon won the contest.

The resentful Polytechnus resolved on revenge. He went to Ephesus and asked his father-in-law to allow him to take Chelidon, Aedon's sister, to stay with her. On the journey he ravished her, gave her the clothes of a slave, cut off her hair and threatened her with death if she told her sister who she was. When he got back to Aedon he gave Chelidon to her as a serving maid. She stayed in her sister's service for some time without being recognized, but one day when she was lamenting her misfortunes at the well Aedon overheard and recognized her and they both resolved to take their revenge. They killed Itys, served his body on a dish for his father to eat, and fled towards Miletus. Polytechnus, learning from a neighbour the nature of the food he had eaten, immediately left in pursuit of them but was stopped by the servants of Pandareus, whose daughters had told him the whole story. Polytechnus was arrested, smeared all over with honey and laid out in a meadow. Plagued by flies, he aroused the pity of Aedon who drove off the flies. Her brothers and sisters, enraged by this, wanted to kill her immediately, but Zeus took pity on this heartbroken family and changed them all into birds, Pandareus into a sea-eagle, Harmothoe, Aedon's mother, into a halcyon, Polytechnus into a green woodpecker, because Hephaestus had previously given him a woodpecker, Aedon's brother into a hoopoe, Aedon herself, as her name shows, into a nightingale, and Chelidon into a swallow (for which the Greek word is χελίδων). Through an act of special kindness on the part of Artemis (to whom she had cried for help when her brother-in-law was ravishing her), Chelidon was granted the right to live among humans.

Aeetes (Αἰήτης) The son of Helios and the sea-nymph Perseis (Table 14). He was given the kingdom of Corinth by his father but soon left for Colchis, a country lying at the foot of the Caucasus, on the coast of the Black Sea. His sisters were the sorceress Circe, who gave Odysseus such an unexpected reception and Pasiphae, the wife of Minos. The traditions about the name of Aeetes' wife are inconsistent. One says she was Eurylyte, another makes her the Nereid Neaera, a third the sea-nymph Idyia, the daughter of Oceanus, and the last Hecate the sorceress, his own niece and daughter of Perseus, king of Tauris (see MEDEA).

In Colchis Aeetes ruled over Aea and his capital was the town of Phasis on the banks of the river of the same name. When Phrixus arrived at Colchis, having fled with his sister Helle on a ram with a golden fleece which carried them over land and sea, he was welcomed by the king, who gave him in marriage one of his daughters, Chalciope (Table 33). Phrixus sacrificed the miraculous ram to Zeus and gave the fleece to Aeetes, who nailed it to an oak tree in a wood dedicated to Ares, the god of war. Jason, being ordered by Pelias to bring him the Golden Fleece, went with his companions in search of it. When they reached Aea, after a very adventurous voyage (see ARGONAUTS), the king promised them the fleece provided that Jason succeeded in accomplishing various feats, thinking by this means to get rid of him. But Jason, with the help of Medea, Aeetes' own daughter, succeeded in taming huge bulls and in overcoming other tests which were set him. Aeetes then openly refused to let him have the fleece and tried to burn the *Argo*. Jason took the fleece by force and fled, taking Medea with him. Aeetes went in pursuit of them but his daughter took her little brother, Apsyrtus whom she killed and dismembered, scattering the limbs on the sea. Aeetes, by waiting to gather them up, allowed Jason to escape. He lost heart and gave up the chase. At a later date Aeetes is said to have been dethroned by his brother Perses, and restored to his rights by Medea, who had returned without being recognized.

Aegaeon (Αἰγαίων) Among the hundred-handed giants (the Hecatoncheires) there was one called Briareus by the gods and Aegaeon by mortals. Together with his brothers he took part in the struggle against the Titans in alliance with the Olympians. Sometimes he is portrayed in the role of warder of the Titans in their underground prison, together with his two brothers, and sometimes it is said that Poseidon rewarded him for his courage in the struggle by giving him the hand of his daughter Cymopolea and exempting him from keeping guard over the Titans. When the Olympians Hera, Athena and Poseidon wanted to put Zeus in chains it was to Aegaeon that Thetis turned for help, and his mere presence and the fear of his prodigious strength was enough to deter them from their plan.

Oddly enough, one tradition claims that this faithful friend and loyal adherent of Zeus was an ally of the Titans, with whom he is said to have fought against the Olympians.

Aegestes (Αἰγέστης) Aegestes, or Acestes, was the son of the Sicilian river-god Crimisus and a Trojan woman named Aegesta or Segesta, who received Aeneas and the Trojans hospitably when they reached Sicily. There are a number of differing explanations of how this Trojan female deity first arrived in Sicily, so far from her native land. According to Servius, after Laomedon refused to pay the fee he owed to Apollo and Poseidon for building the wall around Troy the gods inflicted calamities on the country: Poseidon sent a sea-monster to lay waste to the land while Apollo caused an epidemic to break out, and, when questioned, made it clear that to banish the epidemic, the youngest generation of noble families must be given up to feed the monster. Many Trojans hastily sent their offspring abroad, and Hippotes, or Hippostratus, entrusted his daughter Aegesta to merchants who brought her to Sicily. There the river-god Crimisus coupled with her in the shape of a dog or a bear and she gave birth to Aegestes who founded the town of Aegestes or Segestes. According to Lycophron, Aegesta was the daughter of Phoenodamas, a Trojan who advised his fellow-Trojans to give Hesione, the daughter of Laomedon, to the monster. In revenge Laomedon handed over Phoenodamas' three daughters to some sailors with instructions that they should be left out in the open in Sicily where the wild beasts could eat them. Thanks to Aphrodite's intervention the three girls escaped death. One of them, Aegesta, married the river-god Crimisus. In this version, her son, Segestes, founded the three towns of Segestes, Eryx and Entella. According to one tradition Aegesta, the daughter of Hippotes, returned from Sicily to Troy where she married Capys and gave birth to a son, Anchises.

According to Dionysus of Halicarnassus, a grandfather of Aegesta who quarrelled with Laomedon and roused the Trojans against him was put to death by the king, together with all the male members of his family. Laomedin was reluctant to have the females of the family killed, and gave them to merchants. A young Trojan embarked with them and followed them to Sicily; there he married one of them and fathered Aegestes who was brought up in Sicily and adopted the customs and language of the country. After Troy was attacked, he returned to defend it with Priam's permission, but when the city was lost he went back to Sicily, taking with him Elymus, an illegitimate son of Anchises. Lastly, Strabo says that the companions of Philoctetes helped him to found Segestes.

Another Aegestes was a priest at Lanuvium.

After the founding of the city of Alba the images of the Penates, taken to Alba from Lanuvium, kept miraculously returning to Lanuvium. Aegestes was sent from Alba to Lanuvium to practise the worship of the Penates at the place where the gods wished to remain.

Aegeus (Αἰγεύς) A king of Athens and father of Theseus. He was himself the son of Pandion, the successor of Cecrops (Table 11). Pandion was forced to leave Athens by the sons of Metion as the result of a revolution and withdrew to Megara where he married Pylia, the daughter of king Pylas, and ultimately took his father-in-law's place on the throne. At Megara Pandion's four sons, Aegeus, Pallas, Nisus and Lycus were born. After Pandion's death his sons marched on Athens and regained power, the eldest Aegeus exercising the largest share, together with sovereignty over Attica. Another tradition makes Aegeus the son of Scyrius and only the adopted son of Pandion; this lay behind the argument of the descendants of Pallas in opposition to Theseus, the legitimacy of whose power they disputed.

Aegeus married first Meta, daughter of Hoples, and secondly Chalciope, the daughter of Rhexenor (or, in another version, Chalcodon). Despite these two marriages he was unable to have a child, a fact which he put down to the anger of Aphrodite Urania, the goddess born of Uranus (see APHRODITE), and he introduced her cult into Athens. Then he went to seek the advice of the Delphic oracle, and the Pythia gave him a baffling reply which ran as follows: 'Do not, thou most excellent of men, unloose the opening which causes wine to gush out from the wine bottle before you have reached the highest point in the city of Athens.' Aegeus returned towards Athens but on the way he stopped at Troezen with Pittheus, the son of Pelops. Pittheus understood what the oracle meant and made haste to make Aegeus drunk and to leave him with his own daughter Aethra on the same night in which the god Poseidon also visited the girl. When he went on his way, Aegeus instructed Aethra that should she give birth to a son she must bring him up without telling him the name of his father, but he left his sandals and his sword under a certain rock, saying that when the child was big enough to move the rock he would have the means to trace his father. The child in question was THESEUS.

Medea came in search of Aegeus and promised him that if he married her the sterility from which he suffered would be at an end. He did so and she gave him a son, Medus. When Theseus on reaching maturity returned to Athens, Medea, whose magical powers enabled her to know who he was, wanted at first to have him killed by Aegeus, but he recognized the boy and it was Medea who had to fly with her own son. Theseus arrived just in time; the sons of Pallas, urged on to revolt against Aegeus, tried to dethrone him, but they were crushed by Theseus.

Aegeus was guilty of the murder of Androgeos and Minos then invaded Attica. The annual tribute imposed of fifty young men and fifty girls gave rise to Theseus' expedition against the Minotaur. This was the undertaking during which Aegeus, by then an old man, lost his life. Theseus promised to hoist white flags on his fleet if he came back victorious but if the ships returned without him, they were to run up black flags. Driven to distraction by the curses of Ariadne, whom he deserted on Naxos, Theseus forgot to change the colour of the sails. Aegeus, who was waiting for his return on the shore, believed that his son was dead and threw himself into the sea which has ever since born his name, the Aegean Sea.

Aegiale (Αἰγιάλεια) The fourth daughter of Adrastus, she married Diomedes, king of Argos but shortly afterwards he left to fight against Thebes and then against Troy. Aegiale remained faithful to him for a long time but later had intrigues with various heroes of whom the last was Sthenelus' son, Cometes. One explanation sometimes given for her behaviour is that Aphrodite, who was wounded by Diomedes in the fighting before Troy, sought her revenge by implanting in Aegiale passions which she was unable to control: alternatively, Aegiale's changed attitude was attributed to the slanders of Nauplius, the father of Palamedes whom the Greeks had stoned to death. In revenge Nauplius went from town to town saying that the husbands were making preparations to bring back from Troy concubines who would take the places of the legitimate wives.

When Diomedes finally returned from Troy he had to extricate himself from the traps set for him by Aegiale and her lover, and escaped to Hesperia in the western Mediterranean.

Aegimius (Αἰγιμιός) The son of Dorus, the mythical ancestor of the Dorians, to whom he gave a legal system while he was living in the valley of the Peneus in northern Thessaly. When the Dorians were driven out by the Lapiths, led by

Coronus, Aegimius appealed to Heracles, whose assistance ensured their victory. By way of gratitude Aegimius adopted Hyllus, Heracles' son, and gave him an equal share of the country with his own sons Dymas and Pamphylus, after whom the three Dorian tribes Hylleans, Dymanes and Pamphylians were named.

Aegina (Αἴγινα) The daughter of the river god Asopus. She was loved by Zeus and abducted by him. Her father travelled all over Greece, hunting for her and he discovered the truth through Sisyphus who wished to have a spring on his acropolis at Corinth. Asopus gave him the Spring of Pirene as a reward but Sisyphus later paid for this treachery in the Underworld. When Asopus returned to his original bed Zeus struck him with lightning and later still, lumps of coal could be found in the bed of the Asopus. Zeus took Aegina away to the island of Oenone and fathered a son (see AEACUS and Table 30). The island subsequently took her name. Later Aegina went to Thessaly, where she married Actor and gave birth to another son, Menoetius, who was to be the father of Patroclus.

Aegisthus (Αἴγισθος) The son of the incestuous relationship between Thyestes and his daughter Pelopia (Table 2). Thyestes was banished by his brother Atreus and lived at Sicyon, a long way from Mycenae. He spent his time thinking of ways in which he could avenge himself on his brother, who had killed his sons, and an oracle told him that he would find an avenger in the form of a son by his own daughter. Accordingly he waited for Pelopia while she was performing a sacrifice by night at Sicyon and secretly raped her when she returned. Then he disappeared, but during the rape Pelopia stole his sword. Later, Atreus married Pelopia without knowing who she was. Pelopia abandoned the incestuously conceived infant after his birth but Atreus discovered the child among shepherds who had taken him in and fed him with goat's milk (the source of his name since αἰζ means 'goat'). Atreus took the child back with him and brought him up as his son. When he became a young man Atreus told him to go to Delphi, capture Thyestes and bring him back, since he intended to put Thyestes to death. (Another version of this story, written by a tragic poet, says that Agamemnon and Menelaus, Atreus' two sons by Aerope, were charged with this mission.) Aegisthus obeyed, brought back Thyestes and was ordered to kill him. Aegisthus

was wearing a sword which his mother had given him, the same sword which had been stolen on the night of the rape. When Thyestes saw the sword, he asked Aegisthus who had given it to him. The young man replied that it was a gift from his mother. Thyestes then begged for Pelopia to be summoned, and he then disclosed the secret of Aegisthus' birth. Pelopia seized the sword and stabbed herself in the breast; Aegisthus pulled it out and went to find Atreus, who was conducting a sacrifice on the shore, believing that his brother was already dead, and delighted at having caused the death. Aegisthus killed him and thereafter he and Thyestes ruled Mycenae.

When Agamemnon and Menelaus were at Troy, Aegisthus, who had stayed behind in the Peloponnese, tried to seduce Clytemnestra. For a long time he had no success, as she had an old seer named Demodocus with her, left behind by Agamemnon, but eventually Aegisthus disposed of Demodocus, and Clytemnestra offered no more resistance. Aegisthus lived with her until Agamemnon returned. Aegisthus posted watchers on the shore to give early notice of Agamemnon's homecoming and when the latter did return, he was received with great demonstrations of friendship and happiness. A great feast was prepared for him, during which he was killed by Clytemnestra. Aegisthus subsequently reigned for seven more years over Mycenae before he was killed by Orestes, Agamemnon's son. Aegisthus had two children, Aletes and Erigone.

Aegypius (Αἰγυπιός) The son of Antheus and Boulis. His mistress was a widow named Timandra whose son, Neophron, was consumed with jealousy and arranged for Aegypius to spend the night with his own mother under the impression that he was with Timandra. When Boulis realized the crime which her son had committed she wanted to tear his eyes out, but Zeus took pity on the family and changed them into birds. Aegypius and Neophron became vultures, Boulis a diver – a bird which traditionally eats only the eyes of its prey, and Timandra became a tit.

Aegyptus (Αἴγυπτος) The hero who gave his name to Egypt, the son of Belus and Anchinoe (Table 3). On his father's side he was a direct descendant of Poseidon, and on his mother's a descendant of the river Nile. He had a brother, Danaus. Belus, who reigned over the lands of Africa, established Danaus in Libya and gave Arabia to Aegyptus who also conquered the land of the Melampodes (meaning, literally, 'black feet') which he renamed Egypt. Aegyptus had fifty sons by different women, and his brother Danaus had fifty daughters (see DANAIDES). The two brothers quarrelled and eventually Danaus fled to the Argolid. Aegyptus' sons went to meet Danaus there and asked permission for his daughters to marry them; Danaus agreed, but on the eve of this marriage he contrived for all the sons to be killed by their intended wives. Aegyptus, his sons all dead, became afraid of his brother and he retired to Aroe where he died.

Aeneas (Αἰνείας) A Trojan hero, the son of Anchises and Aphrodite. Through his father, the son of Capys, Aeneas was a descendant of the race of Dardanus, and hence of Zeus himself (Table 7). For the circumstances of his birth, see ANCHISES. In early childhood Aeneas was brought up in the mountains; when he was five he was taken to the city by his father and entrusted to his brother-in-law Alcathus (husband of his sister Hippodamia) who took charge of his education. Later Aeneas stood out as the bravest of the Trojans after Hector. He was not a member of the reigning house, but predictions had been made at his birth which foretold that power would one day be his. Indeed when Aphrodite revealed her identity to Anchises, after he had coupled with her she said: 'You will have a son, who will rule over the Trojans, and sons will be born to his sons, and so on for all eternity.'

The first encounter between Aeneas and Achilles during the Trojan War took place on Mount Ida, during a series of raids mounted by Achilles on Aeneas' herds. Aeneas' attempts to stand up to the hero were in vain and he had to seek refuge at Lyrnessos, whence he was rescued by Zeus' protecting hand when Achilles sacked the city. On several occasions Aeneas took part in the fighting around Troy. Once he was wounded by Diomedes; Aphrodite tried to save him but she herself received a wound. Apollo then hid Aeneas in a cloud and spirited him far away from the battlefield, but he soon returned to the fray, where he slew Crethon and Orsilocus. He was equally successful during the attack on the Achaean camp. He confronted Idomeneus, though without achieving victory. Then he killed a large number of Greeks and was at Hector's side when the latter put the Achaeans to flight. He was among those fighting around the body of Patroclus, and crossed swords again with Achilles, who of all the Greeks was the only one who was likely to succeed in

killing him, but in the nick of time Poseidon snatched Aeneas away from his enemy by enveloping him in a cloud, having remembered Aphrodite's prophecy that Aeneas would one day reign over the Trojans, and that his children and his children's children would keep this position of supremacy. So in the Homeric saga Aeneas appeared as a hero protected by the gods (whom he obeyed with due respect) and destined for a

Aeneas carrying his father Anchises and the Palladium from the sack of Troy. Silver denarius of Julius Caesar, reverse.

great role: in him lay the future of the Trojan race. All these components were woven together by Virgil in the *Aeneid*, and given expression within the framework of the Roman legend.

Poets after Homer showed Aeneas taking part in the final struggles around Troy, filling the role of the dead Hector in the defence of the city; after the fall of Troy his importance increased still further. Following the extraordinary events surrounding LAOCOON and his sons, he realized that the fall of the city was imminent, and on the advice of his father Anchises and with Aphrodite to guide him, he made his escape to the mountains with Anchises, his wife Creusa and his little son Ascanius. A more fanciful version of the legend claimed that Aeneas was taken by surprise by the Greek attack on the city. He made his escape amid the flames, with old Anchises on his back and Ascanius in his arms – carrying in addition the Penates, the most sacred of the Trojan gods, and also the Palladium. With these relics he withdrew to Mount Ida where he gathered together the scattered Trojans who had survived the massacre and founded another city over which he reigned, thus fulfilling the prediction of Aphrodite – who, it was said, had instigated the Trojan War only in order to strip Priam of the throne and give it to her own descendants (see also ASCANIUS).

The most widely circulated legend, the one which formed the basis for Virgil's epic poem, was the story of Aeneas' travels. After a short stay on Mount Ida (see OXYNIUS), the hero left for Hesperia – the lands of the western Mediterranean. The stages of his journey were as follows: after calling at Samothrace, he went to Thrace and Macedonia, then on to Crete via Delos, and thence to Cythera and so on into Laconia and Arcadia; from there he went to Zacynthus, then to Leucas, and so up the coast of Epirus, landing at Bothrotum, where he met Helenus and Andromache. Finally he reached southern Italy where he harried the many Greek colonies that had been established throughout the region. He then decided to sail round Sicily, avoiding the Straits of Messina (the habitat of Scylla and Charybdis), and making a stop at Drepanum, where Anchises died. When he set sail again, a storm cast him onto the Carthaginian coast (see DIDO). From there he resumed his journey at the order of the gods, who had no wish for him to establish himself peacefully in the city destined to be Rome's rival; he landed at Cumae, which Virgil made the scene of Aeneas' visit to the Sybil and his descent into Hades. He soon left Cumae, and made his way along the shores of Italy to the north-west. He stopped at Caieta (Gaeta) to pay his last respects to his old nurse (see CAIETA), carefully avoided a stop at Circe's island, and finally reached the mouth of the Tiber, where he became embroiled in a series of battles with the Rutuli. Leaving the majority of his companions in the camp that had been set up on the coast, Aeneas himself went up the Tiber as far as the city of Pallanteum, which was later to become the site of the city of Rome (the Palatine); there he sought an alliance with old king Evander, who was of Arcadian origin, but who had in former days been the guest of Anchises, and as such was not hostile to the Trojans. Evander gave Aeneas a warm welcome and sent a body of troops to his rescue, led by his own son Pallas. On Evander's advice Aeneas then went to Agylla, in Etruria, where he encouraged the rebellious subjects of King Mezentius to take up arms against their ruler. But in his absence the troops of Turnus, the Rutulian king, attacked the Trojans' camp and tried to set fire to their fleet. The battle was about to go against the Trojans when the arrival of Aeneas with the allied troops reversed the situation.

Aeneas soon killed his enemy Turnus in single combat. Virgil's epic poem comes to an end with this victory of Aeneas; it makes no direct reference to the later events recorded by the historians – the founding of Lavinium, the struggles against the various local tribes, and the disappearance of Aeneas during a storm. According to these legends, the founder of Rome was merely one of Aeneas' descendants, Romulus. Aeneas' son Ascanius (or Iulus) founded Alba Longa, the metropolis of Rome. For the versions of the legend before Virgil, see LATINUS. Some obscure traditions speak of Aeneas as the direct founder of Rome (see NANUS, and ODYSSEUS); others gave him four sons – Ascanius, Euryleon, Romulus, and REMUS. It is apparent that Virgil's version set the tradition for all the later writers, and that it was the only one still current after the first century AD. The legend of Aeneas had the merit of giving Rome the stamp of respectability by tracing its founders' race back to the very beginnings of recorded time, and attributing to it divine ancestors – Zeus and Aphrodite. Furthermore Rome's grandeur seemed to have been foretold by Homer himself. Finally, in the heart of its empire, Rome seemed to have effected the reconciliation of the two enemy races, the Trojans and the Greeks.

Aeolia (Αἰολία)

1. In the *Odyssey* the island of Aeolia is the home of Aeolus, the Lord of the Winds. It was a rocky floating island, surrounded by a wall of bronze. In later days it was sometimes identified as the island of Strongyle (today's Stromboli), and sometimes as the island of Lipari, both of which belong to the group of the Aeolian Islands.

2. The name Aeolia was also borne by a legendary heroine, daughter of Amythaon and wife of Calydon (Table 1).

Aeolus (Αἴολος)

Several characters are known under this name, though they are not easy to distinguish:

1. The first is the son of Hellen and the Nymph Orseis (Table 8), and hence the grandson of Deucalion and Pyrrha. Dorus and Xuthus were his brothers. His descendants became known as the Aeolians. Aeolus was king of Magnesia, in Thessaly. He married Aenarete, the daughter of Deimachus, by whom he had seven sons: Cretheus, Sisyphus, Athamas, Salmoneus, Deion, Magnes, and Perieres – to whom certain traditions added Macareus, Aethlius, and Mimas. He also had five daughters: Canace, Alcyone, Pisidice,

Calyce, and Perimede (according to some authors Tanagra and Arne were also his daughters). This Aeolus was sometimes identified with the Lord of the Winds (see below), but this title is more often given to Aeolus 2. Aeolus played a part in the tragic love affair of his daughter Canace with Macareus.

2. Aeolus, son of Arne and Poseidon, was the grandson of Aeolus the son of Hellen. His mother is often given the name of Melanippe rather than Arne (and this was the tradition followed in particular by Euripides in his two lost tragedies of *Melanippe*). Melanippe (or Arne) had twins by Poseidon – Aeolus and Boeotus. At their birth, Melanippe's father blinded his daughter and imprisoned her in a dungeon. Then he ordered the twins to be exposed on the mountain. A cow came and fed them with its milk, until some shepherds who had witnessed this miracle took Aeolus and Boeotus in and brought them up as their own sons. Now Metapontus, king of Icaria (according to Hyginus, this should read: 'king of Italy') was unable to have a child by his wife Theano, whose sterility caused him to threaten her with divorce. Theano asked the shepherds to provide her with infants which she could pass off as her own and they gave her Aeolus and Boeotus, whom she presented to Metapontus, making him believe they were his sons. But then Theano herself bore twin sons and became anxious to get rid of the two strangers she had so imprudently introduced into her house – especially since their beauty had made them her husband's favourites. One day when Metapontus had gone to sacrifice to Diana Metapontina, Theano told her sons the secret of Aeolus' and Boeotus' birth. As a result of this, and at her encouragement of her own sons, the four youths fought on a mountain while out hunting and, thanks to Poseidon's help, Aeolus and Boeotus were the victors. They killed Theano's sons, then fled to seek asylum with the shepherds who had taken them in before. There Poseidon disclosed to them that he was their father, and told them that their mother was still a prisoner. The young men hastened to her rescue. Poseidon restored her sight and her sons took her to Metapontum, where they revealed Theano's crimes to King Metapontus. The king married Melanippe, and the two young men left to found cities – one of them Boeotia in Thrace and the other Aeolia in Propontis.

There are other versions of this legend. One of them has Arne-Melanippe, pregnant by Poseidon, not imprisoned by her father, but handed over to an inhabitant of Metapontum, who was passing through Thessaly and who adopted the two children, Aeolus and Boeotus, when he reached home, on the advice of an oracle. When they were grown men Arne's two sons seized the throne of Metapontum, thanks to a revolution. Then they slew their adoptive father's wife (Autolyta, or perhaps Siris), who had begun to quarrel with their mother. After this murder they were forced to flee. Aeolus took himself off to the islands of the Aeolian sea, and there founded the city of Lipara. Boeotus went to Aeolis, later known as Thessaly.

The legend also told how after Aeolus had left Metapontum he was welcomed in the Aeolian Islands by King Liparus, the son of Auson, who gave him both his daughter Cyane in marriage, and his throne while he himself went to Sorrento, on the Gulf of Naples. Aeolus had six sons by Cyane: Astyochus, Xouthus, Androcles, Pheraemon, Iocastus, and Agathyrnus.

Aeolus, son of Poseidon, was often identified with Aeolus the Lord of the Winds who appears in the *Odyssey* (see 1, above). When Odysseus landed on the island of Aeolia during his travels Aeolus received him in friendly fashion, and kept him at his side for a month. When Odysseus left Aeolus gave him a goatskin bottle which contained all the winds except one – the one which would take him straight back to Ithaca. But while Odysseus was asleep, his companions opened the bottle, thinking it was full of wine; the winds escaped, and caused a storm which drove the ship back to the shores of Aeolia. Aeolus assumed that the hero was the victim of divine wrath; he refused to have anything more to do with him, and sent him packing.

Aepytus (Αἴπυτος) The name of several heroes.
1. One was an Arcadian, son of Hippothous and father of Cypselus. One day he attempted to force his way into the temple of Poseidon at Mantinea where he was blinded by the god and died.
2. Another Aepytus was the great-grandson of the first. His father was Cresphontes and his mother was Merope, the daughter of Cypselus (Table 16). During a riot his father and his brothers were killed. Aepytus managed to escape and took refuge with his grandfather. When he had grown up he returned with the help of the Arcadians and the Dorian princes, the sons of Aristodemus and Isthmius, and avenged his father and his brothers. He slew Polyphontes, the leader of the riot who, after the death of Cresphontes had

forcibly taken and married his wife MEROPE. Aepytus freed his mother and reigned over the country. His reputation for virtue and wisdom was so great that his descendants, who till then had called themselves the Heraclids, were given the name of Aepytidae. His immediate successor to the throne was King Glaucus.

3.   Still another Aepytus, the son of Elatus or, in some versions, of Arcas (Table 9) ruled over the whole of Arcadia. He was bitten by a snake while hunting and died. His tomb was not far from Mount Cyllene. He brought up as his daughter Evadne, the daughter of Poseidon, whom Pitane had entrusted to him. Evadne had a son, Iamus by Apollo.

Aerope (Ἀερόπη)
1.   One of the daughters of Catreus, son of Minos. She had two sisters, Clymene and Apemosyne, and one brother, Althaemenes. Catreus asked the oracle to tell him how he would die and the oracle had answered that he was destined to die at the hands of one of his children. Catreus tried to keep the oracle secret, but he could not prevent Althaemenes from knowing of it. Althaemenes promptly fled with one sister Apemosyne. Catreus gave Aerope and her other sister Clymene to Nauplius the traveller, with orders to sell them overseas. Nauplius took the two girls to Argos, where Aerope married Pleisthenes, the country's king. Their marriage resulted in the birth of Agamemnon and Menelaus (Table 2).

According to another tradition Catreus handed over Aerope to Nauplius not from fear that she might kill him but because she had had an affair with a slave, and he told Nauplius to drown her. Moreover Aerope was said to have married not Pleisthenes but Atreus, making him the father of Agamemnon and Menelaus. In an attempt to reconcile the two traditions it has been suggested that Atreus was either the son or the father of Pleisthenes and that Aerope married Pleisthenes first and after his death Atreus, and that the two children, whose father was Pleisthenes, were brought up by Atreus.

While she was married to Atreus, Aerope allowed herself to be seduced by her brother-in-law Thyestes and secretly gave him the golden lamb which guaranteed Atreus his royal power. In spite of this Atreus managed to keep his throne with the help of Zeus, and to punish his wife he threw her into the sea.

2.   Pausanias knew of another Aerope, daughter of Cepheus, who was loved by Ares and died while giving birth to a son. But Ares ensured that the child could continue to suck at his mother's breast.

Aesacus (Αἴσακος) The son of Priam and Arisbe (Table 34), and grandson of Merops from whom he inherited the gift of interpreting dreams. Accordingly when Hecuba, who was pregnant with Paris, dreamt that she gave birth to a blazing brand who set the whole city of Troy on fire, people asked Aesacus the meaning of such a strange dream. He replied that the forthcoming child would be the cause of the destruction of the whole city and advised that it should be killed as soon as it was born. Aesacus' wife died from a snake-bite, and he threw himself into the sea. In pity Thetis changed him into a bird, probably a kind of diver.

Aeson (Αἴσων) A son of Cretheus (Tables 1 and 21). By marrying Polymede, the daughter of Antolycus, he became the great-uncle of Odysseus, but other traditions make him marry Alcimede, daughter of Phylacus (Table 20). He was the half-brother of Pelias and the father of Jason. Pelias robbed him of the kingdom of Iolcos, which had been left him by Cretheus and sent Jason to win the Golden Fleece. When the rumour spread that the Argonauts had been lost, Pelias, no longer fearful, wanted to kill Aeson. The latter asked to be allowed to choose the manner of his death, and poisoned himself with bull's blood. Ovid has a quite different story, in which Aeson saw his son again and was magically restored to youth by the magic of Medea.

Aethalides (Αἰθαλίδης) Son of Hermes and Eupolemia, the daughter of Myrmidon. Aethalides was an exceptional archer. He took part in the Argonauts' expedition, in which he acted as herald. He had inherited from his father an exceptionally good memory, which he retained in Hades after his death. Moreover he did not always stay among the dead but came back to live among men for short periods.

Aether (Αἰθήρ) The personification of the upper sky, where the light is clearer than it is in the lower levels nearer the earth. According to Hesiod Aether was the son of Erebus and Nyx (Darkness and Night) and the brother of Hemera or Daylight. According to other traditions, when united with Day he begot not only Earth, Sky and

Sea, but a number of abstract qualities, among them Grief, Anger, and Falsehood, as well as Oceanus, Themis, Tartarus, Briareus, Gyges, Steropes (which Hesiod considered to be Cyclopes), Atlas, Hyperion, Saturn, Ops, Moreta, Dione and the Three Furies. Among this list, recorded by Hyginus, are perceptible traces borrowed from the Uranus legend. According to Cicero Aether was the father of Jupiter and Caelus (another name for Uranus, the sky personified) and grandfather of the Sun.

Aethilla (Αἴθιλλα) Daughter of Laomedon, she was one of the Trojan women captured when the city fell into the hands of the Greeks. She was given to the companions of Protesilaus and when his ships had to sail along the coast of Thrace at Pallene to take on water after a storm, Aethilla incited her fellow captives to revolt by reminding them of the sufferings they had undergone up to that point and describing the still worse ones which were awaiting them if they reached Greece. She urged them to burn the ships and they did so. The Greeks, having no option but to stay in the country, founded the town of Scione.

Aethra (Αἴθρα) Daughter of Pittheus, king of Troezen, and thus grand-daughter of Pelops (Table 2). She was the mother of Theseus, who through her was the rightful possessor of the throne of Troezen.

Aethra was first wooed by Bellerophon. But when Aegeus arrived at Troezen from Delphi, where he had sought advice from the oracle on how he could best ensure that his line did not die out, King Pittheus, who understood the meaning of the oracle's reply (see AEGEUS), arranged to bring together his daughter and his guest without the latter's knowledge. From this union Theseus was born. It is also said that on the eve of the day on which Aegeus was to arrive Athena inspired Aethra in a dream to go to a neighbouring island and offer a sacrifice to the hero Sphaerus who had been the driver of Pelops' chariot. There she was surprised by Poseidon and ravished by him. The same night she slept with Aegeus, so Theseus could pass as the son of the god as much as that of the man.

When Aegeus returned to Athens Aethra remained at Troezen where she brought up her son (see THESEUS). Later Theseus, having become King of Athens, entrusted to his mother the case of the young Helen, whom he had abducted. The girl's two brothers Castor and Pollux came to rescue her and took Aethra prisoner. She followed Helen to Troy as a slave, voluntarily it is said, and indeed some authors hold that she advised Helen to leave Menelaus and follow Paris. At Troy Aethra brought up her great-grandson Munitus. When the city was taken she was recognized by her grandsons Demophon and Acamas who secured her release.

It is said that at the death of Theseus Aethra killed herself for grief.

Aetna (Αἴτνη) Aetna, whose name eventually became that of the volcano which dominates the town of Catania, was the daughter of Uranus and Ge (Earth) or, by some ancient accounts, of Briareus, the hundred-handed giant. When Hephaestus and Demeter were quarrelling over the ownership of Sicily (land of volcanoes and corn) Aetna stepped in to act as arbitrator. She is sometimes regarded as the mother of the Palici, whom she is supposed to have borne by Hephaestus.

Aetolus (Αἰτωλός) The son of Endymion and a Nymph, Aetolus was king of Elis in the Peloponnese. His brothers and sisters were Paeon, Epeius, Eurydice (or Eurypyle), Naxos and Pisus. In order to settle which of his sons should succeed him Endymion decided to make them run a race against each other at Olympia and to nominate the winner as the future king. Epeius was the winner. Paeon fled to Macedonia. Aetolus stayed in the Peloponnese and succeeded to the throne on Epeius' death, but as he had killed Apis the king of the country he was forced by his victim's sons to go into exile. He went north of the Gulf of Corinth to the mouth of the river Achelous. There, having been received as a guest by Dorus, Laodocus and Polypoctes, he killed them and seized the throne, after first driving out the Curetes. The country was named Aetolia after him. He married Pronoe, daughter of Phorbas, by whom he had two sons, Pleuron and Calydon. (See ENDYMION, ELIS, and Table 24).

Agamedes (Ἀγαμήδης) A famous architect, the son of Stymphalus and great-grandson of Arcas, from whom the name Arcadia is derived (Table 9). His wife was Epicaste, who is said to have had a son by Apollo named Trophonius, whom she brought to Agamedes. She then bore him a son, Cercyon. All three, Agamedes, Trophonius and Cercyon, were equally clever architects who constructed many famous buildings in archaic Greece.

To them were attributed, most notably, the marriage chamber of Alcmene at Thebes, the temples of Apollo at Delphi and of Poseidon in Arcadia, on the road from Mantinea to Tegea, and a royal treasury for Hyrieus, king of Hyria in Boeotia. The following legend is told about this treasury: Agamedes and Trophonius, who had been commissioned to build it, placed a stone so skilfully that they could easily remove it and in the night take what they wanted from the king's treasures. The king discovered the thefts and sought Daedalus' advice on how to catch the criminals. He arranged a trap in which Agamedes was caught. Trophonius cut off his head, so that he could not give away his accomplice's name, but the earth opened and swallowed up Trophonius. In the wood of Lebadeus there was a hole and a stele bearing the name of Agamedes. There stood the oracle of Trophonius, to which offerings were brought and where the name of Agamedes was also invoked.

In a slightly different version of this legend the king in question was not Hyrieus but Augias of Elis. Cercyon, who took part in the theft, fled with Trophonius to Orchomenus but when they were pursued by Daedelus and Augias, Cercyon sought refuge in Athens and Trophonius at Lebadeus.

According to yet another legend Agamedes and Trophonius had built a temple to Apollo, and when they asked the god to pay them, he promised to do so at the end of a week and advised them to lead a happy life in the meantime. On the eighth night the two architects died peacefully, this being the best payment the god could make them.

Agamemnon (Ἀγαμέμνων) Agamemnon appears in the legends primarily as the king placed, in the *Iliad*, in supreme command of the Achaean army. He is sometimes described as a descendant of Atreus, sometimes of Pelops or again of Tantalus (Table 2). In the *Iliad* he appears as king of Argos, or sometimes of Mycenae, and gives the throne of Argos to Diomedes (this last version comes in the Catalogue of Ships, a section which has been interpolated and is later than the rest of the poem). Finally, in the last version of all, Agamemnon was said to be the king of the country Lacedaemon, with his capital of Amyclae.

For his ancestry, see Aerope and Atreus. Agamemnon was married to Clytemnestra, who plays a very large part in his story. She was the sister of Helen and, like her, a daughter of Leda and Tyndareus (Table 19). She was first married to Tantalus the son of Thyestes, but Agamemnon simultaneously killed both Tantalus and a newly born son of Tantalus and Clytemnestra. After this double murder and the marriage of Clytemnestra to Agamemnon, which was far from welcome, her brothers, the Dioscuri, Castor and Pollux, pursued Agamemnon who had to take shelter with his father-in-law Tyndareus. Eventually Castor and Pollux agreed to make their peace with Agamemnon, but Clytemnestra's marriage, which had started with a crime, was under a curse, as the unfolding of the legend proves.

Once married to Clytemnestra, Agamemnon had three daughters, Chrysothemis, Laodice and Iphianassa, and a son, Orestes, the last child to be born. This is the earliest version of the legend. Subsequently there appeared on the scene Iphigenia (not the same person as Iphianassa) and finally, in place of Laodice, the tragic poets name Electra, a figure completely unknown to the author of the *Iliad*. Of all these children, the tragedians were most vividly aware of Iphigenia, Electra and Orestes.

The Trojan War When a crowd of suitors was seeking to win Helen, Tyndareus, on the advice of Ulysses, bound them on oath to respect her decision and not to argue with the chosen suitor about who should have her hand. Furthermore, should he be attacked, the others were obliged to come to his aid. After Paris had abducted Helen Menelaus came to Agamemnon to ask for his help, and Agamemnon reminded the former suitors of the oath they had taken and they formed the nucleus of the army which later attacked Troy. Agamemnon was unanimously chosen as commander-in-chief, either because of his personal bravery or as the result of a clever electoral campaign. The forces gathered at Aulis. In the *Iliad* Zeus immediately sent a favourable omen: after a sacrifice to Apollo, a snake leapt from the altar towards a nearby tree and swallowed eight small sparrows in the nest with their mother, making nine in all. Then the snake turned into a stone. The seer Calchas interpreted this as meaning that Zeus was intentionally giving a sign that Troy would be captured after ten years. Aeschylus had heard of another magic sign: a doe-hare big with young, torn to pieces by two eagles. Calchas interpreted this as meaning that Troy would be destroyed but that Artemis would be hostile to the Greeks.

According to a poem later than the *Iliad* (doubtless the *Cypriot Songs*), the Greeks, who did not know the way to Troy, made their first landing in Mysia and, after various skirmishes, were scattered by a storm, each man making his way back to his own country (see ACHILLES). Eight years after this setback the Greeks gathered at Aulis, but the ships could not sail because of a persistent calm. Calchas, when asked for the reason, replied that the calm was due to the wrath of Artemis. This anger had several possible causes: either that Agamemnon, when he killed a doe, had claimed that Artemis could have done no better, or that Atreus had not sacrificed the golden lamb to Artemis (see ATREUS), or that Agamemnon had promised to sacrifice the most beautiful produce of the year to Artemis in the year in which his daughter Iphigenia had been born and had on that account not carried out his promise. For all these reasons the goddess required a sacrifice, namely Iphigenia. Agamemnon agreed to this either out of ambition or from anxiety for the general good and it swelled still further the grievances of Clytemnestra against her husband.

Once the expedition was under way the fleet put in at Tenedos where the latent hostility between Achilles and Agamemnon surfaced for the first time in a quarrel which foreshadowed the enmity which was to put the Greeks in grave danger before Troy. On Lemnos at about the same time, Agamemnon abandoned Philoctetes because his wound was malodorous and his cries disturbed the sacrifices.

There followed the first nine years of the siege. In the tenth year Agamemnon and Achilles took part in various piratical expeditions against the neighbouring villages. From the spoils they brought back, Achilles took Briseis and Agamemnon took Chryseis, the daughter of Chryses, the priest of Apollo. Chryses asked to be able to ransom his daughter but Agamemnon refused the request and, to punish him, Apollo caused a plague in the Greek army. At this point the *Iliad* begins. The general opinion of the army compelled Agamemnon to give up Chryseis but in return he demanded that Achilles should give him Briseis. This was the pretext for Achilles' anger; he refused and retired to his tent. Agamemnon then took steps to demand Briseis formally through two heralds, Talthybius and Eurybates. Achilles had no option but to give the girl back but he refused to fight. In compliance with a request from Thetis Zeus caused Agamemnon to have a misleading dream which allowed him to believe that he would be able to capture Troy without Achilles. Moreover, there was an ancient

oracle which told Agamemnon that Troy would fall when discord arose in the Achaean camp.

The fighting began: Agamemnon took part in person and performed a number of remarkable feats but was wounded and had to withdraw from the battle. After the attack on the camp, he realized that total defeat faced him unless Achilles returned to fight alongside him; he made his peace with Achilles, restoring Briseis, promising him the hand of one of his daughters, and giving him rich gifts. From this moment onwards Agamemnon is hardly mentioned in the *Iliad* and Achilles becomes the central figure.

Later epics speak of other occasions on which Agamemnon was involved in the events which followed Hector's and Achilles' deaths, especially the fighting which broke out over Achilles' body and the disputes over who should have his weapons (see AJAX, son of Telamon, and ODYSSEUS). The *Odyssey* tells how, after the capture of Troy, Agamemnon had as part of his share Cassandra, the prophetess and daughter of Priam, who bore him twins, Teledamus and Pelops.

The return of Agamemnon and his departure from the Troad also gave rise to epic narratives. The *Odyssey* refers to a quarrel between him and Menelaus, who wanted to leave as soon as the war was ended, while Agamemnon wanted to stay on for a while to win the favour of Athena by giving her gifts. Poems about Agamemnon's return also told how, on the very point of embarking, he saw the ghost of Achilles who sought to make him stay by predicting all his future misfortunes. At the same time the apparition called for the sacrifice of Polyxena, one of the daughters of Priam.

When Agamemnon arrived back in his own country a spy, stationed by Aegisthus, his wife's lover, was on the look-out for him. Aegisthus invited Agamemnon to a great feast and, assisted by twenty men hidden in the banqueting hall, killed him and his companions. Other versions of the same legend speak of Clytemnestra taking part in Agamemnon's murder as well as that of her rival Cassandra. Pindar adds that she hated the whole family of Agamemnon so bitterly that she wanted to kill Orestes, her own son, as well. The accounts given by the tragic poets differ from each other. Sometimes, following Homer, Agamemnon is struck down while at table; sometimes he is killed in his bath, hampered by the shirt with sewn-up sleeves which Clytemnestra had given him. Hyginus says that the main figure in the murder was Oeax who was trying by these means to avenge his brother Palamedes; the latter had been stoned to death on Agamemnon's orders. Oeax seems to have told Clytemnestra that Agamemnon was preparing to replace her by Cassandra, and made her resolve to resort to crime. She is said to have killed him with an axe while he was sacrificing, and to have killed Cassandra at the same time. This story bears a very close resemblance to that of Aegiale and Diomedes.

Eventually Agamemnon was avenged by his son ORESTES.

Agapenor (Ἀγαπήνωρ) Mentioned in the *Iliad's* Catalogue of Ships, as the leader of the Arcadian contingent. He lived at Tegea and was the son of Ancaea and Ios and the grandson of Lycurgus (Table 26). As a former suitor of Helen, bound by an oath sworn to Tyndareus, (see AGAMEMNON) he took part in the Trojan expedition. On his way back from the siege his ship was wrecked and he was cast up on the island of Cyprus where he founded the town of Paphos and built a temple to Aphrodite. While Agapenor was still at Tegea the sons of Phegeus, Agenor and Pronous, met at his house the two sons of Alcmaeon, who killed them in revenge for their father's murder.

Agave (Ἀγαυή) The daughter of Cadmus king of Thebes, and his wife Harmonia. Her sisters were Ino, Semele and Autonoe. She married Echion and had a son Pentheus. After Semele had been killed by a thunderbolt after she rashly asked her lover Zeus to show her how powerful he could be, Agave spread a rumour that Semele had had a liaison with a mortal and that Zeus had punished her for having claimed that she was pregnant by him. Later Dionysus, Semele's son, avenged his mother and punished Agave grievously for her slander. When Dionysus returned to Thebes, where Agave's son Pentheus was then ruling, he ordered all the women in the town to assemble on the mountain of Cytheron to celebrate his mysteries. Pentheus, who was opposed to the introduction of the ritual, tried to spy upon the Bacchantes. He was glimpsed by Agave who took him for a wild beast and tore him limb from limb. When she had returned to her senses she fled terrified from Thebes to Illyria, to the presence of Lycotherses, the king of the country, whom she married. But later she killed him, to ensure that her father Cadmus should possess the kingdom.

Agdistis (Ἄγδιστις) The legend of Agdistis is an eastern tale, coming originally from Pessinus, the country of Cybele the Great Mother of the Gods, and recorded for us by Pausanias. It begins with Zeus having a dream, in the course of which he spilt some semen on the earth which begot a hermaphrodite being called Agdistis. The other gods seized Agdistis and castrated him, and from his penis sprang an almond tree. The daughter of the river-god Sangarius picked one almond from the tree and placed it in her womb. She became pregnant and gave birth to a male child called Attis whom she abandoned in the open. He was cared for and fed by a goat. He grew and became so beautiful that Agdistis (who by that time had become purely female) fell in love with him. To hide him from her advances Attis was sent to Pessinus to marry the king's daughter. The marriage hymn had already been sung when Agdistis appeared whereupon Attis went mad and castrated himself, then the king of Pessinus did the same. Agdistis was so grieved that she was granted as a favour that the body of Attis, who had died of his wound, should remain incorruptible.

Another version of the story has it that on the borders of Phrygia there was an uninhabited cliff called Agdos where Cybele was worshipped in the form of a stone. Zeus, who loved her, tried vainly to marry her but since he could not do so he let some of his semen fall on a nearby rock. This in time begot Agdistis, a hermaphrodite, whom Dionysus made drunk and castrated. From his blood grew a pomegranate tree, from which Nana, the daughter of the god Sangarius, inserted one of the fruits in her womb and became pregnant. This was how Attis came to be born. Sangarius bade her abandon the infant. He was gathered up by some passers-by and reared on honey and billy-goat's milk (*sic*), from which he was called Attis, which in Phrygian means either he-goat (*attagus*) or beautiful. During an argument between Cybele and Agdistis, Attis (who had grown very handsome and to whom Midas king of Pessinus determined to marry his daughter) and his attendants were struck with such madness that Attis castrated himself beneath a pine tree, and died. Cybele buried his body but from the blood which had fallen from his wounds violets grew all round the pine tree. Midas' daughter killed herself in her despair and violets grew from her blood too. Cybele buried her as well and an almond tree grew up over her tomb. Zeus, moved by Agdistis' pleading, granted that Attis' body should remain incorruptible, his hair should continue to grow and his little finger should move. Agdistis then took the corpse to Pessinus, where he buried it and founded a community of priests and a festival in Attis' honour.

Agenor (Ἀγήνωρ) A descendant, through Io and her son Epaphus, of Zeus himself. Epaphus had a daughter, Libya who by Poseidon had twin sons Agenor and Belus (Table 3). While Belus was king of Egypt Agenor settled in Syria and ruled over Tyre or Sidon. He married Telephassa and had by her a daughter Europa and three sons Cadmus, Phoenix and Cilix. When Europa was carried off by Zeus in the likeness of a bull Agenor sent his sons in search of her, with orders not to come back until they had found her, and as one by one the young men regarded their search as being in vain, they founded towns where they set themselves up – in Cilicia, at Thebes and at Thasos in Thrace. Phoenix chose Phoenicia. The traditions about the names of Agenor's sons are not always consistent. Euripides calls them Cilix, Phoenix and Thasos: Pausanias gives the name of Thasos, and Herodotus speaks of Phoenician colonies established in the island of that name, as well as a colony set up in the island of Thera by Cadmus. Diodorus Siculus knew of a colony in Rhodes also set up by Cadmus. These are local legends keeping alive the memory of Phoenician settlements, of whose expansion they are a sign.

Agenor's wife is sometimes said to be Argiope and not Telephassa, or sometimes Antiope her niece, the daughter of Belus.

Aglaurus (Ἄγλαυρος or Ἄγραυλος) Legend knows of two figures of this name.
1. The daughter of Actaeus first king of Athens, and the wife of Cecrops by whom she had a son, Erysichthon, and three daughters Aglaurus, Herse and Pandrosus (Table 4).
2. The daughter of the first, she was loved by Ares, by whom she had a daughter Alcippe. Aglaurus and her sisters come into the legend of Ericthonius. Athena had secretly preserved the life of the little Ericthonius, born of the desire that Hephaestus had shown for her. She hid the infant in a basket and entrusted him to the three daughters of Cecrops, especially Pandrosus. The sisters were too full of curiosity to refrain from opening the basket, in which they saw the child in the coils of a snake. Overcome with fear they all three became mad and threw themselves off the highest rocks of the Acropolis. A crow came to tell Athena of this rash deed.

Ovid tells a different story, saying that Aglaurus, though she was most to blame, was not struck with madness. Some time later Ovid shows her to be jealous of her sister Herse, who was loved by Hermes. The god finally changed her into a stone statue (see CERYX).

Agron (Ἄγρων) On the island of Cos lived Eumelus the son of Merops. He had two daughters, Byssa and Meropis, and a son Agron, all of whom were extremely haughty. They lived on an isolated estate, farming and producing excellent crops. In consequence they restricted themselves to worshipping the goddess of Earth and disregarded the other gods. If the girls were invited to a festival of Athena the brother would take it on himself to refuse on their behalf, saying that he disliked women with eyes like those of owls (Athena had eyes of this colour); if they were invited to a festival of Hermes he would say that he disliked gods who were thieves; if it was a feast for Artemis he said that he disliked women who ran by night. In short he sent back nothing but insults. Artemis, Hermes and Athena decided to get their revenge and one evening they all met at the family's house. Athena and Artemis had assumed the appearance of girls, and Hermes that of a shepherd. Hermes invited father and son to a banquet which, he said, the shepherds were giving in honour of Hermes, and he asked them to send Byssa and Meropis to the wood of Athena and Artemis. When she heard the name Athena Meropis began to insult her. She was immediately changed into an owl. Byssa became the bird of Leucothea (a seagull), Eumelus a crow, and Agron a plover.

Aius Locutius This name twice embraces the idea of speech (*aio* and *loquor*) and belongs to a mysterious god who revealed himself on only one occasion, at the time of the Gallic invasion in 390 BC, in the form of a voice announcing the approach of the enemy. No one took any notice of it, but after the Gauls had been put to flight the dictator Camillus, in order to make amends for the disrespect which had been culpably offered to this divine voice, built a shrine to him at the northern angle of the Palatine hill, the place where the voice had been heard.

Ajax (Αἴας)
1. Ajax of Locri is called the son of Oileus or the Lesser Ajax to distinguish him from Ajax the son of Telamon, or Great Ajax. He was one of the heroes who fought against Troy as commander of

Amphora with Ajax and Achilles playing draughts, painted by Exekias, c. 550–540 BC. Vatican Museum.

the Locrians, bringing with him forty ships. He fought beside his namesake the son of Telamon, but whereas the latter was heavily armed, the son of Oileus was armed only with a breastplate of linen and a bow. He was a participant in all the great battles mentioned in the *Iliad*, and took part in the drawing of lots for the intended duel with Hector; he fought in the battles around the ships, and around the body of Patroclus, and competed in the funerary games given in honour of Patroclus by Achilles.

He is said to have been a man of bad character, and he is also compared unfavourably with his namesake in being arrogant, cruel to his enemies, and quarrelsome, as well as impious. His misdeeds led to the loss of a large part of the Greek army; he committed serious sacrilege against Athena, which brought the goddess's wrath down upon him. During the capture of Troy Cassandra had sought refuge near Athena's altar. Ajax wanted to use force to tear her from the statue which she was clasping, and he carried off both girl and statue. The Achaeans wanted to stone him for this failure to observe the laws governing religious practice,

but Ajax in his turn sought safety near the altar of Athena and so escaped death. But on the return journey, near the island of Myconos in the Cyclades, Athena sent a storm which wrecked a large number of Achaean ships including the one in which Ajax was travelling. Nevertheless he was saved by Poseidon, who brought him back to the surface. Ajax boasted that he had survived in spite of the goddess's wrath, whereupon Athena insisted that he should be destroyed, so Poseidon took his trident and broke the rock on which Ajax had taken refuge and drowned him. There is also a story that Athena herself destroyed him with a thunderbolt, using the weapon of her father Zeus.

But the sacrilege committed by Ajax continued to oppress the Locrians his countrymen. Three years after the return of the heroes from Troy epidemics broke out in Locris and there was a series of bad harvests. On being questioned the oracle replied that these calamities were a sign of the divine wrath, and that Athena would only be appeased if the Locrians sent two girls chosen by lot to Troy each year, for a thousand years, to expiate the rape and the violation of Cassandra. This was done. The Trojans killed the first pair and scattered their ashes on the sea. Their successors thereafter were better treated in the service of Athena but the custom on their arrival was continued: they were pursued by the populace, armed with sticks and seeking to put them to death. If they escaped they repaired barefooted to the shrine of Athena and there they stayed, unmarried, to a very advanced age. This was how the sacrilege against the priestess Cassandra by the son of Oileus was expiated, long after his own death.

2.   Ajax son of Telamon (Table 30) is the Great Ajax. He reigned over Salamis and came to Troy leading the island's contingent of twelve ships. In the Achaean camp he commanded the left wing. Next to Achilles he was the most powerful and the bravest hero in the whole army. Strong, large and very handsome, he was calm and self-controlled. He was heavily armed and his remarkable shield was made of seven layers of oxhides, the eighth and outermost coating being a sheet of bronze.

In terms of morality the son of Telamon was the opposite of the Lesser Ajax, not saying much, benevolent and god-fearing. But if he was steadier than Achilles, with whom he shared many characteristics, he completely lacked the sensitivity, love of music, and kindness of Thetis' son. He was first and foremost a man of war, not without an element of roughness.

Ajax was the hero chosen by lot to fight Hector in single combat. He struck him to the ground with a stone, but the heralds then intervened to stop the fight. During the Achaean defeats he tried again to stop Hector but was wounded and had to leave the field. When Hector launched his attack on the ships Ajax was at the heart of the Achaean defence; and the uneasy Poseidon had recourse to ask him to redouble his efforts. He wounded Hector once more with a stone but the latter returned with new energy and forced him to defend himself on his own ship. When Hector broke his spear on him he acknowledged the will of the gods and took flight. This was the moment at which Patroclus came on the scene and forced the Trojans to turn back. Ajax returned to the battle after the death of Patroclus; Hector was about to attack him and would have done so had not Zeus, in deference to the fate which ordained that Hector should fall under Achilles' blows, enveloped them both in a cloud.

During the funerary games given by Achilles Ajax fought against Odysseus, but neither vanquished the other and Achilles gave them both the prize. When fencing against Diomedes Ajax was not defeated, but neither did he succeed in overcoming his opponent. He did not throw the discus so far as did one of the other competitors.

Legends later in date than the *Iliad* glorified Ajax's reputation and put him nearly on a par with Achilles. He was, like Achilles, made out to be the grandson of Aeacus (see TELAMON). In Attica his mother was said to be Periboea, one of the girls sent by Aegeus to Crete as tribute to Minos, whom Theseus had saved from death when he killed the Minotaur.

When Heracles, came to invite Ajax' father Telamon to take part in his expedition against Troy, he found Telamon in the middle of a banquet. Heracles stretched his lion-skin beneath him and begged Zeus to grant Telamon a son as brave as himself and as strong as the lion to whose skin he pointed. Zeus heard his prayer and, as a sign that he would accede to it, sent an eagle (the origin of the child's name, since Ajax is reminiscent of the Greek word for eagle which is αἰετός). According to another legend Ajax had already been born at the time of the visit of Heracles and the hero wrapped him in his lion-skin, asking Zeus to make him invulnerable with the result that the child grew up to be so, except for those parts which on the body of Heracles supported the quiver: armpit, hip and shoulder.

Gradually Ajax' character as portrayed in the *Iliad* acquired new features. When he left for Troy his father advised him to fight first of all with the spear, but also with the help of the gods. Ajax replied that 'the coward as well could be victorious with the help of the gods'. Then he seems to have removed the picture of Athena from his shield, thereby incurring the goddess's wrath.

There is no account in the *Iliad* but tradition insists that Ajax played an important part in the preliminary expeditions. Having been the first to arrive at the mustering at Argos, with his brother Teucer, he was appointed to command the fleet together with Achilles and Phoenix. He even replaced Agamemnon as commander-in-chief when the latter was removed from that position for having killed the sacred doe of Artemis. After the landing in Mysia, Ajax and Achilles took charge of the operations and, while Achilles was wounding Telephus, Ajax killed Teuthranius, the latter's brother.

During the first nine years of the fighting before Troy Ajax took part in the armed raids against the Asian towns. He attacked the town of the Phrygian king Teleutas, and carried off his daughter Tecmessa. He also laid waste the Thracian Chersonese (now known as the Gallipoli peninsula) of which Polymestor, a son-in-law of Priam, was king. Polymestor surrendered Polydorus, one of his father-in-law's children, of whom he had custody. Ajax also hunted the Trojan flocks, both on Mount Ida and in the countryside.

But it was after Achilles' death, during the final stages of the war, that legends expanded the exploits of Ajax; he is described as welcoming Achilles' son, Neoptolemus Pyrrhus, treating him as his own son and fighting alongside him. He also fought beside the archer Philoctetes, just as, in the *Iliad*, he fought beside the archer Teucer. Once the city had been captured, he demanded that Helen should be punished for her adultery by being put to death, but this roused the sons of Atreus to anger against him, and Odysseus secured her return to Menelaus. Then Ajax demanded the Palladium as his share of the spoils, but Odysseus, under pressure from the Atrides, managed to prevent him taking it. This episode gave rise to dissension. Ajax threatened to take vengeance on Menelaus and Agamemnon. The Atrides surrounded themselves with guards and on the morning of the following day Ajax was found stabbed with his own sword.

Another account of his death, and one better known to the tragic poets, tells how Ajax went mad after being refused not the Palladium but the arms of Achilles. These arms had been destined by Thetis for the bravest of the Greeks or at least for whoever had inspired most fear in the Trojans. To discover who this was the Trojan prisoners were questioned and they, in resentment, named not Ajax but Odysseus and he received the arms. During the night Ajax went mad, slaughtered the flocks which were to feed the Greeks and killed himself in the morning when he realized the state of distraction into which he had fallen.

Ajax was not cremated, as was the normal practice, but placed in a coffin and buried. The Athenians offered him divine honours every year at Salamis.

Alalcomeneus (Ἀλαλκομένευς) A hero supposed to be the founder of the town of Alalcomenes in Boeotia. He is said to have been the founder of the hierogamies of Zeus and Hera, that is, the religious ceremonies symbolizing a marriage between the two. The story was that when the goddess Hera, deceived by Zeus, complained to Alalcomeneus, who had been made responsible for bringing up Athena, about her husband's infidelities, he had advised her to have a statue of herself made of oak and to have it wheeled solemnly through the streets, attended by a retinue, as was done for a marriage. Hera did so, and from this arose a ceremony called the festival of Daedalus. In popular belief this ritual was supposed to revive and renew the divine marriage and to restore its effectiveness by a kind of sympathetic magic.

Alcathus (Ἀλκάθοος) The son of Pelops, king of Elis and his wife Hippodamia, and so the brother of Atreus and Thyestes (Table 2).

King Megareus had a son who had been killed by a lion and had promised the hand of his daughter to anyone who could slay the beast. Alcathus came forward, managed to do away with the lion, and gained the promised reward. He deserted his first wife Pyrgo, and married Eraechme the daughter of Megareus. He simultaneously gained the throne of Onchestus.

Subsequently, when the Cretans sacked the town of Megara, Alcathus, with Apollo's help, rebuilt the ruined walls and in the historical period the stone on which Apollo laid his lyre while he worked on the wall was still pointed out. This stone had kept some extraordinary qualities; when it was struck with a pebble, it reverberated and gave out a musical sound.

One of Alcathus' sons Ischepolis took part in the hunt for the wild boar of Calydon and was killed. His brother Callipolis, who was the first to hear of it, rushed to tell his father and found him performing a sacrifice to Apollo on the citadel. In his haste Callipolis interrupted the ceremony and disturbed the prescribed order of the sacred pyre. Alcathus, angered and thinking that his son wanted to offend the gods, struck him to death with a blow from a burning log (see POLYIDUS).

Alcathus also had a daughter Iphinoe, whose tomb could be seen at Megara.

Alcestis (Ἄλκηστις) One of the daughters of Pelias, king of Iolcos, and his wife Anaxibia (Table 21). She was the most beautiful and pious of women, and the only one of Pelias' children who had no hand in his murder when Medea, by means of tricks and spells, brought about his death at the hands of his own sons (see JASON). When Admetus, king of Pheres in Thessaly, appeared to ask for the hand of Alcestis, Pelias forced him to accept certain conditions which, with the help of Apollo, he met. Euripides tells us that their marriage was a model of connubial bliss, to the extent that Alcestis agreed to die in place of her husband. But after her death Heracles plunged into Hades and he brought her back more beautiful and younger than ever. There was also a story that Persephone, moved by Alcestis' devotion, had spontaneously returned her to the land of the living.

Alcinoe (Ἀλκινόη) A Corinthian woman, married to Polybus, son of Dryas. She incurred the wrath of Athena for the following reason: she had hired a woman to spin for her and when the work was completed refused to pay the agreed sum. The woman uttered curses, calling Athena to witness the dishonesty of Alcinoe. Athena was the patroness and protector of women who spun, and she struck Alcinoe with madness. Immediately the young woman fell in love with a guest, a stranger from Samos, called Xanthus. In pursuit of him she abandoned her husband and children, but in mid journey she came to her senses and in despair, calling on her children and husband, she cast herself into the sea.

Alcinous (Ἀλκίνοος) King of an island which Homer refers to as Scheria; it is probably Corfu. Alcinous was said to be the grandson of Poseidon and his father was called Nausithous. Alcinous himself had five sons and one daughter, NAUSICAA.

Alcinous' wife, who was also his niece, was called Arete (which means indescribable in Greek). She lived in the palace with her husband and children surrounded by honour and respect. Their palace was surrounded by a wonderful orchard, where fruit of every kind ripened all the year round. Arete and Alcinous were beloved by their people, hospitable to strangers and especially to victims of shipwreck, whose lot they tried to alleviate.

One of these victims was Odysseus who was shipwrecked when returning from Calypso's island. Having refreshed Odysseus and listened, during a banquet, to the long tale of his adventures, Alcinous gave him a ship on which to return to Ithaca, which is not far from Corfu, and loaded him with gifts.

In the *Argonautica*, Medea and the Argonauts landed in Alcinous' country and found, at his court, a group of envoys from Medea's father, Arete, with orders to bring Medea back to him. Alcinous was chosen to arbitrate between the two sides. He decided that if Medea was still a virgin, she should be sent back to her father; if not she should be left with Jason. Faced with this decision, Arete hastened to marry the young couple and so save Medea from the punishment which awaited her at Colchis (see ARGONAUTS). Not daring to appear before their king the natives of Colchis settled in Corfu, while the Argonauts made their way back home, after Arete had offered gifts to the young couple.

Alcmaeon (Ἀλκμάιων)

1. The eldest son of the soothsayer Amphiaraus (for his ancestry, see Table 1) and elder brother of Amphilochus. When Amphiaraus, under strong pressure from his wife Eriphyle, had to leave for the war against Thebes knowing from his powers of divination that he must die there, he charged his children to avenge him when they reached manhood. To achieve this they were to undertake an expedition against Thebes and also kill their mother. Alcmaeon therefore in due course took part, as a follower of ADRASTUS, in the campaign of the Epigoni. An oracle had promised the Epigoni that they would be victorious if they were led by Alcmaeon.

But in spite of the oracle and the duty which his father had imposed on him before he left Alcmaeon showed no enthusiasm for leaving to fight against Thebes. He was finally persuaded to do so by his mother who had been lured by the gift from Thersandrus son of Polynices of the robe of Harmony (see ERIPHYLE). In the earliest fighting

Alcmaeon with his own hands killed Laodamas, son of Eteocles and king of Thebes. In a state of demoralization the beleaguered Thebans fled during the night on the advice of their soothsayer Tiresias, and on the following day the victorious troops entered the town and sacked and pillaged it. They dedicated part of the booty to Apollo and put Thersandrus in charge of the town.

After the battle had been won Alcmaeon went to the Delphic oracle to ask about the second duty he had to discharge, the murder of his mother. The oracle replied that he must do this without fail since not only had Eriphyle allowed herself to be corrupted in order to drive her husband to his death, but she had done the same thing again with his children in deciding that they should go on the second expedition against Thebes. That made up Alcmaeon's mind and he killed Eriphyle, either with the help of his brother Amphilochus or, more probably, by himself. After this the avenging Furies pursued him as they had pursued Orestes when he had killed Clytemnestra. In his distraction he went first to his grandfather Oecles in Arcadia and then later to Psophis and the protection of Phegeus. The latter purified him, brought him back to health and gave him his daughter Arsinoe (or in other accounts Alphesiboea) in marriage. Alcmaeon gave her the necklace and the robe of Harmony which in bygone days had been used to corrupt Eriphyle. But the land of Psophis was struck by barrenness and the oracle directed that in order to get rid of this curse Alcmaeon must be purified again, this time by the river-god Achelous. Alcmaeon resumed his wanderings. He went first to Oeneus at Calydon where he was received as a welcome guest. In contrast the Thesprotes in Epirus, to whom he went next, drove him from their country. Eventually, in compliance with the terms of the oracle, he found at the mouth of the Achelous a piece of ground 'created after his mother's murder' and there the river-god purified him and gave him his daughter Callirhoe in marriage. But Callirhoe demanded the presents of the robe and necklace of Harmony as a condition of their living together. In order to comply with her wishes Alcmaeon set off again to Phegeus at Psophis and demanded that his first wife should return the presents which he had previously given her. He made the excuse that, in accordance with the command of the oracle, he had to dedicate them to Apollo of Delphi to gain final pardon for the murder of his mother. Phegeus permitted his daughter to return the gifts, but one of Alcmaeon's servants disclosed to the king the true purpose of his master and where they were to go. In his indignation Phegeus ordered his sons Pronous and Agenor (sometimes said to be Temenus and Axion) to set a trap for Alcmaeon and kill him. (Phegeus could not do this himself since Alcmaeon was his guest.)

In the time of Pausanias, Alcmaeon's tomb was to be seen, surrounded by huge cypress trees, in a high valley above Psophis. His sons, however, lost no time in avenging their father (see ACARNAN). A separate tradition, mentioned only by Propertius, had it that this revenge was carried out by Alcmaeon's first wife herself (who, in this version is called Alphesiboea).

Another tradition, which was used by Euripides, has it that during his madness when he was being pursued by the Furies, Alcmaeon had two children, a boy, Amphilochus, and a girl, Tisiphone, by Manto, the daughter of Tiresias. Subsequently he brought them both to Corinth and entrusted them to Creon, the king of the town, to bring up. But Tisiphone became so exceptionally beautiful that the queen was offended and, fearing that the king might make her his wife, she had her sold as a slave. The girl was bought by her true father, Alcmaeon, who did not recognize her. Then when Alcmaeon returned to Corinth he demanded his children back. The king could give back only his son, but it was later realized that the slave that Alcmaeon had bought was Tisiphone and in this way Alcmaeon regained his two children.

2. For another Alcmaeon, son of Sillus, see SILLUS.

Alcmene (Ἀλκμήνη) The wife of AMPHITRYON and mother of Heracles (Table 31). She belonged to the line of Perseus. A girl of exceptional beauty, she had been married to Amphitryon but had not allowed him to consummate the marriage until he had carried out a certain act of vengeance. Meanwhile she lived in exile with him in Thebes. Amphitryon left on an expedition against the Teleboeans, and, at the very moment of his return, Zeus seduced her: in order to accomplish his purpose the god had assumed the appearance of Amphitryon, since Alcmene's chastity was well known to him. One tradition has it that Zeus caused the nuptial night to last for three full days, having ordered the sun not to rise before that length of time had passed. (Alcmene was said to have been the last of the mortal women with

whom Zeus was united.) When Amphitryon returned he was astonished not to be welcomed more joyfully. When he began to tell Alcmene of his campaign she replied that she already knew all the details of it. Tiresias was consulted on this mystery and told Amphitryon of his extraordinary misfortune. Amphitryon first decided to punish his wife by burning her on a pyre but Zeus caused a downpour which put the flames out. Faced with this direct divine intervention, Amphitryon forgave her. Alcmene gave birth to two male twins, on successive days, Heracles, the son of Zeus, and Iphicles, the son of Amphitryon.

As the time of the birth drew near Hera, as goddess of childbirth, out of jealousy for her mortal rival made every effort to prolong Alcmene's pregnancy as long as possible. She had another reason for doing so: an oracle of Zeus allowed her, in arranging the moment when the birth should take place, to make Heracles a slave of EURYSTHEUS.

Later on Alcmene became a widow and she went with Heracles, once his Labours had been accomplished, when the hero, with his brother Iphicles and the latter's son Iolaus, tried to recapture Tiryns, their original native land. But Heracles was thwarted by Eurystheus. Nonetheless, at the time of the apotheosis of Heracles, Alcmene was settled in Tiryns with some of her grandchildren (the others were at Corinth and Trachis). Once Heracles was dead Eurystheus forced Alcmene to leave Corinth and persuaded Ceyx, the king of Trachis, to undertake to expel the descendants of Heracles who were in his realm. All of them fled to Athens, where they found protection. When Eurystheus demanded that the Athenians should also expel the descendants of Heracles, they refused, and in the war which followed, Eurystheus was killed. His head was carried to Alcmene, who tore out his eyes with spindles. Thereafter Alcmene lived at Thebes with the descendants of Heracles. She was very old when she died. When she was dead Zeus sent Hermes to look for her body in order to take it to the Islands of the Blessed where she married Rhadamanthys. Other accounts say that she was raised to Olympus, where she shared in the divine honours of her son. It is also sometimes asserted that after the death of Amphitryon, killed in a battle beside Heracles, Alcmene married Rhadamanthys, at that time in exile, and lived with him at Ocaleus in Boeotia.

Alcon (Ἄλκων) A Cretan archer and a companion of Heracles. His arrows never missed their mark: he could make them go through rings placed on a man's head and could split an arrow in half by striking a blade set up as a target. One day, when his son had been attacked by a snake, Alcon put an arrow through it, without hurting the child.

This latter story was also told about the father of Phalerus, one of the Argonauts. Phalerus' father, an Athenian, and a son of Erechtheus, was also called Alcon and the two heroes were frequently confused. (See Table 11).

Alcyone (Ἀλκυόνη) The daughter of Aeolus, the king of winds. She married Ceyx, the son of the morning star, Eosphorus or Lucifer. Their household was so happy that they compared themselves to Zeus and Hera. Annoyed at such pride, the gods changed them both into birds, a diver and a halcyon respectively. Since Alcyone made her nest on the edge of the sea and the waves relentlessly destroyed it Zeus took pity on her and commanded that the waves should be calm during the seven days before and after the winter solstice, the period when the halcyon was hatching her eggs. These are called the halcyon days, when storms are unknown.

Ovid tells a perceptibly different tale. Ceyx, the husband of Alcyone, had decided to go away to consult an oracle. During his voyage he ran into a sudden storm, his ship was wrecked and he himself drowned. His body was washed by the flood tide on to the coast where it was found by his wife. In her despair she was changed into a bird with a mournful song and the gods granted her husband a similar change.

Alcyoneus (Ἀλκυονεύς)

1. Among the gods begotten by Ge (Earth) in her marriage to the Sky (Uranus), Alcyoneus was exceptional for his height and tremendous strength. It was he who played the leading part in the struggle between the Giants and the Gods, which took place in the Phlegrean Fields (at Pallene in Macedonia). Alcyoneus could not be killed so long as he fought on the earth where he had been born. Accordingly, on the advice of Athena, HERACLES took him far away from Pallene and eventually shot him dead with an arrow after he had crushed to death twenty-four of Heracles' companions with a single blow from an enormous

rock. The Alcyonids, daughters of Alcyoncus, in despair at the death of their father, cast themselves into the sea. They were changed into birds (the halcyons).

2. Legend tells of another Alcyoncus, from Delphi, a young and exceptionally handsome man with exemplary manners. There was in those days on the slopes of Cirphis, a mountain near Delphi, a cavern which was the haunt of a monster called Lamia or Sybaris. This monster used to emerge from its cavern and carry off men and flocks from the fields nearby. The inhabitants asked the oracle how to rid themselves of this scourge. Apollo told them to offer a young man from the town as a sacrifice to the monster, and the lot fell upon Alcyoneus. The priests crowned him and led him in a procession towards the monster. On the way they unexpectedly met Eurybatus, son of Euphemus, a noble young man of the race of the river Axius. When he saw that the priests were escorting a young man he asked the reason for the ceremony, and when he learnt that Alcyoneus was to be sacrificed he was overcome by love for him and, unable to release him by force, demanded to be substituted for him. The priests gave their consent and Eurybatus was crowned and led towards the monster. When he had reached the mouth of the cavern he entered it boldly and grasping the monster he dragged it into the open and threw it violently on the rocks, where its head was shattered. After that the monster was seen no more and in his place a spring gushed forth, called Sybaris. The town which the Locrians later founded in Italy was called after that spring.

Alebion (Ἀλεβίων) The son of Poseidon, he lived in Liguria with his brother Dercynus. When Heracles passed through their country with the herds of oxen which he was bringing back from his expedition against Geryon the brothers tried to take the oxen away from him. The two thieves were both killed by Heracles. (See also LIGYS).

Alectryon (Ἀλεκτρυών) During his secret love affair with APHRODITE, Ares stationed a sentry named Alectryon (the cock) with orders to warn him when day was breaking. One morning the sentry went to sleep and thus the Sun took the two lovers by surprise and lost no time in telling Hephaistus, Aphrodite's husband. This was the occasion when Hephaestus had decided to set a trap for his unfaithful wife.

Aletes (Ἀλήτης)

1. Through his father HIPPOTES Aletes was descended from Heracles who was his great-grandfather. On his mother's side he was descended from Iolaus, Heracles' nephew (Table 31). His name, which means wanderer, had been given him by his father because he was born at the time of the migration of Heracles' descendants, when Hippotes had been banished for murder and was travelling from town to town (see HERACLIDAE). When Aletes reached manhood he decided to seize Corinth and expel the Ionians and the descendants of Sisyphus, who were reigning there. Before putting this plan into action he went to consult the oracle of Dodona, who promised that he would succeed if he fulfilled two conditions: first, that someone should give him a lump of Corinthian earth, and second that he should attack the town 'on a day when crowns were being worn'. The first condition was fulfilled when Aletes, having asked an inhabitant of Corinth for a piece of bread, was given, as a gesture of scorn, only a clod of earth. To satisfy the second condition he marched against the town on a day when the inhabitants were celebrating a festival in honour of the dead and were all wearing crowns, as was customary on such an occasion. Aletes had persuaded the daughter of Creon, the king, to open the gates of the town to him on that very day by promising to marry her. The girl had agreed to the bargain and duly surrendered the town to him.

Subsequently Aletes undertook an expedition against Athens. The oracle had in fact promised that he would be victorious if he spared the life of the king. But the Athenians, who knew what the oracle had said, persuaded their king, Codrus, who was sixty-six years old, to sacrifice himself for his people and so Aletes failed in his undertaking.

2. Another Aletes, son of Aegisthus, figured in the legend of ORESTES and ELECTRA.

Alexander See PARIS.

Aloadae (Ἀλωάδαι)

The name given to the sons of Poseidon by Iphimedia the daughter of Triops. Iphimedia was in fact married to Aloeus, himself the son of Poseidon and of Canace of the house of Deucalion (Tables 10 and 8). Iphimedia had fallen in love with Poseidon and it was her custom to walk along the seashore scooping up the waves in her hand and emptying the water into her bosom. Eventually Poseidon succumbed to her love and gave her two sons, Otus and Ephialtes, who were giants; indeed each year they grew a cubit in breadth and a fathom in height. When they were nine years old, nine cubits (about four metres) broad and nine fathoms (nearly seventeen metres) tall, they decided to make war on the gods. For this purpose they put Ossa on Mount Olympus and Pelion on top of both, threatening to climb up to the sky. Next they announced that they would fill the sea with the mountains to make it dry and put the sea on what had hitherto been dry land. In addition they declared their love for the goddesses, Ephialtes being in love with Hera and Otus with Artemis. Finally, as they were angry with Ares, who had caused the death of Adonis while hunting, they shut him in a brazen cauldron, having first bound him with chains, and left him there for three months until Hermes eventually managed to rescue him. All these outrageous actions brought the wrath of the gods on the two brothers. Sometimes the story is that Zeus struck them with lightning; others have it that Artemis changed herself into a doe and rushed between them when they were hunting one day in the island of Naxos and in their haste to hit her they killed each other. When they reached Hades their punishment continued. They were bound with snakes to a pillar where an owl, perpetually screeching, came to torment them.

Various towns are said to have been founded by the Aloadae: Aloion in Thrace and Ascia on Helicon, where they were supposed to have restored a cult to the Muses. Their presence on Naxos at the time of their death was explained by an errand for which their foster-father Aloeus had made them responsible. It consisted of searching for their mother and their sister Pancratis, who had been carried off by Scellis and Cassamenus (see IPHIMEDIA).

Alope (Ἀλόπη)

Cercyon the robber who ruled at Eleusis, had a daughter called Alope who, unbeknown to her father, was loved by Poseidon, by whom she had a child which her own nurse left to die in the forest. A mare (an animal sacred to Poseidon) came to suckle the child who was found, wrapped in magnificent swaddling clothes, by a shepherd. The shepherd sheltered the child but another shepherd wanted to take it. The first one handed over the child but kept the swaddling clothes for himself. The second shepherd went in anger to Cercyon who, on seeing the swaddling clothes, suspected what had happened and compelled the nurse to tell the whole story. Alope was put to death and the child was once more put out to die, whereupon a mare returned and again suckled it. A shepherd again gathered it up and gave it the name Hippothoon. Later, Hippothoon gave his name to the Attic clan of the Hippothoontis and, when Theseus had put Cercyon to death, Hippothoon came to him to ask for his grandfather's kingdom, which Theseus readily gave him. As for Alope, after Cercyon had killed her Poseidon changed her into a spring.

Alphesiboea (Ἀλφεσίβοια)

1. A nymph from Asia who was loved by Dionysus. But the god could not succeed in seducing her until one day when he had the idea of changing himself into a tiger. In terror Alphesiboea agreed to allow herself to be seduced by the god in order to cross the river (then known by the name of Sollax) to the banks of which she had fled. By Dionysus she had a son, Medus, who afterwards gave his name to the Medes and called the river on whose banks his mother had been forced to yield to Dionysus the Tigris.
2. Alphesiboea was also the name of the daughter of Phegeus, otherwise known as Arsinoe.

Alpheus (Ἀλφειός)

The god of the river of that name, which runs between Elis and Arcadia in the Peloponnese. Like all rivers, he is the son of Oceanus and Tethys. His children are said to be Orsilochus, the father of Diocles, the king of Pheres in Messenia and, in some accounts, PHEGEUS of Arcadia. Various legends tell of the attempts by Alpheus to seduce Artemis and the Nymphs. Alpheus loved Artemis but she resisted his advances, so he decided to seize her by force. One day when Artemis and her Nymphs were celebrating a festival at Letrinoi he tried to approach her but she smeared her face with mud and he failed to recognize her. Another version of the story says that Alpheus pursued Artemis as far as the island of Ortygia which lies in the middle of the harbour of Syracuse. Alpheus also loved one of the followers of Artemis, called Arethusa, and he turned himself into a hunter in order to follow her. To escape him she fled to Syracuse and the isle of Ortygia, and Alpheus went after her. Arethusa was changed into a spring and for love of her Alpheus mingled his waters with hers. (See another version of this legend under NAIADS.)

Alpos (Ἄλπος)

A giant from Sicily who lived on the Pelorus mountains (today called Mount Faro). His legend appears only in the DIONYSIACS of Nonnus. Like every giant he was a son of Earth. He had many arms and his head was covered by a hundred vipers. He used to lie in wait for travellers wandering in the mountain passes, crush them beneath the rocks and then eat them. The mountains were silent and deserted: Pan and the Nymphs, and even Echo, never risked going there. This state of affairs continued until Dionysus came into the district. Alpos attacked him, protected by a breastplate of a lump of rock, while his weapons of attack were whole trees. Dionysus hurled his thyrsus against Alpos, hitting him in the throat. Alpos was struck down and fell into the sea, beside the island under which Typhon lies buried.

Althaea (Ἀλθαία)

The daughter of Thestius, and the wife of Oeneus, King of Calydon, and mother of Deianeira and Meleager (Tables 24 and 27). When her son Meleager was seven days old the Fates came to Althaea and predicted that he would die if the log which was then burning on the hearth was burnt to ashes. Althaea immediately seized the log, put it out and hid it in a chest. According to other traditions this magic log was supposed to be an olive branch to which Althaea had given birth at the same time as her son.

It so happened that during the hunt on Calydon Meleager killed his uncles, Althaea's brothers. In her anger she threw on the fire the log on which her son's life depended. Meleager instantly died, and in her despair Althaea hanged herself.

A story was sometimes told that the two children of Althaea were not really the sons of Oeneus, but of two gods, Meleager being the son of Ares and Deianeira the daughter of Dionysus. The latter had fallen in love with Althaea and Oeneus, who had become aware of it, lent him his wife. In gratitude the god gave him a plan of a vineyard and showed him how to cultivate and use it.

Amalthea (Ἀμάλθεια)

The name of the nurse who, on Mount Ida in Crete, fed the infant Zeus and brought him up in secrecy to keep him safe from Cronus, who was searching for him and wanted to eat him. In some sources, Amalthea is the she-goat who suckled the child, and in others she is a Nymph, the most usual form of the story. It was said that Amalthea had hung the baby in a tree to prevent his father from finding him 'in heaven, or on earth, or in the sea', and that she had gathered the Curetes round him so that their songs and noisy dances should drown his cries. The goat that gave its milk was simply called Aix (a she-goat). She was a terrifying beast, descended from Helios (the Sun) and the Titans were so frightened by her mere appearance that the Earth, at their request, had hidden her in a cave in the Cretan mountains. Later, when Zeus was fighting the Titans, he made himself armour from her skin. This armour was called the aegis. There is also a story that one day, while at play, Zeus took one of the goat's horns and gave it as a present to Amalthea, promising her that this horn would be miraculously filled with all the kinds of fruit she wanted. This is the Horn of Amalthea or the Horn of Plenty (see ACHELOUS).

Amata (Ἀμάτα) The wife of LATINUS and the mother of LAVINIA. From the many suitors of Lavinia Amata had chosen Turnus, the young king of the Rutuli. So when Aeneas arrived and Latinus decided to give his daughter's hand to the stranger, Amata tried to prevent the marriage by rousing the women of Laurentium against the Trojans. When she heard of the Trojan victory and the death of Turnus she hanged herself.

Amata was also the cult name of the Vestal Virgin in Rome, after her consecration by the Pontifax Maximus.

Amazons (Ἀμαζόνες) A race of women descended from Ares the god of war, and the Nymph Harmonia. Their kingdom was believed to lie in the north, either on the slopes of the Caucasus, or in Thrace, or yet again in southern Scythia, in the plains on the left bank of the Danube. They conducted their own government; they were ruled by a queen. They could not stand the presence of men except as servants for the most menial jobs, and at certain times had intercourse with strangers to preserve their race keeping only the baby girls. According to some accounts they mutilated the male children at birth by blinding them or making them lame. According to others, they killed them. They removed one of the breasts of the infant girls so that they should be unencumbered and able to shoot with the bow or to handle a spear, and it was from this custom that they were given the name of ἀ-μαζών (those who have no breasts). Their main love was war.

A number of legends tell of Greek heroes fighting these strange women. Bellerophon fought them at the command of Iobates. Heracles received from Eurysthenes the mission of going to the bank of the river Thermodon in Cappadocia and taking the girdle of Hippolyta, the queen of the Amazons. Hippolyta would have been willing to give him the girdle but Hera, in jealousy, incited the Amazons to mutiny and Heracles was forced to kill Hippolyta. On this expedition he was accompanied by Theseus, who abducted an Amazon called Antiope. In search of revenge the Amazons marched against Athens and the battle took place in Athens itself, where the Amazons set up camp on the hill later to be called the Areopagus (the hill of Ares). They were defeated by the Athenians led by Theseus. There was also a story that the Amazons had sent a contingent commanded by their queen, Penthesilea, to help Priam. But Achilles lost no time in killing her, though her last look aroused his love for her.

The goddess worshipped above all by the Amazons was, naturally, Artemis, whose legends have so much in common with the life attributed to these huntresses and female warriors. They were sometimes regarded as the founders of Ephesus and the builders of the great Temple of Artemis.

Ampelus (Ἄμπελος) A youth beloved by Dionysus. He was the son of a Nymph and a Satyr, and his name means vine stick. The god presented him with a vine laden with grapes which hung from the branches of an elm tree. Anxious to pick the fruit the youth climbed the elm, but fell while he was picking and was killed. Dionysus changed him into a constellation.

Amphiaraus (Ἀμφιάραος) The son of Oecles and Hypermestra (for his descent and breeding, see Table 1). His sons were Alcmaeon and Amphilocus, to whom other traditions add three heroes of Roman legend, Tiburtus, Coras and Catillus, the founders of the town of Tibur near Rome, the modern Tivoli.

Amphiaraus was a seer, under the protection of Zeus and Apollo. He was also a warrior renowned for his integrity and courage, as well as his piety. In the quarrels which marked the beginning of his reign in Argos Amphiaraus killed Talaus, the father of Adrastus, and drove out Adrastus. Later on the two cousins made up their differences, but while Amphiaraus was sincere about it, Adrastus harboured a sense of resentment. Adrastus gave Amphiaraus his sister Eriphyle in marriage, stipulating that if the cousins quarrelled, the issue should be settled by referring the matter to the girl's judgement, and it was this agreement that brought about the death of Amphiaraus. After Adrastus had promised Polynices to restore him to the throne of Thebes he asked his brother-in-law Amphiaraus to take part in the expedition which he was preparing against the town. Amphiarus, warned by his powers of divination of the disastrous outcome of this war, tried to dissuade Adrastus from the enterprise. But Polynices, on the advice of Iphis, offered Eriphyle the necklace of Harmonia (see CADMUS). Swayed by this gift, Eriphyle, when called on to arbitrate between Adrastus and Amphiaraus, pronounced in favour of the war, and Amphiaraus, bound as he was by his promise, had reluctantly to march against Thebes. Before leaving, he made his two young sons swear to avenge him later by killing their mother and raising a second expedition against Thebes which could not fail to be victorious (see ALCMAEON: this was called the expedition of the Epigoni).

On the road to Thebes they met with their first adventure. While they were passing through Nemea the heroes asked HYPSIPYLE, the slave girl who was in charge of Opheltes, the infant son of the king, to show them a stream where they could quench their thirst. Hypsipyle momentarily put down the baby, whom an oracle had ordained must not be laid on the ground before he could walk, near a spring whose guardian serpent immediately attacked the infant and stifled it. Amphiaraus explained to them that this deadly omen meant that the expedition was doomed to disaster and that the chiefs would die. Nonetheless, the heroes continued on their way, after founding games in honour of Opheltes, who they called Archemorus or the star of Fate. They themselves took part in these games which were later called the Nemean Games, and Amphiaraus won prizes for jumping and throwing the discus. His skilful talk and his wisdom succeeded in securing a pardon for Hypsipyle from the parents of Opheltes. The Seven then reached Thebes.

Amphiaraus played a leading part in the fighting which developed in front of the town's seven gates. When one of the Seven, Tydeus, had been wounded in the stomach by Melanippus, Amphiaraus killed Melanippus, beheaded him, and carried the bleeding head to Tydeus who broke it open and ate the brains. Athena, who had intended to make Tydeus immortal, was so shocked by this cannibalism that she gave up her intention. In the rout which marked the end of the campaign, Amphiaraus fled to the banks of the Ismenus. Just as he was about to be joined by Periclymenus, Zeus, with a clap of thunder, caused the earth to open beneath him and swallow up Amphiaraus, with his horses, his chariot and his driver. As late as Pausanias' day, the spot where this happened was still pointed out. Zeus granted Amphiaraus immortality and he continued to utter oracles at Oropus in Attica.

Amphictyon (Ἀμφικτύων) The second son of Deucalion and Pyrrha (Table 8). He had married one of the daughters of Cranaus, king of Athens, and expelled his father-in-law in order to reign in his stead (see also COLAENUS). He was himself banished, after a reign of ten years, by Erichthonius. Some traditions say that it was he who gave Athens its name and dedicated the city to the goddess Athena. It was also during his reign that Dionysus came to Attica, where he was the king's guest. The foundation of the Amphictyonic League, the religious association in which envoys of all the Greek cities met periodically, is sometimes attributed to him. Before he assumed the throne of Athens, he is said to have been king of Thermopylae, one of the two places (the other being Delphi) where the association met. Amphictyon had a son Itonus, whose children play a part in Boeotian legends. One of his daughters was the mother of Cercyon (Table 8: see also LOCRUS).

Amphilochus (Ἀμφίλοχος) The two characters of this name are not at all clearly distinguished in the different traditions.
1.   The first was the younger son of AMPHIARAUS and brother of ALCMAEON (Table 1). He was very young when his father left for Thebes and played a minor part, if any at all, in the murder of his mother Eriphyle and had little hand in the other revenge exacted by Amphiaraus. Also, unlike his brother, he was not pursued by the Furies. He is mentioned as one of the suitors of Helen and in virtue of this he took part in the expedition against Troy after his return from the war of the Epigoni against Thebes. His name, however, is not mentioned in the *Iliad* but had to be brought into the poems about the *Homecomings*. At Troy Amphilochus, who had inherited his father's gift, helped the seer Calchas and, with him, was said to have established a number of oracles on the coast of Asia Minor.
2.   The second Amphilochus was nephew of the first and son of Alcmaeon and Manto, who was herself the daughter of the Theban seer Tiresias. Many of the later accomplishments of the first Amphilocus are attributed to him. In addition this younger Amphilochus was the founder of Argos

in Aetolia (not to be confused with the Argos in the Argolid, which was older and much more famous). He also went to Troy and, together with the seer Mopsus, founded the town of Mallos in Cilicia. Then, moved by a wish to revisit the town of Argos which he had founded he is supposed to have departed from Mallos, leaving it in the hands of Mopsus. But when he reached Argos he was dissatisfied with the state in which he found the town and returned to Mallos. On his arrival he asked Mopsus to return it to his control, but Mopsus refused. Thereupon the two seers engaged in single combat and both of them were killed.

Amphion (Ἀμφίων) The son of Zeus and Antiope and the twin brother of Zethus. The twins were born at Eleutherae in Boeotia and immediately after their birth were abandoned on the mountainside by Lycus their great-uncle. The two infants were rescued by a shepherd who brought them up. Zethus applied himself to pursuits involving force and the use of his hands such as fighting, agriculture and animal husbandry, while Amphion, who had been given a lyre by Hermes, devoted himself to music. There is a story that the two young men used to quarrel over the merits of their respective pursuits. Amphion, who was milder in temperament than his brother, often yielded to him, even to the point of sometimes giving up his music. Their mother ANTIOPE, was a prisoner of her uncle Lycus, and treated as a slave by Dirce his wife, who was jealous of her beauty. But one day the shackles which held her miraculously fell off and, unseen by anyone, she reached the cottage in which her sons lived. The twins took their revenge by killing Lycus and Dirce. Dirce's death was dreadful: while still alive she was tied to a bull which dragged her and tore her to pieces on the rocks. After this the two brothers reigned in Thebes, in place of Lycus. They built walls round the town, Zethus carrying the stones on his back while Amphion restricted himself to bringing them to him, accompanied by the strains of his lyre. Amphion later married NIOBE, the daughter of Tantalus. Some say that he, together with his children, was killed by Apollo. According to others, he went mad and tried to destroy a temple of Apollo, so the god shot him with an arrow.

Amphisthenes (Ἀμφισθένης) A Lacedaemonian, grandson of Agis and son of Amphicles. He had a son Irbus, whose two children Astrabacus and Alopecus discovered the statue of Artemis Orthia which had long been lost (the story goes that it was the one that Orestes and Iphigenia had brought from Tauris). The two children found it hidden in a thicket, and as punishment for having set eyes on the sacred statue they both went mad. This was the statue in front of which the young Spartans were beaten every year until their blood flowed.

Amphitrite (Ἀμφιτρίτη) The Queen of the Sea, she who encircles the Earth. She was a member of the circle of the daughters of Nereus and Doris known as the Nereids, and it was she who led their chorus. One day when they were all dancing near the island of Naxos Poseidon saw her and carried her off. There is also a story that Poseidon had been in love with her for a long time but that she would have nothing to do with him and hid herself in the depths of the Ocean beyond the Pillars of Hercules. She was discovered by the Dolphins and brought back by them in a great procession to Poseidon, who married her. She played the same part in the company of the god as Hera with Zeus and Persephone with the god of the dead. She was frequently depicted surrounded by a large retinue of divinities of the sea.

Amphitryon (Ἀμφιτρύων) The son of Alceus, king of Tiryns and Astydamia, the daughter of Pelops (Tables 2 and 31). He took part in the war between his uncle and brother-in-law Electryon and the latter's great-nephew, Pterelas; Electryon was king of Mycenae, but Pterelas claimed the kingdom by virtue of his descent from Mestor, one of the brothers of Electryon. The sons of Pterelas came at the head of an army of Paphians who lived on the island of Paphos (which lies off the coast of Acarnania) to lay waste Mycenean territory and to carry off the flocks of Electryon. All the sons of Electryon and of Pterelas lost their lives in the fighting except for one from each family: Licymnius of the former and Eueres of the latter. The men of Paphos managed to escape, taking with them the flocks which they entrusted to Polyxenus, the king of Elis. But Amphitryon managed to recover them by paying a ransom and brought them back to Mycenae. Then Electryon determined to avenge his sons by mounting a campaign against Pterelas and his people the Teleboeans. While he was away he entrusted his kingdom and his daughter Alcmene to Amphitryon, who swore to respect her until the king returned. But Electryon did not in the end go to war. Just as Amphitryon was returning the stolen flocks to him, a cow went mad and when Amphitryon threw the staff which he had in his hand at it, the staff bounced off the cow's horns and in so doing hit and killed Electryon. Sthenelas the overlord of Argos, to whom the kingdom of Mycenae belonged, took the opportunity to banish Amphitryon who fled, with Alcmene and Licymnius, to Thebes where he was purified of his murder by Creon, the king. But Amphitryon was still bound by his oath and so could not marry Alcmene while she also refused to agree to the marriage until her brothers' deaths had been avenged. Accordingly Amphitryon had to mount an expedition against Pterelas and the Teleboeans for which he asked Creon's help. Creon did not refuse but made it a pre-condition that Amphitryon should rid Thebes of a fox which was laying the country waste. This fox, the fox of Teumessa, could not be caught by running, so Amphitryon asked for the hound of Procris, an animal native to Crete, which was reputed to run faster than anything that it chased. However the hound was unable to outpace the fox so Zeus, out of respect for the Fates and in order to find a way out, changed both the animals into stone statues.

Amphitryon, having thus met the condition laid down by Creon, secured the Thebans as allies against the Teleboeans, and with other contingents, including those led by Cephalus of Attica, Panopeus of Phocis, and Heleius from the Argolid (who was a son of Perseus), laid waste the island of Paphos. But there again he came up against a magic obstruction. So long as Pterelas lived the town of Paphos could not be captured, and Pterelas' life was linked with a single golden hair hidden among the rest on his head. His daughter Comaetho, however, fell in love with Amphitryon and cut the fatal hair from her father's head. Pterelas died, and Amphitryon was able to take possession of the whole island of Paphos. Thereafter, he killed Comaetho and returned to Thebes laden with booty. At this point Zeus, with the features of Amphitryon, came to Alcmene and obtained what Amphitryon himself had asked for in vain. However that same night Amphitryon returned and consummated his marriage with Alcmene who simultaneously conceived Iphicles by Amphitryon and Heracles by Zeus. When her unconscious infidelity was disclosed to him by the seer Tiresias, Amphitryon's first impulse was to punish her, but Zeus intervened and prevented him. Once reconciled with his wife, Amphitryon took an active part in bringing up Heracles by

teaching him how to drive a chariot. There is also a story that, in order to tell which child was his and which that of Zeus, he brought two snakes into their room when they were ten months old. Iphicles was frightened but Heracles strangled both snakes and this showed that Iphicles was of mortal and Heracles of divine descent. Another tradition has it that the two snakes were sent by Hera. Later, when Heracles was displaying the violence of his inherited disposition by killing his music teacher Linus, Amphitryon, fearing a similar fate if he annoyed the boy, sent him into the country to look after the oxen. This was how the hero came to kill the lion which was attacking Amphitryon's flocks in the mountains of Cithaeron. Amphitryon met his death while fighting at Heracles' side in the struggle which the Thebans were conducting against the Minyans of Orchomenos, a town near Thebes (see also ERGINUS).

Amulius (Ἀμύλιυς) The fifteenth king of Albalonga, the son of Procas and brother of NUMITOR. Before his death Procas had divided the royal inheritance into two parts: one consisted of the treasure, the other of the kingdom. Numitor chose the latter but Amulius, relying on the wealth which had fallen to him, had no difficulty in driving out his brother and usurping his place. However despite all his precautions he was unable to prevent his niece Rhea from giving birth to the twins, Romulus and Remus, who eventually dethroned him, put him to death and restored power to their grandfather Numitor.

Amyce (Ἀμύκη) The daughter of Salaminus, king of Cyprus. She established a colony of Cypriots at Antioch on the Orontes, where she married Casus, a son of Inachus. She died there and was buried not far from the town, in a place called Amyce.

Amycus (Ἄμυκος) A giant, a son of Poseidon and king of the Berbryces in Bithynia. Savage by nature, he invented the sports of boxing and fighting with the cestus. He used to attack strangers who landed on the Bithynian coast and would put them to death with a single blow of his fist. When the Argonauts landed in his country Amycus met them and challenged them to fight. Pollux took up the challenge and the fight began. Despite his huge height and brute strength, Amycus was defeated by the skill and suppleness of Pollux. Each of the contestants had staked his own body on the outcome and Amycus, had he been the victor, would have killed his opponent, but having beaten him Pollux was satisfied with making the giant promise that he would refrain from harming strangers in future.

Amymone (Ἀμυμώνη) One of the fifty daughters of King Danaus. Her mother was Europa. When DANAUS left Libya with his children, Amymone went with him and together they settled in Argos. But the country had no water owing to the wrath of Poseidon who was angry that it had been allotted to Hera when he wanted it himself. After Danaus had become king he sent his daughters in search of water and Amymone went with them. Tired out by walking, she went to sleep at the wayside; a Satyr came upon her and tried forcibly to ravish her. The girl called on Poseidon who immediately appeared and with one blow from his trident drove the Satyr away. Amymone then granted Poseidon what she had refused the Satyr. But the trident had struck the rock and a stream with three springs gushed from it. Another version of the story is that after Poseidon, who was in love with Amymone, had come to her rescue he showed her the existence of the spring of Lerna. Amymone had a son by Poseidon, the hero Nauplius.

Ananke (Ἀνάγκη) Ananke or Necessity, the personification of absolute obligation and of the constraining force of the decrees of destiny, was an 'intellectual' divinity. In Greece she appears under the name of Ananke only in the Orphic theogony where, with her daughter Adrastia, she is the nurse of the little Zeus. She herself was a daughter of Cronus, like Justitia. Her children were Aether, Chaos and Erebus.

Ananke occurs in the cosmological and metaphysical constructions of the philosophers. For example, in Plato's myth in the *Republic*, Ananke is the mother of the Moirai. Gradually, and particularly in popular tradition, Ananke became a goddess of death, but in the works of the poets, particularly the tragedians, she remained the incarnation of the ultimate Force which even the gods must obey. In Rome, Ananke became *Necessitas*, a poetic allegory, which seems not to have had an existence of its own outside purely literary allusions.

Anaxagoras (Ἀναξαγόρας) The son of Megapenthes, who was himself the son of Proetus, king of Argos, whom he succeeded (Table 36).

According to a tradition recorded by both Pausanias and Diodorus it was during Anaxagoras' reign, and not that of his grandfather Proetus, that all the Argive women were struck with a madness which was cured by MELAMPUS. As a reward Anaxagoras gave Melampus a third of his kingdom, giving another third to Melampus' brother Bias, and keeping the remaining third for himself. His descendants, the Anaxagorides, ruled under this sytem until the son of Sthenelus, Cylarabes, reunited the whole kingdom of Argos under his own sway. The last descendant of Melampus, Amphilochus, went into voluntary exile after his return from the Trojan War. Of the descendants of Bias the last, Cyanippus son of Aegialeus (or, according to other versions, his younger brother; see Table 1) died childless, as did Cylarabes, and it was ORESTES, the son of Agamemnon, who gained control of Argos and at the same time of Sparta.

Anaxarete (Ἀναξαρέτη) A Cypriot girl, a member of a noble family, descendants of Teucer, who founded Salamis in Cyprus. A young Cypriot called Iphis fell hopelessly in love with Anaxarete, but she was cruel to him. In his despair Iphis hanged himself at her door. She, far from being moved by the sight, merely wanted to watch the funeral procession as it passed beneath her window, because of the great number of people which Iphis' suicide had brought together, and the laments of the whole town which had been deeply touched by so moving a fate. Aphrodite, angered by Anaxarete's lack of feeling, changed her into a stone statue in the position she had taken up in order to look out of the window. This statue, known as Venus Prospiciens (Venus leaning forward to see) was placed in a temple in Salamis in Cyprus.

Anchemolus (Ἀγχημολος) The son of Rhoetus, king of the Italian tribe of the Marruvians (named after a city in the district of Marses, in central Italy on the edge of Lake Fucinus). Anchemolus had been the lover of his stepmother Casperia. When Rhoetus came to hear of it he wanted to kill his son, who fled and found shelter with Daunus the father of Turnus. He fought beside Turnus in the war against Aeneas and died in the thick of the fighting.

Anchises (Ἀγχίσης) The father of Aeneas and son of Capys and Themiste (Table 7). He was loved by Aphrodite who saw him looking after his flocks on Mount Ida, near Troy. She approached him claiming to be the daughter of Otreus, king of Phrygia, and to have been abducted by Hermes and carried off to the pastures of Ida. By this device she married him. Later, she told Anchises who she really was and predicted that she would bear him a son (Aeneas), but begged him not to tell anyone that his son was the child of a goddess, for if Zeus should come to hear of it he would strike the child with lightning. But Anchises drank too much wine one feast day and boasted of his love affairs. Zeus punished him by making him lame with a blast from a thunderbolt or, in other traditions, blind. Anchises is also said to have been the father of Lyrnus. A hazy tradition gives Anchises a mortal wife named Eriopis, by whom he is said to have had several daughters, the eldest being Hippodamia.

On one occasion Zeus sent Tros some divine stallions; Anchises had these mated with his mares and obtained six colts, two of which he gave to Aeneas.

When Troy had been captured Aeneas snatched his father from the fire and slaughter and made him his companion on his wanderings. The place of Anchises' death (he was eighty years old when he left Troy) is attributed to different sites by various writers. Sometimes his grave is said to be on Ida itself where he had once looked after the flocks; alternatively it is placed near the peninsula of Pallene in Macedonia, in Arcadia, in Epirus, in southern Italy, and on Cape Drepanon in Sicily. Aeneas, according to Virgil, established in his honour the funeral games that were the origin of the Trojan Games that were held in Rome until the beginning of the Empire. Other writers make Anchises live on until Aeneas arrived in Latium, at the time of the war against Mezentius (see also AEGESTES).

Anchurus (Ἄγχουρος) The son of Midas and king of Phrygia. When a yawning chasm opened near his capital and threatened to engulf the town Anchurus asked the oracle how to bring the threat to an end. The oracle replied that he had to cast into it whatever he held most dear. Gold and jewels were thrown into it without any result. At last Anchurus threw himself in whereupon the chasm immediately closed up.

Androclus (Ἄνδροκλος) The son of Codrus and the leader of the Ionian colonists who drove out the Leleges and the Carians who had settled in the area round Ephesus. He himself was supposed to have founded the city. He also conquered the island of Samos. A story told about the foundation of Ephesus was that an oracle had foretold that the site of the city would be revealed to the colonists by a wild boar and a fish. One evening, when they were preparing their meal, a fish that they were cooking jumped off the fire, taking with it a burning piece of charcoal which set fire to a thicket out of which ran a wild boar, which Androclus killed. Realizing that the oracle had been proved accurate by this odd coincidence Androclus founded the town on that spot.

Androgeos (Ἀνδρόγεως) One of the sons of Minos and Pasiphae (Table 28). He excelled in all athletic sports, took part in the meeting held by Aegeus at Athens, and beat all the other competitors. Aegeus was jealous of him and sent him to fight the bull of Marathon, which was laying waste the countryside, but Androgeos perished. In other versions Androgeos is said to have been on his way to compete in the games at Thebes, after his victories at Athens, when he was attacked on the road by his unsuccessful competitors and killed. Whatever the truth, the news was brought to Minos just as he was celebrating a sacrifice to the Graces on the island of Paros. Although he did not interrupt the celebration of the festival he wished to show a sign of his grief so threw his crown off his head and asked his flute-players to stop playing. This is said to be the origin of the ceremony, peculiar to Paros, which banned crowns of flowers and ritual flute music in sacrifices to the Graces. As soon as the festival was over Minos collected a fleet and left to attack Athens, starting on his way by capturing Megara which, lying on the gulf of Salamis, is the key to Attica. He took the town thanks to the treachery of Scylla, the daughter of King Nisus. From there he marched on Athens. But the war dragged on and, wanting it to end, Minos prayed to Zeus to avenge him on the Athenians, and plague and famine struck the city. The sacrifice of several virgins (the Hyacinthides) having proved fruitless, the Athenians consulted the oracle, which replied that if the Athenians wanted the calamities to cease they would have to concede to Minos' demand of an annual tribute of seven girls and seven young men to be handed over as food for the Minotaur, the hideous son of Pasiphae. It was from this tribute that Theseus freed Attica.

One tradition claims that Androgeos had been brought back to life by Asclepius (this is possibly a mistake for GLAUCUS). Androgeos had two sons, Alceus and Sthenelus, who settled in Paros, with their uncles, the sons of Minos and Paria (see NEPHALION).

Andromache (Ἀνδρομάχη) The daughter of Eetion, king of Thebes in Mysia, whose town was sacked by Achilles before the beginning of the ninth year of the Trojan War. Andromache, the wife of Hector and daughter-in-law of Priam, lost her father and seven brothers, all killed by Achilles during the Greek raid on the town where she was born. By Hector she had an only son, Astyanax. After the death of her husband and the sack of Troy Andromache fell, as part of his share of the Trojan booty, to Neoptolemus, Achilles' son. Neoptolemus, having killed Astyanax, according to some accounts, but not having done so according to others, brought Andromache to Epirus, of which he was king. There Andromache bore him three sons, Molossus, Piclus and Pergamus. When Neoptolemus was killed at Delphi, whither he had gone to consult the oracle, he bequeathed his kingdom and his wife to Helenus, brother of Hector (see MOLOSSUS, which follows the story as told by Euripides).

During Aeneas' travels in Epirus Andromache reigned peacefully with Helenus. On the latter's death she was said to have gone with her son Pergamus as far as Mysia, where he founded a town bearing his name, Pergamum. Tradition has it that Andromache was a tall, dark woman with a dominating character.

Andromeda (Ἀνδρομέδη) The daughter of Cepheus, king of Ethiopia, and Cassiopia who claimed to be more beautiful than all the Nereids put together. In jealousy the Nereids asked Poseidon to avenge this insult and to humour them he sent a monster to lay waste the country of Cepheus. When consulted by the king, the oracle of Ammon had predicted that Ethiopia would be freed from this scourge if Cassiopia's daughter were to be abandoned as a victim in expiation. The inhabitants of the country forced Cepheus to agree to this sacrifice and Andromeda was bound to a rock. Here Perseus, on his way back from his expedition against the Gorgon, saw her, fell in love with her and promised Cepheus to free her if she could become his wife. Cepheus agreed and Perseus killed the dragon and married Andromeda. But Phineus, a brother of Cepheus who had been betrothed to his niece Andromeda, plotted against Perseus, who realized what was happening and turned the Gorgon's head towards them, turning them to stone. When Perseus left Ethiopia he took Andromeda first to Argos and later to Tiryns, where they had several sons and a daughter (Table 31).

Conon offers what might be called the rationalist explanation of the legend. According to him Cepheus ruled over the country later to be called Phoenicia (but then known as Joppa from the name of the town on its coast). His kingdom stretched from the Mediterranean to Arabia and the Red Sea. Cepheus had a very beautiful daughter called Andromeda, who was wooed by Phoenix, who gave his name to Phoenicia, and his uncle Phineus, the brother of Cepheus. After a great deal of beating about the bush Cepheus decided to give his daughter's hand to Phoenix but, unwilling to give the impression that he was refusing his brother, pretended that she had been abducted. She was taken to a small island where she was in the habit of sacrificing to Aphrodite, and Phoenix carried her off on a boat called the *Whale*. But Andromeda had no idea that this was merely a device to deceive her uncle; she cried aloud and shouted for help. At that very moment Perseus, son of Danae, happened to be passing by. He saw the girl being abducted, took one look at her and fell in love with her. He leapt forward, upset the boat, left the sailors 'turned to stone' with astonishment and carried off Andromeda, whom he married, and thereafter reigned peacefully in Argos.

Anius (Ἄνιος) A son of Apollo who was reigning at Delos during the time of the Trojan War. His mother was RHOEO ('the pomegranate'), and through her father Staphylus ('the bunch of grapes') she was a descendant of Dionysus. When Staphylus had seen that his daughter was in an advanced state of pregnancy, he could not believe that Apollo was responsible for her condition but blamed some common mortal, and he put the girl in a chest and set it adrift on the sea. It came to rest on the shore of Euboea but as soon as the child was born, Apollo caused mother and child to be transported to the sacred island of Delos which he gave the child the power to rule. At the same time he granted him the gift of prophecy.

By Dorippa Anius had three daughters who had been granted by Dionysus, their ancestor, the power to make oil, corn and wine spring from the earth. There is a story that their father offered their services to the Greeks on the eve of the Trojan War, for as a prophet he knew that the war would last for ten years. Initially the Greeks refused to seek the help of the three sisters; then, as the war dragged on for longer than they had expected, Agamemnon sent Odysseus and Menelaus to look for them in Delos and entrust them with the task of supplying the army. They came readily, but then grew weary and decamped. When the Greeks pursued them they begged Dionysus to give them his protection and he changed them to doves. This is the reason why doves could not be killed in Delos.

The Anius legend does not appear in the Homeric poems, but is to be found only in the Cyclical Poems and was developed in the Hellenistic period. For information about Anius, father of Lavinia, see LAVINIA.

Anna Perenna A very ancient Roman goddess, worshipped in a sacred wood lying directly north of Rome, on the Via Flaminia. She was depicted as having the features of an old woman. When the Plebs migrated to the Sacred Mountain and had not enough to live on Anna Perenna was said to have made cakes which she came and sold every day to the people, thus averting famine. That is the reason why she was paid divine honours once the political troubles had been overcome and the Plebs had returned to Rome.

Another tradition, developed at the same time as the story of Aeneas, made Anna the sister of Queen DIDO. After the latter had killed herself the kingdom of Carthage had been invaded by the natives under the leadership of IARBAS and Anna had been forced to flee. She first found refuge with the king of Melite, an island off the African coast. But Pygmalion, the Syrian king, had asked the king of Melite to surrender the fugitive to him. She took ship and fled from the island, but was caught by a storm and cast up on the shores of Latium. It so happened that at that time Aeneas was ruling the town of Laurentum, exactly where the girl landed. Aeneas was walking by the sea with his friend Achates, who recognized Anna. Aeneas wept as he welcomed her, bewailed Dido's sad death and set Anna up in his palace. But this action greatly displeased Aeneas' wife Lavinia, who did not look at all kindly on the arrival of this evidence of her husband's past. Anna was warned in a dream to be alarmed at the traps that Lavinia would set for her and at the dead of night she fled from the palace. While she was wandering she met Numicius, the god of a nearby stream who carried her off to his bed. The servants of Aeneas searched for Anna and followed her tracks to the river bank, and, while they wondered where to go next a shape rose from the water and revealed to

them that Anna, once an exile, had become a water nymph, whose new name, Perenna, signified eternity. Aeneas' servants in their joy scattered among the fields and passed the day in feasting and festivities, which became established as an annual celebration of the festival of Anna Perenna.

In her old age Anna was chosen by Mars as an intermediary between Minerva and himself. Mars loved Minerva, but the maiden goddess resisted his advances. He accordingly conceived the notion of entrusting to the aged Anna the traditional role of duenna. Anna, who knew that her task could not possibly be accomplished since the goddess would never succumb, deceived the god with falsehoods, gave him false hopes and finally put herself in Minerva's place in a meeting with the god by night. When the lover was ushered into the bridal chamber she lifted the veil over her face: Mars recognized the old woman who was ridiculing him and spoke extremely angrily. This is what is said to lie behind the obscenities which were sung at the Festival of Anna.

Antaeus (Ἀνταῖος) A giant, son of Poseidon and Gaia (The Earth). He lived in Libya (not far from Utica, according to Lucan, but in Morocco according to most writers) and made all travellers fight with him. After he had defeated and killed them he decorated his father's temple with their corpses. Antaeus was invulnerable so long as he kept in touch with his mother (that is, the ground), but Heracles, when he was passing through Libya in his search for the Golden Apples, fought with him and choked him to death by hoisting him on his shoulders (see also TINGE).

Anteia (Ἄντεια) see Stheneboea.

Antenor (Ἀντήνωρ) An old Trojan, a companion and adviser to the aged Priam. Before the Trojan War he had some close friends among the Greek chiefs, including Menelaus and Odysseus who visited him before the siege on a mission to negotiate a friendly settlement. In the *Iliad* Antenor can be seen urging moderation on the Trojans. As a believer in peaceful solutions he tried to get the war decided by a duel between Paris and Menelaus. When Troy fell Lycaon, one of his sons who had been wounded, was recognized by Odysseus who conducted him, together with his brother Glaucus, through the Greek army to a safe place. While the city was being sacked the Greeks hung a leopard-skin over the door of

Antenor's house, to show that it should be spared.

With the development of the Trojan cycle Antenor appears as an entirely different character: he became a traitor to his country who helped the Greeks to steal the Palladium and opened the gates of the wooden horse for the soldiers who were shut inside. After Troy was captured he and his son were said to have gone through Thrace and from there to have reached northern Italy. He was said to be the ancestor of the Veneti, who lived in the lower valley of the Po.

Antheias (Ἀνθείας) A hero from Patras and son of Enmelus (see TRIPTOLEMUS).

Antheus (Ἀνθεύς) A young native of Halicarnassus, of royal stock, who lived as a hostage at the court of Phobius, the tyrant of Miletus. The wife of Phobius, Cleoboea (called by other writers Philaechme) fell in love with him, but the young man would not yield to her. In the end Cleoboea determined to take her revenge by destroying him. She threw a golden cup into a deep well and bade Antheus go down and look for it, then, when he was at the bottom, she threw an enormous stone on him which crushed him. In remorse at the murder she had committed she hanged herself (see also PHRYGIUS).

Anticleia (Ἀντίκλεια) The mother of Odysseus and wife of Laertes. She was the daughter of Autolycus, the most cunning of men (Table 35). When Autolycus stole cattle from Sisyphus the latter went to Autolycus to get them back, and it was during this visit that Anticleia secretly gave herself to Sisyphus before marrying Laertes. This explains why Odysseus is sometimes regarded as Sisyphus' son. During Odysseus' absence Anticleia, tired of waiting for him to come back and consumed with worry, killed herself.

Antigone (Ἀντιγόνη) There are two heroines with this name.
1. The best known was the daughter of Oedipus, sister of Ismene, Polynices and Eteocles (Table 29). The earliest legends call her the daughter of Eurygania, who was herself the daughter of the king of the Phlegeans, a people of Boeotia. But the most usual version (used by the tragic writers) says that she was the daughter of Jocasta and the consequence of the incest committed by Oedipus with his own mother. When Oedipus, enlightened about his crimes by the

oracle of Tiresias, blinded himself and exiled himself from Thebes, Antigone made herself his companion. Their wanderings took them to Colonus in Attica where Oedipus died. After her father's death Antigone returned to Thebes where she lived with her sister Ismene. There she met with a fresh trial. During the War of the Seven Chiefs her two brothers, Eteocles and Polynices, found themselves on opposite sides, the former in the Theban army and the latter in the army attacking his native land. In the course of the fighting which took place before the gates of Thebes, each brother died at the other's hands. Creon the king, the uncle of Eteocles, Polynices and the girls, granted a solemn funeral service for Eteocles but forbade anyone to bury Polynices, who had called in strangers against his own country. Antigone was unwilling to comply with this order. Believing that it was a sacred duty, laid down by the gods and the unwritten laws, to bury the dead and especially her close kin, she broke Creon's ban and scattered a handful of dust over Polynices' body, a ritual gesture which was enough to fulfil the duty imposed by religion. For this act of piety she was condemned to death by Creon and walled up while still alive, in the tomb of Labdacus, from whom she was descended. In her confinement she hanged herself and Haemon, son of Creon and her betrothed, killed himself on her corpse while Creon's wife Eurydice, for her part, committed suicide in despair.
2. Another Antigone is also known to legend. She was Priam's sister and a most lovely girl. She was very proud of her hair, which she claimed was more beautiful than Hera's. In a fit of rage the goddess turned Antigone's hair into snakes. But the gods took pity on the unhappy girl and turned her into a stork, the enemy of snakes.

Antilochus (Ἀντίλοχος) The son of Nestor, with whom he went to the Trojan War. Being handsome and a swift runner he was loved by ACHILLES, second in his affection only to Patroclus. It was he who told Achilles of the death of Patroclus and wept with him for his death. But Antilochus himself was soon destined to die, either, according to varying sources, at the hands of Memnon the son of Aurora, or at those of Hector or indeed perhaps at the same time as Achilles, killed by an arrow shot by Paris. A variant of this legend describes Antilochus coming to his father's rescue when he was on the point of being overwhelmed by his enemies. Antilochus made a rampart of his own body but while he saved his father, he was himself killed. His ashes were laid to rest beside those of Patroclus and Achilles. The three heroes were said to pass their time after death in fighting and feasting on the White Island.

Antinoe (Ἀντινόη) Two women bear this name.
1. A daughter of Cepheus from Mantinea. On the advice of an oracle she followed a snake and led the inhabitants of Mantinea to a spot where they founded a new town on the banks of the little stream Ophis (which means snake in Greek).
2. According to some writers this was also the name of one of the daughters of Pelias. After the unintentional murder of her father (see PELIAS and MEDEA) she fled, overcome with horror, as far as Arcadia. Her tomb could be seen near Mantinea.

Antinous (Ἀντίνοος)
1. The leader of the suitors who invaded Odysseus' palace while he was away and tried to wed Penelope. Antinous was especially notorious

Antinous was Hadrian's favourite and was renowned for his outstanding beauty. He was drowned while accompanying the Emperor up the Nile in AD 130 and subsequently deified at Hadrian's instigation. Delphi, Museum.

for his violence, brutality, pride and hard-heartedness. He tried to cause Telemachus' death, led his companions in the scramble for Odysseus' possessions, insulted Eumaus when the old swineherd admitted Odysseus into the palace, and incited the beggar Irus against Odysseus, whom he did not recognize. He was finally killed by the first arrow loosed by Odysseus, at the very moment when he was raising a cup to his lips. This could well have been the origin of the expression 'There's many a slip twixt the cup and the lip.' (See also CALCHAS.)
2. A better known Antinous was the favourite of the Emperor Hadrian. After he accidentally drowned he was deified and cults and festivals were established in his honour.

Antiochus (Ἀντίοχος) A son of Heracles and ancestor of Hippotes (see HYLLUS 3 and 4).

Antiope (Ἀντιόπη) One of the daughters of the river-god Asopus or perhaps, as some writers claim, of Nycteus the Theban (Table 25). Exceptionally beautiful, she was loved by Zeus who wooed her in the guise of a Satyr. By him she had two children, Amphion and Zethus. Before her children were born Antiope had fled from her home in fear of her father's wrath, and had taken refuge with the king of Sicyon, Epopeus (see LAMEDON). In his despair at his daughter's leaving him Nycteus killed himself, but on his deathbed he charged his brother, Lycus, with the task of avenging him. Lycus attacked and took Sicyon, killed Epopeus, and brought Antiope as a prisoner to Thebes. It was on the road between Sicyon and Thebes, at Eleutherae, that she gave birth to her two children. They were left on the mountain to die by the order of their great-uncle, Lycus, but were found by shepherds (see AMPHION). After their arrival at Thebes Lycus and his wife Dirce treated Antiope cruelly, but one night the chains in which she had been bound fell off of their own accord and she fled as fast as she could to the cottage where her children were living. They did not recognize her at first and even handed her over to Dirce, who had come to look for her. But soon the shepherd who had rescued the twins told them that Antiope was their mother. Amphion and Zethus freed her and took their revenge on Dirce and Lycus. Subsequently Antiope was smitten with madness by Dionysus, who was angered at Dirce's death, and she started wandering all over Greece until the day when she was cured and married by PHOCUS. Variations of the legend are also to be found under LYCUS.

Aphrodite (Ἀφροδίτη) The goddess of love, identified in Rome with the ancient Italic goddess Venus. There are two different accounts of her birth: sometimes she is said to be the daughter of Zeus and Dione, and sometimes a daughter of Uranus (the Sky) whose sexual organs, cut off by Cronos, fell in the sea and begot the goddess, 'she who was born of the sea' or 'she who was born of the god's seed'. Aphrodite had scarcely emerged from the sea when she was carried by the Zephyrs first to Cythera and then to the coast of Cyprus. There she was welcomed by the Seasons (the Horae), dressed and adorned and led by them to the home of the Immortals. Lucian records a legend which has it that she was first brought up by Nereus (compare HERA). Later Plato formulated the idea of there having been two Aphrodites, the daughter of Uranus, Aphrodite Urania and the goddess of pure love, and the daughter of Dione, Aphrodite Pandemia or Aphrodite of the populace, goddess of common love. But this distinction is a late philosophical concept, unknown in the early forms of the myths about the goddess.

Various legends formed round Aphrodite, consisting not of a coherent story but of different episodes in which the goddess played a part. Aphrodite was married to Hephaestus, the lame god of Lemnos, but she loved Ares the god of war. Homer tells how the two lovers were caught by surprise one morning by the Sun, who told Hephaestus of their affair. The latter set a secret trap in the form of a magic net which only he could handle. One night when the two lovers were both in Aphrodite's bed, Hephaestus closed the net over them and summoned all the Olympian gods, which caused them to rejoice exceedingly. At Poseidon's earnest request, Hephaestus agreed to draw the net back and Aphrodite, covered with shame, fled to Cyprus. The love affair between Aphrodite and Ares resulted in the birth of Eros and Anterus, Deimos and Phobos (Terror and Fear) and Harmonia (who later became the wife of Cadmus at Thebes). To these names is sometimes added Priapus, the god of Lampsacus (the protecting deity of gardens), for some traditions describe Aphrodite as the goddess of gardens, but this is true principally of her Italian character Venus.

The love affairs of Aphrodite were not confined to Ares. When Myrrha, who had become a tree, had given birth to ADONIS, Aphrodite gave shelter to the child, who was very beautiful, and put him in the care of Persephone. But the latter would not give him back. The matter was submitted to Zeus to adjudicate and he decided that the youth should spend a third of the year with Persephone, a third with Aphrodite and a third where he wanted. But Adonis actually spent a third of the year with Persephone and two-thirds with Aphrodite. Soon afterwards Adonis was wounded by a wild boar and died, possibly a victim of the jealousy of Ares.

Aphrodite also had a love affair with ANCHISES, on Mount Ida in the Troad, and by him she had two sons, Aeneas and, according to some traditions, Lyrnus.

Aphrodite's outbursts of anger and her curses were famous. It was she who inspired Eos (the Dawn) with an irresistible love for Orion, in order to punish her for having yielded to Ares, and she vented her anger on the women of Lemnos for not honouring her by making them smell so horribly that their husbands abandoned them for Thracian slave girls. The women of Lemnos in their turn then killed all the men on the island and established a community of women, until the day came when the Argonauts arrived to enable them to beget sons (see THOAS). Aphrodite also punished the daughters of Cinyras in Paphos by compelling them to become prostitutes for strangers (see also PHAEDRA, PASIPHAE, etc).

It was equally dangerous to be in Aphrodite's favour. One day Discord threw an apple intended to be given to whichever of the three goddesses Hera, Athena and Aphrodite, was the most beautiful. Zeus bade Hermes lead all three up to Mount Ida in the Troad, where they were to be judged by Alexander (known later as Paris). The three goddesses began to argue in his presence, each boasting of her beauty and promising him gifts. Hera offered him worldwide sovereignty; Athena offered to make him invincible in war; Aphrodite promised him the hand of Helen. He chose Aphrodite and thus it was that she was the underlying cause of the Trojan War. Throughout the war she granted her protection to the Trojans, and to Paris in particular. When Paris took on Menelaus in single combat and was about to yield, it was she who snatched him from danger and so caused the incident which reopened the general fighting. Later she similarly protected Aeneas when he was on the point of being killed by Diomedes, who actually wounded her. But the protection offered by Aphrodite could not avert the fall of Troy and the death of Paris. Nevertheless she succeeded in preserving the Trojan race and it was thanks to her that AENEAS, with his father and son and bearing the Penates of Troy, managed to escape from the burning city and seek a country where he could acquire a new fatherland. This was how Aphrodite-Venus became the special protectress of Rome. She was regarded as the ancestress of the Julii, who claimed descent from Iulus, his father Aeneas, and consequently the goddess. For this reason Caesar built a temple in her honour under the protection of Mother Venus or Venus Genetrix.

Her favourite creatures were doves, a flock of which drew her chariot. Her plants were rose and myrtle.

Apis (Ἄπις) According to the tradition recorded by Apollodorus, Apis was the son of Phoroneus and the grandson of Inachus. His mother was the Nymph Teledice. From his father he inherited power over the whole Peloponnese, which was called Apia after him. But he acted like a tyrant and was killed, according to some by Aetolus, the hero who gave his name to Aetolia, according to others by Thelxion and Telchis. He was subsequently deified and worshipped under the name of Sarapis. His death was avenged by Argos. According to Aeschylus, Apis was a physician with the gift of prophecy, a son of Apollo who had come from Naupactus to purify the Peloponnese.

In another version of the legend, recorded by Pausanias, Apis is said to be the son of Telchis of Sicyon and father of Thelxion (Table 22).

Apollo (Ἀπόλλων) A god of the second generation of Olympians, son of Zeus and Leto and brother of the goddess Artemis. Hera, in her jealousy of Leto, had pursued the young woman all round the world. Wearied by her wanderings Leto searched for a place where she could give birth to the children with whom she was pregnant; and the whole world refused to welcome her for fear of Hera's wrath. Only a bare, floating island called Ortygia (the Island of Quails) or later Asteria agreed to shelter the unhappy Leto. That was where Apollo was born; in gratitude the god laid it down as the centre of the Greek world and named it Delos the brilliant. There, at the foot of a palm, the only tree on the island, Leto waited nine days and nights for the birth to take place. Hera kept back with her on Olympus Eilithyia, the goddess who presided over happy deliveries. All the goddesses, and especially Athena, were close to Leto but could do nothing to help her without Hera's agreement. Eventually they decided to send Iris to ask Hera for permission for the birth to take place, offering her, to assuage her wrath, a necklace of gold and amber, nine cubits thick. This gift was large enough for Hera to agree to Eilithyia's coming down from Olympus and going to Delos. Leto knelt at the foot of the palm tree and gave birth first to Artemis and then, with Eilithyia's help, to Apollo. At the moment of the god's birth, sacred swans came and flew round the island seven times in succession, for it was the seventh day of the month. Zeus at once gave his son gifts – a golden mitre, a lyre and a chariot drawn by swans – and bade him go at once to Delphi. But the swans first took Apollo to their own country, on the shores of the Ocean, beyond the country of the North Wind, to the land of the Hyperboreans. There the god spent a year, receiving the response of the Hyperboreans, then he returned to Greece and made his way to Delphi at midsummer among feasting and song. Even Nature was in festive mood for him: cicadas and nightingales sang to honour him, and the springs were clearer. Each year at Delphi the arrival of the god was celebrated with hecatombs.

At Delphi Apollo slew a dragon, sometimes called Python, and sometimes Delphyne, which had the task of protecting an ancient oracle of Themis, but which had given itself over to every kind of theft in the countryside, muddying the springs and the streams, carrying off the flocks and the villagers, laying waste the fertile plain of Crissa and terrorizing the Nymphs. This monster had issued from Earth and there is also a story that Hera had bidden it to pursue Leto before Apollo and Artemis were born. Apollo rid the country of it but, in memory of his exploit (or perhaps to calm down the monster's anger after its death), he founded funerary games in its honour, which took the name of the Pythian Games and were held at Delphi. After that he took possession of the oracle of Themis and dedicated a tripod in the shrine. The tripod is one of Apollo's symbols and the Pythian was seated on one when her oracles were uttered. The inhabitants of Delphi celebrated the god's victory and his taking possession of the shrine with songs of triumph. For the first time they sang the Paean, which is essentially a hymn in honour of Apollo. But Apollo himself had to go to the Vale of Tempe, in Thessaly, to cleanse himself of the pollution resulting from the slaying of the dragon. Every eight years a solemn festival was held at Delphi in memory of the killing of the Python and the purification of Apollo. There is a story that the god had once again to defend his oracle, this time against Heracles, who had come to question it and, when it refused to give him any answer, tried to ransack the temple, carry off the tripod and establish an oracle of his own elsewhere. Apollo engaged him in conflict which remained indecisive since Zeus separated the opponents (who were both his sons) by hurling a thunderbolt between them. But the oracle remained at Delphi.

Apollo was depicted as a god of extreme beauty and great stature, especially distinguished for his long curling, black hair with tinges of blue like the petals of a viola. He also had a great many love affairs, with both Nymphs and mortal women.

Apollo was represented as a god of ideal mature beauty in antique art. Bronze Apollo of c. 500 BC found at Piraeus. Athens, National Museum.

He fell in love with the Nymph Daphne, daughter of the river god Peneus in Thessaly. His love for her had been fired by the malice of Eros, angered in turn by the taunts of Apollo who had derided him for practising archery (the bow was in fact Apollo's special weapon). Daphne remained unmoved by his advances. She fled into the mountains and when she was pursued by the god and on the point of being captured she uttered a prayer to her father, begging him to change her so that she might escape from Apollo's embrace. Her father did as she wished and turned her into a laurel, the tree sacred to Apollo.

He fared better with the Nymph Cyrene by whom he begot the demigod Aristaeus. He also had love affairs with the Muses, whose cult was closely linked with his own. He is said to have been, through Thalia, the father of the Corybantes, the demons who formed part of the following of Dionysus. By Urania he is supposed to have begotten the musicians Linus and Orpheus, though other versions ascribe them to Oeagrus and the Muse Calliope. One of his most famous love affairs is that relating to the birth of ASCLEPIUS, in which he was the victim of the unfaithfulness of Coronis. He suffered a similar misfortune with Marpessa, the daughter of Evenus. Apollo loved her but she was carried off by Idas, the son of Amphiaraus, in a winged chariot which was a gift from Poseidon. Idas took the girl to Messina, where he and Apollo fought each other, but once again Zeus parted them. Marpessa was given the right to choose between her two suitors and her choice fell on Idas, fearing, so the story goes, that she would be deserted in her old age if she married Apollo. His love for Cassandra, the daughter of Priam, had equally unhappy results. Apollo loved Cassandra and, in order to seduce her, promised to teach her the art of divination. She underwent the lessons but, when she had learned them, she refused to yield to him. Apollo took his revenge by withdrawing from her the gift of inspiring confidence in her divinations, and so the unhappy Cassandra made her most accurate predictions in vain, for no one would believe her.

This may have been about the time when Apollo was loved by Hecuba, Priam's wife and Cassandra's mother, and she presented him with a son, Troilus. Similarly at Colophon, in Asia, Apollo was believed to have had a son by the female soothsayer Manto, in the shape of the seer Mopsus, who overcame the Greek seer Calchas in a contest after the Trojan War. Also in Asia, Apollo had a son called Miletus by a woman variously called Aria, Acacallis or Acalle. This Miletus subsequently founded the town of that name.

In Greece itself Apollo was generally regarded as the lover of Phthia, who gave her name to the eponymous area of Thessaly, and three children were believed to have been born to them – Dorus, Laodocus and Polypoetes, all of whom were killed by Aetolus. Finally by Rhoeo he begot Anius, who ruled over Delos. Tenes, who was killed by Achilles in the island of Tenedos and whose death began the unfolding of the Fates which finally led to the death of Achilles himself, is sometimes said to be the son of Apollo and sometimes of Cycnus.

Apollo did not confine his love affairs to young women, for he also loved young men. The best known are the heroes Hyacinthus and Cyparissus whose deaths or rather metamorphoses (the former became a martagon lily or a hyacinth, while the second became a cypress) distressed the god very deeply.

There is a story that on two occasions Apollo was put to an unusual test, and had to put himself in the position of a slave in the service of mortal masters. The first occasion followed a conspiracy in which he had joined Poseidon, Hera and Athena to bind Zeus in iron chains and hang him in the sky (see AEGEON). After the failure of this plot Apollo and Poseidon were compelled to work for Laomedon, king of Troy, on the task of building the walls of the city though, according to some writers, Poseidon worked by himself on the walls while Apollo looked after the king's flocks on Mount Ida. When the time of their servitude was up Laomedon refused to pay the two gods their agreed wages. Moreover, when they protested he threatened to cut off their ears and sell them as slaves. When Apollo had regained his divine appearance and power he sent a plague to Troy which laid the land waste. (See HESIONE and HERACLES.)

The legend of Apollo in the role of a shepherd recurs in the second test which the god underwent. When Apollo's son Asclepius had advanced so far in the art of medicine that he succeeded in bringing corpses back to life Zeus struck him with lightning. This was an appalling blow for Apollo who, since he could not exact revenge from Zeus himself, killed with his arrows the Cyclopes who made the lightning. Zeus for a moment had it in mind to punish him by plunging him down into Tartarus, but in response to Leto's pleas he agreed to inflict a lighter punishment and commanded

Apollo was also the god of music and poetry and is shown in this Roman wall painting holding his lyre.

that Apollo should serve a mortal master as a slave for a year. In compliance Apollo made his way to Pheres, to the court of King Admetus, and served him as a herdsman. Thanks to him the cows produced two calves at a time, and he brought general prosperity to the family (see ALCESTIS).

Apollo can sometimes be found as a cowherd working for himself. His oxen were stolen by the young Hermes while he was still in swaddling clothes, proof of his precocity. Apollo recovered his possessions on Mount Cyllene. But, so the story goes, the infant Hermes had invented the lyre and Apollo was so delighted with it that in exchange for it he let Hermes keep his cattle. When Hermes subsequently invented the flute Apollo bought it from him for a golden staff (the Caduceus of Hermes) and moreover instructed him in the art of soothsaying.

The story of Marsyas is another legend about Apollo in which the flute plays a part. Marsyas the Satyr, who was the son of Olympus, found a flute which had been thrown away by Athena. (She had tried to play it but had immediately given it up when she had realized how much it put her mouth out of shape and gave her an ugly expression.) When Marsyas found that he could make delight-ful music with it he challenged Apollo and claimed to make sweeter music with his flute than Apollo with his lyre. Marsyas was the loser and Apollo first hanged him from a pine tree and then flayed him.

It was as the god of music and poetry that Apollo was portrayed on Mount Parnassus, where he presided over the pastimes of the Muses. His oracular pronouncements were generally in the form of verse and he was thought to provide inspiration for seers as well as for poets. This office he shared with Dionysus, but inspiration by Apollo differed from that of Dionysus since it was more temperate.

As well as being the god of soothsaying, of music, and of nature, his love affairs with the Nymphs and the young people who became flowers and trees linked him intimately with plant growth and Nature. Apollo was also a warrior god who could, like his sister Artemis, bring a swift and easy death from afar with his bow and arrows. Together they took part in the massacre of Niobe's children to avenge the honour of Leto. Apollo brought down on the Greeks before Troy a plague which decimated their army, in order to compel Agamemnon to return to his priest Chryses the young Chryseis who was still held in captivity. He also slew the Cyclopes, the snake

Python and the giant Tityus. He took part, on the side of the Olympians, in their struggle against the Giants (the Gigantomachia). In the *Iliad* we find him fighting for the Trojans against the Greeks and protecting Paris, and it was said to be his direct or indirect involvement which led to the death of Achilles.

Certain animals were especially dedicated to Apollo: the wolf, which was sometimes sacrificed as an offering to him, and which is often depicted, together with him, on coins; the roebuck or hind which also plays a part in the cult of Artemis; among birds the swan, the kite, the vulture and the crow, whose flight could convey omens. Among sea creatures there was the dolphin, whose name recalls that of Delphi, home of the main shrine of Apollo. The bay laurel was the plant of Apollo above all others. It was a bay leaf that the Pythia chewed during her prophetic trances.

The roles and symbols of Apollo are multifa-rious, and their study belongs to the history of religion rather than to mythology. Apollo gradually became the god of the Orphic religion, and with his name was associated a whole system of thought and belief, half religious and half moral, which promised safety and eternal life to its initiates (see ZAGREUS and ORPHEUS). Apollo was believed to be the father of Pythagoras, to whose name similar doctrines were often attached. Apollo (and especially Hyperborean Apollo) was often seen as ruling over the Isles of the Blessed, which were the Paradise of Orphism and neo-Pythagoreanism. It is by virtue of this that myths of Apollo are so often to be found on the walls of the Basilica of the Porta Maxima in Rome, as well as on carved Roman sarcophagi. Augustus, the first Roman Emperor, took Apollo as his personal guardian and ascribed to him the naval victory which he had won over Antony and Cleopatra at Actium in 31 BC. It was the general belief among the populace that Atia, Augustus' mother, had conceived him through the instrument of the god on a night when she had slept in his temple. Augustus built a temple of Apollo beside his own house on the Palatine, and established a private cult in his honour. It was largely in Apollo's honour that the Ludi Saeculares at which the *Carmen Saeculare* of Horace was sung, were cele-brated in 17 BC. In the *Carmen* Apollo and his sister Artemis are presented as deities forming a channel between the Roman people and Jupiter, and they are the ones who transmit and spread heavenly blessings.

Apriate (Ἀπριάτη) The girl without price, a heroine of Lesbos, who was loved by TRAMBELUS, the son of Telamon, but did not return his love. The young man loved her so desperately that he decided to abduct her while she was walking with her attendants in an estate which belonged to her father. The girl put up a fight so Trambelus threw her into the sea. Some say that she threw herself in, but anyway she was drowned. Soon afterwards heaven punished Trambelus.

Apsyrtos (Ἄψυρτος) See ARGONAUTS.

Arachne (Ἀράχνη) A Lydian girl whose father, Idmon of Colophon, was a dyer. While quite young she gained a great reputation for weaving and embroidery. The tapestries she designed were so beautiful that the Nymphs from the countryside around used to come to gaze at them. Her skill gained her the reputation of having been Athena's pupil, for she was the goddess of spinners and embroiderers. But Arachne was unwilling to attribute her talent to anyone but herself. She challenged the goddess, who accepted the challenge and appeared to her in the guise of an old woman. At first Athena did no more than warn Arachne and advise her to behave with greater modesty: otherwise she would have to fear the goddess's wrath. Arachne replied only with insults, at which point the goddess threw off her disguise and the contest began. The design of Pallas' tapestry showed the twelve Olympian gods in all their majesty, and as a warning to her rival, in each of the corners, Athena wove pictures showing the defeat of mortals who had dared to defy the gods. Arachne's theme on her tapestry was the least creditable love affairs of the gods: Zeus and Europa, Zeus and Danae, and so on. Her work was perfect, but Athena was so angry that she tore it up and struck her rival with the shuttle. At this abuse Arachne lost heart and hanged herself, but Athena would not let her die and changed her into a spider which continues to spin and weave until it has no more thread (for another tradition, see PHALANX).

Arcas (Ἀρκάς) The son of Zeus and Callisto, the Nymph of the hunt and the companion of Artemis. Another version of the myth makes him the son of Pan. When CALLISTO who was loved by Zeus, died, or, in the most familiar form of the legend, was changed into a she-bear, Zeus entrusted the child to Maia, the mother of Hermes, who brought him up. On his mother's side Arcas was the grandson of King Lycaon, who reigned over the country later known as Arcadia. One day Lycaon, in order to test the perspicacity of Zeus, is said to have served up the limbs of little Arcas, cooked and ready to be eaten. Zeus was not in the least taken in. He overturned the table and struck the house of Lycaon with lightning. Lycaon himself was changed into a wolf and Zeus put Arcas' limbs together again and restored him to life.

When Arcas was grown up, one day while he was out hunting he met his mother in the shape of a bear, and chased her. The animal took shelter in the temple of 'Lycian' Zeus. Arcas, following her, made his way into the sacred precinct. There was then a law of the country which made this kind of invasion punishable by death, but Zeus had pity on them both and to save their lives he changed them into the constellation of Ursa and its guardian, Arcturus.

Arcas was the ruler of the Pelasgians of the Peloponnese, who were called Arcadians after him. He was the successor of Nyctimus, the son of Lycaon. He taught his people to grow corn, to make bread and to spin wool. He married Meganira, the daughter of Amyclas (see Table 6 and CROCON) by whom he had two sons, Elatus and Aphidas (for a different version, see CHRYSOPELIA). By the Nymph Erato he had a third son, Azan, and divided Arcadia between the three of them (Table 9).

Archelaus (Ἀρχέλαος) The son of Temenus and a descendant of Heracles (Table 16). He was banished from the town of Argos and made his way to the court of King Cisseus in Macedonia. At the time Cisseus was besieged by his enemies, who were on the point of overwhelming him. He promised Archelaus both his daughter and his throne in return for deliverance. Archelaus, true to the example of his ancestor Heracles, remedied the situation in a single battle and saved Cisseus. But the latter, under the influence of wicked advisers, refused to grant the promised reward and, in order to wipe out all trace of his bad faith, planned to put Archelaus to death. For this purpose he had a huge pit prepared, filled with glowing coals and covered with a layer of branches. But Archelaus, warned of the plot by one of the king's slaves, asked for a secret interview with Cisseus and threw him into the pit. Then, in obedience to a command from Apollo, he left the town and followed a she-goat which he met on his way. The goat led him to a place in Macedonia where he founded a town and named it Aege in honour of the goat which had led him there (αἴζ, goat). Archelaus was said to be a direct ancestor of Alexander of Macedon.

Archemorus (Ἀρχήμορος) See AMPHIARAUS.

Areion (Ἀρείων) The name of Adrastus' horse in the first expedition against Thebes. The horse saved the life of Adrastus, when all the other heroes who had taken part in the war were killed. After the defeat of the Argive army Areion carried his master quickly away from the battlefield and left him in safety near Colonus in Attica. The speed of Areion had already been displayed in the funerary games founded in honour of Archemorus (see AMPHIARAUS).

The following story was told about Arion's breeding. When Demeter was searching for her daughter, who had been abducted by her uncle, Hades (see PERSEPHONE), Poseidon, who was in love with Demeter, followed her everywhere she went. To rid herself of him, Demeter had the idea of changing herself into a mare and hiding among the horses of King Oncus, at Thelpusa in Arcadia. But Poseidon was not taken in. He himself assumed the likeness of a horse and in this guise mated with her. From this union was born a daughter whose name could not be uttered (she was known as the Lady or the Mistress) and a horse, Areion. This horse belonged first to Oncus, and then to Heracles, who used it in the expedition against Elis and the struggle against Cycnus.

Ares (Ἄρης) The Greek god of war, the equivalent of Mars in Italy. He was the son of Zeus and Hera and, like Apollo, Hermes and others, belongs to the second generation of the Olympian deities (Table 38). He is one of the twelve great gods, unlike his sisters Hebe and Eilithyia, who are minor deities. From the Homeric period Ares was pre-eminently the god of war, the spirit of battle delighting in slaughter and blood. In the fighting at Troy he was generally on the side of the Trojans, but had little regard for the justice of the cause he was backing. He is represented wearing armour and a helmet, and carrying a shield, spear and sword. He was of more than human height and uttered terrible cries. He normally fought on foot but he could be found in a chariot drawn by four chargers. He was attended by demons who served him as squires, especially Deimos and Phobos (Fear and Terror), his

children, and also sometimes Eris (Strife) and Enyo.

Ares lived in Thrace, a half-wild country with a harsh climate, rich in horses and traversed by warlike peoples. Thrace was also, at least traditionally, the home of the Amazons, who were Ares' daughters. In Greece proper he was the object of a special cult in Thebes, where he was believed to have been the ancestor of the descendants of Cadmus. In fact Mars had a spring in Thebes, guarded by a dragon of which he was the father. When CADMUS, in order to perform a sacrifice, wanted to draw some water from the spring, the dragon tried to stop him. Cadmus killed it and, in expiation of the murder, had to serve Ares as a slave for eight years. At the end of that time the gods married Cadmus to Harmonia, the daughter of Ares and Aphrodite.

Most of the myths in which Ares featured are, naturally, about war and stories of fighting. But the god is far from being always the victor. It seems, on the contrary, that the Greeks, ever since the Homeric age, took pleasure in presenting the brute strength of Ares as being restrained or deceived by the wiser strength displayed by Heracles or the manly wisdom of Athena. One day, on the battlefield before Troy, Ares was fighting alongside Hector when he found himself confronting Diomedes. He at once attacked him but Athena, rendered invisible by the magic helmet of Hades, was successful in turning Ares' spear aside and he was wounded by Diomedes. The god uttered a terrible cry, heard by the whole army, and fled back to Olympus, where Zeus had his wound dressed. On another occasion, in the confused fighting of the gods which took place before Troy, Athena was once more doing battle with Ares and got the better of him by stunning him with a blow from a stone.

The antagonism between Ares and Athena was not confined to the Trojan cycle. When Ares wanted to defend his son Cycnus in battle against Heracles, Athena invited Ares to submit to Fate which decreed that Cycnus would be slain by Heracles unless the hero were first killed by someone else. But Athena's words were of no avail and she had to intervene directly in order to turn aside Ares' spear. Heracles, taking advantage of Ares' failure to protect himself properly, wounded him in the thigh and Ares fled with ignominy to Olympus. This was, moreover, the second time that Heracles had wounded Ares: the first occasion was at Pylos where Heracles had even stripped him of his weapons. When the Amazon Penthesilea, Ares' daughter, was killed before Troy, Ares wanted to rush headlong to avenge her without any regard to the Fates, and Zeus had to stop him with a thunderbolt. Yet another misfortune of Ares was to be imprisoned by the Aloadae who kept him for thirteen months, chained up in a bronze vessel.

It was an act of violence on the part of Ares which associated him with the Areopagus, the hill in Athens which was the meeting place of the court responsible for trying crimes of a religious character. There was a spring at the foot of the hill and it was there that Ares saw Halirrhothius, the son of Poseidon and the nymph Euryte, trying to rape Alcippe, his daughter by Aglaurus. In a fit of anger Ares killed Halirrhothius; Poseidon made him appear before a court of the Olympians, on the hill at whose foot the murder had taken place. The gods acquitted the murderer.

There are many legends about Ares' love affairs. The best known is without doubt the one in which he was found having a secret affair with the goddess Aphrodite. But he also had many children by mortal women. Most of them turned into violent and unfriendly men who attacked travellers and killed them or gave themselves over to a variety of acts of cruelty. By Pyrene he had three sons, Cycnus, Diomedes of Thrace, whose mares ate human flesh, and Lycaon. All three of them were killed by Heracles. Ares was also said to have been the father of Meleager and of Dryas, who took part with Meleager in the hunt in Calydon. Finally it was Ares who was said to have given his son Oenomaus the weapons with which he slaughtered his daughter's suitors (see PELOPS and HIPPODAMIA).

The animals dedicated to Ares were the dog and the vulture.

Arethusa (Ἀρέθουσα)

A nymph of the Peloponnese and of Sicily (see ALPHEUS and the NAIADS).

Argennus (Ἄργεννος)

A youth of great beauty, son of Pisidice, the daughter of Leucon (Table 33). He lived in Boeotia on the shores of Lake Copais. One day when he was bathing in the Cephisus, Agamemnon, who was then at Aulis, where he was waiting for favourable winds before embarking, caught sight of him and fell in love with him. Argennus fled and Agamemnon pursued him. At the end of his strength, Argennus threw himself into the river and drowned. Agamemnon

Arethusa was loved by the river god Alpheus and to escape him she fled to Syracuse where she was changed into a spring. Decadrachm signed by Evainetos 395–380 BC.

arranged a splendid funeral for him and founded a temple of Artemis Argennis in his honour.

Argonauts (Ἀργοναῦται)

The name given to the companions of Jason in his search for the Golden Fleece (for the origins of this expedition, see JASON). They were so called after the *Argo*, the name of the ship they sailed in, which means swift but also evokes the name of its builder (see ARGOS).

1. *The Argonauts.* A number of catalogues have preserved the list of names of the Argonauts who had come running at the news, proclaimed by heralds throughout Greece, that Jason was preparing an expedition to Colchis. These lists have obvious differences, reflecting their various ages. Two of them are especially interesting because they are largely independent of each other, namely those of Apollonius of Rhodes and of Apollodorus. The number of the Argonauts is fairly constant at fifty to fifty-five. The ship was built for forty oarsmen. A certain number of names occur in both lists and represent the firmest basis for the legend. Apart from Jason, who was in command of the expedition, there was Argos the son of Phrixus (or, in other versions, of Arestor) who built the ship, and Tiphys, son of Hagnias, who was the helmsman. He had taken on this duty on the orders of Athena who had taught him the art of navigation, previously unknown. When

Hagnias died in the land of the Mariandyni (see below) his place was taken by Erginus, the son of Poseidon. Then there was Orpheus, the music-maker from Thrace, whose task it was to set the rhythm for the oarsmen. The gods were said to have bidden him to sail on the ship so that his singing might counter the allurements of the Sirens. The crew numbered several soothsayers – Idmon, the son of Abas, Amphiaraus and, at least in the list of Apollonius, the Lapith Mopsus. Then there were the two sons of Boreas, Zetes and Calais, the two sons of Zeus and Leda, Castor and Pollux, and their two cousins, the sons of Aphareus, Idas and Lynceus. The herald of the expedition was Aethalides, a son of Hermes, whose name does not occur in Apollodorus. All these heroes played an active part in the *Argo*'s adventures. The following generally played minor parts: Admetus, the son of Pheres; Acastus, son of Pelias, who had accompanied his cousin Jason in defiance of his father's orders; Periclymenus, the son of Neleus; Asterius (or Asterion), the son of

Antique bas-relief depicting the building of the ship Argo. *Rome, Villa Albani.*

Cometes; the Lapith Polyphemus, the son of Elatus; Caeneus, or sometimes his son Coronus; Eurytus, the son of Hermes and (according to Apollonius) his brother Echion; Augias, son of Helios and king of Elis, the brother of Aeetes, who took part in the expedition, according to tradition, from a desire to see his brother, whom he did not know; Cepheus, the son of Aleus and (only in Apollonius' account) his brother Amphidamas; Palaemonius, the son of Hephaestus or of Aetolus; Euphemus, son of Poseidon; Peleus and his brother Telamon, both sons of Aeacus; Iphitus, son of Naubolus; Poeas, father of Philoctetes, is mentioned by Valerius Flaccus and Hyginus. There were also Iphiclus, son of Thestius, and his nephew, Meleager; Butes, son of Teleon and, in Apollonius only, Eribotes, the son of another Teleon. Apollonius and Apollodorus both include Heracles, whose name occurs in the incident concerning the abduction of Hylas, but about whom the traditions are widely at variance. Finally, both Apollonius and Apollodorus include Anceus, son of Lycurgus.

The following names are not mentioned by Apollodorus: three of the sons of Pero, Talaus, Areius and Leodocus (Table 1); Iphiclus, son of Phylacus; Eurydamas, son of Ctimenus; Phalerus, son of Alcon; an Athenian Philias or Phlius, son of Dionysus (Apollodorus records instead two other sons of Dionysus, Phanus and Staphylus); Nauplius, whom Apollonius distinguishes, on chronological grounds, from the father of Palamedes; Oileus, the father of Ajax the lesser. Among the relatives of Meleager, Apollonius adds to the names already listed Laocoon, the son of Porthaon, who is not mentioned by Apollodorus. There were also Eurytion, the son of Irus; Clytius and Iphitus, the sons of Eurytus; Canthus, the son of Canethus; and Asterius and Amphion, the sons of Hyperasius.

On the other hand, Apollodorus names the following heroes who are not mentioned by Apollonius: besides Phanus and Staphylus (see above); Actor, son of Hippasus; Laertes, and his father-in-law Antolycus; Euryalus, son of Mecisteus, who is to be found in the Trojan cycle, like Peneleos the son of Hippalmus, Leitus, son of Alectryon, then Atalanta, the only female member of the expedition, Theseus, in whose legend it is only an episode introduced as a contrived and late device, Menoetius, the son of Actor (see above) and finally Ascalaphus and Ialmenus, two sons of Ares.

The imagination of differing scholars and later poets ended by including among the Argonauts impressive names which were not accepted by either Apollonius or Apollodorus. For example Tydeus, Asclepius the healer, Philammon the musician, Nestor, who is mentioned only in the poem of Valerius Flaccus, Pirithous, Theseus' inseparable companion, who is there only because of the latter's presence in the legend, just as the mention of Heracles brings in his son Hyllus in direct contradiction of the generally accepted chronologies, together with Iolaus, Iphis the brother of Eurystheus and even, but only in Hyginus, Iphicles, the twin brother of Heracles. Valerius Flaccus gives the name of a certain Clymenus, uncle of Meleager, generally thought to be one of his brothers (Table 27). Finally Hyginus is the only writer to mention Hippalcimus, the son of Pelops and Hippodamia, who finds no place in the generally accepted genealogies, Deucalion of Crete, the father of Idomeneus, and a hero whose twisted name seems to be Thersanor, son of the Leucothoe who was changed into a sunflower or heliotrope (see CLYTIA).

2. *The Voyage.* The ship was built at Pagasae, a Thessalian port, by Argos (see ARGOS 4) with the help of the goddess Athena. The wood came from Pelion save for the prow, which was a piece of the sacred oak of Dodona brought by the goddess. She herself had cut it and given it the power of speech, to such a degree that it could prophesy.

The *Argo* was launched by the heroes, amid a great crowd of onlookers, on the beach of Pagasae and they embarked, after sacrificing to Apollo. The omens were good; they were interpreted by Idmon and disclosed that everyone would return safe and sound, except for Idmon himself who was fated to die during the voyage.

The first port of call was the island of Lemnos. At that period it was inhabited only by women, since they had put all the men to death (see APHRODITE, HYPSIPYLE, THOAS and others). The Argonauts coupled with them and fathered sons. When they left, they set sail towards the island of Samothrace where, on the advice of Orpheus, they were initiated into the Orphic mysteries. Then they made their way into the Hellespont; they reached the island of Cyzicus in the country of the Delians whose king was called Cyzicus. These people also received them hospitably and the king invited them to a feast and gave them many tokens of his friendship. The following evening the heroes set sail, but during the night adverse winds got up and blew them back before dawn once again on the Delian coast. The inhabitants, who did not realize that the Argonauts were their guests of the previous night, took them for Pelasgian pirates. Battle was joined. When he heard the noise King Cyzicus came in haste to lend assistance to his subjects and was immediately killed by Jason himself, who ran him through the chest with his spear. The other heroes inflicted great slaughter on their enemies, but when dawn broke and the two sides realized their mistake there was universal grief. Jason arranged a magnificent funeral for King Cyzicus. For three days the Argonauts carried on their rites of lamentation and arranged games in his honour, but Clete, Cyzicus' young wife, hanged herself in her despair. The Nymphs wept so deeply for her that from their tears there sprang a fountain which was called Clete. Before they left, as a storm prevented them from putting to sea again, the Argonauts erected a statue of Cybele, the mother of the gods, on Mount Dindymus, which overlooks Cyzicus.

The next stage of their voyage took them further east to the coast of Mysia. The inhabitants welcomed them and gave them gifts. While the heroes were busy preparing a banquet Heracles, who had broken his oar with the power of his rowing during the crossing, went into the nearby forest to find a tree from which to make another. At the same time Hylas, a young man whom he loved, and who had embarked on the *Argo* with him, had been sent to look for fresh water in preparation for the feast. At the edge of a spring he met the Nymphs, and, overcome by his good looks, they lured him to the spring where he drowned. Polyphemus, another of the Argonauts, heard the boy's cry just as he was disappearing beneath the water. He rushed off to help him and on the road met Heracles returning from the forest. They both spent the whole night searching in the forest for Hylas and when the ship left before dawn they were not on board. Accordingly the Argonauts had to resume their voyage without Heracles and Polyphemus, for Fate had not decreed that the two heroes should take part in the capture of the Golden Fleece. Polyphemus founded the nearby town of Clios and Heracles went on to carry out his exploits single-handed.

The *Argo* arrived next at the country of the Bebryces, ruled by King Amycus. According to some traditions, after Amycus had been defeated by Pollux, the fighting between the Argonauts and the Bebryces became general. Many of the latter were killed and finally they fled in every direction.

On the following day the Argonauts left again and, swept along by the wind, they put in on the coast of Thrace, that is to say on the European bank of the Hellespont, before they could make their way into the Bosphorus. There they found themselves in the land of Phineus, a son of Poseidon, and a blind seer on whom the gods had visited an extraordinary curse: every time a table laden with food was set before him, the Harpies, creatures half woman and half bird, swooped on the food, taking part of it and leaving the remainder polluted with their droppings. The Argonauts asked Phineus to tell them what the outcome of their expedition would be but the seer refused to give them an answer before they had rid him of the Harpies. The Argonauts bade him sit at their table and when the Harpies swooped down, Calais and Zetes, who had wings as they were the sons of a god of the wind, launched themselves in pursuit, until the Harpies were exhausted and promised by the Styx not to molest King Phineus any more. Once his curse had been lifted Phineus revealed that part of the Argonauts' future which they were allowed to know. He warned them against a danger which would soon threaten them on their journey, namely the Blue Rocks, moving reefs which collided with each other. To know whether they would be able to pass between them, Phineus advised them to get a dove to fly in front of them. If it succeeded in passing through the straits in safety they would be able to follow it without danger. But if the reefs closed on it the will of the gods was against them and the wise course of action would be to abandon their attempt. Then he gave them some hints about the main landmarks on the route.

After hearing this oracle the Argonauts went on their way. When they arrived at the Blue Rocks, also known as the Symplegades, meaning the Colliding Rocks, they let loose a dove which managed to get through the channel. But the rocks, closing up again, gripped the longest feathers of its tail. The heroes waited until the rocks had parted again and then made the passage in their turn. The ship got through safe and sound, but the stern was slightly damaged, like the tail of the dove. Ever since then the Blue Rocks have remained motionless, for fate had decreed that once a ship passed them safely they could move no more.

Having thus made their way into the Euxine or Black Sea, the Argonauts reached the land of the Mariandyni whose king, Lycus, received them favourably. It was there, during a hunt, that the seer Idmon was wounded by a boar and died. There too their steersman Tiphys, died. His place at the helm was taken by Ancaea. Then the Argonauts passed the mouth of the Thermodon (the river on the banks of which the Amazons were sometimes said to live) then skirted the Caucasus and arrived at the mouth of the river Phasis, which was the goal of their voyage.

The heroes disembarked and Jason presented himself to King Aeetes, to whom he explained the mission with which Pelias had entrusted him. The king did not refuse to give him the Golden Fleece, but added as a condition that he should yoke, unaided, two bulls with brazen hoofs which breathed fire from their nostrils. These huge bulls, which Hephaestus had given Aeetes, had never known the yoke. When he had finished this first test Jason would have to plough a field and sow the teeth of a dragon. These were the rest of the teeth of Ares' dragon at Thebes, which Athena had given to Aeetes (see CADMUS and ARES).

Jason was wondering how he could yoke these monstrous beasts when Medea, the king's daughter, who had fallen deeply in love with him, came to help him. She began by making him promise that he would marry her and take her to Greece if she allowed him to succeed in the tests which her father had set him – a promise which Jason made. Medea then gave him magic balsam (for she was very skilled in all the occult arts) with which he was to cover his body and his shield before he attacked the bulls of Hephaestus. This balm had the property of making anyone covered by it invulnerable for a whole day to harm from iron or fire. Furthermore, it showed him that the dragon's teeth would give birth to a crop of armed men who would try to kill the hero, but he had only to throw a stone into their midst from a distance and the men would start to attack each other, each accusing his neighbour of having thrown the stone, and they would all be killed by each other's blows.

Jason, thus forewarned, managed to yoke and harness the oxen, and then to plough the field and finally he sowed the dragon's teeth. Then he concealed himself and from a distance stoned the warriors who had sprung from this strange seed. They began to fight each other and, taking advantage of their failure to notice him, Jason slew them.

Aeetes, however, did not keep his promise: he tried to burn the *Argo* and kill her crew. But before he had time to do so Jason, acting on Medea's advice, had already secured the Fleece (Medea had put a spell on the dragon which was guarding it) and made his escape.

When Aeetes discovered that Jason had fled taking with him both the Fleece and his daughter, he set out in haste to try to overtake the ship. Medea, who had foreseen that this would happen, killed her brother, Apsyrtus, whom she had taken with her, and scattered his limbs along the way. Aeetes spent some time picking them up and by the time he had done so it was too late to overtake the fugitives. Accordingly, taking with him his sons's limbs, he put in at the nearest port, which was Tomi, on the western shore of the Black Sea, and buried his son there. But before he returned to Colchis he sent out several groups of his subjects in pursuit of the *Argo* warning them that if they returned without Medea they would be put to death in her stead.

Another version of the story says that Apsyrtus had been sent by Aeetes in pursuit of his sister but that Jason, with the help of Medea, had killed him in a temple dedicated to Artemis which lies at the mouth of the Danube. Whatever the truth may be the Argonauts went on their way towards the Danube and followed the river upstream until they reached the Adriatic (at the date of this story the Danube, or Istros, was regarded as a river artery, linking the Black Sea and the Adriatic). Zeus, roused to anger by the murder of Apsyrtus, sent a storm which blew the ship off course. At this point the ship itself began to speak, and made Zeus' anger clear, adding that this would not cease before the Argonauts had been purified by Circe. Accordingly the ship went upstream on the Eridanus (the Po) and the Rhône, through the territories of the Ligurians and the Celts. From there the Argonauts got back into the Mediterranean, skirted Sardinia and reached the island of Aeaea, the kingdom of Circe (which was no doubt the peninsula of Monte Circeo, north of Gaeta, between Latium and Campania). There the sorceress, who, like Aeetes, was a child of the Sun and thus the aunt of Medea, purified the hero and had a long conversation with Medea, but refused point-blank to offer Jason hospitality in her palace. The ship set forth yet again on its erratic course and, guided by Thetis in person, at Hera's bidding, it crossed the sea of the SIRENS. At this point Orpheus sang so sweetly that the heroes had no wish to respond to the Sirens' call. Only one of them, Butes, swam to their rock, but Aphrodite saved him by extracting him and settling him at Lilybaeum (the modern Marsala) on the west coast of Sicily.

Thereafter the *Argo* passed through the straits of Scylla and Charybdis, then the Wandering Isles (no doubt the Lipari islands) above which hung a cloud of black smoke. Finally they arrived at Corcyra (the modern Corfu) in the land of the Phaeacians, where Alcinous was king. There they met a band of the men of Colchis who had been despatched by Aeetes in pursuit of them. The men of Colchis demanded that Alcinous should hand over Medea to them. Alcinous, after consulting his wife Arete, replied that he would agree if Medea, on being examined, appeared to be a virgin. If, however, she was already Jason's wife she should stay with him. Arete confided Alcinous' decision secretly to Medea, and Jason lost no time in making sure that the condition which would save Medea was satisfied. Alcinous could do nothing but refuse to hand the girl over. The men of Colchis, who dared not return to their own country, settled in Phaeacia and the Argonauts took to the sea once again.

They had hardly left Corcyra before a storm drove them towards the Syrtes, on the Libyan coast. There they had to carry the ship on their shoulders until they reached Lake Tritonis. Thanks to Triton, the spirit of the lake, they found a channel to the sea and continued their voyage towards Crete. But during this phase they lost two of their company, Canthus and Mopsus, though they are not mentioned in all the lists of the Argonauts traditionally recorded (see above).

Just as they were disembarking in Crete, the Argonauts came into conflict with a giant named Talos, a kind of monstrous automaton created by Hephaestus whom Minos had charged with the responsibility for stopping anyone from landing on the island. He used to tear huge rocks from the coast and throw them at passing ships to make them turn away from the shore. He used to walk all round the island three times every day. This giant was invulnerable except that in his ankle, beneath a very thick skin, he had a vein which was his life spring and if it was opened he would die. Medea got the better of him by means of her spells. She gave him delusions which made him so wild with rage that he tore the vein in his ankle against a rock and instantly died. So the Argonauts reached land and spent the night on the beach. On the following day they built a shrine to Athena of Minos and went on their way.

On the Cretan Sea, they were suddenly overtaken by a black night of mysterious impenetrability which caused them to run into the greatest dangers. Jason prayed to Phoebus, asking him to show them their way in this darkness. In response Phoebus-Apollo threw out a shaft of flame which showed them that the boat was very close to a small island of the Sporades where they could cast anchor. They called the island Anaphe (the Isle of Discovery) and raised on it a shrine to Phoebus the Radiant. But on this rocky islet the offerings for celebrating the inaugural sacrifice worthily were lacking and they had to make their ritual libations with wine rather than water. When the female Phaeacian servants given by Arete to Medea as a wedding present saw this, they began to laugh and made robust jokes about the Argonauts. The latter responded in kind and a merry scene ensued, which was repeated every time a sacrifice in honour of Apollo was made on this tiny island.

Next the Argonauts called at Aegina and, coasting along Euboea, they arrived back at Iolcos, having accomplished their round voyage in four months, and bringing the Golden Fleece with them. Jason then sailed the *Argo* to Corinth where he dedicated it to Poseidon as an *ex voto*.

The core of this highly complex legend is earlier than the composition of the *Odyssey*, which shows familiarity with the exploits of Jason. For modern readers it is exceptionally famous on account of the long and learned poem by Apollonius of Rhodes, who tells the story in detail. It was extremely popular in the ancient world and ended by forming a cycle to which a number of local legends became attached. It is possible to extract from the adventures of the *Argo*, as from the *Iliad*, plots for plays and poetry of every description. The story of Medea, in particular, caught the imagination of the poets (see MEDEA and JASON).

Argos (Ἄργος) Several characters bear this name.
1. The first Argos was the son of Zeus and Niobe and on his mother's side descended from Oceanus and Tethys (Table 17). Niobe was the first mortal to have children by Zeus. Argos received as his share the sovereignty of the Peloponnese, which he called Argos (a name which stayed attached to the city of that name, and the Argolid, the area round it). He married Evadne, the daughter of Strymon and Neaera (or alternatively of Peitho, a daughter of Oceanus) and had four sons (Table 18 and, to illustrate another tradition, Table 17). Argos was supposed to have introduced the practice of tilling the soil and planting corn into Greece.
2. The best known Argos, generally known by

the Latinized form of his name, Argus, was the great-grandson of the first. Some versions of the story give him a single eye, while others say he had four, two looking forward and two backwards. Yet other traditions ascribe to him a large number of eyes all over his body. Endowed with prodigious strength, he freed Arcadia from a bull which was laying the country waste. He then flayed it and clothed himself in its hide. Next he killed a Satyr which was harming the Arcadians and carrying off their flocks. Then he slew Echidna, the monstrous daughter of Tartarus who was seizing passers-by, by overcoming her in her sleep. Hera then enjoined him to watch over the heifer Io, of whom she was jealous. In order to do this, Argos tethered it to an olive tree which was growing in a sacred wood at Mycenae. Thanks to his many eyes, of which only half were ever shut at one time, so that as many were always open as were shut, he could keep a watch on it. But Hermes was bidden by Zeus to free Io, whom he loved. As usual with Hermes, there are varying accounts of how he achieved this task: sometimes he is said to have killed Argos by throwing a stone from a distance, sometimes to have sent him to sleep by playing to him on Pan pipes; and in another version he plunged him into a magic sleep with his divine wand. In any event Hermes killed Argos. Hera, to give immortality to her faithful servant, moved his eyes to the tail of the bird that was sacred to him, the peacock.

3. The third Argos was the son of Phrixus and Chalciope. He was born and brought up in Colchis, but left to go and claim his inheritance from his grandfather, Athamas. He was shipwrecked on the island of Aria, where he was sheltered by the Argonauts, together with his brothers Phrontis, Melas and Cytissorus. Another version says that he met Jason at the house of Aeetes, in Colchis. It was he who, through the agency of his mother, is said to have brought about the first meeting between Jason and Medea. He came back with the Argonauts. In Greece he married Perimele, the daughter of Admetus, and by her he had a son, Magnes (Table 33).

4 The Argos who built the ship *Argo* (see ARGONAUTS) and took part in the expedition in search of the Golden Fleece, seems to have been yet a fourth character. However he is sometimes regarded as being the son of Arestor, a relationship also claimed for Argos 2, and sometimes confused with the son of Phrixus (Argos 3).

Argynnus A variant spelling of Argennus.

Argyra (Ἀργυρᾶ) A Nymph of an Arcadian spring. She loved a handsome young shepherd called Selemnus. Her love for him lasted while he was young, but when he was no longer handsome she abandoned him. In his despair Selemnus died and was turned into a stream by Aphrodite. But when he still suffered from his love in spite of undergoing this change, Aphrodite granted him the gift of oblivion. That is why all who bathed in the Selemnus were able to forget the sorrows of love.

Ariadne (Ἀριάδνη) The daughter of Minos and Pasiphae (Table 28). When Theseus arrived in Crete to do battle with the Minotaur Ariadne saw him and immediately fell deeply in love with him; to enable him to find his way in the labyrinth where the Minotaur was confined she gave him a ball of thread, which he unwound to show him the way to return. She then fled with him to escape the wrath of Minos but she did not reach Athens because when they stopped on the island of Naxos Theseus abandoned her while she slept on the shore. Different authors give varying accounts of this act of betrayal: sometimes Theseus is said to have left her because he was in love with another woman; other versions say that Theseus acted on the command of the gods because fate would not allow him to marry her. Ariadne woke up in the morning to see the sails of her lover's ship vanishing over the horizon, but she did not remain for long in her grief, for Dionysus and his retinue soon appeared on the scene, the god's chariot drawn by a team of panthers. Overcome by her youthful beauty, Dionysus married her and carried her off to dwell on Olympus. As a wedding present he gave her a golden diadem, made by Hephaestus, which later became a constellation. Ariadne had four children by Dionysus, named Thoas, Staphylus, Oenopion and Peparethus. Another tradition tells how Ariadne was killed on the island of Dia (later identified with Naxos) by the goddess Artemis at the bidding of Dionysus (for alternative versions of the legend about Ariadne, see THESEUS).

Arion (Ἀρίων) A musician from Lesbos who had been given leave by his master, the tyrant of Corinth, Periander, to travel all over Magna Graecia and Sicily, earning money from his singing. After some time he wanted to go back to Corinth, but the slaves and the crew of the ship in which he was travelling conspired to kill him and appropriate his money. Instantly Apollo appeared to Arion in a dream in the guise of a lyre-player and told him to look out for his enemies, promising his help. When Arion was attacked by the conspirators he asked them for the favour of allowing him to sing once more. They granted this request and when the dolphins, Apollo's favourites, heard his voice, they gathered round and Arion, putting his trust in the god, leaped into the sea. A dolphin picked him up and carried him on its back to Cape Tenaros. Once he was safely on shore, the musician dedicated an *ex voto* to Apollo and made his way to Corinth where he told his story to the tyrant. The ship containing the would-be assassins soon arrived at Corinth whereupon Periander asked the sailors where Arion was and they replied that he had died on the voyage. Arion then appeared in person and the conspirators were crucified or, according to some accounts, impaled. To commemorate the story, Apollo changed Arion's lyre and the dolphins which had taken pity on him into constellations.

Aristaeus (Ἀρισταῖος) The son of the Nymph Cyrene, the daughter of Hypseus, the king of the Lapiths who was himself the son of the Naiad Creusa . and the Thessalian river-god Peneus (Table 23). One day when Apollo was hunting in a valley of Pelion, he saw Cyrene and transported her in his golden chariot to Libya where she bore him a son named Aristaeus. When the child was born, Apollo placed him in the care of his great-grandmother Gaia (Creusa was the daughter of Gaia and Poseidon) and of the Seasons (the Horae). According to another tradition, Aristaeus was brought up by Chiron, the Centaur. Then the Muses completed his education by teaching him the arts of medicine and divination. They entrusted him with the care of their flocks of sheep which grazed in the plain of Phthia in Thessaly. The nymphs also taught him the arts of dairy farming and bee-keeping, as well as the culture of the vine. In his turn, he taught men the skills that the goddesses had taught him.

Aristaeus married Autonoe, the daughter of Cadmus and fathered a son named Actaeon. He is also credited with a whole range of discoveries about hunting, notably the use of pits and netting. Actaeon in due course became a hunter like him and thereby met his death. Virgil tells how Aristaeus one day pursued Orpheus' wife Eurydice along a river. In her flight, Eurydice was bitten by a snake and died. Her death brought on Aristaeus the wrath of the gods, who punished him by causing an illness among his bees. Aris-

taeus, in despair, called for help on his mother, the Nymph Cyrene, who dwelt in a crystal palace beneath the waters of the Peneus. When he was admitted to her presence she told him that the only person who could say what was causing his misfortune was the sea-god Proteus. Aristaeus went off to question Proteus and caught him resting on a rock, surrounded by a herd of seals which he was looking after on behalf of Poseidon. Taking advantage of the fact that Proteus was asleep, Aristaeus tied him up and forced him to answer, for Proteus did not like questioners. On this occasion, he told Aristaeus that the gods were punishing him for Eurydice's death and gave him advice on how to get some new swarms of bees.

There is also a story that Aristaeus took part in the conquest of India with Dionysus at the head of an Arcadian army. During a plague which caused much damage to the Cyclades at the time of year when the star Sirius brings back the hottest days, the inhabitants asked Aristaeus for help and he settled in Ceos. There he built a great altar to Zeus and every day he offered sacrifices to Sirius and Zeus on the mountains. Zeus, moved by his prayers, sent the Etesian winds, which cooled the atmosphere and blew away the unhealthy air. Ever since then, each year these winds rise at the hot season and purify the air of the Cyclades. Aristaeus was held in honour in Arcadia, where he had introduced bee-keeping. He was also honoured in Libya, in the region of Cyrene, whither he was said to have followed his mother and where he planted the precious herb called Silphium, which produced both a cure and a spice.

Aristeas (Ἀριστέας) The poet of Proconnesus, a character half mythical and half historical who died in a fuller's workshop. When his friends came to look for his body it could not be found but on the same day some travellers arrived in the town and said that on their way they had met Aristeas going towards Cyzicus. He used to appear at different times in different places. Seven years after his supposed death Aristeas returned and wrote his poem, the *Arimaspes*. During his seven years' absence he was said to have gone with Apollo to the mysterious land of the Hyperboreans. Once his poem was finished, he disappeared again.

Aristodemus (Ἀριστόδημος) One of the descendants of Heracles, the son of Aristomachus, who was himself the great-grandson of Heracles (Table 16). His brothers were Temenus and Chresphontes, who conquered the Peloponnese. When he was with his brother Temenus at Naupactus when the fleet and army for this campaign were being prepared, Aristodemus was struck by a thunderbolt at the request of Apollo, who wanted to punish him for not having first consulted the Delphic oracle. Another tradition says that he was killed by Medon and Strophius, the children of Pylades and Electra. In yet another version it is said that he had not been killed but took part with his brothers in the successful campaign, and was awarded Laconia as his share. He reigned there, leaving his throne after his death to his two sons, Eurysthenes and Procles whose mother was Argia the daughter of Autesion (see THERAS and Table 37).

Artemis (Ἄρτεμις) Identified by the Romans with the Italian and Latin Diana. Although she is sometimes said to have been the daughter of Demeter, she is generally regarded as the twin sister of Apollo, their parents being Zeus and Leto. Artemis, the elder twin, was born in Delos and as soon as she was born she helped her mother to give birth to her brother. Artemis was always a virgin and eternally young, an untamed girl with no interests beyond hunting. Like her brother, her weapon was the bow which she used while she was hunting stags as well as mortals, and she inflicted pain on women who died in childbirth. Her arrows were said to inflict sudden death, especially when they caused no pain. She was vindictive and there were many who suffered from her anger. One of her first actions, together with her brother, was to kill the children of NIOBE. While Apollo was killing the six boys in turn when he hunted on Mount Cithaeron, Artemis was killing the six daughters who had stayed at home. They took this action out of love for their mother, who had been insulted by Niobe and it was in defence of Leto again that Artemis and Apollo, though scarcely born, killed the dragon which had come to attack them; in the same way they attacked and killed Tityus, who was trying to violate Leto.

Artemis took part in the battle against the Giants, where her opponent was the giant Gration whom she killed with the help of Heracles. She destroyed two other monsters in the shape of the ALOADAE and is said to have killed the monster Bouphagus (the eater of oxen) in Arcadia. Other victims of Artemis included Orion, the giant huntsman. The reasons which drove her to kill him differ in various traditions. In some accounts

he is said to have incurred her wrath by challenging her at throwing the discus and in others by trying to kidnap Opis one of her companions whom she had forced to leave his home with the Hyperboreans. In still other accounts, Orion is supposed to have tried to ravish Artemis herself and she sent a scorpion which bit and killed him. Actaeon, the son of Aristaeus, who was another hunter, owed his death to the wrath of Artemis, and she was the instigator of the hunt for the wild boar of Calydon, which was fated to lead to the death of the huntsman MELEAGER. Artemis sent the wild boar of exceptional size to Oeneus' country because he had forgotten to sacrifice to her when he was offering the first fruits of his crops to all the gods and goddesses. Artemis is sometimes said to have been responsible for the death of Callisto whom she killed with an arrow either at Hera's request or as a punishment for having let herself be seduced by Zeus; Callisto was then changed into a she-bear. All these legends relate to hunting, giving a picture of a ferocious goddess of the woods and mountains, who usually kept company with wild beasts.

An account of the Labours of HERACLES tells how he had been ordered by Eurystheus to bring back the stag with the golden horns which was sacred to Artemis. Unwilling either to wound or to kill the sacred beast Heracles pursued it for a whole year but ultimately he became exhausted and killed it. Immediately Artemis and Apollo appeared before him, asking for an explanation. Heracles managed to appease them by blaming Eurystheus for the hunt. The same theme recurs in the story of Iphigenia: the wrath of Artemis against the family was already of long standing (see ATREUS) but it was renewed by an unfortunate utterance of Agamemnon who after hunting and killing a stag when he was waiting at Aulis for a favourable wind to enable him to leave for Troy, cried out: 'Artemis herself could not have killed a stag like that'. Artemis promptly sent a calm which kept the whole fleet from sailing and the soothsayer Tiresias disclosed the reason for this setback, adding that the only remedy was to sacrifice Iphigenia, the king's virgin daughter, to Artemis. Artemis would not have this sacrifice and at the last moment she substituted a doe for the girl, removed her and took her away to Tauris (the modern Crimea) to serve as the priestess of her cult in that distant land.

Artemis was held in honour in all the wild and mountainous areas of Greece, in Arcadia and in the country of Sparta, in Laconia on the mountain of Taygetus and in Elis. Her most famous shrine in the Greek world was the one at Ephesus, where she was integrated with a very ancient Asiatic fertility goddess. Antiquity explained Artemis as a personification of the Moon which roams in the mountains and her brother Apollo was also generally regarded as a personification of the Sun, but not all the Artemis cults had lunar significance, furthermore the goddess took the place of the Lady of the Wild Beasts displayed on Cretan religious monuments in the Hellenic Pantheon. Artemis absorbed some barbarous cults which involved human sacrifice such as that practised in Tauris. (See AMPHISTHENES.) Artemis was also the protecting deity of the Amazons who were warriors and huntresses like her and resembled her too in being independent of men. For her relationship with magic, see HECATE.

Ascalabus (Ἀσκάλαβος) When Demeter was searching far and wide for her daughter she passed through Attica. She was very thirsty and a woman called Misme gave her a drink; she swallowed it in one gulp, so eagerly that Misme's small son Ascalabus burst out laughing. Demeter was so annoyed that she threw the rest of the water over him and the little boy became a spotted lizard.

Ascalaphus (Ασκάλαφος)
1. The son of a Nymph of the Styx and the Acheron; he was in the garden of Hades when PERSEPHONE was eating a pomegranate seed, thus breaking her fast and unknowingly making any hope of returning to the light of day impossible. Ascalaphus saw this and denounced it. Demeter in her anger changed him into an owl. Another version of the story has it that Ascalaphus was first made to lie under a large stone, which Heracles moved when he descended into Hades whereupon Ascalaphus, as a second punishment, was changed into an owl.
2. For Ascalaphus, son of Ares, see IALMENUS.

Ascanius (Ἀσκάνιος) The son of Aeneas and Creusa. He was the grandson of Priam on his mother's side and on his father's the grandson of Aphrodite (see ANCHISES and Table 34). Another tradition makes his mother Lavinia, daughter of King Latinus in which case he could not have been born until after the arrival of Aeneas in Italy. In the oldest version of the story Ascanius is said to have been taken away by his father, together with Creusa and Anchises, after the fall of Troy. Thereafter he is said to have been sent by his father

to the Propontis where he ruled until the day he returned to the Troad with Scamandrius, the son of Hector, to refound the city of Troy, though according to another tradition Ascanius lived with his father in Italy. Aeneas in his old age is supposed to have come back to Asia with him, ruled in Troy and on his death left the kingdom to his son. The strongest tradition and the one related to the Roman legend of Aeneas, depicts Ascanius as settled in Italy, where he was the first of his line.

The character of the young Ascanius is most highly developed in the *Aeneid*, where Virgil depicts him as an adolescent, still just a child, but about to reach manhood. He competes in the Trojan Games, founded in honour of Anchises after his death, goes hunting in the forests of Latium and unwisely kills a sacred roe deer, which triggers off hostilities with the native population. He is dearly loved by his father, embodies the hopes of the outlawed Trojans and is much spoilt by his grandmother, Venus. Legend says that after Aeneas' death, Ascanius ruled over the Latini. He is shown fighting hard against the Etruscans, and is said to have won a victory over them on the shores of Lake Numicius. Thirty years after the foundation of Lavinium by Aeneas Ascanius founded Alba Longa, the mother city of Rome, on the spot where Aeneas had sacrificed a white sow and her litter of thirty piglets long before. He was compelled to do so by the hostility of the Latini, who took the side of Lavinia, the widow of Aeneas and stepmother of Ascanius, against him. Lavinia, pregnant after the death of Aeneas, had fled into the forest since she was afraid that her stepson might kill her unborn child. She sought refuge with a shepherd called Tyrrhus, or Tyrrhenus, and her child Silvius was born in his home. Tyrrhus roused the people of Latium to anger against Ascanius and, on his death, Ascanius was succeeded on the throne of Alba by Silvius. Ascanius is often referred to as Iulus and this was the name which allowed the Roman family of the Iulii (Julii) to claim him as their ancestor (see APHRODITE).

Asclepius (Ἀσκληπιός) In Latin Aesculapius, the god of medicine, he was the son of Apollo, but the stories about his birth differ considerably: generally, and especially in the account given by Pindar, it is said that Apollo loved Coronis, the daughter of the Thessalian king Phlegyas and fathered a son, but before the child was born, Coronis had yielded her love to a mortal, Ischys, the son of Elatus. Apollo, warned of her misdeed by a careless crow, or by his gift of divination, killed the faithless girl and just as her body was lying on the pyre and was on the point of being burnt, Apollo tore the child, still alive, from her womb and that is how Asclepius was born. According to another tradition, intended to explain why Asclepius was the great god of Epidaurus in the Peloponnese, Phlegyas who was a thief on a grand scale, came to the country to discover the wealth it contained and how he could appropriate it. His daughter accompanied him and during their travels was seduced by Apollo, and secretly gave birth to a son in Epidaurus, at the foot of Mount Myrtion. There she had abandoned him but a she-goat came to suckle the infant and a dog protected him. The shepherd Aresthanas who owned both animals found the child and was astounded by the brilliant light in which he was bathed. He knew full well that he was confronted by a mystery and did not dare to pick up the infant, who followed his divine destiny alone. Another version of the story makes Arsinoe, the daughter of Leucippus, the child's mother. This is the Messenian tradition which attempted to reconcile itself with the others by asserting that the child was Arsinoe's, but that he had been brought up by Coronis.

Asclepius was entrusted by his father to the Centaur Chiron, who taught him medicine and soon Asclepius developed exceptional skill in the art. He even discovered how to revive the dead. He was given the blood which had flowed in the Gorgon's veins by Athena, and while the blood from its left side spread a fatal poison, that from the right was beneficial, and Asclepius knew how to use it to restore the dead to life. By this method he revived many people, including Capaneus, Lycurgus (probably during the war against Thebes, where two characters of that name are recorded as victims), Glaucus, the son of Minos, and Hippolytus, the son of Theseus, the most frequently mentioned of all (see PHAEDRA). Zeus, confronted by resurrections on this scale feared that Asclepius might upset the natural order of things and struck him with a thunderbolt. To avenge him Apollo killed the Cyclopes. After his death Asclepius was changed into a constellation and became the plant serpentaria. Several late pieces of so-called evidence show Asclepius taking part in the Calydonian hunt and the Argonauts' expedition, but generally speaking he stands outside the legendary cycles.

He is said to have had two children, Podalirius and Machaon, whose names are found as early as the *Iliad*. The later forms of the legend give him a wife, Epione, and five daughters, Aceso, Iase, Panacea, Aglaea and Hygieia. The cult of Asclepius, which is vouched for at Tricea in Thessaly (where it may have originated) was centred on Epidaurus in the Peloponnese, where what can properly be called a school of medicine flourished. This was based primarily on magical practices but also laid the foundations for a more scientific form of medicine. This art was practised by the Asclepiades or descendants of Asclepius, the best known of these being Hippocrates. The usual symbols of Asclepius were snakes twined round a staff, together with pine-cones, crowns of laurel and sometimes a nanny-goat or a dog.

Asia (Ἀσία) The daughter of Oceanus and Tethys (Table 38) who gave her name to the Asian continent. She was married to Iapetus and had four children, Atlas, Prometheus, Epimetheus and Menoetius.

Asopus (Ἀσωπός) The god of the river of the same name. Writers claim that he was the son of Poseidon and Pero, of Zeus and Eurynome, or, like all other rivers, of Oceanus and Tethys. He married Metope, the daughter of the river Ladon, and fathered two sons named Ismenus and Pelagon and twenty daughters. Diodorus gives the names of only twelve: Corcyra, Salamis, Aegina, Pirene, Cleone, Thebe, Tanagra, Thespia, Asopis, Sinope, Oenia (or Ornia) and Chalcis. He is also in some accounts said to be the father of Antiope, in her turn the mother of Zethus and Amphion, and Plataea, after whom the city is named (see ISMENE and AEGINA).

Aspalis (Ἀσπαλίς) Meliteus, the son of Zeus and the Nymph Othreis, was miraculously fed by a swarm of bees in the woods where his mother had left him to die. He went to Thessaly to found a town called Melitaea and there he ruled like a tyrant, abducting young girls and taking possession of them. He was greatly attracted to one of them, Aspalis, the daughter of one Argaeus and ordered her to be brought to him. The girl hanged herself before the soldiers came to take her away. Her brother, Astygites, put on his sister's clothes, beneath which he hid a sword, and allowed himself to be taken away as if he was Aspalis and as soon as he came into the presence of the tyrant, he killed him. The inhabitants of the town threw the corpse into the river and set Astygites to rule over them. When a search was made for the body of Aspalis, it was found to have vanished. The gods had replaced her with a wooden statue and this became an object of worship.

Assaon (Ἀσσάων) The father of Niobe in the Lydian version of the legend. After his son-in-law, Philottus, was killed on Mount Sipylus, Assaon wanted to have an incestuous relationship with his own daughter but Niobe was unwilling. Assaon then invited Niobe's twenty children to a banquet and brought about their deaths by fire. In her despair Niobe threw herself from the top of a cliff; Assaon went mad and killed himself.

Asteria (Ἀστερία)
1. The daughter of the Titan Coeus and Phoebe, the sister of Leto and grand-daughter of Uranus (the Sky) and Gaia (the Earth). Zeus loved her but she changed herself into a quail to escape his pursuit of her, and threw herself into the sea, where she became an island called Ortygia (Quail Island) which was subsequently called Delos after Leto had given birth to her two children there. This Asteria was the mother of Hecate by Perses (Table 32).
2. Another Asteria (or Asteropia), the daughter of Deion and Diomedes, married Phocus, the son of Aeacus. She was the mother of Panopeus and Crisus (Tables 20 and 30).

Asterion (Ἀστερίων) (or Asterius) The son of Tectamus or Dorus and a daughter of Cretheus, was a king of Crete who married Europa after she had been seduced by Zeus. Asterion adopted the children of this liaison, Minos, Sarpedon and Rhadamanthys (Table 28).

Astraea (Ἀστραία) The daughter of Zeus and Themis (Justice) and sister of Modesty (Pudicitia). She spread the feelings of justice and virtue among mankind in the Golden Age, but after mankind lost its high ideals, and wickedness took possession of the world, Astraea returned to heaven, where she became the constellation Virgo. It is sometimes said that before she left the earth she lingered for a time among peasants in the country. (See also IUSTITIA.)

Astyanax (Ἀστυάναξ) The son of Hector and Andromache. His father called him Scamandrius, after the name of the river which flowed by Troy but the common people called him Astyanax (Prince of the City), out of gratitude to Hector. He features as a baby in his mother's arms, playing innocently with the plume on his father's helmet, when Hector and Andromache were bidding each other farewell. After Hector's death and the fall of Troy Astyanax was seized by the Greeks led by Odysseus, who put him to death by throwing him from the top of a tower. According to a later tradition Astyanax was not killed, but founded a new Troy (see ASCANIUS).

Astymedusa (Ἀστυμέδουσα) The daughter of Sthenelus (Table 31) who, in an obscure version of the Oedipus legend, was married to Oedipus after the death of Jocasta. She is supposed to have slandered her two stepsons Eteocles and Polynices in the presence of their father by claiming that they wished him ill. Oedipus cursed them both and this was said to be the origin of the quarrel between the two princes.

Atalanta (Ἀταλάντη) A heroine who featured in some accounts in the Arcadian cycle and also in connection with Boeotian legends. She is occasionally regarded as the daughter of Iasus (or Iasius), who was himself the son of Lycurgus and a descendant of Arcas (in which case his mother was Clymene, the daughter of Minyas, king of Orchomenus). In some versions (in Euripides for

Hellenistic bronze statue showing Atalanta holding one of the golden apples of the Hesperides. Oxford, Ashmolean Museum.

example) Atalanta's father was Menalus, who gave his name to Mount Menalus, and in others again (and this is the account most commonly followed since Hesiod) she is said to have been the daughter of Schoeneus, one of the sons of Athamas and Themisto after whom the Boetian town of Schoenontes was named (Table 33). Since her father wanted to have only sons, Atalanta was put out to die at birth on Mount Parthenon. A she-bear fed her until one day she was found by some huntsmen who brought her up among themselves. When she reached girlhood, Atalanta had no wish to marry but remained a virgin and devoted herself, like her protectress Artemis, to hunting in the woods. She took a leading part in the hunt for the Calydonian boar (see MELEAGER). At the funeral games held in honour of Pelias she won the prize either for the race or for wrestling against Peleus.

Atalanta was unwilling to marry, either because of her devotion to Artemis or because an oracle had told her that if she did marry she would be changed into an animal. Accordingly, to keep her suitors at a distance she had made it known that she would only marry a man who could beat her in a race. If she won, she would put the claimant to death. Now she was nimble and could run very fast. There is a story that she would begin by giving her opponent a slight start and would then set off in pursuit, carrying a spear with which she would pierce him when she caught up with him. Many young men had met their death in this way when a new challenger arrived, in some accounts called Hippomenes, the son of Megareus, in others Melanion or Milanion, the son of Amphidamas, and her first cousin (Table 26). This new arrival brought some golden apples with him; these had been given to him by Aphrodite. They came either from a shrine of the goddess in Cyprus or from the garden of the Hesperides. During the race, just as the young man was on the point of being caught, he threw the golden apples, one by one, in front of Atalanta. She, out of curiosity, though, (perhaps also through love of her opponent, and because she was happy to cheat herself) stopped to pick them up, and Melanion (or Hippomenes) won and received the agreed prize. Some time later during a hunt, the couple entered a shrine of Zeus (or, in another version, Cybele) and gave themselves over to the ecstasies of love. Furious at such sacrilege, Zeus changed them both into lions (which explains the belief that lions do not mate with each other, but with leopards). A spring known as the Spring of

Atalanta, could also be seen in the region of Epidaurus where Atalanta, in search of water to quench her thirst, had struck the rock with her pike and a spring had gushed forth. Atalanta had, by her husband, or perhaps by Ares or Meleager, a son called Parthenopaeus, who took part in the first expedition against Thebes.

Ate (Ἄτη) The personification of Error. A goddess of lightness whose feet rested only on the heads of mortals, and that without their knowing it. When Zeus made the oath in which he pledged himself to give pre-eminence to the first descendant of Perseus to be born, and in this way exalted Eurystheus above Heracles, Ate deceived him. Zeus took his revenge on her by casting her down from the summit of Olympus. Ate fell to earth in Phrygia, on the hill which took the name of the Hill of Error. That was the spot where Ilus built the fortress of Ilium (Troy). When Zeus cast Ate down from high heaven he forbade her ever to stay in Olympus and that is why Error is the sad lot of mankind.

Athamas (Ἀθάμας) A Boeotian king who reigned over the land of Croneus or, in some accounts, Thebes itself. He was the son of Aeolus and grandson of Hellen (Table 8). His legend which was the theme of many tragedies was the subject of complicated and sometimes contradictory stories. Athamas was married three times, and these marriages provide the basis for the romantic development of an older myth. In the best known version, which undoubtedly goes back to the *Phrixus* of Euripides, now lost, Athamas first married Nephele and fathered a son, PHRIXUS, and a daughter, HELLE. Later he discarded Nephele and married Ino, the daughter of Cadmus. There were two sons of this marriage, Learchus and Melicertes. Ino, who was jealous of the children of Athamas' first marriage, formed the idea of killing them and devised the following trick. She began by persuading the women of the country to roast the seeds of corn which were to be sown. The men sowed the seed, but none of it came up. Naturally Athamas, confronted by this apparent phenomenon, sent messengers to seek the advice of the Delphic oracle. Ino bribed them to report that the god required the sacrifice of Phrixus. The ruse almost succeeded. Phrixus was brought to the altar (together, according to some versions, with his sister) and was about to be killed, when Nephele gave him a ram with a golden mane, a gift from Hermes, which wafted the children into the air and snatched them from danger. Phrixus succeeded in reaching Colchis, while his sister drowned herself. There is another tradition which claims that the messenger who had been bribed by Ino pitied Phrixus and revealed the plan to Athamas who, when he learned of the plot of which his wife had been guilty, gave orders that she should be sacrificed in place of Phrixus, along with her son, little Melicertes. When they were being led to the altar, however, Dionysus had pity on his former nurse (see below) and enveloped her in a cloud which made her invisible and allowed her to escape with Melicertes. He then caused Athamas to go mad and kill his younger son, Learchus, by throwing him into a cauldron of boiling water. Ino, in turn, killed herself together with Melicertes (see LEUCOTHEA). This version is a tragic form of the legend, designed to reconcile two themes, the hatred of Ino towards the children of Nephele and her own death – two episodes which seem originally to have had nothing to do with each other.

Euripides wrote a second tragedy, *Ino* in which he dealt with the third marriage of Athamas with Themisto, the daughter of Hypseus. In this play Ino departed (no doubt after the failed sacrifice of Phrixus) into the mountains to rejoin the Bacchantes in the service of Dionysus. Athamas, who believed that she was dead, married Themisto, and fathered two children, Orchomenus and Sphingius, but Ino returned secretly. She made herself known to Athamas who brought her into the palace in the guise of a servant. Themisto discovered that her rival was not dead, but could not learn where she was hiding. She set about killing Ino's children and to achieve that end she took the new servant as her confidante. She ordered her to make Ino's children wear black clothes and her own children white so that they could be recognized in the dark. The servant changed the clothes round so that Themisto killed her two sons and Ino's children were unharmed and when she discovered her mistake Themisto killed herself. This legend is probably mostly an invention of Euripides. The more common story was that the wrath of Hera had fallen on Athamas after the sacrifice of Phrixus because he agreed to bring up the young Dionysus who had been entrusted to Ino, the sister of Semele. Struck with madness by the goddess, he killed the little Learchus. At this Ino killed Melicertes and then threw herself into the sea with his body (see LEUCOTHEA).

After he was banished from Boeotia because of this crime Athamas took to a wanderer's life. He asked the oracle where he should settle, and received the answer that he should stop at the place where the wild beasts would feed him. When he reached Thessaly he found wolves engaged in eating a sheep's carcass. When they saw him they ran off, leaving the carcass behind and thus the oracle was fulfilled. Athamas settled in that region, which he called Athamantia, and there he founded the town of Alos or Halos. There he was said to have married Themisto, Hypseus' daughter, by whom he had four sons: Leucon, Erythrius, Schoeneus and Ptous (Tables 23 and 33). Later, Athamas was on the point of being sacrificed by his subjects for having broken a religious prohibition, but he was saved by his grandson Cytissorus. This final episode in the legend was dramatized by Sophocles in his lost tragedy of *Athamas Crowned*, and it seems likely that the hero's sacrifice was plotted by Nephele as an act of vengeance. Athamas was said to have been saved not by Cytissorus but by Heracles.

Athena (Ἀθηνᾶ) A goddess identified in Rome with Minerva, the daughter of Zeus and Metis. Metis was pregnant and was about to give birth to a daughter when Zeus swallowed it; he did so on the advice of Uranus and Gaia who disclosed to him that if Metis had a daughter, she would afterwards have a son, who would deprive Zeus of his heavenly kingdom. When the time for the child to be born arrived Zeus bade Hephaestus to personally split open his head with a blow from an axe. A girl in full armour sprang forth from his head: it was the goddess Athena. The place where the birth took place is generally said to be the shore of Lake Tritonis in Libya. As she leaped out, she uttered a war-cry which resounded in heaven and earth. Athena, the warrior goddess, armed with spear and aegis (a kind of goat-skin breast-plate) played an important part in the struggle against the Giants. She killed Pallas and Encelades. She flayed the former and made herself a breast-plate from the skin and she pursued Encelades as far as Sicily and put him out of action by chasing him over the whole island. In the *Iliad*, she participated in the fighting on the side of the Achaeans (she was hostile to the Trojans ever since Paris, on Mount Ida, had refused to award her the prize for beauty). She supported Diomedes, Odysseus, Achilles and Menelaus in the Trojan War. Similarly, she protected Heracles in the fighting and she also began to arm Heracles, just as he was about to undertake his Labours. She

Votive relief c. 470–450 BC of the 'Mourning Athena' represented with her attributes of spear and helmet. Athens, Acropolis Museum.

quite sure that the girl should at this meeting obtain a boat for Odysseus to return to his native land. She also begged Zeus to show Odysseus his favour, and caused the order to be given to Calypso to release Odysseus and supply him with the means to put to sea again. The assistance given to Odysseus and Heracles is a symbol of the help brought by the mind to the brute strength and personal courage of the heroes. For Athena was regarded, both in the Greek world at large, and especially in her own city of Athens as the goddess of Reason. She presided over the arts and literature, in which position she tended to encroach on the role of the Muses but she was more closely connected with philosophy than with poetry and music in the true sense. In her role of the goddess of intelligent activity she was also the patroness of spinners, weavers, embroiderers and similar occupations (see ARACHNE). Her ingenuity, allied with her warlike spirit, led her to invent the quadriga and the war chariot; she was also in overall charge of the building of the ship *Argo*, the biggest ever built up to that time. She also applied her ingenuity to the arts of peace and in Attica she was blessed for the discovery of olive oil, among other kind actions, and even the introduction of the olive tree itself which she was said to have given in order to deserve being regarded as its ruler: Poseidon disputed the sovereignty of Attica with her and each of them tried to give Attica the best present they could, to increase their status. Poseidon, with one blow from his trident, made a salt-water spring gush forth on the Acropolis and Athena made an olive tree grow there. The twelve gods called in to judge decided that the olive tree was the better of the two and they gave Athena sovereignty over Attica.

Athena was often adopted as protectress and patroness of towns. Apart from Athens, to which she gave her name, there were temples dedicated to her in the citadels of cities such as Sparta, Megara, Argos and others. At Troy she was especially worshipped in the form of a very ancient idol called the PALLADIUM. Troy could not be captured before the Palladium had been taken, and this is the reason why Diomedes and Odysseus made their way by night into Troy and stole it, thus removing the city's protection. This was the same Palladium which was kept in the post-classical era in the temple of Vesta in Rome, where it performed its original function. Athena remained a virgin though she was said to have had a son in the following way: she went to pay a visit to Hephaestus in his smithy to acquire

gave him the bronze castanets with which he scared the birds of Lake Stymphalos, enabling him to shoot them down with his arrows. In return, Heracles offered Athena the golden apples of the Hesperides when Eurystheus gave them up to him, and he fought beside her in the struggle against the Giants.

Athena also helped Odysseus to return to Ithaca. In the *Odyssey* she is an active figure intervening under the disguise of various human forms, to give assistance to the hero. Athena also sent dreams: to Nausicaa, for example, to give her the idea of taking her washing to the river on the day that she knew that Odysseus was due to land in the island of Phaeacia. She endowed her favourite with supernatural good looks, to make some weapons. He, who had been deserted by Aphrodite, fell in love with Athena at first sight and began to chase her. She fled but although he was lame Hephaestus caught up with her and embraced her. She did not yield to his advances but in his passion Hephaestus wetted the goddess' leg. In her revulsion she wiped her leg with some wool and threw the dirty piece on the ground. From the earth which was fertilized in this way Ericthonius was born, and Athena regarded him as her son. She brought him up without the other gods knowing and in her desire to make him immortal she shut him in a chest, set a serpent to guard him, and entrusted it to the daughters of the kings of Athens (see AGLAURUS).

Athena's attributes were the spear, the helmet and the aegis, which she shared with Zeus. She attached the Gorgon's head which Perseus had given her to her shield, and this had the special quality of turning to stone every living thing that looked at it. Her favourite animal was the owl and her favourite plant the olive tree. She was tall, with calm features, majestic rather than beautiful, and was traditionally described as 'the goddess with grey eyes'. (For her name of PALLAS see that entry.)

Atlantis (Ἀτλαντίς) In two of his Dialogues Plato tells that Solon, in the course of his travels in Egypt, questioned the priests and that one of them, who lived at Saïs in the Nile delta, told him of very ancient traditions which related to a war waged in the distant past by Athens against the people of Atlantis. This story which starts in the *Timaeus* is resumed and elaborated in the fragment we possess of the *Critias*. The people of Atlantis, according to the priest, used to live on an island which lay beyond the Pillars of Heracles, where the Mediterranean ended and Ocean began. When the gods were sharing out the earth, Athens fell to Athena and Hephaestus, but Atlantis became the kingdom of Poseidon. In Atlantis lived Clito, a girl who had lost both her parents, Evenor and Leucippe. Poseidon fell in love with her. Clito lived on a mountain in the middle of the island and around her dwelling Poseidon raised a barrier consisting of walls and moats full of water, and there he lived with her for a long time. They had five pairs of twin sons, the eldest son of all being called Atlas, to whom Poseidon gave supremacy. He divided the whole island into ten areas. Atlas reigned on the mountain in the centre and it was from there that he wielded his power. The island of Atlantis was extremely rich both in vegetation

and mineral wealth. There were not only many deposits of gold, copper, iron and other metals, but also orichalc, a metal which blazed like fire. The kings of Atlantis built magnificent cities with great numbers of vaults, bridges, canals and tortuous passages, for ease of both defence and trade. In each of the ten districts there reigned the descendants of the ten original kings, the sons of Poseidon and Clito, all ruled over by the descendant of Atlas. Each year they all met in the capital for a special ceremony, during which they gave themselves over to a ritual bull-hunt and joined together in drinking the blood of the bull which they had slaughtered. Then they all passed judgement on each other, clad in flowing gowns of dark blue in the middle of the night seated among the embers still hot from the sacrifice, after which all the lamps were put out. At this point the Dialogue ends.

These men of Atlantis had tried to conquer the world, but they were defeated by the Athenians nine thousand years before the time of Plato. According to a considerably different tradition, recorded by Diodorus Siculus, the men of Atlantis were neighbours of the Libyans and had been attacked by the Amazons (see MYRINA), but in Plato's belief, the men of Atlantis and their island had disappeared for ever, submerged by a disastrous flood.

Atlas (Ἄτλας) A giant, the son of Iapetus and the sea-nymph Clymene (or in some versions of the sea-nymph Asia). He was the brother of Menoetius, Prometheus and and Epimetheus, 'the men of violence' (Tables 25 and 38). According to some traditions he was the son of Uranus and thus the brother of Cronus. He belongs to the generation of monstrous and unbridled divinities which preceded the Olympians. He took part in the struggle between the Gods and the Giants and Zeus sentenced him to carrying the vault of the sky on his shoulders as a punishment. His dwelling was generally regarded as in the very far west, in the country of the Hesperides, though it was sometimes said to be 'among the Hyperboreans'. Herodotus was the first person to refer to Atlas as a mountain in North Africa. PERSEUS was said to have turned Atlas into a rock on returning after slaying the Gorgon, by confronting him with Medusa's head.

Atlas is said to have had several children: the Pleiades and the Hyades by Pleione, and the Hesperides by Hesperis. Dione was also regarded as his daughter and his sons were Hyas and

Hesperus. Late conjectures regarded Atlas as an astronomer who taught men the laws governing celestial bodies and he was deified for that reason. Sometimes it was said that there were three separate figures, all known as Atlas, one African, one Italian and one Arcadian, the father of Maia and hence the grandfather of Hermes. For the Atlas who gave his name to Atlantis, see ATLANTIS.

Atreus (Ἀτρεύς) The son of Pelops and Hippodamia whose younger brother was Thyestes (Table 2). The theme underlying the legend about him is the hatred between the two brothers and the appalling forms of revenge they took on each other. This hatred, however, was apparently not yet known in the Homeric poems; it is sometimes said to have its origin in a curse of Pelops since Atreus and Thyestes, together with their mother Hippodamia, killed their half-brother Chrysippus, whom the Nymph Axioche bore to Pelops. As a punishment Pelops banished the two youths and cursed them. They took refuge in Mycenae, with Eurystheus, the nephew of Atreus, or, according to the most usual version, with Sthenelus, the father of Eurystheus. After Sthenelus had driven Amphitryon from his part of the Argolid he entrusted the city and land of Midea to Atreus and Thyestes. Later, when Eurystheus died childless beneath the blows of Heracles, an oracle advised the inhabitants of Mycenae to take a son of Pelops as their king. They accordingly summoned Atreus and Thyestes and each of the two brothers began to state the grounds for his claim to the kingship: this was the moment when their hatred showed itself. Atreus had some time previously found a lamb with a golden fleece in his flock and although he had vowed that year to sacrifice the finest produce of his flock to Artemis, he kept the lamb back for himself and hid the fleece in a chest. His wife, Aerope who was Thyestes' lover, had secretly given the miraculous fleece to Thyestes however. In the debate before the inhabitants of Mycenae, Thyestes proposed that the throne should go to whoever could display a golden fleece. Atreus accepted the challenge, for he knew nothing of Thyestes' theft. Thyestes produced it and was chosen, but Zeus through Hermes warned Atreus to agree with Thyestes that the real king should be identified by another miracle: if the sun were to change its course, it would be Atreus who would rule over Mycenae; if it did not, then Thyestes would remain in power. Thyestes accepted and the sun immediately set in the east. Accordingly, Atreus who was clearly favoured

Entrance to the Treasury of Atreus at Mycenae.

by the gods, finally reigned over Mycenae. He hurriedly banished Thyestes from the kingdom, but subsequently, learning of Aerope's affair with Thyestes he pretended to make up his quarrel with the latter and recalled him from exile. When Thyestes was in Mycenae, Atreus secretly killed Thyestes' three sons, Aglaus, Callileon and Orchomenus, even though they had sought protection as suppliants at the altar of Zeus. Then, to compound this crime, he had the children cut up, boiled and served in a dish to their father during a feast. After Thyestes had eaten, Atreus showed him the heads of his children, making clear the true nature of the meal and then he hounded Thyestes out of the country. Thyestes took refuge in Sicyon. There, on the advice of an oracle, he begot, by his own daughter but without her knowledge, a son named Aegisthus. Subsequently Pelopia, the daughter of Thyestes, married Atreus, her uncle and Aegisthus, whose real father was unknown to Atreus, was brought up by him. When Aegisthus grew up, Atreus charged him with the task of killing Thyestes, but Aegisthus found out in time that Thyestes was his father and, on returning to Mycenae, he killed Atreus and then gave the kingdom to Thyestes. Atreus had two sons, Agamemnon and Menelaus, though these children are sometimes attributed to Pleisthenes, who was said to be a son of Atreus who died young and whose children were taken in by their grandfather (see PLEISTHENES).

Attis (Ἄττις) A Phrygian god, the companion of Cybele who was the Mother of the Gods, whose legend developed with the spread of his cult through the Hellenic world and later in Rome. He was regarded originally as the son of the hermaphrodite Agdistis and Nana the Nymph, or daughter, of the river Sangarius (for the circumstances of this birth see AGDISTIS). Attis was loved by Agdistis himself, who later struck him with madness; in this state he castrated himself during an orgy and those who saw him followed his example. This part of the myth is a transposition of the rites which belong to the Asiatic cult practices of Cybele. In his own legend, Attis died of self-mutilation, but, though dead, he still retained a kind of regenerated life, and flowers grew from his tomb. Ovid tells a markedly different version of the Attis legend. According to him, a boy lived in the Phrygian woods who was so handsome that he was deservedly loved by Cybele with a chaste passion. She resolved never to let him leave her and to make him the guardian of her temple but she laid down a condition, that he should retain his virginity. Attis however, could not reject the love felt for him by the Nymph Sagaritis, whose name echoes that of the river Sangarius. Cybele in her rage felled a tree to which the Nymph's life was closely bound and she struck Attis with madness. During a violent fit, he castrated himself. After his self-inflicted injury Attis seems to have been once more taken into Cybele's service. He was generally portrayed with Cybele in her chariot crossing the Phrygian mountains.

Aucnus (or Ocnus) An Etruscan hero, associated with the origin of Bologna. He was the son of Fannus or, in other versions, of the god Tiber, and his mother was Manto, the daughter of Tiresias or, in some accounts, of Heracles. Aucnus was a native of Perugia but left the city in order not to overshadow his brother Aulestes who had founded it, crossed the Apennines and was the founder of Felsina, the Etruscan town which was later to be Bologna. His companions founded other cities in the plain of the river Po, including, among others, Mantua.

Auge (Αὔγη) The daughter of Aleus, the king of the city of Tegea, and Neaera, the daughter of Pereus (Table 9). Her legend is linked to the Heracles cycle and, through Telephus, to that of Troy. One of the oldest verified versions described Auge as living at the court of Laomedon, the king of Troy, where she was loved by Heracles when the hero came to capture the city. From there, for some unknown reason, she went to the court of Teuthras, the king of Mysia. But the most common version, which goes back to the *Auge* of Euripides as well as the *Mysians* and the *Aleades* of Sophocles is as follows.

An oracle warned Aleus that his daughter would have a son who would kill his uncles (the Aleades) and reign in their stead. The king accordingly dedicated his daughter to the goddess Athena and forbade her to marry, on pain of death, but Heracles, who was passing through Tegea on his way to Elis to make war on Augias, was welcomed by Aleus. While he was there, he became drunk at a large banquet and violated Auge (who he did not know was the king's daughter). The rape took place either in the shrine of Athena or beside a neighbouring stream. When the king learned that his daughter was pregnant he wanted to kill her, and he either put Auge and her child in a chest which he cast into the sea or entrusted them to Nauplius, the helmsman, with orders to throw them into the sea. Nauplius, as he had done before for Aerope and her sister, saved the girl and her baby son. He sold them both to slave merchants who carried them off to Mysia. The king of the country, who was childless, married Auge and adopted her little son Telephus. Another version says that Auge was sold before her son was born and that he stayed in Arcadia, where he had been put out to die on a mountain, and was suckled by a doe. Later, after taking the advice of the Delphic oracle, Telephus came to the court of Teuthras in Mysia and met his mother again.

Augias (Αὐγείας) The king of Elis in the Peloponnese. He was generally regarded as the son of the Sun (Helios), although there is evidence for other versions of his descent. He is said, for example, to be the son of the Lapith Phorbas, or of Poseidon, or of Eleius, the hero from whom Elis took its name. His mother was Hyrmine, the daughter of Neleus (Tables 14 and 23). All these genealogies say that Actor was his brother. He took part in the expedition of the Argonauts with the purpose, it was said, of getting to know his half-brother,

Aeetes, whom he had never seen. Augias was the owner of very important herds inherited from his father, but through his carelessness, he let the dung pile up in his stables, which damaged the fertility of his lands. Accordingly, when Eurystheus ordered Heracles to clean his stables, Augias was very ready to agree, all the more since Heracles demanded by way of payment a tenth of his herds if he managed to finish the task in a single day, and Augias thought this was impossible. Heracles made an opening in the wall surrounding the stables and caused the waters of the rivers Alpheus and Peneus, which ran very close to each other, to flow through them. The water emerged through the other end of the yard and washed away all the dung. In his anger at seeing the hero perform the task he had boasted of, Augias alleged that he had either been helped by Iolaus or that he was already a servant of Eurystheus and refused to pay the agreed price. On being called as a witness, Augias' son Phyleus swore in front of the judges that his father had indeed promised a tenth of his herds to Heracles in payment for his labour. Before the verdict was pronounced, Augias banished both Heracles and Phyleus from his realm. Later, however, Heracles mustered an army of Arcadian volunteers and marched against Augias, who on hearing that the hero was raising a force against him, commissioned his nephews, the two sons of Actor, or the MOLIONIDAE, to defend him. Since Heracles had fallen ill, the two brothers took advantage of the fact to inflict a defeat on the hero, but shortly after, during a religious ceremony, Heracles killed the Molionidae and captured Elis. He killed Augias and his sons and set Phyleus on the throne of the city. In another tradition, Augias died naturally in extreme old age, and his people were said to have given him divine honours. (For the story of the treasure of Augias, see AGAMEDES.)

Aura (Αὔρα) Whose name means breeze, was the daughter of a Phrygian woman named Periboea and the Titan Lelantus. She was as swift as the wind and was one of Artemis' hunting companions. Dionysus loved her and tried vainly to catch her while she ran but she was lighter and always escaped until, at Dionysus' request, Aphrodite struck her with madness so that she yielded to him. She had twin sons by Dionysus but destroyed them in her madness and threw herself into the river Sangarius. Zeus changed her into a stream. One of her twin sons was INACHUS.

Aurora See EOS.

Auson (Αὔσων) A son fathered by Odysseus during his travels, some traditions say his mother was Circe, others Calypso (Table 39). He is said to have been a brother of Latinus and to have had a son called Liparus. Auson gave his name to the Ausones, who were the first inhabitants of Italy, itself then known as Ausonia. He was the first ruler of the country (see also LEUCASIA).

Autoleon (Αὐτολέων) When the Locrians went into battle they used to leave a gap in the ranks in honour of their compatriot Ajax, in the belief that the hero would come and do battle in their midst. One day, when they were fighting against the inhabitants of Crotona, one of the adversaries, named Autoleon, sought to pass through this gap in the Locrian lines but he was severely wounded in the thigh by a ghost and the wound would not heal. On being consulted, the oracle directed him to go to the White Island, at the mouth of the Danube (see ACHILLES), there to offer sacrifices to the heroes and especially to Ajax of Locri. There he saw Helen, who entrusted him with a message to the poet Stesichorus, who had been struck by blindness for having spoken evil of her in one of his poems. Helen told him to tell Stesichorus that he would regain his sight if he sang a recantation: he did, and his sight was restored. This is the version given by Conon, but Pausanias, who also tells this story, calls its hero Leonymus.

Autolycus (Αὐτόλυκος) The son of Hermes and Chione or Stilbe, the daughter of Eosphorus (see DAEDALION and Chione and Table 3). He is said to have married Maestra, the daughter of Erysichthon but this is certainly a late tradition. He was the grandfather of Odysseus by his daughter Anticleia (Tables 35 and 39). He inherited the gift of stealing without ever being caught from his father, Hermes, and his thefts were very numerous. He stole a leather helmet from Amyntor, and gave it to Achilles, who wore it during his nocturnal expedition with Diomedes against Troy. Then he stole some flocks in Euboea from Eurytus and he also, but unsuccessfully, stole some beasts from Sisyphus. To make his thefts impossible to detect he excelled in disguising the beasts, for example, by dyeing the skins of the oxen. According to some writers he even had the gift of transforming himself, and he taught Heracles the art of fighting. When Sisyphus was visiting in an attempt to recover his cattle,

Autolycus married him secretly to his daughter Anticleia just as she was on the point of marrying Laertes.

Autolycus took part in the Argonauts' expedition. He was in some accounts said to be the grandfather of Jason since his daughter, Polynede, had married Aeson.

Automedon (Αὐτομέδων) Achilles' charioteer and his comrade in battle. He came to Troy at the head of ten ships, a contingent from Scyros, and he played an active part in the fighting before Troy. After Achilles' death, he continued to serve under his son, Pyrrhus-Neoptolemus, and took part in the capture of the city.

Auxesia (Αὐξησία) Auxesia and her companion Damia were two Cretan girls who came to Troezen, where they were by chance caught in a riot and were stoned to death by the mob. As an act of atonement they were made the objects of a cult and a festival was held in their honour. Auxesia and Damia were identified with Demeter and Persephone.

Avilius The son of Romulus and HERSILLA.

B

Babys (Βάβυς) The brother of the Phrygian Satyr MARSYAS, who wanted to compete with Apollo in the art of music. Babys also played the flute, but a flute with only one pipe, while his brother played the double flute. Babys was a simpleton, who played so badly that he was spared the god's anger.

Bacchus (Βάκχος) See DIONYSUS.

Baius (Βαῖος) A pilot of ODYSSEUS whose name does not occur in the Odyssey but who in events subsequent to the legend was supposed to have given his name to several places, such as a mountain in the island of Cephallonia in the Ionian sea, and the town of Baiae in Campania. While piloting Odysseus' vessel he met his death in Italian waters.

Balius (Βαλίος)
1. One of Achilles' horses, offspring of Zephyr and the Harpy Podarge. After Achilles' death, Poseidon took back the horse, which was immortal, as well as Xanthos, Achilles' other horse.
2. Balius was also the name given to one of Actaeon's dogs.

Basileia (Βασίλεια) Basileia, whose name means queen was, according to an inconsistent legend, the daughter of Uranus and Titaia and a sister of Rhea and the Titans, who she brought up. She became famous for her wisdom and intellect. She married her brother Hyperion, and had as children Selene (the Moon) and Helios (the Sun). Out of resentment, the other Titans killed Hyperion and immersed Helios in the river Eridanus and in her grief at the loss of her brother, Selene cast herself from the top of the roof of her house. Helios and Selene were then made into heavenly bodies. Basileia learnt of what had happened in a dream, became deranged and, grasping a tambourine and some cymbals which had belonged to her daughter, began to scour the country banging on the tambourine and clashing the cymbals until some one, out of pity, stopped her. Then a great storm broke and Basileia vanished. A cult was practised in her honour, under the name of the Great Goddess, which identifies her with Cybele. The name of Basileia also means royalty, personified and deified.

Baton (Βάτων) The chariot-driver of Amphiaraus, the Theban hero. He, like Amphiaraus, was also descended from Melampus. Fighting before Thebes, Baton shared the fate of his master and was swallowed up by the earth just as Amphiaraus was about to be struck by an enemy. He was given divine honours. A different tradition claims that Baton withdrew to a town in Illyria called Harpyia after the death of Amphiaraus.

Battus (Βάττος)
1. The name of an old man who played a part in the story of the theft of Apollo's oxen by Hermes. When Apollo was completely absorbed by his love for Hymenaeus, the son of Magnes, he neglected his flocks and Hermes stole a certain number of beasts from him and removed them to the outskirts of Menale in the Peloponnese. There, meeting an old man who lived on the mountain, he was afraid that his theft might be disclosed and he promised the old man whose name was Battus a heifer if he agreed to keep silent. The old man gave his promise but Hermes after putting the cattle in a safe place changed his shape and returned to Battus, pretending that he was looking for his cattle, and asking him if he had not seen a herd pass by, promising him a reward if he would help him to find them. Battus broke his promise and told him, and Hermes in anger changed him into a rock.
2. Battus was also the name of a mythical or historical character, the founder of the colony of Cyrene on the coast of Libya. His father was Polymnestus, a descendant of the Argonaut EUPHEMUS. He belonged to the race known as Minyans who were descended from the Argonauts (see MINYAS). Having left Lemnos for Lacedaemonia, they were obliged to leave Lacedaemonia and settle in Thera, following the Lacedaemonian Theras. His mother was called Phronime and was a native-born Cretan. In the commonest tradition Battus was only a nickname given to a hero because he stammered; however, Herodotus tells us that Battus means king in the

Bacchus, the god of wine and inspiration is represented in this Roman wall painting as a bunch of grapes; he holds his attribute, the thyrsus, and a panther – one of the wild species sacred to him – is at his feet. The serpent approaching an altar with food placed on it represents the tutelary spirit of the house coming to partake of the offering. Vesuvius is shown in the centre of the painting. From a household shrine in the House of the Centenary, Pompeii. Naples, National Museum.

language spoken in Libya. Battus' real name is said by some to be Aristoteles, by others, Aristaeus (the latter has perhaps been confused with Aristaeus, the son of the Nymph Cyrene). According to Pausanias, Battus regained the power of speech after the foundation of Cyrene.

Baubo (Βαυβώ) The wife of Dysaules who lived at Eleusis. Demeter sought for her daughter throughout the Greek world and during her search she arrived at Eleusis, accompanied by her small son, Iacchus. Dysaules and Baubo welcomed them warmly and Baubo, to comfort Demeter, offered her some soup, which the goddess in her grief refused. Then Baubo, either to show her displeasure or to amuse the goddess, tucked up her clothes and showed her buttocks. When Iacchus saw this, he began to cheer. The goddess was amused, began to laugh and accepted the soup. Dysaules and Baubo had two sons: Triptolemus (who is more frequently said to be the son of Celeus and Metanira) and Eubouleus, and two daughters, Protonoe and Nisa.

Baucis (Βαύκις) A Phrygian woman who was married to Philemon, a very poor peasant. They welcomed Zeus and Hermes to their cottage one day when the latter were making their way through Phrygia in the guise of travellers. The rest of the inhabitants would not take the two strangers in and Baucis and Philemon were the only ones to offer hospitality. In their anger, the gods sent a storm over the whole country which left the cottage with the two old people unharmed. The cottage became a temple and because Baucis and Philemon had asked to end their days together Zeus and Hermes turned them into two trees which stood side by side in front of the temple.

Bellerophon (Βελλεροφόντης) A descendant of the royal house of Corinth. He was a son of Poseidon but his human father was Glaucus, the son of Sisyphus (Table 35). His mother was a daughter of Nisus, king of Megara, sometimes called Eurymede and sometimes Eurynome. His exploits began with the accidental murder of a man, sometimes known as Deliades and said to have been his true brother, and sometimes Piren (whose name recalls that of the spring PIRENE at Corinth), or Alcimenes, or Bellerus, which offers an etymology for his own name, as Bellerophon was understood to mean 'the killer of Bellerus', a tyrant of Corinth. After this murder Bellerophon had to leave the city and went to Tiryns to the court of King Proetus, who cleansed him. Stheneboea (called by Homer Anteia), who was the wife of Proetus, asked Bellerophon to meet her secretly, and when he refused, she complained that the young man had tried to seduce her. Proetus at once sent Bellerophon to find his father-in-law Iobates, the king of Lycia and gave him a letter in which he demanded that the bearer be put to death. Proetus was unwilling to kill Bellerophon as he was his guest and an ancient custom forbade anyone to kill a man with whom he had eaten. After reading the letter, Iobates ordered Bellerophon to kill the CHIMAERA, a monster which had the fore-quarters of a lion, the hind-quarters of a dragon and a goat's head which breathed out flames. This monster was laying waste the country and carrying off the flocks. Iobates thought that Bellerophon would never be able to kill it by himself but Bellerophon mounted PEGASUS, the winged horse, which he had found one day while he was drinking at the fountain called Pirene in Corinth and, rising in the air, swooped straight down on the Chimaera, and slew it with a single blow. Iobates then sent Bellerophon to fight against the Solymes, a neighbouring people who were especially warlike and ferocious but he was once more successful against them. Next Iobates sent him to fight the Amazons, and he killed many of them. Finally Iobates mustered a band of the bravest of the Lydians and ordered them to lay an ambush to kill Bellerophon, but he instead killed all of them. Iobates realized that Bellerophon was of divine descent and full of admiration for his exploits, he showed him the letter from Proetus and made him promise to stay at his court. Moreover, he gave him his daughter Philonoe (in some versions called Anticleia) and at his death bequeathed him his kingdom (for an account of the revenge of Bellerophon, see STHENEBOEA).

Bellerophon had two sons by Iobates' daughter, Isandrus and Hippolochus, and a daughter, Laodamia, who by Zeus was the mother of the hero Sarpedon. Later, Bellerophon, swollen with pride, tried to ride on his winged horse up to the domain of Zeus, but Zeus hurled him back to earth, where he was killed. He was held in honour as a hero in Corinth and Lycia. There is a reference in the *Iliad* to the bonds of hospitality which are supposed to have existed between Bellerophon and Oeneus, king of Calydon.

Bellona The Roman goddess of war, who was for a long time ill defined and regarded as a personification of mere force, but gradually became identified with the Greek goddess of war, Enyo. She was sometimes portrayed as the wife of the god Mars and was also depicted as driving her own chariot in terrible guise, holding a torch, sword or spear in her hand, greatly resembling the traditional representation of the Furies.

Belus (Βῆλος) One of Poseidon's twin sons by the Nymph Libya. The other twin was Agenor (Table 3) and while the latter went to Syria, Belus remained in Egypt, where he was king and married Anchinoe, the daughter of the god Nile. He had twin sons, Egyptus and Danaus and in occasional references is said to have fathered Cepheus and Phineus. Writers also note a number of Assyrian and Babylonian heroes of this name; one of these found a place in the genealogy of Queen Dido of Carthage.

Bia (Βία) Bia, whose name means violence, personified this concept. She was regarded as the daughter of the giant Pallas and the Styx. In the struggle between the Gods and the Giants she fought on the side of Zeus. Her sister was Nike (Victory) and her brothers, Zelus (Ardour) and Cratus (Strength) (Table 32), and together with them she was the constant companion of Zeus. She helped to tie down Prometheus in the Caucasus.

Bianna (Βίαννα) A girl who gave her name to the town of Vienna in the Dauphine. She arrived from her native Crete following a famine which forced many Cretans to leave their country. During a dance she was engulfed by an abyss which opened in the ground and her name was given to the town built by the immigrants.

Bianor (Βιάνωρ) A Mantuan hero, and the son of the Tiber and the Nymph Manto (see AUCNUS). He founded the city of Mantua which he named in memory of his mother. He is sometimes identified with Aucnus.

Bias (Βίας) The son of Amythaon and Idomene, the daughter of Pheres. His brother was Melampus, the seer, who is closely associated with his adventures (Tables 1 and 21). When Bias wanted to marry Pero, the daughter of Neleus, he had to perform a task imposed by her father, namely, to steal the herds of Phylacus. The oxen were well guarded by a fierce dog but Melampus agreed to steal them on behalf of his brother and, when he

had been granted the hand of Pero by Neleus, he gave her up to Bias. Subsequently, after Melampus had cured the daughters of King Proetus of their madness, he secured a third of the latter's kingdom for Bias, who set himself up in it (see ANAXAGORAS). When married to Pero, Bias fathered Talaus, the father of Adrastus (Table 1), Perialces, Laodocus, Areius and Alphesiboea. Later, when he was settled in Argos in the kingdom of Proetus, he married the latter's daughter, Lysippe. She was certainly the mother of his daughter Anaxibia who, according to some accounts, later married Pelias.

Bona Dea A Roman divinity, closely associated with the cult of Faunus. Her legend, which is fairly concise, was devised to explain some details of her cult. In the earliest version, Bona Dea was the daughter of Faunus. He fell in love with her but she was unwilling to yield to his desires, even after he had made her drunk with wine, and he chastised her with switches of myrtle (this is given as the explanation of why myrtle could not be brought into her temple). He finally succeeded in having intercourse with her in the guise of a snake. Another version of the legend claims that Bona Dea was the wife of Faunus, a woman highly skilled in all the domestic arts and so chaste that she never left her room and saw no other man than her husband. One day she found a jug of wine, drank it and became inebriated. Her husband beat her so severely with switches of myrtle that she died. In remorse, he granted her divine honours. In Rome, Bona Dea had her shrine under the Aventine Hill and there the women and girls annually celebrated the mysteries of the Good Goddess, which no man was allowed to attend. Hercules, who had himself been shut out by way of revenge, founded ceremonies which no woman could take part in at his Great Altar, which was not far away.

Boreades (Βορεάδαι) The name by which the children of the North Wind, or Boreas, were generally referred to. More strictly, it was the name of his twin sons, Calais and Zetes whose mother was Orithyia, the daughter of Erectheus, who had been abducted by the god on the banks of the Ilyssus (Table 11). The two young men had wings, attached in some versions to their heels and in others to their sides like birds. Like their father, they were the spirits of the winds, whose names were added in antiquity to the verb 'to blow'. Calais was 'he who blows gently' and Zetes was 'he who blows strongly'. Like their father again, they were born in Thrace, and their main characteristic was speed. They took part in the expedition of the Argonauts and played an especially important part during their stay with King Phineus by pursuing the Harpies, who were tormenting the king. There are, however, different traditions about this incident. In some versions they freed the king by forcing the Harpies to fly away and making them promise to leave Phineus in peace in the future and in others they killed two or three of them. Some accounts make no mention of the Harpies and claim that the Boreades inflicted punishment on Phineus, who had blinded the children he had had by their sister, Cleopatra.

There are also different accounts of their deaths. One claims that they failed to catch the Harpies and died on their way back; but according to the most common one they took part in the whole of the Argonauts' expedition and were present at the funerary games held in honour of Pelias (see JASON). There they won the prize for running, but they were killed shortly after by Heracles who did not forgive them for advising the Argonauts to leave him in Mysia when he was delayed in the search for Hylas. When the Boreades were returning from the funeral rites of Pelias, the hero found them on the island of Tenos and killed them. He erected two pillars to them, which shook every time the north wind blew on the island. Boreas also had two daughters, Cleopatra, who was married to Phineus, and Chione (see BUTES).

Boreas (Βορέας) The god of the North Wind. He lived in Thrace which to the Greeks represented the ultimate in a cold climate. He is depicted as a winged demon, physically extremely strong, bearded and normally clad in a short pleated tunic. In one image he is shown, like the Roman Janus, with two faces looking in opposite directions, no doubt representing the two winds, Boreas and Antiboreas, which blew across the Euripus. Boreas was the son of Eos (the Dawn) and Astraeus, son of Crius and Eurybia and the brother of Zephyrus and Notus (Table 14). He thus belonged to the race of the Titans, who personified the elemental forces of Nature. Among other deeds of violence, he was said to have abducted Orithyia, daughter of Erectheus, the king of Athens, while she was playing with her companions on the banks of the Ilissus. He took her to Thrace where she gave birth to two sons, Calais and Zetes (see BOREADES). Another version

of the legend says that the abduction took place during a procession which was making its way up the Acropolis to the temple of Athena Polias. Sometimes the punishment of Phineus is ascribed to Boreas. Boreas, in the shape of a horse, is said to have sired by the mares of Erichthonius twelve colts so light of foot that when they galloped over a field of wheat, they did not even bend the heads of the wheat, and when they galloped over the sea they did not cause a ripple on the water. Boreas also sired swift horses by one of the Furies as well as by a Harpy. For the background to Boreas as king of the Celts, see CYPARISSA.

Bormos (Βόρμος) A son of Titias (or Tityus), a Mariandyne and a young man of great beauty. One day, when he had gone to draw water for the reapers from a deep spring, he was abducted by the Nymphs (see HYLAS). He is also said to have been killed while he was hunting and his death was commemorated every year, at the time of the harvest, by laments to the sound of the flute.

Botres (Βότρης) A Theban and the son of Eumelus, a strong devotee of Apollo. One day, when Eumelus was sacrificing a lamb to him, his son Botres was near at hand and helped him, but Botres divided the brain of the sacrificial victim before placing it as an offering on the altar. In a fit of rage, his father seized a brand from the funeral pyre and struck his son, who died immediately. On seeing the grief of Botres' mother and father, Apollo changed him into a bird called the Acropus; this means 'the bird with a forbidding look' which nests underground and hovers incessantly.

Boucolos (Βουκόλος) Boucolos, whose name means cowherd, was the son of Colonus of Tanagra in Boeotia and had two brothers Ochemus and Leon, and one sister Ochna, the only daughter. Ochna loved Eunostus but was disdainfully rejected by him. She accused him in front of her brothers of having tried to assault her. The young men killed Eunostus with a blow on the head, then in remorse Ochna confessed the truth. The brothers fled before the threats of Eunostus' father, and the girl herself committed suicide.

Boulis (Βουλίς) See AEGYPIUS.

Bounos (Βοῦνος) A Corinthian hero, the son of Hermes and Alcidamia. Aeetes, on leaving Corinth for Colchos, gave the throne of Corinth to Bounos, bidding him to keep it until either he or his children came back. After the death of Bounus, Epopeus of Sicyon was his successor.

Bouphagus (Βουφάγος) An Arcadian hero whose name literally means 'the eater of oxen'; the son of Iapetus and Thornax. During the war against Augias, he and Promne, his wife, sheltered Iphicles who had been wounded (see HERACLES). Bouphagus cared for Iapetus until his death, after which he became a recluse. Later, he was killed by Artemis who was annoyed by his importunate love when he pursued her on Mount Pholoe in Arcadia.

Branchus (Βράγχος) The son of a hero called Smicrus, who was a native of Delphi. Smicrus had settled at Miletus and married there and, before Branchus was born, his mother had had a vision, in which she saw the sun sink into her mouth, pass through her whole body and come up again out of her belly. The seers interpreted this as a portent of good fortune. The son she gave birth to was called Branchus, meaning bronchus, because it was through that part of her body that she felt the sun go down inside her. When the boy, who was very handsome, was looking after the flocks on the mountain one day, Apollo fell in love with him. Broncho raised an altar to Apollo the Friendly, and, inspired by the god who endowed him with the gift of divination, he founded an oracle south of Miletus, at Didymas, which was regarded until historical times as almost equal in prestige to that of Delphi. It was served by the Branchides (descendants of Branchus). Branchus was supposed to have among his ancestors Machaereus, the man who had killed Neoptolemus at Delphi.

Brangas (Βράγγας) The son of the Thessalian river-god Strymon and the brother of Olynthus. Olynthus was killed by a lion while hunting; Brangas buried him on the spot where he had fallen and called the village which he built nearby Olynthus.

Briseis (Βρισηίς) Briseis, whose real name was Hippodamia, was the daughter of Brises, a priest from the town of Lyrnessus which was captured and looted by ACHILLES. Brises was the brother of Chryses, the father of Chryseis. Hippodamia, who was called Briseis after her father, was married to Mynes. He was killed by Achilles and Briseis was carried off by Achilles. To com-

fort her, Patroclus promised to make sure that Achilles married her, and in effect she became Achilles' favourite slave, dearly loved by him. When the assembly of the Greeks compelled Agamemnon to return Chryseis to her father and Agamemnon demanded in return that Achilles should hand over Briseis, Achilles, in his grief and anger, refused to fight. Agamemnon promised to hand her over first when he sent an embassy in an attempt to appease Achilles; and it was she, and she alone, whom Achilles accepted at the time of his reconciliation with the son of Atreus. Traditions subsequent to Homer portray her as a tall, dark well-dressed woman with sparkling eyes, a clear complexion and eyebrows that nearly met. She is said to have offered the tributes at the funeral of Achilles.

Brises (Βρίσης) The father of BRISEIS. In some accounts he was the king of the Leleges in Caria, but generally, like his brother Chryses, he was thought to be the priest of Apollo in the town of Lyrnessos, which was looted by the Greeks during the Trojan War. He had a son as well as his daughter Hippodamia, generally called BRISEIS, who was named Eetion (not to be confused with the hero of the same name, who was king of Lyrnessos and the father of Andromache). Brises hanged himself when his house was destroyed by Achilles in the course of the sack of the town.

Britomartis (Βριτόμαρτις) A Cretan goddess, whose name meant the gentle virgin. She was the daughter of Zeus and Carme and said to be a virgin Nymph, a companion of Artemis, from Gortyn in Crete. Minos was in love with her and in his lust he pursued her for nine months throughout the mountains and valleys in the island. One day, at the end of that time, she realized that she was about to be caught and she threw herself from the top of a cliff into the sea where she fell into the fishermen's nets and was saved, which was why she acquired the name of Dictynna, 'the daughter of the net'. Another, less miraculous version explains the same epithet by attributing to Britomartis the invention of the nets used for hunting. In yet another story, Britomartis, while out hunting was caught by accident in a net and, after being rescued by Artemis, she was accorded divine honours under the name of Dictynna. Like Artemis she was portrayed as surrounded by hounds, dressed as a huntress, eschewing male company and very fond of solitude.

Bryte (Βρύτη) A daughter of Ares (Mars) and an attendant of Artemis; her legend was identical with that of Britomartis. She was loved by Minos and threw herself into the sea where her body was recovered in a fisherman's net. A plague broke out and the oracle pronounced that to bring it to an end she must be accorded divine honours under the name of Diana Dictynna (Artemis of the net).

Busiris (Βούσιρις) In Greek legend a king of Egypt. His name is not to be found in any of the genealogies of the Pharoahs, but it may be a corruption of the name of the god Osiris. Busiris was a very cruel king and the harshness of his rule forced PROTEUS to flee from Egypt. He had also sent a band of pirates to abduct the Hesperides, who were famous for their beauty. Heracles, while on his journey to get the golden apples, met and killed the pirates. A run of bad harvests fell on Egypt and Phrasius, who was a seer from Cyprus, advised the king to sacrifice a stranger to Zeus each year, to mollify the god and restore prosperity. When Heracles was passing through Egypt, Busiris captured him, bound him, gave him a crown of flowers and led him to the altar as a victim, but Heracles burst his bonds, and killed Busiris, his son Iphidamas (or Amphidamas), Chalbes the herald and all the spectators. Busiris was the son of Poseidon and Lysianassa (Table 3). He had been put on the throne of Egypt by Osiris, when the latter had left on his great expedition round the world.

Butes (Βούτης)
1. A son of BOREAS and the half-brother of Lycurgus. They had different mothers, neither of them being Orithyia, the god's legitimate wife. Butes sought to kill his half-brother Lycurgus, but when his intentions were discovered, he had to flee with his followers and he established himself on Naxos, where he lived by armed robbery and piracy. During one of his forays, he attacked the Phthiotide in Thessaly, in order to abduct the women. On Naxos he encountered the female worshippers of Dionysus; most of them escaped, but the god's nurse, Coronis, was carried off and given to Butes. In answer to the girl's prayers, Butes was struck with madness by Dionysus. He threw himself into a well and died.
2. The son of Pandion, king of Athens, and his wife Zeuxippe (Table 11). His brother was Erechtheus and his sisters Philomela and Procne. On the death of Pandion, his estate was divided between his sons. Erechtheus received the kingship, and Butes the priesthood of Athena and Poseidon. He married the daughter of ERECHTHEUS, Chthonia. It was on his being their ancestor that the priestly family of the Eteoboutades based their claim at Athens.
3. For Butes the Argonaut, who founded the town of Lilyboea in Sicily, see ARGONAUTS and ERYX.

Buzyges (Βουζύγης) Buzyges, or 'he who puts oxen under the yoke' was the mythical inventor of the yoke who had the idea of taming and harnessing bulls, as well as using them for work and ploughing the fields. He was also believed to have been one of the first legislators, and is said to have instituted the ban on killing oxen or bulls since they were so useful in cultivation, which was frequently mentioned in classical antiquity (see also PALLADIUM).

Byblis (Βυβλίς) By her father MILETUS Byblis was the great-granddaughter of Minos (see ACACALLIS) or, in some versions of the story, his granddaughter (Table 28). There are a number of conflicting traditions about her mother's name. Sometimes it is said to have been Cyane, daughter of Meandra, sometimes Tragasia, daughter of Celaeno, or again Idothea, the daughter of the king Eurytus. She had a twin brother named Caunus, and she loved him with a guilty passion. Filled with horror for his sister, Caunus fled from Miletus, his birthplace, and went to found the town of Caunus in Caria. Byblis, overcome with grief, went mad and wandered over the whole of Asia Minor. Just as she was about to cast herself from the summit of a rock and thus put an end to both her misery and her life, the Nymphs, who pitied her, turned her into an inexhaustible stream, like the girl's own tears. There is another contrasting tradition: according to this Caunus conceived a guilty passion for his sister, and this was the reason why he fled from his father's house and why Byblis hung herself. Her name was given to two towns in memory of her, namely Byblis in Caria and Byblos in Phoenicia.

Byzas (Βύζας) The son of Poseidon and Ceroessa. His mother was the daughter of Io and Zeus and he was born not far from the site of the city which was later called Byzantium. He founded the city of Byzantium, which was called after him and fortified it with the help of Apollo and Poseidon. When Haemus, the tyrant of Thrace, made an attack on the city, Byzas defeated him in single combat and pursued his fleeing enemies beyond the boundaries of Thrace. While he was away, however, the city was attacked by Odryses, the king of Scythia. He besieged it, but Phidalia, the wife of Byzas, saved the city with the help of some other women by throwing huge numbers of snakes into the enemy camp. She saved it a second time from attacks by her brother-in-law, Strombus.

C

Caanthus (Κάανθος) A son of Oceanus. After his sister, the Nymph Melia, had been abducted by Apollo near Thebes on the banks of the river Ismenus his father sent him to look for her. He found the pair but could not induce them to part. Enraged by this he set fire to the shrine of Apollo, and by doing so lost his life, for the god slew him with an arrow. His tomb could be seen at Thebes, not far from the spring of Ares.

Cabarnus (Κάβαρνος) When Demeter was searching for her daughter, Persephone, who had been abducted, a man named Cabarnus who lived on Paros told her that the culprit was Hades. As a reward, the goddess assigned to Cabarnus and his descendants the duty of looking after her cult.

Cabiri (Κάβειροι) Mysterious divinities whose main shrine was in Samothrace, though they were widely worshipped, even, according to Herodotus, at Memphis in Egypt. The mythographers of the classical world give widely differing accounts both of their descent and of their essential nature. Hephaestus is most commonly cited, either as their father or at least their ancestor. Acusilaus says that Hephaestus had by Cabiro a son, Cadmilus, who was supposed to have fathered in due course the three Cabiri, who were themselves the fathers of the Nymphs known as the Cabirides. Pherecydes says that the Cabiri were the sons of Hephaestus and Cabiro, the latter being the daughter of Proteus. According to both versions, the Nymphs named Cabirides, three in number, were sisters of the Cabiri (also three in number). Other authors maintain that there were seven Cabiri and that their father had been the Phoenician Sydyk; in this case, Asclepius would have been their brother. A tradition dating back to Mnaseas of Patara names four of the Cabiri: Axierus, Axiokersa, Axiokersus and Cadmilus; in Greek mythology these were identified respectively with Demeter, Persephone, Hades and

Hermes and in Roman mythology with Jupiter, Mercury, Juno and Minerva; but in this tradition their genealogy is not identified. In this version Cabiri was nothing more than a mystical and functional name for the celestial beings invoked and this is how the Cabiri came to be sometimes identified with Jason and Dardanus, the children of Zeus and Electra who were also heroes especially associated with Samothrace.

The Cabiri, as divinities of a mysterious character, could not be named with impunity; they were generally referred to as 'the great gods'. One commentary cites, in addition to the names mentioned above, Alcon and Eurymedon, a 'pair' of Cabiri, the sons of Cabiro and Hephaestus. In the Roman period, the Cabiri were generally regarded as a triad, overlapping with the three Roman divinities Jupiter, Minerva and Mercury. There are virtually no myths about the Cabiri. They are said to have been present at the birth of Zeus on the acropolis of Pergamon and this account is consistent with their identification as demons forming part of the retinue of Rhea. They were the servants of the goddess and because of this were often confused with the Corybantes and Curetes. After the classical era ended they seem to have been regarded as protectors of navigation, with functions similar to those of the Dioscuri, whom they had some affinities with.

Cabiro (Καβειρώ) The daughter of Proteus and Anchinoe and a native of Lemnos, where Hephaestus was worshipped; she was loved by Hephaestus and bore him the Cabiri and the Cabirides.

Caca A very ancient Roman goddess, who is said to have been the sister of the robber Cacus. She may have betrayed her brother by disclosing to Hercules the secret place where Cacus had hidden the stolen oxen (see CACUS). In return Caca became the object of a cult and a flame was kept perpetually alight in her honour, as one was for the goddess Vesta.

Cacus Possibly a fire god or perhaps simply a deity associated with a place, Cacus was one of the heroes local to Rome and his myth is closely linked with that of Hercules. He is said to have been the son of Vulcan, and lived in a cavern on the Aventine Hill. When Hercules returned from his expedition in the western Mediterranean, he brought with him the oxen which he had stolen from Geryon; he left them to graze freely on the place which later became the Forum Boarium while he rested by the banks of the Tiber, and Cacus, though he could not steal the whole herd, much as he wanted to, removed a number of the beasts (said to be four cows and four oxen) and concealed them in his cave. In order to leave no clues he pulled the beasts by their tails, making them walk backwards, so that their tracks seemed to be coming away from the cave and not going towards it. When Hercules awoke and counted his herd he realized that a thief had been at work; he went in search of his possessions and would have been taken in by Cacus's trick if, as some accounts say, the beasts had not lowed when they heard the rest of the herd and thus given away where they were, or if as others maintain, he had not been told what had happened by Caca, Cacus's sister. Whatever the true version, Hercules and Cacus began to fight. Cacus had three heads and blew flames from his three mouths, but Hercules soon got the better of him with his club. In another version of the story Cacus shut himself up in his cave, piling up rocks in front of the entrance to resist the assaults of Hercules, but the latter climbed the hill and tore away the rocks which formed the roof of the cave; he succeeded in reaching his enemy and killed him. Then he offered a sacrifice to Jupiter Inventor, in gratitude for his success. King Evander, then reigning at Pallanteia (the site which later became Rome but was then merely a village on the Palatine hill, inhabited by shepherds) thanked Hercules for having disposed of such a robber as Cacus and promised Hercules that heaven would reward him by conferring divine honours on him.

An obscure version of the legend about Hercules substitutes a robber called Garanus or Recaranus for Cacus. According to one early Roman historian, Cacus was a comrade of King Marsyas, who had come from Phrygia to invade Italy. Marsyas sent him as an ambassador with the Etruscan king Tarchon, but he was taken prisoner by the latter. Cacus managed to free himself and returned to Marsyas. Marsyas and Cacus then seized Campania, the country named Volturna and attacked the region of Rome, where an Arcadian colony had established itself. At this point, however, Hercules allied himself with Tarchon and crushed the invading force.

Finally, Diodorus writes of one Cacius (Κακίος) who was a man of exceptional strength. He lived on the Palatine and had entertained Hercules with hospitality. This Cacius gave his name to a rise on the Palatine known as the *Scalae Caci* (Cacius's steps) near his house (*atrium Caci*).

Cadmus (Κάδμος) A hero in the Theban cycle whose legend, like that of Heracles, spread throughout most of the world of the Mediterranean, Asia Minor, Illyria and Libya in Africa. He was the son of Agenor and Telephassa or, as another tradition maintains, of Argiope (Table 3); he was the brother of Cilix, Phoenix and Europa, though sometimes Phoenix is said to have been the father of Cadmus and Europa. A Boeotian tradition, which is later than the preceding ones, claims that Cadmus was the son of the Theban autochthon Ogygus.

After Europa was abducted, Agenor sent his sons to find her, ordering them not to reappear without her. Their mother, Telephassa, accompanied them and they left the country of Tyre which was ruled over by Agenor. The young men soon realized that their quest was a vain one, however, and while the brothers settled in various countries, Cadmus and Telephassa went to Thrace, where they were kindly received by the inhabitants. When his mother died Cadmus went to consult the Delphic oracle which told him to give up his search for Europa and to found a town; in order to choose its site he would have to follow a cow until it collapsed with fatigue. Cadmus set out to obey the oracle, and as he was crossing Phocis he saw a cow among the herds belonging to Pelagon, the son of Amphidamas, bearing on each flank the sign of the moon, that is, a white circle, which recalled the full moon. He followed the cow, and it led him across Boeotia; finally it stopped at the place which later became Thebes. Cadmus at that moment saw that the oracle had been fulfilled and he wanted to offer the cow as a sacrifice to Athena. He sent some of his companions to look for water from a nearby spring, called the Spring of Ares, but a dragon, which in some accounts is said to be a descendant of Ares himself, was guarding the spring and killed most of the men sent by Cadmus. The latter came to the rescue of his companions and killed the dragon. Athena then appeared and advised him to sow its teeth. Cadmus did so, and at once, armed men sprang out of the ground; these became known as the Spartoi. The miraculous men were menacing and Cadmus had the idea of throwing stones into their midst; the Spartoi, who did not know who was throwing the stones, first accused and then slaughtered each other. Only five survived, namely Echion (who subsequently married Agave, one of Cadmus's daughters), Oudaeus, Chthonius, Hyperenor and Pelorus. The killing of the dragon had still to be atoned for by Cadmus so he served as Ares's slave for eight years, but when his sentence ended he became king of Thebes, through the protection of Athena, and Zeus gave him as a wife the goddess Harmonia, a daughter of Ares and Aphrodite. Their wedding was celebrated with great banquets in which all the gods took part and where the Muses sang. The gods came down from heaven and made their way to the Cadmea, the citadel of Thebes, bearing presents with them: the principal gifts, a wonderful robe, woven by the Graces, and a golden necklace, fashioned by Hephaestus the smith-god, were for Harmonia. According to some accounts, this necklace was given to Cadmus by the god himself, but others say that it was a present from Europa to her brother and Europa herself had been given it by Zeus. The same necklace and robe would later play a large part in the episode of the expedition of the Seven against Thebes (see AMPHIARAUS). Cadmus had several children by Harmonia: four daughters, Autonoe, Ino (who took the name of Leucothea after her deification), Agave and Semele, and one son, Polydorus.

Towards the end of their lives Cadmus and Harmonia left Thebes under mysterious circumstances, leaving the throne to their grandson Pentheus, the son of Agave and Echion. They went to Illyria, to live among the Encheleans who had been attacked by the Illyrians. The Encheleans had been promised victory by an oracle if Cadmus and Harmonia would lead them and as this condition was fulfilled, they were indeed victorious. Cadmus then ruled over the Illyrians and he had another son, named Illyrius. But later Cadmus and Harmonia were turned into serpents and reached the Elysian Fields. Their tomb was to be seen in Illyria. A legend recorded by Nonnus of Panopolis, which may be no more than an invention of a late poet, tells how Cadmus followed the tracks of the bull which had carried off Europa and was enlisted by Zeus in the expedition against the Giant Typhon. He put on the clothing of a shepherd, which had been given to him by his companion, the god Pan, and after Typhon removed the sinews of Zeus, Cadmus bewitched him by playing the lyre and retrieved Zeus' sinews on the pretext of making some strings for his lyre out of them. Cadmus returned them to Zeus, thus enabling him to win the struggle. Cadmus in return received Harmonia as a wife. It was commonly said at Thera, Rhodes, Samothrace, Crete and many other places that Cadmus had founded these cities during his search for Europa.

Caeculus The Roman legend of Praeneste (the modern Palestrina, situated on the hills which mark the border between Latium and the Sabine territory) ascribes the foundation of the town to a hero named Caeculus, the son of Culvan. The legend maintains that at one time there lived in this country two brothers called the Depidii, who were shepherds. They had a sister and one day when she was sitting near the hearth in her house a spark flew out of the fire and jumped onto her bosom; almost at once she felt that she had conceived a child. A son was born to her and she abandoned him near the temple of Jupiter but some young women on their way to fetch water at the spring nearby found the infant beside a lighted fire and took it to the two Depidii. They brought the child up, and called him Caeculus (from *caecus* 'blind') when they first saw him, for the smoke of the fire by which he had been found had made his eyes water and he seemed to be blind. During his upbringing among the shepherds Caeculus lived by pillaging, as was customary in those days. After he had grown up, he and some companions founded the village which was destined to become Praeneste. On the day when the inauguration of the new town was to be celebrated, he invited those who lived nearby and were coming to settle in the town, and to induce them to come he asked his father Vulcan to produce a wonderful spectacle: Vulcan sent down flames, which encircled the crowd and extinguished themselves as soon as Caeculus bade them. This miracle made the town's fortune, for a great many people came to settle there, to be under the protection of the god and his son. The gens *Caecilia* claimed to be descended from Caeculus.

Caeira (Κάειρα) The daughter of a potter of Miletus: she played a part in the legend of NELEUS, the son of Codrus. Before leaving his native land, Neleus asked the oracle where he should settle; the oracle replied that he would find a new home at the place where a girl gave him some earth mixed with water. In the course of his wanderings Neleus arrived one day at Miletus and asked Caeira to give him some soft clay on which to make the imprint of a seal. Caeira complied with his request, and the oracle was fulfilled: Neleus then assumed power in Miletus and founded three towns in the vicinity.

Caelus The Sky (this personification is indicated by the use of the masculine form rather than the neuter, *caelum*); this was not a Roman deity but merely a Latin translation of the name of the Greek god Uranus who played a very important part in Hellenic theogony and mythology.

Caeneus (Καινεύς) He was originally a girl named Caenis, daughter of the Lapith Elatus (Table 9), who was loved by Poseidon. She asked the god to change her into a man who was invulnerable; Poseidon granted this request. In his new embodiment Caeneus took part in the struggle against the Centaurs, but when they could not kill him, they beat him with the trunks of fir trees and finally buried him alive. It is said that after his death Caeneus became a woman again, or, according to another version, a bird with shining wings, a flamingo.

A different tradition tells that after he had become a man Caeneus grew extremely proud: he set up his spear in the market place and ordered the populace to worship his weapon, as if it were a god. To punish him, Zeus roused the Centaurs against him and they finally killed him. His name appears in some of the lists of the Argonauts. His son Coronus was king of the Lapiths at the time of Heracles (see AEGIMIUS).

Caieta The legend about this town (the modern Gaete, which is not far from Terracina, on the southern coast of Latium) tells how it had been founded in memory of Caieta, the nurse of Aeneas (or, according to other versions, of Ascanius, Aeneas's son, or even of Creusa, the wife of Aeneas). Some versions say that she had been buried there and others that she had quelled the fire which was threatening to burn Aeneas' ship. Yet another tradition gives the name of Gaete to Aeetes, the father of Medea, who had come to the district in pursuit of his daughter (see ARGONAUTS). According to this version, the town had originally been called Aeete, but the name was later changed to Gaete.

Calamus (Κάλαμος) The son of the river-god Meander of Phrygia, his name means 'reed'. He was deeply in love with a youth of great beauty named Carpus who was the son of the god Zephyrus and one of the Horae. One day they were both bathing in the Meander and Calamus wanted to show his friend that he was the better swimmer, but in the competition which ensued Carpus was drowned. In his grief Calamus withered to such an extent that he became a reed by the river bank. Carpus (whose name means 'fruit') became the 'fruit of the fields' which dies and is reborn every year.

Calchas (Κάλχας) A seer of Mycenae, or possibly Megara; he was the most gifted person of his time with the ability to read the meaning of the flight of birds and to know the past, present and future: Apollo had given him this gift of prophecy. Calchas was the son of Thestor and through him Apollo's grandson. He acted as soothsayer: at each crucial stage in the preparations for the war and during the war itself he issued a prophecy. When Achilles was nine years old it was Calchas who announced that Troy could not possibly be taken unless the child took part in the conflict and this led Thetis to disguise her son among the daughters of the king of Scyros. At Aulis he interpreted the omen which manifested itself in the shape of the snake which ate the birds on the sacrificial altar, prophesying that the city would be captured in the tenth year of the war (see AGAMEMNON). After the ill-starred landing in Mysia, when Telephus had agreed to lead the fleet to the Troad it was Calchas who confirmed by his predictions that the instructions issued by Telephus were correct. Just as the Greek fleet was ready to leave Aulis for the second time Calchas disclosed that the calm which prevented its departure was due to the wrath of Artemis, who would only be appeased by the sacrifice of Iphigenia. Later, after Achilles had died and Ajax, the son of Telamon, had killed himself, Calchas told the Greeks that Troy would not be taken unless someone could obtain the bow of Heracles: he was thus the instigator of the mission of Odysseus to Philoctetes. When Helenus withdrew into the forests of Mount Ida after the death of Paris, Calchas advised the Greeks to capture him, for only Helenus could tell them the conditions on which they could take the city. Finally, seeing that brute force would not succeed, Calchas suggested that the Greeks should construct a wooden horse, to enable the fighting men to enter the city by stealth; he himself was one of the warriors inside the horse. As they set out he foretold that their return home would not be easy because of the wrath of Athena, who was displeased by the injustice suffered by her protégé Ajax, the son of Telamon, and he did not want to sail with them, since he knew that their convoy would not arrive safely in port. He accordingly embarked with another soothsayer, Amphilochus, the son of Amphiaraus and they took with them the heroes

Leonteus, Podalirius and Polypoetes; their vessel was cast up on the coast of Asia Minor, at Colophon (in other versions they are said to have gone there on foot). Now an oracle, probably spoken of by Helenus, had told Calchas that he would die on the day when he met a diviner better than himself; at Colophon, he came across the seer Mopsus. Near his house there was a fig tree. Calchas asked, 'How many figs does it bear?' and Mopsus replied, 'Ten thousand and one bushels and one fig more'; when it was checked Mopsus was found to be correct. There was also a pregnant sow, and Mopsus asked Calchas, 'How many piglets will there be in her litter and how soon will they be born?' Calchas replied that there would be eight piglets. Mopsus declared that he was wrong, and that she would have not eight but nine piglets, all males, and that they would be born on the next day and at the sixth hour. This is what actually happened, and Calchas was so vexed that he died, or according to some accounts, he killed himself; he was buried at Notion, near Colophon. Conon tells a different story about the contest of skill between the two diviners: the king of Lycia was preparing a military expedition and Mopsus advised him not to undertake it as he would be defeated. Calchas, on the other hand, told the king that he would certainly be victorious. The king set out and was defeated, and this enhanced the reputation of Mopsus but caused Calchas to commit suicide in despair.

There is also a story which tells how Calchas had planted a vine in a grove sacred to Apollo in the wood of Grynium, in Mysia. A seer who lived nearby forecast that he would never drink wine from it, but Calchas ridiculed this idea. The vine grew, bore grapes out of which wine was made, and on the day when the new wine was to be tasted Calchas invited the people who lived nearby as well as the seer who had made the prophecy. At the very moment when his cup was full and Calchas was about to drink, his rival repeated that he would never taste the wine. Calchas began to laugh so heartily that he choked to death and died before the cup had reached his lips (see ANTINOUS). South Italian legends speak of another diviner, also called Calchas, whose tomb could be seen at Siris on the gulf of Tarentum. There was yet another Calchas who had a shrine where people used to sleep in order to learn of the future through their dreams; this shrine was in the neighbourhood of Mount Garganon, on the Adriatic coast. The Calchas of Siris was reported

to have been killed by a blow of Heracles' fist. These various legends are incongruent.

Calchus (Κάλχος) King of the Daunii, an ancient race of the south of Italy; he loved the magician Circe at the time when Odysseus was staying on her island, but she did not want to be loved by Calchus and was in love with Odysseus. When Calchus pressed his suit with her she held a banquet for him and there turned him into a pig; she then shut him up in her pigsty. When their king did not return the Daunians came in force to look for him. Circe agreed to give him back to them, in human form, but on the condition that he would not set foot on her island again.

Callidice (Καλλιδίκη) A queen of the Thesproti who married Odysseus at the time when he was forced to leave Ithaca again to comply with the prophecy of Tiresias. Odysseus fathered a son by her named Polypoetes; he reigned over the country upon his mother's death, and Odysseus returned to Ithaca (Table 39).

Calliope (Καλλιόπη) One of the Muses; she was not originally associated with any one particular art form as were her sisters, but from the start of the Alexandrian period she was regarded as Muse of lyric poetry. Calliope is sometimes said to have been the mother of the Sirens and of Linus and Rhesus. She also appears in some legends as the arbitress in the quarrel over Adonis between Persephone and Aphrodite.

Callipolis (Καλλίπολις) The son of Alcathus; he was killed by his father for interrupting the enactment of a sacrifice. His tomb could be seen at Megara.

Callirhoe (Καλλιρρόη) Several heroines were called by this name, which means 'the lovely stream'.
1. The daughter of Ocean and Tethys who by her marriage to Chrysaor, the son of the Gorgon and Poseidon, gave birth to the monsters Geryon and Echidna (Table 32). She had other children: Minyas, fathered by Poseidon, Chione by Nilus and Cotys by Manes, the first king of Lydia.
2. The daughter of the river god Achelous. She married Alcmaeon, who fathered her two sons, Amphoterus and Acarnan (Table 1). After the death of her husband at the hands of the sons of Phegeus, she was loved by Zeus; she asked him to

make her two sons grow up immediately and to give them the strength to avenge their father. Zeus did as she asked and in this way Alcmaeon was avenged. These misfortunes were due to Callirhoe's desire to own the necklace and gown of Harmonia, the divine gifts which were under a curse.

3.   A Callirhoe, possibly the same as that in 2 above, was associated with the Troad: she was a nymph loved by Paris at the time when he looked after the flocks on Mount Ida, before his intrigue with Helen. Paris left Callirhoe for Helen and Callirhoe is said to have wept bitterly for her lost love.

4.   The river god Scamander also had a daughter called Callirhoe. She married Tros and by him had four children: Cleopatra, Ilus, Assaracus and Ganymede (Table 7).

5.   A daughter of Lycus, king of Libya. After the Trojan War, Diomedes was cast up by a storm on the shores of Libya. Lycus captured him and was on the point of sacrificing him to Ares when Callirhoe, who had fallen in love with the hero, freed him. Diomedes left her, however, and in her despair she hanged herself.

6.   Yet another Callirhoe gave her name to a spring near Calydon. She is said to have been a girl who had rejected the advances of a priest of Dionysus, called Coresus; he complained of his rebuff to Dionysus, who spread an outbreak of madness throughout the land. The inhabitants consulted the oracle of Dodona, which disclosed that, to appease the god, the girl, or someone in her stead, would have to be sacrificed at the altar attended by Coresus. Just as he was about to sacrifice her, Coresus, overcome by his love, lost his resolve and killed himself. Callirhoe, in her shame, committed suicide beside the spring which thereafter bore her name.

Callisto (Καλλιστώ)

1.   The legend of the best-known Callisto is an Arcadian one. According to some writers she was a wood-nymph; to others she was the daughter of King Lycaon, and in some versions the daughter of Nycteus. She had vowed to remain a virgin and spent her life hunting in the mountains with the band of companions of Artemis. Zeus saw her and fell in love with her. He married her in the guise of Artemis, for Callisto shunned the company of all men. According to other writers, he assumed the likeness of Apollo, the god of Arcadia and the brother of Artemis. By Callisto Zeus begot Arcas. She was pregnant with him when one day Artemis and her companions decided to bathe in a spring. Callisto had to undress and her offence was disclosed. Artemis in her anger hunted her and changed her into a she-bear. One variant of this story was that her change was due to the jealousy of Hera, or else to the foresight of Zeus, who wanted to conceal his love and to rescue her, in this shape, from the wrath of his wife. Nevertheless, Hera knew how to find her out, and persuaded Artemis to kill her with an arrow, or it may have been Artemis herself who killed her, in order to punish her for having lost her virginity. Zeus changed her into the constellation of the Great Bear (for other variants of her story, involving Arcas, see Table 9). She was also sometimes said to have had a second son, a twin brother of Arcas, namely the god Pan.

2.   A second Callisto was the sister of Odysseus (Table 39).

Calydnus (Κάλυδνος)

The son of Uranus who according to certain traditions was the first king of Thebes, and predecessor of Ogygus. He is sometimes credited with building the wall surrounding the city and its towers, but the most widely known story is that these works were built by Amphion and Zethus.

Calydon (Καλυδών)

1.   The hero who gave his name to the country of Calydon in Aetolia, north of the Gulf of Corinth; he was the son of Aetolus and Pronoe (Table 24). He married Aeolia, a daughter of Amythaon and fathered two daughters, Epicaste and Protogenia.

2.   Other traditions make Calydon a son of Thestius. The latter returned from a long stay at Sicyon to find Calydon lying near his mother, and believing, wrongly, that they were having an incestuous relationship he killed them. When he later realized his mistake he threw himself into a stream called the Axenus, and it was thereafter called the Thestius, until it was finally renamed the Achelous. Another story claims that Calydon was the son of Ares and Astynome who saw Artemis bathing and was changed into a rock on the mountain of Calydon near the Achelous.

Calypso (Καλυψώ)

1.   A Nymph, who in some versions was a daughter of Atlas and Pleione (see PLEIADES) and in others a daughter of Helios (the Sun) and Perseis and, accordingly, the sister of Aeetes and Circe. She lived on the island of Ogygia, which writers place in the western Mediterranean and which is

securely identified with the modern peninsula of Ceuta, opposite Gibraltar. Calypso (or 'she who conceals') welcomed the shipwrecked Odysseus. The *Odyssey* tells how she loved him and kept him with her for ten years (other versions say either one year or seven) offering him immortality, though vainly. Odysseus in his heart always yearned to return to Ithaca and resisted all attempts to entice him to change his mind. Calypso lived in a deep cave with several rooms, which opened on wild gardens, a sacred wood with great trees and streams which flowed over the turf. She spent her time spinning and weaving with her serving girls who were also Nymphs, and they sang as they worked. In response to Athena's request, Zeus sent Hermes to find Calypso and to ask her to release Odysseus. Calypso sadly let the man she loved depart, giving him wood to make a raft with and food for his journey and showing him the stars by which he could navigate.

According to some legends which follow the *Odyssey*, Calypso and Odysseus had a son called Latinus (though he is usually thought to be the son of Circe), but some writers say that Odysseus had two sons by Circe, Nausinous and Nausithous, whose names are derived from the word meaning 'ship' (Ναῦς). Calypso and Odysseus were also said to have had a son, called Auson, who gave his name to Ausonia (Table 39).

2. Calypso was also the name of one of the daughters of Tethys and Oceanus.

Cambles (Κάμβλης) A king of Lydia, who was so greedy that he ate his own wife. In his remorse, he immediately committed suicide. This king was sometimes called Camblites (see IARDANUS).

Camenae The Camenae were the Nymphs of springs in Rome. Their shrine was in a wood not far from the Camenean Gate, a little south of the Caelian Gate, a site where there was also a temple of Egeria. These Nymphs were identified with the Muses from an early period.

Camers The legendary king of a mythical town Amyclae, which lay between Tercina and Gaete. He was the son of Vulcens. His town had vanished by the classical period after it was visited by a plague of snakes.

Camesus The name of a very early king who according to an obscure tradition was said to have ruled over Latium at the time when the god Janus landed there after he had been exiled from his native country of Thessaly. Camesus welcomed the exile warmly and shared his kingdom with him; they ruled together for some time and when Camesus died, Janus ruled by himself.

Camilla The legend of Camilla is found in Virgil's *Aeneid,* and was undoubtedly based on Italian folk-tales and also derived from the story of Harpalyce. Camilla was the daughter of Metabus of Privernum, the king of the Volsci. After the death of his wife he was driven out of the town by his enemies and fled with his daughter, who was still only a little girl, pursued by armed soldiers. Just as he was about to escape from them he encountered the waters of the Amisenus, a small river in Latium. He had the idea of saving his daughter by tying her to a heavy pike which he was carrying and hurling it onto the far bank. He vowed that he would dedicate Camilla to Diana if she reached safety: Diana granted his prayer and the child reached the far bank. Metabus himself swam across the river, and they both lived for a long time in solitude in the woods. The girl became so accustomed to living like this that she became unable to endure staying in a town. She used to hunt and she engaged in warfare, taking part in the struggle against Aeneas during which she performed several notable deeds just like the Amazons in Greek legend. She was killed by the hero Arruns.

Campe (Κάμπη) A female monster appointed by Cronus in Hades to guard the Cyclopes and the Hecatoncheires whom he had imprisoned in Hades. When an oracle promised Zeus that he would defeat Cronus and the Titans if he had the assistance of the Cyclopes, he killed Campe and freed them.

Canace (Κανάκη) One of the daughters of Aeolus and Aenarete (Table 8). Ovid, undoubtedly following Euripides, tells that she gave birth to a son fathered by her brother Macareus. Her nurse was preparing to remove the child from the palace pretending that she was going out merely to offer a sacrifice, but the child cried out and disclosed its presence to Aeolus. He threw the child to the dogs and sent a sword to his daughter, ordering her to kill herself. Canace also had several children by Poseidon (Table 10).

Canens A Nymph of Latium, the personification of song. She was married to King Picus, who ruled over Laurentum, south of Ostia, and they loved each other deeply. One day during a hunt the sorceress Circe saw Picus and fell in love with him; to separate him from his attendants she changed him into a wild boar, not doubting that she would later be able to change him back to his normal form. Picus, separated from his wife, grieved deeply; when Circe declared her love for him he repulsed her and in her anger she changed him into a green woodpecker. In the meantime Canens despaired; she wandered for six days and nights in search of Picus and finally collapsed, her strength finished, on the banks of the Tiber where she sang for the last time and then vanished into thin air.

Canopus (Κάνωπος) Canopus or Canobus was the hero who gave his name to a town in Egypt and to one of the rivers of the Nile delta (Canope) near Alexandria. He was a native of Amyclae who acted as pilot for Menelaus when the latter came with Helen to Egypt after the capture of Troy. Canopus was young and extremely handsome. Theonoe, the daughter of Proteus the king of Egypt, loved him, but he did not return her love. One day, when Canopus was ashore, he was bitten by a snake and died. Menelaus and Helen buried him building him a tomb on the island of Canope. The plant named helenion sprang from the tears shed by Helen at this event. Another tradition claims that Canopus was the pilot of Osiris, the Egyptian god. He is also said to have steered the *Argo*, and both pilot and ship were placed among the constellations.

Capaneus (Καπανεύς) One of the Argive princes who marched against Thebes in the expedition of the Seven Chiefs; he himself was one of the Seven (see AMPHIARAUS and ADRASTUS). Capaneus was the son of Hipponous, a man of violence and a giant in size. He had no fear of the gods and, at the time of the first attack on Thebes, he rushed forward impelled by his resolve to burn it, but the thunderbolt sent by Zeus killed him just as he was about to scale the Theban walls. His wife Evadne threw herself on the funeral-pyre which consumed his body. Sthenelus, who took part in the Trojan war was his son.

Caphaurus (Κάφαυρος) A Libyan who was the son of Amphithemis (also known as Garamas) and one of the Nymphs of Lake Triton, and so the grandson of Acacallis and Apollo. One day he was looking after his flocks of sheep in Libya not far from Lake Triton when one of the Argonauts,

whose name was Canthus, tried to steal some of them to feed to his hungry companions. Caphaurus killed him but was himself overpowered by the Argonauts and then killed (see CEPHALION).

Caphene (Καφένη) A girl from the town of Cryassus in Caria. A colony of Greeks from Melos, led by Nymphaeus, founded a settlement in their territory and grew in numbers so quickly that they became powerful. The people of Cryassus became disturbed and resolved to suppress their unwanted neighbours. They devised a scheme to invite all the Greeks to a feast and kill them while they were all together, but Caphene was in love with Nymphaeus and told him of the plan. When the Carians invited the Greeks they accepted, but said that their country's custom required that their wives should also be invited. They were, and the men came to the feast unarmed, but each woman hid a sword beneath her clothes. At a signal given during the feast, the Carians fell on the Greeks, but their guests outstripped them and killed all the Carians. They demolished Cryassus and from the ruins built a new one which they called New Cryassus. Caphene married Nymphaeus and great honours were decreed for her.

Caphira (Καφείρα) A daughter of Oceanus. Together with the Telchines, on the island of Rhodes, she brought up Poseidon who had been entrusted to her by Rhea.

Capys (Κάπυς)
1.   The *Iliad* mentions a Capys who was one of the ancestors of Aeneas. He was the son of Assaracus and fathered two sons named Ilus and Anchises by Themiste (Table 7). Later legends give Aeneas a companion of the same name who was supposed to have founded the town of Capua in Campania, but there is also a story that Capua had been founded by one of Aeneas' sons, Rhomus, and that it was called this in memory of his great-grandfather (see AEGESTES). Capys, the companion of Aeneas, was sometimes also regarded as the founder of the town of Caphyes in Arcadia.
  Some writers also say that the founder of Capua was not a Trojan but a Samnite of the same name. It is very probable that the name of Capua may actually have been derived from an Etruscan word meaning 'falcon' and, generally, 'those who have turned-in toes'.

Carcabus (Καρκάβος) The son of Triopas, king of the Perrhaebae who reigned over the area in the north of Greece between Macedonia and Thrace. Triopas was a cruel tyrant and his son killed him to free his country, and after doing this he abdicated voluntarily and was purified by Tros, the king of the Troad, with whom he had sought asylum. Tros also gave him a gift of some land on which Carcabus founded the town of Zeleia. His descendant Pandareus fought on the side of the Trojans.

Carcinus (Καρκίνος) Carcinus, whose name in Greek means 'crayfish' was a crayfish which lived in the Lernean marsh. During the struggle between Heracles and the Hydra, Carcinus bit the hero in the heel. Heracles in his anger crushed her, but Hera, to reward her for helping to harass Heracles, took her up into the sky and in the constellations she is the sign of Cancer.

According to the euhemerist explanation of the myth of Lerna it was believed that Carcinus was a military leader who came to the help of King Lernus when he was attacked by Heracles, and was killed by him.

Carmanor (Καρμάνωρ) A Cretan priest, the father of Euboulus and Chrysothemis. According to the Cretans, Carmanor welcomed Apollo and Artemis after the murder of Python and purified them, and he also allowed the intrigue between Apollo and Acacallis to take place in his house.

Carme (Κάρμη) The mother of Britomartis who was born in Crete and fathered by Zeus. She is said to have been the daughter of Euboulcus, the son of Caramanor. Other writers make her the daughter of Phoenix, one of the sons of Agenor and of Cassiopea (Table 3). She is said to have been taken to Megara as a prisoner in her old age and to have been made nurse to Scylla, the daughter of King Nisus.

Carmenta In Roman legend she was the mother of Evander, she accompanied him from Arcadia when he was exiled and was forced to seek refuge in the west (see EVANDER). It is said that she was not called Carmenta in Arcadia. Writers give her original name variously as Nicostrate, Themis, Timandra or Telpousa. She is said to have been a Nymph, a daughter of the river Ladon. She was given the name of Carmenta at Rome because she possessed the gift of prophecy (derived from the word *carmen*, or 'the magic song'). From her knowlege of oracles and destinies she was able to select the most favourable site from the whole of Rome, on which to establish her son. When Heracles came to Pallanteus on his return from the expedition against Geryon, she told the hero of the fate which lay ahead for him (see CACUS). She lived to be exceptionally old, dying at the age of one hundred and ten. Her son buried her at the foot of the Capitol, close to the Porta Carmentalis, so called in her memory.

According to other traditions Carmenta is said to have been Evander's wife and not his mother, and to explain why women were not allowed to attend the ceremonies of the cult of Hercules at the *Ara Maxima* it was said that Carmenta had refused an invitation from the hero to take part in the sacrifice which he was offering at the foundation of the altar, and that in his annoyance, the hero forbade women to be present at the ceremony thereafter. Some writers on ancient Rome regard Carmenta as a divinity of procreation. She was invoked using the two names Prorsa (head first) and Postversa (feet first) – the two possible positions in which a child can be born.

Carna A Nymph who lived in the country at the place where Rome was built. She dwelt in a sacred wood on the banks of the Tiber, called the *Luccus Helerni*, where the pontiffs still offered sacrifices in the time of Augustus. Ovid says that Carna was originally called Crane and had dedicated herself to virginity. She used to hunt over the hills and in the woods and when a suitor approached her she would make him promise to follow her into the woods. Once there, she would immediately disappear and it would be impossible to find her again. One day, however, Janus the two-faced god saw and fell in love with her; he addressed her and she wanted to baffle him as she had the others, but Janus saw her just as she was trying to conceal herself behind a rock. He caught and ravished her but to make amends for what he had done, he gave her complete power over the hinges of doors and entrusted her with an emblem of his attributes, a branch of flowering hawthorn, a magical spray with the power of excluding all evil spells from the openings of the house. Carna had a special responsibility for keeping away vampires, the semi-human birds which come and suck the blood of new-born babies who are left alone in their cradles by their nurses. According to Ovid, she saved a son of King Procas from death by uttering incantations and performing sacred rites after the vampires had already left their mark on the baby's body.

Carnabon (Καρναβῶν) The king of the Getae, who initially welcomed Triptolemus when he was travelling throughout the world in a chariot drawn by dragons, to teach mankind on behalf of Demeter how to grow corn. Subsequently however, Carnabon attacked Triptolemus and killed one of his dragons but Demeter came to the rescue just as Carnabon was about to kill Triptolemus and carried him off to the stars. She set him among them showing him in the act of killing the dragon, which he holds in his hand.

Carnus (Κάρνος) A seer, born in Acarnania who joined the army of the Heraclids when they had assembled at Naupactus and were preparing to invade the Peloponnese. One of the Heraclids named Hippotes took him for a spy and killed him. A plague then struck the army and the oracle declared that it was a result of the anger of Apollo over the death of his priest. In expiation Hippotes was banished and the Heraclids established a cult of Apollo Carneus. Traditionally there was also a hero called Carnus or Carneus, a son of Zeus and Europa who was loved by Apollo.

Cassandra (Κασσάνδρα) The daughter of Priam and Hecuba and twin sister of Helenus (Table 34). To celebrate the birth of Cassandra and Helenus, Priam and Hecuba gave a feast in the temple of Apollo Thymbrius, which lay some distance outside the gates of Troy. In the evening they left the shrine, but forgot the children, who spent the night there. On the following morning when the parents came to find them they were found asleep and two serpents were licking their sensory organs in order to 'purify' them. On hearing the cries of the terrified parents, the serpents withdrew among the sacred laurels which were growing nearby. The children thereafter displayed the gift of prophecy; this had been given to them by the 'purification' of the serpents. There is a different legend which tells how Cassandra had been given this gift by Apollo himself. The god, who was in love with her, had promised to give her the power to foretell the future if she would yield to his advances. Cassandra accepted the bargain, but once she had received the gift of prophecy she slipped away. Apollo then spat in her mouth, withdrawing from her the ability to persuade people to believe her, but not the gift of prophecy.

Cassandra was generally regarded as an

The Greeks gave the name caryatids to columns or pilasters with shafts carved in the form of draped female forms. Caryatid from the Erechtheum, Athens, c. 420–413 BC. London, British Museum.

'inspired' prophetess as were the Pythian oracle or the Sibyl: the god would take possession of her and she uttered her oracles in a trance. Helenus, on the other hand, foretold the future by interpreting the flight of birds and other external signs. Cassandra's prophecies played a part at every important moment during the history of Troy. At the time of the arrival of Paris, she foretold that the young man (whose real identity was at the time unknown) was fated to cause the downfall of Troy. She was on the point of serving his execution when she realised that he was one of Priam's sons, and this recognition saved his life. Later, when Paris returned to Troy with Helen, she predicted that his abduction of her would lead to the loss of the city but, as usual, no one believed her. She was the first person to know, after Hector had been killed and Priam had gone on his mission to Achilles, that Priam would return with his son's body. She fought as hard as she could with the support of the seer Laocoon against the idea of bringing into the city the wooden horse which the Greeks left on the beach when they pretended to withdraw, and she declared that it was full of armed warriors but Apollo sent snakes which ate up Laocoon and his sons and the Trojans paid no heed to her. Cassandra was also said to have made a number of prophecies about the fate of the Trojan women who had been taken prisoner after the city had been captured and about the future fate of the line of Aeneas. During the sack of Troy, she herself took shelter in the temple of Athena. She was pursued there by Ajax of Locri but though she clung to the statue of the goddess, Ajax tore her from it, and in doing so he loosened the statue from its plinth. Confronted by this act of sacrilege the Greeks were ready to stone Ajax, but he saved himself by sheltering at the altar of the goddess he had just insulted.

When the booty was shared out Cassandra was given to Agamemnon who fell head over heels in love with her. Up to that point Cassandra had remained a virgin, although there had been no lack of suitors for her hand, notably Othryoneus, who had promised Priam to rid Troy of the Greeks if, after his victory, he could be rewarded with her hand; he, however, was killed by Idomeneus.

Cassandra was supposed to have had twin sons, Teledamus and Pelops, by Agamemnon. When Agamemnon returned to Mycenae he was murdered by his wife who, at the same time, killed Cassandra out of jealousy. Indeed, in some versions of the story Agamemnon was killed simply because of the love he had for Cassandra.

Cassandra was sometimes called Alexandra, and it was under this name that Lycophron made her the leading character in a prophetic poem written just as the Romans were about to play an active part in Greek affairs. In Lycophron's poem, Priam, who was unhappy about the prophetic gifts of his daughter and feared the ridicule of the Trojans, shut her up and placed over her a keeper with orders to report to him what she said. The poem was supposed to reproduce the girl's prophecies.

Cassiopia (Κασσιέπεια) The mother of ANDRO-MEDA and so proud of her beauty that she dared to compete with the Nereids or even, according to some writers, with Hera. The goddesses demanded of Poseidon that he should avenge this blow to their self-esteem and he sent a sea-monster which laid waste Cassiopia's land. In order to appease the god's wrath, Andromeda had to be exposed in expiation for the monster to do its worst, but PERSEUS appeared, freed her and bore her off with him. Cassiopia was turned into a constellation.

The traditions about the origin of Cassiopia vary. She is frequently said to have belonged to the family of the Syrian Agenor. She is also said to have been the wife of Phoenix and the mother of Phineus (Table 3). She was the daughter of Arabus, a son of Hermes, who gave his name to the country called Arabia. Her husband is sometimes said not to have been Phoenix, but Epaphus, who is said to have fathered Libya, the mother of Agenor. Finally, she is often said to have been the wife of Cepheus, king of Ethiopia. In every case these genealogies associate the legend of Cassiopia with the countries in the extreme south – Arabia, Ethiopia or southern Egypt.

Cassiphone (Κασσιφόνη) A sister of Telegonus and daughter of Odysseus and the witch Circe (Tables 14 and 39). When Telegonus accidentally killed Odysseus, Circe brought him back to life and Cassiphone married Telemachus, his half-brother, but Cassiphone killed Telemachus to avenge her mother Circe, whom Telemachus had killed.

This legend belongs to the latest layers of the Odysseus legend and its sole evidence is to be found in the commentary by Tzetzes on Lycophron. Generally, Circe herself is said to have been the wife of Telemachus.

Castalia (Κασταλία) A girl from Delphi. When she was being pursued by Apollo, near the god's shrine, she threw herself into the spring which was sacred to Apollo and thereafter bore her name. In another version of the legend, Castalia was the daughter of Achelous and wife of King Delphus. By him she had a son, Castalius, who ruled over the country of Delphi after the death of his father.

Castor (Κάστωρ) One of the DIOSCURI.

Cathetus (Κάθητος) A legendary figure who found a place in Latin mythology in order to explain various names. He was in fact in love with the daughter of the Etruscan king Annius, who was called Salia. When Cathetus abducted her and brought her to Rome Annius tried, without success, to catch the fugitives. In his despair, he cast himself into the nearest river which was thereafter called the Anio (known today as the Aniene, which runs into the Tiber north of Rome). Cathetus married Salia, however, and by his marriage had children, called Latinus and Salius who gave their names respectively to the Latin peoples, and the *Collegium* of the Saliens which annually in Rome performed a sacred dance during a ritual procession.

Catillus A hero associated with the legend of the foundation of the town of Tibur (the modern Tivoli). Roman historians regarded him as a Greek; alternatively Catillus might have come with Evander, whose fleet he commanded, or he might have been the son of the Argive hero Amphiaraus, who after his father's death went at the head of a band of young men to seek his fortune in Italy on the orders of Oecles. There Catillus is said to have had three sons, Tiburtus, Coras and Catinus the younger: and these were the sons who were supposed to have founded the town of Tibur. According to Virgil Catillus the younger was present during the fight of the Rutili against Aeneas.

Catreus (Κατρεύς) One of the four children, born of Pasiphae, whom Minos had fathered and his successor on the throne of Crete (Table 28). An oracle had warned that Catreus would die at the hand of one of his children; he had four, three daughters Aerope, Clymene and Apemosyne, and one son, Althaemenes. Catreus had kept this oracle a secret from his children, but his son and Apemosyne were aware of it. They both fled from Crete to avoid fulfilling what fate had decreed; they went

to Rhodes and founded a town called Cretania, after the island where they were born. Nonetheless, Catreus, from fear of the oracle, gave his two other children, Aerope and her sister, to Nauplius the traveller to be sold as slaves abroad; but in his old age, Catreus wanted to leave his kingdom to his son and he went to Rhodes to find him again. After landing with his followers in a deserted spot, he was attacked by drovers, who thought that they were dealing with pirates. He vainly protested and told them who he was, but the barking of the dogs prevented him from being heard and the drovers stoned him until Althaemenes appeared and killed him with his javelin. When he realized what he had done, Althaemenes was, by his own prayer, swallowed up by the earth.

It was at the time that Menelaus had gone to the funeral of Catreus – his grandfather through his mother Aerope (Table 2) – that Paris abducted Helen. The Arcadians claimed that Catreus was the son not of Minos but of Tegeates, and the grandson of their king, Lycaon.

Caucasus (Καύκασος) A shepherd, who was killed by Cronus. Zeus called the Caucasus after him; this had previously been called 'the Mountain of the North Wind'.

Caucon (Καύκων)
1. One of the sons of LYCAON, king of Arcadia, and thus of the family of Pelasgus. He gave his name to a people, the Caucones, who lived in the west of the Peloponnese. Together with all his brothers and his father, he was struck by lightning by Zeus in retribution for the impiety of Lycaon.
2. A second Caucon, the son of Celaenus and grandson of the Athenian Phylus, was the first to introduce the mysteries of Demeter into Messenia.

Caulon (Καυλών) The son of the Amazon Clete, the nurse of Penthesilea. He came to southern Italy with his mother and founded the town of Cautonia in the vicinity of Locri.

Caunus (Καῦνος) The twin of BYBLIS and the son of Miletus, the founder of the town of that name, and of Idothea. He was the object of his sister's incestuous love and he fled and went to found the town of Caunus in Caria. In another account he loved Byblis who for this reason exiled him. There is also a story that in Lycia he married the Nymph Pronoe and fathered a son called Aegialus.

Aegialus is said to have founded the town of Caucus.

Cecrops (Κέκροψ)

1. One of the mythical kings of Attica, and, according to the commonest tradition, the first. He was born of the very earth of Attica, which thereafter was known as Cecropia, after his name, whereas previously the country had been called Acte. He married Aglaurus, the daughter of Actaeus who was sometimes described as the first king of Attica. Cecrops fathered four children: a son Erysichthon (see second entry under ERYSICHTHON), and three daughters, who played a part in the myth of Erichthonia (see AGLAURUS). Cecrops was a dual character: the upper part of his body was human and the lower took the form of a serpent, which indicated that he was a son of the Earth. During his reign the gods quarrelled about the cities over which they wanted to extend their rule. Athens was coveted by the goddess Athena and Poseidon at the same time. The latter came to Attica and with a single blow of his trident caused a 'sea' of salt water to burst forth from the centre of the Acropolis. Then the goddess appeared and taking Cecrops as a witness she planted an olive tree on the hill. At this point, in order to choose between them, Zeus named the judges, who in some versions of the story are said to be Cecrops and Cranaus, and in others the twelve gods. They gave their verdict in favour of Athena, since Cecrops testified that she had been the first to plant the olive tree in Athens. In a fit of anger Poseidon sent a flood which covered Attica.

Under the reign of Cecrops, who was a peaceful ruler, civilisation made its first positive advances in Attica. Cecrops taught mankind how to build cities and how to bury the dead. He is also sometimes said to have invented writing and the census.

2. The roll of the kings of Attica includes another Cecrops, the son of ERECTHEUS.

Cedalion (Κηδαλίων)

The instructor who taught the god Hephaestus to forge and work metals. After Hephaestus was born at Lemnos his mother Hera placed him in the care of Cedalion who lived at Naxos, and Cedalion taught him his skill. The same Cedalion helped ORION to regain his sight when he became blind. Orion placed him on his shoulders and bade him turn towards the rising sun, which cured him.

Celaeno (Κελαινώ)

The name of three heroines:

1. A daughter of Danaus who by Poseidon gave birth to the hero Celaenus.

2. A daughter of Atlas and Pleione, one of the seven Pleiades. Poseidon fathered her children Lycus, Eurypylus and Triton (Table 25).

3. Celaeno was also the name of one of the Harpies.

Celbidas (Κελβίδας)

A native of Cumae who is said to have left Italy in order to go and found the town of Triteia in Achaea. According to other authors, Triteia was said to have been founded by Melanippus, the son of Ares and Triteia, priestess of Athena and daughter of Triton.

Celeus (Κελεός)

1. The son of Eleusis who was born of the earth and the first ruler of the district of that name (see RARUS). He was ruling over Eleusis at the time when Demeter's daughter was abducted by Hades. The goddess searched far and wide for her daughter and one evening arrived at Eleusis in the guise of an old woman at the time of day when the women used to go to draw water. The daughters of Celeus were there and they led the stranger to their father's house where she was offered the position of a serving-woman. Demeter accepted and she was put in charge of Demophon, the king's youngest son. The goddess discharged her debt in a strange way (see DEMOPHON 1) and finally disclosed her divine nature, but before returning to Olympus she told Celeus the rules of her cult and helped him to build a temple (see also TRIPTOLEMUS and DEMETER). Some versions of the story claim that Celeus was not a king, but a peasant of Eleusis.

2. Celeus was also the name of a Cretan who with his companions Laius, Cerberus and Aegolius tried to steal honey from the sacred cave on Mount Ida in Crete where Rhea had given birth to Zeus. Neither gods or mortals were allowed to enter this cave and each year, on the god's birthday, a mysterious fire was seen to shine from it. The thieves clad themselves in sheets of bronze to protect themselves from the bees whose honey had in days of old been given as food to the god when he was an infant, but when they arrived at the actual site of the god's birth, the sheets of bronze fell off of their own accord and Zeus produced a clap of thunder. He would have struck them with lightning on the spot if the Fates and Themis had not stopped him, saying that there was an absolute ban on killing anything in a sacred

place, which ought to stay completely undefiled. So Zeus changed them into birds: Laius into a thrush, Celeus into a crow and Cerberus into an unidentified bird, which in Greek was called by the same name. Since they came from the sacred cave, these birds were regarded as good omens.

Celeutor (Κελεύτωρ) One of the sons of Agrius of Calydon. Together with his brothers he took part in the campaign against his uncle Oeneus, during which they seized his country and gave it to their father. This is the reason why he was killed by DIOMEDES, the grandson of Agrius (Table 27).

Celmis (Κέλμις) A divinity who was one of the companions of Zeus when he was a child, according to the Cretan legend. At first he was loyal to the god but he offended Rhea and as a result was changed into a lump of diamond (or steel?) by Zeus.

Celtus (Κελτός) The hero from whom the Celts took their name. He was a son of Heracles who begot him by Celtine, the daughter of the king of Great Britain. Heracles was on his way back from his expedition against GERYON with the herds that he had won. He happened to be passing through Great Britain, and there the king's daughter concealed his herds and refused to give them back to him unless he married her. Since he wanted them back and, it was said, because the girl was very beautiful, Heracles willingly assented, and from this union Celtus was born (see also GALATEA). In another tradition, Celtus was the son of Heracles and Sterope, one of the Pleiades.

Centaurs (Κένταυροι) Monstrous beings, half man and half horse. The upper parts of their bodies were human, as were sometimes the front parts of their legs, but the rear part was that of a horse and, at least during the classical period, they each had four horse's hooves and two human arms. They lived in the mountains and forests, their food was raw flesh, and their behaviour was bestial. It was generally accepted that the Centaurs sprang from an intrigue between IXION and a storm cloud, which Zeus had made to resemble Hera and then had directed to Ixion to discover whether he dared to have a sacrilegious relationship with it (see Table 23). Two of the centaurs, Chiron and Pholus, were unlike the others in character and came of different descent. Chiron was the product of the love affair between Philyra and Cronus and Pholus was the son of Silenus and a Nymph of the ash-tree, one of the Meliads. Chiron and Pholus were not brutal like their fellow Centaurs; they were hospitable, charitable and loved their fellows, shunning violence.

Centaurs play a part in several myths. They frequently battled against HERACLES. When he went to hunt the Erymanthian boar he came to the home of Pholus who welcomed him warmly and gave him cooked meat, refraining himself from eating anything but raw meat, and when Heracles asked for wine Pholus replied that he had a large jar of it, but that he dared not open it as it was the common property of all the Centaurs. It had been a gift from Dionysus who had put it in their charge and advised them to open it only if Heracles should be their guest. Heracles told Pholus to open it and not to be afraid. Its smell soon brought the Centaurs from the mountains

Antique relief depicting the battle between the Centaurs and the Lapiths. Vatican Museum.

armed with rocks and fir trees to attack the cave. The two first Centaurs who dared to enter, Anchius and Agrius, were stunned by Heracles with torches, and he pursued the others with arrow shots as far as Cape Malea where they took shelter beside Chiron who had been driven out of Thessaly by the Lapiths and lived there. The Centaurs formed a ring round Chiron, and Heracles shot an arrow which first pierced the arm of one called Elatus and then wounded Chiron in the knee. Heracles tried to dress the wound which he had inadvertently inflicted on the good Chiron, but to no avail. Chiron remained in such pain that though he had been born immortal, he begged to be made mortal: Prometheus agreed to take on his burden of immortality, and Chiron died.

The Centaurs also fought against the Lapiths, a people of Thessaly led by PIRITHOUS and his friend Theseus. Pirithous invited the Centaurs, who regarded themselves as his parents, to his marriage feast, but they were unused to drinking wine and soon became intoxicated. One of them, Eurytus (or Eurytion) tried to violate Hippodamia, whom Pirithous had just married. A general brawl soon broke out, and many were killed on both sides. Ultimately the Lapiths were the victors and forced the Centaurs to leave Thessaly.

One or several Centaurs still feature in other legends concerning abductions. Eurytion tried to abduct Mnesimache from Heracles, who was betrothed to her (see DEXAMENUS); then NESSUS, while crossing a river tried to violate Deianeira; and the Centaurs Hylaeus and Rhoecus tried to violate the virgin ATALANTA. Legend knows of Centauresses, female Centaurs who lived with the Centaurs in the mountains; there also exist accounts or pictures of half-human beings such as the ICHTHYOCENTAURS, which were half-man and half-fish, based on the Centaurs.

Centimani Giants with a hundred hands (see HECATONCHEIRES).

Cephalion (Κεφαλίων) A shepherd in Libya, the son of Amphithemis and a Nymph from Lake Tritonis. He killed two Argonauts, Eribotes and Canthus, who tried to rob him of some of his flock (see CAPHAURUS).

Cephalus (Κέφαλος) The hero of several myths, only loosely connected with each other. Accounts of his origin vary. The commonest of them makes him the son of Deion, who was himself the son of Aeolus, of the line of Deucalion. His mother was Diomede, the daughter of Xuthus and Creusa (Tables 8 and 20). He was in this way a member of the stock of Deucalion on both sides of the family. Other writers claim that he was an Athenian, the son of Herse, one of the daughters of Cecrops, and Hermes (Table 4). Lastly, he was sometimes believed to be the son of Pandion. He was married to Procris, daughter of Erechtheus.

The first of the myths attached to Cephalus tells of his abduction by Aurora (see EOS) who loved him; he was supposed to have fathered her son Phaethon in Syria, but soon abandoned her and returned to Attica, where he married PROCRIS and received from her as a present a dog she had been given by Minos which had the gift, imparted by Zeus, of catching any animal which it chased while hunting. It was this dog that he lent to AMPHITRYON to help him catch the fox of Teumessa. Cephalus' love for Procris was the source of various stories. Procris loved him dearly and her love was reciprocated, but one day Cephalus began to doubt whether his wife was faithful to him. He disguised himself and decided to test his suspicions. Without disclosing who he was, he got himself into her presence when she thought he was away and offered her more and more valuable gifts if she would yield to his advances. The girl held out for a long time but finally temptation overcame her, and she gave way. At this point Cephalus revealed who he was. In her shame and anger Procris fled into the mountains. Cephalus was filled with remorse, went after her and they were eventually reconciled, each of them admitting that they had done wrong. For some time they lived together happily, but then Procris became jealous in her turn. She often saw her husband leave to go hunting, and she wondered whether the mountain Nymphs were attracting him. She asked a servant who used to go with him, who said that after the hunt Cephalus would stop and call for a mysterious 'Brise', asking her to come and renew his vitality. The jealous Procris decided to catch Cephalus' guilty intrigue by surprise: she followed him when he went hunting and Cephalus, hearing some movement in the thicket, launched a spear at it; this had the property of never failing to hit its target. Procris was mortally wounded, but on her deathbed she saw that she had been wrong. Cephalus had always been faithful to her and the 'Brise' for which he called was simply the wind.

Cephalus was tried for murder before the Areopagus and sentenced to exile and he left

Attica. He rejoined Amphitryon and went with him on his expedition against Taphos. After their victory the island of Cephalonia was known as Cephalus after his name. There he married Lysippe and fathered four children who gave their names to the four tribes on the island. The origin of the race of Laertes is also ascribed to him as Acrisius, the father of Laertes, is sometimes regarded as either Cephalus's son or his grandson. Cephalus is said to have consulted the Delphic oracle as to how he could have a son. The oracle told him to marry the first female he met. This happened to be a she-bear but in obedience to the oracle he married it and the bear immediately became a beautiful girl who gave birth to a son called Acrisius (Table 39).

Cepheus (Κηφεύς) Legend knows of two characters of this name:
1. The king of Tegea in Arcadia; he was the son of Aleus and took part in the expedition of the Argonauts, as well as playing a part in the legend of Heracles. When the latter decided to undertake an expedition against the son of Hippocoon in Lacedaemon, he called for an alliance with Cepheus, who had twenty sons but who feared that if he left his town the Argives might take the opportunity of invading his territory. As an inducement to him, Heracles entrusted him with a lock of the Gorgon's hair in a bronze vase. This had been given to him by Athena. Heracles told Cepheus that if his enemies attacked the town while he was away, Sterope his daughter had only to lift up the case and shake the lock of hair over the town walls three times. Provided that she took care not to look behind her, the enemy would be put to flight. Cepheus yielded to these arguments and went to war in Lacedaemon with Heracles and his brother Iphicles. During the fighting, however, Iphicles, Cepheus and his sons all lost their lives, but Heracles emerged the winner. In some versions, Cepheus of Arcadia is represented as the son not of Aleus, but of Lycurgus. In these versions Cepheus is said to have taken part in the hunt for the boar of Calydon.
2. The other Cepheus, the father of ANDROMEDA and husband of CASSIOPIA, was the son of Belus (Table 3). He ruled over the Cephenes, who were sometimes said to live on the banks of the Euphrates and sometimes in Ethiopia. Andromeda was Cepheus' daughter, and after Cepheus died it was his grandson Perses, the son of Perseus, who succeeded him.

Cerambus (Κέραμβος) A shepherd from Othrys, in Thessaly. At the time of the great flood in Deucalion's time he had taken shelter on the mountains to escape the waters, and the Nymphs gave him wings, transforming him into a beetle called Cerambus (see also TERAMBUS).

Ceramus (Κέραμος) An Attic hero who gave his name to a quarter of Athens called the Ceramicus. He was the son of Ariadne and Dionysus and was supposed to have invented the art of pottery, as his name suggests.

Cerberus (Κέρβερος) The dog of Hades, one of the monsters which watched over the realm of the dead and forbade living people to enter it, though his main duty was to prevent any occupant from leaving it. Cerberus is generally described as having three dogs' heads, a serpent for a tail, and on his back innumerable snakes' heads. He is also sometimes said to have had fifty, or even a hundred heads. He was chained up in front of the gate of the Underworld and filled souls with terror as they were entering. One of the labours imposed by Eurystheus on Heracles was to go to the Underworld to find Cerberus and bring him back to earth. Heracles set forth, but not before he had had himself initiated into the mysteries of Eleusis. Hades allowed Heracles to take Cerberus back to earth on condition that he could master him without resorting to his weapons. Heracles struggled with Cerberus using nothing but the strength of his arms, half throttled him and got the better of him. Heracles took him back to Eurystheus who was very frightened and gave orders that Cerberus be taken back to where he came from. Much later, Cerberus succumbed to the charms of Orpheus. Cerberus was believed to be the son of Echidna and Typhon, brother of Orthrus, the monstrous dog of Geryon, of the Hydra of Lerna, and of the Nemean lion.

Cercaphus (Κέρκαφος) One of the seven sons of Helios and Rhode who were known as the Heliads. He married Cydippe, one of the daughters of his brother OCHIMUS, whom he followed on the throne of the island of Rhodes. He had three sons, Ialysus, Lindos and Camirus who shared out the island and founded three towns which took their names (see OCHIMUS).

Cercopes (Κέρκωπες) Two brothers, named in some versions Eurybates and Phrynondas and in others Sillus and Triballus, but more usually known collectively as the Cercopes. Their mother was Theia, one of the daughters of Oceanus. They were a pair of ruffians, huge and exceptionally strong, who robbed passers-by and killed them. Their mother had warned them against a certain hero called Melampygus (the man with the black behind). One day they came on HERACLES, who had gone to sleep by the side of the road, and tried to rob him but the hero woke up, easily overcame them and hung each of them by the feet at the end of a long stick, loading them on his shoulders like kids being brought to market. While they were hanging in this position, they could see that Heracles had a black behind and they understood what their mother had prophesied, but Heracles was so amused by their jokes that he agreed to let them go. Despite this adventure, the Cercopes persisted with their life of plundering and armed robbery until Zeus, enraged by their behaviour, changed them into monkeys and removed them to the islands at the mouth of the bay of Naples, Proscida and Ischia. Their descendants lived there and this is said to have been the origin of the name of the archipelago in antiquity, Pithecoussa, that is Monkey Islands.

Cercyon (Κερκυών)

1. A hero of Eleusis, the son either of Poseidon or of Hephaestus and a daughter of Amphictyon, or of Branchus and the Nymph Argio (see RARUS). He had his lair on the road between Eleusis and Megara and he used to stop travellers and make them fight with him. Then when he had defeated them, he killed them. At last Theseus came past the spot; he was more expert at fighting than Cercyon, lifted his enemy in the air, hurled him to the ground and crushed him. On the road between Eleusis and Megara there was a spot known as 'the wrestling ground of Cercyon' and it was said to be there that the robber used to attack his victims (see ALOPE).

2. Legend also tells of another Cercyon, the son of AGAMEDES.

Cercyra (Κέρκυρα)

Cercyra or Corcyra was one of the daughters of the river Asopus, her mother being the Arcadian Netope. She was abducted by Poseidon who married her on the island of Corcyra (the modern Corfu) which came to be called after her. She bore Poseidon a son, Phaeax who gave his name to the Phaeacians.

Cerebia (Κηρεβία)

The mother of Dictys and Polydectes the two brothers who lived in the island of Seriphos and who played a part in the legend of Perseus. Their father was Poseidon. Other authors hold them to have been the sons not of Poseidon but of Magnes.

Ceres

The Roman name for the Greek goddess Demeter, with whom she is wholly identical. Even if it is etymologically true that Ceres was a very early vegetative force (the name is related to a root-word meaning 'growth') worshipped by the Romans, this very early goddess was completely eclipsed by the other. There is a story that when the Etruscans under Porsenna were attacking the young Roman republic the city was threatened with famine. The Sybilline Books, a selection from Greek oracles, were consulted, and they advised the introduction to Rome of the cults of Dionysus and Demeter. This advice was followed in 496 BC and the two gods were established on the Aventine Hill. For the legends about Ceres, which are simply Latin versions of those about Demeter, see DEMETER.

Ceryx (Κήρυξ)

The son of Eumolpus of Eleusis, his name in Greek means 'the herald'. On the death of his father Eumolpus took over responsibility for the cult of Demeter and it was his 'descendants' who were the 'heralds' (Ceryces) involved in the ritual. Some sources have it that Ceryx was the son of AGLAURUS and Hermes.

Cetes (Κέτης)

A king of Egypt who was able to change himself into every kind of animal or tree, or element such as fire and water. He was said to possess 'the knowledge of breathing', which appears to have underlain his magical powers.

Ceto (Κητώ)

The daughter of Pontus, the Sea, regarded as masculine and Gaia, Earth, her name is reminiscent of marine beasts such as whales and is the generic Greek name for any large sea monster. She was the sister of Nereus, Thaumas and other deities (Tables 12 and 32). She married her own brother Phorcus or Phorcys, by whom she had the GRAEAE, the Gorgons and the dragon which guarded the Apples of the Hesperides as well as the Hesperides themselves.

Ceyx (Κήυξ)

1. King of Trachis in Thessaly and a friend and

relation of Heracles (he was the nephew of Amphitryon). It was with him that Heracles took refuge after he had accidentally killed the young EUNOMUS, and after Heracles' death his children, pursued by the hate of Eurystheus, took refuge with Ceyx in Trachis, until Eurystheus made them leave. The daughter of Ceyx, Themistonoe, was the wife of Cycnus, who was killed by Heracles. It was Ceyx who offered funerary honours to Cycnus after his death. Ceyx was said to have had two sons, Hippasus, who went with Heracles on his expedition against Oechalia and died there, and HYLAS, a companion of Heracles and the Argonauts.

2. Another Ceyx was the son of Eosphorus and was married to ALCYONE and became a bird.

Chalciope (Χαλκιόπη) The name of several heroines.

1. One was the daughter of Eurypylus, king of the island of Cos. By her union with Heracles she had Thessalus (Table 16).

2. Another was the daughter of Aeetes, king of Colchis. She married Phrixus, by whom she had four children, Argos, Melas, Phrontis and Cytissorus (Table 33).

3. A third was the daughter of Rhexenor (or Chalcodon 1). She was the second wife of AEGEUS, king of Athens, the first having been Meta, the daughter of Hopleus. Because Aegeus could not have any children by her he went to Delphi and, while passing through Troezen on his way back, he fathered Theseus by his union with Aethra.

Chalcodon (Χαλκώδων)

1. A Euboean hero, the son of Abas who gave his name to the Abantides, and the father of the hero ELEPHENOR who took part in the Trojan War. Chalcodon died at the hands of Amphitryon during a campaign launched by the Thebans against the Euboeans with the aim of freeing themselves of a tribute which the latter had imposed upon them. His tomb was visible near Chalcis. Besides Elephenor, Chalcodon had a daughter Chalciope, who married Aegeus as his second wife.

2. A second Chalcodon accompanied Heracles on his expedition against Elis.

3. A third was one of the claimants to the hand of Hippodamia, but was killed by OENOMAUS.

4. Yet another Chalcodon was one of the defenders of Cos against Heracles during his attack on Eurypylus. He inflicted a wound on Heracles, who was only saved by the intervention of Zeus,

who removed him just in time from the field of battle.

Chalcon (Χάλκων)

1. A native hero of Cyparissus, on Mount Parnassus. An oracle had advised Nestor to give Chalcon to his son Antilochus to be his armour-bearer and adviser. During the fight between Achilles and Penthesilea, the queen of the Amazons, Chalcon, who was in love with Penthesilea, went to her help. He was killed by Achilles and his corpse was crucified by the Greeks to punish his treachery.

2. The son of Metion (see ABAS 1).

Chaon (Χάων) The hero who gave his name to Chaones, a district in Epirus. He was either a brother or friend of HELENUS and followed him to Neoptolemus' court. On Neoptolemus' death Helenus became king of the country, and after Chaon was killed in a hunting accident Helenus named part of his kingdom after him in commemoration. Sometimes it is said that Chaon had sacrificed himself, offering his life to the gods voluntarily for his countrymen during an epidemic.

Chaos (Χάος) The embodiment of the primeval Void which existed before Creation, at a time when Order had not yet been imposed on the elements of the Earth. Chaos begot Erebus and Night (Nyx) and then Day (Hemera) and Air. In a different version of the myth, Chaos is said to have been the son of Time (Chronus) and the brother of Air.

Chariclo (Χαρικλώ)

1. A daughter of Apollo (in other versions, of Oceanus) who married the Centaur Chiron. She brought up Jason and Achilles.

2. The daughter of Cychreus, the king of Salamis. By her marriage to Sciron, the king of Megara, she had a daughter, Endeis, who married Aeacus.

3. A Nymph named Chariclo was the mother of the seer Tiresias. She was one of the favourite companions of Athena, who often allowed her to ride in her chariot. One day when Athena and Chariclo were bathing in the Hippocrene fountain on Mount Helicon, TIRESIAS who was hunting in the area came upon the spring and he saw Athena there, completely naked. The goddess instantly blinded him and when Chariclo reproached her for her cruelty to her son, Athena explained to her

that every mortal who saw a deity against his or her wishes must lose his sense of sight. In reparation she gave Tiresias some wonderful gifts: she gave him first a dogwood stick, with the help of which he could guide himself as well as if he could see, then she refined his sense of hearing so effectively that he could understand what the birds were saying. Moreover, she promised him that after his death he would retain all his intellectual faculties in Hades and especially his gift of prophecy.

Charila (Χαρίλα) An orphan girl who at one time lived at Delphi. During a famine which was a result of drought, Charila went to the king's door to beg for alms in the form of a small quantity of corn, but the king drove her back by brutally kicking her in the face instead of giving her what she asked. Charila hanged herself in despair, and thereafter the drought worsened. When the oracle was consulted, it replied that the death of Charila must be expiated to break the drought. Accordingly, every nine years a festival was held at Delphi during which corn was distributed and a doll, solemnly named Charila and wearing a string of rushes round its neck, was interred in a tomb hollowed out on the mountain.

Charites (Χάριτες) The Charites, called in Latin the Graces (Gratiae) were goddesses of beauty and perhaps also, in their earliest form, of the powers of vegetation. They spread the joy of Nature in human hearts, and even in those of the gods. They lived on Olympus together with the Muses with whom they sometimes sang and were numbered among the attendants of Apollo, the god of Music. They are generally said to be three sisters named Euphrosyne, Thalia and Aglaea, and represented as naked girls with their hands on each other's shoulders, two looking one way and the one in the middle looking the other. Their father was Zeus and their mother Eurynome, the daughter of Oceanus. According to other writers their mother was not Eurynome, but Hera.

The Graces are said to have exercised all kinds of influence on imaginative and artistic works. They wove the robe of Harmonia with their own hands (see CADMUS). They frequently accompanied Athena, goddess of women's works and of intellectual activity, as well as Aphrodite, Eros and Dionysus.

Charon (Χάρων) Guardian of the Underworld; his duty was to ensure the passage of spirits over the marsh of the Acheron to the other side of the river of the dead. Every dead soul had to pay him an obolus, and this was the source of the custom of putting a coin in the mouth of corpses when they were buried. Charon is represented as a very ugly old man with an unkempt grey beard, wearing a tattered cloak and a round hat. He is said to have steered the boat which carried the corpse but did not row it as this task was given to the souls of the dead. He behaved towards them in a despotic and brutal way, like a slave driver. When Heracles came down to Hades, he compelled Charon to ferry him in his boat and when Charon refused, Heracles seized the ferryman's boathook and beat him so violently that Charon had no alternative but to do as he was ordered. Charon was subsequently punished for allowing a living being to enter the place of the dead by being sentenced to a whole year in chains. On Etruscan tomb-paintings Charon is depicted as a winged demon, his hair entwined with snakes and holding a stout mallet in his hand. It seems likely that for the Etruscans he was really the demon of death who kills the dying man and carries him off to the underworld.

Charops (Χάροψ) A Thracian who warned Dionysus of the harm which LYCURGUS was planning to inflict on him. After punishing Lycurgus, Dionysus replaced him on the throne of Thrace with Charops whom he initiated into the Dionysiac mysteries. Charops was the father of Oeager and accordingly the grandfather of Orpheus. Charops handed down the knowledge of the Dionysiac religion to his descendants.

Charybdis (Χάρυβδις) A monster called Charybdis, who was the daughter of Earth and Poseidon, once lived on the rock near Messina which lies just beside the straits between Italy and Sicily. During her life on earth she showed herself to be extremely greedy: when Heracles passed through the district, bringing with him the flocks of Geryon, Charybdis stole some beasts from him and ate them. Zeus punished her by striking her with a thunderbolt and casting her into the sea, where she became a monster. Three times every day Charybdis drank great quantities of sea water swallowing everything that was floating including any ships which were in the vicinity. She then disgorged the water she had swallowed. When ODYSSEUS passed through the straits for the first time he escaped Charybdis, but after the shipwreck which followed the sacrilege committed against the oxen of the Sun he was caught clinging to the mast of his shipwrecked vessel by the current of Charybdis. He succeeded in grasping hold of a fig tree which was growing at the entrance to the cave where the monster concealed herself and when the mast was spewed out by Charybdis, Ulysses grasped it and continued on his voyage. Within a bowshot of Charybdis, on the other side of the strait, another monster lay in wait for sailors; this was SCYLLA.

Chelidon (Χελιδών) The sister of AEDON; she became a swallow at the same time as Aedon was transformed into a nightingale in the Milesian legend.

Chelone (Χελώνη) The tortoise, who had once been a girl who lived in a house by the edge of a river. When the wedding of Zeus and Hera took place, Hermes invited not only the gods, but also all the humans and even the animals to attend. Chelone was the only person who stayed at home, and this was by mistake. Hermes noticed that she was not there; he came down to earth again, took hold of the house with the girl inside it and cast them both into the water. Chelone was changed into a tortoise which, like her, is inseparable from its house.

Chimaera (Χίμαιρα) A legendary beast which took its shape from both a goat and a lion. In some versions it is said to have had the hindquarters of a snake and the head of a lion on the body of a goat, and in others it is claimed that it had two heads, one of a goat and one of a lion; it breathed fire. It was the offspring of Typhon and Echidna (the Viper) and was brought up by Amisodares, the king of Caria at Patera. The king of Lycia, Iobates, commanded BELLEROPHON to kill it since it made many raids on his kingdom: with the help of Pegasus, the winged horse, Bellerophon succeeded. There is a story that Bellerophon fitted the point of his spear with a piece of lead which melted when exposed to the flames breathed out by the Chimaera and killed it.

Chimaereus (Χιμαιρεύς) One of the two sons of the giant Prometheus and Celaeno, the daughter of Atlas; his brother was Lycus (Table 38). The two brothers were buried at Troy. When a plague broke out in Lacedaemon before the Trojan War, the oracle of Apollo was consulted and replied that it would not cease until a noble Lacedaemonian had offered a sacrifice on the tomb of the son of Prometheus. Menelaus immediately made the journey and offered up the prescribed sacrifice. While staying at Troy he was the guest of Paris, and this was how they first came to meet.

Chione (Χιόνη) The name of several heroines:
1.   The daughter of Boreas, the north wind, and Orithyia (Table 11). She bore Poseidon a son named EUMOLPUS and threw him into the sea; he was saved by his father.
2.   The child of a daughter of Oceanus named Callirhoe and the Nile. During her life on earth Chione was raped by a peasant but at the bidding of Zeus Hermes carried her off and placed her among the clouds.
3.   A daughter of King Daedalion, who both Apollo and Hermes loved at the same time. She was the mother of Autolycus and Philammon.
4.   The mother of the god Priapus.

Chiron (Χείρων) The most famous and wisest of all the Centaurs; he was the son of the god Cronus and Philyra, a daughter of Oceanus, and accordingly was of the same generation of divinities as Zeus and the Olympians. In order to beget him, Cronus coupled with Philyra in the assumed shape of a horse, and this accounts for Chiron's twofold nature. Chiron was born an immortal and lived in a cave on Mount Pelion in Thessaly. He was very friendly with humans and was judicious and kindly. He gave special protection to PELEUS during his adventures at the court of ACASTUS by defending him against the savage treatment given by the other Centaurs. Chiron also advised Peleus to marry Thetis and showed him how to force her into marrying him by preventing her from assuming another form; at their marriage Chiron gave Peleus a spear of ash wood. Peleus entrusted his son ACHILLES to Chiron after his separation from his wife. He also brought up Jason, Asclepius and others; Apollo himself is said to have had lessons from him. His knowledge covered music, the martial arts, hunting, ethics and medicine. Chiron was a famous doctor and actually practised surgery; when ACHILLES as a child had had his ankle burned as a result of magical practices used on him by his mother, Chiron replaced the missing bone with one taken from the skeleton of a giant.

At the time of the massacre of the Centaurs by Heracles, Chiron, who was near the hero, was accidentally wounded by one of his arrows. Chiron tried to treat it with an ointment, but wounds from the arrows of Heracles could not be healed (see PHILOCTETES). Chiron retreated to his cave wanting to die, but since he was immortal he could not until Prometheus, who had been born a mortal, eventually offered to make Chiron himself mortal, and thus Chiron was able to die.

Choricus A king of Arcadia whose two sons, Plexippus and Enetus, devised the art of wrestling. One day they gave a display of it before their father, but their sister Palaestra told her lover Hermes of the new skill. Hermes made himself proficient at it as quickly as he could and taught it to mankind, saying he had first thought of it. The two young men complained to their father about Palaestra's indiscretion but Choricus reproved them for not having taken their revenge on Hermes. One day, therefore when they found the god asleep on Mount Cyllene the two young men cut off his hands. Hermes complained to Zeus, who flayed Choricus and made a leather bottle out of his skin. Hermes gave the new-found art the name of his beloved, Palaestra (Παλαίστρα in Greek means 'wrestling').

Chrysanthis (Χρυσανθίς) A woman from Argolis who in one version of the Demeter legend told the goddess how her daughter had been abducted when she came to Argos in search of her. In this version of the story, the abduction did not take place on the plain of Enna in Sicily, but in the Peloponnese, near Lerna.

Chrysaor (Χρυσάωρ) Chrysaor, which means 'the man with the golden sword', was the son of Poseidon and Medusa (the Gorgon), as was Pegasus, the winged horse: both were born from the neck of the Gorgon which was killed by Perseus. Chrysaor was born brandishing a golden sword. From his marriage to Callirhoe, the daughter of Oceanus, Geryon, the giant with three bodies and the foe of Heracles, and Echidna were born (Table 32).

Chryseis (Χρυσηίς) The daughter of Chryses, the priest of Apollo, who lived in the town of Chryse in the Troad; her real name was Astynome. She was abducted by the Greeks at the time of an expedition against the town of Thebes in Mysia, when she was staying there with Iphinoe, the sister of King Aetion. She was given to Agamemnon as part of the spoils; her father came to ask for her return, but Agamemnon refused. Chryseis thereupon prayed to Apollo to send a plague on the Greeks that would make them change their minds. The god complied and the Greeks forced Agamemnon to surrender Chryseis

but the king demanded Briseis in exchange; this episode was at the root of Achilles' anger. There is a tradition that Chryses subsequently returned Chryseis to Agamemnon of his own free will because she had been well treated. She is said to have had two children by Agamemnon, Iphigenia and Chryses, the latter named after his grandfather. Tradition gives the detailed information that Chryseis was fair, slender and small in stature; in contrast, Briseis was a tall brunette with a dark complexion and a very distinguished appearance. The two girls represent the two different kinds of womanly beauty.

Chryses (Χρύσης) The father of CHRYSEIS. This was also the name given to his grandson, the son of Chryseis and Agamemnon, who plays a part in the Orestes legend. When Chryseis was returned to her father by Agamemnon, she was pregnant, but she claimed that Agamemnon was not responsible and when she gave birth to a son whom she called Chryses, she asserted that the child was Apollo's. After the fall of Troy when Orestes and Iphigenia, fleeing the vengeance of Thoas the king of Tauris, arrived at the house of Chryses in search of safety, the priest wanted to hand them over to their persecutor. At that point his daughter disclosed that Agamemnon was in fact the real father of the young Chryses and because of this the two dynasties were linked by family connections. Chryses dismissed the idea of handing over Orestes and Iphigenia and together with the help of the younger Chryses they killed Thoas.

Chrysippus (Χρύσιππος) The son of Pelops and the Nymph Axioche. When the Theban Laius, who had been exiled by Zethus and Amphion arrived at the court of Pelops, he received a warm welcome; he then fell in love with the young Chrysippus and abducted him. Pelops then ritually cursed Laius, and this was the beginning of the curse of the Labdacides (see OEDIPUS). Chrysippus committed suicide in shame. In another version of the legend Chrysippus was killed by his half-brothers ATREUS and Thyestes at the instigation of his stepmother HIPPODAMIA, who was afraid that her sons might be deposed by outsiders.

Chrysopelia (Χρυσοπέλεια) A Hamadryad Nymph who lived in an oak tree in Arcadia. One day when Arcas was hunting there he saw that the oak tree was about to be swept away by a flood. Chrysopelia begged him to save her so Arcas built a dyke to divert the water, which ensured the safety of the oak. In gratitude Chrysopelia married him, and bore him two sons named Elatus and Aphidas who were the founders of the Arcadian race (Table 9).

Chrysothemis (Χρυσόθεμις) The daughter of the Cretan CARMANOR; she is said to have introduced musical contests, and is supposed to have won the prize in the first competition. She was also the mother of the musician Philammon.

Chthonia (Χθονία)
1.   The daughter of Phoroneus and the sister of Clymenus; with her brother she founded a temple of Demeter at Hermione. An Argive tradition makes Chthonia the daughter of Colontas. In this account Colontas refused to restore a cult in Demeter's honour, and reproached her father for his impiety. The house of Colontas was burned down by the goddess who then removed Chthonia to Hermione. There the girl founded a shrine where Demeter was worshipped under the name of Demeter Chthonia, which means Demeter beneath the earth.
2.   One of the daughters of ERECHTHEUS (Table 11). She married Butes, her uncle, though in another version she is said to have been offered as a sacrificial victim at the time of the struggle between Eumolpus and Eleusis. In another account she is said to have killed herself and her sisters after the eldest, Protogenia, had been sacrificed.

Cichyrus (Κίχυρος) A girl of noble birth called Anthippe lived in Chaones. She was loved by a young man of the country and returned his love and the two young people used to meet each other, without their parents' knowledge, in a sacred wood. One day the son of the king of the country called Cichyrus was hunting a panther which had taken shelter in the wood where the tomb of Epirus was. The two lovers hid in a copse and, seeing the leaves moving, Cichyrus hurled his spear and fatally wounded Anthippe. When he approached and saw the crime he had just committed, he became mad. He remounted his horse, driving it over some rocks and killing himself. The people of Chaonia built a wall around the site of the accident and named the newly-created town Cichyrus.

Cicones (Κίκονες) A Thracian tribe recorded in the *Iliad* as being allies of Priam. Their chief was named Mentes, but does not seem to have played any important part in the struggle. The Cicones play an important part in the *Odyssey*. Odysseus made his first stop after leaving Troy in their country; he reached one of their towns, Ismarus, and sacked it. He spared only a priest of Apollo called MARON who lavished magnificent gifts on him by way of ransom, including a dozen amphorae of a sweet and potent wine – the very wine which later was to enable Odysseus to make Polyphemus drunk and so extricate himself from a difficult predicament. After the town had been looted, Odysseus advised his men to withdraw and to be satisfied with the spoils they had already captured, but the soldiers refused to listen. As a result, the population of the interior had time to come in strength and attack them. Six men from each ship lost their lives and Odysseus had time to do no more than make his escape.

The name Cicones is derived from Cicon, the son of Apollo and Rhodope. Orpheus is said to have lived in their country and was initiated there into the mysteries of Apollo, and it is said that the Ciconian women tore him into pieces. The Cicones were still in existence after the classical period: Herodotus quotes them as being one of the races whose land was crossed by the army of Xerxes during the Persian Wars.

Cilix (Κίλιξ) One of the sons of Agenor, the king of Sidon; he was the brother of Cadmus, Thasos and Europa (Table 3). He accompanied his brothers in their search for Europa after her abduction by Zeus and stopped when he arrived at Cilicia, which took his name. Other authors make him the son of Cassiopia and Phoenix, who in an alternative version was his brother. Cilix joined forces with Sarpedon in an expedition against his neighbours, the Lycians, and after he had gained victory he gave up a part of Lycia to Sarpedon.

Cilla (Κίλλα) A Trojan woman who was a sister of Priam and a daughter of Laomedon and Strymo (Table 7). She bore to THYMOETES a son called Munippus at the time when Hecuba was pregnant with Paris. The seer Aesacus explained a dream of Hecuba's as showing that a child would be born who would destroy Troy, meaning Paris, but Paris misinterpreted the prophecy and had his sister and her child, Munippus, put to death. Sometimes Cilla is said to have been Hecuba's sister and Priam is supposed to have fathered her son.

Cillas (Κίλλας) Pelops' charioteer who ruled the area in the Troad surrounding the town which had taken his name. He drowned during a voyage he was making with Pelops from Lycia to the Peloponnese, where Pelops was to have a chariot race with Oenomaus (see SPHAERUS).

Cimmerians (Κιμμέριοι) A mythical race who lived in a country where the sun was never seen. Odysseus went there to conjure up the dead and to question the prophet Tiresias. Ancient writers hold different views on where this country was located: some say it was in the extreme west and others that it was in the plains which stretch north from the Black Sea. Accordingly, the Cimmerians are regarded sometimes as the ancestors of the Celts and sometimes as the forefathers of the Scythians of southern Russia. Occasionally they are said, rather surprisingly, to live near Cumae; this is no doubt because it was believed that one of the gates of the Underworld was there, and the Cimmerians were supposed to live near the Country of the Dead. They are also said to have lived in underground dwellings, linked with each other by passages, and never to have left their city except at night. This legend may perhaps have derived from a confused recollection of the mining people of central and western Europe, that is Bohemia and Britain, who supplied the merchants from the shores of the Mediterranean with tin and copper at a time when the trade routes were shrouded in mystery.

Cinyras (Κινύρας) Traditionally the first king to rule in Cyprus; but he was not a native of the island, as he came from Asia. His country of origin was Byblos, to the north of Syria. His parentage is uncertain: in some accounts he is described as a son of Apollo and Paphos, and in others as a son of Eurymedon and a nymph from the region of Paphos (see PYGMALION). A different source makes him a member of the house of Cecrops as follows: Cephalus, who was abducted by Eos or the Dawn, fathered Phaethon; his son, Astynous, in due course fathered Sandacus, the father of Cinyras. In this version of his descent Cinyras' mother was Pharnace, the daughter of the king of the Syrians. The stories about his arrival in Cyprus are equally conflicting: some simply say that he came with a band of followers and founded the town of Paphos after marrying Metharme, the daughter of Pygmalion, king of Cyprus. By this marriage he had two sons, Adonis and Oxyporus, and three daughters, Orsedice, Laogora and

Braesia. These daughters were victims of the wrath of Aphrodite who made them serve as prostitutes to strangers who were passing through Cyprus and they ended their lives in Egypt. Another version claims that Cinyras committed incest with his daughter Smyrna and fathered Adonis; Smyrna was then changed into a myrrh tree.

Cinyras was the first to introduce the Aphrodite cult to Cyprus, and it assumed great importance in the island. He is said to have had the gift of prophecy and to have been an exceptionally good musician; his name is sometimes said to have associations with the instrument called the kinnor in Phoenician. An obscure legend tells how he dared to compete with Apollo and was, like Marsyas, put to death by the god. More commonly he is credited with introducing elements of civilization into Cyprus, such as the working of the copper mines which were the basis of the island's wealth, as well as the invention of bronze. He was loved by Aphrodite who gave him substantial wealth and allowed him to live to a great age; he is said to have lived to be a hundred and sixty.

Cinyras was not a warlike man. He was living at the time of the Trojan War and the Greeks encouraged him to join them; Odysseus and Talthybius, the herald of Agamemnon, came on a special mission to Cyprus. Cinyras promised to send them a contingent of fifty ships but he only fitted out one of them and the other forty-nine were made of earth. They were all launched simultaneously and naturally only one arrived at Aulis, but Cinyras had kept his promise. After the war TEUCER, who had been banished from Salamis in Attica, sought refuge in Cyprus where he was kindly received by Cinyras who gave him a gift of some land on which Teucer founded Salamis of Cyprus. Cinyras also gave him the hand of his daughter Eune. This legendary marriage formed the basis of the good relationship in the post-classical period between the Athenians and the Cypriots (see ELATUS and LAODICE).

Cipus A Roman general who at a very early date was returning to Rome at the head of his victorious army when, accidentally casting his eyes on the water of a stream, he saw that his forehead sported horns. Presented with this miracle, he offered up a sacrifice and consulted the entrails of the victim. The soothsayer told him that the omen meant that he would become king, provided that he entered the city at once. Cipus was appalled as he was a loyal Republican and he immediately gathered the population on the Field of Mars and made himself an exile. To show their gratitude for this act, the Senate offered him as much land as he could plough in a day, and to commemorate this extraordinary event a portrait of Cipus, in the form of a head of a man with horns, was carved on the Raudusculan Gate at the foot of the Aventine.

Circe (Κίρκη) The witch who plays a part in the *Odyssey* as well as in the legend of the ARGONAUTS. She was the daughter of the Sun and of Perseis, the daughter of Oceanus or, in some accounts, of Hecate (Table 14). She was the sister of AEETES, the king of Colchis who kept the Golden Fleece, and Pasiphae, the wife of Minos. She lived on the island of Aeaea which ancient writers locate in different places. In the *Odyssey*, this so-called island is said to be in Italy, and is undoubtedly the peninsula of modern Monte Circeo, near Gaeta and Terracina, which dominates the low-lying coast of the Pontine Marsh. After his adventures in the city of Laestrygones Odysseus travelled northwards along the Italian coastline and arrived at Aeaea. He sent half his force under the leadership of Eurylochus to spy out the land. The expedition made its way into a forest and came to a valley where its members saw a gleaming palace; they all entered except for Eurylochus who decided to stay on guard. He hid himself and saw how his companions were received. The Greeks were welcomed by the mistress of the palace, who was Circe. She invited them to sit down and to share in a banquet and the delighted sailors accepted but they had scarcely tasted the food and wine when Eurylochus saw Circe touch the guests with a wand. They were all instantly changed into every kind of animal – pigs, lions and dogs – each one in accordance with his fundamental character and disposition. Then Circe propelled them towards the stables, which were already full of animals. When Eurylochus saw this, he rushed back to Odysseus and described what had happened. Odysseus decided to go and find the witch himself to save his companions and was wandering about in the wood, racking his brains to find a way of delivering his crew, when he saw the god Hermes appear. Hermes told him the secret of breaking Circe's spells: if he were to throw a magic plant called moly into the drink which Circe gave him he would have nothing to fear; it would be enough for him to draw his sword, and Circe would swear any oaths that he wished and free his friends from the enchantment. Hermes also gave him some moly. Accordingly, Odysseus sought out Circe who welcomed him as she had his companions and offered some wine. Odysseus drank it, but first took the precaution of mixing the moly with the contents of the cup. Then, when Circe touched him with her wand, he remained unaffected by her spell. He drew his sword and threatened to kill her but she pacified him, swearing by the Styx to do no harm either to himself or to his men. She accordingly changed the sailors back to their original shapes. Odysseus spent a very pleasant month in her company, some sources say a year. During this period he fathered a son called Telegonus and a daughter called Cassiphone (Table 39). In an Italian legend Telegonus is said to have founded the town of Tusculum.

In other traditions Circe is also said to have borne a son called Latinus who gave his name to the Latins (see CALYPSO) or in other versions, three sons, Romus, Antias and Ardeas, and the three cities of Rome, Antium and Ardea were said to be named after them. Circe is also said to have been involved in intrigues with Picus, the king of the Latins (see CANENS) and with Jupiter, who fathered the god Faunus.

Circe plays a part during the return voyage of the Argonauts. The ship landed on the island of Aeaea, where Medea was received by Circe, who was her aunt. Circe purified Jason and Medea of the murder of Apsyrtus but refused to offer hospitality to Jason, and instead merely talked at length to her niece. Circe is said to have been responsible for the metamorphosis of SCYLLA who was her rival for the love of the sea-deity GLAUCUS.

Cithaeron (Κιθαιρών) A king of Plataea who gave his name to the nearby mountain of Cithaeron. He preceded Asopus (after whom the river was named) on the throne. One account tells how during his reign there was a quarrel between Zeus and Hera: the latter did not want her husband to touch her and fled to Euboea. Zeus was deeply upset and took refuge at Plataea with Cithaeron who was very clever, and thought of the following trick: he advised Zeus to make a statue of a woman, to swathe it in a big cloak and to put it on a cart drawn by oxen. As soon as Hera saw her husband in this contraption she made enquiries and was told that Zeus (this was the rumour which Cithaeron had circulated) was abducting Plataea, the daughter of Asopus and was to make her his wife. Immediately Hera rushed up to it, tore off the cloak and saw that there was nothing under it but a wooden statue. She began to laugh and she and Zeus were reconciled. In memory of this episode a festival which had as its theme the marriage of Zeus and Hera was celebrated annually at Plataea (see ALALCOMENEUS).

There are other legends which allude to the name of Cithaeron. According to one, Cithaeron was a very handsome young man who was sought by Tisiphone, one of the Erinyes, but he spurned her love and she then turned one of her locks of hair into a snake, which bit him. He died and gave his name to the mountain which had previously been called Asterion. In another story Cithaeron and Helicon were two brothers; the latter was gentle and kindly but Cithaeron was violent and cruel. He finally killed his father and hurled his brother from the top of a rock, killing himself in the fall. Two neighbouring mountains came to be called Cithaeron and Helicon, the former in memory of the brutal hero because it was the home of the Erinyes, the latter after the kindly hero because it was the home of the Muses.

Cleomedes (Κλεομήδης) A hero from Astypalaea who during the Olympic Games killed his opponent, Iccus of Epidaurus, when fighting with the cestus. The referees did not announce him as the winner, saying that he had not fought fairly and he became mad. When he returned to his own country he knocked down the pillar which was holding up the roof of a school and some sixty children were killed. Then, pursued by the inhabitants, he took refuge in the temple of Athena. His pursuers decided to capture him there, after some hesitation, and failed to find him, dead or alive. They questioned the oracle which replied that Cleomedes was the last hero to live and that his cult should be established and this was carried out at the seventy-second Olympic Games.

Cleopatra (Κλεοπάτρα) Several heroines of this name are known.
1. The most famous was the daughter of Boreas and Orithyia, the sister of Zetes, Calaïs and Chione (see BOREADES). She was married to Phineus, who fathered two sons, Plexippus and Pandion (Table 11). Cleopatra was imprisoned by her husband and her children were blinded when Phineus married a second wife, Idaea, the daughter of Dardanus, but the Argonauts came to her rescue and (in at least one version of the story) killed Phineus.
2. Another Cleopatra, the daughter of Idas, was

the wife of Meleager. After her husband's death she hanged herself (Table 19).
3. A third Cleopatra was sent to Troy by the Locrians (see PERIBOEA 3).

Cleostratus (Κλεόστρατος) A young man of Thebes who rid his country of a dragon which demanded as tribute the life of a young man every year. Cleostratus had himself been chosen by lot as the prospective victim for the dragon, but his friend Menestratus made for him a metal breastplate studded with iron hooks. Cleostratus put it on and allowed himself to be eaten but the dragon died from the effects and this was the end of a very long sequence of deaths.

Cleothera (Κλευθήρα) A daughter of PANDAREUS and Harmothoe and the sister of Aedon and Merope. After they had lost their parents when they were still small the three sisters were brought up by Aphrodite, Hera and Athena. When they became young women the eldest, Aedon, married Zethus, but Cleothera and Merope were abducted by the Erinyes who made them their servants.

Clesonymus (Κλησώνυμος) The son of Amphidamas of Opontus. In his childhood he used to play with Patroclus but he was accidentally killed by his playmate and as a result of this involuntary murder the boy Patroclus had to leave Opontus. His father placed him in the care of Peleus at Phthia, who brought him up with his own son Achilles and this was the beginning of the close friendship between the two heroes.

Clete (Κλήτη) The nurse of PENTHESILEA, the queen of the Amazons and an Amazon herself. After Penthesilea died, Clete wanted to return home, but she was cast up by a storm on the south coast of Italy where she founded the town of Clete, which was perhaps the neighbour of the town of Caulonia, named after her son CAULON. Some time later she died fighting against the people of Croton who annexed her town.

Clinis (Κλεῖνις) A rich and pious Babylonian who was loved by Apollo and Artemis; his wife was Harpa and he fathered three sons, Lycius, Ortygius and Harpasus, and one daughter, Artemiche. He often used to visit the land of the Hyperboreans with Apollo and there he saw that asses were sacrificed to the gods. He wished to do the same in Babylon but Apollo forbade him to do so on pain of death, telling him to sacrifice only animals which were generally used, such as sheep, oxen and goats. Despite this command, two of his sons, Lycius and Harpasus, disobeyed; they came to the altar with a donkey and were on the point of sacrificing it when Apollo made the beast become deranged. It attacked the two young men and began to tear them in pieces and then did the same to their father and the rest of the family who arrived, drawn by the noise. Apollo and the other gods took pity on them, however, and changed them into birds; Harpe and Harpasus (names which suggest the idea of abduction) became falcons, Clinis an eagle, Lycius a crow, Ortygius a tit and Artemiche either a chaffinch or a variety of skylark.

Clisithera (Κλεισιθήρα) A daughter of Idomeneus and Meda; Idomeneus betrothed her to his adopted son Leucus, who was the son of Talus, but Leucus killed her and his mother while Idomeneus was away at the Trojan War.

Clite (Κλείτη) The young wife of Cyzicus; he was killed by the ARGONAUTS shortly after their marriage and in despair, Clite hung herself. She was the daughter of Merops, the prophet of Percotus, in Mysia.

Clitor (Κλείτωρ) One of the sons of Azan, the grandson of Arcas, the first king of Arcadia. After the death of Azan, Clitor founded the town which subsequently bore his name and he was the most powerful prince in the whole of Arcadia. He died childless and his kingdom was inherited by Aepytus, the son of Elatus (Table 9). Another Clitor, who may be identical with the above, is mentioned as one of the fifty sons of Lycaon.

Clitus (Κλεῖτος) There are two figures with this name:
1. Clitus, the grandson of Melampus, was abducted by Eos (the Dawn) because of his beauty and set by her among the immortals. He had a son called Coeranus and a grandson, Polyidus.
2. Another Clitus married Pallene, daughter of Sithon, a king of Chersonesus in Thrace.

Clymene (Κλυμένη)
1. A daughter of Oceanus and Tethys. She belonged to the first generation of divinities, together with the Titans. By her marriage to Iapetus she gave birth to Atlas, Prometheus and Epimetheus, as well as Menoetius (Table 38). In some versions she is regarded as the mother of

Prometheus and therefore the mother of Hellen, the parent of all Hellenes and of Deucalion. According to other accounts she is said to have married Helios (the Sun) and to have borne him a son, Phaethon, and several daughters, called the HELIADS (Table 14).
2. Another Clymene, also born from the sea, was the daughter of Nereus and Doris.
3. Clymene was also the name of one of the daughters of Minyas, the king of Orchomenus (Table 20). She married Phylacus, the son of Deion, and had two sons, Iphiclus and Alcimedes. In other accounts she is said to have been the wife of Cephalus whom she married after the death of Procris, but is also supposed to have married Iasus, a son of Lycurgus (Table 26), and to have had a daughter, Atalanta.
4. Another Clymene was one of the daughters of Catreus of Crete. She married Nauplius and he fathered three sons, Palamedes, Oeax and Nausimedon.

Clymenus (Κλύμενος) There are three figures of this name:
1. The first Clymenus, a native of the town of Cydonia, in Crete, and the son of Cardys, was a descendant of Heracles (Heracles of Ida, the name by which the hero was known in Crete). He came to Olympus about fifty years after Deucalion's flood and founded the Games there; he also built an altar there to the Curetes and to his ancestor Heracles. Clymenus reigned over the country until ENDYMION stripped him of his power. Endymion introduced a running race into the Olympic Games, and offered his sons the right to succeed him on the throne as the prize.
2. A second Clymenus was a Boeotian hero; he was the son of Presbon and ruled the town of Orchomenus after the death of its eponym who had no children (Table 33). He was stoned to death by the Thebans in the wood which was sacred to Poseidon and in revenge for his death his son ERGINUS forced the Thebans to pay tribute; they were freed from this by Heracles. This Clymenus had six children: Erginus, Stratius, Arrhon, Pyleus, and Azeus, and a daughter named Eurydice who married Nestor.
3. Another Clymenus was an Arcadian and the son of Schoeneus, or possibly of Teleus, king of Arcadia; he fell in love with his daughter, Harpalyce, and with the help of her nurse, had an incestuous relationship with her. Later, he married her to Alastor but, overcome with regret, he abducted her from her husband and kept her

openly by him. In revenge for the wrong he had done her, the girl killed either her young brothers or the son Clymenus had fathered, served them up to Clymenus and made him eat them. When he realized what a strange dish his daughter had given him, Clymenus killed first her and then himself. He is also said to have been turned into a bird (see HARPALYCE 2).

Clytemnestra (Κλυταιμνήστρα) The daughter of Tyndareus and LEDA and the sister of Timandra and Phylonoe, the 'human' daughters of Leda, and of Helen and the Dioscuri, Leda's 'divine' children fathered by Zeus. Although Clytemnestra was Helen's twin sister, Helen was the daughter of Zeus, who coupled with Leda in the form of a swan, while Clytemnestra was the daughter of Tyndareus.

She was first married to Tantalus, the son of Thyestes, but Agamemnon slew her husband and children. The Dioscuri then pursued Agamemnon and forced him to marry Clytemnestra, but this marriage seemed inauspicious. Clytemnestra had several children by AGAMEMNON. During the absence of Menelaus, who had gone to Troy to attempt to recover Helen, Clytemnestra took care of Helen's daughter Hermione, who was then nine years old. After the Greek army had gathered at Aulis, the seer Calchas declared that one of Clytemnestra's daughters, IPHIGENIA, must be sacrificed. Agamemnon sent for Clytemnestra who had remained at Argos (or Mycenae) with her children, on the pretext of betrothing Iphigenia to Achilles; he prepared for Iphigenia's sacrifice secretly, taking great care to conceal his plans from his wife. After Iphigenia had been sacrificed, Agamemnon sent Clytemnestra back to Argos, where she fostered her plans for revenge. When TELEPHUS, wounded by ACHILLES during the expedition to Mysia, came to Argos to ask Achilles to cure him it was Clytemnestra who advised him to threaten Agamemnon by taking the child Orestes hostage.

During Agamemnon's absence at the siege of Troy Clytemnestra was initially faithful to her husband. Agamemnon had left an aged bard named Demodocus at her side, and had instructed him to act as her adviser should the occasion arise, and report back to him. But AEGISTHUS fell in love with her and persisted until he had separated the bard from Clytemnestra, and then she yielded to him. Clytemnestra was perhaps prompted to do this by the urgings of NAUPLIUS, who incessantly tried to revenge himself against the Greeks, who

had killed his son Palamedes, by corrupting their wives; but perhaps she was motivated also by her own desire to have revenge on her husband who had sacrificed Iphigenia, or by jealousy, because she knew of his liaison with Chryseis. Aegisthus thus became master in Agamemnon's palace, and arranged for him to be assassinated on his return from Troy.

In the oldest versions of the legend, those of the epic poets, Clytemnestra played no part in this murder, which was regarded as entirely the work of Aegisthus, but the tragic poets maintain that she was his accomplice and indeed, that she murdered her husband with her own hands. She fashioned a robe for him, sewing up the neck and sleeves, so that as he rose from his bath and attempted to dress, he was encumbered by the garment and she was able to strike him down without risk. She also killed Cassandra, of whom she was jealous, but not until she had heaped insults on her head. According to the tragedians, Clytemnestra visited her hatred upon Agamemnon's children; she had Electra incarcerated, and would have slain Orestes, had the child not been taken away by his tutor. Seven years later, Clytemnestra was killed by Orestes, to avenge the death of his father.

Clytia (Κλυτία) A young girl loved by Helios, the Sun, who then spurned her for love of Leucothoe. Clytia revealed her rival's affair to Leucothoe's father and for this was buried in a deep ditch, where she died. Leucothoe was also punished, for Helios never visited her again. She wasted away with love and turned into a heliotrope, the flower which keeps its face turned always towards the sun, as though she were trying to see her former lover. A son was born from the liaison between Leucothoe and Helios. His name, which appears in some lists of the Argonauts, was Thersanor.

Cnageus (Κναγεύς) Pausanias relates that a Laconian named Cnageus who had been taken prisoner by the Athenians at the battle of Aphidna, where he had fought at the side of the Dioscuri, was later sold as a slave in Crete and placed in the service of the goddess Artemis. After some time he managed to escape, taking with him the priestess, a young girl, and the statue of the goddess. After his return to Laconia, he established the cult of Artemis Cnagia.

Cocalus (Κώκαλος) The king of the town of Camicos, in Sicily (later to become Agrigentum).

Daedalus took refuge with him after he put on wings and flew through the air from Crete, where Minos was holding him prisoner (see ICARUS). When Minos came looking for Daedalus, Cocalus hid Daedalus, but Minos made use of a trick: wherever he went he showed a snail's shell and a length of thread and promised a reward to anyone who could insert the thread into the spirals of the shell. No one could solve the problem until Cocalus, tempted, described the difficulty to Daedalus – who attached the thread to an ant and introduced the tiny creature into this novel labyrinth. When Cocalus brought the threaded shell to Minos, the latter knew that Daedalus, the man of ingenuity above all others, must be close at hand. He had little difficulty in inducing Cocalus to admit this and Cocalus then had to promise to hand Daedalus over; but to save his guest in spite of everything, Cocalus instructed his daughters to scald Minos to death in his bath. Another version says that Cocalus replaced the bath-water with boiling pitch, perhaps at the instigation of Daedalus, who had installed a special system of piping. Thus Minos met his death.

Cocytus (Κωκυτός) The Cocytus or the 'River of Groans' was a tributary of the ACHERON above the ground. According to legend it was one of the rivers of Hell, as was the Acheron. It was an extremely cold watercourse which ran parallel to the Styx, like the Pyriphlegethon or 'River of Flame'. Together, these rivers formed the expanse of water which had to be crossed by the souls of the dead before they could reach the kingdom of Hades (see CHARON).

Codrus (Κόδρος) The son of MELANTHUS and a descendant of Neleus, and hence, of the race of Poseidon. After the invasion of the Peloponnese by the Heraclids, Melanthus was driven from his native land, Pylos in Messenia, and emigrated to Athens. There Thymoetes, the last descendant of Theseus, surrendered the kingship to him as a reward for the help Melanthus had given him in his struggle against Xanthus, the king of Boeotia.

Codrus's destiny followed that of his father, and on the latter's death Codrus succeeded him as king of Athens. During his reign the Peloponnesians declared war on the Athenians, and the oracle of Delphi promised them victory if they refrained from killing the king of Athens. This pronouncement became known to the Athenians through Cleomantis, an inhabitant of Delphi. Codrus then resolved to sacrifice his life for his country: he left

Athens dressed as a beggar, ostensibly in search of wood, and wasted no time in seeking out two of the enemy, with whom he picked a quarrel. He killed one of them, and was himself slain by the other. The Athenians then demanded his body from the Peloponnesians in order to bury it. The Peloponnesians realized they had lost all hope of conquering Athens and returned to their own country.

Codrus's tomb was erected at the place where he died, on the right bank of the Ilissus, outside one of the gates of the city; it became one of the show places of Athens. After his death Codrus was succeeded by his elder son, Medon. His younger son, Neleus, went into exile at Miletus (see NELEUS 2).

Coeranus (Κοίρανος) Several heroes were named Coeranus:
1. Notably the grandson of Melampus (see CLITUS and POLYIDUS).
2. The charioteer of Merion who was slain by Hector outside Troy.
3. A Milesian, about whom a strange story was told. One day he saw a fisherman with a dolphin he had caught; Coeranus bought the animal and returned it to the water. Some time later, when he was shipwrecked, Coeranus alone of all the passengers aboard was saved by dolphins. After his death, when his funeral cortège passed near the port of Miletus, a school of dolphins appeared and accompanied the mourners.

Coeus (Κοῖος) A giant of the race of Titans; he was the son of Uranus (Heaven) and Gaia (Earth). He was the brother of Oceanus, Hyperion, Iapetus, and Cronus, and his sisters were the Titanesses Tethys, Rhea, Themis, Mnemosyne, Phoebe, Dione and Thia. By his own sister, Phoebe, he sired Leto, the mother of Apollo Artemis, and Asteria (Table 38).

Colaenus (Κόλαινος) A descendant of Hermes who was reputedly the first king of Attica. He was overthrown by his brother-in-law Amphictyon; driven out of the city, he settled in the district of Myrrhina, where he consecrated a shrine to Artemis Coelanis; he died there. This is a purely local legend (see CRANAUS and CECROPS).

Comaetho (Κομαιθώ)
1. The daughter of Pterelaus, king of the Teleboians, with whom AMPHITRYON was at war (Table 31). Pterelaus was invincible as long as his

head bore the golden lock of immortality which Poseidon had planted in his hair. Comaetho, who was in love with Amphitryon (or perhaps his ally Cephalus), cut off the magic golden lock, thus assuring the victory of her father's enemies. But Amphitryon did not yield to the girl's amorous advances and had her put to death.

2. There was another Comaetho who was a priestess of Artemis at Patras. She was loved by a young townsman named Melanippus, and she returned his love, though their parents were opposed to this match. The two young lovers used to meet in the priestess's sanctuary and Artemis, angered by this sacrilege, sent a plague upon the land. The oracle of Delphi was consulted, and revealed the cause of Artemis' anger; the sacrifice of the guilty couple was pronounced to be the only means of appeasing her. This was carried out, and furthermore, each year the handsomest youth and the most beautiful girl in the land were sacrificed to Artemis. This custom continued until the arrival of EURYPYLUS, who freed the city from this loathsome tribute.

Comatas (Κομάτας) The legend of Comatas is from southern Italy. He was a shepherd in Thurii, on the gulf of Tarentum, who used to frequently make sacrifices to the Muses. His master (from whose herds Comatas used to select the victims) shut him up in a sarcophagus of cedar-wood, telling him that his favourite goddesses, the Muses, would no doubt find a way to save him. Three months later the sarcophagus was opened, and the young man was found still alive: the goddesses had sent him bees who had nourished him with their honey.

Combe (Κόμβη) The daughter of the river-god Asopus, who seems to have been confused later with the Nymph Chalcis, who gave her name to the town in Euboea. She is said to have had many children, but the legends are not in agreement as to their number; some of them even claim that she had a hundred. Usually seven are attributed to her, the seven Corybantes of Euboea, called Prymneus, Mimas, Acmon, Damneus, Ocythous, Idaeus and Melisseus. She was married to the god Socus or Saocus, who was so violent that she fled from him with her children and took refuge at Cnossus, in Crete. From there, she made her way to Phrygia, and then to Athens, in close proximity to Cecrops. After the death of Socus she returned to Euboea with her children and there, in somewhat mysterious circumstances, but perhaps at the

very moment when her sons were about to kill her, she was changed into a dove (see also CURETES).

Cometes (Κομήτης)
1. The son of Sthenelus. When DIOMEDES left for the Trojan war, he entrusted Cometes with the care of his house, but Cometes betrayed him by seducing his wife AEGIALE. In doing this, Cometes was merely the instrument of the anger of Aphrodite, who had been wounded by the hero. On returning to his fatherland, Diomedes was forced into exile, driven out by the intrigues of Cometes and Aegiale.
2. The son of Tisamenus (see TISAMENUS 1).

Condyleatis (Κονδυλεᾶτις) Long ago a statue of Artemis, called Artemis Condyleatis, stood in a sacred wood not far from the town of Caphyes in Arcadia. One day, a group of children playing there found a length of cord which they at once wound round the neck of the image as if they were going to strangle her. Some of the townsfolk happened to pass by and surprised the children at their game. Horror-stricken, and in an excess of piety, they stoned the children to death, but before long the women of Caphyes fell victim to an inexplicable malady: their babies were all stillborn. When the oracle of Delphi was approached she replied that the goddess was angered by the slaughter of the children and ordered that they be buried reverently and be paid the honours due to heroes. This was done and thereafter this Artemis was called 'The Strangled Artemis' (Ἀπαγχομένη).

Consentes The Etruscans acknowledged the existence of twelve divinities with mysterious names, six gods and six goddesses, who formed Jupiter's privy council and who assisted him when important decisions had to be taken, notably the hurling of certain types of thunderbolt. The Romans adopted this belief, but related it to the twelve major gods of the Hellenic pantheon: Jupiter, Neptune, Mars, Apollo, Vulcan, Mercury, Juno, Minerva, Diana, Venus, Vesta, Ceres, – the Greek Zeus, Poseidon, Ares, Apollo, Hephaestus, Hermes, Hera, Athena, Artemis, Aphrodite, Hestia, Demeter. Their statues stood beneath a portico at the side of the road running from the Forum to the Capitol.

Consus Consus was a very ancient and obscure Roman god who had an underground altar in the

The Temple of Concord at Agrigentum, 5th century BC. Agrigentum was one of the most splendid cities of the ancient world.

middle of the Circus Maximus. This altar was disinterred on each of the god's feast-days, during the *Consualia* and during the horse-races. Curious rites were observed on these feast-days. Draught animals, horses, asses, and mules, were spared from work on these days and garlanded with flowers; horse-races and even mule-races were held. The rape of the Sabine women took place during the first feast-day of Consus, in Romulus' time. Originally Consus was perhaps the god of silos and responsible for the protection of the grain stored underground.

Copreus (Κοπρεύς) The son of Pelops of Elis. After slaying Iphitus, he had to leave his fatherland; he took refuge with EURYSTHEUS in Mycenae, where he served as herald to this king and, more notably, was given the task of conveying Eurystheus' orders to Heracles, as the king was too afraid of his victim to meet him face to face. In the legend, Copreus is presented as an unpleasant man who appears as a base, insolent creature and a coward's lackey. Homer tells us that his son Periphetes, who accompanied Agamemnon to Troy where he was killed by Hector, was far superior to his father both in courage and in strength of character. Eurystheus sent Copreus as his envoy to the Athenians, with the demand that they expel the Heraclids; he behaved with such insolence during this mission that the Athenians slew him, in defiance of the law of nations; but in commemoration and expiation of this crime Athenian youths wore dark-coloured tunics on certain festal days.

Cora (Κόρα) Cora, whose name means 'young girl', was DEMETER's daughter who is better known as PERSEPHONE.

Corcyra (Κόρκυρα) See CERCYRA.

Corinnus (Κόριννος) A legendary poet of Trojan

origin who is said to have written the *Iliad* before Homer, at the actual time of the Trojan war, and to have learnt the art of writing from Palamedes himself. He was also said to have composed an epic poem on the war waged by Dardanus against the Paphlagonians. According to the legend, Homer owed most of his poems to him.

Corinthus (Κόρινθος) Corinthus, after whom the city of Corinth was named, was said by the Corinthians to be one of the sons of Zeus, but the rest of Greece laughed at this pretentious claim until the phrase 'Corinthus, son of Zeus' ultimately became the proverbial expression for a monotonous catch-phrase. Historically, he was said to be the son of MARATHON. He fled to Attica with his father, and on the death of EPOPEUS both father and son returned to Corinth. When Marathon died, Corinthus became king of Corinth (Table 10). He died without issue; after his death the Corinthians called for MEDEA. According to one tradition, he was assassinated by his subjects (see also GORGE 2), and his death was avenged by Sisyphus, who reigned over Corinth after him.

Coroebus (Κόροιβος)
1.   When Crotopus was king of Argos his daughter Psamathe was loved by Apollo, by whom she had a son, Linus. Through fear of her father, she exposed the child, but Crotopus hearing of the story killed his daughter and had the infant eaten by his dogs. The incensed Apollo sent a monster called Poene (which means 'Punishment') to devour the children of the inhabitants of Argos. Eventually a young countryman called Coroebus slew Poene but another scourge was visited upon the Argives. Coroebus recognised this as an expression of divine will and went to Delphi, where he offered to make whatever amends Apollo might demand for his having slain Poene against the god's wishes. The oracle instructed him not to return to Argos, but to take a sacred tripod from the temple at Delphi and set out bearing it upon his back. When the tripod fell from his shoulders he was to stop, and found a city at that place; thus the site for the city of Megara was selected. His tomb was to be seen in the central square of this city.
2.   Coroebus was also the name of a Phrygian, the son of Mygdon (see MYGDON 1), who came to offer help to Priam, if the latter would agree to give him Cassandra's hand in return; but he was killed at the fall of Troy (see CASSANDRA).

Coronides (Κορωνίδες) The Coronides were two young sisters called Metioche and Menippe, the daughters of Orion. They were sacrificed as expiatory victims during a plague which had been visited upon their fatherland, Orchomenus in Boeotia. Their bodies were duly interred, but Hades and Persephone, the gods of the Underworld, took pity on them and transformed their dead bodies into shining stars, in the form of two celestial comets.

Coronis (Κορωνίς)
1.   The most celebrated of the heroines who bore this name was the daughter of Phlegyas, king of the Lapiths. She was loved by Apollo, who fathered her son Asclepius. According to a sacred tradition (vouched for by the Paean of Isyllus, which has been preserved for us by an inscription from Epidaurus), she was really called Aegla and had been given the surname Coronis (the Crow) because of her beauty. In this particular tradition, Phlegyas was not the Thessalian king who shared his name, but an inhabitant of Epidaurus who had married a Thessalian girl, Cleomene, the daughter of a certain Malus (who was perhaps a son of Amphictyon) and of the Muse Erato.
   The legend tells how Coronis was unfaithful to Apollo and married Ischys, son of Elatus; it was said that she was afraid the god would tire of her when she grew old, and would abandon her (see MARPESSA and ASCLEPIUS).
2.   Other legends touch on the association of the name Coronis with crows. In one, for example, another Coronis, daughter of Coronus, was changed into a crow by her protectress Athena to enable her to escape the attentions of Poseidon who was in love with her.
3.   Coronis was also the name of one of the Nymphs who were Dionysus' nurses. She was carried off by Butes, who was then stricken with madness by Dionysus as a punishment and committed suicide by throwing himself down a well (see BUTES 1).

Coronus (Κόρωνος) The son of Caeneus who reigned over the Lapiths in the days of Heracles. King Aegimius appealed to Heracles for help against Coronus and his people, and Heracles slew Coronus (see HERACLES). Coronus had taken part in the expedition of the Argonauts. His son was LEONTEUS.

Corythus (Κόρυθος)
1.   The son of Zeus and Electra, Atlas' daughter.

In one legend Iasion and Dardanus were his sons but according to others, Iasion and Dardanus were actually sons of Zeus and Electra (see Table 7). Corythus reigned over the Tyrrhenians of Italy, the ancestors of the Etruscans, and founded the city of Cortona in Italy. Both his sons emigrated from Cortona, one to Samothrace, the other to the Troad (see DARDANUS).

2. Corythus was also the name of a king of Tegea in Arcadia who rescued and reared TELEPHUS after his mother Auge exposed him on Mount Parthenion.

3. Corythus was also a son of Paris and a nymph of Ida named Oenone. When she learnt of her lover's infidelity Oenone sent her son to find the Greeks and guide them to the Troad. The legend also runs that this Corythus who was even more handsome than his father, was loved by Helen, and returned her love. This was why Paris killed him. (Table 34).

Cragaleus (Κραγαλεύς) The son of Dryops; a shepherd who had a reputation for great wisdom and complete impartiality. One day while he was guarding his flock, three divinities, Artemis, Apollo and Heracles, appeared before him and begged him to arbitrate in a dispute which had arisen among them. They wished to know which of the three of them should rule over the town of Ambracia. Cragaleus decided that the town should belong to Heracles: angered at this, Apollo then turned him into a rock on the very spot where he had announced his decision. Thereafter, the inhabitants of Ambracia offered a sacrifice to him on each of Heracles' feast-days.

Cranaus (Κραναός) One of the first kings of Attica, a 'son of the soil' who succeeded CECROPS. Cecrops' son Erysichthon died young without issue while Cecrops was still alive, and on the latter's death Cranaus came to power, since he was regarded as the most powerful of the city's inhabitants. During his reign the population called themselves Cranaeans and the town of Athens, Cranae. He was married to Pedias, the daughter of the Lacedaemonian Mynes; she bore him three daughters – Cranae, Cranaechme, and Atthis. When the latter died, unmarried, her name was given to the country: thus Cranae became Attica and was so known thereafter. Cranaus, who had given one of his daughters to Amphictyon, one of Deucalion's sons, was overthrown by his son-in-law, who seized power in his place. His tomb was to be seen in Athens.

Cranon (Κράνων) A son of Pelasgus, who gave his name to the town of Cranon, in Thessaly. This town was formerly known as Ephyra, but after Cranon died while trying to win the hand of HIPPODAMIA of Pisa and Elis, the townsfolk over whom he reigned changed the name of Ephyra to Cranon in his memory.

Crantor (Κράντωρ) A Dolopian whom Amyntor, the king of that country, had given to Peleus as a hostage after a defeat. He became Peleus' favourite squire and was at his side at the battle between the Lapiths and the Centaurs. He was killed by a tree hurled at the hero by the Centaurs; his death was avenged by Peleus.

Creon (Κρέων) Two heroes of this name appear in the legends.

1. The first was a king of Corinth, the son of Lycaethus. ALCMAEON entrusted him with the upbringing of his children, a boy and a girl, by Manto the daughter of Tiresias. Creon's most important appearance, however, is in the legend of Jason and Medea. After their expulsion from Iolcos Jason and Medea sought refuge at Creon's court in Corinth. They lived there peacefully for several years until the day Creon conceived the idea of marrying his daughter Glauce (or Creusa) to Jason. The latter accepted the proposal, and repudiated Medea. Medea vowed vengeance, and to that end prepared a special robe which she sent to her rival as a present. Glauce was unwise enough to accept the gift and when she donned the robe she was enveloped in mysterious flames which consumed her. Her father came to her rescue, but he too met the same fate. Some versions of the legend claim that in reality MEDEA set fire to the palace, thus burning father and daughter to death at the same time.

2. Creon the Theban was the son of Menoeceus (Table 29). After Laius the king of Thebes had died at the hands of his own son Oedipus, Creon succeeded him; but the town then fell victim to a scourge in the form of a Sphinx, who set the Thebans riddles and devoured them when they were unable to supply the answers. She devoured many people in this way including, finally, Creon's own son Haemon. The king then offered a reward to the man who could answer the Sphinx's riddle. Oedipus came forward, and gave the correct answer, at which the Sphinx threw herself from the top of the citadel in despair. The riddle went as follows: 'What has only one voice, and walks on four feet, and then on two, and then

on three?' Oedipus found the answer – it was Man, who begins his life on all fours, then walks on his two legs, and finishes up supporting himself on a stick. Bound by his promise, Creon then had to yield the throne to the winner, who had set Thebes free. He also gave him his own sister Jocasta in marriage; she was the widow of the previous king, and happened to be (unknown to anyone) the mother of Oedipus. Later, when Thebes was ravaged by a plague, Oedipus sent Creon to consult the oracle at Delphi. Once Oedipus' incest was revealed Creon replaced him on the throne; Oedipus entrusted his children to Creon's care, and went into exile.

During the war of the Seven Champions against Thebes (see ADRASTUS) Creon offered his own son Megareus as a sacrifice to Ares at the order of Tiresias, and thus saved the city. After the assailants had been defeated Creon decreed that POLYNICES, who had borne arms against his country, should remain unburied (see ETEOCLES); and when ANTIGONE scattered the ritual dust over her brother's body Creon condemned her to death. He had her shut up in the tomb of Labdacus where she committed suicide; and if Sophocles' version of the tale is to be believed, Creon's son Haemon to whom she was affianced killed himself upon her corpse. Creon's wife Eurydice hanged herself in despair. Creon's cruelty towards Antigone and his impiety are highlighted by another legend. After being banished from Thebes, Oedipus sought refuge in the town of Colonus in Attica; Creon, who had originally expelled him quite peremptorily, then tried to make him return to Thebes because the oracle at Delphi had declared that Thebes' prosperity would not be assured until Oedipus had returned there. When Oedipus refused, Creon tried to have him brought back by force, and Theseus had to intervene to prevent him from being seized.

Theseus was also credited with the decisive action which forced Creon to return to the Argives the bodies of their men who had died during the war of the Seven Champions. Some versions even go so far as to say that Theseus slew Creon during the expedition he mounted against Thebes to effect this recovery.

Two further episodes are ascribed to Creon's reign over Thebes: the legend of AMPHITRYON and the Twelve Labours of Heracles. It was in fact Creon who purified Amphitryon when the latter took refuge in Thebes; Creon also required that Amphitryon should slay the Teumessian fox before he could accompany Amphitryon on his expedition against the Teleboeans. Creon was also ruler of Thebes when Heracles, still a young man, rid the city of the tribute imposed by ERGINUS of Orchomenus. As a reward, Creon gave him the hand of his eldest daughter Megara, whilst Iphicles, Heracles' twin brother, was given Creon's youngest daughter in marriage.

Creontiades (Κρεοντιάδης) One of the sons of Heracles and Megara, the daughter of the Theban Creon. He was killed together with his brothers by his own father, who had gone mad. He is usually said to have had two brothers, Therimachus and Deicoon, but some authors list seven children of Heracles and Megara: Polydorus, Anicetus, Mecistophonus, Patrocleus, Toxoclitus, Menebrontes, and Chersibius (see also HERACLES).

Cres (Κρής) Cres, the hero who gave his name to the Cretans, was the son of Zeus and a Nymph of Mount Ida in Crete and was sometimes described as a Cretan 'son of the soil'. He reigned over the first inhabitants of the island, the 'Eteocretans' or 'True Cretans'. He is also said to have provided asylum in the range of Mount Ida to the child Zeus who was threatened with death by his father Cronus. He gave the Cretans a code of laws before the time of Minos, the great lawgiver. He is sometimes presented as the father of Talos, the bronze 'robot' who guarded Crete against all attempts to land (see ARGONAUTS and HEPHAESTUS).

Cresphontes (Κρεσφόντης) One of the Heraclids; he was a son of Aristomachus, and Temenus and Aristodemus were his brothers (Table 16). With them (or perhaps only with Temenus and the sons of Aristodemus, who died before the campaign) he conquered the peninsula of the Peloponnese, at the head of the Dorians. After the conquest the three brothers divided the country up among them. They had agreed to form three portions, for which they would draw lots: the first portion consisted of Argos, the second of Lacedaemonia and the third of Messenia. Each of the brothers had to put a pebble into an urn full of water, and the portions were to be allotted in the order in which each of the pebbles was drawn out. However, Cresphontes wanted Messenia, the richest of the portions, and he put a lump of earth into the water, which disintegrated at once. Thus the two other pebbles were drawn out first and Cresphontes became ruler of Messenia, while Temenus received Argos. Once the lots had been drawn each of the brothers built an altar to Zeus and on these altars each found a sign in keeping with the character of the people over whom he had been chosen to rule: on the altar of the ruler of Argos, a toad; on that of Lacedaemonia, a snake; and on that of Messenia, a fox.

Cresphontes divided the land of Messenia into five regions and entrusted each of them to a viceroy. He granted the indigenous population rights equal to those of the Dorians. He himself chose Stenyclarus as his capital; but the Dorians criticized this choice, and Cresphontes changed his system of government accordingly. He assigned Stenyclarus for occupation exclusively by the Dorians, but then the rich land-owners became discontented; they rose in rebellion and killed the king and two of his children. Cresphontes' wife was Merope, the daughter of Cypselus, and AEPYTUS was his surviving son.

Cretheus (Κρηθεύς) A son of Aeolus and Aenarete (Table 8). His marriage to his niece Tyro, the daughter of Salmoneus, produced three sons: Aeson, Pheres, and Amythaon (Table 21). He adopted Neleus and Pelias, Tyro's two children, fathered by Poseidon before her marriage. He is said to have sired other children: Talaus, father of Adrastus (more commonly said to have been the son of Bias); a daughter, Hippolyta, surnamed Cretheis, who married ACASTUS; and another daughter, Myrina, wife of Thoas the king of Lemnos. Cretheus founded Iolcos, the city of Jason and Pelias.

Creusa (Κρέουσα)
1.   The first heroine of this name was a Thessalonian Naiad, daughter of Mother Earth. She was loved by the River Peneus, who fathered two children, Hypseus, king of the Lapiths, and Stilbe. Andreus is sometimes cited as a child of hers (Table 23).
2.   Another Creusa was the daughter of Erectheus and Praxithea (Table 11). Because of her youth, she escaped the fate of her sisters, who offered themselves voluntarily as expiatory victims for the good of their country at the time of the war against Eumolpus. Grown to maidenhood, she was raped by Apollo in a grotto on the Acropolis at Athens and had a son, Ion. She exposed the child in an open basket at the very spot where she had been surprised by the god. Ion was later carried off to Delphi by Hermes, and brought up in the temple. Creusa married Xuthus. For a long time she was childless, but after a pilgrimage to Delphi where she met her son again,

she presented her husband with Diomedes and Achaeus (Tables 11 and 8).
3.   The daughter of Creon the king of Corinth, who was sometimes called Glauce, was also known as Creusa.
4.   Lastly, Creusa was the name of Aeneas' wife who was the daughter of Priam and Hecuba. Like the traditions about Aeneas, those surrounding Creusa are extremely varied. In the great historical paintings in the Lesche at Delphi, Polygnotus showed her among the Trojan captive women, but she is more frequently considered to have succeeded in escaping when Troy fell. In Virgil's version, Creusa was carried away by Aphrodite (or by Cybele) while Aeneas left the city with Anchises and Ascanius. In his search for her, her husband came back into the city for the express purpose of rescuing her; but her shade appeared to him and foretold his travels in search of a new country. The oldest epics call Aeneas' wife Eurydice instead of Creusa.

Crimisus (Κριμισός) A Sicilian river-god who approached AEGESTA or Segesta, a Trojan woman, in the shape of a bear (or a dog) and fathered Acestes, the founder of the town of Segesta. Virgil and Hyginus refer to him as Crinisus.

Crinis (Κρῖνις) The founder of the temple of Apollo Smintheus at Chrysa in Mysia. Crinis had justly incurred the wrath of Apollo, who then brought down a curse upon his household fields, which were devastated by mice. The god came down one day to Chrysa where he was hospitably welcomed by Ordes, who was Crinis' head shepherd. This appeased Apollo's wrath and to rid the land of his curse, he himself slew the mice with his arrows. He then instructed Ordes to go and find Crinis to tell him to consecrate a shrine in the name of Apollo of the Mice (Apollo Smintheus).

Crisamis (Κρίσαμις) A king of Cos who owned enormous herds. One day a monstrous eel emerged from the sea and stole the most beautiful of all his sheep; Crisamis pursued the eel and killed it. He was then visited by a dream, in which he was instructed to bury the eel, but Crisamis failed to heed this warning and he perished.

Crisus (Κρῖσος) The founder of the city of Crisa on the southern slopes of Mount Parnassus. He was a descendant of Aeacus through his father Phocus. His mother was called Asteria; she was the daughter of Deioneus or Deion, and through her Crisus was connected to the race of Deucalion (Tables 8 and 30). Crisus had a twin brother, PANOPEUS, with whom he was at enmity, since even as infants the two had quarrelled at their mother's breast. However, another tradition maintains that Crisus and Panopeus sprang from different stock: while the latter was the son of Phocus, the former was the son of Tyrranus and Asterodia. Crisus married Antiphatia, daughter of Naubolus, and they had a son, Strophius. Strophius married Anaxibia, Agamemnon's sister, and fathered Pylades, the friend and cousin of Orestes (Table 2).

Critheis (Κριθηίς) A Nymph of Asia Minor who married the River Meles (which runs near Smyrna), and was said to have been the mother of the poet Homer.

Another legend identifies her as the daughter of Apelles, an inhabitant of Cyme. On his death-bed, Apelles entrusted the young girl to his brother Maeon, but Critheis escaped from her uncle's guardianship and gave herself to Phemius, who lived at Smyrna. One day, as she was washing her linen in the River Meles, she gave birth to a son who became the poet Homer. The purpose of this legend was to explain the epithet applied to Homer of Melesigenes, which means 'born of the Meles'.

Lastly, a third version makes Critheis a young maiden of Ios who was loved by a minor spirit in the retinue of the Muses. Captured by pirates, Critheis was taken to Smyrna where Maeon the king of Lydia is said to have married her. She brought the baby Homer into the world on the banks of the Meles, and died immediately after the child was born.

Crocon (Κρόκων) According to a local tradition, Crocon was an early king of the region of Eleusis. His palace lay on the boundary between the two territories of Athens and Eleusis. He was the son of Triptolemus and the brother of Coeron. He was married to Saisara, the daughter of Celeus. Crocon and Coeron were the ancestors of the priestly families, the Croconides and the Coeronides, who played a part in the cult of Demeter. The Croconides had precedence. One of Crocon's daughters, Meganira, married ARCAS.

Crocus (Κρόκος) A young man who was changed into a saffron plant after an unhappy love affair with the Nymph Smilax. Smilax, however,

became the plant of the same name (*Smilax aspera*, the European sarsaparilla).

Cronus (Κρόνος) In the family of the Titans, Cronus was the youngest son of Uranus (Heaven) and Gaia (Mother Earth) (Table 5). As a result, he was a member of the first divine generation, before Zeus and the Olympians. He alone of all his brothers helped his mother wreak vengeance on his father (see URANUS), and castrated Uranus with the flint sickle his mother had given him. Then he took his father's place in Heaven, and lost no time in sending his brothers the Hecatoncheires (the Hundred-handed Giants) and the Cyclops back to Tartarus. Uranus had imprisoned his rebellious sons in Tartarus some time before, and Cronus had freed them in response to the entreaties of their common mother, Gaia. As soon as he became ruler of the world Cronus married his own sister Rhea; and since Uranus and Gaia, the fountainheads of wisdom and knowledge of the future, had foretold that he would be dethroned by one of his own children, he devoured them all in turn as soon as they were born: Hestia, Demeter, Hera, Pluto (Hades), and Poseidon. Enraged at seeing herself thus deprived of all her children, Rhea fled to Crete when she was pregnant with Zeus and there she was delivered of him secretly, in the cave of Dicte. Then she wrapped a stone in swaddling-clothes and gave it to Cronus to devour, which he did without noticing the trick that had been played on him. When he was grown up, Zeus – aided by Metis, one of the daughters of Oceanus, or by Gaia herself – gave Cronus a drug which made him vomit up all the children he had devoured. Led by their youngest brother Zeus, these children then declared war on Cronus, whose allies were his brothers the Titans. The war lasted ten years, but at last Mother Earth promised victory to Zeus if he took those whom Cronus had confined in Tartarus as allies. Zeus set them free and gained the victory. Cronus and the Titans were then confined in Tartarus in place of the Hecatoncheires, who became their warders.

Apart from his children by Rhea, Cronus had become the father by Philyra of the Centaur CHIRON, an immortal being of double nature, half-man, half-horse; (when he coupled with Philyra Cronus had in fact assumed the shape of a horse). Other legends also identify him as the father of Hephaestus by Hera. Yet other legends claim Aphrodite as his daughter, rather than as the daughter of Uranus (Table 38).

In the Orphic religious tradition Cronus

appeared freed from his chains, reconciled with Zeus, and living in the Islands of the Blessed. This reconciliation between Zeus and Cronus (who was considered as a good king, the first to reign over both Heaven and Earth) led to the legends of the GOLDEN AGE. He was said in Greece to have reigned on Olympus in those far-off days. In Italy, where Cronus was identified with Saturn at an early date, his throne was said to have been located on the Capitol. He was also said to have reigned in Africa, in Sicily, and in the whole of the western Mediterranean in general. Later, when mankind had become wicked with the discovery of bronze, and even more so with that of iron, Cronus was relegated to Heaven. By a play on words, Cronus is sometimes considered as Time personified. (Κρόνος does in fact sound like Χρόνος, Time).

A Syrian legend related by Philon of Byblos tells how Cronus, son of Uranus, mutilated his father on the advice of Hermes Trismegistus with the help of his brothers, who were called Betylus, Dagon, and Atlas. This is a later Hellenization of very old Syro-Hittite beliefs.

Croton (Κρότων) The mythical hero credited with the foundation of the city of Crotona in Southern Italy. When HERACLES returned from his quest for Geryon's cattle, Croton welcomed him at the site of the future city, and Heracles became his guest; but Lacinius, a neighbour of Croton's, tried to steal the cattle. Heracles killed him, but also accidentally killed Croton during the fight. In expiation, Heracles built him a huge tomb and prophesied that in time to come, a famous city would rise which would bear the name of Crotona. Croton is sometimes claimed to be the brother of Alcinous, king of the PHAEACIANS. This legend is connected with that of LACINIUS.

Crotopus (Κρότωπος) A son of Agenor, king of Argos. He had two children, Sthenelas and Psamathe (Table 17). Psamathe was loved by Apollo, and he fathered her child, LINUS, whom she exposed at birth. Linus had been rescued by some shepherds, but was later devoured by their dogs. Psamathe could not hide her grief from her father, and told him the whole story. Crotopus was highly displeased; he refused to believe her when she said Apollo was Linus' father, and had her put to death. Apollo was angered by the deaths of both his son and his mistress, and called down a famine upon the Argives. The Argives consulted the oracle, which instructed them to dedicate a cult to Psamathe and Linus. In addition,

Crotopus was exiled, and went to the region of Megaris, where he founded a city. Ovid relates that on Crotopus' death Apollo despatched him to Tartarus, to be with the major criminals (see also COROEBUS).

Crotus (Κρότος) The son of Pan and Eupheme, the nurse of the Muses; he was thus the foster-brother of the Muses, with whom he dwelt on Mount Helicon. He hunted and lived on friendly terms with his foster-sisters: to express his admiration for them, he invented applause. At the instigation of the Muses, Zeus turned him into a constellation in the sky.

Cteatus (Κτέατος) Cteatus and his brother Eurytus were the sons of Actor and Molione; they were known as the MOLIONIDAE. They were slain by HERACLES.

Ctimene (Κτιμένη) Ctimene and her brother Ulysses were the children of Anticleia and Laertes (Table 39). She was brought up with the swineherd Eumaeus. She married Eurylochus, a boon companion of ODYSSEUS, who figured prominently in the episodes of Circe and the oxen of the Sun, and met his death during the journey back to Ithaca.

Curetes (Κούρητες) The legends mention a people of this name who in very ancient times occupied Aetolia; but they also relate how the Curetes were driven from their country by AETOLUS, who came from the Peloponnese (see MELEAGER).

More commonly, the name of Curetes was applied to spirits in Zeus' entourage during his childhood in Crete. There is wide variation in the traditions concerning their origin: sometimes, although infrequently, they were identified with the Curetes of Aetolia but they were more often considered to be the sons of Combe and Socus. According to this latter version, they originated in Euboea and were seven in number: Prymneus, Mimas, Acmon, Damneus, Ocythous, Idaeus, and Melisseus. Driven out from Euboea by their father, together with their mother, they wandered all over the Greek world. After travelling through Crete and the region of Cnossus, they came to Phrygia, where they brought up Dionysus. From Phrygia they went to Attica, where King Cecrops helped them to take their revenge on Socus and return to their own country. Their mother COMBE was also called Chalcis, because she was believed to have introduced the use of bronze weapons (from χαλκός, bronze); and her sons the Curetes used to dance and clash their weapons together, smiting their shields with their spears.

Apart from this Chalcidian tradition, it is said that the Curetes were sons of Mother Earth; or, variously, sons of Zeus and Hera, of Apollo and the Nymph Danais, and so on. Their number also varies according to the different authors, and is sometimes said to be two, or nine, or is unspecified. The most celebrated legend in which they played a part is that of Zeus's childhood. When Rhea gave birth to the baby Zeus in a cave on Mount Ida in Crete, she entrusted him to the Nymph Amalthea; but in order that his crying should not reveal his existence to Cronus, who would at once have devoured him, she asked the Curetes to dance their noisy war-dances around him, which they did, thus allowing the god to grow to manhood.

Certain legends even more obscure maintain that the Curetes had the gift of prophecy, and also that they showed MINOS how he could bring his son Glaucus back to life. At Hera's insistence, they spirited away EPAPHUS, Io's son; and this so angered Zeus, Epaphus' father, that he slew the Curetes with a thunderbolt.

Curtius Marcus Curtius was the hero of a topographical legend about the Roman Forum. During the early days of the Republic, the ground opened in the middle of the Forum, creating an enormous chasm; the Romans tried to fill the gulf by pouring earth into it, but their efforts were in vain. They were forced to consult an oracle, which informed them that the only way for the Romans to close the gulf was for them to throw the most prized of their possessions into it. A young man, Marcus Curtius, realizing that Rome's most prized possessions were its youth and its soldiery, decided to sacrifice himself for the salvation of all: clad in his armour, and mounted on his horse, he dedicated himself to the Infernal Gods, and then, before the assembled populace, he rode his horse into the abyss. It closed above him, leaving only a little lake, to which the name Lake Curtius was given, and round its shores a fig-tree, an olive-tree and a vine sprang up. Under the Empire, it was customary to throw coins into the lake as an offering to Curtius, the genius of the place.

According to another tradition, Curtius was a Sabine who, during the war between Tatius and Romulus, was almost swallowed up in the marshes near the Comitium and had to abandon his horse. This episode gave Lake Curtius its name. On the subject of the role played by water in this phase of the struggle between the Sabines and the Romans, see JANUS.

Cyane (Κυανή.)

1. Cyane, whose name evokes the blue colour of the waters of the sea, was the daughter of Liparus, a very ancient king of the Ausonians (ancestors of the Italians). Liparus was driven from Italy or Ausonia, as it was then, and established himself in the islands to which he gave his name. When Aeolus visited Liparus' kingdom, the latter gave him Cyane's hand in marriage, and shared the throne with him (see AEOLUS 2).

2. Another Cyane was a water-nymph of Syracuse, who tried to prevent the abduction of Persephone by Hades. In his anger, Hades transformed her into a pool of a deep blue colour, like that of the sea.

3. Another legend, again Syracusan, tells of a young girl named Cyane, who was raped by her father while he was drunk. This took place in the dark of night, and the father, whose name was Cyanippus, hoped that he had not been recognized by Cyane; but she had pulled a ring off his finger during the assault and, when day broke, she realized who had been involved. A plague broke out in the city, and the oracle declared that it would only be brought to an end by the sacrifice of a human victim – one who had committed incest. Cyane and her father then killed themselves, in expiation of their crime.

Cyanippus (Κυάνιππος)

1. A son of Aegialeus, and hence a grandson of Adrastus, who ruled over Argos (at that time divided into three parts). According to another tradition, he was the son of Adrastus (Table 1). During his childhood, he was brought up by Diomedes and Euryalus. He took part in the Trojan war, and was one of the heroes inside the wooden horse. He died without issue.

2. Another Cyanippus was a Thessalian, the son of Pharax, who had made a love-match with the daughter of a Thessalian nobleman, a very beautiful girl called Leucone. Cyanippus was a great hunter, and he refused to give up his passion for it after his marriage: he would go out in the morning and come back in the evening so tired that he usually went straight to bed and fell asleep as soon as his head touched the pillow, and as this went on, poor Leucone felt more neglected, and became increasingly bored. One day she decided to follow

her husband secretly when he went out to hunt, hoping to discover what he found so attractive in the woods. She slipped out of the house unbeknown to the servants and before long found herself deep in a thicket, where her husband's hounds discovered her; the half-wild pack fell upon her and tore her to pieces. When he discovered her body Cyanippus was driven to despair. He built a funeral-pyre and laid his wife upon it; then he slew his hounds and threw them on to the pyre and, finally, he slew himself. (See CYANE 3.)

Cybele (Κυβέλη) The principal goddess of Phrygia, often called 'the Mother of the Gods', or 'the Great Mother': she governed the whole of Nature and was, in fact, the personification of Nature's powers of growth. She was worshipped in the mountains of Asia Minor, and from there her cult spread over the whole of the Greek world, and, later, into the Roman world as well, when in 204 BC the Senate of Rome decided to have the 'Black Stone' which symbolized the goddess brought from Pessinus, and to build a temple to her on the Palatine Hill.

Cybele was often regarded by the Greek mythographers as merely an incarnation of or another name for RHEA, the mother of Zeus and the other gods by Cronus. The Rhea worshipped on Mount Cybele in Phrygia was said to be Cybele. She figures little in the myths that have come down to us. The only one worth mentioning is the story of AGDISTIS and ATTIS, and she played only a minor role in that. Attis appeared sometimes as her lover but more often as her companion. It is also possible that her personality was concealed behind that of the hermaphrodite Agdistis, whom all the traditions concur in portraying as the lover of Attis after his emasculation.

Cybele's major importance lay in the orgiastic cult which grew up around her and which survived to a fairly late period under the Roman Empire. She was generally portrayed wearing a crown of towers and accompanied by lions, or riding in a chariot drawn by these animals. Like Rhea, she had as her servants the CURETES, also known as the CORYBANTES.

The goddess Cybele, the personification of Nature's powers of growth, is depicted seated on her throne flanked by lions. Late 2nd century Roman lamp.

Cychreus (Κυχρεύς) The son of Poseidon and Salamis, the daughter of Asopus. Cychreus killed a serpent that was ravaging the island of Salamis, and the islanders made him their king in gratitude. It was also said (and this was the version followed by Hesiod, in a fragment which has come down to us through Strabo) that this monstrous serpent had been raised by Cychreus himself, until it was expelled by Eurylochus: the creature then fled to Eleusis, where Demeter welcomed it as one of her attendants. On the island of Salamis, a cult grew up around Cychreus, as one of its guardian heroes. During the naval battle of Salamis, a serpent appeared among the ships: the oracle at Delphi revealed that this was the incarnation of Cychreus, who had come to aid the Greeks and foretell their victory.

Cychreus had a daughter, Chariclo, who was the mother of Endeis and the mother-in-law of Aeacus. Cychreus died without male issue, and left his kingdom to his great-grandson Telamon, Aeacus's son (Table 30). According to another tradition, Cychreus's daughter was called Glauce; she married Actaeus, and bore his son Telamon – who was thus not only Cychreus's great-grandson in one account, but also his grandson in another.

Cyclopes (Κύκλωπες) Ancient mythographers recognized three different kinds of Cyclopes: the

Uranian Cyclopes, sons of Uranus and Gaia (Heaven and Mother Earth), the Sicilian Cyclopes, companions of Polyphemus, who appear in the *Odyssey*, and the 'master-mason' Cyclopes.

The Uranian Cyclopes belonged to the first divine generation, that of the Giants. They each had only one eye in the middle of the forehead and they were distinguished by their strength and manual dexterity. They were three in number, and were called Brontes, Steropes (or Asteropes), and Arges, names which corresponded to Thunder, Lightning, and Thunderbolt respectively. They were first imprisoned by Uranus and then released by Cronus, but only to be confined once more by him in Tartarus, until Zeus finally released them, warned by an oracle that he could achieve victory only with their aid. In return they provided Zeus with thunder, lightning and thunderbolts; to Hades, they gave a helmet which made him invisible, and to Poseidon, they gave a trident. Thus armed, the Olympian gods defeated the Titans and threw them into Tartarus.

In the legend the Cyclopes continued forging the divine thunderbolts, and thus incurred the wrath of APOLLO, whose son ASCLEPIUS had been slain by Zeus with a thunderbolt for having brought the dead back to life. Unable to revenge himself on Zeus, Apollo slew the Cyclopes (or their sons, according to an obscure tradition), and as a punishment for this he was sentenced to work for ADMETUS as a slave. In this version, accordingly, the Cyclopes appear as mortal beings and not as gods.

In Alexandrine poetry, the Cyclopes are considered merely as subordinate spirits; smiths and craftsmen who made every type of weapon for the gods. Under the direction of Hephaestus, the smith-god, for example, they fashioned the bows and arrows used by Apollo and his sister Artemis. They lived in the Aeolian Islands, or perhaps in Sicily, where they owned an underground forge and made a cacophonous noise as they worked: their panting breath and the constant clanging of their anvils could be heard reverberating deep in the volcanoes of Sicily. The fire of their forge reddened the evening sky at the top of Mount Aetna. These legends linking the Cyclopes to the volcanoes also tend to confuse the Cyclopes with the Giants imprisoned under the mountain masses, whose convulsive struggles sometimes shook the land above.

By the time of the *Odyssey*, the Cyclopes had come to be regarded as a race of gigantic, savage beings, with one single eye and tremendous strength, who lived on the coast of Italy (in the Phlegraean Fields near Naples). They were devoted sheep-breeders and their sole resources consisted of their flocks; they were cannibals by choice, and were strangers to the practice of drinking wine, and indeed to viticulture itself. They lived in caves, and had not learnt how to build cities. In some of their characteristics these Cyclopes tended to resemble the Satyrs, with whom they were sometimes classed (see POLYPHEMUS).

Cyclopes who supposedly came from Lycia were credited with the construction of all the prehistoric monuments to be seen in Greece, Sicily, and elsewhere, made of huge blocks of stone of weight and size which seemed beyond the capacity of mere human strength. The Cyclopes in this account were not the sons of Uranus, but a whole new race, one which had put itself at the service of such legendary heroes as Proteus, for example, in the fortification of Tiryns, and Perseus, in the fortification of Argos, and so on. They were given the curious epithet of 'Gasterocheires', which means, literally, 'those who have hands growing from their stomachs' – a name recalling that of the HECATONCHEIRES, or the hundred-handed giants, who were the brothers of the three Uranian Cyclopes in Hesiodic mythology.

Cycnus (Κύκνος) Many different heroes bore the name Cycnus, which means 'swan':
1. The earliest seems to have been a son of Poseidon and Calyce. His legend belongs to the Trojan cycle, but it only appears in poems written after Homer's day. Cycnus was said to have taken part in the games given before the Trojan War in honour of PARIS, who at that time was believed to have died. As an ally of the Trojans, he came to their aid with a fleet of ships when the Greeks landed; he held the invaders up for a long time, until he encountered Achilles. Cycnus had the gift of invulnerability because of his divine origin, and to overcome him, Achilles had to strike him in the face with the pommel of his sword, and drive him backwards with blows from his shield, until Cycnus stumbled over a stone as he retreated and fell. Achilles then suffocated him as he lay on the ground; but through his father's intercession, Cycnus was transformed into a swan.
2. Another Cycnus was also the son of Poseidon. He ruled over a city called Colonae, which lay at some distance from Troy, opposite the island then called Leucophrys and later known

as Tenedos. His mother Scamandrodice had exposed him at birth on the sea-shore, and a swan had taken care of him. Later, he married Proclea, one of Laomedon's daughters, and fathered two children by her: a boy, TENES, and a girl, Hemithea. Proclea died, and Cycnus then married Philonome, the daughter of Tragasus. Philonome fell in love with her stepson Tenes, but when he failed to respond to her advances she accused him falsely to Cycnus. Believing Tenes to be guilty, Cycnus locked him and his sister Hemithea into a chest and cast them adrift on the sea. Tenes and Hemithea were washed ashore, safe and sound, on the island of Leucophrys, which thereafter was known as Tenedos. Philonome's accusation had been supported before Cycnus by a flute-player named Eumolpus, who had borne false witness against the youth. In due course Cycnus realized he had been deceived; he had Eumolpus stoned to death and Philonome buried alive and then he hastened to Tenedos to make his peace with his son, but the latter refused him welcome, and with a single blow of an axe severed the cable anchoring his father's ship to the shore. Thereafter, all flute-players were banished from Tenedos.

Different versions recorded by Tzetzes maintain that Cycnus settled in Tenedos after a reconciliation with his son; and Cycnus is said to have been killed in Tenedos by Achilles. This Cycnus, the father of Tenes, seemed not always to have been clearly distinguished from the hero of the earlier version, and doubtless this is the explanation for this later variant.

3.   The most celebrated hero to bear the name of Cycnus was the son of Ares and Pelopia, daughter of Pelias. He is represented as being a violent and bloodthirsty man, a brigand who used to waylay travellers and kill them and then offer sacrifices to his father from the ransom he took from them. He preyed in particular upon pilgrims on their way to Delphi; this earned him the hatred of Apollo, who incited the hero Heracles against him. Cycnus and Heracles met in single combat and Cycnus was very soon despatched; but then his father came forward to avenge his death. However, Athena deflected Ares's javelin and Heracles wounded the god in the thigh, forcing him to flee to Olympus. So runs the Hesiodic version.

This fight was generally considered to have taken place at Pagasae in Thessaly, but Apollodorus places it in Macedonia, on the banks of the river Echedorus. According to him Cycnus was the son of Ares and Pyrene; as in the other version, Cycnus was slain, but Apollodorus claims that when Ares intervened, Zeus parted the combatants with a thunderbolt. Apollodorus wrote of yet another Cycnus, this time the son of Ares and Pelopia, who was killed at Itonus, but there is no mention of divine intervention in the fight.

A version given by Stesichorus and Pindar combines the two preceding ones, and states that when Heracles found himself opposed by both Cycnus and Ares during the first engagement, he withdrew. Later, he met Cycnus alone, and slew him. No mention is made of the wound inflicted by Heracles on the god in this account.

4.   Another hero of the same name was a king of Liguria, and a friend of PHAETHON, whom Zeus was compelled to slay with a thunderbolt. Cycnus mourned Phaethon's death so bitterly that he was transformed into a swan. Apollo had given this Cycnus a beautiful voice, and from this account springs the supposition that swans sing songs when on the point of death.

5.   Finally, another swan legend deals with a Cycnus who was the son of Apollo and Thyria, the daughter of Amphinomus. This Cycnus lived in Aetolia, between Pleuron and Calydon. He was very handsome, but harsh and capricious – so much so that one after the other all his friends and lovers grew disheartened. Of all those who paid court to him, only one remained in the end, whose name was PHYLIUS. Cycnus then imposed a series of tasks on him, each more difficult and dangerous than the last. With Heracles's help, he completed them all, after which, his patience exhausted, he abandoned Cycnus. Cycnus, dishonoured and completely alone, threw himself into a lake, followed by his mother. Out of pity, Apollo transformed them both into swans.

Cydnus (Κύδνος) Cydnus was the son of the Nymph Anchiale, and through her, the grandson of Iapetus; he gave his name to the river in Cilicia. One of his sons, called Parthenius, gave the surname Parthenia to the city of Tarsus which lay on the River Cydnus. There was a popular legend in Cilicia, so we are told, which deals with the love-story of Cydnus, half-man half-river in form, and Comaetho: Comaetho fell in love with the river, and ended up by marrying Cydnus.

Cydon (Κύδων) Cydon was the son of Hermes and ACACALLIS. He was reputed to be the founder of the Cretan city of Cydonia. The inhabitants of Tegea in Arcadia believed that in actual fact he was one of the sons of their hero Tegeates; but there were also those who said that Apollo and not Hermes was his father, though his mother was the same Acacallis.

Cylabras (Κυλάβρας) Cylabras was a shepherd of Lycia from whom LACIUS, one of the founders of the town of Phaselis, bought the land on which the town was built, paying for it in salted fish. The inhabitants of Phaselis built a sanctuary to Cylabras, where they offered up salted fish in his honour.

Cyllarus (Κύλλαρος) Cyllarus was a young Centaur of surpassing beauty, who was loved by the she-Centaur Hylonome. He was killed during the brawl which marred the wedding-feast of Pirithous; and not wishing to live without him, Hylonome took her own life.

Cyllene (Κυλλήνη) Cyllene was an Arcadian Nymph, who according to some accounts was the wife of Lycaon, and according to others, his mother. In the latter version, she was married to Pelasgus, the eponym of the people of Pelasgia; she gave her name to Mount Cyllene, where Hermes is said to have been born. Sometimes, indeed, she is said to have brought Hermes up during his infancy.

Cynortas (Κυνόρτας) Cynortas was a Laconian hero, the son of Amyclas, who was himself the son of Lacedaemon, and founder of the town of Amyclae. Cynortas was the elder brother of HYACINTHUS (Table 6). On the death of Amyclas his eldest son Argalus succeeded to the throne of Sparta, but Argalus died childless and was succeeded by Cynortas. Cynortas had a son; according to the legends, he was called Perieres, or perhaps Oebalus, though Perieres was generally considered to have been the son of Aeolus (Table 28). One version omits this generation completely, and makes Tyndareus the son of Cynortas.

Cynosura (Κυνόσουρα) Cynosura was a Nymph on Mount Ida in Crete, and in some legends she and the Nymph Helice were said to have brought up the infant Zeus (see AMALTHEA). When Cronus was in pursuit of them both, Zeus turned them into two constellations, the Great Bear and the Little Bear, while he himself took the form of the Dragon constellation. Cynosura gave her name to a place in Crete, near the town of Histoi.

Cyparissa (Κυπάρισσα) Cyparissa, whose name is simply a feminine version of 'cypress', is said in a somewhat obscure legend to have been the daughter of a 'king of the Celts', named Boreas (thus having the same name as the North Wind), who came from Thrace. This Boreas lost his daughter, who died young, and mourned her very deeply. He built a tomb for her, on which he planted a cypress, a species unknown at that time; in this way, the cypress came to be regarded as a tree sacred to the dead, and it took its name from that of the young girl.

Cyparissi (Κυπάρισσοι) The Cyparissi, or, the Cypresses, are said to have been the daughters of Eteocles, the king of Orchomenus in Boeotia. During a festival in honour of Demeter and Cora they fell into a spring as they were dancing, and drowned; but Mother Earth took pity on them and transformed them into cypresses.

Cyparissus (Κυπάρισσος) The legends tell of two heroes of this name, one of them a Boeotian, the other an inhabitant of the island of Ceos:
1. The son of Minyas and the brother of Orchomenus (Table 20). The town of Cyparissus on Mount Parnassus, between Daulis and Delphi, owed its name to him.
2. A son of Telephus who lived on Ceos, and was loved by Apollo (and according to some accounts, by the god Zephyrus, and possibly by the Roman god Silvanus) on account of his great beauty. His favourite companion was a sacred stag which he had tamed, but one summer's day, as the stag was sleeping, stretched out in the shade, Cyparissus inadvertently killed it with his javelin. Racked by his grief, the young man would have welcomed death. He besought heaven to let his tears flow for all eternity. The gods turned him into a cypress, the tree of sadness.

Cypselus (Κύψελος)
1. The first hero of this name was the son of Aepytus, king of Arcadia. He himself was ruler of this country when the HERACLIDS attacked Peloponnesus for the second time. Cypselus appeased them by giving his daughter Merope to one of their number, Cresphontes, and he was thus able to retain his throne. Later he brought up the son of Cresphontes and Merope, who was called AEPYTUS after his great-grandfather, and allowed him to avenge his father's death. Cypselus lived in the city of Basilis, in the land of the Parrhesians, which he himself had founded; he had raised a

temple and an altar there to Demeter of Eleusis. During this goddess's annual festival, a beauty contest was held among the women of the country; and Herodice, Cypselus's own wife, carried off first prize.

2. Another Cypselus was a Corinthian, the son of Eetion and the father of Periander, one of the Seven Sages; and on the basis of this, he can be considered as a historical rather than a mythical personage, although several elements of his story seem inspired by folklore. Among the votive offerings in the sanctuary at Olympia was a cedar chest, which Cypselus had offered: this was the chest which his mother had hidden him in at birth to conceal him from the Bacchiadae (whom he was later to oust from the throne of Corinth, which they had occupied for the past five generations). As the Corinthian for a chest at that time was 'cypsela', the infant was named accordingly, in commemoration of the episode. This chest, described at some length by Pausanias, who had seen it, carried archaic inscriptions and pictures of mythical scenes.

Cyrene (Κυρήνη) Cyrene was a Thessalian Nymph; she was the daughter of Hypseus, the king of the Lapiths, whose parents were the Naiad Creusa (the daughter of Oceanus and Gaia) and the river-god Peneus (Table 23). Cyrene led a primitive life in the forests under Mount Pindus, and protected her father's flocks against attacks by wild beasts. One day, unarmed, she attacked a lion and overcame it after a hard struggle. Apollo chanced to see her as she was performing this feat, and fell in love with her. He immediately went to look for the Centaur Chiron in his cave, to show him the young maiden and find out from him who she was. Then he lifted her into his golden chariot and took her across the sea to the land of Libya, where he bedded her in a golden palace, and gave her part of the country as her domain: the land of Cyrene. From her union with Apollo she had a son, ARISTAEUS, who was brought up by the Horae and Mother Earth.

According to this version, left to us by Pindar, the legend goes back to a lost poem by Hesiod. In Hellenistic days it was said that after Cyrene's arrival in Libya, where she had been brought by Apollo, she was given the kingdom of Cyrene by Eurypylus, the king of Libya and son of Poseidon. A lion was ravaging the country and Eurypylus promised part of his kingdom to whoever should succeed in slaying it: Cyrene managed to vanquish the savage beast, and this was how she was able to

found her city of Cyrene. In this version of the legend, Cyrene had two children – Aristaeus and Antouchus.

There are many variations of the legend of Cyrene. Sometimes, instead of having come straight from Thessaly, she is said to have stayed in Crete. Other traditions maintain that Apollo coupled with her in the shape of a wolf (there was a cult of Lycian Apollo in Cyrene). When Virgil, in the *Georgics*, told the story of Aristaeus, he described Cyrene as a water-nymph who lived beneath the River Peneus, in the subterranean grotto in which the various tributary streams came together before beginning their flow above the surface; in this way Virgil diminished the characterization of Cyrene as a huntress, and instead stressed her lineage, since she was the granddaughter of a river-god. He made no mention of her arrival in Libya.

Cytissorus (Κυτίσσωρος) Cytissorus was the son fathered by Phrixus after his arrival in Colchis, on one of King Aeetes's daughters, who was sometimes said to have been Chalciope and sometimes Iophassa (Table 33). Through his father, Cytissorus was ATHAMAS' grandson. He had three brothers, Argos, Melas and Presbon and a sister, Phrontis. When he grew up, he went to his grandfather Athamas to receive his inheritance. He reached Alos in Thessaly at the very moment when Athamas' subjects were preparing to sacrifice him to propitiate Zeus. Cytissorus saved him and re-established him on his throne. This earned both him and his descendants Zeus's wrath. In each generation, the eldest son had to avoid the Prytaneum; for if he were found within the council hall, he would have been sacrificed.

Cyzicus (Κύζικος) Cyzicus was a hero of the Propontis, on the Asiatic coast. He played a part in the legend of the ARGONAUTS, who made one of their first landings in his country. Cyzicus is said to have come from northern Greece. He was the son of Aeneas, who was himself the son of Stilbe (Table 23), and of Aenete, a daughter of Eusorus, the king of Thrace. Eusorus had a son called Acamas who commanded the Thracian contingent fighting under the orders of the Trojans against the Greeks. Cyzicus reigned over the Doliones, who traced their origins back to Poseidon. When he first appears in the legend, on the arrival of the Argonauts, he had just married Clite, daughter of the soothsayer Merops. Cyzicus welcomed the sailors warmly, gave them a banquet, and replenished their supplies, but after the Argonauts had set sail a storm came up at night and forced them back to shore; unwittingly, they landed on the coast they had just left. The Doliones thought they were being attacked by pirates, and launched a strong assault against the Argonauts. Cyzicus came to the aid of his men and was slain by Jason.

On the next morning, everyone discovered the mistake. The Argonauts mourned for three days over the king's corpse and then gave him a big funeral in the Grecian style and held funeral games. CLITE was completely overcome by despair, and hanged herself. The city over which Cyzicus had reigned then took his name.

D

Dactyls (Δάκτυλοι) The Dactyls of Mount Ida were Daemons, Cretan or Phrygian in origin, who formed part of Rhea's retinue, or possibly Cybele's. Their name means 'the fingers'. They were so called either on account of their skill at working with their hands - and especially working with metals – or from aetiological tradition. It was said by some that when their mother (Rhea, or perhaps one of the Nymphs of Mount Ida) was giving birth to them she pressed her clenched fingers into the soil to ease her pain, and from the marks so produced the infants took their name. Others say that they sprang from the dust that Zeus' nurses scattered behind them through their fingers.

They were related to the Curetes, and were said, like them, to have watched over Zeus during his infancy. They were five in number, though they are often said to have numbered ten, five males and five females, and sometimes even a hundred. An Elean tradition names the males as follows: Heracles, the oldest (not to be confused with Alcmene's son), Epimedes, Idas (or Acesidas), Paeonius, and Iasus.

The Dactyls were magicians, credited with the spread, and sometimes the invention, of the Mysteries. To amuse the infant Zeus, they organized the first Olympic Games. They were also believed to have taught Paris music on Mount Ida in the Troad.

Dada (Δάδα) The wife of the Cretan hero Samon, who helped SCAMANDER take possession of the Troad. After Samon's death in battle Dada entrusted herself to a herald, asking him to accompany her to a nearby city, where she intended to remarry. On the way the herald violated her and, overcome with shame, Dada ran herself through with her dead husband's sword. When the Cretans learnt of this tragic event they stoned the herald to death at the very place where he had carried out his rape; the place became known thereafter as the Field of Shamelessness.

Daedalion (Δαιδαλίων) The brother of Ceyx and the son of Lucifer, the Morning Star (Eosphorus). A fierce man who loved hunting and fighting, he made many conquests. He had a daughter called Chione, a girl of great beauty, who attracted many suitors. One day Hermes and Apollo saw her as they were passing through her neighbourhood, and they both fell in love with her. She gave them two children from this encounter. The one by Hermes was called AUTOLYCUS and the one by Apollo became the musician Philammon. But Chione overstepped the mark. She had the audacity to set her beauty above that of Artemis, who killed her with an arrow. Daedalion's grief was so intense that Apollo transformed him into a sparrow-hawk, a bird which retained the violent instincts he had had as a man.

Daedalus (Δαίδαλος) An Athenian and a member of the royal family through his descent from Cecrops (Table 4), Daedalus was a skilled and versatile artist, being in turn architect, sculptor, and inventor of mechanical devices. In times of Antiquity he was credited with archaic works of art including some more mythical in character than real, such as the animated statues mentioned by Plato in his *Menon*. According to some legends, Daedalus' father was Eupalamus, and his mother was Alcippe; in others his father was Palaemon, or alternatively METION, grandson of Erechtheus.

Daedalus worked in Athens, where his nephew Talos, son of his sister Perdix, was his pupil. Talos proved so talented that Daedalus became jealous, and when Talos, drawing his inspiration from the jaw-bone of a serpent, invented the saw, Daedalus threw him from the top of the Acropolis. The murder was discovered, and Daedalus was arraigned before the Areopagus, found guilty, and sentenced to exile. He fled to Crete, where he became architect and resident sculptor at the court of King Minos. When Minos' wife PASIPHAE became enamoured of a bull, Daedalus constructed a wooden cow for her. He also built the Labyrinth for Minos – a palace with a maze of corridors in which the Minotaur was confined – and then in due course suggested to Ariadne the trick which saved Theseus when he went to fight the Minotaur. Theseus was to take a ball of thread, which he would unroll as he made his way into the Labyrinth so that he would be able to find his way

Antique bas-relief showing Daedalus and Icarus making wings for their escape from Crete. They attached the wings to their shoulders with wax, but Icarus flew too close to the sun – the wax melted, and he fell into the sea and drowned. Rome, Villa Albani.

back along the same route. When Minos learnt of Theseus' success, and the trick he had used to achieve it, he imprisoned Daedalus in the Labyrinth, as Theseus' accomplice, together with his son ICARUS (whom Daedalus had fathered on a palace slave named Naucrate). But Daedalus made wings for himself and his son, which he attached with wax, and they both flew off. Daedalus reached Cumae safe and sound. Minos hunted him in every country while he lay in hiding at Camicos in Sicily, under the protection of King Cocalus (for the ruse by which Minos discovered Daedalus' hiding-place, see COCALUS). Once Minos had been killed by King Cocalus' daughters, Daedalus showed his gratitude to his host by erecting many buildings.

Daitas (Δαίτας) There were two brothers on Lesbos, Daitas and Thyestes, who hatched a child named Enorches from an egg. Enorches built a temple to Dionysus in which the god was worshipped under the name Enorches, given to him by its original owner.

Damaethus (Δάμαιθος) A king of Caria, where PODALIRIUS, the doctor, landed after being shipwrecked on his way back from Troy. Podalirius was rescued by a goatherd, and taken to the king, Damaethus, whose daughter Syrna happened to be seriously ill. Podalirius cured her, and in gratitude Damaethus gave him Syrna's hand in marriage and granted him a peninsula of land on which Podalirius built two cities.

Damascus (Δαμασκός) The hero who gave his name to the city of Damascus in Syria. There are various legends about him. Some make him out to be the son of Hermes and the Nymph Halimede and to have emigrated from Arcadia to Syria, where he founded the city. Others claim that he was a follower of Dionysus and that he chopped down a vine the god had planted; incensed by this, Dionysus had flayed him on the site of the future city of Damascus. Yet other legends claim that the name Damascus came from a hero named Damas, one of Dionysus' companions, who had put up a tent (σκηνή) on the site of the future city and had placed a statue of the god within it; the city was hence called Damascus (from Δαμᾶ σκηωνή).

Damasen (Δαμασήν) A giant, born of Earth (Gaia), and brought up by Eris (strife). He was born bearded, and immediately after his birth the goddess Eilithyia gave him weapons. He grew to a prodigious size and strength. At the request of the Nymph MORIA, he slew the dragon which had killed Tylus, Moria's brother.

Damastes (Δαμάστης) A giant, more commonly known by his agnomen, PROCRUSTES. He was also called Polypemon.

Damysus (Δάμυσος) The swiftest runner of all the giants. He was buried at Pallene. When entrusted with the infant ACHILLES, the Centaur Chiron disinterred Damysus and took his heelbone to replace the child's, which had been damaged by fire; this was why Achilles was so swift a runner himself. According to one of the legends about his death, his heel-bone came off as he was being pursued by Apollo. Achilles fell, thus giving the god a chance to kill him.

Danae (Δανάη) The daughter of Acrisius king of Argos, and of Eurydice, the daughter of Lacedaemon and Sparto (Table 31). An oracle warned Acrisius that he would be slain by the son of his daughter Danae (for the circumstances in which this son, Perseus, was conceived and born, see ACRISIUS), and after the birth of the child Danae was put into a wooden chest with him and thrown into the sea. Through Zeus' protection, mother and child were washed up on the island of Seriphos, where they were welcomed by Dictys, brother of the tyrant Polydectes. According to some accounts Polydectes then fell in love with Danae, and in order to be rid of Perseus, whose continued presence was hampering his plans, he sent him off to bring back Medusa's head. According to other sources, Dictys himself pushed Danae into the arms of Polydectes, who married her and brought up her son. During Perseus' absence (reverting to the first account) Polydectes tried to rape Danae. When Perseus returned he found Dictys and his mother were suppliants at the altar, trying to evade the tyrant's violent threats. With the head of Medusa Perseus turned Polydectes and his companions into stone; then he placed Dictys on the throne of Seriphos. After that he left the island together with Danae, who went back to Argos to live with her mother, while Perseus went off to hunt down Acrisius.

In an Italian version of the legend Danae and the infant Perseus in the chest were washed up on the coast of Latium. There Danae married Pilumnus and the two of them founded the city of Ardea.

Danaides (Δαναίδες) The fifty daughters of King DANAUS, who accompanied him when he fled from Egypt fearing the fifty sons of his brother Aegyptus, with whom he had quarreled. Once established in Argos, he invited his fifty nephews to visit him. They asked him to forget their quarrel and announced their intention of marrying his fifty daughters; and although he had no faith in this reconciliation, Danaus accepted their proposals. The marriages took place in the following manner: the eldest daughter Hypermnestra married Lynceus, and Gorgophone married Proteus – for Lynceus and Proteus were of the blood royal, through their mother. Busiris, Enceladus, Lycus, and Daiphron drew lots for Danaus' four daughters by Europa – namely Automate, Amymone, Agave, and Scaea. Istrus married Hippodamia; Chalcodon married Rhodia; Agenor married Cleopatra; Chaetus married Asteria; Diocorystes married Philodamia; Alces married Glauce; Alcmenor married Hippomedusa; Hippothous married Gorge; Euchenor married Iphimedusa; Hippolytes married Rhode; Agaptolemus married Pirene; Cercetes married Dorion; Eurydamas married Phartis; Aegius married Mnestra; Argius married Evippe; Archelaus married Anaxibia; Menemachus married Nelo; Clitus married Clite; Sthenelus married Sthenele; and Chrysippus married Chrysippe. Eurylochus, Phantes, Peristhenes, Hermus, Dryas, Potamon, Cisseus, Lixus, Imbrus, Bromius, Polyctor, and Chthonius married respectively Autonoe, Theano, Electra, Cleopatra, Eurydice, Galucippe, Anthelia, Cleodora, Evippe, Erato, Stygne, and Bryce. Periphas married Actaea; Oeneus married Podarces; Aegypius married Dioxippe; Menalces married Adite; Lampus married Ocypete; Idmon married Pylarge; Idas married Hippodice; Daiphron married Adiante; Pandion married Callidice; Arbelus married Oeme; Hyperbius married Celaeno; and Hippocoristes married Hyperippe. Some of these couples were chosen by lot, others were paired because their names were similar.

Danaus gave a great feast to celebrate the weddings, but presented each of his daughters with a dagger and made them all swear to kill their husbands during the night. This they did, except for Hypermnestra, who spared Lynceus because he had spared her maidenhood. When Danaus discovered this he had her arrested and placed under strict guard. The murderesses cut off the heads of their victims, gave their bodies full funeral hon-ours beneath the walls of Argos, and buried the heads at Lerna. At Zeus' order, they were purified of their murders by Hermes and Athena. Danaus later confirmed the union of Hypermnestra and Lynceus and tried to marry off the other daughters, but there were few suitors. He then decided to hold games with his daughters as prizes; would-be suitors were excused the requirement of providing the customary gifts. His daughters thus married young men from their own country; and with them they produced the race of the Danaans, which replaced that of the Pelasgians. Together with their father they were later killed by Lynceus, who thus avenged his brothers' deaths. It is probable that the marriage of the Danaides and the story of their death at the hands of Lynceus represent two different states of the legend, the latter being the older. The Danaides were also said to have been punished in Hades by being compelled everlastingly to refill leaking water-pots (see AMYMONE).

Danaus (Δαναός) One of the two sons of BELUS and Achinoe (see AEGYPTUS, and Table 3), and through his father a descendant of Poseidon and the Nymph Libya. By different wives he had fifty daughters (see DANAIDES). His father had given him Libya as his kingdom, but he fled the country, either after a warning from an oracle or from fear of his brother Aegyptus's fifty sons. He travelled in a ship with fifty banks of oars, which Athena had advised him to build. After a short stop in Rhodes he landed with his daughters in Argos, where the Danaides were said to have built a temple to Athena of Lindos. Gelanor was king of Argos at that time; according to some he yielded his throne to Danaus quite spontaneously, but other stories hold that Danaus obtained the throne only after a long debate or rhetorical battle with Gelanor in the presence of the people of Argos, which was ended by a most auspicious omen. As the two contestants met at dawn to present their final arguments, a wolf came out of the forest and fell upon a herd of cattle that was passing by near the city walls. The wolf attacked the bull, overcame it, and killed it. The Argives were struck by the analogy between this wolf that had come out of its solitude, far from mankind, and Danaus. They saw the effect of divine will in this omen, and chose Danaus as their king. Danaus built a shrine to Lycian Apollo (Wolfish Apollo).

For the way in which Danaus procured water for the land of Argos, which had been deprived of it as a result of Poseidon's anger at the god Inachus see AMYMONE and INACHUS. For the murder of Aegyptus's fifty sons, see DANAIDES.

Danaus was said to have founded the citadel of Argos. He was buried there, and his tomb was still to be seen in Classical times.

Daphne (Δάφνη) A Nymph loved by APOLLO; her name means laurel in Greek. She is sometimes said to have been the daughter of the River Ladon and Earth, sometimes of the Thessalian River Peneus. She was pursued by Apollo and fled; just as she was about to be caught she begged her father to transform her. She became a laurel tree, the plant beloved by the god.

A Laconian version of the legend made Daphne out to be the daughter of Amyclas. Fond of the chase and wild in her ways, she would not live in cities, but spent her time wandering among the mountains. She was the favourite of Artemis. Leucippus, son of King Oenomaus of Elis, fell in love with her, and in order to be closer to her he disguised himself as a girl and joined her companions. Daphne became fond of him in his disguise, and would not leave his side. This made Apollo jealous, and in revenge he inspired Daphne and her companions with a sudden wish to bathe in a mountain pool. When Leucippus hesitated to remove his clothing his companions forcibly undressed him and discovered his imposture. At that, they rushed at him with their lances, but the gods made him invisible. Apollo dashed forward to seize Daphne, but she ran off, and in answer to her prayer, Zeus turned her into a laurel tree.

Daphnis (Δάφνις) A Sicilian demigod, from the bucolic cycle. He was the son of Hermes, the god of cattle, and a Nymph. Daphnis was born in the high Sicilian valleys in a thicket of laurel sacred to the Nymphs, and this gave him his name. He was brought up by the Nymphs, who taught him the herdsman's art. He was extremely beautiful, and was loved by many Nymphs and mortal maidens, as well as by several gods. Pan, in particular, taught him music. Daphnis played the syrinx while his cattle grazed. He also sang songs in the bucolic mode, which he had invented himself. But Daphnis died in the bloom of his youth. The cause of his death was the love of a Nymph, Nomia the Shepherdess, a love which he reciprocated. He had sworn to remain eternally faithful, and he kept this vow until the day when a daughter of the king of

Sicily managed to make him drunk and slept with him. In her anger Nomia blinded him. Indeed, it was sometimes said that she actually killed him. It was generally accepted that the blind Daphnis sang sad songs of mourning for a while, finally bringing his grief to an end by throwing himself off a high rock, or by being transformed into a rock, or by being taken up into heaven by his father Hermes. A fountain kept his memory alive, and each year sacrifices were offered in his honour.

According to another version Daphnis loved a Nymph called Pimplea, or Thalia, who was carried off by pirates. He went to look for her and found her in Phrygia, the slave of LITYERSES. When he tried to rescue her he seemed doomed to share the fate that Lityerses reserved for his guests, but HERACLES arrived in time to save him. Heracles killed the king, and gave his kingdom to Daphnis and Pimplea.

The Alexandrine poet Sositheus composed a satyric drama on this theme.

Dardanus (Δάρδανος) The son of Zeus and Electra, Atlas' daughter. His country of origin was Samothrace, where he lived with his brother IASION. After a flood in which Iasion drowned, Dardanus set out to sea on a raft, which took him to the coast of Asia opposite Samothrace. Here reigned King Teucer, son of the River Scamander and the Nymph Idaea. Teucer received Dardanus hospitably, and gave him part of his kingdom, together with his daughter Batieia. Dardanus built the city that carried his name, and on Teucer's death he called the whole country Dardania. Batieia gave him sons – Ilus, Erichthonius and (some say) Zacynthus, and a daughter Idaea, named after her mother's grandmother (Table 7). Dardanus built the citadel of Troy and reigned over the Troad. He was said to have initiated the Trojans into the mysteries of the gods of Samothrace (the CABIRI; sometimes he was even thought to be one of them) and to have introduced the cult of Cybele into Phrygia. According to one legend Dardanus stole the statue of Pallas called the PALLADIUM, which was kept in Arcadia, and brought it over to Troy.

According to an Italian tradition Dardanus came from the Etruscan city of Cortona in central Italy. He won a victory over the Aborigines, the primitive peoples of Italy, and then founded the city. Later he emigrated to Phrygia, thereby creating a bond between Italy and the Troad. It was in memory of these earliest origins of his race that

Aeneas visited the Italian peninsula after the fall of Troy.

Finally, yet another tradition has it that Dardanus was a connection of Evander and of Pallas, the son of Lycaon (see PALLAS 2).

Dares (Δάρης) A Phrygian who, on the advice of Thymbraean Apollo, the god of Troy, was given to Hector as an adviser, to stop him from fighting Patroclus (for the Fates had decreed that if Hector were to slay Patroclus, he himself would be slain by Achilles). Dares wasted no time in deserting to the Greek camp, where he was put to death by Odysseus.

Daunus (Δαύνιος or Δαῦνος) One of the three sons of the Illyrian Lycaon, his brothers being Iapyx and Peucetius. Together with his brothers, he invaded southern Italy at the head of an Illyrian army, threw out the Ausonians who were living there, and divided the land into three kingdoms, named respectively after the Daunians, the Messapians, and the Peucetians. The territory as a whole was known as the land of the Iapygians.

When Diomedes came to Italy after being exiled from his own country he was given a warm welcome by Daunus, who gave him land and the hand of his daughter. A later tradition tells of dissension between Daunus and Diomedes, the latter being slain by the former (see DIOMEDES, 2).

This Daunus (or a figure with the same name) was the father of TURNUS.

Decelus (Δέκελος) The hero who gave his name to the Attic city of Decelia. When the Dioscuri were looking for their sister Helen, who had been carried off by Theseus, it was Decelus who showed them where she was being held prisoner. It was sometimes held that the revelation was made by the hero ACADEMUS.

Deianeira (Δηιάνειρα) The daughter of King Oeneus of Calydon, and hence the sister of Meleager (Table 27). According to another legend her father was Dionysus, who had been Oeneus' guest in Calydon. Her mother was ALTHAEA. Deianeira knew how to drive a chariot and understood the art of war. When her brother Meleager died, she and her sisters were transformed into guinea-fowl; but at Dionysus' pleading, she and one sister, Gorge, resumed their human forms.

When Heracles went down to Hades in search of Cerberus, he encountered the spirit of Melea-ger, who asked him to marry Deianeira, left without support since Meleager's death. As soon as he returned to earth, Heracles hastened to Calydon where he found Deianeira, who was being wooed by the river-god ACHELOUS. In the ensuing struggle Heracles overthrew his rival.

After his marriage HERACLES stayed some time in Calydon, and Deianeira bore him a son, Hyllus (Table 16). Then Heracles and Deianeira left Calydon. At a river-crossing on their way the Centaur NESSUS tried to rape Deianeira but was slain by Heracles. As he lay dying he gave the young woman a drug mixed with the blood welling from his wound, and he told her that this was a love-potion. At Trachis Heracles and Deianeira were welcomed by King Ceyx, and all three waged war against the Dryopians. When Heracles fell in love with Iole Deianeira grew jealous. In an attempt to re-awaken his love, she soaked a shirt in the drug that Nessus had given her and sent it to Heracles. As soon as the shirt touched his skin, a burning corrosion started eating his flesh away, until finally he could no longer stand the agony, and sought death on a funeral pyre on Mount Oeta. When she realized the true nature of the so-called love-potion, Deianeira killed herself. Her tomb was long to be seen in Trachis.

Deioneus (Δηιονεύς) The father of Dia, and the father-in-law of Ixion. When Deioneus called upon Ixion for the customary bridal gifts, Ixion killed him by throwing him into a pit filled with red-hot charcoals just as he was in the very act of bestowing his daughter's hand.

Deiphobus (Δηίφοβος) The son of Priam and Hecuba, and Hector's favourite brother. It was in the likeness of Deiphobus that Athena appeared to HECTOR at his meeting with ACHILLES, and urged him to fight, thus causing his death. It was also Deiphobus who recognized Paris–Alexander at the funeral games where Paris defeated all his brothers. After Paris had been slain by Philoctetes, Deiphobus won the hand of Helen in competition with his brother HELENUS, even though the latter was the elder. After the sack of Troy, Odysseus and Menelaus seized his house, and Menelaus killed him and mutilated his body. His shade appeared to Aeneas in Hades.

Deiphontes (Δηιφόντης) Through his father Antimachus, Deiphontes was a descendant of Heracles. He married Hyrnetho, the daughter of

another Heraclid, Temenus (Table 16). When the HERACLIDS seized the Peloponnese, Temenus received the city of Argos as his share. Deiphontes joined him there, and was involved with him so closely in the government that Temenus' own sons feared they would be disinherited in favour of their brother-in-law. To avoid this happening all the sons except the youngest decided to kill their father. They attacked him while he was bathing in the river and gave him grievous wounds, but the alarm was sounded, and they took to flight. Temenus died of his wounds, but not before he had had time to leave his kingdom to Deiphontes, and reveal his sons' crime. They were duly banished, but did not abandon hope of one day regaining power in Argos; indeed they succeeded in doing this, thanks to some external aid. Deiphontes, together with his wife Hyrnetho and his brother-in-law Agrius, the youngest of Temenus' sons, who had never turned against him, established himself in Epidaurus and obtained the throne of King Pityreus, a descendant of Ion. While Deiphontes was at Epidaurus his two brothers-in-law Cerynes and Phalces carried off his wife, whom they had enticed outside the city walls and dragged into their chariot. Deiphontes pursued them and killed Cerynes with his lance; but Phalces slew Hyrnetho and made his escape. The young woman's body was buried on the spot, in an olive grove, and divine honours were paid to her.

Deipylus (Δηίπυλος) The son of Polymestor, the king of Thrace, who had married Ilione, Priam's eldest daughter. Priam had entrusted the upbringing of his son Polydorus to Ilione, who had looked after the boy from his birth. Ilione had secretly exchanged the two children, passing her own son Deipylus off as her young brother. She took this precautionary step to ensure that if one of them should die, the other would retain his right to the throne. After the fall of Troy, Agamemnon was anxious to wipe out Priam's race completely, and promised Polymestor his daughter Electra in marriage if he would agree to do away with Polydorus. Polymestor accepted the offer and killed his own son Deipylus under the mistaken assumption that he was killing Polydorus. The day came when Polydorus, quite ignorant as to the details of his birth, went to consult the oracle at Delphi, where

The Tholos at Delphi of c. 370 BC. Delphi was said to be the centre of the earth and was celebrated for its temple and oracle of Apollo.

he was told that his father and mother were dead, and his native land in ashes. Polydorus was astounded, since none of this seemed applicable to what he thought was his family. He questioned Ilione, who told him the truth. On Polydorus' advice, Ilione blinded POLYMESTOR and put him to death.

Delphus (Δελφός) The hero who gave his name to the city of Delphi, famed for the sanctuary and oracle of Apollo. He is said to have been the reigning king of the country when APOLLO arrived to take possession of it. He was sometimes said to be the son sired by Poseidon on Deucalion's daughter Melantho; Poseidon coupled with her in the shape of a dolphin (whence the name of the child). Sometimes he was held to be the son of Apollo himself, either by Celaeno (or Melaenis), or by Thyia, or yet again by Melaena – who were respectively the daughters of Hyamus, Castalius, and Cephisus (Table 8). Delphi owed its original name of Pytho either to Delphus' son King Pythes, or to one of his daughters called Pythis (see also PYTHON).

Delphyne (Δελφύνη) The name of two dragons:
1. The first was charged by TYPHON with keeping watch over Zeus' sinews and muscles, which Typhon had hidden in a cave in Cilicia. But Hermes and Pan managed to outwit Delphyne's surveillance and restored Zeus to his former shape and strength. Delphyne was half woman and half serpent.
2. The other dragon of this name was the one at Delphi, which watched over the fountain near which lay the old oracle taken over by APOLLO. There seem to have been two successive states of the legend, the Python version being later than that of Delphyne.

Demeter (Δημήτηρ) The Mother Goddess of the Earth, belonging to the second divine generation, that of the Olympians. She was the second daughter of Cronus and Rhea, born between Hestia, the eldest, and Hera (Table 38). Both in religion and in mythology her personality is quite distinct from that of GAIA, who was the Earth viewed as a cosmogonic element. Demeter, the divinity of agriculture, is essentially the Corn Goddess. Legends about her were rife in every region of the Hellenic world where wheat was grown. These legends were most prolific on the plains of Eleusis and in Sicily, but they were also found in Crete, in Thrace, and in the Peloponnese.

Demeter, goddess of the earth's fruits and especially of corn, is represented on this Roman terracotta with her attributes – corn, poppies and serpents. Rome, Terme Museum.

Both in her legends and in her cult, Demeter was closely linked to her daughter Persephone, and together they formed a couple often known simply as the Goddesses. The adventures of Demeter and Persephone form the central myth of their legend. Initiation into the Eleusinian Mysteries revealed the profound significance that lay behind the myth.

PERSEPHONE was the daughter of Zeus and Demeter and – at least in the traditional legend – the goddess's only child. She grew up happily among the Nymphs, in company with her sisters Athena and Artemis, Zeus' other daughters, and gave little thought to marriage. But her uncle Hades fell in love with her, and with Zeus' help abducted her. The abduction is generally said to have taken place in the grasslands of Enna, in Sicily, but the Homeric Hymn to Demeter rather vaguely mentions the plain of Mysa – a mythical name, which doubtless had little or no meaning from a geographical point of view. Other tradi-tions place it along the River Cephisus at Eleusis: or in Arcadia, at the foot of Mount Cyllene, where a certain cave was reputed to be one of the entrances to the lower world of Hades: or in Crete, near Cnossus: and so on. Wherever it was, while Persephone was picking a narcissus (or a lily) the ground opened, Hades appeared, and dragged her down into the Nether Regions. Demeter immediately embarked on the long search for her daughter, which was to take her over the whole of the known world. Persephone had cried out as she disappeared into the abyss. Demeter heard her, and terror gripped her heart. She ran towards the sound, but there was no sign of Persephone. For nine days and nine nights, without eating, drinking, bathing, or changing her clothes, the goddess wandered over the world, a lighted torch in either hand. On the tenth day she met Hecate, who had also heard Persephone's cry but had not recognized her abductor, whose head was shrouded in the shadows of the Night.

Only Helios, who sees everything, could tell her what had happened. But according to local tradition, it was the people of Hermione in the Argolid who revealed the culprit to her. The angry goddess decided not to return to heaven, but to stay on earth, abandoning her divine role until her daughter was returned to her. She assumed the shape of an old woman and went to Eleusis. First she rested on a stone which was known thenceforth as the Joyless Stone. Then she went to see King Celeus, the ruler of the country. She fell in with some old women, who invited her to join them, and one of them, IAMBE, made her smile with her comic jokes. The goddess then entered the service of Metanira, Celeus' wife, and was taken on as a wet-nurse. The child entrusted to her was the newly-born DEMOPHON (or, in certain versions, little TRIPTOLEMUS). The goddess tried to make him immortal, but was unsuccessful, through Metanira's untimely intervention. Demeter then made herself known, and charged Triptolemus with the task of going about the world sowing corn everywhere he went. Other legends show the goddess playing the role of wet-nurse for Plemnaeus, king of Sicyon (see ORTHOPOLIS).

Now Demeter's self-imposed exile had made the earth sterile, and in consequence the state of the world had been disrupted, so much so that Zeus ordered Hades to return Persephone. But that was no longer possible. During her stay in the Nether Regions, the girl had broken her fast and eaten a pomegranate seed, in this way binding herself for good to Hades. Finally, a compromise was reached: Demeter would take her place again on Mount Olympus, and Persephone would divide the year between the Nether Regions and her mother. This was why each spring, when the first shoots appeared in the furrows, Persephone would escape from her enforced stay below the ground, and make her way towards the sky, only to bury herself once more among the shades when seed-time came around. And for as long as she remained separated from Demeter, the ground stayed sterile and the dreary season of winter gripped the land.

Various episodes have been woven into the story of Demeter's search, to fit in with local legends. At Sicyon, the goddess was credited with the invention of the mill, and with instructing the inhabitants in its use; elsewhere she is associated with the raising of vegetables, in particular the bean or fruit, especially the fig (see PHYTALUS). Demeter's sanctuaries were to be seen almost everywhere in Greece, and it was invariably claimed that these had been built by those who had been her hosts and given her shelter in bygone days: at Argos, one Mysius and his wife Chrysanthis; at Pheneus, in Arcadia, Trisaules and Damithales; and so on. Poseidon's amorous pursuit of Demeter was also woven into the story of her search for Persephone. To escape from Poseidon, the goddess was said to have assumed the form of a mare; but it was in vain, for she gave birth not only to a horse called AREION but also to a daughter, who was known only as the Mistress.

Another legend, current as early as the *Odyssey*, was the love story of Demeter and IASION, who gave the goddess a son, Plutus.

Demeter battled with Hephaestus for possession of Sicily (see AETNA), and with Dionysus for Campania (this myth, probably of later origin, symbolizes very obviously Campania's wealth in both vines and corn; see also ERYSICHTHON).

Demeter's emblems are the ear of corn, the narcissus, and the poppy. Her bird is the crane and her favourite victim the sow (see EUBOULEUS). She is often portrayed seated, with torches or a serpent.

Demiphon (Δημιφῶν) King of the city of Eleonte in the Thracian Chersonese (the Gallipoli peninsula). Demiphon had been told by an oracle that in order to put an end to an epidemic he must sacrifice each year a young girl chosen from among the city's noble families. Every year he drew a name by lot, but he never put the names of his own daughters into the urn. When Mastusius, one of the city's nobles, refused to allow his daughters to be included in the draw, unless the king's daughters were also included, the tyrant slew Mastusius' daughter without drawing lots at all. Determined to have his revenge, Mastusius later invited the king and his daughters to a sacrifice. The girls arrived first. Mastusius slew them, took their blood, and mixed it with wine in a drinking-bowl, which he offered to Demiphon. When Demiphon realized what it was that he had drunk, he flung both bowl and Mastusius into the sea. Thereafter the sea was known as the Mastusian Sea, and the port was known as Crater, from the name of the bowl (Κρατηρ) in which the blood and the wine had been mixed. It was also said that this crater became the constellation generally known as the Cup.

Demodice (Δημοδίκη) The name of PHRIXUS' aunt, in one version of his legend. She was the wife of Cretheus, Athamas' brother (Tables 8 and 33). Demodice fell in love with Phrixus, who did not respond to her advances, whereupon she made false accusations about him to Cretheus, who persuaded his brother ATHAMAS to have him put to death. But Phrixus' mother Nephele saved him by giving him a wonderful ram, which flew off into the air with Phrixus on its back.

Demodocus (Δημόδοκος) The name borne by two bards who played a role in the Homeric epics.
1.   The first, and the more celebrated, was the one who sang at the court of Alcinous, king of the Phaecians, during the banquet at which Odysseus recounted his adventures. He was loved by the Muses, who had deprived him of his sight, but in return had given him the power of moving men's hearts with his songs.
2.   The second was the bard whom Agamemnon left to look after his wife CLYTEMNESTRA on his departure for the Trojan War. But Demodocus was unable to defend her against seduction by Aegisthus.

Demophon (Δημοφών)
1.   The son of Celeus, king of Eleusis, and his wife Metanira: and the younger brother of Triptolemus. In her search for Persephone Demeter had entered Metanira's service, and was entrusted with Demophon's upbringing. Wishing to make him immortal, she held him over the fire at nights, to burn away his mortal elements. As the child seemed to be growing in miraculous fashion his mother – or perhaps his nurse PRAXITHEA – kept watch on Demeter, and one night saw her starting her magical treatment. She uttered a cry, and Demeter dropped the child to the floor; then she revealed her true identity. According to some, Demophon was burnt up in the fire. According to others he survived, but as a mortal: all he retained was the everlasting glory of having been looked after by a goddess during his infancy.

This episode is sometimes attributed not to Demophon, but to his brother Triptolemus (see TRIPTOLEMUS, ELEUSIS, and CELEUS).
2.   Another Demophon was the brother of Acamas (see ACAMAS 3), and hence the son of Theseus and Phaedra (or, as some said, of Theseus and Ariadne). With his brother he took part in the Trojan War in order to free, or perhaps to ransom, their grandmother AETHRA who was one of Helen's slaves. While Theseus was down in the Nether Regions rescuing Persephone, the Dioscuri – Castor and Pollux – drove Acamas and

Demophon from the throne of Athens, and installed the pretender MENESTHEUS in their place. Acamas and Demophon withdrew to Scyros, where they were joined by their father (see THESEUS); and it was from here that they left for the Trojan War, with Elephenor, the son of Chalcodon. They played a part in the fall of the city, being among the heroes inside the wooden horse.

During the journey back from Troy, Demophon (though this episode was also sometimes attributed to Acamas) had an amorous adventure in Thrace with the daughter of Sithon, the king of Amphipolis. This girl's name was Phyllis; she married him, and as dowry her father made Demophon heir to the throne. But he wished to return to Athens; and after many entreaties from Phyllis and promises to return, he began preparing for his departure. Phyllis accompanied him to a place called the Nine Roads, and when she left him she gave him a casket containing objects sacred to the Great Mother, Rhea. She advised him to open it only when he had abandoned all hope of returning to her. Demophon left her and settled in Cyprus. When the time set for his return had passed, Phyllis invoked a curse on Demophon, and took her own life. Demophon, however, opened the casket, and the sight of its contents terrified him. He leapt on his horse, which bolted with him. Demophon was thrown, and gave himself a mortal wound with his own sword.

The Athenians were indebted to Demophon for the Palladium, the Trojan statue of Pallas Athena (see ATHENA and PALLADIUM). Either Diomedes (and Odysseus) voluntarily gave it to Demophon after carrying it away from Troy, or Demophon acquired it by force of arms, when some roving Argives with Diomedes as their leader landed in error at Phalerum one night, and Demophon, taking them for pirates, attacked them and robbed them of the statue.

It was also during Demophon's reign that Orestes came to Athens, pursued by the Eumenides. And in this same period the HERACLIDS came seeking help against Eurystheus.

Obviously this legend, made up as it is from various poorly recorded incidents, is not entirely coherent; certain features of it contradict each other, hence their attribution, seemingly indiscriminate, to either Acamas or Demophon.

Dendritis (Δενδρῖτις) This was the name that Helen used in Rhodes (from δένδρον tree). A local legend told that after Menelaus' death, Helen, accompanied by the two illegitimate sons of

Menelaus, Nicostratus and Megapenthes, went to Rhodes to stay with POLYXO, Tlepolemus' widow. Polyxo was an Argive by birth, as was her husband, and had accompanied him when he fled to Rhodes from the Argolid. During her son's minority she acted as regent of the island. She welcomed Helen warmly: but nevertheless looked for an opportunity to take her revenge on Helen for the death of her husband, who had fallen during the siege of Troy. Accordingly, when Helen was in her bath one day, Polyxo had her own servants, disguised as Erinyes, take her by surprise; they took Helen away and hanged her on a tree. Underneath this 'tree of Helen' there grew a magical plant, called Helenium, which was a remedy against the bites of snakes.

Dercynus (Δέρκυνος) A Ligurian, the brother of Alebion, together, they tried to steal Geryon's cattle that HERACLES was driving to Eurystheus.

Deucalion (Δευκαλίων) There were two heroes named Deucalion.

1.   The better-known one was the son of Prometheus and Clymene or Celaeno (Table 38). His wife was Pyrrha, the daughter of Epimetheus and PANDORA, the first woman on earth. When Zeus felt that the men of the Bronze Age were so steeped in vice that he had best destroy them, he decided to unleash a great flood upon the world and drown them all. He decided to spare only two decent people, Deucalion and his wife. On Prometheus' advice, Deucalion and Pyrrha built an 'ark', a big chest, and got inside. For nine days and nine nights they floated on the waters of the flood, and finally ran ashore on the mountains of Thessaly. When the flood had abated Zeus sent Hermes down to them, to tell them they could make one wish, and it would be granted. Deucalion wished that they could have some companions. Zeus then told both of them to throw their mothers' bones over their shoulders. Pyrrha was aghast at this impiety, but Deucalion understood that Zeus had meant stones – the bones of the Earth, the great Mother of all. So he threw stones over his shoulder, and from the stones he threw sprang men. Pyrrha followed suit, and from her stones sprang women.

Deucalion and Pyrrha had many descendants (Table 8).

2.   Legend tells of another Deucalion, the son of Minos and Pasiphae, and brother of Catreus, Glaucus, and Androgeos (Table 28). This Deucalion was a friend of Theseus, and took part in the Calydonian hunt. He was the grandfather of MERIONES.

Dexamenus (Δεξαμενός) A king of Olenus in Achaea; his name means the Welcomer. HERACLES sought refuge with him after his defeat by Augias, and was promised the hand of Dexamenus' daughter Mnesimache. Heracles then went off on an expedition, and on his return he found the young girl forcibly betrothed to the Centaur Eurytion, who had compelled Dexamenus to give her to him. Heracles killed the Centaur, and married Mnesimache. A variant of the legend makes Mnesimache identical with DEIANEIRA, and sets the scene in Calydon, at the court of Oeneus, where a similar struggle for possession of the young girl took place between Heracles and Achelous.

Dexamenus gave two of his daughters, Theronice and Theraephone, in marriage to the MOLIONIDAE.

Dexicreon (Δεξικρέων) A merchant in Samos. While briefly in port in Cyprus, he was advised by Aphrodite to load his boat solely with water and to leave as quickly as possible. Then when he got out to sea a flat calm occurred and he was able to sell his water to the becalmed ships at a handsome profit. As a token of his gratitude he put up a statue to the goddess.

Diana The Italo-Roman goddess identified with ARTEMIS. This identification seems to have started very early, perhaps in the sixth century BC, through the Greek colonies in southern Italy, and especially through Cumae. The identification merely overlaid the characteristics of an indigenous goddess, whose own legends were evidently very scanty, for she was worshipped by a people still largely uneducated. The two oldest of her shrines were the one at Capua, where she went by the name of Diana Tifatina, and the one at Aricia (on the shores of Lake Nemi, near Rome), where she was called Diana Nemorensis, Diana of the Woods.

It was said that the Diana of Nemi was Taurian Artemis, brought to Italy by Orestes. This explained the savagery of her rites. Indeed, the priest of Diana of Nemi, who was called Rex Nemorensis, could in certain circumstances be slain by anyone who wished to take his place. The Taurian Goddess was known to welcome human sacrifices. It was also said that Artemis had given sanctuary to Theseus' son HIPPOLYTUS after his death and his resurrection at the hands of Asclepius the doctor. She had brought him to Italy, and hidden him under another name in her sanctuary at Aricia, where she had made him priest in charge. Hippolytus called himself Virbius, which was interpreted to mean 'he who has lived twice'. The origin of this legend probably lay in the prohibition against bringing horses into the sanctuary, a very old taboo in the cult of Diana of Nemi. Since Hippolytus' death had been caused by his horses, according to the legend, this fitted in perfectly with his assumed personality of Virbius, and explained the taboo as being due to rancour against the guilty animals.

At Capua, there was a legend about a hind that was sacred to Diana, an incredibly long-lived animal, whose fate was bound up with the preservation of the city.

Dias (Δίας) In one variant of the complicated traditions about the origins of the Atrides, Dias was the son of Pelops and Hippodamia, and hence the brother of Atreus and Thyestes. He had a daughter Cleola, who married Atreus and gave him a son, Pleisthenes. Pleisthenes was the father of Agamemnon, Menelaus, and their sister Anaxibia. According to another tradition, Dias' daughter Cleola was Pleisthenes' wife and Atreus' daughter-in-law, and it was she who was the mother of Menelaus, Anaxibia, and Agamemnon (Table 2).

Dicte (Δίκτη) Another name for the Cretan Nymph Britomartis. Dicte too was loved by Minos, and she too leapt into the sea and was saved by fishermen's nets (see BRITOMARTIS and BRYTE).

Dictys (Δίκτυς) The brother of POLYDECTES, tyrant of the island of Seriphos, and the protector of DANAE and PERSEUS. His name, which is related to the word meaning net, was well fitted to his role. It was he who, on the shore of Seriphos, caught the chest in which Perseus and his mother were floating. He was sometimes portrayed as a simple fisherman. After Polydectes' death, he ruled over the island.

Dido The story of Dido, queen of Carthage, is well known, thanks largely to the love story included by Virgil in his *Aeneid*. But the legend was in existence before Virgil, and relates an episode of the Phoenician migrations to the western Mediterranean. In its earliest form the legend

ran as follows: Mutto, king of Tyre, had two children, a son Pygmalion, and a daughter Elissa (Elissa was Queen Dido's Tyrian name). When he died, he left his kingdom to his children, and the people recognized Pygmalion as their king, although he was still only an infant. Elissa married her uncle Sicharbas, the priest of Heracles and the second most important personage in the kingdom after the king himself. But Pygmalion had Sicharbas assassinated so that he could seize his treasure. However, Elissa was horrified by her brother's crime; she had Sicharbas' treasure secretly loaded onto boats and fled, accompanied by some disaffected Tyrian nobles. The story went that during the voyage, in order to foil Pygmalion's greed, she had quite openly thrown some sacks into the sea which she said were full of gold, an offering to her husband's spirit, but which in reality were filled with sand. She visited Cyprus, where a priest of Zeus coupled with her, driven to it by an instruction from the gods; and there her companions carried off twenty-four maidens consecrated to Aphrodite and made them their wives. Then the emigrants reached Africa, where they were warmly welcomed by the local inhabitants. When Dido asked these people for some land where she could settle they allowed her to take 'as much as she could enclose in the hide of a bull'. Dido had the hide cut up into the thinnest possible strips, obtaining a long leather thong which enabled her to surround a fairly large plot of land. The inhabitants kept their promise and gave her the land she had enclosed. Soon the citizens of Utica sent presents to the newcomers and encouraged them to found a city. When the workmen started digging on the site first chosen they turned up the head of an ox, which they considered an inauspicious omen. The site was changed, and when they dug again they found a horse's head which seemed to them to augur well for the warlike valour of the future city. An influx of colonists from the motherland gave the city new strength, and a neighbouring indigenous king, Iarbas, expressed his wish to marry Dido, threatening to declare war upon the city if she refused. Dido dared not refuse, but the idea of this proposed new union revolted her. She asked for three months' delay, under the pretence of placating her first husband's spirit with expiatory sacrifices. At the end of this period she mounted a funeral pyre and gave herself up to death.

This was the theme on which Virgil based the story of Aeneas, a story in which the hero was driven by a storm on to the shores of Africa and welcomed by the inhabitants of Carthage, the city founded by Dido. At a banquet given in his honour Aeneas related his adventures and told of the fall of Troy. Then, while his companions were repairing the ships, he became the guest of the queen, who gradually began to fall in love with him. Finally, during a hunting party, they were brought together by a storm which forced them both to take shelter in the same cave, and she became his mistress, through the will of Venus and at Juno's instigation. But soon, King Iarbas, aware of what had happened, and angered at seeing a stranger preferred to himself, asked Jupiter to send Aeneas on his way. Jupiter, aware of what the future held in store, and knowing that Rome must come into being far from the shores of Africa, commanded Aeneas to leave and end this transient relationship. Aeneas departed without seeing the queen again. When Dido learnt that she had been abandoned she built a tall funeral pyre and sought death amid the flames. In Virgil's tale Dido had been married before, as in the earlier version of the legend, but her husband's name was Sychaeus. Her sister Anna also appeared in the story, of whom apparently no mention had been made before (see ANNA PERENNA).

Dimoetes (Διμοίτης) The brother of Troezen, whose daughter Euopis he had taken as his bride. But Euopis loved her own brother. Dimoetes found this out, and told Troezen about it. In her fear and shame the young woman hanged herself, after calling down all sorts of curses on the head of the man who had discovered and betrayed her secret. Some time later Dimoetes came across the body of a wonderfully beautiful woman on the beach, being tossed about by the waves. He fell violently in love with this corpse, and lay with it, but all too soon the corpse began to decompose. Dimoetes built a magnificent tomb for the body, but he was unable to withstand his grief at losing what he had loved, and upon this tomb he ran himself through with his sword.

Diomedes (Διομήδης) The legends mention two heroes of this name:
1. The first was a king of Thrace, the son of Ares and Pyrene, who used to have any strangers who came into his land eaten by his mares. Erystheus gave Heracles the task of putting an end to this practice and bringing the mares back to Mycenae. Heracles left with a troop of volunteers, and after overcoming the grooms in charge of the animals he led them away. But he was attacked on the beach by the local inhabitants sallying forth to defend the mares. When he saw them Heracles entrusted the mares to his companion Abderus, a son of Hermes, born in Opontis in Locris. The mares dragged the young man off and killed him. Heracles vanquished the local inhabitants, slew their king Diomedes, and founded a city on the coast, which he called Abdera in memory of the young man he had loved. Then he brought the mares back to Eurystheus, but Eurystheus set them free, and they were devoured by wild beasts on the slopes of Mount Olympus. Another tradition claims that Heracles slew Diomedes by feeding him to his own mares, which ate him. Then the hero brought the mares to Eurystheus, who consecrated them to Hera. Their descendants were still living in the days of Alexander the Great.

One version of the tradition gives the names of the mares as Podargus, Lampon, Xanthus, and Deinus. They were tethered with iron chains to their mangers, which were bronze.

2. The other Diomedes was an Aetolian hero who took part in the war against Troy. He was the son of Tydeus and Deipyle, one of the daughters of ADRASTUS (Tables 1 and 27), and as such he also took part in the expedition of the Epigoni against Thebes. The first of his legendary deeds was his revenge against the sons of Agrius, who had ousted his grandfather Oeneus from his kingdom of Calydon and given it to their own father (Table 27). Diomedes came secretly from his adopted country Argos (see TYDEUS) with Alcmaeon, and slew all Agrius' sons save Onchestus and Thersites, who fled to the Peloponnese beforehand. Since Oeneus was an old man, Diomedes gave his kingdom to Andraemon, who had married Gorge, one of Oeneus' daughters. When Oeneus, who had retired into the Peloponnese, was killed in an ambush by Agrius' surviving sons, Diomedes gave him a magnificent funeral; and later the city of Oenoe, named after the old man, was raised on the site of his grave. Diomedes then married Aegiale, his aunt (Table 1), though some authors insist she was only his cousin, making her the daughter of Aegialieus rather than Adrastus, and hence Adrastus' grand-daughter.

In the tales of the Trojan cycle, Diomedes is Odysseus' usual companion in most of the latter's important undertakings. He set out with the Atrides as one of Helen's former suitors. Some of the legends show him at Odysseus' side in Scyros, trying to make sure of Achilles' support. He also helped Odysseus persuade Agamemnon to sacrifice his daughter Iphigenia at Aulis, and accompanied him in his mission to Achilles when he was seeking to appease the hero's anger and persuade him to return and fight alongside the Greeks. He also took part in Odysseus' reconnaissance exercise during the night after the mission to Achilles. With Odysseus, he killed the spy Dolon, and also Rhesus, the leader of a Thracian contingent that had arrived the day before, and made off with the latter's horses. Then there was his meeting with Glaucus, grandson of Bellerophon (see GLAUCUS 2). Diomedes competed in the funeral games held in honour of Patroclus. In the legends that came into being after the *Iliad*, he is described as accompanying Odysseus to Lemnos to fetch the wounded PHILOCTETES, whose presence was necessary in order for the Greeks to capture Troy. Diomedes was a sturdy fighter, who wounded the goddess Aphrodite in battle, and thereby incurred her wrath. He was a fluent speaker, who figured in the various war councils of the Achaean chiefs. But he was not slow to anger. When Achilles killed Thersites after the latter's sarcastic remarks about Penthesilea, Diomedes lost his temper with him, and reminded him that Thersites was a relative of his (Table 27). Then he demanded that the Amazon's body be thrown into the Scamander.

Of all the returns from Troy, that of Diomedes was long considered to have been the happiest – a tradition supported by the *Odyssey*. But his adventures began again very quickly after the Trojan War. His wife AEGIALE had been unfaithful to him, and on his return to Argos he barely escaped the traps she had set for him. He sought refuge as a suppliant at Hera's altar, and from there fled to Italy, to the court of King Daunus. His wife's unfaithfulness was a manifestation of the wrath of Aphrodite, who still bore him malice for her wound. In Daunus' service Diomedes fought against the king's enemies, but Daunus denied him the fair reward he had promised him. Diomedes then showered curses on the country, and doomed it to sterility every year that it was not cultivated by his fellow countrymen, the Aetolians. Then he took possession of the country, despite Daunus' resistance. Daunus seems finally to have got the better of the hero and killed him, while his companions were transformed into birds, tame when they encountered Greeks, but ferocious against all other humans.

Diomedes was credited with founding a whole series of cities in southern Italy.

Diomus (Δίομος) An Attic hero, who gave his name to the deme. He was the son of Colyttus, and was loved by Heracles when the latter was Colyttus' guest. After Heracles' deification, Diomus offered him a sacrifice, an animal from his father's herds. A dog came along and dragged the animal's hindquarters away to a place where Diomus then erected the shrine of Cynosargean Heracles.

Dion (Δίων) A Laconian king, who was married to Amphithea, the daughter of Pronax. He had three daughters, Orphe, Lyco, and Carya. When Apollo had visited Laconia, Amphithea had welcomed him with the greatest respect. In return, Apollo had promised her daughters the gift of prophecy, provided that they did not betray the gods and did not try to find out matters that did not concern them. But one day Dionysus also arrived as a guest in Dion's palace. He fell in love with Carya, who loved him in return. When he returned from his travels around the world, he came back again to Dion's palace, driven by his love for the girl. Then her sisters began spying, seeking to discover the god's affairs. Both Apollo and Dionysus gave them solemn warnings, but in vain. They were changed into rocks, except for Carya, beloved of the god, who became a walnut tree, prolific in nuts. A cult sprang up around her, under the name of Artemis Caryatis.

Dione (Διώνη) One of the goddesses of the first divine generation. Her origin varies with different traditions. Sometimes she was made out to be the daughter of Uranus and Gaia, and the sister of Tethys, Rhea, Themis, and the rest; sometimes she was one of the Oceanides, the daughter of Oceanus and Tethys. Sometimes, again, she was numbered among Atlas' daughters. She had children by Tantalus – Niobe and Pelops – and one tradition claimed that she was the mother of APHRODITE.

Dionysus (Διόνυσος) Also called Bacchus (Βάκχος), and identified in Rome with the old Italian god Liber Pater, Dionysus was in the Classic Era essentially the god of the vine, of wine, and of the mystic ecstasy. His is a complex legend, combining as it does various elements borrowed not only from Greece, but also from neighbouring countries. For example, Dionysus absorbed within his person several similar cults originating in Asia Minor; and these partial identifications gave rise to episodes which fitted in, to a greater or lesser degree, with the rest of his story.

Dionysus was the son of Zeus and Semele, the daughter of Cadmus and Harmonia (Table 3). In consequence, he belonged to the second generation of Olympians, like Hermes, Apollo, Artemis, and the others. Semele, beloved of Zeus, asked him to show himself to her in all his majesty, and to please her, the god did so. But Semele was unable to endure the sight of the lightning which flashed around her lover, and was struck dead. Zeus hastened to pluck forth the child she was carrying in her womb, and which was still only in the sixth month. He sewed it up immediately inside his thigh and when it came to term, it emerged alive and perfectly formed. This was the infant Dionysus, the twice-born god. The child was then entrusted to Hermes, who gave him to King Athamas of Orchomenus and his second wife Ino to rear. He bade them dress little Dionysus as a girl in order to deceive the jealous Hera, who sought to destroy the child as the fruit of her husband's adultery. But this time Hera was not deceived, and sent Dionysus' wet-nurse Ino mad, together with her husband Athamas (see INO, PALAEMON and ATHAMAS). Thereupon, Zeus took Dionysus far away from Greece, into the country called Nysa (which some say was in Asia, others in Ethiopia or Africa), and gave him to the Nymphs of that land to rear. To avoid Hera's recognizing him yet again, he transformed him into a kid. This episode explains both Dionysus' ritual epithet of 'kid', and gives an approximate etymology of the name Dionysus, which is fairly close to Nysa. The Nymphs who reared Dionysus later became the stars in the constellation of the Hyades.

When he grew to manhood, Dionysus discovered the vine and its use; but Hera drove him mad, and in his madness the god wandered throughout Egypt and Syria. From there, he went up the Asian coast until he reached Phrygia, where he was made welcome by the goddess Cybele, who initiated him into the rites of her cult. Now cured of his madness, Dionysus went to Thrace, where he met with considerable hostility from King Lycurgus, who ruled over the banks of the River Strymon. Lycurgus tried to take the god prisoner, but without success, for Dionysus sought refuge with Thetis the Nereid, who gave him asylum beneath the sea, although Lycurgus did manage to capture the Bacchantes, who were

escorting the god. Then the Bacchantes were miraculously set free, and Lycurgus himself was driven mad. Thinking he was cutting down a vine – the sacred plant of his enemy Dionysus – he cut his own leg, and he also cut off his own son's hands and feet. Recovering his senses, he realized also that his whole country had been smitten with sterility. The oracle was consulted, and replied that Dionysus could not be appeased unless Lycurgus were put to death. This his subjects duly did. They quartered him by having him torn apart by four horses.

From Thrace, Dionysus went to India, a country which he conquered in an expedition half warlike, half divine. He overcame resistance both by force of arms (for he had an army with him), and also by his enchantments and his mystic powers. Here originated his triumphal train, which thereafter accompanied him everywhere; it consisted of the chariot drawn by panthers and bedecked with vine-branches and ivy; the Sileni and the Bacchantes; the Satyrs, and all sorts of other minor divinities such as Priapus, the god of Lampsacus.

Returning to Greece, Dionysus reached Boeotia, his mother's native land. In Thebes, where PENTHEUS reigned as Cadmus' successor, he introduced the Bacchanalia, his revels in which the whole populace – but especially the women – were seized with mystic ecstasy, and went raging round the countryside, filling the air with ritual cries. The king was against the introduction of rites as dangerous as these; he was duly punished for his opposition, as was his mother AGAVE, Semele's sister, for on Mount Cithaeron Agave tore him limb from limb with her own hands in her madness. Dionysus then went to Argos, where he demonstrated his power in a similar fashion. He drove King Proetus' daughters mad (see MELAMPUS and PROETIDES), as well as the women of the region, who roamed around the countryside making lowing noises as though they had been turned into cows, and even went so far as to devour their suckling children in their frenzy.

The god then decided to go to Naxos, and to this end he hired the services of some Tyrrhenian pirates, asking them to give him passage to that island. The pirates pretended to agree, but headed for Asia, thinking to sell their passenger as a slave. When he realized this, Dionysus turned their oars into serpents, filled their ship with ivy and made it echo with the sound of invisible flutes. He paralysed the vessel with garlands of vine, to such an extent that the pirates went mad with fear and threw themselves overboard, where they became dolphins. This explains why dolphins are so friendly to men, and do all they can to save them when they are shipwrecked; they are repentant pirates. Now Dionysus' power won world-wide recognition, and he was able to go back to heaven, having fulfilled his role on earth and established his cult everywhere.

He decided to go down into the Underworld first, to seek the shade of his mother Semele and restore her to life. He went by way of Lake Lerna, a bottomless lake, which was said to offer the quickest access to Hades. But since he did not know the way, Dionysus had to make enquiries from a man named Prosymnus (or POLYMNUS), who asked certain sexual favours from him as a reward, to be paid on Dionysus' way back. The god was unable to pay him these favours when he returned, for Prosymnus had died meanwhile; so Dionysus did his best to keep his promise by fashioning a stick into the appropriate phallic shape and planting it in Prosymnus' tomb. Down in Hades, Dionysus had asked the god to release his mother. Hades agreed to this, provided that Dionysus gave him in exchange something that he held very dear. From among his favourite plants Dionysus gave up the myrtle, and this is said to be the origin of the custom whereby initiates into Dionysus' mysteries wore crowns of myrtle.

It was as a god, after his ascent to heaven, that Dionysus rescued Ariadne from Naxos (see ARIADNE and THESEUS).

Dionysus also took part in the war of the Gods against the Titans; he killed Eurytus with a blow from his thyrsus (a long staff entwined with ivy), which was his usual emblem.

Dionysus, god of wine and inspiration, was worshipped with tumultuous processions in which the spirits of earth and of fecundity appeared, their likenesses evoked by masks. From these revels evolved the more ordinary representations of the theatre, comedy, tragedy and satyric drama, this last retaining the earmarks of its origins longer than the others. In the Roman era, from the second century BC, the mysteries of Dionysus, with all their licence and their orgiastic character, made their way into Italy, where they took root very quickly among the still somewhat uneducated peoples of southern and central Italy. In 186 BC, the Roman Senate had to forbid the celebration of the Bacchanalia. But various mystic sects retained the Dionysiac tradition none the less. In all probability, Caesar authorized the

Bacchic ceremonies once again, and Dionysus still played an important part in the religion of the Imperial Age.

Diopatra (Διόπατρα) See TERAMBUS.

Dioscuri (Διόσκουροι) Castor and Pollux, the sons of Zeus. Born from the union of Zeus and Leda, they were the brothers of Helen and Clytemnestra (Tables 2 and 6). Leda was married to Tyndareus, the king of Lacedaemonia. On the night when Zeus coupled with Leda in the shape of a swan, Leda lay also with her human husband; and the two pairs of twins that resulted were attributed as follows: Pollux and Helen to Zeus, Castor and Clytemnestra to Tyndareus. This was why the Dioscuri were sometimes referred to as the Tyndarides, or sons of Tyndareus (Table 19). One form of the legend has it that each of these two pairs of twins was born from an egg laid by Leda after Zeus had coupled with her in the shape of a swan. They were said to have been born on Mount Taygetus in Sparta. They were pre-eminently Dorian heroes, which explains certain features of their legend, which portrays them engaged in strife with Theseus the Athenian. When Theseus and Pirithous left for the Underworld to win Persephone's hand, the Dioscuri launched an expedition against Attica, because Theseus had carried off their sister Helen and immured her in the fortress of Aphidna. While Theseus was away, not only did they set their sister free (see ACADEMUS) but they also took Theseus's mother AETHRA back to Sparta with them as a prisoner. They also drove Theseus' sons from the throne of Athens, installing in their place the pretender Menestheus (see DEMOPHON).

The Dioscuri took part in the expedition of the ARGONAUTS, and particularly distinguished themselves against Amycus, king of the Bebryces. They were also present at the Calydonian hunt (see MELEAGER) and they helped JASON and Peleus lay waste Iolcos.

The reason why they did not figure among the combatants in the Trojan War, although they were Helen's brothers, was because they had already become divine, after the following adventures. Tyndareus had two brothers, Aphareus and Leucippus. Aphareus had two sons named Idas and Lynceus (Table 19), who were betrothed to Leucippus' daughters, the LEUCIPPIDAE, Phoebe and Hilaera. Castor and Pollux were invited to the wedding and carried off the two young brides. A struggle ensued in the course of

The Dioscuri watering their horses at the pool of Juturna in the Roman Forum after they had appeared at the battle of Lake Regillus on the side of Rome. Republican silver denarius.

which Castor and Lynceus were slain. This simple version was not the only one known to the mythographers. The Dioscuri did indeed carry off the two Leucippidae, but they had children by them, and there was no enmity between them and their cousins on account of their wives. On the contrary, they mounted an expedition with Idas and Lynceus to steal cattle in Arcadia. As all four were returning with their booty, an argument broke out as to the distribution. The Dioscuri laid an ambush for their cousins; but Castor was slain by Idas, while Pollux killed Lynceus, and was himself wounded. Zeus killed Idas with a thunderbolt and took Pollux up to Heaven. But Pollux was unwilling to accept the immortality offered him by the god, if his brother Castor were compelled to remain in the Underworld. At this, Zeus allowed each of them to spend one day in two among the gods.

Castor and Pollux were two young heroes, both fighters, though Castor was primarily a warrior, while Pollux practised the art of boxing. In Roman legends, they appear as participants in the battle of Lake Regillus alongside the Romans; it was they who came to the city to announce the victory, and watered their horses at the fountain of Juturna, on the Forum. Juturna, the Nymph of this fountain, was said to be their sister. They had a temple hard by this fountain, not far from the temple of Vesta. The name Dioscuri was applied to twin-pointed forms of St Elmo's fire, which seamen regarded as favourable omens.

Dirce (Δίρκη) The wife of Lycus, king of Thebes, who tormented Antiope, the mother of Amphion and Zethus. For her punishment, see AMPHION.

Dis Pater The Father of Riches was a god of the Underworld in Rome. At a very early date, he was positively identified with Pluto, the HADES of the Greeks.

Dolius (Δολίος) The name of the old gardener who, in the *Odyssey*, looked after Odysseus' domain during the latter's absence. He helped Odysseus defeat the suitors.

Dolon (Δόλων) A Trojan, the son of the herald Eumedes. Although not large in stature he was a very swift runner. He was Eumedes' only son, though he had five sisters. When Hector suggested to the Trojans that a spy should be sent into the camp of the Achaeans to find out their plans, and promised to give the man who accepted this mission Achilles' chariot and his two divine horses, Dolon agreed to undertake it. He donned a wolf's pelt and set off at night. But he ran into Diomedes and Odysseus, who took him by surprise and captured him. They forced him to tell them how the Trojan army was positioned, and then Diomedes killed him.

Doris (Δωρίς) The daughter of Oceanus and the wife of Nereus (Table 12). She was the mother of the NEREIDS.

Dorus (Δῶρος) The hero who gave his name to the Dorians, one of the peoples of the Hellenic race. There are two distinct legends attached to this name. The first makes Dorus the son of Hellen and Orseis, hence the grandson of Deucalion and Pyrrha (Table 8). His brother was Aeolus, the eponymous hero of the Aeolians, another great branch of the Hellenic race. In this version Dorus and his descendants first lived in the region of Phthiotis, in Thessaly, and then emigrated to the area round Mount Olympus and Ossa. Then they moved westward into the interior, towards the range of the Pindus, later withdrawing to the area around Mount Oeta, before finally settling in the Peloponnese.

The other version makes Dorus the son of Apollo and Phthia, and the brother of Laodocus and Polypoetes. The three brothers were said to have been slain by AETOLUS, son of ENDYMION, who seized their kingdom of Aetolia, to the north of the Gulf of Corinth.

Drimacus (Δρίμαχος) The inhabitants of the island of Chios were the first people to buy slaves, and this earned them the wrath of the gods. A good number of their slaves escaped and established themselves in the mountains, whence they sallied forth periodically to lay waste the lands of their former masters. Their leader was a certain Drimacus. After many encounters the Chians arranged a truce with him, and in return for an annual tribute, he agreed not to attack them any longer. Despite this, the Chians put a price on his head. Finally Drimacus grew tired of living under such conditions, and persuaded a young man whom he loved to cut his head off and collect the agreed reward from the inhabitants of Chios; and this was done. But after the death of their leader the slaves resumed their brigandage. Then the Chians built a shrine to Drimacus and initiated a cult in his honour. Whenever anyone was about to fall victim to a plot being hatched by his slaves, Drimacus would appear to him in a dream and warn him.

Dryas (Δρύας) The name of a son of Ares who took part in the Calydonian hunt. He must perhaps be identified with the Dryas, also a son of Ares, who was a brother of Tereus. When TEREUS found out through miraculous means that his son Itys was fated to be slain by a near relation, he believed Dryas to be planning to get rid of his nephew and thus to assure succession to the throne for himself. Tereus slew Dryas forthwith, giving him no time to carry out the designs that Tereus imputed to him. But Dryas was innocent: it was PROCNE who soon slew Itys.

For another hero of the same name, see PALLENE.

Dryope (Δρυόπη) The only daughter of King Dryops; she looked after her father's flocks near Mount Oeta. The Hamadryads made her their companion in their games and taught her the songs and dances most pleasing to the gods. Apollo saw her as she was singing with the others and fell in love with her. To come closer to her he turned himself into a tortoise. The girl played with him as though he were a ball, until finally the transformed god found himself in Dryope's lap. He immediately took the shape of a serpent, and coupled with her. The terrified Dryope ran home, but said nothing to her parents. Soon she married Andraemon, Oxylus' son, and before long she gave birth to a son, Amphissus, who as soon as he reached manhood founded a city at the foot of Mount Oeta, to which he gave the name of the mountain. One day when Dryope had gone to sacrifice to her former companions the Hamadryads, near a temple to Apollo built by her son, the Hamadryads, moved by their friendship for her, carried her off and made her one of themselves. A tall poplar sprang up at the place where she was kidnapped, and a spring gushed forth from the ground.

Ovid relates a slightly different version. According to him, when Amphissus was still quite small, Dryope went up into the mountain to a lake of sparkling water. It was her intention to make a sacrifice to the Nymphs, but she saw a tree with beautiful shining flowers and picked some of them for her child to play with. She was unaware that this tree was the transformed body of the Nymph Lotis. Blood ran from the branches, and in her anger the Nymph changed Dryope into a tree like herself. Some girls who were foolish enough to relate the story of Dryope's transformation were themselves transformed into pines, which are sad, gloomy trees.

In the *Aeneid*, Virgil gave the name Dryope to a Nymph beloved of the god Faunus.

Dryops (Δρύοψ) Dryops, whose name recalls the word for tree or oak, gave his name to the Dryopians, who were said to have been one of the first peoples to occupy the Hellenic peninsula. He is sometimes portrayed as the son of the River Spercheius by Polydora, daughter of Danaus, and sometimes as the son of Apollo by Dia, Lycaon's daughter. His descendants, who originally inhabited the region round Mount Parnassus, were expelled from there by the Dorians, who forced them to disperse. Some settled in Euboea, others in Thessaly, still others in the Peloponnese, and even in the island of Cyprus.

In the Arcadian version of his legend, which made him a descendant of King Lycaon, Dryops was said to have had a daughter who was loved by the god Hermes and became the mother of the god Pan. In the Thessalian version, his daughter DRYOPE coupled with Apollo, and gave birth to Amphissus.

E

Echemus (Ἔχεμος) The son of Aeropus and husband of Timandra, the daughter of Tyndareus and Leda (Table 2); he was therefore a brother-in-law of the Dioscuri, Helen and Clytemnestra. Echemus succeeded Lycurgus on the Arcadian throne, and in this capacity he defended the Peloponnese against the Heraclids' first invasion attempt. Echemus agreed to fight with Hyllus, the Heraclids' leader, in single-handed combat: if Echemus were to win, the Heraclids would not invade the Peloponnese again for fifty years (or a hundred, in some versions). This fight took place on the isthmus of Corinth, near Megara. Echemus killed Hyllus, and the Heraclids accordingly withdrew. As a result of the victory the Tegeans (Echemus was a native of Tegea) gained control of a section of the Peloponnesian confederate army. Echemus' tomb is said to have been at Megara, beside Hyllus', but his grave is also supposed to be at Tegea. According to one account, Echemus participated in the expedition led by the Dioscuri against Attica to release Helen from Theseus.

Echetlus (Ἔχετλος) An Attic hero who is mentioned once in literature: during the battle of Marathon he is supposed to have suddenly appeared on the battlefield wearing peasant's clothes and to have killed many Persians. After the victory he disappeared; an oracle revealed that this mysterious combatant was divine, and ordered that a sanctuary should be dedicated to Echetlus.

Echetus (Ἔχετος) A legendary hero of Epirus and an archetypal tyrant. In the *Odyssey* the beggar Irus was threatened with being handed over to Echetus, who would then have had Irus' nose and ears cut off and thrown to his dogs. Echetus had a daughter, Metope, who had an intrigue with a lover; as a punishment Echetus mutilated the lover and blinded Metope by piercing her eyes with bronze needles. He then incarcerated her in a

tower and gave her grains of bronze, promising that she would regain her sight when she had ground these grains into flour.

Echidna (Ἔχιδνα) A monster with the torso of a woman and a serpent's tail instead of human legs. Accounts of her origin differ: according to Hesiod she was the daughter of Phorcys and Ceto; other versions claim that she was descended from Tartarus and Gaia, or from Styx, or from Chrysaor (Tables 12 and 32). Echidna inhabited a cave either in Sicily or in the Peloponnese. She used to devour passers-by until eventually she was killed by Argos. Many monstrous offspring were attributed to her: by Typhon she is said to have given birth to Orthrus, the dog of Geryon; to Cerberus, the guardian of the Underworld; the Lernean Hydra; and the Chimaera. Orthrus allegedly fathered Phix, a Boeotian monster, and the Nemean Lion. The dragons guarding the Golden Fleece and the Garden of the Hesperides are said to have been Echidna's offspring, as was the eagle of Prometheus.

Those who lived in the Greek colonies on the Euxine Sea, used to recount a quite different legend concerning Echidna. According to this version, when Heracles visited Scythia he left his horses to graze while he slept and when he awoke he found they had disappeared. As he searched he came across Echidna in a cave; she promised to return his horses if he agreed to couple with her. He consented, and as a result Echidna gave birth to Agathyrsus, Gelonus and Scythes.

Echion (Ἐχίων)
1. One of the five Spartoi, or men born from the dragon's teeth sown by CADMUS, who were still surviving at the foundation of Thebes. He married Agave, one of Cadmus' daughters. She gave birth to Pentheus, who later ruled over Thebes and tried to oppose the introduction of the Dionysian cult there.
2. One of the Argonauts, the twin brother of Eurytus, son of Hermes and Antianira.
3. For another Echion, see PORTHAEON.

Echo (Ἠχώ) A Nymph of the trees and springs; some of the legends surrounding her provide explanations of the phenomenon of echoes. In one account Echo was vainly loved by Pan and loved a satyr instead, who shunned her; in revenge, Pan sent some shepherds mad, who tore her to pieces. In another account Echo loved Narcissus unrequitedly and pined away; when she died her voice alone remained – this repeated the last syllables of spoken words.

Eetion (Ἠετίων) A king of Thebes in Mysia and the father of Andromache. He was killed by Achilles, together with his sons, when the city was sacked by the Greeks. Achilles admired Eetion's courage to such an extent that he did not strip him of his arms but buried them with his body, giving him lavish funeral rites. The Nymphs planted an elm tree on his grave. His wife was freed on payment of a ransom but soon she too died, pierced by Artemis' arrows.

Egeria A Roman nymph who seems originally to have been a goddess of springs, forming part of the cult of DIANA at Nemi. There was also a cult dedicated to her at Rome itself, near the Porta Capena at the foot of the Caelian Hill. She is said to have advised the devout king Numa; and according to some versions she was either his wife or his lover. She prescribed the religious practices which Numa followed, and taught him the most efficacious prayers and incantations. When Numa died, Egeria wept so copiously in her despair that she became a spring.

Elatus (Ἔλατος)
1. The eldest son of Arcas, the eponym of Arcadia (Table 9). When Arcas divided up his lands Elatus was given the area around Mount Cyllene; he later added Phocis to this when he assisted the natives in their war against the Phlegyans; he then founded the town of Elatea.
2. Like many of the Arcadian heroes Elatus had a Thessalian counterpart; the two are barely distinguishable. This Elatus, from Larissa, was sometimes linked with CAENEUS (see POLYPHEMUS 1).

Electra (Ἠλέκτρα) Several characters of this name figure in mythology.
1. The earliest was one of the daughters of Oceanus and Tethys, who married Thaumas and then gave birth to Iris, the messenger of the gods, and to the Harpies. Electra was one of Persephone's companions, and was present when she was carried off by Hades.
2. One of the PLEIADES, the seven daughters of Pleione, who lived on Samothrace. Zeus fathered her child Dardanus (Table 7), who left Samothrace and went to the Troad, where he founded the royal dynasty of Troy.

Electra had another son, IASION, whose legend is linked to those surrounding Cybele and Demeter.

Electra is also said to have had a third son named Emathion, who ruled over Samothrace, but more frequently this third child of hers by Zeus is named as Harmonia, though conflicting accounts claim that Harmonia's parents were Ares and Aphrodite. In the Italian version of Electra's legend, she was the wife of the Etruscan king Corythus, and Dardanus and Iasion were born in Italy.

Electra is also linked to the legend of the PALLADIUM. When Zeus attempted to rape her she sought refuge close to the divine statue, but in vain; in his anger Zeus threw the Palladium from the vault of Heaven. The statue landed in the Troad and was preserved in a temple at Troy. In other versions Electra herself brought the statue to Dardanus to provide protection for Troy. She was later transformed with her sisters into the constellation of the Pleiades.

3. The most famous Electra was the daughter of Agamemnon and Clytemnestra (Table 2). She is not mentioned by Homer; but in the work of later poets she gradually replaced Laodice, one of Agamemnon's daughters, whose name was not mentioned thereafter. After Agamemnon was murdered by Aegisthus and Clytemnestra, Electra, who had barely escaped death herself, was treated as a slave; she was saved only by the intercession of her mother. According to some accounts, it was Electra who saved the infant Orestes from the murderers and secretly entrusted him to their old tutor, who took him far away from Mycenae. To prevent Electra from giving birth to a son who could avenge Agamemnon's murder, Aegisthus gave her in marriage to a peasant who lived far from the city. According to other authors, however, Electra, who had once been betrothed to Castor and then promised to Polymestor, was imprisoned in the palace at Mycenae after the murder.

On Orestes' return, she recognized her brother at their father's tomb and together they plotted the assassination of Clytemnestra and Aegisthus. Electra played an active part in this double murder and afterwards, when Orestes was being pursued by the Erinyes for his crime, she devoted herself to his welfare.

Electra figures in several episodes in the legend of Orestes as developed by the tragedians. In Euripides' *Orestes* she shared her brother's tribulations and fought at his side against the hostility of the populace, who wished to condemn the murderers to death. In Sophocles' tragedy *Aletes*, which is now lost, Electra was the principal figure. According to Sophocles' play, when Orestes and Pylades went to Tauris in search of the statue of Taurian Artemis it was rumoured at Mycenae that they had died, and that Iphigenia herself had killed her brother. Aegisthus' son Aletes immediately assumed the throne. Electra then went to Delphi, where she met Iphigenia who had come there with Orestes; Electra wished to punish her sister, and was about to blind her with a blazing brand when she suddenly glimpsed her brother. Electra and Orestes returned to Mycenae where they killed Aletes. Orestes married Hermione, Helen's daughter; Electra married Pylades and accompanied him to Phocis; their children were Medon and Strophius.

Electryon ('Ηλεκτρύων) One of the sons of Perseus and Andromeda, and the father of ALCMENE (Table 31). According to a Boeotian genealogy, Electryon was Itonus' son and his own son, who fought at Troy, was called Leitus.

Elephenor ('Ελεφήνωρ) The son of Chalcodon, and through him the grandson of Abas, whom he succeeded on the Euboean throne. One day Elephenor saw his grandfather being ill-treated by a servant; he went to Abas' rescue and aimed a blow at the servant's head but his club struck Abas instead, and killed him. Elephenor went into exile to atone for his involuntary crime. Elephenor was one of Helen's suitors, and as such he took part in the Trojan War, to which he led the Euboean people, the Abantes, in thirty ships. Since he could not set foot on Euboean soil he mustered his troops from a rock which stood some distance from the shore. During the Trojan War Acamas and Demophon were his companions.

Accounts of his ultimate fate vary: according to Homer he was killed by Agenor before Troy; but other versions show him surviving the fall of Troy and settling on Othronus, an island off Sicily, from which he was driven by a serpent. After this he went to Epirus, in the area of Abantia, or Amantia.

Eleusis ('Ελευσίς) The eponymous hero of Eleusis. According to certain accounts he was the son of Hermes and Deianeira, and was married to Cothone; their son was Triptolemus. Demeter tried to make Triptolemus immortal by plunging him into a furnace. On seeing this Eleusis cried out which enraged Demeter and she killed him.

Elis ('Ηλις) The son of Eurypyla and the god Poseidon. Upon the death of his grandfather Endymion, Elis succeeded to the throne and then founded the city to which he gave his name.

Elpenor ('Ελπήνωρ) One of Odysseus' companions; he was changed into a pig by Circe, who later restored his human form. When Odysseus and his men assembled in readiness to leave Circe's island, Elpenor was asleep on the terrace of her palace; when his name was called he started up, half-asleep, and fell to his death from the terrace.

Later Odysseus met the shade of Elpenor in the Underworld and was asked to carry out Elpenor's funeral rites, which he did on his return to the upper world. Elpenor's tomb could be seen at Latium.

Elymus ('Έλυμος) The bastard son of Anchises and the companion of Aegestes, with whom he founded several Sicilian cities. He gave his name to the Trojan colony which had emigrated with him, and which formed the nucleus of the Elymian people.

Empusa ('Έμπουσα) One of the creatures in Hecate's entourage: she belonged to the Underworld and filled the night with terrors. Empusa could assume various shapes and appeared particularly to women and children. She fed on human flesh, and often assumed the form of a young girl to attract her victims.

Enarophorus ('Εναροφόρυς) One of Hippocoon's sons; when he tried to rape Helen, Tyndareus entrusted her to the care of Theseus.

Endymion ('Ενδυμίων) The genealogy of Endymion varies with the authors. He is most frequently depicted as the son of Aethlius (the son of Zeus) and Calyce (Table 24), though sometimes his father is said to have been Zeus himself. He led the Aeolians from Thessaly to Elis, and ruled over them. Then he married (his wife's name also varies from one author to another) and had three sons – Paeon, Epeius, and Aetolus – and a daughter, Eurycyde. Some authors credit him with another daughter, Pisa, who gave her name to the city of Pisa in Elis. The most famous legend about Endymion is that of his intrigue with Selene (the Moon). When Selene saw Endymion, depicted in the legend as a young shepherd of great beauty, she fell violently in love with him and seduced him. At Selene's request Zeus promised to grant Endymion one wish; he chose the gift of eternal

Endymion slept eternally and remained young forever. Selene (the Moon) visited him nightly and this relief shows Endymion sleeping while his dog bays at the moon. Rome, Capitoline Museum.

sleep, and fell asleep, remaining young forever. Some versions claim that it was during this sleep that Selene saw him and fell in love with him. Sometimes the Peloponnese is the location of the legend, and sometimes Caria, not far from Miletus (see also HYPNUS). Endymion is said to have given his lover fifty daughters.

Enipeus (Ἐνιπεύς) A Thessalian river-god with whom Tyro, daughter of Salmoneus and Alcidice, fell violently in love. Poseidon, who loved Tyro, assumed Enipeus' form and fathered her twins, Pelias and Neleus (Table 21).

Entoria (Ἐντωρία) Entoria's story is a Roman legend handed down by Plutarch and dealing with the foundation of the temple of Saturn. The account seems to be a fabrication – and moreover one full of contradictions – modelled on the legend of ERIGONE. When Saturn lived in Italy (see GOLDEN AGE) a peasant named Icarius gave hospitality to the god, who slept with his host's daughter, Entoria, and fathered four children:

Janus, Hymnus, Faustus and Felix. Saturn also taught his host the art of cultivating the vine and making wine; and he advised him to share the skills he had acquired with his neighbours. Icarius invited his neighbours and gave them wine to drink; this made them all fall into a deep sleep. When they awoke they thought they had been poisoned and stoned Icarius to death. His grandsons hanged themselves in grief. An epidemic then broke out among the Romans; when the oracle at Delphi was consulted it declared that the epidemic was the result of Saturn's anger. To appease the god, Lutatius Catulus founded the temple of Saturn at the foot of the Capitol and built an altar decorated with four faces (Entoria's four children); he also gave the month January its Roman name Januarius (the month of Janus). Saturn transformed Icarius' whole family into a constellation.

Enyo (Ἐνυώ) A goddess of war, usually shown as a member of the train of ARES and most frequently depicted as his daughter, though sometimes as his mother or his sister. She appears covered in blood, and striking attitudes of violence. In Rome she was identified with Bellona, the Roman goddess of war.

Eos (Ἠώς) The personification of the Dawn. She belongs to the first divine generation, that of the Titans (Table 14). She was the daughter of Hyperion and Theia and the sister of Helios and Selene, or, according to other traditions, the daughter of PALLAS. By Astraeus, a god of the same race, the son of Crius and Eurybie, and the brother of the giant Pallas (Table 32), she was the mother of the Winds: Zephyrus (West), Boreas (North), and Notus (South); and also of Eosphorus (the Morning Star) and the Stars. She was depicted as a goddess whose rosy fingers opened the gates of heaven to the chariot of the Sun. Her legend consists almost entirely of her intrigues. She first slept with Ares; this earned her the wrath of Aphrodite who punished her by turning her into a nymphomaniac.

Her different lovers were as follows: Orion the Giant, the son of Poseidon, whom she abducted and carried off to Delos; then Cephalus, the son of Deion and Diomede (Xuthus' daughter) or, as some say, the son of Herse and Hermes. She carried him off to Syria, where she bore him a son, PHAETHON (more commonly held to be the son of the Sun). Finally she abducted Tithonus, son of Ilus and Placia (or Leucippe), a Trojan, and took him to Ethiopia, which in the old legends was the land of the Sun. There she bore him two sons, Emathion and MEMNON. The latter, who seemed to have been her favourite son, reigned over the Ethiopians and died before Troy, fighting Achilles. Eos persuaded Zeus to grant Tithonus immortality, but she forgot to ask for eternal youth for him, and as he grew older he was stricken with physical infirmities. In the end Eos shut him up in her palace, where he led a wretched life. Others say that Tithonus grew so old that he lost the appearance of a man and became a dessicated cicada.

Epaphus (Ἔπαφος) After Io, beloved of Zeus, was transformed into a cow, she wandered all over the earth pursued by the wrath of Hera. Finally she found asylum on the banks of the Nile, where she resumed her human form and gave birth to a son, Epaphus, or the 'Touch of Zeus'. However Hera transferred her hatred to this son, and ordered the Curetes to hide him away, which they did so effectively that Io was unable to find him. Zeus killed the Curetes and Io continued her search for her son. She learnt that he was being brought up by the wife of the king of Byblos, in Syria. She went there and took him back with her to Egypt, where she completed his upbringing. When he became a man he succeeded his adoptive father Telegonus as ruler. Epaphus married Memphis, daughter of the river-god Nile. He fathered a daughter, Libya, who gave her name to Egypt's neighbouring country; then he had two more daughters, called Lysianassa and Thebe. Sometimes his wife is said to have been CASSIOPIA, rather than Memphis.

Epeius (Ἐπειός) There are two heroes of this name in the legends.
1. The first was one of the sons of Endymion, the king of Elis, and hence the brother of Paeon and AETOLUS. He succeeded his father and for some time part of the Elian race bore the name of the Epeians after him (Table 24).
2. The second and better known Epeius was the son of Panopeus (Table 30). He took part in the Trojan campaign, leading a fleet of thirty vessels, but he was not a warrior of note. He particularly distinguished himself by his boxing during the funeral games held in Patroclus' honour, but he failed at throwing the discus. His chief claim to fame was that he built the wooden horse which was used to capture Troy. On his way back from Troy Epeius became separated from Nestor, the leader of his party, and landed in Southern Italy,

where he founded the city of Metapontum or its neighbour, Lagaria. There, he dedicated the tools with which he had built the Trojan horse to the goddess Athena. Another tradition depicts him as the founder of Pisa in Central Italy. In this version Epeius had been cast onto the coast of Italy by a storm; when he disembarked, the Trojan captives whom he left aboard set fire to his ships. Losing hope of ever returning to their own country, he and his companions then founded the city of Pisa, which was so named after the Elian city of the same name.

Epeius is also said to have possessed a miraculous statue of Hermes which was worshipped at Ainos in Thrace. This Hermes, sculpted in Troy, was swept away when the River Scamander flooded in an attempt to halt Achilles; it came ashore at Ainos, where some fishermen caught it in their nets. The statue was made of wood, and the fishermen tried to chop it up for firewood, but they only succeeded in making a small cut on one shoulder. Then they put the whole statue in the fire, but it refused to burn so they threw it back into the sea but it once again became caught in their nets. They finally realized it was a divine image and raised a shrine for it. This legend was related by Callimachus in a poem of which only a few fragments have survived.

Ephialtes (Ἐφιάλτης) The name borne by two giants. One of them was a member of the ALOADAE, who fought against the gods in the battle with the Giants. He was killed by Apollo and Heracles who pierced his eyes with their arrows.

Epidius A hero from Nuceria in Italy. One day he disappeared into the River Sarno; later he reappeared with bulls' horns on his forehead, a sign that he had been transformed into a river-god.

Epigeus (Ἐπειγεύς) The son of Agacles, the king of Budeion in Thessaly. He killed his cousin, was exiled, and fled to the court of Peleus. He accompanied Achilles in the expedition against Troy, where he was slain by Hector.

Epigoni (Ἐπίγονοι) The name given to the direct descendants of the Seven Chiefs who took part in the first expedition against Thebes. Though the first expedition ended in failure, the second one, which was undertaken by the Epigoni, culminated in the capture of the city (see ADRASTUS and ALCMAEON). Ten years after the first war had ended in failure, the sons of the heroes who had fallen at Thebes decided to avenge their fathers. They consulted the oracle, which promised them victory if they took Alcmaeon, Amphiaraus' son, as their leader. Despite his reluctance, Alcmaeon accepted this position at the urging of his mother Eriphyle, who was won over by the presents of Thersandrus, the son of Polynices; she had been similarly persuaded on the first occasion by the presents of Polynices himself. Those who took part in the war were as follows: Alcmaeon and Amphilochus, the two sons of Amphiaraus; Aegialeus, son of Adrastus; Diomedes, son of Tydeus; Promachus, son of Parthenopaeus; Sthenelus, son of Capaneus; Theresandrus, son of Polynices; and Euryalus, son of Mecisteus. The Epigoni began their campaign by ravaging the villages around Thebes. The Thebans advanced against them, led by Laodamas, son of Eteocles, and the two sides met at Glissas. Laodamas slew Aegialeus, but was himself slain by Alcmaeon; the Thebans were forced to retreat. During the night the inhabitants of the city fled on the advice of the seer Tiresias. The Epigoni entered the city the next morning and pillaged it; they devoted a large part of the spoils to Pythian Apollo.

Epimelides (Ἐπιμηλίδες) Nymphs who watched over sheep. The Messapians used to recount the following legend about them: one day some country shepherds saw the Nymphs dancing near their shrine. Not realizing that they were goddesses, they jeered at them and pretended that they themselves could surpass them. The offended Nymphs accepted the challenge; and the shepherds, who were unskilled in dancing, were easily beaten by the Nymphs. As punishment the Nymphs turned the shepherds into trees on the very spot where they had been surprised. The local inhabitants claimed thereafter that at nights they could hear the groans of the transformed shepherds issuing from the tree-trunks.

Epimetheus (Ἐπιμηθεύς) One of the four children of Iapetus and of either Oceanus's daughter Clymene, or of Asia (Table 38). He belonged to the race of Titans; his brothers were Atlas, Menoetius, and PROMETHEUS. Epimetheus formed a pair with Prometheus, although he was his complete antithesis. He was the tool used by Zeus to deceive the highly-skilled Prometheus; after the latter had outwitted Zeus on two separate occasions he forbade Epimetheus to accept even the smallest of presents from Zeus. However

Epimetheus could not resist when Zeus, through the agency of Hermes, offered him PANDORA. In this way, Epimetheus became responsible for all the miseries of mankind. Epimetheus and Pandora were the parents of Pyrrha, who became Deucalion's wife.

Epione (Ἠπιόνη) The companion of Asclepius, who was generally considered to have been his wife and the mother of his daughters Iaso, Panacea, Aegle and Aceso. At Epidaurus, her statue stood beside the image of Asclepius. On Cos she was considered to be Asclepius' daughter. She is sometimes described as Merops' daughter.

Epirus (Ἤπειρος) Echion's daughter, who accompanied Cadmus and Harmonia on their journey through the interior of the country when they left Thebes, carrying Pentheus' ashes. She died in Chaonia, and was buried in a sacred grove which features in the legend of Anthippe and CICHYRUS. She gave her name to the region of Epirus.

Epopeus (Ἐπωπεύς)
1. A hero of Sicyon. His genealogy varies according to different legends. In some accounts he is said to have been a son of Aloeus, and hence the grandson of Canace and Poseidon; in others he is considered to have been their son (Table 10). At first he reigned over Sicyon as Corax's heir; but upon the death of Bounos (who had inherited the throne of Corinth from Aeetes after the latter's departure for Colchis) Epopeus succeeded him, thus uniting the two cities under his rule. Epopeus played a role in the legend of ANTIOPE. He welcomed the young woman when she fled from her father's house before giving birth to Zeus' sons Amphion and Zethus. Antiope's uncle Lycus came and attacked Sicyon, and during the fall of the city Epopeus was slain. Epopeus had a son named Marathon who took refuge in Attica while his father was alive. He returned to Corinth after Epopeus' death.
2. There was another Epopeus, a king of Lesbos, who had an incestuous relationship with his daughter NYCTIMENE.

Erato (Ἐρατώ)
1. One of the nine Muses and, like all her sisters, the daughter of Zeus and Mnemosyne. She was the Muse of lyric poetry, and especially of love poetry.
2. Erato was also the name of an Arcadian Dryad,

the mother of Azan by Arcas. She was a prophetess, inspired by the Arcadian god Pan.

Erebus (Ἔρεβος) The name of the infernal Shades. He was personified and given a genealogy as the son of Chaos and the brother of Nyx, the Night.

Erechtheus (Ἐρεχθεύς) Athenian hero, whose legend is linked with the origins of the city. In early accounts he is indistinguishable from ERICHTHONIUS, the son of Hephaestus and Mother Earth. Euripides depicted him as Erichthonius' son. As the legends became more established, he was included in the chronology of the first kings of Athens and identified as the son of PANDION I and Zeuxippe (who was Pandion's maternal aunt). He had a brother, BUTES, and two sisters, Philomela and Procne, who were later transformed into birds (see TEREUS and Table 11). At Pandion's death, Erechtheus and Butes divided the inheritance: Erechtheus took the throne, and Butes became the priest of the city's two protecting deities, Athena and Poseidon. In a different legend Erechtheus came from Egypt at a time when Attica was being ravaged by famine. Erechtheus imported wheat and introduced its culture into the country, thus earning the gratitude of the inhabitants, who made him their king.

Erechtheus married PRAXITHEA, the daughter of Phrasimus and Diogeneia, who was herself the daughter of Cephisus. They had many children; their sons included Cecrops 2, Pandorus, Metion, and also (according to some authors) Alcon, Orenus, Thespius and Eupalamus. Their daughters were Protogenia, Pandora, Procris, Creusa, Chthonia and Orithyia, and possibly Merope.

During a war between the Athenians and the Eleusinians, the latter had the Thracian Eumolpus as their ally. He was the son of Poseidon and Chione (who was herself the daughter of Boreas and Orithyia) and hence Erechtheus' great-grandson (Table 11). Erechtheus asked the oracle at Delphi how he could assure himself of victory. The oracle informed him that he would have to sacrifice one of his daughters. On his return to Athens, he sacrificed a daughter, some say Chthonia, others Protogenia. The victim's sisters, who had sworn not to survive her, all committed suicide. Some authors say they deliberately sacrificed their lives in the interests of their country. Erechtheus and the Athenians were victorious; Eumolpus was killed in battle, but Poseidon was so angered by his son's death that he persuaded Zeus to slay Erechtheus with a thunderbolt. Erechtheus is sometimes credited with the introduction of the feast of the Panathenaea, as well as with the invention of the chariot, under the inspiration of Athena.

Erginus (Ἐργῖνος)
1. The king of the Minyans of Orchomenus, in Boeotia, and the son of Clymenus and Buzyges (Table 33). When his father was killed during Poseidon's festival at Onchestus, by a Theban called Perieres who was Menoeceus' charioteer, Erginus recruited an army and marched on Thebes. After slaying many Thebans he concluded a treaty with the king of the city, under which Thebes would pay him an annual tribute of a hundred cattle for twenty years. When Heracles was on his way home after his successful hunt for the lion of Cithaeron, he met Erginus' heralds as they went to collect the annual tribute for their master. He mutilated them by cutting off their ears and noses, which he hung round their necks; he told them to take these grisly trophies back to Erginus as his tribute. Indignant at this outrage, Erginus marched again on Thebes. Creon, the king of the city, was prepared to surrender, but Heracles called the youth of Thebes to arms. He received a suit of armour from the hands of Athena, took command of the force, and joined battle with Erginus. He conceived the idea of flooding the plain to prevent the enemy's cavalry from advancing. Heracles won the battle, but during the fighting his adoptive father Amphitryon was killed; in revenge, Heracles himself slew Erginus. To reward him for his victory Creon gave him the hand of his eldest daughter, Megara.

According to one isolated tradition Erginus did not die in this battle but concluded a treaty with Heracles, who imposed on the Minyans a tribute which was twice as large as the one imposed on the Thebans before. He then set out to rebuild his fortune from his ravaged kingdom. When he had amassed a sufficient sum, he married a young woman on the advice of the oracle and fathered two children, the architects AGAMEDES and TROPHONIOS.
2. Another Erginus was a son of Poseidon and took part in the expedition of the ARGONAUTS. Sometimes he is identified as the king of Orchomenus, Heracles' enemy. When the pilot Tiphys died, Erginus took his place and thereafter set the *Argo*'s course. Although he was quite young his hair was white, and this provoked derision from the women at Lemnos. In the games

they held at Lemnos, he won the prize for running.

Erichthonius (Ἐριχθόνιος) One of the first kings of Athens. His genealogy varies according to different traditions: sometimes he is described as the son of Atthis, the daughter of CRANAUS; sometimes – and this is the generally accepted version – he is portrayed as the child of Athena, fathered by Hephaestus. Athena visited the god's workshop to order some weapons and Hephaestus was filled with desire for her. She tried to escape but in spite of his lameness the god caught her. Athena defended herself and during the struggle some of the god's semen was spilled on her leg. In disgust, Athena wiped the stain off with a scrap of wool which she then threw to the ground. Impregnated in this way, Mother Earth produced a child, whom Athena accepted, calling him Erichthonius (the first part of this name resembles the Greek word for wool, and the second part the word for earth, from which the child was born). Unbeknown to the gods Athena hid Erichthonius in a basket, which she then entrusted to one of Cecrop's daughters (see AGLAURUS). Filled with curiosity, the girls opened the basket and there they saw the child, with two snakes guarding him. According to certain versions the body of the child himself terminated in a serpent's tail, as was the case with most of Mother Earth's children. Others claim that when he saw the basket opened Erichthonius escaped in the form of a snake and hid behind the goddess's shield. The girls were terrified by this sight: they went mad and killed themselves by throwing themselves off the heights of the Acropolis.

Athena brought up Erichthonius in the sacred precincts of her temple on the Acropolis, and Cecrops later yielded the throne to him. Some authors prefer an alternative version which claims that Erichthonius expelled AMPHICTYON, who held the throne of Athens at the time.

Erichthonius then married a Naiad named Praxithea and by her had a son named Pandion, who succeeded him on the Athenian throne. Erichthonius is generally credited with the invention of the four-horse chariot, the introduction into Attica of the use of silver, and the organization of the Panathenaea, the annual festival in celebration of Athena. Some of these innovations were also attributed to his grandson ERECHTHEUS.

Eridanus (Ἠριδανός) The name of a mythical river-god, one of the sons of Oceanus and Tethys. Traditions concerning his status vary but he is generally considered as a river of the west. He featured in the episode in the legend of Heracles in which the hero asked the Nymphs to show him the way to the Garden of Hesperides, and he also played a part in the voyage of the ARGONAUTS. He was said to have guided *Argo* to the land of the Celts and out into the Adriatic. When geography became more precise, the River Eridanus was identified sometimes with the Po, and sometimes with the Rhone.

Erigone (Ἠριγόνη)
1. The daughter of an Athenian named Icarius, who welcomed Dionysus hospitably when he came down to earth to bring mankind the vine. Dionysus fell in love with her and fathered the hero Staphylus on her. The god presented Icarius with a goat-skin bottle full of wine, telling him to let his neighbours have a taste of it. Icarius shared the wine with some shepherds, who became drunk and suspected that Icarius had poisoned them. They beat him to death and abandoned his dead body. The howling of his dog Maera showed Erigone where her father's corpse lay unburied at the foot of a tree: the sight so shocked Erigone that she hanged herself from the tree. Dionysus took his revenge by afflicting the Athenians with an extraordinary scourge: the young girls of Athens were struck with madness and hanged themselves. When the oracle at Delphi was consulted, it answered that this was the god's way of avenging the hitherto unpunished deaths of Icarius and Erigone. The Athenians then punished the guilty shepherds and instituted a festival in honour of Erigone. During this festival young girls were swung from trees, but later the girls were replaced by masks in the shape of human faces. This was the legendary origin of the rite of the *oscilla*, which was also performed in Rome and throughout Italy at the Liberalia, the festival of Liber Pater, who was the Italian Dionysus.
2. The daughter of Aegisthus and Clytemnestra and the sister of Aletes. She played a part in the legend of ORESTES. It is sometimes claimed that Orestes was betrayed before the tribunal of the Areopagus and tried for his double murder because of Erigone's intervention. When he was acquitted Erigone committed suicide. According to other authorities, Orestes wanted to kill her with her parents, but Artemis whisked her away and took her to Athens, where she made Erigone her priestess. Yet another tradition claims that she married Orestes and gave him a son, Penthilus.

One of the two Erigones (generally agreed as being the daughter of Icarius) was transformed into the constellation of the Virgin, one of the signs of the Zodiac (Virgo).

Erinona A Cypriot girl whose legend has been handed down solely through one of Servius' glosses on Virgil. Her purity and wisdom earned her the friendship of the goddesses Athena and Artemis; Aphrodite, however, tried to make Zeus fall in love with Erinona. To prevent this, Hera contrived for the young girl to be raped by Adonis; but Zeus became enraged and killed Adonis with a thunderbolt. In response to Aphrodite's pleas, he allowed a shade of Adonis to return to the world, with Hermes as his escort. After the rape Artemis transformed Erinona into a peacock, and later gave back her human form. Erinona then married the resurrected Adonis and gave birth to a son named Taleus.

Erinyes (Ἐρινύες) Violent goddesses, whom the Romans identified with their Furies. They were also known as the Eumenides, which means the 'kindly ones'; this was a name intended to flatter them, and thus to avoid bringing down their deadly wrath upon the speaker's head for having given them a hateful name. They were engendered by the drops of blood that was spilt on the earth when URANUS was castrated, and thus they belonged to the oldest generation of divinities in the Hellenic pantheon. The Erinyes were primitive forces who refused to recognize the authority of the gods of the younger generation. They were analogous with the Parcae, or Fates, who had no laws other than their own, which even Zeus had to obey. There was originally an indeterminate number of Erinyes, but later their number and names became more precisely established. It was generally accepted that there were three – Alecto, Tisiphone, and Megaera. They were depicted as winged spirits, with their hair entwined with snakes, and they held whips or torches in their hands. When they caught their victims they tortured them and sent them mad. They lived in Erebus, the darkest pit of Hell.

From the days of the Homeric epic poems, their essential function was to avenge crime and to mete out special punishments for sins against the family. Altheus' crime against MELEAGER was forced upon him by the Erinyes as a punishment for Meleager's murder of his uncles. They also caused the misfortunes that plagued Agamemnon's family after the sacrifice of Iphigenia, and

drove Clytemnestra to kill her husband. Afterwards, they had her punished by her own son, and then persecuted him for murdering his mother. They were equally responsible for Oedipus' curse. As protectresses of the social order, the Erinyes punished all crimes likely to disturb this order; they also punished overwhelming pride, or hubris, which made men forget that they were mortal. They forbade seers and soothsayers to foretell the future too precisely, in case Man should be delivered from his uncertainty and become too like the gods. The Erinyes were an expression of the fundamental Hellenic concept of a world order which had to be protected against the forces of anarchy. One of their essential functions was to punish the murderer, since murder endangered the stability of the social group in which it was committed. A murderer was usually banished from his city and wandered from place to place until someone agreed to purify him of his crime; often he was struck with madness by the Erinyes (see ORESTES and ALCMAEON). The Erinyes slowly came to be considered the divinities of infernal punishment, as belief in an afterlife gradually became established. The first faint intimations of this function are already visible in the works of Homer, but it stands out very clearly in the *Aeneid*. Virgil depicted the Erinyes in the deeps of Tartarus, tormenting the souls of the dead with their whips and terrifying them with their snakes. These gloomy images were perhaps influenced by the Etruscan religion, which peopled its Underworld with monstrous entities which tortured the dead (see CHARON).

Eriphyle (Ἐριφύλη) The daughter of Talaus, king of Argos, and the sister of ADRASTUS. After Adrastus had been reconciled with his cousin AMPHIARAUS, the reconciliation was sealed by the marriage of Eriphyle to Amphiaraus (Table 1). Four children were born of this marriage: two sons, Alcmaeon and Amphilochus, and two daughters, Eurydice and Demonassa.

The legend of Eriphyle is linked with the Theban cycle and the expeditions of the Seven and of the Epigoni. When Amphiaraus was asked by Adrastus to take part in the first of these expeditions on behalf of POLYNICES, he had at first refused, because his gift of prophecy told him that he would perish there. But when he married, he had agreed to accept his wife Eriphyle as arbitress of any disagreement between himself and Adrastus. The dispute was submitted to her for settlement, but instead of making an equitable decision,

Eriphyle allowed herself to be influenced by
POLYNICES' present – HARMONIA's necklace. When
he set out for Thebes, Amphiaraus made his sons
swear to avenge him. When the second expedition, that of the Epigoni, was being prepared
Eriphyle accepted a bribe, as she had done before,
and forced Alcmaeon to accept the command. On
this occasion it was Polynice's son Thersandrus
who bribed her, by giving her Harmonia's robe.
When ALCMAEON returned from this expedition he
killed Eriphyle and dedicated the necklace and the
robe to Apollo in the shrine at Delphi.

Eris (Ἔρις) The personification of Strife, generally considered to be the sister of Ares, and his
companion. Hesiod's *Theogony* places her among
the primordial forces, belonging to the generation
of Nyx, the Night. She gave birth to a number of
abstract concepts, such as Sorrow (Ponos),
Forgetfulness (Lethe), Hunger (Limos), Pain
(Algos), and finally the Oath (Horcus). In his
Works and Days, Hesiod postulates two distinct
and separate Strifes: the first a pernicious daughter
of the Night, and the second merely a spirit of
emulation, placed by Zeus within the world to
give it a healthy sense of competition. Eris was
generally portrayed as a female winged spirit, not
unlike the Erinyes. It was she who threw the apple
intended for the fairest of the goddesses, which
PARIS had the task of awarding; and this was the
origin of the Trojan War.

Eros (Ἔρως) The god of Love. His many-faceted
personality evolved considerably between the
Archaic Era and the age of Alexandria and Rome.
In the oldest theogonies Eros was considered to be
a god born at the same time as Mother Earth,
directly from primitive Chaos; and he was worshipped according to this belief at Thespiae, in the
shape of a simple phallic pillar. Other legends
claim that Eros was born from the primordial egg;
Night had given birth to this egg, which split into
two halves one forming the Earth, and the other
its cover, the Sky. Eros always remained a fundamental world force, even at the time of the
Alexandrine embellishments of his legend. He
ensured the continuity of the species as well as the
internal cohesion of the cosmos. Authors of cosmogonies, philosophers, and poets speculated on
this theme. The tendency to regard Eros as one of
the major gods was countered by the doctrine
presented in the form of a myth by Plato in his
Banquet, a myth which he put into the mouth of a
priestess of Mantinea called Diotime, whom he

*Bronze Hellenistic mirror case showing Eros, the god of
love, with his mother Aphrodite.*

claimed to have been Socrates' instructress.
According to Diotime, Eros was a demon halfway
between god and man. He was born from the
union of Expediency (Poros) and Poverty (Penia)
in the garden of the gods, after a colossal feast to
which all the divinities had been invited. He owed
some significant characteristics to his parents: he
was always busy in search of his objective, like
Poverty, and he could always think of some way
of attaining it, like Expediency; but far from being
an all-powerful god, he was a perpetually dissatisfied and restless force.

Various myths came into being, giving Eros
different genealogies. He is sometimes said to be
the son of Eilithyia or of Iris, or of Hermes and
Chthonian Artemis, or – and this was the generally accepted tradition – of Hermes and Aphrodite. One Eros was the son of Hermes and
Uranian APHRODITE; another, called Anterus
(Opposite, or Reciprocal, Love) was born to Ares
and Aphrodite, daughter of Zeus and Dione. A
third was the son of Hermes and Artemis, daughter of Zeus and Persephone; and this Eros in particular was the winged god well known by poets
and sculptors. Cicero, who listed the different
theories propounded by the various mythographers at the end of his treatise on *The Nature of
the Gods*, had no difficulty in showing their artificial character and that they were invented belatedly to resolve difficulties or contradictions
contained in the primitive legends.

The god Eros gradually assumed his traditional appearance under the influence of the poets. He was depicted as a child, often winged, but also wingless on occasion, whose occupation was to trouble the hearts of men. He either inflamed them with his torch or wounded them with his arrows; he was forever interfering. He attacked Heracles, Apollo (who had poked fun at him for playing the archer), even Zeus, his own mother, and of course mankind. The Alexandrine poets loved to portray him playing at nuts (antiquity's equivalent of the game of marbles) with child divinities, notably Ganymede, and arguing with them or with his brother Anteros. Furthermore, they invented childish scenes that fitted the character they had imagined for the god; these depicted Eros punished and put in the corner by his mother, Eros wounded while plucking roses, careless of the thorns, and so on; the paintings at Pompeii exemplify this concept of him. Invariably – and this too was a favourite theme of the poets – beneath the apparently innocent child could be seen the powerful god capable of inflicting cruel wounds as his whims dictated.

One of the most celebrated legends in which Eros plays a part is the romantic adventure of PSYCHE, which is a story treated as a fable; the origins of this were probably to be found among the Milesian fables.

Erylus A legendary hero of Praeneste (modern Palestrina), known to us only through the *Aeneid*. He was the son of the goddess Feronia, and had three separate lives and three bodies. When Evander came to settle in Latium he fought with Erylus and defeated him in single combat.

Erymanthus (Ἐρύμανθος)
1. A son of Apollo, who was smitten with blindness by Aphrodite, because he had seen her bathing before she went to couple with ADONIS. In revenge Apollo turned himself into a boar and killed Adonis with a staggering blow from his tusks.
2. The god of the river of the same name in Psophis. The mythographers claim that this Erymanthus was a member of the family of Arcas, who gave his name to Arcadia.

Erysichthon (Ἐρυσίχθων)
1. A Thessalian, either the son or brother of King Triopas. He was impious and violent, and cared nothing for the gods' anger. He decided to cut down a sacred grove dedicated to Demeter; even divine warnings could not divert him from this act of sacrilege. To punish him, the goddess condemned him to suffer perpetual hunger; within a few days he had devoured all the wealth of his household. Erysichthon's daughter Mnestra, who possessed the gift of metamorphosis (which she had received as a present from Poseidon), conceived the idea of selling herself as a slave. Once she was sold she assumed another form, and then sold herself again in order to procure funds for her father. Erysichthon eventually became insane and ate himself.
2. A legendary hero of Athens, the son of Cecrops I and Aglaurus who died young, without leaving descendants. All that is known of him is that he went on a journey to Delos, where he carried off a statue of Eilithyia, and that he died on his way home (Table 4).

Erytus (Ἔρυτος) Erytus, or Eurytus was the twin brother of Echion, one of the Argonauts. They were the sons of Antianira, the daughter of Menetus.

Eryx (Ἔρυξ) The hero who gave his name to the Sicilian mountain which was famous because of the shrine of Aphrodite which stood at its summit. He was the son of Aphrodite and Butes the Argonaut who was carried away by the goddess just as he was about to yield to the Sirens' song. In other traditions Eryx was the son of Aphrodite and Poseidon, and in some accounts his father Butes is considered as an indigenous king rather than an Argonaut. Eryx is said to have been responsible for the construction of the temple dedicated to Aphrodite Erycina, and he also played a part in the legend of Heracles. As Heracles was returning home, driving before him the cattle he had stolen from Geryon, Eryx challenged him to a fight, hoping to take the cattle from him. Heracles accepted the challenge and killed him; but instead of keeping Eryx' kingdom for himself, he handed it over to the inhabitants, telling them that one of his descendants would come to take possession in due course. This was fulfilled when the Lacedaemonian Dorieus founded a colony on that site in the historical era.

Eteocles (Ἐτεοκλῆς) One of the heroes of the Theban cycle, the son of Oedipus and Jocasta and the brother of POLYNICES (Tables 29 and 37). According to some traditions, his mother was EURYGANIA, not JOCASTA. After Oedipus' incest was discovered, his two sons banished him from

Thebes. Oedipus cursed them and predicted that they would become estranged and kill each other. To avoid this curse being fulfilled, the two brothers decided to rule alternately, each for a period of a year. Eteocles ruled first and Polynices left Thebes, either of his own free will or because his brother had expelled him. When he returned at the end of the year and demanded his right to the throne, Eteocles refused. Polynices then organized an expedition against his own city with Adrastus' help. Before launching the attack, however, he sent Tydeus as an ambassador to ask Eteocles to respect the agreement they had made together. Eteocles refused once again and Adrastus' army of Argives attacked. Eteocles and Polynices met in single-handed combat and killed each other. After the Thebans were victorious Eteocles received an honourable burial, but Polynices was denied the customary funeral rites (see ANTIGONE). At the time of the expedition of the EPIGONI Thebes was ruled by Laodamas, one of the sons of Eteocles.

Ethemea A Nymph who married a king of Cos called Merops thereby forfeiting her place in Artemis' train. To punish her for her desertion, Artemis shot her with arrows and would have killed her had Persephone not dragged her to Hades while she was still alive. Merops, filled with grief at the loss of his wife, was about to commit suicide, but Hera took pity on him, and transformed him into an eagle. She then placed him among the stars so that in his new form he might forget all human griefs.

Etias (Ἠτίας) According to an obscure legend Etias was a daughter of Aeneas who gave her name to the city of Etis, which lay on the coast of Laconia opposite Cythera.

Eubouleus (Εὐβουλεύς)
1. A brother of TRIPTOLEMUS, and the son of Trochilus, the priest of Demeter who fled from Argos and took refuge in Attica. Certain traditions, however, claim that Triptolemus and Eubouleus were the sons of Dysaules.
2. A swineherd who happened to be with his pigs at the place where Hades dragged Persephone down into the Underworld; some of his animals were engulfed with the two divinities. This incident was the origin of the rite carried out in the Thesmophorian festival at Eleusis, which consisted of sacrificing a certain number of young pigs in Eubouleus' honour, in an underground chamber. The name Eubouleus (meaning 'Good

Counsellor' or 'Benevolent') was one of the epithets of Hades; it was sometimes applied to a divinity born to Zeus and Persephone, and worshipped at Athens conjointly with Tritopatreus and Dionysus.

Euchenor (Εὐχήνωρ) A son of the Corinthian soothsayer Polyidus. His father warned him many times of the fates that awaited him: he could choose between an easy death at home, or a violent death if he went to fight at Troy with the Atrides. He chose to die gloriously and fell on the field of battle, smitten by an arrow from Paris' bow.

Eudorus (Εὔδωρος) A son of Hermes and Polymela, the daughter of Phylas. He was brought up by his grandfather; and during the Trojan War he followed Achilles at the head of one of the five battalions of Myrmidons. When Achilles was sulking in his tent and Patroclus wished to continue fighting without him, Achilles gave him Eudorus as his companion in battle.

Eulimene (Εὐλιμένη) The daughter of Cydon, the king of Crete. Her father arranged for her to marry a man named Apterus, a member of the Cretan aristocracy; but she was really in love with Lycastus, who had been her lover for some considerable time. When several Cretan cities revolted against Cydon, he consulted the oracle and asked what he should do. The oracle replied that he must sacrifice a virgin to his country's heroes. Cydon arranged for the young girls to draw lots, and the lot fell on Eulimene. In an attempt to avert the fate that threatened her, Lycastus confessed the truth about their relationship to Cydon; but this merely made the populace more convinced that Eulimene deserved to die, and she was duly sacrificed. Cydon had her body opened and it was found that she was pregnant. Apterus was afraid of reprisals on the part of Lycastus; so he set a trap for the latter and killed him, and then went into exile at Xanthus, near Termera in Lycia.

Eumaeus (Εὔμαιος) The son of the king Ctesius, who reigned over the island of Syris in the Cyclades. He was entrusted to the care of a Phoenician slave-girl while still only a small child. He was Odysseus' swineherd and he remained loyal to his master's memory, and tried, within Odysseus' domain of Ithaca, to safeguard his master's assets. When Odysseus returned to Ithaca, the first person he approached, on Athena's advice, was Eumaeus, who acted as his intermediary for his reconquest of the palace.

Eumelus (Εὔμηλος)
1. The son of Admetus and Alcestis, who was among the warriors in the war against Troy. He took to Troy the horses which had formerly been looked after by Apollo when he was in bond-service to Admetus. These horses won him a victory at the funeral games held in honour of Patroclus.
2. A hero from the island of Cos, who was transformed into a crow because of his impiety (see AGRON).
3. The father of BOTRES of Corinth, who was transformed into a bird by Apollo.

Eumolpus (Εὔμολπος) According to the generally accepted tradition, Eumolpus was the son of Poseidon and Chione, who was herself the daughter of Boreas and Orithyia (Table 11). Fearing her father's wrath, Chione threw the new-born child into the sea; but Poseidon rescued him and took him to Ethiopia, where he entrusted him to Benthesicyme, a daughter of his by Amphitrite, and she brought him up. When he reached manhood, his adoptive mother's husband gave him one of his daughters as his wife; but Eumolpus attempted to rape one of his sisters-in-law, and was banished. He then went with his son Ismarus to the court of the Thracian king Tegyrius, who gave Ismarus one of his daughters in marriage. Eumolpus took part in a plot against Tegyrius, but was discovered and forced to flee. He took refuge at Eleusis, where he became very popular with the inhabitants. After the death of Ismarus, Eumolpus made his peace with Tegyrius, who recalled him to his court and left him his throne. As soon as Eumolpus became king of Thrace, war broke out between the inhabitants of Eleusis and the Athenians, who were led by ERECHTHEUS. Eumolpus was summoned by his friends and came to their aid at the head of an army of Thracians; but he was defeated and killed by the Athenians. His father Poseidon avenged him by persuading Zeus to kill Erechtheus with his thunderbolts.

Various traditions credit Eumolpus with the institution of the Eleusian Mysteries. Eumolpus purified Heracles after the murder of the Centaurs, and the priestly family of the Eumolpides considered themselves to be his descendants. After his death, his son Ceryx (the Herald) was given a role to perform in the Mysteries. This son was the ancestor of the Ceryces, or Heralds, who presided over initiations at Eleusis.

Some traditions link Eumolpus with Museus, who is sometimes said to be his father, sometimes his son; but authors are far from agreeing about the true identity of Eumolpus, the founder of the Mysteries – some even going so far as to consider him to have been completely distinct from Chione's son, and to claim that he was the son of Deiope and the grandson of Triptolemus.

Euneus (Εὔνεως) The son of Jason and HYPSIPYLE, the queen of Lemnos, who lived at the time when the Lemnian women had killed all the men of the island, and the ARGONAUTS arrived unexpectedly and made the women pregnant. Although he was not with the Achaean army at Troy, he maintained friendly relations with the Greeks, and provided them with wine. He bought Lyacon, one of Priam's sons, from Patroclus, in return for a richly engraved drinking-bowl. When Hypsipyle was sold as a slave to Lycurgus, king of Nemea, Euneus rescued her and brought her back to Lemnos.

Eunomus (Εὔνομος) After Heracles had married Deianeira and was living at the court of his father-in-law Oeneus, the king of Calydon, he accidentally killed a child called Eunomus, who was a cup-bearer, and the son of Architeles, one of Oeneus' kinsmen. Eunomus died when he poured the warm water with which he was supposed to be washing the hero's feet over his hands instead. Heracles gave him what he intended to be a slap, but the force of the blow was so great that it killed the boy. Architeles forgave the hero for this involuntary homicide, but Heracles nevertheless went into exile at Trachis with his wife and his son, Hyllus. Eunomus was sometimes called Cyathus.

Eunostus (Εὔνοστος) A hero from Tanagra in Boeotia. He was the son of Aelieus and Scias and was brought up by the nymph Eunosta. He spurned the love of Ochna, the daughter of Colonus, and this was the cause of his death (see BUCOLUS).

Euphemus (Εὔφημος) One of the ARGONAUTS, and the son of Poseidon, who had given him the gift of walking on water. His mother was Europa, daughter of Tityus. When the Argonauts were passing through the Symplegades, it was Euphemus who launched the dove whose fate was to inform the seamen of the destiny awaiting them. In the episode at Lake Tritonis, Euphemus received a lump of magic earth from the god Triton, as a portent of his descendants' arrival in Cyrenaica. Euphemus threw this sacred lump into the sea, causing the island of Thera to spring up. Battus, who founded the colony of Cyrene, was believed to be a descendant of Euphemus through his grandfather Leucophanes, whom Euphemus fathered on a Lemnian woman named Malache. Euphemus married Heracles' sister, Laonane.

Euphorbus (Εὔφορβος) The son of Panthous and a Trojan hero, who gave Patroclus his first wound. He was slain by Menelaus, who carried off Euphorbus' shield and laid it in Hera's temple at Argos. Pythagoras claimed to have been Euphorbus in a previous life.

Euphorion (Εὐφορίων) After his death, Achilles is said to have lived with Helen in the Islands of the Blessed, where they had a son, Euphorion, who was a supernatural winged entity. Zeus fell in love with him, but his love was not returned, and Euphorion fled to escape him. The god caught up with him on the island of Melos and killed him with a thunderbolt. The Nymphs of the island buried him; this enraged Zeus, who transformed them into frogs.

Euphrates (Εὐφράτης) To explain the origin of the name of the River Euphrates, a legend was created in which a man named Euphrates had a son called Axurtus. Euphrates found this son asleep next to his mother one day; mistaking him for a stranger, he killed him. When he realized his mistake he threw himself in his despair into the River Melos, which thereafter bore the name of Euphrates.

Europa (Εὐρώπη)
1. The daughter of Tityus and mother of EUPHE-MUS by Poseidon.

Europa, the daughter of Agenor, being abducted by Zeus in the disguise of a bull and taken to Crete by the god. Mosaic at the Roman villa of Lullingstone, Kent.

2. One of the daughters of Oceanus and Tethys.
3. The mother of Niobe, wife of Phoroneus.
4. The daughter of the river-god Nile, and one of Danaus' wives.
5. The most celebrated figure of this name was the daughter of Agenor and Telephassa; although she is generally thought to be Agenor's daughter (Table 3), her father is in some accounts said to have been Agenor's son Phoenix. Zeus saw Europa when she was playing with her companions on the beach at Sidon, or Tyre, where her father was king. He was filled with love for her beauty, and transformed himself into a bull of a dazzling whiteness, with horns like a crescent moon. In this form he lay down at Europa's feet. After she had overcome her initial fright, Europa grew bolder and stroked the animal, then sat upon its back. The bull immediately rose to its feet and made for the sea and plunged into the waves and swam away from the shore. They reached Crete and at Gortyna, beside a spring, Zeus lay with the young maiden beneath some plane trees; in memory of this intrigue the trees were granted the privilege of never losing their leaves.

Europa had three sons by Zeus: Minos, Sarpedon, and Rhadamanthys. She is also said to have given birth to Carnus – and perhaps Dodon. Zeus gave her three gifts: the bronze automaton TALOS (see ARGONAUTS), who guarded the coasts of Crete against landings by foreigners; a dog which never let any prey escape it; and a hunting-spear which never missed its mark. Zeus then married her to Asterion, the king of Crete and the son of Tectamus. The marriage proved childless, and Asterion adopted Zeus' sons. After her death, Europa received divine honours. The bull whose form Zeus had taken became a constellation, and was included among the signs of the Zodiac. For the saga of Europa's brothers when they went in search of their sister, see AGENOR and CADMUS.

Eurus (Εὖρος) The south-west wind, the son of Eos (the Dawn) and Astraeus, or perhaps Typhon.

Euryalus (Εὐρύαλος)
1. The son of Mecisteus (Table 1), who took part in the expeditions of the Argonauts and the Epigoni, and in the Trojan War, with Diomedes.
2. One of Odysseus' sons, whose mother was EVIPPE, daughter of Tyrimmas, king of Epirus; he was slain by his own father.
3. One of Aeneas' companions. A youth of great beauty, whose friendship with Nisus was widely known. He died in the fighting against the Rutuli.

Eurycleia (Εὐρύκλεια)
1. Oedipus' mother, in a version of the legend which makes no mention of his incest. Eurycleia was Laius' first wife, and it was the second wife, Jocasta, whom Oedipus married after Laius' death.
2. Eurycleia was also the name of Odysseus' nurse.

Eurydice (Εὐρυδίκη)
1. The most famous of the heroines who bore the name of Eurydice was the Dryad who was Orpheus' wife. She was bitten by a snake as she was walking with her companions, the Naiads, in a meadow in Thrace. In order to link this legend with Aristaeus', Virgil claimed that this accident happened when she was fleeing from Aristaeus, who was trying to catch her and ravish her. Orpheus grieved for her when she died and in his despair plunged boldly into Hades to bring her back. He succeeded in moving the divinities of the Underworld with his music and he was given permission to take her back to the light of day, on condition that he made no attempt to look back at her until they were out in the sunlight. Eurydice followed behind him and they were just about to leave the Underworld when Orpheus was unable to resist the desire to see her again and turned round. Eurydice was immediately dragged back to Hades by an irresistible force and Orpheus had to return to earth alone.
2. The daughter of Lacedaemon and Sparte, upon whom Acrisius fathered Danae (Tables 6 and 31).
3. In Euripides' lost tragedy *Hypsipyle*, Eurydice was the name of the wife of Lycurgus, king of Nemea and the mother of Archemorus.
4. The daughter of Amphiaraus and Eriphyle (Table 1). This Eurydice is possibly identical with the preceding one.
5. The wife of Creon, king of Thebes; she was unable to bear the death of their son Haemon, and hanged herself (see ANTIGONE).

Eurygania (Εὐρυγάνεια)
1. Eurygania or Eurygane are the names of Oedipus' wife in the oldest versions of the legend, which makes no mention of his incestuous relationship with Jocasta. According to these accounts Oedipus had his four children Eteocles, Polynices, Antigone, and Ismene by Eurygania and not Jocasta, after the latter's death.
2. According to a very similar tradition, Eurygania was the daughter of Hyperphas, and it was

by her that OEDIPUS had his children, while Jocasta was his mother's name. In this version Oedipus did marry Jocasta, but had no children by her (see EURYCLEIA).

Eurylochus (Εὐρύλοχος) In the *Odyssey*, Eurylochus was Odysseus' companion and lieutenant. He married Odysseus' sister CTIMENE. On Circe's island, he was chosen by lot to reconnoitre, but he did not enter the enchantress's palace, and instead returned to tell Odysseus of the transformation of his companions. Later in the narrative, Eurylochus advised landing on the island where the cattle of the Sun were grazing and he assumed the blame for the curse which followed the sacrilege committed by Odysseus' companions, who had no hesitation about slaughtering the god's heifers and eating them. Eurylochus died with them.

Eurymachus (Εὐρύμαχος) One of the more notable suitors of PENELOPE in the *Odyssey*. He insulted Odysseus when the latter appeared in the palace disguised as a beggar, and threw a stool at him. When the soothsayer Theoclymenus warned the suitors of the doom that threatened them, Eurymachus mocked him, and accused him of being insane. When given the test of the bow, Eurymachus was unable to bend it, much to his shame. After the death of Antinous, he tried in vain to make his peace with Odysseus. Finally, he drew his sword against him, and was killed by an arrow from Odysseus' bow.

Eurymedon (Εὐρυμέδων)
1. A Giant, who reigned over a race of Giants at the far end of the earth. His violent deeds led to the downfall of him and his people. It was said that while he was still a child he raped Hera and fathered Prometheus on her; this earned him the wrath of Zeus. This somewhat unsound version appears to be a later modification of the legend of PROMETHEUS.
2. A son of Minos and the Nymph Paria: his brothers were Nephalion, Chryses, and Philolaus (Table 28). During his expedition against the Amazons, Heracles landed on Paros. Since two of his companions had been killed by Minos' sons, who lived on this island, Heracles attacked these sons and slew them. He then laid siege to the city; to appease him, the inhabitants begged him to take two of their princes to replace his two companions who had been killed. Heracles took two of Minos' grandsons, Alceus and Sthenelus, the sons of Androgeos.

3. Agamemnon's charioteer, who was slain by Aegisthus at Mycenae, together with his master.

Eurymus (Εὔρυμος) A hero who came from Olenus (probably Olenus in Aetolia), who slandered Castor in Pollux's hearing. Pollux reported this slander to his brother, who slew Eurymus with blows from his fists. Alternatively, it may have been Pollux himself who avenged his brother immediately.

Eurynome (Εὐρυνόμη) One of the goddesses of the first divine generation, that of the Titans; she was the daughter of Oceanus and Tethys (Table 38). Before Cronus seized power, she reigned with Ophion over Olympus; they were expelled by Cronus and Rhea, who replaced them. She and Ophion took refuge in the sea, where, with Thetis, she welcomed HEPHAESTUS when he was thrown from the heights of heaven. She was loved by Zeus, who fathered the Graces, Aglaea, Euphrosyne and Thalia, and the river-god Asopus. A very ancient temple on the outskirts of Phigalia was dedicated to Eurynome: this temple stood in the middle of a grove of cypresses. The statue which represented and was worshipped as Eurynome had the torso of a woman, but from the waist downwards had the form of a fish.

Eurynomus (Εὐρύνομος) Pausanias is our sole source of information about the demon called Eurynomus who ate the flesh from buried bodies, leaving only the bones.

Eurypylus (Εὐρύπυλος)
1. The son of Evemon, and a Thessalian chief who took part in the Trojan War. He killed Hypsenor, Melanthus, and Apisaon. He was himself wounded by Paris, but was rescued by Patroclus.
2. A local hero of Patras on the Gulf of Corinth, very often identified with the preceding Eurypylus. According to the legend, the inhabitants of Patras used to make an annual sacrifice to Artemis of the most beautiful girl and the most handsome boy in the city, in expiation of a former sacrilege in the goddess's temple committed by Melanippus and the priestess Comaetho (see COMAETHO 2). Eurypylus had received a mysterious chest as part of his share of the spoils from Troy; upon opening it he had been stricken with madness. The oracle told him that he would be cured when he came across 'an unusual sacrifice' on his journey home, and went on to say that he must settle in the land where he encountered it. When he reached Patras

he saw the annual sacrifice being offered to Artemis and realized at once that the oracle had been fulfilled. The inhabitants of Patras had also been told by the oracle that their sacrifice would no longer be necessary once it had been witnessed by a leader from another land; and as soon as they saw Eurypylus arrive in the city they knew that Artemis' anger had been appeased. Eurypylus settled in Patras and died there. His tomb could be seen on the city's acropolis.

3. A king of the island of Cos, the son of Poseidon and Astypalaea. When Heracles visited Cos on his return from Troy, Eurypylus and his sons tried to prevent him from landing; but Heracles made his way into the town at night and killed them.

4. The son of Telephus who fought alongside the Trojans. On being cured of his wound, Telephus had promised that neither he nor his descendants would ever fight against the Greeks; but Astyoche, Eurypylus' mother and Priam's sister, allowed herself to be persuaded to send her son to Troy, where he was killed by Neoptolemus. She had been bribed by a present – the golden vine which Zeus had once offered to Ganymede. Eurypylus was the father of GRYNUS.

5. A son of Poseidon who ruled over the land of Cyrene in Libya. It was he who gave Euphemus a welcoming present of a lump of earth, when the Argonauts were passing through Lake Tritonis. According to Pindar, Eurypylus was the incarnation of the god Triton; other authors depict him as Triton's brother, with his mother being Celaeno, one of Atlas' daughters. He was married to Sterope, a daughter of the Sun, and had two sons, Lycaon and Leucippus. During his reign Apollo brought the Nymph CYRENE into the country.

Eurysaces (Εὐρυσάκης) Telamon's son Ajax married a captive at Troy named Tecmessa, who was the daughter of the Phrygian king Teleutas (see AJAX 2); she bore him a son called Eurysaces. Before committing suicide, Ajax entrusted this son to his brother Teucer. After the fall of Troy, Eurysaces returned to his father's homeland, Salamis in Attica; but he was not allowed to travel in the same ship as his uncle Teucer, and this provoked Telamon's anger. After Telamon had banished TEUCER, Eurysaces became his grandfather's heir. Teucer attempted to return when he learnt of Telamon's death, but Eurysaces sent him away. With his brother Philaeus, Eurysaces handed over the island of Salamis to the Athenians; for this gift they were both rewarded with the freedom of the city of Athens. According to other

traditions, Philaeus was Eurysaces' son, not his brother; and it was he rather than Eurysaces who handed his country over to the Athenians – though Eurysaces' family certainly settled in Athens. His descendants included Miltiades, Cimon, Alcibiades, and the historian Thucydides.

Eurystheus (Εὐρυσθεύς) Eurystheus was Perseus' grandson; his mother was Pelops' daughter Nicippe, and he was a first cousin of Amphitryon and his wife Alcmene (Table 31). He reigned over Tiryns, Mycenae and Midea in the Argolid. The throne had come to him because of a prophecy of Zeus, which had been cleverly manipulated by Hera. When Heracles was about to be born, Zeus declared that Mycenae would be ruled by the descendant of Perseus who was about to see the light of day. The jealous Hera persuaded Eilithyia, the goddess of childbirth, to hold back the birth of Heracles (see ALCMENE) and to hasten that of Eurystheus, who was still only in his seventh month. Eurystheus was born first and thus reaped the benefit of Zeus's promise.

In the legend of Heracles, Eurystheus appears as an imperfect man, both physically and morally, who trembled with fear before the hero and did not deserve the power he wielded. When Heracles returned from the expedition against the Minyans of Orchomenus (see ERGINUS), Hera struck him with madness with the result that he killed his own children. He went to consult the Pythian oracle, who instructed him to return to Tiryns and put himself in Eurystheus' service. Eurystheus then made him undertake the Twelve Labours that brought great glory to the hero and led to his deification. Eurystheus refused to allow Heracles within the walls of Mycenae, fearing that he might try to seize power; nor would he show himself to the hero, but instead sent orders to Heracles through his herald Copreus, one of Pelops' sons, who had sought refuge with Eurystheus after he had killed Iphitus. Eurystheus instructed Heracles to leave whatever he brought back from each of his Labours outside the gates of the city.

He had a big bronze jar made for himself to serve as a place of refuge should Heracles attack him. In succession, he ordered Heracles to kill the Nemean lion, kill the Lernaean Hydra, capture the hind of Ceryneia, capture the Erymanthian boar, drive the birds away from the Stymphalian marsh, cleanse Augias's stables, capture the Cretan bull, capture the mares of Diomedes, king of Thrace, fetch the girdle of Hippolyta, queen of the Amazons, steal Geryon's cattle, bring the dog

Cerberus up from Tartarus and fetch the golden apples from the garden of the Hesperides. He refused to recognize the second and third of these Labours as tasks carried out at his orders, on the grounds that Heracles had received payment for them from other sources. When Heracles had completed the Labours, Eurystheus offered a sacrifice, to which he invited the hero; but Eurystheus' sons offered Heracles a portion of meat that was smaller than the rest; Heracles took offence at this and killed three of them. Heracles then wished to settle in Tiryns, but Eurystheus, who still hated him, refused permission. Even after the hero's death his descendants were not out of danger, as Eurystheus tried to persuade Ceyx to hand them over to him; but they found protection in Attica. When Eurystheus marched against the Athenians at the head of an army he was killed in battle. His head was brought to Alcmene, who tore out his eyes.

An odd tradition, dating from the Alexandrian era, asserts that Heracles was Eurystheus' lover, and that the hero undertook the Twelve Labours for love.

Eurytion (Εὐρυτίων)

1. One of the Centaurs who tried to carry off Pirithous' bride; this caused the battle between the Centaurs and the Lapiths.
2. Another Centaur, who was killed by Heracles when he tried to rape Mnesimache, the daughter of DEXAMENUS, king of Olenus.
3. Actor's son (see IRUS), a hero from Phthia, who took part in the Calydonian hunt. PELEUS took refuge at his court after the murder of Phocus (see AEACUS). Eurytion purified him and gave him his daughter Antigone in marriage, together with a third of his kingdom. During the Calydonian hunt, Peleus accidentally killed his father-in-law. After this second homicide he had to seek refuge at the court of ACASTUS.
4. GERYON's herdsman.

Eurytus (Εὔρυτος)

1. One of the Giants who took part in the revolt against the gods. Dionysus killed him with a blow from his thyrsus.
2. King of Oechalia, a city which geographers placed variously in Thessaly, Messenia, or Euboea. He was the son of Melaneus and Stratonice, and a remarkable archer whose skill with the bow had won him the reputation of being a son of Apollo, the divine archer. He was married to Pylon's daughter Antioche, and he had four sons, Deion (or Molion), Clytius, Toxeus and Iphitus,

and one daughter, Iole. Eurytus inherited his father's skill with the bow; and according to the Homeric version of the legend, he challenged Apollo himself, who slew Eurytus before he attained old age, to punish him for his presumption. Eurytus taught Heracles how to use a bow. Iphitus gave Odysseus this bow as a present while Odysseus gave Iphitus a spear and a sword. This was the bow with which Odysseus killed the suitors.

The best-known legend about Eurytus portrays him as Heracles' enemy. Eurytus suggested an archery contest, open to all the Greeks, with the hand of his daughter as the prize for the archer who managed to defeat him. Heracles accepted the challenge, and won; but Eurytus' sons were not prepared to let him have the proffered prize. They were afraid that if Heracles had children by their sister, he might kill them, as he had done earlier in a fit of madness. Only Iphitus took the hero's side. From then on, the legends differ. According to some, Eurytus accused Heracles of stealing some cattle, which had in reality been stolen by Autolycus. In order to clear the hero of this accusation, Iphitus offered to help him look for them; whereupon Heracles was seized with another attack of madness, and threw Iphitus off the top of the ramparts of Tiryns. In other versions, Heracles had stolen the cattle himself, and when Iphitus came to recover the booty, Heracles killed him. In expiation for this murder, Heracles was sold into slavery by Hermes, and bought by Omphalus. Eurytus refused to accept the price Heracles was prepared to pay him as compensation for the death of his son. Later, when his term of slavery had expired, Heracles mounted an expedition against Oechalia. He captured the city, killed Eurytus and his sons, and carried Iole off into captivity.

3. The son of Hermes and brother of Echion and one of the Argonauts (see ERYTUS).

Euthymus (Εὔθυμος)

A hero from Locri in southern Italy, who freed the city of Temesa from a harsh tribute which the citizens had to pay each year to a demon named Alybas. This demon was the spirit of Odysseus' companion, Polites. When Odysseus landed at Temesa, Polites had become drunk and raped a young local girl, and the inhabitants had stoned him to death. Polites' spirit then persecuted them in every possible way: it insisted that they build a shrine dedicated to it, and offer up the most beautiful maiden in the land each year. This tribute was dutifully paid until the arrival of Euthymus, who was a famous boxer.

Euthymus challenged the demon, beat it, and then forced it to leave the country. He married and lived to a ripe old age. Instead of dying, he disappeared in mysterious circumstances.

Evadne (Εὐάδνη)

1. The daughter of Poseidon and Pitane. Her 'mortal' father was Aepytus, king of Arcadia (see AEPYTUS 3). Evadne was loved by Apollo and bore him a son named IAMUS, the ancestor of the priestly family of the Iamides of Olympia.

2. The daughter of Iphis. She was married to Capaneus (Table 36), and on the death of her husband she threw herself into the flames of his funeral pyre.

Evander (Εὔανδρος)

1. Sarpedon's son; he was one of the Lycian warriors who came to help the Trojans against the Greeks.

2. One of Priam's sons.

3. The most famous figure of this name was the founder of Pallantium on the Palatine Hill, before Romulus founded Rome. Evander came from the city of Pallantium in Arcadia. According to some traditions he was the son of Hermes and a Nymph named Telphousa, who was Ladon's daughter and who had the gift of prophecy. His mother was worshipped in Rome under the name of CARMENTA, but other authors also assign her the names Themis, Nicostrate and Tyburtis (this last name links her with the river of Rome, the Tiber). Evander is also said to have been the son of Echemus of Tegea and of Timandra, the daughter of Tyndareus and Leda, and hence a descendant of the family to which the Dioscuri, Helen and Clytemnestra belonged. The reasons given for his leaving Arcadia are also varied. Some say he left of his own free will: others claim he had to go into exile after the murder of his father, whom he had killed to protect his mother; and still others say he had killed his mother.

Evander settled on the left bank of the Tiber, on the Palatine Hill. He was warmly welcomed by Faunus, king of the Aborigines, but he had to fight the king of Praeneste, the giant ERYLUS. He was a benevolent ruler, who helped to civilize the primitive inhabitants of the land. He taught them the hitherto unknown arts of writing and music, as well as various useful skills. He is also said to have introduced a certain number of cults of Arcadian origin into Latium, among them the cults of Ceres (Demeter), Neptune (Poseidon), and especially Lycian Pan – in whose honour he initiated the festival of the Lupercalia. When Heracles came to Pallantium, Evander welcomed him and purified him of the murder of Cacus. He recognized Heracles' divine origin, and instituted the cult of Ara Maxima in his honour, between the Palatine and Aventine Hills. Evander's arrival in Latium is said to have taken place sixty years before the Trojan War: he was thus an old man when AENEAS came to him to seek his help against the Rutuli. Evander remembered that in former days he had been the guest of Anchises, and he welcomed Aeneas warmly. He gave him a contingent of troops under the command of his son Pallas, pleading his advanced age as a reason for being unable to fight himself. Pallas was soon killed. Besides Pallas, Evander had two daughters, Rhome and Dyne, or Dauna. An altar was dedicated to Evander at the foot of the Aventine Hill, not far from the Porta Trigemina. This altar was symmetrical with the one dedicated to his mother Carmenta, which lay at the foot of the Capitol, near the Porta Carmentalis, on the other side of the Forum Boarium.

Evenus (Εὔηνος)

A king of Aetolia, the son of Ares and Demonice (Table 24). He had a daughter, MARPESSA, and he used to kill her suitors and then decorate the temple of Poseidon with their skulls. Marpessa was carried off by Idas; Evenus pursued her abductor, but failed to catch him, since Poseidon had given Idas a winged chariot. Evenus then slew his horses and threw himself into the River Lycormas, which was thereafter called the Evenus.

Evippe (Εὐίππη)

1. After he had killed Penelope's suitors, ODYSSEUS went to Epirus to consult the oracle. There he was welcomed by King Tyrimmas, whose hospitality he repaid in shabby fashion by seducing the king's daughter Evippe and fathering a son called Euryalus. When Euryalus reached manhood, Evippe sent him to Ithaca, with some tablets on which she had written certain symbols to ensure that Euryalus would be recognized by his father. Euryalus reached Ithaca while Odysseus was away. Penelope was aware of her husband's love affair with Evippe; when Odysseus returned, she persuaded him to kill Euryalus, pretending that the young man had come to Ithaca with the intention of assassinating him. Odysseus killed him himself. According to other traditions, the son of Evippe and Odysseus bore the name of Leontophron (Table 9).

2. Also described as the grand-daughter of Athamas (see Table 33).

F

Fama According to Virgil, Earth gave birth to Fama (who was *vox populi*) after Coeus and Enceladus. Fama possessed a great number of eyes and mouths, and moved from place to place by flying very swiftly through the air. Ovid repeated this portrayal of Fama, with further embellishments. He depicted her as living in a palace at the centre of the world, within the limits of Earth, Heaven, and Sea – an echoing palace, pierced with a thousand openings, through which every voice, even the lowest, could penetrate. This palace, made entirely of bronze, was always open and every word that entered it was broadcast forth again, much amplified. Fama lived surrounded by Credulity, Error, Unfounded Joy, Terror, Sedition, and False Rumour, and from her palace she kept watch over the whole world. This creature, an imitation of the giants and other monstrous beings of the first divine generation, is clearly a late allegory rather than a true myth.

Fames The allegory of Hunger. Her name was a translation of Limos, described by Hesiod as one of the daughters of Eris (Strife). Virgil portrayed her in the entrance-hall of Hades, alongside Poverty. Ovid embellished the picture and depicted her as living in Scythia, a desolate land, where she nibbled ceaselessly at what scanty vegetation she could find. At the demand of Ceres, she carried off ERYSICHTHON and drove him to his doom.

Fatum The god of Destiny. Originally this word – from the same root as the verb *fari*, to speak – meant the word of a god, and as such was applied to an irrevocable divine decision. Under the influence of Greek religion, Fatum came to include the divinities of Destiny, such as the MOIRAI, the Parcae, and even the Sibyls. Along the Curia in Rome, near the Rostra, stood three statues, which were called the three Fata: these were statues of the Sibyls. The word Fata was in time mistaken for a feminine singular, and became the origin of the word for fairies in Roman folklore. The lower classes even invented a god Fatus (by making Fatum masculine), who was a sort of personal demon, symbolizing man's individual destiny and analogous to the GENII. Feminine destiny was personified by a Fata, feminine, a later equivalent of the primitive JUNO.

Fauna The sister and wife of the god Faunus. She was worshipped as a fortune-teller and was a divinity of women, identified with BONA DEA, for whom she was perhaps originally merely an epithet: the *favourable* goddess in Latin (*quae favet*). As Bona Dea she appeared in the cycle of the Roman Hercules, in which she was portrayed as being the wife of the Latin King Faunus. Hercules loved her and gave her a son, the future King Latinus, the eponym of Latium. Another tradition, reported by Dionysius of Halicarnassus, depicted Fauna as a young Hyperborean girl who bore Hercules' child Latinus, and then married Faunus after Hercules had left her.

Faunus Seemingly a very ancient Roman god, whose cult was located on the Palatine Hill itself, or in its immediate surroundings. From his name, he was apparently a benevolent god, 'favourable' (in Latin *qui favet*), and in particular the protector of shepherds and their flocks. The influence of Greece made it easy to identify him with the Arcadian god Pan. He then underwent his first transformation: he became associated with the personality of the Arcadian king EVANDER (Εὖ-ἀνήρ, the Good Man) whose name could well have been a translation of his own; and in this way the legends about the Arcadians and their immigration to the area of the Palatine Hill were enabled to take root on Roman soil. Faunus gradually lost his divine character however, and came to be regarded as one of the first kings of Latium, ruling before the arrival of Aeneas and his Trojans, and consequently prior to Romulus' founding of the city. He is sometimes described as the son of Circe and Jupiter. He succeeded King Picus, and was himself succeeded by his son Latinus – who was possibly the son of Hercules (see FAUNA). Yet Faunus' divine personality lived on, though in multiple form, as the Fauns (*Fauni*) of the Classical Age, who were rustic and forest demons, the companions of the shepherds, and the equivalents of the Greek Satyrs. Their nature was twofold: half man, half goat, they were endowed with horns and often had goats' hooves as well.

The cult of Faunus originally included the procession of the Luperci, during which boys ran about half-naked, clad only in goatskins and scouring any women they met with lashes of rawhide; this flagellation was said to bring fertility to the victims. For other legends of Faunus see BONA DEA and FAUNA.

Faustinus One of EVANDER'S companions when he arrived in Italy; his name recalls the root of the adjective *faustus*, meaning 'of good omen'. He was the brother of FAUSTULUS, another of Evander's companions. While Faustulus was shepherd to Amulius, whose flocks he tended on the Palatine Hill, Faustinus looked after Numitor's flocks on the Aventine Hill. Both of them lived during the period when the Trojans from Lavinium were settling at Alba. In one version of the legend of Romulus, Faustinus plays a peculiar role. It was said that when Silvia, the daughter of King Numitor of Alba, gave birth to the twins Romulus and Remus, Numitor substituted another pair of twins for the two infants. These second twins were the ones exposed by Amulius. Numitor then entrusted the grandchildren he had saved in this way to the shepherd Faustulus. Faustinus urged his brother very strongly to attend to their education, which he did.

Plutarch also mentions another brother (whose name was mutilated in the manuscripts) who contributed to the education of the two divine children, and who later took part in the struggle between Romulus and Remus, as did Faustulus himself. Both Faustinus and Faustulus died in this struggle. The rivalry between the two hills, the Aventine and the Palatine, is echoed by the locations of the two shepherds in this legend, as it is by the strife between Romulus and Remus. The legend probably represents a relatively late development of the myth of the founding of the city.

Faustulus The shepherd who sheltered the twins ROMULUS and Remus on the banks of the Tiber, at the foot of the Palatine Hill, and then entrusted them to his wife Acca Larentia to bring up. Faustulus was considered to be a good and charitable man; he was sometimes described as King Amulius' head shepherd. When Amulius ordered the infants to be exposed, Faustulus fortunately happened to be on the same road as the servants who were taking the children away in order to expose them. He waited until the servants had started their way back but then discovered that some shepherds had already found the two in-

fants. He persuaded them to hand the children over to him, on the grounds that his wife had just lost a son and would be happy to have some nurselings. According to another version, Faustulus found the children as they were being suckled by a she-wolf. It is also said that Numitor, Amulius' brother, whom Amulius had dethroned at Alba, had saved Silvia's twin sons from death and entrusted them to Faustulus (see FAUSTINUS). When they had grown up, the twins were sent to Gabii to be given an education to match their rank. They were made welcome there by some of Faustulus' friends.

During the strife between Romulus and Remus, Faustulus tried to intervene and was killed. He was buried in the Forum. Later, the statue of a lion was raised above his tomb. In Classical days, Faustulus' hut was still to be seen on the Palatine Hill preserved as a relic of these mythical times. This hut (*tugurium Faustuli*) stood at the southwest corner of the Palatine, dominating the valley of the Circus Maximus and facing the Aventine Hill. Like his brother Faustinus, and like Faunus too, Faustulus bore a name which was connected with the root of the verb *faveo*, 'to be favourable'. It was a name of good omen. Certain authors also use the form Faustus, the diminutive of which was Faustulus.

Febris The goddess of Fever. She was much feared at Rome, where the low ground (Forum, Velabrum) and even the upper parts of the valleys (between the Quirinal and the Viminal Hills) stayed damp and unhealthy for a long time. Febris had no specific legends but was simply a power, a maleficent *numen* that had to be conciliated. Her oldest shrine seems to have been an archaic altar on the Palatine Hill. Two others were known: one on the plateau of the Esquiline Hill, at the spot where slaves and the lower classes (the *puticuli* of the Classical Age) were buried, and the other in the upper part of the Vicus Longus (at the head of the Quirinal Valley) where there were some springs.

Februus The god to whom the month of February was said to be sacred. In later days he was identified with Dis Pater, the Latin Pluto, god of the kingdom of the dead. During February the city was purified by appeasing the dead with sacrifices and offerings. These purificatory festivals bore the name of Februalia, and Februus was probably nothing more than the personification of these festivals and rites.

Ferentina A Latin Nymph, the goddess of a spring and a sacred wood of uncertain location. Her shrine was a place of worship common to the whole of the Latin confederacy.

Feronia A goddess of springs and woods, whose cult was widespread in Central Italy, especially on Mount Soracte, at Terracina, Furfo and Pisauro, and also in Etruria and other places. Slaves were freed in her temple at Terracina, which explains why she was sometimes identified with LIBERTAS. She is said to have been the mother of ERYLUS of Praeneste, who was endowed with three lives and was slain by Evander.

Fides In Rome the goddess Fides was the personification of good faith. She was portrayed as an old woman with white hair, older than Jupiter himself. This was to emphasize that respect for good faith was the foundation of all social and political order. In this earliest of times Aeneas' granddaughter Rhome is said to have dedicated a temple to her on the Palatine Hill. Sacrifices were offered to her with the right hand wrapped in a white linen cloth.

Flora The vegetative power that makes the trees blossom. She presided over everything that blooms. According to the legends, she was introduced to Rome, as was Fides, by Titus Tatius, together with other Sabine divinities. She was honoured by every race in Italy, Latin and non-Latin alike. The Sabine people dedicated a month to her corresponding to April in the Roman calendar.

Ovid linked a Hellenic myth to Flora's name, suggesting that Flora was a Greek Nymph called Chloris. He relates how one spring day as she was wandering through the fields, Zephyr, the god of the wind, saw her, fell in love with her, and carried her off. He married her properly; in return, and to show his love, he granted her dominion over the flowers – not merely the garden flowers, but also the flowers of the fields. Honey is said to have been one of her gifts to mankind, as well as the seeds of countless varieties of flowers. In Ovid's version of this legend (which he perhaps invented) he refers explicitly to Orithyia's abduction by Boreas. Undoubtedly he used this episode as the model for his account of Flora's abduction; but he added one peculiar touch by attributing the

Wall painting from Pompeii depicting Flora, the Italian goddess of flowers. Naples, National Museum.

birth of Mars to Flora. According to Ovid, Juno had been incensed by Minerva's springing spontaneously from Jupiter's head, and wished herself to conceive a child without recourse to any male assistance. She turned to Flora, who gave her a flower which would make a woman pregnant simply if she touched it. Juno then gave birth to Mars, the god whose name is borne by the first month of Spring, without prior sexual relations with Jupiter.

Flora had her own priest at Rome, one of the dozen minor flamens who were said to have been introduced by Numa. The Floralia were celebrated in her honour; these were marked by games in which courtesans took part.

Fons A god associated with springs; he is also known as Fontus. He is said to have been the son of Janus, but no legend concerning him has been preserved. He had a temple at Rome, perhaps adjacent to the Porta Fontinalis (a gate in the Servian Wall, north of the Capitol). There was another altar sacred to Fons at the foot of the Janiculus, not far from the so-called tomb of Numa. His festival was the festival of springs and bore the name of the Fontinalia.

Fornax The goddess of the oven in which bread is baked. She presided at the festival of the Fornacalia.

Fors The male principle of chance, as opposed to Fortuna, who was the female principle; together they formed a pair. Their two names were linked in the phrase *Fors Fortuna*, which eventually came to be regarded as a single divinity, composed of both male and female elements.

Fortuna In the Roman religion of Classical times Fortuna was more favoured than Fors. She was identified with the Greek TYCHE. She was portrayed with the cornucopia and with a rudder, to symbolize that she steered the course of men's lives. She was sometimes shown seated, sometimes standing, and generally as blind. The introduction of her cult was credited to Servius Tullius, the king who was favoured by Fortune above all others. She was even said to have loved him, although he was a mere mortal, and to have gained access to his chamber through a little window. A statue of Servius stood in the temple of the goddess.

The goddess Fortuna was invoked under many

different names, such as *Redux* (when safe return from a voyage was being sought), *Publica* and *Huiusce Diei* (the special Fortuna of that particular day). During the Imperial period, each Emperor had his own personal Fortuna. Under the influence of Greece, Fortuna gradually became assimilated with other divinities, notably Isis.

Furies In the primitive popular beliefs of the Romans the Furies were demons of the Underworld. They very quickly became assimilated with the Greek ERINYES, whose myths they borrowed.

Furrina The Nymph Furrina was the divinity of a spring and a sacred wood that were located on the right bank of the Tiber, at the foot of the Janiculum. In the Republican era, she was considered to be one of the Furies, but her shrine gradually fell into disuse and was taken over by some Syrians, who introduced their own practices there.

G

Gaia (Γαîα) The Earth conceived as the primordial element from which sprang the divine races. She plays a major part in Hesoid's *Theogony*, but does not appear in Homer's poems. According to Hesoid, Gaia was born immediately after Chaos and just before Eros (Love). Without the aid of any male, she gave birth to Uranus (Heaven), to the Mountains, and also to Pontus, the male personification of the marine element. After the birth of Uranus, she coupled with him, and the children she bore thereafter were no longer simple elementary powers, but actual gods. First came the six Titans – Oceanus, Coeus, Crius, Hyperion, Iapetus and Cronus – and the six Titanesses – Theia, Rhea, Themis, Mnemosyne, Phoebe and Tethys, who were feminine divinities. CRONUS was the youngest of this line (Table 38). Gaia then gave birth to the CYCLOPES, Arges, Steropes, and Brontes, who were divinities associated with thunderbolts, lightning, and thunder. Finally Uranus fathered the Hecatoncheires, who were violent beings each with a hundred huge arms: they were called COTTUS, BRIAREUS and GYGES. All these children lived in terror of their father, who never allowed them to see the light of day but instead forced them to remain entombed in the depths of Mother Earth's body. She was determined to free her children, and asked them to exact vengeance for Uranus' actions; but none of them was willing except for the youngest, Cronus, who agreed because of his hatred of his father. Gaia then entrusted him with a very sharp sickle, and when Uranus came to lie with Gaia that night, Cronus cut off his father's testicles with one blow of his sickle, and threw them over his shoulder. The blood from the wound fell upon Mother Earth and fertilized her once again. As a result Gaia gave birth to the Erinyes, the Giants, the Ash Nymphs and other divinities also associated with trees.

After Uranus' castration, Gaia coupled with another of her children, Pontus, or the Wave. She then gave birth to five marine divinities: Nereus, Thaumas, Phorcys, Ceto and Eurybia. Cronus now ruled the whole world; and it was not long before he showed himself to be as brutal a tyrant as his father. He too imprisoned his brothers in Tartarus, with the result that Gaia started planning a second revolution. Cronus' wife Rhea had seen all her children eaten by Cronus, one after the other, because he had been warned he would be overthrown by one of them. When she was pregnant with Zeus, she went to Gaia and Uranus and asked them how to save the child she was carrying. Gaia and Uranus then revealed the secret of the Fates to her, and showed her how to cheat Cronus. Gaia concealed him at birth and hid him away in a deep cave. In place of the child she gave Cronus a stone wrapped in swaddling-clothes, which the god devoured. In this way ZEUS was able to escape his father's greed and grow to manhood. Later, when Zeus began openly resisting Cronus, Mother Earth told him he could only achieve victory with the Titans as his allies. Zeus then set them free, and in return they gave him arms – thunder, lightning and the thunderbolt – with which weapons he soon drove Cronus from his throne. Nevertheless, Gaia did not completely throw in her lot with Zeus. Displeased by the defeat of the Hecatoncheires, she coupled with Tartarus, the god who personified the abyss of Hell, and by him gave birth to TYPHON, a monster of prodigious strength, who declared war on the gods and held them at bay for a considerable time. She had another child by Tartarus, ECHIDNA, who was also a monster.

In other theogonies she was said to have been the mother of Triptolemus, who was fathered by Oceanus, her own son and one of the Titans. The giant ANTAEUS, who was Heracles' enemy, was also said to have been her son, by the sea-god Poseidon. Indeed, there was hardly a single monster that was not considered by one mythographer or another as the child of Mother Earth: CHARYBDIS, the HARPIES, PYTHON, the dragon that guarded the Golden Fleece in the land of Aeetes, and even Fame, the monster Virgil described under the name of *Fama*.

Earth, the power and inexhaustible reserve of fecundity, gradually became known as the Universal Mother and the mother of the gods. As the Greeks began to personify their gods, Mother Earth became incarnated as divinities such as Demeter or Cybele, whose myths, being more human, appealed more to the imagination; while speculations about Earth as an element passed from the realm of mythology into that of philosophy. Gaia was credited with being the inspiration of numerous oracles, for she possessed the secrets of the Fates, and her oracles were older and even more accurate than those of Apollo.

Galaesus A subject of King Latinus who lived at the time when Aeneas and the Trojans landed in Latium. When Aeneas' son Iulus (or Ascanius) killed a tame hind, almost starting a war between the Latins and the Trojans, Galaesus tried to intervene between the two sides and restore peace, but he failed in his attempt and was killed.

Galatea (Γαλάτεια) Legends mention two persons of this name, the etymology of which is derived from the Greek words meaning 'the whiteness of milk' (γάλα).
1. The first was a daughter of Nereus and a sea-goddess who featured in the popular myths of Sicily. The milk-white maiden Galatea lived in the quiet sea and was loved by Polyphemus, the Sicilian Cyclops with the body of a monster. She did not return his passion, however, and was instead in love with the beautiful Acis, son of the god Pan (or Faunus, in the Latin tradition) and a Nymph. One day when Galatea was lying beside the sea with her lover, Polyphemus saw them. Although Acis tried to flee, the Cyclops threw an enormous boulder at him which crushed him to death. Galatea restored to Acis the nature of his mother the Nymph, and turned him into a stream with sparkling waters.
   The birth of three heroes is sometimes attributed to the love between Polyphemus and Galatea: Galas (see GALATES), CELTUS and ILLYRIUS, the eponyms respectively of the Galatians, the Celts and the Illyrians. One version of Galatea's legend may possibly have told of mutual love between Polyphemus and the Nereid, but no direct evidence has been preserved.
2. The other Galatea was a Cretan girl, the daughter of a certain Eurytius. She was married to Lamprus, a man of a good though poor family, who lived in the city of Phaestus. When Lamprus discovered that his wife was pregnant he told her he wanted only a son; if she gave birth to a girl she would have to expose it. While Lamprus was up on the mountain guarding his flock Galatea gave birth to a girl, but she could not bring herself to expose it. On the advice of soothsayers she dressed the child as a boy and called him Leucippus. In this way she concealed the truth from Lamprus.

However, as time went by, Leucippus became very beautiful, and it became impossible to continue the masquerade. Galatea was stricken with fear, and went to Leto's shrine, where she asked the goddess to change her daughter's sex. Leto let herself be swayed and the young girl became a boy (see IPHIS).

Galates (Γαλατής) When Heracles passed through Gaul on his way back from stealing Geryon's cattle, he founded the city of Alesia. The daughter of a local prince, who had never found a husband worthy of her, loved him; he fathered a son called Galates, whose bravery earned him rule over the whole of Gaul. Later, Galates gave his name to Galatia, the land of the Galatians (see also CELTUS).

Galeotes (Γαλεώτης) The son of Apollo and Themisto, who was herself the daughter of Zabius, king of the Hyperboreans. He was the ancestor of a race of Sicilian soothsayers. With Telmissus, another Hyperborean, Galeotes went to consult the oracle at Dodona. They were instructed to travel, one to the East and the other to the West, until an eagle swooped down and robbed them of the meat of the offering made during a sacrifice. At that place they were to raise an altar. Galeotes went to Sicily and Telmissus stopped in Caria.

Galinthias (Γαλινθίας) The daughter of Galinthias, whose name recalls the Greek word meaning 'weasel', was the Theban Proetus. When Alcmene, a friend of Galinthias, was about to give birth to the baby Heracles, Hera ordered the Moirae and Eilithyia, the divinities of childbirth, to stop her from delivering the child. For nine days and nine nights they sat on the threshold of the house with their arms and legs crossed, holding back the birth with their spells. Galinthias was moved with pity for her friend, fearing that her pains might drive her mad, and tricked the goddesses by telling them that despite their efforts, Alcmene had given birth to a boy, at Zeus' command. Frightened and indignant, believing that their privileges had been abused, the goddesses rose to their feet and abandoned the position which had been holding Alcmene in bondage. She immediately gave birth to her child. The divinities took their revenge by turning Galinthias into a weasel, and as it was her mouth that had uttered the lie that deceived them, they condemned her to give birth through her mouth. Hecate, however, took pity on the poor beast, and took her as her own servant and her sacred animal. When Heracles reached manhood, he remembered the woman who had enabled him to be born, and raised a shrine to her near his home. The Thebans, faithful to Galinthias' memory, used to bring her offerings on the feast of Heracles (see also HISTORIS).

Ganges (Γόγγες) The god of the river Ganges in India, and the son of Indus and the nymph Calauria. One day, while drunk, he unwittingly coupled with his mother. When he came to his senses, he threw himself in despair into the river which had hitherto been called Chliarus, and which was henceforth known as Ganges.

Ganymede (Γανυμήδης) A young hero who belonged to the Trojan royal family and was a descendant of Dardanus (Table 7). He is generally said to have been the youngest son of Tros and Callirhoe and the brother of Cleopatra, Ilus and Assaracus. Other versions, however, make him variously the son of Laomedon (the son of Ilus, who in the traditional genealogy was Ilus' nephew), the son of Ilus, or Assaracus, or even the son of Erichthonius (his grandfather, in the generally accepted tradition). When Ganymede was quite young, barely adolescent, he was guarding his father's flocks in the mountains that lay round the city of Troy, when Zeus carried him off and took him to Olympus. Ganymede was said to have been the most beautiful of mortals, and his

The young Ganymede was carried off to Olympus by Zeus who assumed the disguise of an eagle. 3rd century Roman mosaic in the House of Dionysus, Paphos, Cyprus.

beauty fired the most powerful of the gods with love. On Olympus Ganymede served as a cup-bearer. He used to pour nectar into Zeus' cup and he replaced Hebe, the goddess of Youth, in this service.

Traditions differ as to the details of his abduction. Sometimes Zeus himself is said to have carried the boy off, and sometimes the god is thought to have entrusted the mission to his favourite bird, the eagle, who grasped the boy in his claws and bore him away high into the air. Some accounts say that Zeus himself had taken on the form of the eagle, as he had done with so many different animals and persons in the course of satisfying his amorous passions. Still other versions suggest that the abductor was Minos, or Tantalus, or even Eos (the Dawn). The place of the abduction varies equally with different authors. While the generally accepted location is Mount Ida in the Troad, some versions place it in Crete, or even in Euboea, or in Mysia in the small town of Harpagia. In compensation for this abduction, Zeus presented the boy's father with some divine horses, or perhaps a golden vine, the work of Hephaestus. The eagle that carried off Ganymede became a constellation.

Garanus A shepherd who in an obscure version of the legend of CACUS is said to have slain the latter, thus playing the role generally allotted to Heracles (see RECARANUS).

Garmathone (Γαρμαθόνη) The wife of King Nilus of Egypt. Despite the grief she felt on the death of her son Chrysochoas, she received the goddess Isis hospitably when the latter paid her an unexpected visit. The goddess rewarded her by restoring her son to life.

Gavanes (Γαυάνης) One of three brothers, descendants of Temenus, king of Argos. With his brothers Aeropus and Perdiccas, Gavanes emigrated to Illyria and Macedonia; they became shepherds for the king of Lebaia. Every time the queen baked bread for Perdiccas, the bread rose twice as high as that of the others. The king was so disturbed by this miracle that he discharged the three brothers; and instead of paying them the salary agreed upon offered to give them 'the piece of the sun that came down the chimney'. Quite unabashed, Perdiccas drew his knife, cut out the circle of sunshine traced upon the floor, and put it in his satchel. With that, the three brothers took their leave. The king sent horsemen after them to kill them, but a river rose miraculously to protect them and the horsemen had to withdraw. Gavanes and his brothers settled in Macedonia, where Perdiccas founded the country's royal line.

Gelanor (Γελάνωρ) In the genealogy of the kings of Argos, as set out by Pausanias (Table 17), Gelanor, the son of Sthenelas, was the last of Phoroneus' line to rule. He was dethroned by DANAUS when the latter arrived from Egypt with his fifty daughters. According to certain authors, Gelanor handed the throne over to him quite willingly. For the prodigy of the wolf which was said to have put an end to Gelanor's reign and driven the people to choose Danaus as their king, see DANAUS.

Gelo (Γελώ) An ogre on the island of Lesbos who was the tormented soul of a maiden who had died young and kept returning to earth to steal children.

Genii In Roman mythology the Genii were spirits that represented the inborn power of each individual, locality, and corporation (such as societies, colleges, and cities, for example). The genius was born at the same time as the man or thing to which it was linked, and its essential function was to keep its charge alive. It played a part, albeit a somewhat mysterious one, in the conception of the individual, and also presided at his marriage. There was a genius of the marriage bed, which brought fertility to the couple. As a personification of the being, the personal genius was an interior force that generated optimism. A Latin proverb, *indulgere genio*, 'to yield to one's genius', applied to every act of compliance with one's personal taste, and in particular operated as a euphemism for over-indulgence in drink. Oaths were sworn on one's personal genius or on the genius of others. During the Imperial period, the Emperor's genius wielded formidable power. It took precedence over the personal genii of others in the same way that the Emperor himself took precedence over other men. The genius gradually became identified with the MANES and was considered an immortal element in Man. The tendency to allot a separate genius to every entity was so strong that even the gods had their own genii. Sacrifices, for example, were offered to the genius of Mars and to that of Jupiter. For women, the genius was replaced by the JUNO.

Gerana (Γέρανα) A woman of the Pygmy race, to whom the Pygmies paid divine honours, but who held the true deities in contempt. To punish her, Hera turned her into a crane. Before her transformation, Gerana had had a son called Mopsus. When she became a bird she tried to rejoin him in her former home, but the people of the cranes were at war with the PYGMIES (through Hera's will); and the latter, in arms, made it impossible for Gerana to reach her former home, thus unwittingly adding to the poor woman's torment.

Geryon (Γηρυονεύς) This three-headed giant, who also had a triple body down as far as his hips, was the son of CHRYSAOR, whose parents were Gorgo and Poseidon (Table 32), and of Callirhoe, the daughter of Oceanus. He lived on the island of Erythia, and his wealth consisted of herds of cattle, guarded by a herdsman, Eurytion, and a dog, Orthus (or Orthrus), not far from the place where Menoetes kept watch over the herds of Hades. At Eurystheus' command, HERACLES came to Erythia to steal Geryon's cattle from him. He first encountered the dog, and killed him; and then the herdsman, who met with the same fate. Then Geryon himself came to the help of his servants, and fought with Heracles. He lost the fight and was killed, either by Heracles' arrows or by blows from his club. Heracles brought the cattle back in stages to Greece. Antiquity allotted various sites to the island of Erythia; the most probable location was off Cadiz, in Spain. The name Erythia was supposed to be eponymous with one of the HESPERIDES, whose garden lay near the island. This same name, which means 'the red land', seems to indicate a country situated in the west, the land of the setting sun. Another tradition, however, places Erythia in Epirus, in the region of Ambracia.

Giants (Γίγαντες) The children of GAIA (Mother Earth), born from the blood of her husband Uranus' wound when he was castrated by Cronus (Table 12). Although of divine origin they were mortal – or at least they could be killed if they were slain simultaneously by a god and a mortal. There was a magic herb produced by the Earth which could protect them from the blows of mortals; but Zeus plucked this herb himself before anyone else could lay hands on it. He did this by forbidding the Sun, the Moon and the Dawn to shine so that nobody could see well enough to find the herb before he did. Other traditions claim that some Giants (Alcyoneus, for example, or Porphyrion) were immortal as long as they remained on Earth, where they had been born. The legend of the Giants is dominated by the story of their revolt against the gods, and their defeat. Gaia gave birth to them to avenge the Titans, whom Zeus had imprisoned in Tartarus. The Giants were enormous beings of invincible strength and terrifying appearance. They had thick shocks of hair, bristling beards, and their legs were the bodies of great snakes. Their birthplace was Phlegrae on the peninsula of Pallene in Thrace. As soon as they were born they began threatening heaven by hurling flaming trees up at it and bombarding it with enormous rocks. Faced with this threat, the Olympians girded themselves for battle. The Giants' main adversaries were initially Zeus and Athena. Zeus was armed with his aegis and his thunderbolts, brought to him by his eagles. Athena also had an eagle, and she too launched thunderbolts. Their chief assistant was Heracles, the mortal whose help was needed if the conditions set by the Fates concerning the death of the Giants were to be fulfilled. Heracles stationed himself on Zeus' chariot, and fought from afar with his arrows. Dionysus is sometimes said to have taken an active part in the struggle, armed with his thyrsus and with firebrands, and supported by the Satyrs. Then, as the legend gradually grew more elaborate, various other deities came to be included, such as Ares, Hephaestus, Aphrodite, Eros, and Poseidon.

The mythographers have retained descriptions of the roles played by some of the Giants during the struggle. ALCYONEUS was slain by Heracles with the assistance of Athena, who advised the hero to draw Alcyoneus away from Pallene, his native land, since every time he was felled he drew renewed strength from merely touching the earth from which he had sprung. Porphyrion attacked Heracles and Hera, but Zeus filled him with lust for Hera, and while he was trying to tear her garments off Zeus smote him with a thunderbolt and Heracles killed him with an arrow. Ephialtes was slain by an arrow from Apollo in his left eye and another from Heracles in his right eye; Eurytus was killed by Dionysus with a blow from his thyrsus. Hecate killed Clytius, using firebrands, and Hephaestus dispatched Mimas by throwing lumps of red-hot iron at him. Enceladus fled, but Athena threw the island of Sicily on top of him in mid-flight. She flayed Pallas and used his skin as a breast-plate during the remainder of the battle. Polybotes was chased across the waves by Poseidon until he reached the island of Cos. There the god broke off the part of the isle called Nisyron and crushed the Giant beneath it. Hermes wore Hades' helmet, which made him invisible; he killed Hippolytus during the battle, while Artemis slew Gration. The Moirae, armed with their bronze clubs, killed Agrius and Thoas. Zeus stunned the rest of the Giants with his thunderbolts and Heracles finished them off with his arrows. The site of this battle was generally thought to be on the peninsula of Pallene, but a local tradition placed it in Arcadia, on the banks of the river Alpheus.

Later traditions name even more Giants, but these are generally Titans wrongly included in the category of Giants, or other monsters such as TYPHON, BRIAREUS and ALOADAE who were not true Giants, though their immense size and prodigious strength entitled them to be called 'giants'. The Gigantomachy, or the revolt of the Giants against the gods, was a favourite theme of plastic art in the Classical period, and was particularly used in the decoration of temple pediments. The monsters' bodies, ending in snakes, lent themselves admirably to the filling-in of corners and the final balance of the composition.

Glauce (Γλαύκη)
1. Glauce, which means literally 'the green one', was a Nereid and also an Arcadian Nymph.
2. The same name was borne by the daughter of Creon, king of Thebes: she was also called CREUSA and was Medea's rival for the favours of Jason.

Glaucia (Γλαυκία) The daughter of the Phrygian River Scamander. When Heracles undertook his expedition against Troy he was accompanied by, among others, a Boeotian, Deimachus, the son of Eleon. Glaucia and Deimachus loved each other, and Glaucia became pregnant; but Deimachus was killed before their son's birth. When the child was born his mother called him Scamander, in memory of his grandfather. Heracles took Glaucia and her son to Greece, where he entrusted them to Eleon. Scamander gave his own name to a stream not far from Tanagra; his mother's name, Glaucia, to a second watercourse; and his wife's name, Acidusa, to a nearby spring. He had three daughters by Acidusa, and a cult was consecrated to them under the name of the Three Virgins.

Glaucus (Γλαῦκος) The name of several persons, as well as a sea-god.
1. A Glaucus was the son of the Trojan ANTENOR and Theano: he helped Paris to abduct Helen, and because of this his father drove him out. He

fought in the Trojan ranks against the Greeks, and is sometimes said to have been slain by Agamemnon; but it is more generally thought that he was saved by Odysseus and Menelaus, as the son of Antenor, who was bound to both of them by ties of friendship.

2. Another Glaucus also fought on the side of the Trojans. He was the son of Hippolochus, and with his cousin SARPEDON commanded the Lycian contingent. He was famous for his ingenuity and his gallantry. During the fighting around the city he found himself face to face with Diomedes, but both recalled that their families were bound by ties of friendship. Through his father Hippolochus, Glaucus was in fact the grandson of Bellerophon (Table 35), and in former days Diomedes' grandfather Oeneus had welcomed Bellerophon to his palace. They had exchanged gifts of friendship, Oeneus giving a purple baldric and Bellerophon a gold cup, and their descendants repeated this exchange of presents. Diomedes gave Glaucus his own arms, which were made of bronze, and Glaucus gave him his, which were made of gold; afterwards each returned to his station in the battle. Glaucus then performed several feats. When Sarpedon was wounded he went to assist him, but was stopped by Teucer, wounded, and forced to leave the fray. In answer to his prayer, Apollo cured him in time to go out and bring in Sarpedon's body, though he was unable to stop the Greeks from stripping the corpse of its arms. He then joined Hector in the fight for possession of the body of Patroclus, who had just been killed, but he was slain by Ajax, son of Telamon. At Apollo's orders, his body was carried back to Lycia by the winds. This Glaucus, grandson of Bellerophon, was claimed as the founder of the royal dynasty of Lycia.

3. Glaucus was also the name of the preceding Glaucus' great-grandfather. He was the son of Sisyphus, and succeeded his father to the throne of the city he had founded – Ephyra, which later became Corinth. This Glaucus was especially famous for his death. He took part in the funeral games held in honour of Pelias, but was beaten in the four-horse chariot-race by IOLAUS, son of Iphicles; after this his mares ate him alive. They had been maddened either by the water of a magic well which their master had inadvertently taken them to, or as a result of Aphrodite's anger, for in order to make his mares run faster Glaucus refused to let them breed, and so offended the goddess. In another legend, Glaucus, son of Sisyphus, one day drank from a fountain water which conferred

immortality on the drinker. No one would believe that he had become immortal, however, and to convince people, he threw himself into the sea, where he became a sea-god who wandered at large over the waves. Every sailor who saw him was assured of an early death.

4. There was another sea-god called Glaucus, who was given quite a different genealogy from that of the Glaucus described above. He was a fisherman in the city of Anthedon in Boeotia. He was either the son of the city's founder, Anthedon, and of Alcyone, or perhaps the son of Poseidon and a Naiad. When he was born, he was a mortal; but by chance he ate a herb that made him immortal, and became a sea-god. The sea-goddesses cleansed him of any remaining traces of mortality, and he took on a new form. His shoulders grew broader and the lower part of his body became a powerful fish-tail, while his cheeks became covered with a thick beard, tinted green like the patina on bronze. In addition, he received the gift of prophecy, which he used as he wished in a somewhat capricious fashion. Virgil makes him the father of the Cumaean Sibyl, who was herself a prophetess. Glaucus appeared to Menelaus when the latter was rounding Cape Malea on his way back from Troy. In certain versions of the legend, he was also said to have built the *Argo* and to have accompanied the ship on its voyage, during which he fought beside the Argonauts.

Glaucus also had some famous intrigues. He courted SCYLLA, but in vain, though he was the cause of the girl's transformation into a monster by Circe's spells. Despite this, his love for her remained unquenched, and he turned her into a goddess. Glaucus also tried to win the favours of Ariadne, whom Theseus had abandoned on the shores of Naxos. He did not succeed, but he was included in Dionysus' train when the god took the girl away and made her his wife.

5. The mythographers mention yet another Glaucus, the son of Minos and Pasiphae (Table 28). While still a child he was chasing a mouse when he fell into a jar of honey and drowned. Minos spent a long time looking for him, and thanks to the help of his soothsayers, or of Apollo himself, he finally found his son's corpse. The Curetes then told him that Glaucus could be restored to life by the man who could best describe the colour of a certain cow among his herds which changed its colour three times a day. It first became white, then it turned red, and finally became black, repeating the same cycle every day. Minos collected all of the most clever men in Crete and

asked them to describe the colour of the wonderful cow. Only one of them succeeded – Polyidus, son of Coeranus. He answered that the cow was mulberry-coloured, for the fruit is first white, turns red, and finally goes completely black when fully ripe. Minos felt that Polyidus had solved the problem, and told him to bring Glaucus back to life, shutting him up with Glaucus' body. Polyidus was at his wits' end, until he saw a snake make its way into the room and go over towards the body. Polyidus was afraid that the snake might eat the body or at least damage it, so he killed the animal. Soon a second snake came in and when it saw the first one lying dead it went out, only to return a few moments later carrying in its mouth a herb with which it touched its companion. The snake immediately returned to life. Polyidus wasted no time in picking up the herb and rubbing it on Glaucus, who revived at once. Minos, however, was still not satisfied. Before allowing Polyidus to return to his fatherland, Argos (or Corinth), he demanded that the soothsayer should teach Glaucus his art. This Polyidus did, but when he was finally allowed to go, he spat into his pupil's mouth as he took his leave, and Glaucus immediately lost all the knowledge he had just acquired. In other versions of the legend, it was Asclepius, not Polyidus, who brought Glaucus back to life.

Glyphius (Γλύφιος) While TIRESIAS was still a woman and was living in Troezen, a local inhabitant named Glyphius tried to rape her. Tiresias proved stronger than Glyphius and killed him. Glyphius was loved by Poseidon; to avenge him, Poseidon asked the Moirae to turn Tiresias back into a man and take his gift of prophecy away. The goddesses did this.

Golden Age In his *Works and Days* Hesiod cites a myth telling of the different races which had followed each other since the beginning of mankind. Originally, he says, there was a 'golden race'. This was during the time when Cronus was still ruling in heaven. Men in those days lived like the gods, free from worries and safe from grief and distress. They knew nothing of old age but spent their time, eternally young, in banquets and festivals. When the time came for them to die, they went peacefully to sleep. They were not subject to the necessity of work. Every good thing came to them spontaneously. The soil needed no labour to produce large crops, and men lived in peace in the midst of the countryside. Although this race vanished from the earth with the reign of Zeus, they still remain as good spirits, protectors of mankind and distributors of wealth. This, in its oldest form, is the legend of the Golden Age.

Very soon the myth became a commonplace of morality, which liked to depict the beginnings of mankind as the reign of Justice and Honesty. In Rome, where Cronus was identified with Saturn, the Golden Age was thought to have been in the era when Saturn ruled in Italy, then still called Ausonia. The gods lived in close association with mankind. Doors had not yet been invented, for there was no such thing as theft, and men had nothing to hide. The only food was vegetables and fruit, since the concept of killing had not been thought of. Civilization was in its earliest stages. Saturn introduced the use of the sickle (which was an attribute in representations of the god); he taught men how to make better use of the natural fertility of the soil. It was said in Rome that he reigned on the Capitol, the very spot where the temple of Jupiter Optimus Maximus stood later. Saturn had been welcomed to Italy by the god Janus, who ruled with him and agreed to share his kingdom with the newcomer.

The poets vied with each other in embroidering this theme. They told of wool colouring itself in vivid hues on the sheeps' backs, brambles bearing delicious fruits, and the earth rejoicing in a perpetual spring. The myth of the Golden Age also formed an element in neo-Pythagorean mysticism.

Gordias (Γορδιάς) The king who ruled over Phrygia in mythical times, and founded the city of Gordium there. He kept his chariot in the citadel, and the chariot-pole was attached by a knot so complicated that nobody could untie it. The empire of Asia was promised to whoever should succeed in doing this. Alexander, who was familiar with the oracle, drew his sword and cut through the knot. Gordius had been the lover of Cybele, who bore him a son, Midas.

Gorge (Γοργή)
1. The daughter of Oeneus, king of Calydon, and the sister of Meleager. She had a son named TYDEUS by her own father; and by Andraemon she had another son, Thoas (see THOAS 4). She and her sister Deianeira escaped the metamorphosis into partridges which their sisters underwent (see MELEAGRIDS).
2. Gorge was also the name of one of Megareus' daughters, who was married to Corinthus, the

founder of Corinth. When her children were slaughtered, she threw herself in her despair into a lake, which thereafter took the name of Lake Gorgopis.

Gorgons (Γοργώνες) There were three Gorgons, called Stheno, Euryale, and Medusa, all daughters of two sea-gods, Phorcys and Ceto (Table 32). Only the last of them, Medusa, was mortal; the other two were immortal. The name Gorgon was generally applied to Medusa, who was particularly considered as the Gorgon. These three monsters lived in the far West, not far from the Kingdom of the Dead, the land of the Hesperides, Geryon, etc. Their heads were entwined with snakes; they had huge tusks, like those of a boar, hands of bronze, and golden wings which enabled them to fly. Their eyes flashed and their gaze was so penetrating that anyone who encountered it was turned to stone. They were objects of fear and loathing, not only to every mortal but also to those who were immortal. Poseidon alone was not afraid, for he had coupled with Medusa and fathered a child. Then Perseus set off for the West to kill Medusa – either because Polydectes, the tyrant of Seriphos, had ordered him to do so, or because Athena had advised it. After many adventures, Perseus finally found Medusa's lair. Thanks to his winged sandals, the gift of Hermes, he rose up into the air and succeeded in cutting off Medusa's head. To avoid looking at her, he used his polished breast-plate as a mirror and thereby had nothing to fear from the monster's terrible gaze. To make things even safer, he slaughtered the Gorgon while she was asleep. From the stump of Medusa's neck, two beings sired by Poseidon issued forth: PEGASUS, the winged horse, and CHRYSAOR. Athena made use of Medusa's head by fixing it to her shield, or to the centre of her aegis. In this way, her enemies found themselves turned to stone merely by looking at the goddess. Perseus also gathered up the blood that flowed from the wound, for it had magic properties. The blood which flowed from the vein on the left was a mortal poison, while that from the vein on the right was a remedy capable of restoring the dead to life (see ASCLEPIUS). Furthermore, a single lock of her hair, when held up in the face of an attacking army, would put them all to flight (see CEPHEUS and HERACLES).

By the Hellenistic era, the legend of Medusa had evolved considerably from its original form. At the start, the Gorgon was a monster, one of the primordial deities that belonged to the pre-Olympian generation. Then she came to be considered as the victim of a metamorphosis. It was said that the Gorgon had originally been a beautiful girl, who had dared to set her beauty against that of the goddess Athena. She was especially proud of her beautiful hair; so to punish her, Athena changed her hair into a mass of snakes. In other versions, Athena unleashed her wrath against the girl because Poseidon had ravished her in a temple sacred to the goddess; Medusa had to suffer punishment for this sacrilege. Diodorus Siculus put forward a euhemeristic interpretation of the legend of the Gorgons. The Gorgons, he said, were a warlike people, comparable to the Amazons. They lived in a land that lay on the borders of Atlantis. The inhabitants of Atlantis, who had been conquered by the Amazons, induced Queen Myrina to declare war on the Gorgons, who were proving troublesome neighbours. The Amazons were victorious, but the Gorgons soon recovered from their defeat. They were then attacked by Perseus and finally destroyed by Heracles.

Gorgophone (Γοργοφόνη) The daughter of Perseus and Andromeda (Table 3). She married Perieres and bore two sons, Aphareus and Leucippus. Her other two sons, Icarius and Tyndareus (Tables 6, 19 and 39), were sometimes thought to have been fathered by Perieres and sometimes by Oebalus, who became her second husband after Perieres' death. Gorgophone was the first Grecian widow to remarry. Until then, it was considered that widows should not enter into a second marriage.

Gorgophonus (Γοργοφόνος)
1. A grandson of Perseus (Table 31).
2. Another Gorgophonus was a king of Epidaurus, who had been expelled from his kingdom and instructed by the oracle to found a city at the place where he found the scabbard of a sword (the Greek word is μύκης, which more correctly describes the *hilt* of the sword, which forms the cap of the scabbard). Gorgophonus found this object in the Peloponnese where it had been dropped by Perseus as he fled back after slaying Medusa. He founded the city of Mycenae at the spot.

Gorgopis (Γοργῶπις) In a somewhat obscure legend, Gorgopis is the name of the wife of ATHAMAS; she was PHRIXUS' cruel stepmother, and was more generally known as INO.

Gouneus (Γουνεύς) Ocytus' son who, at Troy, led the contingent of the Aenians and the Perrhaebi from Thessaly. He was one of Helen's suitors, and this was the reason why he took part in the expedition. During the return from Troy, he was shipwrecked on the coast of Libya, where he settled on the banks of the river Cinyps.

Graces *Gratiae* was the Latin name for the CHARITES.

The three Graces, known to the Greeks as the Charites, were prototypes for beauty, grace and artistic inspiration. They were usually depicted, as in this wall painting from Pompeii, with their hands on each others' shoulders, two looking one way and one the other.
Naples, National Museum.

Graeae (Γραῖαι) The 'Old Women' who had never been young, and were born old. Their parents were Phorcys and Ceto (hence the name Phorcides by which they were sometimes known), and they belonged to the generation of pre-Olympian divinities, as did their sisters the three GORGONS (Table 32). They were three in number (only two, in certain traditions), and were called Enyo, Phephredo and Dino; they had only one eye and one tooth between them, and they shared these in rotation. They lived in the far West, in the land of night, where the Sun never shone.

The only myth in which the Graeae play a part is that of PERSEUS. When Perseus set out to slay Medusa, he first met the Graeae on his journey, their task was to bar the road that led to the Gorgons. As they had only one eye, they kept watch in rotation, and the two who did not have the eye slept while awaiting their turn. Perseus managed to steal this eye, and thus plunged all three of them into sleep at the same time; this enabled him to pass them without trouble, and carry out his task. He is said to have thrown the eye into Lake Tritonis.

In another version of the legend, the Graeae were trustees of an oracle: they knew the conditions that had to be fulfilled in order to kill the Gorgon. To do so, three things had to be obtained: some winged sandals from certain Nymphs, a sort of bag called a *kibisis*, and Hades' helmet, which made the wearer invisible. Under the coaching of Hermes and Athena, Perseus deprived the three Old Women of their eye and their tooth, and forced them to reveal their secret to him. They told him where to find the Nymphs, who were more than willing to supply him with the things he needed.

Granicus (Γράνικος) The founder of the Phrygian city of Adramyttus, which stood not far from Troy. When Heracles came to Phrygia Granicus gave the hero his daughter Thebe in marriage; Heracles founded the city of Thebes in Mysia in her honour.

Griffins (Γρῦπες) The *grypes*, or griffins, were fabulous birds with powerful wings and lions' bodies, their heads armed with eagles' beaks.

Griffins were legendary guardians of treasure and possessed wings and lions' bodies. Greek gold coin of Panticapeum on the Black Sea.

They were sacred to Apollo, whose treasures they guarded against the assaults of the Arimaspians in the Scythian desert in the land of the Hyperboreans. Other authors place them among the Ethiopians, still others in India. The griffins were also associated with Dionysus, and were said to be the guardians of his ever-flowing bowl of wine. Later fables relate that the griffins resisted any search for gold in the deserts in the north of India, either because they were charged with guardianship of the precious metal or because their nests lay in the mountains in which it was mined, and they wished to defend their young against every danger.

Grynus (Γϱῦνος) The son of Eurypylus and the grandson of Telephus. After the death of his father, slain at Troy by Neoptolemus, he was attacked by his neighbours, who sought to rob him of his throne of Mysia. He then appealed for help to Pergamus, son of Neoptolemus and Andromache. With Pergamus' help, he triumphed over his enemies, and in memory of this he founded two cities, Pergamum and Grynium.

Gyas (Γύας) The name Gyas occurs twice in the *Aeneid*:
1. In the first case, he was one of Aeneas' companions, who took part in the funeral games held in honour of Anchises.
2. In the second, he was one of Aeneas' opponents, who was slain by the hero together with his brother Cisseus. This Gyas was a Latin, the son of a man called Melampus, who had accompanied Heracles on his expedition against GERYON and had settled in Latium on his return.

Gyges (Γύγης)
1. One of the Hecatoncheires, the giants with a hundred arms, whose parents were Gaia and Uranus (Table 12). He was the brother of Briareus (AEGAEON) and Cottus. With Cottus he took part in the revolt against the Olympians, and was imprisoned by Zeus in Tartarus, where he was guarded by his own brother, Briareus.
2. A king of Lydia, whose story as told by Herodotus contains many elements of folk lore, such as the ring that confers invisibility, the amazing fortune, the discovery of treasure, and the love of a queen. This figure belongs to history rather than to mythology.

Gyrton (Γύϱτων) The brother of Phlegyas, and consequently, in some traditions, the uncle of Ixion. He is said to have founded the city of Gyrton in Thessaly.

H

Hades (Ἅιδης) The god of the dead. Hades was the son of Cronus and Rhea, and brother of Zeus, Poseidon, Hera, Hestia, and Demeter (Table 38). Like Zeus and Poseidon, he was one of the three 'overlords' who shared the empire of the Universe between them after the defeat of the Titans. While Zeus gained Heaven, and Poseidon the Sea, Hades' portion was the world of the Nether Regions – Tartarus, or Hell.

Like his brothers, Hades had been swallowed at birth by Cronus, and later disgorged. He took part in the fight against the Titans and the Cyclopes armed him with a helmet which conferred invisibility on the wearer. This helmet of Hades, like that of Siegfried in German mythology, was subsequently worn by other deities, such as Athena, and even by mortal heroes, such as Perseus.

Down in the Nether Regions, Hades reigned over the Dead. He was a pitiless master, who allowed none of his subjects to return to the Living. He was assisted by many demons and genii who worked under his orders (for example Charon the ferryman). Persephone, who was no less cruel, reigned at his side. Persephone, the daughter of Demeter, was his niece (Table 38). Hades fell in love with her, but her father Zeus would not agree to his marrying her, since Demeter was outraged by the thought of her young daughter being imprisoned for all eternity in the land of shadows. Hades therefore decided to abduct her, and carried her off from the plains of Sicily while she was playing with her companions and picking flowers. He was perhaps even helped in this abduction by Zeus, who became his clandestine accomplice. Be that as it may, Zeus later ordered Hades to return Persephone to her mother; but Hades had taken precautions – he had given Persephone a pomegranate seed to eat. Now, whoever visited the kingdom of the Dead, and ate anything there, could no longer return and dwell among the Living. Persephone was thus obliged to spend a third of each year with Hades. Her marriage with him was apparently childless.

Hades appears infrequently in the legends. Apart from the story of the abduction, which belonged in Demeter's cycle, his name hardly features except in one other myth, in which he is linked with Heracles's legend. In the *Iliad*, it was related that when the hero went down into the Nether Regions, Hades wished to deny him access to his kingdom; he met Heracles at the Gates of Hell, but the hero wounded him with an arrow in the shoulder. Hades had to be rushed up onto Mount Olympus, where the healing god Paean applied a magic ointment which healed his wound immediately. Other versions have Heracles stunning the god with a huge boulder. In any event, Zeus's son Heracles was the victor.

Hades, whose name means 'the Invisible', was usually not named out loud, for fear that his anger might be aroused by hearing himself called by name. Euphemisms were used to describe him instead; he was most commonly called by his surname, Pluto, 'the Rich' – an allusion to the inexhaustible richness of the earth, both the cultivated earth and the mines that lay hidden beneath it. Pluto was often depicted holding a horn of plenty, as a symbol of this richness.

Haemon (Αἵμων) The name of several heroes:
1. The best-known was the son of Creon, king of Thebes. There are two different traditions about him: according to the first, Creon's son Haemon was devoured by the Sphinx, and to avenge his death Creon had promised his kingdom to whoever should deliver Thebes from the monster. According to the second tradition, Haemon was betrothed to Oedipus's daughter Antigone, and slew himself when Creon condemned the young girl to death by being buried alive in the tomb of the Labdacides. This second version was the one used in the tragedies: Sophocles in particular followed it in his *Antigone*. It was sometimes said that Haemon and Antigone had a son, called Maeon. This was the tradition followed in particular by Euripides in his tragedy *Antigone*, which has not survived.
2. Haemon was also the name of the eponymous hero of Haemonia, the old name for Thessaly. This Haemon was the son of Pelasgus and the father of Thessalus, who gave the country its new name. In another genealogy, Haemon was one of the fifty sons of Lycaon, who was himself the son of Pelasgus. In this tradition, Haemon was held to

be not the eponym of Haemonia the country, but the founder of the Arcadian city of Haemonia.

3. An obscure tradition mentions another Haemon who was the grandson of Cadmus and the son of Polydorus (Table 3). This Haemon had accidentally killed one of his companions during a hunt, and had had to seek refuge in Athens. His descendants later emigrated to Rhodes, and thence to Agrigentum, in Sicily. The tyrant Theron claimed descent from them.

4. See also Table 27 for Haemon, son of Thoas and father of Oxylus.

Haemus (Αἷμος)
1. Haemus (or Hemus) was one of the sons of Boreas and Orithyia, and hence a brother of the Boreades, Calais and Zetes (Table 11), although his name only appears in later versions of the tradition. He married Rhodope, daughter of the river-god Strymon, and reigned over Thrace with her. They had a son called Hebrus, who gave his name to the River Hebrus. Haemus and Rhodope made so bold as to initiate a cult dedicated to themselves, calling themselves Zeus and Hera respectively. As punishment for this sacrilege they were transformed into mountains.

2. According to another tradition, Haemus was a tyrant of Thrace who attacked the city of Byzantium during the time of its founder Byzas, and was slain by Byzas in single combat on Mount Haemus.

3. Haemus was also the name of one of Telephus' companions before Troy. Like Telephus, he came from Mysia, and was said to be the son of Ares.

Hagno (Ἁγνώ) In the Arcadian legend of Zeus it was said that the god was born on Mount Lyceus, at a place called Cretea (which enabled the Arcadians to reconcile their legend with that of the god's Cretan origin by claiming that there had been confusion between Cretea and the island of Crete). He had been brought up by three local Nymphs: Hagno, Thisoa, and Neda. Hagno was the Nymph of a spring on Mount Lyceus which was noteworthy for always having water, both in winter and in summer. During a severe drought, which had lasted so long that the crops were endangered, the priest of Lycian Zeus finally addressed solemn prayers to the god: and during a sacrifice he dipped a little twig of oak into the water of the spring. The water immediately went turbid, and started moving to and fro and a great storm sprang up, which drenched the land with copious rain.

Halesus An Italian hero who gave his name to the Faliscians of Falerii (a city which he founded in Etruria, and in which a dialect very closely related to Latin was spoken). The mythographers linked Halesus with Agamemnon, making him out to be the latter's companion, or even his illegitimate son, who had come to Italy at the time of the Trojan War. Other traditions portrayed him as a son of Neptune; and as such he was respected by Morrius, king of Veii, who initiated the *carmen Saliare* in his honour (this was the archaic song chanted by the Salians during certain ceremonies in Rome).

As a descendant of Agamemnon and a native of Argos, Halesus was numbered among the enemies of Aeneas when the latter landed in Italy. Halesus fought alongside Turnus, and was slain by Pallas.

Halia (Ἁλία)
1. A Rhodian heroine, the sister of the Telchines. Married to Poseidon, she had six sons, and a daughter called Rhodus who gave her name to the island of Rhodes. Aphrodite struck Halia's six sons with madness, and they tried to rape their own mother; but Poseidon struck them down and thrust them underground with blows from his trident, whereupon the distraught Halia threw herself into the sea. The inhabitants of Rhodes worshipped her as they would a sea-goddess, under the name of Leucothea.

2. There was also a Nereid whose name was Halia. The name *Halia* was in fact connected with one of the names of the sea, the 'salty element' (ἅλς).

Haliacmon (Ἁλιάκμων)
1. The Haliacmon was a river in Macedonia, the god of which was said to have been the son of Oceanus and Tethys.

2. Another legend has it that an inhabitant of Tiryns named Haliacmon had been smitten with madness and thrown himself into the river known until then as the Carmanor; thereafter the river took the name of Haliacmon. Later still a third name was given to the same river, which then became the Inachus (see INACHUS).

Haliae (Ἁλίαι) The name (meaning Women of the Sea) given to some women whose tomb lay in Argos. They were said to have come from the islands of the Aegean Sea to fight alongside Dionysus against Perseus and the Argives. They were all killed in battle.

Haliartus (Ἁλίαρτος) He and his brother Coronus were the sons of Thesandrus and grandsons of

Sisyphus (Table 35). Their great-uncle Athamas, king of Orchomenus, had lost all his sons (see ATHAMAS), and therefore left his kingdom to them. But later on, when Presbon, one of Phrixus' sons, came back from Colchis and claimed his grandfather's throne (for Phrixus was Athamas' son) Haliartus and Coronus surrendered the throne to him; they then left Orchomenus, and founded two cities, Haliartus and Coronea.

Halirrhotius (Ἁλιρρόθιος) The son of Poseidon and the Nymph Euryte. Near Asclepius's spring in Athens he tried to rape Alcippe, the daughter of Ares, whom the god had fathered on Aglauros. Ares slew Halirrhotius, and Poseidon accused his son's murderer before a tribunal of the gods, which met on a hill thereafter known as the Areopagus (the hill of Ares).

Another version claimed that Halirrhotius, son of Poseidon, was outraged when Attica was allotted to Athena and denied to his father. In his anger, he tried to cut down the olive tree which the goddess had presented to Attica; but his axe flew out of his hands in miraculous fashion and chopped off his head.

Halmus (Ἅλμος) A son of Sisyphus and the brother of Glaucus, Ornytion, and Thessandrus (Table 35). Eteocles, king of Orchomenus, gave Halmus a portion of land on which he founded the city of Halmones. He had two daughters, Chrysogone and Chryse. Chrysogone had a son by Poseidon called Chryses; Chryses had a son by Ares called Phlegyas.

Hals (Ἅλς) Hals (the Sea) was the name of an enchantress, the servant and companion of Circe. She was said to be of Etruscan origin, and to have given her name to some sort of a city called Halos Pyrgos, or the Tower of Hals, in Etruria. When Odysseus paid his second visit to Circe (in the legends which described a sequel to the *Odyssey*) he visited Hals, who used her spells to transform him into a horse. She kept him by her side and fed him well until he died of old age. This legend was intended to explain the mysterious verse in the *Odyssey*, which foretold that death would come to Odysseus 'from the Sea'.

Hamadryads (Ἁμαδρυάδες) The Hamadryads were tree Nymphs. They were born with the trees they protected, and shared their fate. Callimachus, in his *Hymn to Delos*, told of an oak Nymph's anguish for her tree, which had just been struck by lightning. The Nymphs were said to have rejoiced when the trees were watered by the rain from Heaven, and to have grieved when they shed their leaves. It was even maintained that they died at the same time as their trees. They were considered to be intermediate entities between Mortals and Immortals. They lived for a very long time – ten 'palm tree lives', or nine thousand seven hundred and twenty years.

Some legends preserve the memory of Hamadryads who had entreated some hero or another to save their trees (see RHOECUS, and CHRYSOPELIA). Other legends told of the punishments visited on men who had shown contempt for a Nymph's prayers and cut down her tree (see ERYSICHTHON).

For a later legend concerning the origin of the Hamadryads, see OXYLUS 3.

Harmonia (Ἁρμονία) There are two different legends about Harmonia, one of them Theban and the other linked to the worship of the gods of Samothrace. The legends have one point in common: in each of them, Harmonia was the wife of Cadmus.

1. In the Theban legend, Harmonia was the daughter of Ares and Aphrodite. Zeus himself married her to Cadmus; the wedding took place on the Cadmea, the citadel of Thebes, and the gods attended it, as they did later for the marriage of Thetis and Peleus. They brought presents, the most famous of which was a robe and a necklace. The robe was a present from Athena (or Aphrodite), and had been woven by the Charites (Graces); the necklace was Hephaestus' gift. According to other stories, both the necklace and the robe were given to Harmonia by CADMUS himself, who had obtained them from Europa; she had been given them by Zeus as love offerings. Yet another tradition asserts that the robe had been made by Athena and Hephaestus, and were impregnated by these two deities with a philtre which poisoned Harmonia's children. The reason for this unkind action was the hatred Hephaestus and Athena felt for Harmonia, the love-child of Ares and Aphrodite. These two presents from the gods were destined to play an important role later in the legend of the Seven Chiefs (see ALCMAEON, AMPHIARAUS, and ERIPHYLE). Later still they became an ex-voto offering at Delphi, where they were stolen in the days of Philip of Macedon.

2. In the Samothracian traditions, Harmonia was the daughter not of Ares and Aphrodite, but of Zeus and Electra, one of Atlas' daughters; she was therefore the sister of Dardanus and Iasion (Table

7). In these versions Cadmus met her as he made his way through the island, in search of his sister Europa who had been carried off by Zeus. Harmonia's marriage to Cadmus took place in Samothrace, in the same way as in the Theban tradition. It was also said that Cadmus had carried Harmonia off with Athena's help. Cadmus and Harmonia had several children (Table 3). At the end of their lives, they abandoned the throne of Thebes and went to Illyria, where they were eventually transformed into snakes.

The name Harmonia was also applied to the abstract concept of harmony and concord. There are no myths about this Harmonia. She was usually portrayed in the train of the Charites and of Aphrodite.

Harmonides (Ἁρμονίδης) The shipwright who built the ship in which Paris sailed from Troy to Lacedaemon to carry off Helen.

Harpalion (Ἁρπαλίων)
1. The son of Pylaemenes, king of Paphlagonia. He fought alongside the Trojans and was killed by Merion.
2. Another man of this same name was numbered among the ranks of the Greeks during the siege of Troy; he was a Boeotian, the son of Arizelus and Amphinome and the companion of Prothoenor. He was killed by Aeneas.

Harpalyce (Ἁρπαλύκη)
1. A Thracian woman who was King Harpalycus' daughter. Her mother died while she was still a child, and Harpalycus fed her on cow's and mare's milk and taught her how to fight. He planned that she should succeed him on the throne, since he had no son. Harpalyce found this sort of life to her liking, and became a skilled warrior. When Thrace was attacked by the Getae, who were barbarians from the Danubian plains, Harpalycus was surrounded by the enemy and seriously wounded; he would have been killed had his daughter not rushed to his support and saved him. Later Harpalycus was dethroned after an uprising brought on by his own cruelty. He withdrew into the woods, accompanied by his daughter. She provided for their needs by hunting, and by raiding cow-sheds and sheep-folds in the neighbourhood. These raids were so successful that the shepherds eventually set traps for her, as if she were a wild beast; they caught her in hunting-nets and killed her. Harpalyce's death resulted in bloody brawls; when the shepherds caught her,

the girl had a kid with her, the booty from her last robbery; they argued over this kid so violently that several of them were killed. A tomb was built for Harpalyce and a cult grew up around her. At the feast held in her honour, her worshippers would engage in mock battles, in memory, so it was said, of the brawls which had marked her death.
2. Another Harpalyce committed incest with her father Clymenus (see CLYMENUS 3). According to the legend, Harpalyce was either transformed after her crime into a night-bird called χαλκίς, or she committed suicide, or possibly she was killed by Clymenus.
3. The central figure in an unhappy love-affair: she fell in love with Iphicles and when he spurned her advances she killed herself.

Harpalycus (Ἁρπάλυκος) There are legends about four people of this name:
1. HARPALYCE's father.
2. A son of Lycaon.
3. In the *Aeneid*, one of Aeneas' companions, who was slain by Camillus during the campaign against Turnus and the Rutuli.
4. Theocritus mentions another Harpalycus who taught Heracles fencing and gymnastics.

Harpies (Ἅρπυιαι) The Harpies (the 'Snatchers') were winged genii, daughters of Thaumas and Electra, the Oceanid (Table 32). They belonged to the pre-Olympian divine generation. There were usually said to be two of them: Aello (also called Nicothoe) and Ocypete; but a third, Celaeno, was sometimes mentioned too. Their names revealed their nature: Aello – wind-squall; Ocypete – fast flier; Celaeno – obscure (like the sky covered with storm-clouds). They were depicted as winged women, or as birds with women's heads and sharp claws. They are said to have lived in the islands of the Strophades, in the Aegean Sea; later, Virgil placed them at the Gates of the Underworld with all the other monsters.

The Harpies carried off children and souls. They are sometimes depicted on tombs, carrying the soul of the deceased in their claws. The legend in which they figured most prominently was that of the king PHINEUS. A curse had been placed on him, and everything that was put before him was snatched away from him by the Harpies, especially his food; and what they could not carry off, they soiled. When the Argonauts arrived, Phineus begged them to rid him of the Harpies. The Boreades, Zetes and Calais, chased these demons away. It was predicted that the Harpies could die only if they were caught by the sons of Boreas; conversely, the latter would die if they failed to catch the Harpies. During the chase the first Harpy fell into a river in the Peloponnese, which was known thereafter as the Harpys; the other one reached the Echinades Islands, which were known thenceforth as the Strophades or Islands of Return. At that point, Iris appeared before Calais and Zetes and forbade them to kill the Harpies, who were Zeus' servants. In exchange for their lives, the Harpies promised to leave Phineus in peace from then on and hid themselves in a cave in Crete. An obscure tradition says that Boreas' two sons perished during their pursuit of the Harpies, but this is unsubstantiated. The Harpies also figured in the legend of PANDAREOS. They were said to have coupled with the wind-god Zephyrus, and given birth to two pairs of horses: Xanthus and Balius, the two divine horses of Achilles, which went as swiftly as the wind; and Phlogeus and Harpagus, the horses of the Dioscuri.

Harpinna (Ἅρπιννα) One of the daughters of the river-god Asopus, who was married to Aegina's sister. Harpinna was loved by Ares, who fathered her child OENOMAUS. She gave her name to the city of Harpina, which was founded by Oenomaus.

Harpyreia (Ἁρπύρεια) In the euhemeristic version of the legend of Phineus, Harpyreia was the name of one of his daughters; her sister was called Erasia. Both of them lived a dissolute life which endangered their father's fortune. They were carried off by the Boreades, Calais and Zetes, who in this way rid Phineus of all his troubles (see HARPIES).

Hebe (Ἥβη) As her name implies, Hebe was the personification of Youth. She was the daughter of Zeus and Hera, and hence the sister of Ares and Eilithyia (Table 38). Within the divine household her role was that of a serving-maid: she poured the nectar (until replaced in this function by the kidnapped Ganymede), prepared Ares' bath, and helped Hera to harness the horses to her chariot. She danced with the Muses and the Horae to the sound of Apollo's lyre. After Heracles was reconciled with Hera and became a god, the hero married Hebe; the gods celebrated his marriage as a symbol of his having attained the eternal youthfulness peculiar to the gods.

Hecaergus (Ἑκάεργος) Hecaergus and Opis were two Hyperboreans; they were the first to offer a sacrifice to Apollo and Artemis on the island of Delos, whither they had brought the sacred objects. They were responsible for the upbringing of the two divine children, who owed their respective surnames of Hecaergus and Opis to their two guardians. This legend was specifically intended to explain these ritual appellations.

Hecale (Ἑκάλη) When THESEUS was on his way to fight the bull of Marathon, he spent the night in a village in Attica, where he was made welcome by an old woman called Hecale. They spent the evening together by the fire, and the following day, after Theseus' departure, Hecale sacrificed to Zeus to ensure the young man's safe return. After Theseus had killed the bull he went back to Hecale's cottage on his return journey, only to find that the old woman had died. Theseus then raised a shrine to Zeus Hecaleius in her honour and established the Hecalesian Rites.

Hecamede (Ἑκαμήδη) When Achilles captured the island of Tenedos, on his way to the Trojan War, one of his captives was a young girl called Hecamede, who was Arsinous' daughter. She was later given to Nestor.

Hecate (Ἑκάτη) A goddess closely connected with Artemis. There are no myths surrounding her; she was characterized by her functions and attributes rather than by legends in which she played a part. Hesiod portrays her as the offspring of Asteria and Perses, and a direct descendant of the generation of Titans (Table 32). She was therefore independent of the Olympian deities, but Zeus allowed her to retain her existing privileges, and even added to them. She extended her goodwill towards all men, granting them the favours they sought of her. She could grant material prosperity, eloquence in political assemblies, and victory both in battle and in sporting events. She had the power to give fishermen big hauls of fish, and she made cattle grow fat or lean at will; her powers extended over every field. She was most particularly invoked as the 'foster-mother goddess' of youth, as were Artemis and Apollo.

Such were the characteristics of Hecate in the early days; but she gradually assumed different attributes. She came to be considered as the deity presiding over magic and spells, and she was linked to the world of Shades. She appeared to magicians and sorceresses with a torch in each hand, or in the form of various animals, such as a mare, a bitch or a she-wolf. She was credited with the invention of sorcery, and legends included her among the family of superlative magicians such as Aeetes and Medea of Colchis (see PERSES). Later traditions even portray her as CIRCE's mother. (Circe was Medea's aunt; sometimes she was even said to have been her mother.) As a magician, Hecate presided over crossroads, the best of all locations for magic. Here, statues were erected to her, in the form of a woman with three bodies or three heads. These statues were very common in the countryside in antiquity, and votive offerings were placed near them.

Hecaterus (Ἑκάτερος) Hecaterus is mentioned only by Strabo, who quotes from a lost work of Hesiod; the reading is not secure though. According to Hesiod, Hecaterus married one of Phoroneus' daughters, probably Niobe, and fathered a whole series of spirits on her: the Mountain Nymphs, the Satyrs, and the Curetes (though this is only one of many genealogies for the latter).

Hecatoncheires (Ἑκατόγχειρες) Giants who were endowed with a hundred arms and fifty heads. They were three in number: Cottus, Briareus (or AEGAEON), and GYGES (or Gyes). They were sons of Uranus and Gaia (Table 12), and belonged to the same generation as the Cyclopes. Like the latter, they fought on the side of Zeus and the Olympians in the war against the Titans. Euhemeristic interpretations claim that the Hecatoncheires were not giants but men, who lived in the city of Hecatoncheiria in Macedonia. They were supposed to have helped the inhabitants of the city of Olympia in their struggle against the Titans, who were finally expelled from the region.

Hector (Ἕκτωρ) The son of Priam and Hecuba – probably their eldest son, though certain traditions (which go back to Stesichorus) make him Apollo's son. Although Priam was king of Troy, Hector held the real power over his compatriots; he organized the Assembly debates as he pleased, and directed the war effort to suit his own plans. He was much loved by the Trojans, who accorded him almost divine honours; and friends and enemies alike acknowledged him as the principal defender of the city. Agamemnon wished to kill Hector as quickly as possible, for he knew he would not take Troy while Hector was alive. Hector's personality is dealt with at considerable length in the *Iliad*. He appears infrequently in the cyclic epics and the tragedies, so we know little

about him apart from the feats attributed to him during the tenth year of the war, the only year dealt with in the *Iliad*. We know that he was married to ANDROMACHE, daughter of the king of Thebes in Mysia, and that he had one son by her, who was called Astyanax by the Trojans and Scamandrius by his parents. Astyanax was still quite young at the time of his father's death. One aberrant tradition gave Hector and Andromache another son, Laodamas; and yet another version mentions a son called Oxymus.

Until the beginning of the tenth year of the war, Hector avoided fighting in open country, since he knew that Achilles was among the Greeks. Achilles tried once to meet him face to face, but Hector was unwilling to stand his ground and retreated into the city. However, he created considerable carnage among the Greeks when Achilles was not present. He was protected by Ares, until Ares himself was wounded by Diomedes. Mnesthes, Anchialus, Teuthras, Orestes, Trechus, Oenomaus, Helenus and Oresbius were prominent among those he killed.

Hector then returned to the fray, accompanied by his brother Paris. He challenged any Greek hero to single combat; Menelaus came forward, but was held back by Agamemnon; finally Ajax accepted the challenge. The fight went on till night without either man winning. When night fell Ajax and Hector exchanged presents, Ajax giving his baldric, and Hector his sword.

Hector's most brilliant exploit was his attack on the Greek ships; he was in sole command of the raid. The direct intervention of the gods was necessary on several occasions to prevent him from killing such heroes as Nestor or Diomedes. Apollo, for his part, protected Hector and deflected Teucer's arrows away from him; and Zeus expressly instructed the gods and goddesses to let Hector be victorious as long as Achilles refused to join the fray. The situation had become extremely critical for the Greeks when PATROCLUS came to their assistance, with the approval of Achilles. He was soon killed by Hector, who stripped him of his arms, despite the efforts of the Greeks.

Achilles then rejoined the battle and Hector's last moments were at hand. When Achilles slew Polydorus, one of Hector's brothers, Hector tried to avenge him, but his spear fell harmlessly at Achilles' feet. His destiny made him helpless against Achilles, for he was fated to die at the latter's hands. To delay the fatal moment Apollo hid him within a cloud and Achilles sought him in

vain; but when the rest of the Trojan army retreated behind the city walls, Hector stayed behind, alone, at the Scaean Gate. His father and
mother urged him to regain the shelter of the
ramparts; but he refused to listen to their advice,
and waited for Achilles. However when Achilles
drew near, Hector was overcome by fear and fled
from him. The two opponents circled the city
three times, one behind the other, until Athena
assumed the form of Deiphobus and persuaded
Hector to stand and fight, promising to help him.
When Hector accepted the challenge and faced
Achilles, Athena disappeared. Hector then realized
his last hour had come. On Olympus, Zeus used
Destiny's scales to weigh the fates of the two
adversaries, and Hector's proved the heavier: his
scale had sunk towards Hades. Apollo too abandoned Hector, and Achilles dealt him a mortal
blow. As he lay dying, Hector begged Achilles to
return his body to Priam, but Achilles refused.
Then Hector, with the second sight of the dying,
foretold Achilles' own early death. Achilles
pierced the heels of Hector's body and attached it
to his chariot with leather thongs. Then he dragged it right round the city, under the eyes of all the
Trojans. Then the corpse was exposed in the
Greek camp and left with no protection against
dogs and birds of prey, till even the gods took pity
on him. Zeus sent Iris to find Achilles, and
ordered him to hand Hector's corpse over to
Priam. For his part, Priam came to Achilles under
a flag of truce, and ransomed his son's body at a
heavy price. A twelve-day truce allowed the
Trojans to perform their defender's funeral rites
with the dignity he deserved. Andromache, Hecuba and Helen were the chief mourners.

Hecuba (Ἑκάβη) Priam's second wife. Her
genealogy was the subject of much controversy in
antiquity. There are two different traditions:
according to the first, she was the daughter of
Dymas, a king of Phrygia, whose wife was the
Nymph Eunoe; in the other, she was the daughter
of Cisseus, a king of Thrace. In the first case, she
was a descendant of the River Sangarius, and a
variant of this tradition made Sangarius not her
great-grandfather but her father, who fathered her
on the Nymph Evagora. In another variant, her
mother was Glaucippe, Xanthus' daughter.
Authors who held that she was the daughter of
Cisseus the Thracian named Telecleia as her
mother. The tradition linking Hecuba with
Dymas and Phrygia was maintained in the *Iliad*.
The Thracian lineage was preferred by the tragic

poets, especially Euripides. The genealogical
problem of Hecuba's origin was so complex that
the Emperor Tiberius took an ironic pleasure in
presenting it to the grammarians of his day.

Hecuba was renowned for her fecundity. She is
sometimes said to have given birth to nineteen
children, though Euripides raised this number to
fifty. Apollodorus names only fourteen: Hector,
the eldest; Paris, called Alexander, the second son,
whose birth was preceded by a prophetic dream;
then four daughters, Creusa, Laodicea, Polyxena,
and Cassandra (though this last was generally
considered as the twin sister of Troilus, or perhaps
of HELENUS, who also possessed the gift of prophecy). The younger children were all boys:
Deiphobus, Helenus, Pammon, Polites, Antiphus, Hipponous, Polydorus, and TROILUS, the
youngest and the best-loved, the favourite of his
elder brother Hector. Hecuba is also said to have
had a fifteenth child, Polydamas (Table 34).

In Homer's work, Hecuba plays only a modest
role. She appears in the background, curbing
Hector's rash courage, weeping over his corpse,
beseeching Athena to ward off disaster from the
city. In the epic cycles, though, and especially in
the tragedies, Hecuba grew in stature until she
became the symbol of majesty and misfortune.
She was reputed to have had a strange dream just
before giving birth to her second son: she had seen
a torch emerging from her bosom, which set fire
to the whole city of Troy and even the forests of
Mount Ida. When the seers were consulted, they
announced that the infant about to be born would
bring about the ruin of the city. Hecuba refused to
allow her son to be put to death when he was
born, and had him exposed. The child was rescued
and later returned to Troy (see PARIS). Another
version claims that the soothsayers (and especially
AESACHUS, one of Priam's sons) had merely
warned Priam that the child to be born on a certain
day would cause Troy's downfall; they recom-
mended that he should be killed, together with his
mother. On the stated day, two births took place:
that of Paris and that of Munippus, the son of
CILLA and Thymoetes, Priam's brother or brother-
in-law. Priam had Cilla and Munippus put to
death. This legend of Hecuba's dream was
intended to made her responsible for the crime
which destroyed Troy.

When Troy fell, she had already lost nearly all
her sons. One of them, Polydorus, had been
entrusted by Priam to POLYMESTOR, king of the
Chersonese (who, according to one version of the
legend, had married Ilione, one of Priam's daugh-

ters), in order to place him in safe keeping. At the same time, Priam asked Polymestor to take care of some important treasures for his son. When Troy had fallen and Priam was dead, Polymestor decided to appropriate the treasures which had been entrusted to him. He killed Polydorus and threw his body into the sea. (According to another version, he slew his own son DEIPYLUS by mistake.) The body was washed up by the waves on the coast of the Troad, just as Hecuba – who had fallen to Odysseus when lots were drawn for the captured Trojan women – was about to leave Troy. The old queen recognized the body of her son, and immediately plotted her revenge. She sent one of her serving-women with a false message for Polymestor. She was to pretend complete ignorance, merely saying that a buried treasure had been found, which the conquerors had so far overlooked. Polymestor came running, driven by the lure of gold. He joined her, and after the Trojan women captured with her had slain the two children he had brought with him before his eyes, she tore his eyes out. As a punishment for this crime, the Greeks decided to stone her to death; but beneath the mass of stones lay not her corpse, but a bitch with eyes of fire. In another version, Hecuba was transformed into a bitch as she was being pursued by Polydorus' companions, intent on avenging their king. Yet another tradition claims that Hecuba had been transformed aboard the ship that was taking her to Greece, and that she had thrown herself into the sea. For another version of her death, see HELENUS.

Hegeleus ('Ηγέλεως) A grandson of Heracles and the son of Tyrsenus, who was himself the hero's son by Omphale. Tyrsenus is said to have invented the trumpet, and Hegeleus introduced the use of this instrument in war among the Heraclids and the Dorians. He built a temple in Argos to Athena Salpinx (Athena of the Trumpet) (see also MELAS).

Heleius ("Ελειος) The youngest son of Perseus and Andromeda (Table 31), born at Mycenae. He accompanied Amphitryon on the expedition to the island of Taphos, and after the victory shared the sovereignty of the island with Cephalus.

He was said to have founded the city of Helos in Laconia.

Helen ('Ελένη) The wife of Menelaus and the woman for whom the Greeks fought for ten years at Troy. Her legend is a very complicated one, which developed considerably from the days of Homer's epic poems and became complicated with many very different elements which gradually overlaid the original tale. In Homer's epic work, her genealogy was still quite clear: she was the daughter of Zeus and Leda, with Tyndareus as her 'human' father (Table 2). The Dioscuri, Castor and Pollux, were her brothers, and Clytemnestra her sister. Helen was later said to be the daughter of Zeus and NEMESIS. In her flight from Zeus, Nemesis was said to have travelled all over the world, taking all sorts of forms. She eventually transformed herself into a goose. Zeus then changed himself into a swan and coupled with her at Rhamnonte, in Attica. As a result of this union Nemesis laid an egg, which she abandoned in a sacred wood. A shepherd found it and brought it to Leda, who put it in a basket. The egg hatched in due course, producing Helen, whom Leda brought up as her own daughter. The tradition that claims that Leda was Helen's mother recounts in similar way how Zeus lay with her in the form of a swan and how she laid an egg from which Helen issued. In a variant tradition, Leda laid *two* eggs; Helen and Pollux came from one and Clytemnestra and Castor from the other. Yet another version claims that Helen, Castor and Pollux all came from the same egg, while Clytemnestra, Tyndareus' daughter, was born in the normal way. Still other traditions claim that Helen was the daughter of Oceanus or even of Aphrodite. In addition, she has been given other sisters besides Clytemnestra – Timandra and Phylonoe.

A legend unknown to Homer tells of Helen's abduction, when still a young girl, by Theseus and his friend Pirithous, which took place as she was offering a sacrifice to Artemis in Lacedaemon. Theseus and Pirithous drew lots for her and Theseus won. When the Athenians proved unwilling to welcome the young girl among them, Theseus took her to Aphidna, where he entrusted her to his mother, AETHRA; but the Dioscuri arrived to rescue her while Theseus and Pirithous were on their way to the Underworld to bring Persephone back to earth. The people of Decelia showed the Dioscuri where Helen had been hidden (see DECELUS). Other versions attribute this role to the hero ACADEMUS. Castor and Pollux attacked the village of Aphidna and captured it; they then carried off their sister, together with Theseus' mother, whom they took back to Lacedaemon. It was sometimes said that Theseus had respected the girl's virginity. Other versions, on

Greek relief depicting the abduction of Helen by Paris – the event which caused the outbreak of the Trojan War. Rome, Lateran Museum.

the contrary, claimed that he had given her a daughter, none other than IPHIGENIA. On Helen's return to Lacedaemon Tyndareus thought that she should be married. A crowd of suitors appeared, including nearly every prince in Greece. The mythographers have preserved their names; the numbers vary, according to the authors, from twenty-nine to ninety-nine. Almost alone among the heroes of his day, Achilles never appears in any of the lists – doubtless because he was not yet of an age to marry. Tyndareus was embarrassed by this vast horde of suitors, for he was afraid that by choosing one he would antagonize the others and perhaps even run the risk of war. He was only too ready to listen to the advice of Odysseus, which was that he should make all the suitors take an oath to accept Helen's choice and support her betrothed, should need arise. It was this oath that Menelaus invoked some years later, compelling all the Greek leaders to take up arms against Troy. As a reward for the service he had thus rendered Tyndareus, Odysseus received the hand of Penelope in marriage (see ICARIUS). Helen chose Menelaus, and all the suitors bowed to her will. Helen soon gave her husband a daughter, Hermione. According to some traditions, she also had a son called Nicostratus; but he was born only after her return from Troy.

Helen was then carried off to Troy. She was then the most beautiful woman in the world, and Aphrodite had promised PARIS that he should have her if he would award the prize for beauty to herself, Aphrodite. On her advice, he sailed to Amyclae, where he was the guest of the Tyndarides, and then on to Sparta, where he was made welcome at Menelaus' court. When Menelaus had to go to Crete to attend CATREUS' funeral, Helen took his place among the guests. This is how she met Paris; and it was not long before he carried her off. Most authors followed Homer in believing that Helen was a consenting party in this abduction, though some sought to vindicate her by asserting that she had yielded only to force. In some versions it is claimed that Tyndareus himself gave Paris Helen's hand while Menelaus was away. It was even said that Aphrodite had given Paris the face and figure of Menelaus, thus making it easy for him to seduce Helen. But the view generally held was that Paris' beauty and wealth were the significant factors in this abduction. Helen did not leave empty-handed: she took a wealth of treasure with her, and also her personal slaves, including the captive Aethra,

Theseus' mother; however, she left Hermione in Sparta.

Once again, there are differing traditions about the voyage of the two lovers. The Homeric poems give very little information on this matter. The oldest version, which is also the simplest, says that favourable winds enabled Paris to reach Asia Minor in three days. On the other hand, another tradition holds that Paris' ship was driven by a storm, raised by Hera, as far as Sidon in Phoenicia. The *Iliad* mentions this occurrence, and later versions expanded it. Paris was said to have taken the city; although the king welcomed him in friendly fashion, Paris plundered the palace before leaving, pursued by the Phoenicians, with whom he had a fierce and bloody battle. He finally reached Troy with Helen. A closely related tradition claims that, because of his fear that Menelaus would pursue him, Paris spent a considerable time in Phoenicia and Cyprus, and returned to Troy only after a long delay, when he was certain he would not be harassed by Menelaus. In all these differing versions, he kept Helen at his side. Other traditions are somewhat more far-fetched. Indeed, one claims that Hera was annoyed to see Aphrodite preferred to herself in the beauty contest, and decided to deprive Paris of Helen's love. Accordingly she fashioned a cloud that looked exactly like Helen and gave it to Paris, while the real Helen was carried off to Egypt by Hermes and entrusted to Proteus. According to a variant traditon, Zeus himself sent a phantom Helen to Troy to provoke a war. According to Herodotus, when Helen and Paris went to Egypt on their way to Troy, Proteus initially made them welcome, until he found out how they came to be together. In his indignation he banished Paris from his kingdom and kept Helen prisoner in his palace until such time as Menelaus could come to fetch her. Later authors added to the legend by claiming that Proteus was reluctant to send Paris off alone, so he used his magic arts to fashion a simulacrum of Helen to keep Paris company, and it was for this phantom Helen that the Trojan War was fought. The object of these legends seems to have been to free Helen from blame and present her as the instrument of fate. They probably derive from the poet Stesichorus' 'recantation'. Stesichorus, writing in the sixth century BC, had castigated Helen in his verses for her behaviour. Pausanias tells us that Stesichorus went blind; but when Leonymus of Crotona went to Leuce, the White Island in the Euxine Sea, where Helen was said to be enjoying eternal life at the side of ACHILLES, a voice instructed him to set sail for Himera, Stesichorus' city, and inform the poet that Helen's anger was the cause of his blindness. To be cured of it, he must publish a retraction of his libellous remarks. Stesichorus complied, and his sight was restored to him (see AUTOLEON).

According to the Homeric tradition, Helen lived in Troy throughout the whole of the war. She was welcomed by Priam and Hecuba, who were enchanted by her beauty. Before long, however, ambassadors arrived from Greece seeking the fugitive's return: Odysseus and Menelaus, or perhaps Acamas and Diomedes. These missions proved fruitless, and war soon broke out. Helen lived with Paris and was universally looked upon as his wife; but she was generally hated by the Trojan people, who regarded her as the cause of the war. Only Hector and the ageing Priam knew that the war had resulted from the wills of the gods, and they were well disposed towards her. In the *Iliad*, Helen is described as standing on the ramparts, helping the Trojans by pointing out the Greek leaders whom she knew well. Her situation was anomalous: she was a compatriot of the enemy and everybody knew she was sympathetic to their cause; the Trojans thus had good reason to distrust her. Though she was constantly threatened, she faced her difficulties with courage, knowing her beauty would always get her out of trouble. A legend not included in the *Iliad* tells how Achilles, who had never seen Helen, was seized with a desire to meet her, and how the two goddesses Thetis and Artemis arranged a meeting for them. This meeting is sometimes said to have taken place before the outbreak of the war, but it was most frequently placed shortly before Achilles' death. It is possible that Achilles fell in love with her at first sight and coupled with her immediately. This was the view of those mythographers who gave Helen five husbands, making Achilles the fourth, after Theseus, Menelaus and Paris. The fifth, whom she married after Paris' death, was Deiphobus, another of Priam's sons. As soon as Paris was slain, Priam offered Helen as a prize for the bravest man: Deiphobus and HELENUS put themselves forward, as did Idomeneus, another of Priam's sons. All three of them had been in love with her for a long time, but Deiphobus won her. Helenus showed his anger by retiring to Mount Ida, where he was taken prisoner by the Greeks.

When Odysseus, dressed as a beggar, made his way into the city, Helen recognized him, though he had carefully disguised himself by painting scars on his face, or by making Thoas mutilate him; however, she did not betray him. Euripides claimed that she revealed his presence to Hecuba, who contented herself with sending him out of the city, instead of handing him over to the Trojans. Later, Odysseus came back into Troy, once again in disguise, and this time accompanied by Diomedes; their intention was to steal the PALLADIUM. Once again, he was recognized by Helen, but this time, she did not restrict herself merely to keeping silent – she actually helped him. During this escapade, Odysseus reached an understanding with her as to the necessary measures for the capture of the city, which she was to deliver up to the Greeks. On the fateful night, she waved a torch from the citadel, the agreed signal for the return of the Greek fleet, lying in wait off Tenedos. She removed all arms from Deiphobus' house, to make resistance impossible. Having thus proved her loyalty to the Greeks, she awaited the arrival of MENELAUS with confidence. It is said that after he had killed Deiphobus, Menelaus ran at her with raised sword, intending to kill her as well, but she stood her ground and displayed herself to him half-naked, and the sword fell from his hand. It is also said that Helen took refuge in Aphrodite's temple, and made her peace with her first husband from that hallowed and inviolable ground. When the Greeks saw that Helen had survived without injury, they wished to stone her to death. Once again she was saved by her beauty, and the stones fell from the hands of her would-be executioners.

Helen's return to Greece with Menelaus was no easier than that of the principal heroes who had taken part in the war. She took eight years to return to Sparta; she wandered over the eastern Mediterranean, especially Egypt, where she was cast up after her ship was wrecked. Various legends deal with her stay in Egypt: the pilot of her ship, Canobus (or CANOPUS) was bitten by a snake and died; then Helen killed the snake and removed its venom. She gave Canobus a ceremonial funeral, and he became the eponym of Canopus, a city at the mouth of the Nile. It is also said that Thon, or Thonis, the king of the neighbouring city, gave Menelaus and Helen a warm welcome; but he was overcome by Helen's beauty and tried to rape her. Menelaus killed him. A more elaborate form of this tradition claims that when Menelaus went off on an expedition to Ethiopia, he entrusted his wife to King Thonis.

Then POLYDAMNA, Thonis' wife, discovered that her husband was paying court to Helen, so she sent her to the island of Pharos, first supplying her with a herb to protect her against the numerous snakes that infested the island. This herb was helenium.

This stay in Egypt was also explained in quite another way. Helen is said to have fled from Troy before the fall of the city, supposedly bribing a ship's captain named Pharos to carry her back to Lacedaemon; but a storm cast them up onto the coast of Egypt, where a snake bit Pharos and caused his death. Helen buried him and gave his name to the island of Pharos, which lay at the mouth of the Nile. Later on, Menelaus found her in Egypt, after the end of the war.

According to Euripides, before Helen and Menelaus reached Sparta they landed at Argos, on the very day that ORESTES had just slain Clytemnestra and Aegisthus. For safety's sake, Menelaus waited until nightfall before bringing Helen into the palace; neither of them knew what had just happened there. When Orestes set eyes on Helen, surrounded by the women of her train, and clad in the oriental style of Trojan dress, he wanted to kill her because he held her responsible for all the disasters which had befallen his house; however at Zeus' command Apollo carried her away and made her immortal. This legend differs completely from the tradition generally accepted since the *Odyssey*, which shows Helen returning to Sparta at Menelaus' side, and thereafter setting an example of all the domestic virtues. However, the legend of Helen's deification derived a certain amount of authority from the fact that there were many shrines to Helen, in which Menelaus was honoured too. He had been deified in answer to the prayers of Helen, who was anxious to compensate him in some way for all the torments she had inflicted on him during their life together. Her prayers were also believed to be the reason for the deification of her two brothers, Castor and Pollux.

A Rhodian legend related by Pausanias gives a very different ending to Helen's life. After Menelaus' death, his two sons Nicostratus and Megapenthes banished Helen as a belated punishment for her offences. Helen then took refuge in Rhodes with Polyxo, whose husband had been killed while fighting for the Greeks in the Trojan War. Polyxo pretended to give her a friendly welcome, but she planned to have her revenge. She dressed up some serving-women as the Erinyes, and told them to terrify Helen while she was in her bath; they tormented her so effectively that she hanged herself. There are many other traditions about Helen's punishment: for example, Iphigenia was said to have offered her as a sacrifice in Tauris ('poetic vengeance' for Iphigenia's sacrifice in Aulis); or again, Thetis, angered by the death of Achilles, who had fallen because of Helen, was supposed to have killed her during the return voyage. Among the mystical legends about Helen is one that portrays her as married to Achilles and enjoying an eternal life of banquets on Leuce, the White Island that lay in the Black Sea at the mouth of the Danube. Poseidon and the other gods attended her wedding, and it was forbidden for any mortal to set foot on this island (however, see above for Leonymus and the legend of Stesichorus, and also AUTOLEON). Achilles and Helen had a son, a winged being called EUPHORION, who was loved by Zeus.

Helen had several children from her various marriages (Table 13). Only her marriage to Deiphobus was childless. She and Paris were said to have had a long argument as to what they should call their daughter: Alexandra, after her father, or Helena, after her mother. Finally, they decided to let the knuckle-bones make the choice for them; they threw the bones, and Helen won. Helena is said to have been slain by Hecuba. Her four brothers perished during the sack of Troy.

Helenus (Ἕλενος) The son of Priam and Hecuba, and CASSANDRA's twin brother. He acquired the gift of prophecy at the same time as she did, during a night spent in the temple of Thymbrean Apollo. Just as Cassandra was said to have been loved by the god, so too was Helenus a favourite of his; Apollo presented him with an ivory bow, with which he wounded Achilles in the hand. Helenus participated in the funeral games held round Paris' cenotaph, when the latter was presumed to be dead. He had predicted to his brother all the calamities that would take place as a result of his voyage to Greece in which he carried HELEN away. During the first part of the Trojan War and until the death of Paris, Helenus fought bravely alongside Hector; after Hector's death he replaced him as the leader of the Trojans. He was wounded by Menelaus.

After Paris' death, Helenus' attitude changed completely when Priam refused him Helen's hand and gave her to Deiphobus; Helenus refused to take any further part in the fighting, and retired to Mount Ida. The Greek seer Calchas had announced that only Helenus could reveal the conditions under which the city of Troy could be taken. Odysseus then succeeded in capturing Helenus, and under the effect of a mixture of compulsion and bribery Helenus pronounced his oracle. Troy could only be taken if three conditions were fulfilled: firstly, Neoptolemus, Achilles' son, must be fighting with the Greeks; secondly, the Greeks must be in possession of the bones of Pelops; and finally, the Palladium, the miraculous statue which had fallen from the heavens, must be stolen from the Trojans. Other conditions were also said to have been imposed by Helenus, including the return of Philoctetes to the Greeks; Philoctetes must also agree to bring them Heracles' bow and arrows. Helenus is also said to have advised the Greeks to use the wooden horse to smuggle warriors inside the ramparts. In return for all these services, and for his behaviour before the war, when he sought to dissuade Paris from his plan to abduct Helen, and because he had stopped the Trojans from leaving Achilles' body for the birds, Helenus' life was spared, and he was set free after the fall of the city. There are different traditions concerning his adventures thereafter. According to one of them, he went to the Chersonese in Thrace and settled there with Hecuba, Andromache, and Cassandra, who had been allotted to him when the women captives were shared out, and a group of Trojans. Hecuba is said to have been transformed into a bitch there, and to have died; Helenus buried her in a place known thereafter as the Bitch Tomb. According to another version, he and Andromache were allotted to Neoptolemus as spoils of war. His gift of prophecy enabled him to advise Neoptolemus not to go back with the other Greeks by the sea route, but to make his way home by land. Neoptolemus consequently escaped the disaster of Cape Caphareus, where most of the Greek fleet was wrecked. When NEOPTOLEMUS was slain at Delphi by Orestes, Helenus married his widow, ANDROMACHE; they had a son called Cestrinus. He ruled in Neoptolemus' place, but on his death the throne reverted to Molossus, Neoptolemus' son.

Helenus was credited with the founding of Buthrotum and Ilium in Epirus. He gave Chaonia its name, after his brother (see CHAON). In the *Aeneid*, Virgil shows Helenus married to Andromache and extending a warm welcome to any of his compatriots passing through Epirus. A tradition of later origin, which was probably invented for the sole purpose of suppressing the incidents of his capture by the Greeks and his subsequent betrayal of Troy, claims that when Helenus saw Deiphobus being preferred to himself he was so discontented that he sought Priam's permission to leave Troy and go and settle in Greece. He and his companions left the Troad in several ships, and took possession of an area in Epirus, where he established himself as ruler of the Molossians.

Heliades (Ἡλιάδαι and Ἡλιάδες) The sons and daughters of Helios, the Sun. Both groups play a role in two quite separate legends.
1. The daughters of Helios and the Oceanid Clymene were Phaethon's sisters. Their names were Merope, Helia, Phoebe, Aetheria, and Dioxippe (or Lampetia). When their brother was smitten by Zeus' thunderbolt and plunged into the river Eridanus, the Heliades wept for him on the banks of the river, where they were transformed into poplars; their tears became drops of amber. It was also said that their metamorphosis was a punishment because they had given their brother PHAETHON the chariot and horses of the Sun without Helios' permission, with catastrophic results.
2. The sons of Helios had as their mother the nymph Rhodos, who gave her name to the island of Rhodes. There were seven of them, and their names were as follows: Ochimus, Cercaphus, Macareus (or Macar), Actis, Tenages, Triopas and Candalus. They were all expert astrologers, more skilled in this art than all the men of their day. Macareus, Candalus, Actis and Triopas grew jealous of their brother Tenages' skill and killed him. Then they fled, to Lesbos, Cos, Egypt and Caria respectively. Ochimus and Cercaphus stayed in Rhodes. Ochimus, the eldest, seized power and reigned over the island. He married the Nymph Hegetoria and they had a daughter Cydippe. Cydippe was married to her uncle, Cercaphus, who was his brother's heir and ruled after him. Cydippe had three sons – Lindos, Ialysus, and Camirus, who in due course shared the country between them and founded the three cities that bore their names (see CERCAPHUS and also TLEPOLEMUS).

Helicaon (Ἑλικάων) One of the sons of ANTENOR the Trojan. He married Laodice, one of Priam's daughters. He was saved by Odysseus when the city fell, together with his brothers, and accompanied Antenor and Polydamas to northern Italy. Helicaon's dagger was to be seen at Delphi, preserved as an *ex-voto* offering in the shrine.

Helice ('Ελίκη)
1. Selinus' daughter; she married ION, and gave him a daughter, Bura.
2. One of the two Nymphs who nursed Zeus. When Cronus pursued them in order to punish them for bringing up the child, Zeus transformed them into constellations, the Great Bear and the Little Bear. Helice was sometimes identified with the Nymph CALLISTO, who was also said to have been changed into the constellation of the Great Bear through Zeus' intervention.

Helios (Ἥλιος) The Sun was a deity, or at least a demi-god or demon, who had an existence and a personality peculiar to himself alone, which distinguished him from other solar deities such as Apollo. He belonged to the generation of the Titans, and was therefore older than the Olympians. He is considered to have been the son of the Titan Hyperion and the Titaness Theia; he was the brother of Eos (the Dawn) and Selene (the Moon) (Table 38), and a descendant of Uranus and Gaia (Table 12). Helios' wife was Perseis, one of the daughters of Oceanus and Tethys. She bore him several children: Circe the sorceress, Aeetes the king of Colchis, Pasiphae, who was Minos' wife, and a son, Perseus, who dethroned his brother Aeetes, and was himself slain by his own niece, Medea. In addition, Helios coupled with several other women including the Nymph Rhodos, by whom he had seven sons, the HELIADES; Clymene, a sister of his wife, who bore him daughters, also called the Heliades; and Leucothoe, the daughter of Orchamus and Eurynome (see also PHAETHON and CLYTIA).

Helios is portrayed as a young man in the prime of life and of very great beauty: his head was surrounded with rays of light, which gave him a mass of golden hair. He travelled across the sky in a chariot of fire drawn by horses of great swiftness, called Pyrois, Eos, Aethon, and Phlegon. Each morning, preceded by the chariot of Aurora, Helios set out on his journey from the land of the Indians, along a narrow path which crossed the centre of the sky. He travelled throughout the day and in the evening he reached the Ocean, where his weary horses bathed to refresh themselves. He rested in a golden palace, from which he set out again the next morning. His route then ran underground, or along the Ocean stream which encircled the world, on a boat fashioned out of a big hollow bowl (see HERACLES). His journey from west to east was much shorter than his daily passage along the vault of heaven.

These concepts were based on very ancient ideas about the shape of the world, and were gradually abandoned as astronomy progressed; this explains Helios' secondary rank in the Hellenic pantheon. From the days of Homer, Helios was portrayed as the servant of the gods – a type of official, as it were, whose duties were confined to those of a luminary. For example, he was unable to take any revenge himself for the insult done to him by Odysseus' companions, who killed and ate part of his herds in the island of Thrinacia in Sicily. He sought redress from Zeus and the other gods, threatening to withdraw beneath the earth if the culprits were not punished as he requested. These cattle of the Sun, which were eaten by Odysseus' companions, were animals of immaculate whiteness, with gilded horns; they were tended by the daughters of the Sun, the HELIADES. Helios was often thought of as the eye of the world, who saw everything, and in this capacity he cured ORION's blindness. For the quarrel between Helios and Poseidon, see POSEIDON.

Helle (Ἕλλη) Phrixus' sister; her father was ATHAMAS and her mother Nephele. With Phrixus, she fled on the winged ram which was sent to save them from death and from the hatred of their stepmother Ino. Phrixus managed to reach Colchis and the court of King Aeetes, but Helle fell into the sea, in the straits thereafter known as the Hellespont (the Sea of Ḥelle, the modern Sea of Marmara). Another legend says that she was saved from drowning by Poseidon, who fell in love with her, and begot Paeon, Edonus and Almops upon her.

Hellen (Ἕλλην) The hero who gave his name to the whole Greek race, the Hellenes. He was the son of Deucalion, and the brother of Amphictyon and Protogenia (Table 8), though certain authors refer to him as Prometheus' son. He married a mountain Nymph called Orseis, who bore him three sons, DORUS, XUTHUS, and Aeolus, from whom sprang the principal groups of the Hellenes: Dorians, Aeolians, Ionians, and Achaeans (Table 8). Hellen was considered to have been the king of Phthia in Thessaly, which lay between the rivers Peneus and Asopus, the exact place where Deucalion and Pyrrha had settled after the Flood. He was succeeded by Aeolus; his other sons emigrated and settled in different areas of Greece.

Hemera (Ἡμέρα) The personification of the Day. She was considered as a feminine deity (the Greek word for day is feminine) and was the daughter of Erebus and the Night, and the sister of Aether (see AETHER and URANUS).

Hemicynes (Ἡμίκυνες) The 'Half-Dogs' were a legendary race who were said to have lived on the shore of the Euxine Sea (the Black Sea), not far from the countries of the Massagetae and the Hyperboreans. They had the head and the bark of a dog. In all probability they were a troop of monkeys.

Hemithea (Ἡμιθέα)
1. A heroine of this name was honoured at Castabus, in the Thracian Chersonese. She is said to have been the daughter of STAPHYLUS and Chrysothemis (see PARTHENUS).
2. The daughter of Cycnus, the king of the Troad, and the sister of Tenes, the eponymous hero of Tenedos. She was washed ashore with her brother on the island of Tenedos and settled there (see CYCNUS 2 and TENES). When the Greeks landed on the island on their way to Troy, Achilles pursued Hemithea and would have raped her, had not the earth opened up and engulfed her.

Heosphorus (Ἑωσφόρος) Heosphorus or Eosphorus, the Flame of Eos (the Dawn), was the name of the Morning Star. He was the son of Aurora and Astraeus (Table 14) and the father of Telauge. He also had a daughter by Cleoboea, named Philonis (see PHILAMMON).

Hephaestus (Ἥφαιστος) The god of fire, the son of Zeus and Hera. It is sometimes claimed that Hera produced him on her own, out of resentment for the birth of ATHENA, whom Zeus had brought into the world without the assistance of any woman. She then entrusted him to the Naxian Cedalion so that he might learn metalworking; that, at least, is the tradition found in Hesiod. A obscure tradition from Crete makes Hephaestus the son not of Zeus but of TALOS, who was himself the son of Cres, the eponymous hero of the island. In this tradition, Rhadamanthys is said to have been Hephaestus' son.

Hephaestus was a lame god, and various mythical explanations are given for his infirmity. The most usual is the one put forward in the *Iliad*. Hera was quarrelling with Zeus about Heracles and Hephaestus took his mother's side. Zeus then grasped him by the foot and threw him down from Olympus. Hephaestus' fall lasted for a whole day: towards evening, he hit the ground in the island

of Lemnos, and was rescued by the Sintians (a Thracian people who had emigrated to Lemnos) and restored to life, but he remained lame forever after. Another legend about this same infirmity is also to be found in the *Iliad*. Hephaestus was born lame, and in her shame his mother decided to hide him from the sight of the other deities, so she threw him down from Olympus. Hephaestus fell into the Ocean, where he was rescued by Tethys and Eurynome, who saved his life and brought him up for nine years in a cave beneath the sea. He forged and fashioned many pieces of jewellery for them during those nine years, and he remained forever deeply grateful to them for the kindness they had shown him. Attempts have been made to reconcile the two versions. It was suggested that Hephaestus had indeed been cast out by Zeus, but that he had fallen not onto Lemnos but into the sea, where he had been rescued by the marine goddesses. (It will be remembered that HERA herself was already said to have been brought up by Oceanus and Tethys.) To avenge himself on his mother for her having thrown him down from Olympus, Hephaestus secretly fashioned a throne of gold, in which chains were concealed to bind anyone who sat in it. He sent it to his mother, who was foolish enough to sit down in it, only to find herself bound hand and foot and quite unable to free herself from her bonds. No one knew how to undo the chains, for only Hephaestus had the secret. The gods were thus compelled to recall him to Olympus, with the request that he should free the goddess. Dionysus – whom Hephaestus trusted – was chosen to go and fetch him; to convince him, Dionysus made him drunk. Hephaestus made his entry to Olympus mounted, so it was said, upon an ass. Then he released his mother.

In the ranks of the major Olympian gods, Hephaestus was master of the element of fire. He was a powerful god, who used flame as his weapon in the Trojan War; during the Giants' Revolt he had slain the Giant Clytius by smiting him with a mass of red-hot iron. He was also the god of metals and metallurgy. He ruled over the volcanoes, which were his workshops, where he worked with his assistants, the Cyclopes (this at least was the version in the later legends). Thetis turned to him when she wanted arms forged for Achilles. Among the gods, Hephaestus was the equivalent of Daedalus among men, an inventor for whom no technical miracle was impossible. Although he was physically deformed, Hephaestus nevertheless seemed able to win the hearts of women of great beauty. In the *Iliad*, his name is linked with that of Charis, who was Grace personified. Hesiod portrays him as wedded to Aglaea, the youngest of the Charites. He was particularly famous for his amorous adventures with Aphrodite, which are related in the *Odyssey*. Zeus himself had married him to the goddess, but she became Ares' mistress. One day Helios, the Sun, who sees everything, noticed the two lovers lying side by side; he told the husband. Hephaestus said nothing, but he prepared an invisible net, which he spread round his wife's bed. When she went to bed with her lover, the net closed over them, and the two culprits found themselves completely immobilized. Hephaestus then summoned all the gods to come and view the spectacle. When she was released Aphrodite ran off in shame.

Tradition credits Hephaestus with several sons, among them Palaemon the Argonaut, and Ardalus, a legendary sculptor who like Palaemon had inherited his father's manual dexterity. Periphetes is also mentioned; he was a famous brigand, who was killed by Theseus. ERICHTHONIUS, the legendary hero of the Athenians, was born of Mother Earth as a result of Hephaestus' lust for the virgin goddess Athena. Hephaestus also played a part in the creation of PANDORA, whose body he fashioned out of clay. He also contributed to the punishment of PROMETHEUS by fettering him to the Caucasus Mountains as the helpless prey of a vulture which gnawed at his liver every day.

Hera (῞Ηρα) The greatest of all the Olympian goddesses. She was the daughter of Cronus and Rhea, and hence ZEUS' sister. Like all her brothers and sisters except for Zeus, she was swallowed by Cronus, but restored to life by METIS' cunning and Zeus' strength. Hera is said to have been brought up at the ends of the world by Oceanus and Tethys, to whom Rhea had entrusted her during the struggle between Zeus and the Titans. She remained extremely grateful to them, and when Oceanus and Tethys argued she tried to reconcile them. Other traditions credit the HORAE with Hera's upbringing, or the hero Temenus, or the daughters of Asterion.

Hera married Zeus in a formal wedding ceremony. Hesiod says this was the third time the god had contracted a formal marriage. His first bride was Metis and the next was Themis. It was said, however, that the love between Zeus and Hera was of long standing, and that they had coupled secretly in the days when Cronus was still ruling over the Universe, before the war against the

Titans. Four children were born of their marriage: Hephaestus, Ares, Eilithyia and Hebe (Table 38). The scene of their wedding varies according to the differing traditions. The oldest tradition, so it seems, places it in the Garden of the Hesperides, which was the mystical symbol of fertility, in the heart of an eternal spring. Sometimes the mythographers assert that the golden apples of the HESPERIDES were a present given to Hera by Gaia, Mother Earth, on the occasion of her marriage to Zeus, and that the goddess found them so beautiful that she planted them in her garden on the shores of the Ocean. The *Iliad* says that Zeus and Hera were married, not in the Garden of the Hesperides but on the summit of Mount Ida in Phrygia. Other traditions place this mystic marriage in Euboea, where the god and goddess landed when they came from Crete. Festivals purporting to commemorate the marriage of Zeus and Hera used to take place almost everywhere in Greece. The statue of the goddess was dressed in the costume of a young bride and carried in procession through the city to a shrine where a marital bed had been made ready (see ALALCOMENEUS and CITHAERON). As the lawfully wedded wife of the first among the gods, Hera was the protecting deity of wives. She is portrayed as jealous, violent, and vindictive, often angry with Zeus, whose infidelities she regarded as insults. She visited her hatred not only on Zeus' mistresses, but on the children he sired upon them. Among these, HERACLES was the greatest victim of Hera's wrath. The idea of the Twelve Labours was commonly attributed to the goddess. Furthermore, she persecuted him incessantly until his final apotheosis. Her vindictiveness cost her dear, for Zeus sometimes punished her severely. When Heracles returned after he had captured Troy, Hera raised a violent storm against his ship. This displeased Zeus, who hung the goddess from Mount Olympus by her wrists with an anvil fastened to each foot. HEPHAESTUS tried to free his mother, which brought Zeus' wrath down upon him and led to his being cast out into the void. Later, Hera made formal peace with Heracles.

Hera appears in many legends. She persecuted IO, and suggested to the Curetes that they should kill EPAPHUS, her rival's son. She was responsible for SEMELE's tragic fate. She struck ATHAMAS and Ino with madness to punish them for having brought up little DIONYSUS, Zeus' illegitimate son by Semele. She urged Artemis to slay CALLISTO, whom Zeus had seduced, and she tried to stop the birth of Artemis and Apollo when LETO was actually in labour. Zeus was forced to reckon with her: on several occasions he tried to conceal his children to protect them from Hera's jealous anger. He hid Elara underground, for example, and she there gave birth to Tityus. He made use of other tricks as well; for example, he transformed Dionysus into a kid. Hera's anger and her acts of vengeance sometimes had other reasons behind them. There is a story that Hera and Zeus were arguing one day as to whether the man or the woman derived greater pleasure from the sexual act. Zeus said that women enjoyed it more, but Hera maintained that men were actually the luckier sex in this regard. The two deities decided to consult TIRESIAS, who had experienced the sexual act both as a man and as a woman. Tiresias sided with Zeus, saying that if the pleasures of love were divided into ten parts, the man felt only one of those parts, while the woman felt the other nine. Hera was so annoyed at being contradicted in this way that she deprived Tiresias of his sight.

Hera participated in the beauty contest in which she was pitted against Aphrodite and Athena, with Paris acting as judge at the request of the three goddesses. Her anger carried considerable weight in the Trojan War: she sided against the Trojans in revenge for Paris' refusal to award her the prize, even though she had tried to bribe him by promising him the sovereignty of the world if he chose her. Her hostility became evident when Paris abducted HELEN; and on their return journey, when the lovers had left Sparta bound for Troy, Hera raised a storm which drove them onto the Syrian coast at Sidon. Hera found it quite natural that she should become Achilles' protectress, since she had brought THETIS up, and this too was said to be the reason why Thetis had spurned the advances of Zeus, who wanted to make her his wife. Later, Hera extended her protection to MENELAUS, and gave him immortality.

Hera participated in the war against the Giants. She was attacked by Porphyrion, who was consumed with lust for her; but as the Giant was tearing off the goddess's robe, Zeus struck him down with a thunderbolt and Heracles finished him off with an arrow. Hera was attacked again later on by IXION, who wished to abduct her, but Zeus created a cloud which deluded Ixion and Hera was saved (see CENTAURS). Hera also became known as the protectress of the *Argo*, which she helped to pass unscathed between the Cyanean Rocks (see ARGONAUTS) and through the narrows of Scylla and Charybdis. Hera's usual symbol was the peacock, whose plumage was said to represent the eyes of ARGOS, the watcher, whom the goddess had set over Io. Her plants were the immortelle, the pomegranate, and the lily. In Rome, she was identified with JUNO.

Heracles (Ἡρακλῆς) Heracles, known to the Latins as Hercules, is the best-known and the most popular hero in the whole of Classical mythology. The legends in which he appears form a complete cycle which continued to develop from the pre-Hellenic age until the end of Antiquity, so it is extremely difficult to place his various exploits in any rational order. This difficulty was recognized by the Classical mythographers; we shall follow their example by adopting a classification – albeit a somewhat artificial one – which divides the Heraclean legends into three major categories:

1. The cycle of the Twelve Labours.
2. Exploits which were independent of this cycle, while the Labours were usually carried out by Heracles alone or with the help of his nephew Iolaus.
3. Secondary adventures, which happened to him while he was carrying out the Labours.

Before describing the Labours, we shall deal with the legends concerning the hero's infancy and upbringing. These, and the legends concerning his final deification, are the only elements in the Heraclean cycle which can be set into an approximate chronology with any confidence.

1. HERACLES' NAME, ORIGINS AND INFANCY

According to the mythographers, Heracles was not the hero's original name: it was a mystical name given to him by Apollo, either directly or through the agency of the Pythian priestess or Pythoness, when he became Hera's bond-servant and found himself committed to the Labours imposed upon him by her. He was originally called Alcides, a patronym formed from the name of his grandfather Alceus (Table 31), or even Alceus, like his grandfather. The Greek version of his name evokes the idea of physical strength (ἀλκή). When the hero went to the Pythoness to atone for the murder of the children he had by Megara, she gave him various orders including the instruction that henceforth he should take the name of Heracles, meaning 'Hera's Glory' – undoubtedly because the Labours he was about to undertake would result in the goddess's glorification. This name stayed with him, and he is always so designated by authors and on statues. Through his mortal father AMPHITRYON and his mother

ALCMENE, Heracles belonged to the race of the Perseides. His two grandfathers, Alceus on his father's side and Electryon on his mother's, were both sons of Perseus and Andromeda (Table 31). He therefore belonged to the Argive race and his birth at Thebes was quite fortuitous. He always considered the Peloponnese, and in particular the Argolid, as his real fatherland and always wished to return there, despite the wishes of Eurystheus (see below), and his descendants came back to settle there (see HERACLIDAE). Heracles' real father was Zeus, who had profited by Amphitryon's absence on an expedition against the Teleboans. Zeus deceived Alcmene by assuming the face and figure of her husband, and during a long night of love, which was prolonged at his order, she conceived the hero. When Amphitryon returned on the following morning, he gave Alcmene a second son, Iphicles, Heracles' twin brother, who was the younger by one night. It was said that to make Alcmene deceive herself into recognizing him as her husband and to remove any shadow of doubt from her mind, Zeus had made her a present of a gold cup which had belonged to Pterelas, king of the Teleboans. In addition, he told her of the feats accomplished by the real Amphitryon during the expedition and claimed them as his own. On Amphitryon's return, Zeus intervened to make peace between husband and wife, and Amphitryon apparently resigned himself to being merely the foster-father of the divine infant.

Even before Heracles was born, Hera's wrath and her jealousy of Alcmene began to be apparent. Zeus had rashly stated that the first child to be born into the race of the Perseides would one day rule over Argos. Hera immediately arranged with her daughter Eilithyia, the goddess of childbirth, that the birth of Heracles should be held up, while that of his cousin EURYSTHEUS, the son of Sthenelus, should be advanced. Eurystheus was consequently born as a seven-months' baby, while Heracles was carried by his mother for ten months (see GALINTHIAS). There are various different legends which tell how Heracles, while still a babe in arms, sucked at the breast of Hera, his bitterest enemy. This is said to have been the condition which had to be fulfilled if the hero were to achieve immortality, and trickery was necessary in order to achieve it. According to several traditions, Hermes put the babe to the goddess's breast as she lay asleep. When she woke up, she pushed the child away, but it was too late: the milk that spurted from her breast formed a trail of stars in the sky, the Milky Way. Another tradition tells the tale differently. According to this version, Alcmene feared Hera's jealousy; as soon as Heracles was born, she exposed him at a place in Argos known thereafter as the Plain of Heracles. Athena and Hera happened to be passing by; and Athena, struck by the new-born baby's beauty and his vigour, asked Hera to give him the breast. Hera did so, but Heracles sucked with such force that he hurt the goddess. She flung him away from her, but Athena picked him up and took him back to Alcmene, telling the young woman to bring her child up without any further fear.

When Heracles was eight months old, though some say ten, Hera tried to destroy him. One evening, Alcmene put the twins, Heracles and Iphicles, down in their cradle and went to sleep herself. Towards midnight, the goddess introduced two huge snakes into the room, which twined themselves around the babies. Little Iphicles started to cry, but Heracles showed no fear; he grasped the animals by the throat, one in each hand, and strangled them. At Iphicles' screams, Amphitryon came running, sword in hand; but there was no need for him to take any action. It was clear to him now that Heracles was indeed the son of a god. Heracles was given an education comparable to that of Greek children of the Classical Era and similar to the one ACHILLES had received from the Centaur Chiron. His principal tutor was the musician Linus, who was said to have taught him the rudiments of letters and of music. He had his lessons with Iphicles, but while Iphicles proved a quiet and diligent student, Heracles was extremely undisciplined, so much so that Linus always had to call him to order. One day he even tried to beat him, but Heracles had no intention of submitting to that; he lost his temper, snatched up a stool, and dealt his master such a blow that Linus fell dead. Heracles was brought before a tribunal and accused of murder. He defended himself successfully by quoting a judgement of Rhadamanthys, which entitled one to kill an aggressor in self-defence, and was acquitted. Amphitryon was uneasy, however, and feared further fits of rage from his adopted son; so he sent him off to the country as soon as he could and put him in charge of his herds of cattle. There his education was continued, according to tradition, by a Scythian cowherd named Teutarus who taught him archery. It is generally agreed, however, that he received his education from other masters: Amphitryon taught him how to drive a chariot and Eurytus showed him how to use a bow (see EURYTUS 2) – although, in a variant of this tradition, he owed his training in archery to Rhadamanthys, who as a Cretan was highly skilled in that art. He was taught how to handle arms by Castor, who was either one of the Dioscuri or a refugee from Argos, the son of a certain Hippalus. After the death of his tutor his lessons were continued by Eumolpus, the son of Philammon and nephew of Autolycus, who perfected his music.

Meanwhile, Heracles was growing up: he reached the extraordinary height of four cubits and one foot. When he was eighteen, he carried out his first exploit by killing the lion of Cithaeron. This lion, a wild beast of outstanding size and ferocity, caused considerable havoc among the herds of Amphitryon and THESPIUS (who was ruler of a country close to Thebes), for no hunter dared to attack it. Heracles decided to rid the country of the lion and moved into Thespius' domain, where he spent all his days out hunting, returning to the palace only at night to sleep. After fifty days, he finally managed to kill the lion. King Thespius had fifty daughters by his wife Megamede, daughter of Arneus, and was anxious to have grandchildren fathered by Heracles; accordingly he arranged for a different daughter to be waiting each evening in Heracles' bed. Heracles coupled with them all in the darkness, and being tired after his day's hunting, he believed that he was lying with the same girl every evening (Table 15). He had fifty sons by them, who became known as the Thespiades. Some authors placed this first lion-hunt, the precursor of the hunt for the Nemean lion, not on the slopes of Cithaeron but on Mount Helicon, or near Teumessus. Pausanias even accepted a legend which claimed that the lion of Cithaeron was not slain by Heracles, but by ALCATHUS (who was more generally considered to have slain the lion of Megara). A local legend from Lesbos claims that Heracles killed a lion there also.

As Heracles was approaching Thebes on his return from hunting the lion he met the envoys of Erginus, king of Orchomenus, who were on their way to collect the tribute which the Thebans paid to the Orchomenians each year (for the origin of this tribute, see ERGINUS). Heracles mutilated them, cutting off each man's nose and ears and hanging them on a cord round his neck. He then told them to take this tribute back to their master. The enraged Erginus marched against Thebes, but Heracles defeated him, and slew him with the arms that Athena herself had given him. He then imposed on the Minyans of Orchomenus a tribute which was double the one they themselves had

exacted from Thebes. Amphitryon was killed during the battle, fighting bravely alongside his son. However, according to another tradition Amphitryon did not die till later, after leading a successful expedition with Heracles against Chalcodon, the king of Euboea (see CHALCODON 1). For other variants of this legend, see ERGINUS.

Creon, the king of Thebes, wishing to give Heracles a fitting reward for his services to the city, gave him his eldest daughter Megara in marriage, while IPHICLES was given the second daughter to marry. Megara bore the hero several children: eight according to Pindar, but only three according to Apollodorus, who named them Therimachus, Creontiades, and Deicoon. Other traditions claim that there were seven, or five (Antimachus, Clymenus, Glenus, Therimachus, and Creontiades), or even four. Heracles slew all his children, together with two of Iphicles'. This murder is treated in different ways by different authors, and forms the subject of tragedies by Euripides and Seneca. According to some – and this seems to be the oldest of the traditions – Heracles threw his children into the fire. According to others, including Euripides, he killed them with arrows; he even attacked his own father, Amphitryon, and was about to slay him when Athena hit him in the chest with a stone, which sent him into a deep sleep. The explanation usually advanced for this series of murders was an attack of madness for which Hera was responsible. According to certain traditions, Hera wanted to force him to put his services at Eurystheus' disposal, by causing him to commit some defilement which would force him to seek expiation. Despite Zeus' oracle, Heracles was reluctant to go to Argos and acknowledge Eurystheus as his master; but now the goddess had sent him a warning. After he had returned to his senses Heracles no longer wished to live with Megara. He gave her to his nephew Iolaus (even though there was a considerable difference of age between her and the boy, for according to the calculations of the ancient mythographers, she was thirty-three while Iolaus was only sixteen).

Euripides couples the legend of the murder of Megara's children with the story of Lycus, a usurper from Euboea, who killed King Creon and seized the throne of Thebes while Heracles was absent from his journey down to the Underworld. The hero returned in time to kill Lycus, but just as he was about to offer a thanksgiving sacrifice at the altar of Zeus in front of the palace, Hera struck him with an attack of madness. He thought his own children were Eurystheus', and killed them. He mistook his own father for Eurystheus' father Sthenelus and was about to slay him too when Athena struck him and sent him to sleep. When he awoke and realized what he had done, he wanted to commit suicide; but just at that moment Theseus arrived, dissuaded him from his plan, and took him off to Athens. Euripides altered the traditional timing of this incident by placing it after Heracles' journey down to Hades, thus inserting it into the middle of the Labours, instead of making it the first action of the hero's life. Furthermore, Euripides introduces Theseus, the perfect 'philosopher hero', and the symbol of the temperate Attic wisdom which was the antithesis of Dorian violence.

II THE TWELVE LABOURS

These were the exploits carried out by Heracles at the bidding of his cousin EURYSTHEUS. The traditions give different explanations of why the hero submitted to someone who was so far from being his equal, and who was agreed by all to be a contemptible and inadequate person. The *Iliad* describes the trickery of Hera, who turned Zeus' promise around to Eurystheus' advantage; but Heracles did not submit personally to his cousin, although the delaying of his own birth had in fact made him Eurystheus' 'subject'. According to Euripides, Heracles expressed his wish to return to Argos and Eurystheus agreed to this – but on the condition that Heracles should carry out for him certain Labours. The object of the principal ones was to rid the world of a certain number of monsters. This period of bondage was generally considered to be the expiation for Heracles' murder of his children. After the murder, Heracles went to consult Pythian Apollo's oracle at Delphi, where he was instructed to place himself at his cousin's disposal for a period of twelve years. Apollo (and Athena) added that as a reward for his pains he would be granted immortality. These variants were produced by the effect of Greek thinking on the myth and met the need for establishing a moral justification for the trials of a hero popularly regarded as the archetypal 'just man'. These trials are not the earliest examples to be found in mythology. Compare Apollo's enslavement to Admetus, as purification for the murder of the Cyclopes, and, in the Heraclean cycle itself, Heracles' enslavement to Omphale, as purification for the murder of Iphitus. In mystical thinking, Heracles' Labours came to be regarded as tests of his soul, which progressively freed itself from the domination of his body and his passions until his final deification. A variant repeated by the Alexandrine poet Diotimus portrays Heracles as Eurystheus' lover, suggesting that it was a lover's complaisance which made him comply with Eurystheus' every whim. The mythographers of the Hellenic Age established an authoritative list of the Twelve Labours, dividing them into two series of six. The first six took place in the Peloponnese, while the other six were spread over the rest of the world, taking place in Crete, Thrace, Scythia, in the Far West, in the land of the Hesperides, and in the Underworld. The established order of events is the one followed here. There are many variations on the order in which the Labours were carried out and on their number (Apollodorus, for example, recognized only ten).

Heracles' most distinctive weapon was his club, which he fashioned himself during his first Labour, the hunt for the Nemean lion. In some versions he was said to have cut it in Nemea, and in others on Mount Helicon, or on the shores of the Saronic Gulf, from the trunk of a wild olive tree. The rest of his weapons were of divine origin – his sword was given to him by Hermes, his bow and arrows by Apollo, and his gilded breastplate was a present from Hephaestus. Athena added a peplum. According to other traditions, she furnished him with all his weapons except for his club. Finally, his horses were a gift from Poseidon.

The Nemean Lion Heracles' first task was to kill the Nemean lion, a monster, the son of Orthrus and ECHIDNA (Table 32); it was the brother of another monster, the Sphinx of Thebes. Hera (or perhaps Selene, goddess of the Moon) brought it up and set it in the region of Nemea, where it ravaged the land, devouring the inhabitants and their herds. The lion lived in a cave with two exits and was invulnerable. Heracles shot at it with his bow, but this proved useless; then he threatened it with his club, drove it back into its cave, and blocked up one of the exits: then he seized it in his arms and strangled it. When the lion was dead, Heracles flayed it and clad himself in its skin, with the lion's head serving as a helmet. Theocritus says that the hero was baffled for a long time by this skin, which was impervious to both steel and fire. He finally hit upon the idea of using the monster's own claws to cut it, and this proved successful. During the hunt for the Nemean lion the incident of Molorchus occured. Molorchus was a poor peasant who lived near Nemea; his son had been killed by the lion, and he welcomed Heracles warmly when he visited him on his way to fight the lion. To do his guest honour, Molorchus proposed to slaughter the only ram he owned, which was indeed his only possession. Heracles dissuaded him and asked him to wait for thirty days: if he had not returned before the thirty days were up, then Molorchus could consider him dead and sacrifice the ram in his memory; but if he returned victorious before the thirty days were up, then the ram would be sacrificed to Zeus. Heracles had not yet returned by the thirtieth day; Molorchus thought he was dead and prepared to sacrifice the animal, as Heracles had asked, but before the sacrifice was complete he saw Heracles coming, clad in the lion's skin. He offered his ram to Zeus; and on the very spot where the sacrifice took place, Heracles founded the Nemean Games in Zeus' honour; these were later revived by the Seven Chiefs who marched against Thebes (see ADRASTUS). Heracles brought the lion's body back to Mycenae, where Eurystheus was so terrified by the courage of the hero who was able to slay such a monster that he forbade him to enter the city, and ordered him henceforth to leave the fruits of his Labours outside the gates. It is said that Zeus added the lion to the constellations to commemorate Heracles' exploit.

Heracles killing the many-headed monster, the Lernean Hydra. 2nd century Roman lamp.

The Lernaean Hydra Like the Nemean lion, the Lernaean Hydra was a monster, the daughter of Echidna and Typhon (Table 32). It was reared by Hera under a plane-tree near the source of the river Amymone, to serve as a test for Heracles. This Hydra was depicted as a snake with several heads; the number of heads varies with different authors, from five or six up to a hundred; sometimes they were even said to be human heads. The breath that issued from its mouths was so venomous that anyone who approached it, even while it was asleep, invariably died. It used to ravage the countryside, destroying crops and herbs. Heracles used flaming arrows against it, and was also said to have cut off its heads with a short curved sabre. He was helped in this exploit by his nephew Iolaus, whose help was all the more essential since every head he cut off immediately grew back again. To stop the heads growing back, Heracles asked Iolaus to set fire to the nearby grove of trees; he then used burning brands to sear the neck-stumps every time, making it impossible for heads to grow again. According to some authors, the central head was immortal; but Heracles cut it off

nonetheless, buried it, and then set a huge rock on top of it. He finally dipped his arrows in the Hydra's venom (or in its blood), and made them poisonous (see PHILOCTETES). In her spite against Heracles, Hera sent an enormous crab to help the Hydra; this crab nipped the hero on the heel, but he crushed it (see CARCINUS). According to Apollodorus, Eurystheus refused to include this Labour in those that Heracles was to do for him, on the grounds that he had been helped by Iolaus. The mythographers gave a euhemeristic interpretation of the myth of the Lernaean Hydra: they said that the Hydra with the heads that renewed themselves was in reality the marsh of Lerna, which was drained by Heracles. The heads represented the springs which always seeped back, making Heracles' efforts useless. Another interpretation claims that Lernus was really the name of a king and Hydra the name of his capital city. Lernus was surrounded by fifty archers, and when one of them fell, another immediately replaced him.

The Erymanthian Boar The third Labour set by Eurystheus was to bring back alive a monstrous boar that lived on Mount Erymanthus. Heracles' shouts forced the animal to leave its lair; then he drove it into the deep snow which covered the countryside, keeping it on the run until it was exhausted, thus enabling him to capture it. He brought it back to Mycenae across his shoulders. When Eurystheus saw it, he was seized with terror and hid himself in a big jar he had had prepared for himself as a refuge in time of danger. The Erymanthian Boar's tusks could be seen, as an ex-voto offering, at Cumae in Campania. During this Labour, Heracles had his adventure with the Centaur PHOLUS.

The Hind of Ceryneia The fourth Labour was the capture of a hind that lived at Oenoe. Euripides says merely that it was an animal of enormous size, which ravaged the crops. Heracles killed it and consecrated its horns in the temple of Oenoetian Artemis. However, this version is an isolated one, and runs counter to the generally accepted legend; its object was to expunge from the hero's cycle an act which might have been termed impious. In Callimachus' account, this hind was one of five which Artemis had seen in earlier days grazing on Mount Lycaeus. They all had gilded horns, and were bigger than bulls. The goddess captured four of them and harnessed them to her chariot. The fifth, guided by Hera, took refuge on Mount Ceryneia – she was

Heracles capturing the Hind of Ceryneia, which was sacred to Artemis. Reverse of gold Roman medallion of Maximianus from the Arras Treasure, found at Beaurains in 1922.

already planning to use it in due course as one of Heracles' Labours. The animal was sacred to Artemis, and was said to wear a collar round its neck with the inscription: 'Taygete has dedicated me to Artemis' (see TAYGETE). It was therefore an act of impiety to kill it or even to touch it. This hind was very swift; Heracles hunted it for a year without catching it. It finally grew tired and sought refuge on Mount Artemisium. When Heracles continued his pursuit, it tried to cross the river Ladon, in Arcadia. Heracles then wounded it slightly with an arrow, after which he caught it quite easily, and swung it up onto his shoulders. As he was returning through Arcadia he met Artemis and Apollo; the two deities sought to deprive him of the animal, which belonged to them. They accused him of wanting to kill it, which was sacrilege. Heracles extricated himself by putting the blame on to Eurystheus, arguing his case so well that in the end they gave him back the hind and allowed him to continue his journey. Pindar gives a mystic version of the chase. According to him, Heracles hunted the hind towards the north, across the river Ister, into the land of the Hyperboreans, and as far as the Islands of the Blessed, where Artemis gave him a kindly welcome.

The Stymphalian Birds These birds lived in a thick forest on the shores of Lake Stymphalus in Arcadia, whither they had fled in former days before an invasion of wolves. They had multiplied so successfully that they had become a plague to the surrounding territory; they ate the fruit of the fields and ravaged all the crops. Now Eurystheus ordered Heracles to destroy them. The difficulty lay in driving them out of the dense thickets; to achieve this the hero used castanets of bronze, which were either of his own fashioning or the work of Hephaestus, given to him by Athena. Frightened by the noise of these castanets, the birds broke cover, and Heracles had no difficulty in killing them with his arrows. Other traditions portray these creatures as birds of prey, which even devoured men. It is also said in some accounts that their feathers were of sharp metal, and that they shot them at their enemies like arrows. A euhemeristic explanation of this myth makes them the daughters of a hero called Stymphalus, whom Heracles killed because they had refused to welcome him, whereas they gave hospitality to his enemies, the Molionides.

The Stables of Augias Augias was a king of Elis in the Peloponnese; he was the son of Helios, the Sun (Table 14), who had given him great herds of cattle. He made no attempt to clear away the dung that lay in his cattle-sheds; and this neglect was depriving the soil of manure and dooming the land to sterility. Wishing to humiliate the hero by ordering him to do menial labour, Eurystheus ordered Hercules to clean these stables, but before he started work, Heracles and Augias reached agreement about a salary. According to some authors, the king undertook to give Heracles a part of his kingdom if he succeeded in cleaning the stables within one day; according to others, the king promised Heracles a tenth of his herds, on the same condition. Heracles successfully carried out this amazing feat by diverting the flow of two rivers, the Alpheus and the Peneus, through the stable-yard. However, Augias refused to pay Heracles the agreed reward, and even banished him from the kingdom. In due course Heracles waged a successful war against Augias. According to Apollodorus, Eurystheus refused to count this Labour among those that Heracles was to perform for him, his argument being that Heracles had received, or at least asked for, a salary for cleaning out these stables, and therefore was not in Eurystheus' service at the time.

The Cretan Bull The Cretan Bull, according to some versions, was the animal which abducted Europa on Zeus' behalf, though this version does not agree that Zeus transformed himself into the bull; according to others, the Cretan Bull had been the lover of Pasiphae. Another account claims that it was a miraculous bull which rose from the sea after Minos had vowed to sacrifice to Poseidon anything which appeared on the waters. When Minos saw the beauty of the bull, he sent it to his own herd and sacrificed a much less valuable animal to Poseidon, who retaliated by making the animal untameable. Eurystheus ordered Heracles to bring this animal to him alive. Heracles went to Crete and asked Minos to help him; Minos refused but gave him his permission to catch the bull if he could do so unaided. Heracles caught the bull and returned to Greece with it, perhaps even swimming on the beast's back just as it had carried Europa in earlier days. He presented the bull to Eurystheus, who wanted to dedicate it to Hera. However, the goddess refused to accept an offering in the name of Heracles; she freed the bull, which wandered through Argos and the Isthmus of Corinth and eventually reached Attica (see THESEUS and the legend of the bull of Marathon).

The Mares of Diomedes Diomedes was a king of Thrace who owned four mares which fed on

Heracles and the Cretan Bull. Detail of an olpe (wine jug), 500–490 BC. London, British Museum.

human flesh, called Podargus, Lampon, Xanthus and Deinus. Heracles' eighth task was to bring them back to Eurystheus alive. Of the two versions of this legend the oldest claims that Heracles went alone to Thrace by land and there gave Diomedes to the mares to eat. After this the animals became calm and allowed themselves to be led without trouble. The more recent version links the legend with the founding of the town of Abdera (see DIOMEDES 1).

The Girdle of Queen Hippolyta At the order of ADMETE the daughter of Eurystheus, Heracles set off for the kingdom of the Amazons to capture the girdle worn by Hippolyta. This girdle, we are told, had belonged to Ares who gave it to Hippolyta as a symbol of his power over her people. Heracles set sail in one ship with a number of volunteers and arrived after numerous adventures at Themiscyra, the port of the Amazons' country. Hippolyta willingly agreed to give him the belt, but Hera, disguised as an Amazon, provoked a quarrel between Heracles' followers and the Amazons and a battle ensued. Heracles thought that he had been betrayed and killed Hippolyta. Other legends claim that hostilities began as soon as Heracles landed with his followers. One of Hippolyta's friends, Melanippe, was captured in the battle and Hippolyta agreed to hand over her girdle in exchange for Melanippe's freedom.

The Cattle of Geryon Geryon, who was the son of Chrysaor, had an immense herd of cattle which grazed on the island of Erythia, attended by his herdsman, Eurytion. To help him in his task Eurytion had the enormous dog, Orthrus, whose parents were TYPHON and ECHIDNA. The island was situated in the extreme west. Eurystheus ordered Heracles to go there to collect the precious herds. The first difficulty was to cross the ocean: to overcome this Heracles borrowed the Cup of the Sun, a huge vessel in which Helios embarked every evening when he had reached the western ocean to enable him to return to his palace in the east. Helios did not give Heracles the vessel without hesitation: during his passage through the Libyan desert the hero had been so troubled by the extreme heat of the Sun that he had threatened to shoot it with his arrows. The Sun begged him not to shoot and Heracles agreed to this request on condition that the Sun lent him his Cup to enable him to cross the ocean and reach Erythia. Heracles had to threaten Oceanus with his arrows because he buffeted him with great waves. Oceanus became frightened and the waves at once subsided. At Erythia Heracles was seen by the dog Orthrus, which flew at him, but he killed it with a single blow of his club and dealt with Eurytion in the same way. He then set off with the cattle. Menoetes, the herdsman of Hades, saw this take place and ran to warn Geryon who met Heracles on the banks of the river Anthemus, and was killed by the hero's arrows. Heracles then returned to Greece.

During his return Heracles had several adventures in the western Mediterranean. He had freed Libya of many monsters on the outward passage and in memory of his passage to Tartessus he built two columns, one on each side of the strait which separates Libya from Europe, which became known as the Pillars of Heracles (the Rock of Gibraltar and the Rock of Ceuta). On his return journey Heracles was attacked by brigands who tried to rob him of his herd. After he left the southern and the Libyan coasts, Heracles returned by the northern route, passing the coasts of Spain, Gaul, Italy and Sicily before arriving in Greece. This trail was marked by a number of shrines dedicated to Heracles which have local legends attached to them.

Heracles was first attacked in Liguria by belligerent natives and after he had killed large numbers of them his supply of arrows ran out. The country was void of stones and Heracles appealed to Zeus who made stones rain from heaven. Using these missiles Heracles put his enemy to flight. This exploit took place in the plain of Ciran between Marseilles and the Rhone (see LIGYS). Similarly, in Liguria, two brigands – the sons of Poseidon called Alebion and Deticynus – wanted to rob him and he killed them both. He then travelled on through Tyrrhenia. He passed the place at Latium where Rome was later to be built and had to fight CACUS to protect his herd; there he was also entertained by EVANDER. These legends probably refer to the Latin Hercules rather than the Greek Heracles.

At Reggio in Calabria one of his bulls escaped and swam across the strait to Sicily. Some accounts claim that Italy owes its name to this bull (the Latin word *vitulus* means 'calf'). The bull reached the plain of Eryx in the country of the Elymi. At that time the king of the Elymi was ERYX, eponym of the town. Eryx wanted to take possession of the bull but he was killed by Heracles. During this episode the rest of the herd was in the charge of Hephaestus (see CROTON and LACINIUS). When they reached the Greek coast of the Ionian Sea the herd was attacked by gadflies sent by Hera; these flies drove them wild. The herd scattered in the foothills of the mountains of Thrace. Heracles chased them but could only round up some; the remainder stayed wild and became the origin of the wandering Scythian herds. During his pursuit of the bulls Heracles was impeded by the river Strymon, so he cursed it and filled it with stones, transforming it from a navigable river into an impassable torrent. At last, the voyage complete, Heracles gave the surviving bulls to Eurystheus who sacrificed them to Hera. Some variants of this story of the return of Heracles have been reported by various authors: Heracles is said to have crossed the Celtic countries, even Great Britain. These stories developed gradually as the world became better known and Greek travellers and merchants came to know local heroes and gods which they more or less equated with Heracles.

Cerberus The eleventh labour imposed on Heracles by Eurystheus was to descend to Hell and bring back Cerberus the dog. In spite of his courage Heracles would never have succeeded in this had Zeus not ordered Hermes and Athena to help him.

He first had to be initiated into the Mysteries of Eleusis which taught how to cross safely to the other world after death. Heracles followed the path of Tenarus for his descent into Hell. When the Dead saw him arrive in their kingdom, they took fright and fled and only two stayed to wait on him, the Gorgon Medusa and the hero Meleager. Heracles drew his sword against Medusa but Hermes, who was acting as his guide, told him that she was nothing but an empty shade. He drew his bow against MELEAGER but Meleager came up to him and described his death so movingly that Heracles wept. He asked Meleager if he still had a sister and he replied that Deianeira was still alive; Heracles promised to marry her. Further on Heracles met THESEUS and PIRITHOUS who were both still alive but who had been put in chains by Pluto because they had come to carry Persephone away. Heracles freed Theseus with her permission but Pirithous had to stay in Hades as a punishment for his temerity. Heracles then released ASCA-LAPHUS who was held under a huge rock. After his release, Demeter transformed him into an owl. To give some blood to the Dead who could regain a little life Heracles contemplated stealing some animals from the herds of Hell and killing them but their herdsman, Menoetes, wanted to prevent this. Heracles seized his body in his arms and broke several ribs; he would have killed him if Proserpina had not demanded mercy. Heracles finally reached the presence of Pluto and asked for permission to take Cerberus away. Pluto granted his request on condition that he overpowered the dog without using his normal weapons, simply clad in his breastplate and lion skin. Heracles grasped the dog's neck with his hands and, although the dog had a forked tongue at the end of its tail, which stung Heracles several times, he did not release the dog until it was overpowered. He returned to earth using the entrance at Troezen. When Eurystheus saw Cerberus he was so frightened that he hid himself in his jar. Because he did not know what to do with Cerberus, Heracles returned him to Pluto, his master. An Olympian legend describes how Heracles brought the white poplar bark from the Underworld, the only wood allowed when sacrifices were being offered to Olympian Zeus.

The Golden Apples of the Hesperides When Hera married Zeus, Gaia gave her golden apples as a wedding present; Hera found them so lovely that she had them planted in her garden near Mount Atlas. The daughters of Atlas used to come and steal

Heracles' final Labour was to bring the golden apples from the Garden of the Hesperides to Eurystheus. Antique relief showing Heracles seated under the trees bearing the apples, guarded by the dragon Ladon. Rome, Villa Albani.

from the garden so Hera had the apples and the wonderful tree that bore them placed under the protection of an immortal dragon with one hundred heads, the offspring of Typhon and Echmida. Three Nymphs of the evening, the Hesperides, also guarded the apples; they were called Aegle, Erythia and Hesperethusa, which mean 'brightness', 'scarlet' and 'sunset glow' respectively: these names suggest the colours of the sky as the sun sets in the West. Eurystheus ordered Heracles to bring him these golden apples. Heracles' first task was to find the way to the land of the Hesperides. He went north across Macedonia and on his way he first met CYCNUS, Ares' son and challenged him on the banks of the Echedorus. Then he reached the river Eridanus in Illyria where he met the river Nymphs who were the daughters of Themis and Zeus. He questioned them and they replied that the sea god Nereus was the only person who could tell him about the country he sought. They brought him to Nereus while the god slept. Although Nereus repeatedly assumed different shapes, Heracles tied him up tightly and would not release him until he had revealed the position of the garden of the Hesperides. From this point Heracles' route is unclear. Apollodorus describes how from the banks of the Eridanus the hero reached Libya where he fought the giant ANTAEUS; he then crossed Egypt where he barely escaped being sacrificed by BUSIRIS. He passed through Asia and into Arabia where he killed Emathion, the son of Tithonus. He embarked in Helios' cup and reached the other bank at the foot of the Caucasus. Whilst climbing the Caucasus he freed PROMETHEUS, whose liver was eaten away every day by an eagle but always grew again. Prometheus told Heracles out of gratitude that he himself would not be able to collect the miraculous apples: this must be done by Atlas. Heracles continued his journey, finally reaching the country of the Hyperboreans where he found Atlas, the giant who bore the whole weight of the sky on his shoulders. He offered to relieve Atlas of his burden while he went to the garden of the Hesperides to collect three golden apples. Atlas willingly agreed to do this but on his return he told Heracles that he himself would take the apples to Eurystheus if Heracles would continue to carry the weight of the vault of heaven. The hero pretended to agree to this but he asked Atlas to take the weight for only a moment, while he put a cushion on his shoulders. Atlas agreed to do this but once relieved of the burden, Heracles picked up the apples, which Atlas had placed momentarily on the ground and fled.

Other accounts claim that Heracles did not need to call on Atlas for help, but either killed the dragon of the Hesperides or put it to sleep and took possession of the golden fruit himself. It is said that the Hesperides were turned into trees, elm, poplar and willow, because of their despair at the loss of the apples. The Argonauts later found shade under these trees. The dragon was transported to the sky where it became the constellation of the Serpent. When he had the golden apples Heracles fulfilled his duty and gave them to Eurystheus but he did not know what to do with them, so he gave them back to Heracles who presented them to Athena. She returned them to the garden of the Hesperides because divine law decreed that the fruit could only be in the garden of the gods.

III. THE CAMPAIGNS OF HERACLES

It is generally agreed by mythographers that the first of these great expeditions of Heracles' first expedition took him to Troy. On his return journey from the land of the Amazons Heracles landed at Troy. At that time the whole town was suffering the consequences of the anger of APOLLO and Poseidon. With the help of Aeacus these two gods had constructed the town's fortifications but Laomedon refused to pay the money agreed for the work. To punish the king for his breach of faith, Apollo sent a plague and Poseidon a sea monster which devoured the inhabitants; an oracle had revealed that this curse would only be removed if Hesione, the king's daughter, was offered to the sea monster. When Heracles reached Troy, Hesione, who was chained to a rock, was about to be killed by the monster. Heracles immediately told the king that he would free Hesione if the king promised to give him the mares, given to the king by Zeus in payment for GANYMEDE. The king promised and Heracles killed the monster, but when Heracles claimed his reward, the king refused to give it. Heracles left Troy, threatening to return one day to capture the town. The opportunity to fulfil his threat arose several years later, after his twelve Labours were finished. When he was free Heracles recruited an army and set sail for Troy in eighteen ships with fifty oarsmen each. On reaching the port of Ilion he left Oecles to guard the fleet and with his troops he attacked the city. In the meantime Laomedon attacked Heracles' ships and killed Oecles but Heracles came to the rescue of the garrison which was protecting the ships and Laomedon was forced to retreat. The siege of Troy began, but it did not last long: almost at once, Telamon, one of Heracles' most faithful followers, crossed the wall and entered the town but Heracles only entered second and, angry to think that his bravery had been surpassed, he was on the point of killing Telamon when the latter knelt down and filled his hands with stones. This intrigued Heracles who asked him what he was doing: Telamon replied that he was building an altar to Heracles the Conqueror. Heracles thanked him and spared his life. Heracles killed Laomedon and all his children except for Podarces, who was later to rule under the name of Priam. He gave Hesione's hand to Telamon and allowed the girl to chose one of the prisoners. She chose her brother Podarces. As Heracles was telling her that her brother would first have to be a slave and be ransomed by her, she took off her veil and gave it to him as ransom for the child. This gave the child its new name, Priam, (which comes from the root of the Greek word meaning 'to buy').

On his way back fresh adventures awaited Heracles. Hypnus, the god of sleep, was incited by Hera to make Zeus fall into a very deep sleep. Hera took advantage of this to raise a storm which drove Heracles' fleet on to the coast of Cos. The inhabitants believed that they were being attacked by pirates and tried to drive them away by throwing stones; this did not deter Heracles and his men from landing and they captured the town during the night. They killed the king Eurypylus – a son of Poseidon and Astypalaea. Heracles then had an intrigue with Chalciope, a daughter of Eurypylus and she bore a son named THESSALUS. Another account, which contradicts this, tells that Heracles was seriously wounded during the battle by Chalcodon and that only the intervention of Zeus saved him (see CHALCODON 4). There was another account of the landing at Cos: during the storm Heracles had lost all his fleet except his ship by the time he reached the island. On the island he met Eurypylus' son Antagoras who was in charge of a flock of sheep. Heracles was ravenous and asked Antagoras to give him a ram but instead of giving him one ram Antagoras challenged him to a wrestling match, with the ram as the reward for victory. During this match the inhabitants of the island rushed to help Antagoras, thinking that he had been attacked; a fight ensued and Heracles was overcome by his attackers. He escaped and took refuge in a woman's hut where he put on women's clothes to avoid being found. From Cos, Heracles went to Phlegra where he took part in the battle of the Gods against the Giants (see ALCYONE).

The War against Augias When Augias refused to pay the amount agreed and banished Heracles from Elis Heracles gathered an army of Arcadians and marched against Elis. Augias put his two nephews the MOLIONIDAE, Eurytus and Cteatus in command of his army. They annihilated Heracles' army and mortally wounded his brother Iphicles. Much later, at the celebration of the third Isthmian games the inhabitants of Elis sent the Molionidae to represent them. Heracles laid an ambush for them at Cleonae and they were both killed. He then mounted a second expedition against Elis. He captured the town and killed Augias and made Augias' son Phyleus king. After this expedition Heracles founded the Olympic Games and consecrated Altis, the sacred enclosure at Olympia. He dedicated a sanctuary to Pelops there. There was a great deal of local folklore about Heracles' retreat from the Molionidae. According to one story he withdrew as far as Bouprasion and when he saw that he had no pursuers, he lay down near a spring which he thought had very palatable water, which he christened Badys, meaning in the language of Elis 'pleasant'.

The Expedition against Pylos Neleus was king of Pylos in Messenia. He had eleven children; the eldest was Periclymenus, the youngest, Nestor. Heracles was angry with Neleus because after IPHITUS' murder Neleus refused to purify him. Periclymenus had helped to drive him out of the country, whereas Nestor, alone among the children, advised, unheeded, that the hero should be granted his request. Heracles decided to take revenge. During the war against the Minyans of Orchomenus Neleus fought for the king of Orchomenus against Heracles and the Thebans, because Orchomenus was his son-in-law According to another account Neleus tried to steal some of Geryon's herds from Heracles. Heracles turned against Neleus. The main event of the war was the fight between Heracles and Periclymenus. Poseidon was the divine father of Periclymenus and gave him the power to transform himself into whatever creature he chose. He sometimes became a serpent and sometimes an eagle and to attack Heracles he changed himself into a bee and landed on the bridle of Heracles' horse. Athena was watching and she warned Heracles that his enemy was very close and was in the form of a bee, so he killed it. During the same battle Heracles wounded several gods including Hera and Ares. According to the Pindaric version, Poseidon and Apollo also took part in the fight. Heracles captured Pylos soon after Periclymenus' death. He killed Neleus and all his sons except for Nestor, because he had favoured Heracles. Pausanias claims that he put Nestor in charge of Pylos, asking him to look after it until the Heraclids came to claim it.

The War against Sparta Hippocoon ruled Sparta with his twenty sons the Hippocoontides after expelling the rightful ruling family, Icarius and Tyndareus who were half-brothers of Hippocoon. Heracles took action against the usurpers. One of his motives was said to be his wish to reinstate Icarius and Tyndareus but, alternatively, it was his desire to avenge the death of Oeonus who was a great-nephew of Heracles and the son of Lycymnius. This child was passing Hippocoon's palace when a mastiff dashed out and tried to bite him; Oeonus picked up a stone and hit the dog with it. At once the Hippocoontides rushed out and beat him to death. According to another version the Hippocoontides had been Neleus' allies.

Heracles assembled his army in Arcadia and asked CEPHEUS and his twenty sons for help; in spite of some misgivings they agreed to join him. In the course of the decisive battle Cepheus and his sons were killed. Heracles massacred Hippocoon and all his sons and gave the kingdom to TYNDAREUS. During the fight one of Heracles' hands was wounded. It was healed by Asclepius in the temple of Demeter in Eleusis on Mount Taygetus. To celebrate his victory Heracles built two temples in Sparta, one dedicated to Athena and the other to Hera to thank her for having done nothing to make things difficult for him during the war.

The Alliance with Aegimius Although the preceding campaigns took place in the Peloponnese, the three separate wars, undertaken as a result of Heracles' alliance with Aegimius, the king of the Dorians, took place in Thessaly. The first campaign was against the Lapiths, who were led by Coronus, the son of CAENEUS. The Lapiths threatened Aegimius and pressed him so closely that he was forced to fall back on his alliance with Heracles, promising him a third of his kingdom if victorious. Heracles had no difficulty in defeating the Lapiths but he refused his reward, asking Aegimius to set it aside for his heirs. After this first victory Heracles reopened an old dispute with a neighbouring race, the Dryopes, who inhabited the Parnassus range. When Heracles and Deianeira were forced to leave Calydon they took Hyllus their eldest son with them. As they were crossing the country of the Dryopes Hyllus became hungry. At that moment Heracles saw Theiodamas, the king of the country, working with a pair of oxen. He asked him for food for his son but Theiodamas refused; Heracles unyoked one of the oxen, killed it, cut it up and ate it with Deianeira and Hyllus. Theiodamas retreated to the town and returned with an armed party. At first the fight went against Heracles and Deianeira was forced to arm herself and take part. Heracles eventually killed Theiodamas and carried Deianeira away.

Later, after the war with the Lapiths, Heracles attacked the Dryopes because they had been their allies and killed their king, Laogoras, who had been guilty of desecration because he held a banquet in one of Apollo's sanctuaries. Heracles took possession of the kingdom; the inhabitants split into three groups and fled: one group went to Euboea and they founded the town of Carystus, the second group went to Cyprus and the third took refuge in the neighbourhood of Eurystheus

who, because he hated Heracles, received them graciously and allowed them to build the towns of Asine, Hermione and Eiones on his land. The third expedition of this series was the one in which Heracles captured the town of Orminion at the foot of Mount Pelion. The hero had been forbidden by its king, Amyntor, to cross his country but Heracles decided to seize the country and to kill the king. Diodorus gives another version, in which Heracles asked Amyntor for his daughter, Astydamia. When the king refused, Heracles captured the town and abducted Astydamia who bore him a son called Ctesippus.

IV. THE MINOR ADVENTURES

Pholus and the Centaurs The adventures concerning Pholus are generally included in the account of hunting the Erymanthian Boar. While he was tracking the boar, Heracles' path took him across the area where a centaur named Pholus lived. Dionysus had given Pholus a sealed jar of wine telling him not to open it until Heracles came and asked for hospitality. Another version of the story claims that this wine was the common property of the Centaurs and could only be drunk if all were present. When Heracles reached Pholus' home, the latter gave him a friendly welcome and offered him many sorts of meat which he had cooked for his guest, although he himself ate them raw. After eating, Heracles was thirsty and asked for some wine. Pholus said that he regretted that he was not permitted to touch the jar of wine when alone. Heracles persuaded him to open it and both soon began to drink. The aroma of the wine quickly attracted the Centaurs who rushed up angrily, armed with torches, stones and whole trees which they had uprooted. The first two Centaurs to attack were Anchius and Agrius. They fell quickly after being hit by Heracles' arrows. Heracles chased the others to Cape Malea. There, Elatus was wounded in the elbow by an arrow and took refuge with CHIRON. The arrow also wounded Chiron. Most of the Centaurs took refuge in Eleusis. Their mother Nephele, came to their help by causing a rain storm. In the fight Heracles killed Daphnis, Argeius, Amphion, Hippotion, Oreius, Isoples, Melanchaetes, Thereus, Doupon, Phrixus and Homadus. Beside these, Anchius and Agrius were killed at the start of the mêlée and Pholus was killed by accident: while he was burying his brethren, he drew an arrow from a wound and was amazed that such a tiny thing could do such harm; he let it fall on his foot and received a mortal wound. When Heracles returned he was very sad to find his host dead, and gave him a magnificent funeral.

Eurytion The fight with the Centaur Eurytion is usually linked with the Augian adventures. When Heracles was banished from Elis, in the presence of the king DEXAMENUS he sought refuge at Olenus, a town which was either in Achaea or Aetolia. There are different versions but all are based on Eurytion's attempted rape of Dexamenus' daughter, who was sometimes called Hippolyta and sometimes Mnesimache. According to one version Dexamenus had betrothed his daughter to Azan, an Arcadian. Eurytion was invited to the wedding feast, where he tried to kidnap the girl. Heracles arrived in time to prevent this and in so doing killed the Centaur. Heracles then returned the girl back to Azan. In another version Heracles, on his way to Augias, is said to have seduced the girl himself and promised to marry her when he returned. While he was away Eurytion courted the girl, in this version named Deianeira. Dexamenus was terrified and did not dare to refuse her to Eurytion; the wedding was just about to start when Heracles returned. He killed the Centaur and married the girl.

The Resurrection of Alcestis This myth is bound up with the journey Heracles undertook through Thessaly to find the Thracian mares of Diomedes. This was the version which Euripides used in his tragedy *Alcestis*, but Apollodorus includes this episode in the description of the adventures of Heracles and *Iphitus*. Other sources suggest that Heracles' inclusion is a later addition to the legend. In the early account Persephone was moved by Alcestis' devotion and returned her to life; in later versions Heracles forced Thanatos (Death) to surrender his prey.

Cycnus The fight against CYCNUS and his father Ares took place during the journey to the Hesperides according to Apollodorus.

Busiris Heracles' adventures with King Busiris of Egypt were fitted into the story of the search for the golden apples.

Antaeus This story is closely linked with that of Busiris. Like it, it formed an incident in Heracles' journey through Libya in his quest for the golden apples. Like Busiris, Antaeus was sometimes described as being one of Poseidon's sons, and he also killed travellers to offer the spoils to his father Poseidon. Heracles killed him in a fight and then lived with Antaeus' wife Iphinoe; she bore a son

named Palaemon. The Pygmies, a race of midgets who lived in Egypt and Libya, tried to take revenge on Heracles. They attacked the hero when he was asleep and tried to kill him but he awoke and laughed. He caught them all in one hand and after imprisoning them in his lion skin, took them all to Eurystheus.

The Liberation of Prometheus Whilst crossing Caucasia to reach the land of the Hesperides, or on his return journey, Heracles shot the eagle which was devouring Prometheus' liver. This had the sanction of Zeus who wished by this action to increase the fame of his son.

The Fight with Lycaon Lycaon was the son of Ares and Pyrene and the brother of Diomedes of Thrace and Cycnus. He was king of the Crestonians who lived in Macedonia on the border of Echedorus; this country was called Europe after Pyrene's grandfather, Europus. While he was looking for the golden apples, Heracles crossed a grove, sacred to Pyrene. Lycaon attacked Heracles, who killed him.

The Battle with Alcyoneus When Heracles returned from Erythia, bringing Geryon's herds, he was attacked by the giant Alcyoneus who pelted him with stones but the hero killed him with his club. Alcyoneus lived on the Isthmus of Corinth, where enormous boulders were shown as evidence of this struggle.

Slavery under Omphale Following the murder of Iphitus Heracles had a fresh attack of madness, so he went to Delphi to ask the Pythian oracle what he should do to be purified. The oracle refused to answer him. Heracles was angry and threatened to sack the sanctuary. He began by seizing the prophetic tripod, claiming that he would set up his own oracle elsewhere. Apollo came to the aid of his priestess and a fight took place between the hero and his brother, the god. Zeus sent a thunderbolt to separate them and Heracles abandoned his attempt, but the Pythian priestess eventually gave him the information he wanted: to be completely purified, Heracles had to sell himself as a slave and serve one master for three years. The money from the sale was to be given to Eurytus, the father of Iphitus. Heracles submitted. He was bought by Omphale, the queen of Lydia, for three talents. The money was offered to Eurytus but he refused to accept it. Whilst serving Omphale Heracles undertook several adventures. During this period of servitude Heracles was ordered to capture the CERCOPES, two bandits who robbed travellers. This incident formed the basis of a number of farces. Heracles was also sent by Omphale to work in Syleus' vineyard. This was used by Euripides as the plot for a satirical play. Heracles was also commanded to fight Lityerses, the brother of Midas, while he was in Omphale's service.

The mythographers are particularly eloquent in their description of the love affair between the hero and the queen and describe Heracles dressed in Lydian clothes, particularly in women's long dresses. While the queen assumed his dress, the cudgel and the lionskin, Heracles, sitting at her feet, learned how to weave. This changing of clothes between the sexes is a folk theme which has been greatly exploited by moralists and philosophers as an example of transvestism.

Mythographers place the hunt of the Calydonian boar and the exploits of Theseus against the brigands who infested the Isthmus of Corinth during this period. In this way they explained the hero's absence from these events!

V. OTHER MYTHS

There are a number of other myths in which Heracles played a part. He was included among the Argonauts, for example. In one account, however, it is said that the *Argo*, which could speak, refused to allow the hero to come aboard because it was afraid that it could not carry his weight. Other versions agree that he left the expedition before it reached Colchis (See ARGONAUTS and the Hylas episode). When the myth of Heracles gained in importance the hero seems to have been conflated with all the main myths, especially those which included miraculous deeds. As an example, there is a story that Heracles had killed the two sons of Boreas as revenge for their advice to the Argonauts to abandon him on the coast of Asia Minor. This later version was invented to unite the two originally independent cycles of Heracles and the Thessalian myths surrounding Boreas. Similarly, Heracles is supposed to have buried Icarus on the island of Doliche. In return Daedalus carved a statue of the hero which he consecrated at Pisa. Thus the two myths of Heracles and Daedalus were conflated.

VI. LATER YEARS, DEATH AND DEIFICATION

Apart from the myths of his childhood and the Twelve Labours, no other part of the Heraclean tradition is as coherent as the highly dramatic story of the events which led to the hero's deification on Mount Oeta. The establishment of these myths was particularly the result of the work of tragic poets and the *Trachiniae* of Sophocles is the most important and fullest source available for Heracles' end. The connecting thread is the love of Deianeira. This forms the link between such diverse adventures as the fight with Nessus, the death of Iphitus, the bondage to Omphale and finally the catastrophe and death of the hero. The marriage with Deianeira was settled during Heracles' meeting with Meleager in the Underworld. It was not easy for Heracles to gain the girl's hand: he had to win her in a savage fight with the river-god ACHELOUS. For some time Heracles lived with Deianeira at Calydon, close to his father-in-law Oeneus, but fate made him accidentally kill Oeneus's page called EUNOMUS, a son of Architeles, a relation of Oeneus. Although Architeles forgave him for the murder, the hero did not wish to stay any longer in Calydon. He went into exile with his wife and son Hyllus. During this journey he had to fight a centaur Nessus for the third time. Nessus lived on the bank of the Evenus, where he was a ferryman. When Heracles arrived with Deianeira, Nessus ferried him over first and then returned for Deianeira, but while he ferried her, he tried to rape her. Heracles shot Nessus in the heart with an arrow as he landed; as he was dying Nessus called Deianeira and told her that if Heracles ever stopped loving her, she could compel him to love her by giving him a love-potion made of the blood from Nessus' wound. Deianeira believed him and collected his blood. The myths about the composition of this so-called love-potion vary. Some versions say that it contained only Nessus' blood and others that it was mixed with blood from the wounds of the Lernean Hydra or with the sperm ejected by Nessus during his attempted rape. After Heracles had captured Oechalia, he made Iole his mistress. Deianeira was staying with Ceyx and was told by Lichas, a follower of Heracles, that Iole might make Heracles forget her. Deianeira remembered the love-potion which Nessus had given her as he was dying and decided to use it.

After his victory over Eurytus, Heracles wished to consecrate an altar of thanksgiving to Zeus and he sent Lichas to Trachis to ask Deianeira for a new cloak for this ceremony. Deianeira dipped a tunic in Nessus' blood and gave it to Lichas. Heracles put the tunic on and started to make the sacrifice. As the tunic was warmed by his body the poison which it contained became active and attacked his skin. The pain quickly became so great that Heracles, beside himself, threw Lichas into the sea. At the same time he tried to force the fatal garment off but the cloth stuck to his body and tore off strips of skin. In this condition he was taken to Trachis in a boat. When she realised what she had done, Deianeira committed suicide. Heracles made his final arrangements: he gave Hyllus control of Iole, asking him to marry her when he was old enough; he then climbed Mount Oeta, not far from Trachis and built a huge funeral pyre and climbed onto it. When these preparations were finished he ordered his servants to set fire to the wood, but no one would obey him. PHILOCTETES finally obeyed him and as a reward Heracles gave him his bow and arrows. There was a clap of thunder and the hero was raised to the sky on a cloud. One legend is that Heracles made Philoctetes, the only witness of his death, promise not to reveal the location of the bonfire to anybody. Philoctetes was subsequently questioned and refused to speak but when he went to the site he kicked the ground with his foot in a significant way and disobeyed Heracles' prohibition. Later he was punished by receiving a severe wound in the offending foot.

There is another version of Heracles' death: according to this, Heracles did not die on his funeral pyre but set himself alight by the heat of the sun in his agony. He threw himself into a stream and drowned. The stream has remained hot ever since and was thought to be the source of the hot rocks between Thessaly and Phocis where there was, and still is, a hot spring. The death of Heracles is always associated with fire which purged him of the mortal elements he owed to his mother. Once among the gods Heracles was reconciled with Hera and she assumed the role of immortal mother. He married Hebe, the goddess of Youth, and became one of the immortals thereafter.

Heraclids (Ἡρακλειδαί) These were Heracles' descendants. In the Hellenistic period many royal families claimed to be Heraclids and traced their ancestry back to the hero. The designation Heraclids was particularly applied to the direct descendants of Heracles and Deianeira who colonized the Peloponnese. After the apotheosis of Heracles, his children, without his protection and fearing Eurystheus' hatred, took refuge with Ceyx, the king of Trachis, who had always shown kindness to Heracles. Eurystheus, however, demanded their expulsion from Trachis. Ceyx had

always been afraid of Eurystheus, so he sent them away on the pretext that he was not sufficiently strong to ensure their safety if they stayed with him. They then went to Athens where Theseus, or according to others his sons, agreed to protect them against Eurystheus, who then declared war on Athens. In the battle Eurystheus' five sons – Alexander, Iphimedon, Eurybius, Mentor and Perimedes – were killed. Eurystheus fled but he was followed by Hyllus or IOLAUS and killed near the rocks of Sciron (see ALCMENE). The victory was ensured by the Athenians, who sacrificed one of Heracles' daughters, Macaria; she volunteered to die when the oracle announced that Athens would be victorious if a young noble girl was executed.

When Eurystheus was beaten the Heraclids wanted to return to the Peloponnese which was their father's country of origin and where he had always tried in vain to return. With Hyllus in command they captured the Peloponnesian towns and established themselves there. After a year, however, a plague broke out and the oracle revealed that it was the result of divine anger provoked by the return of the Heraclids before the time fixed by fate. The Heraclids obediently left the country and returned to Attica, to the Marathon plain, but they always hoped to be able to return. To avoid divine anger, Hyllus went in their name to consult the oracle at Delphi. The oracle told him that their wish would be granted after 'the third harvest'. At that time, Hyllus was married to his father's mistress Iole; before he died, his father had asked him to look after the young woman. Of all his brothers he was his father's true inheritor. For these reasons the Heraclids looked on Hyllus as their leader and they asked him to lead them to their homeland. Hyllus entered the Isthmus of Corinth but there he ran into the army of Echemus, the king of Tegea. He challenged ECHEMUS to single combat and was killed by him.

His grandson Aristomachus went to question the oracle again. The oracle replied: 'The gods will give you victory if you attack by the narrows' or 'by the narrow path'. The oracle's expression was ambiguous. Aristomachus interpreted the oracle as meaning that it was a matter of attacking by the narrow Isthmus, but this was wrong and he was killed. When Aristomachus' sons were grown up, Temenus, the eldest, went to consult the oracle, which only repeated its two previous answers. Temenus remarked that his father and grandfather had followed the advice of the god and that this very advice had caused their death. The oracle replied that they did not know how to interpret the oracles; it added that 'third harvest' meant 'third generation' and that the 'narrow path' meant the straits between the coast of mainland Greece and the Peloponnese. Temenus was satisfied by this interpretation. To conform to the oracle's second reply he set about building a fleet on the coast of Locri at a town which in consequence became named Naupactus (from two Greek words meaning 'to build a ship'). While there with his army, his youngest brother ARISTODEMUS died after being struck by lightning, leaving twin sons, Eurysthenes and Procles.

A short time later a curse struck the army and the fleet. The Heraclids saw a soothsayer called Carnus approaching the camp. Carnus entertained only friendly feelings for the Heraclids but they thought that he was a magician who was coming to bring them bad luck and that he had been sent by their enemies. One of the Heraclids named HIPPOTES pierced him with a javelin. A storm then arose which scattered and wrecked the fleet. At the same time a famine visited the army which broke ranks and scattered. Temenus had to return once more to the oracle which told him that the calamities were due to divine anger incurred by the death of the soothsayer. The oracle added that the murderer must be banished for ten years and that the Heraclids should take a being with three eyes as a guide. Hippotes was banished and then a being with three eyes presented itself to the Heraclids in the form of a man with one eye mounted on a horse. This man was Oxylus, a king of Elis, who had been banished from his town for a year because of an accidental homicide. Oxylus agreed to be the Heraclids' guide, asking only the return of Elis as a reward. The Heraclids at last defeated the Peloponnesians. They killed King Tisamenus, son of Orestes, and two sons of Aegimius, Pamphylus and Dymas, were also killed. The Heraclids built an altar to Zeus, the father, to demonstrate their gratitude for the victory. They then divided the Peloponnese (see CRESPHONTES for details of the partition).

It was said that only three of the Peloponnesian provinces were split: Argos, Messenia and Laconia. Elis was given to Oxylus, as agreed and Arcadia was spared. An oracle had called upon the Heraclids in their conquest to spare 'those with whom they had shared a meal'. When the Heraclids approached the Arcadian border its king, Cypselus, sent ambassadors with presents. It happened that the ambassadors met Cresphontes'

soldiers just after they had bought food from the local peasants and were eating. They asked the Arcadians to share it with them. During the meal there was a quarrel but the Arcadians felt that it was wrong to quarrel with their hosts. The Heraclids remembered the words of the oracle and made an agreement with the Arcadians, promising to spare their country. Another version of the legend claims that the Heraclids were struck by the abundance of crops on the Arcadian frontier. When Cypselus' envoys presented themselves the Heraclids refused to accept the presents which they had brought because the oracle had forbidden them to make any alliance during the campaign. Cypselus pointed out that they had already received as a present the crops which they had seized, consequently the alliance was already concluded. The Heraclids recognized this and turned away from Arcadia. There is also a story that Cypselus, by giving his daughter in marriage to Cresphontes, succeeded in saving his country (see MEROPE).

Hercules To this name (a latinized form of the Greek Heracles – perhaps of Etruscan origin) was attached a whole collection of Roman legends, particularly aetiological and topographical, which had been integrated into the general thread of the account of Heracles' 'return from Geryon' (see HERACLES). These legends were far from coherent. The best-known episode which fits in with an Augustan theme was the fight between Hercules and CACUS. It is reasonable to suppose that this tale appeared relatively late in time and that it sprang from Hellenic models. In its earliest form, the legend was only meant to represent the reception of the hero as a guest by the barbarian King Faunus, a king whose custom it was to sacrifice to the gods all strangers who visited him. When Faunus attempted to lay his hands on Hercules, Hercules killed him. After this, Hercules continued his journey to Magna Graecia. The usual tradition made Evander treat Hercules kindly and tells that on the advice of his mother, Carmenta, who told him who his guest really was, Evander dedicated an altar to Hercules at the outlet of the valley of the Circus Maximus, between the Aventine and Palatine hills. Evander was supposed to be the Greek form of Faunus.

The myth of the Good Goddess (see BONA DEA) is also part of the legend of Hercules. Propertius tells how, thirsty from his fight with Cacus, Hercules asked the Bona Dea (or Fauna), the goddess who performed sacred rites in the neighbourhood, for a drink. She refused to allow him to approach her sacred spring which was only open to women, and Hercules in anger then closed his shrine to the female sex (see RECARANUS). Finally, some large construction works were attributed to Hercules, notably the erection of a dyke and a road eight stadia long separating the sea from Lake Lucrinus in Campania.

Hercyna (Ἑρκύνα) The Nymph who presided over a spring at Lebadea in Boeotia. There is a legend which tells how she had been a companion of Persephone before her abduction by Hades. One day while Hercyna played with Persephone the goose belonging to the two young girls escaped and hid under a stone in a cave. Persephone chased after it and to recapture it removed the stone. A spring immediately gushed out of the ground; this came to be known as the spring of Hercyna. It was situated not far away from the oracle of Trophonius and all who wanted to consult the oracle had to first bathe in the spring.

Hermaphroditus (Ἑρμαφρόδιτος) The name generally given to all people with both masculine and feminine characteristics and more particularly applied by the mythographers to a son of Aphrodite and Hermes. Hermaphroditus, whose name was composed of both his mother's and his father's names, was brought up by Nymphs in the forests of Ida in Phrygia. He was remarkably handsome. When he reached the age of fifteen he started to travel the world and he first travelled across Asia Minor. One day when in Caria he came to a beautiful lake. There the Nymph of the lake, Salmacis, immediately fell in love with him. She made advances which the young man rebuffed, and appeared to be resigned to his reply, though she was only pretending. Hermaphroditus was attracted by the clearness of the water; he undressed himself and plunged into the lake. When Salmacis saw him in her domain and at her mercy, she joined him and embraced him, Hermaphroditus tried in vain to push her away. She uttered a prayer to the gods begging them to cause their bodies never to be separated; the gods granted this prayer and united them in to one new being with a dual personality. At the same time Hermaphroditus also had a request granted by the gods: this was that anybody who bathed in the lake of Salmacis should lose their virility. At the time of Strabo, the lake was still said to have this power. Hermaphroditus was frequently represented on bas-reliefs as one of the followers of Dionysus.

Bronze Hermaphrodite. The nymph Salmacis fell in love with Hermaphroditus and asked the gods that they might be united forever; the gods granted this wish, creating a hermaphrodite, a being with characteristics of both sexes. This was a common theme in later Greek art.

Hermes (Ἑρμῆς) The son of Zeus and Maia, the youngest of the Pleiades; Maia conceived him by Zeus in the dead of night when both gods and men were asleep. He was born in a cave on Mount Cyllene in southern Arcadia on the fourth day of the month – a day which remained consecrated to him. He was wrapped in bandages as was customary for the new-born and was placed in a winnowing-basket instead of a cot. Even on the day of his birth he showed exceptional precocity. By the sheer effort of moving about he found a way to extricate himself from his bandages and went to Thessaly where his brother, Apollo, was shepherd in charge of the herds of Admetus. At that time Apollo was absorbed by his love-affair with Hymenaeus, son of Magnes, and neglected his duty as shepherd; because of his negligence Hermes was able to steal some of the animals in Apollo's care, namely a dozen cows, a hundred heifers which had never known a halter and a bull. He then tied a branch to each animal's tail (in some accounts he provided clogs for them all), and drove them across Greece to a cavern in Pylos. He was seen by only one witness, an old man called BATTUS. At Pylos, Hermes sacrificed two of the stolen beasts, from which he made twelve portions, one for each of the twelve gods. Then, after concealing the remainder of the herd, he escaped to his cave on Cyllene. There he found a tortoise in front of the entrance; he cleaned it and stretched some strings made of the intestines of the cattle he had sacrificed across the hollow of the shell. In this way the first lyre was constructed.

Meanwhile Apollo was looking everywhere for his missing animals, and finally came to Pylos where Battus showed him the hiding-place. (Some people say, however, that Apollo was already aware of the whole episode because of his power to divine events by watching the flight of birds.) He hurried to Mount Cyllene and complained to Maia about the thefts committed by her son, but showing him the child, prudently wrapped in swaddling bands, Maia asked how he could possibly make such accusations. Apollo then called Zeus to the cave, and in spite of the child's denials, Zeus ordered Hermes to return the stolen animals. Apollo in the interim had seen the lyre in the cave and was so enchanted by the sounds Hermes produced from it that he decided to give his beasts in exchange for the instrument.

A little later, while looking after the herd which he had thus acquired, Hermes invented the flute (the syrinx or flute of Pan). Apollo wanted to buy this new instrument and offered as payment the golden crook which he used when looking after the herd of Admetus. Hermes agreed to this, but in addition asked to be taught the art of soothsaying. Apollo accepted this bargain and it is in this way that the golden rod (the herald's wand) became one of Hermes' attributes. Hermes also learned how to foretell the future by using small pebbles, and Zeus was so pleased with the agility and activity of his youngest son that he made him the herald with particular responsibilities towards Zeus and the gods of the Underworld, Hades and Persephone.

These myths about his childhood were the only ones where Hermes himself had the main part. He more often played a secondary role as a divine agent and a protector of heroes. In the battle against the Giants he wore Hades' helmet which made the wearer invisible; this enabled him to kill the Giant Hippolytus. During the battle of the gods against the ALOADAE, he saved Ares by freeing him from the bronze vessel in which the

One of Hermes' functions was to be the messenger of the gods; this Greek bronze statue shows him resting and wearing the winged sandals which were his attributes. Naples, National Museum.

two giants had imprisoned him. He also saved Zeus during his fight with Typhon: he succeeded in stealing the tendons of Zeus from the monster, which Typhon had hidden in a bearskin and left in charge of Delphyne, a dragon, half woman, half serpent. Without being seen by his enemy he was able to replace the tendons in Zeus' body with the help of Pan, making it possible for Zeus to renew the fight. In all these adventures it was Hermes' skill which enabled him to intervene.

In other episodes Hermes simply interpreted divine will. For example, it was he Deucalion came to after the flood, to ask him what he wanted; from Hermes Nephele received the ram with the golden fleece which saved her children PHRIXUS and ATHAMAS; Hermes gave Amphion his lyre, Heracles his sword, Perseus the helmet of Hades and the talaria which bore him through the air. Hermes took action to save Odysseus on two occasions, once when he gave Calypso the order to release Odysseus and to help him to build a raft strong enough to carry him to Ithaca and the second time, when Odysseus was with CIRCE, and

Hermes showed Odysseus the moly, the magic plant which protected him from enchantment and saved him from the degrading transformation undergone by his companions. In Hades Hermes watched over HERACLES and warned him of his mistake in attempting to attack Medusa's ghost. Hermes also undertook to find someone who would purchase the hero to serve as a slave in order that he would be purified for the murder of Iphitus. Hermes struck the bargain with OMPHALE. The best-known incident in which Hermes was involved was the death of ARGOS, whom Hera had put in charge of IO after she had been turned into a cow. This murder was the explanation for the obscure cognomen 'Argeiphontes' given to Hermes and said to mean 'killer of Argos'. To help Zeus and to thwart the vengeance of Hera he took the young DIONYSUS from one hiding-place to another on Mount Nysa and then to Athamas' estate. Hermes was instructed to take the three goddesses – Hera, Aphrodite and Athena – to Ida in Phrygia at the time of the judgement of Paris. He took them to see PARIS and thus played a decisive part in the incident which was to lead to the Trojan war.

Hermes was considered to be the god of commerce and flight, and the one who guided travellers along their way. His statue used to be set up at crossroads in the form of a pillar of which only the top half was shaped as a human bust but which was provided with very visible male organs. He was said to protect shepherds and was often shown carrying a lamb on his shoulders; it was this which earned him the title, Hermes Criophores. He also had the task of accompanying the spirits of the dead to Hades and because of this he was given the name Psychopompus, which means the 'accompanier of souls'. Legend says that he was the father of several children: the grandfather of Odysseus, Autolycus, who inherited Hermes' ability to steal without being caught; Eurytus, one of the Argonauts; Abderus – a favourite of Heracles, after whom the town of Abdera was named and who was devoured by the mares of Diomedes and Cephalus, borne by Herse when Hermes was in Athens. A story of obscure origin also made him the father of the god Pan by Penelope who was unfaithful to Odysseus; Pan was supposedly conceived in the Arcadian mountains and, like his father, was the god of shepherds. Hermes was most frequently shown wearing winged shoes and a large-brimmed hat and carrying the winged staff, the symbol of his position as divine messenger.

Hermione (Ἑρμιόνη) The only daughter of Menelaus and Helen (Table 3). The oldest legends, in the form in which they occur in the *Odyssey*, tell how Menelaus betrothed Hermione to NEOPTOLEMUS, the son of Achilles, while he was away at Troy. When Neoptolemus returned to Lacedaemon, the marriage took place. The tragedians' version of this story is very different, however. According to their account Menelaus had initially betrothed Hermione to Orestes before the Trojan War. (The mythographers claimed that at the time of Helen's abduction Hermione was nine years old.) Yet, during the Trojan War, Menelaus had given his daughter to Achilles' son instead, since his co-operation was necessary if Troy was to be captured. After the war Orestes was forced to give up Hermione to Neoptolemus. To explain how Hermione, already married to Orestes, could be offered to another man, it was related that the first marriage had taken place without the knowledge of Menelaus, and that it was organized by Tyndareus, Orestes' grandfather, while Menelaus was at Troy. In any event, Hermione became the source of contention between Orestes and Neoptolemus. The marriage of Hermione and Neoptolemus produced no children and during the visit he made to Delphi to discover the reason for the sterility, Neoptolemus was killed during a riot either by Orestes himself or by another at Orestes' behest. Orestes then married Hermione who bore him a son TISAMENUS.

Hermochares (Ἑρμοχάρης) A young Athenian who fell in love with a young girl from the island of Chios called Ctesylla when he saw her dancing at the altar of the Pythian Apollo. He wrote an oath on an apple; Ctesylla saw the apple which he had thrown in the temple of Artemis and read the words aloud, thus becoming bound to him by oath. In shame Ctesylla threw the apple away. Following this, Hermochares went to see her father Alcidamas and asked for permission to marry Ctesylla. He agreed to this and promised his daughter in marriage by calling on Apollo as witness and touching the sacred laurel.

Time passed, and Alcidamas, forgetting his solemn oath, betrothed his daughter to another man. One day, while Ctesylla was offering a sacrifice to Artemis to celebrate the engagement, Hermochares hurried to the temple. Ctesylla saw him and immediately fell in love with him (thus following the wish of Artemis) and with her nurse's help, absconded with Hermochares without the knowledge of Alcidamas. The two lovers travelled to Athens where they were married. Soon afterwards they had a child, but Apollo wished Ctesylla to die in childbirth to expiate her father's perjury towards him. At the funeral the mourners saw a dove fly away from the bier, and discovered that the body of Ctesylla had disappeared. Hermochares and the inhabitants of Chios consulted the oracle about the meaning of this event and were instructed to worship Aphrodite Ctesylla, the new name of the girl who had been deified.

Hermus (Ἕρμος) An Athenian noble who accompanied Theseus on his expedition against the Amazons. On his way home, Theseus founded the town of Pythopolis in the Nicaean region, and left Hermus and two of his companions to establish laws and regulations for the new town.

Hero (Ἡρώ) The young girl whom LEANDER loved and for whom every night he swam across the strait between Sestos and Abydos. One night a storm extinguished the light she used to guide him and he drowned; she then threw herself into the sea after him.

Herophile (Ἡροφίλη) The second SIBYL. She was born in Troy, the daughter of a Nymph and a human father called Theodorus, who was a shepherd on Mount Ida; her precise birthplace was Marpessus. Her first prophecies said that the fall of Troy would come from a woman nourished in Sparta. She travelled to Claros, Samos, Delos and Delphi and in each place she made a prophecy, standing on a stone which she carried with her. She died in the Troad where her tomb could be seen in the wood of Apollo Smintheus.

Herse (Ἕρση) One of the three daughters of Cecrops and Aglaurus and therefore a member of the Athenian royal family (Table 4). Her two sisters were Aglaurus and Pandrosus. Athena entrusted the baby ERICHTHONIUS to them. She and her sisters behaved indiscreetly by opening the basket in which the baby was hidden. As a punishment, Athena sent Herse mad; she threw herself from the top of the rocks of the Acropolis. There is another version of this story which ascribes all the blame to Aglaurus. In this account Herse is said to have escaped punishment and to have been seduced by Hermes by whom she had a son called CEPHALUS.

Hersilia A Roman heroine of the period of Romulus. She was a Sabine and one of the highest born of the Sabine women abducted by Romulus' Romans. According to a story told by Plutarch, she was the only one of the abducted Sabine women who was married. Her husband was called Hostilius; he was killed during the war which broke out between the two peoples. It was also said that she was married to one of Romulus' followers, also called Hostilius, by whom she had a son called Hostus Hostilius who was father of the king Tullus Hostilius. During the war between the Sabines and the Romans she was one of the most active of the mediators who intervened between the two opponents and brought about peace. Another legend made Hersilia the wife of Romulus by whom she had two children: a daughter, Prima, and a son, Aollius, who was later called Avilius. After the apotheosis of her husband, Hersilia was struck by heavenly fire and in her turn deified with the name of Hora Quirini and associated with the cult of Romulus, who, after his death, was assimilated with the god Quirinus.

Hesione (Ἡσιόνη) The name of three legendary heroines, all connected with the sea. The first, according to Aeschylus, was one of the Oceanides and wife of Prometheus. She was not however included in Hesiod's list of the daughters of the sea. The second was the wife of Nauplius, the sailor. She was the mother of Palamedes, Oeax and Nausimedon. The third and best known was the daughter of Laomedon, the king of Troy. She married Telamon by whom she had a son called Teucer. The circumstances of her marriage were rather peculiar. Since Laomedon had refused to pay Poseidon and Apollo the amount which he had promised them for building the wall of Troy, the god in fury sent a sea monster against the country, to devour the inhabitants. The people consulted the soothsayer who explained that in order to calm the wrath of Poseidon, the king's own daughter must be sacrificed. Hesione therefore was roped to a rock to wait for the monster to devour her. HERACLES arrived in the Troad at that time and offered to kill the monster on condition that the king would give him his horses. Laomedon consented, but as soon as his daughter was free, refused to keep to the agreed contract. Several years later Heracles organized an expedition in revenge, during which he captured Troy. The first man to scale the wall was Telamon, and as a reward Heracles gave him the hand of Hesione. Among the captives the girl chose to have her brother Podarces, who later took the name of Priam. She took him with her to Greece having ransomed him from Heracles. There was also a story that Hesione, while pregnant by Telamon, fled in a boat and landed at Miletus, where she was welcomed by the king, ARION. There she gave birth to a son TRAMBELUS.

Hesperides (Ἑσπερίδες) The Nymphs of the Setting Sun. In the *Theogony* of Hesiod they were the daughters of the night, but later they were said to be, successively, daughters of Zeus and Themis, of Phorcys and Ceto, and finally of Atlas. The writers did not agree, either, about their number, but most often there were said to be three: Aegle, Erythia and Hesperarethusa, but the last name is often divided into two and applied to two distinct Hesperides: Hesperia and Arethusa (see HERACLES). The Hesperides lived in the extreme west not far from the Island of the Blessed at the edge of the ocean. As the western world became better known, the position of the land of the Hesperides became established and was sited at the foot of Mount Atlas. Their main function, with the help of a dragon, the son of Phorcys and Ceto (or possibly of Typhon and Echidna), was to guard the garden of the gods where the golden apples grew, a gift given earlier to Hera when she married Zeus. They sang in chorus near gushing springs which spurted forth ambrosia. The Hesperides were linked with the story of Heracles. To their dwelling-place the hero went to seek the fruits of immortality and his search for the golden apples was already the symbol of his apotheosis.

The euhemerist interpretation of the myth of the Hesperides is as follows. The Hesperides were seven young girls, daughters of Atlas and Hesperia, Atlas' niece. They had large herds of sheep (by a play on words the Greek word μῆλα can either mean apples or sheep). Busiris, king of Egypt, who was their neighbour, sent brigands to raid their herds and abduct the girls. When Heracles came into the country he killed the brigands, seized their booty, freed the Hesperides and gave them back to Atlas. As a reward Atlas gave the hero 'what he had come to find' (we do not know whether he wanted apples or sheep), and in addition he taught him astronomy (in the euhemerist interpretation of the ATLAS story he was said to be the first astronomer).

Hesperus (Ἕσπερος) The spirit of the evening star, said to be the son or the brother of Atlas. He was the first to climb Mount Atlas to watch the stars; from there a storm swept him away, causing him to disappear without trace. Because of his kindness, men supposed that he had been transformed into the friendly evening star which every evening brought the peace of night. Thereafter they called the star Hesperus. In the euhemerist interpretation of the Atlas legends, Hesperus was said to be the father of Hesperis who, as Atlas' wife, bore the HESPERIDES as daughters. Hellenistic authors identified Hesperus as the star Phosphorus, called Lucifer by the Romans.

Hestia (Ἑστιά) The goddess of the hearth, which she personified. She was the eldest daughter of Cronus and Rhea, and the sister of Zeus and Hera. Although courted by Apollo and Poseidon, Zeus gave her permission to preserve her virginity, He granted her special honours, causing her to be worshipped in every household and in the temples of all the gods. While other gods travelled throughout the world, Hestia remained quietly on Olympus. In the same way that the domestic hearth was the religious centre of the household, so Hestia was the religious centre of the divine dwelling. Hestia's immobility meant that she played almost no role in myths, however. She remained an abstract idea of hearth and home, rather than a personal divinity.

Hiera (Ἱέρα) Married to TELEPHUS. During the Greeks' first expedition to Troy, when they landed in Mysia (see ACHILLES) she led the women of the country in an attack on the invaders, and was killed by Nireus. Hiera was said to have been more beautiful than Helen. She had two sons by Telephus, Tarchon and Tyrsenus.

Hierax (Ἱέραξ) The Falcon. There were two heroes so called in mythology. One was a gossip who prevented Hermes from snatching Io from Argos and who thus caused the god to kill him. Although our sources fail to tell us what punishment Hierax suffered, it is said that he was transformed into a bird of the same name. A second was a rich landowner of the country of the Mariandyni on the north coast of Asia Minor, a faithful servant of Demeter who rewarded him by making his land fertile and productive. When the wrath of Poseidon caused famine and desolation throughout the Troad, the Trojans turned to Hierax for help. He gave them large quantities of wheat and barley and saved them from starvation, but Poseidon punished him for his actions, turning him into a falcon, a bird well known to mortals but one hated by other birds.

Hilaera (Ἵλαρα) One of the LEUCIPPIDAE, the sister of Phoebe.

Hilebie (Εἰλεβίη) When one of the suitors of Io, Lyrcus, a son of Phoroneus, was instructed by Inachus to go to look for the girl who had been abducted by Zeus (see IO), he set off, and travelled far and wide. He did not find her and was afraid to return to Argos without her, so he settled in Caunus in Caria where he married Hilebie, one of the king's daughters. There were no children from this marriage, however, and in order to know the reason for this LYRCUS consulted an oracle whose ambiguous reply caused him to be unfaithful to his wife. His father-in-law was furious and tried to drive him out of the house, but Hilebie remained loyal and helped her husband to win his case.

Himalia (Ἱμαλία) The miller's wife, a Nymph of Rhodes with whom, after his victory over the Titans, Zeus had intercourse, coming upon her as a shower of rain. She bore him three sons whose names recall three stages in the life of corn: Spartaeus (the sower); Cronius (the ripener); Cytus (perhaps the baker, literally 'the hollow', meaning possibly the container that stores grain). During a downpour which covered all Rhodes, the sons of Himalia and Zeus saved themselves by taking refuge on the island's hills.

Himerus (Ἵμερος) The son of LACEDAEMON, the spirit of Himerus was the personification of sexual desire. He followed Eros in Aphrodite's train. On Olympus he lived next to the Graces and the Muses, but being simply an abstract idea, he did not appear in any of the legends.

Hippe (Ἵππη) The best known of the heroines called Hippe was Chiron the Centaur's daughter, who was seduced by Aeolus, one of Helen's sons. When her time came, she fled into Pelion to give birth to the child without her father's knowledge – but her father followed her. In desperation, Hippe besought the gods to let her bear her child in secret. The gods granted her request and transformed her into a constellation in the shape of a horse (see also MELANIPPE).

Hippo (Ἵππω) At Leuctra a man called Scedasus had two daughters, Hippo and Molpia. The two girls were raped by two Spartans, Phrourarchidas

and Parthenius, and, ashamed of what had happened, hung themselves. Scedasus urged the Spartans to punish the guilty pair, but failed, and having cursed Sparta, he too committed suicide. This, in the time of Epaminondas, was one of the reasons which caused divine anger to fall upon the town.

Hippocoon (Ἱπποκόων) The illegitimate son of Oebalus and a Nymph called Batieia. He was a native of Sparta and the half-brother of Tyndareus and Icarius (Table 19). He was older than they were and when their father died, he banished them from Sparta and seized power. He himself had twelve sons, the Hippocoontides, who assisted him to rob Tyndareus and Icarius. Hippocoon and his sons were men of violence: they succeeded in arousing the anger of Heracles who declared war on them and killed them, restoring Tyndareus to the throne of Sparta. (Note that some traditions maintain that Icarius helped Hippocoon to deprive Tyndareus of his kingdom.)

Hippocrene (Ἱπποκρήνη) The horse PEGASUS was on Helicon not far from the Muses' sacred grove. He struck the rock with his hoof and a spring gushed from the ground. It was called Hippocrene, or the Horse's Spring, and it was round the Hippocrene spring that the Muses gathered to sing and dance, for its water was said to bring poetic inspiration. Pausanias describes another Horse's Spring at Troezen, which also owed its origin to Pegasus.

Hippodamia (Ἱπποδάμεια) The name of several heroines. The most celebrated was the daughter of OENOMAUS, the king of Pisa in Elis. Her mother was known by various names. According to some, Hippodamia was the Pleiad Sterope's daughter; to others the daughter of Eurythoe – the Danaid – or else of Evarete, the sister of Leucippus. She was extremely beautiful and many suitors wished to marry her, but Oenomaus was not willing to give his daughter in marriage. Some versions maintain that an oracle had forecast that his son-in-law would kill him; others that he was himself in love with Hippodamia. Whatever the truth, Oenomaus devised the following plan to get rid of the suitors. He offered his daughter as the prize in a chariot race. Each suitor had to take the girl in his chariot while he, riding in his own chariot, strove to overtake them. The finishing-post was the altar of Poseidon in Corinth. It was said that Oenomaus made Hippodamia ride in the suitors' chariots to make the chariots heavier, or to distract the drivers' attention. Even so, Oenomaus had no difficulty in beating the challengers because he had remarkably fast horses. Once he had won a race Oenomaus would behead the suitor and, it was said, would nail the head to the door of his house to frighten future competitors.

When Pelops arrived to take part in the race, Hippodamia was at once enchanted by the young man's beauty. She enlisted the help of Myrtilus, her father's driver who was also in love with her, and persuaded him to substitute wax lynch pins for those in the wheels of her father's chariot. These quickly gave way during the race, causing an accident that was fatal to Oenomaus (see PELOPS). It is also alleged that, in order to win the co-operation of Myrtilus, Pelops promised him one night with Hippodamia; but others claim that Hippodamia herself gave the driver this promise. Later it was said that Myrtilus tried to rape Hippodamia when she, Pelops and Myrtilus were travelling in their chariot and Pelops had gone for a moment to look for some drinking-water. When he came back, Hippodamia complained to Pelops who threw Myrtilus into the sea. However, another version asserts that during Pelops' absence Hippodamia tried to seduce Myrtilus, and that when Myrtilus refused her advances, she invented the incident to relate to her husband. Pelops killed Myrtilus who as he died cursed the house of Pelops. This then was one of the origins of the misfortunes that struck the house of Pelops (see ATREUS, THYESTES and AGAMEMNON, and Table 2).

Pelops, in honour of Hippodamia, founded the quinquennial festival of Hera, the goddess of marriage, at Olympia. There are various accounts of the children of Hippodamia and Pelops. Sometimes six sons are listed: Atreus, Thyestes, Pittheus, Alcathus, Plisthenes and Chrysippus. Another tradition gives them the following children: Atreus, Thyestes, Dias, Cynosourus, Corinthus, Hippalmus, Hippasus, Cleon, Argeus, Alcathus, Heleius, Pittheus and Troezen, together with three daughters: Nicippe, Lysidice and Astydamia, all of whom were said to have married sons of Perseus (Table 31). However, CHRYSIPPUS is more commonly said to be Hippodamia's son-in-law, whom she had murdered by Atreus and Thyestes. In revenge Pelops was said to have had her put to death.

The murder of Chrysippus was sometimes recounted as follows. Since Atreus and Thyestes refused to murder him, Hippodamia decided to do it herself, using the sword belonging to Laius, who happened to be spending the night with Pelops. She left the weapon piercing Chrysippus' body in an attempt to ensure that suspicion would fall on Laius. But although mortally wounded, Chrysippus had time to reveal the facts before he died. Consequently, Hippodamia was driven out by Pelops and banished from Elis. She took refuge at Midia in Argolis where she was said to have died. Later, as instructed by an oracle, Pelops supposedly had her ashes brought back to Olympia where, in fact, Hippodamia had a memorial chapel in the sacred enclosure, the Altis. Hippodamia was also the name of the daughter of Adrastus (or Butes), the wife of Pirithous. It was on her account that the fight between the Centaurs and the Lapiths took place (see PIRITHOUS and Tables 1 and 23). See also BRISEIS (whose real name was Hippodamia) and PHOENIX.

Hippolochus (Ἱππόλοχος) One Hippolochus was the son of Bellerophon and Philonoe (or Anticleia). His son was Glaucus who commanded the Lycians at the siege of Troy (Table 35). A second was the son of the Trojan Antenor and the brother of Glaucus and Acamas. After the fall of Troy, he went with them and settled in Cyprus.

Hippolyta (Ἱππολύτη) Among heroines with this name the most famous was the queen of the Amazons, whose girdle HERACLES attempted to seize. Her father was Ares and her mother Otrera. Some claimed it was she who organized the expedition against THESEUS. She was even said to be the mother of HIPPOLYTUS. But the point on which sources most frequently agree is that she was murdered by Heracles.

Hippolytus (Ἱππόλυτος) Theseus had a son called Hippolytus. The mother was either the Amazon Melanippe or Antiope, or possibly Hippolyta. From his mother Hippolytus inherited a passion for hunting and vigorous exercise. He was especially devoted to the goddess Artemis, but he scorned Aphrodite. The goddess took cruel revenge on him because of his scorn. She inspired Phaedra, Theseus' second wife, with a passionate love for the young man. Phaedra offered to sleep with Hippolytus, but she was repulsed. Fearing that he would tell Theseus about the incident, Phaedra tore off her clothes and smashed her bedroom door, claiming that Hippolytus had tried to rape her. Theseus was furious, but since he did not want to kill his own son, he turned to Poseidon

Roman mosaic depicting Hippolytus with his stepmother Phaedra. From the House of Dionysus, Paphos, Cyprus.

who had promised him that he would fulfil three requests. In answer to his plea the god sent a sea monster which emerged from the sea as Hippolytus was driving his chariot along the shore at Troezen. It frightened the horses and caused the death of the young man, for Hippolytus fell out of the chariot and, catching his feet in the reins, was dragged across the rocks. When she heard of the tragedy she had caused, Phaedra hung herself. Another story tells how, at the request of Artemis, Asclepius brought the young man back to life. The goddess then carried him off to Italy to her sanctuary at Aricia on the shore of Lake Nemi (see DIANA). Hippolytus was identified with the god Virbius, Diana's companion at Aricia. Hippolytus was also the name of a giant who was killed by Hermes in the Battle of the Giants, for Hermes was helped by the helmet of Hades which made him invisible.

Hippomedon ('Ιππομέδων) One of the seven chiefs who attacked Thebes in alliance with ADRASTUS. He was usually said to be the nephew of Adrastus and the son of Aristomachus, one of the sons of Talaus (Table 1). He was an enormous man, but he was killed during the assault on the town, by Ismarius. He lived in a castle at Lerna, whose ruins were still visible in Pausanias' day. His son Polydorus was one of the Epigoni who captured Thebes under the command of ALCMAEON.

Hippomenes ('Ιππομένης) The story of Hippomenes, son of Megareus and Merope, was the same as that of MELANION. Hippomenes wanted to marry Atalanta, although Atalanta herself wished never to be married. Instead, she forced her suitors to run a race with her, killing those whom she outstripped. This went on for some time until the day Hippomenes raced against Atalanta. He dropped three golden apples given to him by Aphrodite, in front of ATALANTA and this won the race. In his role as Melanion he was transformed into a lion for the same reason, but Cybele took pity on Hippomenes and Atalanta as lions and harnessed them to her chariot.

Hippotes ('Ιππότης) One of the HERACLIDS. He descended from Antiochus, one of Heracles' sons, whom the hero had by Meda, the daughter of PHYLAS, king of the Dryopes. Antiochus' son was also called Phylas, and he was the father of Hippotes. On his mother Leipephile's side, he was descended from Iolaus (Table 31). He took part with Temenus in the Heraclids' expedition against the Peloponnese. At Naupactus he killed a seer by mistake, thinking he was a spy. This aroused Apollo's anger against the army, and Hippotes was banished for ten years as a punishment.

Hippotes had one son called ALETES. Hippotes was also the name of the son of Creon, king of Corinth, who welcomed Jason and Medea when they were banished by Acastus. When Medea murdered Creon and his daughter (see JASON), Hippotes indicted her before an Athenian Court, but she was declared innocent (see MEDUS).

Hippothoe (Ἱπποθόη) Among several heroines with this name the mythographers mentioned the daughter of Mestor, the son of Perseus (Table 31), and Lysidice, a daughter of Pelops. She was abducted by Poseidon and taken to the island of the Echinades. There she bore him a son Taphius, father of Pterelas, king of the Teleboans (see AMPHITRYON).

Hirpi Sorani The 'Wolves of Soracte' were priests who held special ceremonies on Soracte – a mountain north of Rome – during which they danced barefoot on burning wood. There was a curious story about the origin of this fraternity of 'wolves'. When the people of Soracte were offering a sacrifice to Dis Pater, a pack of wolves arrived unexpectedly and snatched pieces of the victims' flesh from the flames. The celebrants protested and dashed off in pursuit and after a long chase finally saw the wolves disappear into a cave from which emerged a dreadful pestilential smell. The fumes were so noxious that they not only killed the pursuers but also spread a plague all over the country. In desperation, the people went to seek the advice of the soothsayer, who told them that in order to appease the gods they must behave like the wolves, and live as predators. (Compare with the Roman rites of the LUPERCI.)

Historis (Ἱστορίς) A local legend said that Historis, the daughter of the Theban soothsayer, Tiresias, worked out a scheme making it possible for GALINTHIAS to hasten the delivery of Alcmene, who had been prevented from giving birth to Heracles by the plots of Hera and EILITHYIA. As Eilithyia was sitting on the doorstep of the house with her hands crossed, thus preventing Alcmene from having her child, Historis suddenly burst out of the house with cries of joy, announcing that Alcmene had given birth at last. The goddess believed her story and stormed off in anger, bringing Alcmene's suffering to an end and Heracles and Iphicles into the world.

Homoloeus (Ὁμολωεύς) One of the sons of Niobe and Amphion, Homoloeus helped his father to build the walls of Thebes, where one of the gates of the city was inscribed with his name.

Homonoia (Ὁμόνοια) A purely abstract personification of harmony; she had an altar at Olympia. In Rome she was called Concordia, an abstraction which often appeared in the official ideology, particularly on coins which marked the ending of a rebellion or the conclusion of a civil war. She also had a temple at the foot of the Capitol dedicated to her by Camillus, which symbolized the agreement finally reached between patricians and commoners.

Honos In Rome Honos was the personification of morality, as Virtus was of warlike bravery, and there were several temples dedicated to her in the city.

Hopladamus (Ὁπλάδαμος) According to Arcadian legend, one of the giants who escorted Rhea, carrying the baby Zeus in her arms, to protect her from Cronus.

Horae (Ὧραι) The daughters of Zeus and Themis and sisters of the Moirai (Destiny). There were three – Eunomia, Dike and Eirene, meaning discipline, justice and peace. However, the Athenians called them Thallo, Auxo and Carpo, three words which denote budding, growth and ripening. They had two different aspects: as goddesses of nature they controlled the growth of plants; as goddesses of order (daughters of Themis, goddess of justice) they maintained the stability of society. On Olympus they had several duties, one of which was to guard the entrance to the divine dwelling. By some they were said to have reared Hera, whose servants they were. They were responsible for unharnessing her horses and occasionally did the same for the god of the sun. They were followers of Aphrodite, like the Graces, and they appeared in the train of Dionysus and also among Persephone's companions. Finally Pan, god of woods and flocks, was said to have enjoyed their companionship. They were customarily represented as three graceful girls, often holding a flower or a plant, but they were considered rather abstract beings of uncertain personality and they had almost no mythical role. It was only in a late allegory that one of them was declared to be the wife of Zephyrus, the west wind, by whom she had a son, Carpus.

Horatii Roman folklore knew of three Horatii, of whom one at least was purely mythical and two were said to be historical. The story of one

Horatius is linked to the war between the Romans and the Etruscans, a war prompted by the struggle between Brutus and Arruns Tarquin. Both sides suffered heavy casualties in the fighting, and after the battle it was not at all clear which country had won. The armies were camped on the battlefield near the forest of Arsia, from which suddenly a divine voice proclaimed: 'The Etruscans have lost one more man than the Romans; the Romans are the victors.' At this, the Etruscans took fright and fled. Horatius emerged from the forest as the hero, for it was his voice that had put the enemy to flight.

A little later, another Horatius, one-eyed Horatius (Horatius Cocles), single-handedly defended the only bridge connecting Rome with the right bank of the Tiber against the Etruscans. During the battle, however, he was wounded in the thigh and permanently lamed. In his honour a statue was erected at the Volcanal at the foot of the Capitol – indeed the origin of the story is probably due to this statue of a one-eyed lame man (possibly of Vulcan). Finally, although the conflict between the three Horatii and the three Curiatii, champions of Alba, is generally considered to be historic, there is good reason to believe that this tale was a transposition of a very old initiation myth of which similar examples are found in Celtic legend.

Hostius Also called Hostus Hostilius, a Roman originally from the colony of Medullia, which was set up by the Albani in Sabine territory. During the reign of Romulus he came and settled in Rome. After the removal of the Sabines he married HERSILIA by whom he had a son who was the father of King Tullus Hostilius. During the Sabine war on the level ground of the Forum, Hostius distinguished himself in the front rank of the Roman army and was the first to be killed. After his death the Romans panicked momentarily until Jupiter Stator intervened to restore order. Hostius had already shown outstanding bravery at the capture of Fidenae for which he was awarded a laurel wreath.

Hyacinthids (Ὑακινθίδες) The name given in Athens to girls who had been sacrificed for the safety of the country. There were two distinct traditions connected with them. According to the first they were daughters of the Lacedaemonian HYACINTHUS who had settled in Athens. There were four of them: Antheis, Aegleis, Lytaea and Orthaea. During Minos' war against Attica, plague and famine struck the country (see MINOS and ANDROGEOS). In accordance with the instructions of an ancient oracle, the Athenians sacrificed young girls, hoping that this would relieve their misery. However these actions had no effect at all and the Athenians were forced finally to accept Minos' terms (see THESEUS). Other mythographers identified the Hyacinthids as the daughters of ERECHTHEUS – Protogenia and Pandora – who were offered in expiation to the gods when the Eleusinian army commanded by EUMOLPUS approached Athens. Thereafter the daughters became known as the Hyacinthids because the sacrifice took place on a hill called Hyacinthus.

Hyacinthus (Ὑάκινθος) Most frequently said to be the son of Amyclas and Diomedes, and on his father's side the grandson of Lacedaemon and Sparta (Table 6). This genealogy makes him the uncle of OEBALUS or of PERIERES depending on the authors. Poets, however, sometimes asserted that Hyacinthus was the son of Oebalus, and an isolated tradition recorded by Athenodorus claimed that he was the son of the Muse Clio and of Pierus, who was the son of Magnes. Hyacinthus was so beautiful that Apollo fell in love with him, but one day while the two of them were practising throwing the discus, a gust of wind caught the discus, causing it to swerve and hit Hyacinthus on the head, killing him at once. (Some accounts relate that the discus hit a rock and rebounded.) Apollo was deeply saddened and to make the name of his friend immortal he transformed the blood which had flowed from the wound into a new flower, the 'hyacinth' (perhaps the martagon lily), of which the petals bore marks recalling either the god's cry of sorrow (Ai) or the initial of the Greek version of the young man's name. According to several authors, the one really responsible for the accident was Zephyrus, the unsuccessful rival of Apollo for Hyacinthus' affection, and it was said to be he who made the discus change direction to get his revenge on both of them. Others declare that it was the action of Boreas, who was also supposed to be in love with the beautiful Hyacinthus. The Lacedaemonian Hyacinthus, father of the Hyacinthids of whom Apollodorus speaks and who is unknown otherwise, must not be identified with the hero whom Apollo loved.

Hyades (Ὑάδες) A group of stars very close to the Pleiades whose appearance coincided with the season of spring rain (whence their name which recalls ὔειν 'to rain'. They were said to have been originally Nymphs, daughters of Atlas and an Oceanid named Aethra or Pleione. Sometimes their father was said to have been the king of Crete, Melisseus, or HYAS, or even Erechtheus, or Cadmus. Their number varies from two to seven, and their names were no less variable. The most usual seem to have been Ambrosia, Eudora, Aesyle (or Phaesyle), Coronis, Dione, Polyxo and Phaeo. Before being transformed into stars they had, as the 'Nymphs of Nysa', nursed Dionysus, but for fear of Hera they were said to have passed their nursling over to Ino and fled to Tethys, their grandmother. There they were reputedly transformed into a constellation by Zeus, but not before Medea had rejuvenated them. There was also a story which told that the death of their brother HYAS made them so sad that they committed suicide, after which they were changed into a constellation.

Hyamus (Ὕαμος) The son of LYCOREUS. He married one of Deucalion's daughters, Melantheia. By her he had a daughter, Melaenis (or sometimes Celaeno), who bore DELPHUS, after whom the Delphians were named. Hyamus was supposed to have founded the town of Hya.

Hyas (Ὕας) A son of Atlas and Pleione and brother of the PLEIADES and the HYADES. One day, while hunting in Libya, he was killed, either by a snake which bit him, or by a lion or a boar. Some of his sisters (traditions said five or seven) died of grief (or committed suicide). They were transformed into stars.

Hybris (Ὕβρις) An abstract conception, the personification of lack of restraint and of insolence. She was either the mother or possibly the daughter of Corus (Surfeit).

Hydne (Ὕδνη) The daughter of Scyllis, a native of Pallene. Both the father and daughter were skilled divers, and when Xerxes' fleet came to invade Greece they cut the anchor cables while the ships were moored, so that many were thrown on to the shore and wrecked. As a reward, the Amphictyons erected statues of them at Delphi. Hydne was also said to have been loved by the sea-god Glaucus.

Hydra of Lerna (Ὕδρα) The offspring of Typhon and Echidna (Table 32), and the monster which Heracles killed (for its description and story

and the various traditions and interpretations of early mythographers, see HERACLES). Heracles used the Hydra's blood to poison his arrows. On one occasion he wounded Chiron or another Centaur with an arrow; the Centaur then bathed in the river Anigrus in Elis and the arrow, becoming dislodged, polluted the waters, giving them a terrible smell and rendering all fish from them inedible. In some versions the Hydra's blood was also used in the so-called love philtre which Nessus gave to DEIANEIRA.

Hyettus (Ὕηττος) Supposedly the first man to have taken bloody revenge on an adulterer. He was a native of Argos and he killed Molourus, the son of Arisbas, when he caught him *in flagrante delicto* with his wife. After the murder Hyettus went into voluntary exile and found refuge with Orchomenus, Minyas' son. There he founded the village which was called after him.

Hygieia (Ὑγίεια) The personification of health. She is often said to have been a daughter of Asclepius. There are no special myths about her; she appears only in the entourage of Asclepius.

Hylaeus (Ὑλαῖος) One of the Arcadian Centaurs who tried to kidnap ATALANTA. He seriously wounded Milanion, one of her suitors, but was killed by one of Atalanta's arrows. Another tradition has it that Hylacus took part in the struggle between the Centaurs and the Lapiths and that he was not killed by Atalanta but by Theseus, or else by HERACLES as a result of a fight at Pholus' home.

Hylas (Ὕλας) Heracles, while fighting the Dryopes, killed their king, Theiodamas, and abducted his son, Hylas, a very beautiful young man with whom Heracles fell in love. Hylas accompanied him on the Argonauts' expedition. During a landing in Mysia Heracles went to cut a tree to make an oar to replace the one he had broken, and in the meantime Hylas had been asked to draw water from a spring in the forest, or from the river (or lake) Ascanius. The Nymphs, seeing his beauty, lured him away, to give him immortality. Polyphemus, who had landed with Hylas and Heracles, was the first to realize that the young man had disappeared. For a long time he called out for him in vain, as did Heracles. Meanwhile, however, the Argonauts raised anchor without waiting for their companions, perhaps on the advice of the BOREADES. Polyphemus founded on that spot the town of Cios. Heracles, suspecting that the Mysians had kidnapped Hylas, took hostages and ordered them to find the young man – this they continued to do in an annual ceremony in which the priests would march in procession towards the neighbouring mountain and call the name of Hylas three times.

Hyllus (Ὕλλος) The son of Heracles and Deianeira, at least according to the most generally accepted tradition (Table 15 and 16). Heracles was said to have given him that name because of a Lydian stream, a tributary of the Hermus, which owed its name to a giant, a son of the Earth, called Hyllus, whose skeleton had been brought to light by a flood. Heracles had encountered this stream during the time of his servitude to Omphale. However this tradition does not follow the usual chronology, because it was generally agreed that Hyllus was born well before Heracles' exile in Lydia. Some mythographers said that Hyllus was the son of Heracles and Omphale, but they were wrong. Equally wrong, and seemingly late, was the legend according to which Hyllus was the son of Heracles and Melite, a Nymph of the Phaeacians, with whom Heracles had an affair during his exile in that country after the murder of his sons (an exile usually ignored by mythographers in the traditional version). This Hyllus afterwards went at the head of a group of Phaeacians to found a settlement in Illyria, where he was killed as a result of a dispute with the local inhabitants over a herd of cattle. Hyllus gave his name to the Hylleans of Epirus. But most often it was agreed that it was Deianeira who gave birth to Hyllus, at Calydon in the early days of her marriage to HERACLES. He was already fully grown at the time of the exile to Ceyx. Heracles, as he was dying, asked him to marry IOLE and when the Heraclids had to take refuge in Attica to escape the hatred of Eurystheus, they gathered round Hyllus who (at least according to some authors) killed Eurystheus with his own hand. He then went to settle in Thebes with his grandmother (see ALCMENE). After that he tried to re-establish the children of Heracles in the Peloponnese, but because he misinterpreted a prophecy (see HERACLIDS) he died in single combat with ECHEMUS. After Heracles' death, Hyllus was adopted by AEGIMIUS, king of the Dorians, and by virtue of this he gave his name to one of the three Dorian tribes.

Hylonome (Ὑλονόμη) During the fight between the Lapiths and the Centaurs at the wedding of Pirithous, Hylonome, the wife of the Centaur Cyllarus, killed herself with the same arrow as had killed her husband, because she did not want to survive him.

Hymenaeus (Ὑμέναιος) The god who led the wedding procession. Originally he seems to have been personified in the bridal song (cf. the god IACCHUS). The stories of his origin vary: sometimes he was said to be the son of a Muse (Calliope, Clio or Urania) and Apollo; sometimes his parents were Dionysus and Aphrodite; at other times his father was said to be Magnes or Pierus. To explain how the name Hymenaeus came to be associated with marriage, several myths were concocted. For example, it was told that he was a young Athenian of such outstanding beauty that he was generally thought to be a girl. Although he was of humble birth, he fell in love with a noble Athenian girl; as he had no hope of ever marrying her, he followed her everywhere at a distance, this was the only way in which his love could find an outlet. One day the girls of noble birth went to Eleusis to offer a sacrifice to Demeter, but some pirates attacked and captured all the girls, and also Hymenaeus, whom they took for a girl. After a long voyage the pirates landed on a deserted beach. As they were tired they fell asleep, and while they were slumbering, Hymenaeus killed them all. Leaving the girls in a safe place, he went alone to Athens where he offered to return them on condition that he was given the hand of the one he loved. The bargain was concluded and the girls were returned to their families. In memory of this episode, the name of Hymenaeus was invoked at every wedding, as being a sign of good luck.

Another legend had a different explanation for the inclusion of Hymenaeus in the wedding ceremony. Hymenaeus was Magnes' son and a very skilful musician. He was singing during the wedding ceremony of Dionysus and Althaea, when he died. In order to perpetuate his memory it was decided that, in future, his name would be brought into every wedding service. Another legend similar to the preceding one told that Hymenaeus, who was very beautiful, had been loved by HESPERUS. While he was singing at the wedding of Ariadne and Dionysus, he suddenly lost his voice. In memory of him, every wedding thereafter had its 'song of Hymenaeus'. In yet another version, Hymenaeus was a very beautiful young man who died on his wedding day, thus finally linking his name with the wedding ceremony. Asclepius would, no doubt, have brought him back to life again soon afterwards. All these legends agree about the young man's beauty. He was loved by Apollo or by Thamyris or Hesperus. (In fact it was when the Evening Star rose that a marriage took place.)

The general attributes of Hymenaeus were a torch, a crown of flowers, and sometimes a flute (like those which provided music for the marriage procession).

Hymnus (Ὕμνος) A Phrygian shepherd who was in love with NICAEA, a companion Nymph of Artemis, who wanted to have nothing to do with love. In the end he decided to declare his passion to her but she was so enraged that she killed him with an arrow. The whole world wept for Hymnus, even Artemis, although she herself knew nothing of love.

Hyperboreans (Ὑπερβόρειοι). A mythical race living in a region beyond the North Wind, or the place where Boreas blew. Their legend is associated with that of Apollo. After Apollo's birth his father Zeus ordered him to go to Delphi, but the god first flew with his team of swans to the land of the Hyperboreans where he remained for some time before making his ceremonial entrance into Delphi. For 19 years he returned to this land, each time at the moment when the stars had completed another revolution in the sky and had returned to their original positions. Each night between the vernal equinox and the rising of the Pleiades he could be heard singing appropriate hymns and accompanying himself on the lyre.

After Apollo had massacred the Cyclopes, who had manufactured the thunderbolt used by Zeus to kill Apollo's son, Asclepius, Apollo hid the arrow he had reserved for revenge in the great round temple dedicated to him which had been built in the centre of the principal Hyperborean city. Some said that this arrow, which was enormous, had flown there of its own accord before forming the constellation of Sagittarius in the sky. A Hyperborean named Abasis travelled throughout the entire world borne by this arrow; he did not need to eat as this wondrous arrow provided all the nourishment which he needed.

Legend relates back to the founders of the Hyperborean race a certain number of practices connected with the cult of Apollo. Leto was supposedly born in this land and then returned to Delos to bear her own children. The sacred objects pertaining to Apollo which were venerated at Delos were said to have come from the Hyper-

borean land. On this subject there are two different traditions, both related by Herodotus. In one the sacred objects were supposedly brought to Delos, wrapped up in straw, by two young girls named Hyperoche and Laodice, who were accompanied by five men. They died at Delos where they were given divine honours. In the other version these sacred objects had been entrusted by the Hyperboreans to their neighbours the Scythians who travelled towards the west until they reached the shores of the Adriatic, and then journeyed to the south, passing from town to town. They travelled to Dodona and then to Carystos in Euboea, and eventually reached Delos via Tenos.

It was also said that two young Hyperborean girls, Arges and Opis, came to Delos at the moment of the birth of Apollo and Artemis bearing offerings to Eilithyia in order to obtain a fast and painless delivery for Leto.

It was said that the Delphic oracles had been established by a Hyperborean named Olen, who was the first prophet of Apollo; he devised the use of the hexameter in the oracles. When the Gauls attacked Delphi, various terrifying supernatural manifestations appeared to them, including two armed phantoms who were none other than the two Hyperborean heroes Hyperochus and Laodocus, whose names recall those of the two young women mentioned in the Delian legend above.

The Hyperboreans figured in the legend of Perseus, in that of Heracles (at least according to the version which situates them in the extreme north of the garden of the Hesperides). Their country was represented – particularly after the Classical period – as an ideal one with a mild climate, inhabited by people with happy temperaments – a Utopian land. There, apparently, the sun produced two crops each year; the inhabitants had civilized customs and lived in the fields and sacred groves to great ages. When the old people considered that they had had a good life they threw themselves joyously into the sea from a high cliff with their heads garlanded with flowers and found a happy end in the waves. The Hyperboreans had a knowledge of magic; they were said to be able to travel in the air and find hidden treasure. Pythagoras was said to be an incarnation of Hyperborean Apollo.

Hyperion (Ὑπερίων) One of the Titans, the son of Uranus and Gaia (Tables 5, 12 and 14). He married his sister the Titanide Theia and fathered the Sun (Helios), the Moon (Selene) and the Dawn

(Eos). Sometimes the name Hyperion was applied to the Sun himself since it means 'he who goes before' (the Earth).

Hypermestra (Ὑπερμήστρα)
1. Hypermestra or Hypermnestra was the only one of the DANAIDS who spared her husband Lynceus; because she disobeyed the orders of her father Danaus she was handed over in judgment to him, but acquitted. She left the country with her husband and subsequently had a son, Abas. Aeschylus portrayed her in a lost tragedy *The Judgment of Hypermestra*.
2. The daughter of Thestius and Eurythemis, sister of Althaea, Leda and Iphiclus (Table 24).
3. A daughter of Thespius and mother of Amphiaraus.

Hyperochus (Ὑπέροχος) Hyperochus and Ladocus were the two phantom defenders of Delphi against the Gauls (see HYPERBOREANS). The father of Oenomaus also had this name.

Hypnus (Ὕπνος) The personification of sleep. He was the son of the night and of Erebus (or perhaps the son of Astraea) and the twin of Thanatos (Death). Hypnus scarcely emerged beyond the stage of a purely abstract concept. Homer made him an inhabitant of Lemnos. Later his home became more remote; in the Underworld according to Virgil, or in the land of the Cimmerians according to Ovid, who gave a full description of his magic palace where everything was asleep. It was often claimed that he had wings, travelling fast over land and sea and lulling humans to sleep. He was the subject of only one legend: he fell in love with Endymion to whom he gave the power of sleeping with open eyes, so that he could continually watch the eyes of his lover.

Hypsicreon (Ὑψικρέων) A citizen of Miletus, as Theophrastus related, who had a friend from Naxos called Promedon. One day when the latter was visiting his friend, Neaera, the wife of the Milesian, fell in love with him. As long as her husband was present she concealed her passion, but one day, when Hypsicreon was away, Promedon came to Miletus, whereupon Neaera took the opportunity to declare her love. Promedon refused to listen to her, reminding her of her sacred duty towards a guest, but she ordered her servants to shut her up in the visitor's room, where she succeeded in getting him to agree to all her demands. The next day, Promedon was so terrified by what had happened that he returned to Naxos, but Neaera followed him. When Hypsicreon heard what had happened, he demanded his wife back. However, she took refuge at the altar of the Prytanaeum and refused to go with her husband. The Naxians advised him to persuade his wife but they forbade the use of any violence to get her away from her sanctuary. Hypsicreon considered that he had been insulted by the Naxians, so he persuaded the people of Miletus to declare war on them.

Hypsipyle (Ὑψιπύλη) The daughter of THOAS and Myrina, and through her father the grandchild of Dionysus and ARIADNE. Through her mother she was descended from Cretheus, and so from Aeolus (Table 8 and 21). Thoas was king of Lemnos. When the women of the island neglected the cult of Aphrodite, the goddess punished them by making them all smell horrible. Consequently, their husbands rejected them, seeking replacements among captives and foreigners. In revenge the women of Lemnos massacred all the men. Hypsipyle could not bring herself to kill her father, however, and on the night of the massacre, she hid him in a chest (in another version she dressed him in the regalia of the statue of Dionysus and took him down to the sea next morning, as if he were the god and she was going to purify him after the murders in the night). She launched him out to sea in this makeshift vessel and as a result THOAS was saved. Because she was the daughter of the old king, Hypsipyle was chosen to be queen by the women of Lemnos. This was at the time when the Argonauts arrived at Lemnos. According to some authors the Argonauts were given a friendly welcome; according to others, the women put up armed resistance to the landing. They softened, however, when the heroes undertook to unite with them, and in this way Hypsipyle became Jason's mistress. Then she gave the funeral games in honour of Thoas (who was officially dead) and all the massacred men of Lemnos. Hypsipyle had two sons by Jason: EUNEUS, who is mentioned in the *Iliad* and a second, sometimes called Nebrophonus (or Nephronius) and sometimes Thoas like his grandfather (Table 21).

Later, after the Argonauts had left, the women of Lemnos discovered that their queen had spared her father and they wanted to kill her because of this act of treachery, as it seemed to them, but Hypsipyle fled during the night and was kidnapped by pirates who sold her as a slave to Lycurgus, the king of the Spartans. She was ordered by him to look after his son, the young Opheltes. The Seven Chiefs passed through and asked her where they could get a drink of water. For a moment she abandoned her guardianship of the child, who was immediately suffocated by an enormous serpent (see ARCHEMORUS and AMPHIARAUS). In his anger Lycurgus wanted to put Hypsipyle to death. In the meantime, Hypsipyle's two sons Euneus and Thoas the younger arrived, both trying to find their mother. Amphiaraus, one of the seven, recognized them because of the gold vine branch which the young men were wearing, which had earlier been given by Dionysus to Thoas, their grandfather. Further, Amphiaraus appeased Lycurgus' wife Eurydice and obtained her agreement for Hypsipyle to return to Lemnos with her sons. This theme was used by Euripides in his tragedy of *Hypsipyle*, part of which is lost. As an explanation of how Hypsipyle came to be separated from her children, Euripides supposed that they had sailed off with the Argonauts when their father had departed, a year after they were born (they were twins). Subsequently they had been taken to Thrace by Orpheus, who had brought them up. It was there that they had found their grandfather, Thoas. These romantic stories obviously are not part of the early legend but are literary inventions of secondary origin.

Hyrieus (Ὑριεύς) The father of Nycteus and Lycus and, according to some traditions, of Orion, and the son of Poseidon and the Pleiad Alcyone. He was the founder of Hyria in Boeotia which he ruled. His wife was the Nymph Clonia (Table 25). His legends, which are late, depict him as an old labourer. He entertained Zeus, Poseidon and Hermes once in his cottage. When they offered to fulfil a wish as a reward, he asked them for a son. The gods gave him one, which they fathered by urinating in the skin of the bull which the old man had sacrificed in their honour. This son was ORION. Some stories claim that it was for Hyrieus that Trophonius and Agamedes built the celebrated treasury which was responsible for their death.

Hyrnetho (Ὑρνηθώ) The daughter of Temenus and wife of DEIPHONTES (Table 6). She was the heroine of a lost tragedy of Euripides, the *Temerides*.

I

Iacchus (Ἴακχος) The god who guided the initiated in the mysteries of Eleusis. 'Iacche' was the ritual cry uttered by the faithful; this cry simply became a name which was given to a god. Traditions vary as to his actual personality, but very broadly, Iacchus, whose name recalls Bacchus, one of Dionysus' names, may be considered to be the go-between of the goddesses of Eleusis and Dionysus. Sometimes he is said to have been DEMETER'S son, who accompanied his mother when she was looking for Persephone. It was he who, by his laughter at the action of the god BAUBO, was said to have cheered her up. But Iacchus was more often regarded as the son of Persephone than of Demeter, in which case he was the reborn ZAGREUS, Persephone's son by Zeus. Hera was jealous of her husband's affairs and, because she could not take revenge herself on him, she incited the Titans to attack young Zagreus while he was playing. Zagreus tried to hide by transforming himself into several different identities, but when he turned himself into a bull his pursuers finally caught him and tore him to pieces. They put his remains into a cauldron and started to cook him. Zeus hurried to help his son but was too late. He killed the criminal Titans with a flash of lightning and ordered Apollo to gather together the scattered pieces of his son. Athena brought him his heart which was still beating. He consumed it and restored Zagreus to life and called him Iacchus.

Some stories made Iacchus Demeter's husband, others the son of Dionysus, born in Phrygia by the Nymph AURA. She in fact had twins by the god, but in her madness she ate one. The other baby, Iacchus, was saved by another Nymph who was loved by the god. She entrusted the baby to the Bacchantes of Eleusis who brought him up. Athena is said to have breast-fed him. Aura in the meantime threw herself into the river Sangarius which turned into a fountain. Sometimes Iacchus and Bacchus were said to be the same person but there is no explanation for their dual nature. Iacchus is depicted in art as a child scarcely adolescent carrying a torch and dancing, and leading the procession of Eleusis.

Iaera (Ἴαιρα) A Nereid. According to Virgil, Iaera was also the name of a Phrygian Dryad from Ida. She bore Alcanor twins, Pandarus and Bitias, who are mentioned among the companions of Aeneas.

Ialemus (Ἰάλεμος) The son of Apollo and Calliope. He was the brother of Hymenaeus and ORPHEUS (according to one version of the latter's story). Just as Hymenaeus is the personification of the marriage anthems, so Ialemus is the personification of the funeral dirge, expressing grief at the death of young people. He is said to have invented this sort of lament. Sometimes he was identified with Linus who died young and about whom this sort of lament was sung.

Ialmenus (Ἰάλμενος) With his brother Ascalaphus a son of Ares. Their mother was Astyoche, the daughter of Actor (Table 33). They were kings of Orchomenus in Boeotia. During their reign the Minyans took part in the expedition against Troy with a force numbering thirty ships. After the capture of Troy, Ialmenus sailed not to his own country but to the coast of the Euxine Sea where he founded an Achaean settlement whose inhabitants, at the time of Strabo, still claimed Orchomenus as their mother city. Ialmenus and his brother were also numbered among the Argonauts. Furthermore, the former was one of HELEN'S suitors and it was because of their communal oath that he had to take part in the war to win her back.

Ialysus (Ἰάλυσος) The eponymous hero of the city of Ialysus in Rhodes. Through his father CERCAPHUS he was descended from the Sun (Helios) and the Nymph Rhode. He married Dotis by whom he had a daughter called Syme, who gave her name to the island between Rhodes and Cnidus.

Iambe (Ἰάμβη) The daughter of Pan and the Nymph Echo. She was a servant at Eleusis in the house of Celeus and Metanira, at the time when Demeter passed through on her search for Persephone. Iambe received her and her jokes amused Demeter. This role was sometimes assigned to BAUBO rather than Iambe.

Iamus (Ἴαμος) An Olympian hero, the mythical founder of the priestly family of the Iamids. His divine ancestry was as follows. Pitane, the daughter of the river-god Eurotas, bore Poseidon a daughter EVADNE, who was brought up by her human 'father' AEPYTUS. Apollo fell in love with Evadne, who bore him a son. Since she was ashamed of having been seduced, Evadne abandoned her child. However, two snakes came and fed the child with honey. One day Evadne found him miraculously safe and sleeping in the middle of some flowering violets. So she called him Iamus (the 'child of the violets'). Aepytus then questioned the oracle of Delphi who replied that little Iamus would be a famous prophet and the founder of a long line of priests and prophets. When he was an adult, Iamus went one night to the banks of the Alpheus and invoked his father Apollo and his grandfather Poseidon. Apollo answered his call and told him to follow the sound of his voice. Apollo then led him to the site of Olympus and told him to settle there and wait for Heracles to come and found the games which would later become famous. Apollo also taught him to understand the language of birds and to interpret the omens from sacrificial victims.

Ianiscus (Ἰάνισκος)
1. According to some traditions a son of Asclepius and therefore the brother of Machaon and Podalirius. He was a native of Thessaly from the area of the Perrhebes.
2. There was another Ianiscus who was descended from the Athenian Clytius. The latter had a daughter called Pheno, whom he gave in marriage to Lamedon, the king of Sicyon. Later, when ADRASTUS, one of Lamedon's successors, abdicated, Ianiscus, who came from Attica, was invited to become king. When he died he was succeeded by PHAESTUS.

Ianthe (Ἰάνθη)
1. One of the Oceanids, 'daughter of the violets'.
2. It was also the name of a Cretan heroine who was the wife of IPHIS.

Iapetus (Ἰαπετός) One of the Titans, the son of Uranus (the sky) and Gaia (the earth) (Table 5). He therefore belonged to the first generation of divinities and was one of the elder brothers of Cronus. According to Hesiod he married Clymene, one of the daughters of Oceanus and Tethys, by whom he had four children, Atlas, Menoetius, Prometheus and Epimetheus. Through Prometheus, Deucalion, father of mankind, was connected with him (Table 38) after the worldwide flood. Other legends say that his wife was Asia, another of the daughters of Oceanus, others maintained that his wife was Asopis, a daughter of Asopus and granddaughter of Oceanus or even Libya. Together with the other Titans he was thrown down into Tartarus by Zeus.

Iapyx (Ἰάπυξ) The hero whose name was adopted by the Iapyges in southern Italy. There are various stories about his origin. Some claimed that he was the son of Lycaon and the brother of Daunus (or Daunius) and Peucetius. Others said that he was a Cretan, the son of DAEDALUS and a Cretan wife, and that he went to Sicily and then southern Italy as a result of the events which followed the death of MINOS. Iapyx was said to have been the leader of the Cretans who had followed Minos; after the latter's death they tried unsuccessfully to return to Crete. They were caught in a storm and forced to land in the Tarentum district, where they established themselves. A variation of this story simply said that Iapyx was a Cretan who was the brother of ICADIUS. He went to southern Italy whereas his brother was carried off by a dolphin to the foot of Mount Parnassus, where he founded Delphi.

Iarbas (Ἰάρβας) A native African king. He was a son of Jupiter Ammon and a Nymph from the country of the Garamantes. He reigned over the Gaetuli. He granted DIDO the land on which she founded Carthage, but being in love with the queen and jealous of Aeneas he attacked the new city after Dido's death and drove out Dido's sister ANNA.

Iardanus (Ἰάρδανος) Sometimes called Iardanas, a king of Lydia, the father of Omphale. One tradition has it that he was a magician who by his spells caused Camblites or Cambles to eat his own wife by making him insatiably hungry.

Iasion (Ἰασίων) A son of Zeus and Electra (Tables 7 and 25). Through his mother he was a descendant of Atlas. He lived with his brother, Dardanus, in Samothrace, though some legends said that he was a Cretan. A common thread in all these legends was his love for Demeter, but sometimes this love was unrequited, so he tried to hurt the goddess (or perhaps an image of her, see IXION). This at once aroused Zeus' anger and he killed him with a thunderbolt. It was more often claimed that this love was mutual, however, and that Iasion united with Demeter on a strip of fallow land which had been ploughed three times. She bore a son, Plutus (Wealth), who went round the world spreading abundance everywhere. Diodorus claimed that Iasion was the brother not only of Dardanus but also of Harmonia. Zeus taught him the secrets of the island, which he passed on to numerous heroes. After his sister had married Cadmus he met Demeter, who was attracted to him and gave him wheat-seed. Later Iasion married Cybele by whom he had a son called Corybas, eponym of the Corybantes.

Iaso (Ἰασώ) The healer, said to be a daughter of Asclepius, the god of medicine, and a sister of Hygieia. Her sanctuary was at Oropus.

Iasus (Ἴασος) Or Iasius, a name given to a number of heroes.
1. One of them was the king of Argos, but legend does not agree about his father's name. In some accounts Iasus was one of the sons of Triopas (Table 17); in others he was the son of Argos and grandson of Agenor, the father of Io, the lover of Zeus. In the legend which made him the son of Triopas he shared the Peloponnesian territory with his brothers. His share was in the west and included Elis. Pelasgus had land in the east and founded Larissa. However, Agenor inherited his father's cavalry, and with its help he wasted no time in driving out his two brothers.
2. Another Iasus was a son of King Lycurgus (Table 26). He belonged to the Arcadian dynasty since he was the grandson of Arcas. His daughter was ATALANTA.
3. The same name belonged to a Boeotian who was the father of Amphion, king of Orchomenus. He was married to Persephone, the daughter of Minyas.
4. Finally, Iasus or Iasius was often used instead of the name IASION.

Icadius (Ἰκάδιος) The son of Apollo and the Nymph Lycia. Born in Asia, he gave his mother's name, Lycia, to the place of his birth. He there founded the town of Patara where he set up Apollo's oracle. Later he sailed for Italy but was shipwrecked. A dolphin carried him to the foot of Mount Parnassus where he founded a town which he called Delphi in memory of the dolphin (in Greek δελφίς). It was also said that this Icadius was a Cretan and a brother of Iapyx who gave his name to the Iapyges.

Icarius (Ἰκάριος)
1. The first hero with this name was an Athenian, the father of ERIGONE, who was said to have spread vines throughout Greece during the reign of King Pandion.
2. Another Icarius was said to be the son of Perieres and thus a descendant of the hero Lacedaemon. Alternatively, Oebalus was his father, Perieres his grandfather and Aeolus his great-grandfather. Icarius and Tyndareus, his brother, had a half-brother Hippocoon, the result of their father's affair with a Nymph Batieia. With the help of his sons Hippocoon drove them out of Sparta. They took refuge in Pleuron near Thestius and stayed there until HERACLES killed Hippocoon and his sons (see also CEPHEUS). Tyndareus then returned to Sparta and resumed power, while Icarius stayed in Acarnania, where he married Polycasta, a daughter of Lygaeus, by whom he had three children: a daughter, Penelope, and two sons, Alyzeus and Leucadius, who gave his name to the island of Leucadia. Another version says that Icarius returned to Sparta with his brother and that he married Periboea, a Naiad, who bore five sons: Thoas, Damasippus, Imeusimus, Aletes, Perileus and a daughter, Penelope (Table 19). It is said that Icarius offered his daughter as the prize in a race which he organized for her suitors, and Odysseus was the winner. It is also said that Helen's father and Penelope's uncle Tyndareus made this marriage: Odysseus suggested that the suitors be made to swear on oath not to fight once Helen had made her choice, and Tyndareus, grateful for the good advice, obtained his niece's hand for the wily hero. After the marriage Icarius asked Odysseus to settle near to him with his wife, but Odysseus refused. Icarius continued to press, however, so Odysseus asked Penelope to choose between her father and her husband. Penelope remained silent and blushed, and for modesty she covered her face with her veil. Icarius understood that his daughter had made her choice, so he withdrew and built a sanctuary to Modesty on the site of this incident.
   A Spartan tradition claimed that Icarius turned against his brother TYNDAREUS by taking sides with Hippocoon. By raising a revolution he helped

Hippocoon to expel Tyndareus from Sparta. As a result Tyndareus was said to have taken refuge in Pellene.

Icarus (Ἴκαρος) The son of Daedalus and one of Minos' slaves called Naucrates. When Daedalus explained to ARIADNE how Theseus could find his way out of the labyrinth, and Theseus killed the Minotaur, Minos was angry, so he shut Daedalus and his son in the labyrinth. Daedalus still had something in reserve: he made sets of wings for Icarus and himself, and fixed them to their shoulders with wax; they then both took flight. Before taking off, Daedalus had adviced Icarus not to fly too near the ground or too high in the sky. Icarus was full of pride and did not listen to his father's advice. He flew upwards so near to the sun that the wax melted and the foolish youth was cast into the sea, which was thereafter called the Sea of Icarus (it surrounds the island of Samos). According to another version, after killing his nephew and pupil Talus, DAEDALUS flew from Athens. At the same time his son Icarus was banished and set out to find his father. However he was ship-wrecked and drowned off Samos and the sea was given his name. His body was washed ashore on the island of Icaria where he was buried by Heracles. It is also related that Icarus and Daedalus fled from Crete by sailing boat. Each had his own boat and Daedalus had just invented the use of sails. Icarus, however, did not know how to control his sails and he capsized. Another version states that as he was approaching Icaria he jumped clumsily from his boat and was drowned. Icarus' tomb could be seen on a headland in the Aegean. Daedalus was also said to have erected two pillars, one in honour of his son and the other bearing his own name. These were in the Amber islands. Also, on the doors of the temple of Cumae, which he dedicated to Apollo, he was said to have por-trayed with his own hands the sad fate of his son. Icarus is occasionally said to have invented wood-work and carpentry.

There was a legend about another Icarus who was king of Caria. His lover was THEONOE, Thestor's daughter and Calchas' sister.

Ichthyocentaurs (Ἰχθυοκένταυροι) Fish Cen-, taurs, maritime creatures which seem to have had no place in local myth. However, they were quite widely depicted in Hellenistic and Roman plastic art. The body down to the waist had a human form like that of the Centaurs; however the lower part was shaped like a fish. These creatures often had lion's feet. They appear in processions of sea-gods alongside hippocampi and sea-horses.

Icmalius (Ἰκμάλιος) A craftsman of Ithaca who made Penelope's couch, which he decorated with ivory and silver.

Ida (Ἴδη)
1. One of Melisseus' daughters, who with her sister Adrastea fed the baby Zeus in Crete. Her name was also that of a mountain in Crete where ZEUS spent his childhood (see also AMALTHEA).
2. Ida was also a daughter of Corybas. She married Lycastus, the king of Crete, and bore him a son called Minos the Younger.

Idaea (Ἰδαία) This is a name which means 'she who comes from Ida' or 'she who lives on Ida'. Several heroines have the name, including:
1. A Nymph who from her union with the river-god Scamander gave birth to Teucer, the king of the Teucrians on the coast of Asia Minor opposite Samothrace (Table 7).
2. One of the daughters of Dardanus and so a great-granddaughter of the preceding Idaea. She married Phineus, the king of Thrace, as his second wife. She was responsible for the misfortunes that fell on PHINEUS by her slandering of the children of his first wife, Cleopatra, the daughter of Boreas (see BOREADES).

Idaeus (Ἰδαῖος) The name of several heroes con-nected either with Ida in Crete or with the Troad. People known to have this name were:
1. One of Priam's sons.
2. A son of Paris and Helen.
3. One of Priam's chariot-drivers.
4. A son of Dares, a Trojan hero.
5. One of the Corybantes.
6. In an obscure verions of the legend of Dardanus, he had two sons by Chryse, Dimas and Idaeus. The latter settled on the Phrygian coast at the foot of the mountain which was to be called Ida after him. He introduced to that country the cult of CYBELE, the Mother of the Gods.

Idas (Ἴδας) According to the *Iliad*, the strongest and bravest man and, through his father, Aphareus, a member of Perieres' family. His mother was Arena, a daughter of Oebalus. He had two brothers, Lynceus and Pisus (Table 19). Idas was a cousin of the Dioscuri as well as the Leucip-pides, Hilaera and Phoebe, and Penelope. Idas and Lynceus sailed with Jason and the Argonauts.

During the voyage, Idas played a special part on two occasions. When they were with King Lycus and the Mariandyni, the soothsayer Idmon was killed by a boar. Idas took revenge for the death of his companion by killing the boar. Then he tried unsuccessfully to seize the kingdom of Teuthras, the king of Mysia. He was defeated by TELEPHUS (see also AUGE). Idas and Lynceus both appear among the hunters of the boar of Calydon, Idas as father-in-law of Meleager (who had married his daughter, Cleopatra Alcyone).

Idas abducted Marpessa, the daughter of Evenus, Ares' son, on a winged chariot given to him by Poseidon. EVENUS pursued him but could not catch him and so committed suicide. Idas returned without difficulty to his native Messenia. APOLLO, however, was in love with Marpessa and wanted to steal her from her husband. When Idas defended himself and threatened the god, Zeus intervened, separated the two combatants and gave the girl the choice of loving which of the two she desired. Marpessa chose Idas. Another slightly different legend said that Apollo stole Marpessa from her husband and held her for some time and she did not protest. The kidnapping of Marpessa by Idas was sometimes replaced in the legend by a chariot race in which the girl was the prize (cf. PENELOPE and HIPPODAMIA). Evenus, who won, killed the other contestants.

Idas was also well known for his struggle with his cousins Castor and Pollux. This conflict fell into two distinct episodes, at times separate, at others more or less firmly connected. Castor and Pollux had organized a raid on Arcadia, with Idas and Lynceus, in which they stole some flocks. The division of the spoils was entrusted to Idas. He killed a bull and divided it into four pieces and decided that whoever was the first to eat his portion should have half the carcass; the second to finish should have the rest. Then he immediately ate his part of the bull and also, without delay, that of his brother. So he took possession of all the booty. In annoyance, the Dioscuri attacked Messenia, their cousins' country, and carried off the cattle which were the cause of the trouble and many more besides. They then set up an ambush, waiting for Idas and his brother. The latter saw Castor hidden in the crack of an old chestnut tree. He pointed him out to Idas who killed him with a spear. Pollux chased them and killed Lynceus but Idas attacked him with a large stone said to have been taken from the tomb of Aphareus, his father, and rendered him unconscious. Zeus came to the aid of his son, killed Idas with a thunderbolt and

took Pollux up to the sky. The other episode in the contest was related to the abduction of the Leucippidae. Lynceus and Idas were engaged to their cousins Hilaera and Phoebe, who were daughters of Leucippus, but the DIOSCURI kidnapped the girls. Idas and Lynceus decided to take revenge. Lynceus killed Castor and was in turn killed by Pollux. Idas was about to kill Pollux when Zeus put an end to the fight in the same way as in the previous incident. Other versions have different accounts of the fight. Castor and Lynceus decided to settle the problem by single combat. Castor won and killed his adversary. Idas wanted to avenge his brother and was on the point of felling Castor when he was killed by a thunderbolt from Zeus. Pollux played no part in this version. Hyginus said that Lynceus was killed by Castor and that, as Idas wanted to bury him, Castor tried to stop him on the pretext that Lynceus had not shown courage in the fight and that he 'died like a woman'. Enraged, Idas snatched the sword which Castor had in his belt and struck him in the groin. In another account he attacked him under the column which he was building on Lynceus' tomb and was in turn quickly killed by Pollux.

Idmon (Ἴδμων) One of the Argonauts, the soothsayer whose duty was to interpret the forecasts for the expedition. He is said to have been a son of Apollo, but his mortal father was Abas, the son of Melampus (Table 1). His mother was Asteria or Cyrene. Sometimes Idmon was identified as Thestor, the son of Apollo and Laothoe, and the father of Calchas. Idmon would thus be only an epithet of the root meaning 'to see'. In fact Idmon means 'the man with second sight'. His adventures with the ARGONAUTS were told in different ways. Some accounts agreed that he reached Colchis; others said that he was killed by a boar during a landing in the territory of the Mariandyni. Idmon had foreseen his own death but nevertheless had not hesitated to join the expedition.

Idomeneus (Ἰδομενεύς) A king of Crete, the son of Deucalion and grandson of Minos (Table 28). He was a half-brother of Molus, who was a son of Deucalion and a concubine. Molus was the father of his brother-in-arms MERION, of whom Idomeneus was thus uncle. Idomeneus was one of the suitors of Helen. Bound by the common oath, he had to take part in the Trojan war, where he stood out among the heroes of the first order. He was in command of the Cretan contingent with 80 ships from the towns of: Cnossos, Gortyn, Lyctus, Lycastus, Phaestus and Rhytion. He was one of the nine leaders who volunteered to fight Hector in single combat when it was thought that this was the way to settle the quarrel between the Trojans and the Achaeans. He killed numerous adversaries on the battlefield; he was outstanding in his defence of the ships. His main opponent was Deiphobus and then he faced Aeneas in combat. During the fight round the body of Patroclus he intended to attack Hector but he fled when the latter, charging towards him, killed Coeranus, Merion's charioteer. Idomeneus sought safety in the camp. After the adventures described in the *Iliad*, Idomeneus won a victory in the boxing at the funeral games for Achilles. He was one of the heroes who entered the town in the wooden horse and was one of the judges who had to dispose of Achilles' arms.

Among the homecomings related in the *Odyssey*, that of Idomeneus was one of the happiest. Although his tomb was said to be in Crete, his legend includes a number of dramatic events marking the end of his life which suggest otherwise.

An early story tells how Meda, his wife, was influenced by Nauplius to yield to the love of Leucus. Leucus was a son of Talus who had been abandoned at birth but had been brought up by Idomeneus; the latter had entrusted Leucus with the safekeeping of his house during his absence. Then Leucus killed Meda, and also the daughter of Idomeneus and Meda, called Clisithera, who was sometimes said to have had two sons, Iphiclus and Lycus. When he got back, Idomeneus was said to have blinded Leucus and regained his throne, but other versions say that Leucus harried and drove him into exile. Yet another version said that, during the voyage from Troy to Crete, Idomeneus' fleet was struck by a storm. The king swore to sacrifice the first human being he met in his kingdom if he returned safely, but the first person he saw as he approached the harbour was his son. True to his oath, Idomeneus sacrificed him, though some authors maintain that he only pretended to commit the sacrifice. A plague soon broke out which spread throughout Crete and, to appease the gods, Idomeneus was banished because his cruelty had caused the god's anger. Idomeneus went to southern Italy where he established himself in Salentinum and built a temple dedicated to Athena. There was also the following story about Idomeneus. Thetis and Medea were quarrelling about the prize for beauty. They asked Idomeneus to be the umpire. He decided in favour of Thetis. This made Medea angry. She said 'all Cretans were liars' and cursed the race of Idomeneus, condemning it to never telling the truth. That was the start of the proverb 'All Cretans are liars'.

Idothea (Εἰδοθέα) Several heroines had this name.
1. One of them was the daughter of Proteus. She advised Menelaus to question her father, in Egypt.
2. Another was the daughter of Eurytus, king of Caria and the wife of Miletus who founded the town of Miletus. She was the mother of CAUNUS and Byblis.
3. It was also the name of the second wife of the blind King Phineus. She was the sister of Cadmus. For her hatred of her stepsons and her punishment, see PHINEUS. Phineus' second wife was sometimes called Eurytia or Idaea, not Idothea.

Idyia (Ἰδυῖα) An Oceanid who was the second wife of AEETES, king of Colchis, and the mother of Medea. Generally she was also regarded as the mother of Apsyrtus. However, in some versions she was said to be Aeetes' first wife and so the mother of both his children.

Ieoud (Ἰεούδ) In a Phoenician legend he was the eldest or perhaps the only son of Cronus. A Nymph called Anobret was his mother. During a war, which was devastating the country, Cronus dressed his son in royal regalia and sacrificed him.

Ilia (Ἰλία) The name frequently given to Rhea Silvia, the mother of Romulus and Remus. Some ancient mythographers have made efforts, in the various versions of the story of the foundation of Rome, to distinguish between those where the mother of Romulus was called RHEA and others calling her Ilia , that is, the Trojan woman, wife of Ilion. The name Ilia was reserved for the legends in which the mother of Romulus was the daughter of Aeneas and Lavinia. The legend remained the same whatever the heredity. Rhea/Ilia was always loved by Mars, who was the father of the twins; and Amulius, king of Alba, who condemned her to be a Vestal Virgin because he was frightened of the children which she might have if she married, either kept her prisoner, or even had her thrown into the Tiber. It was also said that the river-god caused her to be made divine and married her.

Ilione (Ἰλιόνη) The beloved daughter of Priam and Hecuba. She married POLYMESTOR (see also DEIPYLUS).

Ilioneus (Ἰλιονεύς)
1. The youngest son of Niobe and Amphion.
2. The son of the Trojan Phorbas.
3. A companion of Aeneas.
4. An old Trojan who was killed by Diomedes during the sack of the city.

Illyrius (Ἰλλύριος) The youngest son of Cadmus and Harmonia. He was born during their expedition against the Illyrians. It is from him that the country got its name (see also GALATEA).

Ilus (Ἶλος) This name occurs twice in the Trojan royal family.
1. The first hero with this name was one of Dardanus' four children (Table 7). He died without issue.
2. The name reappeared two generations later carried by one of the four children of Tros and Callirhoe (Table 7): they were Cleopatra, Ilus, Assaracus and Ganymede. Ilus married Eurydice who was said by Apollodorus to be a daughter of Adrastus. He had one son, Laomedon, who himself had five sons among whom was Podarces called Priam, and three daughters of whom one was Hesione. Besides Laomedon, Ilus had a daughter, Themiste, who married Capys (son of Assaracus), and as a result was the grandmother of Aeneas. It was this Ilus who was the common ancestor of the family of Priam. He founded the town of Troy (Ilion) in the following circumstances; being a native of the Troad he had gone to Phrygia to take part in some games which the king of that country had organized. He won the prize which consisted of fifty young slaves of each sex. The king, under guidance of an oracle, added a dappled cow and advised Ilus to follow the cow and to found a city in the place where it stopped. The cow went north, and stopped on the so-called Hill of Ate in Phrygia. ATE had fallen there when Zeus threw her out of the sky. Ilus built a town there which he called Ilion (the future Troy). This town was set in the valley of the Scamander not far from Dardanus, the town on Mount Ida founded by Dardanus.

Some time after the foundation of Ilion, Zeus, at the request of Ilus, sent a sign to witness his goodwill and to confirm the choice of the site. One morning Ilus found outside his tent a statue, the PALLADIUM, which had miraculously fallen from the sky. It was three cubits high and its feet were joined together; a spear was in its right hand, a spindle and distaff in its left. It was the image of the goddess Pallas Athena. Ilus built a temple to shelter the statue; this was the great temple of Athena at Troy. According to other accounts the statue fell on the roof of the temple before it was finished and took the central position for itself. Another version maintains that during a fire in the temple Ilus saved the statue by removing it from the flames. However, in the process he was struck blind because it was forbidden to look upon this divine likeness. Nevertheless, Athena yielded to his prayers and restored his sight because his sacrilege had been justified.

According to some authors Ilus fought against Tantalus and Pelops because of their abduction of Ganymede, and had them banished.
3. A third Ilus was mentioned in the *Odyssey* as being a member of Jason's family. He was generally said to be the son of Mermerus and the grandson of Pheres II who was himself a son of Jason and Medea. In this version of the legend, Mermerus and Pheres are no longer the two sons of MEDEA, who were killed by her (or the Corinthians) after the murder of Glauce (see also JASON and Table 21).

This Ilus reigned at Ephyra. From his ancestor Medea he inherited knowledge of deadly poisons. Before he set off for Troy, Odysseus went to ask him for a poison in which to dip his arrowheads to make them more lethal, but Ilus, for fear of the divine laws, refused to give it to him.

Imbrasus (Ἴμβρασος)
1. A river on the island of Samos of which the eponymous god was the son of Apollo and the Nymph Ocyrrhoe.
2. It was also the name of a Thracian chief whose son Pirous played a part in the *Iliad*.

Inachus (Ἴναχος) A river-god of the Argolid. It was said that at one time he was king of Argos and that by Melia – a daughter of Oceanus – he had two sons, Phoroneus and Aegialeus (Table 17). He was a son of Oceanus and Tethys. According to the Argives he lived before the beginning of the human era and his son Phoroneus was the first man. Other legends claim that he was a contemporary of ERICHTHONIUS and EUMOLPUS. Alternatively, he supposedly gathered together people after the Deucalion flood and resettled them in the valley of the river, which was given his name in gratitude for his action. When Hera and Poseidon quarrelled over the overlordship of the country, Inachus was chosen as arbitrator together with Cephisus and Asterion. His decision was in favour of Hera. Poseidon was angry and cursed him so thoroughly that Inachus' river-bed became completely dry during the whole summer and did not start to fill until the autumn rains came. Inachus or his son Phoroneus built the first temple to Hera in Argos.

Besides his sons Phoroneus and Aegialeus it is said that Inachus had a daughter, Mycenae, who gave her name to the town. Sometimes he is also said to have had two other sons, Argos and Pelasgus (Table 17 gives their more usual family tree), and also Casus (see AMYCE). More often (and this was the version favoured by the tragedians) he is said to have been the father of IO, who was alternatively regarded as the daughter of Iasus. Her adventures caused him great unhappiness. It is said that he even tried to pursue Zeus, who had raped her. Zeus sent Tisiphone, one of the Fates, against him. She tormented him so much that he threw himself into the river which up till then had been called Haliacmon. Thereafter the river was called Inachus. Another version says that Zeus struck him with thunder which caused the river-bed to dry up.

Incubi The devils of Roman folklore who were said to come out at night to sit on the chests of sleeping people, by which means they caused the sleepers to have nightmares. Sometimes they were said to have intercourse with sleeping women.

Indigetes An extremely numerous type of deity at Rome. They comprised those whose function was limited to the performance of a specific act and normally did not exist apart from that act. Thus among them there were powers which accompanied the human being from birth (and even from conception) until death, from Consevius (the god of conception) to Nenia (the goddess of mourning at the funeral). There was the goddess who taught children how to walk; Abeona, who directed a child's first steps away from its parents' home; Adeona who led it back home; and Potina, the goddess who made it drink. Similarly, there was a whole series of rural gods who watched over the different stages of growing and vegetation, including Segetia (from *Segetes* meaning harvests) and Lactarius who caused the 'milk' to rise in the ears of growing corn. Some of these deities, like FLORA and PROSERPINA, gradually

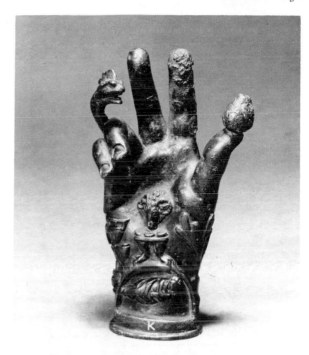

Bronze magical hand embellished with religious charms to increase its power and avert the evil eye. Late Roman period. London, British Museum.

acquired a more specific personality under the influence of Greek mythology.

Others of the Indigetes had specific domains: Janus belonged to doors, Clivicola to sloping streets, and Cardea to door hinges. There were divinities of this sort everywhere: in kitchens, prisons and other places as well. Some were detailed to see that travellers did not lose their way. With these Indigetes we are close to the 'magic mentality' which supposes a supernatural presence in everything we do.

Indus (Ἰνδός)
1. The hero after whom India was named. He was the son of Earth, who was said to have been killed by Zeus, but that was a late legend. Similarly the legend which made the same man the husband of the Nymph Calauria, and would make him the father of the river Ganges (see AEGYPTUS and NILUS), is a modern version.
2. Another Indus was a very handsome young Indian who raped the daughter of King Oxyalces and escaped punishment by throwing himself into the river Mausolus which was thereafter called the Indus.

3.   Hyginus says that a king of Scythia called Indus invented silver, whose use was said to have been introduced into Greece by Erechtheus.

Ino (Ἰνώ) See LEUCOTHEA.

Io (Ἰώ) A young Argive girl, a priestess of Hera of Argos, with whom Zeus was in love. Traditions about the name of her father varied, but all agreed that she was a princess of the royal family of Argos and a descendant of Inachus, the son of Oceanus. Some said that her father was Iasus (Table 1); others (and this was the story which the tragedians preferred) that he was Inachus, the river-god himself. Alternatively her father was said to have been Piren (probably the brother of Bellerophon, in which case Io would have been a member of the Corinthian royal family). If she was a daughter of Inachus, her mother was Melia. If her father was Iasus, Leucane was her mother.

Zeus' love for Io was either due to her beauty or to the spells of Iynx, one of Echo's daughters. It was said that in a dream told Io was told to go to the Lernean lake and to surrender to the embraces of Zeus. Io told her father about her dream. He consulted the oracles of Dodona and Delphi. Both told him to obey if he did not want himself and his whole family to be struck by a thunderbolt. Zeus started an affair with the girl and Hera soon became suspicious. Accordingly, to save Io from his wife's jealousy, Zeus transformed her into an exceptionally white heifer. He swore to Hera that he had never loved this animal. Hera demanded that he should give her the heifer. So Io found herself consecrated to her rival who put Argus of the hundred eyes, one of her relatives, in charge of her.

This was the start of Io's trials. She wandered to Mycenae and then to Euboea. Everywhere she went the earth produced new plants for her. Zeus was sorry for his love (it is said that he sometimes went to visit her in the shape of a bull) and he ordered Hermes to help her escape from her gaoler. With one flash of his magic bracelet Hermes put fifty of Argus' eyes to sleep while the other fifty were having their normal sleep. He then killed him with his javelin. The death of Argus was of no avail to Io, for Hera sent a horsefly to torment her. The insect stuck to her flanks and made her mad. Io set off across Greece. She began by going along the coast of the gulf which became known as the Ionian gulf. She crossed the sea at the strait which divides Europe from Asia and she gave this strait the name Bosphorus ('cow cros-

sing'). In Asia her wanderings continued and she finally arrived in Egypt where she was well received and bore the son of whom Zeus was the father, EPAPHUS, who was said to be the founder of a race (Table 3) which included the Danaides. She resumed her original form and, after a final attempt to find her son, who had on Hera's orders been abducted by the Curetes, she returned to rule in Egypt, where, under the name of Isis, she was worshipped.

Historians in antiquity tried to interpret the legend in historical terms and concluded that Io was a daughter of King Inachus and that she had been abducted by Phoenician pirates who took her to Egypt. Some say that she was the mistress of the captain of the Phoenician ship and went willingly. It is also said that after she was abducted by pirates, Io was taken to Egypt where she was bought by the king who in recompense sent a bull to Inachus led by ambassadors. By the time they reached Greece, Inachus was dead. The ambassadors did not know what to do with the bull, so they exhibited it for an entrance fee to the local people, who had never seen one before. After her life on earth, Io became a constellation. The underlying source of these stories of Io and her family tree was an epic, the *Danais* which has been lost.

Iobates (Ἰοβάτης) A king of Lycia who played an important part in the legends of Acrisius and of Bellerophon. ACRISIUS drove his twin brother Proetus from the kingdom of Argos. Proetus took refuge in Lycia near Iobates, who gave him his daughter Anteia (also called STHENBOEA) in marriage, and organized an expedition with Proetus to help him to regain his kingdom. Thus Acrisius ruled in Argos and Proetus in Tiryns. However, Proetus, suspecting that BELLEROPHON, who was then living in Tiryns, wanted to seduce his wife, sent him to Iobates with a secret request to put him to death. Bellerophon easily withstood the trials set up by the king however, and married Iobates' second daughter called either Philonoe, Cassandra, Alcimene or Anticleia. When Iobates died he bequeathed his kingdom to Bellerophon.

Iobes (Ἰόβης) One of Heracles' sons whose mother was Certhe, one of the daughters of Thespius.

Iocastus (Ἰόκαστος) A son of Aeolus who ruled in Italy. He was said to have founded Rhegium in Calabria; nevertheless another tradition recorded that it was founded by the people of Chalcis who were driven from their own country by famine and set themselves up 'near the tomb of Iocastus', more exactly at a place which fulfilled an oracle's forecast, where there was a woman embracing a man, that is, a vine climbing a green oak. Iocastus was killed by a snake bite.

Iodama (Ἰοδάμα) The daughter of Itonus and consequently the granddaughter of Amphictyon from the family of Deucalion (Table 8). She was the priestess of Athena Itonia at Coronoea in Boeotia. One night the goddess visited her, bearing a shield, and she was turned to stone. In the temple she had an altar and every day, even as late as Pausanias' time, a woman carrying the ritual fire repeated three times 'Iodama is alive and wants a burnt offering'. Zeus loved Iodama and had a child by her who was called THEBE. Zeus married her to Ogygus. A curious legend recorded by Tzetzes claims that Iodama was Athena's sister; Athena supposedly killed Iodama accidentally when they were practising swordplay; this is similar to the myth of Pallas.

Iolaus (Ἰόλαος) A nephew of Heracles; the son of Iphicles, Heracles' half-brother and Automedusa, a daughter of Alcathus. All his life he travelled with his uncle on his Labours and served as his chariot-driver. He participated in the fight with the Lernean Hydra and, later, in the duel with Cycnus, he went with Heracles on his expedition to bring back Geryon's cattle, and was involved in the struggle against Troy. Even if literary sources do not mention his presence in some of the episodes of the Herculean epic, in art, sculptured monuments do not fail to show him at Heracles' side, for example, among the Hesperides, in the battle against Antaeus, in the search for Cerberus and in the Underworld. He accompanied him on the voyage of the Argonauts and was one of the hunters of Calydon. With the use of the hero's team-harness he won the chariot prize at the first Olympic Games established by Heracles, as well as the prize at the funeral games in honour of Pelias (see GLAUCUS 3). When Heracles wanted to marry Iole he gave up his wife Megara to Iolaus; he married her and she then had a daughter called Leipephile (or 'love of the abandoned' which alludes to Megara's state). Iolaus also joined his uncle in the exile imposed by Eurystheus. He left Tiryns with HERACLES and took refuge in Arcadia. He also accompanied him when he ascended Mount Oeta for the final sacrifice and his apotheosis.

After the death of Heracles he went to help the HERACLIDS and took much trouble to settle them. He took many of them to Sardinia – notably most of the grandsons of King Thespius and also some Athenians. He founded several towns, notably Olbia. He commissioned Daedalus to build magnificent buildings which were still standing at the time of Diodorus. It is said that he either died in Sardinia or returned to Sicily where he established a number of sanctuaries dedicated to the deified Heracles. In his old age, or even after his death, rising from the dead especially for this deed, he punished Eurystheus who had attacked the Heraclids out of hatred. Some myths say that he killed Eurystheus. At his request Zeus and Hera gave him one day of strength and youth.

Iole (Ἰόλη) A daughter of the king of Oechalia, EURYTUS, who offered her as the prize in an archery competition. HERACLES won but the king did not give Iole to him because he was afraid that Heracles would become mad, as had previously happened to him, and would kill any children whom he had by Iole. Heracles had to storm Oechalia and seize the young girl, whom he took away captive. When she heard about this, Deianeira sent Heracles the fatal tunic, so Iole was the indirect cause of the hero's death. On his funeral pyre Heracles assigned her to his son Hyllus. Some versions allege that Iole resisted the advances of the victorious Heracles and that rather than yield she preferred to see him massacre her parents before her very eyes. In some versions she tried to commit suicide by throwing herself from the top of the wall after the capture of the town. Her flowing clothes supported her, however, and she was unhurt by her fall. Heracles then sent her to Deianeira, but when Deianeira saw this beautiful girl she prepared Heracles' tunic, without realising that it would be deadly to him.

Ion (Ἴων) The hero who gave his name to the Ionians. He was of the family of Deucalion, a nephew of Dorus and Aeolus, and a son of Xuthus and Creusa, a daughter of Erechtheus (Tables 8 and 11). His father was driven out of Thessaly by Aeolus and Dorus. He settled at Athens where he married Creusa. When his father-in-law Erechtheus died he was driven out of Attica and settled on the north coast of the Peloponnese (in the country of Aegialus.) After his death, his two sons Achaeus and Ion separated, Achaeus returning to Thessaly, while Ion prepared to attack the Aegialians. Their king, Selinus, then gave Ion his only daughter, Helice in marriage and named him as his successor. When Selinus died, Ion assumed power. He founded a town which he called Helice after his wife and gave the inhabitants of his kingdom the name Ionians. Meanwhile the Athenians, who were at war with Eleusis, called on Ion for help and made him their leader. Ion complied with their request but died in Attica. His descendants retained power in Aegialia until the descendants of Achaeus returned from Thessaly, drove them out and changed the name of the country to Achaea. This is the story as told by Pausanias.

Strabo has given us a slightly different one which equally explains the many migrations of the Hellenic people. After he married Erechtheus' daughter, Xuthus founded the Tetrapolis in Attica, which comprised four small towns, Oenoe, Marathon, Probalinthus and Tricorynth. Achaeus, one of his sons, committed an accidental murder and fled to Sparta. He gave the people of this area the name of Achaeans. Meanwhile Ion overcame the Thracians who were fighting under orders of EUMOLPUS. This earned him such a reputation that the Athenians made him their king. Ion divided Attica into four provinces and organized the country politically. When he died this area assumed his name. Later the Athenians sent a colonizing expedition to Aegialus and the country thereafter was called Ionia. These colonists were driven out at the time of the Heraclids by the Achaeans who changed its name to Achaea.

Euripides wrote a tragedy *Ion* which deals with these myths. In it Ion was not the son of Xuthus, but the son of Apollo and Creusa, the youngest daughter of Erectheus. They conceived a child in a cave on the Acropolis where the child was also born. Creusa did not want to rear the child, and immediately after its birth she abandoned it among the rocks in a basket, thinking that Apollo would know how to look after it. The baby was taken to Delphi by Hermes and put in the care of the temple priestess. Later Creusa married Xuthus out of gratitude for the help which he had given to her family in the war against the descendants of Chalcodon. This marriage remained infertile, however, so Xuthus and Creusa went to Delphi to consult the oracle. The oracle told Xuthus to adopt as his son the first child he saw when entering the temple. This turned out to be the son of Creusa. In obedience, Xuthus adopted it, but Creusa had no wish to welcome a child which she did not know and even considered poisoning it, but finally, because of the basket in which the child had been found and which the priestess had

kept, Creusa came to recognize her son, in whom the blood of the Erechthids was revived.

Ionius ('Ιόνιος)
1. The eponym of the Ionian Sea (whose name was more often, particularly by Aeschylus, attributed to Io's voyage; previously the Ionian Gulf was thought to have been called the sea of Cronus and Rhea). Ionius was the son of King Adrias of Illyria, who gave his name to the Adriatic.
2. Ionius was also said to have been a son of Dyrrhachus, eponym of the town of Dyrrhachium (modern Durazzo). When Dyrrhachus was attacked by his own brothers, Heracles, who was passing through the country, came to his aid, but in the fight the hero killed his ally's son by mistake. The corpse was cast into the sea, which thereafter was called the Ionian Sea.

Iope ('Ιόπη)
1. The alleged daughter of Iphicles, the twin brother of Heracles, and the wife of Theseus. This story is obscure, however, and perhaps it was simply an attempt to give the two monster-killing heroes a common ancestry.
2. One of Aeolus' daughters, the wife of Cepheus, who in an obscure form of the legend was Andromeda's father. More often ANDROMEDA's mother was called Cassiopia. But in this rarer case she was not an Ethiopian queen but a Phoenician one. Iope was the eponym for the town of Ioppe.

Ioxus ('Ίωξος) A grandson of Theseus, and a son of Melanippus and Perigoune, daughter of Sinis the brigand. Ioxus' descendants regarded the pimpernel as a sacred plant because at the time Theseus was killing Sinis, Perigoune hid in clumps of this plant and swore that if they concealed her successfully, she would never do them any harm.

Iphianassa ('Ιφιάνασσα)
1. A daughter of King Proetus of Argos, she went mad, with her sister, and was cured by Melampus (see PROETIDES and Table 1).
2. One of AGAMEMNON's daughters in the earliest version of his legend (Table 2). At first there was a distinction between her and Iphigenia but as time went on they became confused.
3. It was also the name of Endymion's wife, the mother of Aetolus.

Iphicles ('Ιφικλῆς) A son of Amphitryon and Alcmene (Table 3) and a twin brother to HERACLES,

though the latter was fathered by Zeus. This difference between the brothers was clear at the first trial which Heracles had to undergo. Hera sent two snakes to the bedroom where the two babies slept; when Iphicles saw the snakes he was frightened and screamed, Heracles seized the two snakes and strangled them both. Later, Iphicles joined Heracles on several of his Labours. He fought with him against the Orchomenians and Creon rewarded him by giving him his youngest daughter in marriage, while at the same time Heracles married Megara, the king's eldest daughter; in order to do this Iphicles had to abandon Automedusa, his first wife, who had borne his son IOLAUS. During his period of insanity Heracles killed not only his own children but also two of the sons of Iphicles. The latter succeeded in saving the lives of his eldest son Iolaus and Megara. Although EURYSTHEUS treated Heracles cruelly, he showed kindness to Iphicles who nevertheless had to do him service. According to a story in Hesiod Iphicles voluntarily gave his service to Eurystheus whilst Iolaus remained faithful to his uncle.

Iphicles went with Heracles on his expedition against Troy, and is also included among the hunters of Calydon. He died in the war against Hippocoon's sons, by his brother's side. In other accounts it is said that he died from a wound received in the struggle against the MOLIONIDAE (see also BOUPHAGUS). His tomb could be seen at Pheneus in Arcadia.

Iphiclus (Ἴφικλος)

1. The son of Phylacus, king of Phylacae in Thessaly. Through Deion, his paternal grandfather, he was descended from Deucalion and Aeolus (Tables 20 and 8). He was the hero of a curious adventure. As a young man he was struck with impotence. His father questioned the soothsayer MELAMPUS, who was his second cousin, and at that time in his power (see also BIAS), about a remedy for this affliction. Melampus sacrificed two bulls which he dismembered and left for the birds. He then stayed to hear what the vultures said as they devoured the flesh: they said that at a earlier date, when he was castrating rams, Phylacus had put his bloody knife beside Iphiclus; the child was frightened and stole the weapon, and then drove it into a sacred oak tree. The bark grew round the blade and covered it completely. The vultures said that if the knife were found and a drink prepared with the rust which covered it, and if he took doses of this liquid for ten days, Iphiclus would be cured, and he would then have a son. Melampus found

the knife and prepared the liquid as prescribed and Iphiclus had a son who was called Podarces. Iphiclus was famous for his speed of foot. He could run over a field without breaking the stalks. He also won the running race at the funeral games in honour of Pelias. He took part in the voyage of the *Argo*

2. The son of Thestius and brother of Althaea. He participated in the hunt for the Calydonian boar and also sailed on the *Argo*.

3. Iphiclus was also a son of IDOMENEUS, the king of Crete. While the king was away Iphiclus was killed by Leucus.

4. The same name also appeared in a legend of Rhodes. It was that of a leader of the Dorian invaders who put an end to Phoenician domination in the following way: the Phoenicians had lost almost all of the island and only one garrison was left in the citadel of Ialysus under the command of the Phoenician prince Phalanthus. An oracle had promised Phalanthus that he would not be driven from his position as long as the crows were black and there were no fish in the well from which the garrison drew its water. Iphiclus learned of this oracle and decided to undermine the confidence of the enemy. He bribed one of Phalanthus' servants (though others said that Dorcia, a daughter of Phalanthus, took part in the enterprise because of her love for Iphiclus), and with his help released over the fortress crows whose wings were whitened with plaster. He then secretly had some fish put into the well. When he saw this, Phalanthus lost courage and surrendered, and this was the end of Phoenician domination of Rhodes.

Iphidamas (Ἰφιδάμας)

1. One of the children of the Trojan ANTENOR and Theano, daughter of King Cisseus of Thrace. He was brought up by the king and married one of his daughters, who was also his aunt. Soon after his marriage he went to Troy with twelve ships and was killed by Agamemnon. His elder brother Coon tried to avenge him, but succeeded only in wounding the king who temporarily withdrew from the battle. Coon was killed on the corpse of his brother.

2. A son of King Busiris who was killed by Heracles on the altar of Zeus at the same time as his father.

Iphigenia (Ἰφιγένεια) One of the daughters of Agamemnon and Clytemnestra (Table 2) but she does not appear, at least under this name, in the Homeric legend. It is only in the epic cycles that

her legend develops, and particularly in the tragedies. Agamemnon incurred the anger of Artemis
who prevented the Achaean fleet from sailing
from Aulis against Troy by inducing a prolonged
calm. The soothsayer Calchas was consulted and
replied that the anger of the goddess would only
be appeased if Agamemnon agreed to sacrifice his
daughter Iphigenia to her; she was then in
Mycenae with her mother. At first Agamemnon
refused, but, under the influence of public opinion
and particularly that of Menelaus and Odysseus,
he gave in. He ordered his daughter to be fetched
on the pretext that she was to be betrothed to
Achilles, and then Calchas offered her to Artemis
on the goddess's altar. However, at the last moment the goddess took pity on the girl; she spirited
her away in a cloud and put a deer in her place. She
took her to Tauris where she made her a priestess.
That was the story in its simplest and best-known
form. There have been a great number of variations and changes of meaning however. In some
accounts the place of sacrifice was different, not
Aulis but an area called Brauron in Attica. It was
also said that the goddess substituted a bear as
victim in place of the deer, or that Iphigenia was
changed into a bull, or a mare, or a she-bear, or
even into an old woman, at the moment of sacrifice, and in one of these forms she disappeared.
Her disappearance was explained by the fact that
all the participants averted their eyes to avoid
seeing such a horrible murder committed.

Iphigenia stayed for many years in Tauris in the
service of the goddess; her duty was to sacrifice all
foreigners brought to the country after shipwreck.
One day she recognized two strangers who had
been brought to her for sacrifice as her brother
Orestes and Pylades; they had been sent by the
Delphic oracle to look for the statue of Artemis.
She gave them the statue and, abandoning her
priesthood, fled with them to Greece. During this
journey an adventure took place which was developed by Sophocles into his tragedy (now lost)
Chryses. Iphigenia, with her brother and Pylades,
landed at the town of Sminthion on the coast of
the Troad, where Chryses was the priest of
Apollo. CHRYSES had a son of his daughter
Chryseis and Agamemnon with him, whom she
had conceived during her captivity in the Greek
camp. This son had the same name as his grandfather and he succeeded him as high priest. When
the fugitives arrived with Thoas, the king of
Tauris, in pursuit, the younger Chryses arrested
them and prepared to hand them over to Thoas.
However, when his grandfather told him who his
father was, Chryses killed Thoas and then accompanied his sister and brother to Mycenae. Another
version even made Iphigenia not the daughter of
Clytemnestra but of Chryseis. In this account she
was kidnapped by Scythian pirates on her return
journey, when Agamemnon returned to Greece
after the capture of Troy. Another variation
claimed that Iphigenia was the daughter whom
THESEUS had by HELEN when he carried her off
before her marriage. When she was rescued by her
brothers the Dioscuri, Helen swore to them that
she was still a virgin but in fact she had given birth
in secret to a daughter, Iphigenia, whom she entrusted to her sister Clytemnestra, who brought
her up as if she were her own child.

It is sometimes said that Iphigenia died in
Megara where she had a sanctuary, and at other
times that Artemis had immortalized her as the
goddess Hecate.

Iphimedia (Ἰφιμέδεια) A daughter of Triops
from the family of Canace who married her uncle
Aloeus and bore three children, two sons called
the Aloadae – EPHIALTES and OTUS – and a daughter, Pancratis. Iphimedia was in love with
Poseidon and she frequently went into the sea and
poured water on her breasts. He finally answered
her prayers and gave her two sons whose human
father was Aloeus. Other authors claimed that the
Aloadae were the children of the Earth like most
giants and that Iphimedia had only been their
nurse. One day when Iphimedia and her daughter
PANCRATIS were celebrating the feast of Dionysus
on Mount Drios in Achaea, they were kidnapped
by two pirates from the island of Naxos (then
called Strongyle). They were of Thracian descent
and called either Scellis and Cassamenus or Sicelus
and Hegetorus. Driven on by their love for these
two women, they had a fight and killed each other
simultaneously. The king of Naxos, Agassamenus, gave Iphimedia to one of his friends and kept
Pancratis for himself. Aloeus sent his two sons to
look for Pancratis and her mother. The two giants
attacked the island of Naxos, drove out the
Thracians who had settled there and became rulers
of the island. The tomb of Iphimedia could be seen
at Anthedon.

Iphis I (Ἰφις)
1. An Argive hero, the son of Alector. He was the
father of Eteoclus (Table 36), one of the Seven
Chiefs who attacked Thebes, and of Evadne, the
wife of Capaneus. According to another tradition
recorded by Pausanias, Iphis was the son of Alec-

tor and the brother of Capaneus. His two children and Capaneus all had an unhappy ending. Eteoclus was killed outside Thebes and Evadne threw herself on her husband's funeral pyre. He had been struck by lightning as he was starting to assault the wall. As he had no more children he left his kingdom to Sthenelus, a son of Capaneus, when he died.

2. The son of a different Sthenelus, who was the son of Perseus. Iphis was the brother of Eurystheus (Table 31), who took part in the Argonauts' expedition.

3. The lover of Anaxarete, the girl from Salamis in Cyprus who was turned into stone by Aphrodite.

Iphis II This was also a woman's name:

1. One of the fifty daughters of Thespius, who slept with Heracles when he was a guest in their father's house.

2. A captive girl from Scyros who was loved by Patroclus.

3. The daughter of Ligdus and Telethousa, two Cretans from Phaestus. Before the birth Ligdus instructed Telethousa to abandon the child should it be a girl. When she was about to give birth she had a vision in which Isis appeared to her and ordered her to rear her child whatever its sex. When she gave birth to a girl she decided to disguise it as a boy. She called her Iphis, a name common to both sexes and dressed her in boys' clothes. But Iphis soon inspired the love of a girl called Ianthe who made the common mistake of thinking the child was a boy. The two girls became engaged. Iphis' mother was very embarrassed; she postponed the marriage for various reasons but finally she could not defer it any longer. She then begged Isis to help her out of her predicament. The goddess took pity on her and turned Iphis into a boy, so the marriage took place (see GALATEA).

Iphitus (Ἴφιτος)

1. The son of Eurytus was the best-known Iphitus. He belonged to the Heracles cycle. His story is complex: at times he appeared with CLYTIUS among the Argonauts and as a son of EURYTUS, king of Oechalia. He himself was a celebrated archer; the *Odyssey* relates that after his father's death he inherited the divine bow used by his father, who had been given it by Apollo. Iphitus presented the bow to Odysseus. It was part of the gift-exchange between the two heroes when they met at Orsilochus' house in Messinia. Odysseus, for his part, gave Iphitus a sword and a spear.

When Odysseus returned from Troy he used the bow to kill Penelope's suitors. In this version of the legend Eurytus died before his son. He was killed by Apollo whom he had tried to rival in archery. Sometimes Heracles was said to have killed him along with his four sons (including Iphitus) at the capture of Oechalia (see IOLE). It was also said that Iphitus was the only one of the brothers who took Heracles' side and that he intended to give Iole, whom he had won in an archery competition, to Heracles: for this reason he survived the massacre after the town was captured. Even in this version he was eventually killed by Heracles. When Odysseus met him in Messinia, Iphitus was searching for some mares, or perhaps cattle, which Heracles had stolen, or which Autolycus had stolen and entrusted to Heracles. The latter refused to give up the animals and he killed Iphitus. Another version says that Heracles was only suspected of the theft and that Iphitus came to enlist his aid in finding his herd. Heracles promised to help but then had a fit of madness such as he had already had, and threw the young man from the top of the walls of Tiryns. To atone for this murder Heracles had to be sold as a slave (see OMPHALE).

2. The son of Naubolus, a prince of Phocis; he was the father of Schedius and Epistrophus who were leaders of the Phocian contingent in the attack on Troy. He went with Jason on the Argonauts' expedition.

3. Another Iphitus was killed by Copreus, the herald of Eurystheus.

4. At the beginning of the historical period there was another Iphitus, the king of Elis, a contemporary of Lycurgus, the Spartan lawgiver. He revived the Olympic Games which had not taken place since the death of King Oxylus. Iphitus, who had gone to consult the Delphic oracle about a remedy for the many plagues, epidemics and political quarrels which were destroying Greece, was advised to reinstate the Olympic Games. At the same time he persuaded the people of Elis to initiate a cult of Heracles whom they had always regarded as their enemy. Through cordial relations with Lycurgus, Iphitus achieved the beginning of Panhellenic union. This was the first step towards curing the political fragmentation from which Greece had always suffered.

Iris (Ἶρις) The daughter of Thaumas and Electra; on both her paternal and maternal sides she was descended from Oceanus. Consequently she was the sister of the Harpies (Table 32). She was the personification of the rainbow and more generally of the relationship between heaven and earth, and between gods and men, which the rainbow represents. She was most often shown with wings, dressed in thin silk, which in sunlight had the colours of the rainbow. Sometimes she was said to be the wife of Zephyrus and mother of Eros. It was Iris who was responsible, like Hermes, for carrying messages, orders or advice from the gods. She was particularly at the call of Zeus and Hera.

Irus (Ἶρος)
1. A son of Actor, king of Opontus, and the father of the Argonauts Eurydamas and EURYTION. When Peleus accidentally killed Eurytion, whose daughter he had married, he offered sheep and cattle to Irus as compensation but Irus refused to accept them. An oracle then advised Peleus to leave the herds at liberty. A wolf attacked them and ate them but divine intervention caused the wolf to be turned into stone. The statue was displayed on the frontier between Locri and Phocis.
2. Irus was also the affronted beggar mentioned in the *Odyssey*, whom Odysseus fought to amuse the suitors.

Ischenus (Ἴσχενος) An inhabitant of Olympia. He was a son of Gigas, himself a son of Hermes and Hiereia. During a famine an oracle prophesied that it would come to an end if a noble man were sacrificed. At once Ischenus voluntarily offered himself as the victim. He was buried on the hill of Cronus not far from the games stadium. Funeral games were held in his honour. After his death the Olympians gave him the name Taraxippus – horse-frightener – because horses always became uncontrollable near his tomb during races. This was attributed to his magical influence or, sometimes, to the shadow of a laurel bush which happened to have seeded itself there.

Ischys (Ἴσχυς) An Arcadian whose father was Elatus, the grandson of Arcas (see LAPITHS). He married Coronis, a daughter of King Phlegyas, when she was already pregnant by Apollo and carrying ASCLEPIUS. For this crime Ischys and his wife were both killed by Apollo.

Isis (Ἶσις) Although Isis was an Egyptian goddess and did not have a place either in Greek or Roman mythology, her cult, and its myths, were so widespread in the Graeco-Roman world at the start of our era that it is impossible not to mention her. In the Egyptian pantheon Isis was the wife of Osiris and the mother of Horus the sun-god. Seth, the god of darkness, killed Osiris and scattered his dismembered body throughout Egypt. Isis searched for Osiris (see NEMANUS) and her lamentations were loud until Horus took revenge for her. Isis, as mother of the gods, and victorious over the powers of darkness, very quickly became endowed with mystical powers and took on various identities in Hellenic religion. The story of IO was assimilated into Isis' myth and iconography (Iris was often shown as a cow carrying the lunar symbol). Isis was compared to Demeter who also searched for her daughter, abducted by Hades, the god of the Underworld. Isis, in the form in which she appeared at the time of Apuleius, represented the female principle: she ruled the sea, the fruits of the earth and the dead. As goddess of magic, she controlled the transformation of things and beings, and the elements. The religious syncretism of the second century AD developed around her.

Ismene (Ἰσμήνη)
1. The mother of Iasus in the genealogy which made him a son of Argos (Table 18). She was a daughter of Asopus.
2. The sister of Antigone and the daughter of Oedipus and Jocasta (Table 29). According to an obscure story Ismene was loved by Theoclymenus, a young Theban, but during a meeting with him she was killed by TYDEUS at the instigation of Athena.

Ismenus (Ἰσμηνός)
1. The god of the river of the same name in Boeotia. Like all rivers he was a son of Oceanus and Tethys. Occasionally he was said to be a son of Asopus and Metope.
2. Another legend mentions another Ismenus (or Ismenius), also a Theban, and a son of Apollo and the Nymph MELIA. He had two daughters, Dirce and Strophia, two Theban springs.
3. The eldest son of Niobe and Amphion. He was killed, together with the rest of Niobe's children, by Apollo's arrows. As he was dying he threw himself into a river which consequently adopted his name.

Isola Tiberina It was said in Rome that after the expulsion of the Tarquins, the area of their lands immediately to the north of the city was dedicated to Mars and became the Campus Martius. Since it was then harvest time and the area was covered with ripe wheat, it was decided to throw this wheat into the river, as it was dedicated to the god and could not be eaten without sacrilege. The water was low and the sheaves became grounded on the sandbanks, forming the beginning of the Isola Tiberina at the foot of the Palatine. A different version maintained that the field of Mars did not belong to the Tarquins, but that it was voluntarily consecrated by its owner, the Vestal Tarquinia.

Issa (Ἴσσα) A young Lesbian girl, whose father was called Macareus. She gave her name to the town of Issa in her own country. She was loved by a god, either Hermes or Apollo.

Isthmiades (Ἰσθμιάδης) The husband of Pelarge, the daughter of Potneus. After the cult of the Cabiri was disrupted by the attack on Thebes by the Seven Chiefs, he and his wife established it again in Boeotia. When Pelarge died, the oracle at Dodona ordered that she should be given divine honours because of her zeal for the gods.

Istrus (Ἴστρος) The personification of the river which is the modern Danube. Like all rivers he was the son of Oceanus and Tethys. Two of his sons, Helorus and Actaeus, fought in Mysia on the side of Telephus at the time of the Greek invasion.

Italus (Ἰταλός) The hero who gave his name to Italy. Legends about his origin and his native land vary. Sometimes it was claimed that he was king of a country situated at the extreme south of Bruttium. In this version Italus was of Oenotrian descent. He ruled the country with such justice and wisdom, giving laws to his people and civilizing them so well, that in gratitude his kingdom was given the name of *Italia*. Others claimed that Italus was of Sicilian origin (or Lucanian or Ligurian or Corcyrean) or yet again a grandson of Minos, being the son of his daughter SATYRIA. These legends were extremely confused. An Italus also played a part in the epic of ODYSSEUS and CIRCE: he would be a son of Penelope and Telegonus (see also LEUCARIA).

Ithacus (Ἴθακος) The hero who gave his name to the island of Ithaca, he was the son of Pterelas and Amphimedes and a kinsman of Zeus. He had two brothers, Neritus and Polyctor, who emigrated with him from Corcyra and founded with him the town of Ithaca on the island of that name. The Ithacans particularly owe the development and consecration of the

source of their water supply to him and his brothers.

Ithome (Ἰθώμη) A Nymph of the mountain of the same name in Messenia. According to local legend she was given the task of rearing the infant Zeus. She was helped by another Nymph called Neda. Both Nymphs used to bathe him in the spring Clepsydra which was nearby. There was a sanctuary of Zeus Ithomas to which, in memory of the god, water was brought every day from the Clepsydra. Zeus Ithomas could also pronounce oracles.

Itonus (Ἴτωνος) A son of Amphictyon (Table 8) and consequently a kinsman of Deucalion. By the Nymph Melanippe he had three children: Boeotus, Chromia and Iodama. He was sometimes said to have been the founder of the cult of Athena Itonia. (See IODAMA.)

Itylus (Ἴτυλος) The son of AEDON and the Theban Zethus, in the Theban version of the legend of the nightingale. He was killed by his mother who thought that she was killing Amaleus, Niobe's eldest son. She was jealous of Niobe because she had many children, whilst she herself only had two, Itylus and Neis.

Itys (Ἴτυς) The son of Procne in the latest version of the legend of the nightingale, the one most commonly used as a source by tragedians. His father was no longer Zethus as in the previous version (see ITYLUS) but Tereus, the king of Thrace who had married Procne, a daughter of Pandion, king of Athens. In the case of Itys, the legend is no longer a Theban but an Attic one. Itys was killed; his flesh was given as a meal to Tereus, and he was then transformed into a bird (possibly a pheasant). There was also a very similar Milesian legend of which AEDON was the heroine. In this version Aedon was turned into a bird but her son Itys does not seem to have undergone a similar change.

Iulus Another name for ASCANIUS. The Julians traced back their ancestry to Iulus; Caesar and, by adoption, Augustus belonged to this family. Iulus founded the town of Alba in Latium, the mother country of the Romans. The origin of this name was explained as follows: during the fighting which followed the disappearance of Aeneas, Ascanius took command of the confederate Latin army (composed of natives and Trojan soldiers) and was victorious over the Rutulians and their

Etruscan allies (see MEZENTIUS). As a reward he was given the surname of Iobum though perhaps it should read Iolum or Iovlum, the diminutive of Jupiter. This etymology was recorded as early as Cato's *Origins*. It is significant that King Latinus at his death was said to have been identified with the god of the Latin confederation, Latin Jupiter. Sometimes Iulus was distinguished from Ascanius and was said to be the grandson of Aeneas and the son of Ascanius himself. After his father's death he was driven from the throne of Alba by his uncle Silvius, a son of Aeneas and Lavinia, who made him a priest.

Iustitia The personification of justice in Roman thought rather than a mythological figure as such. She was not however, the equivalent of Greek THEMIS, but of Dike and Astraea. When mortal wrong-doing put Iustitia to flight and forced her to leave the earth where she was living amicably with the mortals, she took refuge in the sky and became the constellation of Virgo.

Iuventus (or *Iuventas* or *Iuventa*: the official form, in names of temples and so on, was *Iuventas*). The goddess of youth and in particular the protector of adolescents at the time when they started to wear adult clothes and ceased to be children. She had a shrine in the interior of the *cella* of Minerva in the temple of the Capitoline Triad. This shrine preceded the establishment of the Triad, which demonstrates how old the worship of Iuventus was in Rome. Later, Iuventus was more or less identified with HEBE but she always retained her Roman characteristics. Under the Empire, young men's associations – pre-military bodies upon which imperial policy relied – were founded under the auspices of Iuventus. When a youth started to wear a man's toga, it was customary to give a coin as an offering to the goddess.

Ixion (Ἰξίων) Writers give widely differing accounts of the genealogy of Ixion. Most often he was said to be the son of Phlegyas and therefore the brother of CORONIS but sometimes he was said to be the son of Ares, or of Aeton, or of Antion, or of Pision. His mother was Perimele (Table 23). Ixion was a Thessalian king who ruled over the Lapiths. He married Dia, a daughter of King Deioneus. When he requested the hand of the young girl he made great promises to the king, but when the latter claimed the agreed presents after the wedding Ixion treacherously threw him into a ditch full of burning coal, making himself guilty not only of perjury but also of the murder of a member of his family; for when members of one family are united by a religious bond and sacrifice to the same guardian divinities, such a murder becomes sacrilege. The horror caused by this crime was so great that nobody would purify Ixion according to the normal practice. Of all the gods Zeus alone took pity on him; he purified Ixion and delivered him from the madness which had come upon him as a result of his crime. Ixion showed extreme ingratitude to his benefactor, however. He fell in love with Hera and tried to rape her; Zeus shaped a cloud which resembled the goddess and Ixion lay with this phantom, which bore him a son, Centaurus, the father of the Centaurs. In view of this new sacrilege, Zeus decided to punish Ixion: he fastened him to a burning wheel which rotated continuously; Zeus also gave him a draught of magic liquor which made him immortal, so Ixion had to suffer his punishment with no hope of it ever ending. Ixion's punishment is often said to have taken place in the Underworld, in Tartarus, alongside that of the worst criminals.

Iynx (Ἴυγξ) A daughter of Pan and the Nymph Echo who is said to have aroused Zeus' love for Io by giving him a love potion. As a punishment, Hera turned her either into a stone statue or into a bird called Iynx which took part in lovers' intrigues.

J

Janus One of the oldest of the gods in the Roman pantheon. He was represented as having two faces, one looking forwards and the other backwards. His legends were purely Roman and were bound up with those dealing with the origin of the town. According to some mythographers, Janus was a native of Rome where at some point he had ruled with Camesus, a mythical king of whom nothing is known. Others claimed that Janus was a foreigner, a native of Thessaly, who was sent as an exile to Rome where he was welcomed by King Camesus, who shared his kingdom with him. Janus was supposed to have built a city on a hill, which was consequently called Janiculum. He came to Italy with his wife Camise or Camasenca and they had children, the best-known being Tiber, eponym of the river Tiber. After the death of Camesus, he ruled Latium alone. Janus received Saturn when he was driven from Greece by his son Jupiter (see CRONUS and ZEUS). While Janus ruled on the Janiculum Saturn ruled over Saturnia, a village situated on the heights of the Capitol. The reign of Janus was said to have had all the features of the Golden Age: men were perfectly honest; there was plenty; and there was also complete peace. Janus was said to have invented the use of money. The oldest bronze Roman coins indeed had the effigy of Janus on the right side and the prow of a boat on the reverse. Janus was said to have civilized the first natives of Latium, although this was sometimes attributed to Saturn.

When Janus died he was deified. Other legends were attached to him: one miracle in particular was attributed to him, which saved Rome from being conquered by the Sabines. After Romulus and his companions had carried off the Sabine women, Titus Tatius and the Sabines attacked the city again. One night Tarpeia, the daughter of the Warden of the Capitol, delivered the citadel into the hands of Sabines. They scaled the heights of the Capitol and were just about to turn on the

One of the oldest gods in the Roman Pantheon, Janus was represented as having two faces. He was supposed to have invented the use of money and was often depicted on coins. Roman Republican bronze as.

defenders when Janus launched a jet of hot water in front of the attackers which frightened them and put them to flight. To commemorate this miracle it was decided that in time of war the door of the Temple of Janus should always be left open so that the god could come to the aid of the Romans. It was only closed if the Roman Empire was at peace. Janus was also said to have married the Nymph Juturna whose shrine and spring were not far from his own temple in the Forum. He was said to have had a son by her, the god FONS or Fontus, the god of springs. In his satiric poem about the transformation of the Emperor Claudius into a pumpkin (*Apocolocyntosis*), Seneca tells how Janus, a skilful speaker and an *habitué* of the forum, and expert in the ability to see forwards and backwards, pleaded in defence of Claudius.

Jason (Ἰάσων) The son of AESON. He was a native of Iolcos and a descendant of Aeolus (Tables 21 and 1). There were various traditions for his mother's name. Generally she was called Alcimede, daughter of Phylacus, or, in other versions, Polymede, daughter of Autolycus and consequently an aunt of Odysseus. At Iolcos, according to the most generally accepted legend, Aeson, to whom power legally belonged, had been deposed by his half-brother Pelias, the son of Tyro and Poseidon. Another version says that Aeson had entrusted power to Pelias until his son came of age. His son was brought up by the Centaur Chiron, who taught him medicine. When he reached manhood Jason left Pelion, where the Centaur lived, and returned to Iolcos strangely dressed in a tiger skin with a lance in each hand, and no shoe on his left foot. In this outfit he arrived in the main square of Iolcos just as his uncle Pelias was offering a sacrifice. Pelias saw him, but did not recognize him, and was alarmed because an oracle had told him to 'mistrust a man who had only one shoe'. Jason stayed five days and five nights at his father's house and on the sixth day he called on Pelias and claimed the power which was his by right. Pelias ordered him to bring him the fleece of the ram which had carried Phrixus through the air: this was a golden fleece consecrated by Aeetes, king of Colchis, to Ares, and guarded by a dragon. Pelias was certain that

Medea demonstrating to Jason how she can restore lost youth to a living body by cutting up a ram, putting it in boiling water and adding a magic potion. The ram emerges, restored. Greek vase, c. 470 BC. London, British Museum.

Jason would never return from this expedition. Another version claims that Jason forced himself to undergo this trial: Pelias asked Jason what punishment he would give to somebody who was guilty of treason; Jason said that he would send him to fetch the Golden Fleece. The poets claim that the idea of this test had been suggested to Jason by Hera who wanted to find a way of bringing Medea to Colchis so that she could kill Pelias with whom she was angry because he had not given Hera the honours which she thought were due to her.

Jason sought the help of Argos, the son of Phrixus, and on the advice of Athena, Argos built a boat, the *Argo*, which was to take Jason and his companions to Colchis (see ARGONAUTS).

When Jason came back from Colchis with the Golden Fleece, he married MEDEA, and gave the fleece to Pelias. From that point onwards there were various versions. In some he ruled instead of Pelias; in others he lived quietly in Iolcos, and fathered a son called Medeius; a third version claimed that by her magic Medea was the cause of the death of Pelias; she persuaded his daughters to boil him in a cauldron, telling them that this would rejuvenate him. With the exception of Alcestis, the youngest, all Pelias' daughters took part in this murder. The murder of Pelias was said to be Jason's revenge either for the usurpation which he had suffered or because of the death of AESON who had been driven to commit suicide by Pelias. After Pelias' death Medea and Jason were driven out of Iolcos and took refuge in Corinth. They lived happily and quietly there for ten years, but Jason grew weary of Medea and transferred his affections to Glauce (or Creusa) the daughter of King Creon. Medea called as witnesses the gods by whom Jason had earlier sworn fidelity to her, and she sent as a present to Glauce a wedding dress which made her veins burn violently. In the meantime Medea murdered the two children whom she had had by Jason and she fled into the sky in a chariot given to her by the Sun. Jason then wished to go back to Iolcos where Acastus, the son of Pelias, was king. He made an alliance with PELEUS who had been wronged by Acastes, and with the help of the Dioscuri laid the town to waste. Thereafter either Jason or his son Thessalus ruled over Iolcos. Jason was also among those who took part in the hunt of the Calydonian Boar.

Jocasta (’Ιοκάστη) The name given by the tragedians to the wife and mother of OEDIPUS. In the Homeric tradition, she was called Epicaste. She was the daughter of the Theban Menoeceus and the sister of Hipponome and Creon. She was first married to Laius by whom she had Oedipus. Later, without recognizing her son, or his recognizing her, she married Oedipus by whom she had several children (Table 29). When she discovered her incest she hanged herself. Another tradition says that Jocasta and Oedipus had two sons, Phrastor and Laonytus, who were killed in the war against Orchomenus and the Minyads.

Julia Luperca Tzetes, referring to the sacrifice of Iphigenia, states that a similar miracle to the one which saved her at the last minute took place in Rome. The heroine of this story was Julia Luperca. She was a young Roman girl who was to be an expiatory sacrifice in an official ceremony. At the moment when the priest raised the knife against her, an eagle swooped on the priest and snatched the knife, then he let it fall on a mare which was grazing near the temple. The mare was immediately sacrificed and Julia Luperca was saved.

Juno The Roman equivalent of Hera. Originally and in the Roman tradition, she personified the lunar cycle and was one of the three divinities originally honoured on the Quirinal and then on the Capitol, namely Jupiter, Juno and Minerva. She also had other sanctuaries, notably under the name of Moneta 'the goddess who alerts people' or 'she who makes people remember'. She was worshipped in the citadel, or Arx (the north-east point of the Capitol). The saving of Rome at the time of the Gallic invasion in 390 BC was attributed to Juno Moneta. Geese which were reared in her sanctuary sounded the alarm and made it possible for Manlius Capitolinus to save the hill and to force the invaders to retreat.

Juno was honoured for her other attributes. Under the name of Lucina she watched over childbirth and in this role she was more like the Greek Artemis than Hera (see however in the story of HERACLES an incantation of Hera to delay the delivery of Alcmene's child). It was forbidden to take part in offerings to Juno Lucina unless all knots were untied, because the presence of a bond, belt, knot or the like on the bodies of any participants could hinder the happy delivery of the woman for whom the sacrifice was offered. In a general way Juno was the protector of women and particularly of those who were legally married. A festival, the *Matronalia*, in her honour took place on the calends (first) of March. The date of this festival was explained in various ways: sometimes it was said to be the birthday of Mars, the god of war and the son of Juno (the Greek Ares, son of Hera), and sometimes said to be the anniversary of the end of the Roman-Sabine war. The festival recalled the part played by the Sabine women in throwing themselves between their fathers and their young husbands and re-establishing harmony between the two peoples.

While every man had his 'Genius' so every woman had her 'Juno' – a divine double which personified and protected her femininity. The goddesses themselves had their Juno. Inscriptions record a Juno of the goddess Dia and of the goddess Virtus, and so on. Juno also figured in the legend of the Horatii. It was to her, as Juno Sororia, the protector of Horatius' sister, that Horatius had to make a sacrifice of purification after the murder (see HORATII).

Jupiter The Roman equivalent of Zeus. He was the greatest god in the Roman pantheon and appeared as the god of the sky, of daylight, of the weather, which he produced, and particularly of thunder and lightning. In Rome he ruled on the Capitol, which was consecrated to him, and more especially on its south-east summit (the Capitol proper). Virgil tells how at one time this area was covered with oak trees (oaks were especially sacred to Jupiter). Before Rome became predominant, the principal worship of the Latin confederation was always of Jupiter Latialis whose sanctuary was not built at Rome but on the top of the modern Monte Cavo, a wooded mountain which overlooks the lakes of Nemi and Albano. The Capitoline Jupiter was to a large extent the descendant of this older Jupiter, the chief god of the confederation of Latin towns (see LATINUS). On the Roman Capitol there were several cults of Jupiter in his different aspects, the best known, which finally displaced the others, being that of Jupiter Optimus Maximus. This was not, however, the oldest; it was transferred comparatively late from the Quirinal to the Capitol at the same time as those of the other two divinities of the Triad, Juno and Minerva. Previously on the Capitol there had been a temple to Jupiter Feretrius where the Spolia Opima were consecrated – that is, the weapons of all enemy leaders killed by Roman commanders. This temple is said to have been built by Romulus and is considered to have been one of the oldest temples in Rome. Romulus was said to have been the first to consecrate Spolia Opima: those of King Acron. The memory of the second consecration was also preserved – A.

Jupiter was the greatest god in the Roman pantheon and is depicted here on a large gold medallion produced during the emperor Diocletian's rule.

Cornelius Cossus in 426 BC presented the spoils of Tolumnius, the king of the Veians. Romulus was also said to have built another temple to Jupiter in which the god was called Jupiter Stator. This name was attributed to quasi-historical legend: during the battle between Romulus and the Sabines, whose women had been abducted, the Sabines gained the advantage and drove the Romans back across the Forum. Then Romulus, raising his hands to the sky, promised Jupiter that he would build a temple dedicated to him on that spot, if he stopped the enemy. The Sabines immediately began to retreat and were driven off. Romulus kept his promise; the temple of Jupiter Stator (Jupiter who stays or halts) was situated at the bottom of the Palatine where the arch of Titus was later built. A similar legend was told in later years; it was said that M. Atilius Regulus made a vow similar to that of Romulus when he was fighting the Samnites in 294 BC.

As the political framework of Rome grew and strengthened, Jupiter's place in Roman religion became increasingly important. He was seen as the supreme power, the 'president' of the council of gods, the source of all authority. It may be that this conception, which owed a lot to his identification with Zeus, was originally influenced by Etruscan religious ideas. This predominance of Jupiter was shown by the importance of the position given to his priest the flamen Dialis, whose wife was *flaminica* of Juno. The marriage of the flamen and his wife operated as a symbol of the union of the divine couple; it had to be celebrated in the most solemn manner and could not be undone by divorce. As god of the Capitol, under the Republic, Jupiter was the god to whom the consul first offered his prayers on entering office. The victors in solemn procession carried their triumphal crown and consecrated their ritual sacrifices to him. Jupiter guaranteed that treaties would be honoured; he oversaw international relations through the mediation of the college of priests. Less and less meaningful in their original sense became the 'meteorological' attributes of which the memory was kept only in odd expressions like *sub Iove* meaning 'in open air' (literally, under Jupiter).

During the Empire the emperors willingly placed themselves under the protection of Jupiter and some wished to be considered his incarnation. Augustus, the first emperor, for example, claimed to have dreams sent directly by the god and he readily related how he had been miraculously saved from a flash of lightning during the war which he was fighting in Spain against the Cantabrians: the little slave who was walking, torch in hand, in front of his litter was killed whereas he, inside the litter, was spared. In gratitude Augustus had a temple to Jupiter the Thunderer built on the Capitol. Later, Caligula arrogated to himself the two epithets of the Capitoline Jupiter, Optimus Maximus (Best and Greatest). He had his palace on the Palatine joined to the god's temple on the Capitol by a special passage. In every provincial city the first task of the Roman architects was to create a Capitol similar to the one in Rome; there they installed the Triad with Jupiter enthroned in the centre. Thus the god represented the political bond between Rome, the mother city, and the daughter cities which were each a small copy of her (or 'smaller edition').

Juturna In earlier days her name was Diuturna. She was a Nymph of the springs who was originally worshipped on the bank of the Numicius not far from Lavinium. Later her cult was moved to Rome when that city came to predominate over the Latin confederation. The Spring of Juturna was situated in the Roman Forum not far from the temple of Vesta and very close to the temple of Castor and Pollux whose sister she was said to be. Like most of the goddesses of springs Juturna was considered to be a healer. A temple dedicated to her was built on the Campus Martius in a marshy area which was waterlogged until it was drained by Agrippa in the reign of Augustus.

K

Keres (Κῆρες) The Keres or Fates were spirits which played an important part in the *Iliad*. They appeared generally in scenes of battle and violence and controlled the destiny of each hero. They were said to be horrible, black, winged creatures, with big white teeth and long pointed nails. They tore corpses into pieces and drank the blood of the wounded and dead. Their garments were stained with human blood. Some allusions made by Homer show that the Keres were Destinies co-existing with each human being and personifying not only how he would die but also what kind of life would fall to his lot. For example, Achilles had two fates to choose from: one would give him a long and happy life in his native land, far removed from glory and war, and the other, which in fact he chose, would earn him eternal renown at Troy at the price of early death. Similarly, Zeus weighed the fates of Achilles and Hector on scales in front of the gods to determine which of them should die in the duel which faced them. The scale containing the fate of Hector descended towards Hades and therefore Apollo immediately abandoned the hero to his unavoidable destiny.

The Keres are given a genealogy in the *Theogony* of Hesiod. There they appear as 'daughters of Night'; but in the same passage some verses later the poet names a Fate, a sister of Thanatos and Moros (Death and Doom), and several Fates, sisters of the Moirai (in Latin Parcae).

In the classical era the Keres seem to have existed chiefly as literary memories; they tend to be mixed with other similar deities, the Moirai and even the Erinyes, whom they resemble because of their diabolical and savage character. In a poetic passage Plato considers that they are evil genii which, like the Harpies, sully everything which they touch in human life. Popular tradition eventually identified them with the evil spirits of the dead which had to be appeased by sacrifices, such as, for example, took place at the festival of the Anthesteria.

L

Labdacus (Λάβδακος) Son of Polydorus and grandson of Cadmus (Tables 3 and 29) and on Nycteis, his mother's side, the grandson of Chthonius, one of the men born from the teeth of the dragon killed by CADMUS (see also SPARTOI). His father Polydorus died when he was only one year old and his grandfather Nycteus became regent; when he too died, his brother Lycus became regent. Labdacus finally obtained power. After his reign the title passed to his son LAIUS, father of Oedipus. The reign of Labdacus is notable for a war with King Pandion of Athens over a question of the position of the frontier. During this war, TEREUS, king of Thrace, came to help Pandion. According to a legend only recorded by Apollodorus, Labdacus, like Pentheus, was torn to pieces by the Bacchantes because he too had fought against the introduction of the cult of Bacchus.

Labrandus (Λάβρανδος) One of the Curetes. Together with his comrades Panamorus and Palaxus he came to Caria where he spent the first night on the bank of a river which, because of this, was called Heudonus (from the verb ἔυδειν) meaning to sleep).

Lacedaemon (Λακεδαίμων) The son of Zeus and Taygete (Tables 6 and 25). He married Sparta, the daughter of Eurotas, who died without sons and left his kingdom to his son-in-law. He gave the people his name – Lacedaemonians – and the capital of the country took his wife's name – Sparta. His children were Amyclas, who succeeded him as king of Sparta, and Eurydice the wife of Acrisius. In some versions Asine and Himerus were added. The latter was said to have assaulted his sister and in remorse he threw himself into the river Marathon, which was thereafter called the Himerus until its name was changed to Eurotas.

Lacestades (Λακεστάδης) When Phalces, the son of Temenus, took possession of Sicyon, Laces-

tades, the king of the town, who, like his father Hippolytus, had been a vassal of Argos, reigned jointly with him.

Lacinius (Λακίνιος) The hero who gave his name to Cape Lacinium in the territory of the Greek colony of Croton in southern Italy. In some accounts he was said to have been a king of the country, who came from Corcyra, and welcomed Croton when he arrived as a wandering exile; in others he was described as a brigand, a son of the Nymph Cyrene, who had tried to rob HERACLES of his cattle when the hero returned from Erythia with the herds of Geryon. After Heracles had killed Lacinius he built a temple to Hera – the temple of the Hera Lacinia – on the promontory of the same name.

Lacius (Λάκιος) He and his brother Antiphemus had received an order from the Delphic oracle to go, one to the east and the other to the west, and to found a town. Antiphemus founded Gela in Sicily; Lacius founded Phaselis on the frontier between Lycia and Pamphylia. He bought the land needed for his town by the sale of salt fish (see CYLABRAS).

Lacon (Λάκων) A son of King Lapathus, his brother being Achaeus. When the king died he divided his kingdom between them. One part took the name Laconia and the other Achaea. One of Lacon's descendants was King Thespius.

Ladon (Λάδων)
1. The god of the river of that name in Arcadia and the son of Oceanus and Tethys. He married Stymphalis and had two daughters, DAPHNE and Metope, wife of the river-god ASOPUS. It was also said that Daphne was not the daughter of Stymphalis but of Gaia (Earth).
2. Ladon was also the name of the dragon, the son of Phorcys and Ceto, which guarded the golden apples of the Hesperides. Other myths said that this dragon was the son of Typhon and Echidna or sometimes the son of Gaia. He had a hundred heads. After he had been killed by Heracles, Hera turned him into a constellation.

Laertes (Λαέρτης) Particularly celebrated because he was the father of Odysseus. He was the son of Arcisius and Chalcomedusa (Table 39) and consequently of the family of Deucalion through his grandfather Deion. His family came originally from Cephalonia; his maternal grandfather was

CEPHALUS after whom the island was named. Laertes married ANTICLEIA, the daughter of Autolycus, though she had previously been married to Sisyphus, so that occasionally Odysseus was regarded as the son of Sisyphus rather than of Laertes. During Odysseus' absence Laertes was in despair and had an unhappy old age. He withdrew to his estate in the country; his only company was an old maidservant and her husband Dolius and their children. Odysseus went to join him there when he returned. Athena gave him a magic bath which rejuvenated him and gave him the strength to help his son repulse the parents of the suitors who had been put to death. He killed Eupithes, the father of Antinous, with a javelin. The marriage of Laertes and Anticleia produced a daughter called CTIMENE although in some accounts Odysseus was said to be the only son of Laertes.

Laestrygonians (Λαιστρυγόνες) After six days of being buffeted by Aeolus, the god of the winds, Odysseus arrived in the country of the Laestrygonians, giant cannibals who devoured foreigners. They inhabited a town which was said to have been founded by a character called Lamus. When Odysseus arrived, he brought his ships into a large and apparently safe harbour where he anchored. He landed and sent two of his men to explore the area. At the gate of a town they soon met a girl drawing water from a well. They asked who was the king. The girl took them to her home and called her father, Antiphates, who immediately killed one of the two sailors. Then he called all his compatriots to gather together. They dashed to the harbour and bombarded the ships with enormous rocks. All the ships were wrecked except the one which held Odysseus, who managed to escape. It may well be correct to identify the country of the Laestrygonians with Formiae in the south of Latium, on the Campanian boundary.

Laethusa In Hyginus' version of the myth of TEREUS and PROCNE, Laethusa was the wife of Lynceus, the king of Thrace, to whom Tereus had entrusted his sister-in-law Philomela. Laethusa, a friend of Procne, revealed to her the serious crime which her husband had committed and incited her to revenge.

Laius (Λάιος) The son of Labdacus, the king of Thebes, and great-grandson of Cadmus and the father of Oedipus (Tables 3 and 29). Labdacus died while Laius was still young and Lycus, the brother of Nycteus, became regent, but Lycus was killed by Zethus and AMPHION to avenge their mother ANTIOPE; they then seized the kingdom of Thebes. Laius fled and took refuge with Pelops. There he developed a passion for young Chrysippus, a son of Pelops, so introducing, at least according to some writers, the practice of unnatural love. He abducted the young man and was cursed by Pelops. When Amphion and Zethus disappeared in their turn – Amphion after the disaster of the Niobides, Zethus from sorrow at the death of his son – Laius was recalled as king by the Thebans. Laius married the daughter of Menoeceus, Jocasta (or Epicaste) or EURYCLEIA, the daughter of Ecphas, and future mother of OEDIPUS. In this second version, Jocasta was Laius' second wife, so Oedipus only married his mother-in-law and not his real mother. Other names were given to Oedipus' mother and Laius' wife such as EURYGANIA, a daughter of Hyperphas, Euryanassa, also a daughter of Hyperphas, and finally ASTYMEDUSA, daughter of Sthenelus (see also EPICASTE).

See Oedipus for the circumstances of his conception and birth. Laius could not escape what the oracle had predicted, namely that he would be killed by his son. He was killed by Oedipus not far from Delphi, at the crossing of the roads to Daulis and Thebes.

Lamedon (Λαμέδων) A king of Sicyon, a descendant of Aegialeus (Table 22). Coronus was his father and Corax his brother. Corax died childless and Epopeus the Thessalian succeeded him as king of Sicyon. Epopeus was mortally wounded in the fight which he had to undertake against Nycteus on behalf of ANTIOPE, and when he died Lamedon succeeded him. Lamedon was the last in the direct line of Aegialeus at Sicyon. He gave his daughter Zeuxippe in marriage to SICYON, whom he had called in to help in his struggle with the Achaeans. He himself married an Athenian girl, Pheno, a daughter of Clytius, which explains why at a later date IANISCUS, an Athenian who was a descendant of Clytius, reigned over Sicyon.

Lamia (Λαμία)
1. A daughter of Poseidon who bore by Zeus the Libyan SIBYL.
2. A female monster who was said to steal children and was a terror to nurses. There were various stories on this theme. In one account Lamia was a young girl of Libyan origin, the daughter of Belus and Libya. Zeus loved her and had an affair with her, but every time she gave birth to a child, Hera, out of jealousy, arranged for it to die. Lamia hid

herself in a solitary cave; in despair she became a monster jealous of mothers more fortunate than herself, and she seized and devoured their children. In order to punish her yet more, Hera made it impossible for her to sleep, but Zeus, having pity on her, gave her the power to take out her eyes and replace them when she wished. Female spirits which attached themselves to children in order to suck their blood were also called Lamiae. The legend of ALCYONEUS mentioned a monster called Lamia which lived in the mountains near Delphi. Lamia was also another name for the monster Gelo.

Lampetus (Λάμπετος) A hero of Lesbos, son of Irus. He was killed by Achilles, together with Hicetaon and Hypsipylus, the sons of Lepetymnus, at the time of the capture of Methymna.

Lampsace (Λαμψάκη) The daughter of Mandron, king of the Bebryces, who ruled in the town which was then called Pityusa. In the absence of the king, some settlers from Phocis whom he had established there were about to be massacred by the inhabitants, who had formed a conspiracy against them. Lampsace warned the settlers secretly and they succeeded in killing all the natives and taking possession of the town. At that point, Lampsace died; they gave her divine honours and thereafter called the town Lampsacus.

Lampus (Λάμπος) The son of Laomedon, the Trojan. He was the father of Dolops. The town of Lamponia in the Troad bore the hero's name.

Lamus (Λάμος)
1. King of the Laestrygones, who were cannibals and lived, according to the *Odyssey*, on the Italian coast near Formiae. The family of Aelii Lamia in Rome asserted that their noble origins could be traced back to Lamus.
2. A son of Heracles and Omphale. The Greek town of Lamia was called after him.

Lampetia (Λαμπετίη)
1. Helios and the Nymph Naera produced two daughters – Lampetia and Phaethusa (Table 14). These two girls tended the flocks of their father in Thrinacia. They went to Helios to tell him that Odysseus and his followers had killed and eaten his oxen.
2. An isolated legend claimed that Lampetia was the wife of Asclepius and mother of Machaon, Podalirius, Iaso, Panacea and Aegle.

3. One of the HELIADS, according to some traditions.

Laocoon (Λαοκόων)
1. The son of Capys, according to an improbable surmise, or, more likely, of Antenor, according to Tzetzes. He was the priest of Thymbrean Apollo at Troy; he was married to Antiope and by her he had two sons, Ethron and Melanthus, sometimes called Antiphas and Thymbraeus. Laocoon aroused the god's anger because he lay with his wife before the sacred statue, which was sacrilege.
. When the Greeks pretended to prepare for departure from Troy, leaving a wooden horse on the shore, Laocoon opposed the introduction of the wooden horse into the town, and incurred Apollo's wrath again. The Trojans ordered Laocoon to offer a sacrifice to Poseidon, asking him to cause storms and tempests on the route of the enemy fleet but, just as the priest was about to sacrifice a huge bull, two enormous serpents sent by Apollo came out of the sea and twined themselves round Laocoon and his two sons. All three were crushed by the creatures, which then coiled up at the foot of Athena's statue in the

Laocoon, the priest of Apollo, and his sons dying in agony as the two sea-serpents coil themselves round their limbs. Copy of antique sculpture. Florence, Uffizi.

citadel temple. The Trojans, realizing that Lao-coon had angered Apollo, though unaware of his earlier sacrilege, made haste to dedicate the horse to Apollo, and that led eventually to the town's destruction. Tradition has preserved the names of the two snakes as Porce and Chariboea.

2. There was another Laocoon, brother to Oeneus of Calydon and son of Portheus and a slave-girl. He joined the Argonauts with Meleager (Tables 27 and 24).

Laodamas (Λαοδάμας) A son of Eteocles who belonged to the generation of the Epigoni (Table 37). After the regency of Creon, he became king of Thebes and sustained the attack of the second expedition against the city (see ALCMAEON). One legend told that he died at the battle of Glissas after he had killed Aegialeus, son of Adrastus. Another version claims that he escaped on the night of the battle with part of the Theban army and that he took refuge in Illyria.

Laodamia (Λαοδάμεια)
1. A daughter of Bellerophon who had a son, Sarpedon, by Zeus – at least according to the Homeric tradition (Table 35), though generally Sarpedon was said to be a son of Zeus and Europa (Table 28). She died young, killed by arrows shot by Artemis who was angry with her.
2. Another Laodamia, the daughter of Acastus, was the wife of PROTESILAUS, the first Greek hero to be killed at Troy. She was just married when her husband set off for Troy and she loved him deeply. When she learned of his death she begged the gods to allow her to have just three hours with him; Protesilaus had made the same request. When Protesilaus, brought back to life for the stipulated period, had to return once more to Hades, Laodamia killed herself in his arms. Another version related that Laodamia made a wax image of her dead husband which she used secretly to embrace. Her father discovered this and threw the image into the fire. Laodamia followed it, and was burned alive. Euripides dealt with the romance of Laodamia and Protesilaus in a tragedy which is now lost.
3. A daughter of Alcmaeon.

Laodice (Λαοδίκη)
1. The wife of ELATUS and a daughter of Cinyras, king of Cyprus.
2. A daughter of Agapenor of Arcadia, who on his return from Troy was shipwrecked off Cyprus, where he founded the town of Paphos. Laodice had sent a robe as an offering to Athena from Cyprus to Tegea, her birthplace. She also founded a temple to Aphrodite of Paphosa at Tegea.
3. One of the daughters of Agamemnon and Clytemnestra was a Laodice, who in tragedies and in the most modern form of the legend was renamed ELECTRA (Table 2).
4. Laodice was also the name of 'the most beautiful daughter of Priam and Hecuba'. She was married to Helicaon. Authors writing later than Homer recount that while still a young girl she fell in love with ACAMAS, one of Theseus' sons, when he came to Troy as ambassador to demand Helen's return. She had a son, Munitus, fathered by Acamas. Later, after the capture of Troy, Laodice, while escaping from the victors, was swallowed up by the earth.

Laodocus (Λαόδοκος) Among the various heroes with this name the most celebrated was one of the three sons of Apollo and Phthia. His brothers were Dorus and Polypoetes. With them he ruled the country of the Curetes, north of the gulf of Corinth. The three brothers welcomed Aetolus when he was driven from Elis, but were badly rewarded for their hospitality since he killed them all and seized the kingdom.

Laomedon (Λαομέδων) One of the first kings of Troy, the son of Ilus and Eurydice (Table 7). He had several children, including Priam, who was at first called Podarces, and HESIONE. Legends about the name of his wife vary: she was variously called Strymo, or Strymon, Rhoeo, Placia, Thousa, Leucippe and Zeuxippe. He succeeded his father as king of Troy. He had the walls of the fortress built with the aid of APOLLO and Poseidon, who were said to have been helped by a mortal called AEACUS. The legend of Laomedon concerns his perjuries: he refused to pay the gods the sum which had been agreed for the construction of the walls and this brought disaster to his country. After Heracles killed the sea monster sent by Poseidon as punishment, and freed HESIONE, Laomedon refused to give HERACLES the divine horses which he owned and which he had promised in payment. So Heracles returned at the head of an army, captured Troy with Telamon's help and killed not only Laomedon but all his sons except Priam. A later version recorded by Diodorus Siculus was that Heracles sent Telamon and Iphiclus to Laomedon as ambassadors to claim Hesione and the horses which he had promised, but Laomedon put the envoys in prison and tried to wreck the Argonauts, among them Heracles. All Laomedon's sons except Priam (Podarces) participated in this conspiracy. Priam opposed the action and declared that one should treat guests fairly, but nobody took his side. Priam sent two swords to the prison where Telamon and Iphiclus were held, and told them what Laomedon had in mind. Thus armed, the two prisoners cut the throats of their gaolers and returned to the Argonauts, who then attacked Troy. Heracles killed Laomedon, captured the town, killed his enemies and put young Priam on the throne. After that, with his companions he continued the search for the Golden Fleece.

Laomedon's tomb at Troy was in front of the Scaean Gates; a prophecy maintained that as long as the tomb was intact the town could not be captured. Sometimes Laomedon was regarded as the father of GANYMEDE, and it was to recompense Laomedon for the abduction of his son that Zeus was said to have given him either a vine carved in gold or the divine horses – precisely those which he offered Heracles as a reward.

Laonome (Λαονόμη)
1. In a little-known version of the Heracles legend the hero had a sister called Laonome, who was the daughter of Alcmene and Amphitryon. She married an Argonaut, sometimes called Euphemus and sometimes Polyphemus.
2. Amphitryon's mother was sometimes called Laonome. She was said to have been the daughter of Gouneus.

Laonytus (Λαόνυτος) Some mythographers claim that Oedipus and Jocasta had two sons called Laonytus and Phrastor; both were killed in the war between the Thebans and the Minyans and their king, ERGINUS. In this version Oedipus is said to have had a second wife, Eurygania, who bore him Eteocles, Polynices, Antigone and Ismene. His third wife was Astymedusa.

Lapiths (Λαπίθαι) A Thessalian people who have a place both in history and mythology. They originally inhabited the mountain ranges of Pindus, Pelion and Ossa. They drove out the Pelasgians who were the first inhabitants. Lapiths were also mentioned at Olenos and at Elis, at Rhodes and at Cnidos. The Lapiths were said to have been descendants of a river-god of Thessaly, Peneus, and the Nymph Creusa (or Philyra). Peneus had two sons, Hypseus and Andreus, and a daughter who,

by Apollo, gave birth to Lapithes (the eponym of the Lapiths). He, in his turn, sired Phorbas, Periphas and Triopas, and Lesbos (at least if the myth about him which is told by Diodorus Siculus is not corrupt). Periphas was supposedly the ancestor of IXION, but more often Ixion can be linked with the family of Phlegyas. The Lapiths were also related to CAENEUS and his son Coronus. Caeneus had a brother Ischys, who was, like him, the son of Elatus (Table 9). These names recur in the Arcadian legends (see CORONIS). The Lapiths appear in various myths, of which the main one described their struggle against the CENTAURS. HERACLES also fought them on behalf of their enemy AEGIMIUS. Mythographers included Lapiths amongst the hunters of Calydon (see MELEAGER) and the Argonauts (notably Caeneus, Coronus, Mopsus, Pirithous – friend of Theseus – Asterion, Polyphemus, Leonteus, Polypoetes and Phalerus).

Lara According to Ovid, a Nymph of Latium, whose real name was Lala, that is to say, the Gossip. Jupiter loved Juturna, who sought all ways of avoiding him; therefore he brought all the Nymphs of the country together and requested their help. They were to hold their sister and stop her jumping into the water when he was chasing her. All gave their agreement but Lara went everywhere talking about Jupiter's intentions. She warned Juturna and told Juno everything. Enraged, Jupiter tore out her tongue and gave her into Mercury's hands, to be conveyed down to Hades where she would be the water Nymph in the kingdom of the dead. On the journey Mercury raped her and begot twins, the LARES.

Larentia See Acca Larentia.

Lares Roman tutelary gods, doubtless of Etruscan origin, particularly charged with watching over crossroads and domestic property. The story of their birth as it is told by Ovid (see LARA) claims that they were sons of Mercury and gives them duties similar to those of Mercury/Hermes, the god of crossroads and prosperity. It is also said that the Lar Familiaris (protector of each household) was the father of King Servius Tullius. One day when a slave of Tarquin's wife, Tanaquil, was near the fire, a phallus made of ash rose from the hearth. The man who later was destined to become King Servius was born from the union of this with the slave.

Bronze Lares. The lares were Roman tutelary gods; each family honoured its lares by putting small statues of them in the hearth.

A larium or household shrine to the lares from the House of Meander at Pompeii.

Larinus (Λάϱινος) A herdsman of Epirus. When Heracles was travelling with the bulls of Geryon, Larinus was either given some as a present, or stole them. He preserved them and their breed was famous in the classical period.

Larissa (Λάϱισσα) A heroine sometimes said to be from Argos and sometimes from Thessaly. She was also said to have been the eponym of the cities in Thessaly called Larissa and of the fortress of Argos. In some versions she was the mother of Pelasgus by her union with Zeus, or with Poseidon, and in others she was regarded as the daughter of Pelasgus (Table 17). In the first legend she had two sons besides Pelasgus, Achaeus and Phthius; they emigrated from Argos and went to Thessaly.

Las (Λᾶς) A very old local hero of the peninsula of Taygete in the Peloponnese. The locals said that he was killed by Achilles (or Patroclus) when he entered the country to ask Tyndareus for the hand of his daughter Helen. Achilles, however, does not appear as one of Helen's suitors in the most widely used version.

Latinus In Roman tradition, the king of the Aborigines (the very earliest population of Italy) and the hero who gave his name to the Latins. His legend was given a Greek context at a very early date and was linked to the Trojan cycles at the time of the composition of the Roman myths of AENEAS. Nevertheless a number of mythographers, and Virgil in particular, made every effort to preserve his native character. This is why there are two quite different traditions regarding the origin of Latinus. In the Greek version, he was the son of Circe and Odysseus, or alternatively the latter's grandson, in which case his father was Telemachus and his mother was Circe: in the Latin one by contrast he was said to be the son of the old native god Faunus and the goddess of Minturnae, Marica. As the legend of Heracles developed, another genealogy came to be superimposed on the other two: when Heracles returned from staying with Geryon he brought with him a young Hyperborean girl whom he had received as a hostage for her father. During the course of his journey through Italy he gave her as a wife to King Faunus of the Aborigines. This girl was called Palanto. She was considered to be the eponym of the Palatine or of the Palatina (the earliest part of Rome – the village of the palace, founded, it was said, by Evander). When she married Faunus,

Palanto was already pregnant by Heracles. She bore a son, who was King Latinus. Other versions described Heracles as siring Latinus by the king's wife, or even by his daughter.

The tradition dealing with the adventures of Latinus is no less complex. There are two principal, conflicting accounts. In one of them, Latinus received Aeneas with friendliness when he landed on the Latin coast, in the other one he attacked him. He spontaneously gave the immigrants 680 hectares of land, according to Cato, in an extract preserved by Servius in his commentary on the *Aeneid*. In addition he offered his daughter, Lavinia, in marriage to Aeneas. The Trojans were said to have started to raid the neighbouring country-side so heavily that Latinus had to put up a defence, and to this end he formed an alliance with Turnus, the king of the Rutuli. During a decisive battle both Latinus and Turnus were said to have been killed. The capital of the Aborigines, in this version called Laurolavinium, was said to have been captured, and Aeneas became its king. The two peoples, Aborigines and Trojan immigrants, united and became one nation which adopted the name of Latium in memory of the king.

According to the second tradition, Aeneas reached the coast of Latium two years after the fall of Troy and immediately started the task of building a town. Latinus, who was already at war with the Rutuli, approached immediately at the head of a large army to take steps to prevent the establishing of a Trojan colony in his kingdom. He reached the Trojan camp in the evening and when he saw the troops of Aeneas armed in Greek style and in battle position he decided not to attack until morning. During the night he saw in a dream a native god who warned him that an alliance with the strangers would be to his advantage. Aeneas was urged by his own gods, the Penates, to conclude a treaty with Latinus. In the morning the alliance was arranged. The Aborigines gave a piece of land to the Trojans who, for their part, undertook to help them in the war against the Rutuli. Aeneas married Lavinia and called his new town Lavinium. However, this marriage was a cause of war against Turnus who in this version was not a Rutulian but apparently an Etruscan and a nephew of Queen Amata, the wife of Latinus. During the fight which ensued, Latinus and Turnus were both killed and Aeneas, as husband of Lavinia, became king of the Aborigines. As in the preceding legend, the people adopted the name Latin.

In the *Aeneid* Virgil constructed a version unit-ing the two variants. In it Aeneas was well received by Latinus who had been advised by the soothsayers to give his daughter to a heroic stranger. When the envoys of Aeneas arrived in his capital the king realized that the prophecy must be fulfilled and he immediately offered Lavinia's hand to the stranger. Before the alliance between Latinus and the Trojans could be completed there was an accident. Ascanius, Aeneas' son, killed a tame deer on a hunt. This led to a fight between the Trojans who accompanied the young man and the local herdsmen who were annoyed by the murder. Amata, who wanted to marry Lavinia to Turnus, king of the Rutuli, and Turnus himself urged Latinus to fight the Trojans. Latinus refused and shut himself in the depths of his palace. Meanwhile Juno herself opened the doors of the temple of war (the temple of Janus in Rome was closed in times of peace and was only opened at the outbreak of war – this is a case of Virgil transferring to Latinus' town a Roman custom), and Turnus climbed the citadel and ran up the banner which called the people to arms. During the war which followed, Latinus kept apart, confining himself to requesting a truce from the Trojans, so that they might bury their dead, and trying to deflect Turnus from his plan to challenge Aeneas to single combat. After the death of Turnus, Latinus made peace with the Trojans. Two pieces of evidence tell of a legend according to which King Latinus disappeared during a campaign against Mezentius, the king of Caere, and became the god Jupiter Latinus, who in historic times was worshipped by the Latin confederation on the mountain which overlooks Lake Nemi.

Latinus Silvius In the royal line of Alba, he was the fourth king after Ascanius. His father was Aeneas Silvius, his grandfather Postumus Silvius, and his great grandfather Ascanius. He reigned for fifty years and founded a number of cities which were members of the Latin confederation.

Lausus A son of Mezentius (king of Caere) who was an ally of Turnus in his war against Aeneas. He was killed by the latter (see MEZENTIUS). The name recurs in the chronicle of the kings of Alba. It was the name of a son of Numitor who was killed by Amulius.

Lavinia The daughter of King LATINUS and Amata. Before the arrival of AENEAS in Latium she was engaged to Turnus. Her father gave her to the Trojan. In her honour Aeneas named the town which he founded Lavinium. According to one legend her marriage with Aeneas resulted in the birth of Ascanius, but in the *Aeneid* Ascanius is only her step-son who was already a youth when Aeneas arrived. The *Aeneid* does not mention any children of Aeneas and Lavinia, but the mythographers said that after the death of Aeneas Lavinia gave birth to a posthumous son of the hero, Silvius (see ASCANIUS), in the home of the herdsman Tyrrhus or Tyrrhenus, with whom she had taken refuge. Ascanius then handed over Lavinium to his half-brother and went to found Alba, but because he died without children he named Silvius as his successor.

The short legend of the foundation of Rome (which excludes the kings between Aeneas and Romulus) says that Lavinia was the mother of Aemilia, who, after an affair with Mars, gave birth to Romulus. A myth of purely Greek origin related that Lavinia was a daughter of the priest ANIUS who had followed Aeneas as a soothsayer on his trip to the west and who had died in the area where the hero founded Lavinium. (This myth must be based on a play on words, Lavinia being connected with wine (vinum) and related to the word 'oeno' which is the Greek root with the same meaning. The three daughters of Anius were, we know, called the Oenotrophes (the wine growers).)

Leagrus (Λεάγρος) An ally of the Heraclid Temenus. With the help of his friend Ergiaeus, a descendant of Diomedes, and at the instigation of Temenus, he stole the PALLADIUM which was kept at Argos. After quarrelling with Temenus he then offered the statue to the kings of Sparta who accepted the relic very willingly, since it ensured the safety of the town where it lay. They placed it near the town, by the sanctuary of the Leucippidae. As the Delphic oracle had advised them to give the Palladium, as a protector, the guardian-hero of those who had helped to steal it, they erected just by it a temple to Odysseus, who, for them, was almost a national hero because PENELOPE had originally come from Sparta.

Leander (Λέανδρος) A young man of Abydos who was in love with a priestess of Aphrodite called Hero, who lived at Sestos, a town on the other side of the Hellespont. Every night he swam across the river guided by a lamp which Hero placed high on the tower of the house where she lived. One stormy night the lamp was blown out and Leander could not find the shore in the dark.

The next day Hero discovered his corpse at the base of her tower. Not wishing to survive her lover she threw herself off the balcony.

Learchus (Λέαρχος) A son of Ino and Athamas, his brother being Melicertes. When Athamas was driven mad by Hera, who wanted to punish him because he had brought up the little Dionysus in secret, he killed Learchus with an arrow, mistaking him for a deer. According to another account he mistook him for a young lion and threw him off a rock. Another version maintains that Athamas learned of the crime which Ino had committed against Phrixus and Helle, his children by Nephele and, intending to kill her, he killed Learchus by mistake (Tables 3 and 33). Euripides wrote a tragedy about it.

Lebeadus (Λεβέαδος) Of Lycaon's sons Eleuther and Lebeadus were the only ones who did not take part in their father's blasphemy, when he offered Zeus the flesh of a child to test his perceptiveness. After the resulting disaster they fled to Boeotia where they founded the towns of Lebadea and Eleutherae. This was the origin of the old friendship between the Arcadians and the inhabitants of these towns.

Leda (Λήδα) According to the most familiar tradition Leda was a daughter of the king of Aetolia, Thestius, and his wife Eurythemis. She was therefore a descendant of Aetolus and, through her father, of Calyce, one of Aeolus' daughters. She was a member of Deucalion's family (Tables 2, 13, 19 and 24). Her sisters were Althaea, the mother of Meleager, and Hypermestra, though some legends quote her as having Clytia and Melanippe as sisters. It was said that Glaucus, a son of Sisyphus, passed through Lacedaemon looking for horses which he had lost, and there had an affair with Pantidyia who at the same time was married to Thestius; she had a daughter called Leda, whom she passed off as a daughter of Thestius (compare the legend of the birth of ODYSSEUS, who was said to be a product of one of Sisyphus' secret intrigues). When Tyndareus was driven from Lacedaemon by Hippocoon and his sons he took refuge in Aetolia at the court of Thestius who welcomed him and gave him his daughter Leda as wife. When Heracles restored Tyndareus as king of Sparta she went with him. By Tyndareus Leda had several children: Timandra who married ECHEMUS; CLYTEMNESTRA, who married Agamemnon; HELEN and the DIOSCURI.

Leda and Zeus, who assumed the disguise of a swan. 2nd century Roman lamp.

Among all these children (to whom the tragic writers added Phoebe), some were begotten by Zeus, who changed himself into a swan in order to unite with her. It was also said that Helen was really the daughter of Zeus and Nemesis: the goddess supposedly tried to avoid the attentions of the Father of the Gods and changed herself into a goose in order to escape him. Zeus immediately transformed himself into a swan and embraced her. As a result Nemesis laid an egg which she abandoned. A herdsman found it and took it to Leda who put it carefully into a casket. When Helen emerged from it, Leda claimed that she was her child, because of her great beauty. More often, and particularly from Euripides onwards, it was accepted that Leda, because of her love for Zeus, laid an egg, or occasionally two eggs, from which emerged the two pairs of children: Pollux and Clytemnestra, Helen and Castor (see DIOSCURI). In Sparta at the temple of the Leucippidae fragments of an enormous shell were said to be part of the egg laid by Leda.

Leimon (Λειμών) When Apollo and Artemis wanted to avenge the rejections suffered by their mother when she had been pregnant with them and had been given hospitality by nobody, they came to the Peloponnese into the kingdom of Tegeates. There they were received by Scephrus, one of Apollo's sons, who spoke to the god secretly. He was seen by one of his brothers, Leimon, who imagined that he was slandering him to the god and in anger killed him; however, at the same time, Artemis shot him with an arrow. When they knew the gods were there, Tegeates and his wife Maera offered them sacrifices, but Apollo and Artemis would not relent; they departed, leaving a famine behind them. When Tegeates consulted the Delphic oracle it replied that they must give Scephrus full funeral honours. In consequence an annual festival was started at Tegea in his honour, and one of the scenes enacted during the festival depicted the priestess of the goddess Artemis chasing Leimon.

Leimone (Λειμώνη) The heroine of an obscure Athenian legend. She was a daughter of Hippomenes, an Athenian noble and perhaps even the king of the town. When her father realized that she had not preserved her virginity and had had an affair before she was married, he shut her up with a horse in a lonely house and gave them no food or water. There the horse grew mad with hunger and ate the young woman.

Leipephile (Λειπεφίλη) The daughter of Iolaus, a nephew of Heracles. Through her marriage to Phylas – a son of Antiochus, himself a son of Heracles – she united two strands of Heraclean descent in her son HIPPOTES (see also ALETES and Table 31).

Leitus (Λήιτος) A Theban chieftain, a son of Alectryon (or Alector). He commanded a contingent in the Trojan war. The *Iliad* describes his killing of the Trojan Phylacus and his being wounded by Hector. He brought back the ashes of Archesilaus from Troy. He was one of the Argonauts.

Lelex (Λέλεξ) The hero who gave his name to the Leleges. He was the first king of Laconia and a child of the sun. He had two sons called Myles and Polycaon; Myles succeeded him on the throne of Laconia, which he later bequeathed to his own son, Eurotas, the river-god. The younger son, Polycaon, married MESSENE the daughter of

Triopas, king of Argos. He gained the kingdom, which he called Messenia after his wife. Another legend made Lelex the father rather than the grandfather of Eurotas.

Lelex was also regarded as a hero of Leucas and the grandfather of Teleboas (eponym of the Teleboeans) (see AMPHITRYON). The same name appeared in the legends of Megara where Lelex was said to be a son of Poseidon and Libya who came from Egypt to rule over Megara. He had a son, Cleson, whose daughters, Cleso and Tauropolis, received the body of Ino when it was brought to Megara by the sea after the young woman's suicide (see PALAEMON).

Lemures The spirits of the dead which were exorcized annually at the Festival of the Lemuria in Rome on 9 May and the two following odd days, 11 and 13. This festival was celebrated at night. The father of the family came bare-footed out of the house and washed his hands in the water of a spring and threw into the darkness some kidney beans (or broad beans), turning his head and saying 'By these beans, I redeem myself and my own'. He repeated this nine times without looking backwards, while, it was believed, the Lemures gathered the beans. The celebrant then purified his hands again and knocked on some bronze saying 'Shadows of my ancestors, be gone'. He could then look behind himself. The Lemures had gone away satisfied for a year. Concerning the origin of the name Lemuria, Ovid says that this festival was originally called the Remuria and that it was celebrated in memory of the spirit of Remus who was killed by Romulus, but this is evidently a description based on an etymological pun.

Leonassa (Λεώνασσα) The Lioness, and the granddaughter of Hyllus according to an obscure myth (Table 16). She was said to have married Neoptolemus and to have had several children by him: Argos, Pergamos, Pandarus, Dorieus, Genous, Eurylochus and Danae, all heroes and heroines who normally have other family histories.

Leonteus (Λεοντεύς) A chief of the Lapiths, the son of Coronus and grandson of Caeneus (Table 9). He went with another Lapith, Polypoetes, the son of Pirithous) to the Trojan War. Under this name he is alluded to several times in the *Iliad* and is named among the warriors who manned the wooden horse. Myths also include him in the list of the suitors of Helen. After the capture of Troy,

he followed CALCHAS on the land road. After the death of the seer he returned to Troy, whence he returned to his own country. Mythographers mention a brother of Leonteus, Andraemon, who married Amphinome, one of Pelias' daughters, and a sister called Lyside.

Leontichus (Λεόντιχος) Leontichus and Rhadinea are the subjects of a love story told by Stesichorus. Rhadinea was a young girl of Triphylia in Samos. She was betrothed to a tyrant in Corinth but she loved a young fellow-countryman called Leontichus. When she sailed to Corinth to marry her fiancé, Leonticus took the land route. The tyrant killed them both, however, and returned their bodies on a chariot. He then regretted his cruelty and buried them in an enclosure which he dedicated to them. In the time of Strabo rejected lovers still went there to ask for happiness in their love.

Leontophonus (Λεοντοφόνος) After the murder of the claimants to the throne in Ithaca, it was said that Odysseus, when accused by their parents, submitted the matter to the arbitration of Neoptolemus who condemned him to exile. Odysseus withdrew to Aetolia, and took refuge with Thoas, the son of Andraemon, whose daughter he married. Leontophonus was born from this marriage. He was a lion-killer, a hero about whom we have otherwise no information. Another legend mentions a son of Odysseus called Leontophron, whose mother was Evippe.

Leos (Λέως) The eponymous hero of the tribe of Leontis. He was a son of Orpheus, and he had a son called Clyanthus and three daughters called Phasithea, Theope and Euboule. Once when Athens was suffering from a famine he sacrificed his three daughters willingly because the Delphic oracle demanded human sacrifice to overcome the famine. The girls were honoured by the Athenians who erected a shrine in the Ceramicus in their memory.

Lepreus (Λέπρεος) His myth formed part of the legendary cycle of Heracles, especially in connection with the hero's adventures during his stay with Augias. Lepreus was the son of Caucon and Astydamia, herself the daughter of Phorbas and consequently a sister of Augias (Table 23). He advised Augias not to pay to Heracles the money which he had promised for cleaning the king's stables. He further suggested that he should put

Heracles into chains and imprison him. Also, when Heracles returned to take revenge on Augias and called on Caucon so that he could punish Lepreus, he let himself be side-tracked by the entreaties of Astydamia and contented himself with organizing a contest between himself and Lepreus of eating, drinking and discus throwing. Lepreus was beaten at everything. In his rage he took up arms and they both fought until Lepreus was killed.

Lesbos (Λέσβος) The son of Lapithes (Table 23). On the order of the oracle he went into voluntary exile in Lesbos, where he married Methymna, the daughter of King Macareus (or Macar). He gave his name to the island.

Lethaea (Ληθαία) According to a reference in Ovid it seems that there was a myth, now lost, which stated that she was the wife of Olenus. She claimed to rival a goddess in beauty and her husband tried to save her from punishment by assuming the blame, but both were transformed into stone statues.

Lethe (Λήθη) Oblivion, the daughter of Eris (Discord), and according to one myth the mother of the Charites (the Graces). She gave her name to the river of Oblivion in the Underworld. The dead drank this to make them forget their earthly life. In the same way, in the thinking of philosophers, before returning to life and finding a body, spirits drank this liquid which removed any memory of what they had seen when they were underground. Near the oracle of Trophonius at Lebadia in Boeotia there were two springs which those consulting the oracle had to drink – the spring of forgetfulness (Lethe) and the spring of memory (Mnemosyne). Lethe became a personification of Oblivion, sister of Death and Sleep. It is by this title that poets often refer to her.

Leto (Λητώ) The mother of Apollo and Artemis, of whom Zeus was the father, and a member of the first generation of gods. Her father was, indeed, the Titan Coeus and her mother the Titan Phoebe. Her sisters were Asteria and Ortygia (Table 38). It was said that when Leto was about to produce her divine twins, Hera, being jealous, forbade everywhere in the world to offer her shelter where she might give birth. So Leto wandered about without being able to find a resting place. Finally Ortygia, which until then was a barren floating island agreed to receive her. As a reward the island was fixed to the sea bed by four columns which kept it in position. Also it changed its name: because the god of light first saw daylight on its soil it was called Delos, the Brilliant. Another legend claimed that Hera had sworn that Leto could not give birth in any place which was reached by the sun's rays. On Zeus' order Boreas brought the young woman to Poseidon who, by raising waves, made a sort of liquid arch above the island. So, shaded from the sun, Leto was able to give birth to her children in spite of her enemy's oath. The birth pains lasted nine days and nights. All the goddesses came to help Leto except Hera and Eilithyia, the goddess of birth, who remained on Olympus and her absence hindered the event. In the end Iris was sent by the goddesses and by promising Eilithyia a necklace in gold and amber, nine cubits long, persuaded her to help the suffering Leto. The two divine children were then born.

To escape Hera, Leto assumed the shape of a she-wolf and she fled from the land of the Hyperboreans where she usually lived. This would explain the curious epithet Lycogenes (Son of a Wolf), which was sometimes given to Apollo. Similarly, it was in Lycia, 'the country of the wolves', that another episode connected with the birth was placed. Leto went to Lycia with her two new-born babies. She stopped there by a spring or a pond to wash the children but the neighbouring herdsmen hindered her from reaching it and the goddess turned them into frogs.

Leto later became a much loved mother of her children, who made every effort to defend her in all possible ways. They slaughtered the sons and daughters of NIOBE for her. They killed Tityus, the giant, because he tried to rape her; and because the Python had threatened her, Apollo killed it at Delphi.

Leucadius (Λευκάδιος) According to a legend recorded by Strabo, Leucadius, Alyzeus and Penelope were all three children of Icarius and Polycaste (see PENELOPE and Table 19 for a different legend). ICARIUS had been driven by Hippocoon from Lacedaemonia where he was ruling with his brother Tyndareus. But when Tyndareus was restored to Lacedaemonia by Heracles, Icarius stayed in Acarnania where he established a small state. His son Leucadius gave his name to the town of Leucas and Alyzeus gave his to the town of Alyzia.

Leucaria (Λευκαρία) The wife of King Italus and the mother of Auson, who gave his name to Ausonia (the old name for Italy). In another legend she was the mother of Romus, the eponym in some traditions of Rome. She was said to be the daughter of King Latinus and to have married Aeneas (consequently she is identified with LAVINIA).

Leucaspis (Λεύκασπις) A prince of Sicyon who fought Heracles when he crossed Sicily on his return from his time with Geryon. He was killed, as were also a large number of his fellow nobles, in the fight against the hero. He was given divine honours.

Leucatas (Λευκάτας) A young man who was loved by Apollo. To escape from the attentions of the god he threw himself into the sea from the top of a cliff on the island of Leucas and thus gave his name to it.

Leuce (Λεύκη)
1. Leuce or the 'white one' was a Nymph and daughter of Oceanus and Tethys. Hades fell in love with her and carried her off to the Underworld. Leuce was not immortal, however, and she died. In order to make her immortal Hades changed her into a white poplar which he placed in the Elysian fields. From this tree Heracles gathered the garland with which he wreathed his head when he returned from the Underworld.
2. The white island in the Black Sea at the mouth of the Danube. ACHILLES, accompanied by some heroes, enjoyed with Helen (or Iphigenia or Medea) an after-life of feasting and fighting there.

Leucippe (Λευκίππη)
1. The wife of Laomedon and mother of Priam, according to some legends (Table 7).
2. The wife of King Thestius and mother of IPHICLUS.
3. The daughter of Thestor and the sister of Calchas and THEONOE.
4. The mother of Eurystheus.

Leucippidae (Λευκίππιδαι) The daughters of Leucippus who was the brother of Tyndareus, Icarius and Aphareus (Table 19). In fact Leucippus had two daughters, Hilaera and Phoebe; they married Castor and Pollux, their first cousins (see DIOSCURI). The story of the Leucippidae centres on the conflict which arose between the Dioscuri and two of the sons of Aphareus, Idas and Lynceus. This myth appears in several very different forms of which the oldest seems to be the following: at the time of a festival in Sparta given by the Dios-

curi in honour of Aeneas and Paris who were visiting Menelaus with the secret intention of kidnapping Helen, the sons of Aphareus, inflamed by wine, reproached their cousins Castor and Pollux for having married their wives without paying the usual dowry. Castor and Pollux replied to this insult and the quarrel degenerated into a fight. One of the Dioscuri was killed and Idas and Lynceus were both killed. In the latest forms of the legend the Leucippidae were engaged to the two sons of Aphareus and were kidnapped by the Dioscuri. This is the version accepted by Theocritus in his idyll of the Dioscuri. In another version the Dioscuri kidnapped the Leucippidae during the marriage ceremony. According to a local legend recorded by Pausanias the Leucippidae were daughters of Apollo and Leucippus was only their human father.

Leucippus (Λεύκιππος)
1. This was the name of many mythical figures of whom the most famous was the father of the LEUCIPPIDAE, Hilaera and Phoebe (Table 19). He was a son of Perieres (or Oebalus) and Gorgophone, one of the daughters of Perseus, and his wife was Philodice, a daughter of Inachus. Besides Hilaera and Phoebe he had another daughter called Arsinoe, who, according to one legend, was a lover of Apollo, who fathered her child Asclepius (see CORONIS). Leucippus was king of Messenia.
2. The son of Oenomaus of Pisa. He was in love with DAPHNE and disguised himself as a girl but died as a consequence of this scheme.
3. The son of a king of Sicyon, Thurimachus. He had a daughter called Calchinia who had a son by Poseidon called Peratus. Leucippus adopted him because he had no children of his own, and he succeeded him to the throne of Sicyon.
4. The son of Naxos, eponym of the island. He had a son called Smerdius; it was during his reign that THESEUS abandoned ARIADNE.
5. The hero of a love story told by Parthenius from a plot by Hermesianax. This Leucippus was a son of Xanthius, a descendant of Bellerophon. He had great strength and was an excellent warrior, whose reputation was well known throughout Lycia. The wrath of Aphrodite fell upon him, however, and he fell in love with his sister. For some time he restrained his passion but he soon recognized that it was irresistible: he asked his mother to have pity on him and to help him satisfy his desire. His mother agreed and Leucippus became his sister's lover, but the man she was to marry discovered the truth; he went to see Xanth-

ius, accompanied by his father and by leading men of the country, and told him that his daughter had a lover; he did not specify that the lover was Leucippus. Xanthius became very angry and swore that he would punish his daughter's lover if he caught him in the act. He went to his daughter's bedroom and when she saw him enter she hid; Xanthius thought that he had caught the culprit and without recognizing her he struck her with his sword. Leucippus dashed in and, not realizing that the attacker was his father, killed him. Leucippus then went into exile in Crete. Later he was driven out by his companions and he returned to Asia Minor where he founded the town of Cretinaeon in the neighbourhood of Miletus. It is said that Leucophryne, the daughter of Mandrolytus, betrayed her city, Magnesia on the Meander, to enemies commanded by Leucippus, because she was in love with him.

Leucon (Λεύκων) One of ATHAMAS' sons, whose mother was Themisto, a daughter of Hypseus. His brothers were Erythrius, Schoeneus and Ptous. Leucon had a son called Erythras, who founded the town of Erythrae in Boeotia, and two daughters, Evippe, the wife of Andreus, and Pisidice, the mother of Argennus (Table 33).

Leucophanes (Λευκοφάνης) The son of EUPHEMUS, an Argonaut and the ancestor of the Battiades of Cyrene.

Leucosia (Λευκόσια) A siren who gave her name to an island opposite the gulf of Paestum.

Leucothea (Λευκοθέα) The name of Ino, a daughter of Cadmus, after her transformation into a sea-goddess (Table 3). She was married to Athamas and was his second wife; Athamas' first wife was Nephele. After the death of her sister Semele, Ino persuaded Athamas to receive the child DIONYSUS and to bring him up with their children Learchus and Melicertes. Hera was angry because they had received a son born of the adulterous affair of Zeus, and made both Athamas and Ino mad. Ino threw Melicertes into a cauldron of boiling water, while Athamas killed Learchus with a spear imagining that he was a deer. Ino threw herself into the sea with Melicertes' corpse. The sea-gods had pity on her and transformed her into a Nereid; the child became the young god PALAEMON. Ino became Leucothea, the White Goddess or the goddess of the spray. She and Palaemon guided sailors in storms. Sisyphus founded the Isthmian games in honour of Melicertes. In Rome Leucothea was identified with Mater Matuta, whose temple was situated in the Forum Boarium not far from the port of Rome. Palaemon was identified with the god Portunus, the god of ports, who had his temple in the same neighbourhood. There was another Leucothea, also a sea-goddess, who came from Rhodes (see HALIA).

Leucothoe (Λευκοθόη) The name sometimes given to LEUCOTHEA. It is also the name of the rival of CLYTIA, the lover of the sun, who was transformed into a heliotrope.

Leucus (Λεῦκος) A Cretan, son of Talus, who was exposed by his father at birth. Idomeneus rescued him and brought him up as if he were his own son. When Idomeneus went to the Trojan war he placed Leucus in charge of his kingdom and his family, promising him the hand of his daughter Clisithera, but Leucus was influenced by NAUPLIUS, who wanted to avenge the death of his son Palamedes by destroying the Greek leaders. Leucus seduced Meda, the wife of Idomeneus, killed her together with all Idomeneus' children and then usurped the island's throne. When Idomeneus returned, Leucus attacked him and drove him into exile.

Liber The Italian equivalent of Dionysus. He was given this identity at a very early date. His name, which means 'Free' in Latin, was derived from one of Dionysus' common nicknames, Lyaeus, or the Liberator. The Liberalia were celebrated in his honour. Like most of the earliest rustic Latin gods, Liber did not have his own mythology but appears simply as the equivalent of Dionysus. Liber had a female counterpart Libera, who was often linked with Ceres. Latin mythographers identified her with the deified Ariadne.

Libitina The Roman goddess concerned with supervising the rites that were paid to the dead. She had her shrine in a sacred wood, probably south of Rome on the Aventine. All the undertakers (Libitinarii) assembled there. By a piece of erroneous etymology Libitina was confused with Libido (sensual passion): this very ancient goddess was integrated with Venus and the name Libitina became a common name for her. There are no specific myths about her.

Libya The Nymph who gave her name to North Africa including Cyrene. She was normally linked with Io her grandmother but she was a daughter of Epaphus, who was a son of Io and Zeus (Table 3). By Poseidon she bore two sons, Agenor and Belus, the two mythical heroes of Phoenicia and Egypt. A number of variations were introduced into this genealogy. Sometimes Libya was said to be Io's daughter and not her granddaughter. Besides Belus and Agenor, her children were Enyalius (which is only an epithet of Ares), Lelex, BUSIRIS the Egyptian tyrant, Phoenix (though he was also considered to be her grandson, and the son of Agenor) and even ATLAS, the giant who carried the world on his shoulders. A late and 'rationalising' tradition made Libya the daughter of Oceanus and sister of Asia, Europe and Thrace.

Lichas (Λίχας) A companion of HERACLES who remained with him until his death on Oeta. During the war with Oechalia he served as herald. Heracles ordered him to go to find Deianeira, after his victory, to ask her for a new robe so that he could be suitably clad when he made a sacrifice to Zeus. Also, according to some versions, Lichas led Iole as a prisoner to Deianeira or alternatively he told Deianeira that her husband was in love with Iole. Deianeira gave him the tunic steeped in Nessus' blood. When Heracles had put on the poisoned tunic he went first to Lichas and, seizing one of his legs, threw him into the sky; Lichas was changed into stone and became the Lichadian islands (the islands of the shellfish).

Licymnius (Λικύμνιος) A son of Electryon (himself a son of Perseus) and Media, a Phrygian slave (Table 31), and therefore the half-brother of Alcmene, and uncle of Heracles. His story forms part of the Heracles cycles. Licymnius spent his childhood at Mycenae with his father. During the war which the Taphians fought against Electryon, Licymnius, who was still only young, was the only one of his children to escape massacre. When AMPHITRYON accidentally killed Electryon, Licymnius went with him in exile to Thebes with his sister Alcmene. There he married Perimede, a sister of Amphitryon; they had several children: Oeonus (who was later killed by the sons of Hippocoon at Sparta and whose death was the reason for the expedition of HERACLES against Sparta), Argeius and Melas; the latter accompanied Heracles against Oechalia and were killed in battle. Heracles had promised Licymnius to bring him back his son, so he cremated the corpse of Argeius and returned the ashes in an urn.

After Heracles' death Licymnius shared the fate of the other HERACLIDS. He took refuge in Trachis and fought in the battle against Eurystheus. He later joined Hyllus in the first and disastrous expedition against the Peloponnese. The Argives invited Licymnius and Tlepolemus – one of Heracles' sons – to settle in their city. In the course of a quarrel Licymnius was struck down by Tlepolemus, or, alternatively, he was killed accidentally by Tlepolemus.

Ligys (Λίγυς) The eponymous hero of the Ligurians and the brother of Alebion. When HERACLES on his return from the land of Geryon crossed southern Gaul, Ligys tried to get hold of the flock which the hero was bringing back with him. Ligys and his fellow Ligarians attacked Heracles. He began to run short of arrows, and when he was on the point of being overpowered by his attackers he uttered a prayer to his father, who sent him piles of stones which he used to repulse his enemies. The plain of Crau still bears witness to this event, by the vast number of rocks and stones which cover it.

Lilaeus (Λίλαιος) An Indian shepherd, who would acknowledge only Selene (the moon) of all the immortals. The other gods were angry with him, so they set two lions against him which ate him up, but Selene changed him into a mountain called Mount Lilaeon.

Limos (Λίμος) The personification of hunger. She was said to have been a daughter of Eris. She was a purely abstract conception with no legend.

Lindos (Λίνδος) A hero who gave his name to Lindos in Rhodes (see CERCAPHUS).

Linus (Λίνος) There were several legends about Linus, which all had a common thread, in that he was either a singer or the object of a celebrated song.
1. Psamathe, daughter of Crotopus, the king of Argos, had a child by Apollo (Table 17). After his birth this infant, Linus, was exposed by his mother and brought up by shepherds. Some said that Crotopus heard of the incident and caused the child to be eaten by dogs; others that the shepherds' dogs killed him by mistake. Psamathe herself was killed by her father. Apollo was angry and brought a plague down on Argos (see CROTOPUS and COREOBUS). On the advice of the oracle, the custom was introduced of singing a dirge to

celebrate the sad story of Psamathe and Linus. During this ceremony any dogs found in the street or on the square were killed.

2. Theban legend mentions a second Linus, the son of Amphimarus and a Muse (generally Urania, but sometimes Calliope or Terpsichore), who was a remarkable musician. He had the idea of changing the linen strings previously used on lyres for strings of gut. When he dared to compete with Apollo as a singer, the god was angry and killed him. The invention of rhyme and of melody was attributed to this Linus. It is sometimes said that he learned the Phoenician alphabet from Cadmus but gave each letter its definitive name and shape himself. One legend claimed that this Linus (or another man of the same name) had been the music master of Heracles but his pupil was unmusical. Linus often smacked his pupil until one day Heracles became irritated by this treatment and taking a big stone struck his master down. It is also said that he killed him with the plectrum, the instrument used to pluck the strings of the lyre.

Linus' name was given to various philosophical and mystical treatises. As his personality evolved, so his genealogy was altered; he was said to be a son of Hermes, because Hermes was the god of science, particularly the science of language. At other times he was regarded as the son of Oeagrus, and the brother of Orpheus with whom he became increasingly assimilated.

Liparus (Λίπαρος) One of the sons of Auson, the mythical king of Italy. He was driven out of his country by his brothers and fled with some soldiers to an island which he called Lipara, off the Sicilian coast. There he established a community which prospered. Later he welcomed Aeolus when he came to the island and gave him Cyane, his daughter, in marriage. In return Aeolus arranged for him to return to Italy, which he was eager to revisit. Liparus landed on the coast at Sorrento where he was made a king by the inhabitants. When he died, his new subjects gave him divine honours.

Lityerses (Λιτυέρσης) A son of King Midas, and an accomplished harvester. He received travellers who crossed his territory and asked them to go harvesting with him; if they refused he killed them or at least he forced them by violence to work for him. Then in the evening after a day spent harvesting he beheaded them and put their bodies in a stook. Sometimes he forced them to compete with him to see who was the quickest harvester.

He always won and would then behead his opponent. When Heracles was in the service of Omphale he passed Lityerses' estate. He accepted the ruffian's challenge and after making him drowsy by a song, he cut off his head. Heracles killed him because Lityerses was keeping as a slave DAPHNIS the herdsman who was searching for his lover, Pimplea. Harvesters in Phrygia (Lityerses' country) used to sing while working a song dedicated to the exploits of Lityerses in which they boasted of his skill as a harvester. This song was called *Lityerse*.

Locrus (Λοκρός)
1. The son of Zeus and Maera, herself the daughter of Proetus, king of Argos, and Anteia. Maera was a companion of Artemis and after her intrigue with Zeus she was killed by an arrow of the angry goddess. Together with AMPHION and ZETHUS Locrus built Thebes.

2. The figure who gave his name to Locri. His genealogy is given differently by different authors. Some say that he was a son of Physcus and consequently a grandson of Aetolus and a great-grandson of Amphictyon; others claim that he was the son of Amphictyon and the grandson of Deucalion (Table 8). He ruled over the Leleges and gave them the name of Locrians. The legends about the wife of Locrus are no less diverse. It is said, for example, that Opus, a king of Elis, had a daughter called Cabye of exceptional beauty. Zeus abducted her and took her to Mount Menalus. She became pregnant and Zeus took her to Locrus who had no children and gave her to him as a wife. Locrus reared the child which she bore and called it Opus after his grandfather. It was usually said that Locrus was married to Protogenia, a daughter of Deucalion. After an affair with Zeus, Protogenia gave birth to the hero Aethlius.

Locrus had a quarrel with Opus and he decided to relinquish power to him, and to go with some of his subjects to set himself up elsewhere. Locrus asked the oracle where he should go; the oracle told him to stop at a place where he was bitten by a 'bitch of the woods'. When he had reached the western slopes of Parnassus he stepped accidentally on the thorns of a wild rose (in Greek 'dog rose') and could not walk for several days. He realized that the oracle had been fulfilled and he settled in this country, which was also called Locris after him. This legend was meant to explain amongst other things why there were two places called Locris, one in the east and the other to the west of Parnassus.

Lotis (Λωτίς) A Nymph loved by Priapus; she obstinately refused the god's advances. He nearly entrapped her on several occasions but she always escaped. One night when she was sleeping among the Maenads, the companions of Dionysus, Priapus, who was one of the same band, tried to reach her and take her by surprise, but at the moment when he was just already touching her Silenus' donkey began to bray so loudly that everybody woke up; Lotis escaped leaving Priapus abashed while everybody there laughed at his bad luck. Later Lotis asked to be changed into a plant and she became a shrub with red flowers called a Lotus (see also DRYOPE).

Lotophagi (Λωτοφάγοι) The Lotus-eaters, a people amongst whom Odysseus landed when he was driven off course by a violent north wind which sent him south of Cyprus. They welcomed the hero and his men hospitably and gave them the fruit of the Lotus which makes people lose their memory. Odysseus' companions soon lost their desire to return to Ithaca, and Odysseus had to force them to put to sea again. It is possible that the Lotophagi's country was located on the coast of Cyrene.

Lua A very old Roman goddess associated with Saturn, and connected with the *devotio* or offering of enemy spoils. She seems to have been a goddess of the plague or, more often, a magic defilement by which one hoped to see one's enemies struck.

Lucifer This was the Latin name for PHOSPHORUS.

Luna The Roman goddess of the moon. Her temple in Rome was on the Aventine. She seems always to have been regarded as a goddess of the second rank. She was integrated with Diana, whose temple was adjacent to hers. She has no individual legends: in passages where she is alluded to in literature she is merely an equivalent of Selene.

Luperci A community of priests in Rome who celebrated the cult of Faunus Lupercus with a festival called the Lupercalia. This was a procession which took place every year on 15 February. During this ceremony they paraded naked round the Palatine and scourged any women they met on their way with the hair of a specially sacrificed goat. They believed that women would become fertile in this way. Before the procession the priest sacrificed the goat and with the bloody knife marked the foreheads of the Luperci. The marks were removed by being wiped with a wisp of wool soaked in milk, then the Luperci uttered a peal of ritual laughter. The sacrifice also included the immolation of a dog. The shrine of Faunus Lupercus was the cave of Lupercal situated on the north-west slope of the Palatine. According to legend, the she-wolf suckled Romulus and Remus there. This sacred cave, the cradle of Rome, was shaded by a fig tree, the Ruminal fig tree (see ROMULUS). A spring flowed from it. It was restored by Augustus when the cult of the Luperci was reorganized (see also HIRPI SORANI).

Lycaon (Λυκάων)
1. One of the sons of Priam and Laothoe (Table 34). He was captured by Achilles one night when he was cutting branches in Priam's orchard. Achilles subsequently sold him to Lemnos but Eetion of Imbros bought him back and secretly returned him to Troy. Twelve days after his return he met Achilles on the battlefield, on the banks of the Scamander. Although he offered a ransom, the Greek killed him mercilessly.

2. Another Lycaon more famous than the former was an Arcadian hero, a son of Pelasgus. His mother was either Meliboea a daughter of Oceanus, or the Nymph Cyllene (Table 18). Lycaon succeeded his father as king of Arcadia. He had some fifty sons, but the mythographers do not agree on the names or the exact number of the sons. Pausanias and Apollodorus give remarkably different lists: Pausanias for example makes Nyctimus the eldest; whereas, according to Apollodorus he was the youngest and Maenalus the eldest. Here is the list as given by Apollodorus: Maenalus, Thesprotus, Helix, Nyctimus, Peucetius, Caucon, Mecisteus, Hopleus, Macareus, Macednus, Horus, Polichus, Acontes, Evaemon, Ancyor, Archebates, Carteron, Aegaeon, Pallas, Canethus, Prothous, Linus, Corethon, Teleboas, Physius, Phassus, Phthius, Lycius, Halipherus, Genetor, Boucolion, Socleus, Phineus, Eumetes, Harpaleus, Portheus, Platon, Haemon, Cynaethus, Leon, Harpalycus, Heraeeus, Titanas, Mantinous, Cleitor, Stymphalus, Orchomenus. It is said that generally the sons of Lycaon were the eponymous heroes of a great number of towns in the Peloponnese. Pausanias lists: Maenalus, Helisson, Nyctimus, Macareus, Pallas, Lycius, Halipherus, Heraeeus, Mantineus, Orchomenus, Orestheus, Phigalus, Trapezus, Daseatas, Acacus, Thocnus, Hypsas, Tegeates, Cromus, Charisius,

Tricolonus, Peraethus, Aseatas, Sumateus, Oenotrus. Dionysius of Halicarnassus mentions Peucetius who went with Oenotrus his brother to Italy where they gave their name to two races, the Oenotrians and the Peucetians. Dionysius of Halicarnassus also makes a distinction between two Lycaons: one was the son of Aezeius and father of Deianeira; this Deianeira was said to have married Pelasgus by whom she had the second Lycaon, the father of the fifty children whose mother was the Nymph Cyllene. Like all genealogical legends this one is very complicated and seems to have changed with the times and the cities according to the needs of explanation and local data.

Lycaon was a very pious king like his father Pelasgus and was frequently visited by the gods. His sons wanted to know if the strangers who came to visit their father really were gods. So they murdered a child and mixed its flesh with that which had been prepared for the banquet. In horror the gods sent a tornado which destroyed the guilty. But more often, Lycaon, as well as his sons was said to have been impious. One day Zeus wanted personally to establish the extent of their impiety and, disguised as a peasant, he came to ask the king for hospitality. The king received him but because he wanted to discover if his guest was a god, he gave him a child's flesh to eat, either that of a hostage which he had held at court or even one of his own sons, Nyctimus, or indeed of his grandson Arcas. Zeus, enraged by such a meal, turned the table over and in his anger struck Lycaon and his children with lightning, one after the other. Gaia intervened in time to save the youngest, Nyctimus, who succeeded Lycaon as king. Other legends say that Lycaon was transformed into a wolf by Zeus. This version was devised to correspond to the custom of human sacrifice in honour of the Lycian Zeus in Arcadia. There a human victim was sacrificed, and the attendants 'took communion' by eating its entrails.

3. A son of Ares and Pyrene who was killed by HERACLES.

Lycastus (Λύκαστος)

1. A Cretan hero in a legend for which Diodorus is the main source. He was the father of Minos 2, whom he sired on Ida, daughter of Corybas. In this version he was himself the son of Minos 1 and Itone, the daughter of Lyctius.

2. The son of Ares and Phylonome. She was a daughter of Nyctimus; she gave birth to him and Parrhasius secretly at the same time. She aban-

doned both on Mount Erymanthus because she was afraid of her father. They were reared by shepherds and later ruled in Arcadia.

3. For another hero of the same name, see EULIMENE.

Lycius (Λύκιος) The son of CLINIS, a Babylonian, who was turned into a crow because against the wish of Apollo he had sacrificed an ass on the latter's altar, according to the custom of the Hyperboreans. The crow was originally white but it turned black because of his mistake (see CORONIS). Lycius was also an epithet of Apollo.

Lyco (Λυκώ) One of the two sisters of Carya, the daughter of King Dion of Lacedaemon. She and her sister were given the power of prophecy by Apollo. She tried to interfere in the love affair between Carya and Dionysus and was turned into a stone.

Lycomedes (Λυκομήδης) King of the Dolopians who lived on the island of Scyros. Lycomedes was king at the time of the Trojan War and it was to Scyros that Thetis went with Achilles, to help him escape his destiny; for she knew that if he went to the war against Troy he would be killed. Lycomedes dressed him in woman's clothes and concealed him in his harem among his daughters. Achilles fell in love with one of the daughters, Deidamia, by whom he had a child, NEOPTOLEMUS, known as Pyrrhus. Among the women Achilles was known as Pyrrha or Issa or even Cercysera. Lycomedes also played a part in the legend of THESEUS. When Theseus took refuge with him after the murder of the Pallantidae – or the death of Hippolytus, or for other reasons, according to the mythographers – Lycomedes was afraid that the newcomer might earn the affection and admiration of his subjects and would steal his kingdom. Under the cover of friendship he took Theseus with him to the top of a cliff and pushed him down off it.

Lycopeus (Λυκωπεύς) One of the sons of Agrius; the brother of Thersites, Onchestus, Prothous, Celeutor and Melanippus (Tables 24 and 27). With them he took part in an expedition against Oeneus. They captured the kingdom of Calydon from Oeneus but Lycopeus was later killed by DIOMEDES who had come to Argos to help Oeneus.

Lycophron (Λυκόφρων) A son of Mestor. After committing a murder he had to leave Cythera, his home country. He accompanied Ajax, the son of Telamon, to Troy, where he was killed by Hector.

Lycoreus (Λυκωρεύς) The son of Apollo and the Nymph Corycia, who gave her name to a cave on Mount Parnassus, situated above Delphi. He was the king and founder of a town called Lycoreia at the top of Parnassus. He had a son, HYAMUS, whose daughter, Celaeno, had a son by Apollo who was called DELPHUS.

Lycurgus (Λυκοῦργος)
1. A son of Aleus and Neaera and so descended from Arcas (Table 9). When his father died he followed him as king of Arcadia and lived to a very great age. Through his son, Iasus, he was the grandfather of Atalanta, at least in one version of her story, and of Melanion, who succeeded in marrying her (Table 20).
2. A king of Thrace who played a part in the legend of Dionysus. The *Iliad* quoted him as an example of the punishments which awaited those who challenged the gods. Lycurgus drove away Dionysus who had arrived in Thrace with his nurses. He frightened Dionysus so much that he jumped into the sea, where he was rescued by Thetis. The gods however, punished him: Zeus made him blind. In the tragedies Dionysus was represented as grown up. Lycurgus was the king of the Edones in Thrace and a son of Dryas. When Dionysus wanted to cross Thrace on his way to attack the Indians, Lycurgus refused permission. He captured the Bacchantes and the Satyrs in Dionysus' train. Dionysus took refuge in the sea with Thetis, the daughter of Nereus. The Bacchantes were freed miraculously from their chains and Lycurgus went mad; thinking that his son Dryas was a vine, Lycurgus struck him with an axe and killed him. Once this murder had taken place, Lycurgus regained his sanity; but the ground became barren and the oracle told the people that it would become fertile again only if Lycurgus was killed. On Mount Pangeus his subjects tied him to four horses which tore him to pieces.

The legend as related by Hyginus differs greatly from the previous one. Lycurgus drove Dionysus out of his kingdom, calling his divinity into question. Then, after drinking wine he tried to rape his own mother in his drunkenness. To stop a recurrence of such disgraceful behaviour he tried to uproot all the vines, but Dionysus made him mad

and he killed his wife and son. Then Dionysus exposed him to the panthers on Mount Rhodope.

Diodorus knew a variation to this legend. In his opinion Lycurgus was the king of the area of Thrace adjoining the Hellespont. Dionysus had decided to go from Asia to Europe with his army and made a treaty with Lycurgus to this end. Relying on this, the Bacchantes crossed the water and entered Thrace, but during the night Lycurgus ordered his soldiers to kill Dionysus and the Bacchantes. A person called CHAROPS told the god about the plot. The latter was frightened so he decided to leave most of his troops in Asia, and he himself crossed back. In his absence Lycurgus attacked the Bacchantes and put them to death, but Dionysus returned in force and routed the Thracian army. He captured Lycurgus and tore out his eyes. After much torture he crucified him. Diodorus says that this episode was not always set in Thrace but sometimes in Nysa in Ethiopia. Nonnus, in his Dionysiacs, overdeveloped the episode of Lycurgus, describing a Bacchante called Ambrosia, who changed herself into a vine shoot so that she could encircle and throttle him. Hera had to rescue him by brandishing the sword of Ares above the Bacchante.
3. Another Lycurgus, sometimes also called Lycus, was king of Nemea. He was one of Pheres' sons (or alternatively of PRONAX) and either by Amphithea or Eurydice he had a child called Opheltes. This child was put in the charge of its nurse Hypsipyle, but was strangled by a serpent near a spring (see AMPHIARAUS). The tomb of this Lycurgus was to be seen at Nemea in Zeus' sacred wood.

Lycus (Λύκος) Several heroes had this name. Three of them were related to Atlas and the Pleiades (Table 25).
1. The son of Celaeno and Poseidon. He was taken by his father to the Island of the Blessed.
2. According to another tradition, the second was the son of the same Celaeno and Prometheus, and the brother of CHIMAEREUS (Table 38). It was while he was taking an offering to the tombs of Chimaereus and Lycus that Menelaus became the guest of Paris.
3. The best-known of the heroes called Lycus was a grandson of the Pleiad Alcyone and Poseidon (Table 25). He was the son of Hyrieus and the Nymph Clonia and, at least according to the most common legend, the uncle of Antiope. A different version claimed that Nycteus and Lycus were sons

of Chthonius, one of the 'Spartoi', that is the warriors born from the teeth of the dragon killed by CADMUS. Antiope is sometimes said to be the daughter and not the niece of Lycus. Lycus is said to have captured the town of Sicyon to avenge the rape of Antiope, but some accounts claim that Lycus undertook it to avenge his brother's death.

Apollodorus tells how Nycteus and Lycus had to flee from Euboea, their native land, because they had killed Phlegyas, the son of Ares and Doris. The two men took refuge in Hyria in Boeotia; then they went to Thebes, where king Pentheus welcomed them. Pentheus made Lycus commander of the army. When Pentheus died, Lycus took power. Another legend maintained that Lycus became regent on the death of Labdacus because the latter's son, LAIUS, was too young to be king. Another legend, recorded by Hyginus and taken from a later tragic poet, makes Lycus the husband of Antiope. Lycus renounced her because she had an affair with Epaphus and subsequently was loved by Zeus. Lycus then married Dirce but she was jealous of Antiope who, she suspected, had not severed all relationship with her first husband, so she had her imprisoned. Antiope was miraculously freed from her bonds on the orders of Zeus and she fled to Cithaeron where she bore two sons, Amphion and Zethus. These two later took their revenge on Dirce and Lycus. On the revenge of Amphion and Zethus, some accounts say that they killed Lycus and others that, under orders from Hermes, they merely drove him out of his kingdom.

In *Heracles Maddened* by Euripides, the poet introduced a character also called Lycus who in Heracles' absence seized the kingdom of Thebes and was on the point of exiling Megara when Heracles returned. The usurper had come from Euboea and was a descendant of the son of Nycteus who had the same name. It is probable that Euripides based the character wholly on this Lycus.

4. One of the Telchines, the first people to live on Rhodes. Lycus had a premonition that there would be a flood (this was at the time of Deucalion), and took flight with his brothers. He landed in Lycia, where he introduced the worship of the Lycian Apollo in the valley of the Xanthus.

5. One of the four sons of Pandion and a brother of Aegeus. When Pandion's sons returned to Athens, Lycus was given some land in Attica but shortly afterwards he was driven out of it by Aegeus and

took refuge in Messenia. He was a well-known priest and seer. The foundation of the cult of the Lycian Apollo was attributed to him. He introduced Aphareus to the mysteries of the Great Gods. Another account says that he emigrated to Lycia and that the country owed its name to him.

6. A king of the Mariandyni on the western coast of Asia Minor who received the Argonauts hospitably when they stopped there. He was a son of Dascylus and therefore a grandson of Tantalus, which explains his fellow feeling for the Greeks. He provided a magnificent funeral for Tiphys and Idmon, two Argonauts who died, and he provided his son Dascylus to guide the *Argo*. Lycus, who had suffered from pillaging by his neighbours, the Bebryces, was grateful to the ARGONAUTS for killing their king, Amycus, the more so because Amycus had killed his brother Otreus and he was himself engaged in an expedition against them in reprisal when the arrival of the Argonauts relieved him of his enemy. HERACLES, on returning from his expedition to the country of the Amazons, supported Lycus in a war with the Bebryces and killed Mygdon, Amycus' brother. Heracles also gave Lycus a part of the country of the Bebryces.

The legend also mentioned a Lycus who was a son of Ares, king of Libya, who made a practice of sacrificing strangers to his father. Returning from Troy, Diomedes was shipwrecked on the coast. Lycus took him prisoner and was about to sacrifice him when Callirhoe, his daughter, took pity on the prisoner and set him free. Diomedes did not reciprocate the young girl's love, however; he fled, and realizing that she was abandoned she hung herself.

Lydus (Λυδός) This figure gave his name to the Lydians of Asia Minor. He was said, in the account given by Herodotus, to be a son of Atys, who was himself the son of Manes. Dionysius of Halicarnassus gives him a more complex genealogy. Manes was said to be a son of Zeus and Gaia; he had an intrigue with the Nymph Callirhoe and by her had a son called Cotys, who married Halie (or Halia) a daughter of the family of Tullus. Cotys had two sons, Adies and Atys. Atys married Callithea, by whom he had Lydus and Tyrrhenus. Lydus was king before the arrival of the Heraclids. His brother was TYRRHENUS, the hero who gave his name to the Tyrrhenians, or Etruscans. Some versions claim that Lydus was a member of the dynasty of the Heraclids, the offspring of Heracles and Omphale, who seized power after Manes' dynasty.

Lymphae These in popular Latin mythology were divinities of springs. They were identified with the NYMPHS at an early stage. The Lymphae could make anybody who saw them become mad, hence the Latin word *lymphatus* meaning 'fool'.

Lynceus (Λυγκεύς)
1. The son of Aegyptus, and husband of HYPERMES-TRA, one of the DANAIDS. He was spared by his fianceé at the time of the massacre. She was put on trial by Danaus for disobeying her father's orders but thanks to Aphrodite's help she was acquitted. In gratitude she dedicated a statue to the goddess. Lynceus took refuge on a hill near Argos after being spared by Hypermestra and waited to learn if it was safe for him to return to the town. Hypermestra let him know by waving a torch. In memory of this action, the Argives had a torchlight festival on the hill which was called Lyrceia (from the name of Lyrcus who was the son of Lynceus, see LYRCUS 2). Lynceus became reconciled with his father-in-law later and succeeded Danaus as king of Argos. By Hypermestra he had one son, Abas, the father of ACRISIUS and Proetus (Table 31). Another legend claims that Lynceus killed his father-in-law. Lynceus was buried in Argos.
2. The brother of Idas, and the son of Aphareus (Table 9). Through his grandmother Gorgophone he was a member of Perseus' family. He took part in the Calydonian hunt (see MELEAGER) and in the ARGONAUTS' expedition where he was distinguished by his keen sight. His most celebrated actions relate to his fight against the DIOSCURI on behalf of the LEUCIPPIDAE (see also IDAS). The euhemeristic mythographers invented an interpretation of the Lyncean legend which claimed that he was the first miner. He dug up the ground and with the help of a lamp followed the veins of metals. His ability to bring the metal to the surface gave him the reputation for being able to see underground.

Lyncus (Λύγχος) A king of Scythia with whom Triptolemus stayed when he was sent by Demeter to spread the cultivation of wheat. During the night Lyncus, who was jealous, tried to kill him, but Demeter transformed the king into a lynx and so saved Triptolemus.

Lyrcus (Λύρκος)
1. The hero of an incident recorded by Parthenius, according to Nicaenetus and Apollonius of Rhodes. He was a son of Phoroneus, and with several other young men he was sent by Inachus to look for Io when she had been kidnapped by Zeus. He failed to find her and was afraid to return to Argos; so he settled in Caunus where Aegialus gave him the hand of his daughter Hilebie and a part of his kingdom. Hilebie saw Lyrcus, fell in love with him, and asked her father to arrange the marriage. For a long time Lyrcus stayed in Caunus with his wife but they had no children. He finally went to the oracle at Dodona and asked what he should do to be sure of having children. The oracle replied that the first woman with whom he slept would give him a son. Lyrcus was delighted and set off home believing that the prediction referred to his wife, but on the journey he stopped at Bybastus in the land of Staphylus, the son of Dionysus. There he became drunk at a banquet, and during the night Staphylus put one of his daughters, Hemithea, in the room with Lyrcus because he had been told about the oracle's prediction and he was very keen to have male heirs. According to the legend, Rhoeo and Hemithea quarrelled about who should spent the night with the guest, for Lyrcus had attracted them both, but Hemithea won. On the following morning Lyrcus realized what he had done and reproached Staphylus bitterly, saying that he had been deceived by him. In the end he gave his belt to Hemithea so that when her son was born she could give it to him as a sign of recognition. He then returned to Caunus. Aegialus was angry at what had happened and exiled Lyrcus; there was then a civil war between the supporters of Lyrcus and the king. Hilebie took her husband's part against her father and helped to win him the final victory. Some years later, the son of Hemithea and Lyrcus, who was called Basilus, came to Caunus and found his father, whom he succeeded.
2. A son of Lynceus, himself a son of Aegyptus; he established himself after his father's death in the village of Lynceia near Argos and changed its name to Lyrceia (see LYNCEUS 1). Some accounts claim that Lyrcus was not the son of Lynceus but a bastard of King Abas.

Lysidice (Λυσιδίκη) The daughter of Pelops. She was the wife of Mestor and bore him Hippothoe. According to another myth she was the wife of Alceus and the mother of Amphitryon (Alceus' wife was more usually called Astydamia or Laonome) (Table 31). Other versions say that she was the mother of Alcmene and consequently the wife of Electryon.

Lysippe (Λυσίππη) One of the Proetides, daughters of Proetus, who were made mad by Hera and cured by MELAMPUS. It was also the name of the wife of CEPHALUS in Cephalonia.

M

Macar (Μάκαρ) In the *Iliad*, a king of the island of Lesbos. Traditions vary about his origin: in some accounts he is said to have been one of the sons of Helios and Rhodus (see HELIADES), who fled from Rhodes after the murder of his brother Tenages and took refuge in Lesbos. Some authors call him Macareus rather than Macar. In other versions he is said to have been a son of Crinacus and therefore a grandson of Zeus. He was also said to have been a native of Olenus in Achaea. After the flood associated with Deucalion, Macar came to Lesbos at the head of a group of Ionians and other settlers from various places. Macar's settlement flourished and he assumed power over the neighbouring islands which then were uninhabited. At about the same time LESBOS, the son of Lapithes, arrived in Lesbos. He came with some companions in obedience to an instruction from the Pythian oracle to settle on Macar's island. He married Methymna, a daughter of Macar. The two groups of people, those who came with Thessalian Lesbos and the Ionians of Macar inhabited the island jointly. The island later became known as Lesbos. Macar had another daughter, Mytilene, besides Methymna. Each of them gave her name to a town in Lesbos. Another tradition made Macar a son of Aeolus (see MACAREUS). One of his daughters gave her name, Amphissa, to the town in Locris. It is said that she had an intrigue with Apollo.

Macareus (Μακαρεύς)
1. The son of Aeolus who had an incestuous affair with his sister CANACE. When this became known he committed suicide. This Macareus has sometimes been confused with MACAR, king of Lesbos.
2. The name of a priest of Dionysus at Mytilene, who suffered a series of catastrophes because he committed an act of sacrilege. A stranger had entrusted gold to the god and had deposited it in the temple. Macareus seized the treasure and when the stranger came to reclaim it, Macareus killed him in the sanctuary itself. Macareus' two sons were playing shortly after the festival of Trieterides. They amused themselves by imitating the sacrifice which their father had just offered. The elder took the sacred knife and stabbed his brother in the neck. Then in spite of his brother's screams he burned him on the altar which was still hot. In anger his mother struck him down. Macareus killed his wife with a blow of a thyrsus.

Macaria (Μακαρία) Macaria, which means 'the blessed' was the daughter of Heracles and Deianeira. Macaria slew her father's killer on Oeta. She later took refuge, with her brothers, in Trachis, and then in Athens and when the oracle had pronounced that victory over Eurystheus demanded a human sacrifice, Macaria immediately offered herself, thus ensuring victory (see HERACLES). To honour her there was a spring near Marathon in Attica which was named after her.

Macedon (Μακέδων) The hero who gave Macedonia its name. There are many different versions of his ancestry. In some he was said to be a native; in others he was either a brother of Magnes, a son of Zeus and Thyia, or one of Aeolus' ten sons, or a son of Lycaon, or, finally, a son of the god Osiris, who was established by his father as king of Macedonia when Osiris conquered the world. In this last version, reported by Diodorus, Macedon was the brother of Anubis. He was dressed in a breastplate of wolf-skin and wore this animal's head as a mask on his face.

Macello (Μακελλώ) The heroine of an obscure, and probably Rhodian legend. She and her sister Dexithea invited Apollo, Zeus and Poseidon to eat with them. When Poseidon or Zeus destroyed either the Phlegians or the Telchines for having poisoned wheat seed with water from the Styx, he spared the two women and did not strike them with his trident. Macello and Dexithea were daughters of a man called Damon. Dexithea married Minos and bore him a son Euxanthius. At the place where Macello and her sister received the gods Euxanthius built the town of Coresus, 'the city of young girls'.

Machaereus (Μαχαιρεύς) 'The man with the knife', one of the priests of Delphi, and a son of Daitas who killed NEOPTOLEMUS because the latter complained about the custom of the Delphic priests of taking the flesh of victims sacrificed to Apollo (see ORESTES).

Machaon (Μαχάων) A son of Asclepius and a brother of Podalirius. Normally his mother was said to be Epione, the daughter of Merope, though various myths refer to her as Arsinoe, Xanthe, Lampetia, the daughter of Helios, or even Coronis. Machaon was one of Helen's suitors and in this role he took part in the Trojan War. With Podalirius his brother he ruled over three towns in Thessaly: Tricca, Ithome and Oechalia. He was in command of thirty ships. At Troy, with Podalirius, he dedicated himself to the practice of medicine, a skill which he inherited from his father. He was so useful to those fighting that he was soon relieved of all military duty. Among other cures, that of TELEPHUS' wound was attributed to him and also that of Menelaus, who was wounded by one of Pandarus' arrows. He himself was wounded by an arrow shot by Paris. He was taken to Nestor's tent and nursed by Hecamede, the captive taken earlier by Achilles at Tenedos, though subsequently allotted to Nestor. He is principally known for curing a wound inflicted on PHILOCTETES by Heracles.

Machaon's name appeared in the list of warriors who were in the wooden horse. He was killed either by the Amazon Penthesilea or by the hand of EURYPYLUS, the son of Telephus. Nestor brought his ashes back to Gerenia. He was buried with his brother Podalirius at Tricca, where there was a joint memorial. He married Anticleia, a daughter of Diocles. They had two sons, Nicomachus and Gorgasus. Other known sons of Machaon were Alexanor, Polemocrates, Sphyrus and Alcon. Traditionally, Machaon was essentially a surgeon while Podalirius was a physician. His name, connected perhaps with the Greek for 'knife' (μάχαιρα) explains this idea.

Macistus (Μάκιστος) The brother of Phrixus and, like him, a son of Athamas. He founded the town of Macistus, in Elis of Triphylia.

Macris (Μάκρις) A daughter of Aristeus of Euboea. She and her father reared the baby Dionysus who had been entrusted to them by Hermes. When Hera, who ruled the island, drove the god away, he took refuge in the island of Corcyra (Corfu) which became known as Macris. There he lived in a cave with two entrances where, later on, Jason and Medea were to celebrate their wedding (see ALCINOUS).

Maenads (Μαινάδες) The Maenads ('the possessed') were the divine Bacchantes, the female followers of Dionysus. They were depicted as being naked or dressed in thin veils which scarcely covered their nakedness; they wore wreaths of ivy on their heads and carried a thyrsus or sometimes a cantharus (two-handled urn) in their hands. They were also depicted as playing the double flute or striking a tambourine as they performed a hectic

Maenads were female followers of Dionysus often depicted playing a double flute or striking a tambourine. This antique relief shows Dionysus with Pan and a Maenad in procession. Naples, National Museum.

dance. The Maenads were an expression of the orgiastic forces in nature. According to legend, the first Maenads were the Nymphs who nurtured DIONYSUS. Possessed by the god and inspired by him with a mystical frenzy, they roamed about the countryside, drinking at springs and imagining that they drank milk or honey. The human Bacchantes, female followers of the cult of Dionysus, sought to imitate their frenetic conduct. They had power over wild animals: they were depicted as riding panthers and holding wolf-cubs in their arms. The Maenads appear in a number of legends, such as those of Lycurgus, Orpheus, Pentheus and the daughters of Minyas.

Maenalus (Μαίναλος) The hero who gave his name to the Arcadian mountain and to the city of Maenalon. He was the eldest son of LYCAON; according to one tradition it was he who advised his father to offer Zeus the limbs of a child cooked as if it were ordinary meat, as a way of testing the god. He and his father were both struck down by a thunderbolt. According to another tradition Maenalus was not the son of Lycaon, but of Arcas, king of Arcadia, and therefore was the brother of ATALANTA.

Maeon (Μαίων)
1. A Theban, a son of Haemon, who fought against the Seven Chiefs. With Lycophontes he led the unfortunate ambush set against TYDEUS. Maeon was the only one of the ambush party who was not killed, as Tydeus spared him. When Tydeus died at the siege of Thebes Maeon buried him. A tradition used by Euripides made Maeon a son of Haemon and Antigone though Haemon was more often said to be her fiancé.
2. Another Maeon gave his name to the family to which Homer belonged. In poetry he was often described as Maeonides. This relationship with the poet varies from author to author: some say he was his father, married to CRITHEIS and the brother of Dius, who was the father of Hesiod. At other times he is said to have been not the husband but the guardian of Critheis, or even the grandfather of Homer, or the adoptive father of the poet who was said to be the son of a demon.

Maera (Μαῖρα)
1. The mother of LOCRUS I.
2. A heroine of Arcadia who was thought to be the daughter of Atlas and the wife of Tegeates, one of Lycaon's sons who gave his name to the town of Tegea. Her tomb, as well as that of her husband, was in the town's main square. Maera, the wife of Tegeates, was the mother of LEIMON and Scephrus, as well as Cydon, Archedius and Gortys.
3. A dog owned by the hero ICARIUS, who brought the vine into Attica, and was torn apart by drunken peasants. Maera's barking led ERIGONE to her father's grave. After Erigone's suicide, the dog stayed on the grave and died of despair or perhaps committed suicide by throwing itself into the Onigrus spring. Dionysus turned this faithful dog into a constellation – 'the Dog'. In some accounts Maera was one of ORION's dogs.

Magnes (Μάγνης) A Thessalian hero who gave his name to Magnesia. His genealogy varies from author to author. He is thought most often to be the son of Aeolus and Aenarete (Table 8). He married a Naiad and had two sons, Polydectes and Dictys, who played a part in the legend of Perseus (see DANAE). Various legends say that he had other sons: Einoeus, Alector, Eurynomus and Pierus. Other mythographers made him a son of Zeus and Thyia and the brother of MACEDON. Hesiod, according to Antoninus Liberalis, claimed that he was a son of Argos and Perimele, one of the daughters of Admetus (Table 35). In that case he would be the father of Hymenaeus. It was sometimes claimed that Magnes did not have as his son Hymenaeus but the latter's father, Pierus.

Maia (Μαῖα)
1. A daughter of Atlas and mother of Hermes (Table 25). Her mother was Pleione which meant that she was one of the Pleiades. There was another legend which claims that her mother was Sterope. Maia was a Nymph of Mount Cyllene in Arcadia, and there in an affair with Zeus she conceived Hermes. Her legend is very insubstantial. Apart from her link with Hermes she only appears as Arcas' nurse after the death of Callisto.
2. In very early times in Rome there was a goddess called Maia who probably had no connection, originally, with the Greek Maia. She appears to have been the supporter of Vulcan the fire god, to whom the month of May was particularly dedicated. After the introduction of Hellenism she became identified with her namesake and was said to be the mother of Mercury.

Malcandrus (Μάλκανδρος) A king of Byblos in whose service Isis was a slave, as nurse to the queen of Byblos, who was called either Astarte or

Saosis or Nemanous. This was at the time when Isis was searching for the body of Osiris.

Mamercus

1. A Latin name in which can be seen traces of the italic name of Mars: Mamers. There are two legends in which a hero with this name appears. The first makes him a son of Pythagoras, nicknamed Aemilius ('the courteous') because of the sweetness of his manners. This Mamercus Aemilius is said to have been the ancestor of the Gens Aemilia. A variation claimed that he was the son not of Pythagoras but of NUMA, whose connections with Pythagoras and Pythagoranism were well known.

2. The second legend is in Plutarch and was obviously inspired by the myth of Meleager. Mars, disguised as a herdsman, had made Sylvia, the wife of Septimius Marcellus pregnant. He gave her a lance, with a note setting out the destiny of the unborn child attached to it. When this son was born he was called Mamers Mamercus. He fell in love with the daughter of Tuscinus who was later killed by Septimius, his mortal father. When Mamers Mamercus was out hunting he slew an enormous boar which had been sent by Ceres. He gave his lover the head and the feet, but his mother's two brothers, Scymbrathes and Muthias, were annoyed and snatched the trophies back. Mamercus then killed his uncles but to punish him Sylvia burned the lance and Mamercus died.

Mamurius Jupiter had sent a sacred shield to Numa as a pledge of victory for the city of Rome. To hinder any attempts at theft Numa had eleven other shields made as exact copies. He entrusted these to the Salii. The workman who made the shields was an Oscan called Mamurius who asked as payment only that his name should be included in the song sung by the Salii at the festival of the shields. Numa granted his request. There used to be a festival in Rome during which an old man, called for the occasion Mamurius, was ritually beaten with white sticks and driven out of the city. It was known as the Mamuralia, celebrated on 14 March.

Mandylas (Μανδύλας) A shepherd of Dodona who stole one of the best sheep belonging to a neighbouring shepherd and kept it hidden in his stable. The poor man searched everywhere for his sheep and failed to find it, so he finally asked Zeus (the god of Dodona). The sacred oak made a comprehensible reply, telling him that the culprit was the youngest shepherd in the country. Mandylas was forced to return the sheep but, angry with the oracle, he was about to aim his axe at the sacred oak when a dove flew out of the tree and he changed his mind.

Manes (Μάνης) A legendary Phrygian king. According to some legends he was the son of Zeus and Ge. He married Callirhoe and their children were Atys, Cotys and Acmon (see LYDUS and TYRRHENUS).

Manes In Roman belief, the souls of the dead. Manes is an old Latin word meaning 'the Benevolent', and they were so called in the hope that they could be made well disposed simply by addressing them with innocent flattery. The Manes were the centre of a cult. They were offered wine, honey, milk and flowers. Two festivals were specially dedicated to them: the rose festival (or the violet festival) when graves were covered with roses or violets, and the Parentalia celebrated from 18 to 21 February. The custom of the Parentalia is said to have been introduced to Italy by Aeneas, who established it in honour of his father Anchises. It is also said that one year this festival of the dead was forgotten in Rome. The dead took revenge by invading the city and were only appeased when the ritual was carried out. Sometimes the Manes were given a common ancestress, the goddess Mania, or Mother of the Manes. This obscure divinity belonged to the group of popular spirits. She was worshipped at the Compitalia, the festival of the spirits of the crossroads.

Mania (Μανία) The personification of madness. She is analogous to the Erinyes and all infernal spirits and to semi-divinities and semi-abstract ideas, such as Ate (Error), who were instruments of divine anger. She was sent to people who neglected their ritual duties.

Manto (Μαντώ) This name evoked the idea of prophecy. She was a daughter of Tiresias, and, like her father, she had the gift of prophecy. Legend portrayed her leading her blind father along the roads of Boeotia after the capture of Thebes by the Epigoni. However, Tiresias died at Haliartus before reaching Delphi, which Manto was making for. The victorious Argives had promised Apollo, before capturing the town, that he should be given the finest piece of booty and Manto was marked out as an offering for him. She stayed a long time in Delphi, perfecting her skill in prophecy and playing the part of a Sibyl, until the god sent her to Asia Minor where she founded the town of Claros and married the Cretan Rhacius. By him she had one son (whose father, according to some mythographers, was Apollo), the prophet MOPSUS, famous for his rivalry with CALCHAS. A different legend shows Manto as married to Alcmaeon by whom she had a son AMPHILOCHUS the younger, who had the same name as his uncle (Table 1). But Manto, the wife of Alcmaeon, was not thought to be the daughter of Tiresias. This was another Manto, who was the daughter of Polyidus. Virgil also refers to another Manto, after whom the Italian town of Mantua was named (see AUCNUS and BIANOR).

Marathon (Μαραθών) The son of Epopeus (Table 10), king of Sicyon. While his father was still alive he left Sicyon, driven away by Epopeus' injustice and violence. He took refuge in Attica where he introduced the first laws. When EPOPEUS died he returned to his own country. Under his rule he reunited Sicyon and Corinth. He had two sons who gave their names to these towns of Sicyon and Corinth. Marathon was the hero of the Attic deme of Marathon (see also MARATHUS).

Marathus (Μάραθος) A hero of this name was an Arcadian who went with Echedemus on the expedition of the DIOSCURI against Attica. Marathus sacrificed himself of his own free will since an oracle had demanded a human sacrifice to ensure the victory of the attackers. His name was given to the township called Marathon.

Mariandynus (Μαριανδυνός) The king and hero who gave his name to the Mariandyni, a tribe who lived in Bithynia. He was of Aeolian descent. He also ruled over part of Paphlagonia and annexed the country of the Bebryces. He is said to have been a son of PHINEUS 3 and therefore a Thracian; his mother was said to be Idaea. He was also thought to be a son of Cimmerius, or in other versions of Phrixus, or simply a son of Zeus.

Marica A Nymph of Minturnae in Latium where there was a wood dedicated to her. Virgil described her as the mother of King Latinus and wife of the god Faunus. Marica was said to be simply Circe deified.

Marmax (Μάρμαξ) One of HIPPODAMIA's suitors. He was killed by Oenomaus and buried with his two horses, Parthenias and Eriphas.

Maron (Μάρων) In the *Odyssey* he is the son of Evanthes and a priest of Apollo in the Thracian town of Ismarus. Since Odysseus defended him and his family from being plundered, he presented him with some very strong and rare sweet wine. ODYSSEUS made the Cyclops POLYPHEMUS drunk with this wine and thus eventually escaped him. As the son of Evanthes, Maron was also the grandson of Dionysus. According to Euripides, he was the son of the god and the companion of Silenus. In Nonnus this integration with the Dionysian story is even more complete: Maron was the son of Silenus and he accompanied Dionysus on his expedition against India. He appeared in the poem as an old man with tottering limbs, who could only summon up strength to drink and sing in praise of Dionysus. Maron was the personification of the drunkard. There was a statue of him on a fountain at the Pompeian gate in Rome.

Marpessa (Μαρπήσσα) The daughter of Evenus and Demonice and the granddaughter of Ares. She was sometimes said to be the daughter of Oenomaus and Alcippe. When she was engaged to IDAS she was abducted by APOLLO but Idas attacked the god and it was only by the intervention of Zeus that they were separated. Marpessa was allowed to choose which of the two suitors she preferred. She chose Idas because she feared that when she grew old Apollo would desert her (see CORONIS 1). Idas and Marpessa had a daughter called either Cleopatra or Alcyone in memory of the rape of Marpessa (Table 19, and see MELEAGER).

Mars The Roman god identified with the Greek Ares, but he existed in Italic religions before the arrival of Ares. Most of the legends in which he features in classical literature are only transpositions of Greek myths. The love of Mars and Venus celebrated by Lucretius at the beginning of his poem *De Rerum Natura* was based on the account of the intrigue between Aphrodite and Ares as told by Homer. The same was true of the legend which claimed that Mars was the son of Juno, just as Ares was the son of Hera. A curious legend quoted by Ovid asserts that Juno conceived Mars without Jupiter's aid, using a magic flower with fertile properties which FLORA had obtained for her. It is difficult to recognize the traces of genuinely Italian legends. Mars' adventure with ANNA PERENNA is perhaps related to the legend of Mamurius Veturius, the personification of the old year which goes when the new one starts, at the

Mars was not only a god of war but also presided over agriculture. In this Roman wall painting both these functions seem to be represented – he is depicted with his warlike attributes against a background of vegetation. From the House of the Marine Venus at Pompeii.

beginning of March, according to the old Roman calendar.

In the classical period Mars made his appearance in Rome as the god of war, but this was not the only function ascribed to him. His festivals, generally grouped in the month which was dedicated to him, displayed clearly agrarian characteristics, which has led some modern mythographers to conclude that Mars was originally the god of agricultural functions. Mars supposedly guided the young to emigrate from the Sabine cities to go to found new towns. The Sabines indeed had a custom of consecrating to Mars a whole age-group of young people who emigrated, guided on their way by a woodpecker or a wolf (both were dedicated to Mars). This is perhaps the explanation of the part played by the she-wolf, the animal of Mars, in the legend of earliest Rome (see ROMULUS). Early mythographers compiled the history of Mars, who was the father of Romulus and Remus, whose mother was RHEA. The two children were later abandoned on a mountain (in this case, the Palatine) – a frequent occurrence in Greek legend – were nursed by a she-wolf – sacred animal sent by their father (see also among other examples, TELEPHUS fed by a doe) – and sheltered by shepherds. This was in explanation of how the young Romuleans could be called 'children of the Wolf' or 'the children of Mars'. These legends developed round a very old statue showing a wolf and, sheltering under it, two men, symbolizing, in accordance with the date, either the Sabines and the Latin peoples (the two ethnic groups united in primitive Rome, according to Roman historians) or the Roman and the Campanian peoples, after the alliance of Rome and Capua against the Italic population in the interior.

Other people besides the Romans were supposedly descended from the god: the Marsians – the Sabelline people whom Rome fought for a long time – the Marrucians, the Mamertines and others whose names indicated their connection with the god.

Marsyas (Μαρσύας) A mythical character whose legend was located in Phrygia. He is usually said to have been the inventor of the double flute (in contrast with the syrinx or flute of Pan). He was supposedly one of the followers of Cybele because they also played the flute and the tambourine. Marsyas was the son of Hyagnis and Olympus or, alternatively, Oeagrus. It was said in Athens that the flute was actually invented by Athena. When she saw a reflection of herself in water while she was playing and realized how distorted her cheeks were, she threw it away in disgust. A variant of this myth claims that the goddess invented the first flute out of deer's bones at a banquet of the gods, but when Hera and Aphrodite saw her blowing they laughed so much at the appearance which it gave to her face that Athena went to Phrygia immediately so that she could see her reflection in a stream. There she saw that the two goddesses were right and she threw the flute away, threatening anyone who picked it up with dire penalties. Marsyas found it; proud of his discovery and judging that the music of the flute was the loveliest in the world, Marsyas actually challenged Apollo to produce music which was equally beautiful on his lyre. Apollo accepted the challenge on condition that the winner would be free to make the loser undergo any punishment he wished. The first trial was a draw but Apollo challenged his opponent to play his flute upside down as he could with his lyre. Marsyas was declared to be the loser. Apollo tied him to a pine tree (according to Pliny a plane) and flayed him alive. Afterwards he regretted his anger and was said to have broken his lyre. He turned Marsyas into a river. The flaying of Marsyas was a theme frequently used in Hellenistic and Western art. For a brother of Marsyas, see BABYS.

Mecisteus (Μηκιστεύς) One of the children of Talaus and Lysimache and consequently a brother of Adrastus (Table 1). His son was EURYALUS. He was one of the Seven Chiefs whereas his son was one of the Epigoni. Mecisteus was killed by Melanippus outside Thebes.

Mecon (Μήκων) An Athenian who was loved by Demeter. She turned him into a poppy, a plant which was sacred to Demeter.

Medea (Μήδεια) The daughter of AEETES, king of Colchis, and therefore the granddaughter of Helios and the niece of the sorceress Circe. Her mother was the Oceanid Idyia. In some accounts Hecate, the patroness of all magicians, is said to have been her mother. In Alexandrine and Roman literature Medea became the archetypal sorceress. She already had this role in Attic tragedy and in the legend of the Argonauts.

Without Medea, Jason would have failed to win the Golden Fleece; she gave him the ointment to protect him from being burnt by the bulls of Hephaestus (see ARGONAUTS) and with her spells sent the dragon to sleep. A later legend, related by

Diodorus, informs us that in reality Medea was a princess of great humanity and much opposed to her father's policy of killing all foreigners who arrived in his country. Annoyed by her mute opposition, Aeetes imprisoned her but she easily freed herself. This happened on the day that the Argonauts landed on the coast of Colchis. She threw in her lot with theirs, persuading Jason to promise to marry her if she ensured the success of his enterprise and made him lord of the Golden Fleece which he sought. Jason promised and she opened the temple where the precious remains were preserved. As soon as the fleece was gained, Medea took flight with Jason and the Argonauts. He had promised to marry her and all the subsequent crimes of Medea were excused, or at least explained, by Jason's perjury. To follow him and give him victory Medea had not only betrayed and abandoned her father but she had taken as a hostage her brother, Apsyrtus, whom she did not hesitate to kill and to cut into pieces to delay the pursuit of Aeetes.

Jason and Medea did not marry immediately in Colchis. The marriage was postponed until the call on ALCINOUS and was to some extent forced on Jason and Medea by Arete, the wife of Alcinous, king of the Phaeacians; Alcinous had decided to give Medea up to Aeetes' envoys who demanded her return so that she could be punished for her crime, but only if she was still a virgin. Arete told Medea secretly about the king's decision and Jason slept with her in the cave of MACRIS. There is a much later legend according to which Jason was married in Colchis, where he stayed for four years before carrying out the exploits for which he had come to the country. Like Iphigenia in Tauris, Medea, as priestess of Artemis/Hecate, was responsible for putting to death all foreigners who entered Colchis. When she saw Jason she was overcome with immediate love, inspired by Aphrodite, and the scene of the sacrifice was said to have ended with a wedding. This version seems to have been inspired by the story of Iphigenia and Orestes. Hesiod gave Jason and Medea a son called MEDEIUS. Other authors name a daughter, Eriopis. Later, in the tradition used by the tragedians, Pheres and Mermerus were said to have been their two sons. Finally, Diodorus named Thessalus, Alcimenes and Tisandrus.

While returning to Iolchus with JASON, Medea started her campaign of revenge against PELIAS who had tried to destroy Jason by making him search for the Golden Fleece. She persuaded the king's daughters that she could rejuvenate any

living being if she wished to do so, by boiling it in a magic liquid. Under their eyes she cut up an old ram, threw the pieces into a large cauldron which she had put on the fire and presently a fresh young lamb emerged. Convinced by this example of her magic skill, the daughters of Pelias cut him up and threw the pieces into a cauldron provided by Medea; Pelias did not emerge, however. After this murder, Acastus, Pelias' son, banished Jason and Medea from his kingdom.

Corinth was the native city of AEETES. There was a cult at Corinth of 'the children of Medea' which may have been responsible for the following episode in the legend of the woman of Colchis. Jason and Medea lived for some time in Corinth, until CREON wanted to marry his daughter Creusa to Jason. He banished Medea but she obtained a day's delay, which she spent in preparing her revenge. She dipped a dress in poison, together with ornaments and jewels. With the help of her children she delivered them to Creusa; when Creusa put them on she was encircled by a mysterious fire, as was her father when he came to help her. Meanwhile Medea killed her own children in the temple of Hera. She then fled to Athens in a chariot driven by winged horses which were a present of her ancestor, Helios. Euripides was the first author to claim that she killed her children; the earlier version claims that they were stoned by the Corinthians because they had brought the dress and jewels to Creusa (see MERMERUS).

It was said that Medea fled to Athens because before she murdered her children AEGEUS had promised to help her. She assured him that she could bear him a son if he married her. She tried unsuccessfully to kill Theseus when he came to obtain recognition from his father. She was then banished from Athens and made her way back to Asia, taking her son by Aegeus, Medus, who gave his name to the Medes. She later returned to Colchis where Perseus had dethroned Aeetes. She had Perseus killed, and gave the kingdom back to her own father. In one legend Medea was transported to Elysium where she was united with Achilles (compare IPHIGENIA, HELEN and POLYXENA).

Medeus (Μήδειος) He was a son of Jason and Medea, who was brought up by Chiron. No further legend about him is known.

Medon (Μέδων)
1. The natural son of Oileus and Rhene. He was a native of Phthiotis but had to go into exile after the murder of his parents by his mother-in-law

Eriopis. When Philoctetes was left on the island of Lemnos because he was wounded, Medon took command of the contingents of Methone, Thaumacia, Meliboea and Olizon. He was killed at Troy by Aeneas.

2. A herald of the suitors at Ithaca. When they decided to set a trap for Telemachus on his return from his search for Odysseus, Medon told Penelope about the plot; he was therefore spared by Odysseus when the suitors were slaughtered. Ovid and Apollodorus mention him as being one of the suitors but apart from that, the two versions are not incompatible.

3. A son of Pylades and Electra and the brother of Strophius (Table 30).

Medus (Μῆδος)

1. The son of Medea and, according to the most well-known legend, of Aegeus. In some traditions he is the son of an Asian king whom Medea married when she was driven out of Athens upon the return of Theseus. In both versions Medus gave his name to the Medes. The Attic tragedians complicated the story of Medus. Adopting the tradition according to which he was the son of Aegeus, they assumed that Medus fled from Athens with his mother but that he was held up by a storm which landed him on the coast of the kingdom of his great-uncle Perseus. The latter had been warned by an oracle to mistrust the descendants of Aeetes. Medus, who knew of this warning when he was taken to the king by the soldiers who had captured him, concealed his identity. He told the king that he was Hippotes, the son of Creon, the king of Thebes and that he was searching for Medea to punish her for having murdered Creon and Creusa. Perseus did not take him at his word and imprisoned him while further enquiry was made. Meanwhile a famine struck the country. MEDEA arrived at Perseus' palace in a chariot drawn by dragons, claiming that she was a priestess of Artemis who had come to free the country from the famine which was overwhelming it. The king, in good faith, told her that he was holding in prison Hippotes, the son of the king of Thebes. Medea asked the king to hand him over to her. When she saw him she recognized her own son. She drew him aside and gave him a weapon; he killed Perseus and became king in his place.

2. There was also a Medus, son of ALPHESIBOEA.

Mefitis In Rome and other Italian towns this goddess presided over the outbreaks of sulphurous fumes which are so common in Italy. It was claimed that these fumes were responsible for plagues and epidemics, so that sometimes Mefitis was said to be the goddess of plague. In Rome she had a temple on the Esquiline.

Megaclo (Μεγακλώ) One of the daughters of King Macar of Lesbos. As he was bad-tempered, dour, and ill-treated his wife frequently, Megaclo took the Seven Muses of Lesbos (The Seven Virgins of Lesbos) as handmaids, and taught them to sing to the lyre. Once they had been taught, the girls gave concerts to Macar; his character softened and he eventually treated his wife kindly.

Megapenthes (Μεγαπένθης)

1. The name (meaning 'great sorrow') of an illegitimate son of Menelaus, who was born while Helen was away. His mother was a slave, in some versions called Pieris and in others Tereis (Table 13). Menelaus married him to the daughter of Alector of Sparta. Since he was illegitimate, the Lacedaemonians would not let him succeed Menelaus. The throne went to Orestes. Another story said that after the death of Menelaus, when Orestes was still mad and being pursued by the Erinyes, Megapenthes and his half-brother Nicostratus (the son of Menelaus and Helen; but see MENELAUS) had driven HELEN out. She had found safety in Rhodes with Polyxo.

2. The son of Proetus, who had him during the time when his daughters were mad. According to the legends he was the father of Anaxagoras and Iphianira. He ruled Tiryns as successor to his father Proetus; but after Acrisius' death Perseus exchanged the kingdom of Argos for that of Tiryns.

Megara (Μέγαρα)

1. The most celebrated of the heroines bearing this name was the daughter of Creon, king of Thebes, who gave her in marriage to Heracles as payment for his victory over the Minyans of Orchomenus. This marriage had a tragic ending: Heracles, driven mad by Hera, killed the children he had by Megara. The version of this story used by Euripides (set out in *Heracles Maddened* and repeated by Seneca under the same title) has remained the standard one. Euripides tells how during the absence of Heracles, who had gone to hell to find Cerberus on behalf of Eurystheus, a man called Lycus had come to Euboea to dethrone Creon and had killed him. He was similarly on the point of murdering Megara and her children when Heracles returned. The hero began by killing Lycus, but Hera made

him mad and he shot his own children and also Megara with his arrows. He was on the point of doing the same to Amphitryon when Athena intervened and sent him into a deep sleep.

This story was, however, not the only one known to mythographers; some did not accept that Megara was killed in the massacre and claimed that HERACLES wanted to break up the marriage which he had stained with blood and that he married Megara to Iolaus his nephew. Alternatively, it was said that after the killing, Heracles left Thebes for a year in exile. At the end of the year he was recalled by Iphicles and Licymnius but he did not wish to go. Iphicles and Licymnius, accompanied by Megara, went in search of him. They met in Tiryns. The version which claims that the children of Heracles and Megara were killed by Lycus (who would thus be the father of Megara, driven mad by Hera as punishment for having given his daughter to the hero) is completely unauthoritative.

At Thebes the tombs of the children could be seen and they had a cult. According to different authors there were between three and eight of them. In the same way their names differ and are given variously as Therimachus, Deicoon, Creontiades (Table 15), Oneites, Oxeus, Aristodemus, Clymenus, Glenus, Polydorus, Aniectus, Mecistophonus, Patrocles, Toxoclitus, Menebrontes and Chersibius. These various names were grouped according to the varying traditions. 2. Another isolated and late legend spoke of another Megara, who was said to have been killed by Phorbas and Polymelus because she refused their advances. Ixion was said later to have avenged her death.

Megareus (Μεγαρεύς) The son of Poseidon and Ocnope, who was the daughter of Epopeus (Table 10). He was a native of the town of Onchestus in Boeotia. Sometimes he was said to be the son of Apollo or of Aegeus. He had several children: the eldest, Timalcus, was killed by Theseus during the expedition of the Dioscuri against Attica: the youngest, Evippus, was killed by the Lion of Cithaeron. To avenge him, Megareus offered to give the hand of his daughter Evaechme and the right of succession to the hero who put an end to the monster. ALCATHUS offered to do so and killed the lion. Several authors claimed that he married Merope and that his third son, HIPPOMENES, overcame Atalanta. When Minos besieged King Nisus in his town, which was then called Nisa, he called on Megareus for assistance. Megareus was

killed in the battle, fighting for his ally. Later, when his successor, Alcathus, rebuilt the citadel of Nisa in honour of his father-in-law, he called it Megara.

Another story of Megarean origin denied that the city was ever captured. According to this account Megareus had succeeded Nisus because Iphinoe was his wife and the daughter of Nisus. Alcathus had naturally succeeded Megareus because he was his son-in-law.

Meges (Μέγης) The son of PHYLEUS and Ctimene who was a daughter of Laertes and therefore a sister of Odysseus. Through his father he was a descendant of Augias. Other accounts say that his mother was Timandra, a sister of Helen and Clytemnestra, a daughter of Tyndareus (Table 19). He appears among Helen's suitors; because of this, he took part in the siege of Troy. He commanded the contingent from Dulichium and the Echinades. Before Troy he killed Pedaeus, Croesmus and Amphiclus. He was said to have been killed at Troy but this is not mentioned in the *Iliad*. The tradition followed by Polygnotus in the great fresco at Delphi depicted him among the Greeks who had returned from Troy, but it was accepted that he had been wounded and perhaps he died during the voyage.

Melampus (Μελάμπους) 'The man with the black feet', so called because when he was born his mother had put him in the shade but had unintentionally left his feet in the sun. He was the son of Amphythaon and Idomene, and the grandson of Cretheus and Tyro (Tables 21 and 1). He married one of the daughters of Proetus by whom he had the following sons: Mantius, Antiphates and Abas, and also daughters, Pronoe and Manto. Diodorus claims that he actually married Iphianira, a daughter of MEGAPENTHES who was a son of King Proetus. In his childhood Melampus acquired the power of prophecy in the following way: he found a dead snake which he burnt on a pyre. The children of the snake were grateful to him because he took care of them and brought them up; so they purified his ears with their tongues, so that afterwards he could understand the language of birds and that of animals in general (see POLYPHATES). Melampus was not only a prophet but also a doctor capable of cleansing the sick and also of restoring them to health; he also knew about herbs, both magical and medicinal. Melampus and his brother Bias left Thessaly, their home country, and stayed with their uncle Neleus at Pylos in Messenia.

There Bias wanted to marry Pero, a daughter of Neleus but the latter would only give his consent if he brought as a wedding present the herds of Phylacus (others said of IPHICLUS, but Iphiclus was the son of Phylacus and plays a definite part in the legend). These herds were at Phylace in Thessaly and they were guarded fiercely by a dog which neither man nor beast could approach. Since Bias could not steal the herds by himself, he asked Melampus for help. He agreed to do so and forecast that he would succeed, but that he would be caught and would be imprisoned for a year. Then he went to Phylace and as he had predicted, he was caught and incarcerated. He had been in prison for nearly a year when he heard the worms which were in the wood of one of the roof beams ask each other how long the beam would hold before it collapsed. One of them said that the beam had become extremely thin and would break very soon. Melampus immediately asked to be moved to a different prison and in fact, very soon after, the roof collapsed. Then Phylacus realized that Melampus was a prophet and he asked for his help in curing his son, IPHICLUS, of impotence. As a reward he gave Melampus the herds he desired, which Melampus took back to Pylos where Neleus gave to Bias the hand of his daughter Pero. Another legend, recounted only by Propertius, maintained that Melampus was in love with Pero.

Later, Proetus, the king of Argos, called on Melampus to cure his daughters, the PROETIDES, who were suffering from collective madness. They wandered all over the Peloponnese in the belief that they had been turned to cows. Melampus promised their father that he would cure them if, in return, the king would give him a third of his kingdom but Proetus refused. The illness became worse and Proetus had to approach Melampus again. This time as payment Melampus not only asked for a third of the kingdom for himself but a third for his brother as well. Proetus accepted these conditions. Melampus, with the help of young people dancing and shouting, chased the girls out of the mountains and forced them to return to Sicyon. There he purified them with magic rites and they were cured, though the eldest, Iphinoe, died. Proetus gave his other two daughters, Iphianassa and Lysippe, in marriage to Bias and Melampus and he gave them each a third of his kingdom. This is how the descendants of Amythaon came to reign over the Argolid. For the consequences of the division of the kingdom, see ADRASTUS.

Melampygus (Μελάμπυγος) 'The man with a black back', a mysterious man against whom the CERCOPES had been put on their guard by their mother. He turned out to be none other than HERACLES.

Melancraera (Μελάγκραιρα) 'Black head', the nickname of the Sybil of Cumae. This nickname was explained in various ways. Either it is an allusion to the obscure utterances of the Sybil or to her melancholy or possibly to her physical characteristics.

Melaneus (Μελανεύς) The son of Apollo and a famous archer. By Oechalia he had a son called EURYTUS. He is said to have founded the town of Oechalia in Messenia on land granted to him by Perieres. In another Euboean legend he is the son of Arcesilaus and the founder of the town of Eretria which was originally called Melaneis after him. Antoninus Liberalis records that another Melaneus was a son of Apollo and the father of Eurytus and Ambracia (who gave his name to the town of Ambracia). He was the king of the Dryopes and seized Epirus, over which he then also reigned.

Melanippe (Μελανίππη)
1. In one legend, the daughter of the first Aeolus, the son of Helen (Table 8). She had two sons by Poseidon, Boeotus and Aeolus II. She was the heroine of two tragedies of Euripides, now lost: *Melanippe in Chains* and *Melanippe the Philosopher*. In another tradition, recalled by Pausanias, Melanippe was a Nymph who married Itonus, the son of Amphictyon, and bore a son, Boeotus. HIPPE, the mother of Melanippe, was a daughter of Chiron and was seduced by Aeolus on Mount Pelion.
2. A daughter of Ares and a sister of the queen of the Amazons, Hippolyta. Melanippe was captured by HERACLES but Hippolyta obtained her release by agreeing to the conditions of the captor. In the fight which followed the breakdown of the armistice, Hippolyta was killed by Heracles, while Melanippe fell under the attack of his companion, Telamon.

Melanippus (Μελάνιππος)
1. A son of Ares and of the goddess Triteia, a daughter of the god Triton. He founded the town of Triteia in Achaea and called it after his mother.
2. A Theban, the son of Astacus, who was one of the warriors born from the teeth of the dragon of

CADMUS. He fought on the side of the Thebans in the war of the Seven Chiefs. He killed Mecisteus, the brother of Adrastus, and mortally wounded Tydeus before he himself was killed by AMPHIARAUS. Amphiaraus beheaded his corpse and took the head to the dying Tydeus, who split the skull open and ate the brains. As a result Athena, who had decided to make Tydeus immortal, was horrified and abandoned her idea. Amphiaraus, had foreseen what would happen and had deliberately given the head to Tydeus, because he knew how savage he was. Amphiaraus was hostile to Tydeus because he had forced them to undertake this expedition, which Amphiaraus knew was doomed to be disastrous. The tomb of Melanippus could be seen at Thebes, but in historical times the tyrant of Sicyon, Cleisthenes, transferred the ashes of Melanippus from Thebes to Sicyon and put them in the place of those of Adrastus.

3. One of the sons of Agrius, who deposed Oeneus at Calydon (see DIOMEDES).

4. The son Theseus had by Perigoune, daughter of SINIS. He was among the winners at the Nemean games in the time of the Epigoni.

5. Several Trojans with this name fell while fighting before Troy.

6. See also COMAETHO 2.

Melanthius (Μελάνθιος)

An Ithacan goatherd, a son of Dolius and a brother of the servant MELANTHO. Like his sister, he betrayed the interests of his real masters Penelope and Odysseus. When Odysseus arrived in Ithaca disguised as a beggar he met Melanthius who insulted him and took the side of the suitors. During the massacre he tried in vain to give arms to the suitors. He was locked in the room where the weapons were and when the servants had been hung he was taken into the courtyard where his nose and ears were cut off and given to the dogs to eat.

Melantho (Μελανθώ)

1. A daughter of Deucalion, according to one tradition. After an intrigue with Poseidon, who took the shape of a dolphin, she gave birth to Delphus after whom Delphi was named. Other versions give the daughter of Deucalion the name of Melantheia not Melantho, and make her the grandmother and not the mother of Delphus. She also had by the river-god Cephisus, or perhaps by HYAMUS, a daughter variously called Melaena or Melaenis or Celaeno, who was herself said to be the mother of DELPHUS (Table 8).

2. Melantho was also the name of a serving maid of Penelope, whom the latter had nursed as a child, but who took the side of the suitors. She was the mistress of Eurymachus. She was hung, along with the other serving women, after the slaughter of the suitors. She was the sister of MELANTHIUS.

3. Another Melantho was the wife of Criasus and the mother of Phorbas and Cleoboea.

Melanthus (Μέλανθος)

A descendant of Neleus, the king of Messenia, through his father Andropompus. He was driven out of Pylos by the arrival of the Heraclids and on the advice of the oracle he settled down in Attica where he was adopted as a citizen and became a magistrate. At that time the ruler of Attica was a descendant of Theseus called Thymoetes and the Athenians were at war with the Boeotians in a dispute over the town of Oenoe. They decided to settle the quarrel by single combat between the two kings. The king of Athens was afraid of pitting himself against Xanthus, the king of Thebes. He therefore announced in his kingdom that he was willing to abdicate in favour of anyone who could defeat the king of Thebes in single combat. Melanthus accepted the offer and the combat took place. Just as they were about to begin battle Melanthus saw the figure of a warrior dressed in black armour behind Xanthus. It was in fact Dionysus Melanaegis (Dionysus with the black shield) but Melanthus took him for a combatant. Therefore he accused the king of breaking the terms of the duel and of having brought in outside help. Xanthus was surprised and looked around to see who had come to help him, and Melanthus took advantage of this to stab him with a lance. He became their king. The Athenians built a sanctuary to Dionysus whose help had been so useful.

There was another legend which is known to us through Athenaeus. When Melanthus had been driven out of Pylos, he received from the Pythian oracle the advice that he should settle in the area where he was offered a head and feet to eat. When he arrived in Eleusis the priests offered him all that remained of the sacrifice which had just been carried out – the head and the feet. He realized that the oracle was fulfilled and settled in Eleusis. Melanthus also gave his name to an Attic deme and was the brother of CODRUS.

Melas (Μήλας)

1. A son of Heracles and Omphale and the counterpart of HEGELEUS. Like him, he supposedly introduced the use of the bugle at the time of the expedition of the Heraclids.

2. Another Melas (Μέλας) was the son of Phrixus and Chalciope.

Meleager (Μελέαγρος) The son of Oeneus, king of the Aetolians of Calydon, and of Althaea, a sister of Leda (Tables 24 and 27). He was the hero of the Calydonian boar-hunt, as it is known. This exploit was mentioned in the *Iliad*, when Phoenix tried to arouse Achilles, and make him change his mind about not taking part in the fighting against the Trojans, by telling him of the tragic misfortune which befell Meleager, who himself was equally obstinate. Oeneus offered a sacrifice after the harvest to all the gods except Artemis. The goddess then sent against the country an enormous boar which ravaged the fields in Calydon. Meleager organized hunters drawn from all the towns of the neighbourhood. The boar killed several of them but finally fell to Meleager. Artemis was still angry and she fomented a quarrel between the Aetolians and the Curetes (because hunters from both tribes had taken part in the chase) concerning the division of the boar's skin and head. So long as Meleager fought with his fellow Aetolians they had the upper hand, but when he killed his mother's brothers, she cursed him, calling down on him the wrath of the infernal gods with the most violent imprecations. Then Meleager, dreading the effect of his mother's words and fearing that if he continued to fight the Erinyes would strike him, withdrew to his house and refused to help his fellow countrymen. The Aetolians were driven back behind the walls of Calydon and were soon under siege. The oldest of the Aetolians came to plead with Meleager, but in vain. He resisted successively the pleading of the most important of the town's priests, his family, his closest friends. This lasted until the town began to burn and the enemy was on the point of sacking his house. His wife Cleopatra Alcyone, the daughter of Idas and Marpessa, took refuge with him and explained the fate which would be visited on the besieged if the enemy won the victory. Meleager was finally moved by this terrible picture which she painted and put on his armour. His people won, but he died in the fight.

Later his legend developed and became more complicated with variations. The war against the Curetes took second place, and the hunt itself became the most important episode. Meleager was said to be the son not of Oeneus but of Ares. When he was seven days old the Fates supposedly appeared to his mother Althaea and forecast that the fate of the little child would be bound up with

that of the log which was burning on the hearth. If the log burnt itself out Meleager would die. Althaea hastened to take the log off the fire and extinguish it. She then hid it in a chest. Later, when Meleager was grown up, he took it upon himself to rid the country of the monstrous boar which had been sent by Artemis. This account is different from the earlier one; he assembled a large number of heroes, the list of whom was preserved by mythographers. They were Dryas, a son of Ares, Idas and Lynceus, the two sons of Aphareus, who came from Messene; Castor and Pollux, the Dioscuri, from Sparta (they were cousins of Meleager); Theseus from Athens; Admetus from Pherae in Thessaly; Anceus and Cepheus, the sons of Lycurgus of Arcadia; Jason from Iolcos; Iphicles, twin brother of Heracles, from Thebes; Pirithous, the son of Ixion and the friend of Theseus, from Larissa in Thessaly; Telamon, the son of Aeacus, from Salamis; Peleus, his brother from Phthia, who during the hunt killed his brother-in-law, Eurytion, son of Actor; Amphiaraus, son of Oecles, came from Argos, as did the sons of Thestius, uncles of Meleager (Table 24). There was also one huntress, Atalanta, the daughter of Schoeneus who came from Arcadia. All these huntsmen were fêted by Oeneus for nine days. On the tenth day they set off on the hunt, not without resistance from some who found it repugnant to have a woman in the troop. But Meleager managed to make them change their minds because he was in love with Atalanta by whom he wanted to have a child although he was married to Cleopatra.

When the beast was brought to bay, Hyleus and Anchaeus were killed and Peleus accidentally struck Eurytion with a javelin and killed him. Atalanta was the first to wound the boar: she struck it with an arrow and then Amphiaraus shot an arrow into one of its eyes. Meleager finally killed it by stabbing its side with a knife, thus earning the spoils of the animal. As a token of respect he gave them to Atalanta. However the sons of Thestius, who were Meleager's uncles, were annoyed by this gesture. They asserted that if Meleager did not want the remains he should have given them to them, since they were his nearest relations on the hunt. Meleager killed his uncles in rage and thus assured for Atalanta the possession of the remains. Angered by this murder, Althaea immediately threw the magic log on the fire and Meleager died. When, in calmer mood, she realized the consequences of her action, she hanged herself together with the hero's wife

Cleopatra. It was also said that Meleager was in-vulnerable and that Apollo had to shoot an arrow to kill him. This version corresponds to the Homeric one, which claims that Apollo had fought on the side of the Curetes. Among other exploits attributed to Meleager is a victory at the funeral games in honour of Pelias. He was also presented (in the account given by Diodorus) as fighting with the Argonauts at Colchis, where he killed Aeetes. For his meeting with Heracles in hell, see HERACLES and DEIANEIRA.

Meleagrids (Μελεαγρίδες) Meleager's sisters: Gorge, Eurymede, Deianeira and Melanippe, who wept so bitterly at the death of their brother that Artemis out of compassion turned them into guinea fowl. At the request of Dionysus two of them, Gorge and Deianeira, preserved their human form; or, alternatively, Dionysus restored it to them after their transformation. Artemis took the new birds to the island of Leros. The mythog-raphers increased the number of Meleagrids. Be-sides the four already named they included Phoebe, Eurydice, Menesto, Erato, Antiope and Hippodamia. According to a note by Suidas, a legend which originated at Leros considered that the guinea fowls were companions of Iocallis, a local divinity analogous to Artemis. Guinea fowl were reared as sacred birds in the precinct of the temple of Artemis at Leros. The tears of the Meleagrids, like those of the Heliades, were said to have turned into drops of amber.

Meles (Μέλης) A young Athenian for whom Timagoras, a foreigner living in Athens, had a passion. However, Meles despised such a passion; he made Timagoras tolerate all his whims and when he finally challenged him to throw himself from the top of the rocks on the Acropolis, Tima-goras jumped without hesitation and killed him-self. Horrified by what he had done, Meles in his turn threw himself from the top of the rock. An altar was built in honour of Anteros (Love Rejected) to commemorate the incident, and fore-igners living in Athens celebrated a cult related to this. According to another version recorded by Suidas, Timagoras was the beloved and Melitus (instead of Meles) the lover, who was rejected by the object of his passion. In despair Melitus threw himself from the top of the rock. Timagoras fol-lowed him and committed suicide on his body.

Melia (Μελία)
1. A daughter of Oceanus and a sister of Ismenus.

After an affair with Apollo she gave birth to Ismenius and Tenarus. She was worshipped in the temple of Apollo Ismenius near Thebes and at Thebes there was a spring called after her.
2. There was another daughter of Oceanus called Melia. She married Inachus by whom she had three sons, Aegialeus, Phegeus and Phoroneus (Table 17).

Meliads (Μελίαδες) Nymphs of the ash tree who were born from drops of blood spread by Uranus after he had been wounded by Cronus (Table 12). In memory of their birth in blood, deadly lances were made from the wood of the ash trees in which they lived. The bronze age race supposedly sprang from ash trees. This was the third age of people who inhabited the earth and was warlike and harsh.

Meliboea (Μελίβοια)
1. A daughter of Oceanus. She married Pelasgus, by whom she bore Lycaon (Table 18).
2. One of the children of NIOBE. With her brother Amyclas she escaped the massacre of the Niobids in answer to Leto's prayer. They took refuge in Argos and there they built a temple dedicated to Leto. In her terror during the massacre of her brothers and sisters Meliboea turned pale, so she adopted the surname Chloris (the green one) which she kept throughout her life.
3. A girl who had promised to marry a young man called Alexis whom she loved and who loved her. Her parents promised her to another man and in despair Alexis went into exile. On her wedding day Meliboea threw herself off the roof. She wanted to kill herself but she did not hurt herself at all, so she immediately fled to the port, where she embarked on a boat whose sails immediately spread themselves; it then took to sea. The boat carried her to a place where she found her lover, Alexis, preparing a banquet. They were married and, full of gratitude to the gods, they built a shrine to Artemis at Ephesus under the names of Automate and Epidiaita (because the boat had sailed by itself - Automate - and because she had arrived to take her place at the banquet - which is what Epidiaita means).

Meliboeus (Μελίβοιος) A shepherd who found the infant Oedipus abandoned on a mountain and who brought him up.

Melicertes (Μελικέρτης) The younger son of Ino, who took him down with her when she drowned herself. Ino became the goddess Leucothea and Melicertes became the god Palaemon (see LEUCOTHEA; Tables 3 and 33). There are differing versions of the death and apotheosis of Melicertes. In one version Athamas his father threw him into a cauldron of boiling water from which his mother snatched him before committing suicide with him. According to another version, Ino herself threw him into the cauldron and then hurled herself into the sea with his dead body in her arms. In yet another version she fled with the still living child and drowned both him and herself together. The Isthmian Games were held in honour of Palaemon-Melicertes. It is said that at the place where Ino cast herself into the sea, between Megara and Corinth, the body of Melicertes was retrieved by a dolphin, which hung it upon a pine tree. Sisyphus, then the ruler of Corinth and brother of Athamas, found the body and had it buried. In obedience to the instructions of a Nereid, he instituted the worship of the boy under the name of PALAEMON, and founded the Isthmian Games as funeral games in his honour.

Melissa (Μέλισσα)
1. The sister of Amalthea, who was nursemaid to the infant Zeus on Mount Ida in Crete (see MELISSEUS).
2. An elderly priestess of Demeter initiated into her mysteries by the goddess herself. Her neighbours tried to make her reveal details of her initiation but Melissa remained silent; the other women tore her to pieces. Demeter sent a plague upon them and caused bees to be born from the dead woman's body. The name Melissa is Greek for 'bee'.

Melisseus (Μελισσεύς)
1. The king of Crete at the time of Zeus' birth. He had two daughters, Amalthea and Melissa; to their care Rhea entrusted the nurture of the infant god, whom she had hidden in a cave on Mount Ida. Melisseus was the first man to offer sacrifices to the gods. He made his daughter Melissa the first priestess of Rhea.
2. One of the Curetes, the spirits who protected the cradle of the infant Zeus.
3. A king of the Chersonese in Caria, who gave hospitality to Triopas, the son of Helios, and purified him of the murder of his brother Tenages.

Melissus (Μέλισσος)
An Argive who fled to Corinth because of the tyranny of Phidon, the king of Argos. Melissus had a son, Actaeon, whom one of the Heraclids, Archias, tried to abduct forcibly. Actaeon died during this escapade and Melissus committed suicide after invoking the protection of the gods, and cursing his son's murderer. A famine and plagues struck Corinth. Archias, at the head of a deputation, went to ask the oracle the cause of these disasters and was informed that the gods were punishing the city for the murder of the young Actaeon. Archias went into voluntary exile to free the city from the curse which he had brought upon it and he founded the city of Syracuse.

Melite (Μελίτη)
Amongst other heroines of this name there was a Nymph of Corcyra, who had an intrigue with Heracles while he was in exile in her country. She bore him a son named HYLLUS.

Meliteus (Μελιτεύς)
The son of the Nymph Othreis, fathered by Zeus. When he was born, his mother abandoned him in the woods because she was afraid of Hera's wrath. Zeus had him fed by bees and through the agency of an oracle he instructed a shepherd called Phagrus, a son of the same Nymph by Apollo, to bring up the child that he would find being fed by bees. Phagrus obeyed; Meliteus became a sturdy young hero, who conquered the neighbouring peoples and founded the city of Melitaea in Thessaly (for the continuation of his legend, see ASPALIS).

Melus (Μῆλος)
A young Delian who left his homeland to go to Cyprus at the time when Cinyras was king there. Cinyras had a son called ADONIS and he gave Melus to him as a companion. The king also married him to one of his own relatives, named Pelia. A child was born of this marriage, named Melus like his father. Aphrodite, who loved Adonis, was well disposed towards the boy; she took him under her protection and had him brought up in her temple. When Adonis was gored by a wild boar and died, Melus, the father, hanged himself from a tree, which from then on was named after Melus – 'mēlea' being an apple tree in Greek. Pelia hanged herself from the same tree. Aphrodite took pity on them, transforming Melus into an apple and Pelia into a dove (the bird sacred to the goddess).

When Aphrodite saw that the younger Melus had grown to manhood and that he was the sole survivor of the race of Cinyras, she ordered him to go to Delos. There Melus gained control and founded the city of Melos. He first taught people the art of sheep-shearing and of making clothes from wool. As a result sheep took the name 'mēla' (μῆλα). Thus one single legend served to explain three different etymologies.

Melpomene (Μελπομένη) One of the MUSES.

Membliarus (Μεμβλίαρος) A Phoenician who accompanied Cadmus in the search for his sister Europa. Cadmus left him on the island of Thera (then called Calliste, meaning 'the most beautiful'); he was placed in charge of a colony that Cadmus founded there. The island of Anaphe, close to Thera, is sometimes referred to as Membliarus, and was apparently named after the same hero.

Memnon (Μέμνων) The son of Eos (the Dawn) and Tithonus, one of the sons of Laomedon and a brother of Priam (Tables 7 and 14). He was brought up by the Hesperides and reigned over the Ethiopians. At the time of the Trojan War, Memnon came to Priam's aid. His exploits at Troy and his death are recounted in the *Little Iliad* and in the poem *Aethiopis*. Memnon matched himself against Ajax but, as in the battle between Ajax and Hector, there was no decisive outcome to the encounter. On the battlefield he fought Nestor's son ANTILOCHUS when Nestor called his son to his aid. Antilochus saved Nestor's life at the cost of his own but Achilles came swiftly up to avenge his friend's death. A battle began between Memnon, son of Eos, and Achilles, son of Thetis. The two goddesses, anxious over the fate of their offspring, hastened to Zeus, who weighed the destinies of the two heroes in the divine balance, and found that Memnon's weighed the heavier (for a similar weighing of scales see HECTOR). Achilles was soon victorious, but Eos persuaded Zeus to grant her son immortality; she flew off to gather up his body and carry it away to Ethiopia. The tears that Eos shed are the drops of dew which we see each morning in the fields.

One tradition places the tomb of Memnon on the estuary of the river Aesopus, on the banks of the Hellespont. Every year birds could be seen gathering there to lament the hero's death; these birds, called the Memnonides, were supposed to be either the companions of Memnon transformed after his death or his ashes which had acquired a sort of immortality. Every year the birds divided into two groups and fought each other until half of them had been killed.

Legends differ about the land of Memnon's birth. Some say it was Syria, some Susa and the area of Bactria in central Asia; others suggest Thebes in Egypt. This last identification led to the attribution of the name 'Colossus of Memnon' to one of the huge statues raised by Amenhotep III. When the first rays of the dawn struck this statue it was supposed to emit sweet music as though to greet his mother's light (see TEUTAMUS).

Memphis (Μέμφις) The daughter of Nilus, god of the Nile. She was married to Epaphus and gave birth to a daughter, LIBYA (Table 3). She was therefore an ancestor of the family of Cadmus. The Egyptian city of Memphis was named in her honour.

Menelaus (Μενέλαος) The brother of Agamemnon and the husband of Helen. According to the accepted version of the story which is followed by the *Iliad* Menelaus was the son of Atreus, king of Mycenae, and a member of the race of Pelops (Table 2). His mother was the Cretan AEROPE, the daughter of Catreus, who was brought to Mycenae by Nauplius after her father had turned her out of his house for having an intrigue with a slave. A later tradition gives PLEISTHENES, one of the sons of ATREUS, as the father of Agamemnon and Menelaus rather than Atreus himself, but even the authors who support this view agree that Pleisthenes died young and that Menelaus and his brother were brought up by Atreus.

When young Agamemnon and Menelaus were sent by Atreus to search for Thyestes, Atreus' brother, they found him in Delphi and brought him to Mycenae. Atreus imprisoned him and tried to have him killed by AEGISTHUS, who recognized his father and killed Atreus instead. Agamemnon and Menelaus were then expelled from Mycenae by Aegisthus. They took refuge with Tyndareus in Sparta, and there married his two daughters, Agamemnon taking Clytemnestra, and Menelaus HELEN. Menelaus was chosen from the numerous suitors either by Tyndareus or by Helen herself. The suitors had previously sworn to help whichever of their number was chosen, should any man try to dispute his possession of Helen. After the death of the Dioscuri, Tyndareus bequeathed his kingdom to Menelaus. The children of this marriage were Hermione (the only child acknowledged by the *Iliad* and the *Odyssey*) and a son, Nicostratus (Table 13). Late authors give the names of other children as Aethiolas, Thronius, Morrhaphius, Pleisthenes the younger and Melita. Nicostratus and Aethiolas were worshipped in Sparta in the historical period. During Helen's absence Menelaus had a son, MEGAPENTHES, by a slave girl. He gave him this name because of the great grief he felt at having been abandoned by his wife. He also had another son, Xenodamus, by another slave girl, called Cnossia (doubtless a Cretan, whose name indicated that her birthplace was the city of Cnossos). The legend that Helen was banished by Nicostratus and Megapenthes after the death of Menelaus derives from this tradition.

For several years (it was said that Hermione was nine years old at the time of Helen's abduction) Menelaus and Helen lived peacefully in Sparta in the luxurious surroundings of a hospitable court. This happiness was destroyed by Paris, who arrived while Menelaus was in Crete attending the funeral of his grandfather CATREUS, and abducted Helen. According to one tradition Menelaus was responsible for Paris' appearance in Sparta: an epidemic and the curse of sterility had afflicted the land of Sparta, and on the advice of the oracle Menelaus went to Troy to offer a sacrifice on the tombs of LYCUS and CHIMAEREUS, the two sons of Prometheus. At Troy he was the guest of Paris. As a result of an accidental killing, Paris was exiled from Troy and sought refuge at Menelaus' court; Menelaus purified him and repaid his hospitality but during the king's absence Paris abducted Helen.

Menelaus received news of his misfortune from Iris; he hastily left Crete and returned to Sparta. He then called together all the suitors who had sworn Tyndareus' oath and sought help from Agamemnon, Nestor, Palamedes and ODYSSEUS. Achilles was sent for and discovered by Diomedes and Odysseus in the harem of LYCOMEDES on Scyros. Menelaus and Odysseus went to Delphi to ask the oracle whether they would successfully undertake an expedition against Troy. The oracle told them that they should first offer to Athena Pronoia a necklace which Aphrodite had once given to Helen. Then Hera aligned herself with Menelaus and united all the Greeks against Paris, her personal enemy. Menelaus took part in the expedition with a force of sixty ships. He did not win the supreme command however. This honour fell to AGAMEMNON. Although Menelaus was a valiant warrior, he is always in the background in accounts of the war. He was less violent than the other heroes assembled against Troy and his enemies were quick to mock him, reproaching him with accusations of cowardice. This gentleness in Menelaus was manifested in the pardon which he eventually granted Helen.

Immediately after the Greeks had disembarked,

or, according to other traditions, while the fleet was at Tenedos, Menelaus and Odysseus went into Troy as ambassadors, to ask for the return of Helen and the treasures carried off by Paris. They were received by Antenor, who brought them before the Trojan assembly. Paris and his supporters ensured that any attempt at compromise was rejected. Antimachus, a friend of Paris, who had been bribed by the latter, even tried to provoke the people into killing Menelaus, but Antenor succeeded in saving him. According to the account given in the *Iliad*, Paris and Menelaus initially faced each other in single combat. The latter wounded his enemy so heavily that, to save Paris, Aphrodite had to cover him with a cloud and carry him off. Agamemnon pointed out to the Trojans who were watching the fight that his brother was clearly the victor: he asked them to carry out the terms agreed before the fight, according to which Helen would belong to the winner. As the Trojans hesitated, Pandarus fired an arrow at Menelaus and grazed him; a general battle then broke out. Soon Menelaus killed Scamandrius and had an indecisive encounter with Aeneas. That evening Hector issued a challenge to any Greek who cared to face him in single combat. Menelaus stepped forward and was about to accept when he was restrained by Agamemnon and the other Greek chiefs. In the course of the fighting which took place around the ships Menelaus wounded Helenus and killed Pisandrus, then Hyperenor, Dolops and, lastly, Thoas. After Patroclus' death Menelaus was the first to come forward and fight to regain his body; in the course of this combat he killed Euphorbus and Podes. Menelaus sent Antilochus to Achilles with the news of his friend's death, and dragged Patroclus' corpse from the battlefield. Thereafter he makes almost no appearance in the closing books of the *Iliad*, only participating in the chariot race during the funeral games held in Patroclus' honour.

Menelaus appeared again in the events subsequent to the *Iliad*. After Paris was killed by one of Philoctetes' arrows, Menelaus had his corpse mutilated; he then figured among the warriors inside the wooden horse. During the capture of the city Menelaus ran to DEIPHOBUS' house, where he knew Helen was, since after Paris' death she had married Deiphobus. There he was involved in further intense fighting but eventually killed Deiphobus and entered the house. There are several accounts of the meeting of Menelaus and Helen. According to Virgil, Helen called Menelaus and Odysseus into the house, after concealing all weapons, ensuring that her first husband would win. Other accounts state that, after killing Deiphobus, Menelaus rushed into the house and dragged Helen off to the ships as his prisoner. The Greeks assigned her to him as part of his plunder, without drawing lots for her as for the other captive women. It was left to Menelaus to put her to death but Odysseus intervened, saving Helen. According to a still more dramatic version Helen sought refuge at the household altar where Menelaus rushed upon her with raised sword. At the sight of her beauty he fell deeply in love with her again and made his peace with her.

After the victory Menelaus returned to Sparta while his brother stayed at Troy to offer a sacrifice to Athena, whose anger he feared, because of the episode of CASSANDRA. Menelaus went to Tenedos, then Lesbos, then sailed over to Euboea and on towards Cape Sounion. Phrontis his pilot died there and Menelaus turned back to pay him his funeral honours while Nestor and Diomedes continued homewards. When Menelaus set sail again, and reached a point level with Cape Malea, he was caught by a storm that carried him to Crete, where most of his ships foundered. He went on to Egypt, where he stayed for five years, acquiring great riches according to the *Odyssey*. On leaving Egypt, Menelaus was becalmed on the island of Pharos at the mouth of the Nile. The sea-goddess IDOTHEA, daughter of the sea-god Proteus, then appeared to him, advising him to consult her father about how to return to Sparta. Proteus told him to return to Egypt and there offer up sacrifices to the gods. Menelaus did this and finally arrived in Sparta with Helen eight years after leaving Troy and eighteen years after the start of the war.

According to another version, Menelaus found the real Helen in Egypt; she had been kept there by Proteus, who was a king rather than a sea-god, since the time when she and Paris had landed in that country. According to this legend, Paris had only taken a ghost to Troy with him, a Helen made of clouds. The whole Trojan War had taken place then merely for the possession of a cloud. The explanation behind this is that Zeus wanted the war as a means of exalting the race of demigods, the heroes born of the union of immortals and mortals: Helen, his own daughter; Paris, also one of his kinsmen, and Achilles, son of Thetis. This tradition seems to derive from Stesichorus and was used, with some modifications, by Euripides, in his tragedy *Helen*. In this work Hera deceives Paris by giving him a false Helen; the real

Helen is abducted by Hermes, on Zeus' instructions, and taken to Proteus in Egypt. When Menelaus arrives in Egypt with the false Helen, she vanishes and he recovers his real wife.

At the end of his life, Menelaus was carried off alive to the Elysian fields, an honour bestowed on him by Zeus because he was his son-in-law. A late legend, invented seemingly without reference to any previous tradition, tells how Menelaus and Helen went to Tauris in search of Orestes and there were sacrificed by Iphigenia on the altar of Artemis. At the time of Pausanias, visitors to Sparta were still shown the house where Menelaus had supposedly once lived. He was worshipped as if he were a god; men would come and ask him for strength in battle, while women appealed to Helen for beauty and gracefulness.

Menestheus (Μενεσθεύς) A member of Erechtheus' family whose father, Peteus, was the grandson of Erechtheus. Menestheus was in exile at the time of the expedition of the Dioscuri against Attica when THESEUS was in Hades with Pirithous. The Dioscuri brought him back and installed him on the throne of Athens. After Theseus' return Menestheus is said to have withdrawn to Scyros. Other traditions concerning Menestheus exist. The Catalogue of Ships in the *Iliad* gives Menestheus as the leader of the Athenian contingent; he was also one of the warriors inside the wooden horse. After the fall of Troy he went to Melos, where he succeeded Polyanax on the throne. He is also said to have founded Scylletion, between Croton and Caulonia on the coast of Bruttium. Strabo cites a 'Port of Menestheus' on the coast of Baetica not far from Gades.

Menesthius (Μενέσθιος) One of the warriors who fought at Troy under the direct command of Achilles, his uncle. He was the son of Polydora, the daughter of Peleus by the river-god Spercheius. According to one tradition Polydora was not Peleus' daughter but his wife, however, and Peleus would accordingly be the human father of Menesthius and Spercheius his divine father. According to another version, the human father of Menesthius was Borus, a son of Perieres.

Menoeceus (Μενοικεύς)
1. An early hero who was a grandson of Pentheus by his father Oclasus. He was the father of Creon and Jocasta (see OEDIPUS and Table 29).
2. The grandson of Menoeceus 1, the son of Creon.

At the time of the expedition of the Seven against Thebes, Tiresias announced that Thebes would be assured of victory only if Menoeceus, the king's son, were sacrificed. Creon was divided between paternal love and patriotic duty and advised his son to flee without explaining the reason, but Menoeceus discovered why his father wanted to send him away and volunteered himself to be sacrificed. This is the tragic version of the story as recounted in the *Phoenician Women* of Euripides. According to other traditions, Menoeceus was eaten by the Sphinx, or sacrificed by Creon himself. Eteocles and Polynices fought their deadly duel close to his tomb. On the tomb of Menoeceus a pomegranate tree grew with fruit the colour of blood.

Menoetes (Μενοίτης) The name of several heroes of the Trojan epic, and also the herdsman whose task it was to guard the flocks of Hades on the island of Erythia (see GERYON). Menoetes warned Geryon of Heracles' theft. Menoetes met Heracles later in the cycle, when Heracles went down to Hades to bring back Cerberus. Menoetes tried to prevent Heracles from stealing one of his steers, but failed; his ribs were broken during the encounter and he would have suffered a more terrible fate had not Persephone intervened and asked Heracles to release him.

Menoetius (Μενοίτιος)
1. The father of Patroclus and the son of ACTOR and AEGINA (Table 30). Aegina married Actor after giving birth to her son by Zeus, Aeacus, who was an ancestor of Achilles; this established kinship between Patroclus and Achilles. Menoetius lived at Opus. He sent his son to stay with Peleus after Patroclus had accidentally killed one of his comrades, Clitonymus, during a game of dice. Patroclus' mother was Sthenele, the daughter of Acastus, but in some accounts his mother is Periopis, the daughter of Pheres, and in others, Polymela, the daughter of Peleus, which would make Achilles and Patroclus first cousins. Menoetius was one of the Argonauts but played no significant part in the legend. He is said to have first worshipped Heracles as a god at Opus. One of Menoetius' daughters, Myrto, is supposed to have had a daughter by Heracles, named Euclea. She was honoured by the Boeotians and Locrians under the name of Artemis Euclea.
2. A giant who was the son of Iapetus by Clymene, one of the daughters of Oceanus, or Asia, according to another tradition, and brother of Atlas,

Prometheus and Epimetheus (Table 38). He was struck down by a thunderbolt from Zeus and plunged into Tartarus because of his arrogance and brutality.

Menthe (Μένθη) A Nymph of the Underworld, beloved of Hades. She was ill-treated by the jealous Persephone and the god changed her into a plant, mint. This transformation took place on Mount Triphyle in Bithynia.

Mentor (Μέντωρ) The son of an Ithacan named Alcimus. He was a faithful friend of Odysseus, who, on leaving for Troy, entrusted him with the protection of his interests. The goddess Athena adopted the outward guise of Mentor on several occasions, notably when he accompanied Telemachus to help Odysseus during the battle with the suitors.

Mercury The Roman god Mercurius, or Mercury, was identified with the Greek Hermes; like Hermes, he protected merchants in particular (his name contains the root of the word *merx*, meaning *merchandise*), and travellers in general. After the hellenization of his cult, he was depicted as the messenger of Jupiter and even, in a humorous context, as his servant in his amorous exploits (as in Plautus' *Amphytrion*, for example, where Mercury is indistinguishable from Hermes). The first temple of Mercury in Rome was built in the valley of the Circus Maximus not far from the port of Rome, where the commercial centre lay. The date traditionally assigned to the founding of this temple is 496 BC. The temple of Mercury was built three years earlier than Ceres' shrine, which was established in the same area. These two sanctuaries were built outside the *pomerium*, the religious boundary of the city, which suggests that the cult of this god was of foreign origin. As in the case of Hermes, Mercury's attributes are the caduceus (the wand), broad-brimmed hat, winged sandals and the purse, the symbol of the profit to be derived from trade.

Mercury has no myth, in the strict sense, being merely a transposition of a hellenic figure: when he intervenes in a legend, it is to play the part of Hermes. This practice is exemplified in the traditions which make him the father of EVANDER. Mercury was also said to be the father of the LARES. This can perhaps be explained by the fact that the Lares, like Mercury-Hermes, were gods of the crossroads.

Meriones (Μηριόνης) The son of Molus, a Cretan and himself the illegitimate son of DEUCALION of Crete. At Troy Meriones was the most faithful of Idomeneus' companions and commanded the Cretan contingent with him. He is mentioned in the list of Helen's suitors. At Troy Meriones performed several noteworthy deeds: he was present at the nocturnal council of war; he wounded Deiphobus, killed Adamas and Acamas, Harpalion, Moris, Hippotion and Laogone and escaped from the blows of Aeneas. He participated in the skirmishes over the body of Patroclus, collected the wood for Patroclus' funeral pyre and competed in three events in the funeral games given by Achilles, namely the chariot race, the archery contest, which he won, and the javelin-throwing. After the fall of Troy, Meriones accompanied Idomeneus back to Cnossos. Earlier legend shows him travelling to Sicily, where he was welcomed by the Cretan colonists established at Heraclea Minoa and Engyon. There he was worshipped as a god. He was also credited with the founding of Cressa in Paphlagonia. Meriones was supposedly an outstanding dancer.

Mermerus (Μέρμερος) One of the two sons of Jason and Medea. He was killed with his brother, Pheres, in Corinth by MEDEA to punish JASON for his infidelity (Table 21). According to another tradition, Mermerus and Pheres were stoned by the Corinthians because they had brought poisoned gifts to Creusa, the daughter of Creon, causing the death of her and her father. Mermerus, the elder son, is said to have died differently; after following his father to Corcyra, where he had gone into exile after Pelias' murder, he was killed by a lioness while hunting in Epirus.

Merope (Μερόπη)
1. One of the Pleiades, a daughter of Atlas and Pleione, and married to a mortal, Sisyphus (Table 25), king of Corinth, by whom she had a son GLAUCUS. Merope was the only Pleiad to marry a mortal and the star that she became in the constellation shines less brightly than those which represent her sisters.
2. The daughter of Cypselus, the king of Arcadia, who married the Heraclid Cresphontes (Table 16). Cypselus gave her in marriage to Cresphontes to seal his alliance with the HERACLIDS and safeguard his kingdom. When the Peloponnese was divided among the Heraclids, Cresphontes obtained Messenia. Merope was the protagonist in a series of events on which Euripides based a play, now

lost. The plot can be reconstructed, however: according to other traditions Cresphontes was killed by an uprising of his subjects, but in Euripides' tragedy, he was assassinated by Polyphontes, another Heraclid. At the same time Polyphontes killed Cresphontes' two elder sons and married his widow, Merope, against her will. Merope saved her youngest son, Aepytus, by sending him to be brought up in Aetolia. She communicated with him through an old and faithful servant. Polyphontes knew that young Aepytus was still alive; this fact disquieted him and he tried to track him down to prevent him from coming to exact his vengeance. He offered a large reward to anyone who killed Aepytus.

Aepytus grew up and planned to avenge his father and brothers. He went to Polyphontes calling himself Telephontes and claimed the reward, declaring he had killed Aepytus. The king refused to believe him but asked him to remain at his court as his guest; he then made enquiries into his claim. In the meantime Merope received a visit from the servant who acted as intermediary between herself and her son. The old man told her that he did not know where Aepytus was for he had mysteriously disappeared a few days previously. Merope was convinced that the stranger whom the king had received was, as he claimed, her son's murderer, so at night she entered the room where the so-called Telephontes was sleeping, with the intention of killing him. At the moment that she raised her dagger over him the old servant arrived and caught her arm, recognizing him as Merope's son. The mother and son then planned their revenge. Merope went into full mourning and Polyphontes was convinced that her son really was dead. Merope until then had behaved in a hostile way towards Polyphontes, but she seemed reconciled to him, as if she had abandoned all hope and was resigned to her lot. The king prepared to hold sacrificial rites of thanksgiving and invited the man he believed to be Telephontes as a guest of honour, asking him to perform the sacrifice himself. Instead of killing the sacrificial victim the young man struck down Polyphontes. He then succeeded to the throne.

Mesopotamia (Μεσοποταμία) The female personification of the country of that name. According to legend she was the daughter of a priestess of Aphrodite, and the sister of Tigris and Euphrates. At her birth Aphrodite endowed her with great beauty. Mesopotamia had three suitors for her hand and to decide between them she deferred to the judgement of Bochorus, a man renowned for his rectitude and justness. Mesopotamia gave gifts to the young men: to one she gave a goblet; to another her own crown; she embraced the third. Bochorus considered that this last gift was the most serious proof of love and he decided in favour of the third suitor. The young rivals rejected his decision; they fought until they were all dead and Mesopotamia remained unmarried.

Messapus (Μέσσαπος) A Boeotian hero who gave his name to Mount Messapion on the coast of Boeotia facing Euboea. He visited southern Italy where he similarly gave his name to the territory of the Messapii. There was also an Illyrian hero named Messapus or Messapius, who according to another tradition was the man after whom the Messapian region was named.

Messene (Μεσσήνη) The daughter of Triopas, the king of Argos and the granddaughter of Phorbas, though according to another tradition she was his daughter (Table 17). She married Polycaon, the younger son of Lelex, king of Sparta. Lelex' elder son Myles inherited his father's kingdom and Messene urged her husband to acquire a kingdom elsewhere. With the help of Spartan and Argive soldiers Polycaon conquered an area which he named Messenia after his wife. The capital of the region was established at Andania where Polycaon established the worship of Demeter and Persephone, cults brought back from Eleusis by Caucon. Polycaon and Messene were later worshipped as gods in Messenia.

Mestra (Μήστρα) The daughter of ERYSICHTHON. Demeter had afflicted Erysichthon with an insatiable appetite and Mestra used to sell herself as a slave to obtain food for her father. Mestra's lover Poseidon gave her the ability to change shape at will; each time she would escape from her master and return home, only to start again.

Meta (Μήτα) The first wife of Aegeus, who was unable to have children. She was a daughter of Hopleus, one of the children of Ion who gave his name to one of the tribes of Attica.

Metabus (Μέταβος) In the *Aeneid* Metabus was an Etruscan by birth, a king of the Volsci and ruler of the city of Privernum. He was the father of CAMILLA and was exiled with her by his subjects. Servius associates this barbarian king with METAPONTUS who gave his name to the city of Metapontum or Metapontium. According to Greek legend Metabus was the son of Alybas.

Metanira (Μετάνειρα) The wife of CELEUS, the king of Eleusis. She took DEMETER into her house when the goddess was looking for her daughter and employed her as a servant. Metanira is said to have been the wife of Hippothoon, an Attic hero, son of Poseidon and Alope, who gave his name to the Athenian tribe, the Hippothontes.

Metapontus (Μετάποντος) The eponymous hero of the city of Metapontum or Metapontium, west of Tarentum. In its barbarian form the name is METABUS and the city is thought to have been called Metabon before it became Metapontion. Metapontus is said to have been the son of Sisyphus and grandson of Aeolus, but he was more often said to be the adoptive father of the younger Aeolus and of Boeotus. He took in Arne, the daughter of the elder Aeolus when she was pregnant and her father had sent her into exile. For Arne's sake Metapontus sent Siris his first wife to live in the city which took her name. Arne's sons killed Siris at their mother's instigation, and fled, one to Boeotia, to which he gave his name, and the other to the Aeolian islands (see AEOLUS 2). Other versions of the same legends were used by Euripides in his lost tragedy *Melanippe in Chains*.

Methymna (Μηθύμνα) This figure gave her name to the city of Methymna on the island of Lesbos. She was the daughter of Macar, married Lepetymnus and bore Hicetaon and Helicaon, who were both killed by Achilles when he captured Lesbos.

Metiochus (Μητίοχος) A young man of Phrygian birth who fell in love with a girl named Parthenope, who had taken a vow of chastity. Parthenope loved Metiochus in return but refused to break her vow. She cut her hair and went into exile in Campania; there she dedicated herself to the worship of Dionysus. Naples owes its Greek name of Parthenope to her.

Metion (Μητίων) An Attic hero whose genealogy has several variants. He is generally listed amongst the sons of Erechtheus and Praxithea (Table 11). His children by Alcippe drove Pandion II off the throne of Athens, and reigned in his stead. According to this tradition Metion was the father of Eupalamus and the grandfather of DAEDALUS. In another legend Metion was the son rather than the father of Eupalamus and the grandson rather than the son of Erechtheus. He was married to Iphinoe and was supposedly the father of Daedalus. He is also credited with being the father of Musaeus. Metion played an indirect role in the tradition of the city of Sicyon in that he is said to have been the father of SICYON who was summoned by Lamedon to succeed him on the throne of the city (Table 22).

Metis (Μῆτις) Metis, whose name means either prudence or, in a pejorative sense, treachery, was a daughter of Oceanus and Tethys. She is said to have been the first wife, or mistress, of Zeus; she gave him the drug which forced CRONUS to regurgitate all the children he had swallowed. When Metis became pregnant, Gaia and Uranus informed Zeus that after giving birth to a daughter, Metis would then have another child fathered by him who would later dethrone him, just as he had dethroned Cronus. On the advice of Gaia, Zeus swallowed Metis, and thus gave birth to Athena.

Mezentius In the legend of the foundation of Rome Mezentius was an Etruscan king who reigned at Caere and fought against Aeneas. The accounts concerning him take various forms. In the oldest tradition, which is included in the treatise *Origines* written by Cato in the 2nd century BC and now lost, Mezentius was summoned by Turnus after the latter's first defeat at the hands of Aeneas and Latinus. In order to persuade Mezentius to help him, Turnus supposedly promised half of all the wine produced that year in Latium and in his own territory. Aeneas had made the same vow to Jupiter; this vow made to the god carried more weight than Turnus' promise, and both Mezentius and Turnus were killed. During the battle Aeneas was called to take his place among the gods and mysteriously disappeared; his son Ascanius succeeded him. The promise made to Jupiter was kept and this explains the origin of the festival of the *Vinalia*, celebrated annually, during which the first of the year's wine was offered up to Jupiter.

The version of this story given by Dionysus of Halicarnassus is substantially different. After Aeneas' marriage to Lavinia, and the building of Lavinium, he and Latinus had to ward off the attacks of the Rutuli led by Turnus. In the first battle Turnus and Latinus were killed. The Rutuli then called Mezentius and the Etruscans to their aid. A battle took place and at nightfall the outcome was still uncertain. It was then noticed that Aeneas had disappeared. Ascanius assumed the command but the Trojans and Latins were in difficulties. Ascanius then asked for peace terms. Mezentius demanded all the wine produced in Latium. Ascanius then vowed the same wine to Jupiter, and, profiting by a moonless night, made an attack which was completely successful. Mezentius' son Lausus was killed and the Etruscan army fell back in disorder. Mezentius learnt of his defeat and his son's death at the same moment. When he asked for terms, Ascanius granted him safe conduct with the rest of his army and thereafter Mezentius remained an ally of the Latins.

In Virgil's version the figure of Mezentius is more complex, but the legend itself is simplified. Mezentius is still ruler of Caere but has been driven out by his subjects because of his tyranny and has taken refuge at Turnus' court. He fights at Turnus' side with Lausus. Both are killed by Aeneas. Virgil makes no reference to the promise to give the wine of Latium to either Mezentius or Jupiter and in his account it is only Mezentius who is Aeneas' enemy: the Etruscans support the Trojans. This can be explained by the fact that Virgil's patron Maecenas was an Etruscan and at the time when Virgil wrote his epic, Maecenas was a close friend of Augustus.

Midas (Μίδας) The king of Phrygia and a hero of several popular legends. According to one, he came across Silenus one day in a remote place, sleeping off the effects of copious libations. After the god had awoken, Midas asked him to talk to him and teach him wisdom. Silenus then recounted the story of two cities, outside our world, called Eusebes or the city of piety, and Machimus, the city of war. The inhabitants of the first were always happy and died laughing, whereas the citizens of Machimus were born fully armed and spent their lives fighting. These two peoples were very rich: they possessed so much gold and silver that these precious metals were to them as common as iron is to us. They decided to come and visit our world; they crossed the Ocean and arrived in the land of the HYPERBOREANS, who were the happiest of mortals. When they saw the miserable condition of the Hyperboreans and learnt that these were the happiest people in our world, they wanted to see no more and returned back to their own lands. This was the parable of disillusionment told by Silenus to Midas.

There is another version of the king's encounter with Silenus, told by Ovid in his *Metamorphoses*. Silenus had strayed away from the retinue of

Dionysus and fell asleep in the mountains of Phrygia. Some peasants found him and, not recognizing him, brought him in chains to their king. Midas, who had once been initiated into the Mysteries, at once realized who his guest was. He had Silenus untied, received him with great honours and went off with him to rejoin Dionysus who thanked the king courteously and offered to fulfil any wish he might make. Midas at once asked that anything he touched should turn to gold. When the god had granted his request, he went home rejoicing and tried out his new gift. When Midas wanted to eat, everything turned to gold; the wine, too, changed into metal. Midas begged Dionysus to take away his destructive gift. Dionysus agreed, and told him to wash his head and hands in the spring at the source of the river Pactolus. Midas did so and was at once freed from his gift. The waters of the Pactolus were thereafter full of grains of gold.

Another very similar tale is recounted by Plutarch. Midas went to visit a distant province of his kingdom, and became lost in the middle of a desert. There was no water to quench his thirst but, taking pity on him, the earth sent forth a spring. This spring spouted gold instead of water and Midas begged Dionysus for his aid. The god changed the spring of gold into a fountain, which was accordingly called the Spring of Midas.

Midas plays a part in another legend, that of Pan, or Marsyas, and Apollo. Midas happened to be on Mount Tmolus just as the god of the mountain was judging the competition. Tmolus had just passed judgement and declared Apollo the winner; without being asked for his opinion Midas declared that the judgement was unfair, whereupon Apollo, in a fit of anger, made a pair of ass's ears grow out of his head. According to another version Midas was one of several judges and was the only one to decide in Marsyas' favour. Midas himself is credited with the invention of the so-called pan-pipes. Midas hid his cumbersome ears under his head-dress and only his barber knew the secret. He was forbidden, on pain of death, to tell anyone, but the poor man, weighed down under this secret could finally contain himself no longer and, digging a hole in the ground, he confided to the earth that Midas had monstrous ears. The reeds which grew in the area then started repeating the king's secret and whispered to the wind that ruffled them: 'King Midas has ass's ears'.

Midias (Μειδίας) A Thessalian, whose son Eurydamas killed Thrasyllus. Thrasyllus' brother Simon then killed Eurydamas and dragged his body around his brother's tomb. This is said to have been the origin of the Thessalian custom of dragging the corpse of a murderer around the tomb of his victim. Achilles did this when he dragged the body of Hector round the tomb of Patroclus. This duty was generally left to the victim's best friend or to his nearest relative.

Miletus (Μίλητος) The eponymous hero and founder of the city of Miletus in Asia Minor. Traditions differ as to his genealogy. According to Ovid he was the son of Apollo and Deione; Minos expelled him from Crete and he went into exile in Asia Minor, where he founded Miletus. There he married Cyane, daughter of the river-god Meander, and had two children by her, CAUNUS and BYBLIS.

According to another tradition he was the son of ACACALLIS and Apollo (Table 28). His mother had exposed him at birth because she was afraid of Minos. He was fed by a wolf, and then taken in by shepherds. Later Minos was struck by his beauty and wanted to force his attentions on him. On the advice of Sarpedon, Miletus fled during the night to Caria, where he founded the city of Miletus. In this version he there married Idothea, daughter of Eurytus, who bore Caunus and Byblis.

Miletus is also said to have been the son of Aria, the daughter of Cleochus, and Apollo. At his birth he was exposed by his mother, but Cleochus took him in and brought him up. He became very beautiful and Minos wanted to force his attentions on him, so he fled to Samos, where he founded a first city called Miletus, and from there went to Caria, where he founded a second city of the same name.

Mimas (Μίμας) One of the Giants who fought against the gods. He was either struck down by a thunderbolt sent by Zeus or was killed by Hephaestus who hurled red-hot metal projectiles at him.

Minerva The Roman goddess identified with the Greek Athena; she appeared first in Etruria and was then introduced into the Capitoline Triad, with Jupiter and Juno. One of her earliest temples was built on Mons Caelius, the hill where the Etruscan contingent which came to the aid of Romulus, under the orders of Caelius Vibenna, was traditionally said to have stationed itself. This temple bore the name Minerva Capta and it may have been built to house a statue of Minerva captured at Falerii during the Roman conquest of the city. According to one tradition Minerva was one of the gods brought to Rome by Numa. The festival of Minerva was celebrated in March at the Quinquatria. The attributes of the goddess are analogous to those of the Greek Pallas Athena. She presided over intellectual and, in particular, academic activity. On the Esquiline there was a chapel dedicated to Minerva Medica, Minerva the healer; votive offerings have been found there which prove that the cult was still extant under the Empire. Minerva plays no part in any specifically Roman legend (see, however, NERIO and ANNA PERENNA).

Minos (Μίνως) A king of Crete, said to have lived three generations before the Trojan War. He is regarded as the son of Europa and Zeus and was brought up by Asterion, or Asterius, king of Crete. He is also said to have been a son of Asterion, however (Tables 3 and 28). After Asterion's death Minos became the sole ruler of Crete. When he announced his intention of assuming the throne his brothers raised objections: Minos replied that the gods meant the kingdom to be his, and, to prove it, he claimed that heaven would grant whatever he requested. He offered up a sacrifice to Poseidon, asking the god to make a bull emerge from the sea, promising to sacrifice the animal to the god in return. Poseidon sent the bull, and Minos won his kingdom without opposition, but the king refused to sacrifice the animal, since he wanted to breed from it. He accordingly sent it off to his herds, but Poseidon took his vengeance by sending the bull mad. HERACLES had to kill it, at Minos' request. Pasiphae, Minos' wife, later fell in love with this bull and conceived the MINOTAUR.

Minos married Pasiphae, daughter of Helios and Perseis (Table 14). His legitimate children were Catreus, Deucalion, Glaucus, Androgeus (also known as Eurygyes), Acalle (also known as Acacallis), Xenodice, Ariadne and Phaedra. He also had illegitimate children. A Nymph called Paria conceived his children EURYMEDON, Chryses, Nephalion and Philolaus, and by another Nymph, Dexithea, Minos had another son, Euxanthius. Other children are also attributed to him in obscure legends. Minos had a large number of amorous adventures and is said to have been the originator of homosexuality. In one tradition Minos rather than Zeus abducted Ganymede. He is also said to have been the lover of Theseus and was supposedly reconciled with him after

Silver tetradrachm of Cnossos, c. 200 BC depicting Minos, king of Crete.

Ariadne's abduction, and gave him his second daughter Phaedra in marriage. Minos loved BRITOMARTIS, but she threw herself in the sea rather than give in to him. His mistresses were so numerous that Pasiphae became angry; she cast a spell on him which caused all the women whom he possessed to die, devoured by the scorpions and snakes which emerged from his body. He was cured of this curse by PROCRIS, who agreed to sleep with him on condition that he gave her a magic dog and javelin which he owned.

Minos is said to have been the first man to civilize the Cretans and to rule them with justice and equity. Minos' laws were so remarkable that they were thought to have been directly inspired by Zeus: it is said that every nine years Minos consulted Zeus in the cave on Ida where Zeus had been brought up. In his legislative functions Minos is often compared with his brother Rhadamanthys, whom he is said to have expelled from Crete out of jealousy, and whose work he supposedly imitated. In the Underworld both Minos and Rhadamanthys sat in judgement over the souls of the dead, assisted by AEACUS.

The figure of Minos personifies the Cretan domination of the sea which existed from the second millenium BC. Mythographers credit him with dominion over a large number of islands around Crete, and as far away as Caria. Minos is said to have been in charge of several military expeditions, notably one against Athens to avenge Androgeos' death, in which he captured the city of Megara (see NISUS and SCYLLA). He was victorious, as a result of a plague which weakened Athens, and he demanded an annual tribute of seven young men and seven girls to be fed to the Minotaur.

Later Minos went to Sicily at the head of an army to recapture DAEDALUS, whom he found at the court of COCALUS. There Minos was killed in his bath by one of the king's daughters at the instigation of Daedalus. The Cretan soldiers he had brought with him founded the Sicilian city of Heraclea Minoa. Later the Cretans organized an expedition against Sicily but were defeated and driven back onto their boats. A storm cast them among the Iapyges and they established themselves with this colony. Later some of them, forced to go into exile because of internal disagreements, went to Macedonia. An oracle ordered them to settle at the place where they were offered a meal of earth and water. When they reached Bottiaea, a district of Macedonia, they found some children making mud pies. The children solemnly offered them their mud pies to eat and the immigrants saw that the words of the oracle had been fulfilled and settled there.

At Heraclea Minoa there was a 'tomb of Minos', said to be the tomb built by Minos' companions in honour of their king. The ashes of Minos were preserved in an inner chamber. There was a sanctuary consecrated to Aphrodite in a second chamber. This tomb was knocked down by Theron at the time of the founding of Agrigentum and Minos' ashes were then carried off to Crete.

Minotaur (Μινώταυρος) This name was given to a monster with the body of a man and the head of a bull whose real name was Asterius, or Asterion. He was the son of Pasiphae, the wife of MINOS, and of the bull sent to Minos by Poseidon. Minos commissioned the Athenian architect, Daedalus, who was then at his court, to build a vast palace (the Labyrinth) comprising such a maze of rooms and corridors that only the architect could find his way. Minos shut the monster in the Labyrinth and every year Minos fed him with seven young men and seven girls who were the tribute exacted by

Theseus killing the Minotaur. Athenian vase of the 1st half of the 6th century BC found in Italy. London, British Museum.

Minos from Athens. THESEUS offered himself voluntarily as one of the young victims, and with the help of ARIADNE he succeeded not only in killing the beast but also in finding his way out of the Labyrinth. The word 'labyrinth' is connected with λάβρυς meaning 'double axe'; this symbol was carved on Minoan monuments.

Minyads (Μινυάδες) The three daughters of king Minyas, ruler of Orchomenus; their names were Leucippe, Arsippe and Alcithoe, or Alcathoe. They were the subject of a legend intended to demonstrate the punishment inflicted by Dionysus on those who refused to join his cult. There are several versions of the legend. All relate that the three sisters remained at home during a festival of Dionysus, busily weaving and embroidering, while the women of Orchomenus were running over the mountains behaving like Bacchantes. The nature of their punishment varied. In some versions ivy and vines began to grow around the stools where the girls were sitting, and milk and wine began to flow down from the roof. Mysterious lights appeared in the rooms, and cries of wild animals, mingled with the sound of flutes and tambourines, rang out. The Minyads were seized with a divine madness; they took hold of the infant Hippasus, Leucippe's son, and tore him to pieces. Then, garlanding their heads with ivy, they joined the other women in the mountains. In other accounts they were transformed into bats.

Another version is quite different and claims that before punishing the Minyads, Dionysus came to find them, in the guise of a young girl, and reproached them for their indifference. They made fun of him; then, before their eyes, Dionysus turned himself into a bull, a panther, and a lion. At the same time milk and wine flowed from the stools and as in the preceding version, the Minyads went mad and tore Hippasus to pieces.

Minyas (Μινύας) Minyas from the Boeotian Orchomenus gave his name to the Minyans, the inhabitants of Orchomenus in the Homeric period. Minyas was either the son or the grandson of Poseidon; in the latter case his father was Chryses, himself a son of the god by Chrysogenia, the daughter of Halmus (Table 20). By Euryanassa, the daughter of Hyperphas, he had a large number of children: his son Orchomenus, the successor to the throne (see CLYMENUS 2), Cyparissus, Leucippe, Arsippe and Alcathoe, the three MINYADS, Elara the mother of TITYUS, Araethyrea, the mother of Phlias by Dionysus and

Clymene, who was the wife of Phylacus and the grandmother of Jason (Table 20).

Misenus (Μισηνός) One of Odysseus' companions who gave his name to Misenum in Campania. According to another tradition he was a follower of Hector, and after his death Misenus became Aeneas' trumpeter and accompanied him on his travels. When the fleet was at anchor off the coast of Campania, Misenus challenged all the gods, claiming that he could play the trumpet better than any of the immortals. The sea-god Triton, who played a conch shell trumpet, caught Misenus unawares and tipped him into the sea, where he drowned. He was buried on the shore of the headland which took his name.

Mnemon (Μνήμων) When Achilles went to the Trojan War his mother gave him a servant called Mnemon, which means 'he who remembers or reminds', whose task was to forestall the events predicted by an oracle. If Achilles should kill one of Apollo's sons, he would die at Troy. It was not known which of Apollo's sons the oracle referred to. Mnemon had constantly to remind Achilles to ensure his victim was not one of Apollo's descendants. On the island of Tenedos, however, Achilles killed Tenes, who was a son of Apollo, and thereafter he could not escape his fate. To punish Mnemon, he killed him with a blow of his spear.

Mnemosyne (Μνημοσύνη) The personification of Memory. She was the daughter of Uranus and Gaia, and belongs to the group of female Titans (Tables 5 and 12). Zeus coupled with her in Pieria for nine consecutive nights and she later gave birth to nine daughters, the Muses. There was a spring dedicated to Mnemosyne before the oracle of Trophonius at Lebadea (see LETHE).

Mnestheus (Μνησθεύς) One of Aeneas' companions who participated in the boat races organized by the hero and won second prize. Virgil claimed he was the eponym of the Roman *gens* of the Memmii, by a play on etymologies (the two names, one Greek, one Latin, both suggest a root meaning 'remember').

Modius Fabidius During a festival of the Sabine god Quirinus celebrated in the area of Reate (the modern *Rieti*) at a time when the original inhabitants still lived there, a girl of noble lineage was dancing in honour of the god. She was inspired by the god and went into the sanctuary from where she emerged, pregnant by him. She gave birth to a son who was named Modius Fabidius who when grown up distinguished himself by his exploits in war. He decided to found a city and gathered together a band of companions. After journeying some distance, they came to rest, and at this spot he founded a city naming it Cures; this etymology seems to derive from the Sabine word 'curis' meaning 'spear' (see QUIRINUS).

Moirae (Μοῖραι) The Moirae, also known as Fates or Parcae, personified the individual's fate; originally each human being had his or her own *moira*, and this abstract notion became transformed into deities who resembled the KERES, without however becoming, as they were, violent and blood-thirsty spirits. The Moirae were as inflexible as destiny; they embodied a law which even the gods could not break without endangering the equilibrium of existence. Gradually the idea of a universal Moira as a force dominating the destiny of humanity as a whole seems to have developed. After the Homeric period a triumvirate of Moirae appeared, consisting of three sisters called Atropus, Clotho and Lachesis, who regulated the length of each individual's life from birth to death by means of a thread which one Moira spun, the second wound up and the third cut, when the life in question was at an end. These three spinners were daughters of Zeus and Themis and sisters of the HORAE. The Moirae do not have a legend in the strict sense of the term; they operate as a symbol of a half-philosophical, half-religious concept of the world.

Molionidae (Μολιονίδαι) Twin brothers named Eurytus and Cteatus; their human father was Actor, brother of Augias, king of Elis and their divine father was Poseidon. Their mother was named Molione, the daughter of Molus. The Molionidae are said to have been born from an egg, comparable to the one from which the children of LEDA emerged. In the *Iliad*, where their early exploits are mentioned, they appear as two separate men, of considerable size and strength, but human. Nestor, in his youth, fought them during the hostilities between Neleus and the Epeioi. Nestor had been on the point of killing them when Poseidon saved them by concealing them in a cloud. Augias called them to his aid when he was attacked by HERACLES. The Molionidae married two of Dexamenus' daughters, Theronice and Theraephone, who bore them two sons named Amphimachus and Thalpius, who led the contingent of the Epeioi at Troy.

Molorchus (Μόλοϱχος) The shepherd who gave hospitality to Heracles when he came to kill the lion that was ravaging Nemea. He was the first man to pay HERACLES divine honours.

Molossus (Μολοσσός) The son of Neoptolemus (Pyrrhus) and hence the grandson of Achilles, he was also known as Mollessus or Molottus. His mother was Andromache, the wife of Hector but given to Neoptolemus as part of his share of the Trojan female captives. The legend of Molossus was staged by Euripides in his tragedy *Andromache*. Born in Phythia, the home of Neoptolemus after the fall of Troy, the infant Molossus was left to die by his mother but he survived and while visiting Delphi Neoptolemus saw and recognized him. Hermione, the wife of Neoptolemus, was jealous of the child since she herself was barren and she persecuted both Andromache and Molossus. Andromache succeeded for a time in hiding her son in the temple of Thetis, but Hermione discovered them and was on the point of killing both mother and son when the intervention of Peleus saved them. When Neoptolemus was later killed by Orestes, Thetis, conscious that the child was the only surviving descendant of the race of Aeacus, instructed Andromache to take him away to Epirus. Andromache did accordingly, and there married Helenus; Molossus later succeeded his step-father on the throne of Epirus. He gave his name to the inhabitants of the region, the Molossians. One version of the legend attributes to Molossus two half-brothers Pielus and Pergamus, sons of Andromache by Pyrrhus.

Molpadia (Μολπαδία) One of the band of Amazons who attacked Attica. She killed Antiope, the Amazon whom Thesus had married, but was then killed herself by Theseus. For another Molpadia, the daughter of Staphylus, see PARTHENOS.

Molpis (Μόλπις) An aristocrat from Elis who during a famine that was devasting his country and in accordance with the instructions of an oracle voluntarily sacrificed himself in order to appease the wrath of the gods. He was awarded divine honours.

Molpos (Μόλπος) A flautist from the island of Tenedos who gave perjured evidence against Tenes, whose step-mother had accused him of having tried to rape her. Thereafter on Tenedos flautists were not allowed into the temple dedicated to Tenes (see CYCNUS).

Molus (Μόλος) A Cretan, the illegitimate son of Deucalion (Table 28) and father of Merion. During a festival celebrated in Crete in Plutarch's time a doll without a head was given the name of Molus and carried in procession. It is said that Molus attempted to rape a Nymph; his headless corpse was discovered some time later, and the rite was established to commemorate these events.

For Molus, the grandfather of the Molionidae, see MOLIONIDAE. This Molus may have been an entirely imaginary figure, invented merely to explain the patronymic (Molionidae), whose meaning remains obscure.

Momus (Μῶμος) The personification of Sarcasm. In Hesiod's *Theogony* she was a daughter of Night and a sister of the Hesperides. When Earth became exhausted by the weight that she was carrying, because the human race was multiplying too swiftly, she asked Zeus to reduce its numbers. Zeus accordingly sent down a war upon mankind: this was the Theban War. It proved insufficient to deal with the problem and Zeus then considered striking men down with thunderbolts or drowning them *en masse*. Momus then suggested a more effective method: Zeus should marry Thetis to a mortal; she would in time give birth to a daughter (Helen) who would set Asia and Europe against one another. This was one of the accounts sometimes given to explain the origins of the Trojan War.

Moneta The Bringer of Warnings: this is the title under which Juno was worshipped on the north peak of the Capitoline hill in Rome. She was given this name because when the Gauls attacked the city in 390 BC the sacred geese which were kept around the sanctuary of the goddess sounded the alarm by cackling after the enemy had attempted to capture the hill in a surprise night assault. The temple of the Juno Moneta stood on the site of the house of Mantius Capitolinus, the defender of the Capitol: the house had been destroyed when its proprietor was condemned to death on suspicion of aspiring to the throne. In this temple coinage was minted. The story was that during the war against Pyrrhus the Romans were afraid that they would run out of money. They asked Juno's advice and she replied that they would never be short of money if their wars were fought accord-

Juno was worshipped under the title of Juno Moneta or Bringer of Warnings on the north peak of the Capitoline Hill. The minting of coins was placed under her auspices. The obverse of this silver denarius of T. Carisius shows the goddess' head and the reverse coining implements.

ing to the principles of justice. In gratitude for this advice it was decided that the minting of coins would be placed under the auspices of the goddess.

Mopsus (Μόψος) Of the various heroes of this name two are particularly well-known; both of them were soothsayers and they are sometimes confused.

1. The first was a Lapith, and the son of Ampyx and Chloris. He took part in the expedition of the Argonauts as a soothsayer, second in importance to Idmon. He appears among the competitors at the funeral games held in honour of Pelias and is listed among the huntsmen who pursued the Calydonian boar. He died of a snake bite during the Argonauts' expedition in Libya. He gave his name to the Thessalian city of Mopsion.

2. The second Mopsus, son of Manto, was a grandson of Tiresias. Traditions vary greatly as to who his father was. He is often described as the son of Apollo, but that is the standard attribution of parentage in the case of most seers. His human father is sometimes said to have been the Argive Rhacius, whom Manto met when leaving the temple at Delphi and who had thus been marked out by the god as her intended husband. She is said to have gone away with Rhacius to Claros. According to another tradition Manto left for Claros alone, on Apollo's instructions, and was abducted on her way by Cretan pirates who took her to their leader Rhacius. Mopsus was the fruit of this union.

Mopsus was credited with the founding of the city of Colophon. He was the soothsayer of the oracle of Apollo at Claros and he competed against the other great seer of his day (after his grandfather Tiresias) Calchas who was on his way back from the Trojan War. Mopsus won easily, and Calchas committed suicide in his disappointment. After the death of Calchas, Mopsus joined forces with Amphilochus while their followers dispersed throughout Pamphylia, Cilicia and Syria. Mopsus and Amphilochus founded the city of Mallos. On their relationship and their death in a duel see AMPHILOCHUS.

Morges (Μόργης) When King Italus grew old he named as his successor a certain Morges, who reigned over the region bounded by Tarentum and Paestum, which was at that time called 'Italy'. During his reign his subjects took the name of the Morgetes. One day an exile from Rome named Sicelus visited Morges, who took him in and gave him part of his kingdom. In this area the inhabitants took the name Siculi. Morges had a daughter Siris who married Metabus (also called Metapoitus). He was the founder of several cities including Morgantina.

Moria (Μορία) A Lydian woman and the heroine of a supernatural adventure which is reminiscent of the story of the resurrection of Glaucus, the son of Minos. One day when her brother Tylus was walking along the banks of the river Hermos he accidentally touched a snake. The creature bit him on the face, and Tylus died at once. Moria, who was some way off, saw her brother's terrible fate and summoned Damasen, a giant and son of Earth. Damasen plucked up a tree by the roots, and crushed the snake; its mate was then seen to rush off to a neighbouring wood and bring back in her mouth a herb which she placed in the corpse's nostrils. At once it came back to life and immediately fled. Moria, learning from the snake, picked some of the herb and used it to bring back Tylus to life. This herb was apparently called balis.

Mormo (Μορμώ) A female demon whose name was used to frighten small children. She was accused of biting children in general, and naughty children in particular, and making them lame. She is sometimes identified with Gelo or Lamia.

Mormolyke (Μορμολύκη) The She-Wolf Mormo, or Mormolyke, was, like Mormo, an evil spirit whose name was used to frighten children. She is said to have been the nursemaid of the Acheron, so in popular belief she was connected with the world of the dead and of ghosts.

Morpheus (Μορφεύς) One of the thousand children of Sleep (Hypnus). His name (which is derived from the Greek word for form) indicates his function: to take the shape of human beings and to show himself to people during their dreams. Like the majority of divinities associated with sleep and dreams Morpheus was winged. He had large swift wings which beat silently and could carry him in seconds to the ends of the earth.

Mors In Greece Death was personified by the masculine spirit Thanatos. In Rome it was the goddess Mors, or rather a pure personified abstract. There is no specific legend attached to Mors.

Mothone (Μοθώνη) According to a local legend of Messenia she was the daughter of Deneus and gave her name to the city of Mothone, which was called Pedasos in the Homeric epics. After the fall of Troy Diomedes brought his grandfather Deneus to Messenia. Mothone was the fruit of Oeneus' union with a local woman, and in honour of his daughter Oeneus changed the name of the city from Pedasos to Mothone.

Mucius Scaevola After the expulsion of the Tarquins Rome was besieged by the Etruscan King Porsenna, and a man named Mucius decided to kill him. He slipped into the enemy camp but wrongly identified the king and stabbed another of the enemy instead. He was at once arrested and brought before Porsenna. At this moment a brazier full of burning coals happened to be carried in for use in the celebration of a sacrifice: Mucius held his right hand on the flames and of his own free will let it burn away. Filled with admiration Porsenna had the brazier removed and himself gave back to his enemy the sword that had been taken from him. Mucius then told him that three hundred Romans like himself were waiting for the chance to succeed in the enterprise in which he had just failed and that he had simply been chosen by lot for the first attempt. This was untrue but Porsenna, much dismayed, at once concluded an armistice with Rome.

Mucius, one-armed as a result of his sacrifice, took the name of Scaevola or the left-handed.

Munichus (Μούνιχος)

1. In Athens Munichus was the eponymous hero of Munichia, one of the military harbours of Piraeus. He is said to have been a king of Attica and son of Panteuces. It is thought that he gave refuge to the Minyans when they were driven out by a Thracian invasion, and gave them land around the harbour which they named after him.
2. Another Munichus was the hero of an Illyrian legend. He was the son of Dryas who succeeded his father as king of the Molossians (see MOLOSSUS). He was an excellent soothsayer and a just man. By his wife Lelante he had three sons; Alcandrus, who was an even better seer than his father, Megaletor and Philaeus, and a daughter Hyperippe. They were all good and virtuous and the gods loved them for their piety. One night brigands attacked the city; Munichus and his people were unable to withstand the attack so the marauders hurled all the family from the top of the tower and set fire to the house. Zeus did not let such devout people die in such a fashion and changed them into birds. Hyperippe who was afraid of the fire and threw herself into the water became a diver (or gull); Munichus became a falcon, Alcandrus a golden-crested wren, Megaletor and Philaeus who fled through a wall and hid in the sand became two sparrows; their mother Lelante was transformed into either a lark or a green woodpecker.

Munitus (Μούνιτος)

The son born of the clandestine relationship between Laodice, the most beautiful of Priam's daughters, and Acamas, one of Theseus's sons who had come with a deputation to Troy to recover Helen before the war started. The infant was entrusted to his grandmother Aethra and after the fall of Troy she handed him back to his father. Munitus later died of a snake-bite during a hunting expedition in Thessaly.

Musaeus (Μουσαῖος)

According to various traditions, Musaeus was the friend, pupil, master, son, or simply contemporary of Orpheus. He seems simply to have been Orpheus' counterpart in Attic legend. According to this tradition his father was Antiphemus, or Eumolpus; these names indicate that they were singers (Antiphemus' name suggests that he was the inventor of the part-song) just as Musaeus' name suggests that he was the archetypal musician. His mother was Selene, and he was brought up by the Nymphs. Musaeus is said to have been a great musician, capable of healing the sick with his music. He was also a seer and he is sometimes credited with having introduced the Eleusinian mysteries into Attica. Various poems of mystic inspiration were attributed to him.

Muses (Μοῦσαι)

The Muses were the daughters of Mnemosyne and Zeus, the fruits of nine nights of love-making. Other traditions claim that they are the daughters of Harmony, or the daughters of Uranus and Ge (Heaven and Earth). All these genealogies are clearly symbolic and relate more or less directly to philosophical ideas concerning the primacy of music in the Universe. The Muses were not only divine singers, whose chorales and hymns delighted Zeus and other gods; they also presided over thought in all its forms: eloquence, persuasion, knowledge, history, mathematics, astronomy. Hesiod praises their services to mankind; claiming that they accompany kings and inspire them with the persuasive words necessary to settle quarrels and re-establish peace among men and give kings the gift of gentleness which makes them dear to their subjects. Similarly, according to Hesiod, a singer (in other words a servant of the Muses) has only to celebrate the deeds of men of former days or to sing of the gods and any man beset by troubles or sorrows will forget them instantly. The oldest song of the Muses is the one sung after the victory of the Olympians over the Titans to celebrate the birth of a new order.

There were two main groups of Muses; the Thracians from Pieria, and the Boeotians from the slopes of Mount Helicon. The former, neighbours of Olympus, are often referred to in poetry as the Pierides. They are connected with the myth of Orpheus and with the cult of Dionysus, which was particularly strong in Thrace. The Muses of Helicon were placed directly under the control of Apollo who is said to have conducted their singing around the Hippocrene spring. There were other

The nine Muses, the inspiring deities of song, depicted with their various attributes on an antique sarcophagus. Paris, Louvre.

groups of Muses in other regions. Sometimes these groups contain only three figures, analogous to the Graces, which is notably the case at Delphi and at Sicyon. At Lesbos there was a cult of Seven Muses. From the classical period the number of Muses was standardized to nine, and the following list was generally accepted: Calliope, the first of them all in dignity, then Clio, Polyhymnia, Euterpe, Terpsichore, Erato, Melpomene, Thalia and Urania. It was only gradually that each came to be attributed with a specific function, and these vary from one author to another. Broadly speaking, Calliope was said to be the Muse of epic poetry, Clio of history, Polyhymnia of mime, Euterpe of the flute, Terpsichore of light verse and dance, Erato of lyric choral poetry, Melpomene of tragedy, Thalia of comedy and Urania of astronomy. The Muses do not have a cycle of legend peculiar to themselves. They took part as singers in all the great celebrations held by the gods and they were present at the marriages of Peleus and Thetis, and of Harmony and Cadmus.

Myceneus (Μυχηνεύς) The hero who founded the city of Mycene and gave it his name. Certain traditions (expressly described as dubious by Pausanias) claim that he was the grandson of Phoroneus and the son of Sparton.

Myenus (Μύηνος) The son of Telestor and Alphesiboea. His step-mother falsely accused him in the presence of his father of having conceived an incestuous passion for her. Myenus withdrew into the mountains and, pursued by his father with a band of servants, threw himself from the top of a cliff. A mountain was then named after him.

Mygdon (Μύγδων)
1. The *Iliad* mentions a King Mygdon who ruled over a part of Phrygia which lay on the banks of the River Sangarius. During an attack by the Amazons, Mygdon was helped by Priam and in gratitude he in turn came to the aid of Troy when the city was attacked by the Greeks. He was the father of the hero Coroebus.
2. Another Mygdon was the brother of Amycus, and like him king of the Bebryces. He was defeated by Heracles, the ally of Lycus with whom Mygdon was at war. After the defeat of Mygdon's kingdom Heracles founded the city of Heracleia.

Mylas (Μύλας) One of the Telchines, said to have invented the corn mill. He also gave his name to a mountain on the island of Rhodes.

Myles (Μύλης) A Laconian hero, said to have invented the corn mill (but cf. Mylas). In Laconian tradition Myles was the son of Lelex the king of Lacedaemon, and of Peridia; he was the brother of Polycaon, Boumolchus and Therapne and the father of Eurotas. Other traditions omit him completely, claiming instead that Eurotas was the son of Lelex (see Table 6).

Myrice (Μυρίκη) A daughter of Cinyras king of Cyprus. She was changed into a tamarisk, whose name she bears. Compare the legend of MYRRHA who was also a daughter of Cinyras.

Myrina (Μύρινα) An Amazon who led her race to great victories. She declared war on the Atlantes who lived in a land on the shores of Ocean, where the gods were said to have been born. With the help of an army of three thousand Amazons fighting on foot and twenty thousand on horseback, she first conquered the territory of an Atlantic city called Cerne. She captured the city itself, slaughtered all the able-bodied males and took the women and children into captivity. She then razed the city to the ground and the other Atlantes at once surrendered in terror. Myrina treated them generously, she made a treaty of alliance with them, built a city in the place of the one she had destroyed which she called Myrina, and gave it to the prisoners and to all those willing to live there. The Atlantes then asked Myrina to help them fight the Gorgons. In the first battle, which was hard-fought, Myrina was victorious but many of the Gorgons escaped. One night the Gorgons imprisoned in the Amazon camp seized weapons from their guards and killed many of them before the Amazons rallied and massacred the rebels. Myrina paid great honours to those of her subjects who had perished in the fight, and raised a tomb to them made of three hillocks of equal height known as the Tombs of the Amazons. Despite this defeat the Gorgons succeeded in re-establishing their power, and later Perseus and then Heracles are said to have fought them.

The exploits attributed to Myrina are not confined to these two wars. After conquering the greater part of Libya, she later went on to Egypt where Hors, the son of Isis, reigned. She made a treaty of friendship with him, then organized an expedition against the Arabs, ravaged Syria and, returning northwards, was met by a delegation from the Cilicians who voluntarily surrendered to her. She crossed the range of the Taurus mountains, clearing her way through the passes by force, crossed Phrygia and reached the area of the River Caicus, which was the aim of her expedition. Myrina was eventually killed by King Mopsus, a Thracian who had been driven out of his homeland by Lycurgus. This legend is a 'historical' construction, and does not constitute a myth in the strict sense: it offers an interpretation of mythical elements combined to form a more or less coherent account (see also GORGONS) in which,

alongside the myths, the work of the 'rationalist' euhemerist mythographers can be detected. Myrina, the queen of the Amazons, is named in the *Iliad*, but there her name is said to be Myrina 'among the gods' only, her human name being Batieia. She was supposed to have married King Dardanus (see Table 7) and to have been the daughter of Teucer. There is enormous confusion in the traditions relating to this heroine: most of the evidence is of a late provenance.

Myrmex (Μύρμηξ) A young Athenian girl who won the esteem and affection of the goddess Athena because of her upright life and her skill with her hands. Myrmex claimed to have invented the plough, but this was really the invention of Athena, and to punish Myrmex the goddess turned her into a burrowing ant, harmful to crop-growing. Zeus later returned her to human form, together with all the race of ants on the island of Oenone (see AEACUS).

Myrmidon (Μυρμιδών) The ancestor of the Myrmidons (a Thessalian people later ruled by Achilles) and the son of Zeus by Eurymedusa. He was the father of Actor and Antiphus by Pisidice, one of the daughters of Aeolus (see Table 8). Through his daughter Eupolemia, he was the grandfather of the Argonaut Aethalides. Another tradition makes him the son of Dioplethes and the grandson of Pericres, also through his wife Polydora, the son-in-law of Peleus.

Myrrha (Μύρρα) The daughter of Cinyras king of Cyprus. For her legend see ADONIS. She is also sometimes called Smyrna.

Myrsus (Μύρσος) The hero of a legend recorded only by Nonnius in his *Dionysiaca*. He was one of the sons of Aretus who, against his father's wishes marched against Dionysus. Myrsus' brothers were Lycus, Glaucus, Periphas and Melaneus. These sons were all dumb, it having happened that during the wedding of Aretus and his bride Laobia, just as the customary sacrifice to Aphrodite was being made, a sow gave birth with a great cry to a litter of fish and a soothsayer revealed that this portended an equivalent number of dumb children for Aretus and Laobia. After his victory, Dionysus granted the gift of speech to Aretus' children.

Myrtilus (Μυρτίλος) In the versions of the legend of Pelops used by the dramatists Myrtilus is the coachman of Oenomaus who took the axle-pin out of his master's chariot-wheel and replaced it with a wax peg so that Pelops won a victory over Oenomaus, whose divine horses could not otherwise have been beaten (see HIPPODAMIA). Myrtilus was the son of Hermes and Phaethusa, one of the daughters of Danäus, or of Clymene. The motives given for his treachery are various: it is suggested either that he was in love with Hippodamia, or that he had been won over by her, or that he had been bribed by Pelops. After his victory and the abduction of Hippodamia, Pelops killed Myrtilus by throwing him into the sea. (Myrtilus, according to certain authors, is the eponym of the Sea of Myrto which washes the southern coastline of Attica.) Two principal reasons for his death are given: one is that he tried to rape Hippodamia, the other that Pelops killed him to avoid having to pay him the price agreed for his treachery. As he died Myrtilus cursed Pelops and all his race: this is supposed to have been the origin of the misfortunes which overwhelmed Pelops' descendants (see Table 2). After his death Myrtilus was changed by his father Hermes into a constellation, the Charioteer.

Myrto (Μυρτώ) Among the many who bore this name was a daughter of Menoetius and consequently the sister of Patroclus. She gave birth to a daughter fathered by Heracles, named Eucleia (but see MACARIA). Eucleia died a virgin and was often associated with Artemis in the numerous sanctuaries in Boeotia and Locris.

Myscelus (Μύσκελος) The founder of the city of Croton, in Italy. Several legends exist about him.

According to the oldest he was an Achaean, a native of Rhypes, who wanted to found a colony in Graecia Magna. Apollo instructed him through the Delphic oracle to found Croton, but when he arrived in the country he saw the city of Sybaris which already existed and went back to ask the god if it was really necessary to found a new city in the same region. To which the oracle replied: 'Myscelus of the short back [for he was somewhat hunch-backed], if you act against the god's instructions, you will reap a harvest of tears. Accept the gift that he is making you.' Myscelus obeyed. Another tradition, recorded by Ovid, says that the foundation of Croton was due to the intervention of Heracles who had been given hospitality by Croton when on his way back from his encounter with Geryon. In return for this hospitality Heracles had promised Croton that a city would later be built which would bear his name. Accordingly, he advised Myscelus in a dream to go and found a colony in Graecia Magna, but since the laws of Argos at that time forbade its citizens to go abroad, so Myscelus paid no attention to his dream. Heracles returned threatening him with terrible punishments and Myscelus resigned himself to breaking the law. He was brought to court and the judges all voted against him by each putting into an urn the black pebble which would condemn him to death. Myscelus begged Heracles to rescue him and miraculously all the black pebbles at once turned white. Myscelus was acquitted and allowed to leave. He then founded his colony and established himself at the site of Croton.

N

Naiads (Ναἱαδες) The Naiads are water Nymphs, femal beings granted very long life but still mortal (see HAMADRYADS and NYMPHS). Just as the Hamadryads personify the mysterious life of the trees to which they are bound, so the Naiads incarnate the divinity of the spring or stream which they inhabit. Sometimes there is only a single Nymph who is the Nymph of the spring, sometimes the same spring has several Nymphs considered as sisters who are equal in status.

Their genealogy is variable in both myth and legend. Homer calls them 'daughters of Zeus'. Elsewhere they are part of the race of Ocean, more often they are simply the daughters of the god of the river in which they live. The daughters of Asopus are Naiads. Every famous spring has its own Naiad, who has her own particular name and legend. At Syracuse there was the beautiful Nymph Arethusa, who was said to have been a Nymph of Achaea, a companion of Artemis and, like her protectress, scornful of Love. One day she came across a river with fresh, clear water and wanted to bathe in it. As she was swimming, thinking herself alone, she heard the voice of Alpheus, the god of the river, who had conceived a passion for her. Arethusa fled in terror just as she was. The god pursued her and the chase went on a long time, until Arethusa, her strength flagging, called on Artemis to save her. The goddess enveloped her in a cloud and in her fear (for Alpheus refused to leave the spot where he had seen her disappear) she turned into a fountain. The earth then opened to prevent the river god from mingling his own waters with those of the spring that Arethusa had become and thus succeed in uniting with her in this new form. Guided by Artemis, Arethusa went through underground channels to Syracuse, on the island of Ortygia, which is dedicated to Artemis.

The late character of this legend, an invention of the Alexandrian poets, is obvious. It is intended to explain the homonymy of two springs, one in Elis, the other in Sicily. It has been designed according to the traditional formula of passionate pursuit and metamorphosis. Such inventions, however, were only possible because the Naiads were beings familiar to the Greek imagination and each spring and stream possessed its own.

The Naiads were often said to have healing powers. The sick drank the waters of springs consecrated to them or, more rarely, bathed in them. Sometimes bathing was considered sacrilegious and whoever dared to try it risked the anger and vengeance of the goddesses, manifested by some mysterious illness. At Rome Nero himself, when bathing in the Mariam Spring (one of the most highly valued of the city aqueducts) was attacked by a sort of paralysis and fever which beset him for a few days. These disorders were attributed to the displeasure of the Naiads, the protecting spirits of the holy water. Another risk run by those who offended the Naiads was madness. Whoever caught sight of the Naiads, for example, was 'possessed' by them and driven mad (see LYMPHAE).

Many genealogies feature a Naiad as foundress of a family: for example, the wife of Endymion, mother of Aetolus; and the wives of Magnes, Lelex, Oebalus, Icarius, Erichthonius, Thyestes and others. They therefore have an important role in local legend and a further intermediary role in larger legends by attaching this or that hero to the soil of a given city or region. The Naiads are particularly numerous in the Peloponnese.

Nana In the Phrygian legend of Attis Nana is the daughter of the river-god Sangarius. She took to her breast the magic fruit which made her pregnant (see AGDISTIS and ATTIS).

Nanas (Νάνας) The son of Teutamides, a king of the Pelasgians of Thessalia. He was a descendant of Pelasgus by Phrastor, his great-grandfather, and Amyntor, his grandfather. During his reign before the Trojan War, the Pelasgians were driven out of Thessaly by the Greek invasions, crossed the Adriatic, captured the city of Croton and established themselves in Italy. Changing their name they thenceforth called themselves Tyrrhenians. Herodotus distinguishes these Pelasgians who emigrated to Italy from the Tyrrhenians who, according to him, originally came from Asia Minor.

Nannacus (Νάνναχος) A king of Phrygia who lived long long ago before Deucalion's flood. He had foreseen the flood and organized public prayers to try to avert the catastrophe. These prayers were accompanied by tears and lamentations, the proverbial 'tears of Nannacus'. Another legend attached to this name recounted that Nannacus lived for three hundred years and that an oracle had predicted that when he died all his people would die with him. When he eventually died his subjects loudly bewailed their fate. The flood occurred soon afterwards and the oracle was fulfilled.

Nanus (Νάνος)
1. The native ruler of Massalia whose daughter married Euxenus, the chief of the Phocian immigrants.
2. According to Tzetzes, Nanus is also the 'Tyrrhenian' name for Odysseus and in that language means wanderer. On the adventures of Odysseus in Italy and his legendary contacts with the Tyrrhenian world see ODYSSEUS.

Narcissus (Νάρκισσος) A handsome young man who despised love. His legend is recorded in different ways by different authors. The best-known version is that of Ovid's *Metamorphoses* in which Narcissus is the son of the god of Cephicos and of the Nymph Liriope. When he was born his parents questioned the seer Tiresias who told them that the child 'would live to an old age if it did not look at itself'. When he reached manhood Narcissus was the object of the passions of a large number of girls and Nymphs but he was indifferent to all this. Eventually the Nymph Echo fell in love with him but she could get no more from him than the others. In despair she withdrew into a lonely spot where she faded away until all there was left of her was a plaintive voice. The girls rejected by Narcissus asked the heavens for vengeance. Nemesis heard them and arranged matters so that one very hot day, after he had been hunting, Narcissus bent over a stream to take a drink from it and saw his own face, which was so handsome that he immediately fell in love with it. Thenceforward indifferent to the world he stayed watching his own reflection and let himself die, when he even tried to make out the beloved features in the waters of the Styx. On the spot where he died there later grew a flower which was given his name.

The Boeotian version of the legend was substantially different. Narcissus was said to be an inhabitant of the city of Thespiae, not far from Helicon. He was young and very handsome but scorned the joys of love. He was loved by a young man called Ameinias, but did not love him in return, kept rejecting him and finally sent him a present of a sword. Obediently Ameinias committed suicide with this sword in front of Narcissus' door. As he died Ameinias called down the curses of the gods upon the cruel Narcissus. Then one day when Narcissus saw himself in a spring he fell in love with himself and, made desperate by his passion, killed himself. The Thespians worshipped Love, whose power this story illustrates. In the place where Narcissus killed himself and where the grass had been impregnated with his blood there grew a flower which was named after him.

Pausanias on the other hand records that Narcissus had a twin sister whom he closely resembled in looks. Both were very handsome. The girl died; Narcissus, who had loved her very much, was deeply upset and one day seeing himself in a stream, thought he saw his sister, which allayed his sorrow. Although he knew perfectly well that he was not seeing his sister, he fell into the habit of looking at himself in streams to console himself for her loss. This, says Pausanias, was the probable source of the legend as it is usually related. This version is an attempt at a rationalizing interpretation of the pre-existing myth.

Finally, there was an obscure tradition according to which Narcissus was a native of Eretria in Euboea. A certain Epops (or Eupo?) was supposed to have killed him, and from his blood the homonymous flower was born.

Nauplius (Ναύπλιος) Tradition records two heroes of this name, who are often confused with each other.
1. The first, an ancestor of the second, was the son of Poseidon by Amymone, one of the daughters of Danäus. This first Nauplius was considered to have been founder of the city of Nauplion. His sons were Damastor, grandfather of Dictys, and Polydectes, and Proetus, grandfather of Naubolus and accordingly great-grandfather of the second Nauplius.
2. Nauplius II, or Nauplius the Younger, is much the better known of the two. He was descended from Nauplius I as follows: Nauplius I – Proetus – Lernus – Naubolus – Clytoneus – Nauplius II. He took part in the expedition of the Argonauts, whose pilot he became after the death of Tiphys. Some of the mythographers name him as the father of Palamedes, but others, notably Apollodorus, take the father of Palamedes to be Nauplius

I and in so doing get caught up in chronological difficulties since the adventures of Palamedes and consequently the misdeeds of his father (see below) occur at the period of the Trojan War and stretch from the time of Agamemnon's birth to the return of the Greeks from Troy which would give an implausibly long duration to the lifetime of Nauplius I, particularly if this same Nauplius is also made a grandson of Danaos. It is probably to get round this impossible situation that the tradition emerged of two homonymous characters separated by five generations.

Nauplius II (whether or not he is distinguished from Nauplius I) is notable principally for being the father of Palamedes, his wife being either Philyra or Hesione or Clymene in which last case she is the daughter of Catreus. The two other sons of Nauplius II were Oeax and Nausimedon.

Nauplius is the typical example of the traveller-hero. He was a remarkable navigator, and several kings had recourse to his services to take into exile some errant family member. We find two similar legends in which he plays the same role. The first is the legend of Telephus whose mother Auge was seduced by Heracles. Her father Aleus gave Nauplius instructions to drown her, but while he was conveying her to Nauplion she gave birth to Telephus. Nauplius took pity on her and gave her to some merchants who took her off to Mysia.

In the second legend Catreus entrusted Nauplius with two of his daughters with orders to drown them either because they had slept with slaves or because an oracle had told him that he would be killed by one of his children. But Nauplius gave Aerope to Atreus (or Plisthenes, according to different traditions) and himself married Clymene.

Nauplius' son Palamedes joined the Greek army to fight against Troy but was stoned to death by the Greeks on a charge of treachery. The life of Nauplius was from then onwards devoted to avenging his son. He began by persuading the wives of the absent heroes to take lovers and was notably successful with Clytemnestra the wife of Agamemnon, with Meda the wife of Idomeneus, and with Aegiale the wife of Diomedes. Later he even tackled Penelope, but to no avail. Meanwhile he had exacted another and still more horrible form of vengeance from a large number of the Greek leaders. When the main convoy of the Greek army, on its way back from Troy, arrived level with the Gyroi (the Round Rocks near Cape Caphareus in the south of Euboea) Nauplius lit a huge fire on the reefs during the night. The Greeks, thinking they were near a harbour, headed for the light and their ships were broken up. It was in this shipwreck that Ajax son of Oileus died.

According to Apollodorus the death of Nauplius was caused by an act of treachery similar to that of which he had himself been guilty in respect of the Greek fleet but we do not know the details of this adventure. It is also said that on the occasion of his attempt to throw Penelope into the arms of the suitors Nauplius was deceived by Anticlea the mother of Odysseus. She told him of the death of his sons, and in his grief Nauplius committed suicide.

Naus (Ναός) Said to have been a great-great-grandson of Eumolpus, king of Eleusis (see EUMOLPUS). On the instruction of the Delphic oracle he introduced the mysteries of Demeter into Arcadia (though according to Arcadian traditions these mysteries were introduced into the region by Demeter herself).

Nausicaa (Ναυσικάα) The heroine of one of the most famous legends recounted in the *Odyssey*. She is the daughter of the King Alcinous, of the Phaeacians and of Arete. It was she whom Athena used to persuade the Phaeacians to provide Odysseus with the means of returning to Ithaca. Odysseus, in fact, had been the victim of another shipwreck after leaving Calypso's island and was thrown ashore, battered and bruised after a long time in the water, on the coast of an island unknown to him. He fell asleep in a wood on the banks of a stream and during his sleep, Athena sent a dream to Nausicaa. The young girl dreamt that one of her friends chided her for her negligence and asked her to go down as early as possible and wash all the family linen in the river. In the morning Nausicaa asked her parents for permission to go and do this washing. They were happy to let her do so and she went off for the whole day with the female servants in a carriage drawn by mules. The young girls washed the clothes and while these lay stretched out on the grass to dry they began to play ball on the river bank. Suddenly the ball went astray and rolled into the water. The girls gave a loud cry and woke Odysseus. He, being totally naked, swiftly covered himself with branches and made his appearance. The servants fled in terror, but Nausicaa stayed where she was and it was to her that Odysseus addressed himself. He pretended to take her for a goddess or a Nymph of the stream; Nausicaa promised him her help. She gave him something to eat, lent him some clothes and scolded her servants for having felt scared instead of welcoming a guest sent by the gods. When evening fell Nausicaa returned to the city, having shown Odysseus the way to the palace; she herself rode in the carriage with her servants. There her role stops, but she had been touched by the hero's misfortune and in particular by his beauty and she expressly admitted to herself that she would like to marry him. Alcinous was ready to permit this but Odysseus had a wife in Ithaca and could not entertain the thought of another marriage. On this note the episode ends.

The mythographers invented a later marriage between Telemachus and Nausicaa, by which she was said to have had a son named Persepolis.

Nausithous (Ναυσίθοος) The name of several heroes whose legend is connected with the sea.
1. One is the son of Poseidon and of Periboea, herself the daughter of King Eurymedon who reigned over a race of giants. He was king of the Phaeacians while they were still in Hyperia, and it was under his leadership that, driven out by the Cyclops, they established themselves at Scheria (Corfu). Nausithous was the father of Alcinous and of Rhexemor, and by the latter the grandfather of Arete, Alcinous' wife.
2. Another Nausithous piloted the boat which took Theseus to Crete to fight the Minotaur. Theseus built a chapel to him.
3. Lastly, Nausithous is the name of one of the children of Odysseus and Calypso. He had a brother named Nausinous. One tradition makes him the son of Odysseus and Circe and the brother of Telegonus.

Nautes (Ναύτης) An elderly Trojan who accompanied Aeneas on his emigration. In Sicily he advised Aeneas not to stay on the island but to go on to Latium. A tradition independent of the *Aeneid* says that it was he who received back the Palladium from Diomedes when the oracle ordered its return to the Trojans. The Roman family of the Nautii was said to be made up of his descendants.

Naxos (Νάξος) The hero who gave his name to the island. At least three separate traditions exist as to who he was. According to one he was a Carian, son of Polemon who, two generations before Theseus, had installed himself on the island at the head of a Carian colony. The island was then called Dia, and it was Naxos who gave it his own name. According to another legend he was the son of Endymion and Selene. A third version says that he was the son of Apollo and Acacallis; this legend represents the 'Cretan' version.

Neda (Νέδα) Afer Rhea had given birth to Zeus in the mountains of Arcadia, she wanted to purify herself and bathe the child, but the river-beds were completely dry. In her distress Rhea struck the ground with her sceptre, calling on Gaia (the Earth) for help. At once a plentiful spring burst forth, close to the place where the city of Lepreion later was to stand. Rhea gave it the name of Neda in honour of the Nymph, the oldest of the daughters of Ocean after Styx and Philyra.

Neleus (Νηλεύς)
1. Son of Tyro and Poseidon (see Table 21). On his mother's side he was descended from Salmoneus and therefore from Aeolus; he was the twin brother of Pelias and half-brother of Tyro's children by Cretheus, that is, Aeson, Pheres and Amythaon. At their birth Neleus and Pelias were abandoned by their mother and were fed by a mare sent by Poseidon. According to one tradition one of the children was marked on the face by a kick from the mare and both were taken in by horse-dealers who named the child with the scar Pelias (from the Greek word *pelion* meaning livid) and named the other child Neleus. When the young men grew up they found their mother again and she was being badly treated by her step-mother, Sidero. Pelias and Neleus attacked Sidero but were unable to kill her at first because she took refuge in the temple of Hera. Pelias, however, violated the sanctuary and murdered Sidero at the altar. Much later the two brothers fought among themselves to decide who should rule. Neleus was exiled by his brother and went to Messenia, where he founded the city of Pylos. He married Chloris, a daughter of Amphion, and by her he had a daughter Pero and twelve sons named Taurus, Asterius, Pylaon, Deimachus, Eurybius, Epilaus, Phrasius, Eurymenes, Evagoras, Alastor, Nestor and Periclymenus.

Neleus played a role in the Heracles cycle. Heracles led an expedition against him, on the pretext that Neleus had refused to purify him of the murder of Iphitus. In this war, eleven of Neleus' sons were killed, only Nestor escaping the massacre. According to some traditions Neleus himself was also one of the victims but others claim that he outlived his sons. In the latter versions he is said to have died of an illness at Corinth and to have been buried there. On the other wars waged by Neleus, notably against the Epeians, see NESTOR and MOLIONIDAE.

2. A second Neleus was a descendant of the previous one and a son of Codrus, king of Athens. He is credited with the foundation of Miletus. He headed a colony of Ionians who came from Attica and joined up with some Messenians who had been driven from their country by the invasion of the Heraclids.

Nemanus (Νεμανοῦς) In the legend of Isis, the wife of the king of Byblos who gave hospitality to the goddess when she was searching for the coffin containing Osiris' body. Isis had learnt that the coffin had been thrown up by the sea onto the coast of Byblos and had landed on a tree which had grown and lifted it above the ground. This tree had been cut down by Malcandrus the king of Byblos, and used as a column to hold up the palace roof. This was how, unknown to anyone, the coffin came to be concealed at roof height in the palace. Isis arrived at Byblos and in order to make her way into the king's presence, she became acquainted with the serving-women in the palace. She disguised herself as a poor woman and gave the servants a perfume which impregnated their hair with so ambrosial a scent that the queen wanted to meet this woman who had the power to impart to hair so powerful a charm. She took Isis into her service as a children's nurse. At night the goddess used to put the youngest child in the fire in order to rid him of the mortal part of his body and make him immortal. While he was in the fire she would change into a swallow and circle around the column bearing Osiris' coffin, making plaintive cries. During one of these strange scenes Nemanus appeared and let out a cry of anguish at seeing her son amid the flames. Isis at once revealed her true identity to the queen but warned her that her son would never be immortal. She explained the reason for her own presence at Byblos and was at once given Osiris' body. When she opened the coffin she started to scream so violently that the youngest son of Nemanus died of shock. Then she left with the coffin and took the eldest son of Nemanus with her, but he also died as a result of having seen the goddess grieving over the corpse of her husband.

Nemesis (Νέμεσις) Both a goddess and an abstract concept. In her divine form she is attributed with a myth: she who was one of the daughters of Nyx (the Night) and was beloved by Zeus but tried to evade the god's embrace, assuming a thousand different forms and finally changing herself into a goose. Zeus became a swan however and coupled with her. Nemesis laid an egg which some shepherds picked up and gave to Leda. From this egg came Helen and the Dioscuri. This legend shows the symbolic value of Nemesis who personifies divine vengeance. Sometimes she is the goddess who, like the Erinyes, punishes crime, but more often she is the power charged with curbing all excess, such as excessive good fortune, for example, or the pride of kings. This illustrates a basic concept in Greek thought: any man who rises above his condition, for good or ill, exposes himself to reprisals from the gods since he risks overthrowing the order of the world and must therefore be punished. That is why Croesus, who was too wealthy and powerful, was enticed by Nemesis into his expedition against Cyrus, which ruined him.

At Rhamnus, a small town in Attica not far from Marathon, on the coast of the straits which divide Attica from Euboea, Nemesis had a famous sanctuary. A statue of the goddess was carved by Phidias from a block of Parian marble acquired by the Persians, who intended to make it a trophy after they had captured Athens. In this they showed themselves too sure of their victory, a sign of inordinate pride, and consequently their attempt to take Athens was unsuccessful. The Nemesis of Rhamnus encouraged the Athenian army at Marathon.

Neoptolemus (Νεοπτόλεμος) Also known as the Young Warrior and as Pyrrhus, he was the son of Achilles and Deidamia who was a daughter of Lycomedes king of Scyros. Neoptolemus was born during the time when Achilles was concealed in Lycomedes' harem. As Achilles was then disguised as a girl and called Pyrrha the name of Pyrrhus remained attached to his son. The legend acknowledges him equally under both names. Neoptolemus was born after his father had left for the Trojan War and was brought up by his grandfather Lycomedes. After Achilles' death and the capture of the seer Helenus the Greeks discovered through Helenus that the city could never be captured unless Neoptolemus came to fight on the Greek side. Another condition of their success was the possession of Heracles' bow and arrows. The Greeks sent a first embassy of Odysseus, Phoenix and Diomedes to find Neoptolemus on Scyros and bring him back. Lycomedes opposed his departure, but Neoptolemus was faithful to the tradition of his father and followed the Greek ambassadors. On the journey to Troy he accompanied them to Lemnos, where Philoctetes lay ill. He was the possessor of Heracles' arms and Neoptolemus, supported by Odysseus and Phoenix, tried to persuade him to let them carry him off to Troy. Eventually he was successful.

Before the walls of Troy the Greek army found in Neoptolemus a second Achilles. He accomplished numerous deeds of valour; he killed Eurypylus, the son of Telephus, and in his delight he invented the Pyrrhic war dance which is named after him. He was among the heroes who entered Troy in the wooden horse and captured the city. During the decisive battles, he killed Elasus and Astynous, wounded Coroebus and Agenos, then hurled Astyanax from the top of the tower. Thus Hector was killed by Achilles, and his son was killed by Neoptolemus. As part of his share of the plunder Neoptolemus was given Hector's widow Andromache. To honour his father's memory, he offered up Polyxena to him as a sacrifice on his tomb. This part of the legend is told in approximately the same way by all the sources, but from the return journey from Troy onwards the versions start to diverge considerably. The Homeric tradition is simple. In this version Neoptolemus had a happy home-coming like Menelaus. Menelaus married him to his daughter Hermione, and Neoptolemus and Hermione went to live in Phthiotis, in the land of Peleus and Achilles. Other accounts of the return say that Neoptolemus escaped the common fate of the Greeks, thanks to the intervention of Thetis, who advised him to remain for a few days longer at Troy and to return by land. That is why Neoptolemus went via Thrace, where he met Odysseus and from there made his way to Epirus to the area which later took the name of the 'Country of the Molossians' (see MOLOSSUS). Another tradition, recorded by Servius in his commentary on the *Aeneid*, says that it was not Thetis but the seer Helenus who gave this advice to Neoptolemus, and that Helenus voluntarily accompanied him. This is supposed to be the origin of the friendship between the two men which led Neoptolemus on his deathbed to entrust Andromache to Helenus, asking him to marry her. To explain why Neoptolemus did not establish himself in his father's kingdom in Phthiotis, this version supposes that during Achilles' absence Peleus had lost his throne to Acastus, so Neoptolemus went straight to Epirus. On this point too the legends are at variance however. For example it is said in one account that in Epirus Neoptolemus had abducted a grand-

daughter of Heracles, named Leonassa, and that they had eight children who established themselves in the region and became the ancestors of the Epirots. It is said in other accounts that after disembarking in Thessaly on his return from Troy, Neoptolemus burnt his ships on the advice of Thetis and then settled in Epirus because this region fulfilled Helenus' oracle. Helenus had advised him to settle in a country where the houses had iron foundations, wooden walls and canvas roofs, and in Epirus the natives lived in tents with stakes that were tipped with iron points, walls covered in wood and roofs of canvas.

In most of the preceding versions Neoptolemus married Hermione but his marriage was barren, whereas from his union with Andromache three sons were born, Molossus, Pielus and Pergamus. Jealous of the fertility of a mere concubine, Hermione summoned Orestes, whom she was to have married, to avenge her. In the simplest of the versions, Orestes killed Neoptolemus at Phthia, or in Epirus. In the account adopted by the tragedians the legend is more complex: Orestes carried out his revenge at Delphi, and his motive was double because in killing Neoptolemus, he not only avenged Hermione, but also punished his rival for having deprived him of his wife. Neoptolemus had gone to Delphi to consult the oracle as to why his marriage with Hermione was still barren. Other accounts suggest that he had gone there to dedicate to the god part of the booty he had brought back from Troy, or to ask Apollo the reason for his hostility towards his father, Achilles – a hostility which had brought about the latter's death since it was Apollo who had guided Paris' arrow. Orestes is said to have fomented a riot, in the course of which Neoptolemus was killed.

There is also a completely different legend in which Orestes plays no part. It was the custom at Delphi for the priests to take the greater part of the meat of the animals offered up as sacrifices: almost none was left for the person making the sacrifice. Neoptolemus was angered by this custom and tried to prevent the priests from taking away the animal he had sacrificed. One of the priests named Machaereus killed him with a blow to protect the status of the privileges enjoyed by the priesthood. A final version claims that the Delphians killed Neoptolemus on the instruction of the Pythia herself and that Apollo was carrying his anger against

The so-called 'Temple of Neptune' of the 5th century BC at Paestum. Modern scholars now dispute this dedication and argue that the temple was in fact dedicated to Hera.

Achilles into the second generation. Neoptolemus was buried beneath the threshold of the temple of Delphi and divine honours were paid to him.

Nephalion (Νηφαλίων) One of the sons of Minos and the Nymph Paria (see Table 28). He settled in Paros with his brothers Eurymedon, Chryses and Philolaus, as well as his nephews Alceus and Sthenelus, the two sons of Androgeos. This took place at about the time when Heracles set off to the land of the Amazons to look for the girdle of the Amazon queen, Hippolyta. Heracles stopped at Paros and Minos' sons killed two of his companions. In his indignation Heracles immediately retaliated by killing the sons: the rest of the island's inhabitants sent a deputation to him offering in compensation two of them to replace the two he had lost. The choice of men was to be his. Heracles accepted the proposal and took Alceus and Sthenelus.

Nephele (Νεφέλη) The name Nephele, meaning Cloud, is given to several heroines:
1. The most famous is the first wife of Athamas, the mother of Phrixus and Helle. Athamas abandoned her and married Ino.
2. Nephele is also sometimes used with its literal meaning and refers to the magic Cloud fashioned by Zeus to resemble Hera in order to cheat the unlawful passion of Ixion. Mating with him, the Cloud produced the Centaurs.

The Clouds played a definite part in mythology. Aristophanes uses them as characters in one of his comedies, and equips them with a genealogy: they are the daughters of Oceanus (like all water divinities); they sometimes live on the peaks of Olympus, sometimes in the gardens of Oceanus in the Hesperides, sometimes at the distant sources of the Nile, in the land of the Ethiopians. Aristophanes is perhaps making a reference to Orphic beliefs but it is more probable that he is creating a personal poetic myth using ill-defined elements of folklore.

In the legend of CEPHALUS it was sometimes the Cloud (Nephele), rather than the Breeze, who was summoned by the huntsman and it is over this name that Procris made her mistake.

Neptune The Roman god identified with Poseidon. The etymology of his name is obscure but it seems to derive from a very early stage of the language. He was the god of water, but had no legend specific to himself before his assimilation

with Poseidon. His festival was celebrated at the height of summer (on 23rd July) during the season of the greatest dryness. He had a sanctuary in the valley of the Circus Maximus between the Palatine and Aventine hills at the precise spot where a stream had once flowed. In Roman tradition Neptune was said to have had a companion spirit, whose name is sometimes given as Salacia, sometimes as Venilia.

Nereus (Νηρεύς) One of the so-called Old Men of the Sea and sometimes the archetypal Old Man of the Sea. He was a son of Pontus (the High Seas) and Gaia (the Earth) and accordingly brother of Thaumas, Phorcys, Ceto, and Eurybia (see Table 32). His wife was Doris, another daughter of Oceanus, and by her he fathered the Nereids. Nereus was one of the figures who are mentioned most often in Greek folklore about the sea. Other than Poseidon, who belongs to the generation of the Olympian gods, he ranks among the gods who represented the elementary forces of the world. Like the majority of marine deities, he had the power to change himself into all sorts of animals and beings. This power was particularly useful when he tried to escape the questions put to him by Heracles, who wished to learn how to reach the land of the Hesperides. In general Nereus was considered a benevolent and beneficent god as far as sailors are concerned. He was represented as bearded (his beard often white) armed with a trident and riding a Triton.

Nereids (Νηρηίδες) Sea-deities, daughters of Nereus and Doris, and grand-daughters of Oceanus (see Table 32). They can possibly be said to personify the countless waves of the sea. Their number is usually set as fifty, but in some accounts they are thought to be as many as a hundred. There are four separate lists of Nereids which are mutually complementary. The list which follows has been compounded from a comparison of all sources:

Actea, Agave, Amathea, Amphinome, Amphithoe, Amphitrite, Apseudes, Antonoe, Callianassa, Callinira, Calypson, Ceto, Clymene, Cranto, Cymatolege, Cymo, Cymodoce, Cymothoe, Dero, Dexamene, Dione, Doris, Doto, Dynamene, Eione, Erato, Eucrate, Eudore, Eulimene, Eumolpe, Eunice, Eupompe, Evagore, Evarne, Galatea, Galene, Glauce, Glauconome, Halia, Halimede, Hipponoe, Hippothoe, Iaera, Ianassa, Ianira, Ione, Laomedia, Liagore, Limmorea, Lysianassa, Maera, Melite, Menippe,

Nausithoe, Nemertes, Neomeris, Nesaea, Neso, Orithyia, Panope, Pasithea, Pherousa, Plexaure, Polynoe, Pontomedousa, Pontoporeia, Pronoe, Protho, Proto, Protomedia, Psamathe, Sao, Speio, Thalia, Themisto, Thetis, Thoe. The size of this overall list shows how various the traditions are, depending on the whim of individual mythographers and poets. Vase paintings name other Nereids such as Calyce, Choro, Cymatothea, Eudia, Iresia, Nao, Pontomeda.

Some of the Nereids who rarely play any individual role in legends have nonetheless more definitely drawn personalities than their sisters: these include Thetis, mother of Achilles, Amphitrite, wife of Poseidon, Galatea, and Orithyia who is widely described as the daughter of Erechtheus, king of Athens. The Nereids are said to have lived at the bottom of the sea, seated on golden thrones in their father's palace. They were all very beautiful and they spent their time spinning, weaving and singing. The poets picture them playing in the waves, letting their hair float around them, and swimming to and fro amid the Tritons and dolphins. They appear most frequently in legends as spectators, rarely taking part in the action. They wept for the deaths of Achilles and Patroclus with their sister Thetis; they told Heracles how to extract from Nereus the information he needed about the route to the land of the Hesperides, they were present at the freeing of Andromeda by Perseus.

Nerio In Roman tradition (and doubtless in Italian tradition too) Nerio was the wife of Mars. She was the personification of Valour (which is what her name, derived from an old Indo-European root means). Sometimes the spoils taken from an enemy were dedicated to her in the same way as they were to Mars or Vulcan. In certain traditions she seems to have been identified with Minerva who was also a warrior-goddess like the Greek Pallas. For the amorous escapades of Mars and Minerva-Nerio see MARS and ANNA PERENNA.

Nerites (Νηρίτης) The son of Nereus and Doris. He is the hero of sailors' legends and in particular he is said to have been a very handsome young man who excited the love of Aphrodite in the days when she still lived in the sea. When the goddess flew off to Olympus, however, Nerites refused to follow her, even though she had given him wings. In anger and indignation Aphrodite changed him into a shell-fish, attached to a rock and incapable of moving. She then gave his wings to Eros who agreed to be her companion. Another version of Nerites' legend goes as follows: beloved of Poseidon he went about with his friend whose passion he returned, but Helios (the Sun) was jealous of the swiftness with which he could cut through the waves and turned him into a shellfish.

Nessus (Νέσσος) A Centaur and, like all the Centaurs, a son of Ixion and Nephele. He took part in the fight against Pholus and Heracles and, driven off by the hero, settled by the banks of the river Evenus where he acted as ferryman. There he met Heracles for a second time when the latter came with Deianeira to cross the river. Heracles swam over but gave Deianeira to the ferryman who tried to rape her on the way across. She called for help and Heracles struck the Centaur down with an arrow. As he died he told Deianeira a supposed secret to avenge himself on Heracles, giving her a liquid which was composed of a mixture of his own blood and the semen he had spilled during the attempted rape, he assured her that if ever her husband began to love her less she had only to steep an article of clothing in it and the garment would act as a love-philtre and would make him faithful again. This was the way in which Heracles' death was accounted for, since the liquid was in fact a strong poison. When Heracles put on the tunic which had been steeped in it, it attached itself to his body. Every time he tried to tear it off he pulled off strips of flesh with it and he finally burned himself alive to escape the terrible pain.

Nestor (Νέστωρ) The youngest of the sons of Neleus and Chloris (see Table 21). He was the only one to survive the massacre by Heracles. He lived to a very great age (more than three generations) by the grace of Apollo. His mother Chloris was one of the Niobids, the daughters of Amphion and Niobe. His brothers and sisters were killed by Apollo and Artemis, but to make some sort of restitution for this murder Apollo granted Nestor the right to live the number of years of which his uncles and aunts had been deprived. There are various explanations as to why the young Nestor was not killed by Heracles. Some sources say that he was brought up far away from his brothers at Gerenia in Messenia, whereas others claim that Neleus and his other eleven sons had tried to take the oxen of Geryon which Heracles was driving with great difficulty and Nestor alone had refused to take part in the undertaking.

As he appears in both the *Iliad* and the *Odyssey* Nestor is the archetypal wise old man, still valiant on the battlefield but above all excellent in counsel. He reigned at Pylos. Nestor played a leading role in the battles between his compatriots the men of Pylos and their neighbours the Epeians. He attacked them several times to punish them for their raids on his territory. During one of these battles he was on the point of killing the Molionidae and would have done so had not Poseidon wrapped them in a cloud to save them. He was also credited with killing the giant Ereuthalion in Arcadia, after challenging him to single combat. He participated in the fight of the Lapiths and the Centaurs, in the hunting of the Calydonian boar, and, in certain late versions, in the expedition of the Argonauts. Above all his extraordinary longevity allowed him to play an important role in the Trojan War. Menelaus sought his advice after Helen's departure and Nestor accompanied him on his trip around Greece to assemble the heroes. He himself provided a fleet of ninety ships and set off accompanied by his sons Antilochus and Thrasymedes. We know that he took part in the capture of Tenedos by Achilles before the events recounted in the *Iliad*. His share of the booty was Hecamede, the daughter of Arsinous. He acted as intermediary in the dispute between Achilles and Agamemnon and to the end strove to bring harmony to the Greek camp. The epic poems also tell of how Nestor was attacked by Memnon and defended by Antilochus who sacrificed his own life to save him. Achilles finally killed Memnon and avenged Antilochus.

After the fall of Troy Nestor returned safely to Pylos, one of the few heroes to return without mishap. His wife (Eurydice, daughter of Clymenus (see Table 33) according to the *Odyssey*, but Anaxibia, daughter of Cratieus, according to Apollodorus) was still alive. Telemachus went to ask Nestor's advice when he was worried as to what had befallen his father. No tradition about the manner of his death has survived, though his tomb was an object of interest at Pylos. The sons of Nestor were Perseus, Stratichius, Aretus, Echephron, Pisistratus, Antilochus and Thrasymedes. His daughters were Pisidice and Polycaste.

Nicaea (Νικαία) A Naiad, the daughter of the river Sangarius and the goddess Cybele. She was devoted to hunting and spurned love, so when a Phrygian shepherd Hymnus was attentive to her, he was met only with disdain. He refused to resign himself to his failure, however, and Nicaea killed him with an arrow. Whereupon Eros, who was indignant at this act of violence as were all the Gods, inspired Dionysus, who had seen Nicaea bathing naked, with a passion for her. Nicaea was still unwilling to yield and threatened the god with the same fate as Hymnus if he would not leave her alone. Dionysus then changed the water in the spring where she drank into wine and when she had become drunk he had no difficulty in overpowering her. The fruit of their union was a daughter Telete. At first Nicaea wanted to kill herself, but eventually she made her peace with Dionysus and they had other children including a son called Satyrus. When he returned from his expedition to India, Dionysus built the city of Nicaea in her honour.

Nicomachus (Νικόμαχος) A grandson of Asclepius, through his father Machaon. His mother was Anticleia, daughter of Diocles. After the latter's death Nicomachus and his brother Gorgasus became rulers of the city of Pheres in Messenia. Later Isthmus son of Glaucus built a sanctuary to them as two warrior heroes.

Nicostrate (Νικοστράτη) One of the names given in Greece to the mother of Evander. She is sometimes said to have been Evander's wife and the daughter of Hermes. In Rome she was known as Carmenta.

Nicostratus (Νικόστρατος) The son of Helen and Menelaus. Since the Homeric poems affirm several times that Hermione was Helen's only child, Nicostratus is generally said to have been born after the return from Troy. In an attempt to solve this same difficulty he is sometimes presented as the son of Menelaus by a slave, in which case he would be the brother of Megapenthes (see Table 13).

Nike (Νίκη) The personification of Victory. She is represented as winged and flying at great speed. Hesiod makes her the daughter of the Titan Pallas and Styx, so she therefore belongs to the first divine race and is older than the Olympians. Later traditions makes her a playmate of Pallas Athena instead. She is supposed to have been brought up by Palans (in this tradition the eponymous hero of the Palatine) who consecrated a temple to her on the top of his hill, the Palatine, at Rome. This was the temple which in the historical period stood on the edge of the Clivus Victoriae, the Mount of Victory, near the church of San Teodoro. This legend derives from accounts which at Athens combined the goddess Athena and Nike. It also derives from the homonymy of the two Pallases, the Titan and the goddess (or her 'double'). At Athens Nike was in fact only an epithet of Athena.

Nileus (Νειλεύς) In the euhemerist tradition followed by Diodorus Siculus, King Nileus was a man who ruled over Egypt. He gave his name to the River Nile which had previously been called Aegyptus. This honour was awarded to him by his grateful people in recognition of the substantial irrigation work undertaken by him with the aim of increasing the fertility of the land.

Nilus (Νεῖλος) In Greek traditions Nilus is the god of the Nile, the Egyptian river. Like all rivers he was said to be a son of Oceanus, but a more precise legend grew up which associated the river with the cycle of Io. Epaphus the son of Io was said to have married Memphis the daughter of Nilus. From their union was born Libya, mother of the race of Agenor and Belus (see Table 3). The Greeks represented Nilus as a king who had made Egypt fertile by regulating the course of the river, constructing dykes and so on (see above NILEUS).

Ninus (Νίνος) The mythical founder of the city of Nineveh and of the Babylonian Empire. He is said to have been the son of Belus or of Cronus (Belus, the god Baal, is in fact identified with the Greek god Cronus). Ninus is supposed to have invented the art of warfare and to have been the first to assemble huge armies. He took as his ally Ariaeus king of Arabia, and with him conquered all Asia except for India. Bactria resisted him for a long time but he was finally able to conquer it thanks to a ruse of the wife of one of his viziers. This woman was SEMIRAMIS, whom he later married. After his death she took the throne herself. Herodotus gives a genealogy for King Ninus, which makes him a descendant of Heracles through his grandfather Alceus who was the son of Heracles and Omphale, but this makes Ninus several generations too young and is an 'historical' interpretation of earlier legends.

Niobe (Νιόβη) The name of two quite separate heroines whom the traditions tend to confuse.
1. The first is an Argive, daughter of Phoroneus by the Nymph Teledice (or Cero, or Peitho). She was the first mortal woman with whom Zeus mated, the 'mother of mankind', and by him she

gave birth to Argos and (according to Acousilaus) Pelasgus (see Tables 17 and 18).

2. The other Niobe was the daughter of Tantalus and therefore Pelops' sister. She married Amphion and bore him seven sons and seven daughters according to most mythographers, though the number varies from author to author. The seven sons were named Sipylus, Eupinytus, Ismenus, Damasichthon, Agenor, Phaedinus and Tantalus; the daughters were Ethodaea (or Neaera), Cleodoxa, Astyoche, Phthia, Pelopia, Astycratia, and Ogygia. In the Homeric tradition there were twelve children, six of each sex; in the tragedians' version there were twenty, ten sons and ten daughters; and Herodorus of Heraclea gave only five, two boys and three girls. By her marriage Niobe figures among the Theban heroines.

Happy, and proud of her children, Niobe one day declared that she was superior to Leto who had only one son and one daughter. The goddess heard her, felt offended, and asked Apollo and Artemis to avenge her. The two deities did so, slaughtering the children of Niobe with their arrows. Artemis killed the girls, Apollo the boys. Only two of them were saved it seems, one boy and one girl. The latter became pallid as a result of the terror she felt at the death of her brothers and sisters; she then took the name Chloris and later married Neleus. In the version of the legend given in the *Iliad* the children of Niobe remained unburied for ten days. On the eleventh the gods themselves buried them. In the more recent version Niobe in her grief fled to her father Tantalus, at Sipylus (or to Mount Sipylis in Asia Minor), where she was changed into a rock by the gods. Her eyes continued to weep however, and people were shown the rock which had once been Niobe and from which a spring now flowed.

There was another version of the Niobe legend which gave a different explanation of the murder of her children. In this account Niobe was the daughter of Assaon, who had married her to an Assyrian named Philottus. The latter was killed during a hunt, and Assaon became enamoured of his own daughter. She refused to yield herself to him and Assaon then asked his twenty grandchildren to a feast during which he set fire to the palace and burned them all alive. Stricken with remorse Assaon killed himself. Niobe was either changed into stone or threw herself from the top of a rock.

Nireus (Νιρεύς)

1. The first Nireus figures among the suitors of Helen. He was very handsome but of humble birth, the son of Charopos and the nymph Aglaea. He reigned over the island of Syme and is included in the Catalogue of Ships as being the commander of a fleet of only three ships. During the battle between Achilles and Telephus in Mysia (at the time of the first expedition and the failed disembarkation) Nireus killed Hiera, the wife of Telephus, who was fighting at her husband's side. Nireus was killed by Telephus' son Eurypylus before the walls of Troy. His tomb was to be seen in the Troad. Another tradition includes him in the travels of Thoas after the fall of Troy.

2. Another Nireus, a native of Catania, threw himself from the top of the promontory at Leurodia after he had been disappointed in love. He was miraculously saved by fishermen who on pulling him out of the water in their net also brought up a chest full of gold. Nireus claimed the gold as his own, but Apollo appeared to him in a dream and advised him to be content with his life and not to lay claim to treasure that did not belong to him.

Nisus (Νῖσος)

1. One of the four sons of the second Pandion, king of Athens (Table 11). He was born at Megara while his father was in exile, having been expelled from Athens by the sons of Metion. His mother was Pylia, daughter of the king of Megara. After his father's death Nisus returned with his brothers to conquer Megara (see also SCIRON).

Although some traditions attribute to Nisus a daughter named Iphinoe who married Megareus son of Poseidon, usually and in the best known version of the legend Nisus' daughter was Scylla, who betrayed her father for love of Minos. In this legend Nisus was changed into a sea eagle.

2. The name of a companion of Aeneas famous for his friendship with Euryalus. His legend seems to stem from Virgil. At the funeral games celebrated in honour of Anchises, Nisus ensured that his friend was the victor. During the war against the Rutuli, Nisus and Euryalus went into the enemy camp to reconnoitre during the night. They killed Rhamnes, but on their way back were pursued by a troop of cavalry. They sought refuge in the woods but became separated. Feeling that his friend was threatened Nisus left his hiding place and died trying to avenge the death of Euryalus.

Nixi The Nixi were three kneeling female statues which could be seen at Rome, on the Capitol, in front of the *cella* of the Capitoline Minerva. They represented in the popular mind the pains experienced by women at the moment when they bring a child into the world.

Notus (Νότος) The god of the South Wind, a warm and very moist wind. He was the son of Eos (the Dawn) and Astraeus (Table 14). He rarely appears as a character in mythology, unlike his brothers BOREAS and ZEPHYRUS.

Numa Pompilius Numa, a Sabine by birth, was the second king of Rome in the legends of the foundation of the city. He was born on the day Romulus founded Rome, and married Tatia, the daughter of Titus Tatius. He was represented as the religious king *par excellence*; he was credited with creating most of the cults and sacred institutions. He began by paying divine honours to ROMULUS, under the title of Quirinus; then he created the colleges of the Flamines, the Augurs, the Vestals, the Salii, the Fetiales, and the Pontiffs, and introduced a large number of deities, for example the cults of Jupiter Terminus, of Jupiter Elicius, of Fides and Dius Fidius and of the Sabine gods. It was claimed that he was Pythagorean by persuasion, or, alternatively, that his religious policy was inspired by the Nymph EGERIA. She was supposed to have come at night to give him advice in the grotto of the Camenae near a sacred spring. All cultural and religious reforms are attributed to his name, such as the institution of a calendar based on the phases of the moon, and the distinction between *dies fasti* and *dies nefasti*.

Numa possessed magic powers. During a banquet which he was presiding over, for example, the tables suddenly filled with costly dishes and delicious wines which nobody had brought in. It was also said that he had captured Picus and Faunus on the Aventine by mixing honey and wine with the water of the spring at which they used to drink. When he had them in his power, he forced them to talk, although they took on the shapes of all manner of terrifying beings. In the end they admitted themselves defeated and revealed various secrets to him, such as charms against thunder. He is also said to have had a conversation with Jupiter on this topic during which he persuaded the god to content himself with turning thunder aside with onion heads, instead of using the heads of men, horses and fish. Numa is supposed to have had several sons, Pompo, Pinus, Calpus and Mamercus, each of whom was said to have been the ancestor of a Roman *gens*. He also had a daughter, Pompilia, either by Tatia, the daughter of the King Titus Tatius, or by Lucretia, whom he married after his accession to the throne. This Pompilia married a Sabine called Marcius, who accompanied Numa to Rome and became a member of the Senate. King Ancus Marcius was the grandson of Numa through Marcius. He was born five years before Numa's death. Numa died at an extremely old age and was buried on the right bank of the river, on the Taniculum. At the same time the sacred books that he had written in his own hand were placed beside him, in a separate coffin. About 400 years later, under the consulate of P. Cornelius and M. Baebius, a violent rainstorm unearthed the two coffins. Numa's coffin was empty. The other contained the manuscripts; these were burnt in the Comitium in front of the Curia.

Numitor The elder son of Procas, king of Alba, and himself sixteenth king of the Aenead dynasty. His young brother AMULIUS seized the throne on their father's death and expelled Numitor. Then, to be sure that no one could exact vengeance for his crime, he killed Numitor's son and dedicated his daughter Rhea Silvia to the service of Vesta, so that she would be obliged to stay celibate beyond the age of childbearing. Rhea was loved by the god Mars, however, and gave birth to twins, Romulus and Remus. On Amulius' orders the two children were exposed on the banks of the Tiber, but they did not die: the swollen river set down the basket which contained them at the foot of the Germalus (the north-west crest of the Palatine). The children were taken in by the shepherd FAUSTULUS who reared them on the Palatine. When they were older they lived as shepherds and occasionally committed acts of brigandage. One day there was a fight between them and Numitor's shepherds, who were pasturing their flocks on the Aventine. Remus was taken prisoner and taken off to Alba. When brought before the king he behaved so proudly that the king was intrigued, but Remus, who did not know his origins, could not satisfy Amulius' curiosity. Romulus, who had been let into the secret of their birth by Faustulus, came to his brother's help with a troop of countryfolk. He killed his great-uncle, took possession of the palace and re-established his grandfather Numitor on the throne.

Another version gives Numitor a greater role in saving and bringing up the twins. In this account Numitor was supposed to have known about his daughter Rhea's pregnancy and to have contrived to substitute two children for those of his daughter. Rhea's two sons were sent by him to the shepherd Faustulus on the Palatine. They were suckled by Faustulus' wife Larentia who had once upon a time made a trade of her physical charms and thereby earned the title of 'she-wolf' (a term applied to women of easy virtue). Once they had been weaned, they were sent to Gabii to be educated in Greek there. When they came back to the Palatine, to the man they thought was their father, Numitor contrived a quarrel between them and his shepherds; he then complained to Amulius of these insolent young men who were ravaging his flocks in conjunction with the local peasantry. Amulius, without suspecting anything, summoned everyone to Alba to judge the trial. Numitor, helped by this crowd of young men, had no difficulty in overthrowing his brother and regaining the throne. Then he gave his grandsons a piece of ground on which to found a city, the precise spot where they had been brought up by Faustulus.

A number of variants of the legend of Amulius and Numitor exist. For example, both are said to have been sons of the hero Aventinus, or even his grandsons (Procas being their father). In one version their inheritance from their father was shared: one chose power (Amulius), the other chose riches (Numitor). Or in an alternative account, Procas advised them to govern after the manner of the Roman Consuls, by forming a college of two equal kings, but Amulius took the reins of power into his hands alone.

Nycteus (Νυκτεύς) The name of several heroes, the best known being the father of ANTIOPE. He is generally considered to have been the brother of Lycus and the son of Hyrieus and Clonia (Table 25). He is therefore a descendant of Poseidon and the Pleiades; but the mythographers, confusing the two figures, both named Lycus – one the son of Poseidon and Celaeno, the other the son of Hyrieus and the grandson of Poseidon and Alcyone (Table 25) – have sometimes made Nycteus the son of Poseidon and Celaeno. Other versions exist which are apparently irreconcilable with the preceding one. For example, Lycus and Nycteus are said to have been the sons of Chthonius, one of the men born of the teeth of the dragon killed by CADMUS. In this version they both fled to Euboea (probably a Boeotian village of that name) because they had killed PHLEGYAS, and there they became friendly with the king, Pentheus. The even acted as regents for a certain time (see LAIUS and LABDACUS). When Nycteus' daughter

ANTIOPE fled to Sicyon to be with Epopeus, Nycteus killed himself and entrusted LYCUS with the task of avenging his dishonour. A variant of the same tradition given by Pausanias says that Nycteus was slain on the battlefield in an expedition against Sicyon which was mounted to punish the king of that city, Epopeus, who had abducted Antiope. Epopeus was also wounded in the same battle and died soon after.

Nyctimene (Νυκτιμένη) The daughter of Epopeus, the king of Lesbos, or a king of Ethiopia named Nycteus. Her father fell in love with her and she either shared his incestuous passion, or was forced into it by him. In shame she fled to the woods, where Athena had pity on her and turned her into an owl. That is why owls avoid the light, do not like to be seen, and only come out at night.

Nyctimus (Νύκτιμος) The only one of the sons of LYCAON whom the prayers of Ge saved from the vengeance of Zeus. He succeeded his father on the throne of Arcadia. Deucalion's flood occurred during his reign. Nyctimus was succeeded by ARCAS.

Nymphs (Νύμφαι) The Nymphs were who peopled the countryside, woods and streams. They were the spirits of the fields and of nature in general, personifying its fecundity and gracefulness. In the Homeric epics they are said to have been the daughters of Zeus They were considered secondary deities, to whom prayers were addressed and who were sometimes to be feared. They lived in grottos where they spent their time spinning and singing. Often they were depicted as the attendants of a great goddess (particularly Artemis), or of another Nymph of higher status. Thus Calypso and Circe had attendant Nymphs.

There are several categories of Nymphs which correspond to their habitats. The Nymphs of the ash trees, the MELIADS, seem to be the most ancient; they were the daughters of Uranus, not of Zeus. There were also the NAIADS, who lived in springs and streams. The Nereids were often considered to be the Nymphs of the calm sea. Often the Naiads of a given river were said to have been the daughters of the appropriate river-god, such as the daughters of the Asopus, for example. In the mountains lived a special type of Nymph, the Oreads. The Nymphs called Alseids lived in the groves (from the Greek ἄλσος: 'sacred wood'). Other Nymphs were attached to a specific spot or even a given tree, such as the HAMADRYADS. The

Nymphs play a large role in legends. Being deities familiar in the popular imagination they appear, like our fairies, in many folk stories. They are often found as wives of the eponymous hero of a city or district (see, for example, the legend of Aegina and Aeacus, the legend of the Nymph Taygete). They also frequently occur in myths with a love motif (see, for example, the stories of Daphne, Echo and Callisto). Their usual lovers were male nature spirits, such as Pan, the Satyrs and Priapus, but the greater gods did not spurn their favours: they attracted the attentions of Zeus, Apollo, Hermes, Dionysus and others. In some accounts they themselves are said to have fallen in love and abducted handsome young boys, such as Hylas.

Nysa (Νῦσα) One of the Nymphs who brought up Dionysus as a child on Mount Nysa. She is sometimes said to have been the daughter of Aristeus. With the god's other nursemaids she was, at his request, given back her youthfulness by Medea.

Nysus (Νῦσος) According to some traditions, all apparently late, Nysus was the adoptive father of Dionysus, who derived his name from him. During his expedition to India, the god entrusted Nysus with the city of Thebes but on his return, Nysus refused to give the city back to him. The god did not wish to start a struggle with him; he waited for a favourable opportunity, and three years later one presented iself. Dionysus apparently been reconciled with Nysus. He asked his permission to celebrate in Thebes the triennial festival that he had previously introduced there. Nysus agreed. Dionysus disguised his soldiers as Bacchantes and brought them into the city. With their help he had no difficulty in overwhelming Nysus and taking command of the city again.

Nyx (Νύξ) The personification of the night, and its goddess. She was the daughter of Chaos in the Hesiodic *Theogony*, and mother of two elements, Aether and Hemera (Day), and also of a whole series of abstract forces: Morus (Destiny), the Keres, Hypnus (Sleep), the Dreams, Momus (Sarcasm), Distress, the Moirae (Fates), Nemesis, Apate (Deceit), Philotes (Tenderness), Geras (Old Age), Eris (Discord), and lastly the Hesperides, who were the Daughters of Evening. Her realm was in the far West beyond the land of Atlas. She was the sister of Erebus, who personifies subterranean darkness.

O

Oaxes (Ὀάξης) A Cretan hero, son of Anchiale and eponym of the city of Oaxos in Crete. He is mentioned by Virgil in *Eclogue* I, but the text is corrupt and his name may have been confused with that of the river Oxus.

Oaxus (Ὀαξος) In certain traditions Oaxus was a son of Acacallis and founder of the city of Oaxos in Crete. He is probably the same person as Oaxos.

Oceanus (Ὠκεανός) The personification of the water that according to early Greek thought surrounded the world. Oceanus is represented as a river flowing around the flat disk of the Earth and marking its furthest limits to North, South, West and East. This provides an explanation of the topography of some stories, such as the legend of HERACLES and the Hesperides and the account of his adventures with Geryon. As knowledge of the world grew more precise, these notions changed and the name Oceanus referred only to the Atlantic Ocean, the western boundary of the Ancient World.

Oceanus was the eldest of the Titans, and a son of Uranus and Gaia (Tables 5 and 12). He is coupled with his sister Tethys, who represents the sea's female power of fertility. As a deity, Oceanus was the father of all rivers. In the *Theogony* Hesiod names among his offspring: the Nile, the Alpheus, the Eridanus, the Strymon, the Meander, the Istrus, the Phasis, the Rhesus, the Achelous, the Nessus, the Rhodius, the Haliacmon, the Heptaporus, the Granicus, the Aesopus, the Simois, the Peneus, the Hermus, the Caicus, Sangarius, the Ladon, the Parthenius, the Evenus, the Ardescus, and the Scamander. Hesiod himself warns us that this list is far from exhaustive. At least 3,000 other names would have to be added in order to list all the rivers that he fathered upon Tethys. By Tethys he had as many daughters, the Oceanides, who were the lovers of a great many gods and some mortals, and gave birth to numerous children. They personify the rivers and springs. Hesiod gives the names of 41 of them. The eldest is Styx, then came Peitho, Admete, Ianthe, Electra, Doris, Prymno, Urania, Hippo, Clymene, Rhodea, Callirhoe, Zeuxo, Clytia, Idya, Pasithoe, Plexaure, Galaxaure, Dione, Melobosis, Thoe, Polydore, Cerceis, Plouto, Perseis, Ianira, Axaste, Xanthe, Petrea, Menestho, Europa, Metis, Eurynome, Telesto, Chryseis, Asia, Calypso, Eudore, Tyche, Amphirho and Ocyrrhoe. To this list other authors add other names: in particular Philyra, mother of the Centaur Chiron, Camarina and Arethusa.

Ochimus (Ὄχιμος) One of the seven sons of Helios and the Nymph Rhodus (see HELIADES and Table 14). Ochimus and his brother Cercaphus lived at Rhodes, but their brothers Macar, Actis, Candalus and Triopas fled after killing the seventh brother, Tenages. Ochimus, the eldest, reigned over the island of Rhodes. He married a local Nymph, named Hegetoria, and by her had Cydippe. She married her uncle CERCAPHUS, who succeeded his brother to the throne. Another tradition recounts that Ochimus had engaged his daughter Cydippe to a man named Ocridion, but when the latter sent a herald to fetch his bride-to-be Cercaphus, who was in love with his niece, abducted her from the herald and fled abroad with her. He came back later, when Ochimus was an old man. This legend was used to explain the custom of forbidding heralds to go into the sanctuary of Ocrideon at Rhodes.

Ocnus (Ὄκνος) Ocnus the rope-maker is a symbolic character, represented as being in Hades weaving a rope that a female donkey eats as fast as he can make it. The real meaning of the legend is unclear, though it was usually interpreted as meaning that Ocnus was a very hardworking man who had married a spendthrift wife.

Ocrisia Mother of the king Servius Tullius and daughter of the king of Corniculum. She was brought to Rome as a slave, after the conquest of her native land, becoming a maid servant in the house of old Tarquin. There she gave birth to a child in mysterious circumstances. The most famous tradition says that she had seen a male sexual organ appear in the cinders of the hearth while she was taking the ritual offering to the household god. In terror she recounted this vision to her mistress, Tanaquil, who advised her to put on bridal trappings and to shut herself in the room where she had seen this manifestation of the deity. Ocrisia did this, and during the night her divine lover coupled with her; the child born of the union was Servius Tullius. Another version says that Ocrisia arrived in Rome pregnant and was not the daughter but the wife of the king of Corniculum. It was also said that Ocrisia's lover was not a god, but a hanger-on of the royal household.

Ocyrrhoē (Ὠκυρρόη) This is the name of several Nymphs or deities connected with water and springs:

1. One of the daughters of Oceanus, who was said to have coupled with the Sun (Helios) and borne him a son called Phasis. Phasis one day caught her with a lover and killed her, and then threw himself into the river Arcturus, which was thereafter called the Phasis.

2. Ocyrrhoe was also a Nymph of Samos, daughter of the Nymph Chesias and the river Imbrasus. One day, when she journeyed to Miletus, Apollo fell in love with her and wanted to abduct her. Ocyrrhoe had asked a friend of her father, a sailor called Pompilus, to escort her. As they approached Samos, under the impression that they had escaped from Apollo, the god appeared, took the girl, transformed Pompilus' boat into a rock and changed Pompilus himself into a fish.

3. Another Ocyrrhoe was the daughter of Chiron and the Nymph Chariclo. She owed her name to the place of her birth: her mother had given birth to her in a stream with swiftly flowing water. At birth she received the gift of the power of divination, but she used it without discretion. Against the gods' orders she revealed to the little Asclepius and his father the secrets of the gods. She was punished for it by metamorphosis: the gods changed her into a horse and thereafter she was called Hippo.

Odysseus (Ὀδυσσεύς) Odysseus (this is its Greek form; the Latin name is Ulixes, or Ulysses, a dialect form) was the most famous hero of all antiquity. His legend, the subject of *Odyssey,* was reworked, added to and commented on until the end of the period. It has lent itself to symbolic and mystical interpretations even more than the legend of Achilles. For example, Odysseus is often cited as the archetypal wise man.

I. BIRTH
The genealogy of Odyssey is relatively consistent. Authors agree on the name of his father, Laertes,

and on that of his mother, Anticleia. This is the parentage given by the *Odyssey*. Variations are only introduced with the names of his earlier ancestors. On the paternal side, his grandfather was Arcisius (as given in the *Odyssey*) but Arcisius is sometimes said to be the son of Zeus and Euryodia, sometimes of CEPHALUS, or even of Cileus who was himself a son of Cephalus. On the maternal side, the *Odyssey* gives AUTOLYCUS as grandfather, and Hermes as great-grandfather; but there is a tradition according to which Anticleia was seduced by SISYPHUS before her marriage to Laertes, and Odysseus was the son from his affair. This version was embodied in the work of the tragic writers but is not found in the Homeric poems.

Odysseus was born in Ithaca, an island on the western coast of Greece, north-east of Cephalonia, in the Ionian Sea. Anticleia is said to have given birth to him on Mount Neriton one day when she was caught by the rain and she found her path cut off by the water. The origin of this anecdote was a pun on the name Odysseus, which was interpreted as a fragment of the Greek phrase meaning 'Zeus rained the road' (Καιὰ τήν ὁδόν ύσεν ὁ Χεύς). But the *Odyssey* gives another interpretation of the name of the hero: Sisyphus named the child Odysseus because he was himself 'hated by many people' (Odysseus is similar to ὀδύσσομαι, 'to hate'). In the tradition which makes Odysseus the son of Sisyphus, Anticleia gave birth to him at Alalcomenes in Boeotia, while on her way to Ithaca with Laertes, and it was in memory of the place of his birth that Odysseus gave the name of Alalcomenes to a village in Ithaca.

II BEFORE THE TROJAN WAR
Odysseus made several voyages in his youth. A late tradition maintains that, like Achilles, he was one of the pupils of the Centaur Chiron. Homer does not mention this. The *Odyssey* only alludes to a boar hunt which he took part in on Parnassus while staying with Autolycus. During the hunt he was wounded in the knee, and the resulting scar was permanent. It was much later to be the sign by which he was recognized on his return from Troy. In the time of Pausanias, the guides of the sanctuary stated that Odysseus had received this wound on the site of the gymnasium of Delphi. Odysseus made journeys on Laertes' behalf. In particular, he went to Messenia to reclaim the sheep which had been stolen from him. At Lacedaemonia he met Iphitus who had been his guest, and received as a present for his hospitality the

bow of Eurytus, which he was later to use to kill the suitors.

On reaching manhood, Laertes gave Odysseus the throne of Ithaca along with all the wealth of the royal house, which consisted primarily of flocks of sheep. In accounts later than the *Odyssey* it is at this period that his attempt to marry Helen, daughter of Tyndareus, took place. Seeing the very considerable number of suitors, he gave up his claim to Helen in order to make a match that was almost as advantageous by marrying PENELOPE, Helen's cousin, and daughter of Icarius. Wanting to arouse Tyndareus' gratitude, he devised a plan to extricate him from the embarrassing situation created by the great number of Helen's suitors. Odysseus advised Tyndareus to demand each of the suitors to swear to respect the choice which was made and to assist whoever was chosen to safeguard his wife, should anyone else come to lay claim to her. The grateful Tyndareus easily obtained the hand of Penelope for Odysseus. According to other authors, she was the prize in a race which Odysseus won easily.

There was one son of this marriage, Telemachus. He was still very young when the news spread that Paris had abducted Helen and that Menelaus was asking for help against the aggressor. It was only with difficulty that Odysseus persuaded himself to keep his oath, and it was related by poets later than Homer that he had even feigned madness in order to avoid participating in the expedition. PALAMEDES saw through this trick, incurring the hero's resentment. When he realized that he had failed, Odysseus accepted the inevitable and set off for Troy. Earlier his father had given him an adviser, Myiscus, whose task was to watch over him during the war, according to some accounts, but this Myiscus is not mentioned in the Homeric poems. From that moment, Odysseus enthusiastically embraced the cause of the Atrides. He accompanied Menelaus to Delphi to consult the oracle and even, according to certain traditions, went with him on an early trip to Troy to demand Helen's return (see below). He went in search of the young ACHILLES whose assistance was said by the Fates to be indispensable if the city were to be taken. He found him finally at Scyros and, either alone or accompanied by other heroes (Nestor and Phoenix, Nestor and Palamedes or Diomedes, depending on the tradition), he disguised himself as a merchant and went into King Lycomedes' women's quarters, where Achilles lived. There he included materials and arms amongst the poor quality goods he offered for sale, and recognized Achilles by the eagerness with which he chose the arms. In another version, Odysseus forced Achilles to reveal himself by sounding the war trumpet and observing Achilles' reaction. During this preparatory period, we find Odysseus as ambassador of the Atrides to the court of CINYRAS in Cyprus.

III THE TROJAN WAR

The role of Odysseus in the first expedition which resulted in the landing in Mysia (and which is not mentioned by the Homeric poems) seems to have been insignificant, and to be limited to interpreting correctly the oracle which stated that TELEPHUS could be healed only by 'the person who caused the wound'. Although Achilles denied that he could help, Odysseus observed that it was in fact the lance and not the warrior which was in question here. It was in the second expedition, the Trojan War itself, that Odysseus played a greater part. He acted as an intermediary for Agamemnon and made IPHIGENIA come to Aulis on a pretext.

Odysseus commanded a contingent of a dozen ships on the voyage to Troy. He was one of the heroes who met in council, and was regarded as the equal of the greatest of them. On the way to Troy, he accepted the challenge made to him by Philomelides, the king of Lesbos, and killed him in the fight. This episode, to which the *Odyssey* alludes, was made by later authors an assassination in which Odysseus was aided by Diomedes, his usual companion or accomplice. During their stay on Lemnos, Odysseus, according to the *Odyssey*, quarrelled with Achilles during the banquet held for the leaders. Odysseus was praising prudence, Achilles, bravery. Agamemnon, to whom Apollo had predicted that the Greeks would take Troy when discord broke out among the assailants, saw this discussion as an omen of quick victory. This episode has been distorted by later mythographers, who imagined a dispute between Agamemnon and Achilles, and interpreted it as the first sign of the quarrel which nine years later was to pit the two heroes against each other and which forms the subject of the *Iliad*. Odysseus was said to have reconciled them. Instead of taking place on Lemnos, this episode was later transferred to Tenedos. It was on Lemnos, or on the neighbouring small island of Chrysa, which has now disappeared, that Philoctetes was abandoned on Odysseus' advice.

Another episode during this voyage to Troy was introduced by poets writing later than Homer: the mission from Tenedos to demand the return of Helen after she had been abducted. Odysseus and Menelaus had already made one trip to Troy, accompanied by Palamedes, to try to settle the matter peacefully. They renewed these negotiations, but again it was in vain, and they were threatened by the Trojans, only escaping because of the intervention of Antenor (see MENELAUS).

During the siege, Odysseus proved to be a fighter of the greatest bravery, as well as a wise and effective adviser. He was used in any mission which demanded skill in oratory: for example, in the *Iliad*, he was placed in charge of the mission to Achilles when Agamemnon wanted a reconciliation with the latter. By then he had already brought the prisoner Chryseis back to her father, concluded an armistice with the Trojans, organized the single combat between Paris and Menelaus, reduced Thersites to silence during the meeting of the soldiers and persuaded the Greeks to remain in the Troad.

To this diplomatic ability, in the form in which it is presented in the *Iliad*, later poets, indeed from the *Odyssey* onwards) have added various episodes: the mission to ANIUS to persuade him to agree to send his daughters and thus to ensure the replenishment of the army; the mission to PHILOCTETES when Helenus (captured and interrogated by Odysseus) revealed that Heracles' arrows were needed to ensure the capture of the city, and the mission to NEOPTOLEMUS in which he was accompanied either by Diomedes or Phoenix.

Other, often less honourable actions, such as espionage operations, were attributed to Odysseus. The *Iliad* shows him taking part in a night reconnaissance exercise with DIOMEDES, in the episode of the capture of DOLON, during which he killed Dolon and captured RHESUS' horses. There was a later episode modelled on that of Dolon, the removal of the Palladium. The intrigue which brought about the death of Palamedes was also attributed to Odysseus, as was the idea of building the wooden horse; the success of this trick was ensured by a particularly bold expedition mentioned in the *Odyssey*. First of all, Odysseus had himself whipped by Thoas, son of Andraemon (see THOAS 4), to make himself unrecognizable and then, dressed in rags, he appeared in the city claiming to be a deserter. He then made his way to Helen who since Paris' death had married Deiphobus, and persuaded her to agree to betray the Trojans. It was said that Helen had warned Hecuba of Odysseus' presence, but he had so touched the queen by his entreaties, tears and guileful speech

that she swore to maintain secrecy. He was able to escape, but not without having killed several Trojans, notably the guards on the gate.

Odysseus' exploits during the war were numerous. His victims were Democoon, Caerane, Alastor, Chronius, Alcander, Halius, Noemon, Prytanis, Pidytes, Molion, Hippodamus, Hyperochus, Deiopites, Thoon, Ennomus, Chersidamas, Charops and Socus. He protected Diomedes when he was wounded and covered his retreat. He commanded the detachment inside the wooden horse, and warned his companions of Helen's trick of imitating the voices of their wives outside the horse. He was the first to leap out and accompanied Menelaus who wanted to seize his wife from Deiphobus as soon as possible and, according to one version, he prevented the outraged husband from killing his wife on the spot. According to another version, he waited for the Greeks' anger to die down and saved the young woman from being stoned, as the Greeks had wanted. He also saved one of Antenor's sons, HELICAON.

For Odysseus' role in the division of Achilles' arms, and his intrigues against Ajax, see AJAX. Odysseus was also responsible for the death of Astyanax and the sacrifice of Polyxena. Hecuba fell to him in the sharing out of the captive Trojan women and, following the tradition according to which the old queen was stoned, it was Odysseus who threw the first stone, even though she had on an earlier occasion saved him (see above).

IV RETURN TO ITHACA

This part of the adventures of Odysseus forms the subject of the *Odyssey*, but even here the legend has undergone later reworkings and additions.

We know that MENELAUS and AGAMEMNON did not agree on the date of departure for the army's return to Greece. Menelaus set off first with Nestor. Odysseus followed them, but quarrelled with them at Tenedos and returned to Troy to join up with Agamemnon. When the latter put to sea, Odysseus alone of all the Greek princes followed him, but was soon separated from him by a storm. He landed in Thrace in the country of the Cicones where he took the city of Ismarus. He only spared one of the inhabitants, Maron, who was a priest of Apollo. In gratitude, Maron gave him 12 earthenware jars of a strong, sweet wine, which were later to be extremely useful to him in the land of the Cyclopes. In the course of this landing, Odysseus lost six men from each of his ships and when the Cicones launched a counter-attack from land, he put to sea again.

Heading south, two days later, he arrived in sight of Cape Malea, but a violent north wind drove him out to sea off Cythera and, two days later, he landed in the country of the Lotophagi. He sent some of his men off to make enquiries about the inhabitants, who received them favourably. They gave them the fruit of their country to taste, the lotus, which was their staple food. This fruit had the effect of making the eater forget his own country and the Greeks did not want to leave; Odysseus had to force them to embark. Ancient geographers situated this country on the coast of Tripoli.

Making towards the north again, Odysseus and his companions landed on an island which abounded in goats where they were able to replenish their food supplies. From there, they moved on to the land of the Cyclopes, which has always been identified with Sicily. Odysseus disembarked, accompanied by twelve men, and went into a cave. He had been careful to take with him goatskins full of wine, as a gesture of hospitality

Odysseus offering wine to the Cyclops Polyphemus to make him drunk. 2nd century AD Roman lamp.

towards the people whom he might encounter. In the cave, they found quantities of cheese, fresh milk and curds. Odysseus' companions urged him to take these and leave but he was reluctant to. When the inhabitant of the cave, the Cyclops POLYPHEMUS, returned he seized the strangers and shut them away; he then began to devour them in pairs, but Odysseus gave him some of Maron's wine. The Cyclops had never drunk wine before, he found it so excellent and drank so much of it that he became more good-natured. He then asked Odysseus his name, to which the latter replied: 'Nobody'. Out of gratitude for the wine the Cyclops promised to eat him last. Made drowsy by the wine, he fell asleep and Odysseus, using a stake hardened in the fire, pierced the giant's only eye and, at daybreak managed to slip out of the cave under the belly of a ram. Polyphemus appealed to his fellow Cyclopes for help, but when they asked him who was attacking him, he was forced to reply: 'Nobody'. Not understanding the meaning of his answer, the other Cyclopes thought he was mad, and went away. We can trace the hatred felt by Poseidon, Polyphemus' father, for Odysseus to this incident.

Having escaped from the Cyclopes, Odysseus reached the island of Aeolus, the Warden of the Winds. He was received hospitably and given a cattle-skin bag containing all the winds except for a favourable breeze which would bring him straight back to Ithaca. They were already in sight of the fires lit by shepherds on the island when Odysseus fell asleep. His companions, thinking that Aeolus' bag contained gold, untied it. The winds escaped in a hurricane and drove the boat in the opposite direction. Again, the boat landed on Aeolus' island, and once more Odysseus went to see the king to ask for a favourable wind. Aeolus replied that he could not do anything more for him and that the gods had clearly shown their hostility to his return. Odysseus then put to sea again, trusting to fortune, and heading north he reached the country of the Laestrygonians, which was generally identified with the coast around Formiae or Gaeta, in the north of Campania. Being cautious as a result of his adventures with the Cyclops, Odysseus sent scouts out to reconnoitre the country. They met the king's daughter who took them to her father Antiphates; he consumed one of them immediately. The others fled to the shore, pursued by the king and the populace. The Laestrygonians stoned the Greeks, breaking up the ships and killing the men. Odysseus managed to cut the hawser of his ship and put to sea.

Reduced to a single vessel and its crew, he continued to sail north and soon landed on the island of Aeaea, where the sorceress CIRCE lived (later identified with the promontory of Circeii in Latium). When he left the island of Aeaea, Odysseus left behind with Circe a son, Telegonus – and in some accounts two of them, Telegonus and Nausithous (see Table 39).

Circe sent him to consult the spirit of Tiresias in order to find out how he could be certain of returning to Ithaca. Tiresias informed him that he would return alone to his homeland on a foreign ship, that he would have to take revenge on the suitors and later set off again, with one oar on his shoulder, in search of a people who knew nothing about sailing. There he must offer an expiatory sacrifice to Poseidon; he would finally die during a happy old age, far from the sea. After encountering a number of heroes called up from the dead, Odysseus returned to Circe. He then set off again, armed with more advice from the goddess. He first sailed along the coast of the island of the SIRENS (near the gulf of Naples); next he had to confront the Wandering Rocks, and the straits between SCYLLA and CHARYBDIS. Some of the sailors were swallowed up by the latter, but the ship escaped and soon reached the island of Sicily where the white cattle belonging to Helios grazed. There the wind began to fail, and the food began to run out. To remedy this shortage, the sailors killed some of the cattle to eat, despite being forbidden to do so by Odysseus, but the Sun saw this, and complained to Zeus, demanding compensation. Accordingly, when the ship put to sea again, a storm sent by Zeus blew up and the ship

Scylla was the sea-monster which lived concealed in the straits of Messina. Coin of Pompey the Great of 36–30 BC showing Scylla wielding an oar.

was struck by lightning. Only Odysseus was saved, as he had refused to take part in the sacrilegious feast. He clung to the mast and was swept by the current across the straits again, escaping Charybdis' whirlpool. He was tossed around by the sea for nine days and then he reached the island of CALYPSO (probably the region of Ceuta on the Moroccan coast, opposite Gibraltar). Although the *Odyssey* does not mention it, later authors stated that Odysseus had one or even several sons by the goddess including Nausithous and Nausinous (see Table 39). His stay with Calypso lasted ten, eight, five or even one year, depending on the source. Finally, at the request of Athena, the hero's protector, Zeus sent Hermes to order Calypso to release Odysseus. Reluctantly, Calypso provided him with enough wood to build a raft and Odysseus set off towards the east.

But Poseidon's anger had not yet abated: he whipped up a storm which broke up the raft, and clinging to a piece of wreckage, the naked hero was washed up on the shores of the island of the Phaeacians, called Scheria in the *Odyssey*, which was probably Corfu. Exhausted, Odysseus fell asleep in the bushes which grew along a river bank. In the morning he was awakened by the shouts and laughter of a group of girls. Nausicaa, the daughter of the king of the island and her servants had come to wash their linen and play on the river bank. Odysseus presented himself to them and asked for their help. Nausicaa told him the way to the palace of her father, King Alcinous, while she, along with her servants, returned separately, so as not to arouse the suspicions of the passers-by.

Odysseus received a friendly and hospitable welcome from Alcinous and his queen, Arete. A great banquet was given in his honour and Odysseus gave a full account of his adventures. He was then showered with presents and since he declined the offer of the hand of Nausicaa and proclaimed his determination to return to Ithaca, a ship was put at his disposal. During the brief voyage, Odysseus fell asleep, and the Phaeacian sailors put him down on a remote spot on the island of Ithaca, with the treasures which he brought back as gifts from Alcinous. The ship returned to Scheria, but just as it reached the island it was turned to stone by Poseidon, who thus took his revenge for the kindness shown to Odysseus without his approval; the city itself was then surrounded by a mountain and thereby ceased to be a port.

Odysseus' absence had lasted twenty years. He

was so transformed by both age and his dangers that nobody recognized him. However, PENELOPE was waiting faithfully for him, according to the version in the *Odyssey*. She had been exposed to the entreaties of the suitors who had moved into the palace and were squandering his wealth in wild excesses. There were 108 suitors in all, and their names have been preserved by mythographers. They came from Dulichium, from Samos, from Zacynthos and from Ithaca itself – these were the countries under Odysseus' rule.

Penelope made every effort to discourage them and to do this had devised a trick which had long been famous. She had promised them an answer on the day she finished weaving a shroud for old Laertes. She worked at this task by day, but at night she unravelled the day's work. As soon as Odysseus was awake, he decided not to go immediately to the palace. First of all, he went to see Eumaeus, his head swineherd, whom he trusted totally. He disclosed his identity to him, and also met his son Telemachus. Father and son then went to the palace, Odysseus disguised as a beggar. No one recognized him except his dog Argus who, at the age of twenty, was dragging out a miserable life. The dog leapt up, overcome with joy on seeing his master and fell down dead.

At the palace, Odysseus asked the suitors for food. They insulted him, and one beggar called Irus, who regularly attended the suitors' feasts, challenged this newcomer to a fight, since he was threatening his own privileges. Odysseus felled him with several blows and was subsequently further insulted by the suitors, and, notably, by the most important of them, Antinous. Penelope, who had heard of the arrival of this foreign beggar, wanted to see him to ask whether he had any news of Odysseus, but he decided to postpone this conversation until the evening. At nightfall, Telemachus, at his father's command, carried all the weapons in the palace to the armoury. Then the meeting between Penelope and Odysseus took place, but he did not reveal his identity to her. He merely uttered encouraging words. She had dreamt that her husband would soon return, but she refused to believe it and proposed to arrange a competition among the suitors the next day, and to marry the victor. She would give them Odysseus' bow and the winner would be the man who was best able to use it. Odysseus encouraged her in this plan.

The competition took place the next day: the object was to shoot an arrow through rings formed by a number of axes placed side by side.

The suitors each took the bow in turn but not one could bend it. Finally, the bow was handed to Odysseus who accomplished the task at the first shot. Odysseus' servants shut the doors of the palace, Telemachus seized weapons, and the massacre of the suitors began. The servant girls, whose behaviour towards the suitors had not been totally appropriate, carried away the bodies, cleaned the hall, and were then hung in the palace courtyard, along with the goatherd Melanthius, who had sided with the suitors against his master. Odysseus at last revealed himself to Penelope and, to remove her lingering doubts, described their nuptial chamber, which was known only to the two of them.

The next day, Odysseus went to the country where his father lived and disclosed his identity to him. The families of the massacred suitors armed themselves and came together to demand recompense from Odysseus, but thanks to the intervention of Athena, disguised as old Mentor, peace soon returned to Ithaca.

Such is the story of the *Odyssey*. Later poets added episodes to it, often romantic in character and with special love interests, for example, the adventures of Odysseus and Polymela on the island of Aeolia. They also completed the *Odyssey*, giving it different endings. Here are the most striking episodes in these legends which are, for the most part, purely literary:

After the massacre of the suitors Odysseus offered a sacrifice to Hades, Persephone and Tiresias and set off on foot across Epirus as far as the land of the Thesproti. There, he offered Poseidon the sacrifice which Tiresias had earlier ordered him to do. The queen of the country, Callidice, urged him to stay with her and offered him her kingdom. Odysseus agreed, and they had a son, Polypoctes. For a while Odysseus reigned jointly with Callidice and won victories over the neighbouring peoples, but when she died, he handed the kingdom over to Polypoetes, and returned to Ithaca, where he found that Penelope had borne him a second son, Poliporthes. Meanwhile, Telegonus, the son of Odysseus and Circe, had learnt from his mother the identity of his father and had set off in search of Odysseus. He landed in Ithaca, and plundered the herds. Odysseus came to the aid of his shepherds and was killed by his son in the ensuing fight. When Telegonus learnt who his victim was, he was grief stricken. He returned to Circe with the body and Penelope.

Other versions relate that Odysseus, accused by the kinsmen of the suitors, submitted the case to

Neoptolemus the king of Ethiopia for judgement. Neoptolemus wished to gain possession of Cephalonia and condemned Odysseus to exile. He later went to Aetolia, to Thoas the son of Andraemon. There he married Thoas' daughter and by her had a son, Leontophonus, and died of old age. Another tradition, related by Plutarch maintains that after the judgement of Neoptolemus, Odysseus went into exile in Italy.

There existed a whole series of traditions about Odysseus' adventures in Italy and the last years of his life which are only known to us through obscure allusions. In particular, there was a story that Odysseus and Aeneas had met in the course of this journey and had become reconciled. Odysseus went to the land of the Tyrrheni (the Etruscans) and founded thirty cities. There he was said to have taken the name NANUS which in Etruscan meant 'the wanderer'. Odysseus died in the Etruscan city of Gortynia, generally identified with Cortona, suffering from grief caused by the deaths of Telemachus and Circe.

Tacitus records (*Germania* III) that Odysseus' voyage had taken him as far as the Rhine and to commemorate this he had built an altar on the banks, which still existed at the time of the Roman conquest. Like the name of Heracles, that of Odysseus was linked to various stages of the discovery of the far West, through the episode of the Cimmerians and the mysterious voyages he accomplished at the end of his life.

The list of Odysseus' children was very varied. It was modified at the whim of genealogists in order to give titles to all the Italian cities in the time of Cato. Thus, he and Circe were said to have had sons like Ardeas, eponym of the Latin city Ardea, and Latinus, eponym of the Latins etc. (See also ROMUS, CASSIPHONE, EVIPPE, and Table 39).

Oeager (Οἴαγρος) Father of Orpheus, whom the mythographers considered to be a river-god, though traditions vary about his genealogy. He is sometimes said to have been the son of Ares, sometimes of Pierus or of CHAROPS (see the euhemerist legend of Dionysus, under LYCURGUS). In this last version he was a king of Thrace. His wife is supposed to have been the Muse Calliope, mother of Orpheus, or one of the Muses, either Polhymnia or Clio. Late authors claim that he was the father of Marsyas, Linus and Cymothon.

Oeax (Οἴαξ) One of the three sons of NAUPLIUS by Clymene, daughter of Catreus. His brothers were Palamedes and Nausimedon. He went with Palamedes to Troy, and when his brother was stoned to death by the Greeks Oeax transmitted the news to Nauplius by writing an account of his brother's death on an oar and throwing it into the sea. He knew that Nauplius, who spent his time sailing his ship, would be sure to find it during one of his voyages. It is also said that Oeax advised Clytemnestra to kill Agamemnon in order to avenge Palamedes' death. He may himself have died at the hand of Orestes or Pylades.

Oebalus (Οἴβαλος)
1. A king of Sparta. He was a descendant of Lelex and Lacedaemon (Table 6). In the Laconian tradition recounted by Pausanias, Oebalus was the son of Cynortas, while in the tradition referred to by Apollodorus, the son of Cynortas was Perieres, not Oebalus. Oebalus only appears as the father of Arena, wife of Aphareus, who was one of Perieres' sons. Accordingly he was the grandfather of Lynceus, Idas and Pisus – whereas in the preceding tradition Aphareus was his son-in-law (the son of Gorgophone and Perieres, who was her first husband). In this second tradition Lynceus, Idas and Pisus are direct descendants of his wife, rather than of Oebalus himself.

Some attempts have been made to reconcile the two genealogies. The simplest consists in making Perieres the son of Cynortas and Oebalus the son of Perieres, but in that case there were two Perieres, one the son of Cynortas and the other of Aeolus. Moreover, Hippocoon was then an illegitimate son of Oebalus by a Nymph called Stratonice. His legitimate children were Icarius, Arne and Tyndareus. These accounts, compounded from local legends that fit poorly together, are some of the most confused legends that exist.
2. Another Oebalus was a Teleboan hero, the son of Telon and the Nymph Sebethis. Telon had emigrated to Capri, where he married Sebethis, daughter of the river-god Sebethus, whose river flowed near Naples. Oebalus established a kingdom for himself at Capri but his son, finding the island too small for his ambitions, went over to Campania and founded a kingdom between the Sarno and Nola. Later, he is mentioned among the allies of Turnus against Aeneas.

Oecles (Οἰκλῆς) A descendant of Melampus, and therefore of the race of Cretheus and Tyro (Table 1). He was the son of Antiphates, although some authors postulate Mantius, another of the sons of Melampus, as his father. He married Hypermestra, one of the daughters of Thespius, and had several children: Iphianira, Polyboea, and, the best known, Amphiaraus. Oecles accompanied HERACLES on the Trojan expedition. He was entrusted with guarding the ships, and with a small band of soldiers had to withstand the counterattack staged by Laomedon. He was killed during the first assault. Oecles is said to have given refuge to his grandson ALCMAEON in the Peloponnese when the latter, to avenge his father, killed his mother Eriphyle, but chronologically the two episodes are incompatible.

Oedipus (Οἰδίπους) The hero of one of the best-known legends in Greek literature after the Trojan cycle. The epic poems this legend inspired are lost, but we do know they existed. The adventures of Oedipus live for us principally in the form given to them by the tragedians. Oedipus belonged to the race of Cadmus (Table 3). His great-grandfather Polydorus was one of Cadmus' sons. His grandfather was Labdacus, son of Polydorus and Nycteis, herself a descendant, via her father Nycteus, of CHTHONIUS, one of the Spartoi, the men from the dragon's teeth. His father was Laius, son of Labdacus. All Oedipus' ancestors ruled Thebes – with some interruptions, according to the standard version of the tradition – during the time before Laius came of age (see LYCUS).

Oedipus' mother has a very important role in the legend. Her name is given in many different forms. In the *Odyssey* she is called Epicaste; in the tragedies she is Jocasta. She is usually said to have been related to Pentheus, and through him to ECHION, another of the Spartoi. Her father was Menoecceus and her grandfather Oclasus (Table 29). In the epic version of the Oedipus cycle, the hero's mother was called Eurygania, or Euryanassa, and she was the daughter of Hyperphas, Periphas (the Lapith) or Teuthras. Another variant gives her the name Astymedusa, and makes her the daughter of Sthenelus. The aim of this variant was to attach Oedipus, via his mother, to the cycle of myths about Heracles. Apart from these divergent traditions about Oedipus' mother, there are others that mix genealogical elements, using them arbitrarily to resolve contradictions within the legend itself or between its various versions.

At his birth, Oedipus was already marked by a curse. In the tradition represented by Sophocles, the curse took the form of an oracle which had declared that the child Jocasta was bearing 'would kill his father'. According to Aeschylus and Euripides, however, the oracle was supposed to have spoken before the child was even conceived. It had told Laius not to father any children, predicting that if he had a son, this son would not only kill him but would also be the cause of a terrible succession of misfortunes which would bring ruin upon his house. Laius took no notice of this advice and fathered Oedipus. He was punished for this later. To avoid the fulfilment of the oracle, Laius exposed the child as soon as it was born. He had the boy's ankles pierced, so as to join them together with a strap. It was the swelling caused by this wound that won the child its name of Oedipus (swollen foot). There exist two different versions of this episode. It is sometimes said that the little Oedipus was put in a basket and thrown into the sea; at other times he is said to have been exposed on Mount Cithaeron near Thebes. In the first version, the site is given as the north coast of the Peloponnese, or at Sicyon or Corinth. There he was found by Periboea, wife of King Polybus, who took him in and raised him. In the second version the child is supposed to have been exposed in a pot, in the middle of winter. Corinthian shepherds who happened to be in the area with their flocks picked him up and took him to their king, whom they knew was childless and wanted children. In the version followed by Sophocles, Laius ordered his servant to expose the child, but the servant instead gave it to the strange shepherds. Whatever the version, the name of Oedipus' stepfather is always Polybus, though he is sometimes the king of Corinth, sometimes of Sicyon, Anthedon or Plataea.

Oedipus stayed at the court of Polybus throughout his childhood and adolescence, under the impression that he was the king's real son, but when he reached manhood he left his adoptive parents, for a reason that varies from author to author. The oldest version seems to be the following: Oedipus left in search of stolen horses and in the process unwittingly came across his real father, Laius. Later the tragedians introduced more complex psychological reasons. During a quarrel a Corinthian revealed to Oedipus that he was not the king's son but a foundling, in order to insult him. Oedipus questioned Polybus, who eventually confessed that this was indeed the case, though he kept many things secret from him. Oedipus then went off to ask the Delphic oracle who his real parents were. Whatever the circumstances, on his travels Oedipus met Laius. The place of their encounter is given differently by different authors. Some say it was Laphystion, on the road that took Oedipus to Orchomenus in pursuit of the horses; others place it at the Potniai crossroads, or in Phocis at a crossroads now called the Crossroads of Megas, where the roads from Daulis and Thebes meet and make the road that climbs up along the valley to Delphi. There the road is hemmed in by rocks and the space is narrow. When Laius' herald Polyphontes (or Polypoetes) ordered Oedipus to make way for the king, and killed one of his horses because he was slow to obey, Oedipus in his anger slew both Polyphontes and Laius. Thus he fulfilled the prediction of the oracle. In the last version Oedipus was on his way back from Delphi, where the oracle had told him that he would kill his father and marry his mother. Frightened, and believing himself to be the son of Polybus, he decided to go into voluntary exile – which is why he was on the road to Thebes when Laius, by causing him to be insulted or, in some versions, by insulting him himself, drew down his son's wrath upon himself.

When he arrived at Thebes, Oedipus met the Sphinx. It was a monster, half lion, half woman, who asked riddles of those who passed and ate those who could not answer them. In particular it asked 'What is the creature which walks sometimes on two legs, sometimes on three, sometimes on four and which, contrary to the general law of nature, is at its weakest when it uses the most legs?' There was also another riddle: 'There are two sisters: one gives birth to the other and she in turn gives birth to the first'. The answer to the first riddle is 'Man' (because as a baby he walks on four legs, then on two, and ends up by leaning on a stick). The answer to the second riddle is 'Day and Night' (day and night are both feminine nouns in Greek and are therefore 'sisters'). Nobody in Thebes had ever been able to solve these riddles, and the Sphinx was devouring them one after another. Oedipus guessed the answers at once, and the monster, in a fit of pique, threw itself off the rock on which it was perched – or, alternatively, Oedipus pushed it. A version which is perhaps older gives the story as follows: each day the Thebans assembled in the city square to try to solve the riddle together, but without success, and each day, at the end of such a session, the Sphinx would eat one of them. Certain mythographers said that it even ate the young Haemon, son of Creon. By killing the Sphinx and freeing the Thebans of the monster, Oedipus earned himself the favour of the whole city. In their gratitude the Thebans gave him the hand of Laius' widow and made him king. It is also sometimes said that Jocasta's brother Creon had been acting as regent

since the death of Laius and had voluntarily conceded the throne to Oedipus to thank him for having avenged the death of his son.

Soon, however, the secret of Oedipus' birth came to light. In one version it was the scars on his ankles that gave away his identity to Jocasta. This version was modified by Sophocles when he built his tragedy *Oedipus Rex* around the recognition of Oedipus. In that play a plague is ravaging the city of Thebes, and Oedipus has sent Creon to ask the Delphic oracle what the cause of the pestilence is. Creon brings back the Pythia's reply: the plague will not cease before Laius' death is avenged. Oedipus then pronounces a curse upon the author of this crime, a curse which will eventually descend on himself. He asks the seer Tiresias who the guilty man is. Tiresias, who knows the whole story through his seer's powers, tries to avoid giving a reply. Oedipus thinks that Tiresias and Creon must be responsible for the murder. A quarrel arises between Oedipus and Creon. Jocasta arrives, and to reconcile them throws doubt on Tiresias' powers. She gives as proof of his incompetence the oracle which he had once pronounced on the child she had by Laius, whom the king had exposed, fearing that it would kill him. And yet, she says, Laius was killed by brigands at a crossroads. At this mention of a crossroads Oedipus asks for a description of Laius and the carriage in which he was riding. He also asks for details of the spot where the murders took place, and he is soon seized by a terrible suspicion: could he not be the murderer himself? He recalls from the countryside one of the servants who had been with Laius and had seen the murder; this shepherd is none other than the one who had long ago exposed Oedipus on Laius' orders. In the midst of all this a messenger arrives from Corinth to tell Oedipus of the death of Polybus and to ask him to come back and take the throne. Polybus had died of natural causes. However, the second part of the threat remains. Does Oedipus run the risk of incest with the wife of Polybus? To reassure him the Corinthian envoy tells him that he is a foundling and that Polybus was not his father. Thus the net gradually closes on Oedipus. The account that is given of the finding the child leaves Jocasta with no doubts: her own son has killed his father and she has committed incest with him. She flees into the palace and kills herself. Oedipus then blinds himself.

This version, immortalized by Sophocles, was modified by Euripides in a lost play which gave a more important role to Creon. In this play, Creon sets up a conspiracy against Oedipus, whom he thinks is a usurper. He arranges to have him convicted of the murder of Laius and then to have him blinded, but Periboea, Polybus' wife, arrives with the news of her husband's death. From her account of the discovery of the baby Oedipus on Cithaeron, Jocasta realizes that her second husband is none other than her own son. As in the preceding version, she commits suicide.

In the epic versions of the Oedipus legend Jocasta's death does not interrupt Oedipus' reign. He stays on the throne and only dies in the course of a war against his neighbours (Erginus and the Minyans). But in the works of the tragedians Oedipus, who falls victim to the curse he himself had pronounced against Laius' murderer, is banished from the city and begins a vagabond life. He is accompanied by his daughter Antigone, as his two sons have refused to intervene in his favour and have as a result themselves been cursed by him. After long and painful travels Oedipus comes to Attica, the village of Colonus, where he dies. An oracle has declared that the land which contains the tomb of Oedipus will be blessed by the gods. Creon and Polynices have separately tried to persuade the dying Oedipus to go back to Thebes but Oedipus, having been hospitably received by King Theseus, refuses and decides that his ashes should stay in Attica.

Oeneus (Οἰνεύς) King of Calydon. His name is cognate with the Greek word for wine (οἰνεύς). Dionysus presented the first vine stock planted in Greece to him (see ALTHAEA). Another version claims that one of his shepherds, called Orista (or Staphylus), had noticed that one of the billy-goats in his flock often went off and started grazing on the fruit of a plant that he did not recognize. Eventually the shepherd went and gathered some of the berries, pressed the juice from them and mixed it with water from the river Achelous. Oeneus then gave this liquid a name derived from his own.

Although some traditions make him a descendant of Deucalion (see ORESTHEUS) he is more often said to have been a descendant of Endymion and Pronoe. He was the great-grandson of Pleuron, the grandson of Agenor and the son of Porthaon, or Portheus or Euryte (Table 24). He was king of Aetolia (Pleuron was in fact the son of Aetolus, eponymous hero of the region). He had several brothers: Agrius, Alcathus, Melas, Leucopeus and one sister, Sterope (see also Table 27). Oeneus' first wife was ALTHAEA, daughter of Thetis. By her

he had several children: Toxeus, whom he killed for having leaped over a certain ditch although forbidden to; Thyreus, Clymenus and Meleager; then two daughters, Gorge and Deianeira, to whom Eurymede and Melanippe are sometimes added. Some mythographers give him further sons: Phereus, Ageleus, Periphas (see MELEAGRIDS). After the death of Althaea, who committed suicide for having killed her son Meleager in a fit of rage, Oeneus remarried. His second wife was Periboea, daughter of Hipponous, the king of Olenus. Several traditions exist concerning this marriage. The first says that Periboea was taken by Oeneus when he won a victory over Hipponous, and was part of his share of the spoils. Another says that Hipponous voluntarily sent his daughter to Oeneus because she had been seduced by a certain Hippostratus (or by the god Ares). Alternatively, the seducer was none other than Oeneus himself, and when Hipponous gave his daughter away to his swineherds, Oeneus took her away from them. By Periboea Oeneus had one son, Tydeus, who was the father of Diomedes (Table 27).

There are three main episodes among the adventures attributed to Oeneus. He was the unwitting cause of the scourge sent by Artemis upon Calydon because he forgot to name her during the sacrifices to celebrate the end of harvesting (see MELEAGER). Also, as father of Deianeira he played a part in the cycle of Heracles. Heracles spent several years of his life at his palace after carrying out his twelve Labours. He was driven from it as the result of an involuntary murder. Oeneus also makes an appearance in the legend concerning his grandson Diomedes. In old age Oeneus was dispossessed of his kingdom by his nephews, the sons of Agrius. Diomedes, helped by Alcmaeon, killed them, gave the kingdom of Calydon to Andraemon, husband of Gorge and accordingly one of Oeneus' sons-in-law, and took the old man away with him as his great age made him incapable of defending his kingdom. It was also said that during the journey two of Agrius' sons, who had survived, killed Oeneus as he was passing through Arcadia. Oeneus also plays a part in some versions of the legend of AGAMEMNON and MENELAUS. He was said to have given hospitality to the two princes in their youth when they were driven from their kingdom.

Oenoclus (Οἴνοκλος) King of the Aenians. He led his people as far as Cyrrha, where he was stoned to death because the oracle of Apollo pronounced his sacrifice necessary in order to end the famine afflicting the land.

Oenomaus (Οἰνόμαος) A king of Pisa, in Elis; he was the son of Ares by one of the daughters of the river-god Asopus, called Harpinna (or Eurythoe), or by the Pleiad Sterope. His father is sometimes given as the hero Hyperochus. By Sterope (or Evarete, daughter of Acrisius) he had a daughter, Hippodamia. Hippodamia was the object of numerous marriage proposals, but Oenomaus refused to give her hand to any suitor. He was either in love with her himself or an oracle had warned him that he would die at the hand of his son-in-law – both explanations are offered by the mythographers. To discourage suitors he demanded that anyone who wanted to marry Hippodamia had to compete with him in a chariot race to the altar of POSEIDON at Corinth. Before setting off, Oenomaus would sacrifice a ram to Zeus, while the suitor began the race. Oenomaus though delayed by the sacrifice, speedily overtook his rival, whom he then slew. His horses had been given to him by ARES, and were in fact divine, so no ordinary chariot team could hope to win against them. The mythographers give the names of the twelve (or thirteen) suitors killed by Oenomaus: Mermnus, Hippothous, Eurylochus, Automedon, Pelops of Opus, Acarnan, Eurymachus, Lasius, Chalcon, Tricoronus, Alcathous, son of Porthaon, Aristomachus and Crotalus. Oenomaus had already nailed the heads of twelve unsuccessful contestants to his palace door, when PELOPS offered himself. Hippodamia fell in love with Pelops and helped him to win the confidence of her father's charioteer, MYRTILUS, who tampered with the axle of Oenomaus' chariot so that it would break during the race. Oenomaus became tangled in the reins, was dragged by his own horses and he was then killed by Pelops.

Oenone (Οἰνώνη) During his youth Paris was sent away from Troy and lived in the mountains. There he became the lover of a Nymph called Oenone, daughter of the river-god Cebren. By her he had a son, CORYTHUS. When Paris gave his famous judgement between the goddesses he wanted to abandon Oenone for the love of HELEN, promised him by APHRODITE. Oenone, knowing the future, tried in vain to dissuade him. Then she told him that if he were wounded he would have to come back to her, since she alone would know how to heal him. In exchange for her virginity, Apollo had given her the gift of knowledge of herbal medicine. Paris abandoned Oenone for Helen. Some years later, during the last years of the siege of Troy, he was wounded by one of Philoctetes' arrows. Despairing of being cured of his wound, he remembered Oenone's promise. He went to find her – or sent messengers to her – asking her to heal him, but angered at having been abandoned, Oenone refused to help, and Paris died. Repenting of her harshness, Oenone soon hastened off with her remedies, expecting to find her former lover still alive. When she learned of his death she killed herself, either by hanging herself or by throwing herself onto Paris' funeral pyre.

Oenopion (Οἰνοπίων) The wine-drinker, a son of Ariadne and Dionysus (or of Ariadne and Theseus). He was ruler of the island of Chios, to which he introduced red wine. He came from Crete, Lemnos or Naxos. Oenopion had several children: Evanthes, Staphylus, Maron, Talus and a daughter, Merope, whose hand in marriage was sought by ORION when he came to Chios to chase wild beasts. Oenopion, who did not want to give Orion his daughter, made him drink and blinded him in his stupor.

Oenotrus (Οἴνωτρος) One of the sons of Lycaon and Cyllene. Discontented with the lot that had fallen to him when the Peloponnese was divided up between him and his brothers. Oenotrus left the country with his brother Peucetius. Both went to Italy. Peucetius gave his name to the Peucetians; Oenotrus gave his to the Oenotrians. Another tradition, going back as far as Varro, makes Oenotrus a Sabine king. He was also sometimes thought to be the brother of King Italus.

Oeonus (Οἰωνός) A nephew of Alcmene. He was the son of Licymnius and therefore the cousin of Heracles whom he accompanied on his expeditions in the Peloponnese. He was the victor in the running race in the Olympic Games, which Heracles founded. He was killed by Hippocoon and his sons; it was to avenge Oeonus' death that Heracles undertook his expedition against Sparta.

Ogygus (Ὤγυγος)
1. According to Boeotian tradition Ogygus was one of the original native kings of the area who had reigned over the land at a very early period. Other authors made him the son of the hero Boeotus, who had given his name to Boeotia; yet others made him the son of Poseidon and Alistra.

Ogygus was king of the Ectenians, who were the first inhabitants of the earth in the days before Deucalion's flood. One of the gates of Thebes was named after him. He was said to have had several children, notably three daughters who gave their names to Theban villages: Alalcomenia, Anlis and Thelxinoia. During his reign there was a first flood which covered Boeotia. A tradition made this Theban Ogygus the father of Cadmus and Phoenix.

2. Another Ogygus in Eleusinian tradition was the father of the hero Eleusis.

3. Ogygus was also the name given, in certain obscure traditions, to the Titan king who, together with all his subjects, was defeated by Zeus.

Oileus (Οἰλεύς) King of the Locrians of Opus, known principally for being the father of the 'little' Ajax. He took part in the expedition of the Argonauts, and was said to have been wounded in the shoulder by a feather of one of the Stymphalian birds. Apart from Ajax, whose mother was Eriopus, Oileus had an illegitimate son, Medon, by a woman named Rhene. He is sometimes also associated with Alcimache, the sister of Telamon.

Oileus was the son of Hodoedocus, the grandson of Cynus and the great-grandson of Opus. His mother was Laonome.

Olus A legendary giant about whom nothing is known but his name. This was revealed by an Etruscan seer when workmen digging on the top of the Capitol in Rome, in order to lay the foundations of the temple of Jupiter Optimus Maximus, found an enormous skull in the ground. It was attributed to a giant Olus, thus giving the Capitol its name of Caput-Oli, which was supposed to have been 'corrupted' into Capitolium. The find was interpreted as a sign of the future greatness of Rome, destined to become the centre of the world. This legend thus combines two elements: the buried skull as a portent and the etymological punning on the name of the hill.

Olymbrus (Ὄλυμβρος) According to an isolated tradition he was one of the sons of Gaia and Uranus and the brother of Adanus, Ostasus, Sandus, Cronus, Japhet and Rhea. The tradition is independent of Hesiod's *Theogony* and was probably eastern in provenance.

Olympus (Ὄλυμπος)

1. The Greek world contained many mountains called Olympus: in Mysia, Cilicia, Elis, Arcadia and (the best-known) on the borders of Macedonia and Thessaly. From the time of the Homeric epics Olympus was considered to be the home of the gods, particularly Zeus. It was there for example that Zeus weighed in the balance the destinies of Achilles and Hector, and it was from Olympus that he hurled Hephaestus who had tried to intervene on Hera's behalf. Gradually, however, the home of the gods became a concept distinct from the Thessalian mountain itself, and the word 'Olympus' was applied in a general way to the 'heavenly dwelling place' where the gods resided.

2. The name Olympus was given to numerous heroes. One of them was a son of Cres, the eponymous hero of Crete. Cronus gave Zeus to him to look after and Zeus was reared by him, but Olympus later suggested to the Giants that they should dethrone Zeus. Zeus struck him down with a thunderbolt, but immediately afterwards repented of having killed him, and gave his own name to the tomb of Olympus in Crete.

3. Another Olympus, according to Diodorus Siculus, was the first husband of Cybele, whose second husband was Iasion though this was probably part of a euhemerist interpretation of the legend of Cybele, which was associated with the Mount Olympus in Mysia.

4. The last Olympus was a famous flautist, said to be the father (or, more often, the son) and pupil of Marsyas. When Apollo slew Marsyas, Olympus buried him and wept for him.

Olynthus (Ὄλυνθος) There are two legends about Olynthus, the eponymous hero of the Macedonian city. According to one he was the son of King Strymon and brother of Brangas and Rhesus. During a hunt he was killed by a lion and buried on the same spot by Brangas. According to another tradition Olynthus was the son of Heracles by the Nymph Bolbe.

Omphale (Ὀμφάλη) The legend of Heracles and Omphale in its best-known form makes the latter a queen of Lydia and daughter of King Iardanus in whose palace Heracles was serving as a slave. Originally the myth of Omphale seems to have been local to Epirus, where she appears as the eponym of the city of Omphalion, but the myth soon spread to Lydia where it acquired the full flavour of oriental picturesque which was liberally exploited by Hellenistic poets and artists.

As well as the genealogy given above, there is a tradition in certain authors that Omphale was the daughter or widow of King Tmolus who bequeathed his kingdom to her. She enjoined upon her new slave, Heracles, a number of tasks, asking him to clear her kingdom of robbers and monsters. Heracles fought with the Cercopes and with Syleus, and he waged war on the Itones who were ravaging the lands that belonged to Omphale. He captured the city that was their lair, destroyed it and enslaved its inhabitants. Omphale, admiring her slave's exploits and learning of his parentage, freed him and married him. By him she had a son called Lamon. This is the 'historical' version of the tale, recounted by Diodorus Siculus. According to a 'romantic' version Omphale immediately became Heracles' mistress, and the days of his enslavement were spent in ease and indolence. Omphale took to wearing the hero's lion-skin and to brandishing his club. Heracles, by contrast, wore a long Lydian robe and spun linen thread at the queen's feet. When this period was over Heracles left Lydia and came back to Greece where he accomplished numerous feats before his death.

Oneiros (Ὄνειρος) A demon in the form of a dream sent by Zeus to deceive Agamemnon. Dreams are not generally personified. They can represent a multitude of various specific demons, depending on the imagination of different poets (see also MORPHEUS).

Opheltes (Ὀφέλτης) See ARCHEMORUS.

Ophion (Ὀφίων)
1. According to what is probably an Orphic tradition Ophion and his female companion, Eurynome, a daughter of Oceanus, reigned over the Titans before Cronus and Rhea who eventually seized power and cast Ophion and Eurynome into Tartarus.
2. There was another Ophion, one of the giants who attacked Zeus. Zeus crushed him beneath a mountain called Ophionion.

Opus (Ὀποῦς) The eponymous hero of the Locrian Opus. He is said to have been either the son of Locrus and Protogenia, the daughter of Deucalion and Pyrrha (see Table 8), or the son of Zeus by the daughter of another Opus, a king of Elis, the boy taking his grandfather's name. In this second version little Opus was entrusted by Zeus to Locrus, who was childless and who raised the boy as his own.

Ops The Roman goddess of Plenty and the companion of Saturn, she was therefore often iden-

tified by the Romans with Rhea, wife of Cronus, who is himself identified with Saturn. Ops, who had a temple dedicated to her on the Capitol, was said to be one of the Sabine deities brought to Rome by Titus Tatius, a familiar tradition associated with many agrarian gods and goddesses.

Orcus In Roman popular belief Orcus was the spirit that presided over death, barely distinguishable from Hades itself as the realm of the dead. He appears in funerary paintings in Etruscan tombs as a bearded, hairy giant. Gradually this spirit was absorbed into the Greek pantheon and Orcus was used as another name for Pluto or Dis Pater. Orcus survived in the language of the common people however, whereas the other two deities fell into disuse and became part of 'intellectual' mythology.

Orestes (Ὀρέστης) The son of Agamemnon and Clytemnestra (see Table 2). His legend gradually evolved, as did that of his sister Iphigenia, as their names became linked with a growing number of events. However, the broad outlines were fixed by the period of the Homeric epics, in which Orestes appears as the avenger of his father's death (although Homer seems not to have known of the murder of Clytemnestra by her son). It is in the work of the tragedians, particularly Aeschylus, that Orestes became a major figure. The first episode in Orestes' life is associated with the Troy legend after the first expedition, which ended in Mysia in the kingdom of Telephus (see ACHILLES and AGAMEMNON). Telephus, having been wounded by Achilles, was told by an oracle that he could be healed only by the rust from Achilles' same lance. So he went to Aulis, where the Greek army had gathered for the second time, was captured by soldiers and treated as a spy. To save himself he seized the little Orestes, the youngest of Agamemnon's children, and threatened to kill the child if he himself were badly treated. In this way he managed to obtain a hearing, and his wound was healed. (The tragedians, particularly Euripides, liked to portray the child Orestes as arriving at Aulis with his mother and with Iphigenia at the moment when the latter was to be sacrificed to Artemis.)

When Agamemnon returned from Troy and was assassinated by Aegisthus and Clytemnestra, Orestes was saved from death by his sister Electra, who secretly took him away to the house of Strophus, the child's uncle-by-marriage, who was married to Agamemnon's sister Anaxibia and who lived in the city of Cirrha, near Delphia. Strophus brought up Orestes with his own son, Pylades. Thus began the legendary friendship which bound Orestes and Pylades together. (There are other versions of Orestes' escape from massacre. Sometimes a nursemaid, a tutor or an old family retainer is credited with having rescued him.)

When he reached manhood, Orestes was ordered by Apollo to avenge his father's death by killing Aegisthus and Clytemnestra. (According to Sophocles it was Electra who had maintained contact with her brother, and urged him to avenge Agamemnon; Orestes then asked Apollo's advice and was told that this act of vengeance was permissible.) With Pylades at his side Orestes went to the tomb of Agamemnon at Argos and offered up a dedicatory lock of his hair. Electra visited the tomb herself and recognized her brother's hair. This means of recognition, which occurs in the version followed by Aeschylus, seemed implausible both to Euripides, who substituted the intervention of an old man, and to Sophocles, who brought into the story a gold ring which once belonged to Agamemnon and which Orestes showed to his sister.

Orestes presented himself to Clytemnestra in the guise of a traveller on his way from Phocis to Argos, charged by Strophius to bring news of the death of Orestes and to ask whether the dead man's ashes should be brought to Argos or left in Cyrrha. Clytemnestra, thereby freed from her fear of seeing her crimes punished, was overjoyed and sent for Aegisthus. As soon as Aegisthus arrived at the palace he was felled by Orestes. Hearing his dying cry, Clytemnestra ran to him and found her son, sword in hand. She begged him to spare the woman who suckled him, and Orestes was about to yield when Pylades reminded him of Apollo's instructions and of the sacred nature of his vengeance. Orestes killed her. In Euripides Orestes killed Aegisthus while the latter was in his garden offering a sacrifice to the Nymphs; Orestes revealed his identity to Aegisthus' guards who, though they wanted to punish their master's assassin, were unwilling to lift their hands against the son of Agamemnon.

Soon after his parents' death Orestes went mad. Moreover he was haunted by the Erinyes, who pursued him from the very day of Clytemnestra's funeral. He sought asylum and absolution. Aeschylus says that, on Apollo's instruction, Orestes fled to Delphi and was purified by Apollo himself, but many other sanctuaries in Greece claimed the same honour. Purification did not free him from the Erinyes, however: that could happen only after a formal trial, which took place eventually in Athens, on the spot where the Areopagus was later sited. (The judgement of Orestes was taken, symbolically, to be the first verdict which that body delivered.)

Traditions vary as to the identity of the prosecutor. Some say it was the Erinyes in person who arraigned Orestes before the Athenian court; others that it was Tyndareus, the father of Clytemnestra; yet others that it was Erigone, the daughter of Aegisthus and Clytemnestra. Instead of Tyndareus, who was said to be dead by this time, some of the mythographers of antiquity named Perileus, a cousin of Clytemnestra (see Table 19). The judges were equally divided on the verdict. Consequently Orestes was acquitted, for Athena, who was presiding over the court, gave her casting vote to those advocating acquittal. In gratitude Orestes built an altar to her on the hill of the Areopagus.

It is to the period when Orestes was in Athens that the origin of the 'Day of the Jugs' is attributed. During the Athenian festival of the Anthesteria King Demiphon (or, alternatively, King Pandion II), who was then on the throne, was embarrassed by Orestes' arrival in the city. Because of the shame and dishonour inevitably associated with matricide the king did not want to let Orestes take part in the festival or enter the temple but on the other hand he did not want to insult him. So he devised the plan of closing the temple and serving, on separate tables outside, a jug of wine for each of those present. This gave rise to the Festival of the Jugs.

There was another, purely Argive, tradition which placed the trial of Orestes in the Argolid rather than in Athens. Oeax and Tyndareus were supposed to have brought Orestes to trial before the citizens of Argos who condemned him to death, leaving to him the choice of method, whereas the people of Mycenae merely condemned him to banishment. The Aeschylean version is far more widespread.

After his acquittal Orestes asked Apollo what he ought to do. The god replied that he would be rid of his madness if he went to Tauris in search of the statue of Artemis. Here a new episode in the Orestes legend begins: his adventures with Pylades and the return of Iphigenia. This myth was used by Euripides in *Iphigeneia in Tauris*. When they arrived in Tauris, Orestes and Pylades were imprisoned by the inhabitants, who sacrificed all strangers to their goddess. They were brought before Thoas, the king of the region, and then taken to Iphigenia, who turned out to be the priestess of Artemis. Iphigenia untied them and asked them about their homeland. She soons realized who they were. Orestes told her why he had come to Tauris and on whose orders. Iphigenia decided to help him to steal the statue of Artemis and then to flee with him. Accordingly, she persuaded King Thoas that she could not sacrifice the stranger, who had had to leave his own land because of matricide, until she had purified both victim and statue in sea water. Thoas agreed to this, and Iphigenia went to the seashore with Orestes and Pylades, not far from where their boat lay. Iphigenia induced the Scythian guards to withdraw, on the pretext that the purificatory rites must remain secret; she then boarded the ship with her brother Pylades and the statue. But Poseidon cast the ship back on to the shore, and Thoas was about to recapture them all when Athene manifested herself and ordered him to withdraw. Orestes, Pylades and Iphigenia all sailed to Attica, where they built a temple to Artemis. (For a further episode on this return journey see CHRYSES 2.)

The last element in the Orestes legend concerns his settling in the Argolid and his marriage. When he was still a child, his father plighted him to his cousin Hermione, the daughter of Menelaus and Helen. But at Troy Menelaus broke his promise and offered Hermione's hand to Neoptolemus. When he returned from Tauris, Orestes went to visit Hermione while Neoptolemus was at Delphi (whither he had gone to consult the oracle) and abducted her. He was also said to have killed Neoptolemus at Delphi, on Hermione's advice. To do this he provoked a riot during which his rival was found dead. By Hermione Orestes had a son called Tisamenus. Orestes reigned over Argos, where he succeeded Cylarabes, who died without an heir (see ANAXAGORAS), and also at Sparta, as successor to Menelaus. Shortly before Menelaus's death a plague ravaged his kingdom. The oracle declared that the scourge would abate only if the cities destroyed during the Trojan War were rebuilt, and if the gods of those cities had restored to them the honours of which they had been deprived. Orestes sent colonies to Asia Minor to reconstruct the destroyed cities. He died at the advanced age of ninety, after seventy years on the throne. He was paid divine honours.

Orestes' tomb was believed by some to be at Tegea; in Rome it was said that Orestes died at Aricia (one of the places where the cult of the Taurian Arterus was said to survive) and that his bones had been transferred to Rome and buried beneath the Temple of Saturn.

Orestheus (Ὀρεσθεύς) Son of Deucalion, brother of Pronous and Marathonus and king of Aetolia. One of his bitches gave birth to a piece of wood. Orestheus had it buried and from this stump there immediately grew a magnificent vine bearing huge grapes. Faced with this miracle Orestheus gave his son the name Phytius (derived from the Greek verb 'to grow'). This Phytius was the father of King Oeneus.

Orion (Ὠρίων) A giant huntsman, the son of Euryale and Poseidon or of Hyrieus. He was also, like almost all the giants, said to be a son of Gaia. From his father he received the gift of walking on the sea. He was very handsome and prodigiously strong. He married Side, who was so lovely and so proud of her beauty that she claimed to outshine Hera; this prompted the goddess to hurl her into Tartarus. Deprived of his wife, Orion went to Chios, perhaps summoned there by Oenopion, who asked him to rid the island of the wild beasts that infested it. There Orion fell in love with Oenopion's daughter, Merope. Her father was opposed to the match.

At this point the different versions of the myth diverge. Some say that Orion became drunk and tried to rape Merope, others that Oenopion himself got Orion drunk. Whatever the case, Oenopion put out Orion's eyes while he was asleep on the shore. Orion then went to Hephaestus' forge and, taking a child called Cedalion, hoisted him on his shoulders and asked the boy to lead him in the direction of the rising sun. Immediately Orion's sight returned. He hurried off to take his revenge upon Oenopion but failed, for Hephaestus had made him an underground chamber, where he took refuge.

Aurora (the Dawn) fell in love with Orion, abducted him and carried him off to Delor. Her happiness was shortlived, however: Orion was killed by Artemis, either because he imprudently challenged her to a discus competition or because he tried to rape one of her attendants, the Hyperborean virgin Opis. The most widespread account of his death goes as follows: Orion had tried to rape Artemis herself, and the goddess set a scorpion on him, which bit him in the head. As a reward for the service to Artemis, the scorpion was changed into a constellation: Orion underwent a similar metamorphosis. That is why the constellation of Orion is eternally fleeing before the constellation of Scorpio (see also CORONIDES).

Orithyia (Ὀρείθυια)
1. One of the daughters of Erechtheus, king of Athens. She was abducted by Boreas.
2. In another tradition Orithyia was the daughter of Cecrops by a Macedonian woman, who also bore him a son called Europus, the eponym of the village of that name in Macedonia.

Ornythus (Ὄρνυτος)
1. An Arcadian hero (also called Teuthis) who led a contingent of Arcadians from the city of Teuthis to join the Greek side at Troy. When the winds remained unfavourable at Aulis, Ornythus decided to return home. The goddess Athena then appeared, in the form of Molus, son of Ops, and asked him to stay. But he became angry and wounded the goddess in the thigh. Then he returned to the city. There the goddess appeared to him in a dream with her wounded thigh, and he was instantly struck down with a sickness which made him weak and listless; the city fell victim to a famine. When the oracle at Dodona was asked for a solution it said that the remedy consisted in raising a statue to Athena, complete with the wound in her thigh dressed with a purple bandage.
2. Another hero of the same name was a son of Sisyphus who fought on the side of the Locrians of Opus for the possession of Daphnous. He carved himself out a kingdom which he handed on to his son, Phocus, who gave his name to the Phocians. Ornythus and his second son, Thoas, retired to Corinth.

Orontes (Ὀρόντης)
The name is given to two characters who represent two entirely separate legends about the river Orontes in Syria.
1. The first is a Hindu hero, son of Didnasus. He commanded an army for the Hindu king Deriades at the time of Dionysus' expedition to India. He was a giant 20 cubits tall, and a redoubtable warrior. Eventually he was wounded by Dionysus and killed himself. His body was carried away by the waters of the Orontes, which took the hero's name. In Roman times the course of the Orontes was temporarily diverted so that work could be carried out on the banks of the old river-bed. During these works a long plaster sarcophagus was found, containing a human skeleton of enormous size. The oracle at Clarus affirmed that this was the body of the hero Orontes.

2. Orontes is also the name of the god of the river who, like all the river-gods, was a son of Oceanus and Tethys. He fell in love with the Nymph Meliboea, one of the daughters of Oceanus, and the river overflowed its banks, flooding the countryside, until it was brought under control by Heracles.

Orpheus (Ὀρφεύς)
The myth of Orpheus is one of the most obscure and the most highly symbolic in Greek mythology. There are traces of it at a very early date, and it developed into a full scale theology with its own plentiful, and for the most part, esoteric, literature. The Orpheus myth was not without a certain influence on the formation of early Christian belief: there are traces of it in Christian iconography.

Orpheus is said by all authorities to have been the son of Oeagrus. Traditions differ over the identity of his mother. She is usually said to have been Calliope, chief of the nine Muses, though occasionally she is Polhymnia or, more rarely, Menippe, daughter of Thamyris. Orpheus is Thracian in origin. Like the Muses he therefore lived in a region bordering on Olympus, and in paintings and sculptures is often depicted singing there in Thracian dress. The mythographers make him a king of the Bistonians, the Oaryses, the Macedonians, etc.

Orpheus is the 'type' of the singer, musician and poet. He plays the lyre and the cithara, which he is often said to have invented. If not given this distinction, he is accorded that of having increased the number of strings on the instrument from seven to nine 'because of the number of the Muses'. Whatever the truth of that, Orpheus could sing so sweetly that wild beasts would follow him about; trees and plants would bow down to him and the wildest of men would become gentle.

Orpheus took part in the expedition of the Argonauts. Being weaker than the other heroes, however, he could not row and so acted as coxswain for the oarsmen. During a storm he calmed the crew and stilled the waves with his singing. As he alone was an initiate of the Samothracian Mysteries, he made supplication to the Cabiri (the gods of these Mysteries) on his companions' behalf and persuaded the latter to become initiates too. His main role consisted in singing while the Sirens were trying to seduce the Argonauts, and he managed to restrain the latter by surpassing the Sirens' voices in sweetness.

The most famous myth about Orpheus is that

of his descent into the Underworld to fetch his wife Eurydice. As a literary theme this seems to have been developed mainly in the Alexandrian period. It is the fourth book of Virgil's *Georgics* which give us the richest and most complete version of the story. Eurydice herself was a Nymph (a Dryad) or a daughter of Apollo. One day, as she was walking beside a river in Thrace, she was pursued by Aristaeus who desired her. But she stepped on a snake which bit her, and she died. Orpheus, who was inconsolable, went down to the Underworld to find his wife. With the music of his lyre he charmed not only the monsters of Hades but even the Underworld gods. The poets strive to outdo each other in imaginative descriptions of the effects of this divine music: Ixion's wheel ceased to turn; Sisyphus' stone remained poised without support; Tantalus forgot his hunger and thirst; even the Danaides forgot about trying to fill their sieve. Hades and Persephone agreed to restore Eurydice to her husband because he had showed such proof of love. But they set a condition; Orpheus was to return to the world of light, followed by his wife, without looking back at her before they left the kingdom of the Underworld. Orpheus accepted and set out. He had almost reached daylight when a terrible doubt seized him. Had Persephone been playing a trick on him? Was Eurydice really behind him? At last he turned around. Eurydice fainted and died a second time. Orpheus tried to rescue her a second time, but Charon was inflexible, and the entry to Hell was barred to Orpheus. He had to return to the human world unconsoled.

The death of Orpheus has given rise to a large number of traditions. It was generally said that he was killed by the women of Thrace, but the reasons behind this are many and various. Sometimes the women resent his fidelity to the memory of Eurydice, interpreting it as an insult to themselves. It was also said that Orpheus wanted to have nothing to do with women and surrounded himself with young men: it was even suggested that he was the inventor of pederasty and that his lover was Calais, son of Boreas. Some authorities insisted that on his return from the

Orpheus and Eurydice in the Underworld with the ferryman Charon. Attic lecythos, 425–400 BC. Athens, National Museum.

Underworld Orpheus instituted mysteries based on his experiences there but forbade the admission of women. The men met him in a locked house, leaving their weapons outside. One night the women took the weapons and when the men came out killed Orpheus and his close associates. Another explanation was based on a curse of Aphrodite. When she quarrelled with Persephone about Adonis, Aphrodite had, on Zeus' instruction, to submit herself to the arbitration of Calliope, who decided that each goddess should keep Adonis for alternate parts of the year. Aphrodite was angered by this decision and, being unable to take revenge on Calliope herself, made the women of Thrace fall in love with Orpheus, but as none was willing to stand aside in favour of any of the others they all tore him apart. An entirely different tradition said that Orpheus was killed with a thunderbolt by Zeus, angered by the mystic revelations which Orpheus had made to those initiated into his mysteries.

According to the standard account of Orpheus' death, when the Thracian women had torn his body to pieces they threw his remains into the river, which bore them down to the sea. The poet's head and his lyre arrived at Lesbos, whose inhabitants paid funerary honours to the poet and constructed a tomb for him. This is why the island of Lesbos excelled in lyric poetry. Other areas also laid claim to the tomb of Orpheus – Asia Minor, for example, at the mouth of the River Meles.

It was said that after the murder of Orpheus a plague spread throughout Thrace. When consulted, the oracle declared that this was a punishment for the poet's murder and that to rid the land of the pestilence the inhabitants would have to seek Orpheus' head in order to pay it due honour. After searching far and wide some fishermen finally found the head buried in sand at the mouth of the Meles. It was bloody and still singing, as in life. In Thessaly there was another strange legend concerning the tomb. It was said that this had once been at Leibethra and that an oracle of the Thracian Dionysus had predicted that if the ashes of Orpheus saw the sun the city would be ravaged by a pig. The inhabitants laughed at this prediction, thinking that it would be impossible for a pig to destroy their city. Now one summer day a shepherd fell asleep on Orpheus' tomb. In his sleep the shepherd, who was deeply imbued with the spirit of Orpheus, started to sing Orphic hymns in a melodious voice. When they heard this music the men labouring in the fields broke off from their work and gathered round the tomb in

such a crowd that the columns of the monument collapsed on to the sarcophagus containing the hero's ashes. The following night a violent storm arose, swelling the waters of the river Sys (which means 'pig' in Greek) on the banks of which the city stood. Thus the mysterious prediction of the oracle was fulfilled.

After Orpheus' death his lyre was borne up to heaven and became a constellation. The soul of Orpheus was taken to the Elysian Fields where, dressed in a long white robe, it continued to sing for the benefit of the Blessed Ones. It was around this myth that Orphic theology formed. Orpheus was thought to have brought back from his descent into the Underworld information both about how to reach the land of the Blessed Ones and about how to avoid the obstacles which threaten the soul after death. A large number of poems are attributed to Orpheus, ranging from stereotyped, popular verses that people would inscribe on plaques and bury with the dead to hymns, a theogony and a long epic, the *Argonautica*. Orpheus was sometimes said to have shared with Dionysus the founding of the Eleusinian Mysteries.

A tradition recorded by various authors makes Orpheus the ancestor of Homer and Hesiod.

Orthopolis (Ὀρθόπολις) The son of Plemnaeus, and the king of Sicyon. None of this king's previous children had survived birth: as soon as they gave their first cry they died. Demeter took pity on him and, dressing herself as a foreigner, made her way to his court, where she lifted the curse and reared the king's only surviving child. Orthopolis, the boy thus miraculously saved, had a daughter, Chrysorthe, who bore Apollo a son named Coronus.

Orthros (Ὄρθρος) Geryon's dog, which Heracles killed when he made off with Geryon's flocks. He was the offspring of Typhon and Echidna and therefore brother of Cerberus. By mating with his own mother Echidna, he fathered the Theban Sphinx. The descriptions of Orthros vary. Sometimes he is said to have several heads, sometimes a snake's body.

Osinius In the *Aeneid* Osinius was a prince of Clusium in Italy, and part of the contingent sent to Aeneas by Tarchon, king of the Etruscans, as an ally against Turnus.

Otos (Ὦτος) See ALOADAE.

Otreus (Ὀτρεύς) King of Phrygia, who came to Priam's aid against the Amazons. Aphrodite passed herself off as his daughter, who had been abducted by Hermes, when she gave herself to Anchises.

Oxylus (Ὄξυλος) The name of several heroes, two of whom belong to Aetolian legend.
1. The first Oxylus, not known in any other context, was a son of Ares by Protogenia and thereby grandson of Calydon and great-grandson of the hero Aetolus, eponym of the Aetolians (see Table 24).
2. The other Oxylus is generally described as son of Haemon, himself the son of Thoas. He also had Aetolus as a forebear, ten (or nine) generations back. Apollodorus, who makes him the son of Andraemon, says that his mother was Deianeira's sister Gorge (see Table 27). He is therefore related to the Heraclids, being the cousin of Hyllus, the son of Deianeira.

It is very possible that these two Oxyluses, the son of Haemon (or Andraemon) and the son of Ares and Protogenia, are the same person. Both are descended from Aetolus and, through him, from Endymion. To Oxylus is attached the legend of the return of the descendants of Aetolus to Elis. Aetolus, a native of Elis, in the Peloponnese, had to leave his homeland and obtained for himself the gift of a kingdom on the north side of the Gulf of Corinth in the land of Curetes, which took the name of Aetolia after him.

Oxylus accidentally killed his brother, Thermos, with a discus and had to leave the country. He took refuge in Elis. When the time fixed for his exile (a year) was over, he set out for Aetolia. It happened that at that very moment the Heraclids, in response to the words of an oracle, were expecting to find a guide 'with three eyes' who would lead them into the Peloponnese. Oxylus, who was said to be either one-eyed himself (having lost the other as a result of an arrow wound) or was whole-sighted himself but riding a horse or mule which was one-eyed, rode towards them, and the Heraclids realized that in the combination of man and mount the oracle had been fulfilled. They asked him to take them to their 'promised land' and Oxylus agreed. He brought them their victory but claimed as a reward the kingdom of Elis which had belonged to his ancestors. Fearing, however, that if the Heraclids saw how beautiful Elis was they would be loath to give it up to him, he led them through Arcadia. When the Heraclids had divided up the conquered lands

among themselves Oxylus presented himself at the frontiers of Elis with his Aetolians. There he clashed with King Elius. As the forces of the two parties were equal it was decided to settle the matter by single combat. The Eleans chose as their champion an archer called Degmenus. The Aetolians chose a sling-thrower, Pyraechmes, who won the contest.

That is how Oxylus won back the throne of his ancestors in Elis. He allowed the native inhabitants to retain their lands but installed Aetolian colonists who intermarried with the Eleans. Oxylus maintained the old religious cults of the country and distinguished himself by his wise government. Under his rule the city of Elis became strikingly beautiful, and usury was forbidden within his territories. He was also a protector of the Achaeans, who were ill-treated by the invading Dorians (the Heraclids). The Olympic Games, founded by Heracles, had fallen into abeyance. Oxylus restored them, and his name was so closely associated with them that he was sometimes said to be their founder.

Oxylus married Pieria, by whom he had two sons, Aetolus the Younger and Laias. Aetolus died when very young and was buried beneath one of the gates of the city of Elis, through which ran the Sacred Way, in order to satisfy an oracle which said that the child should be buried neither inside nor outside the city. Laias succeeded his brother to the throne.
3. A third Oxylus, the son of Oreius, married his own sister, Hamadryas, and fathered on her the tree Nymphs Carya, Balanus, Crania, Morea, Aeigirus, Ptelea, Ampelus and Syce, whose names evoke various trees including the hazel, the mulberry, the vine and the fig.

Oxynius (Ὀξύνιος) In an obscure legend, recorded by Conon, Oxynius and Scamandrius were two sons of Hector whom Priam had sent for safety to Lydia when Troy fell. After the destruction of Troy, Aeneas, who had taken refuge on Mount Ida, reigned over the country, but soon Oxynius and Scamandrius returned to claim possession of their grandfather's kingdom.

Oxynthes (Ὀξύντης) A king of Athens, the son of Demophon and, accordingly, a member of the Theseid clan. His sons were Apheidas and Thymoetes. Apheidas the elder inherited the throne from him, but was soon dethroned and murdered by his brother.

P

Pactolus (Πακτωλός) The god of the river of that name in Asia Minor. He was said to be the son of Zeus and Leucothea. He himself was father of Euryanassa and, according to one tradition, grandfather of Pelops. During the Mysteries of Aphrodite he unwittingly deflowered his own sister, Demodice. When he realized what he had done he threw himself into the River Chrysorhoas (the 'golden stream', so called because its water has spangles of gold in it). In memory of this suicide the river afterwards took the name of Pactolus (see also MIDAS).

Paean (Παιάν) In the cults of the classical period 'Paean' is frequently no more than the ritual epithet of Apollo the healer. In the Homeric poems, however, an independent god of healing named Paean or Paeon appears, noted for using herbs in his healing. It was he who took care of Hades when the latter was wounded. Paean was gradually superseded both by Apollo and, in some respects, by Asclepius.

Paeon (Παίων) There were several heroes called Paeon (apart from the 'healer' Paeon or Paean mentioned above).
1. One is the eponym of the race of the Paeonians. In the tradition recorded by Pausanias he is one of the brothers of Endymion and therefore a brother of Aetolus, Epeius and Eurycyde (see Table 24). Another tradition, recorded by Hyginus, makes him a son of Poseidon and Helle.
2. Another Paeon is a son of Antilochus and therefore a grandson of Nestor. His children were driven out of Messenia, together with the other descendants of Neleus, at the time of the return of the Heraclids. With his cousins he settled in Athens and from him was descended the Athenian clan of the Paeonids.

Palaemon (Παλαίμων)
1. Palaemon, 'the Wrestler', is the name of a son of Heracles (see Table 15), so called because of a wrestling match fought by his father.
2. Palaemon is also the name of one of the Argonauts in the list given by Apollodorus. This Palaemon was the son of Aetolus (or of Hephaetlus). Like the son of Heracles (see 1, above) he owed his name to the wrestling skills of his father.
3. The best-known bearer of the name is the son of Ino-Leucothea. In his human childhood this Palaemon was called Melicertes; his father was Athamas. On his mother's side Palaemon was the first cousin of Dionysus, since Ino was the daughter of Cadmus and the sister of Semele, Dionysus' mother (see Table 3). After the suicide of his mother, who threw herself from the top of the cliffs near Megara, taking the boy with her, Melicertes became the sea-god Palaemon and Ino the goddess Leucothea. The Megarians said that though the body of the mother was cast up onto the shore near their city and buried by the daughters of Cleson (who was a son of the Egyptian Lelex), the body of the child was borne by a dolphin as far as the Isthmus of Corinth. There it was recovered by Sisyphus who buried it, raised an altar to the boy near a pine tree and paid divine honours under the name Palaemon to mark the child's divine patronage of the Isthmian games.

At Rome Palaemon was identified with the god Portunus.

Palaestra (Παλαίστρα) The personification of wrestling, said to be a young girl beloved of Hermes. She is also sometimes said to be the daughter of Choricus, king of Arcadia, and sometimes the daughter of Pandocus of Cephalonia. This Pandocus (whose name means 'the wellcoming') lived at a crossroads. He used to invite passers-by to come in and would then kill them. One day Hermes happened to pass and was invited in by Pandocus, but Palaestra fell in love with the young god and warned him to kill Pandocus immediately.

Palamedes (Παλαμήδης) One of the three sons of Nauplius and Clymene, the daughter of Catreus. His two brothers were Oeax and Nausimedon. His legend developed independently of the Homeric poems. He appeared among the pupils taught by the Centaur Chiron, along with Achilles, Ajax and Heracles, and he took part in the preliminaries of the Trojan War. At the time of the abduction of Helen he consoled Menelaus (to whom he was related on his mother's side: see Table 2). According to certain authors he then took part in an embassy to Troy to try to negotiate a peaceful settlement of the war. He was even supposed to have carried a personal letter to Helen from Clytemnestra, asking her to come back to her husband. In a second embassy, sent from Tenedos, Palamedes appears alongside Menelaus, Odysseus, Diomedes and Acamas. But the enthusiasm shown by Palamedes for the cause of Menelaus was to bring about his downfall.

As Helen's former suitors were preparing to go to Troy to bring the young woman back, Odysseus, though bound by the oath he had made to Tyndareus, tried to escape his obligation. When Menelaus and Palamedes came to fetch him he pretended to be mad: he harnessed his plough to an ass and an ox, yoked together, and started sowing salt. But Palamedes refused to be hoodwinked by this stratagem and in order to force Odysseus to reveal that he was quite sane he placed little Telemachus in front of the plough. Odysseus could not withstand the test and he stopped his team before it killed the child. A variant of this tradition said that Palamedes threatened the little Telemachus with his sword. Either way it was Palamedes who saw through Odysseus' ruse and thus obliged him to join the expedition of Menelaus and Agamemnon. Odysseus never forgave him.

It was also said that Palamedes took part in the search for Achilles, who was hiding on Scyros at the court of Lycurgus. Similarly it was Palamedes whom Menelaus sent as herald to summon Oinopion and Cinyras. He revealed the true identity of a woman, Epipole of Carystos, the daughter of Trachion, who had dressed up as a man in order to sail with the Greek army. She was stoned to death.

During its early days Palamedes did the expedition army force a great many services: he raised the morale of the soldiers when they were disquieted by unfavourable omens, in particular by an eclipse; he tried to avert the plague which threatened the Greek camp; and he foresaw the arrival in the camp of a wolf (Apollo's animal) which had come from the forests of Mount Ida. He also guarded against a drought by sending for the 'Vine-growers', the three daughters of Oenopion.

Eventually Odysseus contrived his revenge. The versions of this intrigue vary, but all bear witness to the fact that Palamedes was the victim of treachery. One version claimed that Odysseus, having captured a Trojan prisoner, forced him to write a letter, supposedly from Priam, alleging that Palamedes had offered to betray the Greeks.

Then Odysseus bribed one of Palamedes' slaves to hide gold under his master's mattress. Finally, he dropped the letter in the camp. It was found by Agamemnon, who had Palamedes arrested and handed over to the men for punishment. Palamedes was stoned to death. Another version told how Odysseus and Diomedes persuaded Palamedes to descend into a pit and then threw rocks down onto him so that he was crushed to death. Palamedes' end became the archetypal example of an unjust death, the result of the intrigues of evil men against someone of greater worth. The death was avenged, however, by Nauplius.

Tradition credited Palamedes with a great number of inventions, in particular, one or more letters of the alphabet. It was even said that the order of the alphabet had been invented by him, the letters themselves having been created by Cadmus. It was most frequently claimed that Palamedes had the idea for the letter Y when watching a flock of cranes in flight. He is occasionally credited with the invention of numbers, an honour which he shares with Musaeus or Prometheus. His other discoveries include the use of coinage, the calculation of the lengths of months according to the movement of the stars, the game of draughts (which he devised during a famine to prevent people from thinking too much about food), the game of dice and the game of five-stones.

Palans A Roman hero, one of the numerous eponyms of the Palatine. His legend is recounted by Dionysus of Halicarnassus. This Palans was the son of Hercules and Dyna, the daughter of Evander. He died while still young, and his grandfather buried him on the hill to which he gave his name (see also PALLAS 3).

Palanto The daughter of Hyperborean and beloved of Hercules. She bore him a son, who became King Latinus. That at any rate is the obscure tradition recorded by Varro, intended to explain the name of the Palatine.

Pales A guardian spirit of flocks who was worshipped at Rome. Sometimes he is a male deity, sometimes a goddess. In his or her honour the festival of the Parilia was celebrated on 21 April, when the shepherds lit huge straw and brushwood fires through which they leapt. A popular etymology attached the name of this festival to that of the deity, the Parilia having supposedly once been called 'Palilia', but probably this was simply a play on words. The day of the Parilia was said to be the anniversary of the foundation of Rome by Romulus. The name of Pales was also said to be connected with that of the Palatine, but for no good reason. This deity, a simple 'spirit' typifying pastoral life, has no legend of its own.

Palici (Παλιχοί) Twin gods, originating in Sicily. They were sometimes said to have been the sons of Zeus by Thaleia the daughter of Hephaestus, sometimes the sons of Zeus by Aetna. While she was pregnant with the twins Thaleia, fearing Hera's jealousy, hid in the earth and when the time came the twin boys emerged from the ground, which explains their name 'the Returners' (from the Greek παλίν, 'again'). Their place of worship was close to the Lago di Naftia, not far from Leontini and was the site of various volcanic phenomena. For example a fountain of warm water spouted in the lake itself, forming a dome which then fell back into the basin without spilling a drop outside it. A strong smell of sulphur floated over the lake and it was even said that the birds which flew over it died at once and that men who approached it incautiously died within three days.

Such is the site of the Palici, redoubtable deities by whom the Sicilians swore their solemn oaths: when someone wanted to support an assertion with an oath he would write it on a tablet which he threw on to the waters of the lake. If the tablet floated, the oath was sincere; if it sank the oath was clearly invalid. It was said that the Palici struck blind all liars who falsely called upon their name.

Palinurus (Παλίνουρος) Aeneas' pilot. When the Greek fleet left Sicily for Italy Venus promised her son a successful voyage. Only one man's life would be lost, she said, and his death would ensure the safety of all the others. The man in question was Palinurus, who was steering the ship at night when, as Virgil describes it, the god of sleep afflicted him with an irresistible weariness. In vain the poor fellow tried to keep his eyes fixed on the stars; in vain he clung to the tiller. A sudden sharp movement of the boat knocked him into the sea. Everyone aboard was asleep: no one heard the cry he gave as he fell. When Aeneas awoke he discovered that his pilot had vanished, and he wept for him. But he was to see Palinurus again.

When he arrived in the Underworld, whither he was led by the Cumaean Sibyl, Aeneas saw on the banks of the Styx the crowd of the unburied dead to whom Charon pitilessly refused passage.

Among them was Palinurus, who told Aeneas what had happened to him since he fell into the sea. For three days and nights he had swum until he reached the Italian coast. But hardly had he set foot ashore when he was murdered by the barbaric inhabitants of the area, who left his body at the sea's edge. Palinurus asked Aeneas, when he got back to the world above, to go to Velia (on the Lucanian coast, to the south of the Gulf of Paestum) and to pay him his due funeral honours. The Sibyl then promised Palinurus that strange and terrible things would destroy the coastland of Lucania (probably a plague) and that the inhabitants would, of their own accord, collect up the body, pay it divine honours and give Palinurus' name to a local headland.

Palladium (Παλλάδιον) A divine statue, endowed with magical properties, which was thought to represent the goddess Pallas. Its legend, which is labyrinthine, acquired various accretions after the period of the epic cycles, during which it was connected with the story of Troy. The Palladium does not appear in the Homeric poems. In the *Iliad* the ritual statue of Athena honoured in Troy turns out to be the statue of a seated figure, whereas the Palladium is a standing deity, with the rigidity of the old *xoana* (idols from the archaic era). The legend grew gradually more complex and eventually became involved in the story of the origins of Rome. The Palladium had the power to guarantee the safety of the city which possessed it and worshipped it, and for ten years it preserved Troy. Several other cities then claimed to possess it, which conferred on them a priceless reputation for inviolability. Consequently miraculous statues of Pallas appeared in large numbers, and the legends became correspondingly convoluted.

Traditions differ about even the origin of the statue. They all agree that it had a divine origin, but the details vary. In Apollodorus, for example, we read that the goddess Athena was brought up as a child by the god Triton, who had a daughter named Pallas. The two little girls practised warfare together, but one day they quarrelled. Just as Pallas was about to strike Athena, Zeus was afraid for his daughter and placed himself between the two girls. He held the aegis before Pallas, who was frightened, failed to parry the blow that Athena was aiming at her and fell, mortally wounded. To make amends Athena carved a statue in the likeness of her friend, equipped it with the aegis which had frightened her and had indirectly caused her death, and placed her at

Diomedes carrying the Palladium away from Troy; the Palladium is here shown as an archaic statuette. Attic red-figure stemless cup from Apulia, name-vase of the Diomed Painter, end of 5th century BC. Oxford, Ashmolean Museum.

Zeus' side, paying honours to her as to a goddess. The statue remained on Olympus until the day when Zeus attempted to rape Electra who sought refuge by the statue, an inviolable place of asylum. But Zeus hurled the Palladium down from Olympus, and it fell on to the hill in the Troad where Ate had once fallen (see ILUS). At that time Ilus was busy founding the city which was later called Troy, though it was then still called Ilion after its founder. The statue which had miraculously fallen from the sky was taken as a sign that the gods approved of the foundation of the city, and in fact had fallen immediately in front of Ilus' tent (or, according to another version, into the unfinished temple of Athena, there being as yet no roof upon it). Of its own accord it occupied the ritual position for the statue of the cult. The Palladium was 3 cubits tall. Its feet were welded together (as can generally be seen in archaic statuary); in its right hand, which was raised, it held a lance, in its left a distaff and a spindle.

Other traditions said that the Palladium was made of bone and had been carved out of Pelops' shoulder blade. It was said to have been stolen from Sparta along with Helen. Finally, a late legend records that Tros, the ancestor of the Trojan race, had received the miraculous statue from a sorcerer called Asius, in honour of whom the continent of Asia was named.

The versions are equally at odds over the adventures of the statue. For example, Dardanus was said to have taken it with him to Samothrace. Perhaps he had got it from Arcadia. And he gave it as a present to his father-in-law, Teucer. It was

also said that the Trojans had had a second Palladium made, identical in every way with the first, so as to deceive robbers who might try to deprive the city of the statue which guaranteed its safety. They placed the false Palladium in the sanctuary, while the real one was kept in the temple treasury. Several legends formed around this theme of the multiplicity of statues. In the epic cycles it was said that the seer Helenus, when captured by Odysseus on Ida, had affirmed that, in accordance with the dictates of the fates, Troy could be captured only if, among other things, the Palladium was seized and removed from the city. Odysseus made it his job to fulfil this part of the prophecy. With Diomedes' help he got into the citadel by night, though on this point the versions differ. In some Odysseus left Diomedes on watch while he disguised himself as a beggar. Recognized by Helen despite his disguise, he succeeded, with her help, in carrying off the Palladium, though only after massacring the guards stationed on the route back. (This is the version found in Apollodorus' *Epitome*.) More often, however, it is Diomedes who plays the more glorious role. In order to scale the city (or temple) wall, Diomedes climbed on to his companion's shoulders, but once on the top of the wall he refused to pull Odysseus up after him. When he had successfully stolen the magic statue, Diomedes returned to Odysseus, and they both set off for camp. Odysseus tried to take the Palladium from Diomedes and to go back alone to the Greeks, so as to receive all the credit for the theft. He walked behind Diomedes and, raising his arm, was about to murder him when the shadow cast on to the ground by his sword (it being full moon) warned Diomedes who turned round and unsheathed his own sword. Odysseus refused to fight, so Diomedes hit him with the flat of his hand and forced him to walk in front of him thereafter. Some traditions record that the two heroes got into the city through a sewer. Others say that Theano, the wife of Antenor, handed the Palladium over to the Greeks on her husband's instructions, Antenor being a Greek sympathizer. However, yet other legends claim that the real Palladium stayed in Troy and that Aeneas, on that fateful night, rescued it just in time from the temple of Athena and carried it off to Ida, then later to Italy. This Palladium was taken to Rome and kept in the temple of Vesta where the Vestal Virgins worshipped it. At Rome, as at Troy, the safety of the city was linked with the safe-keeping of the statue.

The Palladium also appears in the story of Cassandra. When Ajax of Logis tried to abduct her (see AJAX, son of Oileus) it was the Palladium to which she clung. Ajax seized hold of her and in trying to drag her away pulled over the statue, which only priestesses with pure hands had the right to touch. He thus aggravated the already sacrilegious act of violating a suppliant and drew down on himself the wrath of Athena. In this version the true Palladium stayed at Troy until the very end, Odysseus and Diomedes having apparently stolen a false one. Both the statue, which Ajax also abducted, and Cassandra and the girl were restored to Agamemnon.

As for the later fortunes of the statue (in the versions where it was not in the keeping of Aeneas), some traditions claim that Diomedes kept it, others that it went back to Agamemnon. In the first case Diomedes was supposed to have taken it off to southern Italy with him and later to have given it to Aeneas when he came to settle in Latium. In the second case Agamemnon took the Palladium with him to Argos – at least this is what seems to have happened according to Pausanias' account whereby the Argives claim to possess the divine statue (on the Argive Palladium, see also LEAGROS).

Finally, there is an Athenian tradition designed to prove that the real Palladium was in the city of Athens. The Athenians said that Demophon, who took part in the Trojan War, was given the statue by Diomedes as a pledge. Knowing that Agamemnon coveted it Demophon hastily entrusted it to Buzyges, who took it back to Athens. But in order to deceive Agamemnon, Demophon had had an exact copy of the statue made in secret and he placed it in his own tent. After the fall of Troy Agamemnon, at the head of a large force, came to Demophon's tent and asked for the Palladium. Demophon refused to hand it over and fought for long enough to give Agamemnon the impression that he was defending the real talisman. In the end he appeared to capitulate and gave the king the worthless statue. Another version said that on his way back from Troy Diomedes went ashore at night at Phaleron in Attica but, not knowing precisely where he was, attacked the Athenians. Demophon, then king of Attica, came to his subjects' aid and, unaware of the identity of his attacker, he killed many of Diomedes' men and took the Palladium away from him. But on his way back his horse knocked down an Athenian, who died. For this manslaughter Demophon was brought before a special court which took the name of the Court of the Palladium and which, at a later date, continued to sit in judgement in cases of this kind.

Pallantidae (Παλλάντιδαι) The fifty sons of Pallas (see Table 15) and therefore the grandsons of Pandion, king of Athens, the nephews of Aegeus and the first cousins of Theseus. The Pallantidae thought that Aegeus had no children (the existence of Theseus, who was brought up far from Athens, was unknown to them), and hoped to succeed to the throne and to share power in Athens after Aegeus' death. When Theseus arrived from Troezen and was acknowledged by his father, they contested their cousin's legitimacy, but the Athenians overruled their objections and declared Theseus king. They then openly opposed him but were vanquished and slain. According to some authorities, to purify himself of their deaths, Theseus went into voluntary exile for a year at Troezen with his wife Phaedra. Alternatively, Theseus was brought before an Athenian court and absolved of blame.

Pallas (Πάλλας) Generally a stock epithet of the goddess Athena, who was frequently called Pallas Athena. A late legend records an independent story of Pallas. She was a daughter of the god Triton (the spirit of Lake Tritonis). Athena was brought up with her in childhood, and accidentally killed her (see PALLADIUM).

As a masculine name Pallas is borne by several heroes of whom the four listed here are perhaps the most notable.

1. The Titan Pallas, son of Crius and Eurybia and brother of Perses and Astraeus (see Tables 32 and 38). According to Hesiod's *Theogony* he coupled with Styx, the eldest daughter of Oceanus, who bore him four children: Zelos, Nice, Cratos and Bia (Zeal, Victory, Power and Force). Other traditions make him the father of Eos, who is usually considered to be the daughter of the 'solar' Titans Hyperion and THEIA.

2. One of the sons of Lycaon, the king of Arcadia. He is the eponym of the Arcadian city of Pallantion and plays a distant role in the legend of the origins of Rome. He is sometimes said to be the grandfather of Evander. According to Dionysus of Halicarnassus, this Pallas had a daughter named Chryse, whom he gave in marriage to Dardanus, the founder of the Trojan royal dynasty. At the same time Pallas gave his son-in-law the care of various Arcadian deities, including the Palladium, which was to play a role in the story of Troy. In

this way the mythographers established a link between Rome and Troy, even before the migration
of Aeneas and the foundation of the city, since the
eponymous hero of the Palatine (see below Pallas
3) was the nephew of the first queen of Troy (see
DARDANUS).

3. In the *Aeneid* Virgil introduces another Pallas,
the son of Evander and the eponym of the Palatine. This Pallas, who was the companion of
Aeneas in the war against Turnus, was said to
have been killed by Turnus. However, there was
also an earlier tradition that Pallas himself buried
Evander on the Palatine and therefore died after
his father. This Pallas can be compared with the
other Pallas (or Palans), the son of Heracles by a
daughter of Evander (Dyna or Launa?), who died
young and gave his name to the Palatine.

4. Another Pallas is connected not with Arcadian
– Roman legend but with Attic tradition. He was a
giant, the father of the goddess ATHENA (according
to some authors), who tried to rape his own
daughter. Athena killed him, removed his skin
and dressed herself in it. This Pallas had wings,
which Athena fixed to her feet.

5. Last, and also in Attic legend, Pallas was the
youngest son of Pandion (see Table 11). With his
fifty brothers, the Pallantidae, he rebelled against
Theseus, whom he considered a usurper. All fifty
brothers were slain by Theseus.

Pallene (Παλλήνη)

1. The daugher of Sithon, king of the Thracian
Chersonnese, and of either Anchiroe (or Anchi-
noe), herself daughter of Nilus or of the Nymph
Mendeis. Sithon himself was said to be a son of
Ares (or Poseidon). He had another daughter
called Rhoeteia.

Pallene was very beautiful, but Sithon did not
want to give her in marriage to any of her numerous suitors. He forced them to fight against him
and killed them. But when he felt his strength
declining and realized that he must resign himself
to her marriage he offered her as the prize in a
contest to be fought by single combat between the
two suitors who presented themselves at that
time, Dryas and Cleitus. Pallene was in love with
Cleitus, and not daring to reveal her passion she
wept bitterly. Her old teacher noticed her sorrow
and succeeded in making her confess its cause. He
contrived to bribe Dryas' charioteer to take out
the axle pin which secured his master's wheel.
Dryas was killed, but Sithon found out that his
daughter was implicated in the treachery and decided to punish her with death. He had a vast

funeral pyre built for the body of Dryas and persuaded his daughter to climb upon it. A divine
manifestation intervened, however. Either
Aphrodite appeared in person to forestall the
murder of Pallene, or heavy rainfall prevented the
pyre from catching fire. The inhabitants of the
city, recognizing the will of the gods, obtained the
girl's pardon, and she married Cleitus. She gave
her name to the peninsula of Pallene, in the
Thracian Chersonnese.

2. Another Pallene was one of the daughters of
Alcyoneus. She was changed into a bird, along
with her sisters.

Pamphos (Πάμφως)

According to Pausanias
Pamphos was a very early poet who in mythical
times wrote religious hymns for the Athenians.
Pausanias quotes, among others, hymns to
Demeter, Artemis, Poseidon, Eros and the
Graces.

Pamphylus (Πάμφυλος)

One of the sons of
Aegumius, who gave his name to a Dorian tribe,
the Pamphylians. He fought on the Heraclid side
against Tisamenus. He married Orsobia, daughter
of Deiphontes.

Pan (Πάν)

A god of shepherds and flocks. He
apparently originated in Arcadia, although his cult
percolated throughout Greece and even became
widespread outside the Greek world. He was
depicted as a spirit, half-man, half-animal, with a
reed pipe, a shepherd's crook and a branch of pine
or a crown of pine leaves. His bearded face had an
expression of animal cunning with its wrinkles
and its very prominent chin. On his forehead were
two horns. His body was hairy; the lower parts
were those of a male goat, his feet having cloven
hooves and his legs being tough and sinewy. He
had the gift of amazing agility; he was a swift
runner and climbed rocks with ease; he was
equally good at hiding in the bushes, where he
crouched to watch the nymphs or to sleep during
the heat of midday. It was dangerous to disturb
him at these times. He was particularly fond of
cool streams and woodland shade in which he embodied the taste both of the shepherds and of their
flocks. Pan was also a deity endowed with considerable sexual energy who pursued nymphs and
boys with equal ardour. He had the reputation,
when his amorous ambitions were frustrated, of
settling for solitary pleasures. The few legends in
which he figures are usually late ones, invented by
Alexandrian poets who often evoked him in rustic

idylls. The oldest stories about Pan seem to concern his birth.

There is no mention of Pan in the Homeric poems. A so-called Homeric Hymn celebrates him, however, and says that he was the son of the Hermes of Mount Cyllene and of the daughter of Dryops. When he was born his mother was frightened by the monstrous child to which she had given birth but Hermes wrapped the new-born child in a hare pelt and carried him off to Olympus, where he placed him close to Zeus and showed him off to the other gods. Everyone was delighted with the child, particularly Dionysus (in whose cortège Pan, who is very similar to Silenus and the Satyrs, frequently appears), and he was given the name Pan because he made them all feel happy. (This is the popular etymology of Pan, derived from the Greek πᾶν meaning all. This etymology was later taken up by the mythographers, and also by philosophers who saw in the god the embodiment of the Universe, the Totality.)

Other genealogies were supplied for Pan. One of the oddest associates him with the cycle of Odysseus legends. It is sometimes said that Penelope did not remain faithful to Odysseus throughout his long absence but took lovers. According to some versions it was Antinous, the most famous of her suitors, who was supposed to have obtained her favours and on his return Odysseus sent his wife back to her father Icarius; she then went on to Mantinea, where she coupled with Hermes and gave birth to Pan. Other versions say that all the suitors made love to Penelope by turns and that the product of this multiple copulation was the god Pan. When Odysseus came home, in his sorrow at finding his wife unfaithful he decided to go away again and seek new adventures.

Pan was also said to be a son of Zeus and Hybris or of Zeus and Callisto. In the latter version he is the twin brother of Arcas, the eponymous hero of Arcadia. Sometimes he is made out to be the son of Aether and the nymph Oenoe; or of Cronus and Rhea, of Uranus and Ge or simply of a shepherd called Crathis and a nanny-goat.

Pan loved the nymph Echo and the goddess Selene. He obtained the favours of the latter by giving her a present of a herd of white oxen.

At Rome he is sometimes identified in the Palatine legends with the god Faunus or more generally with the woodland god Silvanus.

A legend recorded by Plutarch says that around the period of Augustus' reign a sailor at sea heard mysterious voices announcing the death of the Great Pan.

Panacea (Πανάκεια) A goddess who symbolizes the power of universal healing through herbs. She is said to be one of the daughters of Asclepius and LAMPETIA, who was herself a daughter of Helios. She had two sisters, Iaso (the Healer) and Hygieia, and two brothers, Machaon and Polarius.

Pancratis (Παγκράτις) The daughter of Aloeus and Iphimedia and therefore a sister of the Aloadae (see Table 10). While worshipping Dionysus she and her mother were abducted by Thracians, invading from the base they had established on Naxos (then called Strangyle, the Round Island), who were short of women. Their two main chieftains, Sicelus and Hegetorus (or, according to Parthenius, Scellis and Cassamenus) fought each other for the possession of Pancratis, who was remarkably beautiful. Both men died. Pancratis then fell to the king of the Naxiot Thracians, Agassamenus. Shortly afterwards the Aloadae organized a punitive expedition against Naxos, but Pancratis died soon after being rescued by her brothers.

Pandareus (Πανδάρεως) A number of obsure myths, apparently coming from Crete and Asia Minor, are attached to the name of Pandareus. The oldest testimony to them is a story recorded in the *Odyssey*.

The first episode is known to Antoninus Liberalis and the *scholia* of the *Odyssey*. When Rhea, fearing that Cronus would eat the baby Zeus, hid him in a mountain cave in Crete, she gave him a nanny-goat to suckle him and a magic golden dog to guard him. Once Cronus had been dethroned, the goat was transformed into a constellation and the dog was assigned to guarding the sanctuary of Zeus on Crete. But Pandareus, the son of Merops, stole the dog away and took it to Mount Sipyle in Lydia. He entrusted it to Tantalus and went away. When he returned he asked Tantalus for his dog, but Tantalus swore on oath that he had never seen it. Zeus then intervened; he changed Pandareus into a rock, as a punishment for his theft, and buried Tantalus under Mount Sipyle to punish him for perjury.

Another version goes as follows. The dog had been entrusted to Tantalus, but it was Hermes who came to fetch it for Zeus, and it was to Hermes that Tantalus swore that he had never seen the dog. Hermes, however, managed to find the animal. Zeus then punished Tantalus as in the version of the story recounted above. As for Pandareus, he was said to have been afraid when he learned what had happened to Tantalus and to have fled with his wife Harmothoe, and his daughters. He went first to Athens and from there to Sicily. But Zeus killed both him and his wife; his daughters were abducted by the Harpies.

It is in the context of the fate of the daughters of Pandareus that the *Odyssey* refers to this myth. When she was in despair one day Penelope wished that she could die swiftly, like the daughters of Pandareus. After the death of their parents these girls had no one in the world to help them. The gods were sorry for them and decided to take them under their protection. Aphrodite brought them food, Hera gave them wisdom and beauty, Artemis endowed them with elegance, and Athena equipped them with manual dexterity. Just as their education was nearly complete Aphrodite returned to Olympus to ask Zeus to find them suitable husbands, and in the brief period of her absence the Harpies swooped on the girls, carried them off and gave them as slaves to the Erinyes in the Underworld.

Traditions vary as to the number and names of the daughters of Pandareus; sometimes there are two: Camiro and Clytie, or Cleothera and Merope. Sometimes there are three: Cleothera, Merope and Aedon. This last name links the myth of Pandareus, in the form in which it appears in the *Odyssey*, with the Milesian story of the Swallow and the Nightingale in which Aedon and Chelidon (their names are those of the two birds) are the daughters of a Pandareus who had received from Demeter the gift of never having a stomach disorder no matter how much he ate. (For this legend see AEDON.)

Pandarus (Πάνδαρος) The leader of a troop sent by the Lycians of the Troad to help Priam. He came from the city of Zeleia and was son of an old man called Lycaon (see CARCABUS). Apollo himself had taught him archery. (Virgil makes him the brother of another archer, Eurytion.) Despite his father's advice, Pandarus went to Troy as a foot soldier, refusing (out of parsimony) to take a chariot and horses. During the truce between Trojans and Greeks, when Paris and Menelaus were fighting in single combat, the goddess Athena, disguised as the Trojan Laodocus, incited Pandarus to fire an arrow at Menelaus. In this way the truce was broken and the war restored. Pandarus then fought Diomedes but was killed. His death was thought to be punishment for his treachery in breaking the truce.

Pandion (Πανδίων) The name of two kings of the dynasty of Erichthonius at Athens.
1. The first is the son of Erichthonius and Praxithea (see Table 11), a Naiad. He married his maternal aunt, Zeuxippe, and had two sons and two daughters by her: Erechtheus, Butes, Procne and Philomela. He was also credited with a bastard called Oeneus (not the same as the Calydonian hero), the eponymous hero of the Attic tribe of that name. To his reign was dated the arrival in Attica of Dionysus and Demeter.

Pandion played a role in the legend of Philomela and Procne. It was he who arranged Procne's marriage with Tereus, the king of Thrace, in exchange for a treaty by which Tereus committed himself to helping Pandion in his battles with the Thebans of Labdacus. Pandion was supposed to have died of grief as a result of the misfortunes of his daughters (see PHILOMELA). After Pandion's death power was divided between Erechtheus and Butes. The first received the throne, the second the priesthood.
2. The second king of Athens to be called Pandion was the great-grandson of the preceding one (see Table 11). His father was the second Cecrops, the son of Erechtheus and Praxithea, while his mother was Metiadusa, daughter of Eupalamus. He inherited the throne from his father and was the eighth king of Attica. It was during his reign that Orestes arrived there, having been purged of the stain of his mother's death, and it was to this event that tradition attached Pandion's introduction of the Festival of the Jugs during the Anthesteria. (This anecdote is sometimes assigned to the reign of Demophon, which accords better with the standard chronology since Demophon, son of Theseus, belonged to the generation of the Trojan war and was intermediate in age between Agamemnon and Orestes. It was said that Pandion II was driven from his throne by a rebellion of his cousins, the sons of Metion and fled to Megara, to the court of King Pylas, who gave him his daughter Pylia in marriage. When Pylas in his turn was forced to leave Megara the throne of that city passed to Pandion. (Some accounts date his marriage to Pylia to before the rebellion of Metion and his sons.) By Pylia Pandion had four sons Aegeus, Pallas, Nisus and Lycus.
3. Finally, yet another Pandion was one of the sons of Phineus and Cleopatra. With his brother, Plexippus, he was falsely vilified by his stepmother and blinded by his father.

Pandocus (Πάνδοκος) The father of Palaestra. He was killed by Hermes.

Pandora being created from clay and water and rising from the ground, with Hephaestus beside her. Hermes stands on the left side, holding the germ of falsehood in his hand. Attic red-figure volute-crater, c 450 BC. Oxford, Ashmolean Museum.

Pandora (Πανδώρα)

1. In Hesiodic mythology Pandora was the first woman, created by Hephaestus and Athena, with the help of all the other gods on the instructions of Zeus. Each god and goddess endowed her with a special quality – beauty, grace, dexterity, cogency, etc. Hephaestus' bequests were lying and deceit. Pandora was fashioned in the image of the immortal goddesses, and Zeus destroyed her for the punishment of the human race, to which Prometheus had just given divine fire. Pandora was the gift of the gods to men, designed to bring them misfortune.

In the *Works and Days* Hesiod recounts that Zeus sent Pandora to Epimetheus who, forgetting his brother's advice that he should accept no present from Zeus, was seduced by her beauty and made her his wife. Now Epimetheus had a large earthenware pot, covered with a lid, which contained all evils and one good: hope. Pandora had hardly reached Earth when, overcome with curiosity she lifted the lid of the pot and released all the ills in the world. Only hope, which was at the bottom, was trapped in the pot when Pandora replaced the lid. Other versions of the legend say that the pot contained not all the world's evils but every blessing, and that Pandora had brought it to Epimetheus as a wedding present from Zeus. By opening it carelessly she let all the good things escape and return to the heavens instead of staying among mankind. That is why men are afflicted with every form of evil: only hope, a poor consolation, is left to them.

2. For Pandora, the daughter of Erichtheus; see HYACINTHIDS.

Pandorus (Πάνδωρος) One of the sons of Erichtheus and Praxithea (see Table 11). He was said to have founded the city of Chalchis in Euboea.

Pandrosus (Πάνδροσος) One of the three daughters of Cecrops by Aglaurus, herself daughter of the first eponym of Attica, Actaeus (see Table 4). With her two sisters, Aglaurus (or Agraulus) 2 and Herse, she committed the crime of opening the basket in which Athena had hidden the little Erichthonius. Her punishment was death. (In some accounts a fourth sister, Phoenice, shared in the crime.)

Pandrosus is said to have been the first woman to spin. She was worshipped on the Acropolis and apparently had her own Mysteries.

Pangaeus (Παγγαῖος) A Thracian hero, son of Ares and Critobule. Having unintentionally raped his own daughter he ran himself through with his sword on a mountain, which in memory of him took the name of Mount Pangaeus.

Panides (Πανίδης) King of Chalchis in Euboea and brother to King Amphidamas, at whose funeral games Homer and Hesiod were supposed to have competed against each other. Panides wanted to give the prize to Hesiod whose poetry, being devoted to agriculture, he found more useful than Homer's which talked only of fighting and warfare. But the public rejected Panides' judgement, and the prize went to Homer. A judgement showing lack of taste was commonly called 'a judgement of Panides'.

Panopeus (Πανοπεύς) The eponymous hero of the city of Panopeus in eastern Phocis. Through his father Phocus he belonged to the race of Aeacus, and through his mother Asteria to the descendants of Deucalion via Xuthus (see Tables 8 and 30). He had a twin brother, Crisus, for whom he felt implacable hatred; the two were said to have fought while still at their mother's breast. Panopeus went with Amphitryon on the expedition against the Taphians and swore by Athena and Ares not to help himself to any of the plunder. But he broke his oath and was punished for his perjury through his son Epeius who, though a courageous wrestler, was a poor warrior. Epeius took part in the Trojan War and was the builder of the wooden horse.

Panopeus appears in Sophocles' *Electra* (where he is called Pharoteus); he sided with Aegisthus, whereas Pylades, his great-nephew, was on the side of Orestes. Thus the old hatred between Panopeus and Crisus persisted among their descendants.

Panthous (Πάνθοος) In the *Iliad* Panthous appears as one of the elderly Trojan companions of Priam. He had three sons, Hyperenor, Euphorbus and Polydamas. His wife was Phrontis. It was said that Panthous came from Delphi and had been initiated into the worship of Apollo. According to this legend, when Troy was first captured (by Heracles), Priam sent an envoy to consult the Delphic oracle and the deputation returned bringing Panthous to establish lasting relations between Troy and Delphi. In another version of the story Priam's envoy was said to have been one of the sons of Antenor, who fell in love with Panthous, a priest of Apollo at Delphi. He ravished him and abducted him to Troy. To recompense Panthous Priam made him high priest of Apollo at Troy. He was killed during the capture of the city.

Paphos (Πάφος)
1. In certain traditions Paphos was a Nymph of the city of that name who mated with Apollo and bore Cinyras (see also Pygmalion).
2. Paphos was also a man, the son of Cephalus and Eos and founder of the city of Paphos in Cyprus. He was the father of Cinyras.

Paraebius (Παραίβιος) An inhabitant of the Bosporus district of Thrace, not far from the kingdom of Phineus. Paraebius' father had committed sacrilege by cutting down a pine tree sacred to the Hamadryads although they had begged him to spare it. The Nymphs punished him by condemning him and his son to poverty. But Phineus told Paraebius that he could overcome the curse if he built an altar and made expiatory sacrifical offerings to the Nymphs. This Paraebius did, and the curse was brought to an end. Out of gratitude Paraebius remained one of Phineus' most faithful servants.

Paralus (Πάραλος) An Athenian hero who was supposed to have invented warships. It was in his honour that the official Athenian trireme was called the *Paralos*.

Parcae The three Roman goddesses of Destiny, identified with the Greek Moirai, whose attributes they gradually assumed. In Roman mythology the Parcae were originally the attendant spirits of childbirth, but this primitive trait was soon lost as they became assimilated to the Moirai. They were depicted as spinning thread and measuring out, at whim, the lifespan of all men. Like the Moirai, they were sisters. One presided over birth, one over marriage and the third over death. In the Forum the statues of the three Parcae are popularly called the Three Fates (the *tria Fata* or Destinies).

Paris (Πάρις) The youngest son of Priam and Hecuba who was also called Alexander. His birth was preceded by an omen. Hecuba, at the beginning of her labour, saw herself in a dream giving birth to a torch which set fire to the citadel of Troy. Priam asked Aesacus (his son by another wife, Arisbe) what this dream meant. Aesacus warned him that the child about to be born would cause the destruction of Troy and advised Priam to have it killed at birth. (For another tradition, see HECUBA.) Instead of killing the child Hecuba abandoned him on Mount Ida.

Paris was reared by shepherds who found him and gave him the name of Alexander ('the Protector' or 'the Protected') because he had not died on the mountainside. A variant of the tradition claims that the infant Paris was left out to die on the mountainside by a servant of Priam named Agelaus, and on the king's orders. For five days a female bear came to suckle the child and when Agelaus found Paris still alive at the end of this period, he took the child in and brought him up. Under Agelaus' care Paris developed into a young man of great beauty and courage. He protected his flocks against thieves, thus earning himself the name Alexander by which he was also known. A third legend has it that Priam, misled by an oracle, ordered the death of Munnippus, son of Cilla, in his son's place, thinking that it was Munnippus whom Hecuba's dream had indicated as destined to bring ruin to his city.

Paris returned to Troy and his identity was revealed as follows. One day some of Priam's servants went to fetch a bull of which Paris was particularly fond from the herd that he was guarding. Knowing that the animal was destined to be the prize at the funeral games which had been instituted in memory of Priam's son, who was supposed to have died at an early age (i.e. none other than himself), Paris followed the servants back to the city. He decided to take part in the games himself and to win back his favourite animal. He won all the events, in competition with his own brothers, who did not know who he was. In anger one of them, Deiphobus, drew his sword on Paris and tried to kill him. Paris then sought refuge at the altar of Zeus, where his sister Cassandra the prophetess recognized him; and Priam, happy to be reunited with the son whom he had thought dead, welcomed him and restored to him his proper place in the royal household. In some versions Paris' identity was revealed not through a miraculous act of Cassandra's but through a deliberate move on Paris' part. Having brought with him the garments which he was wearing when he was abandoned, he had no difficulty in proving his identity.

The second episode of the legend of Paris is that of the Judgement out of which the Trojan War was to grow. When the gods met for the wedding of Peleus and Thetis, Eris (Strife) threw a golden apple into their midst, saying that it should be the prize of the most beautiful among three goddesses: Athene, Hera and Aphrodite. An argument arose. No one wanted to take on the task of choosing between the three goddesses. Zeus therefore instructed Hermes to take the three of them to Mount Ida so that Paris could judge. When he saw the goddesses approaching Paris was frightened

Hermes rehearsing Hera, Athena and Aphrodite before Paris arrives to judge the goddesses. Apulian red-figure bell-crater, name-vase of the Rehearsal Painter, c. 375–350 BC. Oxford, Ashmolean Museum.

and tried to run away. But Hermes persuaded him that he had nothing to fear and put the matter to him, ordering him to assume the role of judge, in the name of Zeus. One after another each goddess put her case to him. Each promised him protection and special gifts if he declared in her favour: Hera guaranteed to make him ruler of all Asia; Athene promised him wisdom and victory in all combats, but Aphrodite offered him the love of Helen of Sparta. Paris awarded the golden apple to Aphrodite.

The poets embroidered at will on this theme, which was also taken up by sculptors and painters. Paris was depicted as a shepherd in a woodland setting beside a fountain. Sceptical mythographers sometimes stated that Paris was the dupe of three village maidens wanting proof of their beauty or that he dreamed the whole thing while he was alone with his flocks on the mountainside.

Until the arrival of the goddesses and the Judgement, Paris had loved a Nymph named Oenone. When Aphrodite promised him Helen's love – Helen being the most beautiful of mortal women – he abandoned Oenone and left for Sparta. According to one tradition, he was accompanied on this trip by Aeneas who had been instructed to go with him by Aphrodite herself. In vain did Hecuba and Cassandra predict the outcome of the escapade; no one believed them. When they reached the Peloponnese, Aeneas and Paris were welcomed by Helen's brothers, the Dioscuri, who took them to Menelaus, her husband. Menelaus received them hospitably and introduced them to Helen. Then he himself left for Crete to attend the funeral of Catreus, entrusting the well-being of his guests to his wife, who was told to entertain them at Sparta for as long as they cared to stay.

Soon Paris won Helen's love. He was helped in his seduction by the presents that he lavished on her, by the oriental luxury with which he was surrounded, and by his beauty, which had been enhanced by his protectress, Aphrodite. Helen gathered all the valuables she could lay hands on and eloped with Paris during the night, leaving behind her nine-year-old daughter Hermione. (For their adventures on the voyage from Sparta to Asia Minor, and the various highly differing versions of the legend, see HELEN.)

When he got back to Troy, Paris was very well received by Priam and the whole royal house, despite the dark prophecies of Cassandra.

During the Trojan War itself Paris played an undistinguished role. At the beginning of the *Iliad* the Greeks and Trojans agreed to settle the affair by a single combat between Paris and Menelaus. Paris was defeated and only saved from death by the protection of Aphrodite, who hid him in a thick cloud. Shortly afterwards the battle recommenced. Later, when Paris was absent from the fighting, Hector came to fetch him from Helen's side and ordered him to join the battle. Paris obeyed, killed Menestheus, wounded Diomedes, Machaon and Eurypylus and took part in the attack on the Greek trenches. He killed Euchenor and Deiocus.

The *Iliad* sometimes depicts Paris as wearing heavy armour (cuirass, round shield, spear and sword), but he is usually said to be an archer, and it was as an archer that he played a role in the death of Achilles, the last great episode in the Paris legend before his own death. It was predicted by Hector with his dying breath. When, after killing Memnon, Achilles forced the Trojans to withdraw to the very walls of the city, Paris stopped him with an arrow which wounded the only vulnerable part of his body, his heel. But though the arrow was fired by Paris its path was guided by Apollo himself. Another version says that the archer was not Paris at all, but Apollo, disguised as Paris. Later, when the episode of the love of Achilles and Polyxena was developed, it was said that Achilles was inclined to betray the Greeks for the love of this girl and was even prepared to fight on the Trojan side. The Trojans were therefore able to lure him into an ambush where Paris killed him. The ambush took place in the temple of Thymbraean Apollo, while Paris hid behind a statue of the god. This story was used to explain Hector's dying prophecy that his enemy would be slain by Paris and Apollo together.

Paris himself was killed by one of Philoctetes' arrows which pierced his groin. He was carried off the battlefield mortally wounded and sent to Oenone, who had the gift of healing, for an antidote to the poison with which Philoctetes' arrows were tipped. But Oenone initially refused to save the man who had abandoned her; by the time she took pity on him it was too late.

Parnassus (Παρνασσός) The eponymous hero of Mount Parnassus, which was sacred to Apollo. He was said to be the son by Poseidon of a Nymph named Cleodora. He was also attributed a mortal father named Cleopompus. Parnassus was supposed to have founded the old oracle of Python, which was later occupied by Apollo. He also invented divination by birds.

Parrhasius (Παρράσιος) An Arcadian hero, the son of Lycaon, or alternatively of Zeus, and the father of Arcas, who gave his name to the region. He was supposed to have founded the Arcadian city of Parrhasia. Plutarch records that the Nymph Phylonome, daughter of Nyctimus and Arcadia, had twins by Ares and because she was afraid of her father, abandoned them on Mount Erymanthe. But a she-wolf suckled the two babies, who were later found and taken in by the shepherd Tyliphus. He gave them the names Lycastus and Parrhasius and brought them up as his own sons. Later the twins seized power in Arcadia. There is a clear parallel between this legend, which is probably a late one, and that of Romulus and Remus.

Parsondes (Παρσώνδης) A Persian, and the hero of a strange adventure. He was a brave warrior and fearless hunter, and the favourite of Artaeus, king of the Medes. He several times asked the king to give him the place of the satrap of Babylon, an effeminate fellow named Nanerus, but Artaeus always refused. Eventually Nanerus learned of Parsondes' intentions and decided to take his revenge. He promised a reward for the capture of Parsondes. One day Parsondes lost his way while hunting near Babylon and met some of Nanerus' retinue. They gave him too much to drink, persuaded him to spend the night with them and, when he had fallen asleep, chained him up and delivered him to his enemy. Nanerus handed Parsondes to his eunuchs, so that they could shave him and force him to live the life of a woman in the harem. Parsondes soon learned to play the cithara, dance and adorn himself, and he became one of the satrap's wives. He led this life for seven years, at the end of which he managed to get a message to King Artaeus who had believed him dead. When he learned that his favourite was alive Artaeus sent an embassy to Nanerus to demand Parsondes' freedom. Nanerus declared that he did not know the latter's whereabouts, but when threatened with death by Artaeus, he eventually handed over Parsondes, who had become so like a woman that the king's envoy had the greatest difficulty in recognizing him among Nanerus' 150 wives.

When Parsondes returned to the court of Artaeus, he demanded vengeance, for he said it was the hope of revenge which had kept him going during his long and debasing captivity. Artaeus promised to punish Nanerus, but the latter contrived to corrupt the king with bribes, and Artaeus eventually refused justice to Parsondes.

Parsondes left the Medean court and fled, at the head of 3,000 men, to the land of the Cadusians, for his sister had married one of the most powerful lords of that region. War broke out. Thanks to his skill Parsondes was victorious, the Cadusians made him their king and from that time on there was constant warfare between the Medes and the Cadusians. On Parsondes' death his successor, who had sworn to him never to make peace with his enemies, pursued the same policy. This went on until Cyrus conquered the Cadusians and forced them to become part of his empire.

Parthenopaeus (Παρθενοπαῖος) One of the Seven who marched against Thebes, described sometimes as an Arcadian, sometimes as an Argive. In the first version he was a son of Atalanta, but traditions vary as to the true identity of his father. According to some he was an illegitimate son of Meleager; others claim that he was a legitimate son of Melanion. In the tradition which makes him an Argive, he was the brother of Adrastus and, like him, son of Talaus, and Lysimache (see Tables 1 and 26).

It was said that he was abandoned as an infant with Telephus, accompanied him to Mysia, and then took part in the expedition against Idas (a legend recorded only by Hyginus). In Mysia he married the Nymph Clymene, by whom he had a son, Tlesimenes or Promachus or Stratolaus, who took part in the expedition of the Epigoni.

His name (reminiscent of *parthenos* 'virgin') derived, in the Arcadian version, from the long period during which his mother preserved her virginity. In the Argive version he owed it to having been abandoned in infancy on Mount Parthenion.

Parthenopaeus was both handsome and brave. He took part in the expedition of the Seven, contrary to the advice of Atalanta who foretold that he would thereby die a violent death. At the games held at Nemea in honour of Archemorus-Opheltes (see AMPHIARAUS) he won the archery contest. He was killed before the walls of Thebes by Periclymenus, a son of Poseidon, or by Asphodicus or Amphidicus, according to other sources. Last, Statius follows a tradition according to which it was Dryas, the grandson of Orion, who mortally wounded Parthenopaeus.

Parthenope (Παρθενόπη) One of the Sirens, whose tomb was said to be in Naples. With her sisters she threw herself into the sea; her body was cast up by the waves onto the Neapolitan shore, and a monument was raised to her there.

According to another version of the legend Parthenope was a beautiful girl, a native of Phrygia, who fell in love with Metiochus but did not wish to break the vow of chastity which she had made. To punish herself for her passion she cut off her hair and went into voluntary exile in Campagna, where she dedicated herself to Dionysus. In anger Aphrodite turned her into a Siren.

Parthenos (Παρθένος) The name of several heroines.

1. One of them was a daughter of Staphylus and Chrysothemis. Her sisters were Rhoeo and Molpadia. Staphylus entrusted Molpadia and Parthenos the task of looking after his wine (which was still a recent innovation). But the two girls fell asleep and while they were slumbering the pigs which they were guarding found their way into Staphylus' cellar and broke all the earthenware jars which contained the wine. When the girls awoke and discovered what had happened, in fear of their father's anger, for they knew him to be a pitiless man they fled to the seashore and threw themselves off the top of the rocks into the sea. Apollo, out of affection for them, gathered them up as they fell and bore them away to cities in the Chersonnese, Parthenos went to Boubastos, where she received divine honours, and Molpadia to Castabos, where she was worshipped under the name of HEMITHEA.

2. Parthenos is also the name of the heroine who became the constellation Virgo. Traditions vary as to her identity. One version gives her as the daughter of Apollo and Chrysotherus. She died young and was changed into a constellation by her father. Another version makes her the daughter of Zeus and Themis and identifies her with Dike (Justice), who lived on earth during the Golden Age. This tradition is represented in particular by Virgil, who in *Eclogue* IV sees in the return of the constellation of Virgo a presage of the coming of an age of justice. She was also said to be the daughter of Astreus and Hemera or of Icarius (in which case she was identified with Erigone). Alternatively she was identified with Demeter herself or with Thespia, one of the daughters of the river god Asopus and eponym of Thespiae in Boeotia.

Pasiphae (Πασιφάη) The wife of Minos (see Table 28) and daughter of Helios and Perseis (see Table 14). Her brothers were Perses and Aeetes, king of Colchis, and her sister the enchantress Circe. The most famous Pasiphae legend is set in Crete and concerns her bestial love affair with a bull. The story went that Minos, when reclaiming the Cretan throne, had asked the gods for a sign of the justice of his claim. He made a sacrifice to Poseidon and prayed to the god to send a bull from the sea, promising in return that he would sacrifice it. But when Poseidon granted his prayer Minos refused to fulfil his part of the bargain. To punish him, Poseidon afflicted the bull with madness and later inspired Pasiphae with an irresistible passion for the animal. But this passion was also said to be the revenge of Aphrodite either because Pasiphae had despised the goddess's cult or because Aphrodite was angered by Helios' indiscretion in disclosing to Hephaestus her affair with Ares.

In despair over her love for the bull, Pasiphae sought the help of Daedalus, who constructed a heifer so life-like that the bull was duped. Pasiphae wooed the bull in this disguise and the monstrous coupling took place. The fruit of their mating was the Minotaur, half-man, half-bull. When he found out what had happened Minos was furious with Daedalus and forbade him to leave Crete but Daedalus managed to flee with the complicity of Pasiphae. (For the standard version of the legend of Daedalus and the labyrinth after the victory of Theseus, see DAEDALUS.)

Pasiphae was supposed to be very jealous and to possess great skill as a sorceress, like her sister Circe and her niece Medea, the daughter of Aeetes. To try to prevent Minos from lying with other women, she put a curse on him so that all the women to whom he made love were devoured by the serpents which emerged from all over his body. He was cured of this curse by Procris.

In Laconia there was an oracle of Pasiphae, but it was said that this Pasiphae was actually the Trojan Cassandra or Daphne, or a daughter of Atlas on whom Zeus fathered Ammon, the god of Cyrene, (who was worshipped under the name Zeus-Ammon).

Patroclus (Πάτροκλος) In the *Iliad*, Patroclus was the friend of Achilles. The son of Menoetius, who was himself the son of Aegina and Actor, he was related to Achilles who, through his father Peleus and his grandfather Aeacus, was great-grandson of the same Aegina (see Table 30). (For the name of his mother, see MENOETIUS.) On his father's side Patroclus was a Locrian of Opus. But when he was young he went to Thessaly, to the court of Peleus. The standard explanation is that as a child, in a fit of rage over a game of knucklebones, he killed one of his companions, Clitonymos (or Clisonymos), son of Amphidamas. He then had to go into exile and was given hospitality by Peleus, who accepted him as a companion to his own son, Achilles. The two were brought up together, and together learned the study of medicine. One tradition says that Patroclus was one of the suitors for the hand of Helen, but there is no reason to assume that it was in accordance with the oath made to Tyndareus that he followed his friend to Troy.

The friendship of Patroclus and Achilles was proverbial. Indeed, it was said that the bond between them was deeper than friendship. When Achilles left Mysia to fight Telephus, Patroclus was at his side. With Diomedes he rescued the body of Thersandrus. He was himself wounded by an arrow but was cared for and healed by Achilles.

The exploits of Patroclus before Troy were numerous. He plays a role in all the epic cycles, not just in the *Iliad*. For example, it was he who sold Lycaon, the son of Priam taken prisoner by Achilles at Lemnos. He also took part in the capture of Lyrnessos and in the raid on the island of Scyros. In the *Iliad* he makes several appearances; he restored Briseis to Agamemnon's heralds, and when the embassy of chiefs came to Achilles he stood by his friend. Later, when the Greeks were in difficulty, Achilles sent Patroclus to Nestor for news. There he took care of Eurypylus, who had just been wounded, then returned to Achilles and told him of the critical situation in the Achaean camp. He pressed Achilles to return to the fight or at least to let him, Patroclus, go back and take the Myrmidons with him. Achilles gave him permission to put on his own armour and to join battle. Patroclus wrought havoc among the Trojans. Then when they were in full flight, he was rebuffed by Apollo as he tried to pursue them. He managed to kill Cebrion, Hector's charioteer, but with Apollo's aid Hector himself killed Patroclus. Battle was soon raging between Trojans and Greeks around the body of Patroclus, which his vanquisher stripped of its arms (the divine armour of Achilles). In this long and desperate struggle Menelaus in particular distinguished himself. Antilochus, son of Nestor, told Achilles of the death of his friend and Achilles in his grief went into the thick of battle without his armour. He gave a shout, and, on hearing the voice of the man they most feared, the Trojans fled, leaving Patroclus' body behind.

Achilles, no longer conscious of his resentment against Agamemnon, now thought only of avenging Patroclus. The accounts of the latter's funeral and of the death of Hector comprise the whole of the end of the *Iliad*. The funeral is marked by the sacrifice of twelve young Trojans captured by Achilles beside the Scamander and by the funeral games in which all the Greek leaders took part. Achilles built a tomb to Patroclus on the site of the funeral pyre.

After the death of Achilles, the ashes of the two friends were mingled – though one tradition claimed that Patroclus had survived at Achilles' side, together with Helen, Ajax (son of Telamon) and Antilochus on the White Island in the Danube estuary.

Patron (Πάτρων)

1. A hero named Patron appears in the *Aeneid* where he took part in the funeral games in honour of Anchises. We know from other sources that this figure was an Acarnanian who joined Aeneas during his travels and who eventually settled in Sicily where he founded the city of Alontion.
2. Another hero of this name was a companion of Evander at Rome. As this Patron was willing to give hospitality to people of limited means the Roman custom of patronage was named after him.

Pax

The divine representation of Peace at Rome. Often invoked during the civil wars of the first century BC, she was given an altar by Augustus to sanctify the definitive re-establishment of civil order. Later Vespasian, then Domitian, devoted a temple to her in the Forum, which was named the Forum of Peace in her honour.

Pegasus (Πήγασος)

A winged horse who played a part in several legends, notably those of Perseus and Bellerophon. His name was supposed to be derived from the Greek word for 'spring' (πηγή) and he was said to have been born 'at the springs of the Ocean' (i.e. in the extreme west) at the time of the slaying of the Gorgon by Perseus. Some versions of the legend said that this divine horse had sprung from the Gorgon's neck, in which case he, like Chrysaor who was born at the same time, was the son of Poseidon and the Gorgon. Other versions recorded that he was born of the earth, which was fertilized by the Gorgon's blood. After his birth Pegasus flew up to Olympus and placed himself at the disposal of Zeus to whom he brought thunderbolts.

Versions of the meeting of Bellerophon and Pegasus vary. It was said, for example, that the goddess Athena brought the horse already broken in for Bellerophon to ride, or that Poseidon gave him to the hero, or that Bellerophon found him while he was drinking at the Pirenean spring. Thanks to Pegasus Bellerophon was able to kill the Chimaera and to defeat the Amazons unaided.

After Bellerophon's death Pegasus returned to the gods. During the singing contest between the daughters of Pierus (see PIERIDES) and the Muses, Mount Helicon swelled in pleasure and seemed about to touch the heavens. On Poseidon's order Pegasus struck the mountain with his hoof to instruct it to return to its normal size. Helicon obeyed, but at the spot where Pegasus had struck it there gushed a spring, the Hippocrene or Horse Spring. (A spring at Troezen was also said to have been started by a blow from one of Pegasus' hooves.)

Eventually Pegasus was changed into a constellation. One of his wing feathers fell to earth close to Tarsus giving the city its name.

Peitho (Πειθώ)

1. Persuasion, who usually appears among the troupe of secondary deities who accompany Aphrodite. She is sometimes said to be the daughter of Ate (Error), but other myths, reflecting the civic value of Persuasion, make her the sister of Tyche (Chance) and Eunomia (Good Order) and the daughter of Prometheus.
2. Hesiod mentions a Peitho as one of the daughters of Oceanus and Tethys. She was supposed to have married the first Argos.
3. There is another Peitho in the same Arcadian cycle of legends. She was the wife of Phoroneus and the mother of Aegialeus and Apis.

Pelasgus (Πελασγός)

The name of several heroes who were supposed to have founded the mythical race known as the Pelasgians. These people were said to have occupied Thessaly and the Peloponnese, so heroes of that name are to be found in those two areas.

1. In Arcadian legend there were two distinct genealogies for Pelasgus. One made him the son of Niobe and Zeus (see Table 18). By the Oceanid Meliboea, or by the Nymph Cyllene or by Deianeira he had a son, Lycaon, who in turn had

Antique relief showing Pegasus the winged horse, led by Bellerophon. Rome, Palazzo Spada.

fifty sons, eponymous founders of most of the cities in Arcadia, and one daughter, Callisto, on whom Zeus fathered the hero Arcas, who gave his name to Arcadia itself. An Arcadian legend makes Pelasgus the first man to live in Arcadia: he was supposed to be 'born of the soil' and was the first king of the area. He invented the use of houses, and distinguished between edible and poisonous plants.

2. The second genealogy of Pelasgus is recounted by Pausanias (see Table 17). He is given as the son of Triopas and Sosis (or Sois) and brother of Iasus and Agenor. He is a fourth-generation descendant of Niobe and Zeus and a fifth generation descendant of Phoroneus. This Pelasgus was really Argive, not Arcadian. He offered hospitality to the goddess Demeter when she came in search of her daughter and built the temple of Demeter Pelasgis in her honour. This Pelasgus had a daughter, Larissa, who gave her name to the citadel at Argos.

3. Thessalian legend tells of another Pelasgus who was Larissa's son by Poseidon (see Table 17). He had two brothers, Achaeus and Phthius, with whom he left the Peloponnese, his native region, and took over Thessaly which was then called Haemonia. They drove the natives from the area and divided it into three parts, each named after the brother who appropiated it. Five generations later the descendants of the conquering trio were driven out in their turn by the Curetes and the Leleges (see LELEX). After other vicissitudes some of these Pelasgians emigrated to Italy.

Peleus (Πηλεύς) King of Phthia in Thessaly, who was famous principally as the father of Achilles. He himself was the son of Aeacus and Endeis, daughter of Sciron. In standard accounts he was the brother of Telamon and half-brother of Phocus, the son of Aeacus by the Nereid Psamathe (see Table 30), but the mythographers noted that even in Antiquity Telamon was not universally considered to be Peleus' brother. Sometimes the two were said to be friends, in which case Telamon was the son of Actaeus and Glauce.

Telamon and Peleus who were jealous of Phocus' physical skills, decided to kill him and drew lots to see which of them should carry out the murder. The task fell to Telamon, who slew Phocus by throwing a discus at his head. Some versions present the murder as accidental or claim that the culprit was Peleus. Whatever the truth, Aeacus discovered the murder and banished both Peleus and Telamon from Aegina. Telamon went to Salamis; Peleus went to the court of Eurytion, son of Actor, at Phthia in Thessaly. Eurytion purified him of the murder, gave him his daughter Antigone in marriage and handed over to him a third of the kingdom. By Antigone Peleus had a daughter, Polydora, who married Borus, the son of Perieres.

Even at Phthia Peleus was pursued by the anger of Phocus' mother, Psamathe, who sent a wolf to prey on his flocks, though at the request of Thetis she agreed to change the wolf into a stone statue.

With Eurytion Peleus took part in the hunting of the Calydonian boar but accidentally killed his father-in-law. Again he had to go into exile. This time he sought refuge at Iolcos, at the court of Acastus, the son of Pelias who purified him. There he had an adventure which nearly cost him his life. Astydamia, Acastus' wife, fell in love with him. He rejected her advances so, to get her own back, she sent a message to Antigone, Peleus' wife, telling her that Peleus was about to marry Sterope, Acastus' daughter. (This was a lie.) In despair Antigone hanged herself. Then Astydamia accused Peleus, before Acastus, of trying to rape her. Not daring to kill his guest, whom he had purified of a murder and with whom he therefore had ties of a religious nature, Acastus took Peleus out hunting with him on Mount Pelion. During the hunt Peleus merely cut out the tongues of the animals he killed, while the other huntsmen bagged their game. His companions mocked him, declaring that they had done all the work themselves, but Peleus proved his skill and courage by showing them the tongues. In the evening Peleus fell asleep from exhaustion on the mountainside. Acastus abandoned him there, having first hidden his sword in a dung heap. When he awoke and looked for his sword Peleus found himself surrounded by Centaurs who would have killed him had not one of them, Chiron, given him back his weapon which he had taken from its hiding place. (Another version said that the sword was sent to him by Hephaestus at the critical moment.)

Later Peleus took a cruel revenge on Acastus and Astydamia. With the help of Jason and the Dioscuri, he captured the city of Iolcos, killed Acastus and chopped Astydamia into pieces which he scattered all over the town.

Peleus then married Thetis, the daughter of Nereus. Zeus and Poseidon had been rivals for her hand, but Themis (or Prometheus) warned them that the Parcae had ordained that the son of Thetis would be more powerful than his father. At once the two gods abandoned their courtship and plans were made for marrying Thetis to a mortal, since they themselves would then be unaffected by the fulfilling of the prophecy. Slightly different versions claim that Prometheus told Zeus that if Thetis bore him a son the boy would dethrone him and rule the heavens in his stead; or that Thetis refused to sleep with Zeus out of regard for Hera, who had brought her up, and that in his anger Zeus decided to marry her to a mortal as a punishment. Thetis refused at first. As a sea-goddess she had the gift of taking any shape she pleased, so she adopted a number of disguises: she was transformed into fire, water, wind, a tree, a bird, a tiger, a lion, a snake and finally a cuttle fish. Peleus, who had been advised by Chiron, held on to her firmly, and eventually she became a goddess and woman again. The marriage took place on Mount Pelion. The gods were present; the Muses sang the epithalamium and each brought a gift for the newly-weds. Among the most remarkable of the presents were an ash-wood spear given by Chiron and two immortal horses, Balius and Xanthus, donated by Poseidon. (These horses turn up again later, harnessed to the chariot of Achilles.)

The marriage was not a success. Thetis bore Peleus some children, it is true, but one after another perished as she attempted to make them immortal. When Peleus tried to save Achilles, the youngest child, by snatching him from the fire into which Thetis was plunging him, she fled and thereafter obstinately refused to return.

In his old age, and while Achilles was at Troy, Peleus was attacked by Archandrus and Architeles, the sons of Acastus, just as the war was ending. Driven out of Phthia, he fled to the island of Cos, where he met his grandson Neoptolemus. There he was given hospitality by Molon, a descendant of Abas, and there he died. In another version, represented by Euripides' *Andromache*, Peleus outlived Neopolemus and intervened on Andromache's behalf in the ploys of Hermione (see MOLOSSUS). Perhaps it is to this tradition that we can attach the episode, recorded by Dictys Cretensis, in which Neoptolemus rescued Peleus, who had been imprisoned by the sons of Acastus, and gave him back his kingdom before he himself was killed by Orestes at Delphi.

Peleus also plays a part, though a secondary one, in the cyclic legends such as the adventures of the Argonauts, the expedition of Heracles against Troy (in which he accompanied his brother Telamon) and the Amazon War which is connected with that expedition. He also appears among the contestants at the funeral games held in honour of Pelias. He was defeated in the wrestling competition by ATALANTA.

Pelias (Πελιάς) A son of Tyro by Poseidon or the river god Eripeus whose shape Poseidon had assumed; his twin brother was Neleus. His 'human' father was Cretheus. His half-brothers were Aeson (the father of Jason), Pheres and Amythaon (see Table 21). Tyro kept the birth of her twin sons a secret and abandoned them. Some horse dealers happened to pass the spot where they lay and after a mare had accidentally kicked one of the babies, leaving a purple mark (*pelion*) on his face, the horse dealers rescued and cared for the twins.

Other versions of the legend record that the twins were suckled by a mare. (The horse was sacred to Poseidon.) This was the tradition followed by Sophocles in his last tragedy *Tyro*, in which the twins were taken in by a shepherd and later recognized by Tyro because of the wooden coffer in which they had been left. They then rescued Tyro from Sidero, their step-mother who was ill-treating her. Sidero took refuge at the altar of Hera and Pelias entered the sacred enclosure in pursuit of her and killed her there, spurning the divine power of the goddess, whom thereafter he continued to treat impiously. It was this impiety that eventually brought about his downfall, though after a long life.

Pelias and Neleus fought each other to determine who should rule Thessaly. Neleus, driven out by his brother, withdrew to Pylos in Messenia and Pelias stayed in Thessaly, at Iolcos, and married Anaxibia, the daughter of Bias (or, alternatively, Philomache, the daughter of Amphion). By her he had a son Acastus and four daughters Pisidice, Pelopia, Hippothoe and Alcestis.

One day Pelias decided to make a sacrifice to Poseidon on the seashore and summoned a large number of his subjects, including his nephew Jason, to attend the ceremony. When Jason learned of the king's summons he hurried off to attend the ceremony, but in crossing a river he lost one of his sandals. Now on one occasion when Pelias had consulted the Delphic oracle he had been warned to beware a man who came to him wearing only one shoe. When Pelias saw Jason arrive he remembered the oracle and, going up to Jason, asked him what he would do, if he were king, to a man whom he knew was destined to overthrow him. Jason replied that he would send him off in quest of the Golden Fleece. Perhaps it was Hera who dictated the answer to him, since she planned to bring the enchantress Medea to Iolcos in order to arrange the death of Pelias. Be that as it may, Pelias took Jason at his word and sent him to find the Golden Fleece (for which see ARGONAUTS).

Pelias, thinking that he had got rid of his nephew for good and had made sure of his own position as ruler, next killed his half-brother Aeson. The latter asked to be allowed to choose how he should die and poisoned himself by drinking bull's blood. Alcimede, Jason's mother, put a curse on Pelias and hanged herself leaving a young son, Promachus, whom Pelias also killed. At this point, four months after his departure, Jason returned. Although anxious to avenge the deaths of his parents and his brother he concealed his intentions and went to Corinth where he plotted with Medea how to punish Pelias.

Medea went to the court of Iolcos and persuaded Pelias' daughters that she was able to restore their father's youth to him, for he was beginning to show his age. To prove to them that she possessed this gift she carved up an old ram, boiled the pieces in a cauldron with magic herbs and, after a certain time had elapsed, produced a young lamb. Without further hesitation the daughters of Pelias carved up their father and boiled the pieces, following the recipe given to them by Medea. (According to tradition, only Alcestis was constrained by filial piety and refused to take part.) But the king did not revive. Overcome with horror at the crime they had committed his daughters went into voluntary exile. They fled to Arcadia, and in the time of Pausanias their tomb could be seen near the temple of Poseidon at Mantinea. Another version records that they married: they were not considered guilty since they had been merely the instruments of Medea's crime.

Acastus, Pelias' son, gathered up his father's remains and gave him a solemn funeral, including the games which were to remain famous. Hyginus has preserved for us the list of the winners, which includes Calais and Zetes, the Boreades; Castor and Pollux, the Dioscuri; Telamon and Peleus, the sons of Aeacus; Heracles; Meleager, who won the javelin throwing; Cycnus, son of Ares; Bellerophon, who won the horse race; Iolaus, son of Iphicles, who won the chariot race, beating Glaucus, son of Sisyphus; Eurytus, the son of Hermes, who won the archery contest; Cephalus, son of Deion, who won the sling throwing;

Olympus, the pupil of Marsyas, who took the flute prize and Orpheus who won the prize for the lyre; Linus, son of Apollo, who won the singing competition, and Eumolpus, son of Poseidon, who won the prize for accompanied song (with Olympus as his accompanist). To this list is sometimes added the name of Atalanta who was supposed to have beaten Peleus in the wrestling.

After the murder of his father Acastus outlawed Jason and Medea from the kingdom of Iolcos.

Pelopia (Πελόπεια)

1. The mother of Aegisthus, whom Pelopia bore as the result of involuntary incest with her own father Thyestes. She lived at Sicyon, at the court of King Thesprotus. While pregnant with Aegisthus Pelopia married Atreus (see Table 2). It was through Aegisthus that Thyestes was finally avenged on Atreus.
2. Another Pelopia was one of the daughters of Pelias and Anaxibia) see Table 21). She had a son, CYCNUS, by the god ARES.

Pelops (Πέλοψ)

1. The son of Tantalus (see Table 2). His mother is sometimes given as Clytia, sometimes Euryanassa, Eurysthanassa, Eurythemiste, etc., whose father is identified as a river-god of Asia, Pactolus or Xanthus (the river in the Troad). Being a son of Tantalus, Pelops was a native of Asia Minor, and emigrated to Europe because of the war waged by Ilus against Tantalus. He arrived in Greece bringing with him many treasures, thereby introducing into a hitherto poor country a certain eastern luxury. He was supposed to have been accompanied by Phrygian emigrants whose tombs, it was said, could still be seen in Laconia in historical times.

In his youth Pelops was reputed to have been the victim of a crime committed by his father Tantalus, who had killed him, cut him into small pieces and made him into a stew which had then been served to the gods. Some mythographers claimed that Tantalus had been motivated by piety since there was a famine in his kingdom at the time and he had no other victim to offer to the gods, but it was usually said that he wanted to test how perceptive the gods really were. All the gods recognized the meat and none of them touched it except Demeter who was famished and ate a shoulder before realizing what it was (variants say that it was Ares or Thetis who was guilty of this). The gods reconstructed the body of Pelops and restored it to life. In place of the shoulder which had been eaten they made him an ivory one – a relic which could later been seen in Elis.

After his resurrection Pelops was beloved of Poseidon, taken to heaven by him and became his cup bearer. Soon, however, he was sent back to earth in disgrace because Tantalus had been using him to steal nectar and ambrosia from the gods in order to give it to mortals. Poseidon remained his protector none the less, and made him a present of some winged horses. Poseidon also helped Pelops in his duel with Oenomaus for the possession of Hippodamia (for this part of the legend see MYRTILUS).

Hippodamia and Pelops had a large number of children about whose names the various authorities disagree. All of them list Atreus, Thyestes and Plisthenes. To these is sometimes added Chrysippus (who is also said to be the son of Pelops by a Nymph called Axioche). Among his daughters are Astydamia, sometimes given as the mother of Amphitryon and Hippothoe, the mother of Taphius, eponymous hero of the island of Taphos, by the god Poseidon.

The name of Pelops is associated with the Olympic Games. He was supposed to have been their first founder; the games having been later re-introduced by Heracles in memory of Pelops and in his honour. They were sometimes thought to be funeral games dedicated to the memory of Oenomaus.

At the time of the Trojan War the seer Helenus revealed, among other necessary preconditions, that Troy could not be captured unless the bones of Pelops (or one of his shoulders) were brought to the city. These bones were therefore brought from Pisa to the Troad. On the way back they were lost in a shipwreck, but a fisherman recovered them.

2. Another Pelops was the son of Agamemnon by Cassandra.

Penates Roman deities who guarded hearth and home. For that reason they were often associated with Vesta, but they remained distinct from the Lares. Each home had its own Penates and so did the Roman state. These Penates, represented by two statues of seated youths, were brought to Italy by Aeneas; they had a temple known as the Velia at Rome. There is no myth connected with these deities.

Peneius (Πηνειός) A river god of Thessaly and a son of Oceanus and Thethys; the founder of the Thessalian race of Lapiths. He was married to

Creusa (or Philyra) by whom he had three children, Stilbe, Hypseus and Andreus (see Table 23). He was also said to be the father of Iphis who married Aeolus and bore him Salmoneus, and of Menippe, the wife of Pelasgus. Better known are two other daughters (attributed to him only in late versions of the legend) Daphne and Cyrene, the mother of Aristaeus.

Peneleus (Πηνέλεως) A Boeotian hero, listed among Helen's suitors. He was the son of Hippalcimus or Hippalmus. He is sometimes mentioned as one of the Argonauts but is best known for his appearance in the *Iliad*. He led a Boeotian force with twelve ships to Troy where he killed Ilioneus and Lycon and was himself wounded by Polydamas. The *Iliad* does not refer to his death. Later poems recorded that he died at the hand of Eurypylus, son of Telephus (see TISAMENUS). His loss was lamented by the Greeks; whereas most of the heroes who fell on the battlefield were buried communally, he was honoured by an individual tomb.

A tradition that cannot easily be reconciled with the above names Peneleus as one of the captains who hid in the wooden horse and took part in the capture of Troy.

Penelope (Πηνελόπη) The wife of Odysseus, her fidelity to her husband for whom she waited twenty years while he was at the Trojan War made her universally famous in the legends and literature of Antiquity. She was almost alone among the wives of the heroes who took part in the capture of Troy in resisting the temptation to take a lover. Her legend is recorded principally in the *Odyssey*, but there are a certain number of local or later traditions which differ significantly from the Homeric Vulgate.

Penelope was the daughter of Icarius and therefore niece of Tyndareus, Leucippus and Aphareus (see Table 19). Her mother was Periboea, a Naiad. Through her father, Penelope was a native of Sparta or of Amyclae, but Icarius was driven out by his half-brother Hippocoon and took refuge in Aetolia at the court of King Thestius, where he married Periboea.

The mythographers give two main versions of the circumstances of the marriage between Odysseus and Penelope. In one version Tyndareus, who wanted to reward Odysseus for his good advice, persuaded Icarius to agree to give his daughter to the hero in marriage; in the other version Penelope was the prize offered to the winner of a race from which Odysseus emerged the victor (see ICARIUS). Last, an obsure tradition for which the only authority is a reference in Aristotle, tells us that Penelope's father was not Icarius but a man called Icadius who was wrongly confused with Icarius. This appears to be a local legend, contradicted by the fact that at Sparta there was a temple to Odysseus, built in memory of the Spartan origins of his wife. (In the classical period Sparta was well known as the archetypal land of virtuous wives.) It was also said that when pressed by her father to stay with him in Sparta instead of going to Ithaca with Odysseus Penelope chose to leave with her husband, thus giving the first proof of her love for him.

As for Penelope's mother, although the most common version of the legend gives her as Periboea she is sometimes called Dorodoche or Asterodia. Similarly, the number of Penelope's brothers and sisters, and their names, vary considerably (see, for example, LEUCADIUS).

When Menelaus visited the cities of Greece to remind the former suitors of Helen of the oath they had taken, which obliged them to avenge his dishonour, Odysseus pretended to be mad. What made him reluctant to take part in the Trojan War was not lack of courage but his love for his wife, who had just given him a son, Telemachus. His pretence was discovered, however, and he eventually set off entrusting his house and his wife to his old friend Mentor. Penelope became the sole mistress of Odysseus' fortune – his old mother Anticleia died of grief because her son was so far away, and his father Laertes retired to the country. Soon Penelope was the object of more and more pressing proposals. All the young men of the neighbourhood asked for her hand, and when she refused they moved into Odysseus' palace, hoping

Penelope with her old house-keeper, Eurynome, and two of the maids who were led astray by the suitors. Roman terracotta, 1st century BC. London, British Museum.

that their extravagant revels would force the young woman to give in by bringing about her financial ruin under her very eyes. Penelope reproached them bitterly but they ignored her. Then she thought of a trick. She told them that she would choose a husband from among them when she had finished weaving Laertes' shroud, and the work which she did by day she unravelled by night. After three years of this she was betrayed by a maidservant, and her respite was over.

When Odysseus eventually returned he did not immediately reveal his identity to Penelope. Throughout his battle against the suitors she was sound asleep in her bedchamber and only afterwards did he acknowledge who he was (for this story see ODYSSEUS). Penelope hesitated but eventually recognized her husband, and the goddess Athena graciously lengthened the duration of the night that followed.

It was said – though the episode is not in the *Odyssey* – that Nauplius, in order to avenge the death of Palamedes, spread the rumour that Odysseus had died before the walls of Troy, that it was then that Anticleia committed suicide, and that Penelope threw herself into the sea but was saved by birds (gulls?) who bore her up and brought her back to the shore. To the same post-Homeric cycle belongs the tradition relating to Penelope's adulterous affairs and to her adventures after the return of Odysseus. Among the former traditions there is in particular the legend that Penelope succumbed in succession to all of her 129 suitors and that during this orgy she conceived the god Pan. Another version said that Odysseus on his return realized that Penelope had been unfaithful to him and banished her. She fled to Sparta and from there to Mantinea where she died and where a tomb was raised to her. According to another version Odysseus killed Penelope to punish her for her adultery with Amphinomus, one of the suitors.

According to some traditions Odysseus had a second son, POLIPORTHES, by Penelope after his return. Then he set off for the land of the Thesproti. On his return he was killed by another son Telegonus, who did not recognize him. Telegonus then carried Penelope off to the island of his own mother, CIRCE, and there married her. Circe bore them both off to the Kingdom of the Blessed.

Penia (Πενία) The personification of Poverty, she has only one myth, and that comes from Socrates, reporting the words of Diotima, priestess of Mantinea, in the *Symposium*: after a feast among the gods Penia married Poros and by him gave birth to Eros.

Pentheus (Πενθεύς) A Theban descended directly from Cadmus. He was the son of Echion, one of the Spartoi (the men born of the dragon's teeth), and of Agave, one of Cadmus' daughters (see Table 3). The standard version makes Pentheus the direct heir of Cadmus (for the conditions of this succession see CADMUS), but a variant tradition places Polydorus, an uncle of Pentheus and son of Cadmus, on the throne between Cadmus and Pentheus, who dethroned him. According to yet another version, Pentheus was not king of Thebes.

The Pentheus story is part of the cycle of Dionysus, a Theban god who through his mother Semele was a cousin of Pentheus. Having conquered Asia, Dionysus decided to come back to his homeland, Thebes, to institute the worship of his cult and to punish his mother's sisters, particularly Agave, for having slandered Semele. When he reached Thebes he inflicted madness on all the women, inducing them to go up into the mountains in Bacchant costume and celebrate the god's mysteries. Despite the warning of Cadmus and Tiresias, Pentheus tried to prevent the spread of this violent cult, calling Dionysus a charlatan and an imposter. Despite several miracles, which he witnessed, Pentheus clapped Dionysus in chains but the god freed himself from his bonds and set the royal palace on fire. He then suggested to Pentheus that he should climb the mountain to spy on the women and witness the excesses in which they indulged. Pentheus accepted this suggestion, disguised himself and hid in a pine tree. But the women saw him, uprooted the tree and tore him to pieces. Agave impaled his head on a thyrsus and went back to Thebes, proudly carrying what she thought was a lion's head. Once she reached the city Cadmus enlightened her about her burden and she saw that she had killed her own son.

This myth, which was cast in theatrical form by both Euripides and Aeschylus, was very well known in classical art and literature. The legend was given a religious significance: Pentheus was the typical godless man whose overweening pride called down punishment upon him.

Penthesilea (Πενθεσίλεια) An Amazon, the daughter of Ares and Otrere. She had a son named Caystrus (who gave his name to the river Cayster in Asia Minor) and a grandson Ephesus. After Hector's death Penthesilea went to Troy to help

Priam, taking with her an army of Amazons. She was supposed to have had to leave her homeland because she had accidentally killed someone. At Troy she made her mark in numerous exploits but was soon defeated by Achilles, who wounded her in the right breast and then fell in love with his beautiful victim. Thersites made fun of this passion and thereby called down on himself the wrath of Achilles who slew him.

Penthilus (Πένθιλος) An illegitimate son of Orestes by Erigone, the daughter of Aegisthus. He himself had two sons, Damasios and Echelas or Echelaus, who founded colonies at Lesbos and on the coast of Asia Minor. He was credited in particular with having founded the Lesbian city of Penthile.

Penthus (Πένθος) A deity personifying Grief. It was said that when Zeus allotted their functions to the various gods, Penthus could not be found. By the time he appeared Zeus had already distributed everything, and so had nothing left to entrust to him except the task of presiding over the honours paid to the dead, mourning and tears. Just as other gods protect and favour those who pay the honours due to them, so Penthus favours those who weep for the dead and observe strict mourning. Because they are so good at weeping he sends them the most distressing experiences possible, so the surest way of keeping him at a distance is to moderate distress at inevitable misfortunes.

Peparethus (Πεπάρηθος) One of the four sons of Ariadne by Dionysus. The other three were Thoas, Staphylus and Oenopion. He gave his name to the island of Peparethos.

Peratus (Πέρατος) In the line of kings of Sicyon, Peratus was the successor to Leucippus. As Leucippus' only child was a daughter, named Calchiaia, he gave his kingdom to Peratus, a son of Calchiaia by the god Poseidon. Peratus' own son was Plemnaeus.

Perdix (Πέρδιξ) This name, that of the partridge, belonged to two characters in Attic legend.
1. The first Perdix was a sister of Daedalus and like him a child of Eupalamus. She was also the mother of the second Perdix. When he died, she hanged herself in her grief. She was paid divine honours by the Athenians.
2. The second Perdix is the better known. As a nephew of Daedalus the craftsman he served an apprenticeship in his uncle's workshop and soon surpassed him in skill and inventiveness. In jealousy Daedalus pushed his nephew from the top of the Acropolis. The murder was discovered and Daedalus was brought before the Areopagus. To Perdix was attributed among other things the invention of the saw; he was supposed to have been inspired by a snake's teeth. He is also said to have invented the potter's wheel. This young man is sometimes called Talus or even Calus. He was given the name of Perdix, it was said, because the goddess Athena, taking pity on him as his uncle pushed him off the Acropolis, turned him into a partridge. This bird was supposed to have attended rejoicing the funeral of Icarus, son of Daedalus, who also died of a fall.

Pergamus (Πέργαμος) The eponymous hero of the Asia Minor city of Pergamon, he was said to have been the youngest son of Neoptolemus and Andromache. In this version of the legend he came back from Asia with his mother and in a duel killed Areius, the king of the city of Teuthrania. Pergamus then took the throne himself and gave the city his own name. According to another tradition he came to the help of Gyrnus, a son of Eurypylus and therefore the grandson of Telephus, when he was attacked by his enemies. As a reward Gyrnus gave one of his cities the name Pergamon.

Pergamus is also the name of the citadel of the city of Troy, but in the legends cited above the stories are intended to explain the name of the Hellenistic city of Pergamon, the capital of the kingdom of the Attalids, and not the Trojan citadel.

Periboea (Περίβοια) The name of a large number of heroines, of whom only the most notable are listed.
1. The Naiad who bore Icarus children, including Penelope (see Table 19).
2. The youngest daughter of King Eurymedon who, mating with Poseidon, gave birth to Nausithous, first king of the Phaeacians.
3. One of the first pair of Locrian girls drawn by lot to be sent as slaves of the Athena at Ilion, in order to appease her wrath which had been aroused by the sacrilege committed by Ajax (son of Oileus). This offering went on for a thousand years. The girls who were thus dedicated to the service of the Athena did not approach her but simply cleansed the sanctuary. They wore only a common tunic and went barefoot. If they were

seen outside the sanctuary they could be put to death.

4. The wife of Polybus, king of Corinth, who took in Oedipus and brought him up.

5. The mother of Ajax and wife of Telamon. This Periboea's father was Alcathus, king of Megara (see Table 2). One tradition said that, together with Theseus, she was part of the tribute sent to Minos by Aegeus. Minos fell in love with her, to the great wrath of Theseus, who prevented Minos from having sexual relations with the girl (for this episode see THESEUS).

6. Finally, the Theban cycle has another heroine of this name, the mother of Tydeus (see Table 27). There are several traditions concerning the marriage of this Periboea and Oeneus. Some said that Oeneus had obtained her as his part of the booty after the sacking of Olenos. Others said that she had been seduced by Hippostratus, the son of Amarynceus, and that her father had sent her to Oeneus to be put to death but instead of killing her, Oeneus married her. A third version claimed that the seducer was Oeneus himself and that Hipponous had forced him to marry the girl.

Periclymenus (Περικλύμενος) Two heroes of this name were particularly renowned.

1. One of them belong to the Theban cycle. He was a son of Poseidon and of Chloris the daughter of Tiresias. When the Seven attacked Thebes, he defended the city and it was he who killed Parthenopaeus by throwing a block of stone down on to his head from the top of the city walls. Then, pursuing the fleeing enemy, he singled out Amphiaraus to chase and would have killed him had not Zeus, with a single thunderbolt, made the earth open up and swallow Amphiaraus together with his chariot.

2. The second hero of this name was an inhabitant of Pylos and a son of Neleus, who took part in the expedition of the Argonauts. From his grandfather Poseidon (see Table 21) he had inherited the ability to change his shape (a gift common to many sea-gods and goddesses). When Heracles led his expedition against Pylos, Periclymenus changed himself into a bee to attack the hero, but, thanks to Athena's advice, Heracles recognized him in time and killed him. It was also said that Periclymenus changed into an eagle and was shot down by Heracles with an arrow.

Perieres (Περιήρης)

1. A hero attached to the cycle of Messenian legends, though his genealogy varies considerably from author to author. He is usually a son of Aeolus, of the race of Deucalion (see Table 8), and the hero from whom the Acelians of Messenia were descended. He reigned over Andania, married Gorgophone daughter of Perseus (see Table 31) and had by her Aphareus, Leucippus and sometimes two additional sons, Tyndareus and Icarius (see Table 19). In this tradition Perieres is the common ancestor of the Tyndaridae (the Dioscuri, Helen and Clytemnestra), the Leucippidae (Phoebe and Hilaera) and of Penelope, Lynceus and Idas.

According to another tradition Perieres was the son of Cynortas and consequently belongs not to the race of Deucalion but to that of Lacedaemon and, though him, is directly related to Zeus and Taygete (see Table 6). This tradition derives from the Spartan desire to show themselves as a separate race. The genealogies often give this Perieres the name of Oebalus (see OEBALUS and GORGOPHONE for an attempt to reconcile the two genealogies).

2. The name of a Theban who drove the chariot of Menoeceus. At Onchestos he slew Clymenus, king of the Minyans which led to a war between the Thebans and Minyans (for the outcome of this war, see HERACLES).

Periergos (Περίεργος) The son of Triopas and brother of Phorbas. After the death of Triopas he went with his companions to the island of Rhodes.

Perigoune (Περιγουνή) The daughter of Sinis, who was killed by Theseus. She was beloved of Theseus and by him had a son Melanippus. Theseus later gave her in marriage to Deioneus, the son of Eurytus.

Perimele (Περιμήλη)

1. A daughter of Admetus and Alcestis and sister of Eumelus. She had a son Magnes by Argos, the son of Phrixus (see Table 33).

2. The daughter of Amythaon and the mother of Ixion (see Table 23).

3. In one of the stories in Ovid's *Metamorphoses* Perimele is the name of a girl beloved of the river god Achelous. When the god made her his mistress her father Hippodamas threw her into the sea in indignation. But Achelous persuaded Poseidon to change her into an island, and thus she became immortal.

Periphas (Περίφας) Several heroes are called Periphas, of whom two are particularly notable.

1. A Lapith, the husband of Astyagyia, who had eight children (see Table 23). This Periphas is Ixion's grandfather.

2. A very early king of Attica renowned for his justice and piety. He was a devoted worshipper of Apollo. Men obeyed him as though he were a god and built a temple to him under the name of Zeus. Zeus was angry at this and at first thought of reducing Periphas and his house to ashes with a thunderbolt. But he allowed himself to be moved by Apollo's prayers and merely paid Periphas a visit, then turned him into a eagle, and his wife into a hawk. To reward Periphas for his piety Zeus made him king of all birds and decreed that the eagle should thenceforth be linked with his own worship.

Periphetes (Περιφήτης) One of the brigands slain by Theseus. His father was Hephaestus and his mother Anticleia. He had weak legs and supported himself on a bronze crutch or club, with which he beat to death travellers on the road through Epidaurus. Theseus met him on his return journey to Attica and, having slain him, took his club and kept it for himself.

Peristera (Περιστερά) A Nymph, one of the attendants of Aphrodite. One day Aphrodite and Eros were competing to see who could pick the most flowers and Aphrodite fell behind in the contest. Seeing this, Peristera came to her aid and helped her to win. Eros was angry at this and changed the Nymph into a dove, but to compensate her Aphrodite made the bird her own.

Pero (Πηρώ) A daughter of Neleus and Chloris (see Table 21). Being very beautiful she had many suitors but Neleus, who did not want to part with her, demanded the flocks of Iphiclus as dowry. Thanks to her brother Melampus, Bias (who by his father Amythaon, was Pero's first cousin) was able to satisfy this condition and marry the girl.

Bias and Pero had several children: Perialces, Areius and Alphesiboea, or Talaus, Areius and Leodocus (see Table 1). Pero was later abandoned by Bias who married instead one of the daughters of Proetus, king of Argos.

Perse, Perseis (Πέρση) A daughter of Oceanus and Tethys and the wife of Helios by whom she had several children: Aeetes, king of Colchis, Perses, Circe and Pasiphae (Table 14).

Persephone (Περσεφόνη) The goddess of the Underworld and wife of Hades. She was the daughter of Zeus and Demeter according to the standard version (Table 38), although another tradition makes her the daughter of Zeus and Styx, the Nymph of the river of Hell. The main legend concerning Persephone is the story of her abduction by Hades (brother of Zeus). Hades fell in love with his niece and abducted her while she and her Nymphs were picking flowers on the plain around Etna in Sicily (that is the place generally named). This abduction occurred with the complicity of Zeus and in the absence of Demeter who was travelling all over Greece in search of her daughter. Eventually Zeus ordered Hades to restore Persephone to her mother. But this was no longer possible for the young girl had broken her fast while in the Underworld and had inadvertently (or because she was tempted by Hades), eaten a pomegranate seed which was enough to tie her to the Underworld for ever (see ASCALAPHUS). As a compromise Zeus decided that she should divide her time between the Underworld and the world above. (The proportions vary from author to author: sometimes she spends only a third of the year on earth.) As Hades' wife Persephone plays a part in the legends of Heracles, Orpheus, Theseus and Pirithus. She was furthermore said to have fallen in love with the beautiful Adonis who also had to share his time between Earth and Underworld. She appears, with Demeter, in the Eleusinian Mysteries. At Rome she was identified with PROSERPINA.

Persepolis (Περσέπολις) In certain traditions Persepolis is a son of Odysseus and Nausicaa. In other versions he is the son of Telemachus by Polycaste, a daughter of Nestor.

Perses (Πέρσης) A son of the Titan Crius and of Eurybia. His brothers were Pallas and Astraeus. He himself married Asteria, the daughter of two Titans, Phoebe and Coeus. He had several children by her including the goddess Hecate. Another tradition makes Perses a son of Helios (the Sun) and Perse and thus the brother of Aeetes king of Colchis, of the enchantress Circe and of Pasiphae (see Table 14). He was said to have been king of Tauris before depriving his brother of the kingdom of Colchis, but he was killed by Medus, a son of Medea, on her instigation because he wanted to return the kingdom to Aeetes. Yet another version makes Perses the brother of Aeetes but father of Hecate by a concubine. Hecate was supposed to have married her uncle

Aeetes and to have been mother of Circe and Medea.

Perseus (Περσεύς) An Argive hero in origin: he is given as a direct ancestor of Heracles (see Table 31). His father was Zeus and on his mother's side he was descended from Lynceus and Hypermestra and consequently from Danaus and Aegyptus. Perseus' grandfather Acrisius asked the oracle how he could have sons. The god replied that his daughter Danae would have a son – but that the boy would kill him. Frightened by this prediction Acrisius built a bronze underground chamber and imprisoned Danae in it, but she nevertheless became pregnant. Some said that the father was Proetus, Acrisius' own brother, and that this was the origin of the quarrel between the brothers, but the more common explanation is that Zeus himself seduced the girl by transforming himself into a shower of gold which filtered into the room through a chink in the roof. This version of the myth was often invoked to demonstrate the power of money, which could open the most stoutly defended doors.

Danae had been incarcerated with her nurse and therefore contrived to bear her son Perseus secretly and to keep him in secret for several months. One day, however the child gave a cry which was heard by Acrisius. Unwilling to believe that his daughter had been seduced by Zeus, Acrisius killed the nurse as an accomplice and had his daughter and grandson thrown into the sea in a wooden chest. The chest was cast up on the shores of the island of Seriphos, where the two stranded travellers were taken in by a fisherman named Dictys, who was the brother of the ruler of the island, Polydectes. Dictys welcomed them both into his house and raised the young Perseus, who soon became a handsome and courageous young man. King Polydectes had conceived a passion for Danae which he could not satisfy as Perseus guarded his mother well and the king did not dare resort to violence. One day Polydectes asked all his friends to dinner, including Perseus. During the meal he asked what gift each was willing to offer him. All the other guests said that a horse was a fitting gift for a king, but Perseus declared that he would bring him the head of the Gorgon Medusa if necessary. The next day all the princes brought Polydectes a horse, except for Perseus, who brought nothing. Polydectes then ordered him to fetch Medusa's head, saying that otherwise he would take Danae by force. (According to another version, Polydectes intended to give all these presents to Hippodania, the daughter of Oenomaus, whom he intended to marry.) In this difficult situation Perseus was helped by Hermes and Athena who provided him with the means of keeping his rash promise. On their advice he went first in search of the three daughters of Phorcus, Enyo, Pephredo and Dino, known as the Graeae, who had only one eye and one tooth between them. Perseus took the eye and tooth and refused to return them until the Graeae had shown him the way to the Nymphs, who possessed winged sandals and a shoulder bag called a kibisis, as well as the helmet of Hades which had the property of making its wearer invisible. The Nymphs gave all these objects to Perseus while Hermes armed him with a very hard and very sharp steel bill-hook. Perseus then set off to look for the Gorgons, Stheno, Euryale and Medusa. The Gorgons were monsters whose necks were protected by dragons' scales and tusks like those of wild boars. Their hands were bronze, and they had gold wings with which they could fly. Moreover their eyes were so powerful that they turned to stone anyone on whom the Gorgons looked. Of the three, only Medusa was mortal, which was why Perseus had some hope of decapitating her. Perseus rose into the air on his winged sandals, and while Athena held a shield of polished bronze over Medusa so that it acted as a mirror he struck off her head. From Medusa's mutilated neck sprang a winged horse, Pegasus, and a giant, Chrysaor. Perseus put the head of Medusa in his shoulder bag and set off home. The victim's two sisters pursued him, but to no avail, for Hades' helmet prevented them from seeing him.

On the way back Perseus travelled through Ethiopia where he came across Andromeda. She was being offered as a sacrifice in expiation of the imprudent words spoken by her mother Cassiopia and had been tied to a rock. Perseus fell in love with Andromeda and promised her father Cepheus, that he would release her if he could have her hand in marriage. The bargain was struck and with his magic weapons Perseus had no difficulty in slaying the sea monster who was to have devoured Andromeda. He then restored the girl to her parents. The marriage did not follow without certain difficulties however, Andromeda had an uncle, Phineus, to whom she had supposedly been engaged. Phineus, angered by the prospect of his niece's marriage to Perseus, conspired against him, but Perseus found out about the plot and, showing the Gorgon's head to Phineus and his accomplices, turned them all into stone statues.

Roman mosaic, depicting the head of Medusa, the Gorgon decapitated by Perseus. This head had the power to turn the viewer to stone. Rome, Terme Museum.

After his marriage Perseus returned to Seriphos accompanied by Andromeda. There he found the situation changed. During his absence Polydectes had tried to rape Danae who with Dictys had had to seek refuge at the altars of the gods. Perseus took his revenge on Polydectes by turning the tyrant and his friend to stone. He then handed over the government of Seriphos to his adopted father, Dictys. He gave back the sandals, bag and Hades' helmet to Hermes who returned them to their legitimate owners, the Nymphs. Athena set the head of Medusa in the middle of her own shield. Perseus then left the island of Seriphos with Andromeda and set off for his native land, Argos. He wanted to see his grandfather Acrisius again, but Acrisius, learning of the hero's intentions and still fearing the oracle which had predicted that he would die at the hands of a son of Danae, fled to the land of the Pelasgians. There Teutamides, king

of Larissa, had organized funeral games in honour of his dead father. Perseus arrived to take part and Acrisius was present as a spectator. When Perseus threw the discus, he hit Acrisius on the foot and killed him: filled with grief when he discovered his victim's identity, Perseus paid due funeral honours to Acrisius and buried him outside the city of Larissa. Not daring to return to Argos in order to claim the kingdom of the man he had killed, he exchanged places with his cousin Megapenthes son of Proetus (Table 31). Megapenthes thus became king of Argos and Perseus king of Tiryns. Perseus is supposed to have been responsible for the fortifications of Midea and Mycenae.

An obscure legend makes Perseus the opponent of Dionysus. He is said to have successfully opposed the introduction of the cult of Dionysus into Argos and even to have fought the god and drowned him in the lake at Lerna. This is when Dionysus is supposed to have ended his earthly life and to have taken his place on Olympus, having been reconciled with Hera. Perseus was also said to have killed Ariadne in the same battle.. Another version of the tale gives just Ariadne as Perseus' victim. The hero was supposed then to have made peace with Dionysus, thanks to the intercession of Hermes. The mythographers of the Roman period recorded that after Danae and Perseus had been thrown into the sea by Acrisius they landed not at Seriphos but on the coast of Latium. There some fishermen caught them in their nets and took them to the King Pilumnus, who married Danae and, with her, founded the city of Ardea. Turnus, king of the Rutuli, was supposed to be a descendant of this marriage. It was also said that Danae had two children by Phineus, Argos and Argeus, whom she brought to Italy. She settled with them on the future site of Rome itself. Argos was killed by the Aborigines (the native savages who inhabited the Roman hills) and the place where he died was called the Argiletum 'the death of Argos'.

Peucetius (Πευχέτιος) One of the sons of LYCAON. With his brother Oenotrus he went from Arcadia to southern Italy where he became the ancestor of the Peucetians. Peucetius and Oenotrus were born seventeen generations before the Trojan War.

Phaea (Φαῖα) The sow killed by Theseus at Crommyon. It was named after the old woman who reared it and was descended from Echidna and Typhon.

Phaeacians (Φαίαχες) A mythical nation of sailors. They were the descendants of Phaeax who led them out of the land of Hyperia which they had once inhabited but from which they were driven by the Cyclopes. Phaeax took them to the island of Scheria which from the Classical period onwards has customarily been identified as Corfu. Under King Alcinous the Phaeacians devoted themselves to navigation and trading. Alcinous offered generous hospitality to Odysseus who was cast up on the shore of Scheria and found by Nausicaa. He entertained him liberally, gave him gifts, and eventually provided him with a fully armed ship which was to put him ashore at Ithaca but Poseidon in anger obtained permission from Zeus to punish the Phaeacians. He changed the boat which had carried Odysseus into a rock and surrounded the Phaeacian city with a mountain (see ARETE).

The Argonauts also landed on the island of the Phaeacians and the marriage of Jason and Medea took place there.

Phaeax (Φαίαξ)
1. The eponymous hero of the Phaeacians. He was the son of Poseidon and a Nymph called Cercyra, the daughter of Asopus, who was abducted by Poseidon. He was king of the island of Corfu and had two sons, Alcinous who succeeded him and Locrus who emigrated to Italy where he gave his name to the Locrians. Phaeax is sometimes also said to have been the father of Croton, another hero who gave his name to a city in southern Italy.
2. The man who piloted Theseus' ship when he sailed from Attica to Crete. He was a native of Salamis.

Phaedra (Φαίδρα) The daughter of Minos and Pasiphae and the sister of Ariadne (Table 28). Her brother Deucalion gave her in marriage to Theseus while the latter was king of Athens and despite the fact that he was already married to the Amazon Antiope (or Melanippe, or Hippolyta). This marriage was the occasion of an attack by the Amazons (see THESEUS). Phaedra had two children by Theseus, Acamas and Demophon. She fell in love with Hippolytus, Theseus' son by his Amazon wife, but Hippolytus, who disliked women, refused to give in to his stepmother. Phaedra was afraid that the young man might tell Theseus of the advances she had made to him and she accused Hippolytus of trying to rape her. As a result Theseus called on Poseidon to punish Hippolytus with death. Hippolytus' horses were shortly afterwards frightened by a sea-monster, flung him from his chariot and dragged him to his death. Phaedra hung herself in remorse and despair. The scene of this legend is usually given as Troezen. In his two tragedies on the subject, of which only one survives, Euripides treats the problem of Phaedra's guilt in different ways. In one version, she dies after she has falsely accused her stepson and caused his death and in the other she kills herself after revealing her love.

Phaestus (Φαίστος) A son of Heracles. He succeeded Ianiscus to the throne of Sicyon and then, in response to an oracle, he went to Crete where he founded the city that bore his name. He had a son named Phopalus. His name appears in Pausanias' Cretan genealogy, instead of that of the god Hephaestus, perhaps a scribal error.

Phaethon (Φαέθων) A son of Helios (the Sun). There are two distinct traditions concerning his genealogy. One makes him the son of Eos (the Dawn) and Cephalus (see Table 4); the other makes his father the Sun and his mother the Oceanid Clymene (see Table 14). It is the second version that is associated with the most famous legend in which he plays a part. Phaethon was brought up by his mother who kept his father's identity a secret until the boy reached adolescence. The young man then requested some acknowledgement of his parentage and asked his father to let him drive his chariot across the sky. After much hesitation Helios gave him permission to do so and gave him much advice. Phaethon started to follow his father's route across the vaults of heaven, but he soon felt afraid at finding himself so high up. The sight of the animals who constitute the signs of the Zodiac frightened him and he left his ordained path. He dropped too low and risked setting fire to the Earth; then he rose too high and the stars complained to Zeus. To prevent a universal conflagration Zeus struck the boy down with his thunderbolt and hurled him into the River Eridanus. His sisters, the Heliades, rescued his body and paid him funeral honours. They wept so much that they were turned into poplars.

Phalaecus (Φάλαικος) A Tyrant of Ambracia. Artemis took him hunting and placed a lion cub in his path, but when Phalaecus had captured it a lioness appeared and tore him to pieces. In gratitude the inhabitants of Ambracia raised a statue to the goddess and worshipped her under the title of Artemis the Guide.

Phalanthus (Φάλανθος) The hero who founded Tarentum. One version of his legend tells that during the Messenian war those Lacedaemonians who had not taken part in the expedition were sold into slavery and their children were deprived of their political rights. These people (known as Parthenians) did not accept their lot and they plotted an uprising to take place during the Spartiate festival of the Hyacinthids. Phalanthus was chosen as leader and was supposed to give the signal for the revolt by putting on his cap. The Spartiates got wind of the matter however, and the herald forbade Phalanthus to put on his cap. Their plot discovered, the Parthenians fled, under the leadership of Phalanthus, and went to Tarentum where

on the instructions of the Delphic oracle they founded a colony. It was also said that the Delphic oracle had told Phalanthus that he would be successful in his attempt at escape 'when it rained out of a clear sky'. This oracle was fulfilled when Phalanthus' wife Aethra (whose name means 'clear sky') wept on learning of the initial failure of her husband and his companions.

Phalanx (Φάλαγξ) An Athenian, the brother of Arachne. While Athena was teaching his sister to weave Phalanx was learning how to fight. The brother and sister had an incestuous relationship and the goddess turned them into animals.

Phalces (Φάλκης) One of the sons of Temenus and therefore a Heraclid (see Table 16). His son was Rhegnidas. Phalces seized power in Sicyon one night but agreed to share the government of the city with Lacestades, the previous king, who was also a Heraclid. With his brothers he murdered his father Temenus (see DEIPHONTES).

Phalerus (Φάληρος) An Athenian hero who gave his name to the Attic port of Phaleron in the Piraeus. He was supposed to have been an Argonaut and to have fought the Centaurs at the side of Theseus and Pirithous. In his childhood he had been attacked by a snake but his father Alcon shot the creature with an arrow and saved the child.

Phaon (Φάων) A hero of the island of Lesbos. He was said to have been a ferryman, old, poor and not particularly good-looking, until the day when he ferried the goddess Aphrodite, disguised as an old woman, and did not ask her for payment. As a reward the goddess gave him a phial of oil with which he rubbed himself every day. He became very handsome and was beloved of all the women on the island, especially Sappho. He was said to have scorned Sappho's love and because she could not tolerate his rejection she threw herself into the waves from the Leucadian rock.

Pharos (Φάρος) The pilot of the boat that brought Helen and Menelaus back to Sparta after the Trojan War. He died after a snakebite sustained on the island in the estuary of the Nile which thenceforth bore his name.

Phasis (Φᾶσις) The god of the river of that name in Colchis. He was said to be the son of Helios (the Sun) and of Ocyrrhoe, a daughter of Oceanus.

When he caught his mother committing adultery he killed her, was pursued by the Furies and threw himself into the river Arcturus, which then took the name Phasis.

Phegeus (Φηγεύς) A king of the city of Phegeia (Psophis) in Arcadia, of which he was the founder. He is said to be a brother of Phoroneus in the genealogy that makes him the son of Inachus (see Table 17). It was to his court that Alcmaeon fled after killing his mother. Phegeus had a daughter Arsinoe (also called Alphesiboea) and two sons Pronous and Agenor or, according to Pausanias, Temenus and Axion.

Pheidippus (Φείδιππος) A son of Thessalus and therefore grandson of Heracles who appears in the Catalogue of Ships at the head of a fleet of thirty vessels, provided by Nisiros, Cos, Carpathos and Casos, sailing against Troy. He is also listed as one of Helen's suitors. During the first expedition to Troy Pheidippus was sent as an ambassador to Telephus who was his uncle. He took part in the attack on the city in the wooden horse and after the fall of Troy he settled on the island of Andros, together with the soldiers from Cos whom he had under his command. His brother Antiphus meanwhile established himself among the Pelasgians and gave their region the name of Thessaly.

Phemonoe (Φημονόη) A daughter of Apollo and the first Pythia of the Delphic oracle. She was said to have invented hexameter verse as the form in which to express her prophecies. She is also credited with the famous Delphic maxim: 'Known thyself'.

Pheraea (Φεραία) A title of Hecate. This title gave rise to the legend of a Pheraea the daughter of Aeolus who had mated with Zeus. She had subsequently given birth to the goddess Hecate who was abandoned at birth at a crossroads where she was found and brought up by a shepherd of Pherae.

Phereboea (Φερέβοια) A girl sent with Theseus (who fell in love with her) as part of the tribute paid to the Minotaur by the Athenians (see also PERIBOEA).

Phereclus (Φέρεκλος) Son of Harmonides, a Trojan famed for his manual skills, who built the boat in which Paris sailed when he set off to abduct Helen.

Pheres (Φέρης)
1. One of the sons of Cretheus and Tyro (see Tables 1 and 21) who was the founder of the Thessalian city of Pheres to which he gave his name. Of his children those most often mentioned are Admetus who married Alcestis, and Idomene who married Amythaon but he had another son Lycurgus who was king of Nemea, also a daughter Periopis who, according to another tradition, was the mother of Patroclus. (For Pheres' refusal to die instead of his son Admetus see ADMETUS.)
2. A son of Medea and Jason (see Table 21) who was killed by his mother at the same time as his brother Mermerus.

Philammon (Φιλάμμων) A poet and seer. His father was Apollo but traditions varied as to the identity of his mother. Sometimes he is given as a son of Philonis daughter of Deion or of Heasphorus and Cleoboea or Chrysothemis, but he is more usually said to be the son of Chione, daughter of Daedalion. The story went that Chione (or Philonis) mated with both Hermes and Apollo on the same day. The result was twin boys, Autolycus being the son of Hermes and Philammon that of Apollo. Philammon was very handsome and was loved by the Nymph Argiope, but when she became pregnant he refused to have anything to do with her. Argiope fled to Chalcidice and there gave birth to a son Thamyris.

To Philammon is attributed the invention of girls' choirs and the institution of the Mysteries of Demeter at Lerna. When the Delphians were attacked by the Phlegyans, Philammon came to their rescue at the head of an Argive army. He died during the battle.

Philandrus (Φίλανδρος) The inhabitants of the city of Elyros on Crete deposited in Delphi an *ex-voto* offering depicting a nanny-goat suckling two human babies. These children were thought to be Philandrus and Phylacides, two sons of Acacallis by Apollo.

Philoctetes (Φιλοκτήτης) Son of Poeas and Demonassa (or Methane) and, in legends as early as the period of the Homeric epics, the keeper of the bow and arrow of Heracles. Philoctetes was said to have obtained them either from his father, to whom Heracles had given them, or from Heracles himself as a reward for setting fire to his funeral pyre on Mount Oeta though Heracles had asked Philoctetes to keep the place of his death a secret and he had promised to do so. Later however, when pressed on the subject, Philoctetes went to Oeta and stamped on the spot where Heracles' pyre had stood. He thus broke his oath without actually speaking. Tradition added that he was punished for this act by a terrible wound which opened up on his foot.

Philoctetes, a native of Thessaly, more specifically of the peninsula of Magnesia, was listed among Helen's suitors and with the best of them he joined the Trojan expedition. He led a flotilla of seven ships with fifty archers but he did not reach Troy with the other leaders as he was bitten on the foot by a snake during a sacrifice at Tenedos. The wound soon became so inflamed that an intolerable stench of rotting flesh emanated from it. Odysseus had no difficulty in persuading the other Greek captains to abandon the wounded Philoctetes on the uninhabited island of Lemnos where he lived for ten years.

There were other traditions concerning Philoctetes' wound and the way in which he was abandoned on a desert island. In his tragedy *Philoctetes* Sophocles records that the episode took place not on Tenedos but on the little islet of Chryse, which disappeared during the second century AD and on which there was once an altar to Philoctetes furnished with the bronze image of a snake and a bow. The hero was supposed to have been bitten by a snake hidden in the long grass while he was tending the altar of Chryse, the goddess who had given her name to the island. An entirely aberrant version claims that Philoctetes was hurt not by an animal but by one of Heracles' poisoned arrows which had long before been steeped in the blood of Hydra of Lerna. The arrow struck him in the foot when it accidentally fell out of its quiver and thus caused an incurable wound. (This accident was supposed to be Heracles' revenge for Philoctetes' betrayal of his oath when he revealed where Heracles' pyre had been located on Oeta.) One legend recounts that Philoctetes was abandoned not because of the stench from his wound but because he was unable to suppress his cries of pain which fractured the ritual silence of sacrifices. Another tradition recounts that the Greeks left Philoctetes on Lemnos to tend his wound because there was on the island a cult of Hephaestus, whose priests were particularly skilled at healing snake bites. Philoctetes was indeed cured and was later able to rejoin the army at Troy. The doctor responsible for his recovery was a certain Pylios, a son of Hephaestus. In exchange Pylios learned archery from Philoctetes.

At the end of ten years the Greeks had still not taken the city of Troy. Paris was dead and Helenus, who had been refused the hand of Helen, had fled to the mountains where he had been captured by the Greeks. Half under compulsion, half of his own free will he revealed to the Greeks that one of the necessary preconditions for the capture of Troy was that its enemies should be armed with the arrows of Heracles. These arrows had already conquered the city once (see HERACLES); they alone could repeat the exploit. So Odysseus left for Lemnos, either alone or accompanied by Neoptolemus (in the version used by Sophocles) or Diomedes (according to Euripides), to find Philoctetes and to persuade him to come to Troy. Philoctetes could only be cajoled with some difficulty. There are various accounts of the arguments which Odysseus used. In Euripides for example, Odysseus and Diomedes seized Philoctetes' weapons by a trick and thus forced the unarmed hero to go with them. In another version they deployed the language of patriotism and duty. Alternatively, they promised that he would be healed by the sons of Asclepius, who were doctors to the Greek forces. Indeed, it was said that once Philoctetes arrived at Troy he was tended by either Podalius or Machaon. The story went that Apollo plunged Philoctetes into a deep sleep while Machaon examined the wound, cut out the dead flesh, and then bathed the wound with vinegar before applying to it a herb whose secret Asclepius had obtained from the Centaur Chiron.

The death of Paris is frequently laid at the door of Philoctetes, but this is contradicted by the story of the prophecy of Helenus, since Helenus was not captured until after Paris' death. To get round this difficulty it was said that the prophecy ordering that Philoctetes should be brought from Lemnos to Troy was made by Calchas and that consequently Philoctetes arrived before the death of Paris.

Once Troy had fallen Philoctetes went home. In the *Odyssey* he is one of the lucky heroes who reach home safely, but later legends credit him with further adventures. He was supposed to have founded several cities in the Croton area of southern Italy. In particular he was supposed to have founded Petelia and Macalla, where he dedicated the arrows of Heracles to Apollo. He died on the battlefield, having come to the aid of the Rhodians, who had arrived in the region under the leadership of Tlepolemus and had been attacked by the barbarian native inhabitants. Various places laid claim to his tomb.

Philoetius (Φιλοίτιος) The drover in charge of Odysseus' stock, together with EUMAEUS and MELANTHIUS. Eumaeus was in charge of the pigs, Melanthius of the goats and Philoetius of the cattle. Like Eumaeus and unlike Melanthius he remained faithful to the memory of Odysseus and very much hoped that he would return. He strongly disapproved of the new regime introduced in Odysseus' absence. He gave hospitality to the returned Odysseus whom he did not recognize in his beggar's disguise, and later helped him to overthrow this regime. He killed Pisandrus and Ctesippus, and with Eumaeus was given the task of punishing Melanthius by Odysseus.

Philolaus (Φιλόλαος) One of the four sons of Minos by the Nymph Paria (Table 28). When Heracles stopped at Paros on his expedition to the land of the Amazons Philolaus attacked his companions.

Philomela (Φιλομήλα) One of the two daughters of Pandion, the king of Athens. One of her sisters was called Procne (Table 11). When war broke out between Pandion and his neighbour Labdacus, the king of Thebes, over the question of boundaries, Pandion asked Tereus, a Thracian and the son of Ares, for his help; thanks to Tereus, Pandion was victorious. He then gave his ally the hand of his daughter Procne in marriage. Procne soon gave birth to a son called Itys. Tereus however fell in love with his sister-in-law Philomela. He raped her and then cut out her tongue so that she could not betray him, but she revealed his crime to her sister by embroidering the tale of her misfortunes on a piece of material. Procne then decided to punish Tereus. To do so she killed Itys, boiled his corpse and served it as a stew to the unwitting Tereus. Then she fled with Philomela. When he became aware of the crime, Tereus took an axe and set out in pursuit of the sisters. He found them at Daulis, in Phocis. The two women implored the gods to save them; the gods took pity on them and changed them into birds. Procne became a nightingale and Philomela a swallow. Tereus was also changed into a bird, and became a hoopoe.

There are variant versions of this legend. In one the roles of Procne and her sister are reversed, Philomela being the wife of Tereus. This version is most widely used by the Roman poets, who make Philomela the nightingale and Procne the swallow. This is more in agreement with the etymology of the name Philomela, which evokes the idea of music.

Philomelides (Φιλομηλείδης) A king of Lesbos who forced travellers who came to his island to wrestle with him and killed those he defeated. This custom continued until he himself was killed by Odysseus (or in some accounts by Odysseus and Diomedes) when the Greek fleet stopped at Lesbos on its way to Troy.

Philomelus (Φιλόμηλος) A son of Iasion and Demeter and the brother of Pluto. He invented the practice of harnessing two oxen to one cart. As a reward his mother changed him into the constellation named Butes.

Philotes (Φιλωτᾶς) The personification of Affection. Hesiod describes her as one of the daughters of Night, and sister to Apate (Deceit), Geras (Old Age) and Eris (Discord).

Philotis (Φιλωτίς) After the Gauls had captured Rome, the city was weakened, and the Latins, under Livius Postumius, took advantage of this and attacked it. The Latin army camped close to Rome and sent ambassadors asking the Romans to hand over their wives and daughters in order to strengthen the ancestral links between the two races. The Romans were reluctant to accept this proposal but were unsure how to act. Then a slave girl called Philotis (or Tutola) suggested the following ruse: they should send Philotis and several other pretty slave girls to the Latin camp, dressed as freeborn Roman women. During the night Philotis would signal with a light, then the Romans could come fully armed and massacre the sleeping enemy. This is indeed what happened. Philotis put a lamp in a fig-tree and veiled the light with draped material so that the Latins could not see it. The Romans then hastily came out of the city and slaughtered the Latins. In memory of this event, the Nonae Caprotinae, or Nones of the Fig-tree, were celebrated. On this day people came rushing out of the city, calling each other all sorts of names. Women feasted in makeshift huts made of fig branches. The female servants were free to walk about where they pleased and throw stones at each other, in memory of the role they played in the battle against the Latins.

Other Roman antiquaries explained the ritual as reflecting the events which accompanied the death of Romulus, which happened on the Nones of July when crowds of people gathered in the Campus Martius in the place called the Goat Marsh, or *palus Caprae*.

Philyra (Φιλύρα) The mother of the Centaur CHIRON who was loved by Cronus. There are two versions of this story. In one, Cronus, fearing the jealousy of his wife Rhea, metamorphosed into a horse and mated with Philyra which explains why Chiron was half-horse, half-man. In the second version Philyra, out of modesty, rejected the god's advances and turned herself into a mare to escape from him, but he turned into a stallion and raped her. Chiron was born on Mount Pelion, in Thessaly, where his mother lived with her son in a cave. Later she helped him to rear the children who were entrusted to him, in particular Achilles and Jason.

Phineus (Φινεύς)

1. One of the sons of LYCAON, the king of Arcadia. He was struck down by a thunderbolt together with his brothers.

2. The brother of Cepheus and the uncle of ANDROMEDA (see PERSEUS). He therefore belonged to the race of Bellerophon. This genealogy is far from being coherent in the various versions of the Cepheus legend. The authors are only in agreement on the fact that Phineus wanted to marry his niece and that he tried to foment a conspiracy against Perseus when the latter won her instead. In the battle which broke out between Perseus and Phineus' supporters in the great hall of Cepheus' palace, Phineus was turned to stone by the sight of Medusa's head. That he suffered this fate makes it impossible to identify him with the Phineus who appears in the legend of the Argonauts (see below), but in order to make such an identification possible, certain late mythographers claimed that Phineus was merely blinded by Perseus, not killed by him.

3. The most famous character of this name. He was a king of Thrace. His legend, which is a complicated one, has numerous variants. The standard version is that Phineus, who had powers of divination, chose to have a long life at the cost of losing his sight. He therefore went blind and the Sun, in indignation, sent HARPIES to plague him. In other versions there were other reasons for his punishment: it is said that he abused his gifts as a seer and revealed to mankind the plans of the gods. Another account claims that he had shown PHRIXUS the way to Colchis, or had shown Phrixus' children how to get back to Greece and had thereby incurred divine wrath. When the Argonauts undertook their expedition to Colchis, they went to ask Phineus for directions. Phineus agreed to tell them, but asked first to be freed from the Harpies. The two sons of Boreas, Calais and Zetes, set off in pursuit of the two demons and destroyed them (see BOREADES).

In another legend, independent of the previous one but offering analogous features, Phineus' first wife was Cleopatra, the daughter of Boreas (Table 11). By her he had two sons, whose names are usually given as Plexippus and Pandion. He then married Idaea, daughter of Dardanus (Table 7). Idaea was jealous of her two stepsons and falsely accused them of trying to rape her. Phineus, believing her, had them both blinded; or alternatively Idaea herself had their eyes put out. According to another extremely obscure version, Cleopatra had blinded her sons herself, to punish Phineus for remarrying. When the Argonauts came to Phineus' court, the Boreades, who were Cleopatra's brothers, took their revenge on Phineus by blinding him in his turn. Asclepius restored the eyesight of the two young men but was punished for doing this by Zeus, who struck him with his thunderbolt.

These variant legends were combined by mythographers, who recounted that Phineus had been punished by Zeus for unjustly accusing his children of the crime and blinding them without sufficient proof. He was then plagued by the Harpies and the Argonauts later freed him from them.

Phix (Φίξ) According to Hesiod this was the name of the Sphinx.

Phlegethon (Φλεγέθων) One of the rivers of the Underworld which joined the Cocytus to form the Acheron. There was said to be a huge waterfall where the two rivers met. The name of the river, which the Greeks associated with the verb 'to burn' suggests that it was a river of fire.

Phlegyas (Φλεγύας) The eponymous hero of the Phlegyans who is mentioned in the *Iliad*. He was the son of Ares and either Dotis or Chryse, one of the two daughters of Halmus (Table 20). He is generally considered to be a Thessalian, although the Phlegyans were also mentioned in connection with Boeotia, Phocis and Arcadia. He is said to have had several children, in particular Ixion (see IXION and Table 23 for other genealogies) and Coronis, the mother of Asclepius. According to regional traditions, Phlegyas succeeded Eteocles on the throne of Orchomenus and then founded a new city, Phlegya, where he gathered around him the most warlike of all the Greeks. He died without children. His heir was his nephew Chryses, the son of Poseidon and Chrysogenia, herself a daughter of Halmus. Phlegyas journeyed through the Peloponnese to investigate the land and prepare for a marauding expedition. During this trip his daughter Coronis was seduced by Apollo; this serves to explain why ASCLEPIUS was born at Epidauros.

In one account, Phlegyas attempted to set light to the temple of Apollo at Delphi, probably to avenge the death of his daughter whom Apollo had killed after her infidelity. Virgil depicts Phlegyas in Hell suffering torments for his impiety. Apollodorus recounts that Phlegyas was killed on Euboea by Lycus and Nycteus but he may in fact be referring to a city of that name, situated in Boeotia like Orchomenus. His murderers went into exile at Thebes.

Phlias (Φλίας) A son of Dionysus and Araethyrea, daughter of Minyas (Table 20). He appears in the genealogy of the kings of Sicyon set out by Pausanias (Table 22) as the husband of Chthonophyle, by whom he had a son called Androdamas. Sometimes Chthonophyle is said to have been the mother of Phlias rather than his wife. Phlias is one of the Argonauts and is supposed to have been the eponymous hero of the city of Phlius in the Peloponnese.

Phlogius (Φλόγιος) Amongst other heroes of this name there was a son of the Thessalian Deimachus whose brothers were Deileon and Autolycus. With them he accompanied Heracles on his expedition against the Amazons, but became separated from the hero, as did his brothers, at Sinope. The three of them spent some time in that area until the Argonauts passed by there and agreed to take them with them.

Phobos (Φόβος) The personification of Fear, who accompanied Ares on the battlefield. Phobos is a male deity. He was said to be the son of Ares and the brother of Deimus but there is no specific legend associated with him.

Phocus (Φῶκος)
1. According to Plutarch, Phocus, a native of Glisas in Boeotia, had a daughter called Callirhoe. Thirty men wished to marry her, but her father continually postponed the day on which he would choose his future son-in-law. Eventually he announced that, according to the Delphic oracle, the matter would have to be settled by the use of

arms. The suitors killed him; Callirhoe fled, and as the suitors were chasing her, some peasants hid her in a corn-mill. On the festival of the Boeotian federation Callirhoe came as a suppliant to the altar of Athena Itonia and accused the suitors of murdering her father. They fled to Orchomenus and then to Hippotae. The Boeotians laid siege to them and forced them to give themselves up. Phocus' murderers were then stoned to death. The evening before they gave themselves up, they had heard a voice coming from the mountains, calling 'I am here'. It was the voice of Phocus, telling them of their punishment.

2. The eponymous hero of Phocis. There are several traditions concerning him. In some versions Phocus was a Corinthian, the son of Ornytus, a descendant of Sisyphus, who was said to be of the blood of Poseidon. He came and settled in the area around the foot of Parnassus and the area then became known as Phocis. Other versions say that it was ORNYTUS himself who settled in the area which was to take the name of Phocis. He had fought there against the Locrians and later withdrew, leaving his kingdom to his son. Phocus is said to have been the husband of Antiope. Dionysus, who was angered by the punishment of Dirce, had made Antiope mad. As she was wandering through Greece, Phocus encountered her. He cured her and they then married. Their joint tomb was said to be at Tithorea.

3. The other tradition about Phocus, the eponym of Phocis, claims that he was the son of Aeacus and Psamathe (Table 30). His half-brothers were Peleus and Telamon, the sons of Aeacus by Endeis. Phocus was so called in memory of the metamorphosis of his mother, a daughter of Nereus, a sister of Tethys. To escape from Aeacus' advances Psamathe, who like all marine deities possessed the gift of metamorphosis, changed herself into a seal. This did not prevent Aeacus from coupling with her; this union produced Phocus. When he reached maturity, this Phocus left Salamis, his father's land, and set out for central Greece. He conquered a district which he then called Phocis. He allied himself with one of the natives, Iaseus, and married Asteria, the daughter of Deion and Diomedes (Table 8). Asteria bore him twin sons, Crisus and Panopeus.

Later Phocus returned to Aegina; there he was murdered by his half-brothers, who were jealous of him and were perhaps incited to murder by Aeacus' legitimate wife. Psamathe avenged his death by sending a wolf to destroy Peleus' flocks in Thessaly, where he had taken refuge after his father had sent him into exile. However, at Thetis' entreaty, she agreed to change the wolf to stone. Phocus' tomb was supposed to be beside that of Acacus on Salamis.

Phoebe (Φοίβη)

1. Phoebe, or the Shining One, is the name of one of the Titanides, a daughter of Uranus and Gaia (Tables 5 and 12). She married Coeus and bore him two daughters, Leto and Asteria. She is sometimes said to have founded the oracle at Delphi in her capacity as a handmaiden of Themis and to have given it to her nephew Apollo as a present.

2. One of the Leucippidae (Table 19) and the wife of Pollux. In literature, in the poetry of Propertius for example, Phoebe is assumed to be the wife of Castor.

3. For Phoebe, one of the daughters of Helios, see HELIADES.

Phoebus (Φοῖβος)

An epithet of Apollo. It is in Latin, primarily, that the god is known just as Phoebus.

Phoenix (Φοῖνιξ)

1. A fabulous bird whose legend is connected with sun worship in Egypt. Herodotus was the first writer to talk about the phoenix and, following him, poets, mythographers, astrologers and natural historians all gave details about the bird. It was generally accepted that the phoenix came from Ethiopia. It lived there for a period, assessed by some versions as 500 years and by others as 1,461 or even 12,954 years. It was supposed to look more or less like an eagle, but was of considerable size. Its plumage was adorned with brilliant colouring, scarlet, blue, purple and gold. The authors differ over the distribution of these colours on the bird's body but all assert that the phoenix was infinitely more beautiful than the most splendid peacocks.

The legend of the phoenix is principally concerned with the bird's death and rebirth. It was the only example of its species which could not reproduce normally. When the phoenix felt its death impending it collected aromatic plants, incense and *amomum* (a balsam plant) and made a nest. At this point mythographers divide into two distinct traditions: according to one tradition, the bird set fire to this sweet-scented pyre and a new phoenix rose from the ashes; the other tradition claims that the phoenix settled upon the nest it had made and impregnated it as it died. The new phoenix was then born, gathered up its progeni-

tor's body and after wrapping it in a hollow myrrh log, took it to the city of Heliopolis in southern Egypt where it laid the body down on the altar of the Sun. It was then solemnly burned by the priests. This was the only moment when the phoenix came to Egypt. It was said to come with an escort of other birds and once it had arrived at the altar of the Sun, the phoenix circled around for a moment, waiting for a priest to appear. At the appropriate moment a priest came out of the temple and compared the appearance of the bird with a drawing of it in the sacred books. Then the body of the former phoenix was burned and when the ceremony was over, the young bird returned to Ethiopia, where it lived on incense until its lifespan was completed. The astrologers connected this lifespan with the theory of the 'Great Year', or one complete cycle of the stars. The birth of a phoenix was supposed to mark the beginning of such a year. During the reign of the Emperor Claudius, a phoenix said to have been caught in Egypt was brought to Rome. Claudius put it on public exhibition, but nobody seriously accepted that it was really a phoenix.

2. One of the sons of Agenor, in the best-known version of the legend of Europa and Cadmus (Table 3). With his brothers he was sent by his father in search of Europa, who had been abducted by Zeus. Failing to find her, and being weary of wandering, he settled on the site of the future city of Sidon in Phoenicia. The area owed its name to him. This genealogy is not unanimously accepted by the mythographers, however; he is sometimes considered to have been the son of OGYGUS, or said to be Europa's father, rather than her brother.

3. One of Achilles' companions. He was the son of Amyntor, king of Eleon in Boeotia. His mother's name is variously given as Hippodamia, Cleoboula or Alcimede. Amyntor had a concubine called either Clytia or Phthia and at the request of his mother, who was jealous, Phoenix seduced this concubine. On learning of this crime, Amyntor had his son blinded. In another version Phthia herself tried in vain to seduce Phoenix; when she failed she denounced him to Amyntor on a false charge. The king then blinded his son. Phoenix then took refuge with Peleus, and was taken by him to the Centaur Chiron who restored his sight. Peleus then entrusted his son Achilles to Phoenix and made him king of the Dolopians. Phoenix left for Troy with Achilles, as his counsellor. When Achilles and Agamemnon were estranged, Phoenix tried unsuccessfully to persuade his friend to be reconciled to Agamemnon

but with no success. He was beside him in his tent when Achilles learnt of the death of Patroclus and he also played a part in the funeral games in honour of Patroclus, when he was in charge of the chariot race. After Achilles' death, Phoenix went with Odysseus to fetch Neoptolemus. When the Greeks returned from Troy, he travelled by the land route with Neoptolemus but died on the journey.

Pholus (Φόλος) A Centaur who lived at Pholoe and a son of Silenus by a Nymph of the ash-trees (a genealogy which differs from the usual one ascribed to the Centaurs, who are usually said to be descendants of IXION). When Heracles was hunting Erymanthus' wild boar he visited Pholus: Pholus received the hero hospitably, giving him roast meat to eat whereas he himself ate exclusively raw food. Heracles asked for wine and Pholus told him that there was only one jar, which belonged communally to the Centaurs. Heracles told him to open the jar and not to be anxious. When the Centaurs smelled the wine they rushed to Pholus' cave armed with rocks, tree-trunks and torches and Heracles battled with them. Pholus was killed accidentally: while he was burying one of his fellow-Centaurs, he drew an arrow out of a wound, dropped it on his foot and was mortally wounded. Heracles gave him a magnificent funeral.

Phorbas (Φόρβας)

1. The most famous is the Thessalian Phorbas, a descendant of the Lapiths. In some accounts he is said to be the son of Lapithes by Orsinome (Table 23), in others the son of Triopas, himself son of Lapithes. He first lived in Thessaly, on the plain of Dotion and from there he emigrated to Cnidus, or to Rhodes with his brother Periergus. Phorbas eventually settled in Ialysus and Periergus in Camiros. Like most Thessalian legends there is also a Peloponnesian version of the story of Phorbas. He is said to have emigrated from Thessaly to Olenos in Elis; there Alector, who was afraid of Pelops' power, allied himself with Phorbas and shared his kingdom with him as a reward for his services. The alliance of Phorbas and Alector is said to have been sealed by a double marriage: Alector married Phorbas' daughter Diogenia, and Phorbas married Alector's sister, Hyrmine. Phorbas had two sons, Augias and Actor, and on his death they divided Elis between them.

2. The son of Argos, who appears in an Argive genealogy given by Pausanias (Table 17). This

Phorbas was the father of Triopas. His wife was called Euboea and MESSENE is sometimes listed among his other children, although she is more frequently said to be his granddaughter.

3. A Phlegyan who lived at Panope in Phocis. He used to attack travellers on the road to Delphi and force them to box with him. He generally beat them and would then kill them. One day Apollo appeared in the form of a child; he challenged Phorbas, and vanquished him.

4. The hero who taught Theseus how to drive a chariot. He is sometimes credited with the invention of wrestling, though this is more generally assigned to Theseus himself.

Phorcys (Φόρκυς) One of the sea-gods who were part of the first race of gods. He is most frequently, and from as far back as Hesiod's *Theogony*, said to be the son of Gaia and Pontus (Earth and Sea). He was the brother of Nereus, Thaumas, Eurybia and Ceto. He married Ceto and had children by her, notably the three Phorcides, who play a part in the myth of PERSEUS. He is also sometimes said to have been the father of the sea-monster SCYLLA. In addition, various sources say that Phorcys was the father of Echidna and the Hesperides and sometimes it is claimed that he was the grandfather of the Eumenides. Phorcys lived either in Arymnion, on the coast of Achaea, or on the island of Cephalonia or on Ithaca. In a Roman legend, Phorcys was a very early king of Sardinia and Corsica, who was defeated by Atlas in a naval battle and then drowned. His allies paid divine honours to him, as if he were a sea-god.

Phormion (Φορμίων) Phormion was a Spartan who became owner of the house where Tyndareus had once lived. The Dioscuri, now gods, one day came to him disguised as two travellers, telling him that they had come from Cyrene. They asked him for hospitality and begged him to give them a specific room, one where they had stayed during their childhood. Phormion placed his whole house at their disposal with the exception of the one room which they particularly wanted because it happened to be his daughter's room. During the night the young girl, her servants and the Dioscuri all disappeared and in the girl's room there was a picture of the Dioscuri and on a table some *silphion*, the aromatic plant which was the main product of Cyrene.

Phoroneus (Φορωνεύς) According to Peloponnesian legend, Phoroneus was the first mortal. He was the son of the river-god Inachus and a Nymph named Melia, and he had two brothers, Aegialeus and Phegeus (Table 17). Phoroneus was chosen to judge the quarrel between Hera and Poseidon for possession of the Peloponnese: he decided in Hera's favour. Phoroneus supposedly first taught men to group themselves together in cities and showed them how to use fire. He is said to have brought the cult of the Argive Hera to the Peloponnese. Traditions vary as to the name of his wife: she is sometimes called Cerdo, sometimes Teledice, and sometimes Peitho. Similarly the list of his children varies considerably according to the source. Usually they are given as Car, the first king of Megara, and NIOBE; to these are sometimes added Iasus, Lyrcus, Pelasgus and Agenor.

Phosphorus (Φωσφόρος) The name sometimes given to the morning star which is also called Heosphorus (see under that name). Translated into Latin the name becomes Lucifer. It is often personified in poetry as the star which announces the approach of Aurora, the dawn, and which is the bearer of the light of Day.

Phrasius (Φράσιος) A seer and a native of Cyprus, who visited Egypt during a famine and predicted to BUSIRIS, the king of that country, that the famine would end if a stranger were sacrificed every year. Busiris acted on his advice and began by sacrificing Phrasius.

Phrixus (Φρίξος) One of the offspring of ATHAMAS and Nephele, and the brother of Helle. On the advice of his second wife INO Athamas decided to sacrifice Phrixus and Helle to Zeus Laphystius, but Zeus sent the two children a ram with a golden fleece which carried them off, saving them from being sacrificed. According to another version, it was Nephele rather than Zeus who provided the children with the ram, which she had obtained from Hermes. Phrixus and Helle left Orchomenus and flew off to the East, but Helle fell into the sea and drowned. Her brother arrived safely in Colchis at the court of Aeetes who received him hospitably and gave him the hand of his daughter Chalciope in marriage. In return, Phrixus sacrificed the ram to Zeus and presented the fleece to the king. Aeetes dedicated the fleece to Ares and hung it up on a nail on an oak tree in a wood sacred to that god. It was this fleece which was the prize sought by the Argonauts. By Chalciope Phrixus had several children, notably Argos,

Melas, Phrontis and Cytissorus. Phrixus spent the remainder of his life in Aeetes' palace and died there at an advanced age, whilst his sons went back to Orchomenus where the throne was restored to them.

In another version Aeetes killed Phrixus, because an oracle had predicted that the king would die at the hands of a descendant of Aeolus. This tradition, which is mentioned by Hyginus, is probably part of a reworking of the myth by the tragedians. The same text tells how Phrixus and Helle, having been saved from the sacrifice, were punished with madness by Dionysus for trying to take revenge on Ino.

Phronime (Φρονίμη) The mother of Battus, who founded the colony of Cyrene. She was the daughter of the Cretan king Etearchus, who ruled over the city of Axos. Etearchus remarried and his second wife denounced her step-daughter Phronime, falsely claiming that she led a debauched life; the king believed his wife and coerced one of his guests, a merchant from Thera named Themison, into promising to do whatever he asked of him. Themison swore that he would; the king told Themison to take Phronime away with him and to push her overboard when he reached the open sea. Themison took the girl away with him but was not prepared to kill her, so he merely dipped her in the sea and drew her out immediately. He then took her ashore at Thera and arranged a marriage to a noble of that island, called Polymnestus, who was the father of Battus.

Phrygius (Φρύγιος) A king of Miletus, the successor to King Phobius, who gave up his throne to Phrygius after the death of Cleoboea (see ANTHEUS). When Pieria, a daughter of Phytes of Myonte, came to Miletus for the festival of Artemis, he fell in love with the girl and, by marrying her, put an end to a war between the inhabitants of Myonte and the Milesians.

Phthius (Φθῖος) The hero who founded Phthiotis in Thessaly. There are various genealogies for him. Sometimes he is said to be one of the sons of Lycaon, and king of Arcadia, sometimes thought to be a son of Poseidon by the Thessalian Nymph Larissa. According to the latter genealogy he is the brother of Achaeus and Pelasgus. In another version he is the son of Achaeus; and the husband of Chrysippe, daughter of Irus. His son by Chrysippe was Hellen, founder of the city of Hellas, in Thessaly. Further genealogies relate

Phthius in different ways to the eponymous heroes of the great Hellenic races.

Phthonus (Φθόνος) The personification of Envy. Like most spirits who are abstractions, Phthonus has no specific legend attached to him.

Phylacus (Φύλακος)

1. A Thessalian hero, descended from Aeolus, the son of Deion, or Deioneus and Diomede, herself daughter of Xuthus and a descendant of Deucalion (Tables 8 and 20). He is above all famous for being the father of IPHICLUS and Alcimede, the mother of Jason. Phylacus married Clymene, the daughter of Minyas. He is supposed to have founded and given his name to the city of Phylacae on the river Othrys. He was the owner of a magnificent herd (see MELAMPUS).

2 A Delphian, who appeared in the shape of an armed giant just as the Persians were attacking the sanctuary, and put them to flight, amid lightning and supernatural manifestations. At his side he had another giant, a hero called Autonous (for an analogous legend see HYPERBOREANS).

Phylas (Φύλας) A certain number of legendary heroes of this name are known; nearly all are connected with the Heracles cycle.

1. The king of the Thesprotian city of Ephyra. Heracles made war on him with the citizens of Calydon, captured his city and then killed him. Phylas had a daughter called Astyoche, who was captured by Heracles and bore him a son, Tleptolemus.

2. The father of Polymela; she bore Hermes' child Eudorus, who accompanied Achilles to Troy.

3. The king of the Dryopes, who led his people in an attack on the sanctuary at Delphi. Heracles then made war upon Phylas, killed him and expelled the Dryopes from their territory, which he gave to the Malians. Heracles had a son called Antiochus by Phylas' daughter.

4. The father of Hippotes and therefore grandfather of Aletes, the companion of the HERACLIDS. This Phylas, son of Antiochus, married Leipephile, daughter of Iolaus, who bore him a daughter called Thero. She later gave birth to a son, Chaeron, the eponym of Chaeronea, who was fathered by Apollo.

Phyleus (Φυλεύς) One of the sons of Augias, the king of Elis who was the enemy of HERACLES. He sided with Heracles against his father, over the issue of the payment which the hero requested for cleaning the stables. For this he was banished by his father and settled at Dulichium. There he married TIMANDRA or Ctimene who bore him a son named MEGES and a daughter, Eurydamia, who married Polyidus. After Heracles had conquered Augias, he placed Phyleus on the throne of Elis. Phyleus later gave the throne to his brothers and returned to Dulichium. He took part in the Calydonian boar-hunt.

Phylius (Φύλιος) An Aetolian hero who played a part in the story of CYCNUS. He was in love with the young Cycnus, who lived in the woods between Pleuron and Calydon. Cycnus was handsome but very hard-hearted and treated those who paid court to him with contempt. All apart from Phylius gave him up; Phylius however agreed to carry out all the feats which the whim of Cycnus imposed upon him. He first had to kill a lion without using an iron weapon; his next task was to capture alive some man-eating vultures and, finally, he had to lead a bull to the altar of Zeus with his own hands. He accomplished the first two deeds on his own, but for the third he sought the assistance of Heracles. The god advised him to stop indulging the young man's whims. Phylius accordingly refused to carry out his last task, and in a fury Cycnus threw himself into a pool, where he and his mother were changed into swans.

Phyllis (Φυλλίς) The heroine of a love story of which the hero is either ACAMAS or his brother DEMOPHON, the sons of Theseus. On his way back from Troy Acamas (or Demophon) was washed up on the coast of Thrace, close to the place where the river Strymon joins the sea. There he was given hospitality by the king of the region, whose name was Phyleus, or Ciasus, or Lycurgus. This king had a daughter called Phyllis, who fell in love with the young prince. In one version he married her; in others he promised to marry her, but told her that he had to return to Athens to settle his affairs there before he could live permanently with her. Phyllis agreed to this separation but gave him a casket which she requested him not to open unless he lost all hope of returning to her. She said that it contained sacred objects relating to the worship of the goddess Rhea. The day fixed for his return arrived, but he did not appear. She went down to the harbour nine times to see whether her lover's boat was approaching, but all in vain. In memory of those nine trips the place was given the name of the 'Nine Roads'. Phyllis despaired of her lover ever returning and hanged herself.

On the same day, in Crete, where Acamas had settled and married another woman, the forgetful lover opened the casket and from it a ghost appeared; it frightened his horse, and the horse bolted; the young man fell on his sword and was killed. It is said that Phyllis was changed into a leafless almond tree and that her lover came to Thrace after the girl's death and learnt of her metamorphosis. He embraced the sterile tree which became green and grew leaves. This was supposed to be the origin of the Greek word for leaves which had originally been 'petala' but from that time became 'phylla'. Another version claims that trees had been planted over Phyllis' grave and that at the anniversary of her death, they lost their leaves.

Phytalus (Φύταλος) An Attic hero who lived on the banks of the Ilissus. Demeter visited Attica when she was looking for her daughter, and Phytalus gave the goddess hospitality. In return she gave him some young fig trees. The Phytalids, his descendants, held the sole right to the cultivation of figs for a long time. They entertained THESEUS when he was on his way back from Corinth and at their domestic altar purified him of the murders of Sinis and other brigands. In memory of this service the Phytalids had certain privileges during the celebration of the festivals of Theseus at Athens.

Piasus (Πίασος) A Thessalian king, the father of Larissa, who violated his own daughter. To avenge herself, Larissa pushed him into a butt of wine while he was leaning over it and he drowned.

Picolous (Πικόλοος) A Giant. During the battle of the Giants and the gods he fled to Circe's island and tried to drive the sorceress from it, but Helios, Circe's father, slew Picolous. The *moly* plant grew from his blood. The plant was white (the colour of the Sun) and its root black, as was the Giant's blood (see ODYSSEUS).

Picus A very early king of Latium who ruled the Aborigines who were the first inhabitants of the region. He was said to have been the father of Faunus and the grandfather of Latinus. His father was sometimes said to be a man called Sterces, or Sterculus, whose name suggests the word 'dung-heap'; he was identified with Saturn by the mythographers, however, to invest his myth with more dignity. Picus was supposed to have been an

excellent seer, who possessed a green woodpecker, the pre-eminent prophetic bird. The mythographers claimed that the woodpecker was in fact Picus himself and that he had been changed into that shape by Circe. It is said that he had repulsed Circe's advances because of his love either for his wife Pomona or for the Nymph Canens, the daughter of Janus. The green woodpecker played a part in Roman religion not only as a prophetic bird but also as the bird sacred to Mars. The woodpecker flew around the divine twins, ROMULUS and Remus, and according to some versions was just as instrumental in saving them as was the she-wolf.

Pierides (Πιερίδες) The name Pierides derives from the district of Pieria in Thrace. According to legend the Pierides were nine maidens who wanted to outshine the Muses. They were the daughters of Pierus and Evippe. They possessed especially beautiful singing voices; so they went to Mount Helicon, home of the Muses, and challenged them to a singing contest. They were unsuccessful, and to punish them the Muses changed them into magpies, according to Ovid, or into various birds, according to Nicander. The latter gives the names of the nine Pierides as Colymbas, Iynx, Cenchris, Cissa, Chloris, Acalanthis, Nessa, Pipo and Dracontis. According to Pausanias, the Pierides had the same names as the Muses, and the children attributed to the Muses such as Orpheus, for example, were children of the Pierides, since the Muses remained eternally virgin.

Pierus (Πίερος)
1. The eponym of Pieria, often thought to be the father of the Pierides. He was the son of Macedon and the brother of Amathus. Pierus introduced the cult of the Muses into his region. He is sometimes said to have been the father of Linus or of Oeager, and therefore the grandfather of Orpheus.
2. The son of Magnes and Meliboea. Pierus was loved by the Muse Clio; Aphrodite had inspired her with the passion as a punishment for deriding the goddess' own love for the beautiful Adonis. Their son was in some versions said to be HYACINTHUS.

Pietas The personification of feelings of duty towards the gods, the state and one's family. As an abstraction Pietas has no myth attached to her. The temple dedicated to her, which was built at the foot of the Capitoline, dates from the beginning of the second century BC. During the Empire Pietas was very often depicted on coinage in order to symbolize the moral virtues of the ruling emperor.

Pilumnus A very obscure Roman deity whose function was to protect new-born babies, in their houses, against the evil tricks and wiles of the malevolent spirit Silvanus. Pilumnus shared his functions with two equally obscure goddesses, Intercidona and Deverra. All three deities derived their names from rituals which were performed at the birth of a child. Intercidona took her name from the symbolic axe-blows given to the door post; Deverra derived hers from the broom which was used to sweep the threshold; and Pilumnus was supposed to be named after the *pilum* (pestle) with which the door was struck. Axe, pestle and broom were considered to be the symbols of civilization since the axe cut down trees, the pestle pounded corn and the broom swept the threshing floor. These symbols were considered sufficient to frighten Silvanus, the spirit of the uncivilized wilderness. Pilumnus is also mentioned alongside Picumnus, an obscure deity, whose name is reminiscent of PICUS. Virgil mentions a Pilumnus who is grandfather of Turnus and father of Daunus.

Pindus (Πίνδος) A son of Macedon, in the tradition which regards Macedon as one of the sons of Lycaon. When Pindus was out hunting one day he met a monstrous serpent. The creature did not attack him, however, and to show his gratitude Pindus from time to time brought the serpent part of the fruits of his hunting expeditions. The creature eventually became friendly with the young man and when Pindus was killed by his three brothers, who were jealous of him, the serpent killed them and guarded Pindus' corpse until his relatives arrived and paid him funeral honours.

Piren (Πειρήν)
1. The son of Glaucus, king of Corinth and the brother of BELLEROPHON. His brother accidentally killed him and consequently went into exile.
2. The son of Argos and Evadne. Sometimes his name is given as Piras rather than Piren. In some accounts he is said to be Io's father, but she is more commonly said to be the descendant of his brother ECBASUS (Table 18).

Pirene (Πειρήνη) The figure who gave her name to the Pirenean spring at Corinth. In the euhemer-ist version of the legend of Asopus, Pirene is one of the twelve daughters of the latter, born at Phlius to Metope, the daughter of king Ladon. By Poseidon she had two children, Leches and Cenchrias, who gave their names to the two gates of Corinth. When Artemis accidentally killed Cenchrias, Pirene, in her grief, shed so many tears that she changed into a spring. In another tradition Pirene was the daughter of Oebalus. There was a different legend surrounding the Pirenean spring which claimed that this spring was given to Sisyphus by the river-god Asopus as a reward for revealing to Asopus the name of the man who had raped his daughter AEGINA. According to some accounts, Bellerophon met Pegasus by the Pirenean spring.

Pirithous (Πειρίθοος) A Thessalian hero who was gradually integrated into the Theseus cycle. In the *Iliad* he is cited as the son of Zeus and Dia, but he is more usually considered to be the son of Dia and Ixion (Table 23). His legend is made up of different episodes which accord with each other badly. The principal events are his part in the Calydonian boar-hunt; his wedding to Hippodamia, which was the occasion of the battle with the Centaurs; his meeting with Theseus; his participation in the abduction of Helen and his visit to Hades.

In the Calydonian boar-hunt Pirithous was simply one of the huntsmen and took no special part in the action. In the *Iliad* Pirithous is portrayed as the vanquisher of the Centaurs, an episode which later became assimilated into his marriage to Hippodamia. She, though sometimes said to be the daughter of Adrastus and Amphithea (Table 1), is more generally described as the daughter of Butes. In one tradition Hippodamia was related to the Centaurs, and this seems to explain why Pirithous invited them to his wedding, but as a son of Ixion, Pirithous was himself a 'half-brother' to these monsters. Under the influence of the wine the Centaurs tried to rape Hippodamia and carry off the other women present. A violent battle broke out between the Centaurs and Pirithous' compatriots, the Lapiths, during which many Centaurs were killed. Pirithous and Hippodamia had a son named POLYPOETES.

To explain the friendship between Theseus and Pirithous it was said that the latter, having heard speak of Theseus' exploits, decided to put him to the test, and set himself the task of stealing some flocks belonging to Theseus, in the area of

Pirithous and Theseus abducting Helen. Amphora, c. 500 BC. Paris, Louvre.

Marathon. The two young men met but were amazed by each other's beauty and at the moment when it seemed that they would have to fight one another, Pirithous spontaneously offered to make reparation to Theseus for the stock which he had stolen, and declared himself Theseus' slave. In his desire to match his rival's nobility Theseus was moved to refuse his offer and declared he would forget Pirithous' crime. Their growing friendship was sealed with an oath. Thereafter the two young men carried out their heroic feats together. Theseus and Pirithous swore to have a daughter of Zeus as their joint wife and this is why Pirithous came to take part in Theseus' abduction of HELEN and also explains why Theseus accompanied his friend to Hades to carry off Persephone. The two friends entered Hades but were unable to leave; they were kept prisoners there until Heracles arrived. Heracles succeeded in bringing Theseus back up to the daylight, but when he tried to rescue Pirithous, the earth trembled and realizing that the gods did not want him to free the guilty party, Heracles abandoned his attempt. A euhem-erist version of the legend recounted by Pausanias claims that Theseus and Pirithous in fact went to Epirus to the court of a certain king Haedoneus, whose name became confused with that of Hades. Haedoncus' wife was called Persephone and his daughter Core. They had a very fierce dog called Cerberus. Theseus and Pirithous claimed that they had come to ask for Core's hand in marriage. In fact they intended to abduct both mother and daughter. Core's hand was promised to whichever hero succeeded in overcoming Cerberus, but Haedoneus guessed the true intentions of the two friends and had them arrested. Pirithous, who was considered the most to blame, was handed over to Cerberus who devoured him. Theseus was imprisoned until the day when Heracles, a friend of the family, asked the king to set Theseus free and his request was granted.

Pisaeus (Πισαῖος) An Etruscan hero named after the city where he was born, that is, Pisa in Tuscany. He was supposed to have invented the trumpet, and battle-rams for warships.

Pisidice (Πεισιδίκη)

1. The daughter of the king of the city of Methymna, on Lesbos. At the time when Achilles was besieging the city, Pisidice saw the hero from the top of the ramparts and fell in love with him. She secretly offered to deliver the city to Achilles if he would promise to marry her. Achilles accepted the offer but, once victorious, he had her stoned to death.

2. A similar story is told about another Pisidice who came not from Lesbos but from the city of Monenia in the Troad. While Achilles was besieging and was about to attack, Pisidice threw a note to the hero, stating that the citizens were about to surrender because of lack of water. Achilles was consequently able to capture the city without striking a single blow. The rest of Pisidice's story is unknown.

3. One of the daughters of Aeolus and Aenarete (Table 8).

4. One of the daughters of Nestor and Anaxibia.

Pisistratus (Πεισίστρατος)

The youngest son of NESTOR. He was the same age as Telemachus and went with him on his journey from Pylos to Sparta. The Athenian tyrant Pisistratus is said to have been descended from him.

Pistor

During the siege of the Capitol by the Gauls, the corn began to run out in the citadel and famine was threatening. Jupiter appeared in a dream in the night to the defenders and advised them to throw their most precious possession at the enemy. At once the Romans made all the rest of their flour into loaves and hurled them at the enemy. The Gauls despaired of ever reducing an enemy who seemed so well provisioned to starvation, and raised the siege. In gratitude the Romans built an altar to Jupiter Pistor (Jupiter the Baker).

Pisus (Πῖσος)

1. A son of Perieres, who marked the Arcadian Olympia, and gave his name to the city of Pisa in Elis.

2. Similarly the Italian city of Pisa laid claim, in certain traditions, to an eponymous Pisus, who was a king of the Celts and son of the Hyperborean Apollo.

3. A son of Aphareus (Table 19).

Pitane (Πιτάνη)

1. A daughter of the river-god Eurotas who bore Poseidon a child named Evadne. This child was exposed at birth by her mother and taken in by Aepytus. In other versions Pitane herself secretly took the child to Aepytus. The Spartan city of Pitane was named after her.

2. An Amazon who founded the city of Pitane in Mysia, as well as the cities of Cyme and Priene.

Pittheus (Πιτθεύς)

A son of Pelops and Hippodamia (Table 2) and the brother of Thyestes and Atreus. He succeeded TROEZEN as king of that city. At Troezen he is supposed to have founded the oldest Greek temple, that of Apollo Thearius. Pittheus had a great reputation for wisdom and eloquence. He was also thought an excellent seer. In Aegeus' presence he interpreted the oracle which promised the latter a brave son. He succeeded in making Aegeus intoxicated and arranged for him to spend the night with Pittheus' own daughter Aethra. As a result of this Pittheus became the grandfather of THESEUS and he brought him up. Through Pittheus, Theseus had a claim on the throne of Troezen. Pittheus was also in charge of the education of Hippolytus, the son of Theseus and the Amazon.

Pityreus (Πιτυρεύς)

A descendant of Ion, who was king of Epidaurus, in the Peloponnese, at the time when the Heraclids returned. He gave up his kingdom to the Heraclid Deiphontes without a fight and withdrew with his subjects to Athens. His son Procles led an Ionian colony from Epidaurus to Samos.

Pitys (Πίτυς)

A Nymph whom Pan loved. One day as the girl fled from his advances she was changed into a pine tree (in Greek πίτυς means 'pine'). This perhaps explains why Pan liked to decorate his brow with wreaths of pine leaves. In another version of the story Pitys was loved by both Pan and Boreas and yielded to the former. In a fit of jealousy Boreas hurled her off the top of a rock. The Earth, taking pity on her, changed her body into a pine tree. The soul of Pitys is said to weep as Boreas blows through the branches of pine trees.

Platanus (Πλάτανος)

A sister of the ALOADAE. After the death of her two brothers, she was changed into a plane tree.

Pleiades (Πληιάδες)

The seven sisters who were given divine status and became the seven stars of the constellation of the same name. They were the daughters of the Giant Atlas and Pleione (Table

25) and their names were Taygete, Electra, Alcyone, Asterope, Celaeno, Maia and Merope. There is another tradition about them which is preserved in the sole remaining fragment of a poem by Callimachus. According to this version the Pleiades were the daughters of a queen of the Amazons and were responsible for introducing choral dances and nocturnal festivals. In this poem their names are given as Coccymo, Glaucia, Protis, Parthenia, Maia, Stonychia and Lampado. Calypso and Dione are sometimes included among the Pleiades. All the Pleiades married gods with the exception of Merope, who married Sisyphus; she was ashamed of this fact and this is an explanation of why her star is the least bright in the constellation. The tradition summarized in Table 25 according to the version given by Apollodorus has some variants.

It is said that the Pleiades were in Boeotia one day with their mother Pleione when they met the terrible huntsman Orion, who fell in love with them. He pursued them for five years and eventually they were changed into doves. Zeus then took pity on them and turned them into stars. There are other traditions about them: in one, their transformation was the result of the grief which they felt when their father Atlas was condemned by Zeus to hold up the sky upon his shoulders, and in another version the Pleiades and their five sisters, the HYADES, were changed into stars after the death of their brother Hyas, who was bitten by a snake. When Troy fell, the Pleiad Electra, from whom the Trojan royal house was descended, left her sisters, in despair, and was changed into a comet.

Pleione (Πληιόνη) The mother of the Pleiades and a daughter of Oceanus and Tethys. Her children included the HYADES and HYAS as well as the PLEIADES. Orion fell in love with Pleione as well as her daughters; she too was changed into a star (Tables 6, 7 and 25).

Pleisthenes (Πλεισθένης) Pleisthenes appears in the genealogy of the family of Atreus and of Pelops but his parentage varies from tradition to tradition. He is most frequently said to be a son of Pelops and Hippodamia, and therefore a brother of Thyestes and Atreus (Table 2); another related version claims that he was the son of Pelops by another woman. In some versions Pleisthenes is the son of Atreus and Cleola, the daughter of DIAS, whom Atreus married after he had settled at Macistus in Triphylia, and in others AEROPE is said

to be his mother, but other versions make her his wife. Although Agamemnon and Menelaus are usually considered to be the sons of Atreus, another tradition claims that Pleisthenes was their father. This genealogy seems to have developed in the work of the tragedians in particular. To make the two traditions correspond it was assumed that Pleisthenes was indeed the father of the two heroes, and was himself the son of Atreus, but being by nature sickly he died young, entrusting his two sons and his daughter Anaxibia to their grandfather to bring up. This is why Agamemnon and Menelaus are generally designated under the title Atridae.

A story summarized by Hyginus makes Pleisthenes a son of Thyestes and brother of Tantalus. Pleisthenes and TANTALUS were said to have been killed by Atreus who wanted to avenge himself on his brother THYESTES. This legend is a late one and probably is based on a misconception. Another story claims that Pleisthenes was the son of Atreus and had been brought up by Thyestes, who believed that Pleisthenes was his own son. Thyestes wanted to avenge himself on Atreus and sent Pleisthenes to kill him, but Atreus killed the young man instead, realizing too late that he was his own son. The origin of this legend is probably a tragedy.

Plemnaeus (Πλημναῖος) A king of Sicyon in the tradition recorded by Pausanias. He is the son of Peratus and father of ORTHOPOLIS. He is said to have introduced the cult of Demeter into Sicyon and to have raised a temple to her.

Pleuron (Πλευρών) The brother of Calydon and, like him a son of Aetolus and Pronoe (Table 24). He gave his name to the Aetolian city of Pleuron and married Xanthippe, daughter of Dorus, thus establishing ties between the Aetolians and the Dorians. Pleuron had several children by Xanthippe: Agenor, Sterope, Stratonice and Laophonte. Another tradition attributes to Pleuron two sons, Coures and Calydon. Pleuron was the great-great-grandfather of Leda. There was a sanctuary dedicated to him at Sparta.

Plexippus (Πλήξιππος)
1. One of the uncles of MELEAGER and the brother of Althaea (Table 24). He was killed by his nephew during the Calydonian boar-hunt.
2. One of the two sons of PHINEUS and Cleopatra. He was blinded by his father (Table 11).
3. One of the sons of CHORICUS.

Pluton (Πλούτων) Pluton, or the Rich Man, is simply a ritual title of HADES, god of the Underworld. He was assimilated to the Latin deity Dis Pater who, like him, was originally the god of the fields, because the ground was the source of all wealth (see PLUTUS and DEMETER).

Plutus (Πλοῦτος) Plutus or Wealth, was the son of Demeter and Iasion according to Hesiod's *Theogony*. He was born in Crete. Plutus appears in the procession of Demeter and Persephone either as a young man, or as a child bearing a horn of plenty. Later, as the concept of wealth developed until it became associated with material goods, Plutus was separated from the followers of Demeter and became the personification of wealth in general; he appears in this form in Aristophanes' comedy. Plutus is represented by the writers of comedy, and by popular tradition, as being blind, since he visits the good and the wicked without making any distinction. According to Aristophanes Zeus himself was supposed to have blinded Plutus to prevent him from only rewarding the virtuous and to oblige him to favour the wicked too. This is less a question of mythology than of symbolism, however.

Podalirius (Ποδαλείριος) The brother of Machaon and, like him, a son of Asclepius, the god of Medicine. His mother's name is sometimes given as Epione, sometimes as Lampetia. Podalirius and Machaon were both Helen's suitors and participated in the Trojan War. Both were skilled in healing and played important parts not only in the fighting but also as doctors: Machaon was said to have been principally a surgeon and Podalirius a general practitioner. He was supposed to have cured a large number of people: he dressed the wounds of Acamas and Epeius, who were badly hurt in the boxing contest at the funeral games in honour of Achilles, and also cured Philoctetes. Podalirius outlived his brother, whose death he avenged. After the fall of Troy he returned to Greece with Calchas, Amphilochus, Leonteus and Polypoetes, and reached Colophon by land. After Calchas' death at Colophon Podalirius went to Greece and asked the Delphic oracle where he should settle. The oracle instructed him to choose an area where, if the sky fell around him, he would have nothing to fear. The region corresponding to this description was the Chersonese at Caria which is ringed by mountains around the horizon and Podalirius settled there. Another legend deals with his arrival in Caria: according to

this version he was thrown up on the coast by a storm and rescued by a goatherd who took him to the king of the region whose name was Damaethus. The king's daughter, Syrna, had just fallen from a roof and the king gratefully accepted Podalirius' offer of medical assistance. He cured the girl, married her, and was presented with the Carian peninsula, where he founded the city of Syrnos.

There was also a sanctuary dedicated to Podalirius in Italy at the foot of Mount Drion. There was another sanctuary on the top of the mountain which was dedicated to Calchas. Podalirius was said to have founded it, and it was believed that if one sacrificed a black ram to either Podalirius or Calchas and then slept in the animal's skin one had prophetic dreams.

Podarces (Ποδάρκης)
1. The name given to Priam when he was young (see HERACLES, PRIAM and Table 7).
2. The name of a son of Iphiclus who accompanied his brother Protesilaus to Troy; after the latter's death he succeeded him as commander of the Thessalian contingent from Phylacae. He killed the Amazon Clonia and was himself killed by Penthesilea. The Greeks paid him special funeral honours and gave him a separate tomb (Table 20).

Podarge (Ποδάργη) One of the Harpies. She gave birth to two horses, Xanthus and Balius, the steeds of Achilles, fathered by the wind-god Zephyrus. She is also said to have been the mother of Phlogaius and Harpagus, the two horses belonging either to Diomedes or to the Dioscuri.

Podes (Ποδῆς) A Trojan, and a close friend of Hector, who was killed by Menelaus in the fighting over the body of Patroclus.

Poeas (Ποίας) The son of Thaumacus, or alternatively of Phylacus. He was married to Methone and was the father of Philoctetes. He appears among the Argonauts but plays a very small part in their legend. One tradition makes him the conqueror of Talos, although this role is more generally attributed to MEDEA. Poeas was an archer who was with Heracles in his dying moments. Some mythographers say that it was he who lit the pyre on which Heracles had placed himself when everybody else refused, and in recompense Heracles bequeathed to Poeas his bow and arrows. PHILOCTETES is more frequently attributed with this role, however.

Poemandrus (Ποίμανδρος) A Boeotian hero who was the son of Chaeresilaus and Stratonice. He married Tanagra, who was a daughter either of Aeolus or of the river-god Asopus. Poemandrus was the founder of the city of Poemandria, which later took the name of Tanagra. The inhabitants refused to take part in the Trojan War and Achilles, accordingly, came and attacked them. He carried off Stratonice and killed her grandson. Poemandrus succeeded in escaping and hurriedly began fortifying the city which up to that time had no walls. During the course of this work the builder Polycrithus insulted Poemandrus, who picked up a large stone and hurled it at Polycrithus; his aim missed, but he killed his own son Leucippus instead. As a result of this murder Poemandrus had to leave Boeotia, but since the region was besieged by the enemy, he asked them to let him leave in safety. Achilles agreed to this, and sent Poemandrus to Elephenor, at Chalcis. Elephenor purified Poemandrus and, in gratitude, Poemandrus built a sanctuary to Achilles outside the city.

Poine (Ποινή) The personification of vengeance or punishment; she is sometimes identified with the Erinyes or Furies whom she accompanied. In later Roman mythology Poena is the mother of the Furies and appears among the demons of the Underworld, but this is an allegorical notion invented by the poets and not part of traditional mythology. There was a legend about Poine which portrayed her as a special monster sent by Apollo to avenge the death of Psamathe (compare CROTOPUS and COROEBUS).

Polhymnia (Πολύμνια) One of the nine Muses, and, like her sisters, a daughter of Zeus and Mnemosyne. Various traditions attribute to her several inventions, including the lyre and even agriculture itself. She was sometimes said to be the mother of Triptolemus, supposedly by a son of Ares called Celeus or Cheimarrhous. Her functions are variously given, as with all the Muses: in some accounts she is said to be the Muse of Dancing, in others the Muse of Geometry or even of History. An isolated tradition claims that she was Orpheus' mother by Oeager, although Orpheus' mother is more usually said to be Calliope. Plato refers to a legend in which she is the mother of Eros.

Poliporthes (Πολιπόρθης) Poliporthes or Ptoliporthes was a son of ODYSSEUS and Penelope, born after Odysseus' return to Ithaca while his father was ruling the Thesprotians (Table 39).

Polites (Πολίτης)
1. One of the sons of Priam and Hecuba. He features in several episodes of the *Iliad*; for example, he came to the help of Troilus when he was attacked by Achilles and he took part in the fighting around the ships, when he saved his brother Deiphobus, who had been wounded by Merion. Polites was the last surviving son of Priam. He was killed by Neoptolemus at the palace altar, in his father's presence. Virgil names a son of Polites, called Priamus, among the competitors at the funeral games given for Anchises. The founding of the city of Politorium in Latium was supposed to go back to this son.
2. Another Polites was a companion of Odysseus who was changed into a pig by Circe. For the specific legend of this Polites, see EUTHYMUS.

Pollux (Πολυδεύκης) One of the DIOSCURI, the twin brother of Castor (Table 19).

Poltys (Πόλτυς) A son of Poseidon and king of Aenos in Thrace. He entertained Heracles when he came to Thrace via the Troad on his way back from the land of the Amazons. He had a brother SARPEDON, distinct from Minos' brother of that name, who was slain by Heracles, on the seashore. During the Trojan War the Trojans sent an embassy to Poltys, bearing gifts and asking for his help, but Poltys demanded that Paris should hand Helen over to him in exchange for two other beautiful women and the demand was, of course, rejected.

Polybus (Πόλυβος)
1. The king of Thebes, in Egypt, who gave hospitality to MENELAUS and HELEN.
   It is also the name of a number of heroes, difficult to distinguish one from another, who appear in the genealogies of the Greek royal houses.
2. A king of Sicyon, son of Hermes and Chthonophyle, who was herself a daughter of Zeuxippe and Sicyon. In him mingled the blood of the kings of Argos and of the family of Erechtheus of Athens (Table 22). Polybus had a daughter called Lysianassa, or Lysimache, whom he gave in marriage to Talaus, king of Argos. She had several children by him, including Adrastus and Pronax (Table 1). ADRASTUS fled to the court of Polybus, and when Polybus died without male children he left his kingdom to Adrastus.
3. A king of Corinth who brought up OEDIPUS.

Polybotes (Πολυβώτης) One of the giants who fought the gods. He was chased by Poseidon as far as Cos, where the god tore off a piece of the island and crushed him beneath it, forming the islet of Nisyros.

Polycaon (Πολυκάων) The husband of Messene and the younger brother of Lelex and Peridea. As he had no hope of inheriting any part of his father's kingdom, he decided, on his wife's advice, to obtain a kingdom of his own. Accompanied by people from Argos and Sparta, he founded the city of Andania and colonized the area of the Peloponnese which he named Messenia (see also MESSENE). This Polycaon is to be distinguished from the hero who married Evaechme, the daughter of Hyllus and Iole (Table 16).

Polycaste (Πολυκάστη)
1. One of the daughters of Nestor who, in the *Odyssey*, prepared a bath for Telemachus when he came to Pylos to ask after the fate of his father. In later legend Polycaste was said to have married Telemachus and borne him a son called Persepolis.
2. The wife of ICARIUS, and Penelope's mother, but in some versions Periboea is also given as the wife of Icarius instead of Polycaste (Table 19). This Polycaste was the daughter of Lygaeus, an Acarnanian.

Polycrite (Πολυκρίτη) A heroine of Naxos to whom a cult was devoted. In the course of a war between the Naxians and the inhabitants of Miletus, who were allied to the Erythraeans, Polycrite was said to have been taken prisoner by Diognetus, leader of the Erythraeans. The latter soon fell in love with his captive, who exerted complete power over him. Polycrite was the sister of the leader of the Naxians, Polycles. By means of a note concealed in a cake she managed to warn her brother that she had persuaded her lover to hand over the camp of which he was in charge to the Naxians during the night. The Naxians, forewarned, entered the camp and massacred their enemy, with whom they subsequently concluded an advantageous peace. However, Polycrite, on returning to Naxos, received so many gifts and was so weighed down by wreaths that she suffocated at the gate as she was entering the town. She was buried at the spot on which she died. At Polycrite's request, Diognetus' life had been spared during the attack on the camp, but there was another version of the story in which he was

killed during the fighting and was buried beside Polycrite.

Polycritus (Πολύκριτος) An Aetolian who had been elected leader of the confederation and had subsequently married a young woman of Locris. But he spent only three nights with his wife, and died before the fourth. After nine months, his widow gave birth to a child possessing both male and female sexual characteristics. The terrified mother took the child to the market-place where the people were gathered. It was agreed that this was a divine curse, and that both the mother and the monstrous child should be carried beyond the frontiers of the land and burnt. At this moment Polycritus appeared, dressed in black, and reclaimed his child, adding that he should be handed over to him quickly, as the gods of the Underworld had granted him only a brief freedom. As the frightened populace hesitated to grant his request, he repeated it, and, at their continued delay, seized the child which he tore in pieces and completely devoured, leaving only the head. He then disappeared. The Aetolians began to discuss the possibility of sending an embassy to Delphi to seek advice as to how the effects of this prodigious event could be avoided, but at this moment the head of the child, which had rolled onto the ground, began to prophesy. It forbade the inhabitants to send a delegation to Delphi, and predicted that there would be a war. Finally, it requested that it should not be buried, but placed in a sunlit spot.

Polyctor (Πολύκτωρ) A hero who, with Ithacus and Neritus, made the stream from which the inhabitants of Ithaca obtained their water flow. They were the children of PTERELAS and Amphimede, and thus descended from Zeus. They had originally come from Cephalonia to colonize Ithaca.

Polydamas (Πολυδάμας) A Trojan hero, the son of PANTHOUS and Phrontis (or else Pronome), the daughter of Clytius. He was born the same night as Hector, and the latter's prowess in battle was equalled by Polydamas' soundness in counsel. It was he, for example, who proposed the plan of attack on the wall of the Achaean camp; he suggested to Hector that he should summon the Trojan chiefs; he advised the Trojans, after their defeat, to take refuge in Ilion and, after Hector's death, to hand over Helen rather than obstinately refuse. Furthermore, Polydamas accomplished several feats on the battlefield. He killed Mecisteus and Otus, and wounded Peneleos. Polydamas was said to have had a son called Leocritus.

Polydamna (Πολύδαμνα) According to one tradition the wife of the Egyptian king Thon. In order to protect HELEN from the amorous advances of the king, she took her to the island of Pharos in the Nile delta, and gave her herbs as a protection against the bite of the countless serpents which inhabited the island.

Polydectes (Πολυδέκτης) According to some writers, a son of Magnes, the descendant of Aeolus (Table 8), and one of the Naiads; according to others, he was the son of Peristhenus who was, through his father Damastor, a grandson of Nauplius. In this second version, his mother was Androthea, daughter of Pericastor. He had a brother, Dictys, with whom he settled on the island of Seriphos. It was with Dictys – or, according to the other traditions, with Polydectes himself – that DANAE sought refuge when she and her son PERSEUS were cast up on the shores of the island. Polydectes soon fell in love with Danae, and it was in order to remove Perseus when he came of age that he sent him off to look for the head of Medusa, on the pretext of wishing to give it as a wedding present to Hippodamia. During Perseus' absence, Polydectes tried to assault Danae who, with Dictys, took refuge in the temple. Perseus reappeared and, by means of the Medusa's head, changed Polydectes into a stone statue.

An aberrant version, related by Hyginus, states that it was at the funeral games organized by Perseus in honour of Polydectes that he accidentally killed his grandfather Acrisius (for the more accepted version of this death, see ACRISIUS and PERSEUS).

Polydora (Πολυδώρα) The name of several heroines, amongst whom should be noted in particular the daughter of PELEUS (Table 30) and Antigone, daughter of Eurytion. Polydora had, by the river-god Spercheius, a son named Menesthius. She subsequently married Borus, the son of Perieres. This Borus sometimes passed for the human father of Menesthius. Some accounts give as her mother Polymela, the daughter of Actor, instead of Antigone. There was also a tradition in which Polydora was not the daughter, but the wife of Peleus (see also DRYOPS).

Polydorus (Πολύδωρος)
1. The first hero of this name belongs to the race of Cadmus (Table 3). He was the son of Cadmus and Harmonia, and married Nycteis, the daughter of Nycteus, by whom he had a son, Labdacus, grandfather of Oedipus. Traditions vary on his role in the succession of power from Cadmus to Oedipus. According to some, it was to Polydorus that Cadmus left the throne of Thebes when he set off for Illyria. Certainly Polydorus was at that time the sole son of Cadmus. According to others, Cadmus is said to have left the throne to Pentheus, the son of his daughter Agave. In this version, Polydorus followed his father to Illyria. An intermediate tradition maintained that Pentheus dispossessed Polydorus, the rightful heir, after Cadmus' departure.

2. Another Polydorus was a son of Priam. There were many traditions about him, one of which made him the son of Priam and Laothoe. During the Trojan War, Priam sent him away from the battlefield because of his youth, but Polydorus, trusting in his own speed as a runner, attacked Achilles who killed him. Polydorus was armed with a silver cuirass which Achilles removed from his body. Later, after the death of her son, Thetis presented this trophy to Agamemnon. Such was the Homeric tradition. Later, particularly in the works of the tragic writers and the Alexandrine and Roman poets, Polydorus was considered the son of Priam and Hecuba. Priam entrusted this son, while still young, to his son-in-law Polymestor, the king of Thrace. At the same time he put into his care rich treasures designed, should the need arise, to allow Polydorus to maintain his rank if the war were to turn to the Trojans' disadvantage. Either because Polymestor coveted the treasures or else because he gave way to the demands of the victorious Greeks, he killed Polydorus. He then threw the body into the sea which cast it up on the coast of the Troad, just as a servant of Hecuba (or Hecuba herself) was drawing water for the funeral rites of Polyxena, who had been sacrificed on the tomb of Achilles. Hecuba recognized her son, and obtained Agamemnon's permission to bury him beside Polyxena. For the story of Hecuba's vengeance against Polymestor, see HECUBA.

In the tradition followed by Virgil, Polymestor buried Polydorus on the coast of Thrace. When Aeneas landed in the country, he cut branches from the trees which grew on his tomb in order to decorate the altar on which he was making a sacrifice. Drops of blood oozed from the branches, and a voice was heard, revealing that he was on the site of Polydorus' tomb, and that these trees had sprung from the javelins which had pierced him. The voice recounted how Polymestor had killed the child which had been entrusted to him to get hold of his gold, and advised Aeneas to abandon his plan to found a city on this accursed spot. Aeneas then gave funeral honours to the murdered child, and left the country. Yet another tradition related that Polymestor had handed Polydorus over to Ajax, the son of Telamon, who had ravaged his kingdom. Ajax and the Greeks wanted to use the child as a hostage, and exchange him for Helen, but the Trojans refused. Polydorus was then stoned before Troy's walls, and his body returned to Hecuba. The tragic writers imagined that Polydorus had not been killed by Polymestor, but that the latter had, in error, put his own son, DEIPYLUS, to death. Later Polydorus was to exact vengeance from the disloyal king.

Polygonus (Πολύγονος) He and Telegonus, the two sons of Proteus and Torone, were killed quite justifiably by Heracles. These two bandits used to challenge travellers to a fight, and then kill them.

Polyidus (Πολύειδος)
1. A famous Corinthian soothsayer, and descended from Melampus in the following way: Melampus had, amongst other children, a son called Mantius, father of CLITUS, who in turn had a son Coeranus, the father of Polyidus. The latter married Eurydamia, a grand-daughter of Augias and daughter of Phylus. He had two sons, Euchenor and Clitus, who took part in the expedition of the Epigoni and later accompanied Agamemnon against Troy. Polyidus had predicted to Euchenor that he could choose between two destinies: either to die at home of illness, or else fall at Troy on the field of battle. Euchenor chose the second and died at the hands of Paris.
    A local tradition which grew up at Megara related that Polyidus came to this city where he purified ALCATHUS of the murder of his son Callipolis and built a temple to Dionysus. In this tradition, Polyidus is acknowledged as son of Coeranus and descendant of Melampus, but his grandfather is given as Abas (Table 1).
    Polyidus is supposed to have advised Bellerophon to go to the spring of Pirene and catch Pegasus. He also advised Iphitus, the son of Eurytus, to go to Tiryns to be with Heracles. He saved Teuthras, the king of Mysia, from his madness.

But the most famous story of his intervention is that of the resurrection of GLAUCUS, the son of Minos.
2. A Trojan, the son of the soothsayer Eurydamas, who along with his brother Abas was slain by Diomedes.

Polymede (Πολυμήδη) A daughter of Autolycus who married Aeson and became the mother of Jason (Table 21) When her husband was condemned to death by Pelias, she cursed the latter and hanged herself. She left a small child called Promachus, but Pelias killed him so as to wipe out the race of Aeson. Aeson's wife was also known to mythographers as Alcimede.

Polymela (Πολυμήλα)
1. An early heroine of this name was the daughter of Phylas who became by Hermes the mother of EUDORUS. She later married Echecles, a descendent of Actor.
2. The daughter of Aeolus, the god of winds, She was Odysseus' mistress while he was staying at her father's court and on Odysseus' departure she was so grieved that even her father noticed it. He wanted to punish her, but Diores his son, was in love with his sister and obtained Aeolus' permission to marry her. It seems that the sons and daughters of Aeolus were accustomed to marrying incestuously.
3. A daughter of Actor who, according to certain traditions, seems to have married Peleus before his marriage to Thetis (see POLYDORA). Sometimes she also passes for the daughter of Peleus.

Polymestor (Πολυμήστωρ) The king of Thrace, husband of Iliona, the daughter of Priam. He played a part in the legend of Polydorus and in that of Hecuba. For the different versions of this legend, see DEIPYLUS, HECUBA and POLYDORUS.

Polymnus (Πόλυμνος) When DIONYSUS descended into the Underworld he sought the way from a peasant called Polymnus (or Prosymnus) who gave him the necessary information, but in return asked the god for his favours. Dionysus promised to bestow these on him on his return. However, when he returned, Polymnus was dead. In order to fulfil his promise, the god carved a fig branch into the shape of a phallus and on Polymnus' tomb performed an act designed to satisfy his shade. This obscene legend was devised to explain the role played by the phallus in the worship of Dionysus.

Polynices (Πολυνείκης) One of the two sons of
OEDIPUS. His brother was Eteocles. Traditions
vary about the identity of his mother. Sometimes
he is the son of Euryganla, the second wife of
Oedipus, but according to others, in the tradition
followed by the tragic writers, he is the son of
Jocasta. Eteocles is sometimes given as his elder,
and sometimes as his younger brother. Their
rivalry over Thebes led to the war of the Seven
against Thebes and the expedition of Adrastus
against the city. It was sometimes related that the
origins of their rivalry could be found in their
father's triple curse. When Oedipus blinded himself on discovery of his incest and parricide, his
sons insulted him instead of pitying him. Polynices put before him, despite being expressly forbidden to do so, Cadmus' silver table along with
his gold cup. This was a way of making fun of
him and reminding him of his origins as well as of
his crime. When he noticed this, Oedipus cursed
them both, predicting that they would be incapable of living in peace either during their lifetime
or after death. Later, during a sacrifice, the two
brothers sent their father the thigh bones of the
victim instead of a choice piece. The enraged
Oedipus hurled the bones to the ground and pronounced a second curse against them, predicting
that they would kill each other. Finally, the third
curse was pronounced when the brothers had
locked Oedipus away in a remote dungeon so that
he might be forgotten, and were refusing him the
honours to which he was entitled. He predicted
that they would divide up their heritage by the
sword. More simply, it was said that Oedipus
cursed his sons because they had not tried to save
him when Creon had banished him from Thebes.

Left as the sole rulers of Thebes, Eteocles and
Polynices decided to share the power by reigning
alternately, each for a year. Eteocles was the first
to reign (or the second, depending on whether he
was considered the elder or the younger, in which
case he then took over from Polynices, following
their agreement, after the first year). However, at
the end of a year, he refused to hand over power to
his brother. Thus, evicted from his homeland,
Polynices came to Argos, bearing with him
Harmonia's dress and necklace. At that time it was
Adrastus who reigned in Argos. Polynices presented himself at his palace one stormy night at the
same time as Tydeus, the son of Oeneus, who had
fled from Calydon. The two heroes fought each
other in the courtyard of the palace. The noise
attracted Adrastus, who separated and greeted
them, and gave them his two daughters in mar-

riage (Table 1). Thus Polynices married Argia and
Adrastus promised to help him recover his kingdom. This was the origin of the expedition of the
Seven against Thebes. Amphiaraus, the soothsayer, foreseeing the fate of the expedition, tried
to dissuade Adrastus. In order to get around this
difficulty, Polynices went to IPHIS, the son of Alector, and asked him how it would be possible to
force Amphiaraus to join the expedition. Iphis
revealed that Amphiaraus was bound by an oath
to accept all the decisions of his wife ERIPHYLE.
Polynices then offered her Harmonia's necklace,
asking her in return to persuade her husband.
Thus the expedition was able to be organized. On
their way to Thebes, at Nemea, Polynices won the
wrestling at the funeral games organized in
honour of Archemorus (these were the future Nemean games). During the fighting outside Thebes,
Polynices was killed by his brother, but as he was
dying, Polynices killed Eteocles. Thus Oedipus'
curse was fulfilled. For the circumstances surrounding the burial of Polynices, see ANTIGONE.

Polyphates (Πολυφάτης) A king who played a
part in the legend of MELAMPUS. While the latter
was his guest, a serpent was killed near the altar by
the king's servants in the course of a sacrifice.
Polyphates ordered Melampus, who was still a
young man, to bury the animal. Melampus
obeyed, but the serpent was a female with young
which Melampus kept and raised. When they
were fully grown they gratefully purified the ears
of their benefactor with their tongues, and thus
gave him the gift of prophecy.

Polyphemus (Πολύφημος) The name of two distinct characters.
1. One of the Lapiths, the son of Elatus and Hippe.
Poseidon was his divine father and Caeneus his
brother. He married Laonome who, according to
an obscure tradition, was said to be the sister of
Heracles. This Polyphemus took part in the fight
of the Centaurs and Lapiths. He also participated
in the Argonauts' expedition, but remained in
Mysia where he founded the city of Cios. He died
in the war against the Chalybes.
2. The more famous figure of this name was the
Cyclops who appears in the *Odyssey*. He was the
son of Poseidon and the Nymph Thoosa, herself
the daughter of Phorcys. The Homeric story depicts him as a horrible giant, the most savage of all
the Cyclopes. He was a cave-dwelling shepherd
who lived off the produce of his flock of sheep.
Although he knew how to use fire, he devoured

raw flesh. He knew what wine was, but drank it very rarely and appeared unaware of the effects of drunkenness. He was not completely unsociable since, when in trouble, he summoned the other Cyclopes to his aid, but was incapable of making them understand his misfortune.

Odysseus was captured by him along with a dozen of his companions and imprisoned in his cave. The Cyclops began to devour several of them, promising Odysseus that he would eat him last in gratitude for the delicious wine which the hero had brought from the boat for him. During the night, when the Cyclops was sleeping soundly under the influence of the wine, Odysseus and his companions sharpened an immense stake, hardened it in the fire and drove it into the solitary eye of the giant. In the morning, as the flock of sheep was going out to pasture, the Greeks attached themselves underneath the bellies of the rams so as to escape without being detected by the blinded Cyclops who was guarding the exit by feeling everything that left with his hands. Once free, and when his boat had set sail, Odysseus cried out to Polyphemus that he was Odysseus and taunted him. The Cyclops was in a rage at being duped, for an oracle had once predicted to him that he would be blinded by Odysseus, and he threw enormous rocks at the boat, but in vain. It is from this moment that we can date the hatred of Poseidon, Polyphemus' father, for Odysseus. After the Homeric poems, Polyphemus became, in a rather strange way, the hero of a love story involving the Nereid Galatea. It is in an *Idyll* of Theocritus that we find preserved the most famous picture of the Cyclops in love with a coquette who finds him too brutish. The same theme is taken up by Ovid (see ACIS). There is a variant tradition according to which GALATEA was in love with the Cyclops, and had children by him.

Polyphides (Πολυφείδης)

1. A soothsayer, the son of Mantius according to certain traditions, and consequently descended from Melampus (Table 1). He had received the gift of prophecy from Apollo himself. As a result of a quarrel with his father, he went to settle at Hyperasia in Achaea. He had a son THEOCLYMENUS and a daughter Harmonide.

2. Another hero of the same name was the twenty-fourth king of Sicyon. He was reigning at the time of the Trojan War according to the tradition reported in Eusebius' *Chronicle*, and Menelaus and Agamemnon, while still children, were brought to his court by their nurse to protect them from Thyestes. Polyphides in turn entrusted them to King Oeneus of Aetolia. If, as the *Chronicle* maintains, Polyphides was still reigning at the time of the fall of Troy, he must have lived to an extraordinarily old age.

Polyphonte (Πολυφόντη)

The daughter of Hipponous, a Thracian, and Thrassa, a daughter of Ares and Tereine, who was herself the daughter of Strymon, the river god. Scornful of the gifts of Aphrodite, she attached herself to Artemis, which so irritated Aphrodite that she inspired her with an obsessive passion for a bear. As a punishment for having lost her virginity in this monstrous love affair, Artemis unleashed against her all the mountain beasts. The terrified Polyphonte took refuge with her father and gave birth to two children called Agrius and Orius (Wild Man and Mountain Dweller). These two children grew up and became endowed with a prodigious strength, fearing neither the gods nor men. On meeting a stranger, they would drag him into their house and devour him. Zeus eventually regarded them as such objects of horror that he sent his messenger Hermes to punish them. Hermes determined to cut off their feet and hands, but Ares, their grandfather, wanted to spare them punishment and metamorphosed them. Polyphonte became a night bird, Orius a bird of prey and Agrius a vulture, all animals of sinister omen. The servant girl who, although quite guiltless, was metamorphosed at the same time, asked the gods if she could become a bird well disposed towards men. They granted her wish and turned her into a woodpecker, a bird of good luck to hunters.

Polyphontes (Πολυφόντης)

1. A son of Autophonus, who commanded the fifty Thebans responsible for ambushing Tydeus at the time of the expedition of the Seven against Thebes. Tydeus massacred them all.

2. A Heraclid who killed Cresphontes in order to seize his kingdom and his wife MEROPE. He was in turn killed by the son of the victim (see AEPYTUS).

Polypoetes (Πολυποίτης)

1. A son of Apollo and Phthia. He was killed by AETOLUS with his two brothers, Dorus and Laodocus.

2. Another Polypoetes was one of the Greeks who participated in the Trojan War. He was a son of Pirithous and Hippodamia (Table 23) and was born on the very day when his father chased the Centaurs from Mount Pelion. His mother died

shortly after his birth and his father went to the court of Theseus at Athens. When Polypoetes reached manhood, he succeeded Pirithous on the throne. He and his friend Leonteus figure amongst the suitors of Helen and, because of this, participated in the war to avenge Menelaus, commanding a contingent of forty ships. The death of several hundred Trojan warriors on the battlefield is attributed to him, including Damasus and Dresaeus. He participated in the funeral games in honour of Patroclus, and figures amongst the heroes of the wooden horse. After the fall of Troy he and Leonteus accompanied CALCHAS overland as far as Colophon.

3. The son of ODYSSEUS and Callidice, the queen of the Thesprotians (Table 39). After her death, he succeeded her on the throne, while Odysseus returned to Ithaca.

Polyxena (Πολυξένη) One of the daughters of Priam and Hecuba, and regarded as the youngest of them all. She is not mentioned in the *Iliad* and appears only in later epics where she is connected with the legend of Achilles. There are differing versions of her meeting with the hero. It is sometimes stated that Polyxena was at a fountain where Troilus was watering his horse when Achilles appeared, pursued Troilus and killed him. Polyxena managed to escape, but not before having aroused Achilles' passion. In the form of the legend which seems to have developed particularly in the Hellenistic period, Polyxena is sometimes said to have come with Andromache and Priam to reclaim Hector's body from Achilles. Whereas the hero remained unmoved by the entreaties of the father and the widow of his enemy, Polyxena managed to sway him by offering to remain with him as a slave. The story of Achilles' betrayal is associated with this version of the legend: in order to win the hand of Polyxena, he suggested to Priam that he would abandon the Greeks and return to his own country, or even betray his own people and fight in the Trojan ranks. The negotiations were to be concluded in the temple of the Thymbrean Apollo, but PARIS, hidden behind the statue of the god, killed ACHILLES with an arrow.

There existed, independent of the story of the love of Achilles and Polyxena and perhaps earlier than this legend, that of the death of Polyxena, sacrificed on the tomb of Achilles. In the *Cyprian Songs*, Polyxena died from wounds inflicted by Diomedes and Odysseus during the siege of Troy. She was buried by Neoptolemus. Later, however,

it was accepted that Polyxena had been sacrificed on the tomb of Achilles either by Neoptolemus or by the Greek leaders at the instigation of Odysseus. This is the version followed by the tragic poets, notably Euripides. The aim of this sacrifice was either to ensure a safe crossing for the Achaean ships (akin to the sacrifice of IPHIGENIA, designed to ensure favourable winds for Agamemnon's army) or else to appease the ghost of Achilles which had appeared to his son in a dream, demanding this offering.

Polyxenus (Πολύξενος)
1. Son of Agasthenes and grandson of Augias. He figures among Helen's suitors and commanded a force of Epeians against Troy. After his return from Troy he had a son whom he called Amphimachus after his companion, the son of Cteatus, who had fallen at Troy. Polyxenus' tomb could be seen at Elis. It was said that after the murder of the suitors Odysseus went to stay with Polyxenus as his guest. Amongst other presents, Polyxenus apparently gave him a vase on which the story of Trophonius, Agamedes and Augias was depicted.
2. One of the sons of Jason and Medea (Table 21).
3. The king of Elis with whom the Taphians hid the oxen which they stole from Electryon. AMPHITRYON recovered them for him.

Polyxo (Πολυξώ)
1. The wife of Nycteus and the mother of Antiope (Table 25).
2. Another, much more famous, was the wife of TLEPOLEMUS of Rhodes, the son of Heracles, who died at Troy. To honour the memory of her husband she organized funeral games in which young children took part. The winner received a crown of white poplar. She also found a way to avenge the death of her husband and to punish Helen, who was responsible for the Trojan War, though there are differing accounts of the form her vengeance took. For example, it was related that Menelaus, returning from Egypt with HELEN, arrived within sight of Rhodes where he intended landing. On learning of this, Polyxo gathered all the inhabitants of the island on the shore, armed with torches and stones. Menelaus thought first of avoiding the island, but the wind drove him onto the shore. However, he concealed his wife in the ship, dressed up the most beautiful of his servant girls in Helen's clothing, and allowed the Rhodians to murder the false Helen. Their vengeance appeased, the islanders allowed Menelaus to leave in peace, and Helen was thus saved

from Polyxo. But the most common version of the legend is less fortunate for the Laconian heroine. After the death of Menelaus, and while Orestes was still wandering the world pursued by the Furies, Helen's two stepsons Nicostratus and Megapenthes evicted her from Sparta. She fled to Polyxo, her compatriot, believing her to be a friend. Polyxo was initially well disposed towards her, but while Helen was bathing she dressed her servants up as the Furies and set them upon her. The torments inflicted on her by the servants so terrified her that in a fit of hysteria she hung herself.

3. The nurse of HYPSIPYLE of Lemnos. She advised her to meet the Argonauts.

Pomona The Roman Nymph of fruit. She had a sacred wood, the Pomonal, on the road from Rome to Ostia. A special priest was in charge of her cult, and poets attributed amorous adventures to her. For example, they made her the wife of the legendary king PICUS. It was for love of her that Picus was said to have rejected Circe's passionate advances, which resulted in him being turned into a woodpecker. Ovid makes her the wife of Vertumnus, who was, like her, a divinity linked with the cycle of the seasons and the fertility of the earth.

Pompo (Πόμπων) In the Hellenized Latin legend, a daughter of the king Numa Pompilius and the ancestor of the *gens Pomponia*. According to one tradition the name of Numa's father was Pompilius Pompo.

Pontus (Πόντος) The masculine personification of the sea. He does not possess any particular legend and only figures in theogonic and cosmogonic genealogies. He was regarded as the son of the Earth (Gaia) and Aether, but by Gaia he fathered Nereus, Thaumas, Phorcys, Ceto and Eurybia (Table 12). He is occasionally made the father of Briareus and of four Telchines namely Actaeus, Megalesius, Hormenus and Lycus. For the descendants of Pontus, see Table 32.

Porphyrion (Πορφυρίων) One of the giants who fought against the gods. He fell, along with Typhon, under the arrows of Apollo. There exists

The House of the Faun at Pompeii. The whole city of Pompeii was buried after the eruption of Vesuvius in AD 79 and was not rediscovered until 1748. A large part has now been excavated.

another legend according to which Porphyrion tried to assault Hera but was killed by the combined force of Zeus and Heracles.

Porthaon (Πορθάων) A son of Agenor and Epicaste, and consequently the grandson of Pleuron (Table 24). He ruled over Pleuron and Calydon, and married Euryte by whom he had several children: Oeneus, Agrius, Alcathus, Melas, Leucopeus, Sterope. He was the ancestor of Meleager (Table 27). His name is sometimes written in the form Parthaon or Portheus.

Portheus (Πορθεύς)
1. A form of the name PORTHAON.
2. The father of Echion, the first of the Greek heroes to emerge from the wooden horse, but who fell while jumping out and was killed.

Portunus A very ancient Roman divinity who seems, initially, to have been a god of doors, but who in the historic age was considered to be a god of the sea watching over harbours. He had a priest, and a special festival the *Portunalia*, which was celebrated in his honour on 17 August. His temple was situated in the Forum Boarium, in the immediate vicinity of the Port of Rome. Portunus was identified with the god PALAEMON and thus was regarded as the son of MATER MATUTA, who was herself identified with Leucothea-Ino.

Porus (Πόρος) The personification of expediency and the son of Metis. Married to Penia (Poverty), he gave birth to Eros (Love). Apart from this symbolic myth told by Plato, Porus does not seem to have had any specific legend.

Poseidon (Ποσειδῶν) The god of the sea and one of the Olympians, the son of Cronus and Rhea. According to different traditions, he is sometimes considered older and sometimes younger than his brother Zeus. The oldest legend, in which Zeus on reaching manhood forces his father Cronus to restore to life the children he had swallowed, implies that Zeus is the youngest of the line, just as Cronus himself, who had dethroned his father Uranus, was the youngest son. Gradually, with the development of birthright, Zeus, who was considered the sovereign ruler, assumed the role of eldest son. For this reason, in legends of the Classical period Poseidon was more often considered to be younger than his brother. Poseidon was regarded as having been brought up by the TELCHINES and by Cephira, the daughter of

Oceanus. When he reached manhood he fell in love with HALIA, the sister of the Telchines, and had by her six sons and a daughter called Rhodus. This took place on the island of Rhodes which subsequently took its name from Poseidon's daughter.

From the time of the *Iliad*, Poseidon presided over the Sea, just as Hades ruled over the Underworld and ZEUS over the Sky and the Earth. He could not only command the waves, but could provoke storms, create landslides on the coast with a flourish of his trident, and cause springs to flow. His power seems to have extended over springs and lakes as well as over the sea. Rivers, on the other hand, had their own divinities. His relationship with Zeus was not always friendly. He joined Hera and Athena in the gods' conspiracy to put Zeus in chains, but withdrew before the threats of Briareus (see AEGAEON). For a year Poseidon, with Apollo and the mortal Aeacus, participated in the construction of the walls of Troy. However, LAOMEDON refused to give Poseidon the agreed salary, and in order to take vengeance he summoned a sea-monster which caused havoc among the Trojans. That was the origin of Poseidon's resentment against the Trojans, and that is why we see him intervene during the Trojan War on the side of the Achaeans. However, when at the beginning of the *Iliad* the Achaeans decided to follow Nestor's advice and fortify their camp by surrounding the ships with a wall, Poseidon protested in the assembly of the gods against this decision because he believed it was likely to diminish the glory he had earned in building the walls of Troy. Conciliatory words from Zeus were required to calm him down, although Poseidon promised to destroy the wall built by the Achaeans. For a while, he remained uninvolved in the struggle, but when the Trojans got the upper hand he came to the assistance of the Achaeans, taking on the appearance of Calchas to encourage the two Ajaxes and urge on Teucer and Idomeneus until, on instructions from Zeus, he abandoned the battle. Nevertheless it was Poseidon who saved Aeneas when Achilles was about to kill him. He caused a mist to rise before Achilles' eyes, removed the lance which was stuck in Aeneas' shield, and transported the hero far behind his own lines. His motive in thus saving a Trojan was that destiny did not desire the death of Aeneas; it was also perhaps that Aeneas was not one of the immediate descendants of Laomedon, but was directly linked with Tros, through Anchises, Capys and Assaracus (Table 7). Along with

Poseidon of Artemision of c. *460 BC. Athens, National Museum.*

all the gods, Poseidon sought the destruction of the descendants of Priam and, like them also, spared and protected the descendants of Anchises.

When the mortals were organized into cities, the gods each decided to choose one or several towns where they would each be particularly honoured. It sometimes happened that two or three divinities chose the same city, which provoked conflicts amongst them which they submitted for arbitration either to their peers or even to the mortals. In these judgements, Poseidon was in general unlucky. He entered into a dispute with Helios (the Sun) about the city of Corinth. The giant Briareus, as judge, decided in favour of Helios. Similarly, Poseidon wanted to rule over Aegina, but lost out to Zeus. Dionysus prevailed over him at Naxos, Apollo at Delphi and Athena at Troezen. But the two most famous 'quarrels' were over Athens and Argos. Poseidon had set his heart on Athens and was the first to take possession of the city when he caused sea-water to spring up on the Acropolis by thrusting his trident into the ground (this sea-water was, according to Pausanias, a well of salt water within the precincts of the Erechtheum). He was soon followed by

Athena, who summoned Cecrops as witness to her action: she planted an olive tree, which was still being pointed out in the second century AD in the Pandrosion. Then she demanded possession of the country. This dispute was brought before Zeus, who named the arbitrators. One tradition maintains that they were Cecrops and Cranaus; another, the Olympian gods. Whichever they were, the tribunal decided in favour of Athena because Cecrops testified that she had been the first to plant the olive tree on the rock of the Acropolis. The furious Poseidon flooded the plain of Eleusis.

Phoroneus was appointed to arbitrate in the quarrel between Poseidon and Hera for Argos. Here again, the decision went against Poseidon. In his fury, he blighted the Argolid with a curse and dried up all the rivers of the country. Shortly after, Danaus and his fifty daughters arrived in the Argolid and found no water to drink. Thanks to AMYMONE, one of the Danaides with whom Poseidon was in love, the curse was lifted, and the rivers began to flow again. Another version maintained that Poseidon, irritated with Phoroneus and Inachus, had flooded the Argolid with salt water, but Hera forced him to free the country and to bring the sea back within its bounds. Poseidon did, however, enjoy full possession of a wonderful island, ATLANTIS.

Poseidon was considered to have had numerous love affairs, all fruitful, but whereas the children of Zeus were kindly heroes, Poseidon's children, like those of Ares, were generally evil and violent. For example, by Thoosa he produced the Cyclops Polyphemus; by Medusa, the giant Chrysaor and Pegasus, the winged horse; by Amymone, NAUPLIUS, who did so much harm to the Achaeans; by Iphimedia, the Aloadae. Cercyon, the bandit Sciron who was killed by Theseus, Lamus the king of the Laestrygonians, and the cursed huntsman Orion were all his children. The sons which he had by HALIA committed all sorts of excess and he had to bury them underground in order to save them from punishment.

Poseidon was the progenitor of a great many mythical genealogies (see, for example, Tables 3, 10, 21–22, 25). Particularly noteworthy is the love affair between Poseidon and Demeter, which produced a daughter whose name it was forbidden to utter, and the horse AREION which Adrastus rode in the expedition of the Seven against Thebes. Poseidon had a legitimate wife, the goddess AMPHITRITE, a Nereid, by whom he had no children.

He was represented armed with a trident, which was the weapon used by tuna fishermen, and riding a chariot drawn by monstrous animals, half-horse and half-serpent. This chariot was surrounded by fish, dolphins and all sorts of sea creatures, as well as by the Nereids and various minor divinities, such as Proteus and Glaucus.

Pothos (Πόθος) The personification of love and desire. He appears in Aphrodite's retinue beside Eros and Himerus, from whom he does not greatly differ. He was said to be a son of Aphrodite. In Syrian mythology, under the influence of Semitic beliefs, he was purported to be the son of Cronus and Astarte (Aphrodite). Pothos does not possess any particular myth, and is really an abstract idea.

Prax (Πράξ) A third-generation descendant of Pergamos, the son of Neoptolemus. Prax came back from Illyria to the Peloponnese and gave his name to the region called Prakiai. He consecrated a sanctuary in honour of his ancestor Achilles on the road leading from Sparta to Arcadia.

Praxithea (Πραξιθέα) The name of several heroines of Attic legend, rather hard to distinguish one from the other.
1. The wife of Erechtheus (Table 11). She was regarded by some as the daughter of the river-god Cephisus, and by others as the daughter of Phrasinus and Diogenia, herself a daughter of Cephisus. Praxithea was said to be a model of patriotism because she had agreed to the sacrifice of her daughters after an oracle had declared their death necessary to ensure an Athenian victory (see ERECHTHEUS).
2. The Nymph married to Erichthonius and, by him, mother of Pandion.
3. Metanira, the wife of Celeus and mother of Demophon and Triptolemus, was sometimes called Praxithea. She was also said to be the nurse of Demophon.

Presbon (Πρέσβων) A son of Phrixus and of Iophassa, the daughter of Aeetes, the king of Colchis (see PHRIXUS for other traditions relating to the marriage of Phrixus). Presbon married Buzyges, the daughter of Lycus, by whom he had a son Clymenus (Table 33). After the death of Phrixus, Presbon returned to Orchomenus to reclaim the kingdom of his grandfather, Athamas. The latter had on his death-bed entrusted it to his great-nephews, the grandsons of Sisyphus, because he believed that his own male line was ex-tinct. On learning of Presbon's return, the two grandsons of Sisyphus, Haliartus and Coronus, hastened to welcome him and restore his kingdom to him. They founded the cities of Haliartus and Coronea. Presbon was the grandfather of ERGINUS, the last of the line of Athamas to rule over Orchomenus.

Preugenes (Πρευγένης) An Achaean originating from the valley of the Eurotas in the Peloponnese. He was the son of Agenor and had himself two children, Patreus and Atherion. After the arrival of the Dorians, he withdrew with his sons to Achaea, where he founded the city of Patras. Heroic honours were later bestowed on him and Patreus.

Priam (Πρίαμος) The youngest of the sons of Laomedon (Table 7). He was particularly famous because the Trojan War occurred during his reign, when he was quite elderly. The name of his mother is uncertain: the *Iliad* does not mention her. Later tradition usually made her the daughter of the river-god Scamander and gave her the name Strymo, but other versions called her Placia or Leucippe.

The *Iliad* contains little information about the life of Priam before the siege of Troy. The poem only informs us that he once fought the Amazons as an ally of the Phrygian Otreus, on the banks of Sangarius. It is the mythographers who have preserved for us the most striking episode of his childhood, the taking of Troy by Heracles. At the time of this event Priam, who was still a child, had been taken prisoner by the hero along with his sister Hesione. Heracles gave Hesione in marriage to his friend Telamon, and offered her whatever she wished as a wedding present. She asked for her brother who was then called Podarces. Heracles agreed, and sold him to her in a symbolic fashion. Podarces then took the name of Priam which means 'the ransomed'. Heracles gave him, as the last surviving son of Laomedon, the entire land of Troy. Priam gradually extended his power over all the region and the islands of the Asiatic coast.

Priam married first Arisbe, the daughter of Merops, who bore him a son named AEACUS, but then abandoned her, leaving her to Hyrtaeus in order to take Hecuba as his second wife. It was by the latter that he had the majority and most famous of his children (Table 34). The first born was Hector, the second Paris. Then followed daughters: Creusa, Laodice, Polyxena and Cassandra. Finally, several sons were born: Deiphobus,

Roman sarcophagus relief depicting Priam pleading with Achilles for the return of the body of Hector.

Helenus, Pammon, Polites, Antiphus, Hipponous, Polydorus and Troilus, who was also said to be the son of Apollo. Priam had yet more children by concubines: Melanippus, Gorgythion, Philaemon, Hippothous, Glaucus, Agathon, Chersidamas, Evagoras, Hippodamas, Mestor, Atas, Doryclus, Lycaon, Dryops, Bias, Chromius, Astygonus, Telestas, Evander, Cebrion, Mylius, Archemachus, Laodocus, Echephron, Idomeneus, Hyperion, Ascanius, Democoon, Aretus, Deiopites, Clonius, Echemmon, Hyperochus, Aegeoneus, Lysithous, Polymedon. Apart from the sons, there were also daughters: Medusa, Medesicasta, Lysimache and Aristodeme. Tradition attributes fifty sons to Priam, a number which is not given exactly by any author. Apollodorus' list, which we reproduce here, is the most complete. Those of Antiphon and Dius, given in the *Iliad*, should perhaps be added to it, as well as that of Axion, cited by Pausanias from the *Little Iliad*, which would make the number up to the fifty of the tradition.

Priam plays a rather unobtrusive role in the *Iliad*. As he is too old to take part in the fighting, he presides over councils, but even there his opinion does not always prevail. It is more often Hector who gains the upper hand. He does not appear to be opposed to Paris' plans, nor to the abduction of Helen; he is well disposed towards the latter and accepts what is fated. His essential characteristic is piety, which brings him Zeus' favours. A man of unaffected presence, he dominates events yet is only involved in them despite himself. He sees his children perish one by one, and Hector, one of the last, becomes the most valiant defender of his kingdom. When Hector is killed and borne away by Achilles into the Greek camp, Priam humbles himself and seeks out the victor, offering him an enormous ransom for the body of his son. Epics prior to the *Iliad* related with some force the details of Priam's death. When the old king heard the enemy in his palace, he wanted to take up his arms and defend his family, but Hecuba prevented him and led him off into the depths of the palace to an altar crowned with laurel so that they might both be placed under the protection of the gods. There Priam saw before his very eyes Neoptolemus kill the young Polites who was also trying to reach the safety of the altar. Neoptolemus then seized the old man by the hair, dragged him from the altar and slit his throat. The body remained unburied. A variant source relates that Neoptolemus dragged Priam to the tomb of Achilles outside the city and killed him there.

Priapus (Πρίαπος) The famous god of the Asiatic town of Lampsacus, usually said to be the son of Dionysus and Aphrodite. He was represented in the form of an ithyphallic figure, the protector of vineyards, gardens and, in particular, orchards. His essential attribute was, in fact, the ability to ward off the 'evil eye' and to render harmless the evil spells of envious people attempting to damage the harvest. Moreover, as a symbol of fertility Priapus was a favourable sign, by sympathetic magic, for the plants of any garden where he was found.

As an Asiatic god and god of fertility, Priapus was included in Dionysus' retinue, chiefly because he bore some resemblance to Silenus and the Satyrs. Like Silenus, Priapus was often depicted in the company of an ass. The following legend is told concerning this: during a Dionysiac festival, Priapus had met the nymph Lotis with whom he had fallen in love. At night he attempted to seduce her, but at the very moment he was about to achieve his goal, Silenus' ass began to bray, waking Lotis and all the Bacchic women. The embarrassed Priapus had to abandon his plan. It is as a memory of his incident that he was represented in the company of an ass. There is a Roman variant of this legend in which the goddess Vesta is substituted for Lotis. Just as he was about to assault her an ass began to bray, waking up the goddess who became aware of the danger threatening her. Henceforward, asses were sacrificed to Priapus, but on the feast of Vesta they were crowned with flowers.

Other legends formed around Priapus, and the tradition by which he was the son of Dionysus and Aphrodite was not universally accepted. According to certain mythographers, the physical deformity of Priapus was due to the evil spells of Hera. When Aphrodite left the Ethiopians after her birth, she had amazed all the gods by her beauty. Zeus, who had fallen in love with her, seduced her. Aphrodite was about to give birth

The avenue of Priapus at Delos.

when Hera, fearing that this child would become a threat to the Olympian gods if he possessed the beauty of his mother and the power of his father, and being jealous of her husband's love affairs, touched Aphrodite's womb with the result that the child was born deformed. The infant Priapus was endowed with enormous genitals. On seeing him, Aphrodite was so afraid that both she and her son would become the laughing-stock of all the gods that she abandoned him in the mountains. There the child was discovered by shepherds who brought him up and established a cult to his virility. It is said that for this reason Priapus remained a rustic god.

Another very similar tradition made Priapus the son of Aphrodite and Adonis, attributing likewise his deformity to the malevolence of Hera. In the euhemeristic interpretation of the legend of Priapus, it is said that he was a citizen of the town of Lampsacus; he was banished on account of his deformity, but was received by the gods. He was later made protector of gardens.

According to Diodorus, Priapus was connected with the myth of Osiris. He was said to be the deification by Isis of Osiris' virility. Diodorus also classes Priapus and Hermaphroditus together.

Prochyte (Προχύτη) A Trojan woman related to Aeneas, who died in sight of the Neapolitan coast and was buried on the island of Prochyte (later called Proscida) to which she gave her name.

Procles (Προκλῆς) The son of Heraclid Aristodemus and Argia, and the twin brother of Eurysthenes (Table 16). The two brothers married Lathria and Anaxandra, the daughters of the Heraclid Thersandrus, the king of Cleonae. Procles had a son called Sous who was the father of Eurypon and the ancestor of Lycurgus, the Spartan legislator.

Procne (Πρόκνη) The daughter of Pandion, the king of Athens, and the sister of Philomela (Table 11). For her legend, and the story of her transformation into a nightingale, see PHILOMELA.

Procris (Πρόκρις) One of the daughters of Erechtheus, the king of Athens (Table 11), although a variant of the tradition made her the daughter of Cecrops. Her legend is a very complex one, and includes superimposed elements. She was married to Cephalus, the son of Deion, but deceived him with Pteleon who had bought her favours by presenting her with a golden crown. When Cephalus

became aware of this deception, Procris fled to Minos. The latter fell in love with her and tried to seduce her. Now Minos had been cursed by his wife Pasiphae: on giving himself to another woman, Minos would bring forth serpents and scorpions which would kill his mistress. In order to free him from this spell, Procris gave him a herb which she had got from Circe. Then, as the price for her favours, she demanded two presents: a dog which never let the game he was pursuing escape, and a javelin which never missed its target. Later, Procris, fearing Pasiphae's jealousy, returned to Athens where she was reconciled with Cephalus. However, her love for her husband was not very enduring and being suspicious he decided to put her to the test by disguising himself and offering her presents. Procris did not succumb, but before long it was she who was jealous, which caused her death (see CEPHALUS for these episodes in the legend).

Procrustes (Προκρούστης) A robber, also called Danastes or Polypemon, who lived on the road from Megara to Athens. He used to force all travellers to lie down in one of two beds which he possessed: the tall in the little bed (which required cutting off their feet) and the short in the large bed (they were stretched violently to make them fit). Procrustes was killed by THESEUS.

Proculus Julius Proculus was the name of the Alban noble to whom Romulus appeared after his apotheosis, indicating his wish to be honoured under the name of Quirinus and to have a temple on the Quirinal.

Proetides (Προιτίδες) The daughters of PROETUS, the king of Tiryns (or Argos) and Stheneboea (Table 31). According to some traditions, there were two of them, Lysippe and Iphianassa; other traditions add a third, Iphinoe. When these young girls reached the age of maturity they were stricken with madness by Hera. The reason for this curse is variously reported: it is sometimes stated that they claimed to be more beautiful than the goddess and thus aroused her jealousy. Elsewhere they were said to have mocked her temple, claiming that their father's palace contained greater riches. It was also stated that they had stolen gold from the goddess's dress for their own use. It was believed that they had been metamorphosed into heifers and escaped into the countryside, wandering here and there and refusing to return home. This behaviour, similar to that of the Bacchantes, gave rise to the legend that it was Dionysus who had inflicted them with madness for having refused to adopt his cult. The soothsayer Melampus offered to cure them if Proetus would give him one third of the kingdom of Argos. Proetus refused, finding Melampus' price exorbitant. The Proetides were then seized by a new frenzy and began to run wild over the Argolid and the Peloponnese. Proetus again appealed to Melampus, who demanded this time not only a third of the kingdom for himself, but another third for his brother Bias. Proetus agreed to pay the price asked for, fearing that Melampus' demands would become even more exorbitant if he refused. Melampus, taking with him the most robust young men of Argos, then pursued the young girls into the mountains amid great shouting and wild dancing. During the pursuit, the eldest of the sisters, Iphinoe, died of exhaustion. The two others were purified by herbs which Melampus mixed with the water of a spring where they came to drink. Melampus and Bias then married a daughter each. A different tradition relates that it was later, during the reign of the Proetides' nephew ANAXAGORAS, that Melampus cured the collective madness of the women of Argos.

Proetus (Προῖτος) A king of Tiryns, the son of Abas and Aglaea, the daughter of Mantineus, and the twin brother of Acrisius (Table 31). He was descended from Lynceus and Hypermestra, and, consequently, from Danäus and Aegyptus. From birth Proetus hated his brother Acrisius; even in the womb the two children had fought. On reaching manhood they divided the kingdom, Abas ruling over the territory of the Argolid, Acrisius over Argos, and Proetus over Tiryns. But this decision was not reached without bloody conflicts which remained unresolved between the supporters of each side. It was also said, as an explanation of the hatred which existed between the two brothers, that Proetus had seduced his niece DANAE, the daugher of Acrisius, and had fathered Perseus, thus mortally offending his brother. Once in possession of Tiryns, Proetus fortified the citadel and it is to him that the Cyclopean walls, still existing, were attributed. It was said that he was aided in this task by the CYCLOPES themselves.

There is another version of the struggle between Proetus and Acrisius, according to which the latter was victorious and expelled Proetus, who sought refuge in Asia Minor with Iobates the king of Lycia, or with Amphianax, whose daughter Stheneboea he married. Iobates gave him an army of Lycians with which Proetus recaptured his kingdom. It was only then that the division of the territory between the two brothers took place. Proetus was established at Tiryns, and married, when BELLEROPHON came to seek sanctuary with him and to purify himself of an accidental murder which he had committed. Stheneboea fell in love with Bellerophon but, being unable to make him share her love, denounced him before Proetus who sent him to his father-in-law, Iobates, so that he might put him to death.

Proetus and Stheneboea had, initially, two or three daughters, the PROETIDES, who were afflicted with insanity by Hera (or Dionysus) and cured by Melampus. This necessitated Proetus dividing his territory into three parts; one he kept, and the other two were handed over to Melampus and his brother Bias (see ADRASTUS for the events following on from this division). During the madness of his daughters, Proetus had another child by Stheneboea, a son named Megapenthes (which means 'great sorrow' on account of the grief caused by his daughters' affliction). This Megapenthes later succeeded Proetus on the throne of Tiryns, but exchanged the kingdom with PERSEUS for that of Argos since Perseus, having accidentally killed his grandfather Acrisius, did not want to owe his kingdom to a crime. This accounts for the fact that at the time of the expedition of the Seven against Thebes, Adrastus ruled in Argos, although his ancestor Bias had originally obtained a part of the kingdom of Tiryns (see however ANAXAGORAS for the tradition according to which the division took place after the reign of Megapenthes).

Ovid has preserved for us a completely aberrant tradition of the legend of Proetus; according to this, the latter attacked Acrisius and was besieging him in the citadel of Argos when Perseus came to the help of his grandfather and changed Proetus into a stone statue. This is probably a late fabrication, modelled on other well-known episodes in the legend of Perseus.

Promachus (Πρόμαχος)
1. Promachus and Leucocamas, two youths from Cnossos in Crete, were the heroes of an amorous incident. Promachus loved the handsome Leucocamas, who was however cruel to him and subjected him to many trials. Promachus set about trying to accomplish them, but his hopes of winning the young man's love were not realized. Finally, having accomplished a particularly diffi-

cult task (he had to procure a certain helmet), before Leucocamas' very eyes he handed the object to another more sympathetic young man. Leucocamas, thoroughly put out, ran himself through with his own sword.

2. The son of Aeson and Alcimede (or Perimede) (Table 21), who was killed by Pelias while still very young.

Prometheus (Προμηθεύς) A cousin of Zeus: the son of a Titan, Iapetus, just as Zeus was the son of another Titan, Cronus (Table 38). Traditions vary as to the name of his mother. She is called Asia, daughter of Oceanus, or Clymene, also an Oceanid (Table 38; see also EURYMEDON 1). Prometheus had several brothers: EPIMETHEUS, who was by contrast with him highly incompetent, Atlas and Menoetius. Prometheus in turn was married, the name of his wife varying from author to author: she was most commonly referred to as Celaeno or Clymene. His children were Deucalion, Lycus and Chimaereus, to which were sometimes added the names Aetnaeus, Hellen and Thebe.

Prometheus was said to have created the first men, fashioning them from potter's clay. But this legend does not appear in Hesiod's *Theogony* where Prometheus is simply the benefactor, and not the creator, of mankind. Once at Mecone, during a solemn sacrifice, he cut up a bull and divided it into two parts: one contained the flesh and the intestines wrapped up in the skin, on top of which he placed the animal's stomach; the other consisted of the bones and the fat. Zeus was then asked to choose his share; the rest was to be given to man. Zeus chose the fat and, discovering that it contained nothing but bones, became embittered against Prometheus and mankind, which was to benefit from this trick. As a punishment, he decided to withhold fire from mortals. Once again Prometheus came to their aid: he stole some sparks of fire from the sun's 'wheels' and brought them to earth concealed in a hollow tube. Another tradition maintains that he stole the fire from Hephaestus' forge. Zeus punished mankind by sending them a specially fashioned woman, PANDORA. As for Prometheus, Zeus had him bound by steel chains to a rock in the Caucasus and sent an eagle, the offspring of Echidna and Typhon, to consume his liver which would continually renew itself. He swore by the Styx that Prometheus would never be released. Heracles, however, when passing in the Caucasus region, shot the eagle with an arrow and released Prom-

etheus. Zeus did not protest, being pleased that this exploit added to his son's fame, but to show that his word was not to be taken too lightly, he forced Prometheus to wear a ring made from the steel chains and to carry a piece of the rock to which he had been attached: a steel bond thus continued to unite the Titan and his rock. It was at this time that the Centaur Chiron, who had been wounded by one of Heracles' arrows and was suffering unceasingly, wanted to die. As he was immortal, he had to find someone who would accept his immortality. Prometheus performed this service for him, and became immortal in his place. Zeus accepted the Titan's freedom and immortality all the more readily because Prometheus did him a great favour by revealing an ancient oracle according to which the son of Zeus and Thetis would be more powerful than him and would dethrone him.

Prometheus possessed powers of prophecy. He told Heracles how to get hold of the golden apples, by revealing that Atlas alone could pick them from the garden of the Hesperides. This gift of prophecy was shared with the ancient divinities who were daughters of the Earth, who was herself the archetypal prophetess. Prometheus also showed his son Deucalion how to escape from the great flood which Zeus was planning in order to wipe out the human race, and which he was able to foresee.

Promethus (Πρόμηθος) A son of Codrus, who ruled in Colophon with his brother Damasichthon. He accidentally killed the latter, and fled to Naxos, where he died. His ashes were brought back to Colophon by his nephews, the sons of Damasichthon.

Promne (Πρόμνη) The wife of the Arcadian Bouphagus who welcomed HERACLES' brother, Iphicles, at Pheneus, and cared for him after he had been wounded by the Molionidae.

Pronax (Πρῶναξ) One of the sons of Talaus, himself the son of Bias (Table 1), and so the brother of Adrastus and Eriphyle. He had a daughter, Amphithea, who married ADRASTUS, and was also said to have had a son LYCURGUS, the father of Opheltes. According to one tradition, Pronax was killed by his cousin AMPHIARAUS during a revolt at Argos. It was also said that the Nemean games were originally funeral games in his honour.

Pronus (Πρῶνος) Pronus or Pronesus was the father of a tyrant from Cephalonia who demanded that young girls be brought to him before their marriage. This lasted until Antenor, disguised as a woman, got into the tyrant's bed and killed him with a dagger. Antenor then ruled in his place.

Propodas (Προπόδας) A king of Corinth, the son of Damophon and a descendant of Sisyphus. It was under the reign of his two sons, Doridas and Hyanthidas, that the Dorians led by Aletes came into the country.

Propoetides (Προποιτίδες) Young girls originally from Amathonta, who dared to deny Aphrodite's divinity. The goddess punished them by inflicting them with desires which could not be satisfied. It was claimed that they were the first female prostitutes. They ended up being transformed into stone statues.

Proserpina At Rome, the goddess of the Underworld. Early on she was assimilated to the Greek Persephone, and it was this assimilation which provided the association with the Underworld. Originally, she was certainly a rustic goddess, presiding over germination. Her cult was officially introduced along with that of Dis Pater (assimilated to Hades) in 249 BC. The Tarentine Games were celebrated in their honour, so called after a locality in the Field of Mars – Tarentum – rather than after the city of Tarentum. The following legend was told about Tarentum: the children of a certain Valerius became ill in the course of an epidemic. Their father asked the gods what he must do to save them. The gods replied that he and his children should go down the Tiber as far as Tarentum where he should give them water to drink from the altar of Dis and Proserpina. Valerius thought that the oracle was urging him to travel from Rome to the city of Tarentum and he was very irritated at having to undertake such a voyage. However he set off and on the first evening camped at a bend in the Tiber. The next morning he asked the local people what the place was called, to which they replied 'Tarentum'. Understanding the meaning of the oracle, Valerius took some water from the Tiber and gave it to his children, who drank it and were cured. In gratitude he wanted to raise an altar at this spot to Dis and Proserpina, but while digging the soil to provide a foundation for his altar, he uncovered a stone already bearing an inscription in honour of these two divinities. This was the altar about which the oracle had spoken. It played a particularly important role in the Secular Games.

Prosymna (Πρόσυμνα) One of the daughters of Asterion, a river in the Argolid. She had two sisters, Acraea and Euboea, and all three were the nurses of Hera. She gave her name to the city of Prosymna.

Protesilaus (Πρωτεσίλαος) A Thessalian hero, the eldest son of Iphiclus and Astyoche. He was descended from Minyas, the king of Orchomenos, and through him from Poseidon (Table 20). He was the brother of Podarces. His home was the Thessalian city of Phylace. An obscure tradition make Protesilaus the son of Actor and not Iphiclus, whose cousin he would then be (Table 20). Protesilaus figures among the suitors of Helen. He took part in the Trojan War, in command of a contingent of forty ships. However, he was the first to be killed by the Trojans, as he was leaping from his ship to set foot in Asia, he was struck down by Hector.

It was also related that Protesilaus had played a particularly important role in the first expedition which had resulted in the Mysian landing. It was said to be he who snatched away TELEPHUS' shield, thus allowing ACHILLES to wound him. When he set out for Troy, Protesilaus had only just married Laodamia. The marriage had not been properly celebrated as the ritual sacrifices had not been carried out. It was as a punishment for this sacrilege that Laodamia became a widow. For the story of Laodamia's love for Protesilaus and the latter's resurrection, see LAODAMIA.

Proteus (Πρωτεύς) In the *Odyssey*, a god of the sea, specially charged with tending the flocks of seals and other sea-creatures belonging to Poseidon. He usually lived on the island of Pharos, not far from the mouth of the Nile. He had the ability to change himself into whatever form he desired: he could become not only an animal, but also an element such as water or fire. He used this power particularly when he wanted to elude those asking him questions: for he possessed the gift of prophecy, but refused to provide information to those mortals who sought it from him. On the advice of the sea-goddess Idothea, Proteus' own daughter, MENELAUS went to question him. Although Proteus metamorphosed himself successively into a lion, a serpent, a panther, an enormous boar, water and a tree, Menelaus did not let him escape, with the result that the old man, finally defeated, spoke to him.

The same version is given by Virgil in the episode of Aristaeus in the fourth book of the

Georgics, although the scene is changed from Pharos to Pallene. From Herodotus onwards, Proteus also appears as a king of Egypt, contemporaneous with Menelaus, rather than as a demon of the sea. This Proteus was reigning at Memphis at the time when Helen and Paris were driven by a storm onto the coast of the country. They were brought before him and he decided to send the abductor back to the Troad but to keep Helen with him, as well as the treasure which she had brought from Sparta. However, the Greeks sailed against Troy and, on arrival in the Troad, sent an embassy to Priam to ask for Helen back. Priam told them that she was not there but was in Egypt with Proteus. The Greeks did not believe this and pressed on with the war. Once Troy was taken, they realized that Helen really was not there, and so went off to look for her at Proteus' court. The latter willingly returned her to her husband.

This legend was taken up and modified by Euripides in his *Helen*, where Proteus is no longer the king of Memphis, but of the island of Pharos. His wife is called PSAMATHE and is the daughter of Nereus. Their two children are Theoclymenus and Idothea. While Paris is taking a phantom of Helen, created by Hera, to Troy, the real Helen is entrusted by Hermes to King Proteus. It was also said that it was Proteus who, through his magic arts, had created the phantom Helen and given her to Paris.

A legend related by Conon maintains that Proteus, an Egyptian, had left his country because of the tyranny of BUSIRIS. He supposedly followed the sons of Phoenix in their search for Europa, and settled at Pallene, in Chalcidice, where he married Chrysonoe, the daughter of Clitus, the king of the country. With the latter's help he seized the land of the Bisaltes, barbarians who lived close to Pallene. He reigned there, but his sons, far from resembling him, were violent men who put to death all strangers who set foot in their country until they were themselves killed by Heracles. These two sons were called Polygonus and Telegonus.

Prothous (Πρόθοος) The name of several heroes, including:
1. One of the sons of Agrius (Table 27).
2. The son of Tenthredon, and leader of a contingent of Magnesians at Troy. He came from Thessaly. When the Greeks returned from Troy, he perished in the shipwreck off Cape Caphareus; however, most of his compatriots reached Crete and from there went to settle in Magnesia on the Meander in Asia Minor.

Protogenia (Πρωτογένεια)
1. A daughter of Deucalion and Pyrrha whose name means 'first-born' (Table 8). She and Zeus had two sons, Aethlius and Opus.
2. One of the HYACINTHIDS.
3. The daughter of Calydon and Aeolia, and, by Ares, the mother of Oxylus (Table 24).

Prylis (Πρύλις) A soothsayer from Lesbos, the son of Hermes and the nymph Issa. At the time of the Greeks' expedition against Troy, Prylis, persuaded by presents from Palamedes, revealed to Agamemnon that the city of Troy could only be taken by using a wooden horse.

Psamathe (Ψαμάθη)
1. A Nereid who had a son, by Aeacus, named Phocus (Table 30). She had taken on diverse shapes, notably that of a seal, to escape the advances of Aeacus, but nothing prevented him from achieving his aim. When Phocus was killed by his half-brothers Telamon and PELEUS, Psamathe sent a monstrous wolf against the latter's flocks. Later, Psamathe abandoned Aeacus and married PROTEUS, the king of Egypt.
2. An Argive woman, the daughter of Crotopus, and a member of the race of Phorbas and Triopas (Table 17). By Apollo she had a son Linus whom she abandoned through fear of CROTOPUS who, when he learnt later of the existence of this son, he had his daughter put to death – buried alive according to some writers. It was to avenge her death that Apollo sent a monster called Poine to attack the Argolid (see COROEBUS).

Psophis (Ψῶφις) The eponymous hero or heroine of the city of Psophis in Arcadia who, according to different sources, was:
1. A son of Lycaon.
2. A seventh-generation descendant of Nyctimus.
3. The daughter of Xanthus, himself the son of Erymanthus.
4. The daughter of Eryx, the king of the Sicani. While passing through Sicily Heracles married her, but he then entrusted her to Lycortas, one of his hosts who lived at Phegea. There she gave birth to two sons of Heracles, Echephron and Promachus, who founded the city of Psophis in honour of their mother.

Psyche (Ψυχή) The soul. It is also the name of the heroine of a tale told by Apuleius in his *Metamorphoses*. Psyche, the daughter of a king, had two sisters. All three were of great beauty, but Psyche's beauty was superhuman. People came from far and wide to admire her, but whereas her sisters had found husbands, no one wanted to marry Psyche because her beauty was so daunting. Despairing that she would ever be married, her father consulted the oracle who replied that the young girl must be dressed as if for marriage and exposed on a rock where a horrible monster would come to take possession of her. Her parents were distraught. Nevertheless they prepared the young girl and led her, in the midst of a funeral procession, to the summit of the mountain indicated by the oracle. Then they left her alone and withdrew to their palace. The abandoned Psyche was lamenting her fate when she suddenly felt herself lifted up by the wind and borne away. The wind gently carried her to the bottom of a deep valley and deposited her on a soft lawn. There, Psyche, worn out by emotional stress, fell deeply asleep and, on waking up, found herself in the garden of a magnificent palace made entirely of gold and marble. She went into the rooms which lay before her, and was greeted by voices which guided her and revealed to her that they were slaves and were at her service. The day passed in this manner, her astonishment growing as she went from marvel to marvel. In the evening Psyche became aware of a presence beside her: this was the husband of which the oracle had spoken, which did not seem as monstrous as she had feared. Her husband did not tell her who he was and warned her that if she ever saw him she would run the risk of losing him for ever. This existence continued for several weeks. She was very happy: by day she was alone with the voices in the palace; at night she was joined by her husband. However, after a while she began to miss her family and to feel sorry for her parents who obviously believed her to be dead. She asked her husband for permission to return to them for a little while. Although the danger that this absence would pose was pointed out to her, she managed with much pleading to persuade her husband. Once again the wind bore her to the mountain top where she had been abandoned, from where she easily returned home. She was greeted with much rejoicing, and her married sisters came from afar to visit her. When they saw their sister so happy and received the presents which she had brought them, they were exceedingly jealous. They conspired to sow doubts in her mind, and ended up by forcing her to admit that she had never seen her husband. They finally persuaded her to hide a lamp at night and, while her husband was sleeping, to discover by its light what he looked like.

Psyche returned to the palace and did as she had been advised. She discovered, sleeping beside her, a beautiful youth. Overcome at her discovery her hand trembled so much that she let a drop of boiling oil fall on him. Burnt by the oil, Love (for he was the cruel monster of which the oracle had spoken) woke up and, as he had warned Psyche, fled immediately, never to return. No longer protected by Love, the unhappy Psyche began to wander the world, pursued by the angry Aphrodite, indignant at her beauty. No divinity would agree to welcome her. She was finally caught by the goddess who imprisoned her in her palace, tormenting her in countless ways and giving her different tasks: sorting grain, gathering the wool from wild sheep, and finally going down into the Underworld. There she was to ask Persephone for a flask of the water of youth but was forbidden to open it. Unfortunately on the way back Psyche opened the forbidden flask and fell into a deep sleep. Love, meanwhile, was in despair, being unable to forget Psyche. When he saw her asleep as a result of Aphrodite's magic, he flew to her, awoke her with a prick of one of his arrows, and, returning to Olympus, asked Zeus for permission to marry this mortal. Zeus willingly granted his request, and Psyche was reconciled with Aphrodite.

Pompeian paintings popularized the image of Psyche as a little winged girl, like a butterfly (the soul was often, according to popular belief, thought of as a butterfly which escaped from the body after death), playing with winged Cupids.

Psyllus (Ψύλλος) The king of a tribe from Cyrenaica, the Psylli, who were renowned in antiquity as snake-charmers. Psyllus was thought to be the son of Amphithemis and a Nymph. According to Nonnus, he was the father of Cataegonus and, when in command of a Libyan fleet, had wanted to wreak vengeance on the South Wind, whose breath had destroyed his harvests. But as he was approaching the island of Aeolus, a storm destroyed his ships. His tomb could be seen near Greater Syrtis.

Pterelas (Πτερέλαος) Pterelas belonged to the race of the descendants of Perseus. According to the genealogy most commonly given to him, he was the grandson of Hippothoe and Poseidon, and the son of Taphius (Table 31). There existed another tradition according to which he was the son of Hippothoe and Poseidon and had two sons, TAPHIUS and TELEBOAS. According to a third tradition Teleboas was the father of Pterelas.

Pterelas was especially famous for the war which he waged against Amphitryon and his betrayal by his daughter COMAETHO. This took place when Electryon was ruling over Mycenae, and the sons of Pterelas came to claim this kingdom, which had belonged to their great-grandfather Mestor, a brother of Electryon (Table 31). Electryon rejected their demands, so in revenge they stole the king's flocks. Electryon's sons challenged them to a fight, in the course of which they were almost all killed: there was only one survivor from each family: Licymius, a son of Electryon, and Everes, a son of Pterelas. Electryon planned to go and fight Pterelas, but died himself before being able to set out. It was AMPHITRYON who organized the expedition, out of his love for Alcmene. But there was an oracle which declared that no one could take Taphos, Pterelas' city, while he was still alive. Pterelas was immortal or, at least, his immortality was linked to a golden hair which Poseidon had planted on his head, so he would have been sure of his victory had his daughter, Comaetho, not fallen in love with Amphitryon and plucked the magic hair from her father's head, thus bringing about his death and the loss of his native land.

Ptoliporthos (Πτολίπορθος) The 'Destroyer of Cities', a son of Telemachus and Nausicaa. He was given this name by his grandfather Odysseus. It should be noted that this epithet was frequently attributed to Odysseus himself in the Homeric poems (see POLIPORTHES).

Pygmalion (Πυγμαλίων) Legend acknowledges two people of this name, both of Semitic origin:
1. A king of Tyre, the son of Mutto and brother of Elissa.
2. A king of Cyprus, who fell in love with an ivory statue of a woman. He was sometimes said to have sculpted it himself. Under the influence of this passion, he asked Aphrodite, during a feast in her honour, to grant him a woman resembling the statue. On returning home, he discovered that the statue had come alive. He married her, and they had a daughter called Paphos who in due course became the mother of Cinyras.

Pygmies (Πυγμαῖοι) A race of dwarfs, mentioned in the *Iliad*, who were said to inhabit southern Egypt, or India. Accounts of the Pygmies refer most frequently to their struggles against storks or cranes. The origin of this war was the subject of several legends: for example, it was said that a very beautiful young girl, called Oenoe, was born amongst the Pygmies, but that she was proud and despised the gods. In particular, she had no respect for Artemis and Hera. She married a Pygmy named Nicodamas, by whom she had a son, Mopsus. To celebrate his birth, all the Pygmies brought numerous presents to the parents. Hera, however, because of her hatred for this young woman who did not worship her as she ought, transformed her into a stork. The metamorphosed Oenoe tried to repossess her son who had remained with the Pygmies, but they drove her off by shouting and wielding weapons. Hence the fear which storks aroused in Pygmies (see also GERANA) and the hatred which the storks bore them.

Pygmies have inspired Egyptian art. They appear in mosaics and paintings in the midst of the fauna of the Nile, fighting with birds and various animals, attacking crocodiles, and indulging themselves in human activities which they parody by their ugliness and clumsiness. They are usually depicted with enormous sexual organs. Although the race of Pygmies belongs, according to the geographers of antiquity, to the realm of fable, they probably borrow some characteristics from the native populations of central Africa.

Pylades (Πυλάδης) The great friend of Orestes, just as Achates was that of Aeneas. He was his first cousin, being the son of Strophius and Anaxibia, the sister of Agamemnon (Table 2). Through his father Strophius he was descended from Phocus, Aeacus and Zeus (Table 30). The two cousins were brought up together at Strophius' court, where Orestes had been put in safety while Clytemnestra was living with Aegisthus during Agamemnon's absence. It was the tragic writers in particular who developed the character of Pylades. He advised his friend in his vengeance, and it was said that he fought against the sons of Nauplius when they came to Aegisthus' aid. But it was especially at the time of Orestes' voyage to Tauris that Pylades was of great help to him. Pylades married Electra, the elder sister of Orestes, and had two children by her, Medon and Strophius 2.

Pylaemenes (Πυλαιμένης) Son of Bisaltes (?), a Paphlagonian, and an ally of the Trojans. He was the father of Harpalion, who also fought for the

Trojans and was killed by Meriones. Pylaemenes was himself killed either by Menelaus or by Achilles. Although his death is recounted in Book V of the *Iliad*, he makes an appearance in Book XIII, in the funeral cortège of his son.

Pylaeus (Πυλαῖος) The son of Lethus. With his brother Hippothous he commanded at Troy a contingent of Pelasgians from Larissa.

Pylas (Πύλας) A king of Megara. He was the son of Cleson and, through him, the grandson of LELEX. He gave his daughter Pylia in marriage to Pandion 2, who succeeded Cecrops 2 at Athens, but was driven out as the result of a revolt organized by the sons of Metion. Later Pylas killed Bias, his father's brother, and had to go into exile. He left his kingdom to Pandion, while he himself, at the head of a band of Leleges, entered the Peloponnese and founded the city of Pylos in Messenia. He was driven out of there by Neleus, and then went on to found Pylos in Elis.

Pylenor (Πυλήνωρ) A Centaur, who was wounded by Heracles during the fight at Pholus' home. His wound was infected by the blood of the Lernean Hydra, in which Heracles' arrows had been dipped. He went to wash his wound in the water of the stream Anigrus, and from then on this stream was said to possess evil properties and an unhealthy smell.

Pylia (Πυλία) The wife of Pandion 2 and daughter of PYLAS, the king of Megara (Table 11).

Pylius (Πύλιος) An obscure tradition names a Pylius, son of Hephaestus, as the man who cured PHILOCTETES of his wound in Lemnos, and learned the art of archery from him.

Pyraechmes (Πυραίχμης)

1. In the *Iliad* was one of the two leaders of the Paeonian contingent which had come to help Priam. Pyraechmes killed Eurodorus who, during the battle, played the role of adviser or equerry to Patroclus. He was himself killed either by Patroclus or by Diomedes, and was buried at Troy. The second leader of the Paeonians was Asteropaeus, the son of the river-god Axius.
2. A slinger who ensured OXYLUS' victory over the Eleians.
3. A king of Euboea, who attacked Boeotia but was defeated by Heracles during the latter's youth, and torn apart by his horses. This fight took place

beside a stream called Heracleius, or the stream of Heracles. Horses neighed each time they drank from this water.

Pyramus (Πύραμος) Pyramus and his lover Thisbe were the protagonists of a love story which exists in two independent versions. According to one of them (probably the older) Pyramus and Thisbe loved each other so much that they slept together before they were married with the result that Thisbe became pregnant. In despair, she committed suicide. On learning of this, her lover did likewise. The gods took pity on them and metamorphosed them: Pyramus became the Cicilian river which bore his name, and Thisbe a spring whose water flowed into that river.

The other and much more dramatic version is told by Ovid, and introduces a complex literary elaboration. Pyramus and Thisbe were two young Babylonians who loved each other but could not marry because of parental opposition. They saw each other secretly through a crack in the wall which separated their two houses. One night they arranged a rendezvous at the tomb of Ninus, outside the town. A mulberry tree grew there beside the stream. Thisbe was the first to arrive at the meeting place, and suddenly saw a lioness which came to drink at the spring. Thisbe fled, but lost her scarf which the lioness seized in her mouth, which was still bloody from her meal, and tore it into pieces. She then disappeared. When Pyramus arrived and saw the scarf, he immediately assumed that Thisbe had been eaten by a wild animal, and without further hesitation ran himself through with his sword. When Thisbe returned, she found him dead, and killed herself with her beloved's sword. The fruit of the mulberry, which had until then been white, turned red with all this spilt blood. The ashes of the two lovers were united in the same urn.

Pyrene (Πυρήνη)

1. A young girl whose father was King Bebryx who reigned, in the time of Heracles, over the indigenous peoples of the Narbonne region. Heracles crossed the country on his way to capture Geryon's oxen. At the court of Bebryx he became drunk and raped Pyrene, who gave birth to a serpent. The terrified Pyrene fled to the mountains, where she was torn apart by wild animals. Heracles found her body when he returned from his expedition and gave her funeral honours. In memory of her, Heracles gave the name Pyrenees to the nearby mountains.

2. The mother of CYCNUS, the opponent of HERACLES, and of the Thracian king Diomedes.

Pyreneus (Πυρηνεύς) A king of Daulis who invited the Muses, crossing his country on their way to Helicon, to enter his palace to shelter from a storm. Pyreneus then tried to assault them. The goddesses flew away and Pyreneus, trying to follow them into the atmosphere, fell onto some rocks and was killed.

Pyrgo (Πυργώ)
1. The wife of ALCATHUS, the king of Megara, who was abandoned by him so that he could marry Evaechme, the daughter of Megareus. Her tomb could be seen at Megara, alongside that of Alcathus and his daughter Iphinoe.
2. Pyrgo was also the nurse of Priam's children. As an old woman, she accompanied Aeneas from Troy and it was she who, at the instigation of Iris, advised the Trojan woman to set fire to the ships. The name is perhaps a link with the old name of the Etruscan town of Caere (near Civitavecchia) – Pyrgi or the 'Towers'.

Pyrias (Πυρίας) A boatman from Ithaca who took pity on an old man captured by pirates. The old man was carrying vessels full, apparently, of pitch. These jars later came into the possession of Pyrias who realized that under the pitch they contained jewels and treasures. In his gratitude Pyrias sacrificed an ox to his unknown benefactor. From this came the proverb: 'Pyrias is the only man to have sacrificed an ox to his benefactor.'

Pyrrha (Πύρρα) The Redhead, the name of the daughter of Epimetheus and Pandora. She married Deucalion and became through him the mother of the human race after the flood (Table 8). Deucalion and Pyrrha lived in Phthiotis. After the flood, which deposited them on the top of Parnassus, they created human beings by throwing stones over their shoulders. DEUCALION created men while Pyrrha created women. Pyrrha was also the name which ACHILLES bore when he hid amongst the women of Scyros. Hence the surname of his son Neoptolemus, called Pyrrhus – the Redhead.

Pyrrhicus (Πύρριχος) The name of the person who invented the 'pyrrhic', a war-dance performed with weapons – the lance, shield and flares. Traditions vary as to his identity. Sometimes he is one of the Curetes from Crete, who watched over the infant Zeus, and sometimes a Laconian. The name of this dance is also sometimes associated with that of PYRRHUS.

Pyrrhus (Πύρρος) The Redhead, the surname of NEOPTOLEMUS, Achilles' son, either because his hair was red, or because he blushed easily or, simply, because his father, who was very fair, bore the name of Pyrrha when he hid among the daughters of Lycomedes on Scyros. Pyrrhus was said to have been the eponym of the town of Pyrrhicus in Laconia, and was reputed to have been the inventor of the 'Pyrrhic' war-dance (but see PYRRHICUS).

Pythaeus (Πυθαεύς) A son of Apollo, who came from Delphi to Argos and founded a temple there in honour of the 'Pythian' Apollo.

Python (Πύθων) When Apollo decided to found a sanctuary at the foot of Parnassus, not far from Delphi, he found near a spring a dragon called Python which used to massacre animals and people. Apollo killed it with his arrows. Hera had entrusted the safety of Typhon to this monster who, like most others, was said to be a son of the Earth. As such, Python could pronounce oracles. That is why Apollo had to eliminate this rival before setting up his oracle at Delphi.

Hyginus told a story according to which an oracle had declared that the serpent Python would perish at the hands of a son of Leto. When she heard that the latter was pregnant by Zeus, Hera proclaimed that she could not give birth in any sunlit place. Python himself tried to kill Leto, but Poseidon, at Zeus' request, welcomed and hid her on the island of Ortygia, which was then covered by the waves. There, under a vault formed by the waves, she gave birth out of the sunlight in accordance with Hera's decree. Three days after his birth, Apollo killed Python; he deposited his ashes in a sarcophagus and founded in his honour the Pythian games. Python was also said to be buried under the Omphalos of the temple of Delphi (see also DELPHYNE).

Quirinus A very early Roman god, one of the three archaic divinities whose worship made up the Indo-European background of Roman religion. In hierarchical order, he was the last of the three, behind Jupiter and Mars. On his nature and functions, ancient sources are nearly unanimous in making him a god of war of Sabine origin, deriving his name either from the Sabine town of Cures, or connecting it with the Sabine name for the lance, *curis*. He was apparently the god of the Quirinal hill where, according to tradition, there was a Sabine community.

Relying on the existence of triads analogous with that of Jupiter, Mars and Quirinus in other Indo-European religions, in which each god corresponds to a social class – Jupiter or his equivalent to the priests, the equivalent of Mars to soldiers, the third god to farmers – V.G. Dumézil has put forward the hypothesis that Quirinus, far from being originally a god of war, was essentially the protector of farmers. This is an attractive hypothesis for which there is some evidence in the Roman sphere in the writings of Servius, according to whom Quirinus was a 'peaceful Mars' belonging within the city. Further, according to Dumézil the Quirites, whose name is obviously connected with that of the god, were essentially citizens of the city, and it was known that this name, when applied to soldiers, was a deadly insult. It should finally be noted that certain functions assumed by the priest of Quirinus were directed towards the worship of rural divinities (notably Consus). Myths about Quirinus are rare. One was connected with the foundation of the city of Cures by MODIUS FABIDIUS, a son of the god. The main point concerns the assimilation of Romulus and Quirinus. After an appearance of Romulus to Julius PROCULUS, the Romans built a temple to ROMULUS dedicated to Quirinus. At the same time, HERSILIA, Romulus' wife, took the name Hora Quirini.

R

Ramnes This figure appears in the *Aeneid* as an augur of the Rutilian army, under Turnus' command. He was killed by Nisus while he was asleep. The name of Ramnes was borne by one of the three primitive tribes of Rome.

Rarus (Ῥᾶρος) According to certain authors, the son of Cranaus and the father of Triptolemus, whom he had by Amphictyon, the woman who was the mother of the bandit CERCYON. According to other authors, Rarus was the grandfather of Triptolemus and not his father, and had a son Celeus, who was more usually considered to be the son of Eleusis. It was Rarus who in this tradition supposedly welcomed Demeter while she was looking for her daughter. As a reward for this hospitality, the goddess taught Triptolemus the art of cultivating wheat. Rarus is said to have given his name to the Plain of Rarus (Ῥάριον Πεδίον) near Eleusis, where wheat was cultivated for the first time.

Ratumena An Etruscan and the hero of a Roman legend. Before his expulsion, Tarquinius Superbus had ordered from craftsmen at Veii a clay chariot to adorn the temple of Jupiter Capitolinus which was then being constructed. While in the oven, the clay chariot, instead of drying out as clay normally does when being baked, expanded in such an extraordinary way that the oven had to be taken to pieces in order to remove it. Soothsayers declared that this marvel promised prosperity and power to the people who owned the chariot. Consequently the Veians decided not to hand the chariot over to the Romans on the pretext that, since giving the order, Tarquinius had been deposed as king; the chariot, they said, belonged to the Tarquinii and not to the Romans. The gods found a way of having Supurbus' wishes respected, however: a few days later, during the games being celebrated at Veii, Ratumena won the first prize in chariot racing. As soon as he was crowned, his horses bolted and raced without stopping to Rome, which they entered through the gate later named Porta Ratumena. At this spot Ratumena was thrown from the chariot and killed. The horses, meanwhile, raced on to the Capitol and only stopped on reaching the statue of Jupiter Tonans, to whom they appeared to pay homage for their victory. In their terror the Veians handed over the clay chariot, the work of their artists and the guarantee of the greatness of Rome.

Recaranus Also called Caranus or Garanus in certain texts, a hero who replaced Hercules in the episode with CACUS. It was he who crossed the site of the future Rome with his herd of cattle, which were stolen from him by the robber Cacus. This Recaranus was said to be of Greek origin, and was endowed with immense strength. In a related version of the legend, Cacus was a slave, a thief and an evil subject of King Evander. Recaranus, despairing of finding his herd, would have abandoned his search had Evander not taken the matter in hand and forced his slave to return them. The joyful Recaranus then supposedly set up an altar to Jupiter the Finder at the foot of the Aventine: this would be the Ara Maxima, generally attributed to Hercules. In honour of Jupiter he then sacrificed one tenth of his animals on this altar. This was reputedly the origin of the tithe that was offered to Hercules from all the victims sacrificed at the Ara Maxima.

Remus In the legend of the foundation of Rome, the twin brother of Romulus. According to one isolated and evidently late explanation, the name Remus was given to the child because he was 'slow' in everything – which would explain why he was supplanted by Romulus. In the legend Remus appears as the unfortunate double of his brother. But whereas Greek legends involving twins who are rivals for power generally trace the hostility of the brothers back to their earliest childhood, the legend of Romulus and Remus shows them, on the contrary, from the very start united in brotherly love. For their early years, see ROMULUS.

Remus only begins to play a definite role once the twins have reached manhood, at the time of the quarrel with Numitor's shepherds. Remus was made prisoner, and brought before the king of Alba. In order to rescue him Romulus, instructed by FAUSTULUS, organized an expedition against the town. There then comes the episode of the recognition of the twins by Numitor, and of the death of Amulius. Romulus and Remus gave the throne of Alba to their grandfather Numitor, the rightful heir. They then set off to found a city. They were agreed on the principle that they would found the town at the spot where they had been saved (on the site of the future Rome). But they were not clear exactly where this spot was. In order to be sure, they took Numitor's advice and decided to consult the omens. Romulus settled himself on the Palatine hill, and Remus on the Aventine. The city would be founded at the spot where the signs seemed most favourable. Remus saw six vultures, whereas Romulus saw twelve. The gods having decided in favour of the Palatine (and so in favour of Romulus), the latter set about marking the boundary of his city. The first boundary was a ditch dug by a plough drawn by two oxen. Remus, disappointed at not having been favoured by the gods, made fun of this boundary which could be so easily crossed and, with a jump, leapt inside the line which his brother had just marked out. Romulus was annoyed by this sacrilege, drew his sword, and killed Remus. In the earliest form of the legend, it seems that the murder was the result solely of Remus' sacrilegious action. Romulus was distraught at his crime, and, it is said, contemplated suicide. He buried Remus on the Aventine, at the place which took, as a result of this event, the name of Remoria. It was by the legend of Remus that was explained the fact that until the time of the emperor Claudius in AD 49, the Aventine remained outside the *pomerium*, the religious boundary of Rome. The origin of the funeral feast, the *Lemuria* (see LEMURES), was also connected with the death of Remus.

There existed a version of the legend in which Romulus did not kill his brother but ruled conjointly with him, sharing the power as the consuls were later to do. According to certain historians, notably Dionysus of Chalcis, it was Remus who founded Rome. This Remus was not the son of Rhea, but of Electra, the daughter of King Latinus. His father was either Ascanius or Italus. For other genealogies of Remus, see ROMULUS.

Rhacius ('Ράχιος) A Cretan, the son of Lebes, who married MANTO, and whose son was the soothsayer Mopsus. He emigrated from Crete to Colophon in Asia Minor where he met Manto who, on Apollo's orders, had left Thebes after the capture of the city by the Epigoni. Apart from Mopsus, he is said to have had another child,

Pamphylia, the eponym of the country of that name.

Rhadamanthys ('Ραδάμανθυς) A Cretan hero who was generally considered to be one of the three sons of Zeus and Europa, and brother of Minos and Sarpedon (Table 28). Like his two brothers, he was adopted by the Cretan king Asterion, to whom Zeus had given Europa. But there was also a local tradition which made Rhadamanthys a son of Hephaestus, grandson of Talos and great-grandson of Cres, who gave his name to Crete. Rhadamanthys was renowned for his wisdom and justice. He was said to have organized the Cretan code, which had served as a model for the Greek cities, with such skill that after his death he became one of the judges of the dead in the Underworld, alongside his brother Minos and another son of Zeus, Aeacus.

One tradition maintained that, towards the end of his life, Rhadamanthys fled from Crete and, having arrived in Boeotia, married ALCMENE. In the *Odyssey* there is mention of an episode in the legend of Rhadamanthys which remains obscure: this is the voyage which he made on board the Phaeacian ships to Euboea to look for the giant Tityus. Two children are attributed to Rhadamanthys: Gortys, the eponymous hero of the Cretan town of Gortyn, and Erythrus, the founder of Erythrae in Boeotia.

Rhea ('Ρεία) One of the Titanides, daughters of Gaia and Uranus. She married Cronus, with whom she ruled over the world. According to Hesiod's *Theogony*, they produced six children: Hestia, Demeter, Hera, Hades, Poseidon and Zeus, the youngest. But Cronus, following an oracle from Uranus and Gaia which warned that one of his children would dethrone him, devoured each as soon as it was born. Rhea, wanting to save one of them, hid the infant Zeus and gave Cronus a stone wrapped in swaddling clothes to eat instead of him. There exists an analogous tradition about Poseidon, saved by his mother by a similar trick. During the Roman period, Rhea, a very ancient divinity of the Earth, was assimilated to CYBELE, the mother of the gods.

Rhea Silvia
1. Rhea or Rea Silvia, the mother of Romulus and Remus, and sometimes also called ILIA. There are two main traditions about her origins: according to one she was the daughter of Aeneas, and according to the other she was descended from

him but several generations later, since she was the daughter of NUMITOR, the king of Alba. In these two versions she was secretly loved; it was generally accepted that her lover was the god Mars, although certain authors attribute the paternity of the twins either to a chance encounter with a lover or to Rhea's uncle, Amulius, who had dethroned Numitor. When it became evident that she was going to give birth, Amulius had her put in prison. She escaped immediate death thanks to the intercession of her cousin Antho, Amulius' daughter. She was then either killed immediately after giving birth, or died as a result of the harsh treatment which was meted out to her, or else was rescued by Romulus and Remus, as Antiope was by ZETHUS and AMPHION, when the twins had dealt with Amulius. Rhea was sometimes considered to have received the honour of apotheosis: in the version in which she was killed by Amulius, the latter threw her into the Tiber. The river-god was then seen rising out of the water to greet her and make her his wife. It was also said that it was the god of the Anio (a tributary of the Tiber) who married her.

2. A priestess whom Hercules fell in love with when he was passing through Rome after his labour with Geryon's oxen. She gave him a son, Aventinus, after whom the Aventine hill was named.

Rhesus (Ῥῆσος) A Thracian hero who fought on the side of the Trojans during the Trojan war, and was killed by Odysseus and Diomedes. Traditions vary as to the name of his parents. In Homer his father is called Eioneus, but in later authors Rhesus was said to be the son of the river-god Strymon and the Muse Clio (or else of Terpsichore, or Euterpe, or Calliope). Rhesus was famous for his horses, which were white as snow and swift as the wind. He came to the help of the Trojans during the tenth year of the war, and had only fought for a single day (but one in which he had wrought great havoc amongst the Greeks) when Diomedes and Odysseus set out at night for the Trojan camp. They surprised Rhesus asleep, killed him and took away his horses. This story, as it appears in the *Iliad*, has been dramatized. It is assumed that an oracle had informed Rhesus that if he and his horses drank from the River Scamander, he would be invincible and would take the Greek camp by storm. In order to avoid this coming about, Hera and Athena suggested to Odysseus and Diomedes that they undertake their expedition that night and kill Rhesus before he and his horses drank from the river. According to a tradition related by Conon, Rhesus was the brother of BRANGAS and OLYNTHUS.

Rhode (Ῥόδη) According to certain traditions, a daughter of Poseidon and Amphitrite, and the sister of Triton (Table 38). According to others, she was one of the daughters of the river-god Asopus. All agree that she married Helios (but see RHODUS).

Rhodope (Ῥοδόπη) The heroine of an Ephesian legend. She was a young girl who had sworn to Artemis that she would keep her virginity, and had been chosen by the goddess as a hunting companion. Aphrodite was annoyed at this and made her fall in love with a young hunter who was as shy as she, called Euthynicus. They met in the mountains and indulged their passion. Artemis then punished Rhodope by turning her into a spring called Styx, which welled up in the very cave in which she had lost her virginity. This spring was used as a test for young girls who swore to remain virgins. They would write their promise on a tablet which they hung around their necks, and then went into the spring. The water was normally quite shallow and came up to their knees. But if they were not virgins, as they claimed to be, the water came up to their necks, covering the tablet on which was written their false oath. For another Rhodope see CICONES and HAEMUS.

Rhodopis (Ῥοδῶπις) A young Egyptian girl of great beauty. One day, while she was bathing, an eagle flew off with one of her sandals and dropped it at the feet of the king Psammetichus, who was then ruling in Memphis. Psammetichus was amazed at the finely worked sandal and had the whole of Egypt searched for the girl to whom it belonged. On finding her, they were married. It was sometimes stated that this Rhodopis was in fact called Doricha, and that she was Greek, having come from Thrace to Egypt, following Charaxus, the brother of the poetess Sappho.

Rhodus (Ῥόδος) The wife of Helios who gave her name to the island of Rhodes, and often confused with RHODE by mythographers. She was sometimes described as the daughter of Aphrodite and an unnamed father, and sometimes as the daughter of Poseidon and HALIA. By Helios she had seven sons, the HELIADES (Table 14), one of whom, Cercaphus, ruled over Rhodes after his brother Ochimus and had children who shared the sovereignty of the island.

Rhoecus ('Ροῖκος)

1. The hero of a love story which recalls both that of Arcas and CHRYSOPELIA, and that of Daphnis. There was an oak tree that was so old that it was on the point of falling. Rhoecus had his servants erect a support for it, and thus saved the life of the Hamadryads whose existence was linked to that of the oak. In gratitude, the gods offered him whatever he wanted. He asked for their favours, which they granted him, but warned him against any unfaithfulness to them. They added that a bee would be their messenger. One day, the bee came to find Rhoecus, apparently to bring him a message from the Nymphs. Rhoecus was playing chess and greeted the bee brusquely, with the result that it stung him in the eyes and blinded him. Judging from certain allusions to this legend, it seems that Rhoecus had been unfaithful to the goddesses, and that this was the real reason for his punishment. The story is sometimes set in Assyria, at Ninus (Nineveh).
2. One of the Centaurs killed by ATALANTA.

Rhoeo ('Ροιώ)

The daughter of STAPHYLUS and sister of Hemithea. When LYRCUS was staying with them, she fell in love with him, and she and her sister fought for the honour of becoming his mistress. Zeus later fell in love with her, and she became pregnant by him. Staphylus, thinking that a mere mortal and not a god was responsible for this, locked his daughter in a chest and put it in the sea. The chest was washed up on the coast of Euboea (or Delos). Rhoeo gave birth to a son called ANIUS and then married a mortal called Zarex, the son of Carystus. She had five sons (two according to some). An isolated and aberrant tradition makes Rhoeo the mistress of Aeson and mother of Jason.

Rhoetus ('Ροῖτος)

1. One of the Giants who took part in the struggle against the gods. He was killed by Dionysus.
2. A Centaur who took part in the fight between the Lapiths and the Centaurs, at the time of Pirithous' wedding. Virgil relates that he was killed by Dionysus, perhaps confusing him with the Giant of the same name). Apollodorus also calls one of the Centaurs Rhoetus.

3. At the time of the marriage of Perseus and Andromeda, one of the companions of PHINEUS bore the name Rhoetus. He was killed by the hero.
4. The father of ANCHEMOLUS was also called Rhoetus.

Rhopalus ('Ρόπαλος)

A king of Sicyon. The son of Phaestus, who was himself a son of Heracles, he ruled after Zeuxippus who succeeded PHAESTUS when the latter was exiled to Crete as the result of a prophecy. His son and successor was Hippolytus who surrendered Sicyon to a Mycenaean army which attacked it on Agamemnon's orders. There existed a tradition according to which Rhopalus was a son of Heracles and the father of Phaestus. The name Rhopalus, which means a club, recalls one of Heracles' favourite weapons.

Rhoxane ('Ρωξάνη)

Said to be the daughter of Cordyas, she was raped by Medus, the son of the Persian king Artaxerxes. Medus, through fear of punishment, threw himself into the river which had until then been called the Xarandas. It was subsequently called the Medus, and later the Euphrates.

Rhytia ('Ρυτία)

In the tradition followed by the mythographer Pherecydes, the mother of the nine Corybantes of Samothrace, whose father was Apollo. The genealogies of the Curetes and Corybantes are very diverse.

Robigo

Robigo and Robigus were two divinities, the first feminine, the second masculine, which watched over the growing of wheat and averted blight (robigo in Latin). A festival was celebrated in their honour each year in Rome on 25 April. There was a wood sacred to them five miles north of Rome, on the Via Clodia, beyond the Milvian bridge.

Roma

Roma or Rhome (so spelt after the Greek word meaning 'strength'), according to certain mythographers the name of a heroine who was supposed to have given her name to the city of Rome. Traditions about her identity vary. The most ancient makes her a Trojan prisoner who was accompanying Odysseus and Aeneas when the two heroes, coming from the country of the Molossians (Illyria), reached the banks of the Tiber. Their ships had been driven into the region by a storm, and the captives were tired of wandering the seas. Roma had no difficulty in persuading

The Forum Romanum was the chief public square of Rome built between the foot of the Capitoline and the Velian ridge opposite the north-eastern end of the Palatine. The Forum has been fully excavated.

them to set fire to the ships, which put an end to the voyage. The immigrants settled on the Palatine, where their town prospered to such a degree that, in gratitude, they wanted to honour the name of the heroine. Another tradition makes Rhome the daughter of Ascanius and consequently the granddaughter of Aeneas. When the Trojans had taken possession of the site of the future Rome, Rhome set up a temple of Faith on the Palatine. Hence the town which grew up on this hill bore the name Rome, in memory of the young girl. A variant of this tradition claimed that Rhome was not the daughter, but the wife of Ascanius. She is also mentioned as the wife of Aeneas, being the daughter of TELEPHUS and consequently granddaughter of Heracles. She was also said to be the daughter of Telemachus and sister of Latinus. A tradition independent of the Trojan legend mentions a Roma who was the daughter of King Evander or of King Italus and Leucaria.

Finally, certain writers maintained that Roma was the name of a soothsayer who had advised Evander to choose this spot to found the town of Pallantea, the original nucleus of Rome.

Romis (Ῥῶμις) According to Plutarch, a very early king of the Latins who drove out of Latium the Etruscan immigrants who had come from Thessaly via Lydia, and founded the city of Rome.

Romulus In the most common version of the legend, the eponymous founder of the city of Rome. He was usually said to be a descendant of Aeneas via the kings of Alba. He and his twin brother Remus were sons of RHEA SILVIA (OR ILIA) and grandsons of NUMITOR. But alongside this standard account there are many variants. For example, the series of Alban kings was omitted and Rhea was made the daughter of Aeneas. Some authors made Romulus and Remus the twin sons of Aeneas and Dexithea, the daughter of Phorbas. In this version the two children were brought to Italy when very young. Of the whole fleet the only ship which was spared by the storm was the one which bore them, and it landed safely at the site of the future Rome. Other traditions make Romulus the son of ROMA and of Latinus, who was himself, according to this version, the son of Telemachus. His mother was sometimes called Aemilia and was thus the daughter of Aeneas and Lavinia (for another legend see TARCHETIUS).

According to the most common version, the god Mars was the father of Romulus and Remus. He seduced Rhea Silvia in the sacred wood where she had gone to look for water for the sacrifice (she was one of the Vestal Virgins). It was also said that she had been assaulted by the god while she was asleep. Amulius, Rhea's uncle, noticed that she was pregnant and put her into prison. When the children were born, the king exposed them on the banks of the Tiber, at the foot of the Palatine (the site of the future Rome lay within his territory, and was used as grazing land for the royal flocks). It was also said that a servant of Amulius put the children in a basket which he then floated on the river, but the river had burst its banks because of recent rain, and a counter-current, instead of carrying it towards the sea, had taken it upstream onto the lower slopes of the Germalus (the north-west summit of the Palatine). The basket deposited the two children under a fig tree, the Ficus Ruminalis, which was later held to be sacred (one tradition placed this fig tree on the Comitium, between the Capitol and the Forum, but it was said that it had been transported there by the magic of the augur Attius Navius). There, Romulus and Remus were found by a she-wolf, which had just given birth. She took pity on the two children and suckled them, thus saving them from starvation. The she-wolf was an animal sacred to the Italian god Mars, and it was believed that this wolf must have been sent by the god to look after his children. Moreover, a woodpecker (Mars' bird) helped the wolf to feed them. One of the king's shepherds, FAUSTULUS, appeared and saw the children being fed in this miraculous way; he took pity on them and brought them home to his own wife, ACCA LARENTIA, who brought them up. Certain sceptical mythographers, along with Fathers of the Church later on, claimed that the she-wolf who had taken care of the twins was none other than Acca Larentia, whose misbehaviour had earned her the name of she-wolf

(*lupa*, the Latin for 'wolf', was also a term used to describe prostitutes).

Faustulus sent the two youths to study at Gabii, which was then, supposedly, the great intellectual centre of Latium. Romulus and Remus later came back to the village on the Palatine, where they became involved in robbery. One day Remus, with other youths of the neighbourhood, attacked Amulius' shepherds who were guarding the king's flocks on the Aventine. The shepherds defended themselves; Remus was made a prisoner, taken before the Alban king and interrogated. Meanwhile Romulus, who had been absent at the time of this incident, returned to the Palatine. Faustulus revealed to him the secret of his birth, and asked him to go and save his brother. At the head of a group of young friends of his, Romulus hurried to Alba, overran Amulius' palace, revealed his identity to the king whom he then killed, and freed Remus. He handed sovereignty over to his grandfather Numitor. The twins then decided to found a city (see REMUS for the choice of the site and the early stages of its foundation). Romulus eventually killed Remus, having marked out the boundary of the Palatine town. The city was founded on 21 April, the festival of the Parilia (the festival of Pales). The chronology varies: the year was either 754, 752 or even 772 BC.

Traditions do not agree on the size of Romulus' city. It is usually agreed that it only included the Palatine *pomerium*, that is the hill itself. But several episodes of the legend of Romulus imply that the city also included the Capitol, notably the *asylum* in the hollow which marked the summit of the hill. At this point we find the greatest number of uncertainties in the sources, which reveal numerous reworkings of the legend corresponding to the various stages of the development of Rome. Plutarch even situates the ritual events of the foundation of the city and the consecration of the *mundus* (the centre of augury in the new city) on the Comitium, at the foot of the Arx, north of the Forum.

Romulus' reign, long considered historical, is now considered a tissue of legends, of which the following are the main ones. When the city was founded, Romulus was concerned to populate it. As local resources were insufficient he thought of creating a place of refuge on the Capitol, between the two sacred woods, that of the Arx (the Citadel) and the Capitol itself (the southern summit of the hill). There all the Italian outlaws could take refuge, those who had been exiled, bankrupt, murderers and even runaway slaves. This was the nucleus of the first population of Rome. Rome was not therefore, short of males, but there were no women. Romulus therefore thought of abducting women from his Sabine neighbours. To this end he organized horse races on the Festival of Consus on 21 August (the altar for which was situated in the valley of the Circus Maximus between the Palatine and the Aventine). People from the surrounding area attended, along with their wives and children. At a given signal Romulus' men abducted all the young women, of whom there were either 30 or 527, or even 683. Only one of them, Hersilia, was a married woman. Those whose daughters had been thus abducted were extremely angry and they flocked around the Sabine king, Titus Tatius. An army was soon formed, which marched against Rome. It was then that Tatius managed to get inside the Capitoline citadel by surprise, thanks to the treachery of TARPEIA. One section of the Sabine army then tried to take from the rear the Roman troops of Romulus who were holding a position at the foot of the Capitol facing north. They would have succeeded if the god Janus had not intervened: he made a boiling hot spring gush forth in front of them and cut off their route. However, the Sabine troops maintained their pressure and forced the Romans to retreat. When the latter reached the very foot of the Palatine and, as defeat was threatening to turn into disaster, Romulus prayed to Jupiter and promised to raise a temple to him at this very spot if he would change the fortunes of the battle. Jupiter granted this wish. The Romans ceased to retreat, turned about and put their enemy to flight. This took place between the Palatine and the Velia on the eastern edge of the Forum. The temple promised by Romulus was constructed: this was the temple of Jupiter Stator (that is, Jupiter the Stayer) which stood on the spot where later the arch of Titus was built, on the Via Sacra.

The Romans and Sabines then signed a treaty of friendship uniting the two people. It was said that the Sabine women abducted by the Romans had thrown themselves between the combatants and had begged their fathers, brothers and new husbands to cease this sacrilegious fight. This episode took place, it was said, in the Forum, where the *Regia* later stood. This was how Titus Tatius, the Sabine king, came to be associated with the rule of Romulus, and the union of the two peoples came about. But Tatius died soon and Romulus became sole ruler of the two peoples.

Romulus lived on the Palatine, at the top of the Ladder of Cacus, which linked the hill with the valley of the Circus Maximus. Here there was displayed an enormous dogberry tree said to have grown from a javelin once thrown by Romulus from the Aventine. It had stuck so deeply into the ground that no one had been able to pull it out, and had grown roots. The tree was sacred, and whenever it was seen to be wilting panic spread around the town and everybody came to water it. It was destroyed at the time of the work carried out nearby by the Emperor Caligula. Similarly, at the top of the Ladder of Cacus, a hut said to have been Romulus' house used to be shown to tourists: it was faithfully restored each time it was damaged by fire.

The reign of Romulus lasted for 33 years, and was marked by the development of the young Rome, with the result that the people gave the king the title of Father of the Nation. But Romulus was to end his earthly life in a very curious way at the age of 54. On the Nones (7th) of July he was reviewing his army on the Campus Martius in a part known as the *palus Caprae* (the Goat's pool) when suddenly a terrifying storm broke, accompanied by an eclipse of the sun. Everything disappeared under a deluge. As soon as the storm was over, when everyone emerged from their shelter, the king was found to be missing. He had disappeared off the face of the earth. A Roman, Julius Proculus, claimed that Romulus had appeared to him in a dream and had revealed that he had been abducted by the gods and had become the god QUIRINUS. In addition he had asked that a sanctuary be raised to him on the Quirinal hill. This was done. Sceptical historians of a later period claimed that in fact the senators had had a too popular king assassinated and had made up this story to pacify the *plebs*. This interpretation took on some validity from the fact that, during the classical epoch, there was a 'tomb of Romulus' situated on the Comitium under the Black Stone (*lapis Niger*). For the feast of the *Nonae Caprotinae* commemorating the disappearance of Romulus, see PHILOTIS.

Romus In certain versions of the legend, the eponymous founder of the city of Rome. He was said to have been the son of Imathion who had been sent from Troy by Diomedes (see HERACLES), or else the son of AENEAS. According to other traditions he was the grandson of the latter, and the son of Ascanius (compare ROMA). He was sometimes considered to be one of the children of

Odysseus and Circe. He had two brothers, Antias and Ardeas, the eponymous heroes of the cities Ardea and Antium. A later legend made Romus the son of Roma who was the wife of Latinus. His brothers were thus Romulus and Telegonus.

Rutuli A tribe from central Italy whose capital was the little town of Ardea in Latium. They were said to have been opposed to the arrival of AENEAS, and to have taken up arms against him at the instigation of TURNUS, their king.

S

Sabazius (Σαβάζιος) A Phrygian god, whose worship was orgiastic in character. It was often compared with the cult of Dionysus in the Greek world, and he was considered to be an earlier Dionysus, the son of Zeus and Persephone. The idea of domesticating oxen and yoking them to the plough was attributed to him, and he was therefore depicted with horns on his forehead. It was said that Sabazius was conceived when Zeus took the form of a serpent to sleep with Persephone. The serpent was, in fact, the most sacred animal of the god, and played a role in his mysteries. There is a story that Sabazius himself, in the form of a serpent, slept with one of his priestesses in Asia Minor, and that children were born of this union.

Sabazius did not properly belong to the Greek pantheon. He was an imported god, and did not possess any personal mythic cycle, or at least any exoteric myth. His legend was perhaps richer in the mysteries celebrated in his honour.

Sabbe (Σάββη) According to Pausanias, the Babylonian Sibyl. She was of Hebraic origin, and a daughter of Berosus and Erymanthe.

Sabus According to one tradition, the son of the Roman god SANCUS and the eponymous hero of the Sabines. According to others who traced the descent of the Sabines from the Lacedaemonians, Sabus was a Lacedaemonian (perhaps of Persian origin) who established himself in the region of Reate (modern Rieti).

Sagaris (Σάγαρις)
1. According to a tradition described only by Solinus, the son of Ajax the Locrian and the founder of the city of SYBARIS in southern Italy.
2. Sagaris (or Sangaris) was also a son of Midas who gave his name to the Asiatic river Sangarius. It was said also that this Sagaris was in reality a son

of Mygdon and of Alexirrhoe. The Great Goddess Cybele afflicted him with madness because of his lack of respect for her, and he threw himself into the river Xerabates, which henceforth was known as the Sangarius.

Sagaritis (Σαγαρῖτις) A Hamadryad in Ovid's version of the legend of Attis. The latter had promised the goddess Cybele that he would remain chaste, but he slept with the Nymph Sagaritis. In anger, the goddess caused the Nymph's death by cutting down the tree to whose life that of Sagaritis was attached, and she sent the young Attis mad, with the result that he castrated himself (see ATTIS for other versions of the legend).

Salacia A Roman divinity of the sea, associated with Neptune. She was the personification of salt water, and akin to Venilia, the divinity of coastal water, but distinct from her.

Salambo (Σαλαμβώ) The Babylonian name of Aphrodite (Astarte) when she was lamenting the death of ADONIS.

Salamis (Σαλαμίς) According to the most popular version of the legend, one of the numerous daughters of the river-god ASOPUS. She was abducted by Poseidon, by whom she had a son CYCHREUS (Table 30), to the island which subsequently took the name of Salamis (off the coast of Attica).

Salius (Σάλιος) A companion of Aeneas. He is variously described as coming from Samothrace, from Mantinea in Arcadia, or from Tegea. The war-dance of the Roman college of priests, the *Salii*, was attributed to him (see also CATHETUS).

Salmoneus (Σαλμωνεύς) One of the sons of Aeolus and Aenarete. He was, therefore, descended from Deucalion and Pyrrha (Table 8). He was born and grew up in Thessaly but emigrated to Elis with a number of his compatriots and founded a city there which he called Salmone. He first married Alcidice, the daughter of Aleus, by whom he had a daughter Tyro. After the death of his wife, he married SIDERO, who turned out to be a cruel stepmother. Salmoneus, being extremely arrogant, got the idea that he could imitate Zeus. So he constructed a road paved with bronze and rode upon it in a chariot with copper or iron wheels, dragging chains after it. He thus hoped to imitate the sound of thunder. At the same time, he threw burning torches to right and left in imitation of lightning. Zeus was furious at this impiety and struck him down with a thunderbolt, destroying not only him, but his people and the town of Salmone. It was said that Salmoneus was extremely unpopular and that his subjects complained strongly of having burning torches hurled at them by their king.

Salus In Rome not only the personification of health, but of preservation in general. She had a temple on the Quirinal. She was an abstraction and consequently possessed no legends. During the classical era she was gradually associated with Hygieia, the Hellenic goddess of health and the daughter of Asclepius.

Samon (Σάμων) According to certain traditions, the eponymous hero of the island of Samothrace. He was the son of Hermes and a Nymph called Rhene. He emigrated from Arcadia to Samothrace with DARDANUS, but whereas the latter then went on to the Troad, Samon remained on the island. For another Samon of Cretan origin, see DADA.

Sanape (Σανάπη) This figure gave her name to the town of Sinope, on the Black Sea. She was an Amazon who escaped being massacred at the time of HERACLES' expedition and fled to Paphlagonia, where she married a king of that country. There she proved to have an excessive liking for wine, which earned her the name of Sanape, which meant 'drunkard' in the local dialect. This name was corrupted into Sinope, and became that of the city where her husband ruled.

Sancus His full name was Semo Sancus, a divinity of the earliest Roman religion. By early writers he was also identified with Dius Fidius. His worship was said to have been introduced by the Sabines. He was sometimes considered to be the father of the hero SABUS, the eponym of the Sabine people. A very obscure god, he does not possess any myth but apparently supervised the keeping of oaths.

Sangarius (Σαγγάριος) The god of the river of that name in Asia Minor. Like all river-gods he was considered to be a son of Oceanus and of Tethys. He was sometimes made out to be the father of Hecuba, whom he sired on either Metope or the Nymph Eunoe or the Naiad Evagora. He was also the father of a certain Alphaeus, a Phrygian, who is supposed to have instructed Athena

in the art of playing the flute, but was struck down by a thunderbolt from Zeus when he tried to assault his pupil. The most famous legend in which Sangarius plays a role is that of his daughter NANA and the birth of ATTIS (see also AGDISTIS).

Saon (Σάων) A Boeotian who went to consult the oracle at Delphi during a drought which was ravaging his country. The Pythian oracle ordered him to go to Lebadea to question the oracle of Trophonius. On arriving at Lebadea, he discovered that no one there knew of an oracle, but he saw some bees and, following them, went into a cave where the hero Trophonius gave him all the instructions necessary for the foundation of a cult as well as an oracle in his honour.

Sardo (Σαρδώ)
1. The wife of Tyrrhenus, who emigrated to Italy from Asia Minor. She gave her name to the Lydian city of Sardis, and also to the island of Sardinia.
2. A daughter of Sthenelus. She was the eponym of the city of Sardis.

Sardus (Σάρδος) The son of Maceris, the name the Libyans and Egyptians gave to Heracles. At the head of a force of Libyans, he landed on the island then known as Iehnooussa, which subsequently took the name of Sardinia.

Saron (Σάρων) A legendary king of Troezen, the successor to Althepus. He erected such a magnificent temple to Artemis on the seashore that the Gulf of Troezen was called the Gulf of Phoebe. He was a great hunter; one day a hind which he was chasing leapt into the sea, whereupon he plunged in after it and swam so long in pursuit that his strength failed him and he drowned. His body was washed up by the waves not far from the temple he had founded. The gulf was then called the Saronic Gulf.

Sarpedon (Σαρπηδών)
1. A hero from Cretan myth, although the name also appears in an isolated case as that of a giant, the son of Poseidon, who was killed by Heracles in Thrace (see POLTYS).
2. Sarpedon was usually said to be one of the sons of Europa and Zeus (Tables 3 and 28). He was brought up by Asterius, Minos and Rhadamanthys. He later quarrelled with Minos, either over the question of who would obtain the Cretan throne, or because they were both in love with the

same boy, Miletus. Whichever it was, Sarpedon left Crete, perhaps with Europa, and went to Asia Minor. He settled in the region of Miletus in Lycia. He became king there, and was sometimes credited with the foundation of Miletus (so, likewise, was the young Miletus, who had fled with him).

3. The *Iliad* spoke of a Sarpedon, leader of a Lycian contingent, who fought alongside the Trojans. It was this Sarpedon whom one is tempted to identify as Minos' brother, who was said to be the son of Zeus and Laodamia, herself the daughter of Bellerophon. This Sarpedon played a major role in the attack on the Achaean camp and the assult on the walls. He ended up being killed by Patroclus, and a great battle was fought around his body.

The chronological difficulty in identifying the Cretan Sarpedon with the Sarpedon who took part in the Trojan War led the mythographers to see them as two separate persons. Diodorus constructed their genealogy thus: Sarpedon, the son of Europa, went to Lycia. He had a son called Evander who married Deidamia (or Laodamia) the daughter of Bellerophon. The fruit of this marriage was the second Sarpedon, grandson of the first, and it was he who took part in the Trojan War.

Saturn A very old Italian god who has been identified with CRONUS. He was said to have come from Greece to Italy in very early times, when JUPITER (Zeus) dethroned him and hurled him from the top of Olympus. He established himself on the Capitol, on the site of the future Rome, and founded a fortified village there which (according to tradition) bore the name of Saturnia. It was also said that he had been welcomed there by a god even older than he, who had likewise emigrated from Greece, the god JANUS. The reign of Saturn over Latium (thus called because the god had hidden himself there; from the verb *latere*) was extremely prosperous. This was the GOLDEN AGE. Saturn continued the task of civilization begun by Janus, and in particular taught men how to cultivate the ground. At this time the Italian population was composed of ABORIGINES, who owed their first laws to Saturn. He was depicted armed with a scythe and bill-hook. For this reason his name was associated with the invention and popularization of viticulture. He was however sometimes considered as a god of the Underworld.

The days sacred to Saturn were the *Saturnalia*, the end of December and of the year. They were marked by rather licentious festivals during which the social order was inverted: slaves gave orders to their masters and the latter waited at the table. During the Imperial period, with the developing Romanization of Africa, Saturn represented not just Cronus but, in Carthaginian countries, the great Punic god Baal.

Satyria (Σατυρία) A daughter of Minos, the king of Crete. She was loved by Poseidon, and gave him a son Taras, the eponymous hero of the town of Tarentum. She herself had given her name to a promontory near this town, Cape Satyrion. It was sometimes also claimed that she was the mother of ITALUS.

Satyrs (Σάτυροι) Demons of nature who invariably appeared in Dionysus' train. They were represented in different ways, sometimes with the lower part of the body resembling that of a horse and the upper part that of a man, and sometimes with their animal half in the form of a goat. In both cases they had a long, thick tail, like that of a horse, and a perpetually erect penis of enormous proportions. They were depicted as dancing in the countryside, drinking with Dionysus and pursuing the Maenads and the Nymphs, the more or less reluctant victims of their lechery. They were gradually represented with less and less obviously bestial characteristics: their lower limbs became human, they had feet and not hooves. Only the

Satyr dancing and playing a pan pipe with Maenad playing a double flute. Roman silver dish from the Mildenhall Treasure. 4th century AD.

tail remained, as evidence of their old form. The Satyrs, companions of the gods, only rarely played a particular role in legends. MARSYAS was a Satyr (see also SILENUS)

Saurus (Σαῦρος) A bandit from Elis who robbed travellers until he was killed by Heracles. His name was associated with a locality where both his tomb and a sanctuary to Heracles could be seen.

Scamander (Σκάμανδρος) The river flowing through the plain of Troy. It also bore the name of Xanthus (Tawny), either because of the colour of its water, or else because it was said that its water stained red the fleece of the sheep which bathed in it. It was also said that Aphrodite had dipped her hair in its water to give it golden highlights before submitting herself to the judgement of Paris. The origin of the river was explained by the following legend: Heracles, finding himself in the Troad, was thirsty, and begged Zeus, his father, to show him a spring. Zeus made a little stream well up out of the ground but Heracles found this insufficient. Heracles then dug the ground (in Greek σκάπτω) and found a large reservoir of water which became the source of the Scamander.

In the *Iliad*, the Scamander appears as a god, the son of Zeus. He played a part in Achilles' fight against the Trojans. Indignant at receiving such quantities of bodies and blood in its water, Scamander determined to put an obstacle in the hero's way; so he overflowed his banks and threatened to drown Achilles until Hephaestus forced the river to return within his banks and remain neutral. Scamander had by the Nymph Idaea a son Teucer (Table 7), who became the first king of the Troad. The river-god was thus one of the founders of the royal family of Troy.

Scamandrius (Σκαμάνδριος)
1. The name given by Hector to his son, who was more usually known as ASTYANAX.
2. A Trojan, the son of Strophius, who was killed in battle by Menelaus.

Schedius (Σχέδιος) One of Helen's suitors. He took part in the war against Troy, commanding a force of Phocians together with his brother Epistrophius. They were both sons of Iphitus (himself the son of Naubolus) and Hippolyte. He was killed by Hector and his ashes were taken back to Anticyra in Phocis. After the end of the war, the Phocian contingent which he had been comman-

ding was driven by a storm onto the Italian coast, where the survivors founded the city of Temesa.

Schoeneus (Σχοινεύς)
1. The father of Atalanta and Clymenus. He was supposedly of Boeotian origin, but he emigrated to Arcadia. He gave his name to a town in both countries.
2. A son of Autonous who was changed into a bird (see ACANTHIS).
3. A son of Athamas and Themisto (Table 33).

Sciapodes (Σκίαποδες) An Indian or Ethiopian people whose name in Greek means 'shady feet': they had such enormous feet that in summer they lay down on the ground, raised their feet in the air, and sheltered from the sun, using their feet as parasols.

Sciron (Σκίρων) According to the common version of the legend, Sciron was a Corinthian, the son of Pelops or Poseidon, who settled in a part of Megara at a place called the Scironian Rocks, near the coastal road. He would force travellers to wash his feet and while they were doing so, would push them into the sea where an enormous tortoise tore their bodies to pieces. Theseus, on his way from Troezen to Athens, killed him in the same way as he had killed others. Historians of Megara however claimed that all this was untrue and that Sciron was in fact a kindly hero who was related to the best families. He was married to Chariclo, the daughter of CYCHREUS, the son of Selanius and Poseidon. There was one daughter from this marriage, Endeis, the wife of Aeacus and mother of Telamon and Peleus (Table 30). According to this version Theseus did not kill Sciron on his way home to Athens but when he had become king, while on his way to take Eleusis. According to another tradition, Sciron was said to be the son of Canethus and Henioche, the daughter of Pittheus, and consequently the sister of Aethra, the mother of Theseus. Theseus and Sciron were thus first cousins. It was said that he had founded the Isthmian Games in honour of Sciron to atone for this murder (see also SINIS).

Sciron was also said to be a son of Pylas, the king of Megara. His grandfather was Cleson, and great-grandfather Lelex. He married one of the daughters of Pandion, the king of Athens, during the latter's exile after he had been evicted by the sons of Metion. He clashed with Nisus, one of his brothers-in-law, after Pandion's death, because Nisus had obtained the throne of Megara. Both agreed to abide by Aeacus' decision: he decreed that they share the power between them, giving the kingship to Nisus and control of the army to Sciron.

Scirus (Σκῖρος)

1. A soothsayer from Dodona who arrived at Eleusis during the war between this town and Athens at the time of Erechtheus. He was killed in the fighting and buried on the Sacred Way at Eleusis, at the place which was called Sciron.

2. A Salaminian who gave Theseus some experienced sailors, among them, notably, his helmsman Nausithous, when Theseus set off for Crete on his mission to kill the Minotaur. This Scirus is often confused with SCIRON of Megara.

Scylaceus (Σκυλακεύς) A Lycian who fought at Glaucus' side on behalf of the Trojans. He was wounded by the Locrian Ajax. Of all the Lycians who fought in the Trojan War, he alone returned to his native country. When he arrived there, the women asked for news of their husbands and Scylaceus was forced to admit that they had all perished. The women were so enraged that they stoned him to death, close to the sanctuary of Bellerophon. Long afterwards Scylaceus was accorded divine honours following Apollo's decree.

Scylla (Σκύλλη) The name of two different figures who were sometimes confused by the mythographers though tradition tends to separate them.

1. The first was a sea-monster who lived concealed in the straits of Messina, on the Italian coast. She had the form of a woman with a ring of six dogs' heads around the lower part of her body; these ferocious creatures devoured all that passed within their reach.

When Odysseus' ship passed by the cave where the monster was lying in wait the dogs leapt out and consumed six of the hero's companions: Stesius, Ormenius, Anchimus, Ornytus, Sinopus and Amphinomus. In the *Odyssey* Scylla is described as the daughter of a goddess Crataeis. Elsewhere her father is called Trienus or Phorcys the sea-god. Other genealogies made her the daughter of Phorbas and Hecate, or else of the latter and Phorcys. Like most mythological monsters she was also made the daughter of Typhon and Echidna, or else of Lamia.

As to how Scylla became the frightful monster of the *Odyssey* traditions are equally varied. Ovid related how Glaucus was in love with Scylla and

scorned the love of Circe on this account. The furious magician decided to have revenge on her rival and mixed magic herbs with the water of the fountain where she bathed. Scylla was immediately transformed: the top half of her body remained the same, but six terrifying dogs grew from her groin. It was also claimed that Poseidon fell in love with the young girl and that the jealous Aphrodite persuaded Circe to metamorphose the girl. Another version maintained that Scylla, in love with Glaucus, had refused Poseidon's advances and he had therefore punished her in this way. The death of Scylla was sometimes attributed to Heracles. When he was crossing southern Italy, on his way back from the country of Geryon, she devoured a number of the oxen which he was bringing back with him. Heracles therefore fought with her and killed her but it was claimed that Phorcys returned her to life by magical operations performed by torchlight.

2. The other Scylla was the daughter of Nisus, the king of Megara. When Minos came to lay seige to her city as punishment for the murder of Androgeos, Scylla fell in love with this handsome foreigner. Nisus was invincible as long as he had a purple lock of hair (some sources speak of a lock of golden hair) on his head. In order to ensure victory to the man she loved, Scylla cut off the fatal lock of hair, having made Minos promise that he would marry her if she betrayed her homeland for love of him. Minos thus gained possession of Megara but was so horrified at Scylla's crime that he attached her to the prow of his boat so that she drowned. However the gods pitied her and transformed her into an egret.

Scyphius (Σκύφιος) The first horse, which was fathered by Poseidon. The god moistened a stone with his semen and the fertilized earth produced Scyphius. It was said that this took place in Thessaly.

Scythes (Σκύθης) The eponymous hero of the Scythians. He was sometimes considered to be a son of Heracles and a female monster with a serpent's body, identified with ECHIDNA. His brothers were Agathyrsus and Gelonus. When Heracles left Scythia Echidna asked him what she ought to do with their children once they were grown up. Heracles gave her one of the two bows he was carrying and his baldric on which a golden cup was hanging. He added that whichever of the three children could draw the bow and use the baldric as he could should rule over the country.

Segesta was the principal city of the Elymi in north-west Sicily. The Segestans built at least three Doric temples including this temple which was constructed during the 5th century AD.

The others would have to be exiled. Scythes was the only one of the three able to fulfil the conditions, so his mother handed control of the country over to him and his brothers went into exile. A tradition reported by Diodorus made Zeus himself Scythes' father.

Selene (Σελήνη) The personification of the Moon. She was sometimes said to be the daughter of Hyperion and Theia (Table 14) and sometimes that of the Titan Pallas or else of Helios. She was depicted as a beautiful young girl who rode across the heavens in a silver chariot drawn by two horses. She was famous for her love affairs: she had a daughter, Pandia, by Zeus, and in Arcadia her lover was the god Pan who had given her as a present a herd of white oxen. She was usually described as the lover of ENDYMION, the handsome shepherd by whom she supposedly had 50 daughters. The hero NAXOS was sometimes said to have been born of their union.

Selinus (Σέλινος) A son of Poseidon who ruled over the country of Aegialia (the ancient name for Achaea). When ION wanted to wage war against him, Selinus gave him in marriage his only daughter Helice. Ion succeeded him on the throne.

Semachus (Σήμαχος) The ancestor of the Athenian family the Semachides. His daughters greeted Dionysus hospitably and were in return (both they and their daughters) made priestesses of his cult.

Semele (Σεμέλη) In Theban tradition, Semele was the daughter of Cadmus and Harmonia. She was loved by Zeus and by him conceived Dionysus (Table 3). The jealous Hera suggested to her that she ask her divine lover to appear before her in all his glory. Zeus, who had rashly promised to grant Semele everything she asked for, had to appear before her with his thunderbolts. Semele was immediately burnt to death. Her sisters spread the rumour that she had had a mortal lover but had boasted of having enjoyed Zeus' favours, whereupon the god had struck her down with his lightning as a punishment. For this calumny a curse was laid on the sisters' descendants (see ACTAEON, INO, PENTHEUS). Later, having earned his divinity through his deeds, DIONYSUS went down to the Underworld to look for his mother. Thus revived, Semele was taken up to the heavens where she was given the name of Thyone.

A Laconian version of the birth of Dionysus states that Dionysus was borne by Semele quite normally at Thebes but that Cadmus abandoned mother and son in a chest at sea. The waves threw the chest up on the coast of Laconia where Semele, who had died, was buried. According to this tradition, this was where the god was brought up.

Semiramis (Σεμίραμις) The legend of this Babylonian queen has been preserved for us by Diodorus Siculus. He tells us that at Ascalon in Syria a goddess was worshipped who was said to live in a lake near the town. This goddess, Derceto, had a woman's face but the rest of her body was that of a fish. Aphrodite, who bore a grudge against her, made her fall violently in love with a young Syrian called CAYSTRUS by whom she had a daughter. But after the latter's birth Derceto in her shame exposed her child, did away with the father and hid herself at the bottom of the lake. By a miracle, doves brought up the child, stealing the milk and, later, the cheese which she needed from nearby shepherds. The shepherds finally discovered the little girl, who was of great beauty, and brought her to their chief who gave her the name of Semiramis, which means in Syrian 'the one who comes from the doves'.

Semiramis was still a girl when one of the king's advisers, Onnes, was ordered to inspect the flocks of sheep. He saw Semiramis in the chief shepherd's house and fell in love with her. He took her back with him to Nineveh and married her. They had two children, Hyapate and Hydaspe. Semiramis was very clever and gave her husband such good advice that he succeeded in all his endeavours. At about this time King Ninus, who ruled in Babylon, organized an expedition against Bactria. Knowing that this would not be an easy conquest he collected an army of considerable size. After an initial setback he managed to overwhelm the country by the sheer number of his troops and only the capital, Bactra, held out against him. Semiramis' husband Onnes, who was with the army and was missing his wife,

asked her to join him. She made several remarks about the way in which the siege was being conducted, and noticed that the attack was being directed from the plain, while both attackers and defenders were ignoring the citadel. She took charge of a group of mountain soldiers, scaled the cliffs which defended the site and turned the flank of the enemy defences. The besieged soldiers were terrified and surrendered. Ninus was full of admiration for the courage and skill of Semiramis and very soon her beauty made him want to have her as his wife. He offered to give Onnes his own daughter Sosana in exchange but Onnes refused. Ninus threatened to tear his eyes out, whereupon in despair Onnes hung himself. Ninus then married Semiramis without difficulty and they had a son Ninyas. On the death of Ninus Semiramis succeeded him on the throne.

She began her reign by building a splendid mausoleum to Ninus at Nineveh itself on the Euphrates plain. She then decided to have a city built for herself on the Babylonian plain. The new city was marked out on horseback on the river bank. Its perimeter was 66 kilometres long and six harnessed chariots could ride abreast along the walls. The walls were approximately 100 metres high, though some historians stated that their height was much less. The city was defended by 250 towers. The Euphrates was crossed by a bridge 900 metres long and was lined with great quays for 30 kilometres. At each end of the bridge was built a fortified castle, the queen's residence. They were linked by a subterranean passage under the river, which was diverted in order to carry this out. It was in the citadel of the western castle that the queen had her famous hanging gardens built. However, according to another account it was an Assyrian queen, later than Semiramis and of Persian origin, who asked her husband for a representation of the 'paradises', the vast pleasure-gardens of her homeland. Diodorus tells us that they were created by superimposing square terraces one on top of the other, like the steps in an amphitheatre. Each of these terraces rested on vaulted freestone galleries, covered with a thick layer of lead, on top of which was put rich soil. Inside these galleries, like a number of porticos opening onto a terrace, the royal apartments had been laid out. A system of hydraulic machines brought the water from the river to the gardens.

Semiramis built many more cities on the banks of the Euphrates and the Tigris. She then set out at the head of a large army to go to Media. On the way she built a vast park opposite Mount Bagistan, and then another park near a curiously shaped rock a little further on. She continued on her route, leaving behind her a trail of works of art of all sorts, notably at Ecbatana, which she filled with fountains. Every mound of earth and every ancient road whose origin could not be explained was attributed to her. She travelled in this fashion all over Asia and then went to Egypt to consult the oracle of Ammon. When she asked the oracle when she would die, it replied that she would meet her end when her son Ninyas conspired against her. She then conquered Ethiopia and wearily returned home to Bactra, the site of her first exploits. But she then planned to conquer India, and for several years she made elaborate preparations. She succeeded in crossing the Indus, but her troops were soon put to flight, and she herself was injured; however she managed to escape since her enemies did not dare pursue her across the river. Shortly afterwards her son Ninyas along with the eunuchs of the palace plotted against her. Recalling the prophecy of the oracle of Ammon, Semiramis handed the empire over to the young man and disappeared. It was said that she was changed into a dove and borne up to heaven where she was deified.

Serestus One of Aeneas' companions and commander of one of the Trojan ships. He was separated from Aeneas during a storm but rejoined him at Carthage. On Aeneas' orders he secretly took the fleet away when Aeneas wanted to leave Dido. He guarded the camp at the mouth of the Tiber in Aeneas' absence and later fought alongside him when they had to relieve the camp which was besieged by Turnus.

Sergestus A Trojan companion of Aeneas and commander of a ship. He was separated from Aeneas during a storm and rejoined him at Carthage. During the regattas organized in honour of Anchises, he commanded the *Centaur*. He took part in the final assault against Turnus.

Servius Tullius The sixth king of Rome. The story of his reign is sufficiently corrupted by legend for him to belong to mythology. Even his birth was mysterious. It was said that he was the son of a slave serving in the house of Tarquin the Elder, who conceived him by uniting with a phallus of ash (see LARES). Another version maintained that he was the posthumous son of Servius Tullius who reigned at Corniculum when the town was taken by Tarquin and the Romans. His mother was still carrying him when his father Servius was killed, and it was at Rome when she was prisoner of Tarquin that she gave birth to her son. One day, while the little Servius was sleeping, his head was surrounded by flames. Tarquin's wife, Tanaquil, prevented the child from being woken up or the flames from being extinguished, and when the child did wake up of his own accord, the flames went out. Tanaquil interpreted this phenomenon as a presage of glory and from that point onwards she and her husband Tarquin brought up their captive's son with the greatest of care. When he reached manhood, Tarquin gave him his own daughter in marriage and openly designated him as his successor. When Tarquin was assassinated by the sons of Ancus, Tanaquil took steps to assure that Servius could assume power without difficulty. Later Servius had his elevation ratified by a proper democratic election.

Setaea (Σεταία) According to Lycophron, Setaea was one of the captive Trojan women who during the voyage to Greece were stranded with their ships on the coast of southern Italy near the spot where the town of Sybaris was later to be built. Setaea persuaded her companions to burn the ships to prevent their ever arriving in Greece, for they were afraid of becoming subservient to the legitimate wives of their conquerors. As a punishment for the burning of the ships the Greeks sacrificed Setaea at the place which took the name of Setaeon (see AETHILLA and ROMA). The same legend was told of two other Trojan women, daughters of Laomedon, Astyoche and Medesicaste.

Sevechorus (Σευήχορος) A legendary king of Babylon. An oracle had told him that he would be deprived of his kingdom by a son of his daughter. He consequently locked her up in a tower but this did not prevent her from conceiving a son. The guardians of the tower, fearing for their lives if the king should discover what had happened, hurled the child from the top of the tower as soon as he was born. However, an eagle rescued the child before he hit the ground and carried him off to a garden whose keeper welcomed him, brought him up and gave him the name of Gilgamus. This Gilgamus, the hero Gilgamesh, later ruled over Babylon.

Sibyl (Σιβύλλη) The name of a priestess whose responsibility lay in making known the oracles of

Apollo. There were a great number of legends concerning the Sibyl or Sibyls. According to certain traditions, the first Sibyl was a young girl of this name, the daughter of the Trojan Dardanus and of Neso, herself the daughter of Teucer. Being endowed with the gift of prophecy she had a great reputation as a soothsayer and the name of Sibyl was given generally to all prophetesses. Another tradition maintains that the earliest Sibyl was not this Trojan but a daughter of Zeus and Lamia (Poseidon's daughter) who was called Sibyl by the Libyans and who uttered prophecies. The second Sibyl was Herophile, a native of Marpessus in the Troad and the daughter of a Nymph and a mortal father. She was born before the Trojan war and had predicted that the Troad would be laid waste through the fault of a woman born in Sparta (Helen). There was a hymn sung at Delos which she had composed in honour of Apollo and in which she called herself the 'legitimate wife' of God, and also his 'daughter'. This Sibyl spent most of her life on Samos but also visited Claros, Delos and Delphi. She carried with her a stone which she mounted before prophesying. She died in the Troad, but her stone could be seen at Delphi in the time of Pausanias.

The most famous of all the Greek Sibyls was the one from Erythrae, in Lydia. Her father was Theodorus and her mother was a Nymph. She was said to have been born in a cave on Mount Corycus. Immediately after her birth she grew suddenly and began to prophesy in verse. While still young she was dedicated by her parents (but against her own wishes) to Apollo in his temple. She had predicted that she would be killed by an arrow of her god. She lived, it was said, for the lifetime of nine men, each of 110 years. One tradition maintained that this Sibyl of Erythrae was the same as the Sibyl of Cumae in Campania, who played an important role in Roman legend. This Italian Sibyl was sometimes referred to as Amalthea, sometimes as Demophile or even as Herophile. She pronounced oracles in a cave. Apollo had given her as many years to live as grains of sand she could hold in her hand, but on the condition that she never returned to Erythrae. For this reason she had settled in Cumae. In one version the Erythraeans inadvertently sent her a letter with a seal made from the earth of their country and on seeing this fragment of her homeland she died. It was also related that in asking Apollo, who loved her and had promised to grant her first wish for a long life, she had omitted to ask him at the same time for youth. The god offered it to her in exchange for her virginity but she refused. So as she aged she became smaller and wizened, with the result that she ended up looking like a cicada, and she was hung up in a cage like a bird, in the temple of Apollo at Cumae. Children would ask her: 'Sibyl, what do you want?' and she would reply weary with life 'I want to die'. The Cumaean Sibyl was said to have come to Rome during the reign of Tarquinius Superbus, bringing with her nine collections of prophecies. She offered to sell them to the king but Tarquinius found them too expensive. At each refusal the Sibyl burnt three of them. In the end Tarquinius bought the last three and deposited them in the temple of Capitoline Jupiter. Her mission accomplished, the Sibyl disappeared. During the Republic, and until the time of Augustus, these 'Sibylline books' exerted a great influence over Roman religion. They were consulted in times of trouble or of any marvellous or extraordinary event. Religious instructions were found inside them: the introduction of a new cult, an expiatory sacrifice, etc., all designed to cope with an unforeseen situation. Special magistrates were put in charge of the preservation and consultation of these books. In the *Aeneid*, Virgil made the Cumaean Sibyl Aeneas' guide for his descent into the Underworld. There was another Sibyl of lesser reputation at Samos called Phyto. For the Hebrew Sibyl, see SABBE.

Sicanus (Σικανός) The eponym of the Sicilian people, the Sicans. He was said to be a son of Briareus and a brother of Aetna. He is reputed to have had three sons: Cyclops, Antiphates and Polyphemus.

Sicelus (Σικελός) The eponymous king of the Siceli, who emigrated from southern Italy to Sicily where they drove the Sicani into the western part of the island. According to Dionysus of Halicarnassus, Sicelus originally lived at Rome but was evicted from there. He took refuge with King Morges, who had succeeded King Italus. Morges gave Sicelus part of his kingdom, whose inhabitants then took the name of Siceli. This Sicelus was sometimes considered to be a son of Italus or even of Poseidon.

Sicinnus (Σίκιννος) The name of a Cretan or even of a barbarian who was said to be the inventor of the dance peculiar to the Satyrs, the Sicinnis. This was sometimes also attributed to a Phrygian Nymph Sicinnis, an attendant of Cybele.

Sicyon (Σικυών) The second founder and eponym of the town of Sicyon in the Peloponnese. The town had been founded by Aegialeus, an autochthonous king, whose descendants maintained themselves in power in a direct line down to Laomedon (Table 22). There were several traditions about Sicyon's genealogy. He was sometimes made a son of Marathon and a brother of Corinthus, but he was usually considered to be the son of Metion and grandson of Erechtheus, the king of Athens. He was thus the brother of Daedalus. King Laomedon summoned him as an ally against his Argive enemies, Archandrus and Architeles, and gave to him in marriage his daughter Zeuxippe, by whom Sicyon had one daughter, Chthonophyle.

Side (Σίδη) The Greek word meaning pomegranate, also the name of several heroines.
1. According to one tradition the wife of Belus and thus the mother of Aegyptus and Danäus (Belus' wife was usually called Anchinoe; Table 3). This Side apparently gave her name to the town of Sidon in Phoenicia.
2. One of the daughters of Danäus and eponym of the little town of Side in the Peloponnese, north of Cape Malea.
3. An Asiatic heroine, daughter of the hero Taurus, and wife of Cimolus. She gave her name to the Pamphylian town of Side.
4. According to a legend recorded by Apollodorus, ORION married a woman called Side, who was hurled into the Underworld by Hera for daring to rival the goddess's beauty.
5. There was, finally, another Side, a young girl who committed suicide on her mother's tomb in order to escape the advances of her father. The gods made a pomegranate tree grow from her blood. Her father was changed into a kite, a bird which it was said would never land on a pomegranate tree.

Sidero (Σιδηρώ) The second wife of Salmoneus and stepmother of Tyro. She was a hard, cantankerous woman who maltreated Tyro very badly. She was later killed by Pelias, one of her two sons, in the sanctuary of Hera.

Silenus (Σιληνός) A general term applied to an old Satyr, but it was also the name of a character who was said to have brought up Dionysus. Traditions about his genealogy varied considerably. He was said to be a son of Pan, or of Hermes and a Nymph, or alternatively to have been born

Terracotta plaque from Tarentum depicting Silenus the woodland deity. 5th century BC Oxford, Ashmolean Museum.

from drops of Uranus' blood when he was mutilated by Cronus. This Silenus was exceptionally wise, but had to be forced to reveal this wisdom to men. He was once captured by King Midas to whom he passed on many wise words. In the same way, Virgil imagines in the sixth *Eclogue* that shepherds could force Silenus to sing. Silenus was said to be the father of the Centaur Pholus whom he had by a Nymph of the ash trees. Other legends made him the father of Apollo Nomius, who protects Arcadian shepherds. Silenus was very ugly, with a snub nose, thick lips and the gaze of a bull. He was very fat and was usually described as riding an ass, on which he could barely stay upright as he was so drunk.

Sillus (Σίλλος) A grandson of Nestor through his father Thrasymedes, he had a son named Alcmaeon. At the time of the invasion of the Peloponnese by the Heraclidae, he fled to Attica where his son became the progenitor of the noble Athenian family of the Alcmaeonidae. This Alcmaeon should be distinguished from the other, more famous Alcmaeon, the son of Amphiaraus.

Silvanus A Roman divinity of the woods (*silvae*). He was not clearly distinguished from Faunus, and in the Hellenized Roman pantheon quickly became identified with Pan. He was depicted as an old man, but he did in fact possess all the strength of youth. His worship was linked to that of Heracles and also to the household Lares. As a mere human, Silvanus did not possess any well-developed myths, living ordinarily in sacred woods, near villages or in the open country. A miraculous event was attributed to him, at the time of the expulsion of the Tarquins. The Etruscan and Roman armies had fought each other, and the slaughter on each side had been so great that the result of the day's fighting was unclear. At night a divine voice could be heard proclaiming that the Romans had won as they had lost one man less than the opponents. The Etruscans lost courage and fled, abandoning their camp to the Romans. Once the dead had been counted, it was realized that the mysterious voice – none other than Silvanus' – had spoken the truth (see AIUS LOCUTIUS for an analogous legend).

Silvius This figure, whose name recalls that of the forest (*silva* in Latin), was a son of Aeneas and LAVINIA, and half-brother of Ascanius. He gave his name to all the kings who reigned over Alba. Ascanius had first of all made way for him in Lavinium and, so as not to offend him, had gone off to found Alba. When he died after a reign of 38 years, Ascanius left the throne of Alba to Silvius; the latter ruled for 29 years and left his kingdom on his death to his son, called Aeneas like his grandfather. The kings of this dynasty who reigned from father to son were after this second Aeneas: Latinus, Alba, Capetus, Capys, Calpetus, Tiberinus, Agrippa, Allades, Aventinus, Procas, Amulius and Numitor, in whose reign Rome was founded.

Instead of making Silvius the posthumous son of Aeneas and Lavinia, other traditions make him the son of Ascanius who was himself the son of Aeneas and Lavinia. Finally he was sometimes considered to be the son of Aeneas and Silvia, the wife of Latinus, whom Aeneas married after the latter's death.

Simois (Σιμόεις) A river in the Trojan plain. Like all rivers it is described, in Hesiod, as a son of Oceanus and Tethys. It played a role in the *Iliad*, where the river-god of the SCAMANDER called for his help in driving back ACHILLES and stopping the massacre of the Trojans. The Simois had two daughters: Astyoche and Hieromneme. The first was the wife of Erichthonius and mother of Tros; the second was the wife of Assaracus and mother of Capys (Table 7).

Sinis (Σίνις) One of the robbers killed by THESEUS on the isthmus of Corinth at the time of his journey to Athens. He was said to be a son of Poseidon, and a giant endowed with prodigious strength. He was nicknamed 'the bender of pine-trees', because he used to bend trees to the ground and tie a man between them. He would then let the trees spring up again, which would tear the unfortunate man apart. According to another tradition, he would force any traveller he could catch to help him bend a pine-tree, but would then let the tree go so that the man would be catapulted into the distance and crushed to death on hitting the ground.

It was sometimes asserted that Theseus brought Sinis to justice not on his way to Athens but long afterwards when he was on the throne of the city. It was supposedly in honour of Sinis that he founded the Isthmian games, considered as funeral games for Sinis (for an analogous tradition, see SCIRON). This Sinis had a daughter Perigoune. While Theseus was killing her father, she hid herself in an asparagus patch. She and Theseus then had a child, MELANIPPUS, who in turn had a son Ioxus, whose descendants were particularly fond of asparagus as their ancestor owed her life to this plant.

Sinon (Σίνων) The spy left by the Greeks at Troy when they pretended to raise the siege and leave with their fleet. Sinon was to alert them the moment the Trojans had taken the wooden horse inside the town. He was the son of Aesimus who was himself the brother of Anticleia, the mother of Odysseus. Odysseus and Sinon were therefore first cousins. Their common grandfather was the treacherous Autolycus (Table 39). Sinon's trick is related in full by Virgil in the second book of the *Aeneid*. In despair that they would never take Troy by force, the Greeks thought of constructing an immense wooden horse, large enough to contain a considerable number of armed men. They had to persuade the Trojans to bring this horse into the town. To achieve this, the fleet weighed anchor and slipped away to wait secretly behind the island of Tenedos. Sinon, however, had remained on land, and soon had himself taken prisoner by Trojan shepherds. He was brought in chains before Priam. The hostile crowd demanded his death. Priam however interrogated him and Sinon told him that he had been persecuted by Odysseus and had fled so as not to be offered as a sacrifice to the gods. He claimed to be a relation of PALAMEDES, and to have lost all support once Odysseus in his hatred had condemned the latter to death. Calchas, in league with Odysseus, claimed that the gods, furious with the Greeks, demanded a human sacrifice, and Sinon had been chosen. The sacrifice had been ready when Sinon managed to escape and hide in a marsh, where he waited until the fleet had weighed anchor. In this way, he added, he had fallen into the hands of the Trojans. The latter then asked Sinon why before embarking the Greeks had left such an enormous wooden horse on the shore. Sinon replied that it was an offering to Pallas Athene, as expiation for the sacrilege committed by Odysseus when he stole the PALLADIUM from the Trojan citadel. Various extraordinary happenings had frightened the Greeks, and Calchas had told them that the goddess demanded in atonement that an offering be made to her in the form of a horse which would replace the stolen statue. Instead of building a horse of normal proportions, the Greeks decided to construct an enormous one which the Trojans would only be able to get inside the city by demolishing a part of the walls. Calchas interpreted the gods' wishes as promising the Trojans supremacy over the Greeks if they worshipped the horse in their city. These apparent revelations of Sinon's convinced the Trojans, and the omen and LAOCOON's death soon confirmed their decision. Sinon was set free, a hole was made in the walls and the horse brought into the city. When night fell, Sinon opened the side of the horse and allowed the concealed soldiers to emerge and massacre the sleeping, defenceless Trojans. At the same time, he signalled to the Greek ships by lighting a flare at the highest point of the city.

There were a number of variants of this legend, originating in the literary embellishment added by individual authors. Thus Quintus of Smyrna related that Sinon, when brought before Priam, refused to speak for a long time, and only revealed his supposed secret after his nose and ears had been cut off. So instead of the accomplished traitor depicted by Virgil, Sinon became the classic example of a hero martyred in the service of his country.

Sinope (Σινώπη) The eponymous heroine of the town of Sinope, on the Asiatic coast of the Euxine Sea. She was one of the daughters of Asopus, the river-god. Apollo abducted her and took her to Asia Minor, where she gave birth to a son, Syrus, who gave his name to the Syrians. Another tradition made her a daughter of Ares and Aegina. A curious legend was related about her: Zeus had fallen in love with her and had sworn to grant her whatever she wanted. The girl asked him to preserve her virginity. Zeus, bound by his oath, respected her wishes and gave her the land of Sinope as a dwelling. She later extracted the same promises from Apollo and Halys the river-god, nor did she allow any mortal to take what the gods had not been able to obtain.

Siproetes (Σιπροίτης) A Cretan who, in the course of a hunt, saw Artemis bathing, totally naked, in a fountain. The goddess changed him into a woman.

Sirens (Σειρῆνες) Sea demons, half woman and half bird. They were sometimes said to be the daughters of the Muse Melpomene and the river-god Achelous, and sometimes daughters of Achelous and Sterope, herself the daughter of Porthaon and Euryte (Table 27). Occasionally their parents were said to be Achelous and the Muse Terpsichore, or else Phorcys, the sea-god. Libanius related that they were born of the blood of Achelous when the latter was wounded by Heracles.

The Sirens are first mentioned in the *Odyssey*, where there were two of them. Later traditions recognized four: Teles, Raedne, Molpe and Thelxiope; or three: Pisinoe, Aglaope, Thelxiepia also called Parthenope, Leucosia and Ligia. Mythographers recognized that they were remarkable musicians, and even knew the part which each played in a trio or quartet. According to Apollodorus, one played the lyre, another sang, and the third played the flute. According to the oldest legend, the Sirens lived on an island in the Mediterranean and attracted sailors passing nearby with their music. Ships would thus approach dangerously close to the rocky coast of the island, and thereby come to grief. The Sirens then devoured the imprudent sailors. It is related how the Argonauts sailed close to the Sirens, but Orpheus sang so melodiously while they were within earshot of the Sirens' music that none of the heroes was lured towards them, except for BUTES, who hurled himself into the sea to try and reach them but was saved by Aphrodite (see ERYX). When in the same vicinity, Odysseus, both curious and cautious, ordered all his sailors to block up their ears with wax. He had himself lashed to the mast and forbade his men to untie him no matter how strongly he pleaded with them. Circe had given him this advice, and had warned him of the risk he was taking. As soon as he heard the Siren's voices, Odysseus felt an overwhelming desire to go to them, but was prevented by his companions. In their frustration at having failed, it was said that

Pyxis from Thessaloniki, supported on 3 feet shaped like lion's claws below and in the form of sirens above. 2nd century BC. Oxford, Ashmolean Museum.

the Sirens hurled themselves into the sea and drowned.

From the earliest times mythographers have speculated about the origin and double form of the Sirens. Ovid related that they had not always possessed birds' wings. They were once ordinary girls, companions of Persephone. When she was abducted by Pluto, they asked the gods to give them wings so that they could look for their companion over sea as well as land. However other authors maintained that this transformation was a punishment inflicted on them by Demeter for not having prevented the abduction of her daughter. It was also said that Aphrodite had deprived them of their beauty because they scorned the pleasures of love. It was also said that after their transformation they tried to rival the Muses, who in annoyance removed all their feathers with which they then crowned themselves. Traditionally, the Sirens' island was situated along the coast of southern Italy, off the Sorrentum peninsula (see also the legend of PARTHENOPE, eponym of Naples which was known earlier as Parthenope).

In later eschatological speculations, the Sirens were said to be divinities of the beyond who sang for the blessed in the Blessed Islands. They could play celestial harmonies, and it was because of this that they were often depicted on sarcophagi.

Siris (Σîρις) The eponym of a town on the gulf of Tarentum. She was sometimes said to be the daughter of the old Italian king MORGES, and sometimes the first wife of King METAPONTUS (and

as such was considered one of the Nereids). Metapontus evicted her in order to marry Arne, the daughter of Aeolus. Arne had her killed by her two sons, Boeotus and Aeolus II.

Sisyphus (Σίσυφος) The most cunning and the least scrupulous of mortals. He was the son of Aeolus (Table 8) and belonged to the race of Deucalion. He founded Corinth, then called Ephyra. He was considered to have been CORINTHUS' successor and avenger in this city, or else MEDEA'S successor, from whom he took over government of the city when she was abruptly forced to leave. The legend of Sisyphus includes several episodes, each of which is the story of a trick. Autolycus had stolen his flocks from him. Sisyphus went to get them back, and was able to establish his claim by pointing to his name which he had engraved as a safeguard under the hoof of each of his animals. It so happened that that particular day was the eve of the marriage of Anticleia, the daughter of Autolycus and Laertes, and during the night Sisyphus managed to find his way into the girl's bed. She conceived a son by him, who was to become Odysseus. According to certain mythographers, Autolycus gave his daughter spontaneously to Sisyphus, as he wanted to have a grandson as wily as he.

When Zeus abducted Aegina, the daughter of Asopus, he passed through Corinth on his way from Phliontus to Oenoe, and was sighted by Sisyphus. So when Asopus arrived, seeking the young girl everywhere, Sisyphus promised to reveal the kidnapper's name on condition that Asopus made a spring gush on the citadel of the town. Asopus agreed, and Sisyphus told him that Zeus was the guilty one. It was this that drew down the wrath of the gods onto Sisyphus. One version maintained that Zeus immediately struck him with a thunderbolt and hurled him into the Underworld, where he was condemned to roll an enormous rock eternally up a hill. No sooner had the rock reached the summit than it rolled down the slope and the task had to be begun again. But this punishment, related in the *Odyssey*, was said to have another explanation in which Zeus, annoyed by Sisyphus' denunciation of him, had sent the spirit of Death (Thanatos) to him in order to bring about his end. Sisyphus, however, did not let things drift but took Thanatos by surprise and chained him up, so that for a while no mortal died. Zeus had to intervene and force Sisyphus to free Thanatos so that he could continue his task. The first victim was naturally Sisyphus. Instead of accepting his fate, Sisyphus secretly enjoined his wife not to pay him any funeral honours before he died. On arriving in the Underworld, he was asked by Hades why he did not arrive accompanied by the accepted ritual. Sisyphus complained strongly of his wife's impiety, and obtained the affronted god's permission to return to earth to punish her. Once on earth again, Sisyphus abandoned any idea of returning to the Underworld and lived to a ripe old age. But when he finally died, the gods of the Underworld were anxious to avoid any possible escape, and so set him a task which left him no free time and no possibility of leaving.

There was another episode in the legend of Sisyphus which justified his punishment in another way. It unfortunately has reached us only in a damaged fragment of Hyginus, an incomplete summary of a lost tragedy. Hyginus tells us that Sisyphus hated his brother Salmoneus. He asked the oracle of Apollo how he could kill 'his enemy', namely his brother. Apollo told him that he would find men to take revenge if he slept with his own niece, Tyro, who was Salmoneus' daughter. Sisyphus became the young woman's lover and gave her twins, but Tyro, learning of the oracle, killed her two children while they were young. We do not know what Sisyphus did then. At the end of the lacuna in the text, we find Sisyphus in the Underworld, rolling his stone because of his impiety.

The foundation of the Isthmian Games is sometimes attributed to Sisyphus, in honour of his nephew MELICERTES. Sisyphus was married to Merope, one of the Pleiades and the only one to marry a mortal. His descendants included Glaucus and Bellerophon (Table 35).

Sithon (Σίθων) A king of Thrace and eponym of the Sithonian peninsula, the middle one of the three peninsulas of the Chersonese in Thrace. He was said to be a son of Ares, or of Poseidon and Ossa (the eponymous Nymph of the neighbouring mountain). He married Anchinoe (or Anchiroe), the daughter of Nilus, and had two daughters by her, Rhoeteia and Pallene. A variant related by Nonnus maintained that Dionysus himself fell in love with Pallene and killed Sithon with a stroke of his thyrsus before marrying the girl. An allusion in Ovid seems to suggest that Sithon became a woman, but we do not know under what circumstances.

Smaragus (Σμάραγος) Together with Asbetus,

Sabactes and Omodamus, one of the evil demons who enjoyed shattering vases in potters' kilns. Artisans would pray to them before baking any pottery.

Smerdius (Σμέρδιος) The son of Leucippus, himself the son of Naxos, and the third king of the Carian dynasty which was established on Naxos after the departure of the Thracians, the first colonists of the island. It was during his reign that Theseus, returning from Crete, abandoned Ariadne on Dionysus' orders.

Smicrus (Σμῖκρος) The son of Democlus, an inhabitant of Delphi. Democlus had gone to Miletus, taking Smicrus, who was then only 13, with him, but when he set out to return to Delphi, he forgot about his son and left him in Asia. Smicrus was befriended by a son of Eritharses who was keeping watch over a herd of goats in the country. He was taken to Eritharses who, after interrogating him, offered him a home and treated him as his own son. One day Smicrus and his adopted brother found a swan, and fought with the local children to see to whom the bird would belong. The goddess Leucothea appeared before them, and ordered them to ask the Milesians to set up a gymnastic competition in her honour in which the children would take part. Smicrus later married the daughter of a noble Milesian, by whom he had one son BRANCHUS. Another variant states that the apparition urged the adoptive father of Smicrus to pay the greatest possible attention to the child. Eritharses then gave him his daughter in marriage and it was she who was the mother of Branchus.

Smintheus (Σμινθεύς) One of the companions of Echelas, the son of PENTHILUS, the first colonist to occupy the island of Lesbos. An oracle had foretold that his daughter would be drowned at sea. The young girl's lover, Enalus, hurled himself into the sea with her. Touched by such devotion, the gods changed their minds, and both were saved.

Smyrna (Σμύρνα) One of the first heroes of this name was an Amazon who founded several cities in Asia Minor, notably Ephesus and Smyrna. Smyrna was also the name of the mother of ADONIS, who was also called Myrrha. She was sometimes said to be the daughter of Theias, the son of Belus and the Nymph Orithyia, or the daughter of King Cinyras.

Sol The Sun, a Sabine divinity whose worship was reputedly introduced in Rome at the same time as that of the Moon by the first Sabine king, Titus Tatius. The family of the Aurelii were said to have violated the cult of Sun, from whom they were descended. For the Hellenic legends about the sun, see HELIOS.

Solois (Σολόεις) Euneus, Tholoas and Solois were three young Athenians who accompanied Theseus in his expedition against the Amazons. On his return, Theseus brought back with him Antiope, and while on board Solois fell in love with her. He confided his secret to a friend, who passed the message on to Antiope. She however refused to give in to Solois who, in desperation, threw himself into a river when the boat was in port and was drowned. When Theseus learnt of the young man's suicide and the cause of his grief, he felt deeply sad. He then remembered an oracle of the Pythian priestess by which he had been ordered to found a city and settle some of his companions on the day when he was afflicted by a great sadness during a voyage in a foreign land. Obeying this command, Theseus founded the city of Pythopolis, in Bithynia, which he called by this name in honour of the Pythian Apollo. He called the nearby river Solois, in memory of the young Athenian, whose brothers, along with another Athenian Hermus, he settled in the city.

Solymus (Σόλυμος) A son of Zeus or, according to others, of Ares, and eponym of the Solymes in Asia Minor.

Sopatrus (Σώπατρος) In the distant past when men lived only on fruit and vegetables and did not yet offer blood sacrifices to the gods, a foreigner named Sopatrus lived in Athens, where he owned a field. During a solemn sacrifice, just as Sopatrus had placed his offering on the altar, a bull appeared which consumed the plants and grain of the sacrifice. The angry Sopatrus seized an axe and killed the animal. Then, regretting his action which he considered impious, he went into voluntary exile in Crete. But after his departure the country was struck by famine. When asked, the gods replied that only Sopatrus could provide the remedy. The slaughtered animal had to be brought back to life, during the same festival, and the murderer punished. Envoys were therefore sent in search of Sopatrus and he was discovered conscience-stricken in Crete. When the Athenian envoys asked him what rites should be carried out to appease the gods, Sopatrus, hoping to make his crime more bearable by sharing it, began by asking them for the right to enjoy the privileges of a citizen of the city in return for his advice. This was agreed. So Sopatrus accompanied them home and devised the following plan. During a general meeting of all Athenians, he had a bull like that which he had killed brought in, and girls offered him water with which he purified a knife which had been sharpened by other Athenians. He killed the animal, which was cut up and skinned by others, so that everyone took part in the murder. Afterwards the flesh of the bull was shared out. After the feast, the skin was stuffed with hay, and this artificial bull was then harnessed to a plough. Finally, a tribunal was set up to judge the murderer. Step by step, it was finally proven that the guilty agent was the knife, which was condemned to be hurled into the sea. This was done. The conditions of the prophecy having been fulfilled – the bull 'resurrected' in the form of the stuffed animal and the guilty party executed – the famine ceased. This rite of sacrifice was thus established in Athens, where it was celebrated by Sopatrus' descendants, the Sopatrides.

Sophax (Σόφαξ) When Heracles had murdered Antaeus, he slept with his wife Tinge, the eponym of the city of Tangiers. She gave birth to a son, Sophax, who reigned in Mauretania. This Sophax had a son Diodorus, who extended his father's empire and founded the dynasty of the Mauretanian kings.

Soranus The god worshipped at the summit of Mount Soracte, north of Rome, by the HIRPI SORANI. Soranus, sometimes identified with Dis Pater, was more generally considered to be Apollo, and it is as such that he was invoked by Virgil. This identification was perhaps the result of the cult of the wolf which was linked to that of the god, as with the Lycian Apollo (and also VEIOVIS, likewise compared with an 'infernal' Apollo).

Sosthenes (Σωσθένης) When the Argonauts, returning from Cyzicus, wanted to cross the Bosphorus, they were prevented from doing so by AMYCUS. They took refuge in a little bay, where a winged man of enormous size appeared to them, predicting that they would defeat Amycus. Encouraged by this, the Argonauts attacked Amycus, and easily got the better of him. They built a sanctuary to the protecting spirit and worshipped him under the name of Sosthenes. During the time of Constantine, this sanctuary became a chapel of the archangel St Michael.

Sparta (Σπάρτα) The eponym of the city of Sparta, daughter of the river-god Eurotas and Cleta, and wife of Lacedaemon. She was the mother of AMYCLAS and EURYDICE (Table 6). She was sometimes also said to be the mother of Himerus and Asine.

Spartoi (Σπαρτοί) The 'sown men' were those who sprang up from the teeth of the dragon killed by CADMUS on the site of the future Thebes and which the hero had sown in the ground on the advice of Athena (or Ares). They emerged, armed, from the ground and slew each other. Only five survived: Chthonius, Oudaeus, Pelorus, Hyperenor and Echion. Cadmus admitted them into his city and with their help built the Cadmeia, the citadel of Thebes.

Spercheius (Σπερχειός) The god of the river of the same name and, like all rivers, a son of Oceanus and Tethys. Peleus dedicated Achilles' hair to him to ensure that his son should return safely from the war against Troy. This offering was explained by the fact that Spercheius was Achilles' brother-in-law, because he had married Peleus' daughter, POLYDORA. Spercheius was said to be the father of DRYOPS, ancestor of the Dryopians and perhaps of the Nymphs of the Othrys.

Sphaerus (Σφαῖρος) The name given posthumously to CILLAS, the charioteer of Pelops. He gave his name to the island of Sphaeria, near Troezen, and it was while making a nocturnal sacrifice to him that AETHRA was surprised by Poseidon (see also AEGEUS and THESEUS).

Sphinx (Σφίγξ) A female monster, said to have the face of a woman, the chest, feet and tail of a lion, and wings like a bird of prey. The sphinx was particularly associated with the legend of OEDIPUS and the Theban cycle. This was the reason why it was mentioned as early as Hesiod's *Theogony*. It was sometimes said to be the child of Echidna and Orthrus, Geryon's dog, and thus the brother of the Nemean lion. But it was also said that its father was the monster TYPHON. More curious was the tradition according to which the sphinx was a natural daughter of Laius, king of Thebes, or else of the Boeotian Ucalegon. This monster was sent by Hera to Thebes to punish the city for the crime of LAIUS, who had been guilty of loving CHRYSIPPUS, Pelops' son. The sphinx made its

Legendary Greek sphinx on a silver coin of Chios, 430–420 BC.

home in a mountain to the west of Thebes, just outside the city. It ravaged the countryside there, devouring every mortal who passed by within reach. Above all, it would ask passers-by riddles which they could not solve. It would then kill them. Only Oedipus was able to provide an answer. In despair the monster threw itself from the top of a rock and was killed. It was also claimed that Oedipus had run it through with his spear.

Staphylus (Σταφυλός) Meaning 'a bunch of grapes' in Greek, this was the name of several rather indistinct characters belonging to the cycle of Dionysus, the god of the vine.
1. A shepherd of the Aetolian king Oeneus. Every day he would take the flocks out to pasture; he noticed that one of the goats returned later than the others and seemed more frolicsome. He followed it and saw that it was eating fruit which he did not recognize. He told the king what had happened, and the latter had the idea of pressing the grapes and making wine. This new liquid was given the name of the king (οἶνος in Greek means 'wine'). The fruit itself was then called 'staphylus'.
2. A related legend made Staphylus a son of Silenus, Bacchus' old companion. He was reputedly the first to introduce the custom of mixing water and wine.
3. Usually Staphylus was said to be a child of

Dionysus and Ariadne (Table 28), after the latter had been abandoned by Theseus on Naxos, although one tradition made him the son of Theseus himself. He was the brother of Thoas, Oenopion and Peparethus, to whom were sometimes added Latramys, Evanthes and Tauropolis. Staphylus married Chrysothemis by whom he had three daughters, Molpadia, Rhoeo and Parthenus (and, according to certain authors, a fourth, Hemithea). Through RHOEO he was the grandfather of ANIUS. For the other sisters, see PARTHENOS and LYRCUS. Staphylus was said to be one of the Argonauts. In the *Dionysiaca*, Nonnus introduced the character of Staphylus whose character he expanded without much reference to the earlier legend.

Stentor (Στέντωρ) In the *Iliad* a Stentor is once mentioned who could shout as loudly as 50 men. His name became proverbial and there was little else mentioned of him by the commentators apart from him being a Thracian who had engaged in a shouting match against Hermes (the gods' herald), and when he had lost he was put to death.

Sterope (Στερόπη)
1. A daughter of Atlas and Pleione, and so one of the Pleiades (Table 25). She married Ares by whom she had a son Oenomaus. One tradition maintained that she married Oenomaus himself. Another tradition said she was married to Hyperochus who fathered OENOMAUS.
2. One of the daughters of Pleuron (Table 25).
3. A third Sterope was said to be the mother of the SIRENS and the daughter of Porthaon and Euryte. She married the river-god Achelous.
4. Another Sterope appeared in the story told by Apollodorus of the alliance between Heracles and CEPHEUS, king of Tegea.
5. A daughter of Acastus, the king of Iolcus (Table 21). When PELEUS took refuge at Acastus' court, Astydamia, Acastus' wife, who was in love with the hero, claimed in a letter which she sent to Antigone, Peleus' wife, that Peleus wanted to marry Sterope. This caused Antigone's suicide.

Steropes (Στερόπης) One of the Cyclopes. His name recalls the Greek word meaning 'lightning' (Tables 5 and 12).

Stheneboea (Σθενέβοια) The wife of King Proetus. She was usually said to be the daughter of IOBATES, king of Lycia, and to have married PROETUS when the latter, evicted by ACRISIUS,

emigrated to Asia Minor. But there were other genealogies. She was also said to be the daughter of Amphianax, king of Lycia, or of the Arcadian king Aphidas (Table 9). In the *Iliad*, the same heroine was called Anteia rather than Stheneboea. The latter was the name most commonly used by the tragic writers. It was at Tiryns, as Proetus' wife, that Stheneboea played a role in legend. She had provided the king with several daughters, the PROETIDES, and a son, Megapenthes. Her happiness was disrupted by the arrival in Tiryns of the young hero BELLEROPHON, whose beauty fascinated her. She made advances to him but was rejected. In anger she secretly denounced him to Proetus for having tried to seduce her. Proetus was fond of Bellerophon and had moreover purified him of a murder, and so could not kill him himself without committing a sacrilege. He sent him to Lycia to his father-in-law Iobates, with a letter in which he asked that the bearer be put to death.

The end of the story, after Bellerophon's victories, was dramatized by Euripides in his lost tragedy *Stheneboea*: the hero returned from Lycia determined to avenge himself for the calamities of which he had been a victim, but Proetus stalled for time and allowed Stheneboea to try and escape on Pegasus, Bellerophon's winged horse. In her flight, Stheneboea was unseated by Pegasus, fell into the sea and was killed. Her body was picked up by some fishermen, not far from the island of Melos, and brought back to Tiryns. Another tradition maintained that Stheneboea committed suicide on learning of Bellerophon's return.

Sthenelas (Σθενέλας) A son of Crotopus, of the family of Phorbas (Table 17). He succeeded his father on the throne of Argos. Danaus, on his arrival from Egypt, claimed the throne from Sthenelas' son Gelanor.

Sthenelus (Σθένελος)
1. The son of Actor, and companion of Heracles, whom he followed in his expedition against the Amazons. He was wounded, died on the way back in Paphlagonia and was buried near the coast. Later, when the Argonauts were passing nearby, Persephone granted Sthenelus permission to return briefly to earth to see them. The Argonauts made a sacrifice to him, as to a hero.
2. Another Sthenelus was also linked with the cycle of Heracles. He was a son of Androgeos and consequently a grandson of Minos, and a brother of Alceus. When Heracles landed on the island of

Paros on his quest to seize the Amazon queen's girdle, two of his companions were killed by four of Minos' sons who happened to be there. As a replacement, Heracles took along with him Sthenelus and Alceus. On their return, Heracles landed on Thasos, evicted the Thracians, and gave the island to the two brothers as their kingdom.

3. A Sthenelus, son of Capaneus, was one of the Epigoni who conquered Thebes. His mother was Evadne. He had inherited one third of the kingdom of Argos from IPHIS (his grandfather, or his uncle, according to different traditions). Later his son Cylarabes reunited the whole kingdom under his rule. He figures amongst Helen's suitors and thus took part in the Trojan War. But from the fall of Thebes onwards (prior to the Trojan War), he became the great friend of Diomedes. At Troy he commanded a fleet of 25 ships. He distinguished himself in battle, especially in Diomedes' service, whose squire he seems to have been. He had earlier been wounded in the foot (possibly during the capture of Thebes), and could fight only from a chariot. Later, after returning from Troy, he accompanied DIOMEDES to Aetolia to restore the throne to Oeneus. It was probably the same Sthenelus who was the father of the COMETES who deceived Diomedes with Aegiale.

4. Another Sthenelus, distinct from the others, was one of the sons of Perseus and Andromeda (Table 31). Tradition gave his wife as either Nicippe, the daughter of Pelops, or Artibia (sometimes Antibia), the daughter of Amphidamas. He had several children: Alcinoe (or Alcyone), Medusa, Eurystheus and Iphis (or Iphitus). He ruled over the city of Mycenae, which had been founded by Perseus.

Stilbe (Στίλβη)

1. The daughter of the Thessalian river-god Peneus and of the Nymph Creusa (Table 23). By Apollo she became the mother of two sons, Centaurus and Lapithes, who gave his name to the Thessalian tribe, the Lapiths. She was also said to have had another son Aeneus, the father of the hero Cyzicus.

2. Another Stilbe, the daughter of Eosphorus, was sometimes said to be the mother of Autolycus.

Stirus Or Styrus, an Albanian prince (present-day Daghestan) who claimed the hand of Medea. As the Scythian king Anausis also wanted to marry the girl, they fought and were both wounded. After Medea's abduction by Jason, Stirus followed her, but was drowned in the storm raised by Hera.

Striges In popular belief, the Striges were winged female demons, with talons like those of birds of prey, who fed off the blood and entrails of children (see CARNA).

Strophius (Στρόφιος)

1. The son of CRISUS, and a descendant of Phocus and through him of Aeacus (Table 30). He reigned over the city of Crisa in Phocis. His mother was Antiphatia, the daughter of Naubolus. Through his wife Anaxibia, he was Agamemnon's brother-in-law (Table 2). Pylades was his son. His nephew Orestes was brought up with him, and it was from then that the legendary friendship between ORESTES and PYLADES dated.

2. The grandson of the preceding Strophius, the son of Pylades and Electra (Orestes' sister).

Strymo (Στρυμώ) The daughter of the river-god Scamander. She married Laomedon (Table 7) and was the mother of Priam (Podarces). Sometimes, Priam's mother was said to be Placia or Leucippe instead of Strymo.

Strymon (Στρυμών) The god of the river of the same name in Thrace. He was said to be the father of RHESUS by one of the Muses, whose identity varied depending on the source. Apart from Rhesus, he was described as the father of BRANGAS and OLYNTHUS and of Tereine and Evadne (Table 18). One legend relates that Strymon was a king of Thrace and a son of Ares. When his son Rhesus was killed at Troy, Strymon threw himself in despair into a river, which was then called Palaestinus but which subsequently took his name. One obscure legend refers to a fight between Heracles and Strymon. As the hero was returning from capturing Geryon's oxen, he arrived at the banks of the Strymon which he was unable to cross as there was no ford. Heracles threw enormous boulders into the river, making the river unnavigable for boats.

Stymphalus (Στύμφαλος) One of the five sons of Elatus and Laodice, the daughter of Cinyras (Table 9). He was the eponymous hero of the town of Stymphalus in the Peloponnese, by the lake of the same name (see HERACLES). He had several sons: Agamedes, Gortys, Agelaus and a daughter Parthenope, who bore Heracles a son, Everes. Stymphalus successfully defended Arcadia against the attacks of Pelops until the latter, seeing that a victory was impossible, pretended to effect a reconciliation with Stymphalus but killed him during a feast. He then dismembered him and dispersed the pieces (see AEACUS). According to an obscure tradition, Stymphalus was the husband of Ornis, and the father of the Stymphalides, young girls who were put to death by Heracles because they had welcomed the Molionidae.

Styx (Στύξ) A river of the Underworld. In Hesiod's *Theogony*, Styx was the oldest of the children of Oceanus and Tethys. But the genealogy which Hyginus placed at the beginning of his fables mentioned her as one of the children of Night and Darkness (Erebus). She featured amongst Persephone's childhood companions in the Homeric *Hymn to Demeter*, but there was also a tradition, related by Apollodorus, according to which she rather than Demeter was Persephone's mother. Styx is usually said to be married to Pallas, by whom she became the mother of Zelus (Zeal), Nike (Victory), Cratus (Power) and Bia (Strength). During the fight between Zeus and the Giants, she and her children supported Zeus, and helped to secure his victory. It was in recognition of this that Zeus gave her the honour of being the surety of solemn oaths sworn by the gods. According to another version related in a fragment of Epimenides, Styx conceived a child by a certain Peiras (Πείρας), and gave birth to ECHIDNA. Finally, one of the children attributed to Styx was ASCALAPHUS.

Styx was the name of a spring in Arcadia, not far from the village of Nonacris, near the city of Pheneus. This spring emerged from a rock above ground, then disappeared underground again. Its water was said to have harmful properties: it was poisonous for men and for cattle and could break iron and metal, as well as any pottery which was immersed in it, though a horse's hoof was unharmed by it. Pausanias, who has preserved for us this list of the properties of the water, referred to a legend according to which Alexander was supposedly poisoned by water from this spring. The water of this underworld river was usually said to possess magical properties. It was reputedly in this river that Thetis dipped ACHILLES in order to make him invulnerable. Above all, the water of the Styx was used by the gods for pronouncing solemn oaths. When a god wanted to bind himself by his word Zeus would sent Iris to draw a ewer of water from the Styx, and bring it back to Olympus, so that it 'witnessed' the oath. If the god subsequently perjured himself, a terrible punishment awaited him. He was unable to breathe for an entire year and could not drink either

ambrosia or nectar. At the end of a year, another test was forced on him. For nine years he was shunned by the other gods, and took no part in their deliberations or their feats. He only resumed his privileges in the tenth year. This description of the result of perjury, given in an interpreted passage of the *Theogony*, provides further details about the nature of this fatal water. It was, we are told, a branch of Oceanus and exactly one-tenth of the present river, the other nine parts forming the nine tributaries by which the river surrounded the globe. This figure of nine meanders is found in Virgil's description of the infernal Styx, which meanders around the kingdom of Hades, completely surrounding it (see ACHERON).

Summanus A Roman god associated with Jupiter: he was the god of the nocturnal heaven. He did not possess any particular legend of his own. It was reported that a statue of Summanus existed on the temple of Jupiter on the Capitol, and that its head had been severed by a flash of lighting in 278 BC and hurled into the Tiber. This omen was interpreted as a sign that the god wanted to have a separate temple, and one was consecrated to him on 20 July in the Circus Maximus. Summanus was said to have been introduced to Rome through Sabine forms of worship imported by Titus Tatius.

Sybaris (Σύβαρις)
1. A female monster from Phocis, also called Lamia (see ALCYONEUS). A spring welled up out of the rock at the spot where the monster was killed, and became known as the Sybaris. Locrian settlers gave this name to the town which they founded in southern Italy.
2. A Trojan companion of Aeneas who was killed by Turnus.
3. The same name appears in a Phrygian legend, according to which Sybaris was the father of a young girl, Alia, who slept with a monster in a wood sacred to the goddess Artemis. The race of the Ophiogenians, or the 'sons of the serpent', was the fruit of this union. They lived in the region of Parion on the Hellespont. This tribe cured serpents' bites by their incantations. It was also said that the ancestor of the Ophiogenians was a serpent who had been changed into a man.

Syceus (Συκεύς) According to a local and probably late tradition, one of the Titans who saved his mother Ge as she was being pursued by Zeus. He made a fig tree grow, which she sheltered under to protect herself from Zeus' thunderbolts.

Sychaeus (Συγχαῖος or Συχαῖος) In the earliest version, Queen DIDO's husband was called Sicharbas, but from the *Aeneid* onwards the name Sicharbas was replaced by Sychaeus. Sychaeus was a Phoenician prince, put to death by Pygmalion, brother of Dido, a king of Tyre, who wanted to gain possession of his treasures. According to tradition, the crime took place during a hunt or a sacrifice. Pygmalion left the body unburied and for some time Dido did not know what had happened, but Sychaeus appeared in a dream to his wife and informed her of the plot. He advised her to flee and revealed to her the spot where he had buried a part of his gold. At Carthage, Dido built a sanctuary to Sychaeus in the middle of her palace, and faithfully preserved his memory. Only Aeneas, thanks to Venus, was able to obtain her favours. Full of remorse for her infidelity to Sychaeus' memory, Dido committed suicide after Aeneas had left. She was reunited with her husband in the Underworld. Another tradition, independent of the *Aeneid*, makes Sychaeus not Dido's husband, but that of her sister Anna.

Syleus (Συλεύς) A character belonging to the cycle of Heracles. During Heracles' servitude to Omphale, the hero performed several feats, amongst them the punishment of Syleus. The latter was a wine-grower who would stop passersby and force them to work in his vineyard before putting them to death. Heracles began working for him but instead of tilling the vines he tore them up and performed all sorts of outrageous actions. He then killed Syleus with a hoe. According to one tradition, Syleus had a brother called Dicaeus (or 'the just one'), whose character was, as his name suggests, a complete contrast to his brother's. They were both sons of Poseidon and lived in Thessaly on the Mount Pelion massif. After killing Syleus, Heracles was welcomed by Dicaeus; he then saw Syleus' daughter, who had been brought up with her uncle. Heracles fell in love with the girl and married her. He went away for some time, during which the young girl died, not being able to bear the absence of her lover. On his promised return, the desperate Heracles wanted to throw himself onto his wife's funeral pyre, and it was only with the greatest difficulty that he was dissuaded from doing so.

The region in which Syleus lived was sometimes given as Lydia, and sometimes as Aulis, Thermopylae or Pelion in Thessaly. A tradition existed according to which HERACLES was sold as a slave to Syleus and not to Omphale as a punishment for spilling the blood of Iphitus.

Syme (Σύμη) A daughter of IALYSUS and Dotis, she was abducted by Glaucus, the son of Anthedon and Alcyone. Having taken possession of the island of Syme (present-day Simi) between Rhodes and the Cnidos peninsula, he gave it his wife's name. The island had previously borne the names of Metapontis and Aegle successively. Syme had a son by Poseidon called Chthonius.

Syrinx (Σύριγξ) An Arcadian Hamadryad who was loved by Pan. The god pursued her, but just as he was about to catch her, she changed herself into a reed on the banks of the Ladon river. As the wind's breath was making the reeds sigh, Pan had the idea of joining reeds of different lengths together with wax. He thus made a musical instrument which he called the Syrinx, in memory of the Nymph. It was also related that there was a grotto near Ephesus where Pan had brought the first Syrinx. This grotto was used as a test for young girls who claimed they were virgins. They were shut up in it and, if they really were pure, the melodious sounds of a Syrinx would soon be heard, and the young girl would appear, crowned with pine. If she were not pure, funeral cries could be heard from within and when, after several days, the grotto was opened, the young girl would have disappeared.

Syrna (Σύρνα) The eponym of the city of Syrnos and daughter of Damacthus, the king of Caria. She had fallen from a roof and was in danger of dying when PODALIRIUS appeared: he bled her from both arms and cured her. Damaethus, in gratitude, gave Syrna in marriage to Podalirius.

Syrus (Σύρος) The eponym of the Syrians, but the facts about his legend are obscure and contradictory. According to some he was the son of SINOPE, the daughter of Asopus and Apollo, but according to others Syrus was one of the sons of Agenor and Telephassa, and thus a brother of Cadmus, Phoenix and Cilix. The invention of arithmetic and the introduction of the doctrine of metempsychosis were attributed to him.

T

Tages One day, as an Etruscan labourer was drawing his plough along a furrow, he suddenly saw a clod of earth rise up and become a child which he named Tages. This Tages was said to be the son of the Genius Iovialis. He was gifted with great wisdom and possessed extraordinary powers of prophecy. He lived just long enough to predict the future for the villagers who had come running to the field where he was born for, after instructing them in the rules of haruspication, he died. His words were written down and formed the basis of Etruscan books devoted to prophecy.

Talassio Essentially a ritual cry, made during marriages at the moment when the young bride was carried over the threshold of the nuptial house. This cry of obscure meaning gave rise to the legend of a certain Talassus, who was said to be one of Romulus' companions. At the time of the rape of the Sabine women, the royal shepherds had abducted a particularly beautiful young girl and, on bringing her back, cried out, so that no one should take her from them: 'she is for Talassus' (in Latin: *Talassio*). As Talassus' marriage was a particularly happy one, this cry of good omen was preserved in the marriage ritual. Another explanation was also given, connecting the word with the Greek Ταλασία (wool-spinning). After the rape of the Sabine women, it was agreed between the Sabines and Romans that the women would not be made to perform any menial tasks, but would content themselves with spinning wool. The cry of *Talassio* was said to recall this agreement.

Talaus (Ταλαός) The son of BIAS, above all renowned for having been the father of ADRASTUS. He ruled over a part of the kingdom of Argos which had been allocated to his father by PROETUS. His mother was Pero, the daughter of Neleus. Traditions vary as to the name of Talaus' wife: she is sometimes called Lysimache, and is said to be the daughter of King Abas and consequently his great-niece (Table 1); she is also called Lysianassa, the daughter of POLYBUS, the king of Sicyon. Talaus figures among the Argonauts.

Talos (Τάλως)
1. A figure of Cretan legend, sometimes said to be a human being and sometimes a bronze robot. In the former case, he was a son of Cres, the eponymous hero of the island, and was himself the father of HEPHAESTUS. Hephaestus in turn was the father of Rhadamanthys. An aberrant version gave Oenopion as Talos' father. Otherwise, Talos was considered to be either the work of Hephaestus, who made a present of him to Minos, or of Daedalus, the official artist to the king, or else the last representation on earth of the Bronze Age.

Talos was essentially the guardian of Crete. Indefatigably vigilant, he had been chosen by Minos, or Zeus, for the task of protecting the island of the god's dear Europa. Each day he walked fully armed three times around the island. He prevented strangers from entering it and also the inhabitants from leaving without Minos' permission. It would seem that it was to escape him that DAEDALUS had to take to the skies. Talos' favourite weapons were enormous stones which he hurled great distances. Illegal immigrants had other dangers to fear from him, even if they got through his first barrage: on catching them, Talos would leap into a fire, make himself red-hot in it, and then, leaping on the victims, would embrace and burn them. His entire body was invulnerable except the lower part of his leg, where there was a little vein closed at the top by a nail. When the ARGONAUTS arrived, Medea succeeded through her magic in opening up the vein and Talos died. Another version relates that Philoctetes' father Poeas, who was one of the Argonauts, pierced this vein with an arrow. Talos was said to have had a son Leucus (see IDOMENEUS).
2. There was another Talos, an Athenian of the family of Metion and a nephew of DAEDALUS, who was killed by the latter because he was jealous of his skill.

Talthybius (Ταλθύβιος) One of Agamemnon's heralds who took part with him in the Trojan War. His colleague was the herald Eurybates. In the stories of the *Iliad*, Talthybius frequently plays many roles. He was given the responsibility of taking Briseis away from Achilles, and was sent as ambassador to Machaon. It was also said that he had accompanied Iphigenia to Aulis for the sacrifice, and that he had been part of the embassy to CINYRAS. At Sparta there was a sanctuary to him. He was considered the protector of international law, assuring the free movement of ambassadors.

Tanais (Τάναϊς) The god of the river we know as the Don and the son of Oceanus and Tethys. A late legend asserted that Tanais was a young hero, the son of Berosus and the Amazon Lysippe, who worshipped only Ares amongst the gods and detested women. In a fit of pique, Aphrodite decided to punish him and made him conceive an incestuous love for his mother. The desperate Tanais found no other means of escaping his passion than leaping into the river which had until then been called Amazonios but which was subsequently known as Tanais.

Tantalus (Τάνταλος)
1. Usually said to be a son of Zeus and Pluto, the latter being a daughter of Cronus or of Atlas. He reigned in Phrygia or in Lydia, on Mount Sipylus. He was extremely rich and loved by the gods, who welcomed him to their feasts. He had married one of Atlas' daughters, the Pleiad Dione. But another woman is also mentioned as his wife, Euryanassa, daughter of the river-god Pactolus. Some mythographers also name Clytia, the daughter of Amphidamas and Sterope, another Pleiad. His children were Pelops and Niobe (Table 2); Broteas, Dascylus and several others are sometimes added to this list. Through Pelops, his descendants were the Tantalides, Thyestes, Atreus and, finally, Agamemnon and Menelaus.

The deeds attributed to him by writers during his life are rather insignificant: he perjured himself in order not to hand over Zeus' dog to Hermes, which had been entrusted to him by PANDAREUS. This crime warranted Zeus' anger and Tantalus was shut up under Mount Sipylus before being condemned to the Underworld. Another adventure brought him and Ilus, the founder of the first Troy, together. Ilus reputedly evicted him from Asia Minor after the misfortunes of his daughter Niobe. A final episode makes him the abductor of GANYMEDE. What made Tantalus famous in mythology was the punishment he underwent in the Underworld, a description of which is given in the 'Descent into the Underworld' of the *Odyssey*, one of the latest passages of the poem. Writers were not, however, entirely in agreement over the reason for the punishment. He was accused of pride: he had been invited by the gods to dine with

them, and is supposed to have revealed their divine secrets, which were freely discussed in his presence, to humans. Alternatively he is accused of having stolen nectar and ambrosia during these banquets and having given some to his mortal friends. For another accusation, see PELOPS. Like Lycaon, Tantalus purportedly immolated his son to serve him as a dish to the gods. Whatever his crime, his punishment was memorable, but even this is described in various ways. Sometimes it was said that in the Underworld he was placed under an enormous stone, which was always on the point of falling, but remained continually balanced. According to other versions, his torture was to feel an eternal hunger and thirst: he was plunged into water up to his neck, but could not quench his thirst because the water withdrew whenever he tried to dip his mouth into it. Similarly, a branch laden with fruit hung just above his head, but if he raised his arm the branch abruptly sprang out of reach.
2. Another Tantalus was a son of Thyestes or of Broteas, both sons of Tantalus. His tomb could be seen at Argos. There were two different legends about him: in one, he had been killed by Atreus because of his hatred for Thyestes and served to the latter in a stew; in another, he was said to have been the first husband of CLYTEMNESTRA and was killed by Agamemnon, his nephew (Table 2).
3. The same name was borne by one of the sons of Amphion and Niobe.

Taphius (Τάφιος) A son of Poseidon and Hippothoe, and so ultimately descended from Perseus (Table 31). His son was PTERELAS. Taphius was the eponymous hero of the island of Taphos.

Taras (Τάρας) The eponymous hero of Tarentum in southern Italy. He was a son of Poseidon and a local Nymph Satyra or Satyria, who was often said to be the daughter of Minos (hence the tradition of the Cretan origin of Tarentum). For another founder of Tarentum, see PHALANTHUS.

Taraxippus (Ταράξιππος)
1. 'Horse-troubling', a demon which haunted the racecourse at Olympia and frightened the horses while they were racing near a certain bend where there was an altar. There was a number of legends about this demon. It was said that it was the troubled soul of the hero ISCHENUS, sacrificed to put an end to a famine, or that of Olenius, a famous Olympian chariot-driver or else of Dameon, daughter of Phlious, who had taken part

in Heracles' expedition against Augias and who had been killed by Cteatus at the same time as her horse. Master and animal were buried at this precise spot. It was also said that this Taraxippus was Alcathus, son of Porthaon, who had been put to death by Oenomaus when he tried to obtain the hand of Hippodamia. The same demon had a dual link with the legend of Oenomaus. Firstly, it was said that Pelops had buried at this spot a 'charm' which he had received from an Egyptian and which he used to frighten Oenomaus' horses and thus win the race. The second legend was that Pelops himself had been buried there in the Olympia racecourse and continued to disrupt the races just as he had interfered with those of his future father-in-law. Finally those more practically minded suggested that there was a laurel growing near the altar and that the dancing shadows caused by the leaves blowing in the wind were sufficient to startle horses racing on the track.

2. Another Taraxippus existed on the Corinth racetrack. It was the soul of the hero GLAUCUS, son of Sisyphus, who had been devoured by his horses.

Tarchetius (Ταρχέτιος) His legend was a variant of the birth of Romulus and Remus. Tarchetius was a king of Alba, in whose house a phallus appeared one day, emerging out of the ground. Tarchetius asked the goddess Tethys what he should do. The oracle replied that a young girl should be united with the phallus and that the first child of this union would have a glorious life. Tarchetius sought one of his daughters and ordered her to carry out the goddess's stipulations. The young girl was modest and sent a servant girl in her place. On learning this, Tarchetius was angry and wanted to put both girls to death. The goddess Vesta appeared to him in a dream, however, and persuaded him to change his mind. To punish them, Tarchetius bound the two women to a spinning stool and promised to free them and find husbands for them when they had finished a specified piece of work. They worked by day but at night, when they were asleep, other servants sent by Tarchetius undid their work. Finally the servant who had given herself to the miraculous phallus gave birth to twins. Tarchetius had intended putting them to death but their mother gave them to a man named Teratius who abandoned them on the banks of the river. There a she-wolf suckled them and the twins were saved. Later they dethroned and killed Tarchetius.

Tarchon (Τάρχων) An Etruscan hero said to be the founder of the city of Tarquinia, north of Rome, and of several others, notably Mantua and Cortona. He was sometimes considered to be the brother of Tyrrhenus and son of Telephus. It was he who led the Etruscan immigrants from Lydia to Italy. It was related that he was born with white hair, a sign of great destiny. Virgil gives a role to Tarchon in the *Aeneid*. He makes him an ally of Evander and, consequently, of Aeneas. He marched at the head of the Etruscan contingent (see CARUS).

Tarpeia A Roman heroine, eponym of the Capitol (*Tarpeius Mons*) or, more particularly, of the Tarpeian rock, from which certain criminals were thrown. The most usual form of the legend is as follows: she was the daughter of Sp. Tarpeius, who had been put in charge of the Capitol by Romulus during the war which resulted from the abduction of the Sabine women; while the Sabine king, Tatius, was encamped with his army at the foot of the Capitol (on the site of the future Comitium) Tarpeia glimpsed the hero and fell in love with him. Thanks to the complicity of a servant (or of her nurse), she promised to turn the citadel over to him on the condition that he agreed to marry her. Tatius accepted this offer and Tarpeia let him and his soldiers into the Capitol. But instead of marrying the young girl Tatius had her crushed to death beneath the shields of his men. Thus Tarpeia perished without receiving the reward for her treachery. Another version maintained that she had demanded from Tatius in payment 'what he and his soldiers were wearing on their left arms', in other words, rich gold jewellery, but Tatius pretended that he understood her to be referring to their shields and had her killed in the manner described. It was also said that the Sabines massacred the young girl so that it would not seem as though they owed their success to treason.

Roman mythographers have also tried to prove Tarpeia innocent and a local cult was devoted to her on the Capitol. There was, for example, the story that she was Tatius' daughter and had been abducted by Romulus. Her treason would then be revenge against her abductor. It is then not clear why the Sabines put her to death, although another version explained her punishment by her refusal to reveal to Tatius what Romulus' battle plans were. It was also said that Tarpeia had planned to deliver the Sabines into the hands of the

Silver denarius of Roman Republic, 88 BC,
depicting Tarpeia.

Zeus, who allied himself with them in his fight against the Titans and the Giants. It was now the turn of the Titans to be thrown into Tartarus by Zeus, assisted by his brothers Hades and Poseidon. The newcomers were put in the charge of the HECATONCHEIRES Gyges, Cottus and Briareus. Tartarus remained a place feared by the Olympians. When any one of them defied Zeus he would threaten to lock the rebel away there and the rebel would then hasten to obey him. When APOLLO killed the Cyclopes with his arrows, he only just escaped this punishment because of Leto's pleading. It was agreed that instead of being hurled into Tartarus, her son would only be condemned to enter into the service of a mortal. The ALOADAE and SALMONEUS were thrown into Tartarus. Gradually it became increasingly identified with the Underworld where serious criminals were tortured. Tartarus was the antitype of the Elysian Fields, where the Blessed lived. In Hesiod's *Theogony*, Tartarus is personified and represents one of the primordial elements of the world, along with Eros, Chaos and Gaia (the Earth). By Gaia Tartarus produced several monsters: Typhon, Echidna and, according to some sources, Zeus' eagle and Thanatos (Death) (Table 12).

Tatius Titus Tatius was traditionally second king of Rome. He was of Sabine origin from the town of Cures. He was king there before being appointed commander-in-chief by the Sabine confederacy, which wanted to avenge the abduction of their women and put an end to the progress of a burgeoning Rome (see TARPEIA). Tatius' camp was situated by Dionysus of Halicarnassus as well as by Propertius in the depression which separates the Capitol from the Quirinal in the region of the Comitium. After the two peoples were reconciled through the initiative of Hersilia and the Sabine women, it was decided that the Sabines and Romans would in future be one race and that Tatius and Romulus would share the power in the city which was thus formed. This city would keep the name of Rome from its founder, but its citizens would be called Quirites in memory of Tatius' homeland. Tatius would dwell on the citadel of the Capitol and Romulus on the Palatine. This joint reign lasted for five years during which time Tatius kept a very low profile. But in the fifth year some of his relations and compatriots quarrelled with some Laurentine ambassadors who were on their way to Rome and finally killed

Romans. She had pretended to betray Romulus and had asked in return for her services for what the Sabines were wearing on their left arms. She had thus meant their shields and hoped that once the Sabines had entered the citadel, deprived of their main protection, they would be easily killed by the Romans. Unfortunately the emissary she was using for the negotiations betrayed her. Tatius learnt of the danger in time and when Tarpeia asked for his and his soldiers' shields, he had her crushed to death beneath them. One version of the legend situates it at the time of the Gallic invasion.

Tartarus (Τάρταρος) In the Homeric poems and in Hesiod's *Theogony*, Tartarus appears as the deepest region of the world, placed beneath the Underworld itself. There was the same distance between Hades (the Underworld) and Tartarus as between Heaven and Earth. The former were the very foundation of the universe. Legend shows that it was in Tartarus that successive generations of the gods locked away their enemies. Uranus imprisoned the first children he had by Gaia, the Cyclopes Arges, Steropes and Brontes, there. To free them Gaia incited the Titans to rise against their father. After victory Cronus, the youngest of the Titans, freed the Cyclopes but he was soon to lock them up again. They were finally freed by them after first trying to rob them. Romulus wanted to punish this attack on the rights of his people but Tatius successfully saved his relations. However friends of the victims attacked and killed Tatius during a sacrifice which the two kings were offering at Lavinium. Although Romulus was in their power they did not harm him but escorted him to Rome, boasting of his justice. Romulus brought Tatius' body back to Rome and gave him great funeral honours. He was buried on the Aventine, near the *Armilustrium*, but Romulus took no steps to punish his colleague's murderers. Certain authors even claimed that although the Laurentines handed over the murderers of their own accord, Romulus freed them, saying that justice had been done.

Taurus (Ταῦρος) Meaning 'the Bull', the name given by euhemeristic mythographers to alleged Cretan heroes in order to explain 'rationally' the myths of Europa and the Minotaur:
1. Some mythographers said that Taurus was a prince of Cnossus who led an expedition against Tyre from which he brought back, amongst other prisoners, Europa, the king's daughter. This Taurus was said to be the founder of the Cretan city of Gortyn and the father of Minos.
2. Concerning the myth of Minotaur, it was related that the Minotaur was not an animal but a certain Taurus, leader of Minos' armies and a cruel man. The young people sent from Athens as tribute were not, it was said, put to death by Minos, but proposed as prizes at the funeral games given in honour of Androgeous. The first winner of these games was this very Taurus, who seriously mistreated those whom he won. Theseus undertook the expedition to Crete to take vengeance on him. As for Minos, he was only too happy to be rid of a general who had become a nuisance and who also had fallen in love with the queen Pasiphae. That was why Minos assisted Theseus' enterprise and even gave him his daughter Ariadne in marriage.
3. Another interpretation of the legend maintained that this Taurus was a very beautiful young man with whom Pasiphae fell in love. She slept with him at a time when MINOS, afflicted by a secret ailment, could not procreate (see also PROCRIS). She became pregnant and Minos knew that the new-born child was not his. He did not dare put him to death however but sent him into the mountains. When grown up, the young man, called Minotaurus because of his resemblance to Taurus, refused to obey the shepherds who had received him from the king. The latter decided to

have him arrested but Minotaurus hid himself in a deep cave from where he could easily chase out those who were sent in pursuit of him. People began bringing him all manner of things to eat in his cave: goats and sheep, and Minos even sent him criminals to put to death. It was in this way that Theseus was sent to him, but he had been armed with a sword by Ariadne and killed the Minotaur.

Taygete (Ταυγέτη) Daughter of Atlas and Pleione, and so one of the Pleiades (Table 25). She yielded to Zeus' advances only when unconscious, and was so ashamed when she recovered consciousness that she hid herself under Mount Taygetus, in Laconia. In due course she gave birth to Lacedaemon (Table 6). It was also said that in order to protect her from Zeus' ardour, Artemis disguised the girl as a doe. When she was restored to her original form, Taygete in gratitude dedicated to the goddess the doe with the golden horns which HERACLES caught as one of his Labours.

Tecmessa (Τέκμησσα) The daughter of the Phrygian king Teleutas, who was abducted by Ajax, son of Telamon, during an expedition against his city, and brought into slavery. She journeyed to Troy with the hero and gave him a son, Eurysaces. Tecmessa plays an important role in Sophocles' tragedy *Ajax*, but she is seldom mentioned by mythographers. It is not known what her fate was after Ajax's suicide.

Tectamus (Τέκταμος) Through his father, Dorus, Tectamus was descended from Hellen and Deucalion (Table 8). Diodorus tells us how he invaded Crete at the head of the Pelasgians and Aeolians. There he married the daughter of Cretheus and had by her a son, ASTERIUS. He consolidated his authority over the entire island. This Tectamus represents the Dorian component of the Cretan population.

Tectaphus (Τέκταφος) An Indian prince whose story is related by Nonnus. Taken prisoner by Deriades, he had been locked away underground, without air or light, and left to die in hunger. Guards prevented any communication with the outside world. But Tectaphus' daughter, Aeria, who had just given birth, obtained the guards' permission to go into the prison, simply, she claimed, to see her father and bring him a supreme consolation. She was searched but no food was found on her. She was thus allowed to enter, where she gave her father milk from her breast.

Deriades learned of this act of piety and freed his enemy.

Tegeates (Τεγεάτης) One of the sons of the Arcadian hero Lycaon and founder of the city of Tegea. He was said to have married one of the daughters of Atlas, MAERA. By her he had sons, among whom were Scephrus and Leimon. A local tradition made him also the father of CYDON, Archedius, Gortys and CATREUS who emigrated to Crete, where they founded several cities: Cydonia, Gortyn and Catra. But the Cretans did not accept this legend (see also RHADAMANTHYS).

Tegyrius (Τεγύριος) A king of Thrace, who welcomed EUMOLPUS and Ismarus when they were banished from Ethiopia.

Telamon (Τελαμών) He was famous for being the father of the great Ajax. There are two different traditions about his genealogy. According to that which appears to be the earliest, his parents were Actaeus and Glauce, the latter being the daughter of the king of Salamis, CYCHREUS. More usually, Telamon was described as a son of Aeacus and Endeis (herself the granddaughter of Cychreus), and so brother of Peleus and Alcimache, who later married OILEUS, thus establishing a link between the two Ajaxes (Table 30). For the early childhood of Telamon see PELEUS. After the murder of Phocus, his half-brother, he was exiled along with Peleus and, while his brother reached Thessaly, Telamon settled in Salamis. From there he tried to reinstate himself in his father's favour by sending ambassadors to him, but Aeacus did not allow him to return to Aegina. He was only allowed to come and plead his case from a dyke which he constructed off the island. But despite everything, Telamon's plea was rejected.

At Salamis, Telamon married Glauce, the daughter of King Cychreus, and when Cychreus died without sons he inherited the kingdom. When he became a widower, he married PERIBOEA or Eriboea, daughter of Alcathus, king of Megara (Table 2). By Periboea he had one son, Ajax.

Legend connects Telamon with major exploits of the heroic period: the Calydonian hunt, before his exile from Aegina, and above all the expedition of the ARGONAUTS. In the *Argo*, he rowed alongside Heracles and was his favourite companion. He reproached the Argonauts for abandoning Heracles when the latter, having broken his oar, went to cut another one in a forest during their stop in Bithynia and did not return in time to continue the voyage because he was looking for Hylas. The most famous episode attributed to Telamon is his participation in the taking of Troy by HERACLES. He was the first to enter the city and managed to escape Heracles' anger over this achievement by a skilful reply. The latter gave him HESIONE, the daughter of LAOMEDON. By Hesione he had a son, TEUCER. According to another version his share of the Trojan booty was a slave named Theanira. She conceived a son by her master but managed to escape to Miletus before his birth. There she was greeted by King Arion and she gave birth to the hero Strambelus, or Trambelus, who was later killed by Achilles. Telamon was still alive at the end of the Trojan War in which his two sons Ajax and Teucer took part. When the latter returned without his brother, Telamon threw him out. We only have very vague information about the way in which Telamon died.

Telchines (Τελχῖνες) Demons from Rhodes, sons of the Sea Pontus, and of the Earth according to certain traditions. They had one sister HALIA, who had children by Poseidon. Along with Caphira, they helped to bring up Poseidon. In this task they played the same role as the Curetes did in the upbringing of Zeus. The invention of a number of the arts was attributed to the Telchines, in particular the idea of sculpting statues of the gods. They were also magicians and had the power to cause rain, hail and snow to fall. They also had the ability to take on any form they pleased. They did not like revealing their talents and were very possessive about them. Shortly before the flood, they had a premonition about the catastrophe and left their birthplace, Rhodes, to scatter themselves around the world. One of them, Lycus, came to Lycia where he built the temple of the Lycian Apollo on the banks of the Xanthus river. They were depicted in the form of amphibious beings: either the lower part of their body was in the form of a fish or a serpent or else they were web-footed. Their gaze was terrifying and could cast evil spells. A particular feat attributed to them was that of having watered the island of Rhodes with water from the Styx to make it sterile (see MACELLO). This aroused the gods' anger against them. Apollo killed them with his arrows; or, alternatively, they were struck by Zeus' thunderbolts and hurled to the bottom of the sea.

Telchis (Τελχίς) One of the kings of Sicyon according to the tradition related by Pausanias

(Table 22). He was the son of Europs and father of Apis. In the Argive tradition, related by Apollodorus, Telchis and Thelxion were the two heroes who rid the country of the tyranny of Apis.

Teleboas (Τηλεβόας) The eponymous hero of the Teleboeans who from the neighbouring island of Taphos (present-day Meganisi) took possession of the island of Leucas. This Teleboas was said to be either the son or the father of PTERELAS.

Telecleia (Τηλέκλεια) According to one tradition, the mother of HECUBA. Telecleia was the daughter of Ilus and wife of Cisseus.

Teledamus (Τηλέδαμος)
1. Supposedly the son of Odysseus and Calypso, perhaps to be identified with TELEGONUS.
2. One of the twins born of the love of Cassandra and Agamemnon (Table 2). He was killed while very young, along with his brother, and buried at Mycenae.

Telegonus (Τηλέγονος) The son of the intrigue between Odysseus and Circe (according to one less well-attested version, of Odysseus and Calypso). This Telegonus does not appear in the *Odyssey*, but he inspired an entire epic poem, the *Telegonia*, written by Eugammon of Cyrene.

Telegonus was brought up on the island of his mother, Circe, after Odysseus' departure. On reaching manhood, he learnt who his father was, and went to Ithaca to make himself known. Then he began to raid a herd of cattle belonging to the king. Odysseus set out to defend his property and in the fight was wounded by his son, whose lance was tipped with the bones of a ray (a fish then thought to be deadly). The wound was fatal and Odysseus died. Telegonus then recognized who his victim was and bitterly lamented his crime. He brought back the body, which Penelope insisted on accompanying, to Circe's island. There he married Penelope, and Circe sent both of them to the Isles of the Blessed. It was sometimes claimed that ITALUS, the eponymous hero of Italy, was born of this marriage. The founding of Tusculum (present-day Frascati) and Praeneste (Palestrina) were sometimes attributed to Telegonus.

Telemachus (Τηλέμαχος) The only son of the marriage of Odysseus and Penelope, at least according to the *Odyssey*. He was born shortly before the Trojan War and had never known his father. His legend is developed particularly in the first four books of the *Odyssey*, which form what is sometimes known as the *Telemachia*, but mythographers acknowledged a whole series of Telemachus' adventures both earlier and later than the Homeric story. When ODYSSEUS, bound by his oath, was required to leave for Troy, he feigned madness and, harnessing an ass and an ox to a plough, began ploughing the land which he then sowed with salt. In order to test him, PALAMEDES seized the infant Telemachus and placed him in front of the ploughshare. Odysseus stopped ploughing, thus proving that he was not as mad as he claimed. On another occasion Telemachus, again while a child, had fallen into the sea: he was saved by dolphins and that was why Odysseus' shield bore the emblem of a dolphin.

The events of Telemachus' youth and adolescence are related in the *Odyssey*. Telemachus grew up at the court of Ithaca, under the care of Mentor, Odysseus' old friend. But when he was about 17 the importunities of Penelope's suitors and their pillage of Odysseus' possessions began. Telemachus, feeling that he had reached manhood, determined to evict them. He undertook a voyage to seek news of his father from Nestor, who had come back to Pylos, and from Menelaus, who was at Sparta. In the course of his visit to Nestor, he was greeted by Polycaste, one of the latter's daughters. From Menelaus, he learnt that the god Proteus had once revealed to him that Odysseus was a prisoner of Calypso, on a far-off island. Once back in Ithaca, Telemachus soon saw his father return, disguised as a stranger. Their first meeting was arranged by the herdsman Eumaeus. Then the plot against the suitors was hatched, followed by the massacre.

To these classical adventures, mythographers have added various episodes. The *Telegonia* related, for example, that after Odysseus was killed by TELEGONUS, the latter married Penelope, and Telemachus married Circe. LATINUS was born of this marriage. According to another tradition Rhome, the eponym of Rome, was also born of this marriage. Telemachus was said to have killed Circe (see CASSIPHONE). It was related that after the massacre of the suitors, Odysseus summoned Neoptolemus to judge between him and the relatives of the victims. Neoptolemus condemned Odysseus to exile during his life. He was then succeeded by Telemachus. Conversely there existed another legend, according to which Odysseus had been warned by an oracle to mistrust his son. He therefore had Telemachus exiled to Corcyra (Corfu), where he was kept under guard. In fact, the oracle alluded to Telegonus and nothing could prevent destiny from being fulfilled nor Odysseus from being accidentally killed by the son he and Circe had produced. Telemachus then reigned over Ithaca. An aberrant tradition about which we possess no details whatsoever related that the Sirens recognized Telemachus and killed him to avenge the death of Odysseus.

Telemachus, a secondary figure in the *Odyssey*, had no well-defined legend. He was therefore much used by mythographers who studied and commented on the legend of Odysseus. Thus, developing the Homeric episode of Telemachus and Polycaste, they affirmed the existence of two children born of this union: Persepolis and Homer himself. Similarly, they conceived of a marriage between Telemachus and Nausicaa, from which Persepolis or Ptoliporthos was born. The Attic orator Andocides claimed amongst his distant ancestors Telemachus and Nausicaa. Apart from these late developments, Telemachus remained above all a literary figure: his rather naïve piety and valour were legendary, which allowed Fenelon to develop the *Telemachia* at length in his famous novel, without moving too far away from the traditional psychology of the hero as established in the *Odyssey*.

Telemus (Τήλεμος) A famous soothsayer from the land of the Cyclopes. According to the *Odyssey* he predicted to Polyphemus that Odysseus would blind him.

Telephassa (Τηλέφασσα) The wife of Agenor and the mother of Cadmus, Cilix, Phoenix, Thasos and Europa (Table 3). With her sons, she set off in search of Europa after the latter had been abducted by Zeus. She died in Thrace of exhaustion and was buried by Cadmus.

Telephus (Τήλεφος) The son of Heracles and AUGE, daughter of Aleus, the king of Tegea (Table 9). Of all Heracles' sons, Telephus was the one who most resembled his father. There were two quite distinct series of traditions about the circumstances of his birth; one went back to specifically epic sources, the other to those used by the tragic writers. According to the former, Auge was, after her son's birth, abandoned at sea by Aleus in a chest which drifted and reached the shore of Mysia. Other versions claim that Aleus handed his daughter over to Nauplius who turned her over to merchants instead of drowning her as he had been commanded. She was thus sold in Mysia to King

Teuthras. Telephus was brought up at his court. The second series of legends, on the other hand, separates Auge and Telephus. Aleus gave Auge to Nauplius, whose task it was to drown her. On the way, the young woman gave birth to her son on Mount Parthenion and abandoned him. While Nauplius was selling Auge to merchants, who took her to Mysia, the infant Telephus was being suckled by a hind. He was then found by some shepherds of King Corythus to whom he was presented. Corythus brought him up as his own son and gave him the name Telephus, which recalls the Greek word ἔλαφος, meaning 'deer' or 'hind'. On reaching manhood, Telephus interrogated the oracle at Delphi in order to locate his mother. He was told to go to Mysia, where he found her at the court of King Teuthras. It was said that earlier, while at Tegea, he had accidentally killed his mother's two brothers Hippothous and Pereus without knowing who they were, thus fulfilling an ancient oracle. This murder was the subject of Sophocles' lost tragedy the *Aleadae*. Hounded from Arcadia, Telephus went to consult the Delphic oracle, who ordered him to go to Mysia without uttering a single word during the journey and until Teuthras had purified him.

A tragic episode was developed around the theme of the recognition scene between Telephus and Auge. It was perhaps treated in the *Mysians* of Sophocles. At the same time as Telephus arrived at Teuthras' court, the Argonaut Idas tried to rob Teuthras of his kingdom. The king asked Telephus, who had come into Mysia accompanied by PARTHENOPAEUS, for his help. He promised him, should he win, the hand of Auge, whom he had considered his adopted daughter ever since she had landed in Mysia. Telephus gained victory and the promised marriage was arranged. However Auge, faithful to the memory of Heracles, did not want to marry a mortal, and entered the nuptial chamber carrying a sword. An enormous serpent, sent by the gods, rose up between her and her son and, by divine intervention, Auge and Telephus recognized each other. Incest and crime were avoided, and mother and son returned to Arcadia.

It was more commonly accepted that Telephus, having been recognized by Auge, remained in Mysia, where Teuthras made him his heir and treated him as a son. He soon gave him his daughter Argiope in marriage. It was at this point that a famous episode in the life of Telephus took place – his fight against the Greeks who were going to Troy and the wound he received from Achilles. At the time of this first attempt against the Trojans, the Greeks, being unaware of the correct route, disembarked in Mysia, believing themselves to be in Phrygia. Some authors claim that they did it deliberately, wanting to diminish the power of the Mysians before attacking Troy so as to prevent Priam from seeking help from them. Whatever the case, Telephus went to meet the invaders and killed many of them, notably Thersandrus, son of Polynices, who had tried to make a stand against him. But when Achilles appeared before him, the frightened Telephus fled. In the chase, he caught his foot in a vine and tripped, with the result that Achilles wounded him in the thigh with his lance. It was claimed that Dionysus himself caused him to fall over because Telephus had not paid him the honours to which he was entitled. The Greeks then re-embarked on their ships (see also HIERA).

The Greeks, however, spent eight years gathering another army, which assembled once again at Aulis, but they did not know how to reach the Troad. Telephus, whose wound was not healing, came from Mysia to Aulis, dressed in rags like a beggar (a feature which seems to have belonged specifically to Euripides' *Telephus*) and offered to show the Greeks the way if Achilles agreed to heal him, as Apollo had predicted to Telephus that he who had wounded him would heal him. Once Odysseus had enlightened Achilles as to the true meaning of the oracle, Achilles agreed; he applied some of the rust from his lance to Telephus' wound, which then healed. Telephus kept his promise, and guided the fleet which successfully reached Troy. In his tragedy *Telephus*, Euripides relates how, on Clytemnestra's advice, Telephus seized the infant Orestes from his cradle and threatened to kill him if the Greeks did not agree to having Achilles cure him. But this dramatic episode appears to have been invented by the poet himself.

After the Greeks had arrived in the Troad, Telephus played no part in the Trojan War. His son EURYPYLUS allowed himself to be persuaded by Astyoce to lead a Mysian contingent to help Priam, despite the promise Telephus had expressly made to the Greeks not to fight against them. But by this time Telephus was already dead.

Telephus was linked with Italian myths through his two sons Tarchon and Tyrsenus (or Tyrrhenus). This link appears in Lycophron's *Cassandra* and is confirmed by Tzetzes and Dionysus of Halicarnassus. Tarchon and Tyrsenus were sons of Telephus and Hiera. They emigrated to Etruria after the capture of Troy. Likewise ROMA, one of the heroines to whom the foundation of Rome was attributed, was sometimes considered a daughter of Telephus and wife of Aeneas.

Tellus The personification of the productive power of the earth in Rome. She was sometimes honoured under the name of *Terra Mater*, the Earth Mother, and identified with the Greek goddess GAIA. In the ancient period she was paired with a masculine *numen*, Tellumo. Tellus does not possess any myths. In legends she sometimes takes the place of Gaia and, more frequently, of Ceres-Demeter.

Telphousa (Τέλφουσα) The Nymph of a spring found in Boeotia, between Haliartus and Alalcomenes at the foot of a cliff. It was said that on his return from the Hyperboreans, Apollo was overwhelmed by the coolness of the spot and had wanted to set up his sanctuary there. But the Nymph was afraid that the number of her conquests would diminish if a great god established himself near her, so she advised him to go instead to Delphi. Apollo did this, but at Delphi he had to endure a very hard struggle against Python. After his victory, realizing that he had been tricked, Apollo returned to reproach Telphousa and, as a punishment, concealed the spring under the cliffs. He then dedicated an altar to himself in this place.

Temenus (Τήμενος)
1. A native of Stymphalus in the Peloponnese, known to us only from a local legend related by Pausanias. He was the son of Pelasgus and it was he who brought up the goddess Hera. He dedicated three sanctuaries in her honour: the first was to Hera the Child, the second to Hera the Married Woman, and the third to Hera the Widow, when Hera and Zeus had briefly separated after a quarrel.
2. According to Pausanias, Temenus was the name of one of the two sons of Phegeus. He and his brother Axion killed Alcmaeon. The two sons of Phegeus were more usually called Pronaus and Agenor (Table 17).
3. The most famous of the heroes bearing this name was a Heraclid, the son of Aristomachus, and great-grandson of Hyllus, the son of Heracles and Deianeira (Table 16). Such, at least, was the ordinary genealogy. But there was another tradition which made him the grandson of Hyllus and son of Cleodaeus who, in the tradition just quoted, was his grandfather. Along with his brother CRESPHONTES he was given the task of conquering the Peloponnese. For the details of the

expedition, see the HERACLIDS. Once the conquest was successful, Temenus was given Argos. Temenus asked a descendant of Diomedes called Ergiaeus to remove the Palladium which had been brought by Diomedes to Argos, and he thus deprived the city of its protection. Later this miraculous statue was transported to Sparta (see LEAGRUS). Temenus gave his daughter Hyrnetho in marriage to the Heraclid DEIPHONTES, thus arousing the hatred of his own sons who tried to assassinate him while he was bathing alone in a river. Temenus did not die immediately however; he had time to disinherit his sons and give his kingdom to Deiphontes.

Temon (Τέμων) When the Aenians, evicted from Pelasgiotis by the Lapiths, were wandering across Greece, they wanted to settle on the banks of the Inachus (in Acarnania). There they came up against the Inachians and the Achaeans. An oracle had warned the original inhabitants that they would lose their country if they surrendered the smallest part of it, but, on the other hand, it also promised the Aenians that if the earlier inhabitants gave up as much as a tiny part of their land, then the Aenians could become rulers of the whole country. To resolve the problem, a noble Aenian called Temon disguised himself as a beggar and went to the king of the Inachians, called Hyperochus. The king, a cruel man, made fun of him and gave him a lump of earth instead of bread. Temon took the clod and put it in his sack. On seeing this, old men of the country recalled the ancient oracle, and alerted the king to what he had just done. They asked him to prevent this particular beggar from leaving with a piece of their land. Temon realized what they were trying to do and fled hurriedly, promising Apollo a hecatomb if he extricated him from this difficulty. Apollo protected him and he escaped from his enemies. Later, Phemius, the king of the Aenians, engaged King Hyperochus in single combat. Phemius killed him with a stone when, at his request, Hyperochus turned around to chase away the dog which had accompanied him to the scene of the fight. The Aenians then took possession of the country. In memory of these events, they devoted a special cult to stones and, during the sacrifices, they would offer to the descendants of Temon a fillet selected from the victim: this was called 'the beggar's meat'.

Tenerus (Τήνερος) The king of Thebes, in Boeotia, and son of the Nymph MELIA and Apollo.

He was the brother of the hero Ismenus, who gave his name to the Boeotian river of that name. He was himself a priest of the temple of Apollo Ptoius and a famous soothsayer.

Tenes (Τένης) The eponymous hero of the island of Tenedos, off the Trojan coast. He was generally considered to be the son of CYCNUS and, more rarely, of Apollo. His mother was Procleia, a daughter of Laomedon, and he had one sister, Hemithea. When Procleia died, Cycnus remarried, this time to a woman called Philonome, who slandered Tenes to Cycnus, claiming that the young man had tried to rape her, whereas in fact he had remained unmoved by her advances. Cycnus believed her, and put both his children in a chest which he then abandoned at sea. The chest was protected by the gods, particularly by Poseidon (the grandfather of Tenes), and was washed up on the coast of the island Leucophrys, which was subsequently called Tenedos. The inhabitants of the island took Tenes as their king. Later, when Cycnus realized his error, he tried to bring about a reconciliation with his son, but Tenes refused, and when Cycnus visited Tenedos, he cut the moorings of his father's boat to signify that all was over between them. When the Greeks, sailing to Troy, appeared off Tenedos, Tenes tried to prevent them from disembarking by bombarding them with stones but Achilles wounded him in the chest and he died. Some authors maintain that Cycnus (who, in this version, had apparently been reconciled with his son) was killed in the same conflict, also by Achilles.

There was another legend about the death of Tenes. According to this he was killed by the hero while trying to protect his sister Hemithea from the amorous advances of Achilles. He was supposedly burned at the same spot where his temple was later to stand. No flute player had permission to enter the temple, as a flautist called Eumolpus (or Molpus), bribed by Tenes' step-mother, had slandered him. In the legend of Achilles (or, at least, in its post-Homeric form), the death of Tenes was one of the numerous episodes which linked the hero to his destiny. Thetis had put him on his guard, and warned him that if he killed a 'son of Apollo' he could not himself escape a violent death at Troy.

Terambus (Τέραμβος) Son of Eusirus, himself the son of Poseidon, and of the mountain Nymph Idothea. As a very young man, he lived high up on Mount Othrys, where he kept large flocks.

Gifted with a melodious voice, he was also skilled at playing the shepherds' pipes, and it was claimed that he was the first mortal to sing to his own accompaniment on the lyre. He was thus a favourite of the Nymphs, who came to listen to him. The god Pan himself was well disposed to him. Towards the end of summer, Pan advised him to go back down to the plain along with his flocks, as winter would be early and harsh. Terambus, with the pride and the carelessness of youth, did not listen to him, and even began to spread ironic stories about the Nymphs, claiming that they were not daughters of Zeus, but that they had as their ancestor the river-god Spercheius. He also said that one day Poseidon, who was in love with one of them called Diopatra, had caused the other Nymphs to be rooted to the ground and had for a while transformed them into poplars. Once his passion was satisfied, he returned them to their original form. Such were the stories of Terambus. At first the Nymphs did not say anything, but soon the frosts began and thick snow fell on the mountains; the trees shed their leaves, and Terambus' flock disappeared from sight. He alone remained on the mountain. Then the Nymphs took their revenge by transforming him into a wood-eating stag-beetle which derived sustenance from gnawing the bark of trees. This insect was used by children as a toy and they would cut off its head, which had enormous horns in the shape of a lyre (see CERAMBUS).

Tereus (Τηρεύς) The king of Thrace and son of Ares. The hero of the legend of PHILOMELA and Procne.

Termerus (Τέρμερος) The eponymous hero of the city of Termera in Caria. He was a pirate who plundered not only the coasts of Lycia and Caria, but also the island of Cos. He is probably to be identified with the pirate of whom Plutarch writes that he would kill travellers by head-butting them. This monster was killed by Heracles.

Terminus An old Roman divinity whose chapel stood on the Capitol, inside the temple of Jupiter. His introduction into the Roman religion was attributed to the Sabine Titus Tatius, as were most of the divinities concerned with agriculture. He was in fact the god identified with the boundaries of fields, and was by his very nature immovable. It was said that during the construction of the temple of Jupiter Optimus Maximus on the Capitol, the various divinities of the chapels existing on the chosen site agreed to withdraw to make way for the ruler of the gods. Terminus alone refused to move and his shrine had to be incorporated within the temple. However as Terminus could only exist under the open sky, an opening was made in the roof for his exclusive use. The *Terminalia* were celebrated in honour of Terminus on 23 February each year.

Terpsichore (Τερψιχόρα) One of the nine Muses, and a daughter of Zeus and Mnemosyne. She was sometimes said to be the mother of the SIRENS whom she had by the river-god Achelous, and also of LINUS and of Rhesus. Her duties and characteristics were, originally, no more clearly defined that those of her fellow MUSES.

Tethys (Τηθύς) One of the primordial divinities of the Greek theogonies. She was the personification of the feminine fecundity of the sea, and was the daughter of Uranus and Gaia, and the youngest of the Titanides (Tables 5 and 12). She married Oceanus, one of her brothers, by whom she had more than 3,000 children who were all the rivers of the world. Tethys brought up HERA who had been entrusted to her by Rhea during Zeus' struggle against Cronus. As a sign of her gratitude, Hera managed to reconcile Tethys and Oceanus who had fallen out. Tethys' dwelling was usually situated in the Far West, beyond the country of the Hesperides, in the region where, each evening, the Sun comes to the end of its course.

Teucer (Τεῦκρος) The name of two heroes, both of them connected with the Trojan cycle, but six generations apart.
1. The first was generally considered to be the son of the Phrygian river-god Scamander and Idaea, a Nymph from Mount Ida (Table 7). But there are other traditions which make Teucer a foreigner who emigrated to the Troad. He was, for example, said to have come from Crete, or, more precisely, from Cretan Ida, along with his father Scamander. On their departure, they had consulted an oracle who had commanded them to settle on the spot where they would be attacked by the 'sons of the earth'. It happened that one night while they were camping in the Troad, their weapons, shields and the strings of their bows were gnawed by mice. Realizing that the prophecy had been fulfilled, they founded a temple to the Sminthean Apollo (the Apollo of Mice) at this spot, and settled there. Attic mythographers

claimed that Teucer came originally from their country and that he emigrated to the Troad.

Whatever his immediate origins, Teucer was the ancestor of the Trojan royal family. He welcomed DARDANUS and gave him his daughter Batieia (or Arisbe). From this marriage was born, amongst other children, Erichthonius, the father of Tros.

2. A son of Telamon and Hesione, herself the daughter of Laomedon and sister of Priam (Tables 7 and 30). He was thus Ajax's half-brother but, through his mother, belonged to the Trojan royal family. In the *Iliad* he was considered to be younger than his brother and the best archer in the whole Greek army. With Ajax he took part in the expedition to Troy, even though Priam was his uncle. His exploits were considerable. He killed successively Orsilochus, Ormenus, Ophelestes, Daitor, Chromius, Lycophontes, Amopaon, Melanippus, Gorgythion and Archeptolemus. He wounded Glaucus and was himself wounded by Hector but saved by his brother. In the course of other fights, he killed Imbrius, Prothoon, Periphetus and Clitus, and just failed to kill Hector. Finally, he participated in the funeral games, where he took part in the archery contest.

In later poems, some of his other adventures are described. At the time of Ajax's death he was absent, taking part in a plundering expedition to Mysia, but he returned in time to protect his brother's body against the insults of the Atrides. He was on the verge of committing suicide in despair and was only prevented from doing so by those present. Teucer was named amongst the soldiers inside the wooden horse. His return to Greece was not a happy one. He went as far as Salamis where Telamon reigned, but on the voyage he had been separated from the boat which was carrying his nephew EURYSACES. Telamon gave him an unfriendly reception; he reproached him for not having been able to protect Ajax, and also for not having avenged his death. Teucer was then forced into exile. It was related how, before leaving, he made a speech from on board his boat in the Attic bay of Phreattys to justify himself against the accusations made by Telamon. The custom of exiles trying for a last time to justify themselves at this spot before leaving the country was traced back to this episode.

He went to Syria, where he was welcomed by King Belus who was at that time in the process of conquering the island of Cyprus. Belus settled Teucer on the island, where he founded the new Salamis. He brought with him prisoners from the Trojan War, who formed one part of the population. He married Eune, the daughter of King Cyprus, eponym of the island. By Eune he had one daughter, Asteria. According to another tradition, Teucer settled peacefully on the island, where he married Eune the daughter of CINYRAS. He had by her numerous children, notably the young Ajax, founder of the city of Olbia in Cilicia. From some writers we learn that Teucer lived on Cyprus until he died, or alternatively that he tried to return to Salamis in Attica: he arrived there at the very moment that Telamon was being evicted from his kingdom and had found refuge in Aegina. He was reconciled with his father and re-established him on the throne. But it was also said that he undertook the voyage to Attica after hearing the news of the death of Telamon, but he was unable to land there, being driven off by his nephew Eurysaces. It was then that he went to Spain, where he founded the future Carthagena. He was also traced to Gades (Cadiz).

Teutamus (Τεύταμος) The king of Assyria, the twentieth successor of Ninyas, also called Tautanes. His reign coincided with the period of the Trojan War. Priam sent ambassadors to him to ask for help. Teutamus agreed to his request and gave him a contingent of 10,000 Ethiopians, 10,000 men of Susa and 200 war chariots. This army was placed under the command of MEMNON, son of Tithonus. Such was the 'historical' interpretation of the myth of Memnon.

Teutarus (Τεύταρος) A Scythian and Amphitryon's shepherd, who taught the young HERACLES the art of archery, and presented him with his bow and arrows.

Teuthras (Τεύθρας)
1. A king of Mysia who played a part in the legend of Telephus. His kingdom extended to the mouth of the Caicus. His mother was Lysippe. The story was told that he killed a boar which begged for mercy in a human voice after having taken refuge in the sanctuary of Artemis Orthosia. As a punishment the goddess afflicted him with madness and a sort of leprosy. Lysippe, with the help of the soothsayer Polyidus, managed to appease Artemis' anger and Teuthras recovered his health. The mountain on which Teuthras had this adventure was called Teuthrania in memory of it.

It was Teuthras who welcomed Auge when she was sold by Nauplius. It was sometimes said that he married her and later adopted TELEPHUS as his son. Occasionally it was also claimed that he treated Auge as though she was his daughter. Whichever the case, Teuthras died without any male issue and it was Telephus who succeeded him.

2. There were several other heroes called Teuthras, notably a Greek killed by Hector at Troy.

Thalia (Θαλία) This name, connected with the word implying the idea of vegetation, is that of several divinities, notably a Muse, a Grace and a Nereid.

1. As a Muse, and although she had originally no particular function, she ended up presiding particularly over comedy and light verse. She was said to have borne Apollo sons, the Corybantes. Likewise, one version of the legend of DAPHNIS made her one of the hero's lovers (in this story she is also called Pimplea).

2. As one of the Charites (Graces), Thalia was the daughter of Zeus and Eurynome. She, like her sisters, also presided over vegetation.

3. A Thalia is mentioned by Homer among the Nereids, and was a daughter of Nereus and Doris.

Thalpius (Θάλπιος) Thalpius and his brother Antimachus were two of the leaders who commanded the four contingents of the Epeians from Elis. They were descended from Actor, the son of Phorbas (Table 23), through the MOLIONIDAE, whose sons they were. Thalpius' mother was Theraephone, daughter of Dexamenus, and his father was Eurytus. He does not possess any particular legend but figures amongst the suitors for the hand of Helen and the heroes inside the wooden horse. His tomb could be seen at Elis, along with that of his brother.

Thamyris (Θάμυρις) Thamyris (or Thamyras) was one of the mythical musicians to whom various poems and musical innovations were attributed. He supposedly composed a Theogony, a Cosmogony and a Titanomachy. He was also said to have invented the Dorian mode.

He was supposedly the son of the musician PHILAMMON and the Nymph Argiope, but other traditions made him the son of Aethlius and grandson of Endymion. Similarly, his mother was sometimes one of the Muses, Erato or Melpomene. He was of great beauty and excelled both in the art of singing and of playing the lyre, which Linus himself purportedly taught him. He was sometimes said to be Homer's teacher. Homer relates how he tried to rival the musical talents of the Muses, but was defeated, whereupon the angry goddesses blinded him and deprived him of his musicial skills. He had asked, had he won, to be granted successively the favours of all the Muses. After his misadventure, Thamyris is supposed to have thrown his useless lyre into the Balyra river (whose name contains the words meaning 'to throw' and a 'lyre') in the Peloponnese. The site of his punishment was generally said to be Dorion, near Pylos.

Thanatos (Θάνατος) The masculine winged spirit who personified Death. In the *Iliad* he appears as the brother of Sleep (Hypnos), and this genealogy is taken up by Hesiod, who makes these two spirits the sons of the Night. In the theatre Thanatos was sometimes introduced as a character. This innovation went back to the tragedian Phrynichus in his *Alcestis*, now lost. Euripides imitated him in his play on the same subject. Thanatos did not, properly speaking, possess any myth. His fight with Heracles in Euripides' *Alcestis* and his misadventure with SISYPHUS are only popular stories invented outside any mythical context.

Thasus (Θάσος) The eponymous hero of the island of Thasos. He was of Phoenician origin, sometimes said to be a son of Agenor and brother of Cadmus and his relations (Table 3) and sometimes connected with Europa's family (notably as either a son of Cilix, or of Phoenix). He accompanied Telephassa, Cadmus and the other brothers of Europa in their quest for her. He stopped at Thasos, to which he gave his name.

Thaumas (Θαύμας) One of the sons of Pontus (the Sea) and Gaia (the Earth) (Tables 12 and 32). He was the brother of Nereus, Phorcys, Ceto and Eurybia, and thus belonged to the group of primordial sea divinities. By Electra, the daughter of Oceanus, he had as daughters the Harpies and Iris. He does not possess any personal legend himself.

Theanira (Θεάνειρα) A Trojan woman, one of Heracles' captives when he first took the city of Troy. She was allotted to Telamon by whom she became pregnant. While still in this condition she managed to escape and fled to Miletus where the king, Arion, greeted her kindly, married her and brought up the son to whom she gave birth, who was to become the hero TRAMBELUS.

Theano (Θεανώ)

1. The daughter of the king of Thrace, who mar-

ried the Trojan ANTENOR. Her mother was Telecleia, one of the daughters of Ilus. She had several children from her marriage with Antenor: Iphidamas, Archelochus, Acamas, Glaucus, Eurymachus, Helicaon and Polydamas. She also brought up with the greatest care Pedaeus, whom Antenor had fathered on another woman. At Troy she undertook the functions of a priestess of Athena. At the time of Odysseus' and Menelaus' embassy before the opening of hostilities, she welcomed them in her home as her husband's guests. So, with Antenor and their children, she was spared during the fighting after the capture of the city and was able to leave Asia quite freely and travel to Illyria. A later tradition related that in collusion with Antenor she betrayed the city and handed the Palladium over to the Greeks.

2. Another Theano was the wife of King Metapontus, who ruled in Icaria and who was threatened with rejection by her husband because she gave him no children. To satisfy him, she went off to find some shepherds and asked them to provide her with a child which she could pass off as her own. The shepherds gave her twins whom she presented to the king. But no sooner had she done it than she herself gave birth to two others. She then tried to dispose of the two orphans, who were in fact sons of Melanippe and Poseidon. She ordered her own two children to kill the two aliens, but the latter were victorious and revealed to Metapontus what his wife's crimes were. She was rejected or even perhaps killed by her husband, and replaced by Melanippe (see AEOLUS 2).

Thebe (Θήβη) The name of several heroines, eponyms of the towns called Thebes.

1. & 2. The Thebes in Boeotia was linked sometimes to a Thebe who was the daughter of Prometheus and a Nymph, and sometimes to another who was the daughter of Zeus and Iodama, a descendant of Deucalion (Table 8).

3. Another Thebe, also claimed by the Boeotians, was the youngest daughter of the river-god Asopus and Metope.

4. Thebes in Cilicia had a heroine Thebe, the daughter of Adramys the Pelasgian, eponym of Adramythium, who had promised her hand to whoever could defeat him at running. Heracles managed to do so, and married Thebe. In her memory, he founded a city in Cilicia, and gave it his wife's name (see also GRANICUS). Another genealogy was sometimes given for the same heroine, linking her with the lineage of Cadmus, by making her the daughter of Cilix. The eponym

of the Egyptian Thebes belonged to the same genealogy: she was a granddaughter of Nilus (Table 3).

Theia (Θεία) One of the first generation of the gods, predating the Olympians. She was one of the Titanides, a daughter of Uranus and Gaia (Tables 12 and 5). By Hyperion (Table 14) she had three children: Helios (the Sun), Eos (Dawn) and Selene (the Moon).

Theias (Θείας) In one form of the legend of ADONIS, he was father of the latter and son of the Babylonian king Belus. He married the Nymph Orithyia and had a daughter, Myrrha.

Theiodamas (Θειοδάμας) A hero connected with the Heracles cycle, one whose legend was sometimes associated with the land of the Dryopians and sometimes with Cyprus. In the case of the former he was said to be the father of HYLAS (see also HERACLES).

Thelxion (Θελξίων) The fifth king of Sicyon and a descendant of Aegialeus (Table 22). Another hero of this name, who was possibly the same person, was one of the two murderers of APIS.

Themis (Θέμις) The goddess of Law who belongs to the lineage of the Titans. She was the daughter of Uranus and Gaia (Tables 5 and 12) and sister of the Titanides. As goddess of eternal laws, she featured amongst the divine wives of Zeus, as the second, after METIS. By Zeus, she gave birth to the three Horae (the Hours); to the three Moirai (the Fates), Clotho, Lachesis and Atropus; to the virgin Astraea, the personification of Justice; and to the Nymphs of the river Eridanus, from whom Heracles asked the way to the land of the Hesperides. Sometimes the Hesperides themselves were said to have been born of this union.

One tradition, mentioned only by Aeschylus, made Themis the mother of Prometheus, and the same name was sometimes given to the Arcadian Nymph more usually called Carmenta in the Roman tradition, the mother of Evander. Mythographers and philosophers imagined that, as the personification of Justice or Eternal Law, Themis was Zeus' adviser. She ordered him to clothe himself in the skin of the she-goat Amalthea, the Aegis, and to use it as a breastplate during the fight against the Giants. Sometimes she was also ascribed with having been the first to suggest the Trojan War, which according to some was caused by her, to remedy the overpopulation of the earth. Themis was one of the few amongst the first-generation divinities to be associated with the Olympians and to share their life on Olympus. She owed these honours not only to her relationship with Zeus, but to the services which she had rendered to the gods by giving them oracles, rites and laws. She taught Apollo the technique of prophecy and she possessed the Pythian sanctuary at Delphi before it came to belong to Apollo. A certain number of her oracles are quoted, such as the one warning Atlas that a son of Zeus would steal the golden apples from the Hesperides and the oracle concerning the progeny of Thetis.

Themisto (Θεμιστώ) The most famous heroine of this name was the daughter of Hypseus, himself the son of Peneus, the Thessalian river-god, and Creusa (Table 23). She married ATHAMAS, one of the sons of Aeolus and Aenarete (Table 33). They had four children: Leucon, Erythrius, Schoeneus and Ptous (see LEUCOTHEA).

Theoclymenus (Θεοκλύμενος)
1. A soothsayer, a son of POLYPHIDES and thus descended from Melampus, who plays a part in the *Odyssey*. He was a native of Argos, but had to go into exile after an assassination. He took refuge in Pylos, where he met Telemachus. He accompanied him to Ithaca, and interpreted an omen provided by a bird at the moment they were disembarking. On another occasion he predicted, in Penelope's presence, that Odysseus was not far away. Finally he announced the fate that awaited the suitors.
2. Another hero of this name, a son of Proteus and Psamathe, plays a part in Euripides' *Helen*. After the death of Proteus, who is depicted as a king of lower Egypt, he succeeded him on the throne. He was a cruel man, an enemy of the Greeks, who sacrificed all those on whom he laid hands. He tried to seduce Helen, who had taken refuge at his court, and, when she tricked him, he became violent and tried to kill his own sister, Theonoe, whom he accused of complicity with Helen. He only agreed to spare her on the intervention of the Dioscuri.

Theonoe (Θεονόη)
1. An early heroine of this name was the daughter of Proteus and sister of THEOCLYMENUS 2. In Euripides' *Helen*, she is the sympathetic adviser, whose divine genealogy gave her powers of prophecy. She helped Helen escape from Egypt and, in doing

so, incurred her brother's wrath. She was saved only by the intervention of the Dioscuri. One tradition maintained that she fell in love with Menelaus' pilot, CANOPUS.
2. Another Theonoe was the heroine of a story told to us by Hyginus, undoubtedly taken from a tragedy which is now lost. She was the daughter of Thestor, and had a brother Calchas, the soothsayer, and a sister Leucippe. One day, when she was playing on the beach, she was abducted by pirates and sold to Icarus, the king of Caria. Thestor immediately set out to look for her, but he was shipwrecked and was by chance washed up on the coast of Caria. He was arrested and taken to the king, whose service he entered as a slave. After losing both father and sister, Leucippe decided to set off to look for them, following an order from the oracle of Delphi. She shaved her hair and disguised herself as a priest. She also reached Caria. Theonoe saw her but did not recognize her and, assuming her to be a man, fell in love with her, and through her servants made amorous proposals to her. Hindered by her disguise, Leucippe declined the suggestions, whereupon Theonoe, in her anger, had her arrested and thrown into prison. She then commanded one of her slaves to kill her. This slave was none other than Thestor whom no one had recognized. The latter entered Leucippe's prison and, failing to recognize her, began to lament the fate which forced him, having lost his two daughters, Theonoe and Leucippe, to commit a crime. Leucippe then realized, from this monologue, whom she was dealing with and, just as Thestor raised his sword against her, she snatched it from him, revealed who she was, and determined to kill Theonoe. She was about to succeed when the latter, in her danger, called on her father Thestor, which led to a recognition scene. King Icarus showered them all with presents and sent them back to their own country.

Theophane (Θεοφάνη) A Thracian heroine of very great beauty who was the daughter of King Bisaltes. Many noble suitors wished to marry her but Poseidon fell in love with her and, to remove her from the others, he transported her to the island of Crumissa (an island unknown to geographers, whose name has perhaps been corrupted by tradition). Her suitors learnt where she had been hidden, and set off to look for her. To deceive them, Poseidon transformed the young girl into an exceedingly beautiful ewe and himself into a ram and the inhabitants of the island into sheep.

When the suitors reached the island they found nothing but flocks of sheep and set about eating them. Seeing this, Poseidon turned them into wolves. He and Theophane, in this guise of sheep, produced a son, the ram with the golden fleece which was to bear away Phrixus and Helle.

Theras (Θήρας) The eponymous hero of the island of Thera. He belonged to the family of Cadmus, and was a fifth-generation descendant of Oedipus (Table 37). His father Autesion had settled in Sparta where Argia, Theras' sister, had married the Heraclid Aristodemus, by whom she had two sons, Procles and Eurysthenes. Aristodemus died while his two sons were still very young, and it was Theras who tutored them and became regent in their name. When they were old enough to rule, Theras left the country so as not to live under their orders, and went to settle on the island which was subsequently called Thera, but which was then known as Calliste, or the very beautiful. He had chosen it because it had already been colonized by the Phoenicians, former companions of Cadmus. He embarked with a number of Minyans, descendants of the Argonauts, who had been exiled from Lemnos and had settled in Lacedaemon, and settled on the island which took, after him, the name of Thera.

Thero (Θηρώ) A third-generation descendant of Iphicles, Heracles' twin brother. By Apollo, she had a son Chaeron, the eponymous hero of Chaeronea in Boeotia (Table 31).

Thersandrus (Θέρσανδρος)
1. The son of Sisyphus and Merope (Table 35). He had two sons, Haliartus and Coronus, eponyms of the Boeotian cities of Haliartus and Coronea.
2. A son of Polynices and Argia. The families of Oedipus and Adrastus were thus conjoined in him (Tables 1 and 37). He took part in the expedition of the Epigoni against Thebes, and it was he who gave Harmonia's peplos to ERIPHYLE so that she would persuade her son Alcmaeon to take part in the expedition. After the capture of the city, Thersandrus came to power, and he summoned back to Thebes the inhabitants who had fled when it was being sacked. He married Demonassa, the daughter of Amphiarus, and had by her a son, Tisamenus. He took part in the first expedition against Troy, the one which resulted in the disembarkation at Mysia. He was killed by Telephus, and his funeral rites were celebrated by Diomedes. Virgil, however, refers to another tradition, according to which Thersandrus participated in the Trojan War and figured amongst the soldiers inside the wooden horse.

Thersites (Θερσίτης) The grandson of Porthaon and Euryte and one of the sons of Agrius (Table 27). His brothers were Onchestus, Prothous, Celeutor, Lycopeus and Melanippus; with them he drove their uncle OENEUS from the throne of Calydon (see DIOMEDES), when the old man had become incapable of defending himself. Thersites was especially famous for the less than glorious part he played in the Trojan War as told in the *Iliad*.

According to the *Iliad*, Thersites was the ugliest and most cowardly of the Greeks at Troy. He limped and was bandy-legged, with round shoulders and only the odd hair on his head. When Agamemnon put his men to the test by urging them to lift the seige, Thersites was one of the first to accept this solution and figured amongst the leaders of the revolt which nearly broke out. He was punished by Odysseus, who beat him with his staff. Thersites collapsed, to the accompaniment of the soldiers' jeers. It was also said – but this story was not featured in the *Iliad* – that he had taken part in the hunting of the wild boar of Calydon, but had fled in terror on seeing the animal. The cyclical epics tell us that Thersites died through misfortune: when Penthesilea, the beautiful Amazon, had been killed by Achilles, the latter fell in love with her as he saw her die. Thersites taunted the hero about this love and, with the point of his lance, gouged out the young woman's eyes. Furious at this crime, Achilles beat Thersites to death with his fists. He then went to Lesbos to purify himself of this murder.

Theseus (Θησεύς) The pre-eminent Attic hero, and the counterpart of the Dorian hero Heracles, whose principal exploits took place in the Peloponnese. Our main sources for his legend are the *Life* written by Plutarch, and the references made by Apollodorus and Diodorus. Theseus was said to have lived a generation before the Trojan War, in which his two sons DEMOPHON and ACAMAS took part. He was younger than Heracles by at least a generation, though certain traditions link the two heroes together in the major joint expeditions of the legendary age, namely the quest for the Golden Fleece (see the ARGONAUTS) and the war against the Amazons, but this is an artificial unity designed to make the legend chronologically realistic.

Greek vase showing the deeds of Theseus: Centre – *killing the Minotaur.* Freize – *left to right starting at the top: the Wrestler Cercyon; swinging a double axe to cut Procrustes down to the size of his bed; aiming Chiron's own footbowl at him; capturing the wild bull of Marathon; flinging Sinis to his death from the pine tree; fighting the wild sow. Cylix found at Vulci. 440–430 BC. London, British Museum.*

I. ORIGINS AND CHILDHOOD

There are two traditions about the origins of Theseus: the human and the divine. The first makes him a son of Aegeus and Aethra, thus uniting the families of Erechtheus and, through the latter's father Erichthonius, of Hephaestus (Table 11) with those of Pelops and Tantalus (Table 2). The story was told how Aegeus, not being able to have children from his successive wives, went to seek advice from the oracle at Delphi. The god had replied in obscure verse, forbidding him 'to untie the mouth of his wineskin until he reached the highest point in Athens'. Aegeus did not understand the meaning of this and went out of his way to consult Pittheus, the king of Troezen, one of Pelops' sons. Pittheus immediately understood the oracle and made

Aegeus drunk and, during the night, sent his daughter Aethra to him. She conceived a child, who was to be Theseus. It was also said that Theseus was in fact the son of the god Poseidon. The same night in which Aethra slept with Aegeus she went to offer a sacrifice on an island, following a dream sent to her by Athena, and was raped by Poseidon. The son which she conceived as a result was believed by Aegeus to be his own.

Whichever the case, Theseus spent his early years at Troezen in the care of his grandfather Pittheus, for Aegeus had not wished to bring the child to Athens, fearing his nephews, the PALLANTIDAE. Just before he had left Troezen, Aegeus had hidden a sword and a pair of sandals underneath a great rock, and had confided this secret to Aethra, advising her to reveal it to her son only when he was strong enough to move the rock and take the objects hidden there. Then, wearing the sandals and armed with the sword, he was to set off in search of his father, secretly, so that the Pallantidae would have no chance to plot his downfall. Theseus' tutor was a certain Connidas, to whom Athenians in the historical period still sacrificed a ram the day before the feast of Theseus. A story was also told in Troezen which demonstrated the child's courage: one day, Heracles was Pittheus' guest, and removed his lion's skin which he placed down beside him. The children of the palace, thinking that a real lion had got into the room, fled, shrieking. Theseus however, then aged seven, took a weapon from one of the servants and attacked the monster. When he reached adolescence, Theseus went to Delphi where, following the custom, he offered some of his hair to the god. Instead of entirely shaving his head, however, he only shaved the forepart, in the manner of the Abantes (a war-like people mentioned in the *Iliad*), thus instituting a fashion which was still carried on in the historical period.

II RETURN TO ATHENS

When he was 16, Theseus was so strong that Aethra decided that the moment had come to tell him the secret of his birth. She led him to the rock where Aegeus had hidden the sword and the sandals. The young man moved the rock, not without difficulty, took the objects concealed there, and decided to set off for Athens to make himself known. Aethra, remembering Aegeus' warnings, and wanting to protect her son from any danger, urged him to take the sea route from Troezen to Athens, and Pittheus added his entreaties to hers. He outlined to Theseus all the dangers which awaited him if he travelled overland along the Isthmus of Corinth. At that time Heracles was virtually a captive of Omphale in Lydia and all the monsters which had recently hidden for fear of the hero were now coming to life again and setting about their devastation. Thus the Isthmus was infested with bandits. But Theseus did not want to listen. Envying Heracles' fame, he decided to imitate him. He killed, one after another: Periphetes, at Epidaurus, and took away his club; the bandit SINIS who would tear travellers apart by means of a pine tree at Cenchreae; and the sow of Crommyon, a ferocious animal which had already killed many men. It was said to be the offspring of Typhon and Echidna, and was called Phaea, after the old woman who fed it. Theseus killed the animal with a blow of his sword. When he reached the Sciro-

nian Rocks, he killed the bandit Sciron. Next, he fought and killed Cercyon at Eleusis. Further on, he gave Damastes, surnamed Procrustes, the punishment he deserved.

After overcoming all these obstacles, Theseus reached the banks of the river Cephisus, where he was met by members of the Phytalides, who greeted him warmly, and agreed to purify him of the murders he had committed. Thus purified, Theseus entered Athens. It was the eighth day of the month of Hecatombaeum, and the city was in a state of extreme confusion. Aegeus was then under the spell of the sorceress MEDEA, who had promised to deliver him from his distressing sterility through her spells. Theseus arrived, preceded by a great reputation as a destroyer of monsters, and Medea immediately guessed his real identity. Aegeus, however, unaware that this stranger was his son, was afraid. Medea did nothing to enlighten Aegeus; on the contrary, she persuaded him to invite the young man to dinner on the pretext of honouring him, but in fact in order to dispose of him by poisoning him. Theseus accepted the invitation, but did not want to declare his identity immediately. In the course of the meal, however, he drew the sword which his father had left him to cut his meat. On seeing this, Aegeus knocked over the cup of poison which was already prepared for Theseus, and officially recognized his son before all the assembled citizens. Medea was exiled and denounced by Aegeus.

It was also said that before she tried to poison him, Medea attempted to kill Theseus by sending him to fight a monstrous bull which was wreaking havoc on the plain of Marathon, and which was sometimes described as being none other than the Cretan Bull brought back by HERACLES to the Peloponnese from where it had escaped. This bull breathed fire from its nostrils, but Theseus captured and chained it up, offering it as a sacrifice to Apollo Delphinius. It was said that this sacrifice took place in the presence of Aegeus, and when Theseus (who had not yet declared himself) drew his sword to cut off some hair from the animal's head (according to the usual rite of consecration) Aegeus recognized the weapon which he had left under the rock at Troezen. This version of the recognition scene, incompatible with the account related above, is undoubtedly the invention of a tragic poet. During the pursuit of the bull at Marathon the episode of Hecale, related by Callimachus in a famous little poem, took place.

Hecale was an old woman who lived in a hut in

the country. Theseus spent the night before the capture of the bull with her, being well looked after during his vigil. She promised to make a sacrifice to Zeus if the young man returned alive from his expedition, but when he returned with his prey, Hecale was dead and already lying on the funeral pyre. Theseus then instituted in her honour a cult of Zeus Hecalesius.

Once he had been officially recognized by his father, Theseus had to fight against his cousins, the 50 sons of Pallas. While Aegeus had been without an heir, the Pallantidae had hoped to share his succession, but when they saw this chance elude them with Theseus' return, they rebelled and tried to obtain power by force. After dividing themselves into two groups, one openly attacked the city from the direction of Sphettus, the other laid an ambush at Gargettus in order to take their enemy in the rear. They had with them a herald from Agnous called Leus, who revealed the plan of the Pallantidae to Theseus. Theseus attacked the group which was lying in ambush and massacred them, whereupon the others scattered and the war was over. This anecdote served to explain the fact that people from Agnous never married at Pallene (the village to which Pallas gave his name). It was often said that Theseus was exiled from Athens and had to spend a year at Troezen to expiate this murder of the Pallantidae. This was the version followed by Euripides in his *Hippolytus*; but, as he added that Theseus was then accompanied by Phaedra, and that it was there that she conceived her guilty passion for her stepson, it follows that this involves some modification of the ordinary chronology of events, and that the expedition against the Amazons took place before the massacre of the Pallantidae. This conflicts with the more usual version, and seems to have been an innovation of the poets.

III THE CRETAN CYCLE

Following the death of his son ANDROGEOS, Minos had demanded from the Athenians a tribute payable every nine years, of seven young men and seven young women. When the time came to provide this tribute for the third time, the Athenians began to murmur against Aegeus. Theseus thought about this and, to appease them, offered himself as one of the victims to be sent to Crete. It was also said that Minos himself chose the victims, and that he asked for Theseus, insisting that the young people come unarmed, though he agreed that, if they succeeded in killing the MINOTAUR to whom they were to be thrown, they would have the right to return. Theseus set off on an Athenian boat on the sixth day of the month of Mounichion. The pilot was Nausithous, a man from Salamis, whom the king of that city, Scirus, had given to Theseus since his grandson Menesthes was amongst the young people being sent to Minos. Among the young girls were Eriboea, or Periboea, the daughter of Alcathus, the king of Megara. The following story was told about Periboea: in the version in which Minos himself had come to collect the tribute, he is said to have fallen in love with the girl during the crossing. She called on Theseus to help her, and Theseus told Minos that, as a son of Poseidon, he, Theseus, was as noble as Minos, even though the latter was the son of Zeus. Minos then prayed to his father, who hurled down a lightning flash. To put Theseus to the test, Minos then threw a ring into the sea and ordered him, if he really was the son of Poseidon, to bring it back to him. Theseus immediately dived after it, and was received into the palace of his father, who handed him Minos' ring. Theseus was later said to have married Periboea, who was famous especially for having been the wife of TELAMON.

On his departure, Theseus received two sets of sails for the boat from his father, one black, one white. The black sails were for the outward journey and symbolized its funereal nature. Theseus inspired so much confidence in his bravery in everyone that it was not doubted that he would kill the Minotaur. In the hope that the return journey would be a joyful one, Aegeus provided Theseus with white sails with which to indicate that his mission had been successful. On arriving in Crete, Theseus and his companions were confined in the Minotaur's palace, the Labyrinth. Theseus, however, had already been glimpsed by Ariadne, one of Minos' daughters; she fell in love with him, and gave him a ball of thread so that he would not lose his way in the Labyrinth.

According to another version, Ariadne did not give him a ball of thread, but a luminous crown which she had received as a wedding gift from Dionysus, but this seems to be an anachronism. It was by the light of this crown that Theseus was able to find his way in the dark Labyrinth. This divine crown was sometimes said to be a gift not of Ariadne but of Amphitrite, given to him when he had gone to Poseidon's palace to look for the ring of Minos. As a condition of helping Theseus, Ariadne asked that he might marry her and take her with him to his country. Theseus agreed to this, and kept his promise. After he had killed the

Wall painting from Herculaneum depicting Ariadne, daughter of Minos, abandoned on the island of Naxos while Theseus sails away. 1st century AD.
London, British Museum.

Minotaur he sabotaged the Cretan ships so that no attempt could be made to follow him, and set sail at night, accompanied by Ariadne and the young Athenians who had been saved by his exploit.

According to the most famous version of the legend, Theseus reached Naxos one evening and put into port there. Ariadne fell asleep, and when she awoke, she was alone. On the horizon she saw the retreating form of Theseus' ship. Mythographers have made many suggestions for the cause of this action. Some maintain that Theseus loved another woman, Aegle, the daughter of Panopeus of Phocis, while others claim that Dionysus ordered him to abandon Ariadne, as he had caught sight of her himself and had fallen in love with her. Others say that the god kidnapped her during the night, or even that Athena or Hermes urged

Theseus to abandon Ariadne. Dionysus then married her and took her off to the land of the gods. There are other versions of this episode. One, for example, claims that the ship carrying Ariadne and Theseus was swept by a storm to Cyprus. Ariadne, who was pregnant, and greatly discomforted by seasickness, disembarked. Theseus boarded the ship again to keep watch over it, but a gust of wind dragged it out to sea. The women of the island, taking pity on the abandoned wife, cared for her, and brought her letters which they had written themselves and which they said had come from Theseus. Ariadne died in childbirth. Theseus later returned, gave money to the women, and established a ritual and a sacrifice in honour of Ariadne.

On his return trip Theseus made another stop,

at Delos, where he consecrated in the temple a statue of Aphrodite which Ariadne had given him. There, along with the other young people who were saved, he performed a complicated dance in a circle which represented the windings of the Labyrinth. This rite continued to be enacted until the historical period. Once he arrived in sight of the coast of Attica, Theseus, perhaps still grieving for the loss of Ariadne, forgot to lower the black sails of his boat and to hoist the white sails of victory. Aegeus, waiting on the cliffs for his return, saw the black sail and, believing that his son had died, hurled himself into the sea, which was thereafter called the Aegean. It was also said that the old king was looking out over the sea from the top of the Acropolis, at the spot where now stands the Temple of the Wingless Victory. When he saw the black sail, he fell from the top of the cliff and was killed.

IV POLITICAL ACTIVITY IN ATHENS

Once Theseus had disposed of the PALLANTIDAE after Aegeus' death, he assumed power in Attica. His first act was to bring about federalization, which involved uniting in a single city the inhabitants who had previously been spread around the countryside. Athens became the capital of the state which he then set up. Theseus endowed it with essential political institutions, such as the Prytaneum and the Boule. He instituted the festival of the Panathenaea, a symbol of the political unity of Attica, minted money, and divided society into three classes: the Nobles, the Artisans and the Farmers. He also laid the foundations, in its broad outlines, for the workings of democracy as it existed in the classical period. He conquered the city of Megara and incorporated it into the state he had created. At the frontier between the Peloponnese and Attica, he erected a column to mark the border between the two countries: the Dorian lands on one side, the Ionian on the other. Just as Heracles had founded the Olympic Games in honour of Zeus, so Theseus founded, or rather reorganized, the Isthmian Games at Corinth in honour of Poseidon.

During the reign of Theseus the expedition of the Seven against Thebes took place. For Theseus' role, see ADRASTUS. Theseus had already granted his protection to OEDIPUS when the latter had sought refuge at Colonus; similarly, he guaranteed the burial of heroes who had fallen outside the city. His son Demophon was to carry on the same practice when the HERACLIDS returned.

V THE WAR AGAINST THE AMAZONS

Tradition has preserved the memory of a war which thc inhabitants of Attica were forced to wage against the Amazons, who had invaded their country. Accounts differ as to the origins of this war. It was often said that Theseus had taken part in the expedition of HERACLES and that he had been given Antiope, one of the captured Amazons, as a reward for his exploits, but most mythographers relate that he had gone alone to abduct Antiope. After landing in the kingdom of the Amazons, he was warmly welcomed – these warriors were hospitable towards strangers – and they had sent him presents. Antiope brought these gifts to him, and Theseus invited her to come on board ship, but as soon as she joined him, he treacherously set sail. This was said to be the cause of the war. The Amazons then sailed in force against Athens, took Attica and established their camp in the city itself. The decisive battle took place beside the Pnyx, at the front of the Acropolis, on the day when, in the classical period, the festival of the Boedromia used to be celebrated. The Amazons won an initial success, but when one of their wings was penetrated by the Athenians, they were forced to sign a peace treaty.

Other versions existed of this war, involving many of Theseus' amorous exploits. According to some writers, the Amazons attacked Attica, not to deliver Antiope, but because Theseus rejected Antiope and decided to marry Phaedra, given to him by Deucalion, the son of Minos. Antiope, who had borne a son by Theseus named Hippolytus, wanted vengeance, and organized an expedition against Attica. The attack took place on the day of the marriage of Theseus and Phaedra. Antiope, leading the Amazons, tried to invade the banqueting hall, but the guests managed to close the doors and kill Antiope. In the version which describes the expedition as an attempt by the Amazons to deliver Antiope, Theseus remained faithful to her, and Antiope, who supported Theseus against her sisters, was killed in the battle. In this version, it was only after her death that Theseus married Phaedra. One obscure tradition maintains that, at the command of an oracle, Theseus sacrificially slaughtered Antiope at the beginning of the war, dedicating the sacrifice to Phobus, the god of Fear.

VI FRIENDSHIP WITH PIRITHOUS

Several episodes concerning Theseus' friendship with PIRITHOUS, the Lapith hero, are associated with his middle age. We know how this friendship sprang up: Pirithous was intrigued by Theseus' exploits and reputation and wanted to put him to the test, but just as he was about to attack the hero he was struck with such admiration for him that he refused to fight and declared himself Theseus' slave. Theseus, encouraged to make a similar gesture, offered him his friendship. Theseus took part in the fight of the Lapiths against the Centaurs alongside Pirithous. One day the two friends decided to marry only daughters of Zeus, since they were themselves sons of two of the greatest gods: Theseus, of Poseidon, and Pirithous, of Zeus. So Theseus decided to seek Helen's hand and Pirithous Persephone's.

They began by abducting Helen. Theseus was then 50, and Helen not yet of marriageable age. Certain mythographers, shocked by the disparity between their ages, maintained that Theseus did not abduct her himself and that this was instead carried out by Idas and Lynceus, or alternatively Tyndareus, Helen's father, handed her over to Theseus for her protection afraid that one of the sons of Hippocoon wanted to abduct her. However, the most generally accepted and plausible version is the following: Theseus and Pirithous went together to Sparta, and kidnapped Helen while she was performing a ritual dance in the temple of Artemis Orthia. They then fled and were followed, but their pursuers stopped at Tegea. Once safe, the two companions decided to draw lots for Helen, on the understanding that whoever won would help the other to abduct Persephone. They drew lots and Theseus won, but as Helen was still too young to marry Theseus took her very secretly to Aphidna and left her in the safekeeping of his mother Aethra. He then set out to find Persephone.

During his absence Helen's brothers, Castor and Pollux, invaded Attica at the head of an army of Arcadians and Lacedaemonians. They began by asking the Athenians quite peacefully for the return of their sister, but on learning that the Athenians not only did not have her, but did not know where she was, they became belligerent. A man called Academus, who had learnt where Helen's secret hiding-place was, revealed it to them. During the numerous invasions of Attica by the Lacedaemonians in the historical period, their armies always spared the Academy because it was the funeral garden of the hero Academus. On learning that Helen was hidden at Aphidna, the Dioscuri took the city and recovered their sister,

taking AETHRA prisoner. They then put a great-grandson of Erechtheus, called Menestheus, on the Athenian throne. He gathered around him those, mainly nobles, who were discontented with Theseus' reforms.

In the Underworld, hunting for Persephone, Theseus and Pirithous were victims of their rashness. They were, it seems, well received by Hades, who invited them to sit down with him to join in a great feast. But they found themselves fixed to their seats, unable to rise, and were kept as prisoners. When Heracles went down to the Underworld, he tried to free them, but of the two only Theseus received permission from the gods to return to earth. Pirithous remained permanently seated on the chair of oblivion. For a euhemeristic interpretation of the legend of Theseus and Pirithous in the Underworld, see PIRITHOUS.

VII THE DEATH OF THESEUS
After being rescued from captivity by Heracles, Theseus returned to Athens to find political affairs problematic. Different factions were sharing power, and he was himself king only in name. Finally, in despair at ever being able to restore himself to the throne, he sent his children secretly to Euboea to be with Elephenor, the son of Chalcodon, and went into exile, cursing Athens. It was sometimes said that he tried to take refuge in Crete with Deucalion, his brother-in-law, but that a storm washed him up on the coast of Scyros; it was also said that he went to Scyros of his own accord to find Lycomedes, to whom he was related. Moreover, he had family estates on the island. Lycomedes greeted him with apparent favour but, taking him up to a mountain to show him a view of the island, he treacherously pushed Theseus off a cliff, killing him. Other authors maintain that Lycomedes was not involved in Theseus' death, and that he was killed accidentally, while walking in the mountains one evening after supper. Whichever version is true, his death passed unnoticed at the time. Menestheus continued to reign in Athens, as the Dioscuri had intended, and Theseus' two sons ACAMAS and DEMOPHON took part in the Trojan War as ordinary citizens. On Menestheus' death, they returned, and refounded the kingdom of Athens.

During the battle of Marathon against the Persians, the Athenian soldiers saw a hero of enormous size fighting at their head and realized that it was Theseus. After the Persian wars, the Delphic oracle ordered the Athenians to gather up the ashes of Theseus and give them an honourable burial in the city. Cimon carried out the oracle's instructions. He conquered Scyros and there saw an eagle perched on a mound, scratching the earth with its claws. Inspired by the gods, Cimon realized the significance of this sign. He dug up the mound and found a coffin containing a hero of enormous stature, and alongside him a bronze lance and a sword. Cimon brought these relics back on his trireme and the Athenians greeted their hero's ashes with magnificent celebrations. The ashes were given a wealthy burial in the city, near the site of a refuge for fugitive slaves and poor people who were being persecuted by the rich, for Theseus had been the champion of democracy in his lifetime.

Thespius (Θέσπιος) The eponymous hero of the Boeotian town of Thespiae, and a son of Erechtheus, king of Attica (Table 11). He left Attica and founded a kingdom in Boeotia. He also plays a subsidiary role in the cycle of the legend of HERACLES. It was with him that Heracles, at the age of 18, began his exploits by killing the lion of Cithaeron. Thespius had 50 daughters, either by one woman alone, Megamede, or by various concubines. While the lion hunt was going on, Heracles stayed with Thespius and slept with one of his daughters every night. In fact, the king wanted to have sons from such a hero, and the latter was so exhausted after each day's outing that he was not aware that each night he was sleeping with a different daughter. Other traditions maintained that he slept with all the daughters in seven nights, or even in a single night. Each one conceived a son by Heracles, and the eldest and the youngest had twins (Table 15). Most of the children were, on Heracles' instructions, taken by Iolaus to Sardinia where they settled on the island. Two came back to Thebes, and seven remained in Thespiae. It was related that the sons of Thespius who had settled in Sardinia supposedly did not die but fell into a deep and eternal sleep, and thus escaped the corruption of the tomb and the flames of the funeral pyre. Thespius was also the friend who purified Heracles after the murder of the children he had had by Megara. For Thespius, father of Hypermestra, see THESTIUS.

Thesprotus (Θεσπρωτός) One of the sons of Lycaon. He left Arcadia and settled in Epirus, in the area which took the name of the country of the Thesprotians. In one version of the legend Thyestes took refuge with him.

Thessalus (Θεσσαλός) The name of the eponymous hero of Thessaly. Several differing traditions exist as to his identity:
1. Roman historians recognized a king of this name who came from the country of the Thesprotians, who was said to have conquered Thessaly and have founded his kingdom there. This Thessalus was a son of Graicus to whom the foundation of the city of Thessalonica was sometimes attributed.
2. Another Thessalus was regarded as a son of Heracles and Chalciope, or of Astyoche (in which case he was the brother of Tlepolemus – Table 15). He was king of the island of Cos and sent his two sons Phidippus and Antiphus to take part in the Trojan War. After the sack of Troy, the sons settled in the country which was called Thessaly in memory of their father.
3. Legend also mentioned a Thessalus, who was the son of Medea and Jason; at the time of the death of Adrastus, son of Pelias, he escaped his mother's violence and fled from Corinth to Iolcus, where he assumed power. He too was said to have given his name to Thessaly.
4. There was also a Thessalus, son of HAEMON.

Thestius (Θέστιος) A king of Pleuron and an Aetolian hero. He was generally considered to be the grandson of Agenor, himself a son of Pleuron. His mother was Demonice and his father Ares (Table 24). His wife was sometimes said to be Eurythemis, sometimes Deidamia, daughter of Perieres, or again Laophonte (daughter of Pleuron and therefore, according to the accepted genealogy, his great-aunt). He had numerous children, among whom were Althaea, mother of Meleager, Leda, Hypermestra, Iphiclus, Evippus, Plexippus, Eurypylus and Meleager's uncles, sometimes called the Thestiades, who were killed during the hunt of Calydon. His daughter Hypermestra is perhaps synonymous with the supposed daughter of Thespius of the same name, for the names Thestius and Thespius are often interchanged in the manuscripts. For the legend of Thestius and Calydon, see CALYDON.

Thestor (Θέστωρ) A son of Apollo and Laothoe, and father of the soothsayer Calchas and two daughters, Leucippe and THEONOE. He was himself a priest of Apollo and the hero of a romantic adventure preserved for us by Hyginus.

Thetis (Θέτις) One of the Nereids, daughter of Nereus (the Old Man of the Sea) and Doris. She was therefore an immortal divinity of the sea, and the most famous of all the Nereids. One obscure tradition, however, made her the daughter of the Centaur Chiron. Thetis was brought up by Hera, just as she herself had been by Tethys. In legend, several episodes involving Thetis are explicable in terms of the bonds of affection linking the Nereid and Zeus' wife. For example, it was Thetis who took in HEPHAESTUS after he was hurled from the top of Olympus by Zeus for having tried to intervene on behalf of Hera. Thetis, at Hera's command, took the helm of the *Argo* during the crossing of the Symplegades. Finally, according to some mythographers, she rejected the love of Zeus so as not to distress Hera. Other traditions, it is true, gave a different interpretation of this episode, and claimed that both Zeus and Poseidon had wanted to possess her until it was revealed by an oracle of Themis that the son born to Thetis would be more powerful than his father. The two great gods did not press their suit, and made hasty attempts to give her to a mortal. Other versions attribute this prophecy to Prometheus, who apparently stated explicitly that the son destined to be born of an affair between Zeus and Thetis would one day become ruler of Heaven. Whichever version is true, Thetis could only marry a mortal man, not a god. Chiron the Centaur learnt of this, and quickly advised his protégé Peleus to take advantage of this opportunity to marry a divinity, but Thetis made his task extremely difficult. Like all divinities of the sea, she had the ability to change shape at will, and she used this gift to elude Peleus, though he eventually succeeded in overpowering and marrying her.

Thetis' attempts to obtain immortality for her son ACHILLES brought about the breakdown of the marriage between herself and Peleus, but she did not allow that to diminish her interest in her son. When the latter was nine years old and the soothsayer Calchas announced that Troy could not be taken without the help of Achilles, Thetis, knowing that her son would die at Troy, took him to Lycomedes, on Scyros, and concealed him amongst his daughters. Achilles could not escape his destiny however and he set off for the war. Thetis used all sorts of means to try to protect him, but all were in vain. She provided him with a companion whose task was to prevent Achilles from making fatal errors; one of the errors was the killing of TENES. She forbade him to be the first ashore at Troy because the first hero to disembark would also be the first to fall in battle. She gave him arms and, after the death of Patroclus, had others made for him by Hephaestus who was devoted to him. Finally, she consoled him at every serious moment of his life. In particular, she tried to dissuade him from killing Hector, as he would himself die soon after. Later, after Achilles' death, Thetis took as strong as interest in her grandson NEOPTOLEMUS. She advised him not to return with the other Achaeans, and to wait several days on Tenedos, thus saving his life (see also MOLOSSUS).

Thoas (Θόας)
1. One of the sons of Dionysus and Ariadne (Tables 21 and 28). He was sometimes said to be the son not of Dionysus but of Theseus, as were his brothers Oenopion and Staphylus. He was supposedly born on the island of Lemnos, and he reigned over the city of Myrina, whose eponym was his wife. By her he had a daughter HYPSIPYLE, who played a role in the legend of the Argonauts. When the women of Lemnos decided to massacre all the men on the island as a result of the curse of Aphrodite, Hypsipyle decided to spare Thoas, with the result that he was the only man on Lemnos to survive the massacre. Hypsipyle gave him the sword with which she was supposed to kill him, and brought him in disguise to the temple of Dionysus where she hid him. The next morning she took him to the coast, dressed as Dionysus, on the god's ritual chariot, on the pretext of purifying the god of the night's murders. Thoas managed to put to sea in an old boat, and landed at Tauris. Another tradition claims that he landed on the island of Sicinos (one of the Cyclades), which then bore the name of Oenoe. There was a story that he reached the island of Chios, where his brother Oenopion was ruler. When the women of Lemnos learnt that Thoas had been saved, they sold his daughter Hypsipyle as a slave.
2. A grandson of the preceding Thoas and the son of Jason and HYPSIPYLE. He was twin brother of EUNEUS (Table 21). The twins succeeded in freeing their mother who was a slave of King Lycurgus. In this connection Thoas figured in Euripides' lost tragedy *Hypsipyle*, but surviving fragments do not make it clear exactly what role he played in it.
3. The king of Tauris at the time when Iphigenia became a priestess of Artemis there. This character was sometimes identified with THOAS 1, who found refuge in Tauris after his escape from Lemnos. When Orestes and Pylades came to the

country and encountered Orestes' sister, IPHIGE-
NIA, the king wanted her to sacrifice them, following the local custom, but they fled with Iphigenia
and the goddess's statue to CHRYSES. Thoas pursued them there, but was killed.

4. In the Catalogue of ships, the *Iliad* mentions
another Thoas, son of Andraemon, as leader of an
Aetolian contingent. His mother was Gorge, one
of the daughters of Oeneus and Althea, and thus
one of the sisters of Meleager (Table 27). He was
mentioned as one of Helen's suitors and, at the end
of the war, one of the warriors inside the wooden
horse. On his return from Troy, he settled in
Italy, in the land of the Bruttii according to some
sources, or, according to others, in Aetolia.
ODYSSEUS took refuge with him when evicted
from Ithaca by Neoptolemus; he married his
daughter, by whom he had a son called Leontophonus or the Lion-Slayer (Table 39). This
Thoas did Odysseus the service of mutilating him to
make him unrecognizable for one of his espionage
operations.

5. The grandson of Sisyphus, through his father
Ornytion (Table 35). He was the brother of
Phocus, eponymous hero of Phocis. Whereas his
brother emigrated to Phocis, he remained in
Corinth where he succeeded his father as ruler. He
was in turn succeeded by his own son Damophon,
who maintained his kingship until the coming of
the Heraclids. This, at least, was the Corinthian
tradition.

6. Son of Icarius and brother of Penelope (Table
19).

Thon (Θών) King of Egypt at the time when
Helen went there. His wife POLYDAMNA sent Helen
a potion which would make her forget all her
sorrows.

Thoosa (Θόωσα) The daughter of Phorcys and
beloved of Poseidon, by whom she had a son,
Polyphemus.

Thrace (Θράκη) The eponymous heroine of
Thrace. She was the daughter of Oceanus and
Parthenope, and sister of Europa. It was asserted
that she was a remarkable sorceress, like many of
the women of her country.

Thrasymedes (Θρασυμήδης) One of the sons of
Nestor. He accompanied his father as well as his
brother ANTILOCHUS to the Trojan War, where he
commanded a fleet of 15 ships. He played a part in
several episodes such as the fight around his

brother's body against Memnon, and he was
among the warriors inside the wooden horse. He
returned successfully to Pylos at the end of the war
and welcomed Telemachus there. He had a son
called Sillus and a grandson Alcmaeon, distinct
from Amphiarus' son who bore the same name.
His tomb could be seen near Pylos.

Thriai (Θριαί) The Prophetesses, they were three
sisters, daughters of Zeus, and Nymphs of Parnassus. They were said to have brought up Apollo.
The invention of divination by means of pebbles
was attributed to them. They were very fond of
honey, which was offered to them when their
advice was sought.

Thyestes (Θυέστης) The twin brother of Atreus
and a son of Pelops and Hippodamia (Table 2).
His legend is concerned primarily with his hatred
for Atreus, and the vengeance which the two
brothers alternately wreaked upon one another.
This tragic subject was used by poets and was
complicated by the addition of episodes each more
atrocious than the last. For the broad outline of
this legend, see ATREUS.

At the instigation of Hippodamia, Thyestes and
Atreus in their youth killed Chrysippus, their half-
brother. After the murder they fled to the court of
Sthenelus and became the rulers of Mycenae.
Thyestes became the lover of his sister-in-law
AEROPE. To avenge himself, Atreus conceived the
horrifying plan of making his brother eat his own
children. For this purpose, he killed the children
Thyestes had had by a concubine (three, according
to some writers: Aglaus, Callileon and Orchomenus; two, according to others: Tantalus and Plisthenes) and prepared a dish from them which he
fed to his brother. He then showed him the arms
and the heads. The Sun was so horrified that it
recoiled from its course. Thyestes fled to THESPRO-
TUS who lived in Epirus and from there went to
Sicyon where his daughter Pelopia was living. An
oracle had told him that only a son born incestuously from his daughter could take vengeance
on his brother. This son, AEGISTHUS, managed to
kill Atreus and gave back to Thyestes the kingdom from which he had been ejected.

Thyia (Θυία) According to a Delphic tradition, a
local Nymph, daughter of the river-god Cephiss-
us, or of the hero Castalius, one of the earliest
inhabitants. Thyia was loved by Apollo, by
whom she had a son DELPHUS, the eponym of
Delphi. Thyia was the first person to celebrate the

cult of Dionysus on the slopes of Parnassus and it was in memory of this that the Maenads sometimes bore the name THYADES. It was also said that Poseidon had been in love with her. There existed another tradition about the same heroine which claimed that she was a daughter of Deucalion, and had two sons by Zeus, Magnes and Macedon, who gave their names to Magnesia, in Thessaly, and to Macedonia.

Thymoetes (Θυμοίτης) In a tradition related by Diodorus, he was a son of Laomedon and thus one of Priam's brothers. But this Thymoetes was more usually described as the husband of CILLA and consequently Priam's brother-in-law rather than his brother. Priam, misinterpreting an oracle, had Cilla put to death. Thymoetes did not forgive him, and to take vengeance he was one of the first to bring the wooden horse into the city of Troy.

Thyone (Θυώνη) In some traditions the name of Dionysus' mother, more usually called SEMELE. This difference in name was explained in two ways: either it was not the same Dionysus, or Semele was the 'mortal' name of the mother of the god and Thyone the 'divine' name, which Dionysus gave to her after her apotheosis when he brought her back from the Underworld and placed her among the gods.

Tiberinus

1. In Roman legend he has a dual character: on the one hand he was the god of the Tiber, a poetic abstraction along Greek lines; on the other hand, he was a king of Alba, a tenth-generation descendant of Aeneas. He is said to have died while fighting by the river Albula, which thereafter became known as the Tiber.
2. A different tradition makes Tiberinus a hero and the eponym of the river, but of divine origin and not a descendant of Aeneas. He was thought to be the son of the god Janus and of Camasene, a Nymph from Latium. He drowned in the river to which he gave his name.

Tiburnus Tiburnus, or Tibartus, the eponymous hero and founder of the Latin city of Tibur (Tivoli). He was sometimes considered to be one of the three sons of the Theban hero Amphiaraus who came to Italy after their father's death to found colonies (see also CATILLUS).

Timalcus (Τίμαλχος) The eldest son of Megareus, the king of Megara. When the Dioscuri were looking for their sister, who had been abducted by Theseus, they passed by Megara. Timalcus joined forces with them, and took part in the capture of Aphidna, but was killed by Theseus in the fighting.

Timandra (Τιμάνδρα) One of the daughters of Tyndareus and Leda (Tables 2 and 19). She married ECHEMUS and, according to a tradition related by Servius, by this marriage had a son, EVANDER. She irritated Aphrodite by neglecting to offer ritual sacrifices to her, however, was struck with madness by the goddess, and allowed herself to be abducted by PHYLEUS who took her to live in Dulichium.

Tinge (Τίγγη) The wife of the giant Antaeus who was killed by Heracles. She bore a son SOPHAX who founded the city of Tingis (modern Tangiers) in honour of his mother.

Tiphys (Τῖφυς) The first pilot of the ship *Argo*. He was said to be the son of Hagnias, and was originally from Siphae in Boeotia. He was said to possess a detailed knowledge of such subjects as the winds and the course of the stars which he had learnt from Athena herself, but was never described as participating in fighting on land. Tiphys did not survive the expedition, for he died from an illness while staying with King Lycus in the land of the Mariandyni, on the shores of the Euxine Sea. His successor at the helm was Ancaeus.

Tiresias (Τειρεσίας) A famous soothsayer, who played an analogous role in the Theban cycle to that of Calchas in the Trojan one. Through his father Everes, who was descended from Oudaeus, he belonged to the race of the SPARTOI. His mother was the Nymph CHARICLO. There were various legends about the youth of Tiresias and the means by which he acquired his gift of prophecy. One version stated that he had been blinded by Pallas because he had seen the goddess naked, but at Chariclo's request Pallas gave him the gift of prophecy in compensation. The most famous version was notably different. One day, when he was walking on Mount Cyllene (or Cithaeron), the young Tiresias saw two serpents mating. At this point in the story, writers are not in agreement: the different accounts say variously that Tiresias either separated the serpents, or wounded them, or killed the female. Whichever was the case, the result of his intervention was that he became a woman. Some years later, walking by the same spot, he again saw the serpents mating. He intervened in the same way and regained his former sex. His misfortune had made him famous, and one day when Hera and Zeus were quarrelling over whether the man or the woman experienced the greatest pleasure in love-making, they decided to consult Tiresias, the only individual to have experienced both. Without hesitating, Tiresias assured them that if the enjoyment of love was constituted out of ten parts, the woman possessed nine and the man only one. Hera was so furious at seeing the great secret of her sex revealed that she struck Tiresias blind. Zeus, in compensation, gave him the gift of prophecy and the privilege of living for a long time, for seven human generations it was said.

A number of prophecies concerning the most important events of the Theban legend were attributed to Tiresias. For example, he revealed to Amphitryon the real identity of his rival for Alcmene (see HERACLES); he disclosed the crimes which Oedipus was unwittingly guilty of and advised Creon to drive Oedipus the king from the country in order to free Thebes from the plague which his presence was causing. At the time of the expedition of the Seven against Thebes, he prophesied that the city would be spared if Creon's son MENOECEUS was sacrificed to appease the anger of Ares. Finally, he advised the Thebans, during the expedition against the Epigoni, to conclude an armistice with them and to leave the town secretly at night in order to avoid a general massacre.

In Hellenistic and Roman poetry, Tiresias became the omnipresent soothsayer of Thebes. He advised King Pentheus not to oppose the introduction of the cult of Dionysus in Boeotia, and also revealed the fate of the Nymph Echo after her metamorphosis. He also predicted the death of Narcissus. The legends associated with the *Odyssey* had already given him a particular role: on Circe's advice, Odysseus undertook the journey to Hades in order to consult Tiresias. Zeus had given Tiresias the privilege of retaining his gift of prophecy even after his death. Tiresias had a daughter, the soothsayer Manto, who in her turn was the mother of the soothsayer MOPSUS. The death of Tiresias was closely linked to the capture of Thebes by the Epigoni. He followed the Thebans in their exodus and stopped with them one morning near a spring called Telphoussa. As he was thirsty after the journey, he drank this water which was extremely cold, and then died. According to another version, Tiresias remained in the city with his daughter. They were taken prisoner by the invaders and were sent to Delphi to be consecrated to Apollo, the god of the Epigoni. On the way Tiresias, who was very old, died of exhaustion.

Tisamenus (Τισαμενός) The Avenger, and the name of two heroes in particular:

1. A son of Orestes and Hermione (Table 13), who succeeded Orestes on the throne of Sparta and reigned until Sparta was attacked by the Heraclids. He was killed fighting against them. Another tradition maintains that he was driven out of Argos and Sparta by the Heraclids, but that they allowed him to withdraw in safety, along with his subjects. He then turned to the Ionians, who were settled on the north coast of the Peloponnese, and asked them to accept him and his people. Knowing Tisamenus' warlike valour and wisdom, and fearing that he might one day place them all under his control, the Ionians refused and attacked him instead. Tisamenus was killed in the fighting, but his soldiers were victorious and besieged the Ionians who had withdrawn into the city of Helice. Finally the besieged soldiers obtained permission to go to Attica, where they were received by the Athenians. Tisamenus' companions, now rulers of the country, gave their king a magnificent funeral. His sons established their control over the region taken from the Ionians, which was called Achaea. The eldest son, Cometes, succeeded Tisamenus, and then left to found a colony in Asia. Tisamenus' four other sons were Daimenes, Sparton, Tellis and Leontomenes.

2. The second hero of this name was a son of Thersandrus and Demonassa. He was a third-generation descendant of Oedipus (Table 37). At the time of the second Trojan expedition his father had already died at the house of Telephus during the landing in Mysia (see THERSANDRUS), but Tisamenus was too young to command the Theban contingent. PENELEUS rather than Tisamenus avenged the king's death by killing Telephus' son Eurypylus. When he reached manhood, Tisamenus ruled over Thebes. He had one son, Autesion, who did not succeed him, but had to be exiled, and joined forces with the Heraclids in the Peloponnese. Tisamenus was succeeded by Damasichthon, grandson of Peneleos.

Tisiphone (Τεισιφόνη)

1. The Avenger of Murder, one of the three Erinyes. There is no specific legend surrounding her, apart from the obscure episode which por-

trays her as in love with the young CITHAERON, whom she killed by having him bitten by a snake which she plucked from her hair.

2. A lost tragedy of Euripides, about the adventures of Alcmaeon, calls one of his daughters Tisiphone. She was given by her father to Creon, the king of Corinth, and sold into slavery.

Titans (Τιτᾶνες) This was the generic name borne by six of the male children of Uranus and Gaia (Table 5). They belonged to the earliest generation of the gods; the youngest amongst them was CRONUS from whom the Olympians were descended. They had six sisters, the Titanides, on whom they fathered a whole cycle of divinities (Table 38).

After the castration of Uranus by Cronus, the Titans, who had been removed from Heaven by their father, seized power. Oceanus refused to help Cronus, however, and remained independent. He later helped Zeus to dethrone Cronus. This struggle, which brought the Olympians to power, was known as the Titanomachia and is related in some detail by Hesiod in the *Theogony*, but it is suspected that the passage is an interpolation. Zeus' allies in this struggle were not only the Olympians, such as Athena, Apollo, Hera, Poseidon, and Pluto, but also the Hecatoncheires, who had suffered under the Titans, and even Prometheus, although he was the son of Iapetus and Styx, the first-born of the Oceanides.

Titanides (Τιτανίδες) The name given to six of the daughters of Uranus and Gaia: Theia (or Thia), Rhea, Themis, Mnemosyne, Phoebe and Tethys (Table 12). After they slept with their brothers, the Titans, they gave birth to divinities of different kinds (Table 38). They do not seem to have taken their brothers' side in the Titanomachia.

Tithonus (Τιθωνός) Although an aberrant genealogy often makes him the son of Eos (Dawn) and the Athenian Cephalus, this hero was more usually connected with the Trojan cycle, regarded as one of the sons of Laomedon (Table 7). His mother was Strymo, the daughter of the river-god Scamander. He was therefore the elder brother of Priam. Tithonus was extremely handsome, and was noticed by Eos (Dawn), who fell in love with him and abducted him. They had two sons, Emathion and MEMNON. Motivated by her love for Tithonus, Eos asked Zeus that he might be granted immortality, but she forgot to obtain eternal youth for him. So, while Eos remained unchanged, Tithonus grew older, and shrank to the point where he had to be put in a wicker basket like a child. In the end Eos changed him into a cicada.

Tityus (Τιτυός) A giant, the son of Zeus and Elara (sometimes said to be the daughter of Orchomenus and sometimes of Minyas). Fearing Hera's jealousy, Zeus concealed his lover when she was pregnant in the depths of the earth, from where Tityus emerged at his birth. When Leto gave birth to Zeus' children Artemis and Apollo, the jealous Hera unleashed the monstrous Tityus against her, at the same time filling him with the desire to assault her, but Tityus was struck by one of Zeus' thunderbolts and fell into the Underworld where two snakes or two eagles devoured his liver, which grew again in accordance with the phases of the moon.

According to other authors, it was Leto's two children who protected their mother, and pierced the monster with their arrows. Tityus therefore returned permanently into the ground, where his body covered over two acres. In Euboea there was a cave where a cult was dedicated to Tityus.

Tlepolemus (Τληπόλεμος) A son of Heracles and Astyoche, daughter of Phylas, the king of the Thesprotians (Table 15). Heracles had slept with her after the capture of the city of Ephyra, during an expedition carried out in collaboration with the inhabitants of Calydon. The *Iliad*, however, calls Actor the father of Astyoche.

After Heracles' death, the HERACLIDS tried, vainly, for some time to return to the Peloponnese, but when they were forced after each attempt to withdraw into Attica, Tlepolemus and his great-uncle Licymnius, Alcmene's half-brother (Table 31), along with Licymnius' children, were granted permission by the Argives to settle in Argos. During a quarrel which flared up between Tlepolemus and his great-uncle, the latter was killed by a blow from a stick. According to some authors this was an accidental death; it was said that Tlepolemus had meant either to strike an ox, or to punish a slave, and the stick had unfortunately missed its mark. Whichever the case, the dead man's relations forced Tlepolemus to exile himself from Argos. He left, along with his wife Polyxo, and settled in Rhodes. There he founded three cities, Lindos, Ialysus and Camirus.

Tlepolemus is mentioned as being one of the suitors for the hand of Helen. He set out for the Trojan War in command of nine ships, leaving

POLYXO at Rhodes as regent. He was killed by Sarpedon. On their return from Troy, Tlepolemus' companions landed first in Crete, then went to settle in the Iberian islands.

Tmolus (Τηῶλος)

1. Omphale's widowed husband.
2. A son of Ares and Theogone, king of Lydia, who assaulted a companion of Artemis called Arripe. The goddess had him killed by an enraged bull. His son, Theoclymenus, buried him on the mountain which was thereafter known as Tmolus.

Toxeus (Τοξεύς)

1. The Archer, one of the sons of the king of Oechalia, Eurytus. He was killed by Heracles at the same time as his brothers.
2. The same name was borne by one of the sons of Oeneus, the king of Calydon, and of Althaea (Table 27). Oeneus killed him with his own hand because he was said to have jumped over a ditch (compare the death of REMUS).

Trambelus (Τράμβηλος)

The son of Telamon and the Trojan prisoner THEANIRA. He was brought up at Miletus by King Arion, who had taken in his mother when she was a fugitive. Shortly afterwards, as Achilles was returning from a raid, Trambelus fought against him and was killed. However Achilles, admiring the young man's valour, asked who he was and, on learning that he was a son of Telamon and therefore his kinsman, erected a tomb for him on the beach (see APRIATE).

Tricca (Τρίκκη)

The daughter of the river-god Peneus, in Thessaly, and wife of HYPSEUS (Table 23). She gave her name to the city of Tricca in Thessaly.

Triopas (Τριόπας)

Or Triops, a hero of very uncertain genealogy, who features both in Thessalian and Argive legends. He was sometimes said to be the son of Aeolus and Canace, or of the latter and Poseidon, sometimes of Lapithes and Orsinome (Table 23), or even (and this is in the Argive tradition) of Phorbas and Euboea, of the family of Niobe and Argos (Table 17). The name of Triopas was also borne by one of the sons of Helios and Rhodus (see HELIADES). For the links between the Thessalian and Argive genealogies, see PHORBAS. The foundation of the city of Cnidus was sometimes attributed to Triopas.

Triptolemus (Τριπτόλεμος)

The archetype of the Eleusinian hero linked to the myth of Demeter. In the earliest version of the legend, he was merely considered to be a king of Eleusis. Later he was said to be the son of King Celeus and Metanira and brother of Demophon. Other traditions made him the son of Dysaules and Baubo, or of the hero Eleusis, or perhaps of Gaia and Oceanus (Table 12). In return for the hospitality which Demeter had received at Eleusis from Triptolemus' relations, she gave him a chariot drawn by winged dragons and ordered him to travel throughout the world sowing grains of wheat everywhere.

In some countries Triptolemus encountered strong resistance. The king of the Getae, Carnabon, for example, killed one of his dragons, but Demeter immediately replaced it with another one. At Patras, moreover, Antheias, son of Eumelus, tried to harness the dragons to the goddess' divine chariot while Triptolemus was asleep and

Votive relief from Eleusis showing Triptolemus receiving ears of corn from Demeter while Persephone crowns him with a garland. Athens, National Museum.

to sow the wheat himself, but he fell from the chariot and was killed. Eumelus and Triptolemus founded the city of Antheia in his honour.

Triptolemus later became 'judge of the Dead' in the Underworld and he figured alongside Aeacus, Minos and Rhadamanthys. The introduction of the festival of the Thesmophoria at Athens was attributed to Triptolemus. For Demeter's attempt to give immortality to one of the sons of Celeus, see DEMOPHON. Often, it was Triptolemus who was said to have been the victim of the goddess's spells. For the children attributed to Triptolemus in local traditions, see CROCON.

Triton (Τρίτων) Strictly speaking, a sea-god similar to Nereus, Glaucus and Phorcys. He is usually said to be the son of Poseidon and Amphitrite (Table 38), and so the brother of Rhode. Although his abode was generally the entire sea, he was often considered in late legends to be the god of Tritonis in Libya. At that period a daughter, Pallas, a childhood playmate of Athena, was attributed to him, but she was accidentally killed by the goddess. There was another daughter of Triton known to tradition, a priestess of Athena called Triteia, who was loved by Ares, by whom she had a son, Melanippus.

According to legend, Triton was involved in the expedition of the Argonauts. Disguised as Eurypylus, he gave a clod of earth to EUPHEMUS as a present for his hospitality and indicated to the sailors the route to take in order to regain the Mediterranean. Triton also appeared in a local Boeotian legend, at Tanagra, where it was related how during a festival of Dionysus, Triton attacked the local women while they were bathing in the lake. But in answer to their prayers Dionysus came to them and drove off Triton. It is also said that Triton plundered the shores of the lake, carrying off herds, until the day when a jug of wine appeared on the shore. Drawn by the smell, Triton went up to it and drank. He fell asleep there and then, and was killed with an axe. This was the rational interpretation of the victory of Dionysus over the sea-god. The name of Triton was often applied not just to a single divinity, but to a whole range of beings who made up Poseidon's retinue. The upper half of their bodies took the form of men's bodies, but the lower half were like those of fishes. They were usually depicted as blowing into shells which they used as horns (see MISENUS).

Trochilus (Τροχίλος) An Argive, the son of Io. The invention of the chariot was attributed to

him, and in particular he is said to have invented the sacred chariot used in the Argive cult of Hera. Hounded by Agenor's hatred, he fled from his homeland and took refuge in Attica, where he supposedly married an Eleusinian woman and had two sons, Eubouleus and Triptolemus. Later he was said to have been placed amongst the stars where he formed the constellation of the Charioteer.

Troezen (Τροιζὴν)
1. The eponymous hero of the city of Troezen on the Saronic Gulf. According to the local tradition, he was said to be the son of Pelops and Hippodamia and brother of PITTHEUS (Table 2). During the reign of King Aetius, Pittheus and Troezen emigrated to the city which was to take the latter's name, and the three of them reigned together. Troezen had two sons, Anaphlystus and Sphettus, who emigrated to Attica.
2. Another hero of the same name played a part in the legend of Euopis and Dimoetes.

Troilus (Τρωίλος) The youngest son of Priam and Hecuba, although it was often claimed that Apollo was in fact his father. There was a prophecy which stated that Troy would never be taken if Troilus reached the age of 20, but he was killed by Achilles shortly after the arrival of the Greeks outside the city. Traditions vary as to the circumstances of his death. He was either attacked by Achilles one evening while he was taking his horses to water, not far from the Scaean Gates (see also POLYXENA), or was taken prisoner and sacrificed to the hero. Another variant claimed that Achilles saw him at the fountain and fell in love with him. Troilus fled and took refuge in the temple of the Thymbrean Apollo. Achilles tried in vain to entice him out but finally lost his temper and ran him through with his spear inside the sanctuary itself.

Trophonius (Τροφώνιος) The hero of Lebadea in Boeotia, where there was a very famous oracle. Traditions concerning his genealogy vary. Sometimes he is described as the son of Apollo and Epicaste and thus step-son of AGAMEDES; he was also said to be one of the children of Erginus (Table 33). He was suckled by Demeter. He was particularly well known for his skill as an architect. The construction of several famous buildings was attributed to Agamedes and him: Amphitryon's house at Thebes; one of the temples of Apollo at Delphi; the treasure-houses of Augias at Elis and of Hyrieus at Hyria; and the temple of Poseidon at

Mantinea. He was skilful but when he put his talent to improper use it caused his downfall (see AGAMEDES). There existed, however, several versions of his death. It was often said that this was the price demanded by Apollo for the construction of his temple, as death was the finest reward which the gods could give to man.

Tros (Τρώς) The eponymous hero of the Trojans and of Troy. He was the son of Erichthonius, himself the son of Dardanus, and of Astyoche, daughter of the river-god Simois (Table 7). He married Callirhoe, daughter of the river-god Scamander, and by her had a daughter, Cleopatra, and three sons, Ilus, Assaracus and Ganymede.

Turnus An Italic hero, the king of the Rutuli at the time of the arrival of Aeneas. He was the son of King Daunus, and grandson of Pilumnus. His mother was the Nymph Venilia. Like the legend of Latinus and all the adventures of Aeneas in Latium, the story of Turnus is found in several versions, of which it is difficult to tell which is the earliest. According to the form of the legend which probably goes back to Cato's *Origines*, Turnus became an ally of Latinus after the marriage between the latter's daughter and Aeneas. Latinus had asked for his help in defending himself against Trojan banditry. In an early battle Latinus was killed. Turnus fled to MEZENTIUS at Caere and enlisted his assistance. He then returned to attack Aeneas, but in the course of a second battle he was killed. According to another version, Aeneas and Latinus were allies and were both attacked by Turnus and the Rutuli. During a battle, both Latinus and Turnus were killed.

Virgil developed the character of Turnus, making him the brother of Juturna and engaged to Lavinia, one of Latinus' granddaughters, who had been promised to him by Latinus' wife, Amatra. His hostility towards Aeneas was as much personal as political. Turnus was a violent young man who would not allow foreigners to settle in central Italy and stirred up all the neighbouring peoples against the Trojans. He was eventually killed by Aeneas in single combat.

Tyche (Τύχη) The deified personification of Chance or Fortune. She was unknown in Homeric poems, but later assumed great importance which continually increased into the Hellenistic period and similarly at Rome (see FORTUNA). She possessed no myth, being merely a concept. She eventually became assimilated with certain goddesses,

such as Isis, and was represented as giving birth to a hybrid divinity called Isityche. This figure featured in the religious syncretism of the Imperial period, and was an emblem of the power of the combination of providence and chance to which the world was subjected. Every city had its Tyche, depicted as being crowned with towers to symbolize her role as a guardian of cities. She was sometimes represented as being blind.

Tychius (Τυχίος) A famous cobbler from Boeotia who made the leather shield for Ajax, son of Telamon. He remained the classic example of the skilled cobbler and was often cited as such.

Tydeus (Τυδεύς) An Aetolian hero, son of the second marriage of King Oeneus and Periboea, the daughter of Hipponous (Table 27). Among the various traditions about the marriage of Oeneus and Periboea, there was one according to which Oeneus seduced Periboea before he married her, and abandoned her to the swineherds, amongst whom the young Tydeus grew up. It was also often claimed that Oeneus, on Zeus' orders, seduced his own daughter Gorge, and that Tydeus was in fact the product of this intrigue.

When he reached manhood, Tydeus committed a murder: the name of his victim varies from author to author and was either Oeneus' brother, Alcathus; or the sons of Melas who had plotted against Oeneus, namely Pheneus, Euryalus, Hyperlaus, Antiochus, Eumedes, Sternops, Xanthippus and Sthenelaus; or his own brother Olenias. Whichever it was, Tydeus had to leave his homeland and, after wandering for a while, he arrived to stay with ADRASTUS at the same time as Polynices. Adrastus agreed to purify Tydeus of his murder and, on the strength of an ancient prophecy, gave him one of his daughters, Deipyle, while Polynices married another, Argia. At the same time, Adrastus promised to restore their homelands to his two sons-in-law. It was as a result of this that Tydeus came to take part in the expedition of the Seven, which was motivated by the aim to restore Polynices to the throne of Thebes.

In the episode of Archemorus, Tydeus took Hypsipyle's side and fought against LYCURGUS. Amphiaraus and Adrastus settled the quarrel. Tydeus won the boxing at the games celebrated in honour of Archemorus (these later became the Nemean Games). Tydeus was next sent as an ambassador to Thebes, but Eteocles refused to listen to him. So, to put the Thebans to the test,

Tydeus challenged them individually to single combat, and defeated them one after the other. As he was leaving, the Thebans set an ambush of 50 men for him, but Tydeus killed them all except MAEON. An obscure tradition records an incident, which demonstrates Tydeus' ferocity, that took place during the siege. Ismene, Eteocles' sister, was in love with a young Theban called Theoclymenus, and had arranged to meet him outside the city, near a fountain. Warned by Athena, Tydeus waited for the young couple and took them by surprise. Theoclymenus managed to escape, but Ismene, taken prisoner, tried to arouse Tydeus' pity. He was, however, unmoved, and killed her.

In the decisive battle outside the seven gates of the city, Tydeus' adversary was Melanippus. The latter wounded him mortally in the stomach, but Tydeus nevertheless defeated him. The goddess Athena, protector of Tydeus, was with Zeus' approval getting ready to make him immortal. But when Amphiaraus, who had not forgiven Tydeus for having helped to organize the expedition, learned of the goddess's intentions, he cut off Melanippus' head which he then presented to Tydeus. The latter split the skull of his enemy in two, and devoured the brains. Disgusted by this act, Athena decided to deprive Tydeus of immortality and withdrew from the field of battle. Tydeus' burial was carried out by Maeon, in gratitude to the man who had spared him. Another tradition maintains that the body was carried off by Theseus' Athenians and buried at Eleusis. Tydeus was the father of DIOMEDES.

Tyndareus (Τυνδάρεως) The father of the Dioscuri, of Helen and of Clytemnestra, as well as of Timandra and Phylonoe (Table 19). He was a Lacedaemonian hero. The various traditions differ about his genealogy. According to some, he was the son of Oebalus and the Naiad Batieia or of Gorgophone, one of the daughters of Perseus (Table 6). Sometimes his father was said to be Perieres of Messena instead of Oebalus, or even Cynortas, who was more usually said to be the father of Perieres. In the latter two traditions, Tyndareus' mother was Gorgophone. His brothers or half-brothers, depending on the tradition, were Icarius, Aphareus and Leucippus; sometimes a sister Arena was added to this list.

On the death of Oebalus, Hippocoon drove his brothers out and kept the kingdom of Sparta for himself. Icarius and Tyndareus then fled to the court of Thestius in Calydon, where he married the king's daughter Leda. Later, Heracles, after defeating HIPPOCOON and his sons, restored the kingdom of Sparta to Tyndareus. According to another tradition, Hippocoon and Icarius remained together in Sparta and agreed to evict Tyndareus, who then took refuge at Pellene in Achaea, or with his half-brother Aphareus in Messenia.

Tyndareus played a part in the legend of the Atrides: after the death of Atreus, the children Menelaus and Agamemnon were sent by their nurse to Polyphides, king of Sicyon. He entrusted them to Oeneus at Calydon. When Tyndareus returned from Calydon to Sparta, he took the two children with him, and brought them up in his own house. It was there that the brothers met Helen and Clytemnestra. After the deification of his two sons Castor and Pollux, Tyndareus summoned his son-in-law Menelaus and bequeathed to him the kingdom of Sparta. Tyndareus was still alive at the time of the abduction of Helen and it was during the Trojan War that he gave his granddaughter HERMIONE in marriage to Orestes. It was even sometimes maintained that he outlived Agamemnon and was ORESTES' prosecutor before the Areopagus, or even at Argos before the people's tribunal. Tyndareus is included among those brought back to life by Asclepius. He was honoured as a hero at Sparta.

Typhon (Τυφών) Typhon, or Typheus, was a monster who was the youngest son of Gaia (the Earth) and of Tartarus (Table 12). There are, however, a series of traditions linking Typhon with Hera and Cronus. Gaia, displeased about the defeat of the Giants, slandered Zeus in the presence of Hera, who went to Cronus to ask for a means of taking revenge. Cronus gave her two eggs coated with his own semen: once buried, these eggs would give birth to a demon capable of dethroning Zeus. This monster was Typhon. According to another tradition Typhon was a son of Hera whom she had produced herself without any male assistance, just as she had done with HEPHAESTUS. She gave her monstrous son to a dragon, the serpent PYTHON who lived at Delphi, for him to bring up.

Typhon was half-man and half-animal. He exceeded all the other children of the Gaia in size and in strength; he was higher than the mountains, and his head often touched the stars. When he stretched out his arms, one of his hands reached the East and the other the West. Instead of fingers, he had 100 dragons' heads. From his waist down he was encircled by snakes. His body had wings and his eyes shot forth flames. When the gods saw this being attacking Olympus, they fled to Egypt and hid in the desert where they took on animal forms. For example Apollo became a kite, Hermes an ibis, Ares a fish, Dionysus a goat and Hephaestus an ox. Only Athena and Zeus resisted the monster. Zeus hurled thunderbolts at him from afar and in closer conflict struck him with his steel sickle. This struggle took place on Mount Casius, on the borders of Egypt and Arabia Petraea. Typhon, who was merely wounded, succeeded in wrestling the sickle from Zeus' hands. He cut the tendons in Zeus' arms and legs, put the defenceless god on his shoulders, and carried him off to Cilicia where he shut him up in the Corycian Cave. He concealed Zeus' tendons and muscles in a bearskin and gave them to the female dragon Delphyne for safekeeping. Hermes and Pan, or, in some accounts, Cadmus, stole the tendons and restored them to Zeus' body. He recovered his strength and, ascending to Heaven in a chariot drawn by winged horses, began striking the monster with thunderbolts. Typhon fled and, in the hope of increasing his strength, tried to taste the magic fruits which grew on Mount Nysa after being promised that these would cure him by the Moirai, who wanted to lure him there. Zeus caught up with him there and the pursuit continued. In Thrace, he threw mountains at Zeus, who forced them back onto the monster with his thunderbolts. Mount Haemus derived its name from the blood (in Greek αἷμα) which flowed from one of his wounds. Discouraged once and for all, Typhon fled, and while he was crossing the sea to Sicily, Zeus hurled Mount Etna at him which crushed him. The flames which erupt from Etna are either then those poured forth by the monster or the remains of the thunderbolts with which Zeus struck him down. Typhon was said to be the father of several monsters (the dog Orthrus, the Hydra of Lerna, the Chimaera) whom he had by Echidna, the daughter of Callirhoe and Chrysaor (Table 32).

Tyro (Τυρώ) The daughter of Salmoneus and Alcidice. She was brought up by Salmoneus' brother, Cretheus. While with him she fell in love with the river-god Enipeus, and would often go to his banks to lament her passion. One day the god Poseidon emerged from the water and in the form of Enipeus seduced her. She secretly gave birth to twins, PELIAS and NELEUS. However, her stepmother Sidero, the second wife of Salmoneus, maltreated her. When her children were grown up, they came and delivered her, and killed Sidero. Tyro then married Cretheus, by whom she had three sons: Aeson, Pheres and Amythaon (Table 21). Tyro appears in a quite different legend whose fragmented story has been partly preserved for us by Hyginus. Sisyphus and Salmoneus, who were brothers, hated each other. An oracle had told Sisyphus that he would only be able to take vengeance on his brother by having a child by his niece Tyro. He slept with her and she gave birth to twins whom she killed on learning the fate which awaited them. We do not know what Sisyphus did then. We only know that he was punished in the Underworld because of his incest.

Tyrrhenus (Τυρρηνός) The eponymous hero of the Tyrrhenians (the Etruscans). He was sometimes said to be the brother of Lydus, eponym of the Lydians, and son of Atys and Callithea, and sometimes a son of Heracles, the inventor of the trumpet. In this case, his mother was Omphale. He was also said to be a son of Telephus and Hiera, which makes Tarchon his brother. The Tyrrhenus of Lydian origin was exiled after the fall of Troy – or else during a famine which was ravaging the country – and was thought to have settled in central Italy where he became the progenitor of the Etruscan race.

Tyrrhus The head shepherd of Latinus. He took command of the Latin peasants to avenge the death of the sacred doe killed by the young ASCANIUS. Later, after the death of Aeneas, LAVINIA, frightened of her stepson, took refuge with Tyrrhus to give birth to her son Silvius.

Tyrus (Τύρος) A Phoenician Nymph, loved by Heracles. It is said that her dog one day ate a purple shellfish (a murex) and came back to her with his nose coloured scarlet. Admiring this hue, the young woman told Heracles that she would no longer love him unless he gave her a garment of the same colour. Heracles obediently went off to look and found purple dye, the glory of Tyre.

U

Ucalegon (Οὐκαλέγων)

1. One of the Trojans and a friend of Priam. He appears in the Council of Elders of the city. His house, which was adjacent to Aeneas', was destroyed by fire on the night when Troy fell.

2. In an obscure tradition, a Theban and father of the Sphinx.

Uranus (Οὐρανος) The personification of the Sky as a fertile element. He plays a prominent role in Hesiod's *Theogony* in which he is the son of Gaia. Other poems make him son of AETHER but this tradition (which goes back to the *Titanomachia*) does not name his mother. She was doubtless Hemera, the female personification of Day. In the Orphic *Theogony* Uranus and Gaia are two of the children of Night.

The best-known legends of Uranus are those in which he appears as the husband of Gaia. (The Sky in fact covers the whole Earth, he alone being her match in size.) By her he had a large number of children (see Tables 5, 12 and 38, compiled on the information supplied by Hesiod and Apollodorus), namely six male Titans, the six female Titanides, the three Cyclopes and the three Hecatoncheires. Gaia tired of endless childbirth and wanted to escape from her husband's brutal lovemaking; she asked her sons to protect her against him. They all refused except the youngest, CRONUS, who ambushed his father and, with the help of a sickle which his mother had lent him, cut off Uranus' testicles and threw them into the sea. This act of mutilation is usually said to have taken place at Cape Drepana, which is supposed to have taken its name from Cronus' sickle; sometimes it is situated off Corcyra, the land of the Phaeacians. The island is then said to be none other than the sickle itself, which was thrown into the sea by Cronus and took root there, and the Phaeacians were born of the god's blood. Alternatively, the scene is set in Sicily, which was fertilized by the god's blood, which is why that island is so fertile.

A somewhat different tradition is recorded about Uranus by Diodorus Siculus. In this version he was the first king of the Atlantes, a particularly pious and just race who lived on the shores of the ocean. He was the first to teach them civilization and to initiate them into culture. He was himself a skilled astronomer: he devised the first calendar from the movement of the stars and predicted the principal events which would occur in the world.

On his death divine honours were paid to him. Gradually he became identified with the sky itself. In this tradition Uranus was supposed to have had 45 children, 18 by Titae (who later took the name Gaia): from their mother they took the name Titans. His daughters were Basileia and, later, Cybele and Rhea (who was also called Pandora). Basileia, who was very beautiful, inherited the throne of Uranus and married Hyperion, one of her brothers, by whom she had two children, Helios (the Sun) and Selene (the Moon). Among the other children of Uranus, Diodorus mentions Atlas and Cronus; according to Plato, Oceanus and Tethys are also children of Uranus. The complexity and variety of these genealogies can be explained by the fact that they reflect not precise legends but symbolic interpretations of intellectual cosmogonies. Uranus does not, in fact, play an important role in Greek myths. However, Hesiod preserves the memory of two prophecies attributed jointly to Uranus and Gaia: first, the prophecy which warned Cronus that his reign would end when he had been conquered by one of his sons: second, the prophecy that put ZEUS on his guard against the child he would have by METIS. It was in response to this prophecy that Zeus swallowed Metis when she was pregnant with Athena. There was also a Syrian legend of Uranus and CRONUS, which was recorded by Philon of Byblos.

V

Vacuna The name of a very ancient Sabine goddess who had a ruined sanctuary near Horace's villa, on the banks of the Licenza. She has been identified, rather vaguely, with Diana, with Minerva, and even with Victory. There is no legend attached to her.

Valeria During an epidemic which ravaged the city of Falerii, an oracle commanded that in order to put an end to this scourge a virgin should be sacrificed every year to Juno. The sacrifice took place; but one year the chosen victim was a girl called Valeria Luperca. Just as she was about to kill herself with a sword at the altar, an eagle appeared, plucked the sword from her, and dropped a small stick by the ritual hammer which was lying on the altar. The eagle flew off and let the sword fall on a heifer which was grazing in a nearby field. Valeria grasped the meaning of the signs given by the bird. She sacrificed the heifer and taking the hammer with her, she touched those who had been stricken by the epidemic with it. They were cured immediately.

Veiovis A Roman god, belatedly identified with Apollo, who had a very ancient shrine on the Capitol and another on Isola Tiberina. He was essentially associated with the Underworld, and seems to have presided originally over swamps and volcanic movements. Veiovis has no specific legend surrounding him; he was primarily a god of the *gens Julia*.

Venus A very ancient Latin divinity who had a shrine near Ardea which was established before the foundation of Rome. She was long considered to preside over vegetation and gardens, but is now

regarded by certain authors as a mediating spirit of prayer. All this is, however, very uncertain. In the second century BC she was assimilated into the legend of the Greek Aphrodite. The *gens Julia*, which claimed to be descended from AENEAS, assumed that Venus was one of their ancestors.

Vertumnus A god, probably of Etruscan origin, who had a statue in Rome in the Etruscan district at the entrance to the Forum. Vertumnus personified the idea of change. He was attributed with the ability to take on as many shapes as he wished. Ovid describes a love affair of his with POMONA which probably had its origin in the belief that Vertumnus was in some respects a protector of vegetation and, more particularly, of fruit trees.

Vesta A Roman goddess of a very archaic form who presided over the fire in the domestic hearth. Like the Greek HESTIA, she belonged to the group of the 12 great gods. Her cult was controlled directly by the chief high priest assisted by the Vestal Virgins over whom he exercised paternal authority. The cult of Vesta was introduced to Rome, according to most authors, by Romulus. There are discrepancies in such an account, however, as her temple (round in shape, like the earliest huts of Latium) stood not inside the Palatine city but on the edge of it, in the Roman forum, and consequently outside the boundaries of the city attributed to Romulus. The archaic nature of the goddess was further confirmed by the fact that her sacred animal was the ass, an archetypal Mediterranean animal, rather than the horse which was Indo-European. On the day of the *Vestalia* in mid-June, young asses were garlanded with flowers and did not work. To explain this phenomenon, a legend was belatedly created in which the goddess, chaste above all others, was protected by a donkey from the amorous designs of PRIAPUS. This was a late legend, of Hellenistic origin and completely artificial.

Virbius A demon whose worship was linked with that of Diana, in the sacred woods surrounding Nemi (Aricia). The fact that horses were not allowed to enter this wood gave rise to the belief that Virbius was none other than HIPPOLYTUS, son of Theseus, who had been killed by his horses, revived by Asclepius, and transported by Artemis to Italy. This interpretation was supported by a

Venus and cupids depicted on a wall painting from the House of the Marine Venus at Pompeii.

pun, breaking Virbius up into *vir* (man) and *bis* (twice): thus, he who has been a man twice, and this was seen as an allusion to the resurrection of the hero.

Volturnus An old Roman divinity who possessed a priest and a festival, the *Volturnalia*, on 27 August. One legend maintained that this Volturnus (or the companion river-god of the same name with whom he was perhaps identified) was the father of the Nymph JUTURNA.

Vulcan A Roman deity, possessing a priest and a festival called the *Vulcanalia*, which took place on 23 August. He was said to have been introduced to Rome by Titus Tatius, but there was a tradition which attributes the construction of his first shrine to Romulus, from the spoils of war taken from an enemy. During the festival of Vulcan, little fish and often other animals were sometimes thrown into the fire. These offerings were supposed to represent human lives and they were offered to Vulcan in order to preserve lives. He does not have any specific legend attached to him and has been identified with HEPHAESTUS. However, Vulcan was sometimes said to be the father of CACUS, or of CAECULUS, or even of the mythical king SERVIUS TULLIUS (more usually considered to be the son of the household god or Lar).

Romano–British representations of Vulcan show him dressed in a tunic, standing with hammer and tongs at an anvil. This pose, naked and seated, echoes an Eastern coin type of 2nd–3rd century AD. The felt hat – Vulcan's usual attribute – confirms the identification.
Oxford, Ashmolean Museum.

Z

Zacynthus (Ζάκυνθος) The eponymous hero of the island of Zacynthus (modern Zante) in the Ionian Sea. According to different traditions, this hero was said either to be the son of Dardanus (Table 7) or an Arcadian from the city of Psophis.

Zagreus (Ζαγρεύς) The son of Zeus and Persephone, and considered the 'first Dionysus'. Zeus was said to have taken on the form of a serpent in order to beget him. He had a particular affection for Zagreus, and intended to make him his successor and bestow on him sovereignty over the world, but the Fates decided otherwise. Anticipating Hera's jealousy Zeus entrusted the infant Zagreus to Apollo and the Curetes, who brought him up in the forest of Parnassus, but Hera managed to discover where he was and gave the Titans the task of abducting him. Zagreus tried in vain to escape from them by changing shape, metamorphosing himself, notably into a bull; however the Titans cut him into pieces and ate him partly cooked and partly raw. Pallas could only save the heart, which was still beating. Several scattered pieces of him were gathered up by Apollo, who buried them near the tripod at Delphi. Zeus wanted him restored to life, and this occurred either through Demeter who reconstituted what remained of him, or because Zeus forced Semele to consume Zagreus' heart and then give birth to a 'second Dionysus'. It was also said that Zeus consumed the child's heart (see IACCHUS) before fathering Zagreus/Dionysus on Semele. Zagreus was an Orphic god, and the preceding legend belongs to the theology of Orphic mysteries. The identification of the hero with Dionysus is attributed to Orphism. Aeschylus, on the other hand, called him an underworld Zeus and likened him to Hades.

Zelus (Ζῆλος) Zeal or Emulation, a son of Styx and Oceanus. He was the brother of Victory, Strength and Violence (Table 32).

Zethus (Ζῆθος) See AMPHION.

Zeus (Ζεύς) Generally regarded as the greatest god of the Greek pantheon. He was essentially the son of Light, of clear skies as well as of thunder, but he was not identified with the Sky any more than Apollo was with the Sun or Poseidon with the Sea. In Greek thought the gods lost the cosmic value with which they had been endowed at an earlier stage of their development, and Zeus became pre-eminently only a heroic figure.

His personality, that of the king of men and of gods, enthroned in the luminous heights of the sky, was created in the Homeric poems. Usually he presided at the summit of Mount Olympus, but he also travelled. He could be found, for example, living with the Ethiopians, a pious race above all others, whose sacrifices found particular favour with him. Gradually his abode lost its association with any particular mountain, and the word *Olympus* came to mean merely the ethereal region where the gods lived. Zeus not only presided over celestial manifestations – causing rain, thunder and lightning, powers symbolized by his shield – but above all he maintained order and justice in the world. He was responsible for purifying murderers of the stain of blood, and he ensured that oaths were kept, and that the appropriate duties were carried out to one's hosts. He was the guarantor of royal powers and, more generally, of the social hierarchy. He exercised prerogatives not only towards men, but also towards the gods. He himself was subject to the Moirai, which he interpreted and whom he defended against the whims of the other gods. For example, he considered carefully the destinies of Achilles and Hector, and when the scale bearing the latter went down to Hades, Zeus forbade Apollo to intervene, and abandoned the hero to his enemy. He was a benevolent god, aware of his responsibilities, and did not act solely upon his whims, at least when it was not a matter of passing love affairs, though even these apparent caprices were usually the result of forethought. He was the distributor of good and evil. Homer relates in the *Iliad* that at the gate of his palace there were two jars, one containing good, the other evil. Zeus' custom with each mortal was to take a portion from both jars. But sometimes he only used one of them, and the resulting destiny was either entirely good or, more usually, entirely evil.

This concept of Zeus as a universal power began to develop in the Homeric poems and ended, with the Hellenistic philosophers, in the conception of a single Providence. For the Stoics (notably Chrysippus who dedicated a poem to him), Zeus was the symbol of a single god, the incarnation of the Cosmos. The laws of the world were nothing but the thought of Zeus, but that was the extreme point of the god's evolution, beyond the limits of mythology towards theology and philosophical history where it more properly belongs.

I BIRTH OF ZEUS

Like all the Olympians, Zeus belonged to the second generation of gods. He was the son of the Titan CRONUS and of RHEA, and just as Cronus was the youngest of the line of the Titans, so Zeus was the last-born (Table 38). Cronus was warned by an oracle that one of his children would dethrone him and tried to prevent this threat from coming about by devouring his sons and daughters as Rhea gave birth to them. On the birth of the sixth, Rhea decided to use a trick and save Zeus. She gave birth to him secretly at night and, in the morning, gave Cronus a stone wrapped up in a blanket. Cronus ate this stone which he thought was a child, and Zeus was saved. There were two distinct traditions about the place of Zeus' birth. The most frequently mentioned place was in Crete, on Mount Aegeon or Mount Ida or Mount Dicte. The other tradition, defended by Callimachus in his *Hymn to Zeus*, situates it in Arcadia (see NEDA). Even Callimachus admits that Zeus' earliest years were spent in a Cretan hiding place, where his mother had entrusted him to the CURETES and the Nymphs. His nurse was the Nymph (or goat) Amalthea, who suckled him. It was also said that when this goat died, Zeus used its skin for his shield: this was the *aegis* whose power was first put to the test at the time of the fight against the Titans. The divine child was also nourished on honey: the bees of Mount Ida produced honey especially for him (for the euhemeristic interpretations of this, see MELISSA and MELISSEUS). The Cretans did not merely show the spot where, according to them, Zeus was born; they would also point out a so-called Tomb of Zeus, to the great indignation of mythographers and poets for whom Zeus was the immortal god.

II THE CONQUEST OF POWER

When Zeus reached adulthood, he wanted to seize power from Cronus. He asked METIS (Prudence) for advice, and she gave him a drug which made Cronus vomit up the children which he had swallowed. With the aid of his brothers and sisters now restored to life, Zeus attacked Cronus and the Titans. The struggle lasted ten years. Finally, Zeus and the Olympians were victorious, and the Titans were expelled from Heaven. To win this victory Zeus, on Gaia's advice, had had to liberate the Cyclopes and the Hecatoncheires from Tartarus where Cronus had locked them up. To do this, he killed their guardian Campe. The Cyclopes then gave Zeus thunder and lightning which they had made; they gave Hades a magic helmet which made the wearer of it invisible; Poseidon received a trident, which could shake the sea and the land at a blow. Having won their victory, the gods shared power out among themselves by drawing lots. Zeus obtained Heaven, Poseidon the Sea, Hades the Underworld. In addition Zeus was to preside over the Universe. The victory of Zeus and the Olympians was soon contested. They had to fight against the GIANTS, aroused against them by the Earth who was annoyed at having her sons, the Titans, locked away in Tartarus. Finally, as the last ordeal, Zeus had to overcome Typhon. This was the toughest fight he had to endure. During his long struggle, he was imprisoned and mutilated by the monster, but he was saved by a trick played by Hermes and Pan, and was victorious.

III MARRIAGE AND THE AFFAIRS OF ZEUS

The earliest of his wives was Metis, the daughter of Oceanus. Metis took on several forms in order to try and escape from the god, but in vain. She finally submitted, and conceived a daughter, but Gaia predicted to Zeus that if Metis gave birth to a daughter, she would then produce a son who would dethrone his father. So Zeus swallowed Metis and, when the time came for the delivery of the child, Prometheus or Hephaestus split Zeus' skull with an axe, and the goddess Athena emerged fully armed. Zeus then married Themis, one of the Titanides, and had daughters by her who were called the Seasons (the Horae), named Eirene (Peace), Eunomia (Discipline) and Dike (Justice). Then he fathered the Moirai who were the agents of Destiny. This marriage with Themis (who was the incarnation of eternal order and of law) has an obvious symbolic value, and explains how the omnipotent Zeus can be subject to fate since the Moirai, emanating directly from him, are in reality an aspect of himself.

Zeus then fathered APHRODITE on Dione, one of the Titanides. By Eurynome, daughter of

Oceanus, he fathered the Graces or CHARITES, Aglaea, Euphrosyne and Thalia, who were originally spirits of vegetation. By Mnemosyne, a Titanide who symbolized memory, he had the MUSES. Finally, by Leto, he fathered Apollo and Artemis.

It was only at this moment that, according to Hesiod, the 'sacred marriage' with Hera, his own sister, took place, but it was generally considered to have happened much earlier. Hebe, Eilithyia and Ares were born of this marriage. By another of his sisters, Demeter, Zeus had a daughter, Persephone. Such were Zeus' unions with goddesses but his intrigues with mortals were countless. Only the main ones will be mentioned here (Table 40). There was hardly a region in the Greek world which did not boast an eponymous hero who was a son born of one of Zeus' love affairs. Similarly, most of the great families of legend were connected with Zeus. The Heraclids, for example, were descended not only from the union of the god and Alcmene but also, earlier, from the union of Zeus and Danae (Table 31). Achilles and Ajax were descended from Zeus through the Nymph Aegina (Table 30), and the ancestor of Agamemnon and Menelaus, Tantalus, was said to be the son of Zeus and Pluto (Table 2). Similarly, the race of Cadmus was connected with Zeus through Io and her son Epaphus (Table 3). The Trojans, through their ancestor Dardanus, were born of the affair between Zeus and the Pleiad Electra (Table 7). The Cretans claimed connections with Europa and the three sons she had by Zeus: Minos, Sarpedon and Rhadamanthys. The Arcadians had an ancestor called Arcas, son of Zeus and the Nymph Callisto (Table 9), and their neighbours the Argives took their name from Argos, the son (like his brother Pelasgus, eponym of the Pelasgians) of Zeus and the Argive Niobe (Tables 17 and 18). Finally, the Lacedaemonians claimed descent from the god and the Nymph Taygete (Table 6).

Although mythographers, especially from the Christian period onwards, pretended to consider these affairs merely as acts of debauchery, earlier poets and mythographers were at pains to recognize the deeper reasons which led the god to father children on mortals. The birth of Helen was explained as a desire to diminish the excessive population of Greece and Asia by provoking a bloody conflict. Similarly, the birth of Heracles was intended to provide a hero capable of ridding the world of destructive monsters. In short, procreation for Zeus was an act of providence. The ancient writers had already commented on the fact that many of these unions took place with Zeus disguised as an animal or in some other form: with Europa he took the form of a bull; with Leda a swan; with Danae a shower of gold. These bizarre acts were sometimes explained by the hypothesis that they offered the substitution of Zeus for earlier, local cults in which the divinity being replaced had an animal or fetishist form, but they nevertheless often aroused the indignation of these writers, who tried to give them a symbolic explanation. Thus for Euripides the shower of gold which seduced Danae was an image of the omnipotence of wealth. These adventures often exposed Zeus to Hera's anger. One explanation given by ancient writers for the god's metamorphoses was the desire to be concealed from his wife, but this is obviously a later invention, later than the stories of metamorphosis themselves. Zeus' lovers often took animal forms. Thus Io was metamorphosed into a cow, and Callisto became a she-bear.

IV VARIOUS LEGENDS

Zeus intervened in a great many legends which are not easy to group together. The *Iliad* relates a plot against him by Hera, Athena and Poseidon, which was an attempt to chain him up. He was saved by Aegaeon. On another occasion he hurled Hephaestus into space, making the god lame thereafter, as a punishment for having sided with Hera. He re-established order in the world after PROMETHEUS' theft by chaining the latter to the Caucasian mountains, but, confronted by the wickedness of mankind, he caused the great flood, from which the human race was saved only thanks to DEUCALION. Thus it was to Zeus the Liberator that Deucalion made his first sacrifice once this flood was over.

Zeus intervened in quarrels which frequently arose between Apollo and Heracles concerning the tripod of Delphi; between Apollo and Idas about MARPESSA; between Pallas and Athena, thus bringing about, quite unintentionally, the former's death; between Athena and Poseidon who were fighting over possession of Attica; between Aphrodite and Persephone who were arguing over the beautiful ADONIS. He also punished a number of criminals, notably sacrilegious people such as Salmoneus, Ixion (thus avenging a particular insult) and Lycaon. We see him intervening also in the Labours of Heracles, giving him weapons against his enemies, or removing him from their hands when he is injured. Zeus was said to have abducted the young GANYMEDE in the Troad, and made him his own cup-bearer as a replacement for Hebe. At Rome Zeus was identified with Jupiter, like him god of heaven, and protector of the city in his temple on the Capitol.

Zeuxippe (Ζευξίππη)

1. The wife of Pandion, the king of Attica, and mother of Erechtheus, Butes, Procne and Philomela (Table 11). She was the sister-in-law of her own mother, the Naiad Praxithea, who married Erechtheus.

2. The daughter of Lamedon, king of Sicyon (Table 22). She married Sicyon, by whom she had a daughter Chthonophyle.

3. The daughter of Hippocoon. She married Antiphates, the son of Melampus, and by him had two sons: Oecles and Amphalces (Table 1).

References

A

Abas (1) Homer, *Il.* 2,536ff. and schol.; 4,464; Eustath. p. 281,43; Hyg. *Fab.* 157; Steph.Byz. s.v. Ἀβαντίς and Ἄβαι; Strabo 10,1,3, p. 445; Euripides, *Archelaus* fragments 2,5 Austin (P.Hamb. 118); Nauck, *TGF*, edn 2, unattributed fragments 454; Apoll. Rhod. *Arg.* 1,77ff. with schol. (2) Apollod. *Bibl.* 2,2,1; Paus. 2,12,2; 2,16,2; 10,35,1. (3) Apollod. *Bibl.* 1,9,13; Apoll. Rhod. *Arg.* 1,139ff. with schol.; Paus. 1,43,5.

Aborigines Dionysius of Halicarnassus, *Ant. Rom.* 1,9ff.; 1,72; 2,48f.; Strabo, 5,3,2,p. 228; Cato, *Origines* fragments 5–7; Sall. *Catil.* 6,1; Lyc. *Alex.* 1253; Festus s.v. *Romam*, p. 266 M.; Pliny, *NH* 3,56; Serv. on *Aen.* 8,328. See W. A. Schröder, *M. P. Cato: das erste Buch der Origines*, pp. 102ff.

Acacallis Paus. 8,53,4; Apoll. Rhod.*Arg.* 4,1490ff. with schol. on 1492; Antoninus Liberalis, *Met.* 30. See M. P. Nilsson, *Mycenean Origins* edn 2, p. 539.

Acacos Paus. 8,3,2; 8,36,10; Steph. Byz. s.v. Ἀκακήσιον.

Academus Plutarch, *Thes.* 32; Diog. Laert. 3,7–8; Steph. Byz. s.v. Ἐκαδήμεια (*sic*). See also THESEUS; HELEN.

Acalanthis Antoninus Liberalis, *Met.* 9; Ovid, *Met.* 5,295ff.; 670ff. See also **Pierus**.

Acamas (1) Homer, *Il.* 2,819ff.; 12,99ff.; 14,476ff.; 16,342ff. (2) Homer, *Il.* 2,844; 6,5ff. (3) Sophocles *Phil.* 562; Euripides *Hec.* 123ff.; Plutarch *Thes.* 35; Parthen. *Erot.* 16; Virgil, *Aen.* 2,262; Hyg. *Fab.* 108; Apollod. *Epit.* 1,18; 1,23; 5,22; Paus. 1,5,2; 10,10,1; 10,26,2; Tzetzes on Lyc. *Alex.* 496.

Acanthis Antoninus Liberalis, *Met.* 7.

Acarnan Apollod. *Bibl.* 3,7,5f.; Paus. 8.24.9; Thuc. 2,102,9; Ovid, *Met.* 9,412; schol. on Pind. *Ol.* 1,127.

Acastus Apollod. *Bibl.* 1,9,10; 1,9,16; 1,9,27; 3,13,3; 3,13,7f.; Apoll. Rhod. *Arg.* 1,224 with schol.; 1,326; Val. Flacc. *Arg.* 1,164ff.; 1,484ff.; Hyg. *Fab.* 14; 24; 103; 273; Ovid, *Met.* 7,306; Paus. 1,18,1; 3,18,16; 5,17,9; Pind. *Nem.* 3,34 (59) with schol. on 59; 4,54ff. (88ff.); 5,25ff. (46ff.) with schol. on 50; schol. on Aristophanes *Clouds* 1063; Euripides *Alc.* 732; *Tro.* 1127ff.; Hom. *Il.* 24,488 with schol.; Tzetzes on Lyc. 175; Diod. Sic. 4,53ff. See Frazer's (Loeb) footnote to Apollod. *Bibl.* 3,13,7.

Acca Larentia Plutarch, *Quaest. Rom.* 35, 272; Lact. 1,20,5; Cato quoted in Macr. *Sat.* 1,10,16; Varro *L.L.* 6,23; Plutarch *Rom.* 4ff. See H. J. Rose, *The Roman Questions of Plutarch*, 1924, on the passage cited.

Achates (1) Virgil, *Aen.* 1,120 etc; Ovid, *Fasti* 3,603; schol. Hom. *Il.* 2,701; Eustath. p. 326,4f.; Hom. *Od.* 11,521 with Eustath. ad loc., p. 1697; Tzetzes, *Antehom.* 230ff. (2) Nonnus, *Dion.* 13,309; 37,350; etc.

Achelous Hesiod, *Theog.* 340; Macr. *Sat.* 5,18,10; Serv. on Virgil *Georg.* 1,8; Joann. Malalas, *Chron.* 6,164; Prop. 2,25,33; Ovid, *Met.* 8,550ff.; Hom. *Il.* 21,194; Apollod. *Bibl.* 1,3,4; 1,7,10; 3,7,5; Apoll. Rhod. *Arg.* 4,896; Paus. 2,2,3; 10,8,5; Euripides *Bacch.* 519; Apollod. *Bibl.* 1,8,1; Sophocles *Trach.* 9ff.; Diod. Sic. 4,35,3ff.; Dio Chrysostom 60; Hyg. *Fab.* 31; Ovid, *Met.* 8,577ff.; 9,1ff.

Achaemenides Virgil, *Aen.* 3,614ff.; Ovid, *Met.* 14,160ff.

Acheron Hom. *Od.* 10,513; Euripides, *Alc.* 439ff.; Virgil, *Aen.* 6,295; Ovid, *Met.* 5,534ff.; Apollod. *Bibl.* 1,5,3; Hdt. 5,92,7; Paus. 1,17,5; 5,14,2ff.; 10,28,1f.

Achilles Birth and childhood: Hom. *Il.* 2,681ff.; 11,771ff.; schol. on *Il.* 9,668; 16,37; 19,326; Eustath. on Hom. p. 14; Stat. *Achill.* 1,283ff.; Apollod. *Bibl.* 3,13,6ff.; *Epit.* 3,14; Apoll. Rhod. *Arg.* 4,869ff. and schol. 816; schol. on Aristophanes *Clouds* 1068; Euripides *Women of Scyros* (lost tragedy, Nauck *TGF*, edn 2, pp. 574f.); Paus. 1,22,6; Hyg. *Fab.* 96; Sophocles fragments ed. Pearson II, 191ff.; Ovid, *Met.* 13,162ff.; Ptol. Heph. *Nov. Hist.* 1, p. 183 and 6, p. 195 Westermann; Lyc. *Alex.* 178ff. with Tzetzes ad loc.; Etymol. Magn. s.v.

First expedition: Hom. *Il.* 11,625; Proclus' summary of *Cypria*, Hom. Oxf. Class. Text V, p. 103, schol. on *Il.* 1,59; Apollod. *Epit.* 3,17; Philostr. *Heroicus* 23 (de Lannoy); Dictys Cret. 1,16; 2,1ff., Hyg. *Fab.* 101; Prop. 2,1,63ff.; Ovid, *Pont.* 3,2,26; see also TELEPHUS.

Second expedition: Hom. *Il.*; *Od.* 11,477ff.; 24,36ff.; Proclus' summary of *Aethiopis*, Hom. Oxf. Class. Text V, pp. 105ff.; Pind. *Ol.* 2,81ff. (147ff.); Apollod. *Epit.* 3,22; 3,31ff; Plutarch *Quaest. Gr.* 28,297; Diod. Sic. 2,46; Philostr. *Heroicus* 46ff. (de Lannoy); Tzetzes, *Antehom.* 257ff.; *Posthom.* 100ff.; on Lyc. *Alex.* 174; 999; Quint. Smyrn. *Posthom.* 3,26ff.; 4,468ff.; schol. on Theocr. 16,49; Ovid, *Met.* 12,70ff.; 597ff; Dictys Cret. 2,12; Hyg. *Fab.* 107; 110; Virgil, *Aen.* 6,57ff; schol. on Apoll. Rhod. *Arg.* 4,815; schol. on Euripides *Hec.* 41; on Euripides *Tro.* 16 Pseudo-Lact. Plac. on Stat. *Achill.* 1,134; Nonnus in Westermann *Mythogr.* p. 382. Number 62; Paus. 3,19,11ff.; 3,24,10ff.

Acis Ovid, *Met.* 13,750ff.; Serv. on Virgil *Ecl.* 9,39.

Acontius Ovid, *Her.* 20 and 21; *Trist.* 3,10,73ff.; Antoninus Liberalis *Met.* 1; Plutarch, *Quaest. Gr.* 27,297; Callim. *Aet.* fragments 67–75, with Pfeiffer's notes.

Acrisius Apollod. *Bibl.* 2,2,1ff.; 2,4,4; schol. on Euripides *Orestes* 965; schol on Apoll. Rhod. *Arg.* 4,1091; 1,40; Paus. 2,16,1–3; 2,23,7; 2,25,7; Hyg. *Fab.* 63.

Acron Plutarch, *Romulus* 16; Livy 1.10; Dion. Hal. 2,34; Val. Max. 3,2,3; Florus, 1,1,11; Serv. on Virgil *Aen.* 6,859.

Actaeon Hesiod, *Theog.* 977; Apollod. *Bibl.* 3,4,4; Hyg. *Fab.* 181; Nonnus, *Dion.* 5,287ff.; Ovid, *Met.* 3,131ff., Fulg. *Myth.* 3,3; Paus. 1,44,8; 9,2,3; Euripides *Bacchae* 337; Diod. Sic. 4,81.

Actor (1) Apollod. *Bibl.* 1,7,3; 1,8,2; schol. on Apoll. Rhod. *Arg.* 1,558; 4,816; Diod. Sic. 4,72.

Admetus Apollod. *Bibl.* 1,8,2; 1,9,16; Tibullus 2,3,11ff.; Ovid, *Her.* 5,151; Plutarch, *Numa* 4; Aeschylus, *Eum.* 723ff.; Euripides *Alcestis, passim.*

Admete Athenaeus 15,672a; Paus. 7,4,4.

Adonis Apollod. *Bibl.* 3,14,4; Hyg. *Fab.* 58; 271; Serv. on Virgil, *Ecl.* 10,18; Ovid, *Met.* 10,345ff.; Serv. on Virgil, *Aen.* 5,72; Hyg. *Fab.* 248; Theocr. 1,109; 3,46 with schol.; Prop. 3,5,38; Lucian, *Dea Syra* 8; Strabo 16,2,18–19,p.755; Paus. 6,24,7; Bion, 1,72; Theocr. 15,102; 136ff.; Orphic Hymns 56,9; Ausonius, *Epit. in Glauc.; Cupido crucif.* 57f.; Clem. Alex. *Protrep.* 2,33,8f.

Adrastus Hom. *Il.* 2,572; Pind. *Nem.* 9,9ff. (20ff.); Hdt. 5,67; Apollod. *Bibl.* 3,6,1ff.; schol. on *Od.* 11,326; *Il.* 14,119ff.; 4,376ff.; Paus. 1,43; 9,9,1; Pind. *Ol.* 6,13ff. (19ff.); Plutarch *Thes.* 29; Hyg. *Fab.* 242; Stat. *Theb. passim*; Aeschylus, *Eleusinii* (lost tragedy, Nauck *TGF*, edn 2, p. 18f.).

Aeacus Apollod. *Bibl.* 3,12,6; Diod. Sic. 4,61,1ff.; 4,72,5ff.; Paus. 2,29,2ff.; Hyg. *Fab.* 52; Ovid, *Met.* 7,614ff.; Tzetzes on Lyc. *Alex.* 176; Strabo 8,6,16, p. 375; Hesiod, *Theog.* 1003ff.; Pind. *Nem.* 5,12ff. (21ff.); *Ol.* 8,31ff. (41ff.); Isoc. 9,14; 15; Plato, *Apol.* 41a; Gorg. 523e ff.

Aechmagoras Paus. 8,12,3f.

Aedon Hom. *Od.* 19,518ff.; Antoninus Liberalis, *Met.* 11.

Aeetes Hesiod, *Theog.* 957; 960; Hom. *Od.* 10,136ff.; Apollod. *Bibl.* 1,9,1; 1,9,23; 1,9,28; *Epit.* 7,14; Apoll. Rhod. *Arg.* 3,242 with schol.; Diod. Sic. 4,45; Hyg. *Fab.* 27, etc.; Hdt. 1,2; 7,193; Cic. *Tusc.* 3,12,26. See also ARGONAUTS; THESEUS; MEDEA; JASON.

Aegaeon Hom. *Il.* 1,396ff.; Hesiod, *Theog.* 811; schol. on Apoll. Rhod. *Arg.* 1,1165; Virgil, *Aen.* 10,565ff.

Aegestes Virgil, *Aen.* 1,195; 550ff.; 5,36ff.; 711ff.; Serv. on Virgil, *Aen.* 1,550; 5,30; Lyc. *Alex.* 951ff. with Tzetzes on 953; 471; Dion. Hal. 1,47,2; 1,52,1ff.; 1,67; Strabo 6,1,3, p. 254.

Aegeus Apollod. *Bibl.* 1,9,28; 3,15,5ff.; Tzetzes on Lyc. 494; Plut. *Thes.* 3; 13; Paus. 1,5,3f.; 1,39,4; Strabo 9,1,6, p. 392; schol. on Aristophanes, *Lys.* 58; Hyg. *Fab.* 26; Ovid, *Met.* 7,402ff. See also THESEUS.

Aegiale Hom. *Il.* 5,412; Apollod. *Bibl.* 1,8,6; 1,9,3; *Epit.* 6,9; Stat. *Silv.* 3,5,48.

Aegimius Paus. 2,28,6; Pind. *Pyth.* 1,62ff. (120ff.). See also HERACLIDS.

Aegina Paus. 2,5,1; Apollod. *Bibl.* 1,9,3; 3,12,6; Pind. *Isth.* 7,15 (21); *Ol.* 9,67ff. (104ff.) with schol. on 104; Hdt. 5,80; Hyg. *Fab.* 52; 115; Ovid, *Met.* 6,113.

Aegisthus Hyg. *Fab.* 87; 88; 117; 252; Sophocles, *Aegisthus(?)*; *Aletes; Thyestes* (lost tragedies, Jebb-Pearson I, pp. 21; 62ff.; 185ff.); Aeschylus, *Ag.* 1583ff.; Hom. *Od.* 3,263ff.; 4,517ff. See also ORESTES; ATREUS.

Aegypius Antoninus Liberalis, *Met.* 5.

Aegyptus Apollod. *Bibl.* 2,1,4; schol. on Hom. *Il.* 1,42; Hyg. *Fab.* 170; Paus. 7,21,6.

Aeneas Hesiod, *Theog.* 1008ff.; Homeric Hymn to Aphrodite, esp. 196ff.; Hom. *Il.* 2,819ff.; 5,166ff.; 297ff.; 431ff.; 512ff.; 541ff.; 12,98; 13,458ff.; 540ff.; 15,332ff.; 16,608ff.; 17,333ff.; 491ff.; 752; 761; 20,75ff.; Dion. Hal. 1,46ff.; 1,72; Livy 1,1ff.; Virgil, *Aen.*; Ovid, *Her.* 7; Arnobius, *Adv. Nat.* 2,71. See W. A. Camps, *An Introduction to Virgil's Aeneid*, pp. 75ff.; N. Horsfall, *JRS* 63 (1973), 68ff.

Aeolia (1) Hom. *Od.* 10,1ff.; Strabo 1,2,32, p. 40; Diod. Sic. 5,9. (2) Apollod. *Bibl.* 1,7,7.

Aeolus (1) Apollod. *Bibl.* 1,7,3; Strabo 8,7,1, p. 383; Conon, *Narr.* 27; Paus. 10,8,4; 10,38,4; 9,20,1; 9,40,5; schol. on Pind. *Pyth.* 4,253; Diod. Sic. 4,67,3; Ovid, *Her.* 11; *Trist.* 2,384; Hyg. *Fab.* 125. (2) Euripides, *Aeolus* (lost tragedy, Nauck *TGF*, edn 2, pp. 365ff.); Hyg. *Fab.* 157; 186; schol. on Dion. Perieg. 461; Diod. Sic. 4,67,3ff.; Strabo 6,1,3, p. 256. (3) Hom. *Od.* 10,1ff.; Hyg. *Fab.* 125; Ovid, *Met.* 14,223ff.; Virgil, *Aen.* 1,52ff.; Apoll. Rhod. *Arg.* 4,761ff. with schol. on 764.

Aepytus (1) Paus. 8,5,5; 8,10,3. (2) Paus. 4,3,7ff.; Apollod. *Bibl.* 2,8,5; Hyg. *Fab.* 137; Eur. fragments 449–59, Nauck *TGF*, edn 2, p. 497f.; Müller *FHG* III,377 (Nicolaus of Damascus). (3) Paus. 8,4,4; 8,4,7; 8,16,2f.; Hom. *Il.* 2,603ff.; Pind. *Ol.* 6,27ff. (46ff.).

Aerope (1) Apollod. *Bibl.* 3,2,1; schol. on Hom. *Il.* 1,7; Sophocles, *Ajax* 1297 with schol.; Apollod. *Epit.* 2,7,10; Euripides, *Orestes* 16f.; *Cretans* (lost tragedy, Nauck *TGF*, edn 2, p. 501ff.); Serv. on Virgil, *Aen.* 1,458; Hyg. *Fab.* 86; Paus. 2,18,2; Ovid, *Trist.* 2,391. (2) Paus. 8,44,7.

Aesacus Apollod. *Bibl.* 3,12,5; Ovid, *Met.* 11,763; Tzetzes on Lyc. *Alex.* 224; Serv. on Virgil, *Aen.* 4,254; 5,128.

Aeson Apollod. *Bibl.* 1,9,11; 1,9,16; 1,9,27; Hom. *Od.* 11,259; Apoll. Rhod. *Arg.* 1,46; 1,233; Ovid, *Her.* 6,105; *Met.* 7,163; 250ff.; Hyg. *Fab.* 3; 13; Diod. Sic. 4,50; Val. Flacc. *Arg.* 1,777ff.

Aethalides Apoll. Rhod. *Arg.* 1,54; Val. Flacc. *Arg.* 1,437; Hyg. *Fab.* 14; Apoll. Rhod. *Arg.* 1,641ff. with schol. on 643f.; Diog. Laert. 8,4; Porphyry, *Vit. Pythag.* 45; Tzetzes, *Chil.* 2,722.

Aether Hesiod, *Theog.* 124ff.; Hyg. *Fab.* pref.; Cic. *De Nat. Deor.* 3,44.

Aethilla Conon, *Narr.* 13; Pomp. Mela, 2,2,33; Tzetzes on Lyc. *Alex.* 921.

Aethra Apollod. *Bibl.* 3,10,7; 3,15,7; Hyg. *Fab.* 14; 37; 92; 243; Plut. *Thes.* 3; 6; Paus. 2,33,1ff.; 5,19,3; Hom. *Il.* 3,144; Tzetzes on Lyc. *Alex.* 494f. See also THESEUS; HELEN; ACAMAS.

Aetna Schol. Theocr. 1,65; Serv. on Virgil, *Aen.* 9,584.

Aetolus Apollod. *Bibl.* 1,7,6f.; Paus. 5,1,2ff.; schol. on Pind. *Ol.* 1,28; Conon, *Narr.* 14.

Agamedes Paus. 8,4,8; 8,10,2; 9,11,1; 9,37,3ff.; 9,39,6; Strabo, 9,3,9, p. 421; schol. on Aristophanes, *Clouds* 508; [Plato], *Axiochus* 367c; Homeric Hymn to Apollo 296; Plutarch, *Consol. ad Ap.* 14,109ab; Cic. *Tusc.* 1,114. See also TROPHONIUS.

Agamemnon Euripides, *IA passim*, esp. 1149fff, 337ff.; Apollod. *Epit.* 2,15; 3,7; Paus. 2,18,2; 2,22,2ff.; Hyg. *Fab.* 88; Hom. *Il.* 9,142ff.; Sophocles, *El.* 157; Euripides, *Or.* 23; Hom. *Il.* 2,299f; Cic. *De Div.* 2,30; Ovid, *Met.* 12,11ff.; Aeschylus *Agamemnon passim*; schol. on Hom. *Il.* 1,59; Apollod. *Epit.* 3,17ff.; Sophocles, *El.* 566ff.; Hyg. *Fab.* 98; Euripides, *IA* 88; schol. on Hom. *Il.* 1,108; Tzetzes on Lyc. *Alex.* 183; Sophocles, *Achaion Syllogos* and *Syndeipnoi* (lost tragedies, Jebb-Pearson I p. 94ff. and II p. 198ff.); Sophocles, *Philoct. passim*; Hom. *Il.* 1,366ff.; *Od.* 8,75ff.; *Il.* 2,1ff.; 9,92ff.; 19,56ff.; *Od.* 11,422; 547ff.; 3,141ff.; Paus. 2,16,6; Hom. *Od.* 3,263ff.; 4,524; 11,421ff.; Pind. *Pyth.* 11,17ff. (25ff.); Aeschylus, *Ag.* 1417; Sophocles, *El.* 530; Apollod. *Epit.* 6,23; Seneca, *Ag.* 875ff.; Serv. on Virgil, *Aen.* 11,268ff.; Hyg. *Fab.* 117. See M. Nilsson, *Homer and Mycenae* (London, 1933); P. Mazon, *Iliad* (edn; Paris, 1949), intro.; L. Marrie, *Arch. f. relig. Wiss.* 23, p. 359ff.; D. L. Page, *History and the Homeric Iliad* (Berkeley, 1959), pp. 127f. and 254f.

Agapenor Hom. *Il.* 2,609ff.; Hyg. *Fab.* 97; Apollod. *Bibl.* 3,10,8; 3,7,6ff.; *Epit.* 6,15; 3,11; Paus. 8,5,2; Lyc. *Alex.* 479; Tzetzes on Lyc. *Alex.* 902.

Agave Hesiod, *Theog.* 975ff; Apollod. *Bibl.* 3,4,2f.; Diod. Sic. 4,2,1; Pind. *Ol.* 2,22ff. (38ff.); Euripides, *Bacchae passim*, esp. 1043ff.; Ovid, *Met.* 3,511ff.; Hyg. *Fab.* 184; 240; 254; Serv. on Virgil, *Aen.* 4,469.

Agdistis Paus. 7,17,9ff.; 1,4,5; Arnobius, *Adv. Nat.* 5,5; 5,12f. See also ATTIS; CYBELE.

Agenor Apollod. *Bibl.* 2,1,4; 3,1; Ovid. *Met.* 2,838; 3,51; 97; 257; Hdt. 4,147; 6,46ff; 2,44; Serv. on Virgil, *Aen.* 3,88; schol. on Euripides, *Phoen.* 6; Paus. 5,25,12; Diod. Sic. 5,59,1ff.; Hyg. *Fab.* 6; 178; 179.

Aglaurus Apollod. *Bibl.* 3,14,2; 3,14,6; Hyg. *Fab.* 166; Ovid, *Met.* 2,560ff; 710ff.

Agron Antoninus Liberalis *Met.* 15.

Aius Locutius Cic. *De Div.* I, 101; II, 69; Aul. Gell. *N.A.* XVI, 17; LIVY V, 32, etc.

Ajax (1) Hom. *Il.* 13,46; 23,483; 754; schol. on *Il.* 13,66; *Od.* 4,499ff.; Paus. 10,31,1ff.; Callim. fragments 35 Pfeiffer; Prop. 4,1,117ff.; Cic. *De Or.* 2,66,265; Hyg. *Fab.* 116; Pliny *NH* 35,60; Tzetzes on Lyc. *Alex.* 1141; *Iliu Persis*, Hom. Oxf. Class. Text V, p. 108; Sophocles *Ajax Locr.* (lost tragedy, Jebb-Pearson I, p. 8ff.). (2) Hom. *Il.* 2,557; 7,183; 11,472; 13,46; 23,842; *Od.* 11,469; Sophocles, *Ajax passim*; Plato *Symp.* 219e; Apollod. *Bibl.* 3,12,7; Plutarch, *Thes.* 29; Pind. *Isth.* 5,48; (61); Hyg. *Fab.* 81; Dictys Cretensis 1,13; Ovid, *Met.* 13,384; 284ff.; Quint. Smyrn. *Posthom.* 4,500ff.; *Aethiopis*, Hom. Oxf. Class. Text V, p. 106; Hyg. *Fab.* 107; Apollod. *Epit.* 5,6f.

Alalcomeneus Paus. 9,33,5; Steph. Byz. s.v.; schol. on Hom. *Il.* 4,8; Plutarch, *De Daed. Plat.* 6 (Loeb *Mor.* XV, p. 293).

Alcathus Paus. 1,41,4; 1,42,4; 1,43,4f.; Ovid, *Met.* 8,14ff.; *Trist.* 1,10,39ff.; Pseudo-Virgil, *Ciris* 104f; Pind. *Isth.* 8,74 (148).

Alcestis Euripides, *Alcestis, passim*; Hyg. *Fab.* 51; Diod. Sic. 4,52,2; Apollod. *Bibl.* 1,9,5; Plato, *Symp.* 179c.

Alcinoe Parthenius, *Erot. Path.* 27.

Alcinous Hom. *Od.* 6. and 7, with schol.; Apoll. Rhod. *Arg.* 4,982ff.; Apollod. *Bibl.* 1,9,26.

Antilochus Apollod. *Bibl.* 1,9,9; Hyg. *Fab.* 252; 81; 97; Hom. *Il.* 569ff.; *Od.* 3,111ff.; Sophocles, *Phil.* 424ff.; Hom. *Od.* 24,72ff.; Paus. 10,30,3ff. See also MEMNON.

Antinoe (1) Paus. 8,8,2. (2) Paus. 8,11,3; Hyg. *Fab.* 24.

Antinous Hom. *Od.* 1,383; 2,113ff.; 4,660ff.; 16–24 *passim*; Zenob. 5,71.

Antiope Apollod. *Bibl.* 3,5,5; Paus. 2,6,2ff.; 9,17,4ff.; 10,36,10; Hyg. *Fab.* 7f;. Euripides, *Antiope* (lost tragedy, Nauck *TGF*, edn 2, pp. 410ff.); Ovid, *Met.* 6,111.

Aphrodite Hom. *Od.* 8,266ff.; *Il.* 2,819ff.; 3,15ff.; 4,10ff.; 5,1ff.; 311ff.; 330; Hesiod, *Theog.* 190ff.; Antoninus Liberalis, *Met.* 34; Apollod. *Bibl.* 1,9,17; 1,4,4; 3,2,2; 3,12,2; 3,14,4; *Epit.* 4,1; Lucian, *Podagra* 87ff.

Apis Apollod. *Bibl.* 1,7,6; 2,1,1ff.; Tzetzes on Lyc. *Alex.* 177; Steph. Byz. s.v. 'Απία; schol. on Hom. *Il.* 1,22; 13,218; schol. on Apoll. Rhod. *Arg.* 4,263; Paus. 2,5,7; Arnobius, *Adv. Nat.* 1,36.

Apollo Callim. *Hymns* 2 and 4; Homeric Hymn to Apollo; Hom. *Il.* 7,452ff.; 21,441ff.; etc.; Pind. *Pyth.* 3,8ff. (14ff.) with schol. on 14; Fr. 33 Snell (78–9 Bowra); Aeschylus, *Suppl.* 260ff.; Euripides, *IT* 1250; *Alc.* 1ff. with schol.; Apoll. Rhod. *Arg.* 2,707ff.; 4,616ff.; Serv. on Virgil, *Aen,* 3,73; 8,300; 6,617; on *Georg.* 1,14; Strabo 9,3,2–12, pp. 417–423; Plutarch, *Quaest. Gr.* 12,293bff.; Hyg. *Fab.* 32; 53; 89; 93; 140; 165; 161; 202; 242; Lucian, *Sacrif.* 4; Ovid, *Met.* 1,416ff.; 452ff.; 3,534ff.; 6,382ff.; 10,106ff.; *Fast.* 6,703ff.; Aelian, *VH* 3,1; Antoninus Liberalis, *Met.* 20; 30; Apollod. *Bibl.* 1,4,1ff.; 1,9,15; 1,3,4; 1,7,6ff.; 2,5,9; 2,5,2; 3,1,2; 3,10,1ff.; 3,12,5; *Epit.* 6,3; 3,8; 3,25; Tzetzes on Lyc. *Alex.* 34. See R. D. Miller, *The Origin and Original Nature of Apollo* (1939); K. Kerenyi, *Apollo,* edn 2, (1953).

Apriate Parthenius, *Erot. Path.* 26 (cf. Müller, *FHG* IV, 335,2a); Tzetzes on Lyc. *Alex.* 467.

Arachne Ovid, *Met.* 6,5ff.; Virgil, *Georg.* 4,246 with Serv. ad loc.

Arcas Apollod. *Bibl.* 3,8,2; 3,9,1; Hyg. *Fab.* 224; *Astron.* 2,4; Ovid, *Met.* 2,496ff.; *Fast.* 2,183ff.; Nonnus, *Dion.* 13,295ff.; Paus. 8,4,1ff.; 8,9,3ff.; 8,36,8ff.; 10,9,5ff.; Pseudo-Eratosth. *Catast.* 1.

Archelaus Hyg. *Fab.* 219; Euripides, *Archelaus* (lost tragedy, Nauck *TGF*, edn 2, pp. 426ff.).

Areion Paus. 8,42,1ff.; 8,25,7ff.; Tzetzes on Lyc. *Alex.* 153; 766; Hom. *Il.* 23,356ff. with schol.; Apollod. *Bibl.* 3,6,8.

Ares Hom. *Il.* 2,512ff.; 5,311ff.; 590ff.; 15,110ff.; 20,32ff.; 21,391ff.;13,298ff.; *Od.* 8,266ff.; Hesiod, *Theog.* 922ff.; *Scutum* 109; 191ff.; 424ff.; Homeric Hymn to Ares; Hdt. 5,7; Euripides, *El.* 1258ff.; *IT* 945ff.; Apoll. Rhod. *Arg.* 2,990; Paus. 1,21,4ff.; 1,28,5; Apollod. *Bibl.* 1,4,4; 1,7,4; 1,7,7; 1,8,2; 2,5,8; 2,5,11; 3,4,1ff.; 3,14,2; 3,14,8; Ovid, *Fast.* 5,229ff.; Serv. on Virgil, *Ecl.* 10,18; Hyg. *Fab.* 159; Quint. Smyrn. *Posthom.* 1,675ff.; 8,340ff.; 14,47ff.

Arethusa Ovid, *Met.* 5,576ff.

Argennus Athenaeus 13,603d; Prop. 3,7,31.

Argonauts General: Pindar, *Pyth.* 4; Apollod. *Bibl.* 1,9,16ff.; Apoll. Rhod. *Arg.*; Val. Flacc. *Arg.*; Orphic *Arg.*; Diod. Sic. 4,40ff.; Tzetzes on Lyc. *Alex.* 175; *Hyg. Fab.* 12; 14–23; Ovid, *Met.* 7,1ff.; *Catalogues:* Pind. *Pyth.* 4,171ff. (303ff.); Apoll. Rhod. *Arg.* 1,23ff. with schol. on 77; Hyg. *Fab.* 14; Diod. Sic. 4,41; Stat. *Theb.* 5,398ff.; Val. Flacc. *Arg.* 1,352ff.; Orphic *Arg.* 118ff. *Voyage:* (a) *Lemnos:* Apollod. *Bibl.* 1,9,17; Apoll. Rhod. *Arg.* 1,607ff. with schol. on 609, 615; schol. on Hom. *Il.* 7,468ff.; Val. Flacc. *Arg.* 2,77ff.; Hyg. *Fab.* 15. See also HYPSIPYLE; THOAS. (b) *Cyzicus:* Apollod. *Bibl.* 1,9,18; Apoll. Rhod. *Arg.* 1,935ff.; Val. Flacc. *Arg.* 2,634; 3,1ff.; *Hyg. Fab.* 16. See also CYZICUS. (c) *Hylas:* Apollod. *Bibl.* 1,9,19; Apoll. Rhod. *Arg.* 1,1207ff. with schol. on 1290; Val. Flacc. 3,521ff.;

Theocr. 13; Antoninus Liberalis *Met.* 26; Prop. 1,20,17ff.; Hyg. *Fab.* 14; Steph. Byz. s.v. 'Αρεταί (d) *Bebryces:* Apollod. *Bibl.* 1,9,20; Apoll. Rhod. *Arg.* 2,1ff.; Theocr. 13,27ff.; Val. Flacc. 4,99ff.; Hyg. *Fab.* 17; Pseudo-Lact. Plac. on Stat. *Theb.* 3,353; Serv. on Virgil, *Aen.* 5,373. (e) *Phineus:* Apollod. *Bibl.* 1,9,21; Apoll. Rhod. *Arg.* 2,176ff. with schol. on 177f., 181; schol. on Hom. *Od.* 12,69; Val. Flacc. *Arg.* 4,422; Hyg. *Fab.* 19; Serv. on Virgil, *Aen.* 3,209; Diod. Sic. 4,43ff. See also PHINEUS. (f) *Cyaneae (Clashing Rocks):* Apollod. *Bibl.* 1,9,22; Apoll; Rhod. *Arg.* 2,317ff.; 549ff.; Val. Flacc. *Arg.* 4,561ff.; Hyg. *Fab.* 19. (g) *Colchis:* Apollod. *Bibl.* 1,9,23f.; Apoll. Rhod. *Arg.* 2,720–4,240 with schol.; Val Flacc. *Arg.* 5,1–8,139; Hyg. *Fab.* 14; 18; 23; Tzetzes on Lyc. *Alex.* 890; Diod. Sic. 4,48; Ovid, *Met.* 7,1ff.; Pind. *Pyth.* 4,211ff. (375ff.). See also JASON; MEDEA. (h) *Return:* Apollod. *Bibl.* 1,9,24ff.; Apoll. Rhod. *Arg.* 4,576ff.; Hyg. *Fab.* 14; 23; Diod. Sic. 4,56. See also TALOS; MEDEA; TRITON. On the legend as a whole, see J. Bacon, *The Voyage of the Argo* (1925).

Argos (1) Apollod. *Bibl.* 2,1,1ff.; Hyg. *Fab.* 123; 145; 155; Paus. 2,16,1; 2,22,6; 2,34,5; 3,4,1. (2) Apollod. *Bibl.* 2,1,3; Hyg. *Fab.* 145; Macrob. *Sat.* 1,19,12; Prop. 1,3,20; Ovid, *Met.* 1,583ff. (3) Hyg. *Fab.* 14; Apoll. Rhod. *Arg.*2,1122ff.; Apollod. *Bibl.* 1,8,9. (4) Schol. on Apoll. Rhod., *Arg.* 1,4; Ptol. Heph. 2; Apoll. Rhod. *Arg.* 1,324ff.

Argyra Paus. 7,23,1ff.

Ariadne Apollod. *Epit.* 1,9; Plutarch, *Thes.* 20; Paus. 1,20,3; 10,29,4; Catull. 64,116ff.; Ovid, *Her.* 10; *Met.* 8,174ff.; Hyg. *Fab.* 43; Hom. *Od.* 11,321ff.; Prop. 1,3,1ff.; Pseudo-Eratosth. *Catast.* 5.

Arion Serv. on Virgil, *Ecl.* 8,55; Ovid, *Fast.* 2,79ff.; Hyg. *Astron.* 2,17; *Fab.* 194; schol. on Aratus *Phaen.* p. 165 Br.; Hdt. 1,24.

Aristaeus Paus. 8,2,4; 10,17,3ff.; 10,30,5; Nonnus, *Dion.* 5,229ff.; 13,300ff.; Apoll. Rhod. *Arg.* 2,500ff. with schol.; Hesiod *Theog.* 977; Ovid, *Pont.* 4,2,9; Virgil, *Georg.* 4,317ff.; Cic. *De Div.* 1,57.

Aristeas Plutarch, *Rom.* 28; Hdt. 6,13ff.

Aristodemus Apollod. *Bibl.* 2,8,2; Paus. 2,18,7; 3,1,5f.; 4,3,4f.; Hdt. 6,52; 4,147: See also PROCLES.

Artemis Hom. *Il.* 21,470ff.; Hesiod, *Theog.* 918; Homeric Hymn to Artemis; Apollod. *Bibl.* 1,4,1; 1,6,2; 1,7,5; 1,4,3; 3,4,3; 3,8,2; Hom. *Od.* 5,121ff.; Paus. 8,27,17; etc.; Euripides, *IT*; *LA*; Callim. *Hymn* 3.

Ascalabus Antoninus Liberalis, *Met.* 24; Ovid, *Met.* 5,446ff.

Ascalaphus (1) Apollod. *Bibl.* 1,5,3; 2,5,12; Ovid, *Met.* 5,539. (2) Paus. 9,37,7.

Ascanius Virgil, *Aen. passim*, esp. 7,483ff.; Livy 1,1ff.; Serv. on Virgil, *Aen. passim*; Dion. Hal. 1,53ff.; Conon, *Narr.* 41; Hyg. *Fab.* 254; 273; Arnobius, *Adv. Nat.* 2,71.

Asclepius Homeric Hymn to Asclepius; Pind. *Pyth.* 3, with schol. on 14; 96; Hesiod Fragments 50; 51; 53; 58; 60 M–W; Apollod. *Bibl.* 3,10,3ff.; Diod. Sic. 4,71; 5,74; Ovid, *Met.* 2,535ff.; Serv. on Virgil, *Aen.* 6,617; 7,761; 11,259; Hyg. *Fab.* 202; *Astron.* 2,40; Paus. 2,26,3ff.; 4,3,2; 4,31,12; Hymn to Asclepius, Epidaurian inscription in Collitz/Bechtel, *Samml. der gr. dial. Inschr.* III, p. 162, no.3342; Cic. *De Nat. Deor.* 3,22,57; Apoll. Rhod. *Arg.* 4,526ff.; Pseudo-Lact. Plac. on Stat. *Theb.* 3,506; Antoninus Liberalis *Met.* 20; schol. on Euripides, *Alc.* 1; Ovid, *Fast.* 5,735ff.; Arnobius, *Adv. Nat.* 1,30; 36; 41; 4,15.

Asia Hesiod, *Theog.* 539; Apollod. *Bibl.* 1,2,2f.

Asopus Apollod. *Bibl.* 3,12,6; Diod. Sic. 4,72; schol. on Pind. *Ol.* 6,144; *Isth.* 7,39; Ovid, *Am.* 3,6,3; schol. on Hom. *Il.* 6,153; Euripides, *IA* 697; Antoninus Liberalis, *Met.* 38; Hyg. *Fab.* 52; Paus. 9,3,3.

Aspalis Antoninus Liberalis, *Met.* 13.

Assaon Parthenius, *Erot. Path.* 33; schol. on Hom. *Il.* 24,613; 617; schol. on Euripides, *Phoen.* 159.

Asteria (1) Hesiod, *Theog.* 414ff.; Apollod. *Bibl.* 1,2,2; 1,2,4; Hyg. *Fab.* 53; Serv. on Virgil, *Aen.* 3,73; Ovid, *Met.* 6,108. See also LETO; APOLLO. (2) See CRISUS.

Asterion (1) Apollod. *Bibl.* 3,1,2; Diod. Sic. 4,60. (2) Scholia on Hom. *Il.* 12,292.

Astraea Hyg. *Astron.* 2,25; Ovid, *Met.* 1,149; Juv. 6,19ff.

Astyanax Hom. *Il.* 6,400ff.; 24,734ff.; Euripides, *Tro.* passim; Paus. 10,25,9; Euripides, *Androm.* 10; Ovid, *Met.* 13,415; Hyg. *Fab.* 109; schol. on Hom. *Il.* 24,735.

Astymedusa Scholia on Hom. *Il.* 4,376.

Atalanta Apollod. *Bibl.* 1,8,2; 3,9,2; Callim. *Hymn* 3,215ff.; Diod. Sic. 4,34; 65; schol. on Euripides, *Phoen.* 151; Euripides, *Meleager* (lost tragedy, Nauck *TGF*, edn 2, p. 525); Xen. *Cyneg.* 1,7; Apoll. Rhod. *Arg.* 1,769ff.; Prop. 1,1,9ff.; Ovid, *Met.* 8,316ff.; 10,560ff.; *Ars Am.* 2,185ff.; *Am.* 3,2,29ff.; Serv. on Virgil, *Aen.* 3,113; Paus. 3,24,2; 5,19,2; 8,35,10; 8,45,2; 8,45,6; Hyg. *Fab.* 70; 99; 173f.; 185; 244; 270; Aelian, *VH* 13,1; Palaeph. *Incred.* 13. See also MELEAGER.

Ate Hom. *Il.* 9,503ff., 10,491, 19,85ff.; Lyc. *Alex.* 29 with Tzetzes *ad loc.*; Apollod. *Bibl.* 13,12,3; Steph. Byz. s.v. Ἴλιον.

Athamas Apollod. *Bibl.* 1,9,1f.; 3,4,3; Hyg. *Fab.* 1–4, *Astron.* 2,20; Tzetzes on Lyc. *Alex.* 22; 229; Ovid, *Met.* 4,481ff.; 9,195ff.; Aeschylus, *Athamas* (lost tragedy, Nauck *TGF*, edn 2, pp. 3f.); Euripides, *Ino* and *Phrixus* (lost tragedies, Nauck *TGF*, edn 2, pp. 482ff, and 626ff.); Sophocles, *Athamas* (lost tragedy, Jebb-Pearson, I p. 1); Paus. 1,24,2; 1,44,7; 6,21,11; 7,3,6; 9,23,6 with schol.; 9,24,1; 9,34,5–8; Strabo 9,5,8, p. 433; schol. on Hom. *Il.* 7,86 and Eustath.; schol. on Aristophanes, *Clouds* 257; schol. on Apoll. Rhod. *Arg.* 3,265; 1,763; Serv. on Virgil, *Georg.* 1,219; Ovid, *Fast.* 2,628ff.; 3,853ff.; Diod. Sic. 4,47.

Athena Hesiod, *Theog.* 886ff.; Pind. *Ol.* 7,35ff. (65ff.); Euripides, *Ion* 454ff.; Apollod. *Bibl.* 1,3,6ff.; 1,6,1ff.; 2,4,3; 2,4,11; 3,14,1; 3,14,6; 3,12,3; Virgil *Aen.* 3,578ff.; Hdt. 8,55; Ovid, *Met.* 6,70ff.; Hyg. *Fab.* 164; 166; Serv. on Virgil *Geo.* 1,12; 3,113; schol. on Hom. *Il.* 2,547; Hyg. *Astron.* 2,13; Paus. 1,18,2; Ovid, *Met.* 2,552ff.; Dion. Hal. 1,68ff.; 2,66,6; Conon, *Narr.* 34.

Atlantis Plato, *Timaeus* 21a ff.; *Critias* 108e ff.; Proclus, *Comm. in Tim.* 21a ff.; Strabo 2,3,6, p. 102; Hdt. 4,184; Diod. Sic. 3,54ff.

Atlas Hesiod, *Theog.* 507ff.; Hom. *Od.* 1,52ff.; 7,245; Aeschylus, *PV* 348, 425f.; Pind. *Pyth.* 4,289ff. (516ff.); Euripides, *Ion* 1ff.; *HF* 402; schol. on Apoll. Rhod. *Arg.* 3,106; 1,444; Ovid, *Met.* 2,296; 6,174; Apollod. *Bibl.* 1,2,3; 2,5,11; Hyg. *Fab.* 150; Hdt. 4,185; Serv. on Virgil, *Aen* 8,134. See also HERACLES.

Atreus Hom. *Il.* 2,105ff. with schol. on 107, 106; Pind. *Ol.* 1,89 (144) with schol. on 144; Thuc. 1,9; Paus. 2,16,6; 2,18,1; 3,1,5; 3,24,11; 5,3,6; 9,40,11; 10,26,3; Hyg. *Fab.* 85; 88; Apollod. *Bibl.* 2,4,6; *Epit.* 2,10ff.; Euripides, *El.* 726ff.; 699ff.; schol. on Euripides, *Or.* 41; 811; 995; 998; Dio Chrys. *Or.* 66; Seneca, *Thyest.* 222ff.; Tzetzes, *Chil.* 1,425ff.; Ovid, *Trist.* 2,391ff.; *Ars Am.* 1,327ff.; Martial 3,45,1ff.; Aeschylus *Ag.* 1583ff.; Paus. 2,16,6; 2,18,1; Serv. on Virgil, *Aen.* 1,568; 11,262; Euripides, *Thyestes* (lost tragedy, Nauck *TGF*, edn 2, pp. 480ff.); Sophocles, *Atreus* and *Thyestes* (lost tragedies, Jebb-Pearson, I p. 91 and I p. 185).

Attis Paus. 7,17,10; Arnobius *Adv. Nat.* 5,5ff.; Ovid, *Fast.* 4,223ff.; Diod. Sic. 3,58ff.; Paus. 7,17,9ff.; Serv. on Virgil, *Aen.* 7,761; Lucian, *Sacrif.* 7.

Aucnus Silius Italicus 5,7; 6,109; Virgil, *Aen.* 10,198ff. with Serv. ad loc.; Serv. on Virgil, *Ecl.* 9,60.

Auge Oxyrhynchus Papyrus 11,1329; Apollod. *Bibl.* 2,7,4ff.; 3,9,1; Diod. Sic. 4,33; Strabo 13,1,69, p. 615; Paus. 8,4,8ff.; 8,47,2; 8,48,7; 10,28,8; Hyg. *Fab.* 99; 100; 101; 162; 252; Tzetzes on Lyc. *Alex.* 206; Sophocles, *Aleades, Mysians* and *Telephus* (lost tragedies, Jebb-Pearson, I, p. 46; II, p. 70; II, p. 220); Euripides, *Auge, Telephus* and *Mysians* (lost tragedies, Nauck *TGF*, edn 2, pp. 436ff.; 579ff. and 531); Alcidamas, *Odysseus* 14–16 (Radermacher, *Artium Scriptores* p. 144); Anth. Pal. 3,2. See also TELEPHUS.

Augias Pind. *Ol.* 10,26ff (32ff.) with schol. on 42b; Hom. *Il.* 11,701; schol. on Hom. *Il.* 2,620ff.; 11,700; Apoll. Rhod. *Arg.* 1,172 with schol.; 3,362; Apollod. *Bibl.* 1,9,16; 2,5,5; Hyg. *Fab.* 14; 30; 157; Paus. 5,1,9; 5,2,1ff.; 5,3,1; Diod. Sic. 4,13,3; 4,33,1; Theocr. 25,7; Tzetzes, *Chil.* 2,278.

Aura Nonnus, *Dion.* 48,242ff.; Etymol. Magn. s.v. Δίνδυμον.

Auson Eustath. on Hom. *Od.* p. 1379,10; Serv. on Virgil, *Aen.* 8,328; 3,171; schol. on Apoll. Rhod. *Arg.* 4,553; Steph. Byz. s.v. Λιπάρα; Tzetzes on Lyc. *Alex.* 44.

Autoleon Conon, *Narr.* 18; Paus. 3,19,11ff.

Autolycus Hom. *Il.* 10,267 with schol.; Apollod. *Bibl.* 1,9,16; 2,4,9; 2,6,2; Hyg. *Fab.* 200; 201; 243; Serv. on Virgil, *Aen.* 2,79; Hom. *Od.* 19,394ff.; 21,220; 24,232; Euripides, *Autolycus* (lost satyr-play, Nauck *TGF*, edn 2, pp. 440ff.; Ovid, *Met.* 8,738. See also ODYSSEUS.

Automedon Hom. *Il.* 9,209; 16,145ff.; 19,395ff.; 23,563ff.; 24,473; 574; 625; Ovid, *Ars Am.* 2,738; Hyg. *Fab.* 97; Virgil, *Aen.* 2,476.

Auxesia Paus. 2,30,4; 2,32,2; Hdt. 5,82ff.

B

Babys Plutarch, *De Proverbiis Alexandrinorum* 2 (ed. O. Crusius, 1887).

Baios Strabo 1,2,18, p. 25; 5,4,6, p. 245; Serv. on Virgil, *Aen.* 3,441; 6,107.

Balios (1) Hom. *Il.* 16,148ff.; schol. on *Il.* 19,400ff.; Apollod. *Bibl.* 3,4,4; 3,13,5; Diod. Sic. 6,3. (2) Apollod. *Bibl.* 3,4,4.

Basileia Diod. Sic. 3,57.

Baton Paus. 3,23,2; 5,17,8; 10,10,3; Apollod. *Bibl.* 3,6,8; Steph. Byz. s.v. Ἀρτυαία. See also AMPHIARAUS.

Battus (1) Antoninus Liberalis, *Met.* 23; Ovid, *Met.* 2,676ff. (2) Paus. 3,14,3; 10,15,6f.; Suda s.v.; Hdt. 4,150ff.; Pind. *Pyth.* 5,27ff. (37ff.) with schol. on 35; *Pyth.* 4,1ff.; Justin 13,7; schol. on Callim. *Hymn* 2,65.

Baubo Clement of Alexandria, *Protrep.* 2,20; Arnobius *Adv. Nat.* 5,25; Paus. 1,14,2; Suda s.v. Δυσαύλης.

Baucis Ovid, *Met.* 8,616ff.; Lact. *Narr.* 8,7–9.

Bellerophon Hom. *Il.* 6,155ff. with schol. on 155 and 191; Hesiod Fragments 43a,82 M–W; *Theog.* 319ff.; Pind. *Ol.* 13,60ff. (87ff.); *Isth.* 7,44ff. (63ff.). Apollod. *Bibl.* 1,9,3; 3,3,1ff.; Tzetzes on Lyc. *Alex.* 17; *Chil.* 7,81off.; Euripides *Stheneboea* (lost tragedy, Nauck *TGF*, edn 2, pp. 567ff.); Sophocles *Iobates* (lost tragedy, Jebb-Pearson, I p. 214); Hyg. *Fab.* 56; 157; 243; 273; Paus. 2,2,3ff.; 2,4,1ff.; 2,27,2; 3,18,13; Strabo 8,6,21, p. 379; Diod. Sic. 6,7; schol. on Stat. *Theb.* 4,589; Palaeph. *Incred.* 29; App. *Narr.* 82, p. 388 Westermann; Horace, *Odes* 4,11,26ff. See also CHIMAERA.

Bellona Aulus Gellius, *NA* 13,23ff.; August. *CD* 6,10; Plautus, *Amphit.* 42; Stat. *Theb.* 5,155.

Belus Aeschylus, *Suppl.* 312ff.; Apollod. *Bibl.* 2,1,4; schol. on Apoll. Rhod. *Arg.* 3,1186; schol. on Euripides *Phoen.* 5; 186; 291; 678; Tzetzes, *Chil.* 7,349ff.; Hdt. 7,61; Hyg. *Fab.* 31; 106;

151; Virgil, *Aen.* 1,620ff. with Serv. ad loc.; Ovid, *Met.* 4,216; Paus. 4,23,10; 7,21,13.

Bia Hesiod, *Theog.* 283ff.; Apollod. *Bibl.* 1,2,4; Aeschylus, *PV* 1ff.

Bianna Steph. Byz. s.v. Βιέννος.

Bianor Servius on Virgil, *Ecl.* 9,60.

Bias Hom. *Od.* 15,242ff.; schol. on Hom. *Od.* 11,287; Eustath. on Hom. p. 1685,8ff.; schol. on Pind. *Nem.* 9,30; schol. on Aeschylus, *Suppl.* 569; schol. on Euripides, *Phoen.* 173; Hdt. 9,34; schol. on Theocr. 3,45; schol. on Apoll. Rhod. *Arg.* 1,18; Prop. 2,3,51ff.; Paus. 2,18,4; 2,21,2; 4,34,4; 4,36,3; Apollod. *Bibl.* 1,9,10ff.; 2,2,2. See also MELAMPUS.

Bona Dea Macrob. *Sat.* 1,12,21ff.; Serv. on Virgil, *Aen.* 8,314; Prop. 4,9; Ovid, *Fast.* 5,148ff.; Lact. *Inst. Div.* 1,22; Arnobius, *Adv. Nat.* 5,18.

Boreades Apoll. Rhod. *Arg.* 1,211ff.; 2,273ff.; 1,1298ff.; schol. on Apoll. Rhod. 2,178; schol. on Hom. *Od.* 14,533; 12,69; Hyg. *Fab.* 14,19; 273; Apollod. *Bibl.* 3,15,2ff.; 1,9,21; Ovid, *Met.* 6,711ff.; Serv. on Virgil, *Aen.* 3,209; schol. on Pind. *Pyth.* 4,181.

Boreas Hesiod, *Theog.* 378ff.; 869ff.; Hdt. 7,189; Ovid, *Met.* 6,682ff.; *Trist.* 3,10,45; Hom. *Il.* 20,221ff.; Quint. Smyrn. *Posthom.* 8,241ff.; Nonnus, *Dion.* 37,155ff.; Plato, *Phdr.* 229b ff.; Paus. 5,19,1; Apollod. *Bibl.* 3,15,1f.; schol. on Hom. *Od.* 14,533. See K. Neuser, *Anemoi* (1982).

Bormos Athenaeus 14,3 p. 620a; schol. on Apoll. Rhod. *Arg.* 1,1126; 2,780.

Botres Antoninus Liberalis, *Met.* 18.

Boucolos Plutarch, *Quaest. Gr.* 40, 300d ff.

Boulis Antoninus Liberalis, *Met.* 5.

Bounos Paus. 2,3,10; Theopompus fragment 340 (Müller, *FHG* I); Tzetzes on Lyc. *Alex.* 174.

Bouphagus Paus. 8,14,9; 8,27,17.

Branchus Conon, *Narr.* 33; 44; schol. on Paus. 5,8,8; Strabo 9,3,9, p. 421; 14,1,5, p. 634.

Brangas Conon, *Narr.* 4.

Briseis Hom. *Il.* 1,318ff.; 2,688ff.; 19,291ff.; Quint. Smyrn. *Posthom.* 3,551ff.; schol. on Hom. *Il.* 1,392; Eustath. on Hom. p. 77,30; Tzetzes on Lyc. *Alex.* 365; *Antehom.* 350ff.; Paus. 5,24,11; 10,25,4; Ovid, *Her.* 3.

Britomartis Solinus 11,8; Paus. 2,30,3; 3,14,2; 8,2,4; 9,40,3; Diod. Sic. 5,76; Callim. *Hymn* 3,189ff.; Pseudo-Virgil, *Ciris* 301; Antoninus Liberalis, *Met.* 40; schol. on Aristophanes, *Frogs* 1356; schol. on Euripides, *Hipp.* 146.

Bryte Mythog. Vat. 2,26 (Bode, *Script. Rer. Myth.*).

Busiris Diod. Sic. 1,17,45; 4,18,1; 4,27,3; Apollod. *Bibl.* 2,5,11; Hdt. 2,45; Gellius *NA* 2,6; Macrob. *Sat.* 6,7; Virgil, *Georg.* 3,5 with Serv. ad loc.; Hyg. *Fab.* 31,56; 157; Ovid, *Met.* 9,183; Etymol. Magn. s.v.; Euripides *Busiris* (lost satyr-play Nauck *TGF*, edn 2, pp. 452f.). See A. B. Lloyd, *Herodotus II* (1976) on Hdt. 2,45.

Butes (1) Diod. Sic. 5,20,2ff. (2) Apollod. *Bibl.* 3,14,8.

Buzyges Servius on Virgil, *Georg.* 1,19; Pliny, *NH* 7,57; schol. on Hom. *Il.* 18,483; Hesychius s.v.

Byblis Nonnus, *Dion.* 13,518ff.; Parthen. *Erot. Path.* 11; Antoninus Liberalis, *Met.* 9; Ovid, *Met.* 9,451ff.; Conon, *Narr.* 2; schol. on Theocr. 7,115; Paus. 8,5,10; Steph. Byz. s.v. Καῦνος.

Byzas Diod. Sic. 4,49,1; Steph. Byz. s.v. Βυζάντιον and γυναικῶν λιμήν; Tzetzes, *Chil.* 2,40.

C

Caanthus Paus. 9,10,5f.

Cabarnus Steph. Byz. s.v. Κάβαρνοι.

Cabiri Strabo 10,3,19f.; schol. on Apoll. Rhod. *Arg.* 1,917; Aelius Aristides, *Or.* 53,5, II p. 469 Keil; Philo Bybl. fragment 2,27, Müller *FHG* III p. 569; Nonnus, *Dion.* 14,17ff.; Hdt. 3,37; Varro, *LL* 5,58; Serv. on Virgil, *Aen.* 3,12; 264; 8,679.

Cabirides Strabo 10,3,21.

Cabiro Strabo 10,3,21; Steph. Byz. s.v. Καβειρία.

Caca Lact. *Inst. Div.* 1,20,36; Serv. on Virgil, *Aen.* 8,190; Mythogr. Vat. 2,153; 3,13 (Bode, *Script. Rer. Myth.*).

Cacus Virgil, *Aen.* 8,190ff. with Serv. ad loc.; Livy 1,7,3ff.; Dion. Hal. 1,39ff.; Ovid, *Fast.* 1,543ff.; 5,673ff.; 6,79ff.; Prop. 4,9,1ff.; Tzetzes, *Hist.* 5,21; Serv. on *Aen.* 8,203, citing Valerius Flaccus; Solinus 1,8; Diod. Sic. 4,21.

Cadmus Hesiod, *Theog.* 935ff.; Hom. *Od.* 5,333ff.; schol. on Hom. *Il.* 2,494; Hdt. 4,147; Diod. Sic. 4,2,1ff.; 5,47ff.; 5,59,2ff.; Theognis 15ff.; Hyg. *Fab.* 6; 178f.; Pind. *Pyth.* 3,86ff. (152ff.); *Ol.* 2,22ff. (38ff.); Apoll. Rhod. *Arg.* 4,516ff.; schol. on Apoll. Rhod. *Arg.* 3,1186; Euripides, *Phoen.* 930ff.; 822ff.; *Bacch.* 1330ff.; schol. on Euripides, *Phoen.* 638; schol. on Aeschylus, *Sept.* 469; 486; Apollod. *Bibl.* 3,1,1; 3,4,1; 3,5,2; 3,5,4ff.; Ovid, *Met.* 3,6ff.; 4,563ff.; Paus. 3,1,8; 3,15,8; 3,24,3; 4,7,8; 7,2,5; 9,5,1ff.; 9,10,1; 9,12,1ff.; 9,16,3ff.; 9,26,3f.; 10,17,4; 10,35,5; Strabo 1,2,39, p. 46; 7,7,8, p. 326; Athenaeus 11,426b; Tzetzes, *Chil.* 4,393ff.; Nonnus, *Dion.* 1,140ff.; 350ff.; etc.; Steph. Byz. s.v. Βουθόη.

Caeculus Serv. on Virgil, *Aen.* 7,678; Verona schol. on Virgil, *Aen.* 7,681 (Thilo/Hagen III.2,438); Solinus 2,9; Mythogr. Vat. 1,84 (Bode, *Script. Rer. Myth.*).

Caeira Tzetzes on Lyc. *Alex.* 1379.

Caelus Cic. *De Nat. Deor.* 3,17,44; 3,24,62ff.; Serv. on Virgil, *Aen.* 5,801. See also URANUS.

Caeneus Apollod. *Epit.* 1,22; Apoll. Rhod. *Arg.* 1,57ff. with schol.; schol. on Hom. *Il.* 1,262; Antoninus Liberalis, *Met.* 17; Virgil, *Aen.* 6,448ff. with Serv. ad loc.; Ovid, *Met.* 12,459ff.; Hyg. *Fab.* 14; 242; Palaeph. *Incred.* 11; Oxyrhynchus Papyrus 13,1611,38ff.

Caieta Virgil, *Aen.* 7,1ff. with Serv. ad loc.; Ovid, *Met.* 14,441ff.; Strabo 5,3,6, p. 233; Solinus 2,13; Anon. *De Orig. Gent. Rom.* 10; Dion. Hal. 1,53,3; Diod. Sic. 4,56.

Calamus Serv. on Virgil, *Ecl.* 5,48; Nonnus, *Dion.* 11,370ff.

Calchas Hom. *Il.* 1,69; 92; 2,300ff.; schol. on Hom. *Il.* 2,135; schol. on Apoll. Rhod. *Arg.* 1,139; schol. on Hom. *Od.* 13,159; Paus. 1,43,1; Hyg. *Fab.* 97; 128; 190; Apollod. *Bibl.* 3,13,18; *Epit.* 3,15; 3,21ff.; 5,8ff.; 5,2ff.; Paus. 1,43,1; 7,3,7; 9,19,6; Ovid, *Met.* 12,11ff.; Strabo 14,1,27, p. 642ff.; Serv. on Virgil, *Ecl.* 6,72; *Aen.* 2,166; 3,322; Conon, *Narr.* 34; 6; Quint. Smyrn. *Posthom.* 6,61; 12,3ff.; Virgil *Aen.* 2,185; Tzetzes, *Posthom.* 645; on Lyc. *Alex.* 427; 978ff.; 1047ff.

Calchus Parthenius, *Erot. Path.* 12.

Callidice Apollod. *Epit.* 7,34; Telegoneia, in Homer Oxf. Class. Text V, p. 109.

Calliope Hyg. *Astron.* 2,7; schol. on Hom. *Il.* 10,435; Apollod. *Bibl.* 1,3,4.

Callipolis Paus. 1,47,2; 1,43,5.

Callirhoe (1) Hesiod, *Theog.* 288ff.; Homeric Hymn to Demeter 419; Tzetzes on Lyc. *Alex.* 651; 874; Hyg. *Fab.* 111; Apollod. *Bibl.* 2,5,10; Serv. on Virgil, *Aen.* 4,250; Dion. Hal. 1,27. (2) See ALCMEON; ACARNAN. Apollod. *Bibl.* 3,7,5; Paus. 8,24,9. (3) Apollod. *Bibl.* 3,12,2; schol. on Hom. *Il.* 20,232;

Cephalus Hesiod, *Theog.* 986ff.; Ovid, *Met.* 766iff.; *Her.* 4,93ff.; Hyg. *Fab.* 48; 160; 189; 241; 270; Apollod. *Bibl.* 1,9,4; 2,4,7; 3,14,3; 3,15,1; Suda s.v. Τευμησία; Hom. *Od.* 11,321ff. with Eustath. ad loc.; Pseudo-Eratosth. *Catast.* 32; Hyg. *Astron.* 2,35; Antoninus Liberalis, *Met.* 41; Serv. on Virgil, *Aen.* 6,445; Strabo 10,2,14, p. 456; Paus. 1,37,6; Aristotle, Fragment 504 Rose; schol. on Hom. *Od.* 24,270.

Cepheus (1) Apoll. Rhod. *Arg.* 1,161ff.; Paus. 8,4,8; 8,5,1; 8,8,4; 8,9,5; 8,23,3; 8,47,5; Apollod. *Bibl.* 2,7,3; Diod. Sic. 4,33. (2) Strabo 1,2,35, p. 42; Herodian 7,61; Euripides cited by Pseudo-Eratosth. *Catast.* 15; 36; Hyg. *Astron.* 2,9; Apollod. *Bibl.* 2,1,4; Conon, *Narr.* 40; Tac. *Hist.* 5,2; Pliny, *NH* 6,183; Ovid, *Met.* 5,12ff.; Nonnus, *Dion.* 2,682ff.

Cerambus Ovid, *Met.* 7,533; Antoninus Liberalis, *Met.* 22. See also TERAMBUS.

Ceramus Paus. 1,3,1; Suda s.v. Κέρανος.

Cerberus Hom. *Il.* 8,366ff.; *Od.* 623ff.; Apollod. *Bibl.* 2,5,12; Paus. 3,18,13ff.; 3,25,5ff.; Hesiod, *Theog.* 311; 769ff.; schol. on Pind. *Pyth.* 1,31; Horace, *Odes* 2,13,34; Ovid, *Met.* 7,408ff.; Hyg. *Fab.* 30; 151; 251; Virgil, *Aen.* 6,417 WITH SERV. AD LOC.

Cercaphus Diod. Sic. 5,56ff.; Pind. *Ol.* 7,71ff. (131f.); Strabo 14,2,8, p. 654; Steph. Byz. s.v. Λίνδος.

Cercopes Diod. Sic. 4,31,7; Apollod. *Bibl.* 2,6,3; Nonnus, *Fab.* in Westermann, *Mythogr.* p. 375; Tzetzes, *Chil.* 2,434; on Lyc. *Alex.* 91; Eustath. on Hom. p. 1864,32; Ovid, *Met.* 14,88ff. See Pauly-Wissowa, *RE* III. 1a, 98f., s.v. Σίλλος.

Cercyon (1) Apollod. *Epit.* 1,3; Bacchyl. 17,26; Diod. Sic. 4,59,5; Plutarch, *Thes.* 11; Paus. 1,39,3; schol. on Lucian, *Jup. Trag.* 21 (p. 65 Rabe); Ovid, *Met.* 7,439; Hyg. *Fab.* 38. (2) Paus. 8,5,4; 8,45,7; 8,53,6.

Cercyra Paus. 2,5,2; 5,22,4ff.; schol. on Pind. *Ol.* 6,144; Apoll. Rhod. *Arg.* 4,568; Diod. Sic. 4,72.

Cerebia Tzetzes on Lyc. *Alex.* 838.

Ceres Dion. of Hal. 6,17; 94; Tac. *Ann.* 2,49; Cic. *Pro Balb.* 55.

Ceroessa Steph. Byz. s.v. Βυζάντιον; Procop. *De Aed.* 1,5; Hesychius. fragment 4,9f. (Müller *FHG* IV, p. 148ff.).

Ceryx Paus. 1,38,3; Suda s.v. Κήρυκες.

Cetes Diod. Sic. 1,62; see also PROTEUS.

Ceto Hesiod. *Theog.* 238; 270ff.; 333; Apollod. *Bibl.* 1,2,6; 2,4,2; schol. on Apoll. Rhod. *Arg.* 4,1399.

Ceyx (1) Apollod. *Bibl.* 2,7,6; 2,8,1; Hesiod, *Scutum* 354; 472ff.; schol. on Sophocles, *Trach.* 39; Diod. Sic. 4,36; 4,57; Antoninus Liberalis, *Met.* 26; Paus. 1,32,6. (2) See ALCYONE.

Chalciope (1) Apollod. *Bibl.* 2,7,8; Hom. *Il.* 2,676ff. with schol.; Plutarch, *Quaest. Gr.* 58,304c; Hyg. *Fab.* 254; 97. (2) Apollod. *Bibl.* 1,9,1; Hyg. *Fab.* 3; 14; Apoll. Rhod. *Arg.* 2,1140ff. with schol.; Tzetzes on Lyc. *Alex.* 22. (3) Apollod. *Bibl.* 3,15,6; Athenaeus 13,556f; Tzetzes on Lyc. *Alex.* 454.

Chalcodon (1) Apollod. *Bibl.* 3,10,18; Hom. *Il.* 2,541 with schol. on 536; 4,464; Eustath. on Hom. p. 281,45; Tzetzes on Lyc. *Alex.* 1034; Paus. 8,15,6f.; 9,17,3; 9,19,3. (2) Paus. 8,15,6. (3) Paus. 6,21,7. (4) Apollod. *Bibl.* 2,7,1; Plutarch, *Quaest. Gr.* 58,304c.

Chalcon (1) Eustath. on Hom. p. 1697,54. (2) See ABAS (1).

Chaon Serv. on Virgil, *Aen.* 3,297; 334; 335.

Chaos Hesiod, *Theog.* 116ff.; Plato, *Symp.* 178b; Virgil, *Georg.* 4,347; Ovid, *Met.* 1,7; Hyg. *Fab.* pref.

Chariclo (1) Pind. *Pyth.* 4,102f. (181f.) with schol. on 181; Apoll. Rhod. *Arg.* 1,554 with schol.; 4,813; Ovid, *Met.* 2,636. (2) Plutarch, *Thes.* 10. (3) Apollod. *Bibl.* 3,6,7; Callim. *Hymn* 5,57ff.

Charila Plutarch, *Quaest. Gr.* 12,293b.

Charites Hom. *Il.* 5,338; 18,382; 14,267; *Od.* 8,362ff.; 18,192ff.; Hesiod, *Theog.* 64; 907ff.; Hyg. *Fab.* pref.; Paus. 9,35,5; Apollod. *Bibl.* 1,3,1; Pind. *Ol.* 14,3ff.; Theocr. 16,108;

Sappho fragment 65 Bergk (53 Lobel-Page); Apoll. Rhod. *Arg.* 4,424ff.; Seneca, *De Ben.* 1,3.

Charon Virgil, *Aen.* 6,299 with Serv. ad loc.; ibid 326; Eustath. on Hom. p. 16,34; Diod. Sic. 1,92; 96; Paus. 10,28,2; Aristophanes, *Frogs* 180ff.; *Lys.* 606; *Plut.* 278.

Charops Diod. Sic. 3,65.

Charybdis Hom. *Od.* 12,73ff.; 104ff.; 234ff.; 430ff.; Apoll. Rhod. *Arg.* 4,789; 825 with schol.; 923; Apollod. *Bibl.* 1,9,25; *Epit.* 7,23ff.; Hyg. *Fab.* 125; 199; Serv. on Virgil, *Aen.* 3,420; Tzetzes on Lyc. *Alex.* 45; 743; 818; Ovid, *Met.* 6,63; Virgil, *Aen.* 3,418ff.; 555ff.; Strabo 6,2,3, p. 268.

Chelidon Antoninus Liberalis, *Met.* 11.

Chelone Serv. on Virgil, *Aen.* 1,505.

Chimaera (1) Hom. *Il.* 6,179ff. with schol.; 16,327ff.; Hesiod, *Theog.* 319ff.; Apollod. *Bibl.* 1,9,3; 2,3,1; Ovid, *Met.* 9,647; Tzetzes on Lyc. *Alex.* 17; Hyg. *Fab.* 57. (2) Serv. on Virgil, *Ecl.* 8,63; *App. Narr.* (Westermann, *Mythogr.*) 82, p. 388.

Chimaereus Tzetzes on Lyc. *Alex.* 132; 136; 219; Eustath. on Hom. p. 521,30.

Chione (1) Apollod. *Bibl.* 3,15,2; Hyg. *Fab.* 157; Hom. *Od.* 14,475; Xen. *Anab.* 5,5,3ff.; Paus. 1,38,2. (2) Serv. on Virgil, *Aen.* 4,250. (3) Hyg. *Fab.* 200; Ovid, *Met.* 11,291ff. (4) Schol. on Theocr. 1,21.

Chiron Hom. *Il.* 11,832; Ovid, *Fast.* 5,384; 413; Pind. *Pyth.* 3,1ff.; 9,29ff. (48ff.); Apollod. *Bibl.* 1,2,4; 3,13,5; Pliny, *NH* 7,196; Xen. *Cyneg.* 1,1ff.; schol. on Apoll. Rhod. *Arg.* 1,554; 558; Apoll. Rhod. *Arg.* 1,1231; Pseudo-Eratosth. *Catast.* 40.

Choricus Serv. on Virgil, *Aen.* 8,138.

Chrysanthis Paus. 1,14,2.

Chrysaor Hesiod, *Theog.* 278ff.; 979; Hyg. *Fab.* 151; Apollod. *Bibl.* 2,4,2; 2,5,10; Tzetzes on Lyc. *Alex.* 17; Diod. Sic. 4,17ff.; Ovid, *Met.* 4,782ff.; 6,119ff.

Chryseis Hom. *Il.* 1,9ff.; 366ff.; 451ff.; schol. on *Il.* 18; 392; Hyg. *Fab.* 121; Tzetzes on Lyc. *Alex.* 183; 298; *Antehom.* 349ff.

Chryses (1) See CHRYSEIS. (2) Hyg. *Fab.* 121; Sophocles, *Chryses* (lost tragedy, Jebb-Pearson II, p. 327).

Chrysippus Apollod. *Bibl.* 3,5,5; Athenaeus 13,602ff.; schol. on Euripides, *Phoen.* 1760; *Or.* 5; schol. on Pind. *Ol.* 1,144; Hyg. *Fab.* 85; 243; 271; Aelian, *VH* 6,15; schol. on Apoll. Rhod. *Arg.* 1,517; schol. on Hom. *Il.* 2,103; Paus. 6,20,7; Tzetzes, *Chil.* 1,415ff.; Euripides, *Chrysippus* (lost tragedy, Nauck *TGF*, edn 2, pp. 632ff.).

Chrysopelia Apollod. *Bibl.* 3,9,1; Tzetzes on Lyc. *Alex.* 480; schol. on Euripides, *Or.* 1646; Paus. 8,4,2; Apoll. Rhod. *Arg.* 2,477 with schol.

Chrysothemis Paus. 10,7,2.

Chthonia (1) Paus. 2,35,4ff.; Aelian, *Nat. An.* 11,4. (2) Apollod. *Bibl.* 3,15,1; Hyg. *Fab.* 46; 238.

Cichyrus Parthenius, *Erot. Path.* 32; see also EPIRUS.

Cicones Hom. *Il.* 2,846; 17,73; *Od.* 9,39ff.; 165; 196; 211; Apollod. *Epit.* 7,2; Hyg. *Fab.* 125; Ovid, *Met.* 6,710; Hdt. 7,59; Pliny, *NH* 6,55; Diod. Sic. 5,77,4; Strabo 7, fragment 18.

Cilix Hdt. 7,91; Apollod. *Bibl.* 3,1; Hyg. *Fab.* 178; Serv. on Virgil, *Aen.* 3,88.

Cilla Apollod. *Bibl.* 3,12,3; Tzetzes on Lyc. *Alex.* 224; 314; 315.

Cillas Paus. 5.10,7; schol. on Hom. *Il.* 1,38; Strabo 13,1,63, p. 613.

Cimmerians Hom. *Od.* 11,14; schol. on *Od.* 10,86; Eustath. on Hom. pp. 1667,41; 1670,49; 1671,44; Tzetzes on Lyc. *Alex.* 695; 1427; Cic. *Acad.* 2,61; Plutarch, *Marius* 11; Diod. Sic. 5,32,4; Strabo 7,2,2, p. 293f.; 7,4,5. p. 310f.; Pliny, *NH* 3,61.

Cinyras Hom. *Il.* 11,20ff. with schol. and Eustath.; Pind.

on Apoll. Rhod. *Arg.* 1,49; 121; 143; 601; 2,1162; Paus. 4,2,5; 9,36,8; Tzetzes on Lyc. *Alex.* 175; 284; schol. on Pind. *Pyth.* 4,252; Hyg. *Fab.* 12.

Creusa (1) Pind. *Pyth.* 9,14ff. (25ff.); schol. on Diod. Sic. 4,69; Ovid, *Am.* 3,6,31. (2) Apollod. *Bibl.* 3,15,1ff.; Euripides, *Ion passim*; Paus. 1,28,4. See also ION. (3) Euripides, *Medea passim*, with schol.; Ovid, *Her.* 12,53ff.; Lucian, *De Salt.* 42. (4) Apollod. *Bibl.* 3,12,5; Hyg. *Fab.* 90; Paus. 10,26,1; Virgil, *Aen.* 2,736ff.; Lyc. *Alex.* 1263ff.

Crimisus Virgil, *Aen.* 5,38; Serv. on Virgil, *Aen.* 1,550; 5,30; Tzetzes on Lyc. *Alex.* 471; 953; Hyg. *Fab.* 273,14.

Crinis Schol. and Eustath. on Hom. *Il.* 1,39.

Crisamis Suda s.v.; Hesychius s.v.; Photius, *Lexicon* s.v.

Crisus Paus. 2,29,4; Steph. Byz. s.v. Κρῖσος; schol. on Euripides, *Or.* 33; Tzetzes on Lyc. *Alex.* 53; 939; schol. on Hom. *Il.* 2,520.

Critheis Suda s.v. Ὅμηρος; Pseudo-Plutarch, *De vita et Poesi Homeri* A, 2–3; B, 2 (*Mor.* ed. Bernardakis VII, pp. 329f; 337) = Ephorus, fragment 164 (Müller *FHG* I, p. 277). See also MAEON.

Crocon Paus. 1,38,2; Suda s.v. Κυρωνίδαι; Apollod. *Bibl.* 3,9,1.

Crocus Serv. on Virgil, *Georg.* 4,182; Ovid, *Met.* 4,283; Nonnus, *Dion.* 12,86.

Cronus Hesiod, *Theog.* 167ff.; 485ff.; 617ff.; *Works* 169ff.; Apollod. *Bibl.* 1,2,1ff.; Hom. *Il.* 14,203; 243; 271ff.; 5,896ff.; 15,221ff.; Paus. 5,7,6ff.; 8,36,2ff.; Lydus, *De Mens.* 4,53; Ovid, *Fast.* 4,199ff.; Horace, *Epodes* 16,63; Pind. *Ol.* 2,70 (124); Diod. Sic. 3,61; Varro, *RR* 3,1,5; Plato, *Polit.* 269a; 276a; Hyg. *Fab.* pref. 3.

Croton Diod. Sic. 4,24,7; Heraclides, *De Reb. Publ.* 36 (Müller *FHG* II, 223); Ovid, *Met.* 15,12ff.; schol. on Theocr. 4,33; Tzetzes on Lyc. *Alex.* 1006; Iamblichus, *Vit. Pythag.* 9,50.

Crotopus Conon, *Narr.* 19; Ovid, *Ibis* 574ff.; Paus. 1,43,7; 2,16,1; 2,19,8.

Crotus Hyg. *Fab.* 224; *Astron.* 2,27; Pseudo-Eratosth. *Catast.* 28; schol. on Aratus Latinus 300ff. (Mass. *Comm. in Arat. Rel.* (1898), p. 239).

Cteatus See MOLIONES.

Ctimene Hom. *Od.* 10,441 with schol.; Strabo 10,2,10, p. 453; Eustath. on Hom. pp. 1664,32; 1784,29.

Curetes Strabo 10,3,1ff.; pp. 462ff.; Nonnus, *Dion.* 13,135ff.; Tzetzes on Lyc. *Alex.* 77; Apollod. *Bibl.* 1,1,7; 2,1,3; 3,3,1; Callim. *Hymn* 1,52ff.; Diod. Sic. 5,70,2ff.; 6,1,9; Lucret. 2,633ff.; Virgil, *Georg.* 3,150ff.; Ovid, *Fast.* 4,207ff.; *Met.* 4,282; Hyg. *Fab.* 139; Serv. on Virgil, *Aen.* 3,104.

Curtius Livy 7,6; Pliny, *NH* 15,20,4; Suetonius, *Aug.* 57; Varro, *LL* 5,148; Val. Max. 5,6,2; Dio Cassius Fragment 30,1; Plutarch, *Rom.* 18; Dion. Hal. 2,42ff.

Cyane (1) Diod. Sic. 5,7; Serv. on Virgil, *Aen.* 1,52. (2) Ovid, *Met.* 5,409ff.; Diod. Sic. 5,4; Nonnus, *Dion.* 6,128. (3) Plutarch, *Parallel.* 19.

Cyanippus (1) Paus. 2,18,4ff.; 2,30,10; Tzetzes, *Posthom.* 643. (2) Parthenius, *Erot. Path.* 10; Plutarch, *Parallel.* 21,310e; Stobaeus, *Flor.* 64,33 M = 4,20,70, p. 471 W-H. (3) See CYANE (3).

Cybele Apoll. Rhod. *Arg.* 1,1092ff.; Strabo 10,3,12, p. 469; 12,5,3, p. 567; Aristophanes, *Birds* 875ff.; Lucret. 2,598ff.; Ovid, *Met.* 10,686; Pliny, *NH* 18,16.

Cychreus Apollod. *Bibl.* 3,12,7; Tzetzes on Lyc. *Alex.* 110; 175; 451; Diod. Sic. 4,72,4; Strabo 9,1,9, p. 394; Plutarch, *Solon* 9; *Thes.* 10; Paus. 1,36,1.

Cyclopes Hesiod, *Theog.* 139ff.; 501ff.; with schol. on 139, citing Hellan. fragment 176 (Müller *FHG* I, p. 69); Apollod. *Bibl.* 1,1,2; 1,2,1; 3,10,4; 2,2,1; *Epit.* 7,3ff.; schol. on Euripides, *Alc.* 1; Hyg. *Fab.* 49; Euripides, *Cycl.* 297; Callim. *Hymn*

3,46ff.; Virgil, *Aen.* 8,416ff.; *Georg.* 4,170ff.; Ovid, *Fast.* 4,287ff.; Hom. *Od.* 9,106ff.; Virgil, *Aen.* 3,617ff.; Ovid, *Met.* 13,760ff.; Pind. Fragment 169 Sn. = 152 Bo.; Euripides *HF* 15; 944; *IA* 1500; Paus. 2,25,8; Strabo 8,6,2, p. 369; 8,6,11, p. 373; Pseudo-Lact. Plac. on Stat. *Theb.* 1,251; 630.

Cycnus (1) Schol. on Aristophanes, *Frogs* 972; Pind. *Ol.* 2,81ff. (147ff.) with schol. on 147; *Cypria*, Homer Oxf. Class. Text V, p. 105; schol. on Theocr. 16,49; Athenaeus 9,393e; Hyg. *Fab.* 157; 273; Ovid, *Met.* 12,72ff.; Seneca, *Tro.* 183; *Ag.* 215; Eustath. on Hom. pp. 116,26; 167,23; 1968,45; Palaeph. *Incred.* 12; Tzetzes, *Antehom.* 257. (2) Strabo 13,1,19, p. 589; Tzetzes on Lyc. *Alex.* 232; Paus. 10,14,1ff.; Apollod. *Epit.* 3,23ff.; schol. on Hom. *Il.* 1,38 with Eustathius; Diod. Sic. 5,83; Suda s.v. Τενέδιος ἄνθρωπος; Conon, *Narr.* 28. (3) Apollod. *Bibl.* 2,5,11ff.; 2,7,7; Hesiod, *Scutum* 57ff.; Diod. Sic. 4,37; Stesichorus, fragment 12 Bergk = 207 PMG; Hyg. *Fab.* 31; 159; 269; 273; Pind. *Ol.* 10,15 with schol. on 19; Euripides *HF* 391ff.; Plutarch, *Thes.* 11; Paus. 1,27,6; Tzetzes, *Chil.* 2,467. (4) Hyg. *Fab.* 154; Paus. 1,30,3; Virgil, *Aen.* 10,189 with Serv. ad loc.; Ovid, *Met.* 2,367ff.; Westermann, *Mythogr. Gr.* p. 347. (5) Antoninus Liberalis, *Met.* 12; Ovid, *Met.* 371ff.

Cydnus Steph. Byz. s.v. Ἀγχιάλη; Nonnus, *Dion.* 40,143ff.

Cydon Paus. 8,53,4; schol. on Apoll. Rhod. *Arg.* 4,1492; schol. on Theocr. 7,12; schol. on Hom. *Od.* 19,176; Steph., Byz. s.v. Κυδωνία.

Cylabras Athenaeus 7,277e ff.; Suda and Photius, *Lexicon* s.v. Φασηλίς.

Cyllarus Ovid, *Met.* 12,393ff.

Cyllene Dion. of Hal. 1,13; Apollod. *Bibl.* 3,8,1; Tzetzes on Lyc. *Alex.* 481; Festus p. 52 M.

Cynortas Paus. 3,1,3ff.; Apollod. *Bibl.* 1,9,5; 3,10,3ff.; Tzetzes on Lyc. *Alex.* 511; 1125.

Cynosura Hyg. *Astron.* 2,2; Pseudo-Eratosth. *Catast.* 2; Serv. on Virgil, *Aen.* 1,744; 3,516; *Georg.* 1,246; schol. on Hom. *Od.* 5,272; *Il.* 18,487ff.

Cyparissa Probus on Virgil, *Georg.* 2,84 (Servius ed. Thilo-Hagen, III.2, p. 367f.).

Cyparissi *Geoponica* 11,4.

Cyparissus (1) Scholia on Hom. *Il.* 2,519; Nonnus, *Dion.* 13,123. (2) Ovid, *Met.* 10,106ff.; Serv. on Virgil, *Aen.* 3,64; 680; *Georg.* 1,20; *Ecl.* 10,26; Probus on Virgil, *Georg.* 2,84 (Servius ed. Thilo-Hagen, III.2, p. 367f.); Nonnus, *Dion.* 11,364.

Cypselus (1) Paus. 4,3,6; 4,3,8; 8,5,6; 8,5,13; 8,29,5; Athenaeus 13,609e. (2) Paus. 1,23,1; 2,4,4; 2,28,8; 5,2,3; 5,17,2ff.; 5,17,10; 10,24,1.

Cyrene Pind. *Pyth.* 9 *passim*, with schol.; Apoll. Rhod. *Arg.* 2,502ff. with schol. on 2,498; 500; 4,1661; Virgil, *Georg.* 4,317ff.; Callim. *Hymn* 2,90ff.; Diod. Sic. 4,81; Hyg. *Fab.* 161; Serv. on Virgil, *Aen.* 4,377.

Cytissorus Apollon. Rhod. *Arg.* 2,1155, with schol. on 388, 1122, 1149; Apollod. *Bibl.* 1,9,1ff.; Pseudo-Plato, *Minos* 315c; Hdt. 7,197.

Cyzicus Apoll. Rhod. *Arg.* 1,949ff, with schol.; Conon, *Narr.* 41; Parthenius, *Erot. Path.* 28.

D

Dactyls Strabo 10,3,22, p. 473ff.; Paus. 5,7,6ff.; 5,8,1; 5,14,7ff.; 8,31,3; 9,19,5; Diod. Sic. 5,64; Pollux 2,156; Apoll. Rhod. *Arg.* 1,1129; Pseudo-Plutarch, *De Musica* 15.

Dada Nicolaus of Damascus, fragment 21 Müller (*FHG* III, 369,21).

Daedalion Ovid, *Met.* 11,291ff.; Hyg. *Fab.* 200; Paus. 8,4,6.

Greeks and their Gods (1962), 145ff.; K. Kerényi, *Dionysus* (tr. R. Manheim, 1976).

Dioscuri Apollod. *Bibl.* 3,10,6ff.; 3,11,1ff.; 3,13,7ff.; *Epit.* 1,23ff.; Hom. *Od.* 11,298ff.; *Il.* 3,236ff.; Homeric Hymns 17 and 33; Pind. *Pyth.* 11,61 (94); *Ol.* 3,35 (61); *Nem.* 10,59ff.; (110ff.); Euripides, *Hel.* 16ff.; Lucian, *Dial. Deor.* 22,14; Plut. *Thes.* 31ff.; schol. on Hom. *Il.* 3,242f.; Paus. 3,24,7; Ovid, *Met.* 8,300; *Fast.* 5,699; Theocr. 22,137ff.; Hyg. *Fab.* 80; *Astron.* 2,22; Pliny, *NH* 2,37,101; Seneca, *NQ* 1,1,13; Pseudo-Eratosth. *Catast.* 10.

Dirce See ANTIOPE.

Dolius Hom. *Od.* 4,735; 24,222; 397ff.

Dolon Hom. *Il.* 10,314ff. with schol.; Hyg. *Fab.* 113.

Doris Hesiod, *Theog.* 240ff.; Prop. 1,17,25; 3,7,67.

Dorus Apollod. *Bibl.* 1,7,3; 1,7,6; Hdt. 1,56; Conon, *Narr.* 14; Strabo 8,7,1, p. 383.

Drimacus Athenaeus 6,265b.

Dryas Apollod. *Bibl.* 1,8,2; Ovid, *Met.* 8,307; Hyg. *Fab.* 45; 159.

Dryope Antoninus Liberalis, *Met.* 32; Ovid, *Met.* 9,331ff.; Virgil, *Aen.* 10,550ff.

Dryops Apollod. *Bibl.* 2,7,7; Antoninus Liberalis, *Met.* 32; schol. on Apoll. Rhod. *Arg.* 1,1213; 1218; 1283; Strabo 8,6,13, p. 373; Tzetzes on Lyc. *Alex.* 480; Paus. 4,34,9; Homeric Hymn to Pan.

E

Echemus Paus. 1,41,2; 1,44,10; 8,5,1; 8,45,3; 8,53,10; Diod. Sic. 4,58; Hdt. 9,26; schol. on Pind. *Ol.* 10,79; Steph. Byz. s.v. Ἐκάδημος; Arnobius, *Adv. Nat.* 4,27; 6,3.

Echetlus Paus. 1,32,4; 1,15,3.

Echetus Hom. *Od.* 18,85 with schol.; 116 with schol.; 21,308; Eustath. on Hom. p. 1839; Apoll. Rhod. *Arg.* 4,1092 with schol.

Echidna Hesiod, *Theog.* 295ff.; Epimenides, fragment 6 Diels-Kranz (*Frag. d. Vorsok.* I, p. 34); Paus. 8,18,2; Apollod. *Bibl.* 2,1,2; 2,3,1ff.; 2,5,11; Hdt. 4,9f.; Steph. Byz. s.v. Γελωνοί; Σκύθαι; Diod. Sic. 2,43,3.

Echion (1) Apollod. *Bibl.* 3,4,1f.; 3,5,2; Hyg. *Fab.* 178; Ovid, *Met.* 3,125ff.; 10,686. (2) Pindar, *Pyth.* 4,179 (318); Apoll. Rhod. *Arg.* 1,52; Hyg. *Fab.* 14; Val. Flacc. *Arg.* 1,440; 4,134; Ovid, *Met.* 8.311.

Echo Columella *RR* 9,5; Anth. Pal. 9,27; Moschus, fragment 2 Wilam./Gow; Ovid, *Met.* 3,356ff.; Ptol. Heph. 6; Longus, *Daphnis and Chloe* 3,23.

Eetion Apollod. *Bibl.* 3,12,6; Hom. *Il.* 6,395ff.; Strabo 13,1,7, p. 585f.

Egeria Ovid, *Met.* 15,482ff.; *Fast.* 3,273ff.; Strabo 5,3,12, p. 239; Juv. 3,11ff.; Livy 1,21,3; Plutarch, *Numa* 13; Dion. Hal. 2,60ff.; Arnobius, *Adv. Nat.* 5,1.

Eilithyia Hom. *Il.* 11,271; 19,119; Hesiod, *Theog.* 922; Pind. *Nem.* 7,2; Apollod. *Bibl.* 1,3,1; Diod. Sic. 5,72; Ovid, *Met.* 9,285ff.; Antoninus Liberalis, *Met.* 29; Homeric Hymn to Delos, 98ff.

Elatus (1) and (2) Apollod. *Bibl.* 3,9,1; Paus. 8,4,2ff.; 8,48,6; 10,34,3.

Electra (1) Hesiod, *Theog.* 266; Homeric Hymn to Demeter, 418. (2) Apollod. *Bibl.* 3,10,1; 3,12,1; Conon, *Narr.* 21; Virgil, *Aen.* 3,163ff.; 8,135; Serv. on Virgil, *Aen.* 3,167; 104; 7,207; 10,272; Hellanicus, fragment 56; 129 (Müller *FHG* I, pp. 52; 63); Diod. Sic. 3,48ff.; Euripides, *Phoen.* 1136. (3) Aeschylus, *Ag.* and *Cho.*; Sophocles, *El.*; Euripides, *El.*; Hyg. *Fab.* 108; 117; 122; Hellanicus, fragment 43 (Müller *FHG* I, p. 51).

Electryon Apollod. *Bibl.* 2,4,5f.; schol. on Hom. *Il.* 2,494; 19,116; schol. on Apoll. Rhod. *Arg.* 1,747; Diod. Sic. 4,67,7.

Elephenor Tzetzes on Lyc. *Alex.* 911; 1034; Hyg. *Fab.* 97; Apollod. *Bibl.* 3,10,8; Plutarch, *Thes.* 35; Paus. 1,17,6; Hom. *Il.* 2,540; 4,463.

Eleusis Servius on Virgil, *Georg.* 1,19; Paus. 1,38,7; Hyg. *Fab.* 147.

Elis Conon, *Narr.* 14.

Elpenor Hom. *Od.* 10,550ff.; 11,57ff.; 12,10ff.; Juv. 15,22; Ovid, *Ibis* 487; Theophr. *Hist. Plant.* 5,8,3; Serv. on Virgil, *Aen.* 6,107.

Elymus Dion. Hal. 1,52ff. See also AEGESTES.

Empusa Aristophanes, *Frogs* 294; Philostr. *Vit. Apoll. Tyan.* 2,4; 4,25; Suda and Etymol. Magn. s.v. Ἔμπουσα; schol. on Apoll. Rhod. *Arg.* 3,862.

Enarophorus Apollod. *Bibl.* 3,10,5; Plutarch, *Thes.* 31; Paus. 3,15,1.

Endymion Apollod. *Bibl.* 1,7,5; Apoll. Rhod. *Arg.* 4,57 with schol.; Hyg. *Fab.* 271; Paus. 5,1,2; Plato, *Phaedo* 72c; Cic. *De Fin.* 5,20,25; *Tusc.* 1,38,92.

Enipeus Hom. *Od.* 11,238; Apollod. *Bibl.* 1,9,8; Diod. Sic. 4,68,3; Eustath. on Hom. p. 168; Ovid, *Met.* 6,116. See also TYRO.

Entoria Plutarch, *Parallela* 9,307e; Aratus, *Phaen.* 137.

Enyo Hom. *Il.* 5,592 with schol. on 333; Cornutus 21; Quint. Smyrn. *Posthom.* Paus. 1,8,5.

Eos Apollod. *Bibl.* 1,2,2; 1,4,4; 1,9,4; 3,12,4ff.; 3,14,3; Antoninus Liberalis, *Met.* 41; Hesiod, *Theog.* 371ff.; 378ff.; 986ff.; Hyg. *Fab.* 160; 189; 270; Pind. *Ol.* 2,83 (149); *Nem.* 6,50ff. (84ff.); Homeric Hymn to Aphrodite, 218ff.; Quint. Smyrn. *Posthom.* 2,540ff.; Tzetzes on Lyc. 18; schol. on *Il.* 11,1; Prop. 2,18,7ff.; Hom. *Od.* 5,1ff.; 121ff.; 4,188; Ovid, *Met.* 13,581ff.; 7,690ff.; Euripides, *Hipp.* 454ff.; Paus. 1,3,1.

Epaphus Apollod. *Bibl.* 2,1,3f.; Tzetzes on Lyc. *Alex.* 894; Hyg. *Fab.* 145; 149; Aeschylus, *Suppl.* 41ff.; 580ff.; *PV* 865ff.; Hdt. 2,153; 3,27 (identifying Epaphus with Apis); Ovid, *Met.* 1,748ff.

Epeius (1) Paus. 5,1,4; 5,1,8. See also ELIS, ENDYMION, AETOLUS. (2) Hom. *Od.* 8,492ff.; 11,523; Virgil, *Aen.* 2,264; Serv. on Virgil, *Aen.* 10,179; Hom. *Il.* 23,653ff.; 826ff.; Vell. Pat. 1,1; Justin 20,22,1; Lyc. *Alex.* 930; 946ff. with Tzetzes on 947; Callim. *Iamb* 7 (fragment 197).

Ephialtes Apollod. *Bibl.* 1,6,2.

Epidius Suetonius, *De Rhet.* 4 (Loeb Suet. II, 442f.).

Epigaeus Hom. *Il.* 16,570ff.

Epigoni Apollod. *Bibl.* 3,7,2; Diod. Sic. 4,66; Paus. 9,5,13ff.; 9,8,6; 9,9,4ff.; Hyg. *Fab.* 70; Hdt. 4,32; Aeschylus, *Epigoni* (lost tragedy, Nauck *TGF*, edn 2, p. 19); Sophocles, *Epigoni* (lost tragedy, Jebb-Pearson I, p. 129f.); schol. on Pind. *Pyth.* 8,68. See also ERIPHYLE.

Epimelides Antoninus Liberalis, *Met.* 31; schol. on Hom. *Il.* 20,8; Alciphro 3,11; schol. on Apoll. Rhod. *Arg.* 4,1322.

Epimetheus Hesiod, *Theog.* 511ff.; *Works* 83ff.; Apollod. *Bibl.* 1,2,3; 1,7,2; Pind. *Pyth.* 5,27(35); Plato, *Protag.* 320ff.; Hyg. *Fab.* 142.

Epione Paus. 2,27,5; 2,29,1; Suda s.v.; schol. on Hom. *Il.* 4,195; schol. on Pind. *Pyth.* 3,14.

Epirus Parthenius, *Erot. Path.* 32.

Epopeus (1) Paus. 2,1,1; 2,6,4; 2,11,1; Apollod. *Bibl.* 1,7,4; 3,5,5; schol. on Apoll. Rhod. *Arg.* 4,1090; Hyg. *Fab.* 8. (2) Hyg. *Fab.* 204; 253; Ovid, *Met.* 2,589ff.; Serv. on Virgil, *Georg.* 1,403; Westermann, *Mythogr. Gr.* p. 348.

Erebus Hesiod, *Theog.* 123; 125; Hyg. *Fab.* pref.; Cic. *De Nat. Deor.* 3,17.

Erechtheus Homer, *Il.* 2,547; Apollod. *Bibl.* 1,7,3; 1,9,4;

3,14,8; 3,15,1; 3,15,4f.; Diod. Sic. 1,29,1; 4,76,1; Hdt. 7,189;
8,55; Dion. Hal. 14,2; Paus. 1,5,3; 1,27,4; 1,38,3; 7,1,2ff.;
Lycurg. *In Leocr.* 98ff.; Plutarch, *Parallel.* 20,310d; Cic. *Sest.*
21; 48; *Tusc.* 1,48,116; *De Nat. Deor.* 3,19,50; *De Fin.* 5,22,62;
Hyg. *Fab.* 46; 48; 238; Euripides, *Ion.* 267; 277ff.; 1007;
Erechtheus (lost tragedy, Nauck *TGF*, edn 2, pp. 464ff.); schol.
on Sophocles, *OC* 100; Pseudo-Eratosth. *Catast.* 13.

Erginus (1) Apollod. *Bibl.* 2,4,11; schol. on Apoll. Rhod. *Arg.*
1,185; Pind. *Ol.* 14,4ff.; Tzetzes on Lyc. *Alex.* 874; *Chil.*
2,226ff.; Paus. 9,17,1; 9,37,2; 9,38,4; Diod. Sic. 4,10; Euripides, *HF* 49ff.; 220; Polyaen. *Strateg.* 1,3,5; schol. on Euripides, *Phoen.* 53. (2) Apoll. Rhod. *Arg.* 1,185 with schol.;
2,896; schol. on Pind. *Pyth.* 4,61; Hyg. *Fab.* 14; Val. Flacc. *Arg.*
1,415; 5,65; 8,177; Apollod. *Bibl.* 1,9,16.

Erichthonius Apollod. *Bibl.* 3,14,6ff.; Paus. 1,2,6; 1,14,6;
1,18,2; 1,24,7; schol. on Hom. *Il.* 2,547; Euripides, *Ion* 20ff.,
266ff.; 1001; Plato, *Tim.* 23de; Antig. Caryst. Fragment 12;
Nonnus in Westermann, *Mythogr. Gr* p 539ff.; Tzetzes on
Lyc. *Alex.* 111; Hyg. *Fab.* 166; *Astron.* 2,13; Pseudo-Eratosth.
Catast. 13; Virgil, *Georg.* 3,274; Serv. on Virgil, *Georg.* 3,113;
Ovid, *Met.* 2,552ff.; Pliny, *NH* 7,197.

Eridanus Hesiod, *Theog.* 338; Hdt. 3,115; Pherecydes, Fragment 33 (Müller *FHG* I, p. 78); Apoll. Rhod. *Arg.* 4,627 with
schol. See also ARGONAUTS.

Erigone (1) Hyg. *Fab.* 130; *Astron.* 2,4; Apollod. *Bibl.* 3,14,7;
schol. on Hom. *Il.* 22,29; Aelian, *VH* 7,28; Serv. on Virgil,
Georg. 2,389; Stat. *Theb.* 11,644ff. (2) Paus. 2,18,6f.; Hyg. *Fab.*
122; Apollod. *Epit.* 6,25; 28; Marmor Parium 40; Etymol.
Mag. s.v. Αἰώρα; Tzetzes on Lyc. *Alex.* 1374; Sophocles,
Aletes and *Erigone* (lost tragedies, Jebb-Pearson I, pp. 62ff.;
173ff.).

Erinona Serv. on Virgil, *Ecl.* 10,18.

Erinyes Hesiod, *Theog.* 134ff.; Apollod. *Bibl.* 1,1,4; Hom. *Il.*
9,571; 19,87; Tzetzes on Lyc. *Alex.* 406; Aeschylus, *Eum.*;
Euripides, *Or.*; Virgil, *Aen.* 6,571; 7,324; 12,846.

Eriphyle Apollod. *Bibl.* 1,9,13; 3,6,2; 3,7,5; Tzetzes on Lyc.
Alex. 439; Hom. *Od.* 15,248; 11,326 with schol.; Paus. 5,17,4;
Hyg. *Fab.* 73; Serv. on Virgil, *Aen.* 6,445; Diod. Sic. 4,65ff.;
Sophocles, *Epigoni* or(?) *Eriphyle* (lost tragedy, Jebb-Pearson I,
p. 129ff.); Cic. *De Opt. Gen.* 6,18; Philodemus, *De Mus.* p. 87f
Kemke.

Eris Hom. *Il.* 4,440; 5,518; 740; 11,3; 73; 18,535; 20,48;
Hesiod, *Theog.* 225ff.; *Scutum* 148; 156; *Works* 11ff.; Hyg. *Fab.*
pref; 92; Serv. on Virgil, *Aen.* 1,27; Apul. *Met.* 10; Tzetzes on
Lyc. *Alex.* 93.

Eros Hesiod, *Theog.* 120ff.; Proclus, *Comm. Tim.* 2,54,21ff.
and 3,154,26ff. Diehl; Aristotle, *Met.* 1,4; Plato, *Smp.*, esp.
201d ff.; Aristophanes, *Birds* 695f.; Paus. 8,21,2; 9,27,1ff.;
Nonnus, *Dion.* 7,1ff.; Alcaeus, Fragment 13 B. = 327 PLF;
Anacreon, Fragments 14; 25; 46; 47; 65 B. = 5; 53; 34; 45; 28
D.; Aeschylus, *Suppl.* 1039ff.; Sophocles, *Trach.* 354; 441; *Ant.*
781ff.; Euripides, *Hipp.* 1269ff.; Apoll. Rhod. *Arg.* 3,111ff.;
Bion 1,80ff. Ovid, *Met.* 1,542ff.; 5,363ff.; *Am.* 1,2,23ff.;
Horace, *Odes* 2,8,14; Apul. *Met.* 4,32ff.; 5,1ff.; Cic. *De Nat.
Deor.* 3,23,59ff.

Erylus Virgil, *Aen.* 8,561ff. with Serv. *ad loc.*; Lydus, *De
Mens.* 1,8.

Erymanthus (1) Ptolemy Hephaestion 1. (2) Paus. 8,24,1ff.;
Aelian, *VH* 2,33.

Erysichthon (1) Athenaeus 10,416ff.; Callim. *Hymn* 6,24ff.;
Lyc. *Alex.* 1393 with Tzetzes on 1396; Ovid, *Met.* 8,738ff. (2)
Apollod. *Bibl.* 3,14,1f.; Plato, *Critias* 110a; Athenaeus 9,392d;
Paus. 1,18,6.

Erytus Pindar, *Pyth.* 4,179 (319); Apoll. Rhod. *Arg.* 1,52;
Apollod. *Bibl.* 1,9,16; Hyg. *Fab.* 14; 160.

Eryx Apollod. *Bibl.* 2,5,10; Hyg. *Fab.* 260; Serv. on Virgil,

Aen. 1,570; Apoll. Rhod. *Arg.* 4,910ff.; Diod. Sic. 4,23,2;
4,83,1; Eustath. on Hom. *Il.* 13,43.

Eteocles Apollod. *Bibl.* 3,6,1ff.; Hyg. *Fab.* 68; Paus. 9,5,10ff.;
9,25,2; Euripides, *Phoen.* 63ff. with schol. on 71; Sophocles,
OC 1295; Stat. *Theb. passim*; Aeschylus, *Sept. passim.*

Ethemea Hyg. *Astron.* 2,16.

Etias Paus. 3,22,11.

Euboeleus Paus. 1,14,2; schol. on Lucian, *Dial. Meretr.* 2,1;
Clem. Alex. *Protrep.* 2,17,1; 2,20,2; Paus. 9,8,1; Cic. *De Nat.
Deor.* 3,21,53.

Euchenor Hom. *Il.* 13,663ff.; Pind. *Ol.* 13,75ff. (105ff.); Cic.
De Div. 1,40.

Eudorus Hom. *Il.* 16,179ff.; Eustath. on Hom. p. 1697,56.

Eulimene Parthenius, *Erot. Path.* 35.

Eumaeus Hom. *Od.* 13,404; 14; 15,301ff.; 403ff.; 16,11ff.;
17,182ff., 507ff.; 21,188ff.; 22,157ff.

Eumelus (1) Hom. *Il.* 2,714; 763; 23,376; *Od.* 4,796. (2) and
(3) See AGRON, BOTRES.

Eumolpus Hyg. *Fab.* 157, 273, Apollod. *Bibl.* 2,5,12, 3,14,4,
Steph. Byz. s.v. Αἰθίοψ (Aithiops); schol. on Sophocles, *OC*
1053; Paus. 1,38,2; 2,14,3; schol. on Euripides, *Phoen.* 854;
Photius, *Lex.* s.v. Εὐμολπίδαι (Eumolpidai).

Euneus Apollod. *Bibl.* 1,9,17; Hom. *Il.* 7,467ff.; 21,40ff.;
23,746ff.; Strabo 1,2,33, p. 41.

Eunomus Apollod. *Bibl.* 2,7,6; Diod. Sic. 4,36,2; Paus.
2,13,8; Athenaeus 9,410f; Tzetzes on Lyc. *Alex.* 50ff.; *Chil.*
2,456ff.; schol. on Apoll. Rhod. *Arg.* 1,1212.

Eunostus Plutarch, *Quaest. Gr.* 40,315e.

Euphemus Pind. *Pyth.* 4,44 (79); schol. on *Pyth.* 4,1ff.; Apoll.
Rhod. *Arg.* 1,182; 2,536ff.; 4,1755; Hyg. *Fab.* 14; Tzetzes,
Chil. 2,618; on Lyc. *Alex.* 886.

Euphorbus Hom. *Il.* 16,808; 17,1ff.; 81; Paus. 2,17,3; schol.
on Apoll. Rhod. *Arg.* 1,645; Diog. Laert. *Vit. Phil.* 8,1,4.

Euphorion Ptolemy Hephaestion 4,1

Euphrates Pseudo-Plutarch, *De Fluviis* 20 (*Mor.* ed. Bernardakis VII, p. 317).

Europa (1) See EUPHEMUS. (2) Hesiod, *Theog.* 357; schol. on
Euripides, *Rhes.* 28. (3) Scholia on Euripides, *Or.* 932. (4)
Apollod. *Bibl.* 2,1,5; Tzetzes, *Chil.* 7,371. (5) Hom. *Il.*
14,321ff.; schol. on *Il.* 2,494; 12,292; Apollod. *Bibl.* 2,5,7;
3,1,1ff.; 3,4,2; Conon, *Narr.* 32; 37; Bacchyl. 16,29ff.; Moschus 2; schol. on Plato *Tim.* 24e; schol. on Apoll. Rhod. *Arg*
3,1186; Diod. Sic. 4,60,3; 5,78,1; Ovid, *Met.* 2,836ff.; *Fast.*
5,603ff.; Hyg. *Fab.* 178; Theophr. *Hist. Plant.* 1,15; Pliny, *NH*
12,5; Horace, *Odes* 3,27,25ff.; Apul. *Met.* 6,39; Hesych. s.v.
Καρνεῖος (Karneios); Steph. Byz. s.v. Δωδώνη (Dodone);
Tzetzes, *Antehom.* 101; *Chil.* 1,473; Pseudo-Eratosth. *Catast.*
33; Hyg. *Astron.* 2,35.

Eurus Hom. *Il.* 2,145; 16,765; *Od.* 5,332; 19,206; Nonnus,
Dion. 6,30ff.; Virgil, *Aen.* 1,131ff. with Serv. ad loc.; Ovid,
Met. 1,61.

Euryalus (1) Apollod. *Bibl.* 1,9,13; 1,9,16; 3,7,2; Hom. *Il.*
2,559ff.; 6,20ff.; 23,653ff. (2) Parthenius, *Erot. Path.* 3. (3)
Virgil, *Aen.* 9,179ff.; 433.

Eurycleia (1) Schol. on Euripides, *Phoen.* 13. (2) Hom. *Od.*
1,429; 19,401; Hyg. *Fab.* 125.

Eurydice (1) Seneca, *HF* 569ff.; *Herc. Oet.* 1069ff.; Ovid, *Met.*
10,1ff.; Virgil, *Georg.* 4,454ff. with Serv. ad loc.; Hyg. *Fab.*
251; Apollod. *Bibl.* 1,3,2; Moschus 3,124; Diod. Sic. 4,25;
Conon, *Narr.* 45; Paus. 9,30,6. See also ORPHEUS. (2) Apollod.
Bibl. 2,2,2; 3,10,3. (3) Apollod. *Bibl.* 1,9,14; 3,6,4; Hyg. *Fab.*
273. See also ARCHEMORUS. (4) Paus. 5,17,7. (5) Sophocles, *Ant.*
1180ff.

Eurygania (1) Scholia on Euripides, *Phoen.* 1760; 13. (2)
Apollod. *Bibl.* 3,5,8; Paus. 9,5,5; schol. on Euripides, *Phoen.*
63.

Eurylochus Hom. *Od.* 10,205ff.; 429ff.; 12,278; 339ff.

Eurymachus Hom. *Od.* 2,177; 18,349ff.; 20,359ff.; 21,245ff.; 22,44ff.

Eurymedon (1) Hom. *Od.* 7,58 schol. on *Il.* 14,295. (2) Apollod. *Bibl.* 2,5,9; 3,1,2. (3) Paus. 2,16,6.

Eurymus Hesychius s.v. Εὐρύμας (Eurumas); Plutarch, *Am. Frat.* 11,483c; Liban. *Epist.* 389.

Eurynome Hesiod, *Theog.* 358; 907; Apollod. *Bibl.* 3,12,6; Hom. *Il.* 18,394ff.; Apoll. Rhod. *Arg.* 1,503; Tzetzes on Lyc. *Alex.* 1192; Paus. 8,41,4ff.

Eurynomus Paus. 10,28,4.

Eurypylus (1) Hom. *Il.* 2,734ff.; 5,76ff.; 6,36; 11,575ff.; 806ff.; Hyg. *Fab.* 81; 97; 114; Ovid, *Met.* 13,353 (or EURYPYLUS (3)); Virgil, *Aen.* 2,114. (2) Paus. 7,19,1ff. (3) Hom. *Il.* 2,677; schol. on *Il.* 14,255; Pind. *Nem.* 4,26 (42) with schol. on 42; Apollod. *Bibl.* 2,7,1. (4) Schol. on Juv. 6,654; Hom. *Od.* 11,519 with schol.; Hyg. *Fab.* 112f.; Serv. on Virgil, *Ecl.* 6,72. (5) Pindar, *Pyth.* 4,33 (57) with schol. on 57; Apoll. Rhod. *Arg.* 4,1551; Tzetzes on Lyc. *Alex.* 902; Callim. *Hymn* 2,92.

Eurysaces Sophocles, *Ajax* 530ff.; 972ff.; Serv. on Virgil, *Aen.* 1,619; Tzetzes on Lyc. *Alex.* 53; Justin 44,3; Plut. *Solon* 10; Paus. 1,35,2ff.; 2,29,4.

Eurystheus Hom. *Il.* 15,639ff.; 19,95ff. with schol. on 116; *Od.* 11,621ff.; Apollod. *Bibl.* 2,4,5; 2,5,1ff.; 2,8,1; 3,9,2; Hesiod, *Scutum* 89ff.; Tzetzes, *Chil.* 2,173ff.; 192ff.; Diod. Sic. 4,10,6ff.; Athenaeus 13,603d; 4,157f; schol. on Hom. *Il.* 15,639; Paus. 1,32,6; 4,34,10; Pind. *Pyth.* 9,79ff. (137ff.); Antoninus Liberalis, *Met.* 33.

Eurytion (1) Hom. *Od.* 21,295ff. with schol.; Ovid, *Met.* 12,219; Paus. 5,10,2. (2) Hyg. *Fab.* 31; 33; Apollod. *Bibl.* 2,5,4. See also DEXAMENUS, CENTAURS. (3) Apollod. *Bibl.* 1,8,2; 3,13,1; schol. on Hom. *Il.* 16,175; Tzetzes on Lyc. *Alex.* 175; Antoninus Liberalis, *Met.* 38; Ovid, *Met.* 8,311; Diod. Sic. 4,72,6; schol. on Aristophanes, *Clouds* 1068; Eustath. on Hom. p. 321.

Eurytus (1) Apollod. *Bibl.* 1,6,2; Hyg. *Fab.* pref. (2) Apollod. *Bibl.* 2,6,1ff.; 2,4,9; 2,7,7; Diod. Sic. 4,31; Tzetzes, *Chil.* 2,412ff.; Sophocles, *Trach.* 260ff. with schol. on 266; schol. on Euripides, *Hipp.* 545; schol. on Hom. *Il.* 5,392; *Od.* 8,223ff.; 21,11ff. (3) See ECHION.

Euthymus Hom. *Od.* 10,224; Paus. 6,6,4ff.; Strabo 6,1,5, p. 255; Aelian, *VH* 8,18.

Evadne (1) Pindar, *Ol.* 6,30ff. (50ff.); Hyg. *Fab.* 157. (2) Apollod. *Bibl.* 3,7,1; Hyg. *Fab.* 243; 256; Ovid, *Ars Am.* 3,21ff.; *Pont.* 3,1,111; *Trist.* 5,14,38; Euripides, *Suppl.* 985ff.; Stat. *Theb.* 12,800ff. with Pseudo-Lact. Plac. ad loc.

Evander (1) Diod. Sic. 5,79. (2) Apollod. *Bibl.* 2,13,5. (3) Dion. Hal. 1,31ff.; Livy 1,5,7ff.; Varro, *LL* 5,21,53; Paus. 8,43,2ff.; Ovid, *Fast.* 1,471ff.; Virgil, *Aen.* 8,51ff. with Serv. *ad loc.*; Hyg. *Fab.* 277; Justin 43,1; Solinus 1,4; 2,8; Tac. *Ann.* 11,14; Plutarch, *Quaest. Rom.* 56,278b.

Evenus Apollod. *Bibl.* 1,7,7; schol. on Hom. *Il.* 9,557; Tzetzes on Lyc. *Alex.* 561; Hyg. *Fab.* 242; Simonides, fragment 216 B. = 563 PMG.

Evippe (1) Parthenius, *Erot. Path.* 3; Sophocles, *Euryalus* (lost tragedy, Jebb-Pearson I, p. 145); Eustath. on Hom. 1796,61. (2) See ATHAMAS.

F

Fama Virgil, *Aen.* 4,173ff.; Horace, *Odes* 2,2,7; Ovid, *Met.* 12,39ff.; Val. Flacc. *Arg.* 2,117ff.; Stat. *Theb.* 425ff.

Fames Virgil, *Aen.* 6,275; Seneca, *HF* 690; Sil. Ital. *Pun.* 13,581; Ovid, *Met.* 8,799ff.; Hesiod, *Theog.* 227.

Fatum Cic. *De Div.* 2,7,19ff.; Virgil, *Aen.* 5,703; 7,50; 239ff.; 12,725ff. with Serv. ad loc. and on 10,628 and 12,808; Aul. Gell. *NA* 3,16,9ff.; Procop. *Bell.* 5,25,19ff. (=*Bell. Goth.* 1,25,19ff.); Petron. *Sat.* 42; 71; 77; *CIL* 6,4379; 10127; 11592 (epitaphs).

Fauna Varro, *LL* 7,36; Serv. auc. on Virgil, *Georg.* 1,11; Serv. on *Aen.* 7,47ff; Lact. *Inst. Div.* 1,22; Macrob. *Sat.* 1,12,21ff. Tzetzes on Lyc. *Alex.* 1232; Dion. Hal. 1,43.

Faunus Virgil, *Aen.* 7,45ff.; Serv. on *Aen.* 8,275; Arnobius, *Adv. Nat.* 2,71,1ff.; Lact. *Inst. Div.* 1,22,9; Tzetzes on Lyc. *Alex.* 1232; Aug. *CD* 8,5; 18,15; Ovid, *Fast.* 4,650ff.; Dion. Hal. *Ant. Rom.* 1,33.

Faustinus Plutarch, *Romulus* 10; Dion. Hal. *Ant. Rom.* 1,84.

Faustulus Plutarch, *Romulus* 3ff.; *Dion, Hal. Ant Rom.* 1,79ff.; Ovid, *Fast.* 3,55ff.; Livy 1,4ff.; Tzetzes on Lyc. *Alex.* 1232; Anon. *De Or. Gent. Rom.* 20ff.; Serv. on Virgil, *Aen.* 1,273; Zonaras 7,1ff.; Solinus 1,17; Conon, *Narr.* 48.

Febris Cic. *De Leg.* 2,11,28; *De Nat. Deor.* 3,25,63; Aug. *Civ. Dei.* 3,25; Pliny, *NH* 2,7,16; Aelian, *VH* 12,11; Val. Max. 2,5,6.

Februus Serv. on Virgil, *Georg.* 1,43; Macrob. *Sat.* 1,13,3; Lydus, *De Mens.* 4,20.

Ferentina Livy 1,50,1; 1,52,5; Dion. Hal. 2,34; 51; 4,45.

Feronia Virgil, *Aen.* 8,564ff. with Serv. ad loc.; Livy 22,1; 22,4.

Fides Virgil, *Aen.* 1,292 with Serv. ad loc. and on 8,636; Sil. Ital. *Pun.* 2,484; Festus p. 269 M; Varro, *LL* 5,74; Cic. *De Off.* 3,104; Horace, *Odes* 1,35,21ff.

Flora Ovid, *Fast.* 5,183ff.; Varro, *LL* 5,74; 7,45; *RR* 1,1,6; Pliny, *NH* 18,69,284ff.

Fons Arnobius, *Adv. Nat.* 3,29; Mart. Capella 1,46; Varro, *LL* 6,22; Cic. *De Nat. Deor.* 3,20,52; *De Leg.* 2,22,56.

Fornax Ovid, *Fast.* 2,525ff.; Lact. *Inst. Div.* 1,20,35; Pliny, *NH* 18,2,8.

Fors Cic. *De Leg.* 2,28.

Fortuna Ovid, *Fast.* 6,573ff.; Plutarch *De Fort. Rom.* (316b ff.); *Quaest. Rom.* 36,273b.

Furies Cic. *De Nat. Deor.* 3,18,46; Dion. Hal. 2,75; Mart. Capella 2,164.

Furrina Varro, *LL* 5,84; 6,19; 7,45; Cic. *De Nat. Deor.* 3,46; Plutarch, *C. Gracch.* 17.

G

Gaia Hesiod, *Theog.* 116ff.; Apollod. *Bibl.* 1,1,1ff.; 1,5,2; 2,1,2; Euripides, *Chrysippus* (lost tragedy, Nauck *TGF*, edn 2, pp. 632ff.); Lucret. 1,250ff.; 2,991ff.; Virgil, *Georg.* 2,325ff.; Plato, *Rep.* 2,377e ff.; Cic. *De Nat. Deor.* 2,23,63ff.; Hyg. *Fab.* pref.

Galaesus Virgil, *Aen.* 7,535; 575.

Galatea (1) Hom. *Il.* 18,45; Hesiod, *Theog.* 250; Hyg. *Fab.* pref. 8; Apollod. *Bibl.* 1,2,7; Athenaeus 7,284c; Theocr. 11; Ovid, *Met.* 13,750ff.; Sil. Ital. *Pun.* 14,221ff.; Nonnus, *Dion.* 6,300off.; Serv. on Virgil, *Ecl.* 9,39; Appian, *Illyr.* 2,3. (2) Antoninus Liberalis, *Met.* 17.

Galates Diod. Sic. 5,24; Etymol. Magn. s.v. Γαλατία (Galatia). See also CELTUS.

Galeotes Cicero, *De Div.* 1,20,39; Aelian, *VH* 12,46; Hesych. s.v. Γαλεοι (Galeoi); Steph. Byz. s.v. Γαλεῶται (Galeotai).

Galinthias Ovid, *Met.* 9,284ff.; Antoninus Liberalis, *Met.* 29; Aelian, *Nat. An.* 12,5; schol. on Hom. *Il.* 19,119.

Ganges Pseudo-Plutarch, *De Fluviis* 4 (*Mor.* ed. Bernardakis VII); Philostr. *Vit. Apoll. Tyan.* 3,6.

Ganymede Hom. *Il.* 5,265ff.; 20,232ff.; Eustath. on Hom. p. 1697,31; Pind. *Ol.* 1,43ff. (69ff.); 10,105 (128); Apollod. *Bibl.* 2,5,9; 3,12,2; Cic. *Tusc.* 1,26; Euripides, *Tro.* 822; schol. on Euripides, *Or.* 1377; Tzetzes on Lyc. *Alex.* 34; Hyg. *Fab.* 224; 271; *Astron.* 2,29; Homeric Hymn to Aphrodite, 210ff.; Virgil, *Aen.* 1,28; 5,253; Ovid, *Met.* 10,255; Diod. Sic. 4,74; Paus. 2,22,4; schol. on Apoll. Rhod. *Arg.* 3,115; Strabo 13,1,11, p. 587; Pseudo-Eratosth. *Catast.* 26.

Garanus Serv. on Virgil, *Aen.* 8,203.

Garmathone Pseudo-Plutarch, *De Fluviis* 16,1 (*Mor.* ed. Bernardakis VII).

Gavanes Hdt. 8,137ff.

Gelanor Apollod. *Bibl.* 2,1,4; Paus. 2,16,1; 2,19,3ff.; schol. on Hom. *Il.* 1,42; Eustath. on Hom. p. 37,32; Steph. Byz. s.v. Σουάγελα (Souagela).

Gelo Suda s.v. Γελλοῦς παιδοφιλωτέρας (Gellous paidophiloteras); Hesych. s.v. Γελλώ (Gello); schol. on Theocr. 15,20.

Genii Festus p. 94 M; Censorinus, *De Die Nat.* 3; Serv. on Virgil, *Aen.* 6,743; Apul. *De Deo Socr.* esp. 15,151ff.; Plautus, *Pers.* 263; *Cil* I, edn 2, 756.

Gerana Ovid, *Met.* 6,90; Athenaeus 9,393e; Eustath. on Hom. 1322,50; Aelian, *Hist. An.* 15,29; Antoninus Liberalis, *Met.* 6 (Oenone for Gerana).

Geryon Hesiod, *Theog.* 287ff.; 979ff.; Apollod. *Bibl.* 2,4,5; 2,5,10; Aeschylus, *Ag.* 870; Euripides, *HF* 423ff.; Pind. fragment 169 Sn. = 152 Bo.; *Isth.* 1,13 (15) with schol. on 15; Hdt. 4,8; Diod. Sic. 4,17ff.; Paus. 3,18,13; 4,36,3; Pliny, *NH* 4,20; Serv. on Virgil, *Aen.* 8,300; Ovid, *Met.* 4,782ff.; 6,119ff.; 9,184ff.; Hyg. *Fab.* 30; 151; Strabo 3,2,11 (fragment 5), p. 148; 5,3f., p. 169; 5,7, p. 172; Arrian, *Anab.* 2,16,5; Pseudo-Scylax, *Periplus* 26 (Müller, *Geog. Gr. Min.* I, p. 33).

Giants Hesiod, *Theog.* 183ff.; Apollod. *Bibl.* 1,6,1ff.; Tzetzes on Lyc. *Alex.* 63, Pind. *Nem.* 1,67 (100f.) with schol. on 100f.; Euripides, *HF* 177ff.; *Ion* 216ff.; Horace, *Odes* 3,4,49ff.; Ovid, *Met.* 1,150ff.; *Fast.* 3,438ff.; *Trist.* 4,7,17; Paus. 8,29,1ff.; Lucret. 5,119ff.; Macrob. *Sat.* 1,20,9; Serv. on Virgil, *Aen.* 1,394; 3,578; 9,564; Diod. Sic. 5,71; Strabo 5,4,4, p. 243f.; 6,3,5, p. 281; 7, fragments 25 and 27 (p. 330).

Glauce (1) Hesiod, *Theog.* 244, Hyg. *Fab.* pref. (2) Paus. 8,47,2f.; Apollod. *Bibl.* 1,9,28; Diod. Sic. 4,54; Hyg. *Fab.* 25; Tzetzes on Lyc. *Alex.* 175; 1318.

Glaucia Plutarch, *Quaest. Gr.* 41,301a.

Glaucus (1) Dict. Cret. *Bell. Tro.* 3,26; 4,7; 5,2; Hom. *Il.* 3,312; Paus. 10,27,3ff.; Apollod. *Epit.* 5,21. (2) Dict. Cret. *Bell. Tro.* 2,33; Hom. *Il.* 2,876; 6,119ff.; 12,329ff.; 16,493ff.; 17,140ff.; Hyg. *Fab.* 112f.; Hdt. 1,147. (3) Hom. *Il.* 4,154; Aeschylus, *Glaucus Pontius* and *Glaucus Potnieus* (lost tragedies, Nauck *TGF* edn 2, pp. 11ff.); Eustath. on Hom. p. 269,35; Hyg. *Fab.* 250; 273; Apollod. *Bibl.* 2,3,1; schol. on Apoll. Rhod. *Arg.* 1,46; Paus. 6,20,19; 7,18,2; Aelian, *Nat. An.* 15,25; Strabo 9,2,24, p. 409; Virgil, *Georg.* 3,268 with Serv. ad loc.; schol. on Plato. *Rep.* 10,497,11. (4) Athenaeus 7,297ff.; Palaeph. *Incred.* 2,23; Tzetzes on Lyc. *Alex.* 754; Ovid, *Met.* 13,900ff.; 14,1ff.; Serv. on Virgil, *Georg.* 1,427; Virgil, *Aen.* 6,36; Diod. Sic. 4,486; Euripides, *Or.* 352 with schol. (5) Apollod. *Bibl.* 3,1,3; 3,3,1; Tzetzes on Lyc. *Alex.* 811; Palaeph. *Incred.* 27; Hyg. *Fab.* 49; 136; *Astron.* 2,14; Sophocles, *Manteis* or *Polyidus* (lost tragedy, Jebb-Pearson II, p. 56f.; Euripides, *Polyidus* (lost tragedy, Nauck *TGF*, edn 2, p. 558ff.); Athen. 2,51d; schol. on Pind. *Pyth.* 3,96.

Glyphius Eustath. on Hom. 1665,48ff.

Golden Age Hesiod, *Works and Days* 106ff.; Catull. 64,384ff.; Tibull. 1,3,35ff.; Virgil, *Ecl.* 4, with Servius; Ovid, *Fasti* 1,193; *Met.* 1,89ff.; *Amores* 3,8,35ff.; Horace, *Epodes* 16,41ff.; Paus. 5,7,6. See M. L. West's note on Hesiod, *Works and Days* 106ff.; A. Lovejoy, G. Boas, *Primitivism* (1935).

Gordias Strabo 12,5,3, p. 568; Arrian, *Anab.* 2,3; Plutarch, *Caes.* 9; Hyg. *Fab.* 191; 274.

Gorge (1) Apollod. *Bibl.* 1,8,1; Tzetzes on Lyc. *Alex.* 1011; Hyg. *Fab.* 97; 174; Ovid, *Met.* 13,543; *Her.* 9,165; schol. on Hom. *Il.* 14,114; 9,584; 15,281; Nonnus, *Dion.* 25,84ff. (2) Hesych. s.v. Ἐσχατιῶτις (Eschatiotis); Etymol. Magn. s.v. Γοργῶπις (Gorgopis).

Gorgon Hesiod, *Theog.* 274ff.; *Scutum* 224ff.; Pind. *Pyth.* 12,6ff.; (12ff.); Hom. *Il.* 5,741; 8,349; 11,36; *Od.* 11,623; Apollod. *Bibl.* 2,4,2ff.; 2,7,3; 3,10,3; Ovid, *Met.* 4,765ff.; Aeschylus, *PV* 800; schol. on Apoll. Rhod. *Arg.* 4,1515; Euripides, *Ion* 989; 1003ff.; Serv. on Virgil, *Aen.* 6,289; Diod. Sic. 3,54f.; Pliny, *NH* 6,35.

Gorgophone Paus. 2,21,7; 3,1,4; 4,2,4; Apollod. *Bibl.* 1,9,5; 2,4,5; 3,10,3; Tzetzes on Lyc. *Alex.* 511; 838.

Gorgophonus (1) Apollod. *Bibl.* 2,4,5. (2) Pseudo-Plutarch, *De Fluviis* 18,7 (*Mor.* ed. Bernardakis VII).

Gorgopis Schol. on Pind. *Pyth.* 4,288.

Gouneus Hom. *Il.* 2,748; Hyg. *Fab.* 81; 97; Apollod. *Epit.* 3,14; 6,15; Tzetzes on Lyc. *Alex.* 877; 897; 902; Arist. *Peplos* (Bergk, *PLG*, edn 3, II 654).

Graeae Hesiod, *Theog.* 270ff.; Apollod. *Bibl.* 2,4,2ff.; Aeschylus, *PV* 794ff. with schol. on 793; Pseudo-Eratosth. *Catast.* 22; Ovid, *Met.* 4,774ff.; Hyg. *Astron.* 2,12; Tzetzes on Lyc. *Alex.* 838; 846; schol. on Apoll. Rhod. *Arg.* 4,1515; Palaeph. *Incred.* 32; Aeschylus, *Phorcides* (lost tragedy, Nauck *TGF*, edn 2, pp. 83f.).

Granicus School. on Hom. *Il.* 6,396.

Griffins Hesiod, cited by schol. on Aeschylus, *PV* 830; Hdt. 3,102; 116; Aeschylus, *PV* 803ff.; Aelian, *Hist. An.* 4,27; Pomp. Mela 2,1,1. See J. D. P. Bolton, *Aristeas* (1962), index s.v.

Grynus Serv. on Virgil, *Ecl.* 6,72.

Gyas (1) Virgil, *Aen.* 1,222; 5,118 with Serv. ad loc.; 12,460; Hyg. *Fab.* 273. (2) Virgil, *Aen.* 10,319.

Gyges Hesiod, *Theog.* 149; 618; 714; 734; 817; Ovid, *Fast.* 4,593;. See also HECATONCHEIRES.

Gyrton Stephanus of Byzantium s.v. Γύρτων (Gurton); schol. on Apoll. Rhod. *Arg.* 1,57.

H

Hades Hom. *Il.* 5,395ff.; 9,569ff.; 15,187ff.; 20,61ff.; Homeric Hymn to Demeter; Hesiod, *Theog.* 311; 455; 768; 850; *Works* 153; Aeschylus, *Eum.* 269ff.; schol. on Hom. *Il.* 15,188; Eustath. on Hom. p. 613,24; Apollod. *Bibl.* 1,1,5; 1,2,1; 1,5,1ff.; 1,5,3ff.; Diod. Sic. 5,4,1ff.; 5,68,2; Cic. *Verr.* 2,4,107; Ovid, *Fast.* 4,419ff.; *Met.* 5,346ff.; Hyg. *Fab.* 79; 146; Strabo 3,2,9;, p. 147; Plato, *Crat.* 403a.

Haemon (1) Apollod. *Bibl.* 3,5,8; schol. on Euripides, *Phoen.* 1760; Sophocles, *Ant. passim*, with hypothesis; Euripides, *Phoen.* 944; Hyg. *Fab.* 72; Hom. *Il.* 4,394. (2) Strabo 9,5,23, p. 443ff.; schol. on Apoll. Rhod. *Arg.* 3,1090; Dion. Hal. 1,17; Pliny *NH* 4,7,44; Apollod. *Bibl.* 3,8,1; Paus. 8,44,1ff.; Rhianus, Fragment 25 (Powell, *Coll. Alex.*). (3) Schol. on Pind. *Ol.* 2,14; 16.

Haemus (1) Steph. Byz., s.v. Αἷμος (Haimos); Serv. on Virgil, *Aen.* 1,317; Ovid, *Met.* 6,87f.; Lucian, *De Salt.* 57; Hesych. fragments 4,17 (Müller *FHG* IV, p. 149). (2) Tzetzes, *Antehom.* 273.

Hagno Paus. 8,31,2; 8,38,2ff.; 8,47,3.

Halaesus Virgil, *Aen.* 7,723ff.; 10,352; 10,411ff.; Serv. on Virgil, *Aen.* 7,695; 723; 8,285; Ovid, *Am.* 3,13,31ff.; *Fast.* 4,73ff.; Solinus 2,7; Pliny *NH*.

Halia (1) Diod. Sic. 5,55. (2) Hom. *Il.* 18,40; Apollod. *Bibl.* 1,2,7; Hesiod, *Theog.* 245.

Haliacmon (1) Hesiod, *Theog.* 341. (2) Pseudo-Plutarch, *De Fluviis* 18,1; (*Mor.* ed. Bernardakis, VII).

Haliai Paus. 2,22,1.

Haliartus Paus. 9,34,7ff.; Eustath. on Hom. p. 268,27; schol. on Hom. *Il.* 2,503.

Halirrhothius Apollod. *Bibl.* 3,14,2; Paus. 1,21,7; 1,28,5; Suda and Steph. Byz. s.v. Ἄρειος πάγος (Areios pagos); schol. on Hom. *Il.* 18,483; 490; schol. on Aristophanes, *Clouds* 1006; Serv. on Virgil, *Georg.* 1,18.

Halmus Paus. 2,4,3; 9,34,10ff.; schol. on Apoll. Rhod. *Arg.* 3,1094.

Hals Ptolemy Hephaestion 4, p. 194f Westermann (*Mythogr. Gr.*); Hom. *Od.* 11,134.

Hamadryads Homeric Hymn to Aphrodite, 259ff.; *Anth. Pal.* 6,189; 9,833; Callim. *Hymn* 4,79ff.; Nonnus, *Dion.* 2,92ff.; schol. on Apoll. Rhod. *Arg.* 2,477; Serv. on Virgil, *Aen.* 1,500; 3,34; *Ecl.* 10,62; Eustath. on Hom. p. 652,32; Ovid, *Fast.* 4,231; *Met.* 8,763.

Harmonides Hom. *Il.* 5,60; Tzetzes on Lyc. *Alex.* 93.

Harmonia Hesiod, *Theog.* 937; 975ff.; Pind. *Pyth.* 3,88ff.; (157ff.) with schol. on 167; Euripides, *Phoen.* 822ff. with schol. on 71; Diod. Sic. 4,2,1; 5,48,5; 5,49,1; 16,64; Theognis 15; Paus. 3,18,12; 9,12,3; schol. on Hom. *Il.* 2,494; schol. on Apoll. Rhod. *Arg.* 1,96; Steph. Byz. s.v. Δάρδανος (Dardanos); Athenaeus 6,232ff.; 14,658ff.; Parthenius, *Erot. Path.* 25; Hyg. *Fab.* 148.

Harpalion (1) Hom. *Il.* 13,643ff. with schol. (2) Quint. Smyrn. *Posthom.* 10,70.

Harpalyce (1) Virgil, *Aen.* 1,315ff. with Serv. ad loc.; Hyg. *Fab.* 193; 252; 254. (2) Parthenius, *Erot. Path.* 13; Nonnus, *Dion.* 12,71ff.; Hyg. *Fab.* 206. See also CLYMENUS. (3) Athenaeus 14,11.

Harpalycus (1) See HARPALYCE. (2) Apollod. *Bibl.* 3,8,1. (3) Virgil, *Aen.* 4,615. (4) Theocr. 24,109ff.

Harpinna Diod. Sic. 4,73; Paus. 5,22,6; 6,21,8; schol. on Apoll. Rhod. *Arg.* 1,752; Tzetzes on Lyc. *Alex.* 149.

Harpies Hesiod, *Theog.* 265; Apollod. *Bibl.* 1,2,6; 3,15,2; Hyg. *Fab.* 14; Virgil, *Aen.* 3,209; 6,289; schol. on Apoll. Rhod. *Arg.* 2,285; 2,1089; Serv. on Virgil, *Aen.* 3,252.

Harpyreia Tzetzes, *Chil.* 1,220ff.; on Lyc. *Alex.* 165.

Hebe Hom. *Il.* 4,2; 5,722; 5,905; *Od.* 11,601ff.; Homeric Hymn to Apollo, 195; Hesiod, *Theog.* 922; 950; Pind. *Nem.* 1,71 (109); 10,17ff. (30ff.); *Isth.* 4,65 (101); Paus. 2,13,3; Apollod. *Bibl.* 1,3,1.

Hecaergus Serv. on Virgil, *Aen.* 11,532; 858.

Hecale Callim. *Hecale* (fragments 230ff. Pfeiffer); Plutarch, *Thes.* 14; *Anth. Pal.* 9,546; Steph. Byz. and Etymol. Magn. s.v. Ἑκάλειος (Hekaleios).

Hecamede Hom. *Il.* 11,624; 14,6; Suda s.v.

Hecate Hesiod, *Theog.* 404ff.; Homeric Hymn to Demeter, 24ff.; Apollod. *Bibl.* 1,2,4; schol. on Apoll. Rhod. *Arg.* 3,200; 242; 467; 861; 1035; 4,828; Diod. Sic. 4,45ff.; Apul. *Met.* 11,2; Cic. *De Nat. Deor.* 3,18,46.

Hecaterus Strabo 10,3,19, p. 417; Perhaps a ritual name of Apollo; see HECAERGUS.

Hecatoncheires Apollod. *Bibl.* 1,1,1ff.; Hesiod, *Theog.* 147ff.; Palaeph. *Incred.* 20.

Hector Hom. *Il. passim*, esp. 1,242; 2,416; 788ff.; 3,76ff.; 5,680ff.; 6,102ff.; 7,11ff.; 113ff.; 9,352ff.; 22,433ff.; 24 *passim*; schol. on *Il.* 3,314; Tzetzes on Lyc. *Alex.* 266; Euripides, *Rhes. passim*; Dict. Cret. *Bell. Tro.* 3,20; 6,12.

Hecuba Hom. *Il.* 6,293ff.; 16,718 with schol.; 22,82ff.; 405ff.; 430ff.; 24,200ff.; 283ff.; 746ff.; schol. on *Il.* 3,325; Apollod. *Bibl.* 3,12,5; Euripides, *Hec.*; *Tro.*; schol. on Euripides, *Hec.* 3;

1259; Seneca, *Tro.*; Ovid, *Her.* 16,43ff.; *Met.* 13,422ff.; 533ff.; Tzetzes, *Antehom.* 41ff.; *Posthom.* 366ff.; on Lyc. *Alex.* pref. p. 5 Scheer; 86; 224ff.; 1176; Hyg. *Fab.* 90; 111; 249; Serv. on Virgil, *Aen.* 2,32; 7,320; 10,705; Suetonius, *Tib.* 70.

Hegeleus Paus. 2,21,3.

Heleius Apollod. *Bibl.* 2,4,5; 2,4,7; Strabo 8,5,2, p. 363; Tzetzes on Lyc. *Alex.* 838; schol. on Hom. *Il.* 19,116.

Helen Almost all the ancient authorities recount the legend of Helen, or at least allude to it. The most important passages are: Hom. *Il.* 3,121; 165; 237; schol. on *Il.* 4,276; *Il.* 6,289ff. with schol. on 291; schol. on *Il.* 7,392; 13,517; 626; *Il.* 24,761; *Od.* 3,205; 4,14; 227; 275ff.; 569; schol. on 355; 11,298; Dict. Cret. *Bell. Tro. passim*; Epic Cycle, Homer Oxf. Class. Text V, pp. 102f.; 106f. etc.; Eustath. on Hom. 1488,21; 1493,61; 1946,9; Euripides, *Hel.*; *Or.* 57ff.; schol. on 239; 1274; *IA* 57ff.; 75; 581; *Cycl.* 182; *El.* 1280; *Tro.* 959ff.; *Hec.* 239ff.; schol. on *Andr.*; Paus. 1,33,7ff.; 2,22,6; 3,19,10ff.; 3,20,9; 3,24,10; 5,18,3; Athenaeus 5,190; 8,334c; Apollod. *Bibl.* 3,10,6ff.; 3,11,1; *Epit.* 5,9; 13; 19; 21; Tzetzes on Lyc. 88; 132; 143; 168; 202; 513; 495; 820; 851; *Antehom.* 96ff.; *Posthom.* 600; 729ff.; Hyg. *Fab.* 77ff.; 81; 118; 249; *Astron.* 2,8; Pseudo-Eratosth. *Catast.* 25; Virgil, *Aen.* 2,567ff.; 6,510ff.; Serv. on Virgil, *Aen.* 1,526; 651; 2,601; 166; 592; 6,121; 8,130; 10,91; 11,262; Ovid, *Her.* 16; 17; schol. on Pind. *Nem.* 10,150; *Ol.* 10,79; Ptol. Heph. 4, p. 188f. Westermann (*Mythogr. Gr.*); Aelian, *Nat. An.* 9,21; 15,13; Plut. *Thes.* 31; *Parallel. Min.* 35; Philostr. *Vit. Apoll. Tyan.* 4,16; Aristophanes, *Lys.* 155; schol. on *Wasps* 714; Diod. Sic. 4,63; Parthenius, *Erot. Path.* 16; Antoninus Liberalis, *Met.* 27; Conon, *Narr.* 8; 18; 34; Hdt. 2,112ff.; Plato, *Phaedr.* 243a ff.; *Rep.* 9,586c; Isocr. *Hel.*

Helenus Hom. *Il.* 6,76; 7,44 with schol; 12,94; 13,576; 24,249; Eustath. on Hom. p. 626,24; 663,40; Apollod. *Bibl.* 3,12,5; *Epit.* 5,9ff.; Sophocles, *Phil.* 604ff.; 1337ff.; Ptol. Heph. 6, p. 195,11 Westermann (*Mythogr. Gr.*); Hyg. *Fab.* 273; Virgil, *Aen.* 3,333; Serv. on Virgil, *Aen.* 1,479; 2,166; 3,279; 334; Tzetzes, *Posthom.* 571ff.; on Lyc. *Alex.* 911; 1439; *Chil.* 6,508ff.; Dict. Cret. *Bell. Tro.* 2,18; Paus. 1,11,1; 2,23,6; 5,13,4; Dio Chrys. I, 208 Dindorf = *Or.* 11,137 Loeb.

Heliades (1) Aeschylus, *Heliades* (lost tragedy, Nauck *TGF*, edn 2, pp. 23ff.); Hyg. *Fab.* 152; 154; pref. 38; Ovid, *Met.* 2,340ff.; schol. on Hom. *Od.* 17,208; Virgil, *Ecl.* 6,62; *Aen.* 10,189ff. with Serv. ad loc.; Apoll. Rhod. *Arg.* 4,595ff.; Diod. Sic. 5,23. (2) Pind. *Ol.* 7,71ff. (131ff.) with schol. on 131ff.; Diod. Sic. 5,56ff.; Strabo 14,2,8, p. 654.

Helicaon Hom. *Il.* 3,123; Paus. 10,26,8; Serv. on Virgil, *Aen.* 1,241; Martial 10,93; Athenaeus 6,232c.

Helice (1) Paus. 7,1,3; 7,25,5. (2) Schol. on Hom. *Od.* 5,272; on Apoll. Rhod. *Arg.* 1,936; Serv. on Virgil, *Georg.* 1,67; 138; 246; Hyg. *Astron.* 2,1; 2,2; 2,13; *Fab.* 177; schol. on Aratus, *Phaen.* 27.

Helios Hom. *Od.* 3,1; 10,138; 12,260ff.; esp. 374ff.; Hesiod, *Theog.* 371ff.; 957; Pind. *Ol.* 7,58ff.; (105ff.); Aeschylus, *Prometheus Lyomenes* (lost tragedy, Nauck *TGF*, edn 2, fragment 192, p. 64); Apollod. *Bibl.* 1,2,2; 1,4,3; 1,4,6; 1,9,1; 1,9,25; 3,1,2; Apoll. Rhod. *Arg.* 3,209; 4,591; 964ff.; Euripides, *Tro.* 439; Diod. Sic. 5,56; Tzetzes on Lyc. *Alex.* 174; Ovid, *Met.* 2,119ff.; 4,167ff.; Antoninus Liberalis, *Met.* 41; Hyg. *Fab.* 154; 156; 183; Serv. on Virgil, *Aen.* 6,14.

Helle Schol. on Aeschylus, *Pers.* 70; Hyg. *Fab.* 3; *Astron.* 2,20; Hdt. 7,58; Steph. Byz. s.v. Ἀλμωπία (Almopia).

Hellen Hdt. 1,56; Thuc. 1,3; Strabo 8,7,1, p. 383; Diod. Sic. 4,60; Apollod. *Bibl.* 1,7,2ff.

Hemera Hesiod, *Theog.* 124; 748ff.; Hyg. *Fab.* pref. 1; 2 Rose.

Hemicynes Strabo 1,2,35, p. 43; 7,3,6, p. 229.

Hemithea (1) Diod. Sic. 5,62ff. (2) Paus. 10,14,1; Tzetzes on Lyc. *Alex.* 232; Conon, *Narr.* 28; Serv. on Virgil, *Aen.* 2,21.

Heosphorus Hom. *Il.* 23,226; schol. on *Il.* 11,267; Hesiod, *Theog.* 381; Pind. *Isth.* 3,26 (42); Conon, *Narr.* 17.

Hephaestus Hom. *Il.* 1,571ff. with schol. on 609; 14,338 with schol. on 292; 18,395ff.; Eustath. on Hom. 987,8, Hesiod, *Theog.* 570; 927ff.; *Works* 60; Paus. 1,20,3; 2,31,3; 8,53,5; Hom. *Od.* 8,266ff.; Homeric Hymn to Apollo, 140; 317; Pind. *Ol.* 7,35ff. (65ff.); Apollod. *Bibl.* 1,3,5ff.; 1,6,2; 1,9,16; Serv. on Virgil, *Aen.* 3,35; 8,454; *Ecl.* 4,62; Ovid, *Fast.* 5,229ff.; Hyg. *Fab.* 158; 166; schol. on Theocr. 7,149.

Hera Hom. *Il.* 1,399ff.; 5,392ff.; 721ff.; 889; 8,400ff.; 11,270ff.; 14,153ff.; 15,14ff.; 18,119ff.; 19,96ff.; Homeric Hymn to Apollo, 127; Hom. *Od.* 11,603ff.; schol. on *Od.* 10,494, Hesiod, *Theog.* 921ff.; Aristophanes, *Birds* 1731; schol on *Peace* 1126; Sophocles, *Inachus* fragment 270 (Jebb-Pearson I); Euripides, *Hipp.* 743ff.; Paus. 2,13,3; 2,17,4; 2,36,2; 8,22,2; Apoll. Rhod. *Arg.* 4,790ff.; schol. on *Arg.* 4,1396; Apollod. *Bibl.* 1,3,1; 1,3,5; 1,4,1; 1,6,2; 1,9,22; 1,9,25; 3,5,11; 3,7,1; 3,6,7; 3,13,5; *Epit.* 3,2ff.; 6,29; Ovid, *Fast.* 5,229ff.; Serv. on Virgil, *Aen.* 1,394; 9,584; Tzetzes on Lyc. *Alex.* 683.

Heracles I *Name*: Apollod. *Bibl.* 2,4,12; Sext. Emp. *In Phys.* 1,36 (Loeb III, p. 20); schol. on Pind. *Ol.* 6,115; Prob. on Virgil, *Ecl.* 7,61; Diod. Sic. 1,24,4; 4,10,1; schol. on Hom. *Il.* 11,324; Serv. on Virgil, *Aen.* 6,392; Aelian, *VH* 2,32; schol. on Pind. *Isth.* 4,104.

Ancestry: Hesiod, *Scutum* 1ff.; 27ff.; 79ff.; Euripides, *HF* 16ff.; 1079.; 1258ff.; Paus. 5,18,3; 9,11,1; Athen. 11,474f; 499b; Plautus, *Amphyt.* 112ff.; 760ff.; Lyc. *Alex.* 33 with Tzetzes *ad loc.*; Lucian, *Somn.* 17; Apollod. *Bibl.* 2,4,8; Stat. *Theb.* 12,300ff.; Diod. Sic. 4,9,1ff.; schol. on Hom. *Il.* 14,323; *Od.* 11,266; on Pind. *Nem.* 10,24; Hyg. *Fab.* 29; Pliny, *NH* 7,29; 28,59; Moschus 4,84ff.; Hom. *Il.* 19,98ff.

Childhood: Hyg. *Astron.* 2,43; Lyc. *Alex.* 1328ff.; Diod. Sic. 4,9,6; Pind. *Nem.* 1,33ff. (50ff.); *Anth. Pal.* 9,589; Euripides, *HF* 1266ff.; Theocr. 24; Diod. Sic. 4,10,1; Apollod. *Bibl.* 2,4,8; Hyg. *Fab.* 30; Virgil, *Aen.* 8,288ff.; Ovid, *Her.* 9,21ff.; *Met.* 9,67; Seneca, *HF* 216ff.; *Herc. Oet.* 59; Paus. 1,24,2; Plautus, *Amphyt.* 1123ff.; Pherecydes, fragment 28 (Müller *FHG* I); Pseudo-Eratosth. *Catast.* 44; Apollod. *Bibl.* 2,4,9; 2,4,11; Theocr. 24,103ff.; Diod. Sic. 3,67,2; Paus. 9,29,9; Tzetzes, *Chil.* 2,213ff.; on Lyc. *Alex.* 662; Lyc. *Alex.* 56, Plautus, *Bacch.* 155; Aelian, *VH* 3,32; Athenaeus 4,164b; Apollod. *Bibl.* 2,4,9f.; schol. on Theocr. 13,6b; Stat. *Theb.* 1,484ff.; Tzetzes, *Chil.* 2,221ff.; Seneca, *HF* 478, Hom. *Oct.* 369ff.; Diod. Sic. 4,29,2ff.; Paus. 9,27,6ff.; 1,41,3ff.; Athenaeus 4,556ff.; Diod. Sic. 4,10,3ff.; Paus. 9,37,2ff.; Tzetzes, *Chil.* 2,226ff.; Apollod. *Bibl.* 2,4,11; Isocr. 10,10; Strabo 9,2,40, p. 414; schol. on Pind. *Ol.* 14,2; Euripides, *HF* 220ff.; Hom. *Od.* 11,269ff. with schol.; Pind. *Isth.* 4,12 (18) with schol. on 104; Paus. 9,11,2; Diod. Sic. 4,10,6ff.; 9,11,2; Tzetzes, *Chil.* 2,228; on Lyc. *Alex.* 38; 48; 663; Pherecydes, fragment 30 (Müller *FHG* I, p. 78); Moschus 4,13ff.; Pseudo-Lact. Plac. on Stat. *Theb.* 4,50; Nicol. Damasc. fragment 20 (Müller *FHG* III); Apollod. *Bibl.* 2,4,12; Plutarch, *Amat.* 9,754d.

II *The Twelve Labours*: Paus. 3,17,3; 3,18,13; 5,10,9; 5,25,7; Hyg. *Fab.* 30f.; Serv. on Virgil, *Aen.* 8,299; Hom. *Il.* 8,132ff.; 14,639ff.; 18,117ff.; 19,132ff.; schol. on 14,639; 19,119; Theocr. 24,82ff.; Euripides, *HF* 15ff.; Apollod. *Bibl.* 2,4,12; Sophocles, *Trach.* 1091ff.; Diod. Sic. 4,10ff.; Ovid, *Met.* 9,182ff.; Tzetzes, *Chil.* 229ff.; Hyg. *Fab.* 30; Athenaeus 13,603d; Virgil, *Aen.* 8,287; Quint. Smyrn. *Posthom.* 6,208ff.

Weapons: Apollod. *Bibl.* 2,4,11; Theocr. 25,209ff.; Paus. 2,31,10; Hom. *Il.* 5,393ff.; *Od.* 11,607ff.; Diod. Sic. 4,13,3.

Nemean Lion: Hesiod, *Theog.* 326ff.; Bacchyl. 8,6ff. (9,6ff.); Sophocles, *Trach.* 1091ff.; Theocr. 25,162ff.; Diod. Sic. 4,11,3ff.; Pseudo-Eratosth. *Catast.* 12; Tzetzes, *Chil.* 2,232ff.; Hyg. *Fab.* 30; Apollod. *Bibl.* 2,5,1; Stat. *Theb.* 4,159ff.; Virgil,

Georg. 3,19 with Serv. and Prob. ad loc.; Nonnus, *Dion.* 17,52ff.; Hyg. *Astron.* 2,24; Sen. *HF* 944ff.; Pseudo-Lact. Plac. on Stat. *Theb.* 2,58; Tibull. 4,1,2ff.; Martial 4,64,30; 9,43,13.

Lernaean Hydra: Hesiod, *Theog.* 313ff.; Euripides, *HF* 419ff.; *Ion* 194; schol. on Euripides, *Phoen.* 1137; Diod. Sic. 4,11,5; Paus. 2,37,4; 5,10,9; 5,17,11; Quint. Smyrn. *Posthom.* 6,212ff.; Tzetzes, *Chil.* 2,237ff.; Virgil, *Aen.* 6,803; 8,299ff.; Serv. on *Aen.* 6,287; Ovid, *Met.* 9,69ff.; Apollod. *Bibl.* 2,5,2; schol. on Hesiod, *Theog.* 313, Palaeph. *Incred.* 38; Pseudo-Lact. Plac. on Stat. *Theb.* 1,384; 2,377; Hyg. *Astron.* 2,11; Pseudo-Eratosth. *Catast.* 11; Sophocles, *Trach.* 714ff.

Erymanthian Boar: Sophocles, *Trach.* 1095ff.; Apoll. Rhod. *Arg.* 1,127 with schol.; Diod. Sic. 4,12,1; Apollod. *Bibl.* 2,5,4; Stat. *Theb.* 4,290; Tzetzes, *Chil.* 2,268ff.; Hyg. *Fab.* 30; Paus. 8,24,5.

Cerynean Hind: Pind. *Ol.* 3,29ff. (52ff.) with schol. on 52f.; Callim. *Hymn* 3,89ff.; Euripides *HF* 375ff.; Virgil, *Aen.* 6,801; Tzetzes, *Chil.* 2,265ff.

Stymphalian Birds: Paus. 8,22,4; Apoll. Rhod. *Arg.* 2,382ff.; 1036ff.; schol. on 2,1052; 1054; Diod. Sic. 4,13,2; Euripides *Phrixus* fragment 838 (Nauck *TGF*, edn 2, p. 632); Pliny, *NH* 6,32; Strabo 8,6,8, p. 371; Quint. Smyrn. *Posthom.* 6,227ff.; Tzetzes, *Chil.* 2,291ff.; Hyg. *Fab.* 20; 30; Serv. on Virgil, *Aen.* 8,300; Apollod. *Bibl.* 2,5,6.

Augean Stables: Pind. *Ol.* 10,26ff. (32ff.) with schol. on 32; Apoll. Rhod. *Arg.* 1,172 with schol.; 3,362; Apollod. *Bibl.* 1,9,16; 2,5,5; Hyg. *Fab.* 14; 30; Paus. 5,1,9ff.; 5,3,1ff.; Theocr. 25,7ff.; Diod. Sic. 4,13,3; Tzetzes, *Chil.* 2,278; schol. on Hom. *Il.* 2,629; 11,300; Seneca, *HF* 247ff.

Cretan Bull: Apollod. *Bibl.* 2,5,7; Diod. Sic. 4,13,4; Paus. 1,27,9ff.; 5,10,9; Tzetzes, *Chil.* 2,293ff.; Hyg. *Fab.* 30; Pseudo-Lact. Plac. on Stat. *Theb.* 5,431; Virgil, *Aen.* 8,294ff. with Serv. ad loc.

Mares of Diomedes: Diod. Sic. 4,15,3ff.; Quint. Smyrn. *Posthom.* 6,245ff.; Tzetzes, *Chil.* 2,299ff.; Strabo 7, fragments 44; 47 (p. 331); Hyg. *Fab.* 30; Apollod. *Bibl.* 2,5,8; Euripides, *Alc.* 483; 492ff.; *HF* 380ff.; Steph. Byz. s.v. Ἄβδηρα (Abdera); Lucret. 5,29; Ovid, *Met.* 11,194ff.

Hippolyte's Girdle: Euripides, *HF* 408ff.; Apoll. Rhod. *Arg.* 2,777ff. with schol. on 778; 780; 2,966ff.; Diod. Sic. 4,16; Paus. 5,10,9, Quint. Smyrn. *Posthom.* 6,240ff.; Tzetzes, *Chil.* 2,309ff.; on Lyc. *Alex.* 1327; Hyg. *Fab.* 30; Hellanicus, fragment 33 (Müller *FHG* I, p. 49); Apollod. *Bibl.* 2,59.

Cattle of Geryon: Hesiod, *Theog.* 287; 979; Aeschylus, *Ag.* 870; Pind. fragment 169 Schr. = 152 Bo.; Hdt. 4,8; Euripides, *HF* 423ff.; Plato, *Grg.* 484b; schol. on *Tim.* 24e; Diod. Sic. 4,17ff.; Paus. 3,18,13; 4,36,3; 5,19,1, Athenaeus 9,370e ff.; 11,468e; 469d ff.; 781d; Quint. Smyrn. *Posthom.* 6,249ff.; Tzetzes, *Chil.* 2,322ff.; on Lyc. *Alex.* 652; Lucret. 5,28; Pliny, *NH* 4,20; Horace, *Odes.* 2,14,7ff.; Serv. on Virgil, *Aen.* 8,300; Virgil, *Aen.* 6,289; Ovid, *Met.* 9,184ff.; Solinus 23,12; Apollod. *Bibl.* 2,5,10; Macrob. *Sat.* 5,21,16; 5,21,19; Hyg. *Fab.* 30; 151.

Return from Geryon: Aeschylus, *Prometheus Lyomenos* fragment 199 (Nauck *TGF*, edn 2, p. 66); Strabo 4,1,7, p. 182f.; Dion. Hal. 1,34ff.; Eustath. in Müller, *Geog. Gr. Min.* II, p. 231; Hyg. *Astron.* 2,6; Tzetzes, *Chil.* 2,340ff.; Diod. Sic. 4,20ff.; Seneca, *Apocol.* 7. See also ERYX, ECHIDNA, GALATES, PYRENE, CELTUS.

Cerberus: Hom. *Il.* 8,366ff.; schol. on 5,395; *Od.* 11,623ff.; Bacchyl. 5,56ff.; Euripides, *HF* 23ff.; 1277ff.; Diod. Sic. 4,25,1; 4,26,1; Paus. 2,31,2; 2,35,10; 3,18,13; 3,25,5ff.; 5,26,7; 9,34,5; Apollod. *Bibl.* 2,5,12; Tzetzes, *Chil.* 2,388ff.; Ovid, *Met.* 7,410ff.; Hyg. *Fab.* 31; Seneca, *Ag.* 859ff.; *HF* 50ff.; Xen. *Anab.* 6,2,2; Palaeph. *Incred.* 39.

Apples of the Hesperides: Hesiod, *Theog.* 215ff.; Euripides, *Hipp.* 741ff.; *HF* 394ff.; Apoll. Rhod. *Arg.* 4,1396ff. with schol. on

Illyrius Apollod. *Bibl.* 3,5,4; Steph. Byz. s.v. Ἰλλύρια (Illuria); Strabo 7,7,8, p. 326.

Ilus (1) Apollod. *Bibl.* 3,12,2. (2) Apollod. *Bibl.* 3,12,2; Hom. *Il.* 20,215ff.; 232ff.; Steph. Byz. s.v. Ἀτύλοφος (Atiolophos) and Ἴλιον (Ilion); Lyc. *Alex.* 29 with Tzetzes ad loc.; Diod. Sic. 4,74ff.; Plutarch, *Parallel.* 17,309f; Paus. 2,22,3. (3) Hom. *Od.* 1,259; 3,328; Eustath. on Hom. p. 1415,50ff.; Strabo 8,3,5, p 338

Imbrasus (1) Athenaeus, VII, 283e. (2) Hom. *Il.* IV, 520.

Inachus Apollod. *Bibl.* 2,1,1ff.; Paus. 2,15,4ff.; Tzetzes on Lyc. *Alex.* 178; Hyg. *Fab.* 124; 143; 145; 155; 235; 274; Ovid, *Met.* 1,583; Aeschylus, *PV* 590; 636; 663; 705; Sophocles, *Inachus* (lost satyr-play, Jebb Pearson, I, p. 197ff.); Pseudo-Plutarch, *De Fluviis* 18 (*Mor.* ed. Bernardakis VII). See also IO; PHORONEUS.

Incubi Horace, *Epod.* 5,95ff.; Tertull. *De An.* 44; Macrob. *in Somn. Scip.* 1,3,7; Petron. *Sat.* 38; Pliny. *NH.* 25,4,29; 30,10,84; Aug. *Civ. Dei* 15,23.

Indigetes Aug. *Civ. Dei.* 4,8; 6,1ff.; Tertull. *Ad Nat.* 2,1ff.; Censor. *De Die Nat.* 2,2ff.; Serv. on Virgil, *Georg.* 1,21.

Indus (1) Nonnus, *Dion.* 18,272; Pseudo-Plutarch, *De Fluviis* 4 (*Mor.* ed. Bernardakis VII). (2) Pseudo-Plutarch, *De Fluviis* 25. (3) Hyg. *Fab.* 274.

Io Apollod. *Bibl.* 2,1,3ff.; Paus. 2,16,1; 3,18,3; 1,25,1; Lucian, *Dial. Deor.* 7 (3); Ovid, *Met.* 1,583ff.; Hyg. *Fab.* 145; 149; 155; Aeschylus, *Suppl.* 41ff.; 291ff.; 556ff.; *PV* 589ff.; 640ff.; Suda s.v. Ἰώ (Io) and Ἴσις (Isis); schol. on Apoll. Rhod. *Arg.* 2,168; on Hom. *Od.* 2,120; Pliny, *NH* 16,239; Hesiod, fragments 294 M-W; Diod. Sic. 1,13,5; 1,25; 3,74; 5,60; Parthenius, *Erot. Path.* 1; Martial 11,47,4; Hdt. 1,1; 2,41; Hyg. *Astrom.* 2,21.

Iobates Apollod. *Bibl.* 2,2,1ff.; Hom. *Il.* 6,169 with schol. on 155; Diod. Sic. 6,7,8; Hyg. *Fab.* 57; Sophocles, *Iobates* (lost tragedy, Jebb-Pearson, I, p. 214).

Iobes Apollod. *Bibl.* 2,7,8.

Iocastus Tzetzes on Lyc. *Alex.* 45, 738; Heracl. Lemb. *De Rebus Publicis* 25 (Müller *FHG* II p. 219); Diod. Sic. 5,8; schol. on Hom. *Od.* 2,2; 16.

Iodama Paus. 9,34,1ff.; Tzetzes on Lyc. *Alex.* 355; 1206; Etymol. Magn. s.v. Ἰτωνίς (Itonis). See also ITONUS.

Iolaus Apollod. *Bibl.* 2,4,11; 2,5,2; Paus. 1,19,3; 1,29,5; 1,44,10; 5,8,3ff.; 5,17,11; 7,2,2; 8,14,9; 8,45,6; 9,23,1; 9,40,6; 10,17,5; Hesiod, *Scutum* 74ff.; *Theog.* 317; Tzetzes on Lyc. *Alex.* 830; Diod. Sic. 4,24; 29; 30; 31; 33; 38; 5,15; Pind. *Nem.* 3,36 (61); *Isth.* 1,16 (21); Hyg. *Fab.* 14; 173; 273; Strabo 5,2,7, p. 225; Euripides, *Heracl.* 843ff.; schol. on Pind. *Pyth.* 9,137.

Iole Apollod. *Bibl.* 2,6,1; 2,7,7; Hyg. *Fab.* 31; 35f.; Sophocles, *Trach.* 351–632 with schol. on 266; 354; Diod. Sic. 4,31; Athenaeus 13,560c; Plutarch, *Parallel.* 13,308f.

Ion Hdt. 7,94; Apollod. *Bibl.* 1,7,3; schol. on Hom. *Il.* 1,2; Strabo 8.7.1, p. 383; 9,1,18, p. 397; Paus. 1,31,3; 2,14,2; 2,26,1; 7,1,2ff.; 7,4,2; 7,25,8; Euripides, *Ion*; schol. on Aristophanes, *Clouds* 1468; on *Birds* 1527; Sophocles, *Creusa* (lost tragedy, Jebb-Pearson II, p. 23).

Ionius (1) Schol. on Apoll. Rhod. *Arg.* 4,308; Tzetzes on Lyc. *Alex.* 630; schol. on Pind. *Pyth.* 3,120; Serv. on Virgil, *Aen.* 3,211. (2) Appian, *Bell. Civ.* 2,39.

Iope (1) Plutarch, *Thes.* 29. (2) Steph. Byz. s.v. Ἰόπη (Iope); Dion. Perieg. fragment 910; Conon, *Narr.* 40.

Ioxus Plutarch, *Thes.* 8.

Iphianassa (1) Apollod. *Bibl.* 2,2,2; schol. on Hom. *Od.* 15,225. (2) Hom. *Il.* 9,145; 287; Sophocles, *El.* 157 with schol.; Lucret. 1,85. (3) Apollod. *Bibl.* 1,7,6.

Iphicles Apollod. *Bibl.* 2,4,8ff.; 2,7,3; 1,8,2; schol. on Hom. *Od.* 11,266; 269; on *Il.* 14,323; Tzetzes on Lyc. *Alex.* 33; 38; 839; Hesiod, *Scutum* 48ff.; 87ff.; Theocr. 24; Nic. Damasc.

Iphiclus (1) Apollod. *Bibl.* 1,9,2; 3,19,8; *Epit.* 3,13; Hom. *Od.* 11,287ff. with schol. ad loc.; Eustath. on Hom. p. 1685; Apoll. Rhod. *Arg.* 1,45ff. with schol.; Hyg. *Fab.* 14; 103; 251; Paus. 4,36,2ff.; 5,17,10; 10,31,10. (2) Apoll. Rhod. *Arg.* 1,190ff. with schol. on 201; Apollod. *Bibl.* 1,9,16, Hyg. *Fab.* 14. (3) Tzetzes on Lyc. *Alex.* 1218. (4) Athenaeus 8,360.

Iphidamas (1) Paus. 4,36,4; 5,19,4; Hom. *Il.* 11,221ff.; Eustath. on Hom. p. 840. (2) Apollod. *Bibl.* 2,3,11; schol. on Apoll. Rhod. *Arg.* 4,1396.

Iphigenia Apollod. *Epit.* 3,21ff.; *Cypria*, Homer Oxf. Class. Text V, p. 104; Euripides, *IA; IT*; Tzetzes on Lyc. *Alex.* 103; 143; 148; 194; 1374; *Antehom.* 191; schol. on Hom. *Il.* 1,108; 13,626; Hyg. *Fab.* 98; 120f.; 238; 261; Ovid, *Met.* 12,24ff.; Dict. Cret. *Bell. Tro.* 1,19ff. Paus. 1,33,1; 1,43,1; 2,22,7; 2,35,1; 3,16,7; 7,26,5; 9,19,6; Antoninus Liberalis, *Met.* 27; Serv. on Virgil, *Aen.* 1,116; 11,267; Lucret. 1,85ff.; Cic. *De Off.* 3.25; Aeschylus, *Iphigenia* (lost tragedy, Nauck *TGF*, edn 2, p. 31); Sophocles, *Chryses* (lost tragedy, Jebb-Pearson II, p. 327ff); Steph. Byz. s.v. Χρυσόπολις (Chrusopolis); Etymol. Magn. s.v. Ἴφις (Iphi); Diod. Sic. 4,44; Hdt. 4,104.

Iphimedia Hom. *Od.* 11,305ff.; Pind. *Pyth.* 4,88ff. (156ff.); schol. on Apoll. Rhod. *Arg.* 1,482; on Hom. *Il.* 5,385; Hyg. *Fab.* 28; Diod. Sic. 5,50ff.; Parthenius, *Erot. Path.* 19.

Iphis (I) (1) Paus. 2,18,5; 10,10,3; Apollod. *Bibl.* 3,6,3; Aeschylus, *Sept.* 458ff. (2) Schol. on Apoll. Rhod. *Arg.* 4,223; 228; Diod. Sic. 4,28; Val. Flacc. *Arg.* 1,441; 7,423. (3) See ANAXARETE.

Iphis (II) (1) Apollod. *Bibl.* 2,7,8. (2) Hom. *Il.* 9,667; Paus. 10,25,4. (3) Ovid, *Met.* 9,666ff. See also IANTHE.

Iphitus (1) Apollod. *Bibl.* 1,9,16; Hom. *Il.* 2,518 with schol. on 517; 17,306; Apoll. Rhod. *Arg.* 1,207ff.; Paus. 10,4,2; 10,36,10; Hyg. *Fab.* 14; 97. (2) Apollod. *Bibl.* 2,6,1ff.; Apoll. Rhod. *Arg.* 1,86; 2,114ff.; Hyg. *Fab.* 14; Hom. *Od.* 8,226ff.; 21,11ff.; schol. on 21,22; Sophocles, *Trach.* 270ff.; Tzetzes, *Chil.* 2,417ff.; schol. on Euripides, *Hipp.* 545; on Sophocles, *Trach.* 266; Diod. Sic. 4,31; Paus. 10,13,8. (3) Apollod. *Bibl.* 2,5,1. (4) Paus. 5,4,4ff.; Plutarch, *Lycurg.* 1; 23ff.; Euseb. *Chron.* p. 86 Helm.

Iris Hesiod, *Theog.* 266; 780; 784; Alcaeus, fragment 13 Bergk = 327 PLF; Hom. *Il.* 3,111; 8,397ff.; 18,166; 24,77ff.; 15,143ff.; Homeric Hymn to Apollo, 102; Virgil, *Aen.* 4,694ff.; 9,5ff.; Euripides, *HF* 822ff.; Callim. *Hymn* 4,22ff.; Theocr. 17,134.

Irus (1) Apoll. Rhod. *Arg.* 1,72 with schol.; Tzetzes on Lyc. *Alex.* 175; schol. on Hom. *Il.* 23,88; Antoninus Liberalis, *Met.* 38. (2) Hom. *Od.* 18,1ff.; Hyg. *Fab.* 126.

Ischenus Tzetzes on Lyc. *Alex.* 38; 42ff.; Paus. 6,20,8.

Ischys Pind. *Pyth.* 3,8ff. (14ff.) with schol. on 14ff.; 60; Ovid, *Met.* 2,542ff.; Antoninus Liberalis, *Met.* 20; Cic. *De Nat. Deor.* 3,22. See also ASCLEPIUS.

Isis Plutarch, *De Iside*; Apul. *Met.* 11.

Ismene (1) Apollod. *Bibl.* 2,1,3. (2) Sophocles, *Ant.* with hypothesis; Apollod. *Bibl.* 3,5,8.

Ismenus (1) Hyg. *Fab.* pref.; Apollod. *Bibl.* 3,12,6; Diod. Sic. 4,72. (2) Paus. 9,10,5; Callim. *Hymn* 4,76. (3) Apollod. *Bibl.* 3,5,6; Ovid, *Met.* 6,224; Hyg. *Fab.* 11; Pseudo-Plutarch, *De Fluviis* 2 (*Mor.* ed. Bernardakis VII).

Isola Tiberina Livy 2,5; Plutarch, *Publicola* 8.

Issa (1) Steph. Byz. s,v,; Tzetzes on Lyc. *Alex.* 219; Ovid, *Met.* 6,124. (2) Ptol. Heph. 1.

Isthmiades Paus. 9,25,7ff.

Istrus Hesiod, *Theog.* 339; Tzetzes, *Antehom.* 274.

Italus Dion. Hal. 1,12; 35; 73; Strabo 6,1,4, p. 254; Thuc.

6,44,2; Aristotle, *Pol.* 7,9,2; Tzetzes on Lyc. *Alex.* 1232; Serv. on Virgil, *Aen.* 1,2; 1,533; Hyg. *Fab.* 127.

Ithacus Hom. *Od.* 17,207ff. with schol.; Eustath. on Hom. p. 1817,43.

Ithome Paus. 3,26,6; 4,12,7ff.; 4,33,2ff.

Itonus Paus. 9,1,1; 9,34,1; 5,1,4.

Itylus Hom. *Od.* 19,518ff. with schol.; Eustath. on Hom. p. 1875,15; Paus. 9,5,9; 10,32,11; Hesiod, *Works and Days* 568ff.; Aelian, *VH* 12,20.

Itys Aeschylus, *Suppl.* 57ff.; *Ag.* 141ff.; Hyg. *Fab.* 45; 239; 246; Sophocles, *Tereus* (lost tragedy, Jebb-Pearson II, p. 221); Ovid, *Met.* 6,411ff.; Apollod. *Bibl.* 3,14,8; Conon, *Narr.* 31; schol. on Virgil, *Ecl.* 6,78; *Mythogr. Lat.* (Bode) 1,4,2. p. 217.

Iulus Virgil, *Aen.* 1,288; 4,274; 6,364; Serv. on Virgil, *Georg.* 3,35; Suetonius, *Divus Iulius* 81; Juv. 12,70; Dion. Hal. *Ant. Rom.* 1,70; Festus s.v. *Silvi*, p. 340 M.; Euseb. *Chron.* p. 64 Helm; Anon. *De Orig. Gent. Rom.* 17,4.

Iustitia Ovid, *Fasti* 1,249ff.; *Met.* 1,150; Virgil, *Georg.* 2,474; Serv. on *Ecl.* 4,6; Hyg. *Fab.* 130; *Astr. poet.* 2,25; cf. Aratus, *Phaen.* 96ff.; see ASTRAEA.

Iuventus Dion. Hal. *Rom. Ant.* 3,69; Livy 5,54,7; Florus 1,1; Cic. *De Nat. Deor.* 1,112; Ovid, *Ex Ponto* 1,10,12; Aug. *Civ. Dei* 4,23ff.; 6,1.

Ixion Apollod. *Epit.* 1,20; Pind. *Pyth.* 2,21ff. (40ff.) with schol. on 40; Aeschylus, *Eum.* 440; 718; *Ixion* (lost tragedy, Nauck *TGF*, edn 2, pp. 29f.); Sophocles, *Phil.* 679ff.; schol. on Hom. *Il.* 1,286; Euripides, *Ixion* (lost tragedy, Nauck *TGF*, edn 2, p. 490f.); schol. on Euripides, *Phoen.* 1185; Apoll. Rhod. *Arg.* 3,62 with schol.; Diod. Sic. 4,69; Hyg. *Fab.* 14; 62; Lucian, *Dial. Deor.* 9 (6) with schol. on *Pisc.* 12; Virgil, *Georg.* 4,484; Strabo 9,5,19, p. 439. See also CENTAURS.

Iynx Suda s.v. ἴυγξ (iynx); schol. On Theocr. 2,17; on Pind. *Nem.* 4,56.

J

Janus *Carmen Saliare* in Varro, *De Ling. Lat.* 7,26; Piso, *Annals*, quoted ibid. 5,165; Livy 1,19,2; etc.; Ovid, *Fasti* 1,63–299; *Met.* 14,785ff.; Virgil, *Aen.* 7,180; 7,610; 8,357; 12,198; Serv. on *Aen.* 1,291 and 8,319; Plutarch, *Quaest. Rom.* 41,274e-f; Macrob. *Sat.* 1,7,19; 1,9; Aug. *Civ. Dei* 7,4; Solinus 2,5; Joann. Lyd. *De Mensibus* 4,1–2. Cf. P. Grimal, *Lettres d'Humanité* IV, 1945; L. A. Holland, '*Janus and the Bridge*' in *Papers and Monographs, American Academy in Rome.* 21, 1961.

Jason Hesiod, *Theog.* 992ff.; Pind. *Pythian* 4; Apoll. Rhod. *Argon.* Orphic *Argon.*; Val. Flacc. *Argon.*; Diod. Sic. 4,40ff.; Hyg. *Fab.* 12ff.; Apollod. *Bibl.* 1,8,2; 1,9,16ff.; 3,13,7; Paus. 2,3,8ff.; 5,17,9–10; Lyc. *Alex.* 1309ff. and Tzetzes on ibid. 175; Ovid, *Met.* 7,1ff.; *Heroides* 6 and 12; Stat. *Theb.* 516ff.; Serv. on Virgil, *Ecl.* 4,34; Euripides *Medea*; see also ARGONAUTS; MEDEA.

Jocasta Hom. *Od.* 11,271ff. with scholia; Apollod. *Bibl.* 3,5,7–9 (cf. Frazer's edn, Appendix 8, vol. II p. 370ff.); Sophocles *OT* with schol.; Euripides, *Phoen.* 1–62; 1760; schol. on *Phoen.* 53; Seneca, *Oedipus;* Diod. Sic. 4,64; Paus. 9,5,10ff.; Hyg. *Fab.* 66–7; 70; see also OEDIPUS.

Julia Luperca Tzetzes on Lyc. *Alex.* 183 (fin.).

Juno Varro, *De Ling. Lat.* 5,65ff.; 5,158; Ovid, *Fasti* 3,167ff. (Matronalia); ibid. 6,183 (Moneta); Livy 7,28,6; Cic. *De Nat. Deor.* 2,66; Macrob. *Sat.* 1,12,30; Serv. on Virgil, *Aen.* 4,518; *CIL* VI.i, no.2099; for Lanuvium, Prop. 4,8,3ff.; Aelian, *Nat. An.* 11,16; for Junones corresponding to Genii, Pliny *NH* 2,16; Petron, *Sat.* 25,4; Lygdamus 6,48; Seneca, *Ep.* 110,1. See also HERA.

Jupiter Livy 1,10,5ff.; 1,12,3; 4,20; 10,37,14; 41,16,1ff.; Ovid,

Fasti 3,285ff.; 6,793f.; Plutarch, *Numa* 15; Pliny, *NH* 3,69; Dion. Hal. *Rom. Ant.* 2,50,3; Festus, p. 189 M. Virgil, *Aen.* 8,347ff.; Serv. on *Aen.* 6,855; 12,135; and on *Georg.* 3,332; Suetonius, *Aug.* 29. Cf. C. Koch, *Der römische Juppiter*, 1937; see also ZEUS.

Juturna Cic. *Pro Cluent.* 101; Virgil, *Aen.* 12,134ff., etc.; Serv. ad loc.; Ovid, *Fasti* 1,463ff.; Varro, *De Ling. Lat.* 5,71; Arnobius, *Adv. Nat.* 3,29.

K

Keres Hom. *Il.* 1,228; 1,416ff.; 2,302; 3,454; 8,70ff.; 9,410ff.; 11,330ff.; 18,114ff.; 18,535ff.; 22,102; 22,209ff.; 23,78ff.; Hesiod, *Theog.* 211; 217; *W. & D.* 92; *Scutum* 156; 249ff.; Aeschylus, *Septem* 760; 1055; Sophocles, *OT* 469ff.; *Phil.* 42; 1166; Euripides, *HF* 870; *Elect.* 1298ff.; *Phoen.* 950; Plato, *Laws* 937d; Apoll. Rhod. *Arg.* 4,1485; 1665ff.

L

Labdacus Sophocles, *OT* 224, etc.; *O.C.* 221; *Ant.* 594; Hdt. 5,59; Euripides, *Phoen.* 8; Paus. 2,6,2; 9,5,4ff.; Hyg. *Fab.* 76; Apollod. *Bibl.* 3,5,5.

Labrandus Etym. Magn. p. 389,58.

Lacedaemon Schol. on *Il.* 18,486; on *Od.* 6,103; on Euripides, *Orestes* 615; on Pind. *Pyth.* 3,14 (8); on Apoll. Rhod. *Arg.* 4,1091; Paus. 3,1,2–3; 3,13,8; 3,18,6; 3,20,2; 7,18,5; 9,35,1; Apollod. *Bibl.* 2,2,2; 3,10,3; Hyg. *Fab.* 155; Steph. Byz. s.v. Ἀσίνη (Asine) and Λακεδαίμων (Lacedaemon); Tzetzes on Lyc. *Alex.* 219; Nonnus, *Dion.* 32,66; Pseudo-Plut. *De Fluviis* 17.

Lacestades Paus. 2,6,7.

Lacinius Diod. Sic. 4,24; Steph. Byz. s.v.; Tzetzes on Lyc. *Alex.* 856; 1106; Serv. on Virgil, *Aen.* 3,552; Etym. Magn. p. 555,16; schol. on Theocr. 4,33.

Lacius Steph. Byz. s.v. Γέλα (Gela); Etym. Magn. p. 225,1ff. (on Antiphemus); Athenaeus 7,297e ff.

Lacon John of Antioch, fragment 20 Müller (*FHG* IV, p. 549).

Ladon (1) Hesiod, *Theog.* 344; Apollod. *Bibl.* 3,12,6; Diod. Sic. 4,72; Paus. 8,20,1; 8,43,2; 10,7,8; schol. on Pind. *Ol.* 6,140ff. (83ff.); Serv. on Virgil, *Aen.* 2,513; 3,91; on *Ecl.* 3,63; Tzetzes on Lyc. *Alex.* 6; schol. on Hom. *Il.* 1,14. (2) Hesiod, *Theog.* 333ff. (no name given); schol. on Apoll. Rhod. *Arg.* 4,1396; Apollod. *Bibl.* 2,5,11; Hyg. *Fab.* 30; *Astron.* 2,3.

Laertes Hom. *Il.* 2,173; 3,200 (in the form of the patronymic *Laertiades*); *Od.* 1,189ff.; 11,187ff.; 16,138ff.; 23,359ff.; 24,205ff.; Diod. Sic. 4,48; Cic. *De Senectute* 54; Ovid, *Her.* 1,98; 1,113; Hyg. *Fab.* 173; schol. on Hom. *Od.* 16,118 and 24,270; Eustath. p. 1796,10.

Laestrygones Hom. *Od.* 10,81ff.; 199; 23,318ff.; schol. ad loc.; Hesych., s.v. Λάμος (Lamus); Aul. Gell. *Noct. Att.* 15,21; Lyc. *Alex.* 662, with Tzetzes ad loc.; Ovid, *Met.* 14,233ff.; Hyg. *Fab.* 125.

Laethusa Hyg. *Fab.* 45 (Rose corrects to *Lathusa*).

Laius Hdt. 5,59ff.; Sophocles, *OT* passim; Euripides, *Phoen.* with schol. on lines 13; 26; 39; etc.; Aeschylus, trilogy consisting of *Laius, Oedipus* (both lost) and *Seven against Thebes*, cf. Nauck, *TGF*, edn 2, p. 39; Hyg. *Fab.* 9; 66; 76; Apollod. *Bibl.* 3,5,5ff.; Paus. 4,8,8; 9,2,4; 9,5,6ff.; 10,5,3–4; etc.; Nic. Damasc. fragments 14–15 Müller (*FHG* III, p. 365f.); Athenaeus 13,603a; Plutarch, *Parall.* 33,313e; Stat. *Theb.* 7,354ff.

Lamedon Paus. 2,5,8; 2,6,3ff.

Lamia (1) Paus. 10,12,1; Plutarch, *De Pyth. Orac.* 9,398c. (2) Schol. on Apoll. Rhod. *Arg* 4,828; schol. on Aristophanes, *Peace* 758; *Wasps* 1035; *Knights* 693; Diod. Sic 22,41; Strabo 1,2,8, p. 19; Philostr. *Vit. Apoll.* 4,25; Antoninus Liberalis, *Met.* 8; schol. on Theocr 15,40; Suda and Hesych. s.v.

Lampetia (1) Hom. *Od.* 12,132; 375; Eustath, p. 1717,27ff.; Tzetzes on Lyc. *Alex.* 740; Nonnus, *Dion.* 27,198; 38,170. (2) Schol. on Aristophanes, *Plut.* 701. (3) Hyg. *Fab.* 154; 156; Ovid, *Met.* 2,349; schol. on Hom. *Od.* 17,208.

Lampetus Parthenius, *Erot. Path.* 21.

Lampsace Steph. Byz. s.v. Λάμψακος (Lampsacus); Plutarch, *De Mul. Virt.* 255a ff. (quoting Charon of Lampsacus, = fragment 6 Müller, *FHG* I, p. 33).

Lampus Hom. *Il.* 15,526; 20,238; Eustath, p. 1030,22; Hecataeus, fragment 210 Müller (*FHG* I, p. 14), quoted by Steph. Byz. s.v. Λαμπωνεία (Lamponeia).

Lamus (1) Hom. *Od.* 10,81, and schol. ad loc.; Eustath, p. 1649,10; Ovid, *Met.* 14,233; Horace, *Od.* 3,17; schol. on Aristophanes, *Peace* 758; Suda and Hesych. s.v. (2) Ovid, *Her.* 9,54; Steph. Byz. s.v. Λαμία (Lamia).

Laocoon (1) Arctinus, in *Homer Oxf. Class. Text* 5, p. 107, line 24 (Proclus' summary of the Epic Cycle); Dion. Hal. *Rom. Ant.* 1,48,2; Virgil, *Aen.* 2,40ff. and 199ff. and Serv. ad loc.; Quint. Smyrn. *Posthom.* 12,449ff.; Apollod. *Epit.* 5,17ff.; Tzetzes on Lyc. *Alex.* 347; Hyg. *Fab.* 135; Macrob. *Sat.* 5,2,4; Petron. *Sat.* 89,23ff. (2) Hyg. *Fab.* 14; schol. on Apoll. Rhod. *Arg.* 1,191.

Laodamas Apollod. *Bibl.* 3,7,3; Paus. 1,39,2; 9,5,13; 9,8,6; 9,9,5; 9,10,3; cf. Hdt. 5,61.

Laodamia (1) Hom. *Il.* 6,197ff. with schol.; Apollod. *Bibl.* 3,1,1; Serv. on Virgil, *Aen.* 1,100; Nonnus, *Dion.* 7,127; Diod. Sic. 5,79 (with a variant of the name). (2) Hom. *Il.* 2,698ff. with Eustath p. 325; Ovid, *Ars Am.* 3,17; *Her.* 13; *Trist.* 1,6,20; *Ex Ponto* 3,1,110; *Rem. Am.* 723; Catull. 68,74ff.; Hyg. *Fab.* 103–4; 243; 251; 256; Tzetzes, *Antehom.* 227; 246; *Chil.* 2,52; Serv. on Virgil, *Aen.* 6,447; Apollod. *Epit.* 3,30; Lucian, *Dial. Mort.* 23; schol. on Aristid. p. 671ff.; Euripides, *Protesilaus* (lost tragedy), cf. *TGF*, edn 2, p. 563ff. (3) Schol. on Hom. *Il.* 16,175.

Laodice (1) Apollod. *Bibl.* 3,9,1. (2) Paus. 8,5,3; 8,53,7. (3) Hom. *Il.* 9,145, with schol.; ibid. 287. (4) Hom. *Il.* 3,124; 6,252; Hyg. *Fab.* 90; 101; Apollod. *Bibl.* 3,12,5; *Epit.* 5,23; Parthenius, *Erot. Path.* 16; Tzetzes on Lyc. *Alex.* 314; 447; 495; *Posthom.* 736; Quint. Smyrn. *Posthom.* 13,544ff.; Paus. 10,26,3; Plutarch, *Theseus 34; Cimon* 4.

Laodocus Apollod. *Bibl.* 1,7,6.

Laomedon Hom. *Il.* 6,23; 20,237; 21,441ff., Pind. *Ol.* 8,41 (30) with schol.; Diod. Sic. 4,49; Apollod. *Bibl.* 2,6,4; 3,12,3 and 8; Serv. on Virgil, *Aen.* 2,241; Ovid, *Met.* 11,696; Strabo 13,1,32, p. 596; schol. on Euripides, *Troades* 822; schol. on Euripides, *Orestes* 1391; Tzetzes on Lyc. *Alex.* 34; 523; 1341; Sophocles *Ajax* 1302.

Laonome (1) Schol. on Pind. *Pyth.* 4,76 (43); Tzetzes on Lyc. *Alex.* 886; schol. on Apoll. Rhod. *Arg.* 1,1241. (2) Paus. 8,14,2; Apollod. *Bibl.* 2,4,5; schol. on Hom. *Il.* 19,116.

Laonytus Schol. on Euripides, *Phoen.* 53, quoting Pherecydes (fragment 48 Müller, *FHG* I, p. 85).

Lapiths Hom. *Il.* 2,738ff.; 12,128ff.; 23,836ff.; Pind. *Pyth.* 9,14ff. and schol. ad loc.; Apollod. *Bibl.* 1,8,2; schol. on Hom. *Il.* 1,266; Ovid, *Met.* 8,303ff.; 12,250ff.; Hyg. *Fab.* 173; Diod. Sic. 4,69ff.; cf. 5,81.

Lara Ovid, *Fasti* 2,599ff.; Lact. *Inst. Div.* 1,20,35.

Lares Ovid, *Fasti* 2,599ff.; Varro, *De Ling. Lat.* 9,61; Pliny, *NH* 36,204; Arnobius, *Adv. Nat.* 5,18; cf. Livy 1,39. Cf. E. Tabeling, *Mater Larum*, 1932.

Larinus Athenaeus, 9,376b ff.; schol. on Pind. *Nem.* 4,82 (51); schol. on Aristophanes, *Peace* 925; *Birds* 465; Tzetzes *Chil.* 8,270; Suda and Photius, s.v. Λαρινοὶ βόες (Larinoi boes.)

Larissa Paus. 2,24,1; schol. on Apoll. Rhod. *Arg.* 1,40, quoting Hellanicus, fragment 29, Müller, *FHG* I, p. 49; Serv. on Virgil, *Aen.* 2,197; Dion. Hal. *Ant. Rom.* 1,17; Steph. Byz. s.v. Φθία (Phthia).

Las Paus. 3,24,10.

Latinus Hesiod, *Theog.* 1011ff., id. fragment 5 Merkelbach-West; schol. on Apoll. Rhod. *Arg.* 3,200; Steph. Byz. s.v. Πραίνεστος (Praenestos); Dion. Hal. *Ant. Rom.* 1,43ff.; 1,57ff.; 1,72; Festus pp. 194; 220; 269 M.; Hyg. *Fab.* 127; Plutarch, *Romulus* 2; Livy 1,1,6ff.; Virgil, *Aen.* 7–12; Serv. on *Aen.* 1,267 and 273; 3,148; 4,620; 6,760; etc.; Tzetzes on Lyc. *Alex.* 1232 and 1254; Varro, *De Ling. Lat.* 5,144; Solinus 2,14; Aug. *Civ. Dei* 18,16; schol. Bob. on Cic. *Pro Planc.* 23; Strabo 5,3,2, p. 229. Cf. J. Perret, *La légende troyenne de Rome*, pp. 526ff

Latinus Silvius Ovid, *Met.* 14,611, *Fasti* 4,41ff., Dion. Hal. *Ant. Rom.* 1,71; Diod. Sic. 7,17; Tzetzes on Lyc. *Alex.* 1232; Serv. on Virgil, *Aen.* 6,767.

Lausus Virgil, *Aen.* 7,649; 10,426; 790ff.; Ovid, *Fasti* 4,54; Dion. Hal. *Ant. Rom.* 1,65; Anon. *De Orig. Gent. Rom.* 15 (cf. Müller, *FHG* III, p. 174).

Lavinia Livy 1,1,3; Dion. Hal. *Ant. Rom.* 1,59f.; 1,70; Virgil, *Aen.* 6,764; 7,52ff.; 12,194; Ovid, *Met.* 14,449; 570; Tzetzes on Lyc. *Alex.* 1232; Serv. on Virgil, *Aen.* 1,2; 259; 270; 6,760; 7,51; 484; Plutarch, *Romulus* 2; Aelian, *Nat. An.* 11,16; Strabo 5,3,2, p. 229.

Leagrus Plutarch, *Quaest. Gr.* 48,302d.

Leander Ovid, *Heroides* 18–19; Virgil, *Georg.* 3,258; Musacus, *Hero and Leander*; Anth. Pal. 5,232 (Paulus Silentiarius); 263 (Agathias Scholasticus); 9,215 (Antipater of Macedon); 381 (a Homeric cento).

Learchus Apollod. *Bibl.* 1,9,1ff.; 3,4,3; Paus. 1,44,7; 9,34,7; Tzetzes on Lyc. *Alex.* 21; 229; schol. on Apoll. Rhod. *Arg.* 2,1144; Hyg. *Fab.* 1–2; Ovid, *Met.* 4,512ff.; *Fasti* 6,489ff.; Serv. on Virgil, *Aen.* 5,241; Pseudo-Lact. Plac. on Stat. *Theb.* 1,12.

Lebeadus Plutarch, *Quaest. Gr.* 39,300b.

Leda Apollod. *Bibl.* 1,7,10; 3,10,5ff.; Paus. 3,1,4; 3,13,8; 3,16,1; 3,21,2; Serv. on Virgil, *Aen.* 8,130; schol. on Apoll. Rhod. *Arg.* 1,146; schol. on Euripides, *Or.* 457; Strabo 10,2,24, p. 461; Hyg. *Fab.* 77; Hom. *Od.* 11,298ff.; Euripides, *I.A.* 49ff.; *Helen* 17ff.; 214; 257; 1149; *Or.* 1387; Prop. 1,13,30; John of Antioch, fragment 20 (Müller, *FHG* IV, p. 549); Tzetzes on Lyc. *Alex.* 88; 511; schol. on Pind. *Nem.* 10,150 (80).

Leimon Paus. 8,53,1ff.

Leimone Aeschines, *In Tim.* 182, with schol.; Callim. fragment 94 Trypanis.

Leipephile Hesiod, fragment 252 Merkelbach-West (quoted in Paus. 9,40,6).

Leitus Hom. *Il.* 2,494; 6,35f.; 17,601ff.; Euripides, *IA* 259ff.; Hyg. *Fab.* 97; 114; Paus. 9,39,3; Apollod. *Bibl.* 1,9,16.

Lelex Paus. 1,39,6; 1,42,7; 1,44,3; 3,1,1; 3,12,5; 4,1,2; Steph. Byz. s.v. Λακεδαίμων (Lacedaemon); schol. on Euripides, *Or.* 626; Apollod. *Bibl.* 3,10,3; Strabo 7,7,2, p. 322.

Lemures Ovid, *Fasti* 5,419ff.; Serv. on Virgil, *Aen.* 1,276; 292; Pers. *Sat.* 5,185 with schol.

Leonassa Schol. on Euripides, *Andromache* 24; 32.

Leonteus Hom. *Il.* 2,738ff.; 12,130ff.; 23,837ff.; Hyg. *Fab.* 81; 97; 114; Quint. Smyrn. *Posthom.* 7,487; 12,323; Tzetzes, *Posthom.* 646; on Lyc. *Alex.* 427; 980; 1047; Apollod. *Bibl.* 3,10,8; *Epit.* 6,2; Diod. Sic. 4,53; Steph. Byz. s.v. Φιλαίδαι (Philaidai).

Leontichus Strabo 8,3,20, p. 347, quoting Stesichorus, *Rhadine*, fragment 44 Bergk; Paus. 7,5,13.

Leontophonus Apollod. *Epit.* 7,40; Eustath. p. 1796,51 (Leontophron).

Leos Paus. 1,5,1–2; 10,10,1; Suda and Photius, s.v. ἐπώνυμοι (eponymoi); Suda, Photius and Hesych. s.v. Λεωκόριον (Leocorion); schol. on Thuc. 1,20; Aelian, *Hist. Var.* 12,28; Diod. Sic. 17,15; Cic. *De Nat. Deor.* 3,50; Aelius Aristides, *Or.* 1 (13),87, with schol. (p. 111 Dindorf).

Lepreus Schol. on Callim. *Hymn* 1,39; Athenaeus 10, p. 411c ff.; Aelian, *Hist. Var.* 1,24; Paus. 5,5,4.

Lesbos Diod. Sic. 5,81.

Lethaea Pseudo-Lact. Plac. *Narr. Fab.* Ovid. 10,1; cf. Ovid, *Met.* 10,68ff.

Lethe Hesiod, *Theog.* 227ff.; schol. on Hom. *Il.* 14,276; schol. on *Od.* 11,51; Anth. Pal. 7,25; Plato, *Rep.* 10,621a; Virgil, *Aen.* 6,705ff.; Ovid, *Ex Pont.* 2,4,23; Paus. 9,39,8.

Leto (Latona) Hesiod, *Theog.* 404ff.; Homeric Hymn to Apollo 62; Apollod. *Bibl.* 1,2,2; schol. on Apoll. Rhod. *Arg.* 1,308; Callim. *Hymn to Delos* 4; Pind. fragment 87 Bergk; Hyg. *Fab.* 9; 53; 55; 140; Libanius, *Narrationes* 25 (ed. Foerster, vol. VIII); Antoninus Liberalis, *Met.* 25; Ovid, *Met.* 6,313ff.

Leucadius Strabo 10,2,8, p. 452; 10,2,24, p. 461.

Leucaria Tzetzes on Lyc. *Alex.* 702; Plutarch, *Romulus* 2; Dion. Hal. *Ant. Rom.* 1,72.

Leucaspis Diod. Sic. 4,23.

Leucatas Serv. on Virgil, *Aen.* 3,271.

Leuce (1) Serv. on Virgil, *Ecl.* 7,61. (2) Pind. *Nem.* 4,49; Strabo 2,5,22, p. 125; 7,3,16, p. 306; schol. on Euripides, *IT* 436; Steph. Byz. s.v. Ἀχίλλειος δρόμος (Achilleios dromos); Tzetzes on Lyc. *Alex.* 186–8; Antoninus Liberalis, *Met.* 27; Conon, *Narr.* 18; Pomp. Mela 2,98.

Leucippe (1) Apollod. *Bibl.* 3,12,3; Tzetzes on Lyc. *Alex.* 18. (2) Hyg. *Fab.* 14. (3) Hyg. *Fab.* 190. (4) Schol. on Hom. *Il.* 19,116.

Leucippidae Pind. *Nem.* 10,49ff. with schol.; Lyc. *Alex.* 549; 562ff.; schol. on 535; Apollod. *Bibl.* 3,11,2; Theocr. 22,137ff.; Tzetzes, *Chil.* 2,48; Paus. 3,16,1; Ovid, *Fasti* 5,699ff.; Prop. 1,2,15ff.; Hyg. *Fab.* 80.

Leucippus (1) Apollod. *Bibl.* 1,9,5; 3,10,3ff.; Tzetzes on Lyc. *Alex.* 511; Paus. 1,18,1; 3,12,8, etc.; 4,2,4, etc.; Hyg. *Fab.* 80; Ovid, *Fasti* 5,702; Theocr. 22,137; schol. on Hom. *Il.* 3,243. (2) Paus. 8,20,2; Parthenius, *Erot. Path.* 15. (3) Paus. 2,5,5; schol. on Pind. *Ol.* 6,46ff. (28ff.). (4) Diod. Sic. 5,52. (5) Parthenius, *Erot. Path.* 5.

Leucon Apollod. *Bibl.* 1,9,2; schol. on Apoll. Rhod. *Arg.* 2,1144; Nonnus, *Dion.* 9,312ff.; Paus. 6,21,11; 9,34,5.

Leucophanes Schol. on Pind. *Pyth.* 4,455 (256); Tzetzes on Lyc. *Alex.* 886.

Leucosia Strabo 6,1,1, p. 252; 6,1,6, p. 258; Tzetzes on Lyc. *Alex.* 722.

Leucothea Hom. *Od.* 5,333ff.; with schol.; schol. on *Il.* 8,86; Hyg. *Fab.* 2; Ovid, *Met.* 4,539ff.; *Fasti* 6,480; Hesiod, *Theog.* 976; Pind. *Pyth.* 11,2; *Ol.* 2,28ff.; Euripides, *Medea* 1282ff. with schol.; lost tragedy entitled *Ino* (see Nauck, *TGF*, edn 2, pp. 482ff.); Diod. Sic. 4,2; Tzetzes on Lyc. *Alex.* 107; 229ff.; Paus. 1,44,7; 2,1,3; 9,5,2; Serv. on Virgil, *Aen.* 5,241.

Leucus Tzetzes on Lyc. *Alex.* 384; 431; 1093; 1218ff.; schol. on Hom. *Il.* 2,649; schol. on *Od.* 19,174; Eustath. p. 1860,39.

Leucothoe See CLYTIA.

Liber Cic. *De Nat. Deor.* 2,62; Paulus ex Festus p. 115 M.; Aug. *Civ. Dei* 7,21 (material derived from Varro); Ovid, *Fasti* 3,713ff.; Hyg. *Fab.* 224. See also DIONYSUS.

Libertas Cic. *De Nat. Deor.* II, 61; Ovid, *Fast.* IV, 623ff.

Libitina Plutarch, *Numa* 12.

Libya Aeschylus, *Suppl.* 319; Hdt. 4,45; Apollod. *Bibl.* 2,1,4; Pind. *Pyth.* 4,14 with schol. ad loc.; schol. on Hom. *Il.* 1,42; Eustath. p. 1485,7; Hyg. *Fab.* 149; 157; 160; Paus. 4,23,10;

schol. on Euripides, *Phoen.* 5 and 158; Tzetzes, *Chil.* 7,350; on Lyc. *Alex.* 894 and 1283; Pliny, *NH* 7,56.

Lichas Sophocles, *Trachiniae*; schol. on Apoll. Rhod. *Arg.* 1,1213; Apollod. *Bibl.* 2,7,7; Diod. Sic. 4,38; Strabo 9,4,4, p. 426; Ovid, *Met.* 9,211ff.; Hyg. *Fab.* 36; Seneca, *Hercules Oetaeus* 817ff.

Licymnius Hom. *Il.* 2,662ff. with schol.; Pindar, *Ol.* 7,27ff. with schol.; Diod. Sic. 4,38; 57–8; Apollod. *Bibl.* 2,4,5ff.; 2,7,3 and 7; 2,8,2; Eustath. p. 316,1; Strabo 14,2,6, p. 653; Tzetzes on Hom. *Il.*, p. 103.

Ligys Eustath. on Dion. Perieg. 76.

Lilaeus Pseudo-Plutarch, *De Fluviis* 24,4.

Limos Hesiod, *Theog.* 227; Ovid, *Met.* 8,790ff.

Lindos Pind. *Ol.* 7,74; Diod. Sic. 5,57; Steph. Byz. s.v. Λίνδος (Lindos).

Linus (1) Paus. 1,43,7; Hom. *Il.* 18,570 with schol.; Ovid, *Ibis* 478; Conon, *Narr.* 19; Callim. Fragments 26–8 Trypanis; Aelian, *Nat. An.* 12,34; Stat. *Theb.* 1,562ff.; Serv. on Virgil, *Ecl.* 4,56. (2) Paus. 8,18,1; 9,29,6ff.; Hesiod fragments 305–6 Merkelbach-West; schol. on Euripides, *Rhesus* 347; Hyg. *Fab.* 161; Apollod. *Bibl.* 1,3,2; Diod. Sic. 3,67; Theocr. 24,103; Aelian, *Hist. Var.* 3,32; Tac. *Ann.* 11,14.

Liparus Diod. Sic. 5,8; Steph. Byz. s.v. Λιπάρα (Lipara); Pliny, *NH* 3,14,93.

Lityerses Pollux, *Onom.* 4,54; Athenaeus 10, p. 415; Tzetzes, *Chil.* 2,595; Westermann, *Mythogr. Gr.* p. 346; Serv. on Virgil, *Ecl.* 8,68; schol. on Theocr. 8; Theocr. 10,41; Hesych. s.v. Λιτυέρση (Lityerse).

Locrus (1) Schol. on Hom. *Od.* 11,325; Eustath. p. 1688,64. (2) Hesiod fragment 234 Merkelbach-West (quoted by Strabo, 7,7,2, p. 322); Pind. *Ol.* 9,41ff. with schol.; schol. on Apoll. Rhod. *Arg.* 4,1780; Eustath. p. 277,17; Plutarch, *Qu. Gr.* 15,294e; Steph. Byz. s.v. Φύσκος (Physcos).

Lotis Ovid, *Met.* 9,340ff.; *Fasti* 1,415ff.; Serv. on Virgil, *Georg.* 2,84.

Lotophagi Hom. *Od.* 9,82ff.; Hyg. *Fab.* 125; Pliny, *NH* 5,28; Hdt. 4,177.

Lua Livy 45,33,1; Serv. on Virgil, *Aen.* 3,139.

Luna Varro, *De Ling. Lat.* 5,74; Aug. *Civ. Dei* 4,23; Dion. Hal. *Ant. Rom.* 2,50; Cic. *De Nat. Deor.* 2,27.

Luperci Ovid, *Fasti* 2,381ff.; Dion. Hal. *Ant. Rom.* 1,22,4; 1,79,8; Virgil, *Aen.* 8,343 with Serv. ad loc.; Suetonius, *Aug.* 31; Plutarch, *Romulus* 21; *Res Gestae Divi Augusti*, 19,1. Cf. A. M. Franklin, *The Lupercalia*, 1921.

Lycaon (1) Hom. *Il.* 3,333; 20,81; 21,34ff.; 22,46ff.; 23,746ff.; Apollod. *Bibl.* 3,12,5; *Cypria* (in Proclus' summary, Homer Oxf. Class. Text 5, p. 105). (2) Hesiod fragment 161 Merkelbach-West (cf. Strabo 5,2,4, p. 221); Apollod. *Bibl.* 3,8,1ff.; schol. on Euripides, *Or.* 1642ff.; Paus. 8,2,1ff.; Dion. Hal. *Ant. Rom.* 1,11,13; Hyg. *Fab.* 176; 225; *Astron.* 2,4; Ovid, *Met.* 1,196ff.; Tzetzes on Lyc. *Alex.* 482; Nic. Damasc. fragment 43 Müller (*FHG* III, p. 378); Suda s.v.; Nonnus, *Dion.* 18,20ff.; Eratosthenes, *Catast.* 8.

Lycastus (1) Steph. Byz. s.v.; Eustath. p. 313,13; Diod. Sic. 4,60. (2) Plutarch, *Parall.* 36,314e.

Lycius Antoninus Liberalis, *Met.* 20.

Lyco Serv. on Virgil, *Ecl.* 8,29.

Lycomedes Apollod. *Bibl.* 3,13,8; Ptol. Heph. *Nov. Hist.* 1; Sophocles, *Philoct.* 243; Plutarch, *Theseus* 35; Paus. 1,17,6; Tzetzes on Lyc. *Alex.* 1324.

Lycopeus Apollod. *Bibl.* 1,8,6; Hyg. *Fab.* 175; Diod. Sic. 4,65; Eustath. p. 971,7.

Lycophron Hom. *Il.* 15,429ff.

Lycoreus Paus. 10,6,2; schol. on Apoll. Rhod. *Arg.* 2,711; Euripides, *Bacch.* 559; Steph. Byz. s.v. Λυκώρεια (Lycoreia); Etym. Magn. p. 571,47; Hyg. *Fab.* 161.

Lycurgus (1) Hom. *Il.* 7,142ff.; schol. on *Il.* 2,209 and 7,8; Paus. 8,4,10. (2) Hom. *Il.* 6,129ff. with schol.; Apollod. *Bibl.* 3,5,1; Tzetzes on Lyc. *Alex.* 273; Hyg. *Fab.* 132; Sophocles, *Antigone* 955ff.; Serv. on Virgil, *Aen.* 3,14; Aeschylus, lost tetralogy *Lycurgeia* (Nauck, *TGF*, edn 2, p. 19ff.); Ovid, *Met.* 4,22; Diod. Sic. 1,20; 3,65; Nonnus, *Dion.* 21,1ff. (3) Hyg. *Fab.* 15; 74; 273; Apollod. *Bibl.* 1,9,14; 3,6,4; Paus. 2,15,3; 3,18,12; Stat. *Theb.* 5,660.

Lycus (1) Schol. on Hom. *Il.* 18,486, Eratosthenes, *Catast.* 23, Apollod. *Bibl.* 3,10,1; Hyg. *Astron.* 2,21. (2) Lyc. *Alex.* 132 and Tzetzes *ad loc.*, schol. on Hom. *Il.* 5,64; Eustath. p. 521,27. (3) Apollod. *Bibl.* 3,5,5; 3,10,1; Hyg. *Fab.* 157; *Astron.* 2,21; schol. on Apoll. Rhod. *Arg.* 4,1090; Hyg. *Fab.* 7–8; Euripides, lost tragedy *Antiope*, Nauck *TGF*, edn 2, p. 410ff.; Prop. 4,15,12; schol. on Stat. *Theb.* 4,750; Paus. 2,6,1ff.; 9,5,4ff.; 9,16,7. See also LAMEDON. (4) Euripides, *Heracles* and Seneca, *Hercules Furens*; Serv. on Virgil, *Aen.* 8,300. (5) Diod. Sic. 5,56; Hesych. s.v., Tzetzes, *Chil.* 7,124, 12,836. (6) Strabo 9,1,6, p. 392; Sophocles fragment 24 Jebb-Pearson (872 Nauck, edn 2); Apollod. *Bibl.* 3,15,5ff.; schol. on Aristophanes, *Wasps* 1223; *Lysistrata* 58; Hdt. 1,173; 7,92; Steph. Byz. s.v. Λυκία (Lycia), Paus. 1,19,3, 4,1,6ff., 4,2,6, 4,20,4, 10,12,11. (7) Apollod. *Bibl.* 1,9,23; 2,5,9; Apoll. Rhod. *Arg.* 2,720ff., and schol. on 758ff.; Val. Flacc. *Arg.* 4,733ff.; Hyg. *Fab.* 14; 18; Tzetzes, *Chil.* 3,806ff. (8) Plutarch, *Parall.* 23,311b-c (quoting Juba, cf. Müller, *FHG* III, p. 472).

Lydus Hdt. 1,7 and 94; Dion. Hal. *Ant. Rom.* 1,27ff.; Strabo 5,2,2, p. 219; Tzetzes on Lyc. *Alex.* 1351.

Lymphae Varro, *De Ling. Lat.* 5,71; 7,87; *De Re Rustica* 1,1,6.

Lynceus (1) Apollod. *Bibl.* 2,1,5; Pind. *Nem.* 10,6 and schol. *ad loc.*; Aeschylus, *PV* 865ff.; lost tragedy *Aegyptioi* (Nauck, *TGF*, edn 2, p. 4; it formed a trilogy with *Supplices* and - also lost - *Danaides*); Ovid, *Heroides* 14; Serv. on Virgil, *Aen.* 10,498; Paus. 2,16,1; 2,19,6; 2,20,7; 2,21,1; 2,25,4; schol. on Euripides, *Hec.* 886; Hyg. *Fab.* 168. (2) Pind. *Nem.* 10,61ff. with schol.; Apoll. Rhod. *Arg.* 1,53ff.; Apollod. *Bibl.* 3,10,3; Hyg. *Fab.* 14; Tzetzes on Lyc. *Alex.* 553; Palaeph. *Incr.* 10.

Lyncus Ovid, *Met.* 5,650ff.; Serv. on Virgil, *Aen.* 1,323; Hyg. *Fab.* 259.

Lyrcus (1) Parthenius, *Erot. Path.* 1. (2) Paus. 2,25,5; Hesych. s.v. Λυρκείου δῆμος (Lyrceiou demos).

Lysidice Apollod. *Bibl.* 2,4,5; Tzetzes on Lyc. *Alex.* 932; Paus. 8,14,2; Plutarch, *Theseus* 7; schol. on Pind. *Ol.* 27 (49).

Lysippe Apollod. *Bibl.* 2,2,2; schol. on Hom. *Od.* 15,225; Serv. on Virgil, *Ecl.* 6,48.

M

Macar Schol. on Pind. *Ol.* 7,73 (135); Diod. Sic. 5,56ff.; 5,81ff.; Nonnus, *Dion.* 14,44; Hom. *Il.* 24,544 with schol.; Strabo 8,3,31, p. 356; 13,1,7, p. 586; Paus. 10,38,4; Dion. Hal. *Ant. Rom.* 1,18,1.

Macareus (1) Apollod. *Bibl.* 1,7,3; Serv. on Virgil, *Aen.* 1,75; Hyg. *Fab.* 238; 243; Euripides, lost tragedy *Aeolus* (Nauck, *TGF*, edn 2, p. 365ff.; fragments 14ff.); Ovid, *Heroides* 11; Sostratus *Tyrrhenica* fragment quoted in Plutarch, *Parall.* 28,312c and Stobaeus, *Flor.* 4,20b,72 W-H. (2) Aelian, *Hist. Var.* 13,2.

Macaria Schol. on Plato, *Hipp. Major* 293a; Paus. 1,32,6; Euripides, *Heraclidae* 474ff.; Aristophanes, *Knights* 1151 with schol.; Eustath. p. 1405,36.

Macedon Strabo 7, fragment 11, p. 329; Hesiod, fragment 7 Merkelbach-West; Steph. Byz. s.v. Μακεδονία (Macedonia);

schol. on Hom. *Il.* 14,226; Eustath. on Dion. Perieg. 427; Diod. Sic. 1,18; Aelian, *Nat. An.* 10,48.

Macello Bacchyl. 1 (= 8 Bergk); Nonnus, *Dion.* 18,35ff.; schol. on Ovid, *Ibis* 475; Serv. on Virgil, *Aen.* 6,618. See also TELCHINES.

Machaereus Pind. *Nem.* 7,42 (62) with schol.; schol. on Euripides, *Or.* 1654; Strabo 9,3,9, p. 421, Apollod. *Epit.* 6,14.

Machaon Hom. *Il.* 2,729ff.; 4,193ff. with schol., 11,506ff., 14,2ff., schol. on Pind. *Pyth.* 1,56 (109); 3,7 (14); Hyg. *Fab.* 81; 97; 108; 113; schol. on Aristophanes, *Plut.* 701; Diod. Sic. 4,71; Sophocles, *Philoctetes*; Paus. 2,11,5; 2,23,4; 2,38,6; 3,26,9ff.; 4,30,3; Westermann, *Mythogr. Gr.* p. 128; Quint. Smyrn. *Posthom.* 6,406ff.; Dict. Cret. 2,6ff.; Serv. on Virgil, *Aen.* 2,263; Apollod. *Bibl.* 3,10,8; *Epit.* 5,1; Tzetzes on Lyc. *Alex.* 911; *Posthom.* 520ff.; Prop. 2,1,59.

Macistus Steph. Byz. s.v.

Macris Apoll. Rhod. *Arg.* 4,1131, with schol. ad loc.

Maeander Hesiod, *Theog.* 339; Paus. 7,4,1; Ovid, *Met.* 9,450; Steph. Byz. s.v. Ἀλάβανδα (Alabanda).

Maenads Euripides, *Bacchae*; Sophocles, *Ant.* 1150; Athenaeus 5,198; Diod. Sic. 3,64; 4,3; Nonnus, *Dion.*; etc.

Maenalus Apollod. *Bibl.* 3,8,1; Paus. 8,3,1; schol. on Apoll. Rhod. *Arg.* 1,168; 769; schol. on Theocr. 1,129; Tzetzes on Lyc. *Alex.* 481.

Maeon (1) Hom. *Il.* 4,394; Apollod. *Bibl.* 3,6,5; Stat. *Theb.* 2,693; Paus. 9,18,2; Euripides, lost tragedy *Antigone* (Nauck, *TGF*, edn 2, p. 404ff., fragments 157ff.); Hyg. *Fab.* 72; Diod. Sic. 4,65. (2) See CRITHEIS; cf. Hellanicus, fragment 6 Müller (*FHG* I, p. 46).

Maera (1) See LOCRUS. (2) Paus. 8,48,6; 8,53,2ff. (3) Apollod. *Bibl.* 3,14,7; Hyg. *Fab.* 130; *Astron.* 2,4; Ovid, *Fasti* 4,939ff.

Magnes Apollod. *Bibl.* 1,7,3; 1,9,6; Hyg. *Astron.* 2,2; Paus. 6,21,11; Eustath. p. 338,21; schol. on Euripides, *Phoen.* 1760; Steph. Byz. s.v. Μακεδονία (Macedonia); Antoninus Liberalis, *Met.* 23; Tzetzes on Lyc. *Alex.* 831.

Maia (1) Hom. *Od.* 14,435; Hesiod, *Theog.* 948; Serv. on Virgil, *Aen.* 8,130; schol. on Pind. *Nem.* 2,10 (16); Aeschylus, *Choeph.* 813; Diod. Sic. 3,60; Apollod. *Bibl.* 3,10,1–2; 3,8,2. (2) Aul. Gell. *Noct. Att.* 13,23,1ff.; Censor. *De Die Nat.* 22,12; Macrob. *Sat.* 1,12,19; Joann. Lyd. *De Mensibus* 4,52.

Malcandrus Plutarch, *De Iside et Osiride* 15,357b ff.

Mamercus (1) Plutarch, *Aemilius* 2; Paul. ex. Fest. p. 23 M; Dion. Hal. *Ant. Rom.* 2,76. (2) Plutarch, *Parall.* 26,312a.

Mamurius Plutarch, *Numa* 13; Paul. ex. Fest. p. 131 M.; Ovid, *Fasti* 3,389; Varro, *De Ling. Lat.* 6,45; Dion. Hal., *Ant. Rom.* 2,71; Joann. Lyd. *De Mensibus* 4,3,6; Serv. on Virgil, *Aen.* 7,188.

Mandylas Schol. on Hom. *Od.* 14,327.

Manes (1) Hdt. 1,94; 4,45; Steph. Byz. s.v. Ἀκμονία (Acmonia); Dion. Hal. *Ant. Rom.* 1,27. (2) Varro, *De Ling. Lat.* 6,2; 9,61; Macrob. *Sat.* 1,3,13; 1,7,34ff.; Serv. on Virgil, *Aen.* 1,139; 2,268; 3,63; Ovid, *Fasti* 2,523ff.; Cic. *In Pisonem* 16; *In Vatinium* 14.

Mania Hom. *Il.* 22,460; Quint. Smyrn. *Posthom.* 5,451ff.; Paus. 8,34,1; Plato, *Phaedrus* 265a.

Manto Schol. on Apoll. Rhod. *Arg.* 1,308; Euripides, *Phoen.* 834; 953; Paus. 7,3,1ff.; 9,10,3; 9,33,2; Virgil, *Aen.* 10,199; Ovid, *Met.* 6,157; 9,285ff.; Hyg. *Fab.* 128; Apollod. *Bibl.* 3,7,4 and 7; *Epit.* 6,3; Diod. Sic. 4,66 (there named Daphne); Conon, *Narr.* 6.

Marathon Paus. 1,15,3; 1,32,4; 2,1,1; 2,6,5.

Marathus Plutarch, *Theseus* 32; Suda s.v. Μαραθών (Marathon).

Mariandynus Steph. Byz. s.v. Μαριανδυνία (Mariandynia); Eustath. on Dion. Perieg. p. 787 and 791; Strabo 12,3,4,

30; schol. on Theocr. 7,115; Hyg. *Fab.* 243; schol. on Apoll. Rhod. *Arg.* 1,185; Apollod. *Bibl.* 3,1,2; Paus. 7,2,5.

Mimas Euripides, *Ion* 215; Apoll. Rhod. *Arg.* 3,1227 with schol.; Horace, *Od.* 3,4,53; Apollod. *Bibl.* 1,6,2.

Minerva Varro, *De Ling. Lat.* 5,74; Serv. on Virgil, *Aen.* 1,42; 11,259; Ovid, *Fasti* 3,835ff.; Juv. *Sat.* 10,115ff.

Minos Hom. *Il.* 13,448ff.; 14,322ff.; schol. on 12,292; *Od.* 11,568ff.; Eustath. p. 1699,6; 1830,55; 1860,15; Hdt. 1,171ff.; 7,170ff.; Apoll. Rhod. *Arg.* 2,516; 4,1564, with schol.; schol. on 3,1087; 4,433; Paus. 1,1,2–4; 1,17,3; 1,19,4; 1,22,5, etc.; Hyg. *Fab.* 41; Strabo 6,3,6, p. 282; 10,4,9, p. 477; 12,8,5, p. 573; Diod. Sic. 4,60ff.; 5,78ff.; Plato, *Minos* 318ff.; *Gorgias* 523ff.; Pseudo-Lact. Plac. on Stat. *Theb.* 4,530; 5,441; 7,187; schol. on Callim. *Hymn* 1,8; Tzetzes, *Chil.* 1,473; 546; 2,293ff.; on Lyc. *Alex.* 1301; Antoninus Liberalis, *Met.* 41; Apollod. *Bibl.* 3,1,2ff.; 3,15,1; 2,5,7; Conon, *Narr.* 25; schol. on Euripides, *Or.* 1643; Athenaeus 13,601e ff.; Suda s.v. (Diod. Sic. 4,60 distinguishes two bearers of the name Minos, the former the son of Zeus and the latter, grandson of the former, the subject of the rest of the legends).

Minotaur Apollod. *Bibl.* 3,1,4; 3,15,8; Diod Sic. 1,61; 4,61; 4,77; Plutarch *Theseus* 15ff.; Paus. 1,22,5; 1,24,1; 1,27,10; 3,18,11; 3,18,16; Virgil *Aen.* 5,588 with Serv. ad loc.; 6,21ff.; Hyg. *Fab.* 40–42; cf. Hom. *Il.* 18,590ff.; Ovid, *Met.* 8,167; *Her.* 4,115ff.; Callim. *Hymn* 4,310ff.; Plato, *Phaedo* 58a; Strabo 10,4,8, p. 447.

Minyads Antoninus Liberalis, *Met.* 10; Plutarch, *Quaest. Gr.* 38,299e-f; Aelian, *VH* 3,42; Ovid, *Met.* 4,1ff.

Minyas Paus. 9,36,4ff.; 10,29,6; schol. on Hom. *Il.* 2,511; 22,227; schol. on Pind. *Isthm.* 1,55 (79); *Pyth.* 4,69 (122); schol. on Apoll. Rhod. *Arg.* 1,45; 230; schol. on Hom. *Od.* 11,326; Tzetzes on Lyc. *Alex.* 874.

Misenus Strabo 1,3,18, p. 26; Virgil, *Aen.* 6,163ff.; Serv. on *Aen.* 3,239.

Mnemon Lyc. *Alex.* 241ff., with Tzetzes on line 232; cf. Plutarch, *Quaest. Gr.* 28,297e-f.

Mnemosyne Hesiod, *Theog.* 54ff.; 135; 915ff.

Mnestheus Virgil, *Aen.* 5,116ff. with Serv. ad loc.; ibid. 12,127.

Modius Fabidius Dion. Hal. *Ant. Rom.* 2,48.

Moirai (Fates) Hom. *Il.* 4,517; 5,83; 613; 12,116; 16,433ff.; etc.; *Od.* 3,269; 11,292; Hesiod, *Theog.* 217; 901ff.; Hymn. Orph. 43,7; 59; Stobaeus, *Ecl.* 1,5,12; Pind. *Ol.* 10,52; *Pyth.* 4,145; Aeschylus, *Eum.* 956ff.; *PV* 511ff.; Euripides, *Alc.* 12; 52; Aristophanes, *Birds* 1734ff.; *Frogs* 453. See also PARCAE.

Molionidae Hom. *Il.* 2,621; 11,709ff.; 23,638ff.; schol. on last two passages; Eustath. p. 882,14; Paus. 5,1,10ff.; 5,3,3; 8,14,9; Athenaeus 2,57ff.; Apollod. *Bibl.* 2,7,2; Pind. *Ol.* 10,26ff.; Plutarch, *De Pyth. Orac.* 13,400e.

Molorchus Serv. on Virgil, *Georg.* 3,19; Probus, ibid.; Apollod. *Bibl.* 2,5,1; Callim. *Aetia* 3, fragment 55ff. Trypanis.

Molossus Euripides, *Andromache*; schol. on Hom. *Od.* 3,188; Serv. on Virgil, *Aen.* 3,297; Paus. 1,11,1ff.

Molpadia Paus. 1,2,1.

Molpis Tzetzes on Lyc. *Alex.* 159.

Molpus Plutarch, *Quaest. Gr.* 28,297e-f; Tzetzes on Lyc. *Alex.* 232–4; Steph. Byz. s.v. + ‖∬‖ ‖ | ⌐ (Tenedos); Euripides, los tragedy *Tennes* (Nauck, *TGF*, edn 2, p. 578; rather doubtful); Diod. Sic. 5,83.

Molus Hom. *Il.* 10,269; Diod. Sic. 5,79; Plutarch, *De Defectu Orac.* 14,417e; Apollod. *Bibl.* 3,3,1.

Momus Hesiod, *Theog.* 214; schol. on Hom. *Il.* 1,5ff.

Moneta Livy 4,7,12; 6,20,13; 7,28,6ff.; Plutarch, *Romulus* 20; Ovid, *Fasti* 6,183ff.; Macrob. *Sat.* 1,12,30; Suda s.v.

Mopsus (1) Hesiod, *Scutum* 181; Ovid, *Met.* 8,316; 12,456;

Apoll. Rhod. *Arg.* 1,65 with schol.; 1,80; 4,1518ff.; Hyg. *Fab.* 14; 173; Paus. 5,17,10; Strabo 9,5,22, p. 443; Lyc. *Alex.* 881ff. (2) Strabo 14,1,27, p. 642; 14,4,3, p. 668; 14,5,16, p. 675; Conon, *Narr.* 6; Cic. *De Div.* 1,88; schol. on Apoll. Rhod. *Arg.* 1,308; Paus. 7,3,2; 9,33,1; Serv. on Virgil, *Ecl.* 4,72; Apollod. *Epit.* 6,2; 6,4; 6,19.

Morges Dion. Hal. *Ant. Rom.* 1,12,3; 1,73,4–5; Etym. Magn. p.714,21; Strabo 6,1,6, p. 257.

Moria Nonnus, *Dion.* 25,451ff.; cf. Pliny, *NH* 25,14.

Mormo Xen. *Hellenica* 4,4,17; Theocr. 15,40 with schol.

Mormolyce Strabo 1,2,8, p. 19; Apollod. fragment 10 Müller (*FHG* I, p. 430).

Morpheus Ovid, *Met.* 11,635ff.

Mors See also THANATOS; Cic. *De Nat. Deor.* 3,44; Serv. on Virgil, *Aen.* 11,197.

Mothone Paus. 4,35,1ff.

Mucius Scaevola Plutarch, *Publicola* 27ff.; Livy 2,12ff.

Munichus (1) Euripides, *Hippol.* 761; cf. schol. on Demosth. *De Corona* 73c. (2) Antoninus Liberalis, *Met.* 14; cf. Ovid, *Met.* 13,717.

Munitus Tzetzes on Lyc. *Alex.* 495ff.; Paus. 10,26,8; Parthenius, *Erot. Path.* 16 (= Hegesippus, fragment 4 Müller, *FHG* IV, p. 424).

Musaeus Paus. 1,14,3; 1,22,7; 1,25,8; 4,1,5; 10,5,6; etc.; Strabo 10,3,17, p. 471; Diod. Sic. 4,25; Serv. on Virgil, *Aen.* 6,667; Athenaeus 13,597c; Suda s.v.; Harpocration s.v.; schol. on Aristophanes, *Frogs* 1033; Plato, *Apol.* 41a; Hdt. 2,53.

Muses Hom. *Il.* 1,406; *Od.* 24,60; Hesiod, *Theog.* 35ff.; 915; Homeric Hymn to Hermes, 429; Homeric Hymn to Apollo, 189ff.; Pind. *Pyth.* 3,88ff.; schol. on *Nem.* 3,9 (16); Paus. 1,2,5; 9,29,2ff.; Euripides, *Med.* 834; Diod. Sic. 4,7; Plutarch, *Quaest. conv.* 8,716f; Serv. on Virgil, *Ecl.* 7,21. Cf. P. Boyancé, *Le Culte des Muses*, 1936.

Myceneus Paus. 2,16,4; schol. on Euripides, *Or.* 1239; Steph. Byz. s.v. Μυκῆναι (Mycenae); Eustath. p. 289, 44.

Myenus Pseudo-Plutarch, *De Fluviis* 8,3.

Mygdon (1) Hom. *Il.* 3,185ff. with schol.; Euripides, *Rhes.* 539; Serv. on Virgil, *Aen.* 2,341; Paus. 10,27,1; Pseudo-Plutarch, *De Fluviis* 12,1. (2) Apollod. *Bibl.* 2,5,9; schol. on Apoll. Rhod. *Arg.* 2,786.

Mylas Steph. Byz. s.v. Μυλαντία ἄκρα (Mylantia acra); Hesych. s.v. Μύλας (Mylas).

Myles Paus. 3,1,1; 4,1,1; 3,20,2; schol. on Euripides, *Or.* 615.

Myrice Hesych. s.v.

Myrina Hom. *Il.* 2,814 with schol.; Tzetzes on Lyc. *Alex.* 243; Strabo 13,3,6, p. 623; Diod. Sic. 3,54ff.

Myrmex Serv. on Virgil, *Aen.* 4,402.

Myrmidon Serv. on Virgil, *Aen.* 2,7; schol. on Hom. *Il.* 16,177.

Myrrha See ADONIS.

Myrsus Nonnus, *Dion.* 26,250ff.

Myrtilus Schol. on Hom. *Il.* 2,104; schol. on Apoll. Rhod. *Arg.* 1,752; Sophocles, *Electra* 508ff. and schol.; lost tragedy *Oenomaus* (Jebb-Pearson II, p. 121ff.); Euripides, *Or.* 988ff. with schol.; Hyg. *Fab.* 84; *Astr. Poet.* 2,13; Diod. Sic. 4,73; Ovid, *Ibis* 369ff.; Apollod. *Epit.* 2,6ff.; Paus. 8,14,10ff.; Serv. on Virgil, *Georg.* 3,7.

Myrto Plutarch, *Aristides* 20.

Myscelus Hippys of Rhegium, fragment 4 Müller (*FHG* II, p. 14); Strabo 6,1,12, p. 262; Diod. Sic. 8, fragment 17; Ovid, *Met.* 15,12ff.

N

Naiads Hesych. s.v.; schol. on Hom. *Il.* 20,8; Eustath. p. 622,31; cf. 652,32ff.; 1384,35; Serv. on Virgil, *Ecl.* 10,62; Paus. 3,25,2; 8,4,2; 10,33,4; Callim. *Hymn* 3,13ff.; Ovid, *Met.* 2,441; 5,576ff.; *Fasti* 4,761; Porphyry, *Antrum Nympharum* 10; 13; Pseudo-Lact. Plac. on Stat. *Theb.* 4,684; schol. on Theocr. 13,44; Paul. ex. Fest. p. 120 M.; Anth. Pal. 6,203; Hyg. *Fab.* 182; Tac. *Ann.* 14,22; Apollod. *Bibl.* 1,7,5; 1,9,6; 3,10,3 4; 3,14,6; *Epit.* 2,13.

Nana Arnobius, *Adv. Nat.* 5,6ff.; cf. Paus. 7,17,10; see also ATTIS; AGDISTIS.

Nanas Dion. Hal. *Ant. Rom.* 1,28; cf. Hdt. 1,57.

Nannacus Suda. s.v.; Herodas 3,10; Steph. Byz. s.v. Ἀνναχός (Annacus).

Nanus (1) Athenaeus 13,576a. (2) Lyc. *Alex.* 1242ff. with Tzetzes ad loc.; see also ODYSSEUS.

Narcissus Paus. 9,31,6ff.; Westermann, *Mythogr. Gr.* p. 378; Ovid, *Met.* 3,339ff.; Conon, *Narr.* 24; Myth. Vat. 2,180; Nonnus, *Dion.* 48,582ff.; Tzetzes, *Chil.* 1,9; 1,11; on *Il.* p. 139; Probus on Virgil, *Ecl.* 2,48; Strabo 9,2,10, p. 404.

Nauplius (1 and 2) Paus. 1,22,6; 2,38,2; 4,35,2; 8,48,7; schol. on Apoll. Rhod. *Arg.* 4,1901; Apollod. *Bibl.* 2,1,5; 2,7,4; 3,2,2; *Epit.* 6,7ff.; Hyg. *Fab.* 116-7; 169; 249; 277; Strabo 8,6,2, p. 368; Apoll. Rhod. *Arg.* 1,134ff.; 2,826ff.; schol. Veron. on Virgil, *Aen.* 2,88; Euripides, *IA* 198; Diod. Sic. 4,33; Sophocles, *Ajax* 1295ff.; Aeschylus, lost tragedy *Palamedes* (Nauck, *TGF*, edn 2, p. 59f.); Sophocles, lost tragedy *Nauplius* (Jebb-Pearson II, p. 80ff.); Euripides, *Helen* 767ff.; 1126ff.; schol. on Euripides, *Or.* 432; Lyc. *Alex.* 381ff.; 1093ff.; Tzetzes on *Alex.* 386; 992; 1093; Serv. on Virgil, *Aen.* 11,260; Ovid, *Met.* 14,472ff.; *Tristia* 1,1,83; 5,7,35ff.; Plutarch, *Quaest. Gr.* 33, p. 298d; schol. on Hom. *Od.* 4,797.

Naus Paus. 8,15,1 and 3.

Nausicaa Hom. *Od.* 6-8; Dict. Cret. 6,6.

Nausithous (1) Hom. *Od.* 6,7ff.; 7,56ff. and schol.; 8,565; Apoll. Rhod. *Arg.* 4,539ff. with schol. (2) Plutarch, *Theseus* 17. (3) Hesiod, *Theog.* 1017; cf. Hyg. *Fab.* 125.

Nautes Virgil, *Aen.* 5,704ff.; Serv. on *Aen.* 2,166; 3,407; 5,704; Dion. Hal. *Ant. Rom.* 6,69; Festus p. 166 M.; Myth. Vat. 1,142.

Naxos Diod. Sic. 5,51; Steph. Byz. s.v. Νάξος (Naxos) and Κυδωνία (Cydonia).

Neda Callim. *Hymn* 1,15ff.; Paus. 4,33,1; 8,31,4; 8,38,3; 8,47,3.

Neleus (1) Hom. *Il.* 11,671ff.; *Od.* 11,235ff.; 15,229ff.; Apollod. *Bibl.* 1,9,5ff.; 2,6,2; 2,7,3; Hyg. *Fab.* 10; Diod. Sic. 4,31; 68; schol. on Hom. *Il.* 10,334; Paus. 2,2,2; 4,2,5; 4,3,1ff.; 4,15,8; 4,36,1ff.; etc.; Hesiod, fragment 33 Merkelbach-West; schol. on Pind. *Ol.* 9,3; Ovid, *Met.* 12,530ff. (2) Paus. 7,2,1ff.; 10,10,1; Strabo 14,1,3, p. 633.

Nemanus Plutarch, *De Is. et Osir.* 15,357b.

Nemesis Hom. *Il.* 3,156; 6,335, etc.; *Od.* 1,350; 2,136; 23,40; Hesiod, *Theog.* 223; *W. & D.* 200; Athenaeus 8,334b ff.; Clem. Alex. *Protrept.* 2,26; Apollod. *Bibl.* 3,10,7; Tzetzes on Lyc. *Alex.* 88; Aeschylus, *Septem* 233ff.; Sophocles, *Philoct.* 601ff.; *Electra* 792ff.; Paus. 1,33,2ff.; Hdt. 1,34.

Neoptolemus Hom. *Il.* 19,326ff.; *Od.* 4,5ff. and schol.; 3,188ff.; 11,503ff.; Pind. *Nem.* 7,35ff. (52ff.) and schol.; Apollod. *Bibl.* 3,13,8; *Epit.* 5,10ff.; 6,5; 6,12ff.; 7,40ff.; Eustath. p.1463,36; Sophocles, *Philoct.*; Euripides, *Or.*; *Androm.*

and schol.; *Troades* 1125ff.; Paus. 1,11,1; 1,13,9; 1,33,8; 2,5,5; 2,23,61 etc.; Hyg. *Fab.* 97; 108; 112-4; 122-3; 193; Virgil, *Aen.* 2,500ff.; 3,333; Serv. on Virgil, *Aen.* 2,166; 3,297ff.; Dict. Cret. 6,7ff. See also HERMIONE, PYRRHUS.

Nephalion Apollod. *Bibl.* 2,5,9; 3,1,2.

Neptune Varro, *De Ling. Lat.* 5,72; 6,19; Cic. *De Nat. Deor.* 2,66. See also POSEIDON.

Nereids Hdt. 2,50; Hom. *Il.* 18,31ff.; *Od.* 24,47; Hyg. *Fab.* pref. 8; cf. 59; 64; 96; 106; Apollod. *Bibl.* 1,2,7; cf. Virgil, *Georg.* 4,336; Hesiod, *Theog.* 243ff.; Prop. 3,7,68; Pind. *Isthm.* 6,6, (8), Aeschylus, fragment 174 Nauck edn 2, (= 89 Lloyd-Jones).

Nereus Hom. *Il.* 18,35; 49; 141; Hesiod, *Theog.* 233ff.; Apollod. *Bibl.* 1,2,6; 2,5,11; Hyg. *Fab.* pref. 8 Rose; 157; Aelian, *Nat. An.* 14,28; Arg. Orph. 336.

Nerio Aul. Gell. 13,23; Joann. Lyd. *De Mensibus* 4,60 (42); Plautus, *Truc.* 515; Porphyrion on Horace *Epist.* 2,2,209.

Nerites Aelian, *Nat. An.* 14,28; Etym. Magn. s.v.

Nessus Hyg. *Fab.* 34; Apollod. *Bibl.* 2,5,4; 2,7,6; Sophocles, *Trach.* 580ff.; Seneca, *Hercules Oetaeus* 491ff.; Serv. on Virgil, *Aen.* 8,300; schol. on Stat. *Theb.* 11,235; Ovid, *Met.* 9,101ff.; *Her.* 9,141ff.; schol. on Apoll. Rhod. *Arg.* 1,1212.

Nestor Hom. *Il.* 1,247; 2,76ff.; 2,336ff.; and many other passages; *Od.* 3,165ff.; 452ff.; Hyg. *Fab.* 10; Apollod. *Bibl.* 1,9,9; 2,7,3; *Epit.* 6,1; Paus. 2,2,2; 2,18,7ff.; 3,26,7ff.; 3,26,8 and 10; etc.; Ovid, *Met.* 8,313; 13,210ff.; Proclus' summary of the *Cypria*, Homer Oxf. Class. Text V, p. 103; Quint. Smyrn. *Posthom.* 2,243ff.; Val. Flacc. *Arg.* 1,380; 3,143ff.; 6,569ff.

Nicaea Nonnus, *Dion.* 15,169ff.

Nice Hesiod, *Theog.* 383; Serv. on Virgil, *Aen.* 6,134; Apollod. *Bibl.* 1,2,4; Dion. Hal. *Ant. Rom.* 1,33.

Nicomachus Paus. 4,3,10; 4,30,3.

Nicostrate Plutarch, *Romulus* 21; *Quaest. Rom.* 56,278c; Anon. *De Orig. Gent. Rom.* 5; Serv. on Virgil, *Aen.* 8,51, Solinus 1,10ff.; Strabo 5,3,3, p. 230. See also EVANDER; CARMENTA.

Nicostratus Hesiod, fragment 175 Merkelbach-West; schol. on Hom. *Il.* 3,175; Eustath. p. 400,32; schol. on Sophocles, *El.* 539; Paus. 2,18,6; 3,18,13; 3,19,9.

Nileus Diod. Sic. 1,19; 1,63; schol. on Theocr. 7,114.

Nilus Hesiod, *Theog.* 338; schol. on Lyc. *Alex.* 119 and 576; Tzetzes ibid.; schol. on Apoll. Rhod. *Arg.* 4,276; Apollod. *Bibl.* 2,1,4.

Ninus Hdt. 1,7; Alexander Polyhistor, fragment 2 Müller (*FHG* III, p. 210); Diod. Sic. 2,1ff.; 2,20ff.; Steph. Byz. s.v.; Conon *Narr.* 9.

Niobe (1) Apollod. *Bibl.* 2,1,1; Tzetzes on Lyc. *Alex.* 111; schol. on Euripides, *Or.* 932; Paus. 2,21,2; Hyg. *Fab.* 145; Diod. Sic. 4,14; Dion. Hal. *Ant. Rom.* 1,11; cf. Pliny, *NH* 4,17. (2) Hom. *Il.* 24,599ff.; schol. on 604; Apollod. *Bibl.* 3,5,6; Aelian, *VH* 12,36; Diod. Sic. 4,74; Paus. 1,21,3; 2,21,9; 5,11,2; 5,16,4; 8,2,5 and 7; Ovid, *Met.* 6,146ff.; Pseudo-Lact. Plac. on Stat. *Theb.* 3,191; Euripides, *Phoen.* 159 and schol.; Sophocles, *Antig.* 822ff.; *Electra* 150ff.; Aeschylus, lost tragedy *Niobe* (Nauck, *TGF*, edn 2, pp. 50ff.; 228ff.); Tzetzes on Lyc. *Alex.* 111; schol. on Plato, *Tim.* 22a; Parthenius, *Erot. Path.* 33.

Nireus (1) Hom. *Il.* 2,671ff.; Hyg. *Fab.* 81; 97; Diod. Sic. 5,53; Euripides, *IA* 204; Tzetzes, *Antehom.* 278; on Lyc. *Alex.* 1011; Quint. Smyrn. *Posthom.* 6,372ff.; 7,11ff. (2) Ptol. Heph. 7 (Westermann, *Mythogr. Gr.* p. 159).

Nisus (1) Strabo 9,1,6, p. 392; Hyg. *Fab.* 198; 242; Apollod. *Bibl.* 3,15,5ff.; Plutarch, *Quaest. Gr.* 16,295a; Paus. 1,39,4; 1,19,4; 2,34,7; Suda s.v.; Aeschylus, *Choeph.* 612ff.; Tzetzes on Lyc. *Alex.* 650; Appendix Virgiliana, *Ciris* 378ff.; Virgil. *Georg.* 1,404ff.; Ovid, *Met.* 8,8ff. (2) Virgil, *Aen.* 5,294ff.; 9,176ff.; Hyg. *Fab.* 257; Ovid, *Tristia* 1,5,25; 1,9,33ff.; 5,4,26.

O

Oenopion Paus. 7,4,8ff.; 7,5,13; Hyg. *Astr. Poet.* 2,34; schol. on Apoll. Rhod. *Arg.* 3,997; Parthenius *Erot. Path.* 20; Diod. Sic. 5,79; 84; Aratus, *Phaenomena* 636ff.; Plutarch *Theseus* 20; Apollod. *Bibl.* 1,4,3; *Epit.* 1,9; Athenaeus 1,26b; Serv. on Virgil, *Aen.* 10,763.

Oenotrus Paus. 8,3,5; Dion. Hal. *Ant. Rom.* 1,11ff.; Serv. on Virgil, *Aen.* 1,552.

Oeonus Pind. *Ol.* 10,65ff. (78ff.) and schol.; Paus. 3,15,3; Diod. Sic. 4,33–4, schol. on Hom. *Il.* 1,52; 2,581; Apollod. *Bibl.* 2,7,3; Plutarch *Quaest. Rom.* 90,285f.

Ogygus (1) Paus. 1,38,7; 9,5,1; 9,19,6; 9,33,5; Photius s.v. Ὠγύγιον (Ogygion); Eustath. p. 1393,31; Tzetzes on Lyc. *Alex.* 1206ff. (2) Varro, *De Re Rust.* 3,1,2; schol. on Apoll. Rhod. *Arg.* 3,1178. (3) Tzetzes on Hesiod, *Theog.* 806; Nonnus *Dion.* 3,204ff.; Suda s.v. ὠγύγια κακά (ogygia kaka).

Oileus Hom. *Il.* 2,727f.; schol. on 527, and on 13,694; Eustath. p. 277,10ff.; Hyg. *Fab.* 14; Strabo 9,4,2, p. 425; Apoll. Rhod. *Arg.* 1,74ff.; 2,1030ff.

Olus Arnobius, *Adv. Nat.* 6,7; Serv. on Virgil, *Aen.* 8,345.

Olymbrus Steph. Byz. s.v. Ἄδανα (Adana).

Olympus (Mount) Cf. Hom. *Od.* 6,42ff., etc.; schol. on Apoll. Rhod. *Arg.* 1,598.

Olympus (1) Ptol. Heph. *Nov. Hist.* 2. (2) Diod. Sic. 5,49. (3) Apollod. *Bibl.* 1,4,2; Plato, *Symp.* 215b ff.; Ovid, *Met.* 6,393; Hyg. *Fab.* 273.

Olynthus Conon, *Narr.* 4; Athenaeus 8,334e.

Omphale Apollod. *Bibl.* 2,6,3; 2,7,8; Diod. Sic. 4,31; Ovid, *Her.* 9,55ff.; Sophocles, *Trach.* 247ff.; Lucian, *Dial. Deorum* 13,2; Plutarch *Quaest. Gr.* 45,301f–302a; schol. on Hom. *Od.* 21,22; Hyg. *Fab.* 32.

Oneiros Hom. *Il.* 2,26ff.; Paus. 2,10,2.

Ophion (1) Apoll. Rhod. *Arg.* 1,503; Tzetzes on Lyc. *Alex.* 1192; schol. on Aristophanes, *Clouds* 247. (2) Schol. on Hom. *Il.* 8,479.

Opus Pind. *Ol.* 9,58ff. (86ff.) and schol., Eustath. p. 277,20.

Ops Varro, *De Ling. Lat.* 5,64; 5,74; Aug. *Civ. Dei* 4,23; Livy 39,22,4; Macrob. *Sat.* 1,10,19; Festus p. 186M.

Orcus Lucret. 1,115; 6,763ff.; Aug. *Civ. Dei* 7,16 (derived from Varro); Serv. on Virgil, *Georg.* 1,277; Paul. ex. Fest. p. 128M.; Petron. *Sat.* 34; 45.

Orestes Hom. *Il.* 9,142; schol. on *Il.* 1,7; *Od.* 1,40ff.; 3,193ff.; 306ff.; 4,546ff. and schol.; 11,452ff.; Proclus' summary of *Nostoi*, Homer Oxf. Class. Text V, p. 109; Aeschylus, *Oresteia*; Sophocles, *Electra*; Euripides, *Orestes*; *Electra*; *IT*; Pind. *Pyth.* 11,34ff. (52ff.) and schol.; Hyg. *Fab.* 101; 117; 119–20; 129; Hdt. 4,103; Ovid, *Ex Ponto* 3,2,43ff.; *Her.* 8; Apollod. *Epit.* 6,23ff.; schol. on Aristophanes *Ach.* 332; schol. on Apoll. Rhod. *Arg.* 4,703ff.; Tzetzes on Lyc. *Alex.* 1374; Paus. 1,22,6; 1,28,5; 1,33,8; 1,41,2; 2,16,7; etc.; Serv. on Virgil, *Aen.* 2,116.

Orestheus Athenaeus 2,35b; Paus. 10,38,1.

Orion Hom. *Il.* 18,486ff. and schol.; *Od.* 5,121ff. and schol.; 11,572ff.; Horace, *Odes* 3,4,70ff.; Hyg. *Astron.* 2,34; Pseudo-Eratosth. *Catast* 7; 32; Apollod. *Bibl* 1,4,2ff.; Virgil, *Aen.* 10,763ff.; Serv. *ad loc.*; Hesiod, fragments 148–9 Merkelbach-West; Parthenius, *Erot. Path.* 20.

Orithyia (1) See BOREAS; Apoll. Rhod. *Arg.* 1,213ff. and schol. on 211; Hyg. *Fab.* 14; Hdt. 7,189; Virgil, *Georg.* 4,463ff. (2) Steph. Byz. s.v. Εὔρωπος (Europos).

Ornytus (1) Paus. 8,28,4ff. (2) Schol. on Euripides, *Or.* 1084.

Orontes (1) Nonnus, *Dion.* 17,196ff.; 314; 26,79; 34,179; etc.; Paus. 8,29,3; Steph. Byz. s.v. Βλέμυες (Blemyes). (2) Hyg. *Fab.* pref. 6 Rose; Tzetzes on Lyc. *Alex.* 697.

Orpheus (Cf. the evidence collected in Diels-Kranz, *Die Fragmente der Vorsokratiker*, edn. 7, I, p. 1ff.) Pind. *Pyth.* 4,177; Simonides, fragment 40 Bergk; Aeschylus, *Agam.* 1630; Euri-

pides, *Bacch.* 562ff.; *IA* 1211ff.; *Alc.* 357ff.; schol. on Euripides, *Rhes.* 892; Diod. Sic. 1,96; 3,65; 4,25; 5,77; Conon, *Narr.* 45; Hyg. *Fab.* 14; 164; *Astron.* 2,6ff.; Pseudo-Eratosth. *Catast.* 24; Apollod. *Bibl.* 1,3,2; 1,9,16; 1,9,25; 2,4,9; Paus. 1,14,3; 2,30,2; 3,13,2; etc.; Ovid, *Met.* 10,8ff.; 11,1ff.; Virgil, *Georg.* 4,453ff.; Serv. on Virgil, *Georg.* 524; Strabo 8, fragment 18, p. 330; Tzetzes on Lyc. *Alex.* 831; Apoll. Rhod. *Arg.* 1,23ff. and schol.; Myth. Vat. 2,44; schol. on Arat. *Phaen.* 269; Phanocles, *Erotes,* in J. U. Powell, *Collectanea Alexandria* p. 106 (= Stob. Flor. 4,20,47 W.-H.); Arg. Orph. Cf. W. K. C. Guthrie, *Orpheus and Greek Religion*, 1935.

Orthopolis Paus. 2,5,8; cf. 2,11,2.

Orthrus Hesiod, *Theog.* 309; Apollod. *Bibl.* 2,5,10; schol. on Apoll. Rhod. *Arg.* 4,1399; Tzetzes on Lyc. *Alex.* 653.

Osinius Virgil, *Aen.* 10,166ff.; 655; Serv. ad loc.

Otreus Hom. *Il.* 3,186 and schol.; Hesych. s.v.; Homeric Hymn to Aphrodite 111.

Oxylus (1) Apollod. *Bibl.* 1,7,7. (2) Paus. 5,3,6ff.; 5,8,5; 5,9,4; 5,16,1; etc.; schol. on Pind. *Ol.* 3,12 (21–2); Strabo 8,3,33, p. 357; 10,3,2, p. 463; Apollod. *Bibl.* 2,8,3; Polyaenus, *Strat.* 5,48; Aristotle, *Politics* 6,4,1319a 12. (3) Athenaeus 3,78b.

Oxynius Conon, *Narr.* 46.

Oxyntes Paus. 2,18,9; Athenaeus 53,96d; Nic. Damasc. fragment 50 Müller (FHG III, p. 386); Tzetzes, *Chil.* 1,182.

P

Pactolus Tzetzes on Lyc. *Alex.* 52; Pseudo-Plutarch, *De Fluv.* 7,1; cf. Nonnus, *Dion.* 12,127; 24,52; 43,411.

Paean Hom. *Il.* 5,401; 900 and schol.; *Od.* 4,232 and schol.; Hesiod, fragment 307 Merkelbach-West; Eustath. p. 1494,12; Solon, fragment 13,57 West.

Paeon (1) Paus. 5,1,4ff.; Hyg. *Astron.* 2,20; Pseudo-Eratosth. *Catast.* 19. (2) Paus. 2,18,8.

Palaemon (1) Apollod. *Bibl.* 2,7,8; Tzetzes on Lyc. *Alex.* 662. (2) Apollod. *Bibl.* 1,9,16; cf. Apoll. Rhod. *Arg.* 1,202. (3) Euripides, *Medea* 1284ff.; Paus. 1,44,8; 2,1,8.

Palaestra Serv. on Virgil, *Aen.* 8,138; Etym. Magn. s.v. παλή (pale).

Palamedes Apollod. *Bibl.* 1,1,5; 3,2,2; *Epit.* 3,7–8; 6,8ff.; Dict. Cret. 1,4ff.; 2,15; 2,20; Tzetzes, *Proleg. Alleg. Il.* 405; Antehom. 155; 177; 264ff.; 316ff.; on Iliad, p. 155; on Lyc. *Alex.* 580; 818; Cic. *De Off.* 3,98; Ovid, *Met.* 13,36ff.; Pseudo-Lact. Plac. on Stat. *Achill.* 1,93; Aelian, *VH* 13,12; Hyg. *Fab.* 95; 105; 277; Lucian, *De Domo* 30; Serv. on Virgil, *Aen.* 2,81; schol. on Euripides, *Or.* 432; Ptol. Heph. *Nov. Hist.* 5, p. 192 Westermann; Sophocles, *Palamedes* (lost tragedy, Jebb-Pearson II p. 131); Paus. 10,31,1ff.; Tac. *Ann.* 11,14; Dio Chrys. 13,12.

Palans Dion. Hal. *Ant. Rom.* 1,32ff.

Palanto Varro, *De Ling. Lat.* 5,53; Solinus 1,15.

Pales Varro, *De Ling. Lat.* 6,15; *De Re Rust.* 2,1,9; Serv. on Virgil, *Georg.* 3,1; Probus, ibid.; Ovid, *Fasti* 4,776; Prop. 4,1,19ff.; Arnobius, *Adv. Nat.* 3,40; Cic. *De Div.* 2,98; Plutarch, *Romulus* 12.

Palici Macrob. *Sat,* 5,19,15ff.; Steph. Byz. s.v. Παλίκη (Palice); Diod. Sic. 11,89; Serv. on Virgil, *Aen.* 9,584; Strabo 6,2,9, p. 275; Aeschylus, lost tragedy *Aetnaeae* (TGF, edn. 2, p. 4ff.).

Palinurus Virgil, *Aen.* 3,202; 562; 5,12ff.; 814ff.; 6,337ff.; Serv. on *Aen.* 6,378f.

Palladium Apollod. *Bibl.* 3,12,3; *Epit.* 5,10ff.; Dion. Hal. *Ant. Rom.* 1,68ff.; cf. *Iliu Persis*, Homer Oxf. Class. Text V, p. 137; Clem. Alex. *Protrept.* 4,47; Conon, *Narr.* 34; schol. on Hom. *Il.* 6,311; Suda and Hesych. s.v.; Suda s.v. Διομήδειος

Euripides, *Phoen.* 5; schol. on Aeschylus, *Suppl.* 317; Antoninus Liberalis *Met.* 40; Apollod. *Bibl.* 3,1,1; Hyg. *Fab.* 178; Conon, *Narr.* 32; Lyc. *Alex.* 1106; schol. on Hom. *Il.* 12,292. (2) Apollod. *Bibl.* 3,13,8; *Epit.* 6,12; Hom *Il* 9,168; 430ff.; 658ff.; 16,916; schol. on 9,448; Eustath. p. 762,43ff.; Sophocles and Euripides, lost tragedies *Phoenix* (Jebb-Pearson II, p. 320; Nauck, *TGF*, edn. 2, p. 621ff.); Anth. Pal. 3,3; Tzetzes on Lyc. *Alex.* 421; Prop. 2,1,60.

Pholus Apollod. *Bibl.* 2,5,4ff.; Sophocles, *Trach.* 1095ff.; Diod. Sic. 4,12; Tzetzes, *Chil.* 2,268ff.; Hyg. *Fab.* 30; Theocr. 7,149ff.; Serv. on Virgil, *Aen.* 8,294; Athenaeus 11,499a ff. See also HERACLES.

Phorbas (1) Diod. Sic. 4,69; 5,58; 61; Paus. 5,1,11; 7,26,12; Hyg. *Astron.* 2,14; Athenaeus 6,262e ff.; Callim. *Hymn* 6,24; Eustath. p. 303,8; schol. on Apoll. Rhod. *Arg.* 1,172; Apollod. *Bibl.* 2,5,5. (2) Paus. 2,16,1; 4,1,1; schol. on Euripides, *Or.* 932. (3) Schol. on Hom. *Il.* 23,660; cf. Ovid, *Met.* 11,413. (4) Paus. 1,39,3; Euripides, *Suppl.* 680.

Phorcys Hesiod, *Theog.* 270, 333ff.; Apollod. *Bibl.* 1,2,6; Serv. on Virgil, *Aen.* 5,824; 10,388; Lyc. *Alex.* 47ff.; Apoll. Rhod. *Arg.* 4,828.

Phormion Paus. 3,16,7ff.

Phoroneus Plato, *Timaeus* 22a; Acusilaus, fragment 20 Diels-Kranz, = Clem. Alex. *Strom.* 1,102; Paus. 2,15,5; 2,19,5; Apollod. *Bibl.* 2,1,1; 3,1,1; schol. on Euripides, *Or.* 933; Hyg. *Fab.* 143; Tzetzes on Lyc. *Alex.* 177.

Phosphorus Ovid, *Met.* 4,628; *Her.* 17,112; Hyg. *Fab.* 65; 161.

Phrasius Apollod. *Bibl.* 2,5,11; Hyg. *Fab.* 55; Ovid, *Ars Am.* 1,649.

Phrixus Apoll. Rhod. *Arg.* 2,1140ff.; schol. on 1144; Hdt. 7,197; Palaeph. *Incred.* 31; Paus. 9,34,5; Apollod. *Bibl.* 1,9,1; 1,9,16; 1,9,21; Hyg. *Fab.* 1ff.; 12; 14; 21f.; 188; 245; Pseudo-Eratosth. *Catast.* 19.

Phronime Hdt. 4,154ff.; Suda s.v. Βάττος (Battus).

Phrygius Polyaenus 8,35; Plutarch, *De Mulierum Virtutibus* 16,254a; cf. Parthenius, *Erot. Path.* 14.

Phthius Apollod. *Bibl.* 3,8,1; Tzetzes on Lyc. *Alex.* 481; Dion. Hal. *Ant. Rom.* 1,17; Eustath. p. 320,24; Steph. Byz. s.v. Φθία (Phthia) and Ἑλλάς (Hellas); Serv. on Virgil, *Aen.* 2,197; Hdt. 2,98.

Phthonos Euripides, *Troades* 768ff.; Demosth. 25,52; Lucian, *Calumniae non temere credendum* 5.

Phylacus (1) Apollod. *Bibl.* 1,9,4; 1,9,12; Steph. Byz. s.v. Φυλάκη (Phylace); schol. on Hom. *Il*, 2,695; Eustath. p. 323; schol. on Apoll. Rhod. *Arg.* 1,45; 118; 230; schol. on Hom. *Od.* 11,290; Eustath. p. 1685,33; schol. on Theocr. 3,43. (2) Hdt. 8,36ff.; Paus. 10,8,7.

Phylas (1) Apollod. fl2Bibl. 1,7,6; cf. Diod. Sic. 4,36. (2) Hom. *Iliad* 16,181. (3) Paus. 4,34,9; Diod. Sic. 4,37. (4) Paus. 2,4,3; 9,40,5–6.

Phyleus Hom. *Il.* 2,628; 15,528; 23,637; schol. on 2,629; 11,700; 15,519; 23,637; Eustath. p. 305,9; Euripides, *IA* 285; Apollod. *Bibl.* 2,5,5; 2,7,2; 3,10,8; *Epit.* 3,12; Plutarch, *Quaest. Rom.* 28,271c; Diod. Sic. 4,33; Paus. 5,3,2; Callim. fragment 77, p. 62 (Trypanis); Ovid, *Met.* 8,308.

Phylius Antoninus Liberalis, *Met.* 12; Ovid, *Met.* 7,372ff.

Phyllis Tzetzes on Lyc. *Alex.* 495; Apollod. *Epit.* 6,16; Appendix Vergiliana, *Culex* 131ff.; Ovid, *Her.* 2; *Rem. Am.* 591ff.; *Ars Am.* 3,57; Hyg. *Fab.* 59; cf. 243; Serv. on Virgil, *Ecl.* 5,10.

Phytalus Paus. 1,37,2ff.; Plutarch, *Theseus* 12.

Piasus Schol. on Apoll. Rhod. *Arg.* 1,1063; Eustath. p. 357,43ff.; cf. Parthenius, *Erot. Path.* 28.

Picolous Eustath. p. 1658,48.

Picus Virgil, *Aen.* 7,47; 189; Serv. on *Aen.* 7,190; 10,76; Dion. Hal. *Ant. Rom.* 1,31; Arnobius, *Adv. Nat.* 2,71; Aug. *Civ. Dei*

4,23; 5,10; 18,15; Ovid, *Met.* 14,312ff.; Paul. ex. Fest. p. 212; Strabo 5,4,2, p. 200; Plutarch, *De Fortuna Romanorum* 8,320d; *Quaest. Rom.* 21,268f.

Pierides Antoninus Liberalis, *Met* 9; Ovid, *Met.* 5,669ff.; cf. Paus. 9,29,4.

Pierus (1) Schol. on Hom. *Il.* 14,225; Ovid, *Met.* 5,302; Plutarch, *De Mus.* 3,1132a; Serv. on Virgil, *Ecl.* 7,21, see also PIERIDES. (2) Apollod. *Bibl.* 1,3,3.

Pietas Cic. *De Leg.* 2,28; Livy 40,34,4ff.

Pilumnus Aug. *Civ. Dei* 6,9; Virgil, *Aen.* 10,75ff.; 619; Serv. on *Aen.* 9,3; 10,76; Festus p. 224M.

Pindus Aelian, *Nat. An.* 10,40; Tzetzes, *Chil.* 4,338 and schol. on 333.

Piren (1) Apollod. *Bibl.* 2,3,1; Tzetzes on Lyc. *Alex.* 17. (2) Apollod. *Bibl.* 2,1,3.

Pirene Paus. 2,2,3; 2,3,2ff.; 2,5,1; 2,24,7; Diod. Sic. 4,72; Steph. Byz. s.v. Κέγχριαι (Kenchriai).

Pirithous Hom. *Il.* 1,262ff.; *Od.* 11,631, and schol. on 21,295; Euripides, *Heracles* 619; Diod. Sic. 4,70; Apollod. *Bibl.* 1,8,2; 2,5,12; 3,10,8; *Epit.* 1,16ff.; 21ff.; Paus. 1,2,1; 1,17,4; 1,18,4; 1,30,4; 1,41,5; 2,22,6; etc.; Apoll. Rhod. *Arg.* 1,101ff. and schol. on 107; 3,62; Hyg. *Fab.* 33; Serv. on Virgil, *Aen.* 7,304, Plutarch, *Theseus* 30ff.

Pisaeus Pliny, *NH* 7,57; Photius, *Lex.* s.v. Λῃστοσαλπίγκτας (Lestosalpinktas).

Pisidice (1) Parthenius, *Erot. Path.* 21; cf. schol. on Hom. *Il.* 6,35. (2) Apollod. *Bibl.* 1,9,10; Hyg. *Fab.* 24. (3) Apollod. *Bibl.* 1,7,3. (4) Apollod. *Bibl.* 1,9,9.

Pisistratus Hom. *Od.* 3,36; 400; 415; 482; 15,4ff.; Apollod. *Bibl.* 1,9,9; Paus. 4,3,1; Hdt. 5,65.

Pistor Ovid, *Fasti* 6,350ff.; Lact. *Inst. Div.* 1,20,33.

Pisus (1) Paus. 5,17,9; 6,22,2. (2) Serv. on Virgil, *Aen.* 10,179. (3) Apollod. *Bibl.* 3,10,3.

Pitane (1) Pind. *Ol.* 6,28ff. (46ff.) and schol. (2) Diod. Sic. 3,55.

Pittheus Hom. *Il.* 3,144; schol. on Pind. *Ol.* 1,89 (144); Euripides, *Medea* 680ff.; *Heracles* 107ff.; schol. on Euripides, *Or.* 5; Paus. 1,22,2; 2,30,8; 2,31,6; Strabo 8,6,14, p. 374; Diod. Sic. 4,59; Plutarch, *Theseus* 4 and 34; Hyg. *Fab.* 4, 37, Apollod. *Bibl.* 3,15,7; *Epit.* 2,10.

Pityreus Paus. 2,26,1; 7,4,2.

Pitys Nonnus, *Dion.* 2,108; 118; 42,259; Lucian, *Dial. Deorum* 22,4; *Geoponica* 11,10.

Platanus Westermann, *Mythogr. Gr.* p. 381.

Pleiades Schol. on Hom. *Il.* 18,486; Eustath. p. 1155; Hesiod, *W. & D.* 383; Aeschylus, fragment 312 Nauck, *TGF*, edn. 2 (from an unidentified play); Hyg. *Astron.* 2,21, *Fab.* 192; Pseudo-Eratosth. *Catast.* 23; schol. on Apoll. Rhod. *Arg.* 3,225; Apollod. *Bibl.* 3,10,1; Ovid, *Fasti* 4,172; 5,83ff.; Aratus, *Phaen.* 262ff.; Callim. fragment 693 Pfeiffer (quoted in schol. on Theocr. 13,25); Paus. 2,30,8.

Pleione Apollod. *Bibl.* 3,10,1; schol. on Hom. *Il.* 18,486; schol. on *Od.* 5,272; schol. on Hesiod, *W. & D.* 382; Hyg. *Fab.* 192; 248; *Astron.* 2,21; Tzetzes on Lyc. *Alex.* 149; 219; Ovid, *Fasti* 5,83; *Met.* 2,743.

Pleisthenes Schol. on Euripides, *Or.* 4; schol. on Sophocles, *Ajax* 1297; Apollod. *Bibl.* 3,2,2; Euripides, lost tragedy *Pleisthenes*, Nauck, *TGF*, edn 2, p. 556ff.; Seneca, *Thyestes* 726; Hyg. *Fab.* 86 and 88.

Plemnaeus Paus. 2,5,8; 2,11,2.

Pleuron Schol. on Apoll. Rhod. *Arg.* 1,146; Apollod. *Bibl.* 1,7,7; schol. on Hom. *Il.* 13,218; Paus. 3,13,8.

Plexippus (1) Apollod. *Bibl.* 1,7,10; 1,8,2; Ovid, *Met.* 8,305; 434ff.; schol. on Ovid, *Ibis* 601; schol. on Hom. *Il.* 9,567; Hyg. *Fab.* 173–4; 244; Diod. Sic. 4,34. (2) Apollod. *Bibl.* 3,15,3; schol. on Sophocles, *Antig.* 980. (3) Serv. on Virgil, *Aen.* 8,138.

(quoting Philostephanus, fragment 13 Müller, *FHG* III, p.31); Arnobius, *Adv. Nat.* 6,22; Ovid, *Met.* 10,243ff.

Pygmies Hom. *Il.* 3,3ff., and Eustath. p.371,43; Virgil, *Aen.* 10,264ff.; Hecataeus, fragment 266 Müller, *FHG* I, p.18; Hdt. 2,32; Pliny, *NH* 7,26ff.; Antoninus Liberalis, *Met.* 16; Ovid, *Met.* 6,90ff.; Athenaeus 9,393c ff. See also GERANA.

Pylades Pind. *Pyth.* 11,15 (23); Aeschylus, *Choeph.* 900; Sophocles, *Electra*; Euripides, *Orestes*, and schol. on 764; *Electra*; *IT*; Paus. 1,22,6; 2,16,7; 2,29,9; Hyg. *Fab.* 121–2.

Pylaemenes Apollod. *Epit.* 3,35; Hom. *Il.* 2,851; 5,576ff.; 13,658ff.; Hyg. *Fab.* 113.

Pylaeus Hom. *Il.* 2,840ff.; Strabo 13,3,2, p.620ff.; Dict. Cret. 2,35.

Pylas Apollod. *Bibl.* 3,15,5; Paus. 1,5,3; 1,39,4ff.; 4,36,1; 6,22,5.

Pylenor Paus. 5,5,10; Ovid, *Met.* 15,282ff.; cf. Strabo 8,3,19, p.346.

Pylia Apollod. *Bibl.* 3,15,5.

Pylius Ptol. Heph. in Westermann, *Mythogr. Gr.* p.197.

Pyraechmes (1) Hom. *Il.* 2,848; 16,287; Apollod. *Epit.* 3,34; Eustath. p.359,33ff.; 1697,57; Dict. Cret. 3,4; Porphyry, *Quaest. Hom. ad Il.* 2, p.50 Schrader. (2) Paus. 5,4,2; Eustath. p.311,21. See OXYLUS. (3) Plutarch, *Parall.* 7,307b-c.

Pyramus Westermann, *Mythogr. Gr.* p.384; Ovid, *Met.* 4,55ff.; cf. Serv. on Virgil, *Ecl* 6,22; Hyg. *Fab.* 242–3. Cf. E. Rohde, *Der griechische Roman*, edn. 2, p.153ff.

Pyrene (1) Sil. Ital. 3,420ff.; Pliny, *NH* 3,3,8. (2) Apollod. *Bibl.* 2,5,11.

Pyreneus Ovid, *Met.* 5,274ff.

Pyrgo (1) Paus. 1,43,4. See ALCATHUS. (2) Virgil, *Aen.* 5,645.

Pyrias Heraclides (?Lembus), *De Rebus Publicis*, in Müller, *FHG* II, p.223, fragment 38,2; Plutarch, *Quaest. Gr.* 34,298e.

Pyrrha Hesiod, fragments 2–4 Merkelbach-West; Pind. *Ol.* 9,43 (64)ff.; Apollod. *Bibl.* 1,7,2; Conon, *Narr.* 27; Hyg. *Fab.* 153.

Pyrrhicus Paus. 3,25,2; Strabo 10,4,16, p.480; Athenaeus 14,630e; Pollux 4,99; 104.

Pyrrhus Serv. on Virgil, *Aen.* 2,469; Paus. 1,4,4; 3,25,2. See NEOPTOLEMUS; PYRRHA.

Pythaeus Paus. 2,24,1; 2,35,2.

Python Homeric Hymn to Apollo, 372ff.; Callim. *Hymn* 2,100ff.; Hyg. *Fab.* 140; Ovid, *Met.* 1,438ff.; Euripides, *IT* 1245ff.; Paus. 10,6,5; Aelian, *VH* 3,1; Varro, *De Ling. Lat.* 7,17. Cf. J. Fontenrose, *Python: a study of Delphic myth and its origins*, 1959.

Q

Quirinus Ovid, *Fasti* 2,477ff.; 4,910; Varro, *De Ling. Lat.* 5,51; Festus p.185; 254M.; Paul. ex. Fest. p.49; Macrob. *Sat.* 1,9,16; Serv. on Virgil, *Aen.* 1,292; *CIL* I, edn. 2, p.259 (Fasti Silvii); Plutarch, *Romulus* 29; *Quaest. Rom.* 87,285d; Dion. Hal. *Ant. Rom.* 2,48ff.; Lucilius I, fragment 19–22 Marx; Tertullian, *De Spectaculis* 5; Livy 5,40,7ff.; Cic. *De Leg.* 1,3; *De Rep.* 2,20. Cf. G. Dumézil, *Jupiter, Mars, Quirinus*, 1941.

R

Ramnes Virgil, *Aen.* 9,325ff.; 359; Ovid, *Ibis* 629 and schol.

Rarus Steph. Byz., Hesych. and Phot. s.v.; Suda s.v. Ῥαρίας (Rarias).

Ratumena Plutarch, *Publicola* 13; Pliny, *NH* 8,161; Festus p.274M.

Recaranus Anon. *De Orig. Gent. Rom.* 6 and 8; Serv. on Virgil, *Aen.* 8,203. See HERCULES.

Remus Plutarch, *Romulus* 7ff.; Cic. *De Div.* 1,107ff.; *De Rep.* 1,4; Paul. ex. Fest. p. 276; Festus p. 298M.; Dion. Hal. *Ant. Rom.* 1,72ff.; Strabo 5,3,2, p. 230; Ovid, *Fasti* 3,59ff.; 5,479; Conon, *Narr.* 48; Anon. *De Orig. Gent. Rom.* 21ff.; Serv. on Virgil, *Aen.* 1,273 and 276; 6,777; Livy, 1,5ff. Cf. ROMULUS.

Rhacius Schol. on Apoll. Rhod. *Arg.* 1,308; Paus. 7,3,1.

Rhadamanthys Hom. *Od.* 7,323ff.; *Il.* 14,322; Eustath. p. 989,35; Paus. 7,3,7; 8,53,4ff.; Diod. Sic. 4,60; Pind. *Pyth.* 2,73; *Ol.* 2,75; Antoninus Liberalis, *Met.* 33; Apollod. *Bibl.* 3,1,2.

Rhea Hom. *Il.* 15,187; Hesiod, *Theog.* 453ff.; Apollod. *Bibl.* 1,1,3; Diod. Sic. 5,66ff.; Paus. 8,2,2; Lucret. 2,629; Virgil, *Aen.* 9,83.

Rhea (or Rea) Silvia (1) Dion. Hal. *Ant. Rom.* 1,72ff.; Varro, *De Ling. Lat.* 5,44; Aug. *Civ. Dei* 18,21; Ovid, *Fasti* 2,303 3,20ff.; *Am.* 2,6,45ff.; Serv. on Virgil, *Aen.* 1,273; 6,777; Cic. *De Div.* 1,40; Strabo 5,3,2, p. 229; Livy 1,3ff.; Plutarch, *Romulus* 3; Anon. *De Orig. Gent. Rom.* 20; Justin-Trogus 43,2,2; Horace, *Od.* 4,8,22. (2) Virgil, *Aen.* 7,659 and Serv. ad loc.

Rhesus Hom. *Il.* 10,434ff. and schol.; Eustath. p. 817,26; Serv. on Virgil, *Aen.* 2,13; Conon, *Narr.* 4; Euripides, *Rhesus*, and schol. on 347; Virgil, *Aen.* 1,469ff. and Serv. ad loc.; Apollod. *Bibl.* 1,3,4; *Epit.* 4,4; Hyg. *Fab.* 113.

Rhode Apollod. *Bibl.* 1,4,6; schol. on Hom. *Od.* 17,208; Tzetzes on Lyc. *Alex.* 923.

Rhodope Nicetas Eugenianus 3,263ff. in Herscher, *Scriptores Erotici* II, p. 468; Achilles Tatius 8,12.

Rhodopis Strabo 17,1,33, p. 808; Aelian, *VH* 13,33.

Rhodus Pind. *Ol.* 7,14 (25) ff. and schol.; Diod. Sic. 5,55; Tzetzes, *Chil.* 4,360; Eustath. p. 315,27; Ovid, *Met.* 4,204, and Lact. Plac. *Narr. Fab. Ovid.* 4.

Rhoecus (1) Schol. on Apoll. Rhod. *Arg.* 2,477; schol. on Theocr. 3,13; Plutarch, *Quaest. Nat.* 36 (quoting Pindar, fragment 236 Bergk); Etym. Magn. p. 75,26. (2) See ATALANTA.

Rhoeo Parthenius, *Erot. Path.* 1; Diod. Sic. 5,62; Tzetzes, *Chil.* 6,979ff.; schol. on Lyc. *Alex.* 570 and 580.

Rhoetus (1) Horace, *Od.* 2,19,23; 3,4,55. (2) Virgil, *Georg.* 2,456; Ovid, *Met.* 12,271; Val. Flacc. *Arg.* 1,141; cf. Apollod. *Bibl.* 3,9,2. (3) Ovid, *Met.* 5,38; Apollod. *Bibl.* 3,4,3. (4) Virgil, *Aen.* 10,388 and Serv. ad loc.

Rhopalus Paus. 2,6,7; 2,10,1; Ptol. Heph. *Nov. Hist.* 3 (Westermann, *Myth. Gr.* p. 186).

Rhoxane Pseudo-Plutarch, *De Fluviis* 20,1.

Rhytia Strabo 10,3,21, p. 472.

Robigo Varro, *De Re Rust.* 1,1,6; *CIL* I, edn. 2, p. 316 (Fasti Praenestini); Ovid, *Fasti* 4,905ff.

Roma Dion. Hal. *Ant. Rom.* 1,72ff.; Plutarch, *Romulus* 1; Festus p. 266ff.M.; Solinus 1,1ff.; Serv. on Virgil, *Aen.* 1,273.

Romis Plutarch, *Romulus* 2.

Romulus Livy 1,1ff.; Dion. Hal. 1,76ff.; Plutarch, *Romulus*; *De Fort. Rom.* 8ff., 320b; Cic. *De Div.* 1,40; 107ff.; Strabo 5,3,2, p. 230; Cic. *De Rep.* 2,4; 2,12; Ovid, *Fasti* 2,381ff.; 3,11ff.; 179ff.; 431ff.; Tzetzes on Lyc. *Alex.* 1232; Serv. on Virgil, *Aen.* 1,273ff.; 6,778; 8,635; Anon. *De Orig. Gent. Rom.* 21ff.; Varro, *De Ling. Lat.* 5,54; Tac. *Ann.* 13,58; Pliny, *NH* 15,77ff.; Tertullian, *Apol.* 25; *Ad Nat.* 2,10; Lact. *Inst. Div.* 1,20; 2,6; J. Hubaux, *Les Grands Mythes de Rome*, 1945.

Romus Festus, p. 266; 269M.; Dion. Hal. *Ant. Rom.* 1,72; cf. Plutarch, *Romulus* 2.

Rutuli Virgil, *Aen.* 7, etc.; Livy 1,3,57; Dion. Hal. *Ant. Rom.* 1,57; 59; 64; Strabo 5,3,2, p. 228ff.; Cic. *De Rep.* 2,5.

S

Sabazius Diod. Sic. 4,4,1; Joann. Lyd. *De Mensibus* 4,51; Cic. *De Nat. Deor.* 3,58; Aelian, *Nat. An.* 12,39; Strabo 10,3,15, p. 470 and 18, p. 471; schol. on Aristophanes, *Birds* 874; Macrob. *Sat.* 1,18,11, Clem. Alex. *Prot.* 2,16, cf. Demosth. *De Corona* 259ff. (on the mysteries of Sabazius).

Sabbe Paus. 10,12,9.

Sabus Dion. Hal. *Ant. Rom.* 2,49; cf. Serv. on Virgil, *Aen.* 8,638.

Sagaris (1) Solinus 2,10. (2) Etym. Magn. p. 707,18; Pseudo-Plutarch, *De Fluv.* 12,1.

Sagaritis Ovid, *Fasti* 4,229ff.

Salacia Aul. Gell. *Noctes Atticae* 13,23; Aug. *Civ. Dei.* 4,10; 7,22; Serv. on Virgil, *Georg.* 1,31; on *Aen.* 1,44; 10,76.

Salambo Etym. Magn. p. 747,48; Historia Augusta, *Elagabalus* 7.

Salamis Paus. 1,35,2; Diod. Sic. 4,72; schol. on Pind. *Ol.* 6,84 (144), Tzetzes on Lyc. *Alex.* 110, 175, 451, Apollod. *Bibl.* 3,12,7.

Salius Plutarch, *Numa* 13; Festus p. 329M.; Serv. on Virgil, *Aen.* 8,285; cf. Virg. *Aen.* 5,298ff.

Salmoneus Apollod. *Bibl.* 1,9,7ff.; schol. on Hom. *Od.* 11,236; Diod. Sic. 4,68; Hyg. *Fab.* 61; 250; Virgil, *Aen.* 6,585ff.; Serv. ad loc.; Strabo 7,3,31ff., p. 356; Steph. Byz. s.v. Σαλμώνη (Salmone).

Salus Cic. *De Leg.* 2,28.

Samon Dion. Hal. *Ant. Rom.* 1,61.

Sanape Schol. on Apoll. Rhod. *Arg.* 2,946; Etym. Magn. p. 739,67, s.v. Σινώπη (Sinope).

Sancus Ovid, *Fasti* 6,213ff.; Lact. *Inst. Div.* 1,15,8; Aug. *Civ. Dei.* 18,19; Dion. Hal. *Ant. Rom.* 2,49.

Sangarius Hesiod, *Theog.* 344; Arnobius, *Adv. Nat.* 5,6; Paus. 7,17,11; Apollod. *Bibl.* 3,12,5; schol. on Hom. *Il.* 16,718; Westermann, *Mythogr. Gr.* p. 347.

Saon Paus. 9,40,2.

Sardo (1) Schol. on Plato, *Tim.* 25b. (2) Hyg. *Fab.* 275.

Sardus Paus. 10,17,2; Solinus 10,4,1.

Saron Paus. 2,30,7; Etym. Magn. p. 708,51, schol. on Euripides, *Hippol.* 1200.

Sarpedon (1) Apollod. *Bibl.* 2,5,9. (2) Hesiod, fragments 140–1 Merkelbach-West; Bacchyl. fragment 56 Bergk (quoted in schol. on Hom. *Il.* 12,292); Hdt. 1,173; 4,45; Euripides, *Rhesus* 29; Diod. Sic. 4,60; 5,79; Apollod. *Bibl.* 3,1,1ff.; Hyg. *Fab.* 155; 178; Paus. 7,3,7; schol. on Apoll. Rhod. *Arg.* 1,185; Strabo 12,8,5, p. 573. (3) Hom. *Il.* 2,876ff.; 5,471ff.; 627ff.; 6,198ff.; 12,101ff.; etc.

Saturn Dion. Hal. *Ant. Rom.* 1,34; Virgil, *Georg.* 2,538; *Aen.* 6,794; 8,319ff.; 357ff.; Serv. ad loc.; Ovid, *Fasti* 1,35ff.; Plutarch, *Quaest. Rom.* 34,272e.

Satyria Schol. Bern. on Virgil, *Georg.* 2,197; Probus ibid.; Serv. on *Aen.* 1,533; Paus. 10,10,8.

Satyrs Homeric Hymn to Aphrodite 262; Hesiod, fragment 123 Merkelbach-West (quoted in Strabo 10,3,19, p. 471); Paus. 1,23,5–6.

Saurus Paus. 6,21,3.

Scamander Hom. *Il.* 21,131ff.; schol. on 21,1ff.; Hesiod, *Theog.* 337ff.; Diod. Sic. 4,75; Apollod. *Bibl.* 3,12,1; Aristotle, *Hist. An.* 3,12; Aelian, *Nat. An.* 8,21; Eustath. p. 1197,49ff.

Scamandrius (1) Hom. *Il.* 6,400ff.; see ASTYANAX. (2) Hom. *Il.* 5,49.

Schedius Hyg. *Fab.* 97; Hom. *Il.* 2,517; 17,306; cf. 15,515; Paus. 10,4,2; 10,30,8; 10,36,10; Apollod. *Bibl.* 3,10,8; Lyc. *Alex.* 1067ff. and Tzetzes ad loc.; Strabo 9,3,17, p. 425.

Schoeneus (1) Apollod. *Bibl.* 1,8,2; Tzetzes on Lyc. *Alex.* 22; schol. on Apoll. Rhod. *Arg.* 1,769, 2,1144; Steph. Byz. s.v. Σχοινοῦς (Schoenus); Diod. Sic. 4,34; Hesiod, fragments 75–6 Merkelbach West; schol. on Euripides, *Phoen.* 150; schol. on Theocr. 3,40; Hyg. *Fab.* 173; 185. (2) Antoninus Liberalis, *Met.* 7. (3) Apollod. *Bibl.* 1,9,2.

Sciapodes Pliny, *NH* 7,2,23; Hesych. s.v.; Steph. Byz. s.v.; Philostr. *Vit. Apollon.* 3,47.

Sciron Apollod. *Epit.* 1,2, Plutarch, *Theseus* 10; 25; Bacchyl. 17,24ff.; Diod. Sic. 4,59,4; Paus. 1,44,8; schol. on Euripides, *Hippol.* 979; Ovid, *Met.* 7,443ff.; Hyg. *Fab.* 38; Paus. 1,39,6; 2,29,9.

Scirus (1) Paus. 1,36,4. (2) Plutarch, *Theseus* 17.

Scylaceus Quint. Smyrn. *Posthom.* 10,147ff.

Scylla (1) Hom. *Od.* 12,73ff.; schol. on 12,257; Eustath. p. 1721,8; Lyc. *Alex.* 44ff. and Tzetzes ad loc.; ibid. 668; 738ff.; Pseudo-Virgil, *Ciris*; *Culex*, 331ff.; Dict. Cret. 6,5; Apoll. Rhod. *Arg.* 4,789ff.; 825ff.; schol. on 828; Apollod. *Epit.* 7,20; Hyg. *Fab.* 125; 199; Ovid, *Met.* 7,62ff.; 13,900ff.; Pseudo-Lact. Plac. *Narr. Fab. Ovid.* 14; Serv. on Virgil, *Ecl.* 6,74; on *Aen.* 3,420. (2) Aeschylus, *Choeph.* 613ff.; *Appendix Vergiliana, Ciris,* Virgil, *Georg.* 1,404ff., Serv. on Virgil, *Ecl.* 6,74; Ovid, *Met.* 8,6ff.; Apollod. *Bibl.* 3,15,8; Paus. 1,19,4; 2,34,7; Tzetzes on Lyc. *Alex.* 650, schol. on Euripides, *Hippol.* 1200; Hyg. *Fab.* 198.

Scyphius Schol. on Pind. *Pyth.* 4,138 (246); Tzetzes on Lyc. *Alex.* 766; schol. on Apoll. Rhod. *Arg.* 3,1244; Pseudo-Lact. Plac. on Stat. *Theb.* 4,43.

Scythes Hdt. 4,9–10; Steph. Byz. s.v. Σκύθαι (Scythai); Diod. Sic. 2,43.

Selene Homeric Hymn to Hermes 100; Euripides, *Phoen.* 175 and schol.; Nonnus, *Dion.* 44,191; Virgil, *Georg.* 3,391 and Serv. ad loc.; schol. on Apoll. Rhod. *Arg.* 4,57; schol. on Theocr. 3,49. Cf. LUNA.

Selinus Steph. Byz. s.v. Ἑλίκη (Helice); Paus. 7,24,5.

Semachus Steph. Byz. s.v. Σημαχίδαι (Semachidai); Euseb. *Chron.* p. 44 Helm.

Semele Apollod. *Bibl.* 3,4,2ff.; 3,5,3; Hesiod, *Theog.* 940ff.; Euripides, *Bacch.* 1ff.; 242ff.; 286ff.; Diod. Sic. 4,2,2ff.; 4,25,4; 5,52,2; schol. on Hom. *Il.* 14,325; schol. on Pind. *Ol.* 2,26 (44); Lucian, *Dial. Deorum* 9; Ovid, *Met.* 3,259ff.; Hyg. *Fab.* 167; 179; Pseudo-Lact. Plac. on Stat. *Theb.* 1,12.

Semiramis Diod. Sic. 2,4ff.; 2,13ff.; Hdt. 1,184; 3,155; Hesych. s.v.; Lucian, *De Dea Syria* 14.

Serestus Virgil, *Aen.* 1,611; 4,288; 5,487; 9,171; 10,541 and Serv. ad loc.; 12,549; 561.

Sergestus Virgil, *Aen.* 1,510; 4,288; 5,122; 155ff.; 282ff.; 12,561.

Servius Tullius Livy 1,39ff.; Varro, *De Ling. Lat.* 5,61; Arnobius, *Adv. Nat.* 5,18; Dion. Hal. *Ant. Rom.* 4,1ff.

Setaea Lyc. *Alex.* 1075; Tzetzes ad loc. and on 921; Steph. Byz. s.v. Σηταῖον (Setaion).

Sevechorus Aelian, *Nat. An.* 12,21.

Sibyl Arrian, fragment 64 Müller, *FHG* III, p. 598 (quoted in Eustath., p. 356,28); Clem. Alex. *Strom.* 1,108; Lact. *Inst. Div.* 1,6, quoting Varro; Paus. 10,12,1ff.; Suda s.v.; Hermias on Plato, *Phaedrus* 244b; Euseb. *Or. ad Sanct.* 18; Pseudo-Aristotle, *De Mirab. Ausc.* 95 (97); Serv. on Virgil, *Aen.* 3,441ff.; 6,321; Virgil, *Aen.* 6,10ff.; Petron. *Sat.* 48; Ampelius 8,16; Dion. Hal. *Ant. Rom.* 4,62; Ovid, *Met.* 14,130ff.

Sicanus Solinus 5,7; Isidore, *Etym.* 14,6,32; Steph. Byz. s.v. Τρινακρία (Trinacria); schol. on Theocr. 1,65.

Sicelus Dion. Hal. *Ant. Rom.* 1,22; Isidore, *Etym.* 14,6,32; Solinus 5,7; Serv. on Virgil, *Aen.* 8,328.

Sicinnus Dion. Hal. *Ant. Rom.* 7,72; Athenaeus 14,630b; cf. Eustath. p. 1078,22.

Sicyon Paus. 2,1,1; 2,6,5–6; 2,7,1; 7,1,1.

Side (1) John of Antioch, fragment 6,15 Müller, *FHG* IV, p. 544. (2) Paus. 3,22,11. (3) Steph. Byz. s.v. (4) Apollod. *Bibl.* 1,4,3. (5) Dionysius, *De Avibus* 1,7, in *Poetae Bucolici et Didactici*, Bibl. Script. Graec., 1851, p. 109.

Sidero Apollod. *Bibl.* 1,9,8; Tzetzes on Lyc. *Alex.* 175; Diod. Sic. 4,68; Eustath. p. 158,24; 1940,57.

Silenus Apollod. *Bibl.* 2,5,4; Hdt. 8,138; Virgil, *Ecl.* 6 and Serv. on 6.13; Clem. Alex. *Protr.* 24. See also MIDAS.

Sillus Paus. 2,18,8.

Silvanus Cato, *De Agr.* 83; Virgil, *Ecl.* 2,24ff.; *Georg.* 1,20; *Aen.* 8,597ff.; Ovid, *Met.* 14,639ff.; Plutarch, *Publicola* 9; Livy 2,7.

Silvius Dion. Hal. *Ant. Rom.* 1,70; Virgil, *Aen.* 6,760 and Serv. *ad loc.*; Ovid, *Fasti* 4,41; *Met.* 14,610; Anon. *De Orig. Gent. Rom.* 16ff.; Aul. Gell. *Noct. Att.* 2,16,3; Livy 1,3,6ff.; Zonaras 7,1 (derived from Dio Cassius).

Simois Hom. *Il.* 5,777; 12,19ff.; 21,305ff.; Hesiod, *Theog.* 342ff.; Virgil, *Aen.* 1,100; Apollod. *Bibl.* 3,12,2; Tzetzes on Lyc. *Alex.* 29.

Sinis Plutarch, *Theseus* 8,2; cf. 25,4; Bacchyl. 17,19ff.; Diod. Sic. 4, 59; Apollod. *Bibl.* 3,16,2; Paus. 2,1,4; Ovid, *Met.* 7,440ff.; *Ibis* 403ff.; Hyg. *Fab.* 38; Marmor Parium 36; schol. on Pind., argument to *Isthm.* (ed. Drachmann, III p. 193).

Sinon Apollod. *Epit.* 5,15; 5,19; Tzetzes, *Posthom.* 720ff.; Aristotle, *Poet.* 23, 1459b 7; Plautus, *Bacchides* 937ff.; Virgil, *Aen.* 2,57ff.; Serv. on *Aen.* 2,79; Hyg. *Fab.* 108; Quint. Smyrn. *Posthom.* 12,243ff.; Lyc. *Alex.* 344 and schol. ad loc.

Sinope Diod. Sic. 4,72; Apoll. Rhod. *Arg.* 2,946 and schol. ad loc.

Siproetes Antoninus Liberalis, *Met.* 17.

Sirens Hom. *Od.* 12,1ff.; schol. on 39; Eustath. p. 1709; schol. on Lyc. *Alex.* 653; Paus. 9,34,3; 10,5,12; 10,6,5; Tzetzes on Lyc. *Alex.* 712; Hyg. *Fab.* 125; 141; Apollod. *Bibl.* 1,3,4; 1,7,10; 1,9,25; *Epit.* 7,18ff.; Sophocles, fragment 861 (Jebb-Pearson III, p. 66); Plato, *Rep.* 617b; *Crat.* 403e; Ovid, *Met.* 5,512ff.; Libanius, *Narrationes* 1,31; Plutarch, *Quaest. Conv.* 9,14,6, 745d ff.; Apoll. Rhod. *Arg.* 4,895.

Siris Strabo 6,1,14. p. 264; Athenaeus 12,523; schol. on Dion., Perieg. 461; Etym. Magn. p. 714,12; cf. Diod. Sic. 4,67.

Sisyphus Hom. *Il.* 6,152; schol. ad loc. and on 1,180; *Od.* 11,593ff.; Apollod. *Bibl.* 1,7,3; 1,9,3; 3,4,3; 3,10,1; 3,12,6; Paus. 2,1,3; 2,3,11; 2,5,1; 9,34,7; 10,30,5; Pind. *Ol.* 13,52 (72) schol. on Apoll. Rhod. *Arg.* 3,1240; Tzetzes on Lyc. *Alex.* 107; 176; 229; 284; 344; Aeschylus, (lost tragedy *Sisyphus* Nauck, *TGF*, edn. 2, p. 74ff.); Sophocles, lost tragedy of same title (Jebb-Pearson II, p. 184f.); Critias, in Nauck, *TGF*, edn 2, p. 771ff.; schol. on Sophocles, *Ajax* 190; Suda s.v.; Hyg. *Fab.* 60; 201; Serv. on Virgil, *Georg.* 1,138; and on *Aen.* 6,616.

Sithon Parthenius, *Erot. Path.* 6; Conon, *Narr.* 10; schol. on Lyc. *Alex.* 583; 1161; 1356; Nonnus, *Dion.* 48,183ff.; Ovid, *Met.* 4,279.

Smaragus Homeric Epigrams 14,9, in Baumeister's edition of Homeric Hymns.

Smerdius Diod. Sic. 5,51.

Smicrus Conon, *Narr.* 33; Pseudo-Lact. Plac. on Stat. *Theb.* 8,198.

Smintheus Plutarch, *De Sollertia Animalium* 36,984e.

Smyrna (1) Strabo 11,5,3, p. 505; 12,3,21, p. 550; 14,1,4, p. 633; Steph. Byz. s.v. Ἔφεσος (Ephesus); Tac. *Ann.* 4,56. (2) See ADONIS.

Sol Varro, *De Ling. Lat.* 5,74; Dion. Hal. *Ant. Rom.* 2,50; Aug. *Civ. Dei* 4,23; Paulus ex Festus p. 23M.

Solois Plutarch, *Theseus* 26 (quoting Menecrates, cf. Müller, *FHG* II, p. 345).

Solymus Etym. Magn. p. 721,43ff.

Sopatrus Porphyry, *De Abstinentia* 2,29ff.

Sophax Plutarch, *Sertorius* 9.

Soranus Virgil, *Aen.* 11,785; Serv. ad loc.; Sil. Ital. 5,175ff.; Pliny, *NH* 7,19.

Sosthenes Malalas 4, p. 78ff. Dindorf.

Sparta Apollod. *Bibl.* 3,10,3; Paus. 3,1,2; schol. on Euripides, *Or.* 626.

Spartoi See CADMUS; also schol. on Euripides, *Phoen.* 942; schol. on Apoll. Rhod. *Arg.* 3,1179.

Spercheius Hom. *Il.* 16,174; schol. on 23,142; Antoninus Liberalis, *Met.* 22; 32.

Sphaerus Paus. 2,33,1; 5,10,7; see CILLAS.

Sphinx Hesiod, *Theog.* 326ff. and schol.; Apollod. *Bibl.* 3,5,8; Sophocles, *OT* 391ff.; Euripides, *Phoen.* 45ff.; schol. on 26; 45; 1760; Diod. Sic. 4,63; Paus. 9,26,2ff.; Hyg. *Fab.* 67; Seneca, *Oedipus* 92ff.; Athenaeus 10, p. 456b; Tzetzes on Lyc. *Alex.* 7.

Staphylus (1) Probus on Virgil, *Georg.* 1,9. (2) Pliny, *NH* 7,199. (3) Plutarch, *Theseus* 20; Parthenius, *Erot. Path.* 1; schol. on Apoll. Rhod. *Arg.* 3,997; Apollod. *Bibl.* 1,9,16; *Epit.* 1,9; schol. on Lyc. *Alex.* 570; Diod. Sic. 5,62.

Stentor Hom. *Il.* 5,785; schol. ad loc. and on 2,96, and Eustath. p. 607,27.

Sterope (1) Diod. Sic. 3,60; Apollod. *Bibl.* 3,10,1; Paus. 5,10,6; Pseudo-Eratosth. *Catast.* 23; cf. Tzetzes on Lyc. *Alex.* 149; 219. (2) Apollod. *Bibl.* 1,7,7. (3) Apollod. *Bibl.* 1,7,7; schol. on Hom. *Od.* 12,39; Eustath. p. 1709,38. (4) Apollod. *Bibl.* 2,7,3; Paus. 8,47,5. (5) Apollod. *Bibl.* 3,13,3.

Steropes Hesiod, *Theog.* 141; Callim. *Hymn* 3,68; Virgil, *Aen.* 8,425; Ovid, *Fasti* 4,188; Apollod. *Bibl.* 1,1,2.

Stheneboea Apollod. *Bibl.* 2,2,1; 2,3,1; 3,9,1ff.; Hyg. *Astron.* 2,18; *Fab.* 57; 243; Euripides, lost tragedy *Stheneboea* Nauck, *TGF*, edn. 2, p. 567ff.; schol. on Hom. *Il.* 6,157; 200; schol. on Hom. *Od.* 11,325–6; Apoll. Rhod. *Arg.* 1,161ff.; cf. Hom. *Il.* 6,164 (Anteia); Eustath. p. 634,20.

Sthenelas Paus. 2,16,1; 2,19,3.

Sthenelus (1) Apoll. Rhod. *Arg.* 2,913ff. and schol. (2) Apollod. *Bibl.* 2,5,9. (3) Hom. *Il.* 2,564; 4,367; 5,109ff.; 241; 319ff.; 835; 8,114; etc.; Apollod. *Bibl.* 3,7,1; 3,10,8; Hyg. *Fab.* 97; 257; Serv. on Virgil, *Aen.* 2,261; Paus. 2,30,10; 10,10,4; schol. on Hom. *Il.* 4,106; Westermann, *Mythogr. Gr.* p. 346; Serv. on Virgil, *Aen.* 8,9; Tzetzes on Lyc. *Alex.* 603; 610; 1093. See also COMETES. (4) Hom. *Il.* 19,116 and schol.; Apollod. *Bibl.* 2,4,5; Tzetzes on Lyc. *Alex.* 838; Euripides, *Alc.* 1150; *Heraclidae* 361; Ovid, *Met.* 9,273; schol. on Apoll. Rhod. *Arg.* 4,223; 228.

Stilbe (1) Schol. on Hom. *Il.* 1,266; Diod. Sic. 4,69; 5,61; Ovid, *Am.* 3,6,31ff.; schol. on Apoll. Rhod. *Arg.* 1,948. (2) See AUTOLYCUS.

Stirus Val. Flacc. *Arg.* 3,497; 5,459; 6,265ff.; 8,299ff.; 328ff.

Striges Ovid, *Fasti* 6,131ff.; Petron. *Sat.* 63; cf. Pliny, *NH* 11,232.

Strophius (1) Euripides, *Or.*, argument, and schol. on 33; 765; 1233; Paus. 2,29,4; Pind. *Pyth.* 11,35 (53) and schol.; Ovid, *Ex Ponto* 3,6,25; Aeschylus, *Agam.* 840ff.; Seneca, *Agam.* 920ff. (2) Paus. 2,16,7.

Strymo Apollod. *Bibl.* 3,12,3; schol. Veron. on Hom. *Il.* 11,5; Tzetzes on Lyc. *Alex.* 18.

Strymon Euripides, *Rhesus* 279; 346ff.; schol. on 351; Conon, *Narr.* 4; Pseudo-Plutarch, *De Fluv.* 21,3; Antoninus Liberalis, *Met.* 21; Apollod. *Bibl.* 1,2,5; 2,1,2.

Stymphalus Paus. 2,24,6; 8,4,4; 8,22,1; 8,35,9; Apollod. *Bibl.* 3,9,1; 3,12,6; schol. on Apoll. Rhod. *Arg.* 2,1052.

Styx Hesiod, *Theog.* 361ff.; 383ff.; 775ff.; Callim. *Hymn* 1,36; Hyg. *Fab.* pref. 17 Rose; Homeric Hymn to Demeter, 424; Apollod. *Bibl.* 1,2,1; 1,3,1; Tzetzes on Lyc. *Alex.* 707; Epimenides, fragment 6 Diels-Kranz, quoted by Paus. 8,18,2; Paus. 8,17,6ff.; Virgil, *Aen.* 6,439; Serv. on *Aen.* 4,462; Strabo

8,8,4, p. 389; Hdt. 6,74; Apul. *Met.* 6,13ff.; Aelian, *Nat. An.* 10,40.

Summanus Cic. *De Div.* 1,16; Ovid, *Fasti* 6,729ff.; Pliny, *NH* 2,138; Aug. *Civ. Dei* 4,23; CIL VI, 1207 p. 574 (Acta Arvalium); Varro, *De Ling. Lat.* 5,74.

Sybaris (1) Antoninus Liberalis, *Met.* 8. See ALCYONEUS. (2) Virgil, *Aen.* 12,363. (3) Aelian, *Nat. An.* 12,35; cf. Strabo 13,1,14, p. 588.

Syceus Athenaeus 3,78b, Steph. Byz. s.v., Eustath. p. 1964.

Sychaeus Virgil, *Aen.* 1,343ff.; 4,457ff.; 6,474ff.; Ovid, *Heroides* 7,97; Sil. Ital. *Punica* 1,81; 8,123; Appian, *Punica* 1; Malalas, *Chron.* 6,68; Eustath. on Dion. Perieg. and schol. p 193-5.

Syleus Apollod. *Bibl.* 2,6,3; Diod. Sic. 4,31; Philo, *Quod omnis probus liber sit* 101; Tzetzes, *Chil.* 2,429ff.; Conon, *Narr.* 17; Euripides, lost satyric drama *Syleus*, Nauck, *TGF*, edn. 2, p. 575.

Syme Athenaeus 7,297b ff.; Eustath. p. 518 and 671; Steph. Byz. s.v.; Diod. Sic. 5,53.

Syrinx Ovid, *Met.* 1,689ff.; Theocr. *Syrinx*; Westermann, *Mythogr. Gr.* p. 347; Serv. on Virgil, *Ecl.* 2,31; 10,26; Achilles Tatius 8,6.

Syrna Steph. Byz. s.v.

Syrus (1) Schol. on Apoll. Rhod. *Arg.* 2,946; Diod. Sic. 4,72. (2) Eustath. on Dion. Perieg. 899

T

Tages Cic. *De Div.* 2,23; Ovid, *Met.* 15,553; Censor. *De Die Nat.* 4,13; Festus p. 359M.

Talassio (or *Thalassio*) Serv. on Virgil, *Aen.* 1,651; Plutarch, *Quaest. Rom.* 31; *Romulus* 15; Livy 1,9,12; Catull. 61,127 (134); Festus p. 351M.; Paul. ex. Fest. p. 350.

Talaus Apollod. *Bibl.* 1,9,10; 1,9,12-13; Paus. 2,12,2; Apoll. Rhod. *Arg.* 1,118ff. and schol.; Tzetzes on Lyc. *Alex.* 175.

Talos (1) Paus. 7,4,8; 8,53,5; Apollod. *Bibl.* 1,9,26; Apoll. Rhod. *Arg.* 4,1636ff. and schol.; Eustath. p. 1893; Diod. Sic. 4,76; schol. on Plato, *Rep.* 1, p. 396; Ovid, *Met.* 8,183ff. (2) Apollod. *Bibl.* 3,15,9; Diod. Sic. 4,76; Paus. 1,21,4; 1,26,4; Ovid, *Met.* 8,236ff.; Hyg. *Fab.* 39; 244; 274; Serv. on Virgil, *Aen.* 6,14; and on *Georg.* 1,143.

Talthybius Hom. *Il.* 1,320; 3,118; 4,192ff.; 7,276; etc.; Ovid, *Her.* 3,9ff.; Apollod. *Epit.* 3,22; Hdt. 7,134ff.; Paus. 3,12,7.

Tanais Hyg. *Fab.* pref. 6 Rose; Pseudo-Plutarch, *De Fluv.* 14,1.

Tantalus (1) Hom. *Od.* 11,582ff.; schol. on *Odd.* 19,518 and 20,66; Apollod. *Bibl.* 3,5,6; *Epit.* 2,1; Pind. *Ol.* 1,55 ff. (87 ff.) and schol. on 60 (97); *Isthm.* 8,10 (21); Euripides, *Or.* 4ff.; Plato, *Crat.* 395d ff.; Paus. 10,31,10; Lucian, *Dial. Mort.* 17; Westermann, *Mythogr. Gr.* p. 386; Athenaeus 7,281b ff.; Lucret. 3,980ff.; Cic. *De Fin.* 1,60; *Tusc.* 4,35; Horace, *Epod.* 17,65ff.; *Sat.* 1,1,68ff.; Ovid, *Met.* 4,458ff.; 6,174; Hyg. *Fab.* 9; 82; 155; Antoninus Liberalis *Met.* 36; Pseudo-Lact. Plac. on Stat. *Theb.* 2,436; Diod. Sic. 4,74. (2) Paus. 2,18,2; 2,22,3; Seneca, *Thyestes* 718; Hyg. *Fab.* 88; 244; 296; Euripides, *IA* 1150. (3) Ovid, *Met.* 6,239; Hyg. *Fab.* 11.

Taphius Apollod. *Bibl.* 2,4,5; Tzetzes on Lyc. *Alex.* 932; schol. on Hesiod, *Scutum* 11.

Taras Paus. 10,10,8; 10,13,10; Stat. *Silvae* 1,1,103; Serv. on Virgil, *Aen.* 3,551; Probus on Virgil, *Georg.* 2,176. Cf. P. Wuilleumier, *Tarente*, p. 35ff.

Taraxippus (1) Paus. 6,20,15; Lyc. *Alex.* 42ff. and Tzetzes *ad loc.* (2) Paus. 6,20,19.

Tarchetius Plutarch, *Romulus* 2.

Tarchon Strabo 5,2,2, p. 219; Steph. Byz. s.v. Ταρχυνία (Tarquinia); Serv. on Virgil, *Aen.* 10,179; 198; Tzetzes on Lyc. *Alex.* 1242ff.; 1249; Virgil, *Aen.* 8,503ff.; 10,147ff.

Tarpeia Plutarch, *Romulus* 17; *Parall.* 15,309c; Livy 1,11,7ff.; Dion. Hal. *Ant. Rom.* 2,38ff.; Serv. on Virgil, *Aen.* 8,348; Ovid, *Met.* 14,777; *Fasti* 1,261; Prop. 4,4; Varro, *De Ling. Lat.* 5,41.

Tartarus Hom. *Il.* 8,13ff.; 478ff.; Hesiod, *Theog.* 119ff.; 722ff.; 820ff.; Apollod. *Bibl.* 1,1,4ff.; 1,6,3; 2,1,2; 3,10,2; Paus. 9,27,2; Hyg. *Astron.* 2,15.

Tatius Plutarch, *Romulus* 20 and 23; Dion. Hal. *Ant. Rom.* 2,36ff.; Livy 1,10; 1,14; Prop. 4,4; Ovid, *Fasti* 1,260ff.

Taurus (1) Palaeph. *Incred.* 15; Tzetzes on Lyc. *Alex.* 1297-9. (2) Plutarch, *Theseus* 16 and 19; John of Antioch, fragment 1,16 Müller, *FHG* IV, p. 539. (3) Palaeph. *Incred.* 2; Pseudo-Heraclitus, *Incred.* 7 (6), in *Mythographi Graeci* (Teubner) III. 2, ed. Festa.

Taygete Schol. on Pind. *Ol.* 3,29 (53); *Nem.* 2,10 (16); Hesiod, fragment 169 Merkelbach-West; Hyg. *Fab.* 154; 192; *Astron.* 2,21; Hellanicus, fragment 56 Müller (*FHG* I, p. 52); Apollod. *Bibl.* 3,10,3; Paus. 3,1,2; 3,18,10; 3,20,2; 9,35,1; Pseudo-Eratosth. *Catast.* 23; Tzetzes on Lyc. *Alex.* 219; Ovid, *Fasti* 4,174; Pseudo-Plutarch, *De Fluv.* 17,3.

Tecmessa Sophocles, *Ajax*; Quint. Smyrn. *Posthom.* 5,21ff.; schol. on Hom. *Il.* 1,138; Horace, *Od.* 2,4,5ff.; Ovid, *Ars Am.* 3,517ff.; Serv. on Virgil, *Aen.* 1,619; Plutarch, *Alcibiades* 1.

Tectamus Diod. Sic. 4,60; 5,80.

Tectaphus Nonnus, *Dion.* 26,101ff.

Tegeates Paus. 8,3,4; 8,45,1; 8,48,6; 8,53,2ff.

Tegyrius Apollod. *Bibl.* 3,15,4.

Telamon Hom. *Il.* 11,465; 591; *Od.* 11,553; schol. on *Il.* 16,14; 13,694; Sophocles, *Ajax* 202; 433ff.; Euripides, *Troades* 799; Apollod. *Bibl.* 1,8,2; 1,9,16; 3,12,6ff.; Hyg. *Fab.* 14, 89; 173; Diod. Sic. 4,41; 4,72; Plutarch, *Theseus* 10; 29; Paus. 1,42,4; 2,29,3ff.; 3,19,13; 8,15,6; Ovid, *Met.* 7,476ff.; 8,309ff.; 11,216ff.; 13,151ff.; Apoll. Rhod. *Arg.* 1,93ff.; schol. on 1289; Athenaeus 2,43d; Parthenius, *Erot. Path.* 26; schol. on Lyc. *Alex.* 467.

Telchines Strabo 14,2,7, p. 654; Eustath. p. 771; Diod. Sic. 5,55-6; Tzetzes on Hesiod, *Theog.* 81ff.; *Chil.* 7,126; Serv. on Virgil, *Aen.* 4,377; Ovid, *Met.* 7,367.

Telchis Paus. 2,5,6; Clem. Alex. *Strom.* 1,102; Apollod. *Bibl.* 2,1,1; Tzetzes on Lyc. *Alex.* 177.

Teleboas Strabo 7,7,2, p. 322; Eustath. p. 1472,38; see PTERELAUS.

Telecleia Schol. on Euripides, *Hec.* 3.

Teledamus (1) Eustath. p. 1796,47. (2) Paus. 2,16,6.

Telegonus Hesiod, *Theog.* 1014; Telegoneia, in Homer Oxf. Class. Text vol. V, pp. 109 and 143f.; Eustath. p. 1796,49; Hyg. *Fab.* 125; 127; Sophocles, fragments of tragedy *Odysseus Acanthoplex* (Jebb-Pearson II, p. 105ff.); Serv. on Virgil, *Aen.* 2,44; Apollod. *Epit.* 7,16; 7,36ff.; Lucian, *Vera Historia* 2,35; Parthenius, *Erot. Path.* 3; Tzetzes on Lyc. *Alex.* 794; Horace, *Epod.* 1,29ff.; *Od.* 3,9,8, with Porphyrio ad loc.

Telemachus Hom. *Od.* 1-4, etc.; Eustath. p. 1796; Tzetzes on Lyc. *Alex.* 798; 805; 808; 811; Apollod. *Epit.* 3,7; 7,32ff.; Plutarch, *De Soll. An.* 36,985b; Serv. on Virgil, *Aen.* 1,273; Ptol. Heph. 7.

Telemus Hom. *Od.* 9,508ff.; Ovid, *Met.* 13,771ff.; Theocr. 6,23; Hyg. *Fab.* 125.

Telephassa Apollod. *Bibl.* 3,1,1ff.

Telephus Proclus' summary of *Cypria* (Homer Oxf. Class. Text V, p. 104); Apollod. *Bibl.* 2,7,4ff.; 2,7,8ff.; 3,9,1; *Epit.* 3,17; 5,12; Tzetzes, *Antehom.* 269ff.; Hyg. *Fab.* 99-101; 162; 244; Aristotle, *Poetics* 13, p. 1453a 21; Strabo 12,8,2, p. 571; 13,1,69, p. 615; schol. on Hom. *Il.* 1,59; Paus. 1,4,6; 3,26,10;

8,4,9; 8,47,3; 8,48,7; 10,28,8; Aeschylus, lost tragedy *Mysoi*, Nauck, *TGF*, edn. 2, p. 47; Sophocles, *Aleadai* (Jebb-Pearson I, p. 46ff.); *Mysoi* (ibid. II, p. 70ff.); Euripides, *Telephus*, fragments in Nauck, *TGF*, edn. 2, p. 579ff.; Diod. Sic. 4,33; Philost. *Heroicus* p. 156K.; Dion. Hal. *Ant. Rom.* 1,28; Plutarch, *Romulus* 13; schol. on Aristophanes, *Clouds* 919; Lyc. *Alex.* 1245ff.; Tzetzes ad loc. and on 206.

Tellus Lucret. *De Rerum Nat.* 5,259; Virgil, *Aen.* 7,136, and Serv. on 1,171; Horace, *Carmen Saeculare* 29; Cic. *De Nat. Deor.* 3,52; Aug. *Civ. Dei* 7,32ff.

Telphousa Homeric Hymn to Apollo 244ff.; 377ff.

Temenus (1) Paus. 8,22,2. (2) Paus. 8,24,10. (3) Paus. 2,6,7; 2,11,2; 2,12,6; etc.; 3,1,5; 4,3,3ff.; Apollod. *Bibl.* 2,8,2ff.; Hyg. *Fab.* 124; 219; Tzetzes on Lyc. *Alex.* 804; Plutarch, *Quaest. Gr.* 48,302d; Euripides, lost tragedies *Temenus* and *Temenidae* (Nauck, *TGF*, edn. 2, p. 589ff.).

Temon Plutarch, *Quaest. Gr.* 13,294a ff.

Tenerus Strabo 9,2,34, p. 413; Paus. 9,10,6; 9,26,1; Tzetzes on Lyc. *Alex.* 1211.

Tenes Steph. Byz. s.v. Τένεδος (Tenedos); Suda ibid.; Aristotle, fragment in Müller, *FHG* II, p. 157, fr. 170; Heraclides ?Lembus, Müller, *FHG* II, p. 213,7; Plutarch, *Quaest. Gr.* 28,297d ff.; Paus. 9,14,1ff.; Diod. Sic. 5,83; Conon, *Narr.* 28; Apollod. *Epit.* 3,23ff.; Tzetzes on Lyc. *Alex.* 232ff.; schol. on Hom. *Il.* 1,38; Strabo 13,1,46, p. 604. See also MOLPUS.

Terambus Antoninus Liberalis *Met.* 22.

Tereus Apollod. *Bibl.* 3,14,8; Aeschylus, *Suppl.* 61ff.; Livius Andronicus, lost tragedy *Tereus*, in Warmington, *Remains of Old Latin* II, p. 10ff.; Hyg. *Fab.* 45; 246; Ovid, *Met.* 6,427; Lact. Plac. *Narr. Fab. Ov.* 6. See PHILOMELA.

Termerus Schol. on Euripides, *Rhes.* 509; Plutarch, *Theseus* 2.

Terminus Varro, *De Ling. Lat.* 5,21; 5,74; Dion. Hal. *Ant. Rom.* 2,74; 3,69; Livy 1,55,2; 5,54,7; Plutarch, *Quaest. Rom.* 15,267c; Festus p. 162; *CIL* I, edn. 2, p. 310.

Terpsichore Hesiod, *Theog.* 78; Tzetzes on Lyc. *Alex.* 653; Suda s.v. Λίνος (Linus); argument to Euripides, *Rhesus*.

Tethys Hom. *Il.* 14,201ff.; Hesiod, *Theog.* 136; 237ff.; fragment 343 Merkelbach-West; Ovid, *Fasti* 2,191; *Met.* 2,509; 527ff.; 9,950ff.; Hyg. *Fab.* 177; *Astron.* 2,1; Apollod. *Bibl.* 1,1,3; 2,1,1; Diod. Sic. 4,69; 4,72.

Teucer (1) Apollod. *Bibl.* 3,12,1ff.; Diod. Sic. 4,75; Tzetzes on Lyc. *Alex.* 29; 1302ff.; 1465; Serv. on Virgil, *Aen.* 3,108; Aelian, *Nat. An.* 12,5; Strabo 13,1,48, p. 604; Dion. Hal. *Ant. Rom.* 1,61ff. (2) Hom. *Il.* 6,31; 8,266ff.; 12,370ff.; etc.; Paus. 1,23,8; 1,28,11; Aeschylus, *Salaminiai* and Sophocles, *Teucer* (lost tragedies: Nauck, *TGF*, edn. 2, p. 72 and Jebb-Pearson II, p. 214ff.); Sophocles, *Ajax* 342ff. and schol.; 1008; schol. on 1019; Quint. Smyrn. *Posthom.* 5,500ff.; 12,322; Tzetzes on Lyc. *Alex.* 447; 452; *Posthom.* 645; Virgil, *Aen.* 1,619ff. and Serv. ad loc.; Pind. *Nem.* 4,46 (74) and schol.; schol. on Euripides, *Hel.* 147ff.; Ovid, *Met.* 14,696ff.; Horace, *Od.* 1,7,21ff.; Strabo 14,5,10, p. 672; 14,6,3, p. 682; Athenaeus 6, p. 256b; Sil. Ital. *Pun.* 3,368; 15,192; Philostr. *Vit. Apoll.* 5,1.

Teutamus Diod. Sic. 2,22; cf. Euseb. *Chron.* 1,66.

Teutarus Tzetzes on Lyc. *Alex.* 50; 56; 458; schol. on Theocr. 13,9.

Teuthras (1) Apollod. *Bibl.* 2,7,4; 3,9,1; Paus. 8,4,9; 10,28,8; Steph. Byz. s.v. Τευθρανία (Teuthrania); Diod. Sic. 4,33; Strabo 12,8,2, p. 571ff.; Hyg. *Fab.* 99–100; Pseudo-Plutarch, *De Fluv.* 21,4. (2) Hom. *Il.* 5,705; Tzetzes, *Homerica* 100.

Thalia (1) Hesiod, *Theog.* 77; Diod. Sic. 4,7; Apollod. *Bibl.* 1,3,1 and 4; Plutarch, *Quaest. Conv.* 9,14,7, 746c; Tzetzes on Lyc. *Alex.* 78; Serv. on Virgil, *Ecl.* 8,68; argument to Theocr. 8 and schol. on 92. (2) Hesiod, *Theog.* 909; Paus. 9,35,5; Apollod. *Bibl.* 1,3,1; Tzetzes, *Chil.* 10,516; Plutarch, *Quaest.*

Conv. 9,14,4, 745a. (3) Hom. *Il.* 18,39; Hyg. *Fab.* pref. 8 Rose; Virgil, *Aen.* 5,826; *Georg.* 4,338.

Thalpius Paus. 5,1,11; 5,3,3ff.; Hom. *Il.* 2,618ff.; Eustath. p. 303,4; Quint. Smyrn. *Posthom.* 12,323; Apollod. *Bibl.* 3,10,8.

Thamyris Hom. *Il.* 2,594ff.; Eustath. p. 297,41ff.; Suda s.v.; Tzetzes, *Chil.* 7,92ff.; Plutarch, *De Mus.* 3,1152b; Plato, *Ion* 533b ff.; Pliny, *NH* 7,207; Euseb. *Praep. Ev.* 10,6, p. 476c; Paus. 4,33,3; 10,7,2; schol. on Hesiod, *W. & D.* (Gaisford, *Poet. Lat. Min.* I, p. 25); Apollod. *Bibl.* 4,33,3; schol. on Euripides, *Rhes.* 346; Sophocles, lost tragedy (Jebb-Pearson I, p. 176ff.); Diod. Sic. 3,67; Hyg. *Astron.* 2,6.

Thanatos Hom. *Il.* 11,241; 14,231; Paus. 3,18,1; Hesiod, *Theog.* 211ff.; Serv. on Virgil, *Aen.* 4,694, cf. Phrynichus, fragment 3, Nauck, *TGF*, edn. 2, p. 720; Euripides, *Alcestis*. See also MORS; SISYPHUS.

Thasos Hdt. 6,47; Steph. Byz. s.v.; Apollod. *Bibl.* 3,1,14; Paus. 5,25,12; schol. on Euripides, *Phoen.* 5; 25.

Thaumas Hesiod, *Theog.* 237; 267; Apollod. *Bibl.* 1,2,6; Hyg. *Fab.* pref. 14; Serv. on Virgil, *Aen.* 3,212; 249; Cic. *De Nat. Deor.* 3,51.

Theanira Tzetzes on Lyc. *Alex.* 467, quoting Istrus, fragment 22 Müller, *FHG* I, p. 421; ibid. 469.

Theano (1) Hom. *Il.* 5,69ff.; 6,297ff.; 11,221ff.; schol. on 266; schol. on Euripides, *Andr.* 224; *Hec.* 3; Tzetzes on Lyc. *Alex.* 340; *Posthom.* 516; Apollod. *Epit.* 3,34; Paus. 10,27,3; Serv. on Virgil, *Aen.* 1,242; 480. (2) Hyg. *Fab.* 186.

Thebe (1) and (2) Steph. Byz. s.v.; Tzetzes on Lyc. *Alex.* 1206; cf. Müller, *FHG* IV, p. 657; Pindar, *Isthm.* 8,18 (37)ff.; Paus. 2,5,2; Diod. Sic. 4,72. (3) Schol. on Hom. *Il.* 6,396, quoting Dicaearchus, fragment 11 Müller, *FHG* II, p. 238; Diod. Sic. 5,49,3. (4) Schol. on Hom. *Il.* 9,383; Tzetzes on Lyc. *Alex.* 1206.

Theia Hesiod, *Theog.* 135; 371ff.; Apollod. *Bibl.* 1,1,3; 1,2,2; Pind. *Isthm.* 5,1 and schol. on 1 (2).

Theias Antoninus Liberalis *Met.* 34.

Theiodamas Schol. on Apoll. Rhod. *Arg.* 1,131; Apollod. *Bibl.* 2,7,7; Hyg. *Fab.* 14; argument to Sophocles, *Trach.*; Westermann, *Mythogr. Gr.* p. 370ff.; Conon, *Narr.* 11.

Thelxion (1) Paus. 2,5,7. (2) Apollod. *Bibl.* 2,1; Tzetzes on Lyc. *Alex.* 177.

Themis Hesiod, *Theog.* 135; 901ff.; Diod. Sic. 5,66; Apollod. *Bibl.* 1,1,3; Hyg. *Fab.* pref. 3 and 25 Rose; Pseudo-Eratosth. *Catast.* 9; schol. on Apoll. Rhod. *Arg.* 4,1396; schol. on Euripides, *Hippol.* 742; Aeschylus, *PV* 18; 209; 874; Plutarch, *Quaest. Rom.* 56,278b; Dion. Hal. *Ant. Rom.* 1,31; schol. on Hom. *Il.* 15,299.

Themisto Schol. on Pind. *Pyth.* 9,17 (31); Apollod. *Bibl.* 1,9,2; Tzetzes on Lyc. *Alex.* 22.

Theoclymenus (1) Hom. *Od.* 15,223ff.; 508ff.; 17,72ff.; 151ff.; 20,350ff.; Eustath. p. 1780,10ff. (2) Euripides, *Helen*.

Theonoe (1) Euripides, *Helen*; Conon, *Narr.* 8. (2) Hyg. *Fab.* 190.

Theophane Hyg. *Fab.* 3; 188; cf. Ovid, *Met.* 6,117.

Theras Hdt. 4,147ff.; Paus. 3,1,7ff.; 3,15,6; 4,3,4; 7,2,2; Apoll. Rhod. *Arg.* 4,1755ff. and schol. on 1764; Pind. *Pyth.* 4,257ff.; 5,72ff.; Callim. *Hymn* 2,73.

Thero Paus. 9,40,5.

Thersandrus (1) Paus. 10,30,5; schol. on Hom. *Od.* 11,326. (2) Pind. *Ol.* 2,43 (76) and schol.; Paus. 2,20,5; 3,15,6; 9,5,14ff.; 9,8,7; Apollod. *Bibl.* 3,7,2; Hyg. *Fab.* 69; Serv. on Virgil, *Aen.* 2,261; schol. on Apoll. Rhod. *Arg.* 4,1764; schol. on Euripides, *Phoen.* 135; Eustath. p. 489,37; Stat. *Theb.* 3,683; Lact. Plac. on Stat. *Theb.* 3,697; 12,348; Apollod. *Epit.* 3,17; Dict. Cret. 1,14; Virgil, *Aen.* 2,261.

Thersites Hom. *Il.* 2,211ff.; Quint. Smyrn. *Posthom.* 1,770ff.; Apollod. *Bibl.* 1,7,10; *Epit.* 5,1; Proclus' summary of *Aethiopis*, Homer Oxf. Class. Text V, p. 105; Diod. Sic. 2,46; Ovid, *Ex Ponto* 3,9,9ff.; *Met.* 13,232ff.; Tzetzes on Lyc. *Alex.* 999f.; Antoninus Liberalis *Met.* 37; schol. on Sophocles, *Philoct.* 439ff. and schol. on 445; Eustath. p. 208,2; Chaeremon, lost tragedy or satyric drama *Achilles Thersitoctonus*, Nauck, *TGF*, edn. 2, p. 782ff.

Theseus
Childhood: Plutarch, *Theseus* 3ff.; Apollod. *Bibl.* 3,16,1ff.; Euripides, *Suppl.* 1ff.; Paus. 1,27,7; 2,33,1; schol. on Stat. *Theb.* 5,431; Hyg. *Fab.* 37; Lyc. *Alex.* 494ff.
Return: Plutarch, *Theseus* 6ff.; Apollod. *Bibl.* 2,6,3; 3,16,1ff.; *Epit.* 1,1ff.; Bacchyl. 18,16ff.; Diod. Sic. 4,59; Paus. 1,44,8; 2,1,3ff.; Ovid, *Met.* 7,404ff.; *Ibis* 407ff.; Hyg. *Fab.* 38; schol. on Hom. *Il.* 11,741; Sophocles, *Aegeus* (lost tragedy, Jebb-Pearson I, p. 15ff.); Euripides, *Aegeus* (Nauck, *TGF*, edn. 2, p. 363ff.); Serv. on Virgil, *Aen.* 6,20; 8,294; Strabo 9,1,22, p. 399; Callim. *Hecale*; Euripides, *Hippolytus*.
Cretan Cycle: Hom. *Od.* 11,322ff.; 631; cf. Paus. 1,20,3; 10,28,2ff.; Serv. on Virgil, *Georg.* 1,222; on *Aen.* 3,74; 6,21; Plutarch, *Theseus* 15ff.; schol. on Hom. *Od.* 11,322; schol. on *Il.* 18,590; Hyg. *Fab.* 41–3; *Astron.* 2,5; Lact. Plac. on Stat. *Achill.* 192; Diod. Sic. 4,61; 6,4; Paus. 1,22,5; Catull. 64,215ff.; Pseudo-Eratosth. *Catast.* 5; Ovid, *Met.* 8,174ff.; *Heroides* 10.
Political Activity: Plutarch, *Theseus* 24; Thuc. 2,15; Cic. *De Leg.* 2,5; Isocr. 10,35.
War against the Amazons: Plutarch, *Theseus* 26ff.; Apollod. *Epit.* 1,16ff.; Diod. Sic. 4,28; Paus. 1,2,1; 1,15,2; 1,41,7; 2,32,9; 5,11,4 and 7; Seneca, *Phaedra* 927ff.; Hyg. *Fab.* 30; 241; Tzetzes on Lyc. *Alex.* 1329.
Friendship with Pirithous: Plutarch, *Theseus* 30ff.; Hellanicus, Fragment 74 Müller (*FHG* I, p. 55); Apollod. *Epit.* 1,21ff., Aelian, *VH* 4,5; Paus. 10,29,9; schol. on Aristophanes, *Knights* 1368; Aul. Gell. *Noct. Att.* 10,16,13. See also PIRITHOUS.
Death: Plutarch, *Theseus* 35ff.; Paus. 1,17,6; Diod. Sic. 4,62,4; Apollod. *Epit.* 1,24.
Thespius Eustath. p. 266,6; Apollod. *Bibl.* 2,4,9ff.; 2,7,6ff.; Paus. 1,29,5; 7,2,2; 9,23,1; 9,27,6; 10,17,5–6; Diod. Sic. 1,29ff.; Steph. Byz. s.v. Θέσπεια (Thespeia); schol. on Sophocles, *Trach.* 460; Philoponus, commentary on Aristotle, ed Vitelli, XVII, p. 715,15ff.
Thesprotus Apollod. *Bibl.* 3,8,1; Steph. Byz. s.v. Ἀμβρακία (Ambracia); Tzetzes on Luc. *Alex.* 481; Hyg. *Fab.* 88.
Thessalus (1) Pliny, *NH* 4,28; Velleius Paterculus 1,3,2; cf. Hdt. 7,176. (2) Hom. *Il.* 2,677; cf. Hyg. *Fab.* 97; Apollod. *Epit.* 5,15; Diod. Sic. 5,54; Strabo 9,5,23, p. 443–4. (3) Diod. Sic. 4,34ff.
Thestius Ovid, *Met.* 4,487; Strabo 10,2,24, p. 461; 10,3,6, p. 466; Paus. 3,13,8; Apollod. *Bibl.* 1,7,7. See also ALTHAEA; LEDA; HYPERMESTRA.
Thestor Hom. *Il.* 1,69; Pherecydes, fragment 70 Müller (*FHG* I, p. 88); Tzetzes on Lyc. *Alex.* 427; 980; 1047; Ovid, *Met.* 12,19; Hyg. *Fab.* 97; 128; 190.
Thetis Hom. *Il.* 1,348ff.; 493ff.; 9,140ff.; 18,22ff.; etc.; Hesiod, *Theog.* 240; 1003; Apollod. *Bibl.* 1,2,7; 1,3,5; 1,9,25; 3,5,1; 3,13,4ff.; *Epit.* 3,29; 6,5ff.; Tzetzes, *Prol. All. Il.* 426; 443; 451; *Antehom.* 180; Hyg. *Fab.* 54; 92; 96; 97; 106; 270; *Astron.* 2,18; Ovid, *Met.* 11,423ff.; Apoll. Rhod. *Arg.* 4,790ff.; schol. on ibid. 1,582; Pind. *Nem.* 4,65ff. (107ff.) and schol.; schol. on 3,35 (60); Catull. 64; Euripides, *IA* 701ff. See also PELEUS.
Thoas (1) Apoll. Rhod. *Arg.* 1,634ff.; 4,424ff.; Apollod. *Bibl.* 3,6,4; *Epit.* 1,9; Lact. Plac. on Stat. *Theb.* 4,768; Diod. Sic. 5,79; Ovid, *Her.* 6; Hyg. *Fab.* 15; 74; 120–1; 254; 261; Val.

Flacc. *Arg.* 2,242ff.; Euripides, *Hypsipyle* (fragments ed. G. Bond, 1963). (2) Euripides, *Hypsipyle* (see above). (3) Hyg. *Fab.* 120–1; Sophocles, lost tragedy *Chryses* (Jebb-Pearson II, p. 327ff.). See IPHIGENIA. (4) Hom. *Il.* 2,638ff.; 4,527ff.; 15,281ff.; Tzetzes on Lyc. *Alex.* 780; Hesychius s.v.; Apollod. *Bibl.* 1,8,6; Hyg. *Fab.* 81; 97; 114; Strabo 6,1,5, p. 255; Virgil, *Aen.* 2,262; Apollod. *Epit.* 7,40; Plutarch, *Quaest. Gr.* 14,294c. (5) Paus. 2,4,3; schol. on Euripides, *Or.* 1094. (6) Apollod. *Bibl.* 3,10,6.
Thon Hom. *Od.* 4,228, and Eustath. p. 1493,54.
Thoosa Hom. *Od.* 1,71; Apollod. *Epit.* 7,4.
Thrace Schol. on Aeschylus, *Persae* 185; Steph. Byz. s.v.; Tzetzes on Lyc. *Alex.* 533; Eustath. on Dion. Perieg. 322.
Thrasymedes Hom. *Il.* 9,80ff.; 10,196ff.; 255ff.; 16,317ff.; *Od.* 3,39; 3,442ff.; Quint. Smyrn. *Posthom.* 2,342; 12,319; Apollod. *Bibl.* 1,9,9; Hyg. *Fab.* 97; Paus. 4,31,11; 4,36,2.
Thriai Hesychius s.v.; Steph. Byz. s.v.; Homeric Hymn to Hermes 554ff.; Philochorus, Fragment 196 Müller (*FHG* I, p. 416; cf. IV, p. 637); Callim. *Hymn* 2,45.
Thyestes Hom. *Il.* 2,106ff. and schol.; schol. on Euripides, *Or.* 4; 12; Apollod. *Bibl.* 2,4,6; *Epit.* 2,10; Hyg. *Fab.* 86–8; Seneca, *Thyestes*; Sophocles, lost tragedy *Thyestes* (Jebb-Pearson I, p. 185ff.). See also ATREUS; AEROPE; AEGISTHUS; AGAMEMNON.
Thyia Paus. 10,6,4; cf. 10,29,5; Steph. Byz. s.v. Μακεδονία (Macedonia); Hesiod, fragment 7 Merkelbach-West.
Thymoetes Hom. *Il.* 3,146; Diod. Sic. 3,67; Virgil, *Aen.* 2,32 and Serv. ad loc.
Thyone Oppian, *Cynegetica* 1,27; cf. Horace, *Od.* 1,17,23; Ovid, *Met.* 4,13; Diod. Sic. 3,62; 4,25; Cic. *De Nat. Deor.* 3,58; Apollod. *Bibl.* 3,5,3.
Tiberinus (1) Virgil, *Aen.* 8,31ff. (2) Serv. on Virgil, *Aen.* 8,330; Varro, *De Ling. Lat.* 5,30; Dion. Hal. *Ant. Rom.* 1,71; Diod. Sic. 7,5; Ovid, *Fasti* 2,389ff.; *Met.* 14,614ff.
Tiburnus Virgil, *Aen.* 7,670 and Serv. ad loc.; 11,519; Solinus 2,8; Pliny, *NH* 16,237.
Timalcus Paus. 1,41,3ff.
Timandra Apollod. *Bibl.* 3,10,6; Paus. 8,5,1; schol. on Pind. *Ol.* 10,66 (80); Hesiod, fragment 23,31; 76 Merkelbach-West; Serv. on Virgil, *Aen.* 8,130; Eustath. p. 305,17.
Tinge Plutarch, *Sertorius* 9.
Tiphys Apoll. Rhod. *Arg.* 1,105 and schol.; 2,815ff.; etc.; Hyg. *Fab.* 14; 18; Paus. 9,32,4; Apollod. *Bibl.* 1,9,16; Seneca, *Medea* 2ff.; 617ff.
Tiresias Hom. *Od.* 10,487ff.; 11,84ff.; schol. on 10,494; 23,323; Eustath. p. 1665,41ff.; Apollod. *Bibl.* 2,4,8; 3,4,1; 3,6,7ff.; 3,7,3ff.; Hyg. *Fab.* 67–8; 75; 125; 128; Callim. *Hymn* 5,57ff.; Sophocles, *OT*; Euripides, *Phoen.* 834ff.; 1589ff.; Paus. 9,33,1ff.; Ovid, *Met.* 3,320ff.; Tzetzes on Lyc. *Alex.* 683.
Tisamenus (1) Sophocles, lost tragedy *Hermione* (Jebb-Pearson I, p. 141ff.); Eustath. p. 1479,10ff.; schol. on Euripides, *Or.* 1654; Apollod. *Bibl.* 2,8,2–3; *Epit.* 6,28; Tzetzes on Lyc. *Alex.* 1374; Hyg. *Fab.* 124; Paus. 2,18,6; 7,1,7; 7,6,2; Velleius Paterculus 1,1,4. (2) Paus. 9,5,15.
Tisiphone (1) See ERINYES; CITHAERON. (2) Apollod. *Bibl.* 3,7,7; cf. Euripides, lost tragedy *Alcmeon* (Nauck, *TGF*, edn. 2, p. 379ff.).
Titanides See TITANS.
Titans Hesiod, *Theog.* 132ff.; 531ff.; Apollod. *Bibl.* 1,1,2ff.; Hyg. *Fab.* pref. 3 Rose; 150; 155; Hom. *Il.* 15,224ff.; schol. on 229; Aeschylus, *PV* 201ff.
Tithonus Hom. *Il.* 11,1ff. and schol.; 22,237ff.; *Od.* 5,1 and schol.; Hesiod, *Theog.* 984; Apollod. *Bibl.* 3,12,3; Hyg. *Fab.* 270; Diod. Sic. 3,67; 4,75; Serv. on Virgil, *Georg.* 1,447; 3,48; 3,328; Aelian, *Nat. An.* 5,1; Homeric Hymn to Aphrodite 218ff.; Tzetzes on Lyc. *Alex.* 18.

Tityus Hom. *Od.* 11,576ff.; Pind. *Pyth.* 4,90ff. (160ff.) and schol.; Apollod. *Bibl.* 1,4,1; schol. on Hom. *Od.* 7,324; Eustath. p. 1581; Apoll. Rhod. *Arg.* 1,761 and schol.; Lucret. 3,984ff.; Virgil, *Aen.* 6,595ff.; Appendix Vergiliana, *Aetna* 80; Hyg. *Fab.* 55; Paus. 10,4,5; 10,29,3; Strabo 9,3,14, p. 423; Ovid, *Met.* 4,457ff.

Tlepolemus Hom. *Il.* 2,653ff. and schol.; 5,627ff.; Pind. *Ol.* 7,27 (50); Apollod. *Bibl.* 2,7,6 and 8; *Epit.* 3,13; 6,15; Hyg. *Fab.* 81; 97; 162; Diod. Sic. 4,36; 4,57ff.; Strabo 14,2,6, p. 653; Paus. 3,19,10; Tzetzes on Lyc. *Alex.* 911.

Tmolus (1) Apollod. *Bibl.* 2,6,3. (2) Pseudo-Plutarch, *De Fluv.* 7,5.

Toxeus (1) Hesiod, fragment 26 Merkelbach-West; Diod. Sic. 4,37. (2) Apollod. *Bibl.* 1,8,1.

Trambelus Eustath. p. 343ff.; Lyc. *Alex.* 457ff. and schol.; Parthenius, *Erot. Path.* 26.

Tricca Eustath. p. 330,26; Steph. Byz. s.v.

Triopas Apollod. *Bibl.* 1,7,4; Diod. Sic. 5,61; Callim. *Hymn* 6,96ff.; Paus. 2,16,1; 2,22,1; 4,1,1; 4,3,9; 4,26,8; etc.; schol. on Euripides, *Or.* 932.

Triptolemus Homeric Hymn to Demeter 153; 474; Paus. 1,14,2ff.; 1,38,6; 1,41,2; 7,18,3; Hyg. *Fab.* 147; *Astron..* 2,14; Ovid, *Fasti* 4,549ff.; *Tristia* 3,8,1ff.; Serv. on Virgil, *Georg.* 1,19; 1,163; Lact. Plac. on Stat. *Theb.* 2,382; Apollod. *Bibl.* 1,4,5; Sophocles, lost tragedy *Triptolemus* (Jebb-Pearson II, p. 239ff.); Plato, *Apol.* 41a.

Triton Hesiod, *Theog.* 930ff.; Euripides, *Cyclops* 263ff.; schol. on Euripides, *Or.* 364; Hdt. 4,179; 188; Pind. *Pyth.* 4,19ff.; schol. ad loc.; Apoll. Rhod. *Arg.* 4,1588ff. and schol. on 1,109, etc.; Paus. 7,22,8ff.; 9,20,4ff.; 9,33,7; Apollod. *Bibl.* 1,4,6; 3,12,3; Hyg. *Fab.* pref. 18 Rose; Ovid, *Her.* 7,49; Tzetzes on Lyc. *Alex.* 34; 519; 754; 886; Serv. on Virgil, *Aen.* 1,144; Diod. Sic. 4,56.

Trochilus Paus. 1,14,2; schol. on Aratus, *Phaen.* 161; Hyg. *Astron.* 2,13; Tertullian, *De Spect.* 9.

Troezen (1) Paus. 2,30,8ff.; Steph. Byz. s.v. (2) Parthenius, *Erot. Path.* 31.

Troilus Hom. *Il.* 24,257; Eustath. p. 1348; Apollod. *Bibl.* 3,12,5; *Epit.* 3,32; Lyc. *Alex.* 307 and schol.; schol. on Hom. *Il.* 6,49; Proclus' summary of *Cypria*, Homer Oxf. Class. Text V, p. 105; Virgil, *Aen.* 1,474ff. and Serv. ad loc.; Dio Chrys. *Or.* 11,77; Sophocles, lost tragedy *Troilus* (Jebb-Pearson II, p. 253ff.); Dict. Cret. 4,9.

Trophonius Homeric Hymn to Apollo 296; schol. on Aristophanes, *Clouds* 508; Philostr. *Vit. Apoll.* 8,19; Paus. 8,10,2; 9,11,1; 9,37,4ff.; 9,39,2ff.; 10,5,13; Strabo 9,3,9, p. 421; Cic. *Tusc.* 1,114.

Tros Hom. *Il.* 20,230; Apollod. *Bibl.* 3,12,2; Conon, *Narr.* 12; Diod. Sic. 4,75; Paus. 5,24,5; Tzetzes on Lyc. *Alex.* 1232.

Turnus Dion. Hal. *Ant. Rom.* 1,64; Livy 1,2,1ff.; Virgil, *Aen.* 7–12; Serv. on *Aen.* 1,267; 4,620; 9,742. See AENEAS; MEZENTIUS.

Tyche Paus. 4,30,4. Cf. F. Allegre, *Etude sur la déesse grecque Tyché*, 1889.

Tychius Hom. *Il.* 7,220ff.; Hesych. s.v.; cf. Ovid, *Fasti* 3,824; Pliny, *NH* 7,196.

Tydeus Hom. *Il.* 4,372ff.; 5,126; 800ff.; 6,222ff.; Apollod. *Bibl.* 1,8,4ff.; 3,6,1ff.; 3,10,8; Hyg. *Fab.* 69–71; 97; 175; 257; Paus. 3,18,12; 9,18,1ff.; 10,10,3; Eustath. p. 971; schol. on Hom. *Il.* 5,126; 14,114 and 120; Diod. Sic. 4,65; Stat. *Theb.* 1,401ff.; 669ff.; 2,370ff.; 8,717ff.; etc.; Lact. Plac. *ad loc.*; argument to Sophocles, *Antigone*; Sophocles, *OC* 1315; fragment 799 (Jebb-Pearson III, p. 38); Euripides, *Phoen.* 134; 419; schol. on 135; Tzetzes on Lyc. *Alex.* 1066; schol. on Pind. *Nem.* 10,7 (12), etc.

Tyndareus Hesiod, fragments 23; 196; 199; 204 Merkelbach-West; Eustath. p. 293,11; schol. on Hom. *Il.* 5,81; Tzetzes on Lyc. *Alex.* 1123; *Chil.* 1,456ff.; Hyg. *Fab.* 77–80; 92; 117; 119; Apollod. *Bibl.* 1,9,5; 2,7,3; 3,10,3ff.; *Epit.* 2,15ff.; Paus. 1,17,5; 1,33,7ff.; 2,1,9; 2,18,2ff.; 2,34,10; etc.; Diod. Sic. 4,33; schol. on Euripides, *Or.* 457; Strabo 10,2,24, p. 461; Euripides, *Helen* and *Orestes*.

Typhon Hesiod, *Theog.* 820ff.; Pind. *Pyth.* 1,15ff.; Aeschylus, *PV* 351ff.; Antoninus Liberalis, *Met.* 28; Ovid, *Met.* 5,321ff.; Hyg. *Fab.* 152; Apollod. *Bibl.* 1,6,3; schol. on Hom. *Il.* 2,783; Homeric Hymn to Apollo 306ff.; 352ff.; Nonnus, *Dion.* 1,481ff.

Tyro Hom. *Od.* 2,120; 11,235ff.; Apollod. *Bibl.* 1,9,7ff.; Diod. Sic. 4,68; Sophocles, two lost tragedies *Tyro* (Jebb-Pearson II, p. 270ff.); Hyg. *Fab.* 60; 239; 254; Strabo 8,3,32, p. 356; Prop. 1,13,21.

Tyros Pollux 1,45ff.

Tyrrhenus Dion. Hal. *Ant. Rom.* 1,27ff.; Hdt. 1,94; Hyg. *Fab.* 274; Tzetzes on Lyc. *Alex.* 1239; 1249; Serv. on Virgil, *Aen.* 10,179 and 198; Paus. 2,21,3.

Tyrrhus Virgil, *Aen.* 7,485; 508ff.; Serv. on *Aen.* 7,484; cf. Dion. Hal. *Ant. Rom.* 1,70 (name given as Tyrrhenus).

U

Ucalegon (1) Hom. *Il.* 3,148; Virgil, *Aen.* 2,311ff. and Serv. ad loc. (2) Schol. on Euripides, *Phoen.* 26.

Ulysses See ODYSSEUS.

Uranus Hesiod, *Theog.* 126ff.; 463ff.; 886ff.; 924ff.; fragment 389 Merkelbach-West; cf. Cyclic *Titanomachia*, fragment 1, Homer Oxf. Class. Text V, p. 110; Cic. *De Nat. Deor.* 3,44; Fragm. Orph. 89,1 Abel; Diod. Sic. 3,57ff.; Plato, *Timaeus* 40e; Macrob. *Sat.* 1,8,12; Apollod. *Bibl.* 1,1,1ff.

V

Vacuna Horace, *Epist.* 1,10,49 and schol.

Valeria Plutarch, *Parall.* 35,314d.

Veiovis Cicero, *De Nat. Deor.* 3,62; Aul. Gell. *Noct. Att.* 5,12,8ff.; Ovid, *Fasti* 3,437ff.; Varro, *De Ling. Lat.* 5,74.

Venus Strabo 5,3,5, p. 232; Solinus 2,14; Macrob. *Sat.* 1,12,12ff.; Varro, *De Ling. Lat.* 6,20; 6,33; Festus, p. 265M.; Pliny, *NH* 19,50; Lucret. 1,1ff.; cf. R. Schilling, *La Religion romaine de Vénus*, 1954.

Vertumnus Varro, *De Ling. Lat.* 5,46; Prop. 4,2; Ovid, *Met.* 14,643ff.; *Fasti* 6,410.

Vesta Serv. on Virgil, *Aen.* 8,190; 9,257; Aug. *Civ. Dei* 7,16; Cic. *De Nat. Deor.* 2,67; Cato, *De Agricultura* 143,2; Ovid, *Fasti* 6,319ff.; Lact. *Inst. Div.* 1,21,25ff.; Dion. Hal. *Ant. Rom.* 2,65; Plutarch, *Romulus* 22.

Virbius Ovid, *Met.* 15,545ff.; Serv. on Virgil, *Aen.* 5,95; Virgil, *Aen.* 7,765ff.; Ovid, *Fasti* 3,266ff.

Volturnus Varro, *De Ling. Lat.* 6,21; 7,45; Paul. ex. Fest. p. 379M.; Arnobius, *Adv. Nat.* 3,29.

Vulcan Varro, *De Ling. Lat.* 5,74; 83ff.; 6,20; Macrob. *Sat.* 1,12,18; Pliny, *NH* 16,236; 36,204; Plutarch, *Romulus* 24,5; Virgil, *Aen.* 7,679; 8,190ff.; Paul. ex. Fest. p. 38M.; Ovid, *Fasti* 6,637; H. J. Rose, *Journal of Roman Studies* 1933, p. 46ff.

Z

Zacynthus Steph. Byz. s.v.; Paus. 8,24,1ff.; Dion. Hal. *Ant. Rom.* 1,50.

Zagreus Aeschylus, fragment 5 (from *Aegyptioi*, Nauck, *TGF*, edn. 2, p. 4) and 228 (from *Sisyphus*, Nauck, *TGF*, edn. 2, p. 74); schol. on Pind. *Isthm.* 7,3; Tzetzes on Lyc. *Alex.* 355; cf. 207; Proclus on Plato, *Timaeus* 200d; Macrob. commentary on *Somnium Scipionis*, 1,12; Nonnus, *Dion.* 5,565ff.; 6,155ff.; Hesych. and Suda s.v.; Diod. Sic. 3,62; 64; Callim. fragment 43,117 Pfeiffer (cf. Etym. Magn. s.v.); Ovid, *Met.* 6,114; Clem. Alex. *Protrept.* 2,18; Hyg. *Fab.* 155; 167.

Zeus (only a selection of the more important texts is given here.) Hom. *Il.* 1,396ff.; 8,13ff.; 24,527ff.; schol. on 15,229; 24,615; Hesiod, *Theogony*, esp. 468ff.; Callim. *Hymn* 1; Paus. 8,38,2; 4,33,1; Apollod. *Bibl.* 1,1,6; 1,2,1ff.; Diod. Sic. 5,70ff.; Ovid, *Fasti* 4,207ff.; *Met.* 6,103ff.; Virgil, *Georg.* 4,153; Serv. on Virgil, *Aen.* 3,104; Lucret. 2,629; Hyg. *Fab.* pref. 19ff.; 23ff., 31ff. Rose; 2; 7–8; 14; 19; 29ff.; 46; 52ff.; etc.; Clem. Alex. *Strom.* 5,12ff. See also JUPITER. Cf. A. B. Cook, *Zeus*, 1925.

Zeuxippe (1) Apollod. *Bibl.* 3,14,8; Hyg. *Fab.* 14. (2) Paus. 2,6,5. (3) Diod. Sic. 4,68.

Table of Sources

The principal ancient sources used in compiling the Dictionary are listed here. There is no separate table of abbreviations, but there should be no difficulty in elucidating from this list the abbreviations used in the list of references on pages 471–515. A few sources which occur only once or twice have been omitted from this list; in such cases a complete reference is given in the body of the work. Reference is made here to the editions which are most easily accessible for English readers, and in particular to the Loeb Classical Library wherever it contains an appropriate volume.

Achilles Tatius	S. Gaselee, Loeb, 1917.
Aelian	*De Natura Animalium*. A. Scholfield, Loeb, 3 vols, 1958–9 *Varia Historia*. M. Dilts, Leipzig (Teubner), 1974.
Aelius Anstides	see *Aristides*
Aeschines	G. Adams, Loeb, 1919. Scholia, F. Schultz, Leipzig, 1865 (with text).
Aeschylus	H. Weir Smyth, Loeb, revised edn, 2 vols, 1952–7. Fragments in Nauck, *Tragicorum Graecorum Fragmenta*, edn 2, or in the Loeb edn, vol. II (selected frr. only, edited by H. Lloyd-Jones). Scholia, O. L. Smith, Leipzig (Teubner), 1976– (in process of completion: vols. I, II completed so far); otherwise see A. Wartelle, *Bibliographie . . . d'Eschyle 1518–1974*, Paris, 1978, for edns of individual tragedies with scholia.
Ampelius	E. Assmann, Leipzig (Teubner), 1935.
Anthologia Palatina	W. Paton, Loeb, 5 vols, 1916–18.
Antigonus of Carystus	see *Paradoxographi*.
Antoninus Liberalis	*Metamorphoses*. M. Papathomopoulos, Paris (Budé), 1968, or in Westermann, *Mythographi Graeci* (q.v.).
Apollodorus	*Bibliotheca* and *Epitome*. J. Frazer, Loeb, 2 vols, 1921.
Appian	H. White, Loeb, 4 vols, 1912–13.
Apuleius	*Metamorphoses*. W. Adlington – S. Gaselee, Loeb, 1915.
Aratus	*Phaenomena*. A. and G. Mair, *Callimachus, Lycophron and Aratus*, Loeb, 1921 (see Callimachus, *Hymns*). Scholia, E. Maas, Berlin, 1898.
Aristides	*Orationes* 1–16: F. Lenz – C. Behr, Leiden, 1976; *Or.* 17–53: B. Keil, Berlin, 1898. Scholia, W. Dindorf, Leipzig, 1829.
Aristophanes	B. Rogers, Loeb, 3 vols, 1924.

Aristotle	*Poetics*. W. Hamilton Fyfe, Loeb, 1927. *Historia Animalium*. P. Lovis, Paris (Budé), 3 vols, 1964–9; A Peck, Loeb, 1965– (in process of completion: vols I, II completed). *Politics*. H. Rackham, Loeb, 1932.
ps. – Aristotle	*Mirabiles Auscultationes*, see *Paradoxograhi*.
Arnobius	*Adversus Nationes*. A. Reifferscheid, *Corpus Scriptorum Ecclesiasticorum Latinorum* IV, Vienna, 1875. Translated by G. McCracken, Westminster (Maryland), 1949.
Athenaeus	C. Gulick, Loeb, 7 vols, 1927–41.
Athenagoras	*Legatio pro Christianis*. W. Schoedel, Oxford, 1972.
Augustine	*De Civitate Dei*. G. McCracken and others, Loeb, 7 vols, 1957–72.
Aulus Gellius	see Gellius.
Aurelius Victor	*De Caesaribus*. P. Dufraigne, Paris (Budé), 1975; F. Pichlmayr, Leipzig (Teubner), 1961 (with ps. – Aurelius Victor, *De viris illustribus* and *De origine gentis Romanae*).
Ausonius	H. Evelyn White, Loeb, 2 vols, 1919–21.
Avianus (or Avienus)	*Fabulae*. F. Gaide, Paris (Budé), 1980; J. W. and A. M. Duff, *Minor Latin Poets*, Loeb, 1934.
Babrius	*Fabulae*. B. Perry, Loeb, 1965 (with Phaedrus).
Bacchylides	R. Jebb, Cambridge, 1905.
Bode	see *Mythographi*.
Callimachus	*Hymns*. A. Mair, Loeb, 1921 (with Aratus and Lycophron). Fragments (*Aetia*, *Hecale*, etc.). C. Trypanis, Loeb, 1958 (with Musaeus); R. Pfeiffer, Oxford, 2 vols, 1949–53 (with scholia).
Cato	*De Agricultura*. W. Hooper – H. Ash, Loeb, 1934 (with Varro, *De re rustica*). *Origines* (fragments). H. Peter, *Historicorum Romanorum Reliquiae* I, Leipzig (Teubner), edn 2, 1914.
Catullus	F. Cornish, Loeb, 1913 (with Tibullus and *Pervigilium Veneris*).
Censorinus	*De die natali*. F. Hultsch, Leipzig (Teubner), 1867.
Cicero	Various editors and dates, 22 vols in Loeb series. Scholia Bobiensia, H. Hildebrandt, Leipzig (Teubner), 1907.
CIL	= *Corpus Inscriptionum Latinarum*, 1863–.
Claudian	M. Platnauer, Loeb, 2 vols, 1922.
Clement of Alexandria	*Protrepticus*. G. Butterworth, Loeb, 1919. *Stromateis*. O. Stählin – L. Früchtel, Berlin, 2 vols, 1960–70.
Comicorum Atticorum Fragmenta	T. Kock, Liepzig (Teubner), 3 vols, 1880–8.
Conon	*Narrationes*. In A. Westermann, *Mythographi Graeci* (see *Mythographi*), or in Photius, *Bibliotheca* (cod. 186), R. Henry, Paris (Budé), 1962, vol. III.
Demosthenes	J. H. Vince and others, Loeb, 7 vols, 1926–49. Scholia, W. Dindorf, Oxford, 1851 (*Demosthenes*, vols. VIII–IX).
Dictys Cretensis	W. Eisenhut, Leipzig (Teubner), 1973. Translated by R. Frazer, Bloomington, 1966.
Dio of Prusa (Dio Chrysostom).	J. Cohoon and others, Loeb, 5 vols, 1932–51.
Diodorus Siculus	C. Oldfather and others, Loeb, 12 vols, 1933–67.
Diogenes Laertius	R. Hicks, Loeb, 2 vols, 1925.

Dionysius of Halicarnassus *Antiquitates Romanae.*	E. Cary, Loeb, 7 vols, 1937–50.
ps. – Dionysius of Halicarnassus	*Rhetorica.* In Dionysius *Opuscula* II, II. Usener – L. Radermacher, Leipzig (Teubner), 1904.
Dionysius Periegetes	In G. Bernhardy, *Geographici Graeci Minores* I, Leipzig, 1828 (with scholia). See also Eustathius.
Dionysius Thrax (Scholia Vaticana)	In A. Hilgard, *Grammatici Graeci* I.3, Leipzig (Teubner), 1901.
Dionysius *De Avibus*	F. Lehrs, *Poetae Bucolici et Didactici*, Paris (Didot), 1851.
Dracontius	E. Baehrens, *Poetae Latini Minores*, V, edn 2, Leipzig (Teubner), 1914.
ps. – Eratosthenes	*Catasterismoi*, see *Mythographi.*
Erotici Scriptores Greci	R. Hercher, Leipzig (Teubner), 2 vols, 1858–9.
Etymologicum Magnum	T. Gaisford, Oxford, 1848.
Euripides	A. Way, Loeb, 4 vols, 1912. Fragments in Nauck, *Tragicorum Graecorum Fragmenta*, edn 2. Scholia, E. Schwartz, Berlin, 2 vols, 1887–91.
Eusebius	*Chronicon.* R. Helm, Berlin, 1956. *Praeparatio Evangelica.* K. Mras, Berlin, 2 vols, 1954–6. Translated by E. Gifford, Oxford, 2 vols, 1903. *Oratio ad Sanctos.* I. Heikel, Leipzig, 1902.
Eustathius	*Commentaria in Homeri Iliadem et Odysseam.* G. Stallbaum, Leipzig, 7 vols, 1825–30. *Commentaria in Dionysium Periegetam.* In C. Müller, *Geographici Graeci Minores* II, Paris (Didot), 1861, or G. Bernhardy, Leipzig, 1828 (see Dionysius Periegetes).
Festus	W. Lindsay, Leipzig (Teubner), 1913.
Firmicus Maternus	*Mathesis.* W. Kroll – F. Skutsch, Leipzig (Teubner), 2 vols, 1897–1913. Translated by J. Bram, Park Ridge (New Jersey), 1975.
Fragmenta Historicorum Graecorum	C. Müller, Paris (Didot), 5 vols, 1841–70.
Fulgentius	R. Helm, Leipzig (Teubner), 1898. Translated by L. Whitbread, Ohio State University Press, 1971.
Gellius	*Noctes Atticae.* J. Rolfe, Loeb, 3 vols, 1927.
Greek Anthology	see Anthologia Palatina.
Harpocration	W. Dindorf, Oxford, 1853.
ps. – Heraclitus	*De Incredibilibus*, see *Mythographi.*
Hermias	*Commentaria in Platonis Phaedrum.* P. Couvreur, Paris, 1901.
Herodas	W. Headlam, Cambridge, 1922; A. D. Knox, Loeb, 1929 (with Theophrastus, *Characters*, etc.).
Herodotus	A. D. Godley, Loeb, 4 vols, 1921–5.
Hercher	see *Erotici Scriptores Graeci.*
Hesiod	H. Evelyn White, Loeb, revised edn, 1936. Fragments, R. Merkelbach – M. West, Oxford, 1967. Scholia on *Theogony*, H. Flach, Leipzig (Teubner), 1876; on *Works and Days*, A. Pertusi, Milan, 1955.
Hesychius	*Lexicon.* M. Schmidt, Jena, 4 vols, 1858–62; K. Latte, Copenhagen, 2 vols, 1953–66 (A – O only).
Historia Augusta	D. Magie, Loeb, 3 vols, 1922–33.
Homer	*Iliad* and *Odyssey*, A. Murray, Loeb, 4 vols, 1919–25.

	Homeric Hymns and Epic Cycle, T. W. Allen, Oxford, 1912 (Homer Oxford Classical Text V). Homeric Epigrams, in A. Baumeister, *Hymni Homerici* Leipzig (Teubner), 1897. Scholia on *Iliad*, W. Dindorf, Oxford, 4 vols, 1875–7; H. Erbse, Berlin, 1969– (6 vols to date). Scholia on *Odyssey*, W. Dindorf, Oxford, 2 vols, 1855. See also Eustathius.
Horace	*Odes* and *Epodes*, C. Bennett, Loeb, revised edn, 1927. *Satires, Epistles, Ars Poetica*, H. Fairclough, Loeb, revised edn, 1929. See also Porphyrio.
Hyginus	*Fabulae*. H. Rose, Leiden, 1933, repr. 1963. Translated by M. Grant, Lawrence (Kansas), 1960. *Astronomica Poetica*, B. Bunte, Leipzig, 1875.
Isidore	W. Lindsay, Oxford, 2 vols, 1911.
Isocrates	G. Norlin – L. van Hook, Loeb, 3 vols, 1928–45.
Joannes Lydus	see Lydus.
Justin	*Epitoma Historiarum Pompei Trogi*. O. Seel, Stuttgart (Teubner), edn 2, 1972.
Juvenal	G. Ramsay, Loeb, 1918.
Kock	see *Comicorum Atticorum Fragmenta*.
Lactantius	*Institutiones Divinae*. S. Brandt, Vienna, 1890 (*Corpus Script. Eccl. Lat.* XIX.1).
ps.–Lactantius Placidus	*Commentarii in Statii Thebaida et Achilleida*. R. Jahnke, Leipzig (Teubner), 1898 (Statius, vol. III). *Narrationes Fabularum Ovidianarum*, in H. Magnus, *Ovidi Metamorphoseon Libri XV*, Berlin, 1914.
Libanius	R. Foerster, Leipzig (Teubner), 12 vols, 1903–23.
Lucan	scholia in C. Weber, *Lucani Pharsalia* III, Leipzig, 1831.
Lucian	A. Harmon and others, Loeb, 8 vols, 1913–67. Scholia, H. Rabe, Leipzig (Teubner), 1906.
Lucretius	W. Rouse – M. Smith, Loeb, revised edn, 1975.
Lycophron	*Alexandra*. A. and G. Mair, Loeb, 1921 (see Callimachus, *Hymns*). See also Tzetzes.
Lycurgus	In J. Burtt, *Minor Attic Orators* II, Loeb, 1954.
Lydus	*De Mensibus*. R. Wuensch, Leipzig (Teubner), 1898.
Macrobius	*Saturnalia* and *Commentarii in Somnium Scipionis*, J. Willis, Leipzig (Teubner), 2 vols, 1970. *Sarturnalia* translated by P. Davies, New York, 1969.
Malalas	*Chronographia*. L. Dindorf, Bonn, 1831.
Manilius	*Astronomica*. G. Goold, Loeb, 1977.
Marmor Parium	F. Jacoby, Berlin, 1904.
Mela	*Chorographia*. K. Frick, Leipzig (Teubner), 1880.
Moschus	In J. Edmonds, *The Greek Bucolic Poets*, Loeb, 1912.
Müller	see *Fragmenta Historicorum Graecorum*.
Musaeus.	*Hero and Leander*. C. Whitman, in C. Trypanis, *Callimachus*, Loeb, edn 2, 1975 (see Callimachus, Fragments).
Mythographi Graeci	A. Westermann, Brunswick, 1843, or N. Festa and others, Leipzig (Teubner), 1902.
Mythographi Latini	G. Bode, *Scriptores Rerum Mythicarum Latini Tres*, Celle, 1834.
Nauck	see *Tragicorum Graecorum Fragmenta*.
Nicander	A. Gow – A. Scholfield, Cambridge, 1953. Scholia

	on *Theriaca*, A. Crugnola, Milan, 1971; on *Alexipharmaca*, M. Geymonat, Milan, 1974.
Nonnus	*Dionysiaca*. W. Rouse and others, Loeb, 3 vols, 1940.
	Fabulae, in A. Westermann, *Mythographi Graeci* (see *Mythographi*).
Oppian	A. Mair, Loeb, 1928.
De Origine Gentis Romanae	J.-C. Richard, Paris (Budé), 1983, or in F. Pichlmayr, *Aurelius Victor*, Leipzig (Teubner), 1961 (see Aurelius Victor).
Orphic *Argonautica*	G. Dottin, Paris (Budé), 1930.
Orphic Hymns	W. Quandt, Berlin, 1955.
Orphic Fragments	O. Kern, Berlin, 1922.
Ovid	*Metamorphoses*. F. Miller, Loeb, 2 vols, 1916 (see also ps. – Lactantius Placidus, *Narrationes Fabularum Ovidianarum*). *Fasti*. J. G. Frazer, Loeb, 1931. *Heroides and Amores*. G. Showerman – G. Goold, Loeb, edn 2, 1977. *Ars Amatoria*, etc. J. Mozley – G. Goold, Loeb, edn 2, 1979. *Tristia and Ex Ponto* A. Wheeler, Loeb, 1924.
Oxyrhnchus Papyri	Vols. I–, London, 1898–.
Palaephatus	*Incredibilia*. In N. Festa, *Mythographi Graeci*, III.2 (see *Mythographi*).
Paradoxographi	A. Westermann, 1839; A. Giannini, Milan 1965.
Parthenius	*Erotica Pathemata*. S. Gaselee, in J. Edmonds, *Longus*, Loeb, 1946.
Paulus	*Epitome* of Festus, see Festus.
Pausanias	W. Jones, Loeb, 5 vols, 1918–35.
Petronius	M. Heseltine – E. Warmington, Loeb, 1969.
Philargyrius	See Servis.
Philo of Alexandria	*Quod omnis probus liber sit*. F. Colson, Loeb, 1941, vol. IX.
Philoponus	In *Commentaria in Aristotelem Graeca*, XIII–XVIII, Berlin, 1887–1909.
Philostratus	*Vita Apollonii*. F. Conybeare, Loeb, 2 vols, 1912. *Heroicus*, C. Kayser, Leipzig (Teubner), 1871, vol. II; L. de Lannoy, Leipzig (Teubner), 1977.
Photius	*Lexicon*. R. Porson, London, 1822; S. Naber, Leiden, 1864. *Bibliotheca*, R. Henry, Paris (Budé), 8 vols, 1959–77.
Pindar	J. Sandys, Loeb, revised edn, 1937. Scholia, A. Drachmann, Leipzig (Teubner), 3 vols, 1908–27.
Plato	H. Fowler and others, Loeb, 12 vols, 1914–35. Spurious works in Budé Plato vol. XIII. 3, J. Souilhé, Paris, edn 2, 1962, or Oxford Classical Text, J. Burnet, 1907, vol. V. Scholia, W. Greene, Haverford, 1938.
Plautus	P. Nixon, Loeb, 5 vols, 1916–38.
Pliny the Elder	*Naturalis Historia*. H. Rackham and others, Loeb, 10 vols, 1938–80.
Plutarch	*Moralia*. F. Babbitt and others, Loeb, 15 vols, 1927–69 (vol. XVI still in process of completion). Spurious works in vol. VII of the older Teubner edn, G. Bernardakis, Leipzig, 1896. *Lives*. B. Perrin, Loeb, 11 vols, 1914–26.

Pollux	*Onomasticon*. E. Bethe, Leipzig (Teubner), 3 vols, 1900–37.
Polyaenus	*Strategemata*. E. Wölfflin – I. Melber, Stuttgart (Teubner), 1970.
Pomponius Mela	see Mela.
Porphyrio	*Commentarii in Horatium*. W. Meyer, Leipzig (Teubner), 1874; A. Holder, Innsbruck, 1894 (repr. Arno 1979).
Porphyry	*De Antro Nympharum* and *De Abstinentia*. A. Nauck, Leipzig (Teubner), 1886. Translated by T. Taylor, *Select Works of Porphyry*, London, 1823. *Quaestiones Homericae in Iliadem*, H. Schrader, Leipzig (Teubner), 1880–2.
Priscian	In H. Keil, *Grammatici Latini* II–III, Leipzig, 1855–9.
Probus (scholia on Virgil)	see Servius.
Proclus	*Commentaria in Hesiodi Opera et Dies*. In T. Gaisford, *Poetae Graeci Minores* III, Oxford, 1820. *Commentaria in Platonis Timaeum*. E. Diehl. Leipzig (Teubner), 3 vols, 1903–6.
Propertius	H. Butler, Loeb, 1924.
Ptolemy Hephaestion	*Nova Historiae*. In Westermann, *Mythographi Graeci* (see *Mythographi*); or in Photius, *Bibliotheca* (cod. 190), R. Henry, Paris (Budé), 1962, vol. III.
Quintus Smyrnaeus	*Posthomerica*. A. Way, Loeb, 1913.
Res Gestae Divi Augusti	In F. Shipley, *Velleius Paterculus*, Loeb, 1924.
Seneca	Tragedies, F. Miller, Loeb, 2 vols, 1917. *Epistulae Morales*. R. Gummere, Loeb, 3 vols, 1917–25.
Servius	*Commentarii in Virgilium* (with Probus and Philargyrius). G. Thilo – H. Hagen, Leipzig (Teubner), 3 vols, 1878–1902. Berne scholia on Virgil, H. Hagen, Leipzig (Teubner), 1867 (repr. Hildesheim 1967).
Sextus Empiricus	R. Bury, Loeb, 4 vols, 1933–49.
Silius Italicus	J. Duff, Loeb, 2 vols, 1934.
Solinus	T. Mommsen, Berlin, 1895.
Solon	Fragments in J. Edmonds, *Elegy and Iambus* I, Loeb, 1931.
Sophocles	F. Storr, Loeb, 2 vols. 1912–13. Fragments, R. Jebb – A. Pearson, Cambridge, 3 vols, 1917. Scholia, P. Papageorgiou, Leipzig (Teubner), 1888.
Statius	J. Mozley, Loeb, 2 vols, 1928. For scholia, see ps. – Lactantius Placidus.
Stephanus of Byzantium	L. Hostein and others, Leipzig, 1825; A. Meineke, Berlin, 1849 (one vol. only).
Stobaeus	K. Wachsmuth – O. Hense, Berlin, 5 vols, 1884–1912.
Strabo	H. Jones, Loeb, 8 vols, 1917–32.
Suda	A. Adler, Leipzig (Teubner), 5 vols, 1928–38.
Suetonius	*Vitae Caesarum*. J. Rolfe, Loeb, 2 vols, 1913–14.
Tacitus	*Historiae* and *Annales*. C. Moore – J. Jackson, Loeb, 4 vols, 1925–37. *Agricola, Germania, Dialogus*. M. Hutton and others, Loeb, revised edn, 1970.
Tertullian	F. Oehler, Leipzig, 3 vols, 1853.

Theocritus	J. Edmonds, *The Greek Bucolic Poets*, Loeb, 1912. Scholia, K. Wendel, Lepzig (Teubner), 1914.
Theophrastus	*Historia Plantarum*. A. Hort, Loeb, 2 vols, 1916.
Thucydides	C. Smith, Loeb, 4 vols, 1919–23. Scholia, K. Hude, Leipzig (Teubner), 1927.
Tibullus	In F. Cornish and others, *Catullus, Tebullus, Pervigilium Veneris*, Loeb, 1913, see Catullus.
Tragicorum Graecorum Fragmenta	A. Nauck, Hildesheim, 2nd edn. with supplement by B. Snell, 1964.
Trogus	see Justin.
Tzetzes	*Commentaria in Lycophronis Alexandram*. E. Scheer, *Lycophronis Alexandra* II, Berlin 1908. *Historiarum Variarum Chiliades*. P. Leone, Naples, 1968. *Antehomerica, Homerica, Posthomerica*. F. Lehrs, Paris (Didot), 1840. *Allegoriae Iliadis*. J. Boissonade, Paris, 1851. *Commentaria in Iliadem*. In G. Hermann, *Draco de metris*, Leipzig, 1812, or in G. Bachmann, *Scholia in Homeri Iliadem*, Leipzig, 1835–8. *Commentaria in Hesiodi Theogoniam*. In T. Gaisford, *Poetae Graeci Minores* III, Oxford, 1820, or P. Matranga, *Anecdota Graeca* III, Rome, 1850.
Valerius Flaccus	J. Mozley, Loeb, 1934.
Valerius Maximus	K. Kempf, Leipzig (Teubner), 1888.
Varro	*De Lingua Latina*. R. Kent, Loeb, 2 vols, 1938.
Velleius Paterculus	F. Shipley, Loeb, 1924.
Virgil	H. R. Fairclough, Loeb, 2 vols, edn 2, 1930. For scholia see Servius.
Westermann	see *Mythographi*.
Xenophon	Various editors and dates, 8 vols in Loeb series.
Zenobius	*Epitome*. In E. Leutsch – E. Schneidewin, *Paroemiographi Graeci* I, Göttingen, 1839.
Zonaras	*Lexicon*. J. Tittmann, Leipzig, 2 vols, 1808.

TABLE 1

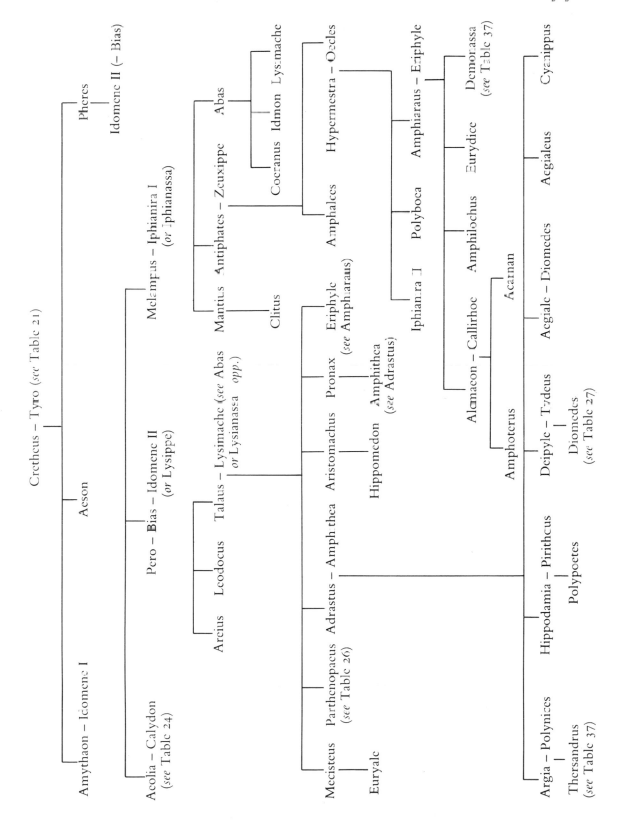

TABLE 2

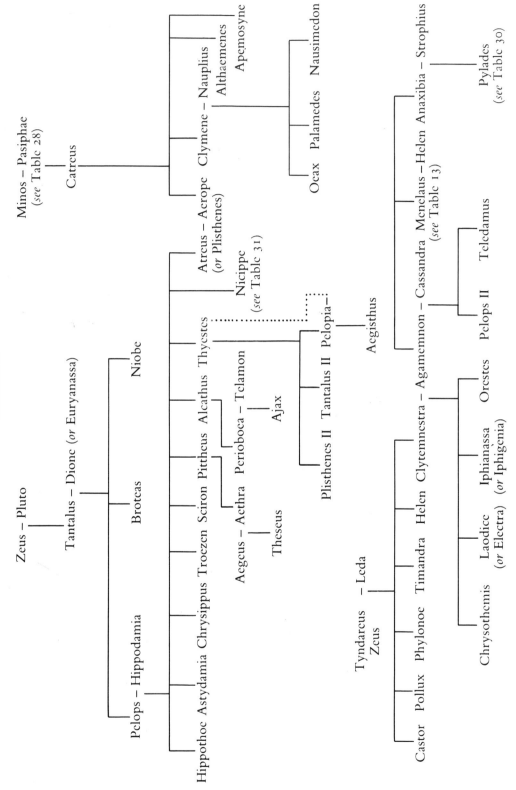

TABLE 3

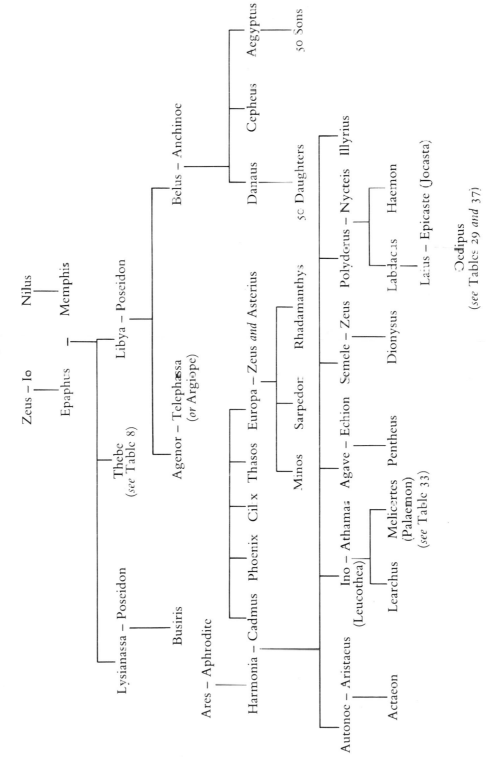

TABLE 4

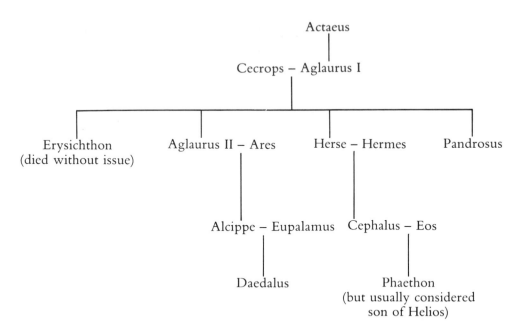

TABLE 5

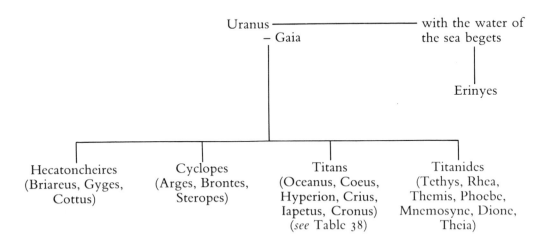

TABLE 6

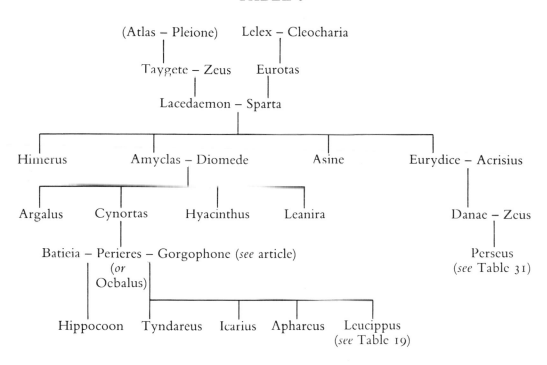

TABLE 7

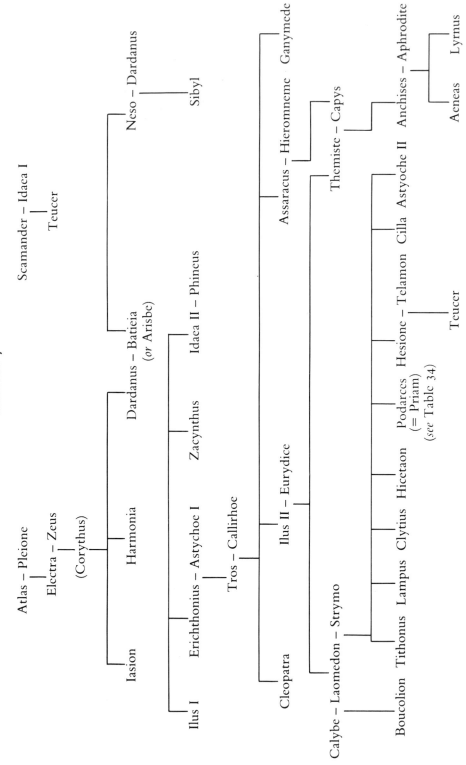

TABLE 8

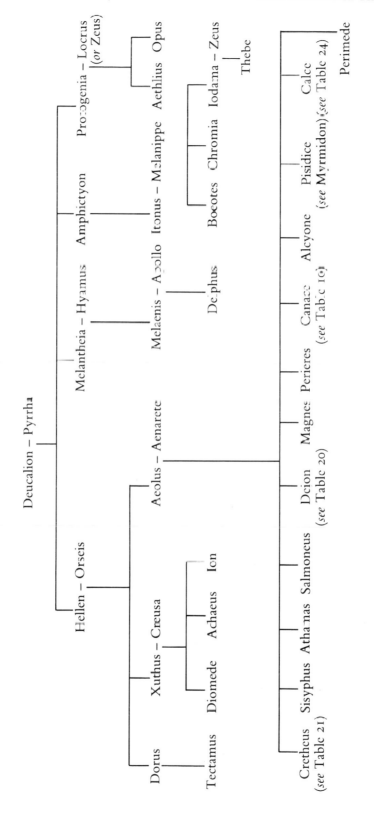

Deucalion – Pyrrha

Hellen – Orseis

Dorus

Xuthus – Creusa

Tectamus   Diomede   Achaeus   Ion

Aeolus – Aenarete

Melantheia – Hyamus   Amphictyon   Proogenia – Locrus (or Zeus)

Melaenis – Apollo   Itonus – Melanippe   Aethlius   Opus

Delphus

Boeotus   Chromia   Iodama – Zeus

Thebe

Cretheus (see Table 21)   Sisyphus   Athamas   Salmoneus   Deion (see Table 20)   Magnes   Perieres   Canace (see Table 19)   Alcyone   Pisidice (see Myrmidon)   Calce (see Table 24)   Perimede

TABLE 9

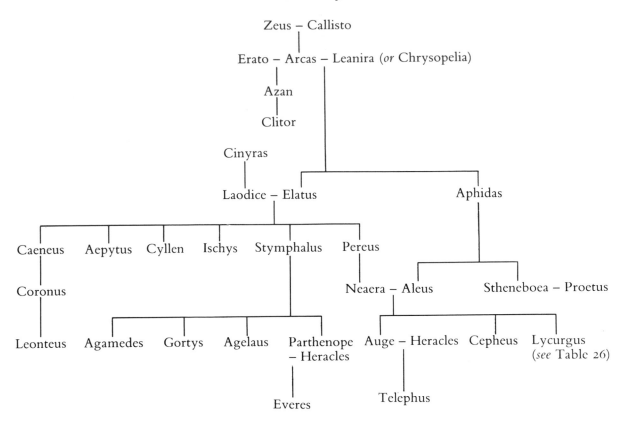

TABLE 10

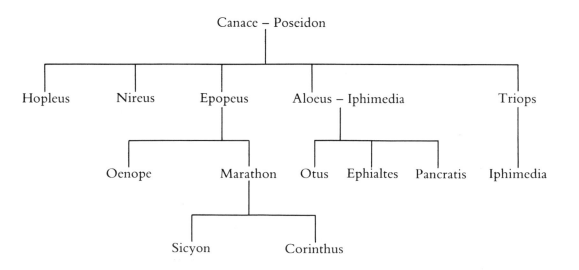

TABLE II

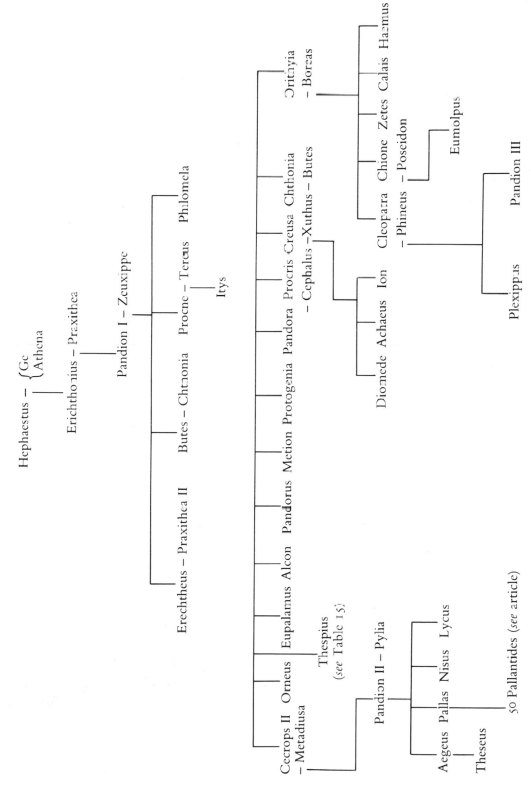

TABLE 12

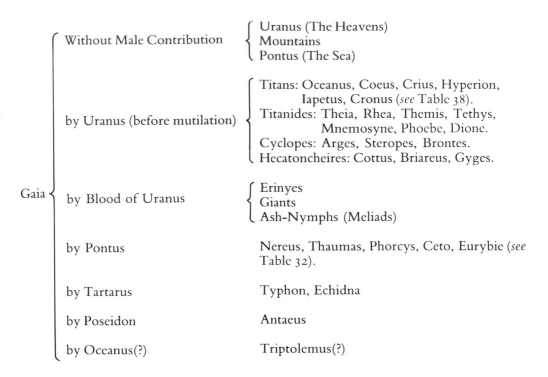

Gaia
- Without Male Contribution
  - Uranus (The Heavens)
  - Mountains
  - Pontus (The Sea)
- by Uranus (before mutilation)
  - Titans: Oceanus, Coeus, Crius, Hyperion, Iapetus, Cronus (*see* Table 38).
  - Titanides: Theia, Rhea, Themis, Tethys, Mnemosyne, Phoebe, Dione.
  - Cyclopes: Arges, Steropes, Brontes.
  - Hecatoncheires: Cottus, Briareus, Gyges.
- by Blood of Uranus
  - Erinyes
  - Giants
  - Ash-Nymphs (Meliads)
- by Pontus
  - Nereus, Thaumas, Phorcys, Ceto, Eurybie (*see* Table 32).
- by Tartarus
  - Typhon, Echidna
- by Poseidon
  - Antaeus
- by Oceanus(?)
  - Triptolemus(?)

TABLE 13

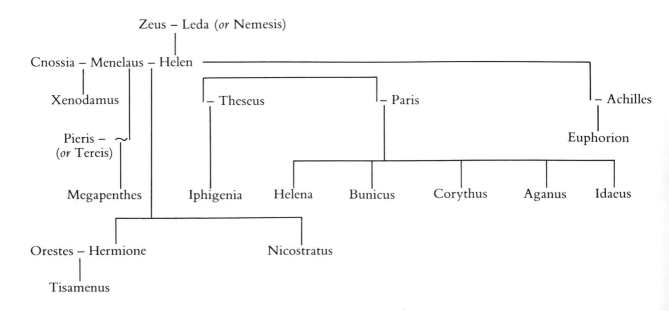

Zeus – Leda (*or* Nemesis)

Cnossia – Menelaus – Helen

Xenodamus

Pieris – ~
(*or* Tereis)

Megapenthes

– Theseus

– Paris

– Achilles

Euphorion

Iphigenia   Helena   Bunicus   Corythus   Aganus   Idaeus

Orestes – Hermione   Nicostratus

Tisamenus

TABLE 15

Heracles
{

50 Daughters of Thespius: 50 Sons: Antileon, Hipeus, Threpsippas, Eumenes, Creon, Astyanax, Iobes, Polylaus, Archemachus, Laomedon, Eurycapys, Eurypylus, Antiades, Onesippus, Laomenes, Teles, Entelides, Hippodromus, Teleutagoras, Capylus, Olympus, Nicodromus, Cleolaus, Eurythras, Homolippus, Antromus, Celeustanor, Antiphus, Alopius, Astybies, Tigasis, Leucones, Archedicus, Dynastes, Mentor, Amestrius, Lycacus, Halocrates, Phalias, Oestrobles, Euryopes, Bouleus, Antimachus, Patroclus, Nephus, Erasippus, Lycurgus, Bucolus, Leucippus, Hippozygus.

Megara: Therimachus, Deicoon, Creontiades.

Astyoche: Tlepolemus (and Thessalus; see below).

Parthenope: Everes.

Epicaste: Thestalus.

Chalciope: Thessalus (sometimes attributed to Astyoche).

Auge: Telephus.

Deianira: Hyllus, Ctesippus, Glenus, Onites (or Hodites), Macaria.

Omphale: Acheles (or Agelaus), Tyrsenus.

Astydamia: Ctesippus.

Autonoe: Palaemon.

Hebe: Alexiares, Anicetus.

Meda (daughter of Phylas): Antiochus.

TABLE 14

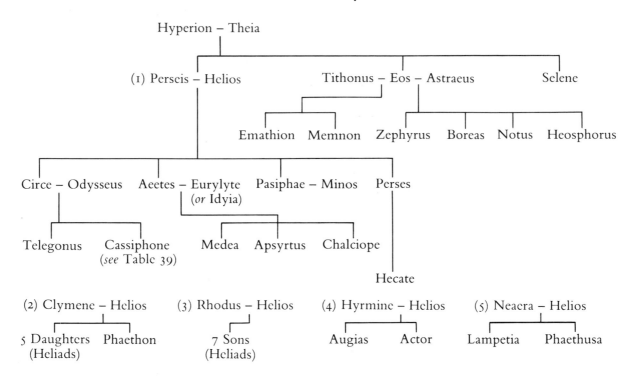

TABLE 16

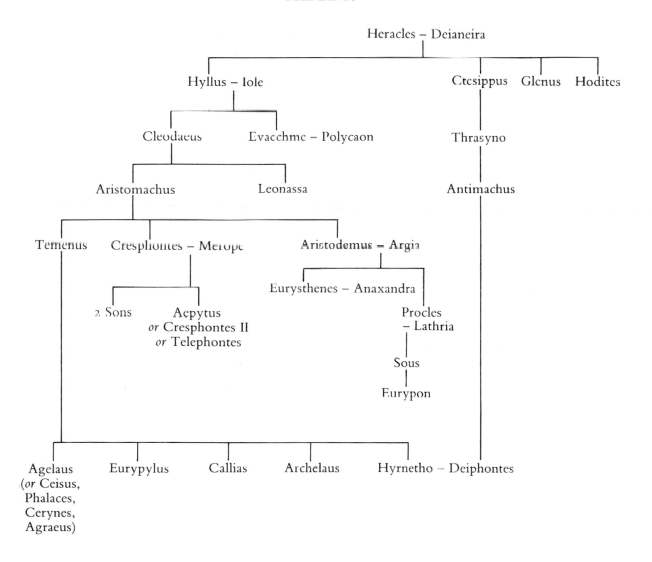

TABLE 17 (after Pausanias)

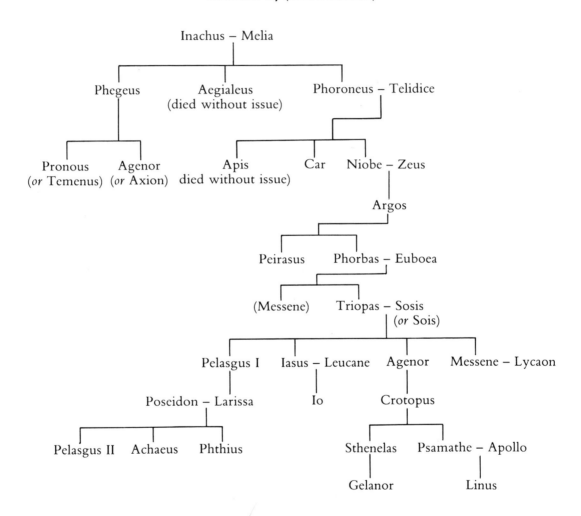

TABLE 18 (after Apollodorus)

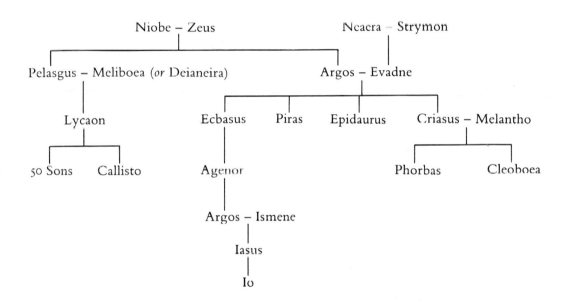

TABLE 19

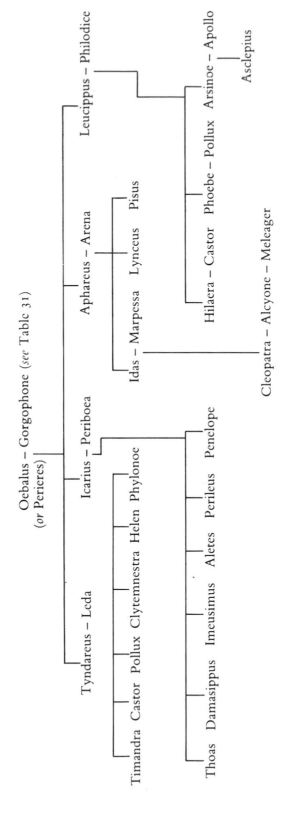

Oebalus – Gorgophone (*see* Table 31)
(*or* Perieres)

TABLE 20

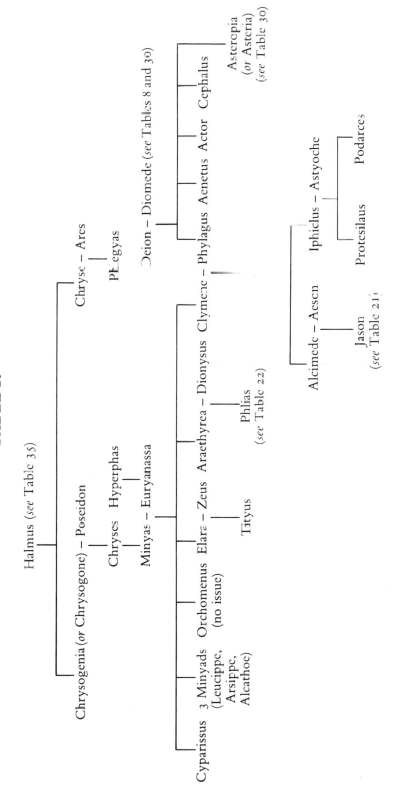

TABLE 21 (*see* also Table 1)

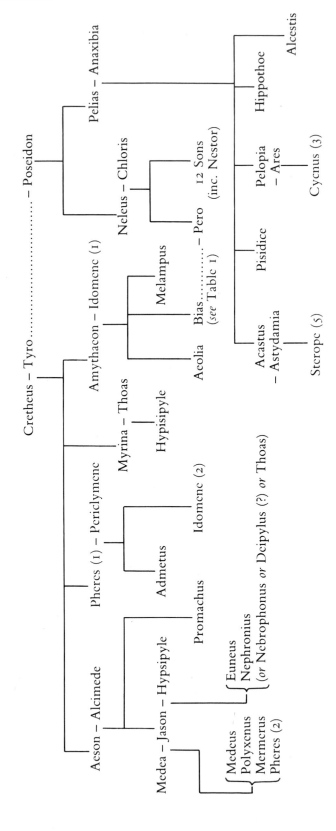

TABLE 22

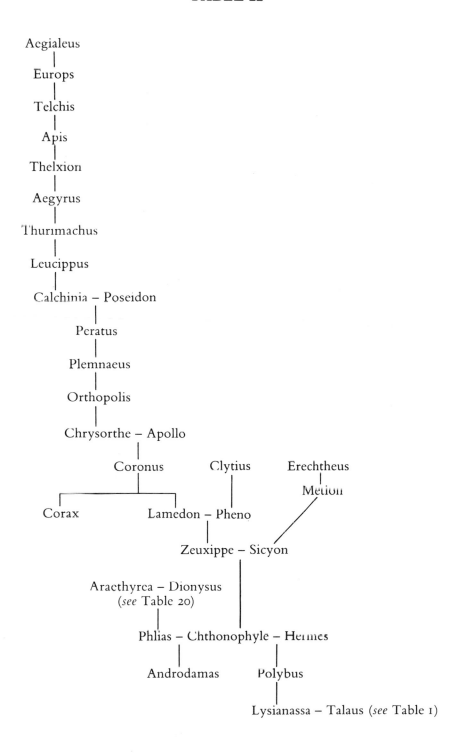

Acgialeus
|
Europs
|
Telchis
|
Apis
|
Thelxion
|
Aegyrus
|
Thurimachus
|
Leucippus
|
Calchinia – Poseidon
|
Peratus
|
Plemnaeus
|
Orthopolis
|
Chrysorthe – Apollo
|
Coronus   Clytius   Erechtheus
| |
                                 Metion

Corax   Lamedon – Pheno
|
Zeuxippe – Sicyon

Araethyrea – Dionysus
(*see* Table 20)
|
Phlias – Chthonophyle – Hermes
| |
Androdamas   Polybus
|
Lysianassa – Talaus (*see* Table 1)

TABLE 23 (*see* article Lapiths)

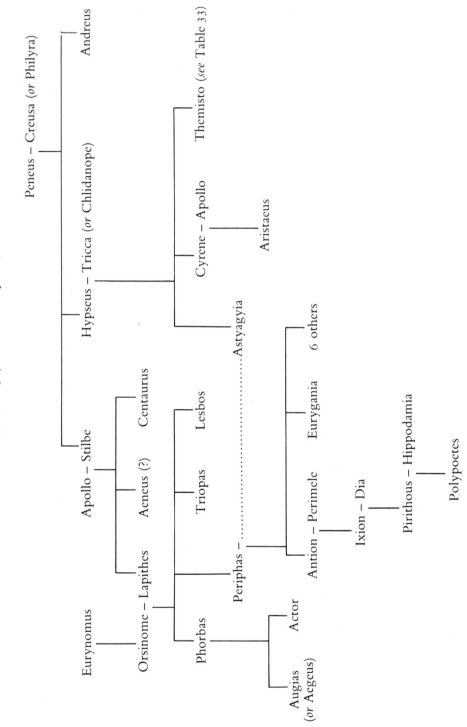

TABLE 24

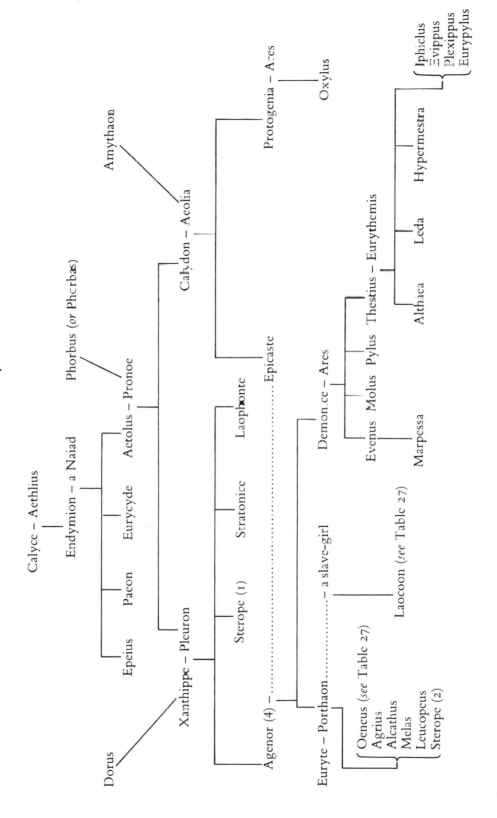

TABLE 25

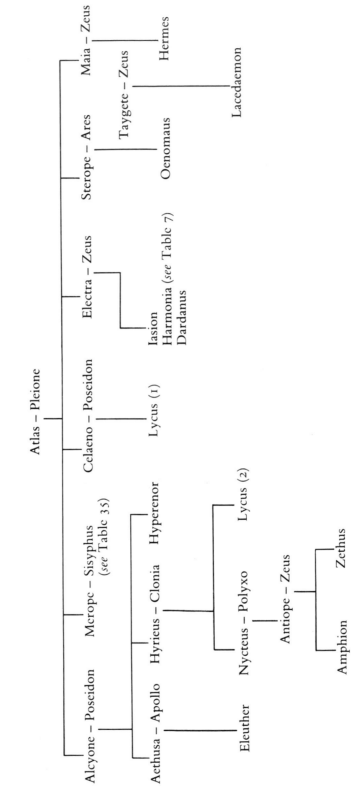

TABLE 26

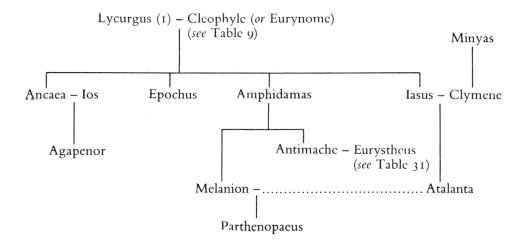

TABLE 27 (cf. Table 24)

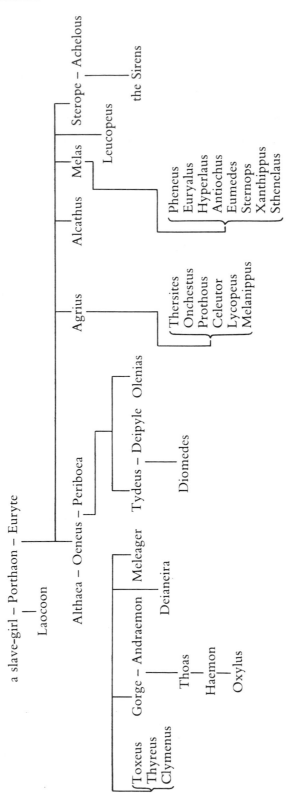

TABLE 28

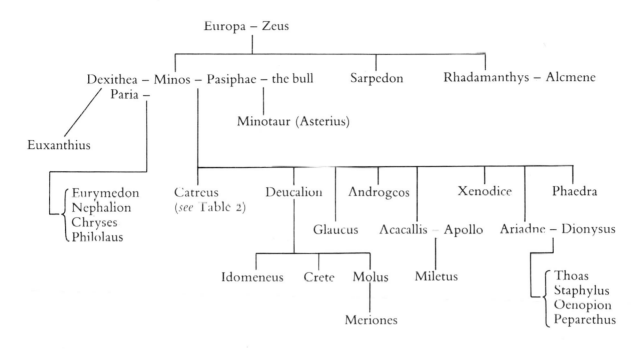

TABLE 29

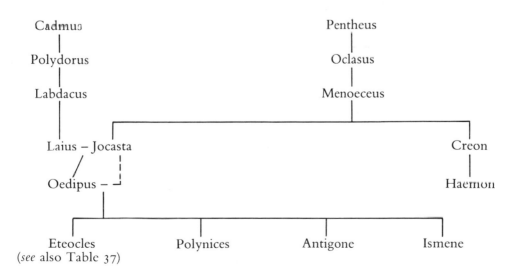

TABLE 30

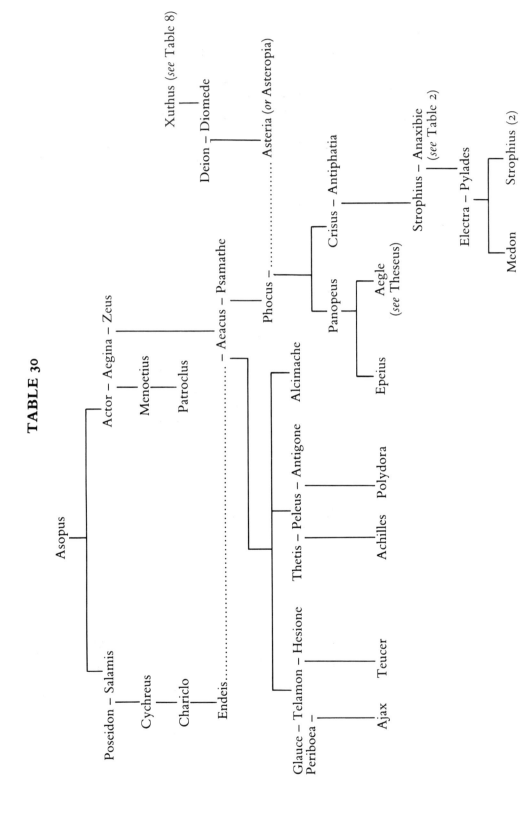

TABLE 31

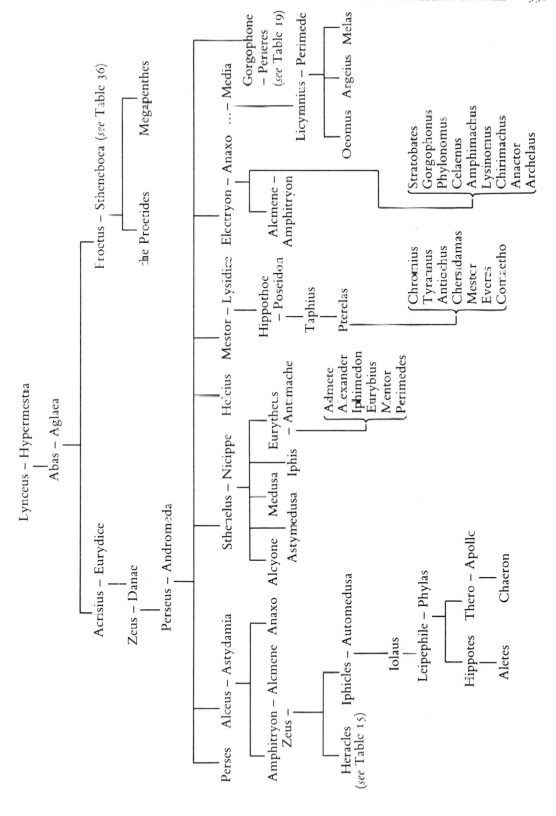

TABLE 32

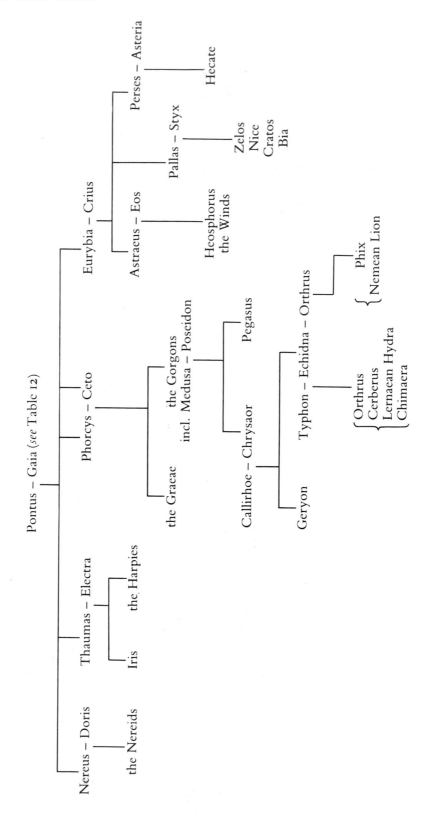

TABLE 33

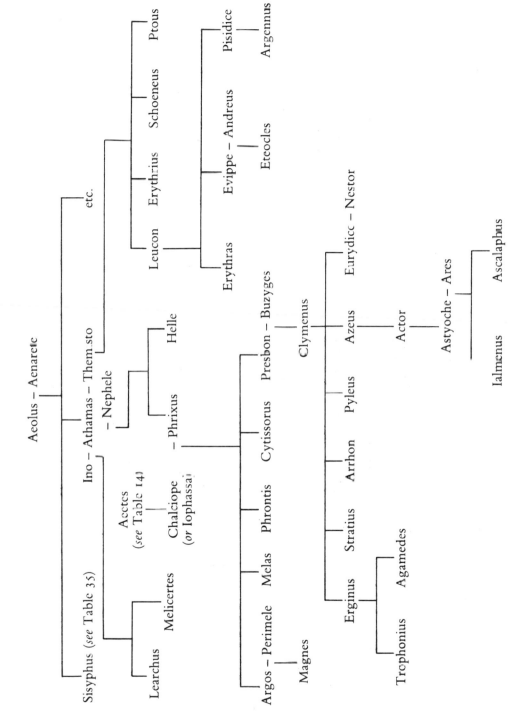

TABLE 34

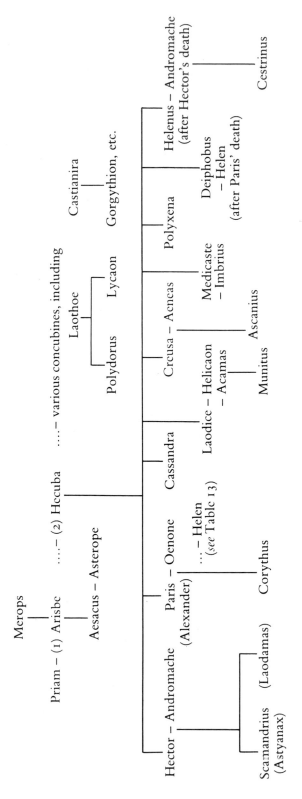

TABLE 35

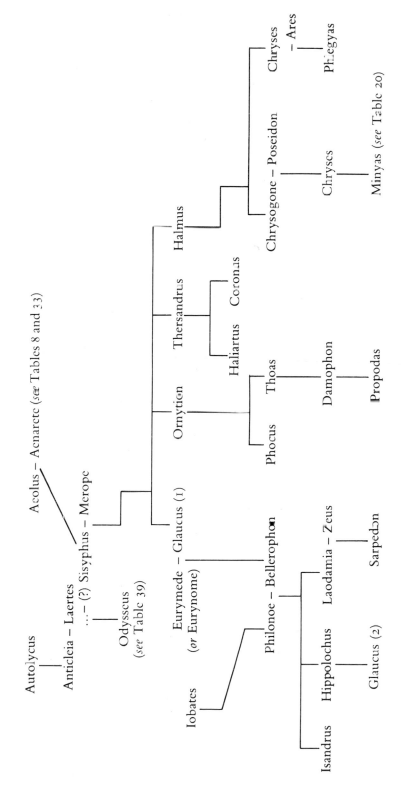

TABLE 36

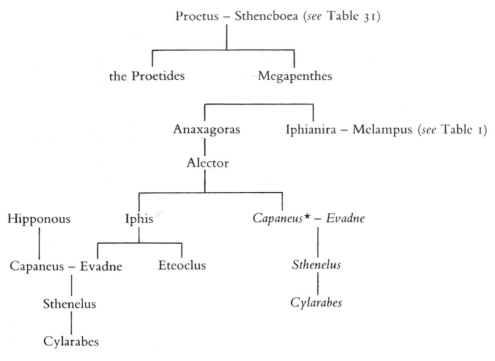

* *variant in Pausanias 2, 18, 5*

TABLE 37

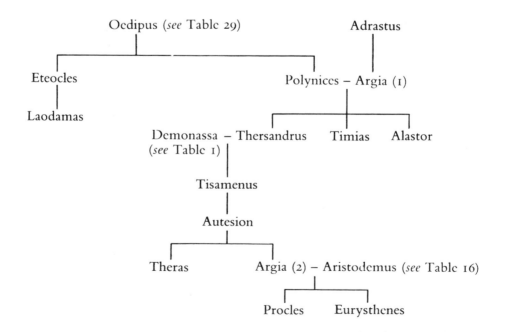

TABLE 38

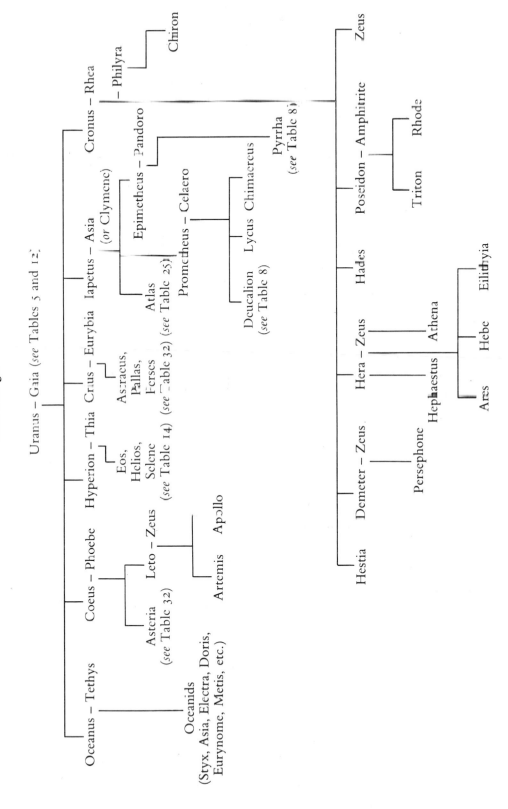

Uranus – Gaia (*see* Tables 5 and 12)

TABLE 39

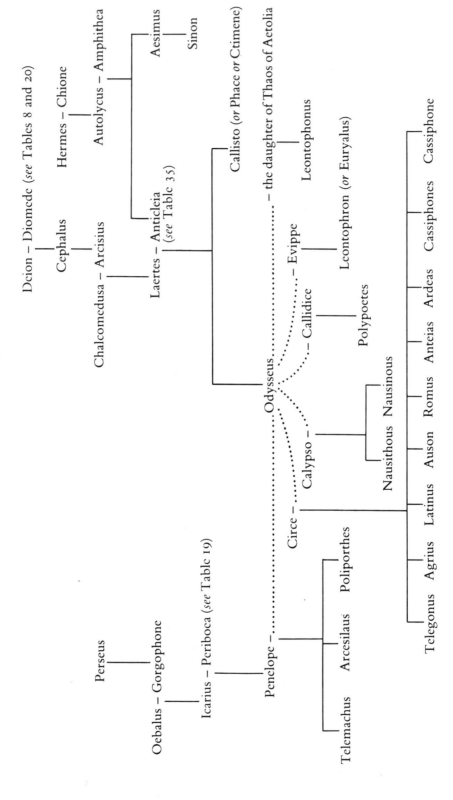

TABLE 40

Zeus

Divine unions
- Metis: Athena.
- Themis: Horae, Fates.
- Dione: Aphrodite
- Eurynome: Graces.
- Mnemosyne: Muses.
- Leto: Apollo, Artemis.
- Demeter: Persephone.
- Hera: Ares, Hebe, Eilithyia; (Hephaestus).

Human unions
- Alcmene: Heracles (Table 31)
- Antiope: Amphion, Zethus (Table 25)
- Callisto: Arcas (Table 9)
- Danae: Perseus (Table 31)
- Aegina: Aeacus (Table 30)
- Electra: Dardanus, Iasion, Harmonia (Table 7)
- Europa: Minos, Sarpedon, Rhadamanthys (Table 28)
- Io: Epaphus (Table 3)
- Laodamia: Sarpedon (Table 35)
- Leda: Helen, Castor and Pollux (Table 2)
- Maia: Hermes (Table 25)
- Niobe: Argos, Pelasgus (Tables 17 and 18)
- Pluto: Tantalus (Table 2)
- Semele: Dionysus (Table 3)
- Taygete: Lacedaemon (Table 6)

Index

Note: The first entry preceding a colon refers to the main dictionary entry. Incidental references follow the colon. The parents of each person are not entered every time in the index. Their names can be discovered by consulting the main entry or the genealogical tables on pages 525–559.